Nineteenth-Century
Literature Criticism

Guide to Thomson Gale Literary Criticism Series

For criticism on	Consult these Thomson Gale series
Authors now living or who died after December 31, 1999	*CONTEMPORARY LITERARY CRITICISM (CLC)*
Authors who died between 1900 and 1999	*TWENTIETH-CENTURY LITERARY CRITICISM (TCLC)*
Authors who died between 1800 and 1899	*NINETEENTH-CENTURY LITERATURE CRITICISM (NCLC)*
Authors who died between 1400 and 1799	*LITERATURE CRITICISM FROM 1400 TO 1800 (LC)* *SHAKESPEAREAN CRITICISM (SC)*
Authors who died before 1400	*CLASSICAL AND MEDIEVAL LITERATURE CRITICISM (CMLC)*
Authors of books for children and young adults	*CHILDREN'S LITERATURE REVIEW (CLR)*
Dramatists	*DRAMA CRITICISM (DC)*
Poets	*POETRY CRITICISM (PC)*
Short story writers	*SHORT STORY CRITICISM (SSC)*
Literary topics and movements	*HARLEM RENAISSANCE: A GALE CRITICAL COMPANION (HR)* *THE BEAT GENERATION: A GALE CRITICAL COMPANION (BG)* *FEMINISM IN LITERATURE: A GALE CRITICAL COMPANION (FL)* *GOTHIC LITERATURE: A GALE CRITICAL COMPANION (GL)*
Asian American writers of the last two hundred years	*ASIAN AMERICAN LITERATURE (AAL)*
Black writers of the past two hundred years	*BLACK LITERATURE CRITICISM (BLC)* *BLACK LITERATURE CRITICISM SUPPLEMENT (BLCS)*
Hispanic writers of the late nineteenth and twentieth centuries	*HISPANIC LITERATURE CRITICISM (HLC)* *HISPANIC LITERATURE CRITICISM SUPPLEMENT (HLCS)*
Native North American writers and orators of the eighteenth, nineteenth, and twentieth centuries	*NATIVE NORTH AMERICAN LITERATURE (NNAL)*
Major authors from the Renaissance to the present	*WORLD LITERATURE CRITICISM, 1500 TO THE PRESENT (WLC)* *WORLD LITERATURE CRITICISM SUPPLEMENT (WLCS)*

ISSN 0732-1864

Volume 185

Nineteenth-Century Literature Criticism

Criticism of the
Works of Novelists, Philosophers, and Other
Creative Writers Who Died between 1800
and 1899, from the First Published Critical
Appraisals to Current Evaluations

Kathy D. Darrow
Russel Whitaker
Project Editors

THOMSON
™
GALE

Detroit • New York • San Francisco • New Haven, Conn. • Waterville, Maine • London

Nineteenth-Century Literature Criticism, Vol. 185

Project Editors
Kathy Darrow and Russel Whitaker

Editorial
Dana Barnes, Thomas Burns, Elizabeth Cranston, Kristen Dorsch, Mandi Rose Hall, Jeffrey W. Hunter, Jelena O. Krstović, Michelle Lee, Thomas J. Schoenberg, Noah Schusterbauer, Catherine Shubert, Lawrence J. Trudeau

Data Capture
Frances Monroe, Gwen Tucker

Indexing Services
Factiva, Inc.

Rights and Acquisitions
Jacqueline Key, Lisa Kincade, Timothy Sisler

Composition and Electronic Capture
Amy Darga

Manufacturing
Cynde Bishop

Associate Product Manager
Marc Cormier

LIBRARY OF CONGRESS CATALOG CARD NUMBER 84-643008

ISBN-13: 978-0-7876-9856-0
ISBN-10: 0-7876-9856-3
ISSN 0732-1864

Contents

Preface vii

Acknowledgments xi

Literary Criticism Series Advisory Board xiii

Preface

Since its inception in 1981, *Nineteenth-Century Literature Criticism* (*NCLC*) has been a valuable resource for students and librarians seeking critical commentary on writers of this transitional period in world history. Designated an "Outstanding Reference Source" by the American Library Association with the publication of is first volume, *NCLC* has since been purchased by over 6,000 school, public, and university libraries. The series has covered more than 500 authors representing 38 nationalities and over 28,000 titles. No other reference source has surveyed the critical reaction to nineteenth-century authors and literature as thoroughly as *NCLC*.

Scope of the Series

NCLC is designed to introduce students and advanced readers to the authors of the nineteenth century and to the most significant interpretations of these authors' works. The great poets, novelists, short story writers, playwrights, and philosophers of this period are frequently studied in high school and college literature courses. By organizing and reprinting commentary written on these authors, *NCLC* helps students develop valuable insight into literary history, promotes a better understanding of the texts, and sparks ideas for papers and assignments. Each entry in *NCLC* presents a comprehensive survey of an author's career or an individual work of literature and provides the user with a multiplicity of interpretations and assessments. Such variety allows students to pursue their own interests; furthermore, it fosters an awareness that literature is dynamic and responsive to many different opinions.

Every fourth volume of *NCLC* is devoted to literary topics that cannot be covered under the author approach used in the rest of the series. Such topics include literary movements, prominent themes in nineteenth-century literature, literary reaction to political and historical events, significant eras in literary history, prominent literary anniversaries, and the literatures of cultures that are often overlooked by English-speaking readers.

NCLC continues the survey of criticism of world literature begun by Thomson Gale's *Contemporary Literary Criticism* (*CLC*) and *Twentieth-Century Literary Criticism* (*TCLC*).

Organization of the Book

An *NCLC* entry consists of the following elements:

- The **Author Heading** cites the name under which the author most commonly wrote, followed by birth and death dates. Also located here are any name variations under which an author wrote, including transliterated forms for authors whose native languages use nonroman alphabets. If the author wrote consistently under a pseudonym, the pseudonym will be listed in the author heading and the author's actual name given in parenthesis on the first line of the biographical and critical information. Uncertain birth or death dates are indicated by question marks. Single-work entries are preceded by a heading that consists of the most common form of the title in English translation (if applicable) and the original date of composition.

- The **Introduction** contains background information that introduces the reader to the author, work, or topic that is the subject of the entry.

- The list of **Principal Works** is ordered chronologically by date of first publication and lists the most important works by the author. The genre and publication date of each work is given. In the case of foreign authors whose works have been translated into English, the list will focus primarily on twentieth-century translations, selecting those works most commonly considered the best by critics. Unless otherwise indicated, dramas are dated by first performance, not first publication. Lists of **Representative Works** by different authors appear with topic entries.

- Reprinted **Criticism** is arranged chronologically in each entry to provide a useful perspective on changes in critical evaluation over time. The critic's name and the date of composition or publication of the critical work are given at the beginning of each piece of criticism. Unsigned criticism is preceded by the title of the source in which it appeared. All titles by the author featured in the text are printed in boldface type. Footnotes are reprinted at the end of each essay or excerpt. In the case of excerpted criticism, only those footnotes that pertain to the excerpted texts are included. Criticism in topic entries is arranged chronologically under a variety of subheadings to facilitate the study of different aspects of the topic.

- A complete **Bibliographical Citation** of the original essay or book precedes each piece of criticism.

- Critical essays are prefaced by brief **Annotations** explicating each piece.

- An annotated bibliography of **Further Reading** appears at the end of each entry and suggests resources for additional study. In some cases, significant essays for which the editors could not obtain reprint rights are included here. Boxed material following the further reading list provides references to other biographical and critical sources on the author in series published by Thomson Gale.

Indexes

Each volume of *NCLC* contains a **Cumulative Author Index** listing all authors who have appeared in a wide variety of reference sources published by Thomson Gale, including *NCLC*. A complete list of these sources is found facing the first page of the Author Index. The index also includes birth and death dates and cross references between pseudonyms and actual names.

A **Cumulative Nationality Index** lists all authors featured in *NCLC* by nationality, followed by the number of the *NCLC* volume in which their entry appears.

A **Cumulative Topic Index** lists the literary themes and topics treated in the series as well as in *Classical and Medieval Literature Criticism, Literature Criticism from 1400 to 1800, Twentieth-Century Literary Criticism,* and the *Contemporary Literary Criticism* Yearbook, which was discontinued in 1998.

An alphabetical **Title Index** accompanies each volume of *NCLC,* with the exception of the Topics volumes. Listings of titles by authors covered in the given volume are followed by the author's name and the corresponding page numbers where the titles are discussed. English translations of foreign titles and variations of titles are cross-referenced to the title under which a work was originally published. Titles of novels, dramas, nonfiction books, and poetry, short story, or essay collections are printed in italics, while individual poems, short stories, and essays are printed in roman type within quotation marks.

In response to numerous suggestions from librarians, Thomson Gale also produces an annual paperbound edition of the *NCLC* cumulative title index. This annual cumulation, which alphabetically lists all titles reviewed in the series, is available to all customers. Additional copies of this index are available upon request. Librarians and patrons will welcome this separate index; it saves shelf space, is easy to use, and is recyclable upon receipt of the next edition.

Citing *Nineteenth-Century Literature Criticism*

When citing criticism reprinted in the Literary Criticism Series, students should provide complete bibliographic information so that the cited essay can be located in the original print or electronic source. Students who quote directly from reprinted criticism may use any accepted bibliographic format, such as University of Chicago Press style or Modern Language Association style.

The examples below follow recommendations for preparing a bibliography set forth in *The Chicago Manual of Style,* 14th ed. (Chicago: The University of Chicago Press, 1993); the first example pertains to material drawn from periodicals, the second to material reprinted from books:

Franklin, J. Jeffrey. "The Victorian Discourse of Gambling: Speculations on *Middlemarch* and *The Duke's Children.*" *ELH* 61, no. 4 (winter 1994): 899-921. Reprinted in *Nineteenth-Century Literature Criticism.* Vol. 168, edited by Jessica Bomarito and Russel Whitaker, 39-51. Detroit: Thomson Gale, 2006.

Frank, Joseph. "*The Gambler*: A Study in Ethnopsychology." In *Freedom and Responsibility in Russian Literature: Essays in Honor of Robert Louis Jackson,* edited by Elizabeth Cheresh Allen and Gary Saul Morson, 69-85. Evanston, Ill.: Northwestern University Press, 1995. Reprinted in *Nineteenth-Century Literature Criticism.* Vol. 168, edited by Jessica Bomarito and Russel Whitaker, 75-84. Detroit: Thomson Gale, 2006.

The examples below follow recommendations for preparing a works cited list set forth in the *MLA Handbook for Writers of Research Papers,* 6th ed. (New York: The Modern Language Association of America, 2003); the first example pertains to material drawn from periodicals, the second to material reprinted from books:

Franklin, J. Jeffrey. "The Victorian Discourse of Gambling: Speculations on *Middlemarch* and *The Duke's Children.*" *ELH* 61.4 (Winter 1994): 899-921. Reprinted in *Nineteenth-Century Literature Criticism.* Eds. Jessica Bomarito and Russel Whitaker. Vol. 168. Detroit: Thomson Gale, 2006. 39-51.

Frank, Joseph. "*The Gambler*: A Study in Ethnopsychology." *Freedom and Responsibility in Russian Literature: Essays in Honor of Robert Louis Jackson.* Eds. Elizabeth Cheresh Allen and Gary Saul Morson. Evanston, Ill.: Northwestern University Press, 1995. 69-85. Reprinted in *Nineteenth-Century Literature Criticism.* Eds. Jessica Bomarito and Russel Whitaker. Vol. 168. Detroit: Thomson Gale, 2006. 75-84.

Suggestions are Welcome

Readers who wish to suggest new features, topics, or authors to appear in future volumes, or who have other suggestions or comments are cordially invited to call, write, or fax the Associate Product Manager:

Associate Product Manager, Literary Criticism Series
Thomson Gale
27500 Drake Road
Farmington Hills, MI 48331-3535
1-800-347-4253 (GALE)
Fax: 248-699-8054

Acknowledgments

The editors wish to thank the copyright holders of the criticism included in this volume and the permissions managers of many book and magazine publishing companies for assisting us in securing reproduction rights. Following is a list of the copyright holders who have granted us permission to reproduce material in this volume of *NCLC*. Every effort has been made to trace copyright, but if omissions have been made, please let us know.

COPYRIGHTED MATERIAL IN *NCLC*, VOLUME 185, WAS REPRODUCED FROM THE FOLLOWING PERIODICALS:

Children's Literature, v. 25, 1997. Copyright © 1997 by Hollins College. The Johns Hopkins University Press. Reproduced by permission.—*Children's Literature in Education,* v. 33, December, 2002. Copyright © 2002. Reproduced with kind permission from Springer Science and Business Media and the author.—*CLA Journal,* v. 45, September, 2001. Copyright, 2001 by The College Language Association. Used by permission of The College Language Association.—*Diacritics,* v. 27, fall, 1997. Copyright © 1997 The Johns Hopkins University Press. Reproduced by permission.—*Eighteenth-Century Studies,* v. 37, fall, 2003. Copyright © 2003 The Johns Hopkins University Press. Reproduced by permission.—*French Forum,* v. 25, January, 2000. Copyright © 2000 by French Forum, Inc. All rights reserved. Reproduced by permission of the University of Nebraska Press.—*Journal of the History of Sexuality,* v. 2, April, 1992 for "Madame Bovary and the Dissolution of Bourgeois Sexuality" by Lawrence Birken. Copyright © 1992 by the University of Texas Press. Reproduced by permission of the University of Texas Press and the author.—*MLN,* v. 94, May, 1979. Copyright © 1979 by The Johns Hopkins University Press. The Johns Hopkins University Press. Reproduced by permission.—*The Modern Language Review,* v. 93, July, 1998. Copyright © Modern Humanities Research Association 1998. Reproduced by permission of the publisher.—*Nineteenth-Century French Studies,* v. 6, spring-summer, 1978; v. 13, winter-spring, 1985. Copyright © 1978, 1985 by *Nineteenth-Century French Studies.* Both reproduced by permission.—*Novel: A Forum on Fiction,* v. 34, spring, 2001. Copyright © NOVEL Corp., 2001. Reproduced with permission.—*Orbis Litterarum,* v. 50, 1995; v. 57, 2002. Copyright © 1995, 2002 Basil Blackwell Ltd. Both reproduced by permission of Blackwell Publishers.—*Philological Quarterly,* v. 77, fall, 1998. Copyright © 1998 University of Iowa. Reproduced by permission.—*Poetics Today,* v. 23, spring, 2002. Copyright, 2002, the Porter Institute for Poetics and Semiotics, Tel Aviv University. All rights reserved. Used by permission of the publisher.—*Romance Notes,* v. 37, spring, 1997. Reproduced by permission.—*Romanic Review,* v. 71, March, 1980. Copyright © 1980 by the Trustees of Columbia University in the City of New York. Reproduced by permission.—*The South Atlantic Quarterly,* v. 55, April, 1956. Copyright, 1956 Duke University Press. Copyright renewed 1986. All rights reserved. Used by permission of the publisher.—*Studies in English Literature, 1500-1900,* v. 34, autumn, 1994. Copyright © 1994 The Johns Hopkins University Press. Reproduced by permission.—*Studies in Philology,* v. 70, January, 1973. Copyright © 1973 by the University of North Carolina Press. Used by permission.—*Studies in Romanticism,* v. 33, winter, 1994; v. 37, spring, 1998; v. 38, winter, 1999; v. 40, fall, 2001; v. 43, summer, 2004. Copyright 1994, 1998, 1999, 2001, 2004 by the Trustees of Boston University. All reproduced by permission.—*Studies in the Novel,* v. 1, spring, 1969. Copyright © 1969 by North Texas State University. Reproduced by permission.—*Symposium,* v. 32, winter, 1978; v. 44, spring, 1990; v. 54, winter, 2001. Copyright © 1978, 1990, 2001 by Helen Dwight Reid Educational Foundation. All reproduced with permission of the Helen Dwight Reid Educational Foundation, published by Heldref Publications, 1319 18th Street, NW, Washington, DC 20036-1802.

COPYRIGHTED MATERIAL IN *NCLC*, VOLUME 185, WAS REPRODUCED FROM THE FOLLOWING BOOKS:

Bowie, Malcolm. From *Madame Bovary: Provincial Manners.* Translated by Margaret Mauldon. Oxford University Press, 2004. Translation © Margaret Mauldon 2004. Introduction © Malcolm Bowie 2004. All rights reserved. Republished with permission of Oxford University Press.—DeRosa, Robin. From "A Criticism of Contradiction: Anna Leticia Barbauld and the 'Problem' of Nineteenth-Century Women's Writing," in *Women as Sites of Culture: Women's Roles in Cultural Formation from the Renaissance to the Twentieth Century.* Edited by Susan Shifrin. Ashgate Publishing Company, 2002. Copyright © 2002 Susan Shifrin. Reproduced by permission.—Favretti, Maggie. From "The Politics of Vision: Anna Barbauld's *Eighteen Hundred and Eleven,*" in *Women's Poetry in the Enlightenment: The Making of a Canon, 1730-1820.* Edited by Isobel Armstrong and Virginia Blain. Macmillan Press Ltd, 1999. Copyright © Macmillan Press Ltd 1999. Reproduced with permission of Palgrave Macmillan.—Levin, Harry. From *The Gates of Horn: A Study of Five French Re-*

Thomson Gale Literature Product Advisory Board

Anna Laetitia Barbauld
1743-1825

English poet, essayist, children's author, and editor.

The following entry presents an overview of Barbauld's life and works. For additional discussion of Barbauld's career, see *NCLC,* Volume 50.

INTRODUCTION

Anna Laetitia Barbauld was among Britain's most influential women authors of the late-eighteenth and early-nineteenth centuries. During a long and distinguished career, she published books of poetry, essays, political writings, and pedagogical lessons, in addition to editing several important anthologies of women's writing. Barbauld first achieved recognition as a poet. According to William McCarthy and Elizabeth Craft, editors of *Anna Letitia Barbauld: Selected Poetry and Prose* (2002), Barbauld's verse embodied the qualities of restraint and elevated diction characteristic of eighteenth-century British poetry while also embracing the ideals of subjectivity and passion that would later form the heart of Romanticism. Barbauld's reputation grew in the 1780s with the publication of her landmark series of educational texts, *Lessons for Children* (1787-88), works that proved influential in both England and the United States. Toward the end of her career, Barbauld also gained prominence as an editor, selecting and introducing works for the fifty-volume *British Novelists* (1810) and editing the 1816 anthology *The Female Speaker; or, Miscellaneous Pieces in Prose and Verse, Selected from the Best Writers.*

Although widely known in her lifetime, Barbauld fell into relative obscurity after her death, and she remains relatively unknown outside of academic circles. Since the 1980s and 1990s, however, Barbauld's writings have undergone an exhaustive reexamination by literature scholars, who have begun to recognize that she played a central role in British literary culture at the beginning of the Romantic age. Today most scholars acknowledge the broad scope of Barbauld's impact on the writing of her era, notably her influence on Coleridge, Wordsworth, and especially William Blake, whose *Songs of Innocence* (1789) and *Songs of Experience* (1794) clearly exhibit the influence of Barbauld's *Hymns in Prose for Children* (1781).

BIOGRAPHICAL INFORMATION

Barbauld was born Anna Laetitia Aikin on June 20, 1743, in the village of Kibworth Harcourt, Leicestershire, the oldest child of John Aikin, a prominent Protestant Dissenter and schoolmaster, and Jane Jennings Aikin. Scholar Leslie Haynsworth has described the young Aiken as a child prodigy, noting that she learned to read by the age of three and mastered Latin and Greek before she reached adolescence. During her childhood, Aikin developed an intimate bond with her younger brother, John, who also demonstrated an early interest in literature; as adults they collaborated on several book projects, and they remained close until her death in 1825.

In 1758 Aikin moved with her family to Warrington, Lancashire, where her father became a tutor at a school for Dissenters. Over the course of her fifteen years at Warrington, Aikin honed her skill as a poet, producing a substantial volume of work and earning the praise of the other residents of the school. These early poems later formed the bulk of her first book, titled simply *Poems,* which she published in 1773. The work gained immediate popularity and went through four editions over the course of the next year. Her first collaboration with her brother, *Miscellaneous Pieces in Prose,* was also published in 1773.

Aikin married Rochemont Barbauld, a clergyman and former student at Warrington, in 1774. The couple moved to Palgrave, Suffolk, where they founded a boys' school. The school proved enormously successful (according to Barbauld's niece and editor, Lucy Aiken, the school's popularity was "doubtless in great measure owing to the literary celebrity attached to the name of Mrs. Barbauld") and produced a number of prominent graduates over the course of its eleven-year existence. Although they had no children of their own, the couple adopted Barbauld's nephew, Charles, in 1777. During her years at Palgrave, Barbauld authored several well-received books for children, including her *Hymns in Prose for Children,* as well as her four-volume *Lessons for Children.*

In 1785 Barbauld and her husband decided to close the school in Palgrave and spent the next year traveling through France. Upon their return to England, Barbauld's husband became the minister of a church in Hampstead. There, Barbauld rededicated herself to writing verse, publishing several new poems in the *Monthly Magazine* over the course of the next decade.

In the early 1790s Barbauld began to play a more active role in British politics, becoming a vocal critic of religious intolerance and the institution of slavery. Her most famous works from this period include *An Address to the Opposers of the Repeal of the Corporation and Test Acts* (1790), a pamphlet attacking the coercive practices of the Anglican Church; and *Epistle to William Wilberforce, Esq., on the Rejection of the Bill for Abolishing the Slave Trade* (1791), a passionate defense of Wilberforce's efforts on behalf of the abolitionist movement. In 1792 Barbauld also began collaborating with her brother in publishing *Evenings at Home; or, The Juvenile Budget Opened* (1792-96), a six-volume series of books for children, to which she also contributed a number of stories and fables.

According to scholar Elizabeth Kraft, Barbauld's life in Hampstead was extremely unhappy, owing to the deteriorating mental health of her husband. Rochemont's behavior became increasingly abusive, and Barbauld began to fear for her safety. In 1802 she convinced her husband to move to Stoke Newington so they could live closer to her brother. Although her domestic life became more stable over the next few years, Rochemont's health continued to decline, culminating with his death by drowning in 1808. After her husband died, a distraught Barbauld immersed herself in the editing of the ambitious fifty-volume series *The British Novelists,* for which she also authored introductory essays.

In 1812 Barbauld published what many scholars consider her most important poem, *Eighteen Hundred and Eleven,* a satire criticizing the arrogance and hubris of British colonial policy. Critical reactions to the poem were so vehement and damning that Barbauld was devastated and stopped writing verse for several years. During the remaining decade of her life, she devoted most of her energies to editing; one of her most noteworthy efforts, *The Female Speaker; or, Miscellaneous Pieces in Prose and Verse, Selected from the Best Writers,* appeared in 1816. In her last years, she published occasional poems in the *Monthly Repository*; her last poems included "Poetical Thought on Death" (1822) and "Life" (1825). Barbauld died on March 9, 1825, in Stoke Newington.

MAJOR WORKS

Barbauld's debut collection of poetry, *Poems,* caused an immediate sensation and included some of her most enduring verses. Among these were "Corsica," her elegiac ode to the island's struggle for independence from France (a poem that, as scholar Mary Beth Wolicky has pointed out, inspired the establishment of a financial assistance program for Corsican exiles), and "The Mouse's Petition," described by Mary Ellen Bellanca as

a sort of spiritual meditation on the medical experiments of her family friend Joseph Priestly. The essays in her *Miscellaneous Pieces in Prose,* published in collaboration with her brother, John Aikin, also earned recognition upon publication, both for their elegant, classical prose style and for their insights into the dominant intellectual and political issues of the day. Barbauld's most important, and controversial, work remains the anti-imperialist poem *Eighteen Hundred and Eleven.* A satirical depiction of British colonial power, the poem examines the relationship between economics and individual liberty and draws a stark contrast between the promise of freedom offered by the New World and the repressive imperialist policies of England. The work elicited a fierce backlash among Britain's more patriotic reviewers.

Throughout the 1790s Barbauld published a number of important political tracts, including *An Address to the Opposers of the Repeal of the Corporation and Test Acts* and *Sins of the Government, Sins of the Nation* (1793). Barbauld's *Hymns in Prose for Children* and *Lessons for Children* exerted a lasting influence on educational practice in both England and the United States. The works were designed to help integrate religious and moral instruction with children's formative educational experiences, introducing concepts of divinity and ethical responsibility into their earliest encounters with reading. In the view of a number of scholars, the books proved revolutionary in two key respects: they employed rhyme and meter as a means of helping young readers memorize the fundamentals of English usage, and they were printed in large type, which helped facilitate reading instruction for beginners. *Hymns in Prose for Children* proved especially popular; it was reprinted thirty times between 1781 and 1849 and was translated into five languages. The hymns also struck a chord with other poets, notably William Blake, who drew from Barbauld's imagery and prose rhythms in the composition of *Songs of Innocence* and *Songs of Experience.*

CRITICAL RECEPTION

During her lifetime, Barbauld was widely recognized as one of the most prominent female authors in England. Reviewing her debut poetry collection in 1773, a commentator for the *Monthly Review* lauded the author as a "great . . . accession to the literary world," while a writer for the *Female Advocate* praised the poet in verse, concluding with the plea, "Proceed, bright maid! and may thy polish'd page / Refine the manners of a trifling age." At the height of her career, she cultivated relationships with a number of promising young poets, among them William Wordsworth and Samuel Taylor Coleridge, who deemed her a "great and excellent woman" and a writer of "great acuteness" and "propriety of mind." William Hazlitt described Barbauld as a "very pretty poetess," as well as a "neat and pointed prose writer," while Samuel Johnson famously commended her writing style in *Miscellaneous Pieces in Prose* for being similar to his own. In spite of these distinguished endorsements, however, Barbauld also had her share of detractors. Many, like Horace Walpole and John Wilson Croker, attacked her on political grounds; in his notoriously scathing review of the poem *Eighteen Hundred and Eleven,* Croker accused Barbauld of allowing political prejudice to compromise her aesthetic judgment. Charles Lamb expressed outrage at Barbauld's children's writings, lamenting that they placed a higher premium on knowledge than on the imagination. In spite of Lamb's complaint, Barbauld's *Lessons for Children* held a central place in school reading lists in both England and the United States throughout the nineteenth century.

With the rise of Romanticism among a new generation of writers, Barbauld's classical literary style began to seem antiquated, and her writings slipped into relative obscurity soon after her death. Except for Jerom Murch's 1877 study *Mrs. Barbauld and Her Contemporaries,* few writings devoted to Barbauld's career appeared until the early 1980s, when her work became the subject of a minor renaissance among literature scholars. Numerous commentators, among them John M. Anderson, Josephine McDonagh, and William Keach, have analyzed the political elements in Barbauld's poetry, paying particular attention to the critique of British economic and colonial practices that underlies her poem *Eighteen Hundred and Eleven.* William McCarthy has written extensively on Barbauld, focusing in particular on the exploration of feminist issues in her work. Along with Elizabeth Kraft, McCarthy also edited *Anna Laetitia Barbauld: Selected Poetry and Prose* (2001); in the work's introduction, McCarthy and Kraft argued that an extensive reevaluation of Barbauld's writings was long overdue. Other recent commentators on Barbauld include John Mee, who examined the unique moral authority and stylistic vigor of Barbauld's writings; Maggie Favretti, who discussed the relationship between gender and politics in the poem *Eighteen Hundred and Eleven*; and Robin DeRosa, who analyzed Barbauld's writings within the framework of British conceptions of female identity during the Enlightenment.

PRINCIPAL WORKS

Miscellaneous Pieces in Prose [as Anna Laetitia Aikin, with John Aikin] (essays) 1773
Poems [as Anna Laetitia Aikin] (poetry) 1773
Hymns in Prose for Children (prose) 1781

Lessons for Children. 4 vols. (essays) 1787-88
An Address to the Opposers of the Repeal of the Corporation and Test Acts (pamphlet) 1790
Epistle to William Wilberforce, Esq., on the Rejection of the Bill for Abolishing the Slave Trade (poem) 1791
Evenings at Home; or, The Juvenile Budget Opened. 6 vols. (prose) 1792-96
Sins of the Government, Sins of the Nation (essay) 1793
The Correspondence of Samuel Richardson [editor] (letters) 1804
The British Novelists. 50 vols. [editor] (novels) 1810
Eighteen Hundred and Eleven (poem) 1812
The Female Speaker; or, Miscellaneous Pieces in Prose and Verse, Selected from the Best Writers [editor] (poetry and prose) 1816
The Works of Anna Laetitia Barbauld. 2 vols. (poetry and prose) 1825
A Legacy for Young Ladies, Consisting of Miscellaneous Pieces, in Prose and Verse [edited by Lucy Aikin] (poetry and prose) 1826
The Poems of Anna Laetitia Barbauld (poetry) 1994

CRITICISM

Horace Walpole (letter date 29 September 1791)

SOURCE: Walpole, Horace. "To Miss Hannah More." In *The Letters of Horace Walpole,* vol. 15: 1791-1797, edited by Mrs. Paget Toynbee, pp. 69-73. Oxford: The Clarendon Press, 1905.

[*In the following excerpt, written on 29 September 1791, Walpole expresses his outrage over Anna Laetitia Barbauld's political beliefs, accusing her of factionalism and hypocrisy.*]

On that charming young woman's chapter I agree with you perfectly; not a jot on Deborah Barbauld [Anna Laetitia Barbauld]: I have neither read her verses, nor will. As I have not your aspen conscience, I cannot forgive the heart of a woman that is *party per pale* blood and tenderness, that curses our clergy and feels for negroes. Can I forget the 14th of July, when she contributed her faggot to the fires that her Presbytyrants (as Lord Melcombe called them) tried to light in every Smithfield in the island; and which, as Price and Priestley applauded in France, it would be folly to suppose they did not only wish, but meant to kindle here? Were they ignorant of the atrocious barbarities, injustice, and violation of oaths committed in France? Did Priestley not know that the clergy there had no option left but between starving and perjury? And what does he think of the poor man executed at Birmingham, who declared at his death he had been provoked by the infamous handbill[1]? I know not who wrote it. No, my good friend: Deborah may cant rhymes of compassion, but she is a hypocrite; and you shall not make me read her, nor, with all your sympathy and candour, can you esteem her. *Your* compassion for the poor blacks is genuine, sincere from your soul, most amiable; hers, a measure of faction. Her party supported the abolition, and regretted the disappointment as a blow to the good cause. I know this. Do not let your piety lead you into the weakness of respecting the bad, only because they hoist the flag of religion, while they carry a stiletto in the flag-staff.

Note

1. A handbill containing revolutionary sentiments had been distributed in Birmingham previous to the celebration of July 14, 1791. Priestley and his friends disclaimed any hand in this paper.

Charles Lamb (letter date 23 October 1802)

SOURCE: Lamb, Charles. "To Samuel Taylor Coleridge." In *The Letters of Charles Lamb,* vol. 1, edited by Alfred Ainger, pp. 237-39. London: Macmillan and Co., Limited, 1904.

[*In the following excerpt from a letter to Coleridge, dated 23 October 1802, Lamb criticizes Barbauld's books for children. Lamb complains that Barbauld's writings are directed toward a child's intellect, while ignoring the imagination.*]

I am glad the snuff and Pi-pos's books please. "Goody Two Shoes" is almost out of print. Mrs. Barbauld's stuff has banished all the old classics of the nursery; and the shopman at Newberry's hardly deigned to reach them off an old exploded corner of a shelf, when Mary asked for them. Mrs. Barbauld's and Mrs. Trimmer's nonsense lay in piles about. Knowledge insignificant and vapid as Mrs. Barbauld's books convey, it seems, must come to a child in the *shape of knowledge*; and his empty noddle must be turned with conceit of his own powers when he has learnt that a horse is an animal, and Billy is better than a horse, and such like; instead of that beautiful interest in wild tales, which made the child a man, while all the time he suspected himself to be no bigger than a child. Science has succeeded to poetry no less in the little walks of children than with men. Is there no possibility of averting this sore evil? Think what you would have been now, if, instead of being fed with tales and old wives' fables in childhood, you had been crammed with geography and natural history!

Hang them!—I mean the cursed Barbauld crew, those blights and blasts of all that is human in man and child.

John Wilson Croker (essay date June 1812)

SOURCE: Croker, John Wilson. "Review of *Eighteen Hundred and Eleven: A Poem.*" *Quarterly Review* 7, no. 14 (June 1812): 309-13.

[*In the following review, Croker levels scathing reproach at the satirical tone of Barbauld's poem. Croker asserts that Barbauld compromises her reputation as a poet by allowing political prejudice to infiltrate her work.*]

Our old acquaintance Mrs. Barbauld turned satirist! The last thing we should have expected, and, now that we have seen her satire, the last thing that we could have desired.

May we (without derogating too much from that reputation of age and gravity of which critics should be so chary) confess that we are yet young enough to have had early obligations to Mrs. Barbauld; and that it really is with no disposition to retaliate on the fair pedagogue of our former life, that on the present occasion, we have called her up to correct her exercise?

But she must excuse us if we think that she has wandered from the course in which she was respectable and useful, and miserably mistaken both her powers and her duty, in exchanging the birchen for the satiric rod, and abandoning the superintendance of the 'ovilia' of the nursery, to wage war on the 'reluctantes dracones,' statesmen, and warriors, whose misdoings have aroused her indignant muse.

We had hoped, indeed, that the empire might have been saved without the intervention of a lady-author: we even flattered ourselves that the interests of Europe and of humanity would in some degree have swayed our public councils, without the descent of (dea ex machina) Mrs. Anna Letitia Barbauld in a quarto, upon the theatre where the great European tragedy is now performing. Not such, however, is her opinion; an irresistible impulse of public duty—a confident sense of commanding talents—have induced her to dash down her shagreen spectacles and her knitting needles, and to sally forth, hand in hand with her renowned compatriot,[1] in the magnanimous resolution of saving a sinking state, by the instrumentality of a pamphlet in prose and a pamphlet in verse.

The poem, for so out of courtesy we shall call it, is entitled *Eighteen Hundred and Eleven,* we suppose, because it was written in the year 1811; but this is a mere conjecture, founded rather on our inability to assign any other reason for the name, than in any particular relation which the poem has to the events of the last year. We do not, we confess, very satisfactorily comprehend the meaning of all the verses which this fatidical spinster has drawn from her poetical distaff; but of what we do understand we very confidently assert that there is not a topic in **Eighteen Hundred and Eleven** which is not quite as applicable to 1810 or 1812, and which, in our opinion, might not, with equal taste and judgment, have been curtailed, or dilated, or transposed, or omitted, without any injustice whatever to the title of the poem, and without producing the slightest discrepancy between the frontispiece and the body of the work.

The poem opens with a piece of information, which, though delivered in phraseology somewhat quaint and obscure, we are not disposed to question, namely, that this country is still at war; but it goes on to make ample amends for the flat veracity of this commonplace, by adding a statement, which startled, as much as the former assertion satisfied, our belief. Mrs. Barbauld does not fear to assert, that the year 1811 was one of extraordinary *natural* plenty, but that, with a most perverse taste,

> Man called to Famine, nor invoked in vain.

We had indeed heard that some mad and mischievous partisans had ventured to charge the scarcity which unhappily exists, upon the political measures of government:—but what does Mrs. Barbauld mean? Does she seriously accuse mankind of wishing for a famine, and interceding for starvation? or does she believe that it is in the power of this country, of what remains of independent Europe, nay, of herself, to arrest the progress of war, and, careless of what Buonaparte or his millions may be about, to beckon back peace and plenty, and to diffuse happiness over the reviving world?

But let us select a specimen of her poetry, which shall be also one of her veracity, prophecy, and patriotism. It is the description of the fallen state of this poor realm.

> Thy baseless wealth dissolves in air away,
> Like mists that melt before the morning ray;
> No more in crowded mart or busy street,
> Friends meeting friends with cheerful hurry greet.
>
> * * *
>
> Yes, thou must droop; thy Midas dream is o'er,
> The golden tide of commerce leaves thy shore,
> Leaves thee to prove th' alternate ills that haunt
> Enfeebling luxury and ghastly want.
>
> —p. 5 [*Eighteen Hundred and Eleven*
> (London: Johnson and Co., 1812)]

We do not know where Mrs. Anna Letitia now resides, though we can venture to assert that it is not on Parnassus: it must, however, be in some equally unfrequented, though less classical region; for the description just quoted is no more like the scene that is really before *our* eyes, than Mrs. Barbauld's satire is like her **Lessons for Children,** or her **Hymns in Prose.**

England, in her prophetic vision, is undone; soon, it seems,

> [. . .] to be only known
> By the gray ruin and the mouldering stone.

while America is to go on increasing and improving in arts, in arms, and even, if that be possible, in virtue! Young Americans will cross the Atlantic to visit the sacred ruins of England, just as our young noblemen go to Greece.

> Then the ingenuous youth, whom fancy fires
> With pictured glories of illustrious sires,
> With duteous zeal their pilgrimage shall take,
> From the blue mountains or Ontario's lake
>
> —p. 10

and pay sentimental visits to Cambridge and Stratford-upon-Avon. These 'ingenuous' Americans are also to come to London, which they are to find in ruins: however, being of bold and aspiring dispositions,

> They of some broken turret, mined by time,
> The broken stair with perilous step shall climb,
> Thence stretch their view the wide horizon round,
> By scatter'd hamlets trace its ancient bound,
> And *choked* no more with fleets, *fair* Thames survey
> Through reeds and sedge pursue his idle way.

This is a sad prospect! but while all our modern edifices are to be in such a lamentable state of dilapidation, Time is to proceed with so cautious and discriminating a step, that Melrose Abbey, which is now pretty well in ruins, is not to grow a bit older, but to continue a beautiful ruin still; this supernatural longevity is conferred upon it in honour of Mr. Scott.

But let not Mr. Scott be too proud of a distinction which he possesses in a very humble degree, compared with him, to whom

> [. . .] belong
> *The* Roman virtue and the Tuscan song.

Which of the virtues, *the . . .* Roman virtue is, Mrs. Barbauld does not condescend to inform us, nor does our acquaintance with Mr. Roscoe enable us to guess any virtue for which he is more particularly famous: so great, however, is to be the enthusiastic reverence which the American youth are to feel for him, that, after visiting the scenes which are to remind them of General Moore, Mr. Clarkson, Lord Chatham, Doctor Davy, Mr. Garrick, and Lord Nelson, they are to pay a visit,

> Where Roscoe, to whose patriot breast belong
> The Roman virtue and the Tuscan song,
> Led Ceres to the black and barren moor,
> Where Ceres never gained a wreath before—

Or, in other words, (as the note kindly informs us,) to Mr. Roscoe's farm in Derbyshire, where, less we apprehend, by the Roman virtue and the Tuscan song, than by the homely process of drainage and manuring, he has brought some hundred acres of Chatmoss into cultivation. O the unequal dispensations of this poetical providence! Chatham and Nelson empty names! Oxford and Cambridge in ruins! London a desert, and the Thames a sedgy brook! while Mr. Roscoe's barns and piggeries are in excellent repair, and objects not only of curiosity but even of reverence and enthusiasm.

Our readers will be curious to know how these prodigies are to be operated: there is, it seems, a mysterious Spirit or Genius who is to do all this, and a great deal more, as we shall presently see; but who or what he is, or whence he comes, does not very clearly appear, even from the following description:

> There walks a Spirit o'er the peopled earth,
> Secret his progress is, unknown his birth,
> Moody and viewless as the changing wind,
> No force arrests his foot, no chains can bind.

—p. 17

This extraordinary personage is prodigiously wise and potent, but withal a little fickle, and somewhat, we think, for so wise a being, unjust and partial. He has hitherto resided in this country, and chiefly in London; Mrs. Barbauld, however, foresees that he is beginning to be tired of us, and is preparing to go out of town: on his departure that desolation is to take place in reality, which is so often metaphorically ascribed to the secession of some great leader of the ton.

But the same Genius has far more extensive powers even than these;—he 'changes nature,' he 'absorbs the Nile,' (we had not heard of the Nile's being absorbed,) and he has of late taken it into his head to travel 'northward,' among the 'Celtic nations,' with a mercantile venture of Turkey carpets, of which speculation the immediate effects are, that the 'vale of Arno' and the 'coast of Baia' are not near so pleasant as the dykes of Batavia; that the Pontine marshes have *lately* become extremely unwholesome, and that Venice is no longer, as she was a short time since, the mistress of the sea. (p. 20, 21.)

This wonderful person is also so condescending as to assist us in divers little offices, in which we are hardly aware of his interference; he is the real author of Dryden's Virgil and Middleton's Cicero, (p. 22,) he dresses 'light forms' in 'transparent muslins,' he 'tutors' young ladies 'to swell the artful note,' and he builds verandas to our balconies; he is, besides, an eminent nursery man, and particularly remarkable for 'acacias' and 'cedars,' and the 'chrystal walls' of his hothouses produce the best grapes and pines about London; (p. 23;) in short, there is nothing good, bad, or indifferent that this Genius does not do: but, alas! good upon England he intends no longer to confer; our muslins, pines, acacias, and even our forte-pianos are in jeopardy;

> For fairest flowers expand but to decay,
> The worm is in thy core, thy glories fade away;
> Arts, arms, and wealth destroy the fruits they bring,
> Commerce, like beauty, knows no second spring;
> Crime walks the streets, fraud earns her unblest bread,
> O'er want and woe thy gorgeous robe is spread.

—p. 24

Upon this melancholy night, however, a bright day dawns, and all the little sense with which Mrs. Barbauld set out, now dissolves away in blissful visions of American glory. This Genius of her's which 'walks the *peopled* earth,' 'viewless and secret,' suddenly *appears* walking on the summit of Chimberaço, (which never was nor can be *peopled,*) displays his '*viewless*' form on the Andes, and '*secretly*' arouses, by loud exclamations, all the nations of the western continent.

> Ardent the Genius fans the noble strife,
> And pours through feeble souls a higher life;
> Shouts to the mingled tribes from sea to sea,
> And *swears*—Thy world, Columbus, shall be free.

—p. 25

And with this oath concludes **Eighteen Hundred and Eleven,** upon which we have already wasted too much time. One word, however, we must seriously add. Mrs. Barbauld's former works have been of some utility; her **Lessons for Children,** her **Hymns in Prose,** her **Selections from the Spectator,** et id genus omne, though they display not much of either taste or talents, are yet something better than harmless: but we must take the liberty of warning her to desist from satire, which indeed is satire on herself alone; and of entreating, with great earnestness, that she will not, for the sake of this ungrateful generation, put herself to the trouble of writing any more party pamphlets in verse. We also assure her, that we should not by any means impute it to want of taste or patriotism on her part, if, for her own country, her fears were less confident, and for America her hopes less ardent; and if she would leave both the victims and the heroes of her political prejudices to the respective judgment which the impartiality of posterity will not fail to pronounce.

Note

1. See Art. II [*Quarterly Review* 7, no. 9 (March and June 1812)].

William Hazlitt (essay date 1818)

SOURCE: Hazlitt, William. "On the Living Poets." In *Lectures on the English Poets and the English Comic Writers,* edited by William Carew Hazlitt, pp. 190-222. London: George Bell and Sons, 1906.

[*In the following excerpt, originally delivered as a lecture and published in 1818 in* Lectures on the English Poets: Delivered at the Surrey Institution, *Hazlitt commends both the poetry and prose writings of Barbauld.*]

The first poetess I can recollect is Mrs. Barbauld, with whose works I became acquainted before those of any other author, male or female, when I was learning to spell words of one syllable in her story-books for children. I became acquainted with her poetical works long after in Enfield's *Speaker,* and remember being much divided in my opinion at that time between her **"Ode to Spring"** and Collins's "Ode to Evening." I wish I could repay my childish debt of gratitude in terms of appropriate praise. She is a very pretty poetess; and, to my fancy, strews the flowers of poetry most agreeably round the borders of religious controversy. She is a neat and pointed prose-writer. Her **"Thoughts on the Inconsistency of Human Expectations,"** is one of the most ingenious and sensible essays in the language.

Maria Edgeworth (letter date 15 March 1825)

SOURCE: Edgeworth, Maria. "To Mrs. Ruxton." In *The Life and Letters of Maria Edgeworth, Volume 2,* edited by Augustus J. C. Hare, p. 478. Boston: Houghton, Mifflin and Company, 1895.

[*In the following letter, written just days after Barbauld's death in March of 1825, Edgeworth laments the loss of a dear friend and a "great writer," praising the "elegance and strength" of Barbauld's style.*]

You have probably seen in the papers the death of our admirable friend Mrs. Barbauld. I have copied for you her last letter to me and some beautiful lines written in her eightieth year. There is a melancholy elegance and force of thought in both. Elegance and strength—qualities rarely uniting without injury to each other—combine most perfectly in her style, and this rare combination, added to their classical purity, form, perhaps, the distinguishing characteristics of her writings. England has lost a great writer, and we a most sincere friend.

Jerom Murch (essay date 1876)

SOURCE: Murch, Jerom. "Part II." In *Mrs. Barbauld and Her Contemporaries: Sketches of Some Eminent Literary and Scientific Englishwomen,* pp. 57-100. London: Longmans, Green and Co., 1876.

[*In the following excerpts, Murch examines the political issues at the heart of Barbauld's controversial poem* Eighteen Hundred and Eleven. *Murch argues that Barbauld's art deserves to be criticized on its own merits, not on the basis of her political convictions.*]

It has been stated with reference to her last important poem, ***Eighteen Hundred and Eleven,*** that her mind had not regained its usual healthy tone. There is no doubt that she long suffered severely, but the poem should be judged on its own merits, and few persons would admit that it deserved the bitter criticism with which it was assailed. Its thesis has been described to be this "that Civilisation had always changed her seat from age to age, and that the time was now come at which she would leave Britain, worn out by perpetual war, and take refuge on the shores of the New World."[1] To understand the feeling on both sides, which was stronger than any that is common even in these days, we must remember that Mrs. Barbauld belonged to the party who admired the American Revolution and deprecated the war with France, while the other party took, on each subject, the precisely opposite side. I do not here attempt to show for a moment which were right; my subject is not the truth or error of Mrs. Barbauld's political opinions but the value of her contributions to English Literature. Still, even with reference to this last point it may be allowable to offer two remarks: First: the Poetess certainly committed an error of judgment in founding on a few military reverses predictions of the permanent decline of the country, especially at the time when the tide of Napoleon's success had already begun to ebb, and when it was evident that England possessed in Wellington a General of most brilliant promise. Secondly: no error of the kind, however, should have so blinded the critics of the day as to lead them to charge Mrs. Barbauld with a want of patriotism, because some of the most impassioned parts of her poem are those which breathe the most ardent love of her native land. From her time to that of Lord Eldon and from Lord Eldon's to the present day, what prophecy has been more common with partizans on all sides than the ruin of the country if their views were not adopted? . . .

Mrs. Barbauld lived fourteen years after the publication of this poem. Her powers were still vigorous; her fancy retained all its brightness, but the harp was hung upon the willows. She felt so deeply the misconstruction of angry critics that she wrote nothing more of much importance, though her kindness and gentleness were more conspicuous than ever. Occasionally she addressed a few beautiful lines to some affectionate friend, or added another exquisite hymn to those in which her deep earnest piety had been expressed from time to time. To dwell upon what she felt and did in this respect would not be desirable; the higher parts of her pure and noble character need not be eulogised on the present occasion. Still, however, is the thought of how she rose above the bitterest trials of our mortal lot a power in many minds; still is the echo of the song of the aged pilgrim going downward to the grave in many hearts:—

> We tread the path our Master trod,
>   We bear the cross he bore,
> And every thorn that wounds our feet,
>   His temples pierced before.
> Our powers are oft dissolved away
>   In ecstasies of love,

> And while our bodies wander here,
> Our souls are fix'd above.

Note

1. *Theological Review* No. xlvi., p. 404.

Porter Williams Jr. (essay date 1980)

SOURCE: Williams, Porter, Jr. "The Influence of Mrs. Barbauld's *Hymns in Prose for Children* upon Blake's *Songs of Innocence and Experience*." In *A Fair Day in the Affections: Literary Essays in Honor of Robert B. White, Jr.*, edited by Jack D. Durant and M. Thomas Hester, pp. 131-46. Raleigh, N.C.: The Winston Press, 1980.

[*In the following essay, Williams discusses the influence of Barbauld's hymns on both the poems and the illustrations in Blake's* Songs of Innocence and Experience.]

A considerable library of material discusses the literary, philosophical, religious, and artistic influences upon Blake's *Songs of Innocence and of Experience,* yet none of these influences except the Bible is important enough to be called a dominant one. The very range of demonstrable influences is so broad that there is never any sign of Blake's individual voice being absorbed, for example, by the conventions of Elizabethan lyrics, contemporary pastoral modes, Swedenborgian symbolism, or even the rich borrowings from the Scriptures. Nevertheless, such influences are of considerable interest and are a part of the richness of the *Songs.* Similarly, the relatively minor but demonstrable influence of Mrs. Barbauld's once popular book ***Hymns in Prose for Children*** (1781) makes its quiet contribution to the effect of the whole and is worthy of study.

Blake was obviously aware of "the dissenting tradition of children's literature from Bunyan through Watts to Mrs. Barbauld"[1] and probably first conceived of *Songs of Innocence* (1789) as a children's book just as his first version of *The Gates of Paradise* (1793) bore the title-page heading, *For Children.* Critical attention is most often given to the influence in the Songs of Isaac Watts' *Divine and Moral Songs for Children* (1720), though, as Kathleen Raine observes, the influence of the moralizing Dr. Watts "was a negative one" as Blake "managed . . . to differ with Watts at every point."[2] The influence of Mrs. Anna Laetitia Barbauld's ***Hymns in Prose for Children*** (1781) is often mentioned but usually with caution, as if her gentle moralizing must also have triggered Blake's antagonism. In actuality her prose ***Hymns*** [*Hymns in Prose for Children*] still make pleasant reading, and there is only a slight indication that Blake wished to satirize some of them. Neverthe-

less the ***Hymns*** continue to suffer from the "bad press" given Mrs. Barbauld by the Romantic poets, especially Coleridge. Professor Pinto more recently characterized her as "a talented, pious prig" and her ***Hymns*** as "conventional in sentiment" and "written in a pseudo-biblical style with many echoes of the Authorized Version of the Psalms and other parts of the Bible."[3]

It is not the aim of the present discussion to assert that the ***Hymns*** are the achievement of neglected genius or that their influence upon Blake was major. I do hope to show, however, that Blake drew from them freely not only for isolated images and phrases but also for some of his important thematic structure. The very fact that Mrs. Barbauld's aims were modest, the translation of complex Biblical sentiments into a simple language pleasing and interesting to children, was of particular use to Blake. Blake needed neither a Watts nor a Barbauld to expound the Scriptures or to suggest visions to him, but he must have profited from observing the degree of success or failure of writers attempting to communicate with young children. Blake's *Songs,* both poems and illustrations, are surprisingly consistent in maintaining on one level a childlike simplicity of language even when expressing upon other levels richly subtle and mature insights. The "Introduction" to *Innocence* is quite sincere in presenting "a book that all may read" and that "Every child may joy to hear" (E. [*The Poetry and Prose of William Blake*] 7),[4] though Blake also meant it when he told Dr. Trusler, "That which can be made Explicit to the Idiot is not worth my care" (E. 676). But on the whole, symbolic complexities lead back to a few clear major themes.

Most writers who try to interpret the Scriptures for children are aware of the need to engage the child's interest with a simple and pleasing style and to convey some sense of the profound richness of Christian doctrine without adopting the patronizing tone of adult admonition. Even Dr. Watts, for example, offered the following challenge on his title page: "A slight specimen of *Moral Songs,* such as I wish some happy and condescending genius would undertake for the use of children, and perform much better. . . . Here the language and measures should be easy, and flowing with cheerfulness, with or without the solemnities of religion . . . that children might find delight and profit together."[5] Mrs. Barbauld accepted this specific challenge. In her Preface to the ***Hymns*** she speaks of the number of children's books designed to "unfold the system, and give a summary of the doctrines of religion," but only Watts' *Hymns* and her own book, she feels, are concerned with assisting children in "devotion." Blake must have scoffed at her idea that poetry should not be "lowered to the capacities of children," but he must have rejoiced in her belief that if a child is "to feel the full force of the idea of God," he must be encouraged to connect religion "with a variety of sensible objects; with all that he sees, all he hears, all that affects his young mind with wonder or delight. . . . For he who has early been accustomed to see the Creator in the visible appearance of all around him, to feel his continual presence, and lean upon his daily protection . . . has made large advances toward that habitual piety, without which religion can scarcely regulate the conduct, and will never warm the heart" (pp. iii-vii).[6] The most pleasing quality in the *Hymns,* even if they occasionally moralize or preach, is that to a large degree they fulfill the promise to delight the senses with a lively variety of images describing the natural world.

In several ways Mrs. Barbauld's Preface anticipates the qualities we admire in Blake's *Songs.* Blake would not have approved of Mrs. Barbauld's desire to "regulate the conduct" and to "refine away" religious "improprieties" by means of the "corrector reason" (p. vii), but her desire to bring before the child whatever delights the senses and warms the heart is at one with Blake's plan to write with his "rural pen" "happy songs / Every child may joy to hear." Above all, Mrs. Barbauld's major concern, the child's capacity to feel God's "continual presence, and lean upon his daily protection" (p. vii), is surely the dominant theme of *Songs of Innocence.* E. D. Hirsch, Jr., anticipates this aspect of my thesis when he explains that beyond borrowing isolated images, Blake gained from Mrs. Barbauld's book the "fundamental conception" of a work asserting the idea of God's personal spiritual guardianship, shown most often in the *Hymns* through "the relationship between Parent and Child" and in the *Songs* through a similar but visionary sense of "Man's sacramental re-enactment of Christ's care for man."[7] A number of parallels to emphasize these similarities of images and themes must serve to represent the most convincing kind of evidence of Mrs. Barbauld's influence upon Blake.[8]

The first two Hymns, after an opening call to praise God, present a lively catalogue of pastoral images illustrating the bounty of creation. Mrs. Barbauld describes the sun and moon, animals great and small, singing birds, spring fields, buds upon the trees, "the crimson blossoms of the peach and the nectarine," young goslings "running upon the green," butterflies, hens and lambs, warblings and bleatings, and above all the playful happiness of creatures "glad to be alive" (p. 9). The third Hymn introduces the dominant theme of parenthood, showing through a series of analogies the guardianship of shepherds over sheep, parents over children, and God, as the Good Shepherd, over all. The opening is a free rendering of the Twenty-Third Psalm:

> Behold the Shepherd of the flock, he taketh care for his sheep, he leadeth them among clear brooks, he guideth them to fresh pasture. . . .

> But who is the shepherd's shepherd? who taketh care for him? who guideth him in the path he should go? . . .

God is the shepherd's shepherd. He is the Shepherd over all . . . the whole earth is his fold: we are all his flock. . . .

> (pp. 12-14)

Blake opens *Songs of Innocence* with this same important theme. The Piper of the "Introduction," ultimately the prophet or bard of all the *Songs,* is visualized on the Frontispiece as a shepherd standing before a flock of sheep.[9] The poem that usually follows, "The Shepherd," is similar to the opening of Mrs. Barbauld's third Hymn and is also based upon the Twenty-Third Psalm:

> How sweet is the Shepherds sweet lot,
> From the morn to the evening he strays:
> He shall follow his sheep all the day
> And his tongue shall be filled with praise.

> (E.7)

With the same simplicity of diction, Blake far more concisely transmits Mrs. Barbauld's message of guardianship. His shepherd brings peace to his flock, but God as the shepherd's shepherd is also present, symbolized in the reference to "the lambs innocent call." Blake is thus making use of the traditional New Testament identification of both lambs and shepherds with Christ, either as the Lamb of God or as the Good Shepherd.

Mrs. Barbauld's method is discursive, and here she chooses to use a catechistic or antiphonal progression of ideas. As her Preface states, the *Hymns* are in "measured prose," often "composed in alternate parts" intended for recitation so as to "give them something of the spirit of social worship" (p. v). Thus in the important third Hymn the antiphonal pattern leads from the description of the shepherd to the dominant theme of parenthood:

> The mother loveth her little child; she bringeth it up on her knees . . . she feedeth its mind with knowledge: if it is sick, she nurseth it with tender love; she watcheth over it when asleep. . . .

> But who is the parent of the mother? who nourisheth her with good things. . . .

> God is the parent of the mother; he is the parent of all. . . .

> (pp. 14-16)

The pattern modulates in **"Hymn IV"** into descriptions of things of beauty, strength, and glory—the "fully blown rose," the roaring lion, and the sun—and for each, God is more beautiful, stronger, or more glorious. **"Hymn V"** returns to the theme of protection. At night mothers shelter their sleeping children, and God in turn protects all, for his "is an eye that never sleepeth" (p. 30). Ultimately the child's universe is surveyed, its beauties and terrors, nature and society, the whole forming a simplified great chain of being with God watching over all. Doubtless the children at Mrs. Barbauld's school at Palgrave enjoyed a happier and more sheltered life than Blake's London waifs, yet enough harsh experience enters the *Hymns* to remind any young reader that he is a "Child of mortality" (p. 77). Just as in Blake's *Songs,* there are in the *Hymns* terrors of the dark forest, wild beasts, sickness, evil men, killing frosts, thorns, worms, suffering, grief, and "DEATH . . . the spoiler . . . among the works of God" (p. 82). The beautiful rose, the stately tree, the sporting insects, and "man in the pride of his strength" must all die. "Therefore do I weep" (pp. 78-82). The progression is still antiphonal, although **"Hymn X"** is almost entirely concerned with the universality of death.

Not until these harsh truths are driven home in what may be called her Hymn of Experience, does Mrs. Barbauld fully develop her theme of renewal. **"Hymn XI,"** in the time-honored tradition of the pastoral elegy, turns first to the idea of cyclic renewal in nature. Each day the sun returns; each year flowers spring forth afresh and the insect "shrouded in the silken cone" bursts from "its tomb" (pp. 83-85). "Thus shall it be with thee, O man! and so shall thy life be renewed" (p. 86). Mrs. Barbauld carefully emphasizes the transition from the idea of naturalistic renewal to that of Christian rebirth. Drawing from the rich imagery of Ezekiel and Revelation, she describes the descent of Jesus on "a fiery cloud" come to open the tomb and "bid the dead awake." He "hath conquered death:—child of immortality! mourn no longer" (pp. 87-89). **"Hymn XII"** completes the transition from natural cycles. Though "the rose is sweet . . . it is surrounded with thorns." The fragrant lily "springeth up amongst the brambles," the pleasant spring "is soon past," and all earthly life "is quickly swallowed up in death." But "There is a land, where the roses are without thorns, where the flowers are not mixed with brambles" (pp. 89-91). Dominant from here on are images from the closing chapters of Revelation, though just as Blake was to do in the *Songs,* Mrs. Barbauld carefully selects the pastoral imagery while avoiding the architectural complexities of the New Jerusalem. Her Edenic landscape in Eternity is dominated by the Tree of Life, holy rivers, unfading flowers, and peaceful animals. All shall dwell in peace with Jesus, "who is gone before" (pp. 91-97).

Most of these images and patterns are found in Blake's *Songs.* It must be conceded that much of this imagery, whether pastoral or scriptural, is quite familiar and available to all. But the fact that Blake so often echoes Mrs. Barbauld's details and arrangements stands as a kind of statistical evidence that her influence, however minor, was a persistent one throughout the *Songs.* Professor Pinto's observation can also be readily conceded, that Blake "transmuted Mrs. Barbauld's tinsel into the gold of authentic poetry."[10]

It should also be pointed out that Blake even made use of the rhetorical structure Mrs. Barbauld emphasized in her Preface, the composing of her *Hymns* "in alternate parts" for recitation. Many of Blake's *Songs* adopt this question-answer device or dramatize a situation with direct address. In "The Lamb," for example, the child asks and answers a series of questions: "Little Lamb who made thee / Dost thou know who made thee . . . / Little Lamb I'll tell thee! / He is called by thy name" (E. 8-9). Similarly, in the "Introduction" to *Innocence* the child makes a series of demands that are all fulfilled, from the piping of "a song about a Lamb" to the composition of a book of songs "that all may read" (E. 7). Contrasting voices come to opposite conclusions about love in "The Clod & the Pebble" (E. 19), and the startled speaker in "The Sick Rose" uses direct address: "O Rose thou art sick" (E. 23).

It is of course the themes and images that provide the most convincing evidence of Mrs. Barbauld's influence, especially when they occur in clusters. Mrs. Barbauld's linking of protective shepherds with parents and with God as "the shepherd's shepherd" or "the parent of all," described in **"Hymn III"** and elsewhere, is found throughout Blake's *Songs,* including of course many of the illustrations. In a sense, as the "Introduction" and the title-page to *Songs of Innocence* suggest, the whole volume is a gift to be read by protective and loving parents to their children.

Both of Blake's "Holy Thursday" poems, as David Erdman shows, are unusually rich in echoing clusters of images from the *Hymns.* In **"Hymn XII"** Mrs. Barbauld describes Heaven as follows: "Myriads of happy spirits are there, and surround the throne of God with a perpetual hymn. The angels with their golden harps sing praises continually, and the cherubim fly on wings of fire!" (p. 92). "Holy Thursday" of *Innocence* similarly describes the charity children in St. Paul's as "multitudes of lambs" raising "to heaven the voice of song" until it thunders among "the seats of heaven" (E. 13). Even the images of "angels" and of fiery "cherubim" that Mrs. Barbauld took from Ezekiel (10:1 ff.) are to be found in Blake's manuscript draft of the poem in *An Island in the Moon* (1784). Blake at one stage compared his singing children to "Cherubim & Seraphim" and before that to "angels," as if he had used and then rejected two more of Mrs. Barbauld's images.[11] Even so, the closing line of the poem does introduce the "angel" comparison through the warning echo from Hebrews not to "drive an angel from your door" (13:2). The angry Blake of "Holy Thursday" of *Experience* also draws from **"Hymn XII"** when he describes England as "a land of poverty" for the children, as a place where "their sun does never shine," "their fields are bleak & bare," "their ways are fill'd with thorns" and where "eternal winter" reigns (E. 19-20). Mrs. Barbauld writes that on earth the rose "is surrounded with thorns" and the lily growing "amongst the brambles." But "There is a land, where the roses are without thorns, where the flowers are not mixed with brambles. In that land, there is eternal spring, and light without any cloud" (pp. 89-91). Blake thus follows Mrs. Barbauld's contrast between what is and what should be in his last two verses. But the turning of Mrs. Barbauld's "eternal spring" into "eternal winter," if this is satire, is really an attack upon those who would rejoice in the children's singing while ignoring their suffering.

The nearest approach to any thematic satire of Mrs. Barbauld is found in the paired songs "The Little Boy Lost" and "The Little Boy Found" (E. 11). The terrified child seeking his father in "the lonely fen" and following the "wand'ring light" of a will-o'-the-wisp has been misled, as Erdman interprets it, by an "impersonal God." The episode might well imply some mockery of **"Hymn VI"** "in which the 'Child of Reason' fails to recognize the voice of God in a forest breeze" (pp. 36-38).[12] It is important to add that in the same hymn Mrs. Barbauld's child also fails to detect God's presence in the frightening thunderstorm. Mrs. Barbauld writes, "Was there nothing bright and terrible, but the lightning? . . . God was in the storm. . . . His terrors were abroad" (pp. 41-42). Blake's illustration of the deceiving "wand'ring light" (Plate 13), a vertical white streak and explosive flame, makes a surprisingly accurate representation of Mrs. Barbauld's bright and terrible "thunderbolt." Likewise, the second drawing, for "The Little Boy Found," showing a personal God leading the child by the hand, may well be intended as a "correction" of Mrs. Barbauld's description of a temporarily frightening or Urizenic God. Whether or not Blake is registering disapproval of Mrs. Barbauld at this point, he does seem to have had **"Hymn VI"** in mind. Not until *Songs of Experience,* however, will Blake launch with unmistakable bitterness his attack upon the concept of a terrifying and cruel God.

Many of Blake's poems and illustrations seem to have been most strongly influenced by Mrs. Barbauld's feel for the lively colors and sounds of nature—the brilliance of flowers, merry voices, seasonal changes, and the adjustments in human activities as day gives way to night. Hymns **"II"** and **"V,"** especially, offer a veritable catalogue of Blakean images. **"Hymn II"** describes the spring fields, the sport of children "upon the new grass," "crimson blossoms," playful lambs, and the sense of joyful thanksgiving "on every hill, and in every green field" (pp. 5-12). **"Hymn V"** describes the coming of night that brings quiet and rest but also its dangers: "The glorious sun is set in the west; the night-dews fall; and the air . . . becomes cool." "Darkness is spread over the skies," the sheep rest, "their loud bleating . . . no more heard amongst the hills," and birds seek their nests. "There is no sound of a number of voices, or of children at play." Mothers watch over sleeping children,

and God watches over all (pp. 25-35). Similarly Blake in "Laughing Song" describes "the voice of joy" in "the green woods" and meadows, while "Nurse's Song," "The Echoing Green," and "Night" first describe the play and laughter of children in the green world and then the descent of the sun, the coming of darkness, the quieting of merry sounds, the return to parental protection, the presence of danger, and the need for spiritual guardianship (E. 8, 11, 13-15). With Blake, however, a single poem, such as "Night," may move in a few compact verses from joyful innocence, to danger or slaughter, and on to a vision of Eternity (E. 13-14).

Except for **"Hymn X"** on death, Mrs. Barbauld does not dwell at length upon the suffering of children although there is a rich array of images that anticipate some of the human and natural harshness found in *Songs of Experience.* Several passages in the **Hymns** speak of sickness and the destructive cold of winter that withers trees and flowers (pp. 15, 73). Thorns and brambles are often emphasized (pp. 89-90). **"Hymn IV"** has a vivid description of the lion rising from his lair to strike terror with his roaring: "the cattle of the field fly, and the wild beasts of the desert hide themselves, for he is very terrible" (pp. 21-22). In the world of man, kings can be "evil" and fearful (pp. 17, 61), and for some there is slavery. The Negro woman "pining in captivity" weeps over her "sick child," and for all there are "dark places" that God must watch (pp. 60, 24). Finally, God himself can be wrathful. "His anger is terrible; he could make us die in a moment" (p. 22).

Many of Blake's poems and illustrations, especially of *Experience,* similarly emphasize wintry harshness and cruel thorns, most often to symbolize human and social evils. Out of Mrs. Barbauld's description of those made "black with the hot sun" and the slave with the sick child (pp. 58-60) Blake has constructed a brilliantly ironic poem of *Innocence* about the capacity to love, "The Little Black Boy" (E. 9). The poem "Night" with its wolves and tigers that "howl for prey" and "rush dreadful" (E. 13-14) recalls Mrs. Barbauld's roaring lion and wild beasts, and even "The Tyger" is a reminder of Mrs. Barbauld's surprisingly harsh images of God's terrors, terrors that are felt as quite real even if Blake is partly satirizing them as the "mind-forg'd" mysteries of Urizen.

Some further emphasis should be placed upon Mrs. Barbauld's flower imagery, especially her fondness for "crimson blossoms" (pp. 6, 70). Blake's many symbolic flower poems and bright flame-flower designs come to mind here, including the illustrations for "The Blossom," "Infant Joy," and "The Divine Image." If for Mrs. Barbauld "every painted flower hath a lesson written on its leaves" (p. 75), for Blake, "Each herb & each tree / Mountain hill Earth & Sea / Cloud Meteor & Star / Are Men Seen Afar" (E. 683). Blake's flame-flowers always contain human or angelic figures and usually symbolize the conception of new life, unless thorns appear to warn of sexual frustration or cruelty.

"The Sick Rose" may be described as the death of a flame-flower. The "crimson joy" of the rose is destroyed by the "dark secret love" of the "invisible worm" who comes in "the howling storm" (E. 23, Plate 39). The illustration shows the literal death of the rose, attacked by worm and caterpillar, and reveals the symbolic implications through the grieving male and female figures draped on the thorny branches. Professor Pinto demonstrates that a cluster of images from the *Hymns* probably suggested the literal level of the poem.[13] "Hymn IX" speaks of the rose drawing "its crimson from the dark brown earth" and of the lily in "shining white" (p. 70). "Hymn X" describes a rose "dying upon its stalk," its "grace," "form" and "loveliness" destroyed. Finally, Blake's "howling storm" and "invisible worm" can be found in Mrs. Barbauld's next paragraph, describing "a stately tree . . . nipt by the east wind" and eaten by the worm that "had made its way into the trunk" until "the heart thereof was decayed" and it "fell to the ground" (pp. 77-79). The flower-and-worm image is universal, but the cluster of vivid details does suggest the influence of the *Hymns*.[14]

Other echoes of Mrs. Barbauld's flower imagery are indicated by the pairing of the rose and "shining white lily," first in the sentence just quoted (p. 70) and again in "Hymn XII" describing the sweet rose "surrounded with thorns" and fragrant lily springing up "amongst the brambles" (pp. 89-90). Similarly Blake in "My Pretty Rose Tree" and "The Lilly," both on Plate 43, describes a jealous Rose-tree greeting her lover with "thorns," a selfishly modest rose who "puts forth a thorn," and a "Lilly white" who shall delight in love because neither "a thorn nor a threat" shall "stain her beauty bright" (E. 25). The two poems exploit Mrs. Barbauld's distinction between the rose responsible for its thorns and the lily innocent of any taint in spite of nearby brambles. Both writers are describing the beauty and hardship of earthly life, but Blake's flowers characteristically symbolize human psychology, and at least one plant grows best in the Human Brain ("The Human Abstract," E. 27).[15]

A final poem, "To Tirzah," should be mentioned. As it is a late addition to the *Songs,* around 1805, and subtly related to the important works of the *Jerusalem* period, it seems unlikely that its composition could have been directly influenced by the *Hymns*. Yet "To Tirzah" is remarkably in tune with Mrs. Barbauld's simplified rendering of the apocalyptic message of the Scriptures. Her three closing *Hymns* describe the need to look beyond an imperfect earth ruled by death and to turn to the promise of immortality through Jesus who "hath conquered death" (pp. 89 ff.). Similarly Blake writes,

Whate'er is Born of Mortal Birth,
Must be consumed with the Earth
To rise from Generation free;
Then what have I to do with thee?

* * *

The Death of Jesus set me free,
Then what have I to do with thee?

(E. 30)

Parts of the poem concern Blake's radical association of the Creation with the Fall, but the lines quoted show Blake remarkably in accord with the Biblical orthodoxies followed by Mrs. Barbauld to bring the *Hymns* to a close on a note of triumph. Blake's illustration reinforces the message (Plate 52). It shows mankind's fallen body about to receive the water of eternal life from a robed figure representing God and Jesus. On the robe is inscribed part of a verse from Paul, "It is sown a natural body; it is raised a spiritual body" (I Cor. [Corinthians] 15:44). The setting is pastoral and symbolic of the New Eden, with the Tree of Life and golden fruit. The body is also that of Christ rising from the dead to become "the firstfruits of them that slept" (15:20). The poem and illustration, in spite of some complexities, contain most of the images selected by Mrs. Barbauld, and they offer a final insight into the reasons for Blake's sympathetic response to nearly the whole range of the *Hymns*.

A few additional remarks should be made concerning the importance of Blake's illustrations to the present discussion. In recent years much critical attention has been devoted to the exploration of the *Songs* as a composite art "in which text and design," as Frye states, "are simultaneously present and contrapuntally related."[16] A picture may expand the thematic range of a poem or may focus upon a single aspect, but one way or another the visual designs collectively orchestrate all of the images and themes of the poems. It therefore follows, as already suggested by several examples, that at least as sound a case can be made to demonstrate Mrs. Barbauld's influence upon the illustrations as has been made for her influence upon the poems. The same principles for making comparisons apply. Evidence is most convincing when parallel images and themes occur in clusters, but no sharp margins between areas of convincing influence and fortuitous paralleling can be drawn, and as always the child-like simplicities flourish in the presence of adult profundities.

A surprisingly large number of Blake's pictures quite accurately illustrate passages from *Hymns*. In fact, a most impressive illustrated edition of the *Hymns* could be produced by using the majority of the illustrations in the *Songs*.[17] The continuity of themes in the *Hymns* would be appropriately echoed, and many times Blake's subtle overtones would apply, especially when Biblical echoes are involved. Some examples should help to reveal areas of significant paralleling and possible influence of the *Hymns*. The title page for *Songs of Innocence* (Plate 3), with its pastoral setting and a mother and children looking at an open book would be equally appropriate as a title page for the *Hymns* or to represent the dominant theme of **"Hymn III"** describing how the mother "feedeth" her Child's mind "with knowledge" and "rejoiceth . . . in its growth" (p. 15). Blake's touches of Experience, such as the book and broken branch, are entirely appropriate to Mrs. Barbauld's later reminders that earthly joys are imperfect and transitory. All of Blake's many scenes showing parental figures watching over infants or young children at play on the echoing green, shepherds watching over sheep, and Christ as the Good Shepherd watching over all would be appropriate illustrations for many passages in the *Hymns*. Plate 17 for "A Cradle Song" even shows the drawn curtain to shade the infant's "tender eyes" (p. 32), and both writers make visual the Twenty-Third Psalm. Although Blake is concerned with the identity of God, man, shepherds, sheep, and infants as one, his drawings must depict them as discrete visual entities, as do the *Hymns*.

Almost all of the fifty-four plates of the *Songs* show or suggest a pastoral Edenic garden as a frame or background, either as richly green and heavenly, earthly and touched by decay, or quite harsh and fallen, sadly brown and dangerously thorny. And so do the *Hymns*. Many of the same animals and plants, domestic or wild, are depicted in both works, and although Mrs. Barbauld does not touch upon the sexual implications of flowers, fruits, and thorns, her many descriptions of parental and heavenly guardianship are easily represented by the human and angelic figures in several of Blake's flame-flowers, especially the Annunciation scene in the crimson flower of Plate 25 for "infant Joy." Many of the harsher pictures of *Experience* quite accurately illustrate equivalent passages in the *Hymns*, particularly those of **"Hymn X"** on death. Blake's title page showing grown children weeping over the bodies of parents, Plate 33 for "Holy Thursday" showing grieving children and the corpses of a man and a child, and Plate 49 for "A Poison Tree" with its impressive cadaver with outstretched arms are all applicable to the *Hymns*. Mrs. Barbauld's weeping "Child of mortality" (p. 77) must place "parents and friends . . . in the cold ground" (p. 95) and see proud man lying "stiff and cold on the bare ground" (pp. 81-82). Finally, several of Blake's pastoral renderings of Eternity, such as the designs for "The Little Black Boy," "The Divine Image" and "To Tirzah" (Plates 10, 18, 52), represent in one way or another Mrs. Barbauld's descriptions of the coming of Jesus "to bid the dead awake" and to preside over a happy and permanent pastoral Heaven (pp. 87 ff.).

Of the fifty-four plates in the *Songs,* less than a dozen seem entirely inapplicable to the *Hymns*; for example the embracing couples, the London scenes, and Urizen entangled in the net of religion.[18] It is true that some of Blake's most caustic attacks upon society, especially upon institutionalized religion, may emerge in drawings that seem at first easily applicable to scenes in the *Hymns*. But it is unlikely that the satire would be directed against Mrs. Barbauld, for she was herself very much in the tradition of religious dissent. Thus the superficially pious scene on Plate 44 for "The Garden of Love," showing a priest leading two children in prayer, is such a bitter attack upon the church that it is inconceivable anything in the *Hymns* about giving thankful prayers could have inspired it. But Plate 39 for "The Sick Rose" echoes the *Hymns* so clearly that it hardly matters if we know that the caterpillar devouring a leaf is often for Blake a symbol of the priest who "lays his curse on the fairest joys" (E. 37). It must be accepted that Blake always transforms what he uses.

Any final conclusions about Mrs. Barbauld's influence upon the poems and illustrations must be cautious ones. But because of the esthetic and thematic unity of Blake's illuminated manuscripts, it does seem clear that as sound a case can be made for an influence upon the illustrations as critics have already made for the influence upon the poems alone. The pictures like the poems echo the *Hymns* over a surprisingly wide range of parallels, and like the poems they seldom lose their naive visual appeal even when symbolically complex. At best the influence may be minor, although readers of Blake should always find Mrs. Barbauld's *Hymns* to be of interest if only to observe how brilliantly tinsel can be transformed into gold.

Notes

1. E. D. Hirsch, Jr., *Innocence and Experience: An Introduction to Blake* (New Haven, 1964), p. 28. We do not find references to Mrs. Barbauld in Blake's letters or annotations; however, we know that early in the 1780s both writers belonged to the circle of "eminent persons" who gathered at the home of the Rev. Anthony Stephen Mathew (Mona Wilson, *The Life of William Blake,* ed. Geoffrey Keynes [London, 1971], pp. 21, 44). More importantly, both were socially and professionally acquainted with the publisher Joseph Johnson during the years Johnson was printing a wide range of popular children's books, including Mrs. Barbauld's *Lessons For Children from Two to Three Years Old* (1778), "which had an impact far beyond her modest purpose," *Lesson for Children Three Years Old* (1778), in a "handsome volume on good paper with large type," and the *Hymns* three years later, also in large type (Gerald P. Tyson, *Joseph Johnson: A Liberal Publisher*

[Iowa City, 1979], pp. 80-84, 112-14). For a broader perspective on children's literature, see Cornelia Meigs, et al., *A Critical History of Children's Literature* (New York, 1953); Harvey Darton, *Children's Books in England* (Cambridge, England, 1932); and Martha Winburn England and John Sparrow, *Hymns Unbidden: Donne, Herbert, Blake, Emily Dickinson and the Hymnographers* (New York, 1966).

2. Kathleen Raine, *Blake and Tradition* (Princeton, 1968), I, 31, and *William Blake* (New York, 1970), pp. 46-47.

3. Vivian de Sola Pinto, "William Blake, Isaac Watts, and Mrs. Barbauld," *The Divine Vision: Studies in the Poetry and Art of William Blake,* ed. V. de S. Pinto (London, 1957), p. 84.

4. References to Blake in parentheses are to *The Poetry and Prose of William Blake,* ed. David V. Erdman (Garden City, N. Y., 1970).

5. Isaac Watts, *Horae Lyricae and Divine Songs* (Boston, 1854), p. 335.

6. References to the *Hymns* in parentheses are to the original edition: Anna Laetitia Barbauld, *Hymns in Prose for Children* (London, 1781). For a detailed discussion of Mrs. Barbauld's career and the composition of the *Hymns,* see Catherine E. Moore, "The Literary Career of Anna Laetitia Barbauld," Diss. University of North Carolina at Chapel Hill, 1969. I am indebted to Miss Moore for the use of this valuable study and for many useful comments on Mrs. Barbauld's ideas about the religious education of young children.

7. Hirsch, pp. 28-30.

8. There are no doubts about the availability of Mrs. Barbauld's *Hymns* to eighteenth-century readers and no evidence that any of Blake's *Songs* were composed before the publication of the *Hymns.* The first edition of the *Hymns* (1781) was highly successful, and various editions were constantly reprinted well into the second half of the nineteenth century by publishers on both sides of the Atlantic ("A Forgotten Children's Book," *Hibbert Journal,* 73 [Autumn 1964], 27-34, and Moore, pp. 255-56). Blake's *Songs* has a complex textual history, but verifiable dates for all of the poems fall between 1784-1805. Early versions of three *Songs of Innocence* appear in the manuscript of *An Island in the Moon* (about Dec. 1784), and eighteen *Songs of Experience* are found in Blake's Notebook (the Rossetti Manuscript) at entries made between 1790-1792. See E. [*The Poetry and Prose of William Blake*] 713-15, 766-67, and *The Notebook of William Blake: A Photographic and Typographic Facsimile,* rev. ed., ed. David V. Erdman (Oxford, 1973; rpt. New York, 1977), pp. 53-ff.

9. For convenience, references to plate numbers are to the fairly standardized arrangement as found in *Songs of Innocence and of Experience,* a reproduction with introduction and commentary by Geoffrey Keynes (New York, 1967). See E. 714.

10. Pinto, p. 84.

11. See David V. Erdman, *Blake: Prophet Against Empire,* 3rd ed. (Princeton, 1977), pp. 124-25, and E. 767.

12. Erdman, pp. 125-26. Erdman is particularly interested in the manuscript version of "The Little Boy Lost" as found in the satirical *An Island in the Moon.* He is skeptical about any conjectural identification of Mrs. Barbauld with Mrs. Nannicantipot, who "sings as if in gentle parody of—or at least derives phrasing, images, and mood from—the second and fifth *Hymns*" (pp. 123-24).

13. Pinto, p. 86.

14. S. Foster Damon, *A Blake Dictionary* [New York, 1965, 1971], s. v. [under the word] "Young," shows that a passage from Edward Young's *Night Thoughts* might have influenced Blake: "Death's subtle Seed within (sly, treach'rous Miner!) working in the Dark, smil'd . . . and beckon'd the Worm to riot on that Rose so red" (i. 335). See also Morton D. Paley, "Blake's *Night Thoughts*: An Exploration of the Fallen World," *William Blake: Essays for S. Foster Damon,* ed. Alvin H. Rosenfeld (Providence, 1969), pp. 134-35.

15. In the early poem "How sweet I roam'd" (E. 404) Blake used these symbolic flowers in a context suggesting sinister sexual possessiveness. Blake first used the lily and the rose to symbolize contrasting sexual attitudes in the *Songs,* and this remains the clearest example emphasizing Mrs. Barbauld's physical distinction between the two flowers. For the whole range of "Blake's Symbolism of Roses and Lilies," see John E. Grant, "Two Flowers in the Garden of Experience," *William Blake: Essays for S. Foster Damon,* pp. 333-67.

16. Northrop Frye, "Poetry and Design in William Blake," *Journal of Aesthetics and Art Criticism,* 10 (September 1951), 36. See Jean H. Hagstrum, *William Blake: Poet and Painter* (Chicago, 1964) and *Blake's Visionary Forms Dramatic,* ed. D. V. Erdman and J. E. Grant (Princeton, 1970).

17. Blake was sometimes employed by Joseph Johnson, publisher of the *Hymns,* to make illustrations for books about children, but there is no evidence that he ever thought of illustrating the *Hymns.*

18. The following plates seem quite inapplicable to the *Hymns*: Plates 1, 19, 30, 34, 37, 41, 43, 44, 46, 47, 50. A few are doubtful: Plates 35, 36, 45, 54.

John M. Anderson (essay date autumn 1994)

SOURCE: Anderson, John M. "'The First Fire': Barbauld Rewrites the Greater Romantic Lyric." *Studies in English Literature, 1500-1900* 34, no. 4 (autumn 1994): 719-38.

[*In the following essay, Anderson analyzes Barbauld's "First Fire" within the framework of M. H. Abrams's conception of the "greater romantic lyric." Examining the work alongside Coleridge's "Frost at Midnight," Anderson argues that Barbauld's poem contains greater social and political relevance than most other romantic writings, primarily because it remains grounded in a specific historical time and context.*]

The current rapid expansion of the literary canon, brought about by a reconsideration of women writers and others writing in a tradition outside the privileged "mainstream," must raise questions about the critical canon as well. How useful in the discussion of such works are the labels devised to describe the products of a rival tradition? Must a new and separate critical idiom be invented before these newly canonized writers can be read, or can such an idiom be developed by modifying existing critical constructs? To what extent must such constructs be modified before they can be applied to the work of a woman poet without doing her or her poetry an injustice? For students of the Romantic period, one of the most influential of these critical constructs has been the form that M. H. Abrams derived after the fact to describe many famous lyrics by the male Romantics, a form Abrams christened the "greater Romantic lyric." **"The First Fire,"** a subtle meditative poem by A. L. Barbauld that has been critically neglected, closely resembles some of the poems Abrams invented his "genre" to describe. (See the appendix for the full text of **"The First Fire."**) What tensions result when one applies Abrams's critical model to Barbauld's poem?

The English poet Anna Laetitia Barbauld (1743-1825) has lately been coming into her own. In 1984 Barbara Brandon Schnorrenberg called her "one of the most neglected writers of her day. . . . [A] far better poet than Anna Seward, she offers imaginative subjects, often portrayed with much humor."[1]

A handful of Barbauld poems have since been reprinted or discussed in articles and anthologies, though these have curiously failed to notice her most ambitious work, such as **"The First Fire,"** or the important political poem *Eighteen Hundred and Eleven*.[2] In *The Contours of Masculine Desire: Romanticism and the Rise of Women's Poetry*—the first book-length critical examination of this period of women's poetry—Marlon Ross gives Barbauld something like her due.[3] His format allows Ross to discuss Barbauld at length: he dedicates a passage of sixteen pages to her exclusively and takes her into account in his discussions of her various contemporaries throughout the book. Ross is especially interested in Barbauld's "conception of female poeticizing" and the limits of her feminism (p. 217). The chief example of these limits is **"The Rights of Women,"** a conservative approach to these topics, in contrast to what Roger Lonsdale, admitting this exception, called Barbauld's "liberal political opinions."[4]

Distracted by such expectations and agendas, no one—not Ross, Schnorrenberg, or the anthologists—has yet sufficiently considered an important Barbauld poem that takes for its shape the most characteristic genre of the canonical Romantic tradition. **"The First Fire: October 1st, 1815"** is a pragmatic, politically activist woman's variation upon what would later be called the greater Romantic lyric.[5] The poem cannot have been conceived in exactly these terms, of course, because this "genre" was not described or named until 1965, when in his famous essay Abrams wrote of "a distinctive and widely practiced variety of the longer Romantic lyric." This variety, Abrams said, "includes some of the greatest Romantic achievements in any form. Coleridge's 'Eolian Harp,' 'Frost at Midnight,' . . . Wordsworth's 'Tintern Abbey,' his 'Ode: Intimations of Immortality' . . . Shelley's 'Stanzas Written in Dejection' . . . and his 'Ode to the West Wind.'" This last poem Abrams designates a "variant" of the form.

Abrams defined the form exemplified by such distinguished works rather precisely.[6] His definition also seems designed for maximum flexibility. Its repeated catalogues of possibilities, its qualifiers like "usually," "sometimes," "more frequently," and "often," and the latitude of such terms as "insight," "moral decision," and "emotional problem": all these encourage wide application, allowing the number of canonical poems that may be fitted into this newly discovered "genre" to be as great as possible. Furthermore, some of the poems from which the definition is extrapolated do not fit all of its few unqualified stipulations. Coleridge's "Frost at Midnight," for instance—the second poem Abrams cites as an example, and one to which he returns for further examination in his essay—does not occur in an "outdoor setting." Finally, when a poem is canonically central and shows some resemblance to the form thus loosely defined, Abrams somewhat arbitrarily labels it a "variant," like "Ode to the West Wind."

Despite such vagaries and vaguenesses, however, the definition is a powerful one, and it provides a context for orientation that is especially useful in discussing a noncanonical work. Any poem that fits or interestingly varies Abrams's outline, however far removed otherwise from the poetry from which the outline was traced, can be seen to have a relation to that poetry. **"The First Fire"** may well be placed in Abrams's broad context, because its exclusion from the canon has let it drift in the disorienting limbo of a critical vacuum. It may be seen as a "variant" of the interesting kind that reflects on the shortcomings of the form it varies, and that therefore varies, as it were, out of principle, for **"The First Fire"** works in a great many ways as a variation on "Frost at Midnight." Thus, long before Abrams extrapolated his influential "genre" from the poetry of the canonical male Romantics, Barbauld, in her response to "Frost at Midnight," had already thrown the ruling terms of that genre into question.

The fact that Barbauld was a woman—unlike any of the poets mentioned by Abrams and unlike any of the canonized Romantics—may introduce questions of gender that never occurred to Abrams in defining the form. Anne K. Mellor, in her recent critical survey *Romanticism and Gender,* points out that women poets were in effect discouraged, for reasons of gender, from writing in "masculine" genres. "Women poets' choice of genre thus exists in contestation both with the eighteenth-century ordering of the arts and the masculinist poetics this hierarchy reflects; they implicitly rejected the egotistical sublime that sustains, however precariously, the Romantic epic and the odal hymn" (p. 11). The "odal hymn" is surely less suffused with the "egotistical sublime" than the typical greater Romantic lyric, and one might infer that women were no more likely to write the latter than the former. Yet such generalizations about gender and genre are hazardous: as Mellor acknowledges, many epic poems were in fact composed by women in the period,[7] and it is possible that being female, in fact, gave Barbauld an advantage in writing a greater Romantic lyric. Frederic Rowton, in his 1853 anthology, might lead one to think so. "Mrs. Barbauld's poetry," Rowton wrote, "exhibits, in a high degree, the characteristic qualities of female genius. The quick intuitive perception, the chaste tenderness, the delicate, *musical* flow of thought, that distinguish the female mind, are very forcibly and fully developed by Mrs. Barbauld."[8] These sound like the characteristics Abrams was to find a hundred years later in "Frost at Midnight," where, he says, "directed especially by the rhythm of the seemingly unnoticed breathing of a sleeping infant, the meditative mind disengages itself from the physical locale, moves back in time to the speaker's childhood, still farther back, to his own infancy, then forward to express, in the intonation of a blessing, the hope that his son shall have the life in nature that his father lacked."[9] The question of gender—clearly not distinguishable thus crudely by voice, and no more explicit in Barbauld's poem than in Coleridge's—is neverthe-

less important in **"The First Fire"** as a grounds for literal political empowerment or disenfranchisement.[10] Sexual potency, moreover, is used as a symbol for active engagement as opposed to passive yearning. Such issues of gender and sexuality are unconventionally and ironically applied by Barbauld. However, before the subtleties of Barbauld's irony and the significance of her departures from the form can be made clear, it is necessary to establish the proximity of **"The First Fire"** to Abrams's greater Romantic lyric, and to explore its relationship to "Frost at Midnight," one of the "genre's" founding texts.

Barbauld's speaker is, in accord with Abrams's definition, "determinate," especially by the idiosyncratic, hearty colloquialism of her voice:

> HA, old acquaintance! many a month has past
> Since last I viewed thy ruddy face; and I,
> Shame on me! had mean time well nigh forgot,
> That such a friend existed. Welcome now!—
>
> (lines 1-4)

This voice, whose "fluent vernacular" is perhaps a bit more thoroughly vernacular than Abrams had in mind, does "rise easily to a more formal speech." The opening declaration that "many a month has past" seems to allude to a biographical fact similar to that at the opening of "Tintern Abbey," except that, because this speaker is located in a "particularized setting" by the title and the date beneath it, we see that this is not a unique but a cyclical occurrence. Similarly, the "first fire" of the title is not the primordial fire of myth but merely the first of the year. (Perhaps there is a domesticated reference to Prometheus here; that would set up expectations for another standard kind of Romantic poem, expectations that are immediately disappointed: the poem forgoes the grand scale of mythology in favor of the greater immediacy of the quotidian.) Besides the cyclical return of autumn signaled by "October 1," however, there is in the same date the unique and remarkable year. It is 1815, and Waterloo is just three months in the past. This "particularized" placement in time is underscored in the first stanza, which mentions "Frenchmen" in a tone of either pity or scorn.

Though the setting is an interior one (as is that of "Frost at Midnight"), it switches in the poem's final lines, as if in anticipation of Abrams's insistence on outdoor settings. Similarly, the speaker apostrophizes the fire, as in the odes Abrams mentions, but there is no "silent human auditor, present or absent," here, until the poem's final lines, which do address a silent auditor—the reader of the poem. But perhaps the most serious objection to reading **"The First Fire"** as an unreconstructed greater Romantic lyric is the style of its "process of memory, thought, anticipation, and feeling which remains closely intervolved with the outer scene" (p. 201). In Barbauld's lyric, thoughts take the form of a series of archetypal vignettes, all interiors, all revolving around the hearth, but ranging across a spectrum of social extremes, from the rich (lines 21-25) to the poor (lines 72-79), from the populous (lines 26-47) to the solitary (lines 47-57). These vignettes are neither memories nor anticipations of the speaker, and though they may be said to reflect her/his thought, they do so in something like the generic style used by Herbert in Abrams's counterexample, the metaphysical poem.[11] But the vignettes in **"The First Fire"** are less the result of what Abrams calls "an inherited typology" and more the sociological typology of a writer aware of class injustices—the same kind of topical typology that informs the protovignette[12] in lines 18-20, which is given the greater part of its force by the recent war.

Finally, Barbauld's poem fits the Abrams requirement in that "[i]n the course of this meditation . . . [it] comes to a moral decision" (p. 201). The poem's ending, in fact, does more than signal, or even enable, a moral decision—it acts upon it by calling others to action. The speech act with which the poem ends thus carries on the vigorous pattern of the poem as a whole by moving decisively from passive meditation into energetic activity.

This movement from meditation to action constitutes one of several differences between the greater Romantic lyric as written by Barbauld and by Coleridge. Barbauld herself underlined this distinction in the following famous encounter, as recalled by Susan Wolfson.

> Today, most readers of *The Rime of the Ancient Mariner* are probably not as bothered as was Coleridge's acquaintance, the poet and essayist Mrs. Barbauld, about the "improbable" nature of his story. The second "fault" of which she complained to the author, however, remains something of a notorious vexation for many modern readers—namely, that the poem "had no moral." Coleridge is willing to cede the point on "probability"; but "as to the want of a moral," he counters, the poem's "chief fault, if I might say so, was the obtrusion of the moral sentiment so openly on the reader as a principle or cause of action in a work of pure imagination."[13]

The objections of "Mrs." Barbauld, as framed in Wolfson's diction, may sound quaint and literal-minded.[14] Or she may sound, in current vocabulary, politically engaged.

Coleridge might have made a similar hyperbolic answer to a complaint about the absence of politics in "Frost at Midnight." The "ministry" of the frost in line 1 works as do other ministries, both civil and religious: aimlessly yet with a florid show of precision; silently, slowly, in the dark, almost unnoticeably; and entirely without the assistance of the apolitical speaker. It is a cold and inorganic force that nonetheless gives the

speaker a feeling of security. This speaker is a sort of universalist, humble, self-effacing radical, fundamentally unhappy with social conditions yet patient in his wait for change. He is optimistic in his wisdom, confident that the frost is performing good service, that the infant now sleeping will, as Abrams says, "have the life in nature that his father lacked." This is an "apolitical" speaker who would have been charmed by the idea of Pantisocracy, and it is a similar escape to an idealized world without political conflict that he wishes for his son.

It is true that Coleridge's poem is far more evocative of mood than Barbauld's. This effect is due in part to the infant's use as a musical device, as mentioned above. In part it arises from the more general use of the infant and of every other element in the poem as a projection of the poet's mind; this view of things proves especially comforting because lacking independent existence, these things cannot have independent political needs and desires. Such a philosophy is useful in sustaining moods because it prevents musings of the sort that would disturb them, such as the reflection that though oneself is cozy there are those within reach who are in need.[15] To approach "Frost at Midnight" in this way is to risk a tone of self-righteousness, or at the least to seem insensitive to the feel of the thing. A consideration of the escapist politics underlying the mood evoked by "Frost at Midnight"—such considerations as are inspired by the contrast of Barbauld's hearty activism—devalues that mood and makes it seem, just for a moment, like the "dreamy twilight of the vacant mind, / Soothed by the whispering shade" that Barbauld perceived in Coleridge the year before he wrote the poem.[16]

Abrams points out the "lyric rondure" or "return-upon-itself" with which "Frost at Midnight" ends,[17] but the ending might also be identified with the kind of understated and comforting millennium characteristic of some of the lyric poems included in the category of Abrams's greater Romantic lyric—notably in "Tintern Abbey"—but also of more politically oriented Romantic poems such as Shelley's sonnet "England in 1819." Such unearned and improbable visions of the future like Coleridge's declared hope that his son will never go to school seem more like lyric-ending techniques than like predictions or recommendations for application in the real world.

The context of **"The First Fire"**—though Barbauld's poem is far less concentrated than Coleridge's upon the mind and mood of the speaker, and though hers ranges abroad into a far wider variety of social settings than his—is in certain ways less universal than that of "Frost at Midnight." The homely image of the fire, one of the several images with which Coleridge begins, suffices Barbauld to the end. Barbauld's context is less dramatic and more schematic than Coleridge's, and in this way less thoroughly localized than his, but her preference for the historical over the universal makes her poem at the same time more precise and particular in its placement.

The historical implications of the date in the subtitle are emphasized in line 10, where "Frenchmen" are twice ambiguously mentioned. It is not clear from the words "As Frenchmen say" how many of the poem's opening lines are to be attributed to Frenchmen—possibly only the theory that sulfur generates spleen, but just as possibly the whole axiomatic passage beginning on line 5. This second possibility is ironic because that passage is placed in the universal language of human nature and centers itself on an all-encompassing "We" (line 7): this language is already problematized by the sudden introduction of the Frenchmen, but it is especially so when the universal assertions turn out retrospectively to have been voiced by one who is definitionally not one of "us." The second mention of Frenchmen in the line is doubly ambiguous. The reader cannot tell if the phrase "never knew" is only disqualification for comment on the fire, or how much its past tense is to be stressed, indicating that the situation is henceforth going to be different. If the "sober comforts of a good coal fire" (line 11) may represent only Britain as opposed to France, it may as well represent the domestic comforts hitherto unavailable to the French lower classes, and worth waging revolutions to attain. We could better determine which interpretation was more likely if we could determine whether the "Frenchman" is to be scorned or pitied for never having experienced such comforts. As it is, the passage is something of an enigma—but in all events it serves as a reminder of the kind of fire with which the French have indeed become familiar.[18] The ambivalence of the passage is politically appropriate: as Mellor has shown, many women writers of Barbauld's day were radically divided on their interpretation of the Revolution, but the "ethic of care" that such writers shared with Barbauld spanned this divide.[19]

The ambiguity surrounding Barbauld's Frenchmen is repeated when the poet returns, again briefly but more explicitly, to the recent war.

> Here a man might stand,
> And say, This is my world! Who would not bleed
> Rather than see thy violated hearth
> Prest by a hostile foot?
>
> (lines 17-20)

The exclamation "This is my world!" though fervent in expression, is curiously difficult to translate out of its metaphorical language. Is the hearth here, for example, England? If so, does the expression mean that everything outside of England ought to be sacrificed for the sake of this "world"? Such nationalism might fit easily with the individualism that would be implied if the

hearth is to be taken as standing only for the private household, an individualism that, though it objects to any intrusive government, often coincides with a strong patriotism. The folly of reducing the world to the "close circle" of a single fireplace troubles the simple emotion of the exclamation, however—especially given the equivocal nature of the fireplace, which only ten lines ago was being mocked for its "grim attire and sooty jaws."

Ambiguities deepen the passage, but the emotional movement is clear enough. The joy in "Friends, brethren, kinsmen . . . All the dear charities of social life" (lines 15-16) inspires a mood, familiar from Coleridge, of snug self-sufficiency; this in turn inspires a rash, universalizing statement; this leads to abstruser musings upon war, rape, and invasion. No wonder the chastened speaker notices at this point that "[t]he winds sing shrill." Nor is the exuberance surprising with which she dispels the chill of such thoughts with "Heap on the fuel!" Neither these thoughts nor this solution occurs to Coleridge, of course; and the sexuality that informs them is absent from "Frost at Midnight" as well. This sexuality is not incidental; rather, it is an image of bodily activity opposed to the passive thoughtfulness more characteristic of the genre, an opposition that we have already met with in its political aspect.

With his infant, evidence of his sexuality, asleep beside him, Coleridge's speaker nods beside the "low-burnt fire" and thinks, like Barbauld's "sire," of his youth. The border areas of infancy and old age, both comparatively asexual, dominate "Frost at Midnight." Coleridge's speaker, in fact, is less sexual than Barbauld's "sire": the latter seats himself not by a "thin blue flame," but "in sunniest nook," in "the grateful warmth" that "thaw[s] the ice / Of fourscore years" (lines 30, 35-36). This old man—whose thoughts of his own youth mark the transition of the narrative to the "young ones" beside him, as Coleridge's speaker is led again to think of the infant beside *him*—seems written in specific contrast to the speaker in "Frost at Midnight," and is the first of a series of speakers in **"The First Fire"** who perform the same function. To these we shall return, but a single further example of the differences between the two lyrics fits better within the present discussion.

It may be argued that the "matron sage" of lines 44-46 reflects the attitude and aspirations (as well as the asexuality) of Coleridge's speaker better than the "sire" does. She is certainly speaking, as the figure in "Frost at Midnight" seems to be doing, and as the "sire" is not; the blue flame of "Frost at Midnight" recurs here, and frost, mentioned only two times in the poem (both of them significant) occurs for the first time here; further, the "matron sage" is speaking within the hearing of the young, but not to them or for their understanding; she is, finally, looking into the fire and drawing inferences from it to the outside world. These characteristics all resemble Coleridge's speaker. There are, however, telling differences. This flame is "scorching," these children "listen," and, of course, this is an old woman. It seems reasonable to speculate that the "matron sage," like the speaker in "Frost at Midnight," is something of a portrait of the artist, a possibility that underscores another irony in the contrast between Barbauld's signals of sexuality and Coleridge's torpid asexuality: Barbauld was seventy-two when she wrote **"The First Fire"**; Coleridge wrote "Frost at Midnight" at the age of twenty-five.

Having thus established to some extent the political and sexual contexts that distinguish **"The First Fire"** from Coleridge's greater Romantic lyrics, we may proceed to explore its incidental strategies for establishing context locally. The main technique Barbauld uses, referred to above as her "vignettes," might perhaps better be called idiosyncratic stereotypes. The portraits are individualized, but with general import. Each also provides a context for the others, progressing in socioeconomic steps that muffle the contrasts and mask the gap that is finally revealed between the first vignette and the last. Thus, when Barbauld employs her variation of Coleridge's lyric rondure, the impact is an especially striking one of "altered mood and deepened understanding," which according to Abrams should result from the "intervening meditation."

The first vignette—following immediately upon the self-comforting command of "Heap on the fuel!"—is a view of the rich, set interestingly in terms similar to those of 1 Corinthians 13.

> Not the costly board,
> Nor sparkling glass, nor wit, nor music, cheer
> Without thy aid.
>
> (lines 21-23)

This passage presents more explicitly, by means of this allusion, the alternate possibility that the fire may be interpreted simply, as love. In particular, the third verse of the famous Pauline chapter is applicable here: "And though I bestow all my goods to feed the poor, and though I give my body to be burned, and have not charity, it profiteth me nothing." This allusion makes the mildness of the discomfort especially amusing in Barbauld's satirical illustration of a wealthy gathering at which the host has skimped on the heat:

> If thrifty thou dispense
> Thy gladdening influence, in the chill saloon
> The silent shrug declares th' unpleased guest.
>
> (lines 23-25)

Such a host—stingy enough to risk but superficial enough to fear that displeased shrug—is rather far from the ecstasy of self-sacrifice with which Paul proposes giving not his extra firewood but his body to be burned.

This scene of wealthy chilliness establishes a context for the next, and most extended, of the vignettes, the scene of the cheerful cottage from which we have already met the "sire" and the "matron sage." The contrast to the previous vignette is striking. The cool luxury of a scene in which there is ample rich furniture ("costly board," "sparkling glass") and a certain amount of disembodied noise ("wit," "music")—but no actual people until the unpleased guest appears, his shrug and displeasure preceding him, in the last word of the passage, is now reversed, and we are presented first with an isolated "traveller / Homeward returning" (lines 26-27) who comes into a scene in which the fire and the people around it predominate. The social class is of course considerably lower, as established by the unprepossessing word "cottage" (line 28), a building that the traveler sees only after remarking the "blaze" (line 27) in its window. The "wicker chair" (line 30) in which the sire sits "enshrined" (line 30) is further evidence of this reduction in class—but this modest chair, unlike the board and glass of the wealthy, serves its purpose so well that it rises into metaphor and becomes indistinguishable from the "privilege" (line 31) that allows the old man his seat by the fire, and that as thoroughly as the chair "supports his limbs" (line 33).

This somewhat sentimentalized domestic scene is the nearest Barbauld comes to the speaker's memory in "Frost at Midnight" of his "sweet birth-place," and its differences from that memory are most apparent. Of course, the Coleridge passage occurs outside and on a "hot Fair-day" (line 30). Moreover, the poor in Coleridge are merely evoked, and in an idealized way. That the church bells are "the poor man's only music" (line 29) is pathetic in the deprivation it implies. But those bells rang "So sweetly, that they stirred and haunted me / With a wild pleasure" (lines 31-32), which is about as much as one can ask of any music, so the deprivation is not great, after all, but in its nearly natural simplicity may be something of an advantage.[20] The music in Barbauld's poem is entirely confined to the wealthy, and though she emphasizes the cheer and gladness of the cottage scene (partially in preparation for depictions still to come of poverty at its bitterest), there is an edge to poverty even here. The "immortal hunger" (line 40) of the fire, for example, seems an image drawn from the human experience of enduring hunger and at the same time marks the resentment of those who must pay for the wood that feeds such a mouth. The rendering "idle" of the personified Winter's "rage" is the chief cultural accomplishment of this group, themselves rendered idle in defense.

The children, too, are very different from Coleridge's "cradled infant." The fire, symbol of Christian charity in the home of the rich, has resumed a demonic aspect here among the poor—an aspect visible in the immortal hunger but also in the image of the flames that "Dart like an adder's tongue upon their prey" (line 42) by which the Biblical context seems to shift from 1 Corinthians to Genesis. And the children feel the allure of this dangerous power. They look at its "face delighted" (line 38) and their faces uncannily begin to mirror it with a "gaze delighted" (line 41) of their own. Thus repeated, the word "delighted," which has only positive connotations outside such a context, becomes something sinister, first by this uncanny mirroring and then by the chiming of the words with the "lighted reed" (line 43) that marks the children's first, tentative, physical contact with the blaze. The "wreaths of smoke" in the same line seem rather funereal, but they have become playthings for these children. There is hope in the fact that these children listen to the "matron sage." If she is in fact Barbauld's representative, perhaps such children represent her ideal audience.

With Winter's rage comes the first stanza break of the poem, and the next three stanzas comprise a series of four vignettes, two of them isolated in stanzas of their own and the last, most wretched two sharing the final stanza. It is appropriate that the first lines to be broken away from the greater part of the poem, which is all of a piece, should concern a figure called "the solitary man." He may be, like the "sire" before him, modeled after Coleridge. He is discovered as he "converses" with the fire, "moralizes" with it (line 50)—social concepts made ironic by his solitude. He is caught "musing" (line 50), just like the speaker of "Frost at Midnight."[21] And his musings cover the range of human thought—from the learned speculations of science, which have deduced the "many aeras of uncounted time" (line 51) since coal "Was green with vegetative life" (line 53), to the "fancies gay" of the fine arts, which people the thinker's solitude with "gay discourse, life, motion, mirth" (line 56). And each of these limits of human imagining is undercut by Barbauld's irony. The scientist is as many "aeras" from green life as the coal upon which he speculates; the artist is motivated to create in an effort to disguise his loneliness and is only partly successful. Both are ridiculous to the extent that they are solitary, are cut off from life-giving society.

The next brief stanza makes the natural step from solitary man to "bashful poet" (line 58). Like Coleridge's speaker, this poet

> loves to sit
> Snug, at the midnight hour with only thee [the fire],
> Of his lone musings conscious.
>
> (lines 59-60)

There is again the key word "musings." And the communion with the fire is arguably an echo of the fire in "Frost at Midnight" when

> its motion in this hush of nature
> Gives it dim sympathies with me who live,
> Making it a companionable form.
>
> (lines 17-19)

There is irony in Barbauld's sympathetic fire, however. Notice, for instance, that the poet himself is not conscious of his own "lone musings": only the fire is. This comic dreaminess explains the "eyes of vacancy" (line 62) with which the poet, just like the poor children, "Gazes . . . on thy [the fire's] bright face" (lines 62-63). It may also partly explain the process by which "Oft he writes, / And blots, and writes again" (lines 60-61)—a realistic treatment of the poetic process which exposes the spontaneity of "conversation poems" as a fiction. The final irony is that the fire reveals that it enjoys the poet's high regard not for any spiritual affinities, not, despite all the "musing" going on, because the flames are muselike, but because of its destructive power. The poet, "Dreading the critic's scorn, to thee [the fire] commits, / Sole confidant and safe, his fancies crude" (lines 64-65).[22]

From the literary realm of satire to the social realm of what we now call human-rights abuses, the stanza break that follows the poet's "fancies crude" marks quite a boundary. The prisoner of line 66 and following may be yet another incarnation of Coleridge's speaker, but he is primarily a social fact—his "narrow cell" is neither the sonnet form, at which Wordsworth's poet, nunlike, strives not to fret, nor the stanza (both "room" and "poetic division") occupied by the Coleridge-like solitary man and bashful poet. It is a prison cell, and the green upon its walls is not the sign of life and hope that it is to the abstract thinker but the signal of "unwholesome dews" (line 68) of the kind upon which a purgatorial fire would have a healthy, "purifying influence" (line 69). But like the Frenchmen with which the poem began, these walls have never felt such an influence. The prisoner is "youthful" (line 70), but his environment, like that of the poor children, has the quality of imparting its own features to him. His life, like the slime on the walls, "stagnates, and the hue of hope" typologically green, though here clearly referring to rosiness, "is fled / From his wan cheek" (lines 71-72). The hue of hope identifies the young man with the green walls around him, and more subtly, so does the slightly greenish tinge of his wan cheek.

Crowded against this prisoner in shared misery is the last of the portraits in **"The First Fire,"** the "Poverty-struck" (line 75). With him, Barbauld moves outside (she was there once before, with the "belated traveller" [line 26], who, however, was bracketed in the poem by "grateful" on the one hand and "Homeward returning" on the other and never felt the full force of the cold). The "Poverty-struck" represents the final, bitterest commentary upon any complacent reliance on the "secret ministry of frost." Because he is outside, and because he must build his fire with peat "or stick plucked from the hedge" (line 76), the frosts he experiences "bite keen" (line 73). Even this wretched man goes inside at the end, but still he sees something different from the frosty patterns on the window glass. Because he lives surrounded by "the dreary fen" (line 78), and because his window does not shut out its evil influences, being in the usual state of disrepair common to the possessions of the poor, another personified abstraction, "Ague, sallow-faced," (we recall the prisoner's "wan cheek") "Stares through the broken pane" (lines 78-79). "Broken pane" is a melancholy pun, implying the agony that causes Ague, as it will cause his victim, to stare.

Like other poems of its time, **"The First Fire"** ends with a sort of millennium, but Barbauld accomplishes her version by stepping out of the poem's frame and addressing the audience directly, identifying us now not with the poor children listening to the "matron sage" but with both the "thrifty" rich (fire is now for the first time explicitly allegorized into "the sun of plenty" [line 80]—not sex or God or love, but money), and the summer-prosperous of the poem's opening lines, who blithely fail to realize that their own winter may not be far away. "Assist him, ye" (line 79)—it has the effect of a socially committed Puck, stepping out of character to ask his audience not for applause but for charity.[23]

Impressed by the number and variety of the women poets in the recent anthologies but perhaps a bit daunted by what they see as the poetry's uninviting strangeness, Romanticists might draw encouragement from this Anna Barbauld: from the subtlety and spirit apparent in her adaptation of the greater Romantic lyric; from her fortification of the form's subjective melancholy by means of a social realism akin to satire; from her application of its powerful, "particularized and usually localized" allegory to inspire and vivify a poetry aware of the real suffering beyond the traceries on the poet's window.

Notes

1. Janet Todd, ed., *A Dictionary of British and American Women Writers, 1660-1800* (New York: Rowman and Littlefield, 1984), p. 37.

2. Stuart Curran assisted in Barbauld's reclamation—though cautiously, commenting at length only on the poem cited by Schnorrenberg, an unambitious little work called "The Mouse's Petition, Found in the TRAP where he had been confin'd all Night [by Dr. Priestly]"—in "Romantic Poetry: The I Altered," in *Romanticism and Feminism,* ed. Anne K. Mellor (Bloomington: Indiana Univ. Press, 1988). In his turn, Roger Lonsdale reprinted this same poem along with eight others in his groundbreaking anthology, *Eighteenth-Century Women Poets* (Oxford: Oxford Univ. Press, 1990). Jennifer Breen has added nothing to the reclamation of

Barbauld: all five of the poems included in her derivative anthology *Romantic Women Poets, 1795-1832* (London: J. M. Dent and Sons; Rutland VT: Charles E. Tuttle-Everyman's Library, 1992) are already in Lonsdale. Breen, however, shows some critical independence in resisting the temptation to include the hitherto ubiquitous "Mouse's Petition" in her own selection. Lonsdale goes far beyond Curran in showing Barbauld's range and depth; he includes an excerpt from her long political blank-verse poem *Corsica* (written in 1769). But he omits *Eighteen Hundred and Eleven,* her mature poem in the same genre, which is much more pointed and courageous.

3. Marlon Ross, *The Contours of Masculine Desire: Romanticism and the Rise of Women's Poetry* (New York: Oxford Univ. Press, 1989).

4. Lonsdale, p. 300. Such designations are in any case not sophisticated enough to characterize the opinions of such politically conscious women as Barbauld, Wollstonecraft, or Helen Maria Williams, who, despite their varying positions on a liberal-conservative continuum, often showed solidarity with one another, as in what Anne K. Mellor calls "feminine Romanticism's primary commitment to the preservation of the domestic affections and the family unit" (*Romanticism and Gender* [New York: Routledge, 1993], p. 65). The intricacies of their politics, beyond my present scope, are traced in Mellor's book and in Donna Landry's *The Muses of Resistance: Laboring-Class Women's Poetry in Britain, 1739-1796* (Cambridge: Cambridge Univ. Press, 1990).

5. My text for this poem is that in *The Works of Anna Laetitia Barbauld: With a Memoir by Lucy Aikin,* 2 vols. (Boston: David Reed, 1826), 1:192-93. See appendix. Curran does mention this poem, but only in passing.

6. Because in exploring another "variant" of this form, I will be using this definition extensively, I quote it here at length.

> Some of the poems are called odes, while the others approach the ode in having lyric magnitude and a serious subject, feeling fully meditated. They present a determinate speaker in a particularized, and usually a localized, outdoor setting, whom we overhear as he carries on, in a fluent vernacular which rises easily to a more formal speech, a sustained colloquy, sometimes with himself or with the outer scene, but more frequently with a silent human auditor, present or absent. The speaker begins with a description of the landscape; an aspect or change of aspect in the landscape evokes a varied but integral process of memory, thought, anticipation and feeling which remains closely interwoved with the outer scene. In the course of this meditation

the lyric speaker achieves an insight, faces up to a tragic loss, comes to a moral decision, or resolves an emotional problem. Often the poem rounds upon itself to end where it began, at the outer scene, but with an altered mood and deepened understanding which is the result of the intervening meditation.

7. Stuart Curran has listed ten women poets, "ranging from the mid-1780s to the mid-1820s, [who] were the authors of poems of epic ambition": "Elizabeth Barrett, Sophia Burrell, Hannah Cowley, Charlotte Elizabeth Dixon, Elizabeth Hands, Margaret Hodson [this is Holford, under her married name, presumably to distinguish her from her mother], Mary Linwood, Eleanor Ann Porden, Elizabeth Smith (of Birmingham), and Helen Maria Williams" (Curran, p. 206 n. 4). Mellor recognizes the women's epics of the period, citing Curran (*Romanticism and Gender,* p. 5).

8. Frederic Rowton, *The Female Poets of Great Britain: Chronologically Arranged with Copious Selections and Critical Remarks,* facsimile of the 1853 edition with a critical introduction and bibliographical appendices by Marilyn L. Williamson (Detroit: Wayne State Univ. Press, 1981), p. 242.

9. Abrams, p. 205. My text for "Frost at Midnight" is from *The Complete Poetical Works,* ed. E. H. Coleridge, 2 vols. (Oxford: Oxford Univ. Press, 1912), 1:240-42.

10. Nancy Armstrong cites Rowton's anthology, in fact, in commenting on the implications of genre on gender politics: "Rowton's preface implies that the social differences between male and female depend on a form of subjectivity that in turn depends on gender differences. His unquestioned belief in the essential difference between the minds of a man and a woman provides the rationale for his publishing *The Female Poets of Great Britain.* If nature decrees women to write 'not as the rivals' but as the 'partners' of men, it follows that women's writing will complement that of men and never be able to engage male writing in a critical manner. A debate between the sexes becomes especially difficult to imagine if genres are rooted in gender. Thus Rowton identifies feminine discourse as personal and subjective rather than political or philosophical in character" (*Desire and Domestic Fiction: A Political History of the Novel* [New York: Oxford Univ. Press, 1987], p. 41).

11. "Herbert's flower is not a specified plant, described by the poet with his eye on the object, but a generic one; it is simply the class of all perennials, in which God has inscribed the invariable signatures of his providential plan" (Abrams, p. 228).

12. I designate it so because it is outside of the patterned sequence of, and separated from, the vignettes that follow.

13. Susan J. Wolfson, "The Language of Interpretation in Romantic Poetry: 'A Strong Working of the Mind,'" in *Romanticism and Language,* ed. Arden Reed (Ithaca: Cornell Univ. Press, 1984), p. 24.

14. Her status as Coleridge's "acquaintance"; the characterization of her as "bothered," and what is worse, more so than we readers would be today; her "complaint about Coleridge's 'fault'" (the latter word in careful quotation marks): all of these combine with the convention, long since outmoded in reference to male authors, of referring to the poet by her title, to make her a relic of a past era.

15. A comment by Anne K. Mellor on a more famous woman of the period underscores this point: "the canonical male-authored autobiographies have been for the most part the production of a leisured, bourgeois, racially dominant class, of men who are at least temporarily free from the physical deprivations of hunger, cold and poverty, and thus have the luxury of constructing a mind detached from a body. In contrast, Dorothy's *Journals* join much African-American, working-class, and female autobiographical writing in an inscription of the body as a determining condition of subjectivity" (*Romanticism and Gender,* p. 157).

16. "To Mr. S. T. Coleridge" in Barbauld, pp. 152-54, lines 22-23. Laurence Hanson, in his biography of Coleridge, shows that the canonical poet was as aware of the noncanonical as she of him. A practical estimate of Barbauld's abilities—and popularity—is this: Coleridge asked Thomas N. Longman in 1800 to send "3 or 4 Copies" of the newly published *Lyrical Ballads* "to different people of eminence," expressly specifying "one to Mrs. Barbauld" (*Collected Letters of Samuel Taylor Coleridge,* ed. Earl Leslie Griggs, 4 vols. [Oxford: Clarendon Press, 1932], 4:1013).

17. Abrams, p. 205.

18. One thinks of the passage about English versus French street lighting in Byron's *Don Juan* (canto 11, strophes xxvi-xxvii):

> The French were not yet a lamp-lighting nation,
> And when they grew so—on their new-found lantern,
> Instead of wicks, they made a wicked man turn.
>
> * * *
>
> A row of gentlemen along the streets
> Suspended may illuminate mankind,
> As also bonfires made of country seats.

19. "Where Wollstonecraft and Mary Shelley could see the French Revolution only as denying an ethic

of care, Williams could see it rather as the final triumph of an ethic of care, a recognition of the right of every citizen to the protection of the state. Thus, despite their directly opposing attitudes to the revolution itself, all these women writers sustained the same ideological commitment to the egalitarian family as the model of good government" (Mellor, *Romanticism and Gender,* p. 77. The term "ethic of care" comes from Carol Gilligan, *In a Different Voice: Psychological Theory and Women's Development* [Cambridge MA: Harvard Univ. Press, 1982], pp. 62-63).

20. This line about the "poor man's only music" is perhaps the most politically explicit line in the poem. It is the only line from "Frost at Midnight" that is quoted by Carl R. Woodring in *Politics in the Poetry of Coleridge* (Madison: Univ. of Wisconsin Press, 1961). This is not an obviously political poem.

21. Or like the Coleridge Barbauld depicts in her own poem: see note 16 above.

22. Such satire would have been particularly telling on the Coleridge of 1815, when his poetic output, so voluminous in 1798, had dwindled pretty thoroughly away.

23. Perhaps Barbauld's inspiration here was the so-called *envoy,* a stanza for concluding ballads that took the form of direct address. The "minor" male Romantics Scott and Southey made good use of this—here ironically—French form.

William Keach (essay date winter 1994)

SOURCE: Keach, William. "A Regency Prophecy and the End of Anna Barbauld's Career." *Studies in Romanticism* 33, no. 4 (winter 1994): 569-77.

[*In the following essay, Keach discusses Barbauld's vision of British cultural and economic decline in the poem* Eighteen Hundred and Eleven. *Keach evaluates the general indifference, and in some cases open hostility, directed toward the poem by Barbauld's contemporaries.*]

When they're seriously unsettled, Tories can be quick to dispense with the traditions of gentlemanly respect and courtesy they say they cherish. In his June 1812 *Quarterly Review* attack on Anna Barbauld's *Eighteen Hundred and Eleven,* John Wilson Croker resorts to sneers even more patronizing than those in his 1818 review of Keats's *Endymion.* Claiming that "it really is with no disposition to retaliate on the fair pedagogue of our former life," Croker insists that he cannot "comprehend the meaning of all the verses which this fatidical

spinster has drawn from her poetical distaff."[1] It was a coarse mistake, even for the likes of Croker, to apply the term "spinster" to the sixty-nine-year-old Barbauld, who had in fact been left a widow less than four years earlier after a long and, near the end, difficult marriage. Whether the mistake is a deliberate slur, or only the inadvertent consequence of Croker's snide pursuit of the pun on "spinster" in his reference to Barbauld's "poetical distaff," hardly matters. What matters is the extremity of his reaction to a poem in which, as he misleadingly but tellingly puts it, "England . . . is undone . . . while America is to go on increasing and improving in arts, in arms, and even, if that be possible, in virtue" (310). Croker ends with what sounds more like an official threat from the Tory Secretary of the Admiralty than the sting of a waspish Tory reviewer:

> Mrs. Barbauld's former works have been of some utility; her ***Lessons for Children,*** her ***Hymns in Prose,*** her ***Selections from the Spectator,*** et id genus omne, though they display not much of either taste or talents, are yet something better than harmless: but we must take the liberty of warning her to desist from satire, which indeed is satire on herself alone; and of entreating, with great earnestness, that she will not, for the sake of this ungrateful generation, put herself to the trouble of writing any more party pamphlets in verse.
>
> (313)

No wonder John Murray told Henry Crabb Robinson, many years later, that "he was more ashamed of [Croker's attack] than of any other article in the *Review.*"[2]

What's striking about the response to *Eighteen Hundred and Eleven,* though, is that it wasn't attacked only by Barbauld's reactionary enemies. Crabb Robinson himself, a devoted friend, says in his *Diaries:* "I certainly wish she had not written it, though it is written in a pleasing style. For the tone and spirit of it are certainly very bad. She does not content herself with expressing her fears lest England should perish in the present struggle; she speaks with the confidence of a prophet of the fall of the country as if she had seen in a vision the very process of its ruin" (*Robinson* [*Henry Crabb Robinson on Books and Their Writers*] 1: 63-64). Years later Crabb Robinson looks back on *Eighteen Hundred and Eleven* and concludes that it "was written more in sorrow than in anger. There was a disheartening and even dastardly tone in it which even I, with all my love for her, could not excuse." Robinson adds: "I find in my journal occasional expressions of displeasure at the unqualified Jacobinism of her politics" (1: 64). Maybe it was the implication of such "unqualified Jacobinism" that upset the one-time Jacobin William Godwin so much. According to Crabb Robinson, "He was full of his censure of Mrs. Barbauld's new poem . . . which he called cowardly, time-serving, Presbyterian, besides a string of epithets which meant only that he found the work wretched" (1: 63).

Maria Edgeworth defended the poem privately, in a letter to Barbauld, but—in a gesture with which some of us are all too familiar—she declined to enter the fray in public:

> I cannot describe to you the indignation, or rather the disgust, that we felt at the manner in which you are treated in the *Quarterly Review,* so ungentlemanlike, so unjust, so insolent a review I never read. My father and I, in the moment of provocation, snatched up our pens to answer it, but a minute's reflection convinced us, that silent contempt is the best answer—that we should not suppose it possible, that it can hurt anybody with the generous British public, but the reviewers themselves. The lines even which they have picked out with most malicious intent, are excellent, and speak for themselves. But it is not their criticism on your poem which incenses me, it is the odious tone in which they dare to speak of the most respectable and elegant female writer that England can boast. The public, the *public* will do you justice![3]

What exactly it would mean on this occasion for the "public," whom Edgeworth confidently invokes but declines directly to address, to do Barbauld justice is not entirely clear.

Edgeworth's letter does raise interesting questions about the moment in cultural history when, as Habermas puts it, "the sphere of the conjugal family became differentiated from the sphere of social reproduction."[4] Edgeworth writes to Barbauld from her position in a distinctive kind of late Enlightenment *Intimsphäre.* The Edgeworth family might appear to constitute a countercase to the separation of the "patriarchal conjugal family" from the "public sphere" developed by Habermas, since for Maria Edgeworth and her father the family was the site from which interventions in the public sphere were launched. Yet in her letter to Barbauld it is just such an intervention that Edgeworth foregoes, deferring instead to "the public" as a source of justice outside the scene of her and her father taking up their pens. Croker, for his part, tries to discredit Barbauld's critical public intervention in *Eighteen Hundred and Eleven* by undermining her claim to the kind of proper domestic or familial identity on which, presumably, she based her earlier claims to modest pedagogical public attention. Now, as a "fatidical spinster," she is placed by Croker outside both the "conjugal family" and the "public sphere" into which she has intruded with a new set of claims for attention and legitimacy.

The *Monthly Repository,* a journal with which Barbauld and her family had long been associated, defended *Eighteen Hundred and Eleven* as a "deeply interesting poem" full of "solemn truths," but even this review ends with an uneasy supplication: "Heaven grant that the melancholy strain may not prove the *voice of prophecy*!"[5] With judgments such as this counting as praising defense, one can understand why Barbauld sadly took

Croker's advice and went him one better: she not only wrote no more of what he calls "satire" and "party pamphlets in verse," she wrote no more for publication at all. A prolific and influential literary career came to an end with Croker's croakings, and the disapproval of both enemies and friends was mainly unanswered.

So what was it about this poem that so upset Barbauld's contemporaries? Crabb Robinson's later characterization treats the extended central section of the poem as if it were the whole: "*1811,* a poem in heroic rhyme in which it is prophesied that on some future day a traveller from the Antipodes will from a broken arch of Blackfriars Bridge contemplate the ruins of St. Paul's!" (1: 64). Robinson here confuses Barbauld's poem with the famous image of "some traveller from New Zealand" to which it ironically gave rise in Macaulay's 1840 *Edinburgh Review* article on Ranke's *History of the Popes.*[6] Barbauld's image of British cultural ruin turns upon not Antipodean but trans-Atlantic visitors, who in the future

> With duteous zeal their pilgrimage shall take
> From the Blue Mountains, or Ontario's lake,
> With fond, adoring steps to press the sod
> By statesman, sages, poets, heroes, trod.[7]

She imagines future U.S. or Canadian tourists visiting the crumbling monuments of Oxford, Cambridge, Stratford, and the Lake District as well as "London's faded glories." (It may be worth thinking for a moment about the bearing of this part of Barbauld's prophecy on the reverse cultural traffic across the Atlantic these days—for instance, on the irony of British scholars coming to "Ontario's lake" to participate in the academic analysis of their own cultural history at a convention which some of them profess to despise.[8]) Barbauld's vision of England's ruins is full of reverence for the traces of what remains, but this reverence is registered mainly by visitors from England's former colonies: "With throbbing bosoms shall the wanderers tread / The hallowed mansions of the silent dead." At the same time, in the still influential vein of Volney's *Ruins of Empire,* she links the internal collapse of British power to the decline and fall of previous empires, relics of whose might are to be found incorporated within Britain's own decay, grim tokens of the desire and the power to appropriate past greatness:

> On spoils from every clime their eyes shall gaze,
> AEgyptian granites and the Etruscan vase;
> And when 'midst fallen London they survey
> The stone where Alexander's ashes lay,
> Shall own with humbled pride the lesson just
> By Time's slow finger written in the dust.

It's clear from what some of Barbauld's contemporaries said that the cultural politics of *Eighteen Hundred and Eleven* disturbed them. They were even more disturbed, though, by her account of the historical and material basis of this vision of cultural collapse and dispersal, a basis which Barbauld emphasizes in the first 60-70 lines of the poem. One of the striking things about *Eighteen Hundred and Eleven*—the year in which the King was declared mentally incapable of ruling, the year of the Luddite uprisings, of massive unemployment, of terrible food shortages and soaring food prices, of mounting sentiment against the war because of its disruptive effect on trade and finance capital—is that it was published and read in 1812—the year in which the Prime Minister was murdered in the House of Commons, the year when the Peninsular War entered its critical phase, when Napoleon invaded Russia with some 500,000 soldiers and retreated with about one-fifth that number, when the author of *Childe Harold's Pilgrimage* (a poem with fascinating links to *Eighteen Hundred and Eleven*) awoke one morning and found himself famous. Barbauld doesn't address every aspect of the unstable mix of economic and political crisis with burgeoning cultural production, but she makes evident many of the key determining forces in the poem's opening movement. First, the war with France is an imperialist war, and Britain must bear its share of the responsibility for it:

> And think'st thou, Britain, still to sit at ease,
> An island queen amidst thy subject seas . . . ?
>   . . . Britain, know,
> That who hast shared the guilt must share the woe.

The pun on "guilt" in this last line may be familiar, but it's effectively deployed. So are the images Barbauld uses to represent the ephemeral power of speculative finance capital, which she understands as at once cause and symptom of the war's devastation:

> Thy baseless wealth dissolves in air away,
> Like mists that melt before the morning ray:
>
> * * *
>
> . . . Thy Midas dream is o'er;
> The golden tide of Commerce leaves thy shore,
> Leaves thee to prove the alternate ills that haunt
> Enfeebling Luxury and ghastly Want.

Though she still writes from the standpoint of that alliance between rationalist Dissent and middle-class commercial interest that Briggs and other historians have described as an emergent anti-war force in the Regency,[9] Barbauld is keenly in touch with heightened class division—with the gap between "Enfeebling Luxury and ghastly Want"—and with the inordinate hardship borne by workers and peasants. This comes out most sharply in the lines about the food shortages of 1811:

> Man calls to Famine, nor invokes in vain,
> Disease and Rapine follow in her train;
> The tramp of marching hosts disturbs the plough,

> The sword, not sickle, reaps the harvest now,
> And where the Soldier gleans the scant supply,
> The helpless Peasant but retires to die;
> No laws his hut from licensed outrage shield,
> And war's least horror is the ensanguined field.

Barbauld's conviction that the famine of 1811 was caused by human, not simply natural, agency infuriated Croker, who predictably blusters: "We had indeed heard that some mad and mischievous partisans had ventured to charge the scarcity which unhappily exists, upon the political measures of government:—but what does Mrs. Barbauld mean? Does she seriously accuse mankind of wishing for a famine, and interceding for starvation?" (310). Of course not: what she means is that the effects of the bad harvest of 1811 were brutally intensified by government policies on food distribution and trade that were driven by the Tory war effort.

Barbauld's vision of Britain's cultural decline is preceded, then, by this account of the economic and social crisis. It is followed by a retrospect of Britain's eighteenth-century mercantile ascendency which casts the vision of cultural decline in a more complex and contradictory light. This section of the poem has its weaknesses: the personified figure of capricious Genius, "Moody and viewless as the changing wind," making his fickle progress from east and south to west and north, needlessly mystifies the historical shifts in cultural power and authority; and the focus on the rise of Britain is somewhat dissipated in the vision of a more generalized flourishing of northern genius during the Enlightenment: "Northward he throws his animating ray, / O'er Celtic nations bursts the mental day." What's strong in this section, by contrast, are the figurings of cultural achievement as cultural appropriation. Barbauld updates Pope's Belinda at her toilet, with her compacted spoils from India and Arabia, "The Tortoise . . . and the Elephant," and counters Pope's sexism in this instance with an almost programmatic effort at gender balance:

> Art plies his tools, and Commerce spreads her sail,
> And wealth is wafted in each shifting gale.
> The sons of Odin tread on Persian looms,
> And Odin's daughters breathe distilled perfumes.

The recurrent tactic here is to show the triumphs of art and commerce implicated with exotic forms of exploitation and commodification:

> . . . crystal walls the tenderer plants confine,
> The fragrant orange and the nectared pine;
> The Syrian grape there hangs her rich festoons,
> Nor asks for purer air or brighter noons:
>
> * * *
>
> London exults:—on London Art bestows
> Her summer ices and her winter rose.

Such images of technological and cultural success as these contain the seeds of their own undoing—and the turn comes quickly:

> But fairest flowers expand but to decay;
> The worm is in thy core, thy glories fade away;
> Arts, arms, and wealth destroy the fruits they bring;
> Commerce, like beauty, knows no second spring.
> Crime walks thy streets, Fraud earns her unblest bread,
> O'er want and woe thy gorgeous robe is spread,
> And angel charities in vain oppose:
> With grandeur's growth the mass of misery grows.

Marlon Ross observes about *Eighteen Hundred and Eleven* that "doom is presented as a foregone conclusion"; Barbauld "does not seem interested in spurring individuals to action."[10] This is accurate enough when it comes to her vision of internal British ruin but not, I think, with respect to those societies across the Atlantic to which Genius is seen to have flown. In the last twelve lines of the poem the focus shifts dramatically from North to South America; there, "On Andes' heights," "On Chimbarazo's summits," a previously fickle and arbitrary Genius issues a decisive and militant call to arms: "Sudden he calls: ''Tis now the hour!' he cries, / Spreads his broad hand, and bids the nations rise." It's in this closing appeal to the colonial nations of Latin America, even more than in the earlier image of the northern European traveler picking his way among the wastes of ancient eastern empires ("Explor[ing] . . . Those limbs disjointed of gigantic power"), that Barbauld reveals her surprising ties with Byron and Percy Shelley and the Regency poetry of national liberation. Barbauld's denunciation of imperialist war doesn't prevent her from heralding the need for an altogether different kind of battle on behalf of freedom:

> Ardent, the Genius fans the noble strife,
> And pours through feeble souls a higher life,
> Shouts to the mingled tribes from sea to sea,
> And swears—Thy world, Columbus, shall be free.

Columbus still possesses this rising world in more than just a grammatical sense in the poem's last line—but not forever, perhaps not for long.

It is, of course, easy to smile at Barbauld's prophecy if we look at what happened in the short or even the middle run. Regency crisis and corruption were hardly the end of British imperial grandeur; for that, the world had to wait more than another century and endure a continuation of British imperialism that made the Georgian version look modest and benign by comparison—and which was responsible, in ways Barbauld couldn't recognize, for the dissemination of British literature around the globe. British cultural achievement was not arrested at Reynolds and Johnson, or at Cowper and Wordsworth. Some political reform, of the kind that William Roscoe gets attacked for advocating in the same number of the *Quarterly Review* that contains

Croker's attack on Barbauld, was eventually won. But in the long run, Barbauld got more things right than she got wrong. England would continue to suffer—has been suffering now for some fourteen years—under the Tories, or the "Conservatives" as Croker himself would be instrumental in getting his party called. When Barbauld lamented the decline of productive economic life in England in *Eighteen Hundred and Eleven,* Croker feigned incredulity and ignorance: "We do not know where Mrs. Anna Letitia now resides, though we can venture to assert that it is not on Parnassus: it must, however, be in some equally unfrequented, though less classical region" (310). Barbauld lived from 1802 until her death in 1825 in Stoke Newington—then a peaceful village just north of London, now a depressed area that has quite recently seen savage police brutality against the black community there. Barbauld wasn't so much wrong as premature in her gloomy vision of the future Britain.

And "the generous British public" did not, as Maria Edgeworth predicted they would, "do [her] justice." It's hard to estimate how widely *Eighteen Hundred and Eleven* was read; I haven't even been able to find out how many copies of the poem were published by Joseph Johnson and Co., Barbauld's publisher since the first edition of her *Poems* (1773). It's understandable that readers accustomed to the views characteristic of Barbauld's previous writing—unwavering in defense of the French Revolution and in opposition to the slave trade but consistently balanced, sensible, moderately reformist (Barbauld's friend Mary Wollstonecraft famously attacks her conventionality on the woman question)—should have been surprised and put off by her version of the ruins of empire. Though rooted in the progressive Dissenting ideology that motivates all her work, *Eighteen Hundred and Eleven* marks a decisive break with the meliorist historical perspective to which that ideology had previously been attached. One would expect that at least some readers would have appreciated rather than deplored the break, but I've found no references to the poem in Byron or Percy Shelley or Hunt.

What we have instead is Hazlitt's disappointing treatment of Barbauld in his 1818 Surrey Institution lecture *On the Living Poets.* He speaks for a spectrum of Regency readers that includes Croker as well as himself when he says, "The first poetess I can recollect is Mrs. Barbauld, with whose works I became acquainted before those of any other author, male or female, when I was learning to spell words of one syllable in her story-books for children." While he recognizes her as "a neat and pointed prose-writer"—her "**Thoughts on the Inconsistency of Human Expectations'** is one of the most ingenious and sensible essays in the language"—he condescends to her as a poet: "She is a very pretty poetess; and, to my fancy, strews the flowers of poetry most agreeably round the borders of religious controversy."[11] It's disturbing to think that Hazlitt may not have read Barbauld's most important and unpretty poem. It's even more disturbing to think that he did read it but was unable to see what it meant—not just for Barbauld, but for the historical crisis that we so unperturbedly call "the Regency."

Notes

1. *The Quarterly Review* 7 (1812): 309. Subsequent page-references to Croker's article are given parenthetically in the text. The article was long thought to have been written by Southey; for evidence of Croker's authorship, see Hill Shine and Helen Chadwick Shine, *The Quarterly Review Under Gifford: Identification of Contributors, 1809-1824* (Chapel Hill: U of North Carolina P, 1949) 31, and Geoffrey Carnall, *Robert Southey and His Age: The Development of a Conservative Mind* (Oxford: Clarendon, 1960) 114.

2. *Henry Crabb Robinson on Books and Their Writers,* ed. Edith J. Morley (London: J. M. Dent, 1938) 1: 64. Subsequent references to this edition are given parenthetically in the text.

3. Quoted in Anna Letitia Le Breton, *Memoir of Mrs. Barbauld, Including Letters and Notices of Her Family and Friends* (London: George Bell, 1874) 155-56.

4. Jürgen Habermas, *The Structural Transformation of the Public Sphere: An Inquiry into a Category of Bourgeois Society,* trans. Thomas Burger, with the assistance of Frederick Lawrence (Cambridge, MA: MIT Press, 1991) 28. Habermas develops this differentiation further under the subheading "The Bourgeois Family and the Institutionalization of a Privateness Oriented to an Audience" (43-51).

5. Quoted in Betsy Rodgers, *Georgian Chronicle: Mrs. Barbauld and her Family* (London: Methuen, 1958) 140.

6. Thomas Babington Macaulay, *Critical and Historical Essays* (London: J. M. Dent, 1907) 1: 39.

7. All quotations are from the first edition, *Eighteen Hundred and Eleven, A Poem* (London: J. Johnson, 1812).

8. See John Sutherland, "The Annual MLA Disaster," *London Review of Books* 16 December 1993.

9. Asa Briggs, *The Age of Improvement 1783-1867* (London: Longman, 1979) 170.

10. *The Contours of Masculine Desire: Romanticism and the Rise of Women's Poetry* (New York: Oxford P, 1989) 224.

11. *Complete Works of William Hazlitt,* ed. P. P. Howe (London: J. M. Dent, 1935) 5: 147.

William McCarthy (essay date 1995)

SOURCE: McCarthy, William. "'We Hoped the *Woman* Was Going to Appear': Repression, Desire, and Gender in Anna Letitia Barbauld's Early Poems." In *Romantic Women Writers: Voices and Countervoices,* edited by Paula R. Feldman and Theresa M. Kelley, pp. 113-37. Hanover, N.H.: University Press of New England, 1995.

[*In the following essay, McCarthy explores issues of feminism and femininity in Barbauld's body of work. McCarthy argues that Barbauld's writing represents a form of "compensation fantasy" through which the author enacts a condition of liberation and equality denied to her in real life.*]

I take my title from William Woodfall's 1773 review of ***Poems*** by Anna Letitia Aikin, later Mrs. Barbauld.[1] It is a piece both admiring and muddled, in almost equal proportions. Few have praised ***Poems*** more highly than Woodfall did: "In some of the pieces we have a smoothness and harmony, equal to that of our best poets; but what is more extraordinary, in others, we observe a justness of thought, and vigour of imagination, inferior only to the works of Milton and Shakespeare" (54). But on one score Woodfall found the poems disappointing. They seemed to him insufficiently "feminine": "We hoped the *Woman* was going to appear; and that while we admired the genius and learning of her graver compositions, we should be affected by the sensibility and passion of the softer pieces." He wished "that she had marked, from her own feelings, the particular distresses of some female situations," that "she had breathed her wishes, her desires, and given, from nature, what has been hitherto only guessed at . . . by the imagination of men" (133). This perceived failure to represent "the *Woman*" Woodfall attributes to Barbauld's having been educated by her father: "she . . . has . . . trod too much in the footsteps of men . . . : if she had taken her views of human life from among her female companions . . . we should have been as much enchanted with her feminine beauties, as we are now . . . astonished by the strength of her imagination, the variety of her knowledge, and the goodness of her heart" (137).

In our time, commentators have shifted this ground slightly and have declared the poems, along with Barbauld herself, disappointingly unfemin*ist*. In part they have been influenced by Mary Wollstonecraft's scorn of one Barbauld poem, **"To a Lady, with some painted Flowers,"** as an example of "the language of men" that degrades women.[2] In part they have been influenced by a letter printed by Lucy Aikin, Barbauld's niece and first memoirist, in which Barbauld deprecates the wisdom of founding a college for women.[3] Citing both Wollstonecraft and this letter, Marilyn Williamson brusquely declares Barbauld "no feminist" and her position on the question of women's intellectuality "almost retrograde." Citing this letter, Marlon Ross holds that "a woman who cannot grant women absolute equal rights with men also cannot grant them the right to write freely from the dictates of their own desire"; the poems themselves suffer from "the limits of Barbauld's feminism."[4]

From Woodfall to Ross, despite its changed vocabulary, the charge is the same: Barbauld neither writes "as a woman" nor affirms womanhood in her writing. The charge, I shall argue, is false. It expresses a spurious essentialism, the idea that there is a "natural" (as Woodfall would say) female view of human life that a person biologically female would adopt if she were not perverted by education. The antidote to this notion is historical inquiry; to understand the relation of Barbauld's work to feminism and gender, we need to study the codes in which matters of gender were encrypted in her time. I reserve for a later page consideration of Wollstonecraft's response to Barbauld, for her response forms part of an attack on the very feminism which, as I read them, Barbauld's poems embody. In contrast to Wollstonecraft, other women found *Poems* thrillingly woman-affirming. Thus "Mira," in the *Gentleman's Magazine* (1774):

> Hail, charming Aikin, hail! thy name inspires
> My glowing bosom with congenial fires.
> Oh! could the Muse her tuneful aid impart,
> And teach to speak the raptures of my heart . . .

Thus Mary Scott, in *The Female Advocate* (also 1774):

> How fair, how beauteous to our gazing eyes
> Thy vivid intellectual paintings rise!
> We feel thy feelings, glow with all thy fires,
> Adopt thy thoughts, and pant with thy desires.

Introduced to *Poems* at age fifteen, Mary Darby (later Robinson) "read them with rapture; I thought them the most beautiful Poems I had ever seen, and considered the woman who could invent such poetry, as the most to be envied of human creatures." In *The Scottish Village* (1786), Hannah Cowley celebrates "glowing Barbauld," "powerful Barbauld," her "fervors" and her "magic glass."[5] For these readers, Barbauld was "a woman speaking to women" and expressing strong emotion. They were moved by the poems' construction of female passion and a female subject; unlike Marlon Ross, they appear to have recognized Barbauld's texts as signs of female desire.

I propose to follow their lead and to explore Barbauld's early poems for the woman who eluded Woodfall and still eludes feminist commentators.[6] I begin by decoding several poems for Barbauld's motives and personal "themes," to illustrate a way of reading them that discloses those themes and explains their disguises. I then consider the poems as feminist texts, finding topics in them that align them with particular kinds of feminism. Finally, I examine Barbauld's constructions of "woman" in the poems, arguing for a feminist understanding of her need to idealize the female in the way she does. At each stage, I read Barbauld's texts biographically, that is, as traces of a subject who was their efficient cause. The case against Barbauld is based on a biographical reading: the presumed inadequacies of her poems are traced to presumed personal failings. The corrective to this bad biography must be better biography. That may seem to imply appeal to "personal" documents (letters, diaries) rather than "literary" ones like poems, but in Barbauld's case it does not. In her case, relatively few "personal" documents survive; apart from some anecdotes by her niece (to which I shall indeed appeal), the main evidence of her youthful subjectivity is her poetry. As I construe them, the poems are Barbauld's experiments in constructing her own subjectivity.[7]

Because Barbauld constructs her subjectivity in terms of gender, the biographical is necessarily the political. Self-construction, however privately carried on, entails entry into a public discourse; or, as Mary Poovey has put it, "because gender roles are part of familial, political, social, and economic relationships, the terms in which femininity is publicly formulated dictate, in large measure, the way femaleness is subjectively experienced." *Poems* thus has a place in the big debate about gender—specifically, about "woman"—that occupied public discourse in the last quarter of the eighteenth century. William St. Clair has observed, following Foucault, that the outpouring of books on the subject of female education and conduct between 1785 and 1820 argues that "women were . . . a problem in Britain" throughout those years; and G. J. Barker-Benfield persuasively holds that "the culture of Sensibility" was a culture dominated by concerns about gender roles.[8] In Barbauld's own life "woman" was similarly a problem: her early poems document her resentment of woman's restricted fate, her imaginative resistance to that fate, and her efforts to conceive a more satisfying idea of her gender. Moreover, in publishing her self-constructions Barbauld performed the political act of inciting other women to observe and emulate. The responses of women readers of *Poems* suggest that they experienced Barbauld's imaginings not as constraints upon, but rather as liberations of, their own subjectivities.

"The Daughter of a Presbyterian Clergyman"

That Woodfall found "the *Woman*" absent from *Poems* is surprising, for "woman" is literally written all over them. Twenty of the thirty-three published poems are addressed to, mention by name, or incorporate as an internal character a person of female gender.[9] Less immediately obvious but nevertheless noticeable is their tendency to gender nouns feminine, not only conventionally feminized nouns such as the soul, nature, pleasure, the earth, the spring, nations and countries, liberty and virtue but even comparatively unexpected nouns such as "the bird of Jove" (i.e., the eagle). In the concluding poem of the volume, **"A Summer Evening's Meditation"** (poem 58), ten of fourteen explicitly gendered nouns in the first-edition text (the one reviewed by Woodfall) are feminine. Woodfall himself censured one of those genderings as mistaken: "there is . . . a slight mark of seeming inattention, where the . . . writer speaks of Saturn in the feminine." He calls this an "offense," albeit a minor one, "against ancient mythology" (*Monthly Review,* 136n), and in so doing he exposes his own bias. The **"Meditation,"** as we shall see, is virtually a gynetopia, but the only female noticed by Woodfall is noticed because, according to patriarchal booklore, she should be "he" and is thus an "error."[10]

Gender pronouns, however, probably did not interest Woodfall. What he wished for were personal confessions, much as Marlon Ross wishes for endorsements of desire. These wishes need not have been disappointed. The poems swarm with signs of "the personal": the first-person pronoun abounds, usually signifying authorial subjectivity; a footnote to **"On the Death of Mrs. Jennings"** (poem 17) identifies Mrs. Jennings as "The Author's Grandmother"; passages in **"The Invitation"** (poem 4), describing the Duke of Bridgewater's Canal and Warrington Academy, situate the author geographically in Lancashire and politically in Protestant Dissent; **"Mrs. P———"** (poem 3), **"Miss B * * * * *"** (poem 4), **"Miss R———"** (poem 8), and **"Lissy"** (poem 39) all appear to signify the author's intimate friends. The poems actually invite a biographical reading, even as they also slightly repel it by making the signs of the personal only partially intelligible (**"Mrs. P———,"** not "Mrs. Priestley"). The effect of half-disclosure is to make the poems seem not really meant for the public eye; our relation to them seems that of overhearers of private musings. This privacy itself may signify gender because in gender convention (and in much social practice) the private was the realm of woman.

Woodfall, who knew something of Barbauld apart from what he saw in *Poems,* in fact initiated reading them biographically. He footnoted lines 61-62 of **"The Groans of the Tankard"** (poem 38), "Unblest the day, and luckless was the hour / Which doom'd me to a Presbyterian's power," with the remark "Miss Aikin is the daughter of a Presbyterian clergyman" (*Monthly Review,* 56n). The Tankard is speaking, but Woodfall's note seems to assign its groans to Barbauld herself. In so doing, whether or not Woodfall understood it, his note points to a deeply personal theme of Barbauld's poems: resentment against repression, amounting to imaginative insurrection. His note also intimates the nature of the code in which the poems inscribe her per-

sonal themes: displacement or, in rhetorical terms, allegory. **"The Groans of the Tankard"** is a fine point of departure for both topics.

In this burlesque poem, the Aikin family tankard interrupts dinner with a miraculous complaint of ill usage. Once the vehicle of port and ale at City feasts and ecclesiastical manses, it has been degraded by its Presbyterian owners to a mere water pitcher. Its lament includes brief but luxuriant description of the gustatory pleasures enjoyed by "the portly Alderman, the stately Mayor," "the gouty Dean, / Or rosy Prebend" (39, 70-71), from which it has been exiled. Because the poem is burlesque, the opposition between the past and present lives of the Tankard courts an ironic reading of the Tankard's groans, one in which Presbyterian purity and sobriety contrast favorably with Establishment booziness and loose living.[11] This contrast is by no means trivial to Barbauld; elsewhere she identifies vigorously with Presbyterian Dissent, victimized as it was by a bigoted and licentious Establishment. But in **"The Groans of the Tankard"** that is only one strand of resentment, and it provides cover for a deeper resentment of Presbyterian Dissent itself—of the very sobriety which, in the ironic reading, is Presbyterianism's honorable distinction. Presbyterianism, the Tankard complains, is joyless, anti-sensual; the Tankard is

> Fated to serve the Puritanick race,
> Whose slender meal is shorter than their grace;
> Whose moping sons no jovial orgies keep;
> Where evening brings no summons—but to sleep;
> No Carnival is even Christmas here,
> And one long Lent involves the meagre year.
>
> (63-68)

Unequivocally, albeit humorously, this poem ratifies *appetite*. At the dinner hour, desire, in the form of hunger, simply overwhelms an entire system of values:

> 'Twas at the solemn, silent, noon-tide hour,
> When hunger rages with despotic power,
> When the lean student quits his Hebrew roots
> For the gross nourishment of English fruits,
> And throws unfinish'd airy systems by
> For solid pudding and substantial pye,
> When hungry poets the glad summons own,
> And leave spare fast to dine with Gods alone . . .
>
> (5-12)

Synecdochically represented by "Hebrew roots" (a pun that links learned philology with low diet) and "airy systems" is the curriculum of study at Warrington Academy. The snub to Milton in line 12 ("spare Fast, that oft with gods doth diet" ["Il Penseroso," line 46]) generalizes to the Dissenting tradition of high-minded seriousness, of which Warrington was the latest and most ambitious effort. The fact that the "lean student" is male further generalizes to gendered provisions for education in patriarchal society. Even the desire acknowledged by these lines is male: men are also allowed to drop their pretensions and feast. Only at "our sober meal" (13) is desire stinted.

Whose desire? The Tankard's, and the Tankard is implicitly gendered female. It is feminized by being given words that parody the speech of Pope's Thalestris to Belinda after the rape of the lock. Was it for this, Thalestris asks, that your sexuality was cultivated? Was it for this, demands the Tankard, that I was born?

> Did I for this my native bed resign,
> In the dark bowels of Potosi's mine?
> Was I for this with violence torn away,
> And drag'd to regions of the upper day?
> For this the rage of torturing furnace bore,
> From foreign dross to purge the bright'ning ore?
> For this have I endur'd the fiery test,
> And was I stamp'd for this with Britain's lofty crest?
>
> (53-60)[12]

A second feminizing move is Barbauld's allusion, in line 5, to a poem by David Mallett, "The Ballad of William and Margaret." At "the silent, solemn hour, / When night and morning meet," Margaret's ghost appears at William's bedside to reproach him for faithlessness.[13] The Tankard utters its—or rather, her—reproach at "the solemn, silent, noon-tide hour."

The character whom the Tankard reproaches—the counterpart to William in the ballad—is the Presbyterian to whose power she is subject, and that person, in Woodfall's reading and in mine, is a character never named in the poem, the Rev. John Aikin.[14] The poem suggests that his faithlessness consists of stinting his daughter's appetite and barring her from the studies of men. The stinting of appetite may be both literal and figurative. It is literal in that, as Barker-Benfield observes, control of desire for food was strongly urged on women: "moralists pushed inexorably against women's . . . expressing appetite."[15] It is figurative if "appetite" is generalized to include other desires, such as hunger for education. The poem protests, but at its close repression is reinstituted. The Tankard's groans are quelled by the appearance of another female,

> An ancient Sybil furrow'd o'er with years;
> Her aspect sour, and stern ungracious look
> With sudden damp the conscious vessel struck;
> Chill'd at her touch its mouth it slowly clos'd,
> And in long silence all its griefs repos'd . . .
>
> (82-86)

In terms of the poem's fiction—it is dinnertime, and the meal is just over—this crone might be a servant, come to clean up. But why should the Tankard be made to feel guilty ("conscious") by a servant? And what is she feeling conscious about, unless about her rebellion? Re-

bellion against a parent is, of course, punishable by a parent; logically, then, the "sour" female who represses complaint is the poet's mother.[16] Commenting on this poem, Woodfall, in another moment of muddled insight, speaks of Barbauld's "chastised and regulated genius," from which he would not have expected her to succeed in burlesque (*Monthly Review*, 57). His words are surprisingly apt, in view of the poem's close. Chastised and regulated, the Tankard shuts up.

A similar but more prosperous insurrection, one not punished by an internalized parent, is the ode **"To Wisdom"** (poem 32). Perhaps its greater success results from its being more heavily encoded. In appearance, the poem simply replays Milton's "L'Allegro," banishing the wisdom that only frowns and inviting pleasure in its place:

> But if thou com'st with frown austere
> To nurse the brood of care and fear;
> To bid our sweetest passions die,
> And leave us in their room a sigh;
>
> * * *
>
> WISDOM, thine empire I disclaim,
> Thou empty boast of pompous name!
>
> * * *
>
> Hail to pleasure's frolic train!
> Hail to fancy's golden reign!
> Festive mirth, and laughter wild,
> Free and sportful as the child!
>
> (7-10, 15-16, 19-22)

But one of Lucy Aikin's anecdotes promotes a more pointed reading. Barbauld, she says, wrote the poem in protest against a ban by the Warrington Academy tutors on amateur theatricals.[17] In this context, "Wisdom" acquires a new, more specific meaning: it virtually personifies the Academy's authorities—who included her father—and thus transforms the poem into an outright repudiation of them. ("Care and fear" are particularly suggestive in this reading, for the Rev. John Aikin was noted for his caution, even timidity: "He is alarmed at every thing," his colleague Joseph Priestley remarked.)[18] Construing "Wisdom" as Barbauld's code name for the local patriarchy is encouraged by an unpublished poem regretting the departure from Warrington of a Mr. and Mrs. Edwards, apparently as a result of conduct that offended the tutors (poem 45).[19] To Barbauld, they are still a "blest pair" in whose company she delights; she loves them for the very gaiety and "careless[ness]" that probably led to their exile, and she sighs for their return "tho Wisdom frown." "Wisdom" serves as a code name for the tutors by metonymy, in congruence with its more customary meaning. Barbauld "patriarchalizes" the word, making it a blocking agent and an object of resistance. In both poems it is placed in opposition to pleasure, and in both its repressive opposition is resisted.

In the published poems the personal is (not surprisingly) encoded in displaced forms so that to read the poems biographically is to allegorize them. Two unpublished poems give us the personal without displacement, although at a price: instead of displacing, they idealize. One of them, **"To [her brother] Dr. Aikin on his Complaining that she neglected him"** (poem 7; 1768), fills a gap at the center of **"The Groans of the Tankard"**: it tells what birthright Barbauld felt herself to have been cheated of. Apologizing to her brother (who is at Manchester studying surgery) for neglecting his letters, she asserts her utter freedom from "angry thoughts" and "envy" (35) and traces their mutual love to their earliest years. But in the very act of denying envy, she repines at the fate patriarchy assigns to her gender, a fate so different from John's:

> Those hours are now no more which smiling flew
> And the same studies saw us both pursue;
> Our path divides—to thee fair fate assign'd
> The nobler labours of a manly mind:
> While mine, more humble works, and lower cares,
> Less shining toils, and meaner praises shares.
> Yet sure in different moulds they were not cast
> Nor stampt with separate sentiments and taste.
> But hush my heart! nor strive to soar too high,
> Nor for the tree of knowledge vainly sigh;
> Check the fond love of science and of fame . . .
>
> (48-58)

Compare "stampt" here with the Tankard's "stamp'd . . . with Britain's lofty crest": both signify one's condition at birth. The Tankard was born to a better fate than it has met. Likewise Barbauld: by birthright she was as capable as John of enjoying literary and medical education. However, she now feels guilty for desiring them and tries to accept her "bounded sphere" (60).[20] The other unpublished poem, **"On Mrs. P[riestley]'s Leaving Warrington"** (poem 1; 1767), is a lamentation at losing two dear friends, Joseph and Mary Priestley, to whose house she has been in the habit of making day-long visits:

> How oft the well-worn path to her abode
> At early dawn with eager steps I've trod,
> And with unwilling feet retired at eve,
> Loath its approach unheeded to believe.
> Oft have I there the social circle joined
> Whose brightening influence raised my pensive mind,
> For none within that circle's magic bound,
> But sprightly spirits move their chearful round.
> No cold reserve, suspicion, sullen care,
> Or dark unfriendly passions enter there,
> But pleasing fires of lively fancy play,
> And wisdom mingles her serener ray.
> Not in that form those stern forbidding airs
> Which seated on the Cynic's brow she wears
> To damp the spirits, each gay hope controul,
> And check the unguarded sallies of the soul,
> But drest in easy smiles with happy art
> She builds the surer empire in the heart.
>
> (37-54)

Barbauld's representation of the "sprightly," "chearful" Priestley household may owe something to contemporary idealizations of the "middle-class family" as a locus of happiness (for example, in Adam Smith's *Theory of Moral Sentiments* [1759]); however, lines 37-45 also suggest a felt contrast between their household and her own, a place of "reserve, suspicion, sullen care" where "wisdom" operates as "controul" and restrains her spontaneity. For her, the Priestleys represent the freedom to be spontaneous; her eager visits to them and reluctant returns home enact the same opposition as that between pleasure and wisdom in **"To Wisdom."**

The woman who can be inferred from these poems and whom I identify with Barbauld the poet is emotionally conflicted, struggling against strong parental and cultural repressions of her energies. Sometimes she is able imaginatively to overthrow the repressions; at other times they resubjugate her. The struggle takes various forms, some of them far displaced. In one form, the overtly political metaphorically represents the personal or simply admits the personal by congruence. Thus, **"Corsica"** (poem 9; 1769) and **"The Times"** (poem 10; c. 1769, unpublished) espouse oppositionist causes and insurrectionary acts in the public sphere. It is not, however, simply the cause of Corsican independence that makes Barbauld's "raptur'd fancy" burn (31). The idea of struggle for freedom itself excites her:

> It is not in the force of mortal arm,
> Scarcely in fate, to bind the struggling soul
> That gall'd by wanton power, indignant swells
> Against oppression; breathing great revenge,
> Careless of life, determin'd to be free.
>
> (102-106)

Obliged in the end to acknowledge Corsica's defeat by superior numbers, she proceeds, characteristically, to feminize it, this time by simile:

> . . . So strives the moon
> In dubious battle with the gathering clouds,
> And strikes a splendour thro' them; till at length
> Storms roll'd on storms involve the face of heaven
> And quench her struggling fires.
>
> (188-92)

The suppression of Corsican nationalism is thus likened to the suppression of the female. Finally, Barbauld herself closes the poem with a move that envelops a "private," "female" meaning within a public, political one:

> There yet remains a freedom, nobler far
> Than kings or senates can destroy or give;
> Beyond the proud oppressor's cruel grasp
> Seated secure; uninjur'd; undestroy'd;
> Worthy of Gods: The freedom of the mind.
>
> (197-201)

This is a compensatory move, asserting an ideal substitute for a failed reality. Hermeneutically, it speaks to two audiences at once. To one, including Woodfall, it speaks the language of Milton ("the mind is its own place") and thus situates Barbauld in a well-defined male tradition of ethical-political discourse. To the other, readers of Mary Astell or Lady Chudleigh, it speaks the language of early feminist quietism: the conclusion that, in Astell's words, since women cannot obtain power in this world, "our only endeavour shall be to be absolute monarchs in our own Bosoms."[21] Thus, Barbauld smuggles her personal themes into these poems under the label of a public discourse. To the reader of **"Corsica"** who, like Woodfall, is prepared only to hear Milton, there will seem to be no woman in the poem.

Elsewhere, protest against Establishment repression of Dissent is the vehicle of her complaints. Barbauld is ambivalent in her relation to Dissent; although she resents its self-denial, rationalism, and emotional low temperature, she also identifies with its deprivations at the hands of the Establishment. In **"The Invitation"** (poem 4), allegorizing the legal obstacles raised by the Establishment against Dissenters' education, she figures Dissent as an eagle, gendered feminine, impeded in her flight by a phallic figure, a snake (99-104). In the same poem, her expressions of enthusiasm for Warrington Academy compare in wistful enviousness with her praise of her brother's achievements in **"To Dr. Aikin . . ."** [**"To Dr. Aikin on his Complaining that she neglected him"**] (poem 7). She intimates that she might appreciate the opportunities open to Warrington students more than they do:

> Ye generous youth who love this studious shade,
> How rich a field is to your hopes display'd!
> Knowledge to you unlocks the classic page;
> And virtue blossoms for a better age.
> Oh golden days! oh bright unvalued hours!
> What bliss (did ye but know that bliss) were yours?
> With richest stores your glowing bosoms fraught,
> Perception quick, and luxury of thought . . .
>
> (111-18)

In a **"Prologue to the Play of Henry the Eighth, spoken by a Warrington Student in his morning Gown"** (poem 30, c. 1772, published 1790), she constructs a contrast between the ancient universities and humble Warrington that parallels the contrast, in **"To Dr. Aikin . . . ,"** between her brother's life prospects and her own. Against the towers and bowers of "illustrious Oxford" and the "growing pride" of Cambridge (3-5), she sets Warrington's "far humbler structures . . . unknown to fame," which "fondly aspire to bear the muses name" (15-16). By analogy, Warrington's relation to the Establishment resembles that of female to male opportunity. The parallel structurings of privilege and denial ("illustrious" and "nobler" against "humble[r]" and "fond[ly]") in the two poems—undisplaced in **"To Dr. Aikin . . . ,"** displaced onto Warrington in the **"Prologue"** [**"Prologue to the Play of Henry the Eighth, spoken by a Warrington Student in his Morning Gown"**]—implicitly align women with Dissenters and patriarchies with Establishments. Here in the **"Prologue"** and in her later pamphlet *An Address to the Opposers of the Repeal of the Corporation and Test Acts* (1790), Barbauld anticipates Virginia Woolf, who in *A Room of One's Own* and *Three Guineas* figures the second-class status of women in terms of the scanty educational provisions made for them by a patriarchy that lavishes treasure on the instruction of its sons.

Once sensitized to Barbauld's pattern of displacement, we can see it in contexts apparently far distant from the biographical. **"On the Backwardness of the Spring 1771"** (poem 18) tells in its figuration a tale of mutilated, grieving womanhood. The rainy spring resembles a woman pilgrim "whose wounded bosom drinks her falling tears" (14). If we assume that Barbauld's grief and sense of "mutilation" arose from her experience of parental "controul" and denial of opportunity, this poem appears to enact child-parent relations. The poem's last stanza, a plea to "indulgent nature" to let spring happen, sounds like a child's plea to a withholding parent. "Indulgent" is one of Barbauld's favorite words in *Poems*; in **"The Invitation,"** in a typical use of it, she flies from winter's rigor to "brighter climes, and more *indulgent* skies" (22; my emphasis). Such passages may be seen as metaphors for harsh and kind parenting—for the "controul" she had endured and the spontaneity she craved.

Perhaps the only undisplaced form in which a young woman would feel licensed to articulate emotional turbulence in the first person was the religious poem. **"An Address to the Deity"** (poem 2) avows "the waves of grief," seemingly chronic, and the "headlong tide" of "impetuous passion" (13, 14). It can avow them because it also surrenders them, longingly, to the "controul" of the superparent. While her family's control was marked by reserve, suspicion, and care, God's is that of an indulgent father:

> His spirit, ever brooding o'er our mind,
> Sees the first wish to better hopes inclin'd;
> Marks the young dawn of every virtuous aim,
> And fans the smoking flax into a flame:
> His ears are open to the softest cry,
> His grace descends to meet the lifted eye;
> He reads the language of a silent tear,
> And sighs are incense from a heart sincere.
>
> (27-34)

Imagining this parenting, Barbauld permits herself a moment's regression to infancy: "Thus shall I rest, unmov'd by all alarms, / Secure within the temple of thine arms" (69-70). Although religious discourse commonly trades in fantasies of infantile regression, this poem may still be treated hermeneutically in the same way as **"Corsica"**; its public discourse of God is an envelope for Barbauld's fantasies of happier relations with her parents. Again, in **"Hymn to Content"** (poem 52) she prays to be "no more by varying passions beat" (13) and to be stilled into stoical indifference. Here the admission of turbulence is licensed by the avowed wish to escape it, a move that had a respectable (and distinctly female) lineage, including, most famously, Elizabeth Carter's translation (1758) of Epictetus, whose work counseled the conquest of passion by self-command.

Read biographically, Barbauld's poems give an impression of reiterated, restless efforts to deal with the same knot of life themes. Their core motive is grief and anger at the deprivation of birthright inflicted by her family's and her culture's oppressive construction of "woman." The complaints they raise are encoded to elude detection by the wrong parties. Because the poems were written for and to Warrington people and circulated in the very milieu of which they complain, we could hardly expect otherwise. Barbauld's way of circulating them tended to emphasize their character as "messages" even while it also often displaced them from herself. Many were sent in letters to her intimate friend Elizabeth Belsham;[22] others were deposited in places where they would be found later. The most famous of the deposited poems is **"The Mouse's Petition"** (poem 19), left in the cage of a mouse that Joseph Priestley had captured for use in an experiment. In the "person" of the mouse it pleads, quite simply, for freedom; it asks for equal treatment under Priestley's code of political liberty, which "spurn[s] a tyrant's chain" (10). No doubt Priestley took the poem literally (he is said to have released the mouse); but had he known Anne Finch's poem "The Bird and the Arras" (1713), he might have divined that fables of animal entrapment are a tradition of feminist complaint. Encoded in these various ways, Barbauld's poems lend themselves to duplicitous readings, often, although not exclusively, along gender lines. Thus, William Woodfall could admire them for carrying on in the tradition of Milton, oblivious to the signs in them of "the *Woman.*" From the ecstatic responses of "Mira," Mary Scott, Mary Robinson, and Hannah Cowley, it would appear that they understood Barbauld's encodings as the postcards from the volcano that they are.[23]

"We . . . Pant with Thy Desires"

The cardboard antifeminist image of Barbauld, purporting to be based on her biography, is a figure of repression pure and simple, an enemy of women's desire. A more thorough biographical reading discloses a far more complicated and interesting woman—and in at least one important respect, a feminist. In a culture that imposes upon women a narrow range of permissible desires and limited means of expressing them, to insist on asserting desire may be, ipso facto, a feminist act.[24] Barbauld's insurrections against repression all assert desire. The objects of her desire vary and thus imply various traditions of feminism. In **"The Groans of the Tankard"** and, more explicitly, in **"To Wisdom,"** the object of desire is pleasure—a more oppositional demand, given the historical tendency of Presbyterianism (of which the Tankard reminds us), than it may seem today, when pleasure (or what at least usually passes for it) appears politically banal. In **"The Invitation"** (poem 4), Barbauld calls upon her friend Elizabeth Belsham to leave the town and join her in pursuing the pleasures of a Lancashire spring:

> From glittering scenes which strike the dazzled sight
> With mimic grandeur and illusive light,
> From idle hurry, and tumultuous noise,
> From hollow friendships, and from sickly joys,
> Will DELIA, at the muse's call retire
> To the pure pleasures rural scenes inspire?
>
> (9-14)

Pleasure is allegorized as a "smiling goddess" whom they will pursue wherever she may lead, through forest or mead or hill or glade, and whom they will never lose because "she cannot fly from friendship, and from you" (33-38). In a twist on the traditional moral exhortation *surge, age* (arise, get going), Barbauld urges her friend to "haste away, / And let us sweetly waste the careless day" (52). This single line epitomizes important Barbauld concerns. *Careless* is a word central to Barbauld's youthful poetic vocabulary; almost always used honorifically, it contrasts with *care,* as in "the brood of care and fear" (**"To Wisdom,"** 8) and thus opposes the patriarchal ideology encoded in the word *wisdom.* "Waste" is gloriously self-indulgent: an exhortation to *haste* that we may *waste* implicitly summons up everything for which Protestant Dissent stood, to snub it utterly. (The gesture is analogous to the gesture in **"The Groans of the Tankard"** that summons up Milton in order to snub him.) Barbauld is seeking not "improvement," not "profit," not power nor responsibility nor rationality, nor even "seriousness"; she is seeking pure enjoyment. Her ethic here resembles that of Aphra Behn's poem "The Golden Age" (1684), in which the only injunction is "to pursue delight," and in our own time that of Marilyn French's *Beyond Power.* This kind of feminism, writes French, "abjures the self-sacrifice . . . patriarchy demands from women, offering instead an ideal of personal integrity and pleasure; it condemns the pursuit of power, stratification, and the repudiation of the body and feeling that patriarchy instills in the public world, offering instead an ideal of felicity."[25] In their short compass, Barbauld's lines indeed do all this. The town's "glittering scenes," "mimic grandeur and illusive light," encode the public world of power and stratification in which women have no place; the invitation to Delia to form a gynetopia of two (or rather three, including Pleasure) repudiates patriarchy. Feeling is present in

Barbauld's love for her friend, and body is honored by the sensuous image of pleasure lying "*wrapt* in careless ease" as in a garment (29; my emphasis).

Although Barbauld's language of pleasure is chaste, it is by no means drained of sensuousness or eroticism. Two of her favorite words, *soft* and *sweet,* serve as shorthand for a range of sensory delights. They can eroticize discourse otherwise seemingly unerotic, as in **"Verses written in an Alcove"** ([earlier, **"Lissy,"**] poem 39), where these two words, together with the pulse of the lines, suggest quick-breathing anticipation:

> Now the moon-beam's trembling lustre
>   Silvers o'er the dewy green,
> And in soft and shadowy colours
>   Sweetly paints the checquer'd scene.
>
>   * * *
>
> Choral songs and sprightly voices
>   Echo from her cell shall call;
> Sweeter, sweeter than the murmur
>   Of the distant water fall.
>
>   * * *
>
> Soft, as when the evening breezes
>   Gently stir the poplar grove;
> Brighter than the smile of summer,
>   Sweeter than the breath of love.
>
>   (1-4, 21-24, 29-32)

The poem appoints a tryst in the alcove, at night, with "Lissy" (Elizabeth Rigby, whose "love creating wiles" are celebrated in another poem [poem 44, unpublished]). Barbauld eroticizes her friendship with Lissy as a way of figuring the delights of that friendship—more probably, of female friendship in general.

The most apparently erotic of the poems are the six "Songs" (poems 22-27). Because they are love songs, they are highly conventionalized and codified, and their eroticism is largely notional. The subject position in most of them is generically male, and the objects of the passions represented in most of them are generically female. First published in John Aikin's *Essays on Song-Writing* (1772) and written in correspondence with him about love songs as a genre, they have a "theoretical" character, as if designed to demonstrate various postures of amorous discourse. There is probably also a measure of dry humor in them; Barbauld has something of Dryden's taste for extravagance verging on parody. Nevertheless, the songs give scope to her genuine desire for passionate rhetoric, for representing hyperbolic emotion. Thus, the "marks" of true love (according to **"Song 1"**) include being "all bath'd in tears," lying "whole ages at a beauty's feet," "kneel[ing]," "languish[ing]," "implor[ing]," and still adoring "tho' she disdain": "It is to do all this and think thy sufferings

sweet." The lover in **"Song 4"** is carried away by destructive passion as a sailor is carried out to sea by the storm surge and drowned. **"Song 6"** envisions a lover who has heedlessly cultivated a passion for a young girl that, now that she is grown, utterly dominates him. To represent his state, Barbauld indulges herself in the language of "Oriental" despotism:

> But now despotic o'er the plains
> The awful noon of beauty reigns,
>   And kneeling crowds adore;
> Its beams arise too fiercely bright,
> Danger and death attend the sight,
>   And I must hope no more.
>
>   (19-24)

The extravagant irrationality of these assertions, their studied imprudence and cultivated rhetoric of self-immolation, must have been highly attractive to a person brought up on rational guard against the "sallies of the soul"; they are best regarded as exertions of a secularized religious enthusiasm.[26] That the subject position of these songs is generically male rather than female is almost inevitable. No "respectable" woman in the late eighteenth century could have addressed such language to a male (other than God or Jesus); in a woman's text, the rhetoric of erotic passion had to be encoded in a form that makes it appear male.[27]

The poems also evince a sporadic but intense interest in childbirth. In **"To Mrs. P[riestley], with some Drawings of Birds and Insects"** (poem 3), this interest is displaced onto the insects, which await their birth in a "heaving tomb" that "distends with vital heat" (78). Their birth is likened to two scenes in Tasso's *Gerusalemme Liberata,* here conflated by Barbauld into one:

> So when Rinaldo struck the conscious rind,
> He found a nymph in every trunk confin'd;
> The forest labours with convulsive throes,
> The bursting trees the lovely births disclose,
> And a gay troop of damsels round him stood,
> Where late was rugged bark and lifeless wood.
>
>   (85-90)

The births follow an act analogous to sexual penetration. This passage, which occurs apropos insects, could give point to Richard Polwhele's horror in *The Unsex'd Females* (1798) at the idea of teaching women natural history; in his view it was a provocation to eroticism.[28] In another Barbauld poem (a "character" of Mary Enfield, published post-humously [poem 46]), a woman who bore twins is figured as an orchard tree, "heavy . . . with fruit" (3). Emphasizing "lovely fruit" (7), "ruddy orchards" (8), and "twin apples blushing on a bough" (9), the poem images the childbearing woman as luxuriantly sensual.

Pleasure and eroticism are not, however, the only objects of desire in Barbauld's poems. In **"Corsica,"** desire is explicitly political: to be free of domination, to be empowered. Lines 102-106 (quoted above) generalize the demand for liberty in terms that could embrace young women in Lancashire as well as male insurgents in Corsica. More than that, the poem's figure of Liberty is amazonian: "the mountain goddess," a female athlete who "loves to range at large" in "lonely scenes / Of unquelled nature," "and on the iron soil / Prints her majestic step" (68-69, 75-77). The sheer power implied by the language of *printing* a step on *iron* soil is noteworthy. Indeed, the female in **"Corsica"** is a notably powerful person, whether encoded as Liberty or—her other incarnation—as Virtue. A virago, she revels in scenes of storm and combat:

> . . . then her tow'ring form
> Dilates with kindling majesty; her mien
> Breathes a diviner spirit, and enlarg'd
> Each spreading feature, with an ampler port
> And bolder tone, exulting, rides the storm,
> And joys amidst the tempest.
>
> * * *
>
> . . . The bold swimmer joys not so
> To feel the proud waves under him, and beat
> With strong repelling arm the billowy surge;
> The generous courser does not so exult
> To toss his floating mane against the wind,
> And neigh amidst the thunder of the war,
> As virtue to oppose her swelling breast
> Like a firm shield against the darts of fate.
>
> (146-51, 160-67)

The two last lines image female joy in aggressive action, in terms anticipating Monique Wittig's *Les Guérillères* (1969).[29] To appreciate just how thrilling these visions of female athleticism must have been to Barbauld and her women readers, we need only recall the impediments to movement with which eighteenth-century women were encumbered. The suppression of bodily activity in girls was, of course, part of their training to be "ladies."[30] In the figures of Liberty and Virtue here and in that of "my soul" in **"Hymn 5"** (poem 37), exhorted to awake and arm herself for Christian battle, Barbauld compensates for the restraints imposed on her gender with robust fantasies of free and powerful movement. That women readers responded to these fantasies is perhaps indicated by Elizabeth Benger's praise of Barbauld in *The Female Geniad* (1791): "she *rambles* o'er the bounties of the globe."[31]

The greatest female freedom of action in **Poems** is found in **"A Summer Evening's Meditation"** (poem 58), an extraordinary poem in the traditions both of Anne Finch's "A Nocturnal Reverie" and of *Paradise Lost*; indeed, it seems to marry them. Like Finch and also as in her own **"Alcove"** verses [**"Verses Written in an Alcove"**], Barbauld claims the night poetically for women, as the time when (in Finch's words) "tyrant *man* doth sleep." At the poem's opening, Diana, rising

while the sun ("the sultry tyrant of the south" [1]) sets, "impatient for the night, . . . seems to push / Her brother down the sky" (9-10; cf. Barbauld's all but avowed envy of her brother). Contemplation is up and about; she is a female who spends her days in dark, hidden places (grottoes or deep woods), feeding on "thoughts unripen'd by the sun" (22) but who at night comes into her own. The stars emerge, at once a sensuous experience by virtue of their beauty and also an accession of knowledge, for they speak divine wisdom to her who watches them.[32] As the poem's narrator contemplates the stars, relishing their beauty and pondering their meaning, she dares to wish to explore them nearer. No sooner is the wish formed than she soars upward, sailing "on fancy's wild and roving wing" (72) past the moon and the planets, launching "fearless . . . into the trackless deeps of space" (81-82), even "to the dread confines of eternal night . . . Where embryo systems and unkindled suns / Sleep in the womb of chaos" (93, 96-97). Her language in this recalls, of course, the Miltonic Satan's journey upward from Hell through Chaos to Earth (*Paradise Lost*, 2:910 ff). Apparently, she is appropriating the Miltonic sublime for a feminist "sally of the soul." Yet in a way, Satan's rebellion against the deity is an archetype of Barbauld's various insurgencies against patriarchy; like him, she will not stay in her assigned place. Having dared thus greatly, the poem backs down at its close. She ceases flight, "abash'd" (111), and returns to earth. Even so, the poem ends with a permitted (because religiously authorized) orgasm of pleasure as she imagines what heaven will offer hereafter "to my ravish'd sense" (121).

In Barbauld's poems, then, desire takes the form of compensatory fantasy. What in life she is denied or discouraged from doing Barbauld asserts in imagination. That the assertions themselves are displaced or variously compromised signifies that the texts in which they occur should be construed as emotional battlegrounds or, in the phrase of materialist feminism, "sites of conflictual discourses." To see them merely as static embodiments of fixed positions (and those positions "unfeminist") is to perpetuate the remarkably unperceptive notion set down long ago, by Henry Crabb Robinson, to the effect that "the felicity of [Barbauld's] life consisted in a passionless serenity of mind," a state that "is not the element of poetry."[33] This notion still lives in Marlon Ross's claim that Barbauld's poetry is limited by her alleged unwillingness to endorse female desire. In fact, Barbauld's mind was neither passionless nor serene. It was turbulent, and a main source of its turbulence was gender.

"The Sunshine That Laughs on Her Brow"

The poem that Mary Wollstonecraft scorned, **"To a Lady, with some painted Flowers"** (poem 55), likens the lady to "flowers sweet, and gay, and delicate" (3), distinguishes flowers, a "luxury," from "loftier forms" to which "rougher tasks [are] assign'd" (7-9), and closes by asserting that "[her] best, [her] sweetest empire is—to please" (18). "On this sensual error," complains Wollstonecraft, ". . . has the false system of female manners been reared, which robs the whole sex of its dignity, and classes the brown and the fair with the smiling flowers that only adorn the land. This has ever been the language of men."[34] Even apart from this poem, many of the other constructions of "woman" that we encounter in *Poems* cannot avoid striking us as proleptic of the Victorian "angel in the house." Miss Rigby ["**Miss R————**"] (poem 8) is an example: honored as a caregiver whose breast is a "pillow" for her declining mother's head (28), she is even called an "angel" (9). Susannah Barbauld Marissal (poem 40) is praised for a sweetness and innocence that feminists today would regard as idiotic; we want something altogether tougher. To say this is, of course, to come up short against the ideological demands of feminist textual commentary today. If we mean to be historians, however, we must be willing to situate the constructions of "woman," so persistent in Barbauld's early poems, not among our discourses but among the discourses of their culture. Further, to understand why Barbauld persisted in constructing these particular ideas of woman, we need to imagine the role they played in her construction of her self.

Because Barbauld's early poems predate the *Vindication* by twenty years, the discourses among which we must situate them do not include Wollstonecraft. Rather, Barbauld's constructions can be seen as reactions against previous or contemporary constructs of "woman" that Barbauld herself would have regarded as misogynist. Her insistence on women's friendships, for example, and on celebrating so many of her friends, looks like a direct response to James Fordyce's *Sermons to Young Women* (1766). She deeply resented Fordyce's insinuation that women's friendships are not sincere (a hoary topic of misogyny) and was tempted "to have burnt the book for that unkind passage."[35] But the writer whom she most answers probably is Pope. Her intimate knowledge of his poems is written all over hers, in the form of echoes and allusions such as the one in "**The Groans of the Tankard**" to *The Rape of the Lock*. Implied by Pope's Belinda, whose eyes are "unfix'd," is an idea of woman as light-minded and unsteady;[36] his essay "Of the Characters of Women" dwells on the supposed incoherence of the female character (or even its nonexistence) and on women's alleged abundance of incontinent, whirling, wasteful energy. In some quarters today, the idea that woman cannot be fixed to any character may have a satisfyingly Foucaultian ring, for we have learned to distrust category divisions as engines of cultural control; in the name of human liberation (from race, class, and gender), we are exhorted to "refuse what we 'are.'"[37] There is some irony in a de-

velopment that can make Pope's misogynist ideology look retrospectively chic. For Pope, "female caprice" signified not the liberation of woman but her inferiority; it was evidence of the "weaker," "softer" material of which woman was made, "matter too soft a lasting mark to bear."[38]

Barbauld could reply to the Popean aspersion in several ways. She could oppose it, counterasserting female integrity and coherence in terms similar to those in which Pope constructs such ideal figures as the "good Critic" or some other character that reconciles oppositions instead of being torn apart by them. Several poems practice this reply. Mary Priestley ["**On Mrs. P[riestley]'s Leaving Warrington**"] (poem 1) reconciles Popean opposites in possessing at once "so cool a judgment, and a heart so warm" (26). Barbauld's cousin and sister-in-law-to-be, Martha Jennings (poem 41), is utterly regular and rational, speaks only "sense and truth," and betrays but one ruling passion, a "generous" excess of love. Sarah Taylor Rigby (poem 42, unpublished) is "prudent, *tho* gay, and active, *yet* serene"; an unnamed lady's handwriting evinces her combination of strong judgment and easy manner, "correct *though* free, and regular *though* fair" (poem 51, my emphases in both). Elizabeth Rowe the poet reconciles "the Christian's meekness and the Poet's fire," and like Pope's good Critic in *Essay on Criticism,* she is "learned without pride" (["**Mrs. Rowe,**"] poem 57).

These "pattern[s] of a female mind" (Barbauld's phrase, poem 40) do not lack precedent, even in satires on women, as Felicity Nussbaum has demonstrated;[39] but whereas in satires—including Pope's "Of the Characters of Women"—the "pattern" woman serves as a rare and scarcely saving exception to the general wreck of the sex, in Barbauld she is the only kind of woman. Where the satires depend on a dialectic in which pattern women are used as sticks to beat the rest of their sex, Barbauld's aim in constructing pattern women appears to be to rebuke that dialectic. From her poems, one might imagine that every woman she knew was a pattern. This holds true even for a certain Mrs. Fenton, whom Barbauld calls "ill fated Flavia," whose history would classify her in satire or homily among the "fallen" and therefore as a typical blot on her sex: she was seduced in youth and abandoned.[40] Barbauld, however, does not renounce her and sympathizes with her sufferings; moreover, she hails Flavia as a heroine who refuses to be defeated by misfortune. Flavia

> Not only bore her wrongs, but strove to hide;
> The griefs she could not quell, she scornd to own,
> And drew resources from herself alone.
> Her active mind above her fortunes rose,
> And smil'd superiour to a weight of woes.
>
> (Poem 48, unpublished)

A second kind of reply to Pope would be to revalue his terms, promoting "soft" (still feminized) and demoting the (masculinized) honorifics "strength," "firmness," and so forth. This kind of move, of which there is a long feminist tradition, amounts, as Marilyn French (following Julia Kristeva) observes, to an attempt "to alter the symbolic dimension of women's position, and the 'sociosymbolic contract' imposed on them" (*Beyond Power,* 454). Although she did not invent it,[41] this is Barbauld's preferred move. (A narrative version of it is the opening of **"A Summer Evening's Meditation,"** where, as we saw, the harsh, masculine sun is expelled in favor of the gentle, feminine moon.) The poem in praise of Susannah Marissal (poem 40) provides the archetype: "soft," "sooth[ing]," "innocent," "endearing," "kind," "pure" and "good"; she is explicitly valued above wealth, wisdom, beauty, or "brutal strength" on the principle that "goodness only can affection move." We can see here another example of the feminism that, like Marilyn French's, would reverse the culture's preference for power over pleasure.

In her poems Barbauld usually associates the female with softness, and softness she always associates with pleasure; **"To a Lady, with some painted Flowers"** is fairly typical, though a bit more aggressive than the others. (There is a suggestion of *épater* in the last line's dash: "Your best, your sweetest empire is—to please."[42]) The constellation of honorifics that compose **"Verses written in an Alcove"**—"soft" and "sweet" primarily, in practically every possible grammatical form—not only sensualize that poem but also feminize it. And like **"The Invitation,"** it too is an intimate gynetopia made up of Barbauld, one female friend, and a goddess, here "that other smiling sister, / With the blue and laughing eye" (45-46), probably personifying Mirth. *Smiling* and *laughing,* words almost as important in Barbauld's early poems as *soft* and *sweet,* should remind us that pleasure need not be passive: the enjoyment that Barbauld wants to associate with woman is outgoing and jovial. In **"The Invitation,"** pleasure itself is feminized as a "smiling goddess." In another poem, her friend Elizabeth Belsham is composed of spring, sunshine, and joy:

> But the sunshine that laughs on her brow
> Unclouded shall ever remain;
> Ease, Wit, and the Graces reside,
> With Betsy the joy of the plain.

(Poem 5, unpublished)

The Rigby sisters, whose actual gaiety seems to have alarmed the Warrington tutors, are celebrated in two unpublished poems for the very frivolity that the tutors condemned. The younger, Elizabeth (**"Lissy"** of the **"Alcove"**), "stands like the laughing year and breathes delight." Her exuberant good health and happiness alone are antidotes to Barbauld's "pensive mind": "Bloom on her cheek and pleasure in her eye / Sorrow and care chear'd when she is by" (poem 44).[43]

The female figures on whom Barbauld confers her honorifics are all, of course, idealizations, all "pattern[s] of a female mind." Once we understand Barbauld's usual form of psychic defense—compensatory fantasy—we can understand these idealizations as so many distress signals. The true subtext of her notorious letter about women's education is that Barbauld was not easy in her gender—that, in many respects, she hated being "woman" as "woman" was constructed in her culture.[44] Unhappy with her mother, unhappy with what she was being compelled to become, she compensated, as adolescent girls classically have compensated, by idealizing other actual women (friends or relatives) into possibilities of a more satisfying self.[45] "Pensive," socially awkward, and depressed in her life, she envisions women who laugh, frolic, and charm. For her, hedonism is a necessary component of feminism. The laughing woman is such a central figure in these poems because she combines so many of Barbauld's life themes. She is spontaneous, able to indulge "the unguarded sallies of the soul"; she is a pleasure seeker and giver, in opposition to Presbyterian "care and fear" and stinted senses; and she is, not least, at ease in her gender.

This last point, perhaps the most important to Barbauld, is, of course, the most problematic for modern feminism—or even for Wollstonecraft's feminism. The same type of objection can be brought against Barbauld's pattern female as has been brought against the late eighteenth-century "feminization of sensibility" itself by some feminists today: "if women were valued for natural, intuitive feeling, so were children and idiots."[46] Barbauld is vulnerable to the criticism that she makes her ideal of woman in purely oppositionist reaction against Presbyterianism, so in seeking to undo its particular deprivations she embraces a conventionally impoverished construct of the female. (Indeed, in one poem she herself identifies pleasure as "the portion of th' inferior kind" [**"To Mrs. P(riestley) . . . ,"** 94].) On the other hand, there are many rooms in the house of feminism, and Wollstonecraft is not its sole proprietor. Take Barbauld's flower-woman, for instance: if classing "the brown and fair with the smiling flowers that only adorn the land . . . has ever [meaning "inevitably," "essentially"?] been the language of men," what would Wollstonecraft have made of Monique Wittig's lesbian warriors, who compare their vulvas to violets?[47] Whatever position one takes on the political wisdom of basing a feminism on "only those metaphors and parts of experience that have already been ceded to women" (French, *Beyond Power,* 455), it must at least be granted that a discourse of flower-women like Barbauld's is not *essentially* "the language of men." It can be appropriated as well by women who identify strongly with women.

We should also be careful, puritans as we ourselves tend to be, not to scorn Barbauld's constructs merely because they identify the female with pleasure. We need to ask, first, pleasure for whom? In Barbauld's poems the answer is usually clear: pleasure for the subject herself, for woman. A comic poem published posthumously, **"Bouts Rimés in Praise of Old Maids"** (poem 16; 1770?), because it is comic can, as usual, assert the point more directly:

> Hail all ye ancient damsels fair or Brown,
> Whose careless minutes dance away on Down,
> No houshold cares your free enjoyments Saddle,
> Thro' life's wide sea your lonely skiff you Paddle
>   . . .
>
>   (1-4)

There follows a list of evils from which the old maid is free: lovers, wedding bells, nurses attending "with Caudle and with Cake" ("Too dearly bought when liberty's at Stake"), fickle and drunken husbands, dying children, "squalling brats." And the poem concludes, grandly: "In pleasure's free career you meet no Stop, / Greatly alone you stand without a Prop" (15-16).[48]

Not that this is Barbauld's last word on "woman." There is a third response to Pope's aspersion of the female: to revalue his notion of woman as a bundle of restless, crazy energy to construct a figure of powerful and purposeful woman—roughly, to see Atossa in "Of the Characters of Women" not as a termagant but as an amazon. To be sure, Pope himself might have called her an amazon and damned her precisely for that character. The problem of revaluation here is greater than with "soft," for energy itself is forbidden to women, and softness is not. In the late eighteenth century, however, together with the "feminization" of culture we see also a tendency to what might be called the "amazonizing" of woman: stories of women who smuggled themselves into army regiments and fought alongside men become topical, and in other ways women come to be imagined in men's roles.[49] Whether the amazon figures in Barbauld's poems result from a revaluation of Pope is impossible to say, but the figures are there: Liberty and Virtue in **"Corsica,"** as we have seen, and "my soul" in **"Hymn 5."** Another is Sarah Vaughan, wife of the patriot Samuel Vaughan. In her "character" (poem 14, post-humously published) elements of the amazon mix with a figuring of woman's domestic roles of wife and mother: Vaughan is likened to "the mighty mothers of immortal Rome" (4). This poem seeks both to "domesticate" the amazon and to "amazonize" the domestic. Strenuous moral agents, Barbauld's amazon figures all exert themselves in scorn of pleasure. Presumably, they would have been more to Wollstonecraft's taste, embodying as they do the kind of feminism that emphasizes moral agency.

It would be nice if we could date Barbauld's poems to construct a satisfying progression from "lower" to "higher" versions of woman and thus represent Bar-

bauld as waxing consistently "stronger" in her imaginings. The arrangement of *Poems* for publication tends, in fact, to do that, since it places in the last position **"A Summer Evening's Meditation,"** a poem in which the woman's pleasure and her power are one. But *Poems* does not reproduce the order of the poems' composition, and for many of them the order is unknown. In any case, the "growth of strength" paradigm is itself an idealization, one favored by the political tradition of optimistic individualism. It is probably better biography to see Barbauld's various constructs as just that: various. She returns to the subject because it is vital to her to do so, but she does not necessarily build on previous imaginings; rather, because she is in deep conflict on all of these subjects she takes different, sometimes contradictory, positions. Alternatively, her various imaginings could be construed as so many different angles of attack on her ongoing problems. They could be understood as her tacit recognition that (to quote Marilyn French one more time) feminists, confronted as they are with massive patriarchal resistance, "must shift and parry, [and] demonstrate imagination, spontaneity, opportunism, and joy in the quick jab" (*Beyond Power,* 487).

Barbauld's feminism can be seen, finally, to give her an important place in Romanticism as well. Her relation to both is bound up with the principal psychic defense encoded in her poems, compensation fantasy. Deprived in life, she seeks in imagination the opposite of her condition. Constrained by the "bounded sphere" (**"To Dr. Aikin . . . ,"** 60) of cultural womanhood as she knows it, she envisions bursting out of it by active opposition; condemned by religion and gender to "controul" and plain living, she revels in ideas of hedonism. Compensation fantasies were necessary to women in a culture that constructed "woman" as a stinted, mutilated being, denied her birthright. As women entered upon the scene of writing in ever greater numbers in the late eighteenth century, it is not surprising that what they committed to paper were precisely such fantasies. The movement that later came to be identified with Wordsworth and his circle began with women committing to print their (inevitably, in this context) feminist fantasies of compensation. In a true history of Romanticism, Anna Letitia Barbauld would be counted among its genuine founders.[50]

Notes

1. William Woodfall, *Monthly Review* 48 (1773): 54-59, 133-37. Anna Letitia Barbauld, *Poems* (London: printed for Joseph Johnson, 1773). Although I am treating the poems Aikin wrote before she became Mrs. Barbauld (1774), I use her married name because it is the name by which she is known to posterity.

2. Mary Wollstonecraft, *Vindication of the Rights of Woman,* ed. Miriam Kramnick (1792; reprint, New

York: Penguin, 1975), 143. Wollstonecraft prints the entire poem in a footnote, asking indignantly, "how could Mrs. Barbauld write the following ignoble comparison?"

3. *Works of Anna Letitia Barbauld. With a Memoir* (London: Longman, 1825), 1:xvii-xxiv. "Some distinguished persons [writes Lucy Aikin], amongst whom was Mrs. Montague, . . . were induced to propose to [Barbauld] to establish under their auspices what might almost have been called a College for young ladies." In the letter that her niece prints, Barbauld argues at length against the project. "Young ladies . . . ought only to have such a general tincture of knowledge as to make them agreeable companions to a man of sense. . . . The best way for women to acquire knowledge is from conversation with a father, a brother or friend . . . and by such a course of reading as they may recommend. . . . I am . . . convinced that to have a too great fondness for books is little favourable to the happiness of a woman." Barbauld gives other reasons also, including personal ones; she feels unfit to teach young women (see n. 44 below). Lucy Aikin lets it appear that this letter was written to Elizabeth Montague, but it was not. The occasion and thrust of the letter are subtly distorted in Aikin's "Memoir," more by omission than by commission; but a footnote is not the place to sort them out, and I do not yet know their full details.

4. Marilyn Williamson, "Who's Afraid of Mrs. Barbauld? The Blue Stockings and Feminism," *International Journal of Women's Studies* 3 (1980): 90-91; Marlon Ross, *The Contours of Masculine Desire: Romanticism and the Rise of Women's Poetry* (New York: Oxford University Press, 1989), 216-17. More sympathetic but making fundamentally the same case is Miriam Leranbaum, "'Mistresses of Orthodoxy': Education in the Lives and Writings of Late Eighteenth-Century Women Writers," *Proceedings of the American Philosophical Society* 121.4 (August 1977): 281-300.

5. "Mira," "To Miss AIKIN, on reading her Poems," *Gentleman's Magazine,* 44 (July 1774): 327; Mary Scott, *The Female Advocate* (London: Johnson, 1774), 35; Mary Robinson, *Memoirs of the late Mrs. Robinson, written by herself* (London: Phillips, 1801), 1:102; Hannah Cowley, *The Scottish Village* (London: Robinson, 1786), 17-20 passim.

6. *Poems* comprises only a selection of the poems Barbauld had written. Because they are the poems known to her public and to us, this essay will emphasize them; but because I aim to understand Barbauld's motives and the nature of her feminism, I take account also of poems written before 1773 but not published until later or not at all.

Texts of the poems are those in *The Poems of Anna Letitia Barbauld,* ed. William McCarthy and Elizabeth Kraft (Athens: University of Georgia Press, 1994). In our edition the poems are numbered; I cite them hereafter by poem and line number.

7. In materialist-feminist commentary, the subject whom I seek would, of course, be only a "subject." The most thorough exercise in that commentary known to me is Felicity Nussbaum, *The Autobiographical Subject: Gender and Ideology in Eighteenth-Century England* (Baltimore: The Johns Hopkins University Press, 1989). That I am constructing from the poems a text that I call a subjectivity and attribute to Barbauld is obvious and inevitable; I agree with Nussbaum that the persons inferred from texts are verbal constructs, subject to all of the influences that act on and in verbal culture. I do not share her (seeming) belief that the persons who wrote the texts are therefore unknowable or even (as she sometimes seems to imply) nonexistent.

8. Mary Poovey, *The Proper Lady and the Woman Writer: Ideology and Style in the Works of Mary Wollstonecraft, Mary Shelley, and Jane Austen* (Chicago: University of Chicago Press, 1984), x; William St. Clair, *The Godwins and the Shelleys: The Biography of a Family* (Baltimore: The Johns Hopkins University Press, 1991), 504-6; G. J. Barker-Benfield, *The Culture of Sensibility* (Chicago: University of Chicago Press, 1992).

9. For example, "Mrs. P———" (poem 3), "Miss B* * * * *" (poem 4), "Miss R———" and her mother (poem 8), "Mrs. Jennings" (poem 17), "Mrs. Rowe" (poem 57), "Lissy" (poem 39), "Chloris" (poem 25), "Araminta" (poem 26), "Delia" (poems 4 and 53), "a Lady" (poems 51 and 55).

10. The lines to which Woodfall objected read, in the first edition: "Where chearless Saturn 'midst her wat'ry moons / . . . majestic sits / . . . like an exil'd queen / Amongst her weeping handmaids." In the third edition, "her" becomes "his," "queen" becomes "monarch," and the handmaids are banished. The changes, presumably Barbauld's, do not necessarily amount to admission of error.

11. A model of this reading is Ann Messenger, *His and Hers: Essays in Restoration and Eighteenth-Century Literature* (Lexington: University Press of Kentucky, 1986), 175-84.

12.
   Was it for this you took such constant Care
   The *Bodkin, Comb,* and *Essence* to prepare;
   For this your Locks in Paper-Durance bound,
   For this with tort'ring Irons wreath'd around?

For this with Fillets strain'd your tender Head,
And bravely bore the double Loads of Lead?

 (Pope, *The Rape of the Lock* 4:97-102 [*Poems,*
 ed. John Butt (New Haven, Conn.: Yale
 University Press, 1963), 235])

13. David Mallett, *Works* (London, 1759), 1:3.

14. As if to confirm this reading, the first edition contains a "Freudian" typographical error in line 2 of the poem: "the wond'rous theme a reveren*d* ear require[s]" (emphasis mine). An errata slip changes it to "reverent." Perhaps Barbauld's manuscript contained the "error." The occasion of the poem, as reported by William Turner in 1825, is suggestive as well: "a large old family-tankard used to stand on her father's sideboard, filled with water, his only beverage. A gentleman dining with the Dr. observed on the degradation to which this noble vessel was subjected, after having been accustomed to pass round the festal board as the vehicle of so much more generous liquors. The hint was taken [by Barbauld] and happily improved" (quoted in McCarthy and Kraft, *Poems of . . . Barbauld,* 257). The tankard, that is, *belongs* to Dr. Aikin, and *his* use of it is the subject of complaint.

15. Barker-Benfield, *The Culture of Sensibility,* 290, quoting John Gregory's popular *A Father's Legacy to his Daughters* (1774): "in your sex [overeating] is beyond expression indelicate and disgusting."

16. That Barbauld in fact experienced her mother as an agent of repression is suggested by Lucy Aikin; see n. 44, below.

17. "Somebody was bold enough to talk of getting up private theatricals. This was a dreadful business! All the wise and grave, the whole tutorhood, cried out, it must not be! The students . . . and . . . my aunt, took the prohibition very sulkily; and my aunt's Ode to Wisdom was the result" (Aikin to Henry Bright, quoted by Bright, *A Historical Sketch of Warrington Academy* [Liverpool: Brakell, 1859], 14).

18. Joseph Priestley to Theophilus Lindsey, 30 July 1770 (Priestley, *Theological and Miscellaneous Works,* ed. J. T. Rutt [New York: Kraus Reprints, 1972], 1:i, 117. According to his son, John Aikin was also "too diffident" to become an author despite his knowledge and ability (Lucy Aikin, *Memoir of John Aikin, M.D.* [London: Baldwin, Cradock and Joy, 1823], 1:13).

19. Bright, *Historical Sketch,* comments, "Mr. Edwards, the lively West Indian, had to slip away from his creditors and leave Warrington for ever" (12).

20. In fairness to the Rev. John Aikin, we need to distinguish "psychic" from historical reality. Aikin did not in fact withhold higher learning from his daughter; however, Lucy Aikin implies that he granted it only reluctantly, after long importunity (*Works of . . . Barbauld,* 1:vii). And of course, medical education would have been unthinkable.

21. Mary Astell, *A Serious Proposal to the Ladies: Part II* (1967; reprint, New York: Source Book Press, 1970), 159.

22. On Barbauld's sending poems to Belsham, see "History of the Poems" in McCarthy and Kraft, *Poems of . . . Barbauld* (xxix).

23. I allude to the title of Sandra Gilbert's 1980 essay, "What Do Feminist Critics Want? A Postcard from the Volcano," reprinted in *The New Feminist Criticism,* ed. Elaine Showalter (New York: Pantheon, 1985), 29-45. The phrase is really Wallace Stevens's, but Gilbert appropriates it with reference to volcano poems by Emily Dickinson.

24. Barker-Benfield argues in *The Culture of Sensibility* that in fact the range of expression permitted to women widened during the century. Certainly it did, albeit against opposition. Its expansion must be regarded as a feminist tendency, and Barbauld should be seen as having contributed to the expansion.

25. Marilyn French, *Beyond Power: On Women, Men, and Morals* (London: Cape, 1985), 487.

26. Barbauld's need for stronger feeling and a more fervent experience of religion, as well as her resentment of Warrington rationality, emerged (to the discomfiture of her co-religionists) in an essay, "Thoughts on the Devotional Taste," published with her selection of psalms in 1775.

27. Barbauld's model for the songs was probably Elizabeth Rowe, to whose muse she dedicates herself in "Verses on Mrs. Rowe" (poem 57); for examples of Rowe, see *Eighteenth-Century Women Poets,* ed. Roger Lonsdale (Oxford: Oxford University Press, 1989). In Barbauld's "Ode to Spring" (poem 56), where female desire for a male object is admitted without displacement, it is admitted only in a "whisper'd sigh" (18-20). A poem of unknown date, published post-humously (poem 157), is an allegory of the passage of the year in the figure of a highly erotic courtship of the earth by the sun. Earth (female, of course) is the speaker.

28. See Polwhele's description of modern girls who "with bliss botanic as their bosoms heave, / Still pluck forbidden fruit, with mother Eve, / For puberty in sighing florets pant, / Or point the prostitution of a plant" (*The Unsex'd Females: A Poem* [London: Cadell & Davies, 1798], 8-9). Pol-

whele's principal targets are Wollstonecraft and Erasmus Darwin's *Botanic Garden.* He speaks kindly (if nervously) of Barbauld and does not quote this poem.

29. "Some [women warriors] laugh out loud and manifest their aggressiveness by thrusting their bare breasts forward brutally" (Wittig, *Les Guérillères,* trans. David Le Vay [Boston: Beacon Press, 1985], 100).

30. Lucy Aikin tells anecdotes of Barbauld's own agility in her youth, agility she would have been expected to inhibit. "In her youth, great bodily activity, and a lively spirit struggled hard against the tight [parental] rein which held her. London cousins wondered sometimes at the gymnastic feats of the country lass" (Aikin's "Family History," in Anna LeBreton, *Memoir of Mrs. Barbauld* [London: Bell, 1874], 25). At age 15, to escape an importunate suitor, Barbauld "ran nimbly up a tree which grew by the garden wall, and let herself down into the lane beyond." (ibid.). See also n. 44, below.

31. Elizabeth Benger, *The Female Geniad* (London: Hookham, 1791), 5 (emphasis mine).

32. The year after *Poems* was published, Hester Mulso Chapone's *Letters on the Improvement of the Mind* (3rd ed. [London, 1774]) would claim astronomy for women. Chapone describes her own rapture at being taught to consider the stars as "worlds formed like ours for a variety of inhabitants," and she urges young women to study the stars in order to "enlarge [the] mind and excite in it the most profound adoration" (2:140-41).

33. Henry Crabb Robinson to Dorothy Wordsworth, 6 January 1826 (MS HCR Letters 6:141, Dr. Williams's Library).

34. Wollstonecraft, *Vindication,* 143.

35. Barbauld to Elizabeth Belsham, February 1771, (*Works . . . of Barbauld,* 2:59). Fordyce wrote that "so far as he has been able to observe, young men have appeared more frequently susceptible of a generous and steady friendship for each other, than females as yet unconnected; especially if the latter have had, or been supposed to have, pretensions to beauty not yet adjusted by the public voice" (*Sermons to Young Women* [reprinted, Boston, 1767], 1:114).

36. Pope, *The Rape of the Lock,* 2:10 (*Poems,* 223).

37. Nussbaum, *Autobiographical Subject,* xxii. Nussbaum does not, in fact, revalue Pope in this way; yet such a revalorization would be deducible from a Foucaultian project like hers.

38. Pope, "Of the Characters of Women," line 3 (*Poems,* 560). Cf. *The British Apollo* (1708):

women "are cast in too soft a mould, are made of too fine, too delicate [a] composure to endure the severity of study" (quoted in Barker-Benfield, *Culture of Sensibility,* 23). In her study of seventeenth- and eighteenth-century misogynist satire, *The Brink of All We Hate* (Louisville: University Press of Kentucky, 1984), Felicity Nussbaum contends that "Of the Characters of Women" is not "finally misogynist" (140) but acknowledges that it was "long seen" as antifeminist (138). As late as 1804, Pope was accused of misogyny by one "Camilla" in the *Monthly Magazine,* 17 (1804): 109-10. "Camilla" is particularly offended by his claims that women have "no character" and that their characters are inconsistent.

39. Nussbaum, *The Brink,* chaps. 7 and 8.

40. The name Flavia may come from William Law's *A Serious Call to a Devout and Holy Life* (London: printed for William Innys, 1729); Law's Flavia is fashionable and dissipated, a cautionary example to women.

41. The general shift in the direction of feminizing culture throughout the eighteenth century is treated in Barker-Benfield's *Culture of Sensibility.*

42. One reading of that line is to see it as bitterly ironic: "Given the low esteem in which women are held, the most you can hope to do is please." I would not summarily reject this reading, given the degree of conflict that Barbauld's texts exhibit; but I would argue that it is not consistent with the general trend in these poems of associating the female with pleasure.

43. In the published poem "To Miss R[igby] . . ." (poem 8), however, Sarah is praised not for frivolity but for self-effacing caregiving. That the Rigby sisters were regarded as troublesome by the Academy authorities is evident from a 1769 incident (details unknown) concerning one of them and a "Mr. G"; the Trustees ordered Mr. Rigby to remove his daughters from Warrington (Warrington Academy "Minutes," 26 January 1769 [MS, Manchester College, Oxford]). A practical joke attributed to them is reported by Bright, *A Historical Sketch,* 23.

44. One reason she declined to manage a college for young women was that she felt incompetent to teach the skills expected in young women of her class: "I know myself remarkably deficient in gracefulness of person, in my air and manner, and in the easy graces of conversation" (*Works . . . of Barbauld,* 1:xxiii). Lucy Aikin's account of Barbauld's education by her mother is guarded but sufficiently informative: To avoid the danger of contamination by the manners of the boys who at-

tended her father's school, "maternal vigilance" instilled into Barbauld "a double portion of bashfulness and maidenly reserve; and she was accustomed to ascribe an uneasy sense of constraint in mixed society . . . to the strictness" of her education (ibid., 1:viii). See also n. 30: the "rein" was her mother's.

45. The "classic" account is by Helene Deutsch; I depend on the summary given by Nancy Chodorow in *The Reproduction of Mothering* (Berkeley: University of California Press, 1978), chap. 8 (esp. 137).

46. Alan Richardson, "Romanticism and the Colonization of the Feminine," in *Romanticism and Feminism,* ed. Anne K. Mellor (Bloomington: Indiana University Press, 1988), 21. Richardson cites Mary Jacobus.

47. Wittig, *Guérillères,* 48.

48. A manuscript text of the poem (Liverpool Record Office 920 NIC 22/5/3) associates it with Sarah Scott's *Millenium* [*sic*] *Hall* (1762) and testifies that Barbauld had probably read that story of a fictional gynetopia.

49. See Dianne Dugaw, *Warrior Women and Popular Balladry 1650-1850* (Cambridge: Cambridge University Press, 1989). The middle-class intellectual *Monthly Magazine* published "An Account of Frances Scanagatti, . . . who served . . . as an Ensign and Lieutenant . . . during the last War" (22 [1806]: 465-68). The youthful Amelia Opie met a sailor named "William Henry Renny," who turned out to be a woman; Opie was both fascinated and repelled by her (Cecilia Brightwell, *Memorials of the Life of Amelia Opie* [Norwich and London, 1854], 18-20). A striking instance of "amazonizing" is Henry Fuseli's illustration, *Lady Macbeth Presenting the Daggers,* in which conventional gender postures are reversed: she strides powerfully toward her husband, and he shrinks back in fear. Ideas about amazons are discussed in Barker-Benfield, *Culture of Sensibility,* 351-59.

50. For advice and criticism I am grateful to Brenda Daly, Paula Feldman, Mitzi Myers, and Rosanne Potter.

Laura Mandell (essay date spring 1998)

SOURCE: Mandell, Laura. "'Those Limbs Disjointed of Gigantic Power': Barbauld's Personifications and the (Mis)Attribution of Political Agency." *Studies in Romanticism* 37, no. 1 (spring 1998): 27-41.

[*In the following essay, Mandell examines the relationship between personification and political empowerment in Barbauld's work.*]

How personification works is crucial to understanding the relation between aesthetics and politics. "Aesthetic ideology," defined by Paul de Man, is "the confusion of linguistic with natural reality," a view with which Terry Eagleton agrees.[1] For both, "the formal move . . . is the ideological move" (Ferguson 119) in two ways. First, aesthetics hides the workings of language, presenting a discursively constructed reality as "natural," independent of human intentions, independent of power. Second, aesthetics is said to resolve contradictions by defining "a universal subject." The aesthetic provides a "dream of reconciliation," of "individuals woven in intimate unity with no detriment to their specificity, of an abstract totality suffused with all the flesh-and-blood reality of the individual being" (Eagleton 25). By smoothing over the contradictions, aesthetic ideology enables individuals to recognize themselves in abstract, universalizing statements, to feel part of the imaginary group of people, class or nation, thus defined.[2]

The workings of personification provide the best test case for the critical purchase that the notion of "aesthetic ideology" gives us in thinking about the relation of the aesthetic to the political. Personification is crucial precisely because it eludes both these paradigms for how form mystifies. As against the allegedly naturalizing tendency of form, personification proclaims its artificiality. "Except in a very few instances the Reader will find no personifications of abstract ideas in these volumes," Wordsworth announced in the 1800 Preface to *Lyrical Ballads*; "I wish to keep my Reader in the company of flesh and blood."[3] For Wordsworth personification is the work of artifice against art; but if so, it also works against ideology in the ways described by de Man: its artificiality advertises the configurative, positing power of language.[4] To Eagleton, however, Wordsworth's distinction poses no difference: aestheticizing discourse endows abstract ideas with "flesh-and-blood reality," or, in Steven Knapp's formulation, "metaphors with the agency of literal persons" (2). As Adela Pinch has noticed, moreover, at the very moment in the Preface when Wordsworth claims a flesh-and-blood reality for his poems, he personifies: "Poetry sheds . . . natural human tears; she can boast of no celestial ichor that distinguishes her vital juices from those of prose; the same human blood circulates through the veins of them both."[5] This personification naturalizes rather than advertises an artificial cultural construct.

Yet the more important yield is the way Wordsworth's Preface reveals both potentialities: personification can both serve and subvert ideological mystification. This contradiction shows us that literary form is not reducible to "aesthetic ideology."[6] In this essay, I discuss the contradictory potential of personification, first its capacity to mystify (its ideological function), then its use to demystify, drawing my demonstration from Anna Letitia Barbauld and Karl Marx.[7] Barbauld and Marx may seem strange bedfellows: an Enlightened dissenter, Barbauld welcomes the commercial developments whose powers of alienation Marx criticizes. Both, however, use personification to stimulate political activism, deploying the figure to challenge a quietism of accepting "things as they are."

In the service of mystification, personification figures the relation of the individual to the particular in two misleading ways. First, it solicits an almost unconscious identification with an imaginary group. When Anna Seward writes, "Pleasure shed all her lustre over the scene," she elides individual difference (Pinch 45). Second, as Seward's syntax suggests, personification elides agency. Thus Coleridge personifies "Freedom":

> When Slumbering Freedom roused by high Disdain,
> With giant fury burst her triple chain!
> Fierce on her front the blasting Dog-star glowed,
> Her banners, like a midnight meteor, flowed;
> Amid the yelling of the storm-rent skies
> She came, and scattered battles from her eyes.
>
> (17-22)[8]

The effect of such personification, argue some, is to mystify agency (who is exerting power over whom?) and furthermore make it seem omnipresent or unlocalizable:

> personification, because adorning a commentary on contemporary political events, serves to misattribute agency: especially it serves to attribute to unchanging, ahistoric forms the powers of action that belong to individuals, groups, classes. The necessities of this kind of gigantism, wherein the complicated and muddled processes of social change are simplified and purified into cosmic battle, indicate an ideological use of hyperbole: "high," "giant," "burst," "fierce," "yelling," and so forth become simultaneously a way of distancing the events from possible experience, and an excuse for the poet's withdrawal.[9]

Imagining formless historical processes as a gigantic form—"Freedom" who "burst[s] her . . . chain"—implies one's own puny insignificance, and tacitly justifies one's "withdrawal" from politics.

Preferring "realistic" description over poetic "mystification," such a critique elides the mystification of "realism" itself. As Catherine Belsey has argued, realism may obscure agency as much as poetic personifications do.[10] It is precisely this question—of a particular agency behind universal, impersonal figures—that animates Barbauld's poetics of personification: by radicalizing the conditions of allegedly non-aesthetic, literal discourse, she exposes its latent gigantism. Disputing the imaginary "nation" advanced by emerging bourgeois ideology, Barbauld uses personification to demystify its "realist" discourse. Her political theories and poetry interrogate the fiction of a non-aesthetic, non-ideological

truth.[11] Her implicit question is, "aesthetic ideology" as opposed to what?[12] "Realistic" discourse also aestheticizes; it just does so differently.[13] While the aesthetic of personification can conceal historical agents behind imaginary totalities, it also can expose such totalizing as fabrication.

In her 1793 pamphlet *Sins of Government, Sins of the Nation,* Barbauld contends that revolutionary reformers can be just as bad as a tyrannical government.[14] Although herself a reformer, Barbauld attacks their refusal of the "principle of subordination" (2.388, 391) by which the minority cedes to majority "will": "It is [the] business [of reformers] to sow the seed, and let it lie patiently in the bosom of the ground—perhaps for ages—to prepare, not to bring about revolutions" (2.390). Yet if here Barbauld sounds a kind of Godwinian gradualism, elsewhere her disgust for revolution is less evident. It is significant that she does not advocate submitting to the law of the land, but to "the general will." Majority opinion is not at all visible through voting—it is precisely the unrepresentativeness of the government that British reformers are protesting during the period of the French Revolution. If voting isn't designed by government so as to express a change in the general will, then only revolution can do so. In her earlier 1790 tract *An Address to the Opposers of the Repeal of the Corporation and Test Acts,* Barbauld describes how gradual reform may at a certain moment tip over into revolt: "The spread of [the] light [of reform] is in general gradual and imperceptible; but there are periods when its progress is accelerated, when it seems with a sudden flash to open the firmament and pour in day at once" (2.371). How can one know the difference between a revolution that imposes a factional, minority point of view on the majority, and one that represents the majority view?

The answer has to do with number. In her **"Lecture on the Use of Words,"** Barbauld faults the use of "unmeaning epithets," as in the case of someone who said, "there will be monstrous few apples this year, and those few will be huge little."[15] The fault here is one of misaligning "being huge" and actual number. For Barbauld, getting people to think about the relation of number to gigantic images has political implications. Certainly in her day the number of people represented by an abstraction was crucial. Burke opens his *Reflections on the Revolution in France* (first published November 1790) by contesting Dr. Richard Price's claim to speak for the people of England. Price's proposal of a "new, and hitherto unheard of bill of rights," Burke says, "though made in the name of the whole people, belongs to those gentlemen and their faction only [i.e., only to Price and the Society for Commemorating the Revolution]. The body of the people of England have no share in it."[16] Burke strategically designates as a "body" numbers of people whom he wants to claim form the largest group: he transforms subscribers to his own political beliefs into a single, gigantic body—i.e., a personification sharing one feeling automatically expressed by government policy. When Barbauld personifies the English people into a body, "the Nation," she distinguishes it from government.

The very issue at stake in *Sins of Government, Sins of the Nation* is the extent to which the Government's decision to wage war against France is backed by the Nation, the English people.[17] She writes this pamphlet in response to the Government's proclamation of a day of fasting on 19 April 1793, designed to promote public unity in the war effort. Protesting this war ("this guilty business" [2.403]), Barbauld asks Britons whether the actions of their "appointed rulers" (2.384) so express their will that they are willing to take responsibility for this policy in the eyes of God, as if they each, individually, enacted it (2.385, 410-12). Is the government a gigantic form that represents them all, or no one? Might "Nation," in its huge numbers, dictate the giant form of "Government"?

Barbauld presses the question of number in *To a Great Nation,* a poem addressed to the French revolutionary army when it was threatened in 1792 by the Duke of Brunswick's counter-revolutionary army.[18] She begins by reversing the typical association of numbers with abstract terms:

> Rise mighty nation! in thy strength,
> And deal thy dreadful vengeance round;
> Let thy great spirit rous'd at length,
> Strike hordes of Despots to the ground.
>
> (1-4, *Poems* 124)

Usually revolutionaries, or "the people," are seen as multitudes. Here, they are seen as a singular "nation" with a single emotion (vengeance), and a single "great spirit," while the forces of tyranny, usually personified by the unitary king, are plural: "hordes of Despots." Why the reversal?

To a Great Nation was published less than a month before The British Convention of the Delegates of the People convened in Edinburgh in order to debate whether its "body" ought, might, or could "exert further extraparliamentary pressure on the government."[19] As the example of the French National Assembly attests,[20] such bodies could suddenly acquire such power, could indeed become "the government," thereby transforming their extra-legal actions into law. All that it would take for a revolution in England would be for people to do to the British conventions what Barbauld does to "nation" in her first stanza: to see members of the Convention as a unified majority body, and the existing government as the enemy hordes. *To a Great Nation* simultaneously dissolves monolithic forms into multiple Despots, and transforms multitudes of revolutionaries into one bigger form, the mythological giant *Briareus:*

> *Briareus*-like, extend thy hands,
> That every hand may crush a foe;
> In millions pour thy generous bands,
> And end a warfare by a blow.
>
> (17-20, *Poems* 124)

That *Briareus* has one hundred hands conveys a powerful image of the revolutionary body as a great and politically effective form, its multiples unified into a giant. Through this personification, the revolutionaries become millions of hands poured into "generous" or numerous bands, all animated to deliver one single, great "blow" that ends the counter-revolutionary assault.

Barbauld thus imagines the nation as "an aggregate body" (2.406) that can be coordinated for action. One form this action may take is conscientious disapprobation. Active disapprobation differs from the sheer passivity of an alienation that sees "Nation" as a gigantic, inert form—a Government imposing its dictates on people. When should passive disapprobation become active insubordination, or even revolution? "There are, indeed, cases of such atrocity that even [passive] concurrence would be criminal," Barbauld realizes, but cautions, "What these are, it is impossible to specify; every man must draw the line for himself" (2.407). When a huge number of people draw the line, this is the moment of revolution: the abstraction, Government, is broken, giving birth to a Nation body that is multitudinous and self-propelled. For revolution to seem thus possible, people must be able to imagine the Nation's actions as a swarm of individual acts unified by a "great spirit" (*Poems* 124).

Barbauld's *Address to the Opposers of the Repeal of the Corporation and Test Acts* describes these two stages of reform. First, gigantic but inanimate forms must be broken apart. The ruling forces have seemed gigantic, have been envisioned as monumental or marmoreal, because they consist in the tyrannic imposition of a minority perspective on the public. But resistant multitudes are bursting through the ice, granite, and marble embodiment:

> Can ye not discern the signs of the times? The minds of men are in movement from the Borysthenes to the Atlantic. Agitated with new and strong emotions, they swell and heave beneath oppression, as the seas within the polar circle, when, at the approach of spring, they grow impatient to burst their icy chains; when what, but an instant before, seemed so firm,—spread for many a dreary league like a floor of solid marble,—at once with a tremendous noise gives way . . . and the air resounds with the clash of floating fragments.
>
> (2.371)

Barbauld is, in effect, breaking up reifications, as Marx would attempt to do. "The establishments of the earth," its governments and religious institutions, are "a floor of solid marble" broken up by a sea of numerous minds: "it is no more in your power to stop" these minds, she says, "than to repel the tide with your naked hand." "Obscure murmurs" of the numerous multitude "penetrat[e] every part of the great body politic," breaking up and "lop[ping] away" whatever is unsound. What emerges takes the form of renovated personifications. After the ice has been broken, "the genius of Philosophy [begins] walking abroad," and "Liberty . . . led by Philosophy, and crowned with the civic wreath, animates men to assert their long-forgotten rights" (2.371-72). A seemingly solid body is turned to fragments, and a new body is born.

These two stages animate Barbauld's abolition polemics of 1793. In *Sins of Government, Sins of the Nation,* she assaults a seemingly monolithic slave trade by envisioning it as multiple enormities, myriad individual acts of cruelty:

> Can we look round from sea to sea . . . and say, that our brother hath not aught against us? . . . Are there not some darker-coloured children of the same family, over whom we assume a hard and unjust controul? And have not these our brethren aught against us? If we suspect they have, . . . if such enormities . . . are still sanctioned by our legislature, defended by our princes— deep is the colour of our guilt.
>
> (2.395)

The still legal slave trade is imaged as "hard" control, a term that echoes her sentence on the same issue in the Test Act pamphlet of 1790: "Liberty . . . animates men to assert their long-forgotten rights . . . and even extends a smile of hope and promise to the poor African, the victim of hard, impenetrable avarice" (2.372). Slavery is a set of practices sanctioned by hard, seemingly immutable law, but actually sustained by individuals: "deep is the colour of *our* guilt." Slavery is not a gigantic external form but a set of multiple "enormities," enacted against individual persons by individual persons in such daily actions as eating sugar, doing business with a slave merchant, and so forth.

The political problem of slavery consists precisely in the distantiating reification of such practices into an abstract term. "Societies [are] composed of individuals," Barbauld insists, and a Nation is the sum of "those affairs in which we act in common, and as a body" (2.385-86). Individuals are guilty in their passive acquiescence, in allowing government to operate through their limbs:

> Many nations are guilty of the crime of permitting oppressive laws and bad governments to remain amongst them, by which the poor are crushed, and the lives of the innocent are laid at the mercy of wicked and arbitrary men. This is a national sin of the deepest dye.
>
> (2.387)

When Barbauld describes the sins of the nation in terms of this "dye" (cf. "deep is the colour of our guilt"), she figures the nation as a body tainted by its business. If it seems to be acceptable to trade Africans like commodities because their bodies seem different ("darker-coloured"), revealing the nation's dark face shows that they are "the same" (2.395). Or, as in Blake's ambiguously tinted picture of "The Little Black Boy," Barbauld insists that dark color is actively painted on a child's face: the skin-color of Africans has been darkened into a racial difference by the projection of Britain's guilt onto someone else's face. Barbauld's personification makes a deeply political, deeply moral point.

A ruling body is conventionally conceived of as an imaginary identity caught in battle with imaginary foes. This allows its individual subjects to de-animate events, depersonalize them into abstractions, and to think of themselves as victims "crushed" by unassailable historical forces (2.387). Barbauld proposes an alternative to such gigantism. *Sins of Government, Sins of the Nation* opens with a call for national religion, a surprising notion for a dissenter.[21] But she does not want another institutional ideology. She wants her readers to extricate from their thoughts those marmoreal personifications that rule them and victimize others—Government, Catholicism, Anglicanism—and to replace these ossified bodies with personifications influenced by their own individual actions, e.g., a Nation. Religious ideology will be replaced by the general will expressed by active participation in national worship. But, if not ideology, what is the "great spirit" that forms numerous people's activities into the unified acts of a Nation?

For Barbauld, there is only one spirit that could possibly unify such a diverse group with opposing interests and overlapping claims: the desire for radical equality. Into her supple personifications she figures huge numbers of people acting in unison—multiple hands becoming one blow—animated by a collective sense of the injustice of "enormities." "Liberty," "Philosophy," or "Equality" embody multiple actions performed in concert because animated by a great spirit. Thus, she defends public worship for the way "the electric fire of correspondent feelings" joins into "one common flame."[22]

> As we have never seen, perhaps we can hardly conceive, the effect which the united voices of a whole congregation, all in the lively expression of one feeling, would have upon the mind. We should then perceive not only that we were doing the same thing in the same place, but that we were doing it with one accord.
>
> (2.460)

Such a spirit is inevitably democratic:

> [H]ere only [the poor man] sees the prostrations of the rich as low as his, and hears them both addressed together in the majestic simplicity of a language that knows no adulation. . . . Every time Social Worship is celebrated, it includes a virtual declaration of the rights of man.
>
> (2.448)

"Social Worship" is not merely a communal event but a personification of what the bill of rights states in abstract terms.

It is an equalizing, commercial spirit that is the great spirit or "Genius" of Enlightened thought in *Eighteen Hundred and Eleven*.[23] The Genius leaves any country (such as England) at the moment when it moves toward despotism, avowed or covert:

> The Genius now forsakes the favoured shore,
> And hates, capricious, what he loved before;
> Then empires fall to dust, then arts decay,
> And wasted realms enfeebled despots sway;
>
> * * *
>
> Then with enthusiast love the pilgrim roves
> To seek his footsteps in forsaken groves,
> Explores the fractured arch, the ruined tower,
> Those limbs disjointed of gigantic power;
>
> (241-44, 251-54, *Poems* 159)

"Gigantic power" is a phrase that Barbauld consistently uses to designate both Napoleon and tyranny in general.[24] To say that Napoleon's imperial ambition disjoins limbs and leaves them "mouldering stones" is to say that tyranny deanimates the social body. Britain is not immune. The spirit of equality leaves this "island Queen" (40) for "distant lands," to "deal the gifts of Heaven with equal hands" (65-66, *Poems* 154). Wherever the equal dealing of multiple hands is possible, there the Nation can be composed of multitudes animated and unified; wherever it is not possible, there the Government is only a reified abstraction, disjointed limbs.

But *Eighteen Hundred and Eleven* does not simply present a theory of personified power; it also enacts it in its personifications. The political purpose was not lost on John Wilson Croker, whose harsh review in the *Quarterly* is said to have ended Barbauld's career of publication.[25] Her visionary poem opens with an attack on Britain's participation in the Continental wars against Napoleon. While Britain "Feeds the fierce strife" by "bend[ing] her ear" to "the stern call" of war, Nature goes on producing bountifully both nourishment and joy (1-4). But "in vain": "Man calls to Famine, nor invokes in vain . . . / The sword, not sickle, reaps the harvest now" (15-18, *Poems* 152). Croker focuses his attack on Barbauld's personified Famine:

What does Mrs. Barbauld mean? Does she seriously accuse mankind of wishing for a famine, and interceding for starvation? or does she believe that it is in the power of this country . . . to arrest the progress of war, and, careless of what Buonaparte or his millions may be about, to beckon back peace and plenty?[26]

What bothers Croker is Barbauld's figure of agency: waging war against an aggressive imperial power, Croker argues, is not the same as "call[ing] to Famine," as actively *asking* to starve to death. But Croker's ridicule of Barbauld's personification elides his own political motives.[27]

Other accounts, moreover, support Barbauld's sense of who is doing what to whom. In *The Wealth of Nations,* Adam Smith sees waging war as indeed calling to famine. Dissenters such as Joseph Priestley and Barbauld might well sympathize with this work, for its attack on military expenditures as "public prodigality and misconduct" is consonant with their opposition to war.[28] According to Smith, commerce is hurt by state prodigality, but it is stimulated by the right kind of private expenditure, a notion that informs *Eighteen Hundred and Eleven.* Extravagant court revelries ("profuse hospitality") do stimulate the production of food, but Smith prefers that aristocrats devote their extravagant expenditures to artworks, books, building, and fashionable commodities: "this expense maintains productive, . . . the other, unproductive hands" (277). Because of war, Barbauld maintains, Britain's "Midas dream is o'er" (61):

> The golden tide of Commerce leaves thy shore,
> Leaves thee to prove the alternate ills that haunt
> Enfeebling Luxury and ghastly Want;
> Leaves thee, perhaps, to visit distant lands,
> And deal the gifts of Heaven with equal hands.
>
> (62-66, *Poems* 154)

She echoes Smith both in argument and in the metonym "hands." The prodigality of war causes desiccation, while the prodigality that spreads money to the hands of producers such as "masons, carpenters, upholsterers, mechanics, &c." (Smith 277) causes a flowering of commerce.

Smith's metonymy has been seen as symptomatic of the alienation that people (whole bodies) feel in the division of labor.[29] Barbauld's personification and metonymy challenge the reader with a veritable thicket obscuring cause and effect: Britain bends an ear to a Colossal power; Nature is wildly producing; a personified man calls to a personified Famine, while a personified Commerce picks up her skirts and strides across the ocean to America. Even Want and Luxury, two class poles, have the agency to enfeeble and grow pale. The reader of this poem is asked to figure out who is doing what to whom: whose hands are these? The whole poem, moreover, is in the conditional mode (see "perhaps" [65]). "If" we do not do something, "if" we proceed on our present course, Britain will become a ruined empire: "Yet, O my Country, . . . / If prayers may not avert, if 'tis thy fate / To rank amongst the names that once were great . . ." (67-72, *Poems* 154). That conditional mode, implying the possibility of averting ruin, makes the answer to the question "whose hands are doing what to whom?"—and perhaps, "what is my hand in this?"—just that much more pressing.

Personification works in *Eighteen Hundred and Eleven* to evoke the uncertainty of agency while the conditional mode insists on people's responsibility for actions performed by gigantic forms. You are responsible, Barbauld says to the people of the Nation on the day of the fast, for wielding an agency that is capricious and moody, whose operations you cannot fully comprehend:

> [I]f you place power in improper hands, you are answerable for the abuse of that power. . . . It is not sufficient, even if our intentions are pure; we must weigh the tendencies of our actions, for we are answerable, in a degree at least, for those remote consequences which, though we did not intend, we might have foreseen.
>
> (2.409-10)

The kind of action one is capable of depends upon the kinds of causality one can imagine. Personifications figure collective agency, a group of hands acting simultaneously in accordance with one principle that will benefit all. But even if personifications do not help us to imagine such agency, they can defamiliarize our habitual modes of attributing agency to individuals, abstractions, and institutions. They help us recover the agency we have projected into "improper hands," limbs that seem gigantic because not *propre*—not our own.

* * *

In her political pamphlets of the 1790s, Barbauld asks, what difference does it make to use one particular *form* of historical discourse as opposed to any other? Her poetry answers with a politics of personification. Sharing Marx's goal of inspiring people to think for themselves about what actually constitutes any abstract term, Barbauld produces a comparable analysis of personification, even though their politics differ.[30] *The German Ideology* and Volume 1 of *Capital* argue that alienation of human labor is accomplished by concealing agency. In *The German Ideology,* Marx and Engels say that when private and public interests are

> divided, man's own deed becomes an alien power opposed to him, which enslaves him instead of being controlled by him. . . . [Alienation involves the] fixation of social activity, this consolidation of what we ourselves produce into an objective power above us, growing out of our control.[31]

Disowning one's own actions by projecting them onto the performance of an insuperable "objective power" is alienating: it reifies one's activity into a gigantic form, just as commodification solidifies social relations into a fetish. Alienation and commodification are thus modes both of *deanimation* (conditions of existence no longer seem to be made by human beings) and of *personification*: human-made conditions of existence are seen as gigantic forms capable of human activity, that is, as monstrous persons. Capitalist oppression works in part, Marx argues, by personification—by rewriting one's own activity as feats perpetrated by an implacable other who wears a black hat.

However, Marx also uses personification to expose reification. In *Capital* he takes a reified form, the commodity, and personifies it: commodities, he says, "attract" money (201) with which they are "in love" (202) and at whom they cast "wooing glances" (205). Saying (insanely) that commodities fall in love with money, Marx rewrites the agency of a perfectly reasonable, realistic proposal: commodities produce money. In both forms, the agency of capitalist exploiters is rendered completely invisible. But, while passively accepting the realistic statement, the reader might be spurred by the outrageous personification to interrogate agency: if commodities don't fall in love, they also don't "produce"; *who* is the agent of production? If "realistic" statements conceal agency—if they mislead about who is doing what to whom—then violating realist discourse demystifies. Both Marx and Barbauld invest personifications with political agency to the extent that these figures expose the mystifications of realist discourse.

Barbauld's *oeuvre* both analyzes habitual depersonification—the deanimation of human forms into stone-like abstractions—and attempts to stimulate personification in people's thinking and actions. She wants her readers to imagine and become a Nation animated by the only "spirit" capable of unifying the diverse intentions of many people: "the spirit of equality." After Huxley, however, the prospect of a Nation unified by a rational idea is perhaps rather chilling to us: doesn't unanimity, even if it is based in radical equality, smack of totalitarianism? And for all Barbauld's talk of Nation, isn't she advocating what we know to be politically insidious, viz., nationalism? Barbauld is indeed a rationalist, and I wouldn't want to deny that rationalism has its dangers. But as to the second charge, Barbauld is not advocating nationalism as we know it: rather, she is promoting her readers' identification with a personification whose limbs they believe to be manipulable by their own limbs. Such a notion differs fundamentally from the nationalist identification with an imaginary group defined by opposition to an aggressor. The alienating imaginary identifications that promote aggression, the gigantism against which Barbauld pits her personifications, form the basis of nationalism as we know it.[32]

In contrast, the vivifying kind of identification proposed by Barbauld will produce a community of active, responsible citizens. The ability to identify with two different kinds of images, images of gigantic stone on the one hand, and images great with spirit on the other, is exercised through reading literature. Barbauld writes her pamphlets and poems to discourage gigantism and encourage imagining oneself as the powerful limb of any gigantic form. Both Barbauld's and Marx's analyses of personification suggest that, if oppression operates by falsely reifying people's own actions into a solid external reality, then teaching people to personify and depersonify abstractions teaches them to revolt. If people can be brought to see themselves as an aggregate of hands personifying Liberty, Equality, and Nation, a legitimate body of people will overturn oppressive forms. Like Marx, Barbauld writes to revise modes of personification that she sees taking place—not in people's writing alone—but in the medium of history.

Notes

1. De Man, *The Resistance to Theory* (Minneapolis: U of Minnesota P, 1986) 11; Eagleton, *The Ideology of the Aesthetic* (Cambridge: Basil Blackwell, 1990) 10, the remark quoted and discussed in Frances Ferguson, "Romantic Studies," *Redrawing the Boundaries: The Transformation of English and American Literary Studies,* ed. Stephen Greenblatt and Giles Gunn (New York: MLA [Modern Language Association], 1992) 119-20.

2. Thus Benedict Anderson defines the nation in *Imagined Communities: Reflections on the Origin and Spread of Nationalism,* rev. ed. (New York: Verso, 1991) 5-6. Eagleton links the formation of aesthetic ideology to nationalism in "Nationalism: Irony and Commitment," in *Nationalism, Colonialism, and Literature,* by Terry Eagleton, Frederic Jameson, and Edward Said (Minneapolis: U of Minnesota P, 1990) 32; see also 28-29. On nationalism and personification, see Steven Knapp, *Personification and the Sublime: Milton to Coleridge* (Cambridge: Harvard UP, 1985) 43-45.

3. *The Prose Works of William Wordsworth,* ed. W. J. B. Owen and Jane Worthington Smyser, 3 vols. (Oxford: Clarendon, 1974) 1.130, cited hereafter in the text as *PW*.

4. De Man argues that allegory reveals and represents the way that language really works, its signifier having only an arbitrary connection to its signified. *Allegories of Reading: Figural Language in Rousseau, Nietzsche, Rilke, and Proust* (New Haven: Yale UP, 1979).

5. *PW* 1.131, 135; Adela Pinch, *Strange Fits of Passion: Epistemologies of Emotion, Hume to Austen* (Stanford: Stanford UP, 1996) 49.

6. George Levine introduces *Aesthetics and Ideology* (New Brunswick, NJ: Rutgers UP, 1994) by questioning "the reductive assimilation of literature to ideology" (1).

7. Like William Jewett, I find that uses of poetic form are historically specific ("*The Fall of Robespierre* and the Sublime Machine of Agency," *ELH* 63.2 [Summer 1996]: 423-52). Unlike Jewett (438), however, I see the deployment of personifications as partly governed by personal and political views.

8. "To a Young Lady, With a Poem on the French Revolution" (1792), *Samuel Taylor Coleridge, The Complete Poems,* ed. William Keach (Middlesex: Penguin, 1997).

9. UEA Studies Group (David Punter, David Aers, Robert Clark, Jonathan Cook, Thomas Elsasser), "Strategies for Representing Revolution," in Francis Barker, et al., ed., *1789: Reading Writing Revolution* (Colchester, England: U of Essex P, 1982) 84.

10. Agency is misattributed as much in the statement "The French won a battle," as it is in the line "Freedom . . . scattered battles from her eyes." Who constitutes "the French"? Who "Freedom"? In *Critical Practice* (New York: Methuen, 1980), Belsey discusses the function of realism (67-79), arguing that the reader's "identification with the subject of enunciation" (the "I" of the unstated "I believe" preceding any realistic statement) is precisely what makes realism "the accomplice of ideology" (79, 73).

11. "The notion of ideology appears to me difficult to make use of [for the reason that,] like it or not, it always stands in virtual opposition to something else which is supposed to count as truth." Michel Foucault, "Truth and Power: An Interview," *Power/Knowledge: Selected Interviews and Other Writings, 1972-1977,* ed. and trans. Colin Gordon (New York: Pantheon, 1980) 118.

12. Stanley Cavell finds a similar problem in the work of Paul de Man: "The Politics of Interpretation (Politics as Opposed to What?)," *Themes Out of School: Effects and Causes* (San Francisco: North Point P, 1984) 60-96.

13. "I realized that what Ian Watt called 'formal realism' was not a way of trying to hide or disguise fictionality [during the eighteenth-century, in the introduction to novels proclaiming to be "true accounts,"]; realism was, rather, understood to be fiction's formal sign," remarks Catherine Gallagher, *Nobody's Story: The Vanishing Acts of Women Writers in the Marketplace, 1670-1820* (Berkeley: U of California P, 1994) xvi-xvii.

14. "The endeavouring to overthrow any system before it is given up by the majority is faction; the endeavouring to keep it after it is given up by them is tyranny; both are equally wrong." *Sins of Government, Sins of the Nation, The Works of Anna Laetitia Barbauld. With a Memoir,* ed. Lucy Aikin, 2 vols. (London: Longman, Hurst, Rees, Orme, Brown, and Green, 1825) 2.390-91. Unless otherwise noted, all citations to Barbauld's pamphlets are from this edition. Vol. 2 is available in Adobe Acrobat at: http://miavx1.muohio.edu/~leaporm/barbauld2.htm

15. This pamphlet is not in the 1825 edition (n. 14), but in *The Works of Anna Laetitia Barbauld. With a Memoir,* ed. Lucy Aikin, 2 vols. (New York: G. & C. Carvill, et al., 1826) 2.218.

16. Burke, *Reflections on the Revolution in France and on the Proceedings in Certain Societies in London Relative to That Event,* ed. Conor Cruise O'Brien (New York: Penguin, 1968) 99.

17. I am indebted to Stuart Curran for forceful clarification of this point; see "Women Readers, Women Writers," in *The Cambridge Companion to British Romanticism,* ed. Stuart Curran (New York: Cambridge UP, 1993) 189. See also Betsy Rodgers, *Georgian Chronicle: Mrs. Barbauld & Her Family* (London: Methuen, 1958) 118-19.

18. See the note in William McCarthy and Elizabeth Kraft, eds., *The Poems of Anna Letitia Barbauld* (Athens: U of Georgia P, 1994) 291, cited hereafter as *Poems,* by line and page number.

19. Albert Goodwin, *The Friends of Liberty: The English Democratic Movement in the Age of the French Revolution* (London: Hutchinson, 1979) 297.

20. During the Treason trials of Erskine and Hardy, the prosecution argued that the Edinburgh convention of delegates from both Scottish and English Corresponding Societies held on 19 November 1793, in its attempt "to frame a reform petition," was in fact "a copy of the French National Convention" (Goodwin 297).

21. Although this pamphlet was originally attributed to an anonymous "Volunteer" in the army, its anti-war sentiment might suggest that a dissenter wrote it.

22. "Remarks on Mr. Gilbert Wakefield's Enquiry into the Expediency and Propriety of Public or Social Worship" (2.413-70), published in May of 1792 (McCarthy and Kraft, xliv-xlv); quotation from 419-20.

23. Marx also connects equality, enlightenment, and commerce: his personified commodity is "a born leveller and a cynic." He argues in *Capital* that the spirit of equality is responsible for alienation insofar as it is what makes labor conceivable in the abstract, and thus susceptible of being exchanged (Volume 1, trans. Ben Fowkes [New York: Vintage, 1977] 179, 152; hereafter cited in the text by page number). It is the essential equality, Marx would say, of the human labor it takes to produce a commodity that makes possible "the conceptual disembodiment that all commodities achieve at the moment of exchange, when their essence appears an abstract value" (Gallagher xv). But whereas for Marx, equality and concomitant exchangeability lead to alienation, for Barbauld they lead to the breakup of gigantic, monumental forms.

24. See McCarthy and Kraft 308, headnote to fragment 123. Barbauld also attacks Calvinism for making God into what she calls "the giant Force" or "Colossal Power"—the image of a tyrant who acts out of "caprice and blind partiality . . . [who is] severe, and unforgiving, except induced to pardon by the importunate intercession of some favourite" (2.465). The conception of a despotic God throttles the vivifying, animating, and unifying "spirit of liberty" which is for Barbauld essential to collective worship and collective action.

25. Anna Letitia Le Breton, *Memoir of Mrs. Barbauld* (London: George Bell, 1874) 156-57.

26. Croker, *Quarterly Review* 7 (1812): 310, quoted in McCarthy and Kraft 312.

27. "Tory journalist" for the *Quarterly,* Croker was so horrified by the spread of democracy that, immediately after passage of the Reform Bill in 1832, he retired from his post as secretary of the admiralty and refused a place in the cabinet (*Dictionary of National Biography* [Oxford: Oxford UP, 1917] 5.123-32).

28. See Smith, *An Inquiry Into the Nature and Causes of the Wealth of Nations,* ed. C. J. Bullock, The Harvard Classics Volume 10 (New York: Collier & Son, 1909) 270. Their anti-war stance "made Dissenters feared and distrusted by the Government," sabotaging efforts for other kinds of reform (Rodgers 117-19). See also J. E. Cookson, *The Friends of Peace: Anti-War Liberalism in England, 1793-1815* (Cambridge, England: Cambridge UP, 1982). According to McCarthy and Kraft, Barbauld was herself consistently opposed to war, the only exception being a *Song for the London Volunteers* in May of 1803 written in anticipation of a French invasion. Barbauld may have read Smith. During the time he was at Warrington Academy (1761-1767), and close friends with Barbauld (then Aikin), Joseph Priestley

taught "the subject of commerce" ("Proposed New Subjects," "An Essay on the Course of Liberal Education for Civil and Active Life," in Ira V. Brown, ed., *Joseph Priestley: Selections from his Writings* [University Park: Penn State UP, 1962] 85). Priestley's willingness to engage the subject could have made *Wealth of Nations* (1776) inviting to Barbauld, who believed that "The best way for a woman to acquire knowledge is from conversation with a father or a brother, and by such a course of reading as they may recommend" (letter to Mrs. Montagu; quoted in Rodgers 62).

29. Wai Chee Dimock, "Class, Gender, and a History of Metonymy," *Rethinking Class: Literary Studies and Social Formations,* ed. Wai Chee Dimock and Michael Gilmore (New York: Columbia UP, 1994) 58.

30. Although Barbauld and Marx both use personification as revolutionary discourse, they have different ideals about what kind of world order the revolution ought to usher in. Barbauld's *Eighteen Hundred and Eleven* seems to portray "Commerce" as a good thing since she allies it with imagination and cultural production of the arts, although, as Susan Wolfson has pointed out to me, her identification of commerce with "Midas" (61) whose touch was solidifying, to say the least, may suggest some ambivalence.

31. Marx and Engels, *The German Ideology* (1965) Part 1, ed. C. J. Arthur (New York: International Publishers, 1988) 53.

32. Julia Kristeva applies to nationalism Lacan's notion of the imaginary in *Nations Without Nationalism* 3, 29. On Lacan's notion of the relation between the imaginary and aggression, see *Écrits,* trans. Alan Sheridan (New York: Norton, 1977) 18-22, and on the relation of the imaginary to space, even nation-space, see 26-28.

Thomas C. Kennedy (essay date fall 1998)

SOURCE: Kennedy, Thomas C. "From Anna Barbauld's *Hymns in Prose* to William Blake's *Songs of Innocence and Experience." Philological Quarterly* 77, no. 4 (fall 1998): 359-76.

[In the following excerpt, Kennedy compares elements of parody in the two poets' works, analyzing the ways in which Blake's verse echoes, and subsequently transcends, Barbauld's poetic language.]

When Northrop Frye refers in *Fearful Symmetry* to the relationship between *Songs of Innocence* and *Songs of Experience* as mutual satire with "double-edged irony,"

he uses the term "satire" in an unusual way. Frye argues that pastoral poetry traditionally satirizes "the artificiality of the court or city."[1] The notion, however, that two texts satirize each other seems to stretch the common meaning of the term. Whether satire is directed at contemporary society or, as in burlesque and parody, at another text, it is usually a one-way street.

Most subsequent criticism has focussed on just one side of Frye's satirical equation, the irony directed against innocence. Thus, for example, Donald A. Dike, in "The Difficult Innocence: Blake's Songs and Pastoral," focuses his attention on irony in *Songs of Innocence* that undercuts innocence and that is therefore not "double-edged."[2] And when David V. Erdman in *Blake: Prophet Against Empire* discusses satire in *Songs of Innocence,* the satire is not directed at *Songs of Experience.* Erdman classifies "Holy Thursday," "Nurse's Song" and "Little Boy Lost" as satirical because they originate in the satirical context of *An Island in the Moon.*[3] With regard to "Nurse's Song," he goes on to suggest, somewhat equivocally, that it is a "gentle parody" of Anna Barbauld's **"Hymn II"** and **"Hymn V"** in **Hymns in Prose for Children.** Erdman replaces Frye's mutual with a regressive satire, so that *Songs of Experience* becomes in effect a parody of a parody.

Although both Erdman and Frye are pointing at something serious and important in *Songs of Innocence,* Erdman himself as much as acknowledges that "parody" is not the right term when he withdraws it immediately: "Mrs. Nan's song is a gentle parody of—or at least derives phrasing, images, and mood from—Mrs. Anna's second and fifth **Hymns in Prose for Children.**"[4] If parody "imitates the serious materials and manner of a particular literary work, or the characteristic style of a particular author . . . and applies this to a lowly or comically inappropriate subject,"[5] then a parody of Barbauld's text would focus our attention on her text as an object of ridicule.

In Mrs. Nannicantipot's song, Blake was particularly influenced by the following passage from **"Hymn V":**

> The little birds have ceased their warbling; they are asleep on the boughs, each one with his head behind his wing.
>
> There is no murmur of bees around the hive, or amongst the honeyed woodbines; they have done their work, and lie close in their waxen cells.
>
> The sheep rest upon their soft fleeces, and their loud bleating is no more heard amongst the hills.
>
> There is no sound of a number of voices, or of children at play, or the trampling of busy feet, and of people hurrying to and fro.
>
> The smith's hammer is not heard upon the anvil; nor the harsh saw of the carpenter.

All men are stretched on their quiet beds; and the child sleeps upon the breast of its mother.

Darkness is spread over the skies, and darkness is upon the ground; every eye is shut, and every hand is still.

Who taketh care of all people when they are sunk in sleep; when they cannot defend themselves, nor see if danger approacheth?

There is an eye that never sleepeth; there is an eye that seeth in dark night, as well as in the bright sun-shine.

When there is no light of the sun, nor of the moon; when there is no lamp in the house, nor any little star twinkling through the thick clouds; that eye seeth every where, in all places, and watcheth continually over all the families of the earth.

The eye that sleepeth not is God's; his hand is always stretched out over us.[6]

A parody of this passage would, for example, take Barbauld's question, "Who taketh care of all people when they are sunk in sleep; when they cannot defend themselves, nor see if danger approacheth?" and make Barbauld's concern seem pompous and silly by reducing it to the relatively trivial worries of an anonymous baby sitter, a mock-heroic Barbauld. But Mrs. Nannicantipot's song does not focus our attention on Barbauld's text as an object of ridicule. Instead it gives sympathetic expression to the feelings of Blake's nurse and children:

Come Come leave off play & let us away
Till the morning appears in the skies
No No let us play for it is yet day . . .[7]

Instead of holding up Barbauld's text to ridicule, Blake creates something else, something equally serious in its own way, something different.

If, as Erdman as much as acknowledges, Mrs. Nannicantipot's song is not a parody, then what is it? The relationship between Blake's text and Barbauld's seems to be something like a mirror image or inversion, a searching after truth through an opposition of thesis and antithesis.

The antithesis stands out against a shared pastoral background. In addition, both Mrs. Nannicantipot's song and Barbauld's **"Hymn V"** express a similar fear of dangers associated with the night. Barbauld expresses this fear as a concern for the individual sleeper's vulnerability while asleep, while unconscious and therefore unprepared to deal with unspecified but harmful threats. In Barbauld's text, the adult voice shares the child's fears, but reassures the fearful child with the idea that God will protect those who are asleep. Barbauld discusses the dangers of night in a general and rational way while Blake dramatizes a particular although universal moment, a particular nurse calling to children. In

Blake's text, the adult voice is divided from the child's voice, and the fear is expressed as the adult's supervisory concern for the child's welfare.

When children speak in **Hymns in Prose** [**Hymns in Prose for Children**], they either speak in unison with the adult voice or they represent visions of the world that are limited theologically, visions that are to be enlarged through Barbauld's patient instruction. Thus the Child of Reason in **"Hymn VI"** sees only material things but is taught by Barbauld to see God in everything:

God is in every place; he speaks in every sound we hear; he is seen in all that our eyes behold: nothing, O child of reason, is without God;—let God therefore be in all thy thoughts.

(**Hymns** [**Hymns in Prose for Children**] 42)

The Child of Mortality in **"Hymn X"** sees death everywhere but is renamed after being taught the doctrine of the resurrection:

Mourn not therefore, child of immortality!—for the spoiler, the cruel spoiler that laid waste the works of God, is subdued: Jesus hath conquered death:—child of immortality! Mourn no longer.

(**Hymns** 88-89)

While these theological ideas, the promise of the resurrection and the transcendental immanence of God, are not contradicted by Blake, the tone and rhetorical strategies are reversed. The children in Mrs. Nannicantipot's song are relatively naturalistic and express a normal and authentic childhood desire to stay up later. Far from having a limited vision that must be enlarged through patient instruction, Blake's children are instructing the fearful adult. They offer, not a theological lesson, but the examples of animals, the birds and the sheep, who are still awake. With these examples, they reassure the adult, convincing her that her fears are exaggerated and enlarging her vision of what is possible.

Thus Barbauld's "The little birds have ceased their warbling; they are asleep on the boughs, each with his head behind his wing" and "The sheep rest upon their soft fleeces, and their loud bleating is no more heard amongst the hills" become Blake's antithetical "Besides in the Sky the little birds fly / And the hills are all coverd with Sheep," with a transference of the description from the adult voice of Barbauld to the voices of Blake's imploring children. Also, Barbauld's further description, "There is no sound of a number of voices, or of children at play," becomes Blake's final "The little ones leaped & shouted & laughd / And all the hills ecchoed" (**Hymns** 26-28, E [*The Complete Poetry and Prose of William Blake*] 463).

This reversal appears even in small details, as when Barbauld's "the night dews fall" becomes Blake's "And the dews of night arise." In having the dew, not fall from heaven as in Barbauld's text, but instead rise up from the earth, Blake anticipates the menacing "dew," "mire," and "vapour" of "The Little Boy Lost," the poem from *Songs of Innocence* that immediately follows Mrs. Nannicantipot's song in *An Island in the Moon* (E 11, 463).

The central action of Mrs. Nannicantipot's song, children playing, is mentioned only twice in *Hymns in Prose*. In **"Hymn VII,"** play is referred to, but not described: "We will think of God when we play, and when we work." Even the idea of "play" seems rather carefully circumscribed between "God" and "work" in Barbauld's text, and the plural voice is the adult voice including and leading the child (*Hymns,* 52).

In **"Hymn VIII,"** Barbauld describes the children of a "labourer" playing:

> See where stands the cottage of the labourer, covered with warm thatch; the mother is spinning at the door; the young children sport before her on the grass.
>
> (*Hymns* 53)

The description is sympathetic and yet distanced. The children playing in front of the cottage are observed as if they were part of nature. They are not the children addressed by Barbauld. As part of the family, they are the first step in a hierarchy that Barbauld describes leading from family to village to nation to God. They are subject matter of, not participants in, the poetic discourse.

In short, Mrs. Nannicantipot's song in *An Island in the Moon* is not a parody of Barbauld's *Hymns in Prose*. Instead, the relationship is something like the relationship that obtains within *Hymns in Prose* between Barbauld and the child voices; in other words, Blake transcends the limitations of Barbauld's vision. He does this, not like Barbauld with theological instruction, but instead with a rhetoric of opposition and reversal. Blake adds conflict by dividing the voices of child and adult, in effect, adding the child's voice as independent and authentic, not merely as understood or paraphrased by an adult. The result is more conflict and more emotional intensity. Barbauld tends to resolve conflict in the calm and rational perspective of the adult. For Blake, the freedom and play of the children express spiritual values that are missing in Barbauld's text.

This reading of the relationship between Blake's text and Barbauld's is further supported by a careful analysis of the relationship between the characterization of Mrs. Nannicantipot and what we know about Barbauld. Erdman acknowledged in the notes to his third edition of *Blake: Prophet Against Empire* that the character of Mrs. Nannicantipot was after all probably not a parody of Barbauld.[8] In fact, on a number of key points, the characterization of Mrs. Nannicantipot is more of an antithesis than a parody.

For example, there is the question of church attendance. In Chapter 4 of *An Island in the Moon,* Mrs. Sinagain says to Mrs. Nannicantipot: "You hinder your husband from going to church," an accusation that Mrs. Nannicantipot does not deny (E 452). That Barbauld might have *habitually* hindered her husband, a dissenting pastor, from attending church seems unlikely. After his death in 1808, she described his church services as "characterized by the rare union of a fervent spirit of devotion, with a pure, sublime philosophy, supported by arguments of metaphysical acuteness."[9]

It is possible that when Blake wrote *An Island in the Moon* in 1784-85, Mrs. Barbauld was less supportive of her husband's vocation, and that what she expressed in 1808 was influenced by a posthumous perspective. Still, she is so completely positive that, in the absence of other evidence, it seems more reasonable to assume that she would have done what she could to make sure that her husband was never prevented from going to church.

The discussion of church attendance continues in *An Island in the Moon*:

> —Ha Ha said Inflammable Gass what dont you like to go to church. no said Mrs Nannicantipot I think a person may be as good at home.
>
> (E 452)

It is true that the author of *Hymns in Prose* does not direct children to go to church for religious instruction but rather directs them to experience religion in nature, "to see the Creator in the visible appearances of all around him, to feel his continual presence."[10] Nevertheless, Barbauld wrote two essays in which she discusses the positive influence of institutional religion on adult religious experience, one before and the other after Blake wrote *An Island in the Moon*. In the first, **"Thoughts on the Devotional Taste and on Sects and Establishments,"** published in 1775, she carefully weighs the advantages and disadvantages of an established church and a dissenting sect and concludes that, whatever the limitations of each, they may, by complementing each other, be "mutually useful," the established church making "the gross of mankind better than they would be without it," and the dissenting sect holding "some one truth in the strongest light."[11]

In the second essay, **"Remarks on Mr. Gilbert Wakefield's Enquiry into the Expediency and Propriety of Public or Social Worship,"** published in 1792, Barbauld addresses the issue of church attendance directly. She argues that, if personal emotions are given public expression in response to a marriage, a birth or a death, then it is also natural for religious emotions to be both personal and public: "If devotion really exists in the heart of each individual, it is morally impossible it should exist there apart and single."[12] This second essay was published seven years after Blake finished *An Island in the Moon,* but it seems unlikely that between 1775 and 1792 Barbauld would have first changed to opposing church attendance and then changed again from opposing to supporting it.

Although Erdman withdrew his original identification of Mrs. Nannicantipot as Barbauld, he nevertheless interpreted Mrs. Nannicantipot's refusal to go to church as a logical reduction satirizing what he referred to as Barbauld's belief "that church going has a certain value as social participation."[13] In other words, if one goes to church only because it is "useful" to do so, then to Blake it might have made better sense not to go to church at all. It is possible that Blake would have reacted to Barbauld's beliefs as Erdman assumes if Blake interpreted those beliefs as Erdman interprets them. This remains, however, rather hypothetical, especially as Erdman's argument does not seem to be based on an accurate reading of Barbauld. Barbauld does not, in fact, justify church attendance primarily on the basis of social participation as an end in itself. Barbauld's tolerant assessment of religious variation and her justification of social worship are utilitarian, but her utilitarianism does not make religion subservient to political, economic, or other non-religious ends. For Barbauld, religion and morality are inseparable, or should be, and both are valued for their own sake. They are the sources of value by which usefulness is measured.

Mrs. Nannicantipot's views on church attendance seem to be not so much a satire of or logical reduction of Barbauld's views as they are a fairly accurate representation of Blake's own. Thus Blake's contemporary, John Thomas Smith, commented in 1828 on Blake's religious practices:

> I have unspeakable pleasure in being able to state, that though I admit he did not for the last forty years attend any place of Divine worship, yet he was not a Free-thinker, as some invidious detractors have thought proper to assert, nor was he ever in any degree irreligious.[14]

If Smith's "forty years" is accurate, then Blake would have last attended church about three years after completing *An Island in the Moon,* and Mrs. Nannicantipot's views anticipate the general tendency of his, not Barbauld's, thinking. In addition to reflecting the tendency of Blake's own views, Mrs. Nannicantipot's opposition to church attendance anticipates the contrast in Blake's subsequent poetry between institutional religion and religion experienced outside of church. Institutional religion is represented, for example, by the church attendance of the parents in "The Chimney Sweeper" in *Songs of Experience* (E 22-23). It contrasts with the religion of Tom Dacre in "The Chimney Sweeper" in *Songs of Innocence,* a religion experienced not in church but in a dream (E 10) and with the religion imagined by

the speaker in "The Little Vagabond" in *Songs of Experience,* a religion that includes the warmth and pleasures of the ale house (E 26).

Finally there is Mrs. Nannicantipot's imagined reaction to a ranting minister. In *An Island in the Moon,* Mrs. Sistagatist describes a minister she likes who "would tear off the sleeve of his Gown, & set his wig on fire & throw it at the people / hed cry & stamp & kick & sweat, and all for the good of their souls." Mrs. Nannicantipot calls this minister "a wicked villain," and "a passionate wretch," and says, "If I was a man Id wait at the bottom of the pulpit stairs & knock him down & run away" (E 452).

Mrs. Nannicantipot's imagined violence is the antithesis of Barbauld's carefully and calmly reasoned tolerance of religious variation. When in *The Marriage of Heaven and Hell* Blake included among the proverbs of Hell "The tygers of wrath are wiser than the horses of instruction" (E 37), he may have considered schoolmistress Barbauld to be one of the horses, and it would seem that in Mrs. Nannicantipot he created a character who imagines herself to be, if she is not in fact, one of the tigers. At the same time, the degeneration of Mrs. Nannicantipot's response into imagined violence may also be Blake's way of indicating the social limitations of rational discourse.[15] Once again, Mrs. Nannicantipot more accurately represents Blake than Barbauld. Note, for example, John Thomas Smith's observation that Blake dropped out of Mrs. Matthew's literary circle "in consequence of his unbending deportment, or what his adherents are pleased to call his manly firmness of opinion, which certainly was not at all times considered pleasing by every one."[16] That Mrs. Nannicantipot imagines the action she would take if she "were a man" is similar to the views of Blake's friends that his unsociable behavior was "manly."[17]

In any case, Mrs. Nannicantipot's song is not a parody of Barbauld's text, and Mrs. Nannicantipot is not a caricature of Barbauld. Instead Mrs. Nannicantipot and her song are both generated by a rhetoric of opposition, transcending what Blake perceived as the limitations of Barbauld and her *Hymns in Prose.* Within the satirical fiction of *An Island in the Moon,* however, Mrs. Nannicantipot's song is generated not in opposition to Barbauld's **"Hymn V"** but, as Erdman points out, in reaction to another of Blake's songs, and Mrs. Nannicantipot's song in turn generates a song in reaction to itself.[18] Thus the freedom of the children in Mrs. Nannicantipot's song is generated in opposition to the regimentation of the children in "Holy Thursday." Then, the carefree attitude of Mrs. Nannicantipot's song generates the cares and concerns of Quid's version of "A Little Boy Lost." In Quid's song, the fears expressed in Mrs. Nannicantipot's song are realized: a child becomes lost in the dark (E 462-63). In this way, the principle of opposition that characterizes the relationship between Barbauld's *Hymns in Prose* and Mrs. Nannicantipot's song serves to generate a sequence of poems.

Notes

1. Northrop Frye, *Fearful Symmetry* (Princeton U. Press, 1947), 237.

2. Donald A. Dike, "The Difficult Innocence: Blake's Songs and Pastoral," *ELH* 28:4 (1961): 353-75.

3. David V. Erdman, *Blake: Prophet Against Empire*, 3rd ed. (Princeton U. Press, 1977), 117-27.

4. Erdman, *Prophet Against Empire*, 113.

5. M. H. Abrams, *A Glossary of Literary Terms*, 5th ed. (New York: Holt Rinehart and Winston, 1985), 166.

6. Anna Laetitia Barbauld, *Hymns in Prose for Children*. (London: J. Johnson, 1781; facsimile rpr., New York: Garland, 1977), 26-31; hereafter referred to in the text as *Hymns*.

7. *The Complete Poetry and Prose of William Blake*, ed. David V. Erdman, rev. ed. (New York: Doubleday, 1982), 463; hereafter referred to in the text as E.

8. Erdman, *Prophet Against Empire*, 123 n. 25.

9. Anna Laetitia Barbauld, *The Works of Anna Laetitia Barbauld*, ed. Lucy Aikin, 2 vols. (London: Longman, 1825), 1: xlvii-xlviii.

10. "Preface," *Hymns in Prose for Children*, vi-vii.

11. *The Works of Anna Laetitia Barbauld*, 2:257-58.

12. *The Works of Anna Laetitia Barbauld*, 2:419-20.

13. Erdman, *Prophet Against Empire*, 109, n. 43.

14. G. E. Bentley, Jr., ed., *Blake Records* (Oxford U. Press, 1969), 458.

15. Erdman, *Prophet Against Empire*, 104, observes that "the breakdown of communication and the substitution of violence for intellectual persuasion is the limit which Blake's fun constantly explores."

16. *Blake Records*, 457.

17. My argument here closely follows Nancy Bogen, "William Blake's 'Island in the Moon' Revisited," *Satire Newsletter* 2 (1968): 110-17, but while Bogen argues that Mrs. Nannicantipot is not Barbauld, I am arguing that she is the antithesis of Barbauld. Bogen suggests that the characterization of Mrs. Nannicantipot might be based on Blake's wife, Catherine, but there is really no evidence for this. It is possible, of course, that in Blake's mind Catherine Blake was in some sense the opposite of the bluestocking Barbauld, but this is rather hypothetical.

18. Erdman, *Prophet Against Empire*, 125-26.

Josephine McDonagh (essay date 1998)

SOURCE: McDonagh, Josephine. "Barbauld's Domestic Economy." In *Romanticism and Gender,* edited by Anne Janowitz, pp. 62-77. Cambridge: D. S. Brewer, 1998.

[*In the following essay, McDonagh contends that adverse contemporary reactions to* Eighteen Hundred and Eleven *derived from deeply embedded prejudices concerning gender roles in early nineteenth-century England. According to McDonagh, the poem represents Barbauld's lament not only over Britain's political and economic crises but also over her own powerlessness, as a woman, to contribute to the search for viable solutions.*]

The swingeing attacks on Anna Letitia Barbauld's late poem, *1811* (1812)—her devastating account of the ruined state of the British nation in the midst of the Napoleonic wars—have acquired lasting notoriety. Croker's lambasting, in the Tory magazine, the *Quarterly,* of the 'fatidical spinster' whom he pictured 'dash[ing] down her shagreen spectacles and her knitting needles . . . to sally forth',[1] is held to have been responsible for the silencing of Barbauld for the rest of her life. Standing accused of abandoning her proper, domestic role, the 'knitting' lady retreated forthwith: *1811* was the last work she published, although she continued to write. As William Keach has observed, however, more striking even than Croker's attack is the fact that criticism of the poem came from all directions, not only from Tories. Even those from whom she might have expected a more sympathetic response found room for complaint.[2] In the *Eclectic Review,* a magazine to which Barbauld had contributed, the tone is one of apologetic embarrassment: '[d]isposed as we are to receive every performance of Mrs Barbauld with peculiar cordiality, yet her choice of a subject in this instance, as well as her manner of treating it, is so unfortunate that we scarcely ever read a poem of equal merit with so little pleasure'.[3] Her friend Crabb Robinson wrote in his diary, 'I certainly wish she had not written it. . . . For the tone and spirit of it are certainly very bad.'[4] In the *Monthly Review,* a magazine to which her brother, John Aikin, was a regular contributor and for which she wrote herself from 1809 to 1815, an otherwise admiring reviewer wrote that, 'the first thought which occurred to us, after our perusal of her poem, was that, instead of purporting to be descriptive of the year 1811, it should have been made to refer to a subsequent period'.[5] Trying to be nice, the reviewer unfortunately misses the point: *1811* does contain a warning about the future—national decline and the transfer of wealth and moral virtue to the New World—but one based on its assessment of the lamentable current state of England.

Barbauld's poem and its gloomy predictions seemed palatable to no one. Its reception, however, provides a useful commentary on the gendered terrain of public discourse in the early decades of the nineteenth century. Throughout the reviews, the tone was one of irritation and embarrassment. The message was emphatic: Mrs Barbauld had spoken out of line, out of place and out of time. In doing so she had exposed herself to criticism, but also, in a more particular sense, exposed *herself*. The criticisms in the reviews tended to focus on her gender and her sex. Nowhere is this more evident than in Croker's review, which concentrates its attacks specifically on the aberrant femininity of this 'spinster' (who was in fact a widow), the 'fair pedagogue' and so forth: she had 'wandered from the course in which she was respectable and useful'.[6] Maria Edgeworth, Barbauld's friend and correspondent, understood the nature of the insults, the lurking suggestion throughout that, by behaving with impropriety, she had encouraged the various assaults she received—the literary equivalent of dressing provocatively.[7] In a private letter to Barbauld, she declared that 'it is not their criticism of your poem which incenses me, it is the odious tone in which they dare to speak of the most respectable and elegant female writer that England can boast'. She called on a chivalric 'public' to redeem Barbauld's soiled reputation: 'The public, the *public* will do you justice!'[8]

The *Eclectic Review*, however, gives another sense of her transgression. The figure of exposure here is different from that in Croker's account—and in fact much more violent. The disturbing image conjured is of Barbauld, not as an ineffectual spinster, but as a matricidal anatomist:

> The whole tone of it is a most extraordinary degree unkindly and unpatriotic—we had almost said unfilial. Such is her eagerness to read a lecture in morbid anatomy, and display her knowledge of the body of her venerable parent, while she is yet in very tolerable health; and in doing this preserves all the while such perfect composure, as is to us absolutely astonishing.[9]

Barbauld has found disease where there was none, and indecently displayed her findings. Another female body is exposed—but this time it is the mother's (England's) body, flayed, its interiors ripped apart.

Interesting here is the way in which emphasis is placed on what is deemed to be Barbauld's excessive, fanatical, and thus unfeminine claims to knowledge. Through the anatomical metaphor, the reviewer draws attention

to the poem's inclusion of a realm of knowledge of public affairs that it is clearly inappropriate for a woman to possess, but also for a poem to evince. Concluding, the reviewer judges the poem to be 'not so much a work of genius as of art and industry; not an emanation, but an edifice of the mind: its words more poetical than its imagery, and its imagery than its sentiment'.[10] The judgement recalls the anti-discursive critical values of Wordsworth—the idea that poetry should be an 'emanation', a powerful overflow of feeling—rather than a sustained engagement with or display of knowledge. Later the notoriously undisciplined writer, Thomas De Quincey, whose obsessions with disciplinary boundaries I have discussed elsewhere, further developed Wordsworth's terms into the idea of two distinct kinds of literature: the 'literature of power' and 'literature of knowledge', the former characterised as the outpourings of poetic genius, while the latter assumed a more expository function, designed to impart information, to instruct rather than to move.[11] De Quincey's terms were influential in the construction and dissemination in Britain of a notion of 'literature' ('the literature of power') as a transcendent category which took hold throughout the century: a depoliticised discursive space for the outpourings of subjective feeling in particular generic forms (especially poetry), in the construction of what would come to be known as the 'Romantic Ideology'. In the *Eclectic*'s critique, Barbauld's mechanical poetry, the work of 'art and industry', rather than effortless 'genius', designates her as a writer of the qualitatively lesser 'literature of knowledge', rather than the superior 'literature of power'.

According to this account, then, Barbauld's misdemeanour is a double one: a gender *and* a genre offence. By displaying a too technical—'anatomical'—knowledge of the state of the nation within the form of poetry, she transgresses the generic rules of the 'literature of power'. But by aspiring to the 'literature of knowledge' as a woman, displaying a knowledge that she should not have, and certainly should not reveal, she transgresses the limits of appropriate female utterance. This observation is a useful one because it points to a distinction in the modes of public discourse available to women in this period. Feminist revisions of Romanticism have shown the amount of poetry by women at this time which was published, circulated and highly regarded, as a conclusive corrective to the received view that, in some vaguely defined 'past', women were excluded from most forms of literary expression—and certainly all public ones. Recent critics have offered a more nuanced and historically convincing account of women's relation to public discourse through using the Habermasian model of the public sphere of letters, which in the eighteenth century was still relatively ungendered. In this respect, Keach usefully comments on Edgeworth's letter to Barbauld, and her application to an undesignated 'public' to redeem Barbauld's soiled reputation. He reads this as an indication of the 'moment in cultural history when, as Habermas puts it, "the sphere of the conjugal family became differentiated from the sphere of social reproduction"'.[12] Other models, however, can also be illuminating in explaining the awkward position of women in relation to public utterance. If women were not excluded from the production of literary works, it is true that they are strikingly and increasingly absent from other kinds of public discourse. This is markedly the case within the new and developing disciplines, the emergence of which, around the beginning of the nineteenth century, Michel Foucault analyses in *The Order of Things,* as indicative of the epistemic shift that characterises modernity.[13] The absence of women as producers of knowledge in the new disciplines of (following Foucault) the biological sciences, political economy and linguistics, is explicable in terms of women's lack of education at the higher levels, and the development of a gendered division of labour in which middle-class women's roles were restricted to the domestic arena.[14] But their presence as producers of *literature* indicates the particular discursive space that literature provides, straddling public and private in intricate and interested ways, but ones in which the exact division is still to be negotiated.

In its critique of *1811,* the *Eclectic Review* alights on the poem's disciplinary transgression—displaying too much knowledge of the wrong kind and in the wrong way. I want to suggest that one way in which we might understand the critical failure of the poem—its out-of-placeness and its consequent exposures—is through its evident inability to observe the strictures of an emerging economy of knowledge, which has precise implications for the gendered division of intellectual labour. To this end, I want to look at Barbauld's work within, or more accurately *around,* one of the newly emerging disciplines—that of political economy. In some ways the choice of political economy is somewhat arbitrary, and at first sight marginal to the poem *1811.* Only in a loose sense does this text engage with issues in political economy; for instance, in its invocation of 'Commerce' as a self-propelling system, dissociated from any particular geographical or social location, able to abandon the shores of England for more hospitable American climes ('The golden tide of Commerce leaves thy shore' [line 62]). However, in this looser sense, *1811,* and many of Barbauld's other writings, do engage with issues that overlap with political economy. In the following discussion, I will consider the implications of the development of a discipline like political economy as a gendered discursive space. For Barbauld, I will suggest, this process of disciplinisation amounts to a stricter regulation of the divisions between private and public utterances, which not only has profound effects for a woman writer, but, as we shall see, also ruptures the organisation of Barbauld's moral universe. This enhanced separation of spheres is seen by her as a lamentable pri-

vatisation of the domestic world, which renders it no longer capable of having the political and public function that it holds in the earlier work. By looking at her treatment of the idea of home, in the final part of the essay I shall examine Barbauld's sense of the political and moral implications of this division, its impact on the formation of the idea of the nation. It is this wresting of public from private that in *1811,* I shall suggest, is held responsible for Britain's sorry decline.

* * *

That Barbauld only latterly became aware of the changing epistemological landscape is evident in a passing remark in her correspondence with Edgeworth. In September, 1817, she writes to Edgeworth, 'I am just entering on *Mrs Marcet's Conversations on Political Economy,* a new subject for a lady's pen.'[15] Jane Marcet's educational works, her 'Conversations' on subjects as diverse as, for instance, chemistry, natural philosophy, the evidence of Christianity, and the history of England were enormously successful in the first half of the century.[16] Ostensibly for children, but also designed to address women, specifically mothers, the works introduced this amateur audience to the technicalities of the new disciplines. Her *Conversations on Political Economy,* first published in 1816, ran to five editions within the space of eight years and came to be recognised as an accomplished and standard introductory work on the subject. J. R. McCulloch, for instance, in his comprehensive bibliography of political economy, wrote in 1845 that this was 'on the whole, perhaps, the best introduction to the science that has yet appeared'.[17] Moreover, Marcet is the only female name to appear in McCulloch's compendious work.

In this sense, Barbauld's observation that political economy is a 'new subject for a lady's pen' is an accurate observation. In other senses, however, this passing remark jars. First, the implication, that Marcet was opening up the field to more female interventions, is not borne out by subsequent works. Although Harriet Martineau consciously followed in Marcet's footsteps with her multi-volumed *Illustrations of Political Economy* (1832-34), women seem to have contributed very little to the expanding field of works of political economy.[18] Second, Barbauld and her correspondent Edgeworth were already no strangers to the discipline of political economy themselves. Both women were immersed in an intellectual culture in which political economy and political economists played a major part. This is evident, for instance, from Barbauld's relations with T. R. Malthus, who had been educated at the Warrington Academy, the dissenting school at which Barbauld's parents had been teachers, and who maintained close ties with the family from then on.[19] Edgeworth had received a thorough education in political economy from her father, Richard Lovell Edgeworth. Both writers' works are steeped in ideas from political economy, even if they sometimes adopt a critical stance in relation to them. In this respect we might note Edgeworth's discussions of rent and land improvement in *Castle Rackrent* (1800); or Barbauld's critique of 'Enfeebling Luxury and ghastly Want' (*1811,* line 64) in poems such as *1811,* and **'West End Fair'**; or, as Isobel Armstrong has recently shown, her critique of Malthusian population theory in 'Inscription for an Ice-House' or her prose piece, 'Dialogue in the Shade'.[20]

Even more pertinent in this context is the fact that Barbauld's immensely successful work for children, *Evenings at Home* (1793), cowritten with her brother, John Aikin, incorporates episodes illustrating themes from political economy. For instance, in volume one, we find **'A Dialogue on Different Situations in Life'**, a conversation in which Mrs Meanwell explains to her daughter, Sally, the nature of wealth and inheritance, the function of poor relief, and the greater virtues of industry and charity; in volume two, there is a conversation **'On Manufactures'** between Father and Henry; and in volume three, **'The Landlord's Visit, a Drama'**, which dramatises the precept that 'good tenants deserve good landlords'.[21] Together these episodes teach the rudiments of economic exchange, production and consumption, and establish connections between wealth, social class and moral virtue, as the middle-class values of industry and sobriety, charity and quiescence are extolled. Thus Mrs Meanwell convinces her daughter of her moral advantages, over those of her daughter's aristocratic friend, the daughter of Sir Thomas, recipient of inherited wealth. 'Let it dwell upon your mind, so as to make you cheerful and contented in your station', she urges, 'which is so much happier than that of many and many other children.'[22]

While the strong moral agenda of Aikin and Barbauld's *Evenings at Home* is less evident in Marcet's work, there are striking similarities between the two works in their use of the Socratic form, in their episodic structure, and pedagogic content.[23] Given the popularity of *Evenings at Home,* it is hard to believe that Marcet was not aware of it when developing her own characteristic conversational form as a mode through which to instruct the uninitiated in political economy. *Evenings at Home* was of course a co-authored work, and indeed it is not the case that all the episodes on political economy themes were penned by Barbauld's 'lady's pen': Lucy Aikin in her memoir of her aunt corrects what she purports to be a widely held view, that all the contributions to *Evenings at Home* were by Barbauld, and lists only fourteen—including **'On Manufactures'**—of the ninety-nine pieces as hers.[24] Nevertheless, despite this, the prominence of pieces on themes in political economy in this work in which Bar-

bauld had a significant hand suggests a certain kind of forgetting on her part when she declares political economy to be 'a new subject for a lady's pen'.

Marcet's work, and Barbauld's recognition of it, however, coincided with a new phase in the growth of the discipline of political economy. The development of political economy as an academic subject can be located at around this time. Malthus's appointment to a chair in political economy in 1805, at the newly established college of the East India Company at Haileybury, marked the first use of political economy to designate an academic office, and demonstrated the discipline's growing prestige; this was further enhanced by the establishment of the Political Economy Club in 1821. Alongside its new institutional status, as Noel Thompson has observed, political economy also gained popularity in the post-war period with a general, unspecialised readership, as society saw the emergence of new economic phenomena which could not be explained in terms of local or natural factors: the activities of bad employers, or harvest failures, wars or plagues, 'factors exogenous to the functioning of the economic system'. In the early nineteenth century, Thompson argues, it became apparent that 'it was not shortage of physical produce which caused hardship . . . but rather the fact that markets were glutted with products which could not secure adequate remuneration for their producers'.[25] Hence political economy provided a widely endorsed explanation for social effects in the post- war period, both for middle-class and working-class audiences. Marcet's work, therefore, was timely in that it provided popular education in a subject of growing relevance to daily life—but also, paradoxically, a subject that was becoming increasingly specialised, abstract, and separate from the kinds of social effects it sought to explain. Indeed, one could see Marcet's work of popularisation as an adjunct to the discipline's new sense of itself as a discrete subject—a specialism, in need of interpretation and mediation.

Marcet's work as a female disseminator of the subject—addressing a distinctly female and infant readership—came at a time when the discipline was becoming institutionalised in ways that, in fact, initiated a more formal exclusion of women, as both producers and consumers of economic knowledge. Barbauld's passing comment, that Marcet wrote on 'a new subject for a woman's pen', thus marks this moment of women's exclusion from the subject in its institutionalised form—from the universities and the Political Economy Club, for instance. Barbauld's comment demonstrates a recognition of a new specialisation in the fields of knowledge that had specific implications for women writers. For the developing academisation, or professionalisation of the disciplines brought with it the increasing separation of spheres and what was imagined as an increasing confinement of women to the private realm of the domestic.

The fundamental irreconcilability of private and public, domestic and national, within the development of political economy, was a problem of wider scope than might at first be apparent. While its original conceptual model was that of the household economy, as is reflected in the derivation of the word economics from the Greek term for the household, οίκος, nevertheless, in its developed form, it engendered a conflict between domestic or private interests and those of the state and the larger society.[26] As Kurt Heinzelman points out, while the economic theorists of the late eighteenth and early nineteenth centuries modelled 'economic production on a household that attains self-sufficiency primarily by means of agricultural labour', they also conceptualised economic consumption on a model of 'individualistic decision-making within a society of duly constituted individuals acting in generally similar, self-interested ways'.[27] The mutual co-operation implicit in the model of production was thus fundamentally at odds with the idea of the competitive market place in which individuals were motivated only by self interest. The moral problem presented by political economy, then, emerged out of the conflict between domestic mutuality and an aggressively individualistic market place. This structure of antagonism is repeated in many other aspects of eighteenth-century and early nineteenth-century culture, in particular in the long tradition of civic humanism that it inherited, in which individuals were considered at risk from the corrupt state.[28]

This intellectual context is useful for understanding an increasingly intense anxiety in Barbauld's work around the divisions between public and private. In her political writings, it is this division that she holds responsible for the political and moral problems of the state. In *Sins of the Government, Sins of the Nation* (1793), for instance, her response to England's declaration of war against the French Republic in February of the same year, she writes: 'the united will of a whole people cannot make wrong right, or sanction one act of rapacity, injustice, or breach of faith. The first principle, therefore, we must lay down is, that we are to submit our public conduct to the same rules by which we are to regulate our private actions . . .'[29] What has been lost, and must be retrieved, is a fundamental congruity between private and public action.

This separation of private and public acts represented a rupture in Barbauld's moral universe. For her, the domestic provided a model for conceptualising social and economic relations within the nation, and beyond. In **'Hymn VIII'** of *Hymns in Prose for Children* (1781), she presents a picture of the cosmos, beginning with the 'cottage of the labourer covered with warm thatch'.

Scanning the scene, we are next introduced to 'the mother [who] is spinning at the door; the young children [who] sport before her on the grass; . . . the father [who] worketh to provide them food. . . . The father is the master (of the family).' This harmonious family unit then provides the basic social building block for the construction of a wider society: '[m]any homes are built together'; '[i]f there are many houses, it is a town—it is governed by a magistrate', who within the symmetry of the vision, occupies the same position as the father. The town is both the aggregate of many families, and an enlarged version of the family. On the same basis, she envisages a kingdom made up of many towns, and a universe made up of many kingdoms, over which God rules like the father, the magistrate or the king over each of their respective domains. 'All are God's family', she goes on, returning us to the beginning, to the first and basic unit in the construction of the cosmos. This is a patriarchal universe, founded on a clear continuity and congruence between the domestic sphere and the public world of affairs of state, and religious belief. Significantly, there is no sense of a market or a developed economy here, except in the blandest sense of 'buy[ing] and sell[ing]' on the village green. Rather, what is represented is an agrarian society in which families are virtually self-sufficient.[30]

Barbauld returns to the idea of home in many of her poems, most famously perhaps in **'Washing-Day'** (1797), a text that manages to find poetic material in the most mundane of domestic activities. Frequently it is the representative capacity of the home that interests her—its function as the basis for an exploration of wider social and political concerns. This is the case in her poem, **'To a Great Nation'** (1793), the 'Nation' in question being France, on the occasion of the invasion of the new republic led by the Duke of Brunswick in September 1792. Although Britain had at this stage not yet declared war with France, nevertheless, Barbauld's continuing support for the revolution is striking at a time when general British opinion had turned against it. The point at issue here, is not, however, Barbauld's political allegiances; rather, more simply, her utilisation of the rhetorical category of the home. In the poem, Barbauld calls on France to '[r]ise', and '[s]trike hordes of Despots to the ground' (line 4) in order that it might 'rise—the model of the world' (line 36).[31] The focus of attention is the different ways in which the nation is represented and the kinds of transformations it must undergo to achieve this representative-'model'-status: first it is a '*Briareus*',[32] a many-armed monster, crushing its enemies; then, after a period of penitence ('wash with sad repentant tears, / Each deed that clouds they glory's page' [lines 21-2]), it is transformed into an altogether more domestic image, as the arms of the monster are transformed into the arms of a mother, embracing 'wretched outcasts where they roam / . . . / O call the child of Misery home' (lines 26-8). This 'home' then becomes a mausoleum, as they 'build the tomb' for those 'who bled in freedom's cause' (lines 29-30); a site of national mourning through which can be established the 'antient [*sic*] laws' of the state. In the end, in this more maternal and domestic cast, national and domestic values are conjoined, and the home, as the nation, achieves a representative capacity—'thy tide of glory stay'd / . . . thy conquering banners furl'd, / Obey the laws thyself has made, / and rise—a model for the world' (lines 33-36).

In other poems, however, this reassembling of domestic and national, or private and public, is not effected; instead they are wrested apart, or come into conflict with each other. Her undated poem **'The Baby-house'** is interesting in this respect.[33] The poem begins by admiring the 'baby-house'—or doll's house—of 'Dear Agatha', with its tiny luxuries, its 'velvet couch', 'tiny cups' and 'sugared meat'. But what begins as a miniature emblem of domestic bliss and bourgeois comfort is appropriated in the course of the poem by national cultures to become a means of oppression of the poor and a tool for class division. As a toy, the Baby-house is a totally different kind of 'model' to that of the home in **'To a Great Nation'**. Thus, the Egyptian pyramid, built by 'some mighty nation's toil', is a 'baby-house to lodge the dead'. The baby-house of Versailles is nothing but a 'dome [. . .] of pomp and folly', the luxurious adjunct of a state in which 'The peasant faints beneath his load, / Nor tastes the grain his hands have sowed.' And finally, the poem claims that 'Baby-houses oft appear / On British ground, of prince or peer':

> Where are they now?
> Gone to the hammer or the plough:
> Then trees, the pride of ages, fall,
> And naked stands the pictured wall;
> And treasured coins from distant lands
> Must feel the touch of sordid hands;
> And gems, of classic stores the boast,
> Fall to the cry of—Who bids most?
> Then do not, Agatha, repine
> That cheaper Baby-house is thine.

> (lines 45-54)

Ultimately, the trappings of luxury are transient, will fall into decay, will be wrested back into circulation ('gone to the hammer' of the auctioneer), 'naked' and soiled. The decline of the baby-house in these final lines is represented in striking terms as a kind of exposure, almost a sexual violation ('naked' and 'touched by sordid hands'), as the small domestic model is dissipated and recirculated back on the market. Agatha's modest, or 'cheaper' baby-house, therefore, presents a preferable image of moderation, but it is one in which the domestic has no public, or national face.

What is described in these visions of national degeneracy is precisely the opposite of the moral universe of the *Hymns* [*Hymns in Prose for Children*], and of what

is achieved in **'To a Great Nation'**. Here—even though the home has only representative status and exists only as a model—it is divested of its representative capacity to become an empty emblem. No continuity is envisaged between the domestic and the national; it can only function as a sign of material excess and moral corruption.

A similar kind of disjunction between domestic and national domains is evident in *1811*. Indeed, the crux of the poem is the realisation that the nation state in fact is responsible for the hardships of domestic life during the war: Britain must share a responsibility in the effects of the war ('Thou who has shared the guilt must share the woe' [line 46]). The 'woe[s]' represented throughout the poem are located in a feminine, natural, and specifically domestic realm, and are exacted by a masculine aggressor: 'famine', 'disease and rapine' are 'called' by 'man', the 'sword not the sickle, reaps the harvest now' and soldiers are seen as taking the 'scant supply' from the peasant, who 'retires to die' (lines 15ff.). The most striking images in the first passages of the poem are of the needless productivities of nature ('[b]ounteous in vain' [line 11]) and women ('[f]ruitful in vain,' [lines 23 and 27]): women's sons, brothers, husbands are slaughtered, their bodies like 'fallen blossoms strew a foreign strand' (line 26). Described here is something close to a Malthusian vision, in which excessive productivity brings only death in (for Malthus) a natural process of realignment between lives and resources. For Barbauld, on the contrary, the emphasis is on men's agency in war, rather than a natural or inevitable overproductivity.[34]

Rather than resolving this conflict between men and nations, on the one hand, and women and nature on the other, Barbauld predicts only their continuing disjunction and the continuing ruin of Britain—'[t]he worm is in thy core, thy glories pass away' (line 314). Instead, focus is shifted to the New World, whence the 'spirit' or 'genius' takes 'his awful form' (line 324) and can flourish. Britain remains scarred by its inability to realign national and domestic values. Images of disjunction abound in the poem: families are riven by a war in which men die in foreign lands; wealth has been accumulated through gathering 'gems' from 'the East' (line 307); luxurious but unnatural goods, like 'summer ices' and the 'winter rose' (line 306), abound; 'commerce' departs, leaving behind 'crime' and 'fraud', and 'grandeur' for the few in the midst of 'the mass of misery' (line 320). All of these images are ones that suggest profound disorder, as people and things are taken from their natural environment, or mixed in unnatural combinations. Within this disordered universe, there is no possibility of finding the cohesive symmetries of her moral universe described in the *Hymns*.

Many of these images are ones which describe a kind of spatial disjunction: for instance, the splitting of families and the separation of mothers from their sons. This kind of dispersal, we might note, has some affinities with the structure of political economy, in which material effects such as hunger and poverty are explained in terms of geographically and conceptually remote economic causes. This kind of dissociation between local effects and their roots in the disinterested and abstract mechanisms of the market is one that in Barbauld's way of thinking would endorse the division between public and private; it makes the domestic household the inevitable and, to a degree, irrelevant, consequence of the larger abstract system, rather than, in her moral universe, the representative unit of social order, the basis of public life.

The importance of the domestic in Barbauld's work should not be under-estimated. Paul Hamilton rightly points out the optimistic cast of her cosmopolitan patriotism expressed in the poem, that 'the alternative [to 'self-serving nationalistic modes'] is to free identity from a fixed patriotism and tie it instead to a cultural centre of gravity that will settle wherever civilization renews itself'.[35] Within this we should remain aware of the structural necessity of the domestic unit in relation to the wider conception of the public and the national.

One of the many responses to the poem was Anne Grant's *1813: A Poem in Two Parts* (1814), designed as a specific rejoinder to Barbauld's 'unpatriotic' poem. One of its striking features is its reaggregation of the domestic and the national: for Grant, the family and the household regain the representative function within the conceptualisation of the nation that is lost in *1811*. Thus unlike Barbauld's uselessly productive mothers, Grant envisages a world populated by British babies, spawned from the great maternal body of the nation:

> Her children spread o'er Earth's remote extremes,
> Or by Columbia's lakes, or Ganges' streams,
> Whether they serve, or suffer, or command,
> Led by the Genius of their native land,
> Shall at their country's hallow'd altars bend,
> And truth and freedom o'er the world extend.[36]

The nation as a mother, no longer 'fruitful in vain', is the effective agent of colonisation, her offspring exporting national values to the 'remote extremes' of the world. Grant's form of maternal nationalism can be seen in a tradition of patriotic poetry written by women throughout the century, such as Felicia Hemans and Adelaide Proctor.[37]

For Barbauld, in 1811, however, this maternal role is sadly not available. The intellectual, social and political conditions for the domestic to maintain this representative capacity have, in her eyes, been lost. It amounts to a kind of displacing of women from a domestic function that provides a model for social relations, to one

that is nothing other than a totally privatised one. This privatisation of the home is in fact an aspect of the degeneracy that she diagnoses in the state of the nation.

To a certain degree, therefore, we might agree with the *Eclectic Review*'s estimation that the poem is 'unfilial', for it recognised the decline of the domestic sphere in relation to the conceptualisation of the national. If Barbauld does kill the mother-nation through her morbid anatomising, as the review suggests, she does so because she finds her already dead—that is, in a context in which the representative bond between domestic and national, private and public has been broken; in which, in a sense, the domestic has lost its meaning. The severe criticisms of *1811* thus come in a context which is characterised by this splitting of private and public, in which women's voices in the public sphere will sound only shrill and shrewish. They mark a particular stage in the negotiation of public and private, and of the proper place for women. They also provide insight into the complex construction of the domestic ideology as it takes shape in the early decades of the nineteenth century, the conservative uses of which have been widely explored. Barbauld's works, however, remind us that shadowing this is a much more radical conception of the domestic.

Notes

1. John Wilson Croker, *Quarterly Review* 7 (1812): 309-13, 309.

2. William Keach, 'A Regency Prophecy and the End of Barbauld's Career', *Studies in Romanticism* 33 (Winter: 1994): 569-577.

3. *Eclectic Review,* 8 part 1 (December 1811): 474.

4. *Henry Crabb Robinson on Books and Their Writers,* ed. Edith J. Morley (London: J. M. Dent, 1938), 1:64. Cited in Keach, 570.

5. *Monthly Review,* new series, 67 (1812): 428. On the Aikin family's contributions to the periodical press, see J. O. Hayden, *The Romantic Reviewers 1802-1824* (London: Routledge & Kegan Paul, 1969), 52-58.

6. Croker, 309. On the sexual character of the criticisms, see Keach, 569-71.

7. Previously she had been admired precisely for her 'propriety'. Coleridge, for instance, wrote: 'The more I see of Mrs Barbauld the more I admire her—that wonderful *Propriety* of Mind!' Coleridge to Estlin, 1 Mar. 1800; *Letters,* 1:578. Cited in William McCarthy and Elizabeth Kraft, *The Poems of Anna Letitia Barbauld* (Athens: University of Georgia Press, 1994), 296. However, later he descended to lewd name calling: 'Mistress Bare and Bold'. See Coleridge, *Notebooks,* 3: 3965. Cited in McCarthy and Craft, xxxiv.

8. Anna Letitia Le Breton, *Memoir of Mrs Barbauld: Including Letters and Notices of her Family and Friends* (London: George Bell, 1874), 157.

9. *Eclectic Review,* 8 part 1 (December 1811): 474.

10. Ibid., 478.

11. Thomas De Quincey, 'Letters to a Young Man' (1823) and 'The Poetry of Pope' (1848), in *Works,* ed. David Masson, 14 vols (Edinburgh: Adam and Charles Black, 1889-90), 10: 47-49, 11: 54-48; Josephine McDonagh, *De Quincey's Disciplines* (Oxford: Clarendon Press, 1994), 72-81.

12. Keach, 571. Citing Jurgen Habermas, *The Structural Transformation of the Public Sphere: An Inquiry into a Category of Bourgeois Society,* trans. Thomas Burger with the assistance of Frederick Lawrence (Cambridge, MA: MIT Press, 1991), 28. Essays by Mary Favret and Ann Mellor in the same *Studies in Romanticism* edition (33[winter 1994]) also offer useful developments of the Habermasian model.

13. Michel Foucault, *The Order of Things,* trans. Alan Sheridan (London: Tavistock Press, 1970).

14. Foucault's analysis of the epistemic turn is useful in considering the *Eclectic Review*'s accusation that Barbauld is a 'morbid anatomist'. This would put her on the side of Marie-François-Xavier Bichat, the French anatomist whose works Foucault held up as ushering in a new, modern understanding of the human body as an organic unit. On this see Michel Foucault, *The Birth of the Clinic,* trans. Alan Sheridan (London: Tavistock, 1973)

15. Le Breton, *Memoir of Mrs Barbauld,* 178.

16. Jane Marcet, *Conversations on Chemistry* (1806), *Conversations on Natural Philosophy* (1819), *Conversations on the Evidence of Christianity* (1826), *Conversations on the History of England* (1842).

17. J. R. McCulloch, *The Literature of Political Economy* (London: Longman, Brown, Green and Longman, 1845), 18.

18. Martineau's works on political economy did not gain the recognition from political economists that Marcet's did. For instance, Martineau did not receive an entry in McCulloch's bibliography. Goldstrum speculates that this was because of Martineau's Unitarian background. He also argues that the impact of both writers was much more limited than is sometimes claimed. Neither 'achieved anything like "household name" status', he argues, and both were overshadowed by the introductory works of Richard Whately which, by mid-century, had become part of the school curriculum. See Max Goldstrum, 'Popular Political Economy and the British Working-Class Reader in the Nineteenth Century', in *Expository Science: Forms and Functions of Popularisation,* ed. T. Shin and R. Whitley (Dordrecht: D. Reidel, 1985), pp. 263-7. Symptomatically, Donald Winch, in his index to *Riches and Poverty: An Intellectual History of Political Economy in Britain, 1750-1834* (Cambridge: Cambridge University Press, 1996), makes an interesting hybrid of 'Harriet Marcet'.

19. See Donald Winch, *Riches and Poverty,* 255.

20. Isobel Armstrong, 'The Gush of the Feminine: How Can We Read Women's Poetry of the Romantic Period?', in *Romantic Women Writers: Voices and Countervoices,* ed. Paula R. Feldman and Theresa M. Kelley (Hanover, NH: University Press of New England, 1995), 13-32. For the context of Barbauld's critique of Malthus, see also Josephine McDonagh, 'Infanticide and the Boundaries of Culture, from Hume to Arnold', in *Inventing Maternity: Politics Science and Literature 1650-1865,* ed. Carol Barash and Susan Greenwood (Lexington, Kentucky: University of Kentucky Press, forthcoming, 1998).

21. John Aikin and Anna Letitia Barbauld, *Evenings at Home: or, the Juvenile Budget Opened, Consisting of a variety of Miscellaneous Pieces for Instruction and Amusement of Young Persons,* 6 vols (10th edition; London: Joseph Johnson, 1814), 3: 15.

22. Ibid., 1: 61.

23. On children's literature in this period, see Alan Richardson, *Literature, Education and Romanticism: Reading as Social Practice, 1780-1832* (Cambridge: Cambridge University Press, 1994), ch. 3, esp. 127-42.

24. Barbauld, *The Works of Anna Letitia Barbauld with a Memoir by Lucy Aikin,* 2 vols (London: Longman, Hurst, Rees, Orme, Browne, and Green, 1825), 1: xxxvi-xxxvii.

25. Noel W. Thompson, *The People's Science: The Popular Political Economy of Exploitation and Crisis 1816-1834* (Cambridge: Cambridge University Press, 1984), 56-7. See also Winch, *Riches and Poverty,* ch. 13.

26. See J. G. A. Pocock, 'The Mobility of Property and the Rise of Eighteenth-Century Sociology', in *Virtue, Commerce, and History: Essays on Political Thought and History, Chiefly in the Eighteenth Century* (Cambridge: Cambridge University Press, 1985), 103 ff.

27. Heinzelman, 'The Cult of Domesticity: Dorothy and William Wordsworth at Grasmere', in Anne

K. Mellor (ed.), *Romanticism and Feminism* (Indiana: Indiana University Press, 1988), 58.

28. Pocock, *Virtue, Commerce and History,* 43-45, 70-71, 114 ff.

29. *Works* 2:387. See J. E. Cookson, *The Friends of Peace: Anti-War Liberalism in England, 1793-1815* (Cambridge: Cambridge University Press, 1982), ch. 4.

30. Barbauld, *Hymns in Prose for Children* (London: Joseph Johnson, 1781), 53-62.

31. All citations from the poems are from McCarthy and Kraft, eds, *Poems.*

32. '*Briareus* was a giant of ancient fable, represented with a hundred hands, and fifty heads.' Barbauld's note, reprinted in McCarthy and Kraft, 292.

33. McCarthy and Kraft remain uncertain as to the date of the poem, but suggest that it came after 'The Wake of the King of Spain' which they tentatively date c. 1819. The post-1811 date for 'The Baby-house' would, however, suggest a progressive disillusionment with the possibility of reassembling private and public.

34. On Barbauld's critique of Malthus, see n. 19 above.

35. Paul Hamilton, 'The New Romanticism: Philosophical Stand-ins in English Romantic Discourse', *Textual Practice* 11 no. 1 (1997): 109-132, 127.

36. Grant, *Eighteen Hundred and Thirteen: A Poem in Two Parts* (Edinburgh, 1814), 62.

37. There are evident links between this kind of maternal nationalism and the proto-eugenic arguments of the 1880s and 1890s in which women's role is defined specifically in terms of their reproductive capacity, to populate the empire with fine English bodies. See Anna Davin, 'Imperialism and Motherhood', *History Workshop Journal* 5 (spring 1978): 9-65; Sally Ledger, *The New Woman: Fiction and Feminism at the Fin de Siècle* (Manchester: Manchester University Press, 1997), ch. 3.

Diego Saglia (essay date winter 1999)

SOURCE: Saglia, Diego. "The Dangers of Over-Refinement: The Language of Luxury in Romantic Poetry by Women, 1793-1811." *Studies in Romanticism* 38, no. 4 (winter 1999): 641-72.

[In the following excerpts, Saglia investigates the economic, political, and allegorical implications of luxury in Barbauld's writings.]

"The riches of Asia have been poured in upon us, and brought with them not only Asiatic luxury, but, I fear, Asiatic principles of government."[1] Thus, in 1770, William Pitt, Earl of Chatham adapted the Livian explanation of Rome's decline to bemoan the changes that had been taking place in politics, society, and the economy during the century. Paradoxically defining progress as a metamorphosis into a backward *other,* this remark encapsulates two recurrent images of the discourse of luxury in eighteenth-century Britain: luxury as a foreign body that must be contained by a qualifying adjective or any other demarcating linguistic device; and luxury as one of the most important principles for the identification of evil in history. Chatham's judgment also exemplifies the flexible status of the discourse and its applicability to an interpretation of the political, social, economic, or cultural phenomena of contemporary Britain. This discursive flexibility owes much to the wide-ranging debate in which the desire to possess rare artifacts and precious commodities was disputed from positions such as mercantilism, civic humanism and the mythology of trade. It is indeed a familiar fact of cultural history that the early eighteenth century saw a profound reorganization of the discourse of luxury, a renewed incitement to talk and write about consumption, and the need to rationalize and regulate its effects. Employing *topoi* as old as the Bible, representations also drew on the increased prominence of luxury items, now more easily obtainable and affordable by wider social groups[2]. . . .

At the end of the eighteenth century, women poets such as Anna Letitia Barbauld, Mary Darby Robinson, and Charlotte Turner Smith consistently and repeatedly turned to the discourse of luxury in poems with a political and public message on the condition of contemporaneity. Their elaboration of luxury represents a culturally significant fact and a discursive climax for a variety of reasons, not least because, around the turn of the century, the literary market was dominated by women poets whose compositions treated public issues with an intensity and an overtness which was to be restricted in the following decades. At this historical juncture, the paramount importance of French revolutionary events determined the ways in which luxury was figured and explained. Linked with the climactic event in contemporary history, luxury became a recurrent topic in the revolutionary controversy from Tom Paine's praise of the seizure of aristocratic luxury in *The Rights of Man* (1791-92) to Arthur Young's denunciation of this doctrine of levelling in *The Example of France* (1793).[3] Additionally, discursive treatments of luxury were attuned to contemporary material conditions and their effects on practices of consumption, as the 1780s and 90s saw a dramatic increase in the inflation rates accompanied by a rise in prices affecting both the macro-economy of the whole nation and the microeconomic spaces of everyday life. A response to changing economic modes, the discourse of luxury in women's writings thus also bore on the preoccupation with disposable incomes, or "money competences," and spending power increasingly identified as prerequisites for independence.[4] Women's verse was then part of an emergent romantic culture which defined new economies of desire and patterns of consumption resulting in what Colin Campbell has described as a "modern autonomous imaginative hedonism."[5]

Involved in a cultural shift towards new ways of producing and consuming commodities, imaginative and non-fictional writing by women started to address commonplace images of luxury as a feminine concept, of consumption as a typically feminine activity, and of female corruption as a symbol employed by both commercial and anti-commercial, civic humanist discourses. As argued by Harriet Guest, this figure of "corrupted femininity . . . needs to be understood primarily as a set of gendered characteristics appropriated to the requirements of the discourse of commerce and its feared inverse, the anti-commercial horrors of profiteering, greed and consumerism run riot."[6] Towards the end of the century, writings by women—from Wollstonecraft's *Vindication of the Rights of Woman* to Hannah More's *Strictures on the Modern System of Female Education*—discussed the idea of woman as flawed consumer and turned it into a field of contention about femininity and gender difference. Addressing the issue of woman's position and figurative role in a capitalist economy, women's verse investigates luxury in order to readjust the gendered discourse of consumption and to transcend the marginalization it implies by probing the public value of the sumptuous. . . .

The language of luxury in late eighteenth-century verse can be approached through Anna Laetitia Barbauld's **"Inscription for an Ice-House"** (c. 1793). Albeit not strictly a representation of luxury, this text is nonetheless centered around a luxury object for, before the invention of the ice-making machine in the 1830s, the comforts offered by ice houses were only to be found on the country estates of the upper bourgeoisie, Indian nabobs, and the aristocracy. As with conservatories or greenhouses for exotic produce, ice houses signalled the owner's wealth and power. Associated with manor houses, their ice rooms were also filled with the produce of kitchen gardens and orchards, game, fish and poultry. Mindful of these multiple functions, Barbauld evokes the ice house as a monument to country-house life and the wealth of the higher classes, and thus places the luxury object in the relation between estate and state. The mansion being both private habitation and center of public power, her text evidences the dependence of literary renditions of the discourse of luxury on a traditional genre such as the country-house poem.[7]

Intended to be placed on the façade of an ice house, Barbauld's **"Inscription"** [**"Inscription for an Ice-House"**] opens by abruptly announcing itself as worthy of the reader's attention and by spectacularizing its text through an apostrophe and the calculated delay of its subject:

> Stranger, approach! within this iron door
> Thrice locked and bolted, this rude arch beneath
> That vaults with ponderous stone the cell; confined
> By man, the great magician, who controuls
> Fire, earth and air, and genii of the storm
>
>   * * *
>
> A giant sits; stern Winter . . .[8]

(1-8)

Although belonging to a commonplace genre in eighteenth-century versification, Barbauld's lines draw attention to the complexity of "inscribing" the ice-house into a text which, shorn of its title, will supposedly end up on the building's surface. The question of inscription is crucial, for the structure of the poem is conditioned by its relation to the object it describes. Even if the aim is illustrating an ice house, and the building is actually named in the title, the text begins by creating a suspension and proceeds through a deferral of this very object.

As with Coleridge's "Ancient Mariner," the poem approaches its readers, sets them as its destined receivers, and monopolizes their attention by forcing them to decode an object which is being wilfully delayed and held back. Even when this is discovered to be Winter, the giant that man has chained to do his bidding, the text does not disclose the primary object of the inscription itself but rather an allegory of the processes inside the ice house. In this textual journey through technological mythology, the interior of the building takes the shape of a magic grotto, a legendary cave, and a frozen garden. Whilst exploring these associations, the text attracts the reader and viewer deeper and deeper into its figurative recesses, creating a literary counterpart of the actual journey into the recesses of the locked room. Supposing the title to be redundant once the inscription is in place, Barbauld's poem withholds the name of its referent, points to itself, and shows the way into the cold room.

The opening lines of the poem accentuate one of the outstanding traits in the writing of luxury, the presence of a gap or an interruption both rhetorical—the vocative in "Stranger, approach!"—and figurative—the "iron door / Thrice locked and bolted." These breaks circumscribe luxury and establish its significance either by setting it off as a meaningful object, or by separating it from other narratives and images in the text. Not so much a fixed rhetorical scheme, the gap is rather an effect of discontinuity in a text where luxury represents a climax. Further, in the space opened by this interruption, Barbauld's poem deploys yet another distinctive device in representations of the sumptuous by way of the list of luxury commodities and their attributes. Once Winter has been identified as the source of energy, the receding *mise en abîme* and game of mirrors of the initial lines is suspended and the practical applications of the ice house are listed:

> The rugged power, fair Pleasure's minister,
> Exerts his art to deck the genial board;
> Congeals the melting peach, the nectarine smooth,
> Burnished and glowing from the sunny wall:
> Darts sudden frost into the crimson veins
> Of the moist berry; moulds the sugared hail:
> Cools with his icy breath our flowing cups;
> Or gives to the fresh dairy's nectared bowls
> A quicker zest . . .
>
> (20-28)

Thus accumulation transmits one of the effects of luxury, which is the multiplication of pleasurable sensations, reproduced in textual form through the natural objects turned into luxuries by the preserving and cooling power of Winter. In addition, accumulation problematizes the conspicuous status of luxury, in that these lines reflect the paradox which saw ice houses as a usually hidden feature of country-estate parks although signs of wealth and social standing. This contradiction of visibility is addressed by the text of the **"Inscription"** which avoids naming the building itself whilst evidencing and rhetorically amplifying the luxury it produces.

In the sensuous procession of food and drink, brute strength is harnessed to ensure modern comfort while primitive forces are yoked to provide pleasures for mankind. Gradually, however, the myth-making and allusive language of the poem annuls the scene of the production of luxury to concentrate on its consumption. In other words, the scheme of accumulation moves luxury from the domain of use-value—the freezing, storing and keeping of food—to a reflection of the social and economic power of its owner. The text thus endows the modern luxury commodity with what Jean Baudrillard has theorized as "sign-value," the object taken as a sign of the discursive and material context that creates it. This sign-object is then a form of "coded difference" which abolishes the actual relations of production and exists only as a sign of the social construction of value and the social logic of exchange.[9] As with the sign-object, Barbauld's ice house signifies the co-responsiveness between state and estate while at a second, but no less important remove, the **"Inscription"** posits luxury not only as the by-product, but as the significant face, of contemporary advancement.[10]

Common features in representations of the sumptuous, images of femininity and masculinity also characterize Barbauld's depiction of the "mechanisms" of the ice house, directing the reader's perceptions of the value of

luxury and its social and moral consequences. With its rather obviously gendered mythology, the **"Inscription"** describes the function of the cold room as the submission of the rugged giant Winter to the commands of fair Pleasure, the building being then magnified through Biblical and Classical allusions. Since Winter is compared to Samson and Hercules, both heroes subjected to women, the gendering of the production of luxury is underscored by an ethical alertness to the emasculating condition of the consumption of luxury products. Samson and Hercules, slaves respectively of "Gaza's wealthy sons" (17) and Queen Omphale, are tamed purveyors of luxuries for effeminate or female masters.

The operations of Barbauld's redistribution of gender acquire particular relief when considered in relation to one of its most authoritative precedents, the description of winter in James Thomson's *Seasons* (1726-30):

> See, Winter comes, to rule the vary'd Year,
> Sullen, and sad, with all his rising Train;
> *Vapours,* and *Clouds,* and *Storms* . . .[11]
>
> (1-3)

Introducing the sublime procession of Winter, Thomson genders this season as masculine. King of the year accompanied by a retinue of meteorological phenomena, Winter is further masculinized through epithets such as "Father of the Tempest" (72) and by the Gothic chromatism of "Wrapt in black Glooms" (73). From the end of autumn his figure rises to dominate the lives of men, his complete sway reconfirmed in the conclusion of the poem: "'Tis done!—Dread WINTER spreads his latest Glooms, / And reigns tremendous o'er the conquer'd Year" (1024-25).

Thomson's gendered theme of dominance and narrative organization are adopted by Barbauld in her conclusion about her own Winter's return to elemental freedom:

> . . . Sullen he [Winter] plies his task,
> And on his shaking fingers counts the weeks
> Of lingering Summer, mindful of his hour
> To rush in whirlwinds forth, and rule the year.
>
> (28-31)

Interestingly, this subscription to the masculine sublimity of Thomson's Winter comes at the end of a sustained discourse on the subjection and feminization of this seasonal force. Indeed, whereas in the *Seasons,* Winter is a "grim Tyrant [who] meditates his Wrath" (898), by contrast, in Barbauld's text Winter, albeit "Indignant," is assimilated to tamed heroes and such household activities as Hercules' weaving and spinning. Also, Thomson's Pindaric lines magnify the dangers of Winter by turning its weather features into as many weapons: he "arms his Winds with all-subduing Frost" (899),

"Moulds his fierce Hail, and treasures up his Snows, / With which he now oppresses half the Globe" (900-901). Disputing Thomson's poetics of gender and military imagery, Barbauld transforms Thomson's terms from arms injurious to humankind into features of Winter's luxury-producing activity. As seen above, Barbauld's domesticated Winter "Darts sudden frost into the crimson veins / Of the moist berry" and "moulds the sugared hail," whereas his "treasured snows" (10) are now enclosed in the safe space of the ice house. By this subversion of Thomson's lexical choices, the **"Inscription"** reduces his mythically destructive Winter into a minor household god which, although still nominally masculine, is tied to domestic chores, his wild energy so tamed that the (feminine) visitor is reassured that the giant will not "wither with his touch the coyest flower / That decks thy scented hair" (13-14).

The compressed demasculinized portraits of Samson and Hercules turn the myth-making language of the "Inscription" into a language of myth-*un*making indicative of the gender compromise of sturdy masculinity being curbed and, in Hercules' case, feminized for the production of pleasure. Also, by this interlacing of masculinity and femininity, luxury becomes the place of an ambiguous construction of gender for, if the pleasurable objects of luxury feminize existence, these very objects are guaranteed by the masculine technology which harnesses Winter inside the chamber of the ice house.[12]

Another important confrontation set up by the **"Inscription"** is that between public and private spheres of action. Writing conspicuous consumption through a varied discourse of celebration, irony, and denigration, Barbauld's text places luxury within a tension between the estate owning the luxury ice house and the larger context in which the luxury object finds its place. As berries, fruits, and cooled wines go to decorate the "genial board," the climactic ritual of the eighteenth-century cult of sociability, Barbauld's poem defines the experience of luxury as that of entering a private, locked space which then opens up to the public in the convivial banquet.[13] As with the issue of the visibility of luxury, Barbauld's text elaborates the country-house poem and its distinctive preoccupation with the aristocratic mansion as an interface between private pastoral and public forum. And, including the country house into contemporary technology, the **"Inscription"** places luxury at a crucial junction between a private dimension of pleasure and a public one of sociability.[14]

Probing the ideological undercurrents in Barbauld's text reveals how luxury is signified through the repetition and multiplication of its components, and by linguistic devices such as accumulation, lists, and verbal augmentation. Further, whilst representing luxury, the tropes and schemes of **"Inscription for an Ice-House"** attempt to reproduce its material effects: the foregrounding of the luxury object through apostrophes, invocations, or exclamations; a gradual penetration and descent into the scene of luxury; the precious commodity as contained, hidden, submerged, or enclosed; a "processional" spelling out of the attributes of luxury; and, finally, the presence of a gap which indicates the outstanding and differential value of the scene of luxury. . . .

In other contemporary poems the explanatory value of luxury becomes significant in relation to the themes of liberty and the slave-trade, and in reflections about the causes and effects of British economic growth. Such an interlocking of representative strategies forcefully emerges in Anna Barbauld's *Epistle to William Wilberforce, Esq. on the Rejection of the Bill for Abolishing the Slave Trade* (1791). There, by way of long-established tropes and figures, luxury is feminized, connected with the slave-system and posited as a cause of the incipient decadence of the British ruling class. Specifically, gaps and verbal accumulations delimit the space where Barbauld may attack the effects of excessive consumption on society through the commonplace personification of luxury as female corruption in commercial and anti-commercial discourses. Conspicuous consumption is thus focused upon as an attribute of the prosperous and unfeeling British nation presented in the shape of a despotic lady:

> Lo! where reclin'd, pale Beauty courts the breeze,
> Diffus'd on sofas of voluptuous ease;
> With anxious awe, her menial train around,
> Catch her faint whispers of half-utter'd sound;
> See her, in monstrous fellowship, unite
> At once the Scythian, and the Sybarite;
> Blending repugnant vices, misally'd,
> Which *frugal* nature purpos'd to divide;
> See her, with indolence to fierceness join'd,
> Of body delicate, infirm of mind,
> With languid tones imperious mandates urge . . .
>
> (57-67)

A familiar grammatical feature, the initial imperative once more represents an interruption in the discursive flow of the poem's argumentation and inaugurates the focusing and penetration into the private spectacle of the pampered, luxurious lady. Conveyed by the geographic and cultural otherness of "Scythian" and "Sybarite," this definition of luxury is modelled upon those attached to the myths of republican Rome and Classical Greece. The epithets of otherness emphasize luxury as import thanks to the actual increase in luxury goods coming to Britain from its colonies and the world. Likewise the passive role of women as consumers (and opposed to men's productive role) combines with love of ostentation and greed to produce an imagery of corrupted and corrupting consumption inevitably figured as feminine. Barbauld, moreover, expands on the pernicious *othering* power of the sumptuous, an enervating and feminizing phenomenon which induces inhuman behavior and exploitation. Indeed the lady is portrayed as a monstrous figure, physically and mentally inept ("Of body delicate, infirm of mind"), embodying classically foreign types of unnatural behavior, and opposite but equally repulsive vices ("Blending repugnant vices, misally'd").

The palatial setting of the passage is then keyed to the country-house poetics seen at work in **"Inscription for an Ice-House"** and throws further light on Barbauld's use of the clichéd icon of female corruption. A figure compatible with both commercial and anti-commercial polemics, it was also taken on board by women writers in their descriptions of the reification of woman in present society, and in their discussions of the socioeconomic regimentation of middle-class women (see Harriet Guest 317-18). By contrast, Barbauld's abolitionist text seems to offer a readjustment of this gendered construct and the specificity of its class connotations. The poem's social denunciation in fact revolves around the allegory of luxury as a lady of quality or a lady from the landed aristocracy and not a middle-class woman or a woman from the lower classes. In terms of literary precedents the text is once again taking on the affiliation of country-house poetics to an aristocratic addressee and patron, whereas its polemical tone recalls Crabbe's critique of the ideological implications of the pastoral in *The Village* (1783). As justly remarked by Marlon Ross, Barbauld's attack on luxury in the *Epistle* [*Epistle to William Wilberforce, Esq., on the Rejection of the Bill for Abolishing the Slave Trade*], is an adaptation of Crabbe's critique of the landed gentleman as a representative of the gentry and minor aristocracy from the countryside:

> Say ye, opprest by some fantastic woes,
> Some jarring nerve that baffles your repose;
> Who press the downy couch, while slaves advance
> With timid eye, to read the distant glance;
>
> * * *
>
> How would ye bear in real pain to lie,
> Despis'd, neglected, left alone to die?
> How would ye bear to draw your latest breath,
> Where all that's wretched paves the way for death?[15]
>
> (250-61)

Whilst Crabbe is here comparing the plight of the sick poor to the hypochondria of the wealthy, in her vignette of luxury Barbauld adapts the image of the excesses of the wealthy as another, metaphorical, kind of disease. The symbol of an unproductive class, the luxurious aristocrat also implies an attack on the civic humanist ideal of landed property. Reversing the discourse of privilege sanctioned by the country-house poem, Barbauld contests its traditional mission of celebrating the civilized grandeur of an aristocratic establishment. Such

patterns of consumption stand accused of mutating the structure of the state by fostering unnatural institutions such as slavery. Thus, reworking the equation of estate and state by way of luxury, Barbauld's text denounces "Old Corruption" and its forms of consumption while, at the same time, contesting its theoretical basis in the shape of those tenets of aristocratic civic humanism which demonized bourgeois acquisitive activities.[16] Once more by way of traditional tropes, excessive aristocratic consumption is then represented as a form of contagion spreading to all social classes and affecting the entire body politic, "The soft luxurious plague alike pervades / The marble palaces, and rural shades" (88-89).

As by the late eighteenth century, the two groups competing for consumption and accumulation of luxury objects were the landed aristocracy and the trading classes, Barbauld's class-specific portrait may be read as an attempt to redefine different types of luxury and to qualify its attack on unproductive expenditure. In this interpretive context, aristocratic *otium* is deplored and bourgeois *negotium* celebrated, in a text which, in more generalized terms, shows the "relation between personal idleness and sociopolitical oppression" (Marlon Ross 222). If Barbauld's text employs the hackneyed figure of the despotic, greedy woman, it also reclaims the female figure from the role of supporting anti-commercial discourse and the tainted cliché of corrupted female consumption which in the 1790s seemed a dominant trope identifying corrupting luxury in the precise social setting of the middle class.[17]

In *Epistle to William Wilberforce* [*Epistle to William Wilberforce, Esq., on the Rejection of the Bill for Abolishing the Slave Trade*] the positive mythology of commerce beckons in the distance, whereas the denunciation of the parasitical and depleting form of consumption of the higher classes indicates the approval given to the invigorating practices of the bourgeoisie. This implicit textual architecture later becomes visible in *Eighteen Hundred and Eleven* (1812) where trade is presented by Barbauld as the driving force behind British expansion and the merchants are celebrated as the unrecognized heroes of contemporary society. The latter text transports the kind of aristocratic and injurious luxury of the *Epistle* into a confrontation with the kind of luxury produced and marketed by the thriving world of British trade. Whilst concluding the argument in the *Epistle,* here Barbauld also avoids representing luxury through the gap or the list in favor of an imagery alternating between expansion and decay, or growth and decline.

Addressing Britain during a period of economic crisis and social unrest, Barbauld remarks that "Sad, on the ground thy princely merchants bend / Their altered looks, and evil days portend" (57-58) whereas in previous, happier times they "Sent forth their mandates to dependant kings" (164). Following an eighteenth-century tradition of praise for the mercantile profession, including such texts as Edward Young's "The Merchant" (1729), Richard Glover's *London* (1739) and Cornelius Arnold's *Commerce* (1751), in Barbauld's poem the figure of the British trader becomes the symbol and guarantor of national welfare and strength. *Eighteen Hundred and Eleven* places luxury within an overtly political and social discourse by engaging with eighteenth-century critiques of political economy and its appreciation of conspicuous consumption, and specifically deploys its sumptuous imagery by way of a contrast between vertical (developing) and horizontal (static) figures. As expected, vertical images convey the effects of progress upon the polity, and thrusting economic development is presented as an upward-thrusting structure:

> Then from its bed is drawn the ponderous ore,
> Then Commerce pours her gifts on every shore,
> Then Babel's towers and terrassed gardens rise,
> And pointed obelisks invade the skies
>
> (227-30)

The upward movement conveys Barbauld's homage to Britain's commercial supremacy which has replaced that of Venice ("Venice the Adriatic weds in vain" 269). As with the Italian republic, Britain rises from the sea, rich products being symbolically poured on her coasts from all the corners of the world ("And wealth is wafted in each shifting gale" 274) in another representation of the spoils of empire: "The sons of Odin tread on Persian looms, / And Odin's daughters breathe distilled perfumes" (275-76). At the same time, this vertical imagery is questioned from the opening section of the poem: "And think'st thou, Britain, still to sit at ease, / An island Queen amidst thy subject seas [?]" (39-40). Throughout the text, figures of growth and towering domination alternate with an imagery of decadence and the end of progress, starting from the initial vista of Napoleon's supremacy over Europe: "Colossal Power with overwhelming force / Bears down each fort of Freedom in its course; / Prostrate she [Britain] lies beneath the Despot's sway" (7-9). Within this generalized decadence, "Enfeebling Luxury" is a factor of inequality and a cause of national crisis together with "ghastly Want" (64), so that the plateau of development depicted by the poem can only be followed by a phase of decline, as "fairest flowers expand but to decay" (313). Scattered around the text, figurations of fallen empires, London's future ruins, and cross-references to the Bible and Volney's *Ruins of Empire* ("In desert solitudes then Tadmor sleeps" 249) point to the crisis of progress and a decline aggravated by economic development and excessive consumption.[18]

With its depiction of luxury as contributing to national decadence, Barbauld's jeremiad must have appeared prophetic to certain readers when, in the year of its publication, the Prime Minister Spencer Perceval was shot by John Bellingham, a bankrupt whose pleas had not been attended to, and who had then been greeted as a hero by disaffected sections of the public. The lesson seemed to be that, if the existing economic system leads to bankruptcy, this, in its turn, fosters political destabilization.

Yet the poetic signs of luxury, here the imagery of expansion and decay, promote a more ambiguous view. *Eighteen Hundred and Eleven* projects a not so distant future when "Europe sit[s] in dust, as Asia now" (126), but in fact also resists the idea of Britain's economic and cultural twilight following the pattern set by the Eastern empires: "if 'tis thy fate / To rank amongst the names that once were great, / Not like the dim cold Crescent shalt thou fade" (71-73). From a hypothetical vantage point in the future, the poem assesses the apogee of British progress as the period of mercantile supremacy, "Where through each vein spontaneous plenty flowed, / Where Wealth enjoyed, and Charity bestowed" (167-68). This secondary agenda in the poem, competing but also collaborating with pessimism, connects luxury to the present and its achievements, and culminates in the poetical set-piece of a panegyric on London:

> London exults:—on London Art bestows
> Her summer ices and her winter rose;
> Gems of the East her mural crown adorn,
> And Plenty at her feet pours forth her horn;
> August she sits, and with extended hands
> Holds forth the book of life to distant lands.
>
> (305-12)

Expansion alternates with decadence, plenty with poverty, and economic supremacy with a future nation in ruins. Developing along a dual imagery, the language of luxury in *Eighteen Hundred and Eleven* is torn between an appreciation and a denunciation of the effects of modernity and the influence of progress. The praise of the merchants and the sympathetic eye Barbauld turns to their plight reveals that it is the luxury thus produced that indicates the wealth of the nation and its economic welfare, its cultural activity and artistic wealth. From its radical, dissenting and mercantile vantage point, *Eighteen Hundred and Eleven* does not contest the importance of this productive kind of luxury linked to new social and economic forces and their trading interests. Whereas actively produced luxury is enhanced by the imagery of growth and expansion, the self-destructive consumption of the present status quo is condemned by the opposite imagery of decay and the transformation of Britain into an *other* nation.[19]

Notes

1. Quoted in H. V. Bowen, "British India, 1765-1813: The Metropolitan Context," in *The Oxford History*

of the British Empire, ed. William Roger Louis, vol. 2: *The Eighteenth Century,* ed. P. J. Marshall (New York: Oxford UP, 1998) 542.

2. On the luxury debate see Gordon Vichert, "The Theory of Conspicuous Consumption in the 18th Century," in *The Varied Pattern: Studies in the 18th Century,* eds. Peter Hughes and David Williams (Toronto: Hakkert, 1971) 253-67; John Sekora, *Luxury: The Concept in Western Thought, Eden to Smollett* (Baltimore and London: Johns Hopkins UP, 1977); J. G. A. Pocock, "The Mobility of Property and the Rise of Eighteenth-Century Sociology," in *Virtue, Commerce, History: Essays on Political Thought and History, Chiefly in the Eighteenth Century* (Cambridge: Cambridge UP, 1985) 103-23; Christopher J. Berry, *The Idea of Luxury: A Conceptual and Historical Investigation* (Cambridge: Cambridge UP, 1994); James Raven, "Defending Conduct and Property: The London Press and the Luxury Debate," in *Early Modern Conceptions of Property,* eds. John Brewer and Susan Staves (New York: Routledge, 1996) 301-19.

3. See *Burke, Paine, Godwin, and the Revolution Controversy,* ed. Marilyn Butler (Cambridge: Cambridge UP, 1984) 108, 109-21.

4. See Edward Copeland, *Women Writing about Money: Women's Fiction in England 1790-1820* (Cambridge: Cambridge UP, 1995).

5. Colin Campbell, *The Romantic Ethic and the Spirit of Modern Consumerism* (Oxford: Blackwell, 1995 [1987]) 77-95.

6. Harriet Guest, "The Dream of a Common Language: Hannah More and Mary Wollstonecraft," *Textual Practice* 9 (1995): 309. On the eighteenth-century feminization of luxury by civic humanism see E. J. Clery, *The Rise of Supernatural Fiction, 1762-1800* (Cambridge: Cambridge UP, 1995) 95-105.

7. Ice houses were a sign of distinction featured in the gardens of most eighteenth-century mansions, and catering to the comforts and tables of the aristocracy, although early in the nineteenth century plans were drawn to extend ice houses also to the lower classes. See Monica Ellis, *Ice and Icehouses through the Ages* (Southampton: Southampton U Archeology Group, 1982) 1-10; Sylvia P. Beamon and Susan Roaf, *The Ice-Houses of Britain* (New York: Routledge, 1990) 24-25.

8. *The Poems of Anna Laetitia Barbauld,* ed. William McCarthy and Elizabeth Kraft (Athens and London: The U of Georgia P, 1994) 126. All further references to Barbauld's poems appear in the text by line number.

9. Jean Baudrillard, *For a Critique of the Political Economy of the Sign,* trans. Charles Levin (St Louis: Telos P, 1981). It is worth remembering that Baudrillard's discourse on the object of consumption is located within his critique of the political economy of the sign, the disappearance of the concept within its representation because commodification and signification both depend on an abstract equivalence between the objects to be exchanged or the signifier and the signified. As Baudrillard's notion of sign-value belongs to his peculiar structuralist attempt to describe the system of objects in the contemporary world, this essay will not understand sign-value as supplanting use and exchange, but rather as developing from, and subsuming, them.

10. On the eighteenth-century luxury debate as a complex reaction to the conditions of modernity, see Christopher J. Berry 140-42.

11. James Thomson, *The Seasons,* ed. James Sambrook (Oxford: Clarendon, 1981) 202. All further references to the poem appear in the text by line number.

12. For an incisive reading of the various levels of the gendered imagery in Barbauld's poem see Isobel Armstrong, "The Gush of the Feminine: How Can We Read Women's Poetry of the Romantic Period," in *Romantic Women Writers: Voices and Countervoices,* eds. Paula R. Feldman and Theresa M. Kelley (Hanover and London: UP of New England, 1995) 13-32.

13. Barbauld draws explicit parallels between state and estate in point 12 of *Sins of Government, Sins of the Nation; or, a Discourse for the Fast, Appointed on April 19, 1793. By a Volunteer* (London: Joseph Johnson, 1793). Early in her review of the socio-political "sins" of Britain, Barbauld denounces the pernicious effects of extravagance on the private estate, and declares that equal ruin awaits any state whose economy is managed in the same unwise ways.

14. On country-house poetics, its celebration of "reciprocal harmony," and luxury as its dark face, see Malcolm Kelsall, *The Great Good Place: The Country House and English Literature* (New York and London: Harvester Wheatsheaf, 1993) 32-35.

15. George Crabbe, *The Complete Poetical Works,* ed. Norma Dalrymple-Champneys and Arthur Pollard (Oxford: Clarendon, 1988) 1: 164. The intertextual links between Crabbe's and Barbauld's texts are examined in Marlon B. Ross, *The Contours of Masculine Desire* (Oxford, New York: Oxford UP, 1989) 221-23.

16. On this principle of civic humanism, see Christopher J. Berry 154-55; see also E. J. Clery, "The

Pleasure of Terror: Paradox in Edmund Burke's Theory of the Sublime," in *Pleasure in the Eighteenth Century*, ed. Roy Porter and Marie Mulvey Roberts (Basingstoke and London: Macmillan, 1996) 171-75.

17. On the socio-economic varieties of luxury in eighteenth-century British theory, see David Spadafora [*The Idea of Progress in Eighteenth-Century Britain* (New Haven and London: Yale UP, 1990)] 276.

18. On the imagery of decadence and "bearing down" in *Eighteen Hundred and Eleven*, see Marlon B. Ross, "Configurations of Feminine Reform: The Woman Writer and the Tradition of Dissent," in *Re-Visioning Romanticism: British Women Writers, 1776-1837*, eds. Carol Shiner Wilson and Joel Haefner (Philadelphia: U of Pennsylvania P, 1994) 105.

19. Paul Hamilton has recently proposed that Barbauld's balanced views in *Eighteen Hundred and Eleven* stem from an "expressive reserve" and a scepticism alien to the expected categories of contestation and subversion. See "The New Romanticism: Philosophical Stand-Ins in English Romantic Discourse," *Textual Practice* 11 (1997): 126-29. For an interpretation which, instead, considers Barbauld's poem as a straightforward denunciation, see Anne K. Mellor, "The Female Poet and the Poetess: Two Traditions of British Women's Poetry, 1780-1830," *SiR* [*Studies in Romanticism*] 36 (1997): 261-76.

Maggie Favretti (essay date 1999)

SOURCE: Favretti, Maggie. "The Politics of Vision: Anna Barbauld's *Eighteen Hundred and Eleven*." In *Women's Poetry in the Enlightenment: The Making of a Canon, 1730-1820*, edited by Isobel Armstrong and Virginia Blain, pp. 99-110. Houndmills, England: Macmillan Press Ltd, 1999.

[*In the following essay, Favretti discusses the relationship between gender and politics in Barbauld's* Eighteen Hundred and Eleven. *Favretti argues that Barbauld's breadth of vision in the poem derives from her position outside of the male-dominated power structure.*]

In her brilliant long poem *Eighteen Hundred and Eleven,* Mrs Anna Aikin Barbauld commandingly stakes out her political position concerning gender and the aetiology of destruction. In doing so she claims for herself an authoritative vantage point of 'disinterestedness', and in skilfully phrased heroic couplets looks out over

time and the disparate elements of society to describe the dismal state of affairs in 1811, to identify what went wrong, and finally to explore what will happen after Britain loses its status as the seat of civilization. By 1811 her neo-classical style was regarded as old-fashioned, but in a successful career of nearly 40 years no-one had publicly questioned her extraordinary ability to use powerful yet accessible allusions to present and argue complex ideas. Yet the reception of this poem was hostile. John Croker wrote in the *Quarterly Review,*

> We think that she has wandered from the course in which she was respectable and useful, and miserably mistaken both her powers and her duty, in exchanging the birchen for the satiric rod, and abandoning the superintendance of the 'ovilia' of the nursery, to wage war on the 'reluctantes dracones', statesmen, and warriors, whose misdoings have aroused her indignant muse.[1]

Since the liberal, Unitarian Anna Barbauld had always been critical of the misdoings of political men, the venom expended in this and other reviews like it reveal a crucial moment in the politics of vision. Barbauld's earlier political poems had been limited to short poems with domestic subjects, and to poems in the form of letters. And although *Eighteen Hundred and Eleven* did not attempt to introduce ideas which are different from those already widely discussed in her work and elsewhere, the poem did mark a very significant step. In *Eighteen Hundred and Eleven* Barbauld shot at the heart of an already crumbling notion of gentlemanly disinterestedness, by choosing for herself a specific elevated promontory from which to view the wide prospect of the world, to investigate the causes of social destruction, and to assign blame.

In their rush to dim the bright light Anna Barbauld focused on the businessmen and politicians of her world, male critics tried to break the poem down into its particulars, to turn the discourse (and direct the attention of the public) away from her broad view. The reviewers nearly all point to her choice of a title as though it is the main symptom of her problem—her perception of time. 'Instead of purporting to be descriptive of the year Eighteen Hundred and Eleven, it should have been made to refer to a subsequent period', writes *The Monthly Review.*[2] John Croker concurs, 'we very confidently assert that there is not a topic in *Eighteen Hundred and Eleven* which is not quite as applicable to 1810 or 1812 . . .'. The critics' dissatisfaction with Barbauld's choice of title reflects their inability to accommodate her elevating her vantage point to a more challenging position. She has stationed herself at a single fixed point, 1811, from which she can survey the broad expense of society and time in all directions. The ability to see the world in this kind of broad prospect taken from a single, secured eminence had been claimed by powerful men. It was these men who claimed a disinterested viewpoint as a way of objectifying all of society, controlling conflicting interests and creating, at least in theory, a stable unity.[3]

In the seventeenth century, conflicting interests were seen as evidence of the instability of human nature and a threat to stable society. So governing was left up to those whose only interest was in the stability of the whole—landholding gentlemen who were free from the narrowing view of any specific trade. Only they could claim the public virtue of 'disinterestedness'. Ironically, as soon as the gentleman left his removed estate and became engaged in furthering legislation or exercising other social or economic authority, his disinterestedness would (by definition) be compromised. But in the seventeenth century the presence of a group of disinterested observers (even if they couldn't *actually* be devoid of interests) had meant that there was always someone society could count on to be able to see the 'big picture'. There was a group of people who could at least sustain the illusion that they could see society as a manageable competition between interests, which they could direct in such a way as to maintain the unity and stability of the whole. It was an illusion that was worth maintaining.

By the eighteenth century very few gentlemen could even come close to making the claim to disinterestedness. More and more, they were supported by marriages into merchant or banking families, connecting them even further with competing interests in commerce. At the same time, economists of the period began to focus on the importance of the separate interests, from Adam Smith's division of labour to Mandeville's argument that private vices such as greed and envy are actually public virtues. The idea was to encourage specialized self-interest in order to enhance the wealth of the whole. For a while the seventeenth-century idea of disinterestedness became an eighteenth-century cult of the gentleman observer, as anxiety set in as to who, if anyone, could understand society. Wealthy men built vantage points on high hills on their estates, from which to survey the scene around them. James Thomson describes Lyttleton's musings in Hagley Park, in *The Seasons* (1730):

> Meantime you gain the Height, from whose fair Brow
> The bursting Prospect spreads immense around;
> And snatch'd o'er Hill and Dale, and Wood and Lawn,
> And verdant Field, and darkening Heath between,
> And Villages embosom'd soft in Trees,
> And spiry Towns by dusky Columns marked
> Of rising Smoak, your eye excursive roams . . .
> . . . And oft, conducted by Historic Truth,
> You tread the long Extent of backward Time:
> Planning, with warm Benevolence of Mind,
> And honest Zeal unwarp'd by Party-rage,
> *Britannia*'s Weal; how from the venal Gulph
> To raise her Virtue, and her Arts revive.[4]

In this way of thinking, the entire scope of society can be held within the gentleman's gaze, including all of time. All of society is feminized as the object of his gaze. Can a woman claim this vantage point?

In her *Strictures on the Modern System of Female Education*, Barbauld's acquaintance Hannah More wrote, 'A woman sees the world, as it were, from a little elevation in her own garden, where she makes an exact survey of home scenes, but takes not in that wider range of distant prospects which he who stands on a loftier eminence commands . . . .'.[5] But in *Eighteen Hundred and Eleven* Anna Barbauld commands the lofty eminence, and what she sees is the present and future of British civilization. She sees the ascendance of the United States and the role Britain can claim in its birth. Perhaps most importantly, she sets forth an engendered explanation for the loss of British hegemony.

In the beginning of *Eighteen Hundred and Eleven* Barbauld establishes that destruction is at hand. The first two lines of the poem read: 'Still the loud death drum, thundering from afar, / O'er the vext nations pours the storm of war . . .'.[6] It is a bloody thunderstorm drenching both European and British life and liberty. It is a corrupt deluge which, in Barbauld's words, '. . . with overwhelming force / Bears down each fort of Freedom in its course . . .'.

And what will happen to Britain, she asks, as it, too, forsakes its democratic principles of free speech and rational politics? For Barbauld the death drum for English liberty had been beating since 1790, when the most recent attempt to repeal the Corporation and Test Acts had failed, an event which perpetuated the denial of full civic participation to Dissenters and other nonconformists. In the same year, Edmund Burke's *Reflections on the Revolution in France* demonized the revolution and linked Dissenters and their associates with radical jacobinism, launching more than a decade of severe restrictions of civil liberties, especially aimed at silencing the voices of Dissenters and reformers such as Barbauld's family and intellectual community. Her friend Joseph Priestley escaped to America after an informal 'Church and King' mob blew up his home and laboratory, and her publisher Joseph Johnson was jailed for printing 'seditious tracts'.

Just prior to the publication of *Eighteen Hundred and Eleven* the death drum signalled more crises for Britain. Four of the seven largest cities had no Parliamentary representation. Governments split repeatedly over the conduct of the war and the issue of a Regency during the King's illness. The maritime economic warfare between Britain and France was escalating tensions with the United States to dangerous levels. The rising price of grain, brought about by blockades, disruption of trade with North America, and a succession of bad harvests encouraged the largest number of enclosures in any single decade. On the Continent the Peninsular Campaign dragged on, subsidized by taxes on consumer goods, further passing the heaviest cost of the war onto the poor. Napoleon's 1806 and 1807 Berlin and Milan Decrees forbade any of his occupied territories from trade with Britain. Britain responded with the Orders in Council, essentially blockading all of the Continent. The war was being fought with starvation and economic disaster as its main weapons. A British population which had grown during the previous 40 years by 50 per cent needed to be fed. By 1811 starvation was a significant enough concern that some factory owners began providing meals. Bread riots were common.[7]

Anna Barbauld identifies the sources of peril as both attack from without in the form of Napoleon's expanding empire, and corruption from within in the forms of repression and exploitation. 'Ruin', she writes, 'is here, / There, the heart-witherings of unuttered fear, / And that sad death, whence most affection bleeds, / Which sickness, only of the soul, precedes.' In these lines the ultimate source of destruction is corruption from within, perhaps in the very nature of man himself. Anna Barbauld uses the tone of the morally responsible woman of the house to further the classical notion of virtue in a constant battle with corruption. Unfortunately for British civilization, once men seek corruption the plunge towards destruction will be irreversible. She writes, '. . . but, Britain, know, / Thou who hast shared the guilt must share the woe'. Where did the soul-sickness come from? When did corruption begin to triumph over virtue?

Barbauld adopts the classical theory that civil society is fragile, and that, in order to sustain it, man's lust after power must be balanced by his civic virtue, or placing the public good over his private interests, claiming 'disinterestedness'. But commerce, and consequently Britain's strength, relied on private initiative, and capitalism offered the incentive. By the 1780s and 1790s, private interests fulfilled were good for Britain, and by the end of the 1790s 'virtue' had come to mean a man's ability to look out for himself and his family. To make wealth produce more wealth was his socially approved goal.[8] Barbauld scathingly critiques the profit motive, when she writes: 'Thy baseless wealth dissolves in air away, / Like mists that melt before the morning ray: / . . . Sad, on the ground thy princely merchants bend / Their altered looks, and evil days portend, / And fold their arms, and watch . . .'. They gave over classical virtue for profit, gave in to soul-sickness and greed, and now must passively observe the hour of destruction approach.

Barbauld's gendering of man's desire for commercial wealth and her placement of it in a Miltonian setting make *Eighteen Hundred and Eleven* a powerful if traditional critique. There are three main characters in her 'course of empire' narrative: the first two, creative masculine Genius and creative feminine Nature join, and 'The steaming marsh is changed to fruitful meads.' Already present is a temptress, the worm, commercial wealth. As Barbauld writes: 'Then from its bed is drawn the ponderous ore. / Then Commerce pours her gifts on every shore, / . . . Then spans the graceful arch the roaring tide, / And stricter bounds the cultured fields divide.' Commerce encourages man to attempt to conquer the roaring power of nature by making a beautiful bridge to cross the tide, and to tame the wilderness by culturing the fields and containing them within strict bounds. Here Barbauld alludes to the loss under the enclosure process of a nostalgic idea of rural life, where the masculine farming image is in harmony with nature. Rather than a relationship of conquest and enclosure, she envisions the pastoral relationship as companionate.

Oliver Goldsmith's well-known poem 'The Deserted Village' views the loss of this pastoral harmony as signifying the end of Britain's cultural moment. Barbauld told H. Crabbe Robinson that 'I shall never tire of reading Goldsmith's "Deserted Village"', and its influence on her and on *Eighteen Hundred and Eleven* is plain.[9] Barbauld herself performs the duties of the 'sad historian', guiding the reader to all of the important 'sites'. Goldsmith accuses commerce and its attendant vices of destroying the harmonious rural lifestyle: 'O luxury! Thou cursed by Heaven's decree, / How ill exchanged are things like these for thee! / . . . Kingdoms, by thee to sickly greatness grown, / Boast of a florid vigour not their own.'

Dr Goldsmith's and Anna Barbauld's thinking is part of a long cultural debate. Very early on, the dangers of commerce were recognized in association with one of the most destructive passions of men, avarice. Originally, people such as St Augustine and Calvin believed that these passions could be coerced under control by the state. Gradually, this idea developed into the eighteenth-century notion (initially Giambattista Vico's, and further developed by Adam Smith and Bernard Mandeville) that destructive passions can be harnessed for the public good: avarice into commerce, ferocity into defence, ambition into politics, and so on. But this idea suggests, like Barbauld's description of Commerce, that a positive drive carries the negative within it. Hume added to this that the soul is a constant battleground where these countervailing passions fight it out.[10]

In *Eighteen Hundred and Eleven* the strategy is simple. Corrupt female Commerce tempts man to subjugate creative female Nature. Anna Barbauld describes the trapping and confining of nature's power for private gain with vivid images.

Where once Bonduca whirled the scythed car,
And the fierce matrons raised the shriek of war,
Light forms beneath transparent muslins float,
. . . While crystal walls the tenderer plants confine
. . . The Syrian grape there hangs her rich festoons,
Nor asks for purer air, or brighter noons.

The creative female Nature of the 'civilized' world is barely even there. These powerful, passionate women have been reduced to substanceless, floating forms. In beautiful vocabulary the 'tenderer plants' (women) are imprisoned behind glass, a substance only the objectifying gaze can penetrate, and there they must stay for others to enjoy their fragrance and nectar. The Syrian grape hangs there, fecund, rich, the exotic and mysterious Other. Colonized by 'civilized' empire, it is unclear whether she breathes the best air and has the best light, or has simply stopped asking for it.

In this part of her poem Barbauld uses western orientalism in order to highlight a shift in Europeans' attitudes towards nature. For nearly 150 years the Renaissance image of the nurturing teacher/parent earth had been replaced by the desire of science to master, manage and possess nature and the earth. In 1661 Boyle wrote: 'Some men care only to know nature, others desire to command her . . . to bring nature to be serviceable to their particular ends, whether of health, or riches, or sensual delight.' In 1668 Glanville proudly confessed the virtues of chemistry in *Plus Ultra*: it could 'eviscerate nature' because it 'forced submission and disclosure by violence of its artful fires'.[11] Anna Barbauld's poetry is sympathetic with views expressed by Bishop Berkeley who, like Barbauld, sees hope in the New World because 'The force of art by nature seems out-done, / And fancied beauties by the true; / . . . Where nature guides and virtue rules'.[12] In the New World, nature and virtue have been restored to their primary importance.

In the last part of *Eighteen Hundred and Eleven,* however, man 'feels finer wants, and burns with new desires'. In order to fully possess Nature and her creative power, he wishes to 'New mould a climate and create the soil, / Subdue the rigour of the northern Bear, / O'er polar climes shed aromatic air, / . . . And ask[s] not gifts but tribute at her hands.' He believes that Nature has become his slave; but instead, he has produced a civilization which, rotten at the centre, will pass away. As Barbauld writes near the end of *Eighteen Hundred and Eleven*:

But fairest flowers expand but to decay;
The worm is in thy core, thy glories pass away;
Arts, arms and wealth destroy the fruits they bring;
Commerce, like beauty, knows no second spring.
Crime walks thy streets, Fraud earns her unblest bread
O'er want and woe thy gorgeous robe is spread . . .
With grandeur's growth the mass of misery grows.

Man has abandoned disinterested virtue and uses Commerce for personal gain. He expands Commerce's own destructive possibilities, and to facilitate Commerce he must (and believes he can) subjugate Nature. Once man subdues Nature and privileges destruction, Genius loses interest, 'The Genius now forsakes the favored shore, / And hates, capricious, what he loved before; / Then empire fall to dust, then arts decay, / And wasted realms enfeebled despots sway; / Even Nature's changed.' Genius had provided the masculine creative power to match Nature's, and once she has been confined and he leaves, there is no creative power available—destruction is inevitable.

Reviewers tried to discredit Barbauld's account of the rise and fall of empire, even though other highly esteemed authors such as Edward Gibbon had provided earlier sympathetic examples. In volume three of *The Decline and Fall of the Roman Empire* Gibbon wrote:

> The decline of Rome was the natural and inevitable result of immoderate greatness. Prosperity ripened the principles of decay; the causes of destruction multiplied with the extent of conquest; and as soon as time or accident had removed the artificial supports, the stupendous fabric yielded to the pressure of its own weight.

Anna Barbauld's assignment of blame for the decline of the British Empire on the shoulders of corrupted men who are susceptible to the wiles of the seductress Commerce seemed to touch a nerve. The *Anti-Jacobin Review* wrote:

> May we be allowed to ask, how does Mrs. Barbauld know . . . ? But we ask pardon . . . Mrs. B. is a *prophet*; and, to prophets it is given to penetrate the veil of futurity. . . . We presume that when Mrs. Barbauld wrote the line ['Thy baseless wealth dissolves in air away'], she had just risen from a perusal of the *alarming* report of the *Bullion Committee!*[13]

The reviewer attacks her ability to interpret society and to make prophecy precisely *because* she is not engaged in trade. Croker takes his attack one step further, casting doubt upon her ability to see at all. In his review Croker draws attention to Barbauld's lack of qualifications to invade the male territory of disinterestedness.

> We had hoped, indeed, that the empire might have been saved without the intervention of a lady-author: we even flattered ourselves that the interests of Europe and of humanity would in some degree have swayed our public councils, without the descent of (dea ex machina) Mrs. Anna Letitia Barbauld . . . [her] confident sense of commanding talents—have induced her to dash down her shagreen spectacles and her knitting needles, and to sally forth. . . .[14]

Croker's comments typify the reaction many reviewers had. They asserted: 'We are the ones who can interpret the interests of Europe and humanity, not an old lady who can barely see'. Croker's acknowledgement of her 'descent' suggests a recognition but not acceptance of the elevated vantage point she has claimed. Barbauld's second main assertion, one common in the cultural discourse of the time, that the New World would renovate and improve on the old one, made reviewers even more furious.[15]

Why, when Barbauld was such a widely respected figure, did critics react so negatively to *Eighteen Hundred and Eleven*? There are no new concepts in the poem that she or other poets had not already addressed. If, then, it was not solely what she said, perhaps the negative reception had more to do with how she said it. Barbauld had always presented her social criticisms in a less threatening form. Her works before 1790 were nearly all in the form of small poems in a 'properly' feminized voice. Even after 1790, when her work became more politically challenging, she still set her challenges in the form of private communication, sermon, or household allegory.

In *Eighteen Hundred and Eleven* Anna Barbauld had clearly made the 'terrible mistake' of engaging in forbidden discourse. She could no longer be considered 'proper', or even be charitably removed from the status of womanhood by being made a 'muse'; now she was a real threat. Croker satirizes the whole idea of a woman being able to interpret 'the interests of Europe'. *The Eclectic Review* is 'astonished' that she can make prophecies concerning the westward course of civilization 'with such perfect composure', and concludes such a poem could only have been the product of an irrational and 'peculiarly frigid' temperament.[16] *The Universal Magazine* objected to its 'cold regularity' and 'frigid observance of what is right'.[17] The very 'disinterested' composure and vision necessary in a gentleman who could claim to interpret the 'interests of Europe' was somehow threatening, emerging as it was from the pen of an old woman.

Why Barbauld made the move into claiming a 'gentlemanly' view is not altogether clear, although one can suggest some possibilities. As the gentleman must withdraw from the world in order to see it as stable and unified, an elderly lady, no longer particularly active, could see herself as in command of a view of time unavailable to a younger person. Further, as a woman who had become responsible for the care of her husband and their affairs long before his death, she had begun to see herself as independent, and her widowed status gave her yet another boost out of the domestic realm.

At the same time, the year 1811 produced more than its share of anxiety about who, if anyone, was capable of controlling competing interests within England. The best suited of all the so-called 'gentlemen' to survey the society widely should have been the King. But George III was pronounced incurably insane, leaving the throne to the questionably responsible Prince Regent.

Perhaps most importantly, just as the viewer of a painting must be outside of it to fully comprehend it, women were situated outside of the political scene. What better position from which to claim a moral authority similar to disinterestedness? In this sense Barbauld's voice is distinctly feminine as far as the feminine role of moralist was developing into the nineteenth century. For the male readers of *Eighteen Hundred and Eleven,* however, the prophecy of the end of the British empire as a result of the gentleman's failure to fully comprehend and stabilize the competing interests in the world struck too close to home. She appropriated the gaze they had claimed but felt slipping away, exposed its illusory nature, and used it to show where both it and they had failed.

Notes

1. [John Wilson Croker], '*Eighteen Hundred and Eleven: A Poem. By Anna Letitia Barbauld*', *The Quarterly Review,* 7 (June 1812), p. 309.

2. '*Eighteen Hundred and Eleven: A Poem. By Anna Laetitia Barbauld*', *The Monthly Review,* 67 (April 1812), p. 428.

3. John Barrell, *English Literature in History, 1730-1780: An Equal Wide Survey* (New York: St Martin's Press, 1983). I am indebted to the ideas in this book for my analysis of Barbauld's viewpoint in *Eighteen Hundred and Eleven* and its critical reception.

4. Quoted in John Dixon Hunt and Peter Willis (eds), *The Genius of the Place: The English Landscape Garden, 1620-1820* (New York: Harper & Row, 1975), p. 195.

5. Hannah More, *Strictures on the Modern System of Female Education* (1799), quoted in Bridget Hill, *Eighteenth-Century Women: An Anthology* (London: Allen & Unwin, 1984).

6. Anna Laetitia Aikin Barbauld, *Eighteen Hundred and Eleven: A Poem* (London: Johnson, 1812) in *The Works of Anna Laetitia Barbauld: with a Memoir, in Three Volumes,* ed. Lucy Aikin, vol. 1 (Boston: David Reed, 1826), pp. 166-77.

7. Roy Porter, *English Society in the Eighteenth Century* (Harmondsworth: Penguin Books, 1982), p. 227.

8. Joyce Appleby, *Capitalism and a New Social Order: The Republican Vision of the 1790s* (New York: New York University Press, 1984), pp. 9-22. See also Adam Smith, *Wealth of Nations* (1776) and Adam Ferguson, *Essay on the History of Civil Society* (1767).

9. Grace A. Ellis, *A Memoir of Mrs Anna Laetitia Barbauld, with Many of her Letters* (Boston: Osgood, 1874), p. 328.

10. Albert O. Hirschman, *The Passions and the Interests: Political Arguments for Capitalism before its Triumph* (Princeton, NJ: Princeton University Press, 1977).

11. Carolyn Merchant, *The Death of Nature: Women, Ecology, and the Scientific Revolution* (New York: Harper & Row, 1980), p. 189.

12. George Berkeley, Bishop of Cloyne, 'Verses on the Prospect of Planting Arts and Learning in America', *The Works of George Berkeley, Bishop of Cloyne*, ed. A. A. Luce and T. E. Jessop (London: Nelson, 1955), and Ernest Lee Tuveson, *Redeemer Nation: The Idea of America's Millennial Role* (Chicago: University of Chicago Press, 1968).

13. 'The Monthly Review for April, 1812; and *Eighteen Hundred and Eleven; A Poem*. By Anna Laetitia Barbauld', *The Anti-Jacobin Review,* 42 (June 1812), p. 205.

14. [Croker] op. cit., p. 309.

15. This is the topic of another essay.

16. '*Eighteen Hundred and Eleven. A Poem*. By Anna Laetitia Barbauld', *The Eclectic Review,* 8 (May 1812), p. 475.

17. 'Original Criticism: *Eighteen Hundred and Eleven. A Poem*. By Anna Laetitia Barbauld', *The Universal Magazine,* 17 (March 1812), p. 217.

Claudia L. Johnson (essay date spring 2001)

SOURCE: Johnson, Claudia L. "'Let me make the novels of a country': Barbauld's *The British Novelists* (1810/1820)." *Novel: A Forum on Fiction* 34, no. 2 (spring 2001): 163-79.

[*In the following excerpt, Johnson evaluates the academic, as well as political, ramifications of Barbauld's* British Novelists.]

The early nineteenth century witnessed a surge in the business of canon-making—modern canons beginning, however they may end, as highly commercialized ventures. In part because of the success of such earlier tomes as *The English Poets,* for which Johnson wrote his famous *Lives of the English Poets,* booksellers issued many extensive collections of earlier literature which had the effect (among other things) of consolidating national self-consciousness and creating a national "literature" as a means of deploying it—one thinks for example of such widely selling sets as the six-volume *Cabinet of Poetry* (1808), Chalmers's 21-volume *The Works of the English Poets from Chaucer to Cowper* (1810), John Bell's 34-volume *British Theatre* (1797) and Elizabeth Inchbald's 25-volume set *The British Theatre* (1806-09), and James Ferguson's 45-volume set of the *British Essayists* (1802-1819)—all of which texts have had a long shelf life. But while collections of poetry, drama, and essays surely had been published before, no one had ventured to assemble a full-scale collection of British fiction until Anna Barbauld did. On the strength of the work she did as Richardson's biographer and the editor of his **Correspondence** (1804), and on the strength of her reputation as a poet, booksellers approached Barbauld in 1809 and commissioned her to edit a selection of British novels and to preface each with a biographical and critical sketch. The result was her monumental 50-volume set published in 1810 under the title **The British Novelists,** selling at the price of 12 guineas for the set, or 50s per volume.

Until the past decade, Romantic scholars have been even more remiss than eighteenth-century scholars in thinking about the fiction of the late eighteenth and early nineteenth centuries—this essay joins others in redressing such inattention. Thanks to the work of scholars like Harriet Guest, Anne K. Mellor, James Chandler, and William Keach, Barbauld's achievement as a poet and as a public intellectual is taken quite seriously now, but her work as an editor of fiction receives relatively little attention.[1] Her **British Novelists** constitutes the first novelistic canon, and it rewards attention on several counts. First, on the score of canonicity, it demonstrates how the work of canon-making is a volatile venture explicitly committed to the business of national culture. John Guillory has shown that Barbauld's criticism of poetry emerges from her effort to assert the increasingly controversial authority of middle-class dissenters to speak on behalf of the nation (103-06). An examination of **The British Novelists,** and its subsequent emendation, helps us figure out what happened to the "Romantic novel" she installed once that authority collapsed, and thus points to the truth of Homer Brown's argument that the novel has many rises, many institutions, which were ideologically loaded from the get-go. In his determination to recover Scott's role in the rise of the novel, however, Brown bypasses Barbauld, whose canon looks different. Indeed, by granting Barbauld's **British Novelists** its due status as one of the instituting moments in a history of the British novel, we can see its diverse, inclusive, and politically vanguard agendas were foreclosed as the novel itself gained in prestige and as novel-writing acquired a respectable professional status.

What does the British novel look like in 1810? If we follow Robert Kiely's example in *The Romantic Novel in England* (1972) and date the "Romantic" novel from as early as the 1760s, we find the "Romantic" novel well represented in Barbauld's selection. Indeed, of the twenty-nine novels Barbauld includes, only seven were published before 1755, though it must be admitted that the early novel being the hefty entity it is, five among these—*Robinson Crusoe* (1719), *Clarissa* (1747-48), *Sir Charles Grandison* (1753-54), *Joseph Andrews* (1742), and *Tom Jones* (1749)—take up a whopping twenty-one volumes. Drawing on Hurd, Beattie, and Warton, and in places cribbing from Clara Reeve's *Progress of Romance* (1785) and John Moore's *Commencement and Progress of Romance* (1797) in its exposition of classical, medieval and renaissance prose fiction, though not her discussions of eighteenth-century novels, Barbauld's introductory essay **"On the Origin and Progress of Novel-Writing"** is one of the most important essays on prose fiction written in the nineteenth century. Although she duly mentions Behn, Haywood, Swift, and Manley, Barbauld gives Defoe, Richardson, and Fielding all the pride of place we've learned to expect—for their general preference of the natural over the marvelous, for their unity of design, and for their powers to move the heart. On this account, Brown praises the first part of Barbauld's collection for "begin-[ning] to resemble the modern canon." But, momentarily begging the questions his own study so brilliantly illuminates, Brown evinces disappointment that the "following volumes are a bit spottier in this regard," for Barbauld's collection seems "spotty" only if we assume the canon we already know (Brown 180). In fact, even Barbauld's early selections are heterodox by today's standards: The two other early novels included in *The British Novelists*—Coventry's *Pompey the Little* (1751) and Charlotte Lennox's *Female Quixote* (1752)—show that Barbauld does not privilege the fictional modes or examples of those later called the "masters." And Barbauld's remaining twenty-two selections go a long way towards satisfying those of us who have felt gypped by the canons that modern scholarship assumed and then produced. She includes: Johnson's *Rasselas* (1759), Johnstone's *Adventures of a Guinea* (1760/65), Hawkesworth's *Almoran and Hamet* (1761), Frances Brooke's *History of Lady Julia Mandeville* (1763), Walpole's *Castle of Otranto* (1764), Goldsmith's *Vicar of Wakefield* (1766), Mackenzie's *Man of Feeling* (1771) and *Juliet de Roubigné* (1777), Smollett's *Humphry Clinker* (1771), Graves's *Spiritual Quixote* (1773), Reeve's *Old English Baron* (1778), Burney's *Evelina* (1778) and *Cecilia* (1882), Moore's *Zeluco* (1786), Smith's *Old Manor House* (1793), Radcliffe's *Romance of the Forest* and *Mysteries of Udolpho* (1794), Bage's *Man As He Is* (1792), Inchbald's *Simple Story* (1791) and *Nature and Art* (1796), and finally Edgeworth's *Belinda* (1801) and *Modern Griselda* (1805).

Before turning to what Barbauld's selection means, some clarification of what it doesn't mean is in order. "This particular selection," Barbauld explains in the collection's introductory essay, "presents a series of some of the most approved novels, from the first regu-

lar productions of the kind to the present time" with attention to "variety in manner" (**"On the Origin and Progress of Novel-Writing,"** *British Novelists* 1.61). Clearly: coverage, variety, and critical esteem condition Barbauld's choices. But so do other considerations. First among these is the booksellers' wish to sell books: "some regard it has been thought proper to pay," she writes, "to the taste and preference of the public, as was but reasonable in an undertaking in which their preference was to indemnify those who are at the expense and risk of the publication" (1.61). One wonders how far Barbauld was willing to go to satisfy booksellers' standards of saleability. When it comes to including Oriental tales, for example, she goes with Hawkesworth's *Almoran and Hamet* (1761) with manifest reluctance, having described its style as "turgid"; Beckford's *Vathek,* she insists, "is the only modern composition which has seized the genuine spirit of the Arabian tales" (26.i). Barbauld, we may infer, cedes to the booksellers' sense that Beckford was too scandalous to ensconce in a collection of British novels designed for family libraries but under an undisguised protest that tells her readers to read *Vathek* in some other publication. "Regard" to the booksellers does not necessarily signify accord even when it forces compliance. Barbauld writes that Reeve's *Old English Baron,* for example, possesses only a "moderate degree of merit"; but it has also been "a great favourite with the public" and is reprinted presumably on this account (22.i). But being already read is no set condition of continuing to be read, i.e., of being canonized. In the case of no less than Richardson himself, Barbauld includes novels despite the fact that their popularity has plummeted enough to require explanation: "It is a truth which cannot be denied, that the works of Richardson are not found to be so attractive to the present generation as they were to the past" because of frankly acknowledged "defects of his style"; but *Clarissa* "will still hold its place" in "the literature of our country" despite its unpopularity (1.xlvi). Clearly, canonicity for Barbauld is neither the purely commercial affair it was in *Harrison's Novelists Magazine,* the closest thing to a precedent which Barbauld probably consulted, since it reprinted anything likely to sell in weekly installments between 1780-88; but nor is it vatically normative. Second, Barbauld reminds us that "[c]opyright also was not to be intruded on" (1.61), and her assemblage might look different had copyright not been at issue. Barbauld singles out, for example, Amelia Opie's novels for ringing praise but includes none, and we may infer that her selection may have included more "Romantic" novels had they not been under copyright in 1810. Finally, because the "number of volumes was determined by the booksellers" (1.61) and because the volumes themselves are the same format and of roughly the same length, Barbauld's initially quite arbitrary task of furnishing so many volumes with so many pages obliges her to fill out volumes with shorter works, and thus her collection gives ample place to fictional kinds—tales, short novels, novellas—rarely even considered in modern academic histories of the novel in England.

Having clarified some of the parameters of Barbauld's project, I will venture some comments on the distinctiveness of Barbauld's selection and how it might help us both to recover a vast stretch of late eighteenth- and early nineteenth-century fiction and to understand how it might have dropped from view. Barbauld's selection is not bottom heavy. Saturated in the radical-leaning traditions of rational dissent pre-dating the French Revolution (the usual watershed for Romantic literary historians), Barbauld has no truck with politically freighted mythoses of origin or for the authority of forefathers. Nor does she imply a respect for the rugged virility of early exemplars, uncorrupted by false refinements. "At length," she writes, "in the reign of George the Second, Richardson, Fielding, and Smollet [*sic*], appeared in quick succession; and their success raised such a demand for this kind of entertainment, that it has ever since been furnished from the press, rather as a regular and necessary supply, than as an occasional gratification" (*British* [**"On the Origin and Progress of Novel-Writing,"** *British Novelists*] 1.38). By this account, Richardson, Fielding, and Smollett came first in the history of modern fiction, and their success enabled later novelists to come after. Sounds vacuously simple, but what comes after "the rise" is precisely what so many subsequent histories of the novel cannot make room for. Relatively indifferent to periodization and epoch-making from the eighteenth century forward—for her (though perhaps not for Austen) there is no such thing as the "Romantic" novel—Barbauld gathers British fiction from 1719 to 1805 into a varied whole, in which the modes of pathos, comedy, terror, picaresque, sentiment, romance, satire, and didacticism are allowed equal generic status as novels.[2]

Second, and related, Barbauld's selection presumes the artistic legitimacy of women novelists. Turning to Johnson's novel *Rasselas*—a work rarely considered a novel today—Barbauld writes "Hercules, it is said, once wielded the distaff; and the Hercules of literature, Dr. Johnson, has not disdained to be the author of a novel" (*British* 26.i). The distaff by Barbauld's account is not restricted to women, nor is it a degradation to be employed by men. The novel is a "polite" form, where polite signifies a heterosocial discursive space, one open to women and men on equal terms. The dignity of women's artistic achievement on this score seems beyond dispute to Barbauld:

> notwithstanding the many paltry books of this kind published in the course of every year, it may safely be affirmed that we have more good writers in this walk living at the present time [i.e., the outset of the nine-

teenth century], than at any period since the days of Richardson and Fielding. A very great proportion of these are ladies: and surely it will not be said that either taste or morals have been losers by their taking the pen in hand. The names of D'Arblay, Edgeworth, Inchbald, Radcliffe, and a number more will vindicate this assertion.

(1.58-59)

In equating the novel with the novel by Radcliffe, Edgeworth, and Burney, Austen (as we have seen) draws on the same survey of the novelistic landscape Barbauld describes here. Barbauld and Austen evince conspicuous confidence in contemporary novels by women, a confidence that would soon be wiped out. A look at numbers underscores this point dramatically: of the twenty-two novelists Barbauld includes, fourteen are men and eight are women. By contrast, in Scott's *Ballantyne's Novelist's Library,* to which I will return later, of the fourteen novelists Scott includes, twelve are men and two are women (Radcliffe and Reeve).

Third, Barbauld's *British Novelists* constructs a diverse, politically self-conscious, and progressive canon always laying bare the work of social dissent and the political associations and interests of authors. Most obviously, she does so by including the texts of authors known to favor dissenting causes—the War of Independence, the abolition of the slave trade (which she never passes up an opportunity to mention), the early stages of the French Revolution, anti-sedition laws). Of these, Moore's *Zeluco,* Bage's *Man As He Is,* Smith's *The Old Manor House,* and Inchbald's *Nature and Art* stand out as examples, and Radcliffe's *Romance of the Forest,* Barbauld's favorite novel by Radcliffe, probably belongs in this group too.[3]

But Barbauld's political commitments inform her enterprise in ways that go beyond a preference for a certain kind of content to underpin her entire sense of the novel's and her readership. She begins her collection with a complaint—"A Collection of novels has a better chance of giving pleasure than of commanding respect" (*British* 1.1)—and continues with a counterclaim: novelists, dramatists, and epic poets all write "fictitious adventures" after all, and good novelists, requiring the same "talents of the highest order" to execute their plots, "ought to be appreciated [*sic*] accordingly" (1.3). Barbauld's arguments on behalf of novelistic art and novelistic pleasure form, I would contend, the rationale for her social and political arguments about the novel. In most respects, Barbauld's ideas about fiction recast Samuel Johnson's *Rambler* #4, on modern fiction,—she wrote a parody-homage of it that Johnson liked a lot—as well as his chapter in *Rasselas* about the dangers of the imagination and its powers of fiction-making and fiction believing.[4] Barbauld's revisions constitute a methodical and quite radical intervention in authoritative Johnsonian dicta on novels and their readers. Though Johnson prefers modern fiction (with its commitment to the probable) over romance (with its indulgence in the marvelous), he is intensely anxious that even (and indeed, especially) probable modern narratives can operate so powerfully and irresistibly on our minds as to take them over and stimulate wishful identificatory fantasies that confuse or overpower the judgment. Fabulous narratives, by this account, pose little or no moral or psychological danger, for "the reader was in very little danger of making any application to himself; the virtues and crimes were equally beyond his sphere of activity; and he amused himself with heroes and with traitors, deliverers and persecutors, as with beings of another species" (Johnson 21). But modern fiction (called here, "familiar histories") can promote delusional thinking, for when the "power of example is so great" the narratives can "take possession of the memory by a kind of violence, and produce effects almost without the intervention of the will" (Johnson 22). Modern novels are thus more dangerous than old romances to the degree that they seem less fictive.

By contrast, Barbauld has no anxiety because modern fiction—a designation including gothic romances, oriental tales, and novels of manners—is always understood to be as fictional as older romance. Thus, Barbauld rehashes the conventional history of narrative fiction by narrating, in David Kaufmann's apt words, "the westering of romance, of its translations from the wilds of Arabia . . . through the superstitious European Middle Ages, to the more sedate, less superstitious and resoundingly modern Britain" (24).[5] Yet, because she insists on the fictiveness of even the most probable of novels, she posits no firm binary between romance and novel, ancient and modern fiction, or probability and improbability. "It is pleasant to the mind," she writes of novel-reading, "to sport in the boundless regions of possibility; to find relief from the sameness of every-day occurrences by expatiating amidst brighter skies and fairer fields" (1.47), thus recasting Imlac's fearful discourse on the "power of fiction" in chapter 44 of *Rasselas,* where this sort of "expatiating" in "boundless futurity" is the first step towards madness. Barbauld can recommend our indulgence in the power of fiction without worry because she imagines novel readers not to be idle, young, too impressionable, or wishful, but to be alert proto-narratologists altogether conscious that a novelist is executing fiction according to discernible designs and in relation to understood conventions:

> Let us suppose a person speculating on the character of Tom Jones as the production of an author whose business it is pleasingly to interest his readers. He has no doubt but that, in spite of his irregularities and distresses, his history will come to an agreeable termination. He has no doubt that his parents will be discov-

> ered in due time . . . And why does he foresee all this? Not from the real tendencies of things, but from what he has discovered of the author's intentions.

> (1.56-57)

Novelistic pleasures are safe to indulge, in other words, because the Barbauldian reader of novels, unlike the Johnsonian one (of both sexes) is not feminized, not passive, uncritical and apt to be overpowered, but rather has the sagacity to know that novels are the artifice of novelists and the self-consciousness to take novel reading as an occasion for the exercise of judgment and criticism.[6]

The space Barbauld creates for a pleasure-taking and critically active readership bears on her sense of what novels are and what they can do politically. Novels, she announces, "take a tincture from the learning and politics of the times, and are made use of successfully to attack or recommend the prevailing systems of the day" (1.2). By this model, novels absorb ideology even as they can also intervene in and alter specific political "systems." The French Revolution, she reminds us, was inspired not only by the grave labors of the encyclopedist, but by novelists like Marmontel, whose fiction diffused "sentiments of toleration, a spirit of free inquiry, and a desire for equal laws and good government over Europe. Happy, if the mighty impulse had permitted them to stop within the bounds of justice and moderation!" (1.24). Writing at the late date of 1809-1810, Barbauld might well be expected to soft-pedal her sympathy with the "mighty impulse" of the French Revolution and her belief that novels can and should stir the public in insurrectional ways. Instead, she foregrounds how recent novels have been devoted to recommending or reprobating what she calls the "systems of philosophy or politics which have raised so much ferment of late years" (1.59). But though she does not include aggressively polemical novels such as Hamilton's "*The Modern Philosophers,* and the novels of Mrs. West" on the one hand, and "Mr. Holcroft's *Anna St. Ives*" on the other, she promotes fiction that has "Some serious end . . . in view" (1.60), and this is in keeping with the rationally involved, judicious readership she envisions for the novel. Indeed, her prefaces highlight the engagement of British novelists and novels not only in the controversies of the 1790s but also in the political civil war of the earlier eighteenth century, calling particular attention to the importance of the Jacobite uprisings in her preface to *Tom Jones.*

Foregrounding the Jacobite Rebellion in *Tom Jones* may sound like small potatoes, but the leading principle of twentieth-century histories of the novel is that novels are narratives of private life, that they turn inward, forming subjectivities that occlude or mystify the political. Such attitudes produced the restricted and serenely apolitical Jane Austen of the New Critics who dominated the scene before Marilyn Butler's pathbreaking *Jane Austen and the War of Ideas*. And so effectively have subsequent Marxist as well as Foucauldian methodologies redefined our very sense of what constitutes the political that, as Homer Brown has shown, the other sort of politics—i.e., the importance of the Jacobite uprising and the freighted thematics of inheritance—have rarely received sustained attention in the criticism of *Tom Jones*. Barbauld's conviction that eighteenth-century novels do not simply encode manners but also represent and contest the politics of civil war seems important. Similarly, her discussion of *Rasselas* calls attention to a charged political narrative underpinning the plot:

> In that country, [Abyssinia] it is said, the younger branches of the royal family, instead of being sacrificed, as in some of the Eastern monarchies, to the jealousy of the reigning sovereign, are secluded from the world in a romantic and beautiful valley, where they are liberally provided with every thing that can gratify their tastes or amuse their solitude.
>
> (26.i)

Stressing the rootedness of Johnson's plot in conflicts about legitimate authority, about the suspiciousness of absolute sovereignty and its draconian stratagems for security, about the instability of claims to succession, Barbauld once again brings politics forward, making Johnson's tale less likely to be read as a purely abstract narrative about the incommensurateness of desire to satisfaction but also as a narrative about rule.

Barbauld's vision of the novel and the canon it supported didn't take. The groundwork of Barbauld's marginalization was established a year after the ***British Novelists*** appeared, when her poem ***Eighteen-Hundred and Eleven*** was savaged by Croker, in part on the grounds that a woman—much less a dissenting woman—has no business delivering opinions about England's welfare at home and abroad. As the dissenting tradition was exiled from the vanguard to the periphery, Barbauld lost the authority she had possessed to define the exemplary.[7] To some degree, this is speculation on my part: Croker in fact has nothing to say about Barbauld's edition of the novels and indeed mockingly enjoins her to return to the busy work of editing or writing children's tales, as though these were contemptible tasks, by implication appropriate to the abilities of fussy old women. What is not speculation is the impact of Sir Walter Scott's 10-volume series of novels, *Ballantyne's Novelist's Library* (1821-24), which, despite its eventual commercial failure, quickly gained a normative status by virtue of Scott's enormous prestige and the durability of his lives of the novelists.[8] Scott, of course, knew and admired Barbauld, and himself wished to edit a collection of novels much like Barbauld's during the first decade of the nineteenth century, only to desist when he learned that she was already doing so and had in a sense scooped him. Nevertheless her series, reissued in 1820, was not merely Scott's competition but also his foundation, his template; it was her choices that he modified, in the process transforming the canon into something we recognize today.

The first and most important revision Scott undertook was to supplement some of her selections so as to make the canon of the British novel the treasury of specific novelists' careers. Barbauld included 29 titles by 22 authors, only occasionally reprinting two novels by any given writer and never more than two; Scott by contrast reprints 37 novels by 14 writers. In other words, fewer novelists are represented and by more novels—indeed often by their complete novels. Highly critical of episodic and digressive plots, Barbauld had for example included only one (late and relatively short) novel by Smollett, *Humphry Clinker*. In perhaps his largest revision to Barbauld's canon, Scott by contrast includes all of Smollett, even translations and his biography of Cervantes. Similarly, he includes all of Fielding's novels, all of Richardson's, all of Mackenzie's, both of Sterne's, and he even jumps the Channel and prints three novels by Le Sage.[9] While Barbauld had printed only two, Scott includes all of Radcliffe's novels, but she is the only woman writer acknowledged to have a career. For Scott, the British novel becomes principally the complete works of a few men who by virtue of his selection become great authors.

Scott's edition makes a history of the novel that proleptically creates and vindicates Scott himself. Barbauld, we remember, like Austen, is testy about the novel, aware that it lacks the cultural prestige of poetry, and this anxiety about the stature of novels and novelizing haunts novelists until well into the twentieth century. The force of her prefatory essay **"On the Origin and Progress of Novel-Writing"** is to dignify novels by linking them to a classical history, an aesthetic integrity, and a nation-making effect. Scott has no such preface. The title of the series replaces that preface as a vindication of novels. That word "Novelist's" in the *Ballantyne's Novelist's Library,* it is often overlooked, is in the singular. Unlike Barbauld, Scott is not only *a* novelist, but he is *the* novelist; it is his library of previous novelists we are being invited to read. Scott's authorship of novels by this time is an open secret, and while the secret attests to the faint disgrace still attending to novel-writing as a profession, the openness attests to its emerging dignity. By creating a canon consisting of gentlemen authors, Scott creates the justificatory illusion that they (too) were professional novelists—when as we know Richardson, Fielding, Smollett, Sterne, and others all came to the novel late in their lives and most often as a sort of last resort after other careers failed. Subsequent literary histories take up Scott's pattern— Taine's chapter on the novel lists Defoe, Richardson,

Fielding, and Sterne (though he briefly mentions Goldsmith and Johnson);[10] and, writing at the outset of WWI, Saintsbury describes Richardson, Fielding, Smollett, and Sterne as the venerably olden, "Four Wheels of the Novel Wain," while other novelists of the period are shunted away under the invidious chapter title "Minor and Later Eighteenth-Century Novel," as if to be *later* were precisely to be *minor*.[11]

As intimated earlier, one glaring feature of the transformation of Barbauld's canon into Scott's is the elimination of most of the women novelists generously represented in the earlier collection. The Romantic-era novel is a casualty of the novel's "rise" to professional dignity during the Romantic period itself with Scott's collection, if not by intention (we know he sincerely admired Edgeworth, for example, as well as Barbauld, despite his irritation with her politics), then by effect, that professionalization entailing a process of "remasculinization" that would refuse Edgeworth, Burney, Radcliffe, and Inchbald a dignity commensurate with their male counterparts.[12]

Particularly considered as a post-Waterloo effort to produce and preserve a national culture, moreover, Scott's *Ballantyne's Novelist's Library* also entails a consolidation and a conjuring of the novel's glorious origins in a remoter and a safer national past. Michael Sadleir long ago described the difference between the Scott and Barbauld canons as one of emancipated sexual morality. As a gentleman, Scott could afford to include (the argument runs) the marvelously full-blooded, ribald English novels, supposedly passed over by Barbauld because she was a "stickler for feminine decorum" (Sadleir 90). But Scott's interventions have more to do with politics and gender than they do with sexual morality. Indeed, in important ways, the *Ballantyne's Novelist's Library* is a diminution and not an expansion of the **The British Novelists.** Scott omits the late-century novels that interest us so much, particular those accommodating to radical politics—Moore's *Zeluco,* Inchbald's *Nature and Art,* for instance, and most glaringly the fiction of Bage. Though Scott actually includes more novels by Bage than Barbauld does (in keeping with his tendency to ensconce novelistic careers), he drops *Man as He Is,* which Barbauld reprinted, omits the radical *Hermsprong,* and vigorously censures his radicalism in the prefatory biographical sketch. The deeply conservative tendencies we now almost reflexively attribute to canon-making were in the case of the British novel clearly reactions to and revisions of an earlier effort in which dissent was broadly a constitutive element.

I started with Austen, and it is fitting to return to her by way of conclusion and to speculate on how her novels might look in the context of Barbauld's or Scott's collections. Austen obviously has no place in Barbauld's **British Novelists**: her first published novel (*Sense and Sensibility*) appeared in 1811, a year after **British Novelists** was published. Judging from the similarities between Austen's defense of fiction and Barbauld's, many of which would have been available to Austen in the preface to Barbauld's edition of the **Correspondence of Samuel Richardson** (1804), Barbauld seems to have been a formative influence, though the dating of *Northanger Abbey*'s tangled publication and revision history makes this claim a very risky venture.[13] At the very least, Barbauld's canon clearly contextualizes Austen's enterprise in exciting ways, and Austen's almost-first published novel, *Northanger Abbey,* in turn helps us to read Barbauld's vision of the novel and the canon she put together. The achievement of *Northanger Abbey* in my view is to put the gothic novel and the novel of manners into conjunction with each other, to unite the horrid with the familiar, the mountainous world of the Alps with the "midland counties of England" (*Northanger* 200), in part by cultivating the sagacious readership Barbauld imagined. This has not been the orthodox reading of the novel, not the reading produced by the novel's "hero" Henry Tilney. Tilney's lesson is that Radcliffe's novels are good but silly reads, for horror is contrary to a "sense of the probable" here in "the country and the age in which we live" (197). Catherine labors deferentially to learn this lesson, a political lesson which clearly bears on one view of how novels should be read and written, but her progress is endearingly shaky:

> Of the Alps and Pyrenees, with their pine forests and their vices, [Radcliffe's novels] might give a faithful delineation; and Italy, Switzerland, and the South of France, might be as fruitful in horrors as they were there represented. Catherine dared not doubt beyond her own country, and even of that, if hard pressed, would have yielded the northern and western extremities. But in the central part of England there was surely some security for the existence of a wife not beloved, in the laws of the land, and the manners of the age. Murder was not tolerated, servants were not slaves, and neither poison nor sleeping potions to be procured, like rhubarb, from every druggist.
>
> (200)

As this passage indicates, even under the sunny dispensation of the probable, the security conferred by English (as distinct from British) national boundaries and national culture is doubtful: Alps and vices close in on Catherine even as she is trying to establish a safety zone coextensive with England's borders: before too long Catherine cedes the northern and western extremities of her island, finding herself circumscribed in the central part of England. And by the novel's end, even that area is not secure, and Catherine finally—if silently—repudiates Henry's lesson altogether: when she learns about General Tilney's greed she feels "that in suspecting General Tilney of either murdering or shutting up his wife, she had scarcely sinned against his character, or magnified his cruelty" (247). Radcliffean gothic, then, is not remote from the "central part of England," and Catherine's intuition that General Tilney is a version of Montoni, as it turns out, is not absurdly exaggerated.

Such is the conjunction Barbauld's collection invites and Scott's forecloses. Scott printed all of Radcliffe's major fiction but none of the politically and polemically charged novels around Radcliffe that might assist us in putting her style of terror in relation to anything, particularly in relation to anything political, least of all to that "neighborhood of voluntary spies" (*Northanger* 197-98) in which Henry Tilney—believing in the benignity of the state's apparatuses of surveillance—wrongly takes such comfort. Indeed, the thrust of Scott's collection as well as his unsigned 1816 review of Austen in the *Quarterly Review* is to interdict that conjunction. Scott places Austen at the head of a newly emerging practice of modern fiction that scrupulously observes the dictates of strict probability in plot as well as character. "[N]either alarming our credulity nor amusing our imagination by wild variety of incident, or by those pictures of Romantic affection and sensibility," such fiction replaces the "excitements" of excess with "the art of copying from nature as she really exists in the common walks of life" (Scott 63). Although Scott's warmly appreciative but at the same time foundationally diminishing review does not address *Northanger Abbey*—which was not published until 1819—it suggests that he would read the novel as Henry Tilney would, by invoking a politically loaded and politically naïve standard of "nature as it really exists in the common walks of life." Whereas *Northanger Abbey* represented the "alarms of romance" and the "anxieties of common life" (*Northanger* 201) as an ultimately false opposition from the legitimate standpoint of a girl like Catherine, Scott enlists Austen in particular and the modern novel in general under the banner of the latter and relegates the former to the improbable—as if Catherine had never repudiated Henry Tilney's trust in the authority of English institutions, had never reaffirmed her judgment against General Tilney, and had never rediscovered the aptness of gothic hyperbole, as if Austen indeed wrote *only* a novel that had nothing to say about the nation as it looked in the middle counties of England, and nothing to suggest about how novels and their criticism can disclose not terribly reassuring things about it.

Barbauld concludes her general preface to **British Novelists** with a defense of the novelist's labor and of her own:

> It was said by Fletcher of Saltoun, "Let me make the ballads of a nation, and I care not who makes the laws." Might it not be said with as much propriety, Let me make the novels of a country, and let who will make the systems?
>
> (1.62)

To make the novels of a country. Is Barbauld referring to the composition of novels or to the editing of them in collections such as her own? The answer seems to be both. In Barbauld's formulation, novelistic canons supplement, critique, or contest political systems rather than displace or stand as alternatives to them. Her first, short-lived tradition of the British novel imagined novel and the nation alike as responsive to dissent (neither constituted by the Reaction to the French Revolution, however much it took cognizance of it, nor by the Napoleonic Wars), as inclusive of difference, and as foundationally inviting to women writers. Without taking her as its *raison d'etre,* this national and generic history produced Austen's pointed (and poignantly uncredited) conviction that it was the Romantic-era novel, not the earlier one, in which "the greatest powers of the mind are displayed, in which the most thorough knowledge of human nature, the happiest delineation of its varieties, the liveliest effusions of wit and humour are conveyed to the world in the best chosen language" (38).

Notes

1. Also, see Catherine Moore, who has paid attention to Barbauld's work as an editor.

2. See Dunlop, *The History of Fiction* (1814) and Raleigh, *The English novel* (1894).

3. See Norton's recent research into Radcliffe, which refutes longstanding assumptions about her genteel Tory conservatism by uncovering her and her husband's ties to progressive dissenting circles.

4. Johnson's essay on fiction was reprinted wholesale without attribution in the early editions of the *Encyclopedia Britannica,* and so entered the realm of common knowledge during the Romantic era. Barbauld wrote a riff on it that Johnson praised, because it imitated not only the style but the sentiments he expressed there. On this subject, see Rogers 27-42.

5. I am indebted to Kaufmann's compelling account, even where I disagree.

6. I am much impressed with Mellor's sense that Barbauld herself is a budding narratologist and I extend that notion to her readers here. See *Mothers of the Nation* 94.

7. McCarthy traces the demise of Barbauld's reputation brilliantly, paying particular attention to the ill-fated repute of the tradition of rational dissent. See his "A High Minded Christian Lady."

8. I am much indebted to Millgate.

9. It is worth pointing out that Defoe's novels don't make it into Scott's collection in part because he had already edited a selection of them.

10. See Taine 151-92. Taine's *History* was first written in 1856-59.

11. Saintsbury's phrases serve as titles to chapters III and IV.

12. On this subject see Ferris 19-59 and Hofkosh. Ferris addresses Barbauld's success in the public sphere before the *Quarterly*'s attacks and also traces its attacks on other women writers.

13. See Harris 40ff. Harris touches upon the similarity of their defenses of the novel and their possible bearing on Austen's revisions to the novels she drafted in the 1790s in order to make a case for the increased importance of Richardson for her oeuvre. A shorter version of Barbauld's essay "On the Origin and Progress of Novel-Writing" appeared in the biography essay appended to her edition of *The Correspondence of Samuel Richardson* (1804). Since *Northanger Abbey* as *Catherine* was sold for publication in 1803, it is impossible that Barbauld had any impact on the novel as it existed at that stage. Austen bought the manuscript back in 1816 and it is possible that she revised it at this time. But since Austen's note to the novel apologizes for the datedness of the allusions, most scholars have assumed that Austen decided not to revise extensively.

Works Cited

Austen, Jane. *Northanger Abbey and Persuasion.* 3rd ed. Ed. R. W. Chapman. Oxford: Clarendon, 1933.

Barbauld, Anna. *The British Novelists; with an Essay and Prefaces, Biographical and Critical.* 50 vols. London: Rivington, 1820.

Brown, Homer Obed. *Institutions of the English Novel from Defoe to Scott.* Philadelphia: U of Pennsylvania P, 1997.

Chandler, James K. *England in 1819: The Politics of Literary Culture and the Case of Romantic Historicism.* Chicago: U of Chicago P, 1998.

Dunlop, John. *The History of Fiction: Being a Critical Account of the Most Celebrated Prose Works of Fiction, from the Earliest Greek Romances to the Novels of the Present Age.* London: n.p., 1814.

Ferris, Ina. *The Achievement of Literary Authority: Gender, History, and the Waverley Novels.* Ithaca: Cornell UP, 1991.

Guest, Harriet. *Small Change: Women, Learning, Patriotism, 1750-1810.* Chicago: U of Chicago P, 2000.

Guillory, John. *Cultural Capital: The Problem of Literary Canon Formation.* Chicago: U of Chicago P, 1993.

Harris, Jocelyn. *Jane Austen's Art of Memory.* New York: Cambridge UP, 1989.

Hofkosh, Sonia. "The Writer's Ravishment: Women and the Romantic Writer—the Example of Byron." *Romanticism and Feminism.* Ed. Anne K. Mellor. Bloomington: Indiana UP, 1988. 93-114.

Johnson, Samuel. *The Rambler.* Ed. W. J. Bate and Albrecht B. Strauss. 19-25. Rpt. in *The Yale Edition of the Works of Samuel Johnson.* Vol. 3. Ed. John H. Middendorf. 16 vols. New Haven: Yale UP, 1958-90.

Kaufmann, David. *The Business of Common Life: Novels and Classical Economics between Revolution and Reform.* Baltimore: Johns Hopkins UP, 1995.

Keach, William. "Barbauld, Romanticism, and the Survival of Dissent." *Essays and Studies* 51 (1998): 44-61.

———. "A Regency Prophecy and the End of Anna Barbauld's Career." *Studies in Romanticism* 33 (1994): 569-77.

McCarthy, William. "A 'high-minded Christian lady': The Posthumous Reception of Anna Letitia Barbauld." *Romanticism and Women Poets: Opening the Doors of Reception.* Ed. Harriet Kramer Linkin and Stephen C. Behrendt. Lexington: UP of Kentucky, 1999. 165-191.

Mellor, Anne K. *Mothers of the Nation: Women's Political Writing in England, 1780-1830.* Bloomington: Indiana UP, 2000.

Millgate, Jane. *Scott's Last Edition: A Study in Publishing History.* Edinburgh: Edinburgh UP, 1987.

Norton, Rictor. *Mistress of Udolpho: The Life of Ann Radcliffe.* New York: Leicester UP, 1999.

Raleigh, Walter. *The English novel; Being a Short Sketch from the Earliest Times to the Appearance of Waverly.* London: Murray, 1894.

Rogers, Katherine. "Anna Barbauld's Criticism of Fiction—Johnsonian Mode, Female Vision." *Studies in Eighteenth-Century Culture* 21 (1991): 27-41.

Sadleir, Michael. *XIX-Century Fiction: A Bibliographical Record.* Vol. 2. London: Constable, 1951.

Saintsbury, George. *The English Novel.* London: J. M. Dent, 1913.

Scott, Walter. Rev. of *Emma,* by Jane Austen. *Quarterly Review* March 1816: 201. Rpt. in *Jane Austen: The Critical Heritage.* Ed. B. C. Southam. London: Routledge, 1968. 58-69.

Taine, Hippolyte. *History of English Literature.* Vol. II. Trans. H. Van Laun. Edinburgh: Edmonston and Douglas, 1871.

Karen Hadley (essay date September 2001)

SOURCE: Hadley, Karen. "'The Wealth of Nations,' or 'The Happiness of Nations'? Barbauld's Malthusian Critique in *Eighteen Hundred and Eleven*." *CLA Journal* 45, no. 1 (September 2001): 87-96.

[*In the following essay, Hadley examines Barbauld's critique of Enlightenment rhetoric in* Eighteen Hundred and Eleven. *In Hadley's reading, the poem's language equates freedom not with an abstract, ungendered conception of individual liberty but with a distinctly masculine cultural and political hegemony.*]

The first great awakeners of the mind seem to be the wants of the body.

—Thomas Malthus,
Essay on the Principle of Population

This account suggests that Anna Letitia Barbauld's apocalyptic vision in her poem *Eighteen Hundred and Eleven* was in fact much broader than it has been credited with, either initially in the early nineteenth century, or more recently. Drawing from early accounts, I argue that she critiques the early nineteenth-century rise of British imperialism and, from more recent accounts, that key aspects of her critique are gendered. Extending these accounts, however, I suggest that her Malthusian-based insights lead her to address not only the British empire exclusively, but also its roots in enlightenment culture and free-market capitalism. Moreover, I suggest that her text challenges some of the gendered stereotypes that her more recent critics have observed, where she addresses the gendered logic of enlightenment hegemony: In what follows, I will trace the evolution of allegorized "Freedom" in the narrative of the poem—what I am calling "Freedom's progress"—suggesting that this trope instances the contemporary justification of masculine desire, in the form of enlightenment rhetoric.

A number of recent accounts have addressed the complex dynamic of Anna Barbauld's *Eighteen Hundred and Eleven,* what Julie Ellison has called, for example, the "self-destructive feedback loop" of history.[1] Ross and Mellor gender the "feedback loop" as essentially a tension between the poem's "natural matron," and its representation of "man's conquesting desire."[2] Ross goes on to identify Barbauld's representation of "freedom" as a "feminine figure," demonstrating her "capacity for a chaste conscience even at the point of rape,"[3] while Mellor laments the disappearance or sacrifice of "freedom" in the poem, to imperialist demands of "war or commerce"[4] These readings are valuable, especially to the extent that the poem's gendered rhetoric operates as a subtext to its socio-economic perspective. And yet, I want to argue, it is exactly such critical (en)gendering which encourages a sustained underreading of the poem's more penetrating insights. Rather, I suggest that in *Eighteen Hundred and Eleven,* Barbauld defies contemporary metaphoric convention and genders her version of "freedom"—associated with the "Genius" and "Power" of Britain—as only initially feminine.

The poem opens describing England's participation in the Napoleonic wars:

To the stern call still Britain bends her ear,
Feeds the fierce strife, the alternate hope and fear;
Bravely, though vainly, dares to strive with Fate,
And seeks by turns to prop each sinking state.
Colossal power with overwhelming force
Bears down each fort of Freedom in its course;
Prostrate she lies beneath the despot's sway,
While the hushed nations curse him—and obey.

(2-10)[5]

The opening lines are by turns both descriptive and interpretive: we get a sense of the "fierce strife," providing "hope and fear" for a nation assisting others under siege. And yet, too, we learn that her efforts are made in "vain," that she strives with "Fate" to assist nations which are in fact "sinking." As it opens, the poem suggests in this manner a general sense of futility, a sense that any effort to change the course of events would be merely an effort to "strive with Fate" (5). And in fact in the first twenty-seven lines of the poem, variations of the term "vain" (in the sense of futility) appear in several lines (5, 11, 13, 15, 23, 27), whether the term is associated with a Britain seeking to confront the "despot's sway," or with Nature herself, "Bounteous in vain," who pours "the means . . . of life; / In vain" (11-13) against the "Disease and Repine" of a country at war (16).

This conflict is gendered in the lines following, rendering masculine the despotic "Colossal power," and feminine the anthropomorphized "Freedom" (signifying the collective effort of Britain and the sinking states). In particular I would highlight the narrative representation of allegorized, feminized "Freedom," which early on in the poem—and in critical accounts, as I suggest—is represented characteristically as a chaste victim of the strife. The poem's early reference to the concept functions in direct contrast to its reference at the conclusion, which suggests a new and contrastive set of associations. I will argue that the term is employed ironically from the beginning, after which its initial interpretation as "chaste conscience" is exploited to expose a similar version of exploitation at work in contemporary Enlightenment discourse.

Following her initial apocalyptic depiction of a doomed Empire, the narrator intercedes with a laudatory ode, "Yet, O my Country, name beloved, revered, / By Every tie that binds the soul endeared . . ." (67-68), an ode in which Britain is praised for her enlightenment qualities:

Thine are the laws surrounding states revere,
Thine the full harvest of the mental year,
Thine the bright stars in Glory's sky that shine,
And arts that make it life to live are thine.
If westward streams the light that leaves thy shores,
Still from thy lamp the streaming radiance pours.

(75-80)

Note in these lines the numerous references to light, for example in Britain's "bright stars . . . that shine," in her "westward stream(ing)" "light," and in her allegorical "lamp," from which "streaming radiance pours" (77, 79, 80). Clearly this light is associated with a culture imbued with enlightenment, reason, or rationality in her "laws," in her reference to the "mental year," and in particular where the developing (and by now standard) conjunction of light and reason is made explicit:

> Thy stores of knowledge the new states shall know,
> And think thy thoughts, and with thy fancy glow;
> Thy Lockes, thy Paleys, shall instruct their youth,
> Thy leading star direct their search for truth.
>
> (87-90)[6]

Another aspect of enlightenment culture, art, or the arts, is in the poem identified as native, (as in "England, seat of the arts" (123)), where it is related to "Genius" or "science," and accompanied by a requisite "finer sense of morals" (236, 241, 299, 86). And yet "art" as an aspect of contemporary culture in the poem is associated not only with an eighteenth-century understanding of rationality and morals, but also with another contemporary phenomenon, the rise of capitalism: "Stirring the soul, the mighty impulse moves; / Art plies his tools, and Commerce spreads her sail, and wealth is wafted in each shifting gale" (272-74). If the function of "art" in the poem is to mediate between enlightenment culture and the rise of capitalism, these lines suggest a direct causality in its role: where "art" sets up camp, "commerce" accompanies her, and "wealth" is not far behind. Likewise, where the poem (notoriously) predicts the decline of the British Empire, these same cultural phenomena undergo a parallel decline:

> . . . fairest flowers expand but to decay;
> The worm is in thy core, thy glories pass away;
> Art, arms, and wealth destroy the fruits they bring;
> Commerce, like beauty, knows no second spring.
>
> (313-16)

Finally, the poem suggests that enlightenment culture and free-market capitalism do not come without a price to the cultures "roused" to the "better life" offered them (220):

> Science and Art urge on the useful toil,
> New mould a climate and create the soil,
> Subdue the rigor of the Northern Bear,
> O'er polar climes shed aromatic air,
> On yielding Nature urge their new demands,
> And ask not gifts, but tribute, at her hands.
>
> (299-304)

The final move in this associative chain has taken us from rationality to desire—that is, to enlightened, capitalist man's desire for "tribute," as one of the fruits of imperial conquest. Coming on the tail of this chain of associations, the reappearance of "freedom" in the final line of the poem, "Thy world, Columbus, shall be free" (334), carries an altered connotation from its mention at the outset: allegorized freedom appears initially as a feminized, chaste victim, whereas the logic of the poem's conclusion suggests that it is tainted by masculine ambition and conquest.

A plausible observation of these lines taken together could be that Barbauld's initial use of "freedom" in the poem is ironic, that we are introduced to the term in its standard, gendered allegorical context only to witness, by the conclusion of the poem, its transformation into a quality which is related by the logic of the poem, but clearly oppositional. This observation leads to a plausible conclusion, that in fact Barbauld constructed the narrative as such to provide a logic which criticizes not only England's actions but also Western bourgeois culture in general: the term "Freedom," in this reading, is used to mediate and even legitimize a culturally sanctioned, unholy alliance between enlightenment thought and, to quote Ross again, "man's conquesting desire." I argue that Barbauld exploits such a rhetoric of "freedom," suggesting thereby that freedom as a bourgeois ideal is used to legitimize man's desire for conquest, in the name of enlightenment thought.

Where Barbauld exposes this substitution of rationality for desire at work in the cultural ideology, she engages a contemporary debate which, by 1811, had gained some notoriety in the general culture. With the combined force of intellectual, political, and industrial revolutions in the eighteenth century, progress and perfectibility increasingly seemed the destiny of mankind. Reflecting this tendency, William Godwin's utopian tract *Enquiry Concerning Political Justice* (1793) prophesied a utopian society in which human life would be prolonged by the "immediate operation of intellect," and all inhabitants would be distinguished by a "cultivated and virtuous mind." In such a society, he argued, the number of inhabitants would never be found, "in the ordinary course of affairs, greatly to increase, beyond the facility of subsistence."[7] To Godwin's ideal vision, Thomas Malthus responded more materially that population, in fact, increases up to the limits of the means of subsistence. In his *Essay on the Principle of Population, as It Affects the Future Improvement of Society: With Remarks on the Speculations of Mr. Godwin, M. Condorcet, and Other Writers* (1798), he argued famously that "the power of population is indefinitely greater than the power in the earth to produce subsistence for man," since population by nature increases geometrically, and subsistence only arithmetically.[8] Much of his argument rested on the assumption, counter to Godwin's, that man was most predictably motivated by the sensual, and only then, perhaps, by the intellectual. Moreover, he suggested the "improbability, that the lower classes of people in any country, should ever be sufficiently free from want and labour, to obtain any high degree of intellectual improvement" (XI.79).⁹

Less recognizable, perhaps, is the segment in which Malthus engages the same argument in addressing Adam Smith, author of *The Wealth of Nations* (1776) and intellectual father of free-market capitalism. Toward the conclusion of the first edition of his *Essay* [*Essay on the Principle of Population, as It Affects the Future Improvement of Society*], he addresses Smith's inquiry into the nature and causes not of the "wealth" of nations, but rather of the "happiness of nations or the happiness and comfort of the lower orders of society, which is the most numerous class in every nation." In particular, he observes that "Dr. Adam Smith . . . has not stopped to take notice of those instances where the wealth of a society may increase . . . without having any tendency to increase the comforts of the labouring part of it" (XVI.109). And as a key instance he cites the commerce of England which, he observes, "has certainly been rapidly advancing during the last century" (XVI.112). "But, upon examination," he continues,

> it will be found that the increase has been chiefly in the produce of labour and not in the produce of land, and therefore, though the wealth of the nation has been advancing with a quick pace, the effectual funds for the maintenance of labour have been increasing very slowly, and the result is such as might be expected. The increasing wealth of the nation has had little or no tendency to better the condition of the labouring poor. They have not, I believe, a greater command of the necessaries and conveniences of life, and a much greater proportion of them than at the period of the revolution is employed in manufactures and crowded together in close and unwholesome rooms, . . . [a situation] unfavorable both to health and virtue.

> (XVI.112, 115)

Thus proceeds Malthus' proto-Marxist argument that the increased wealth of a few, gained from the increased "produce of labour" in the newly manufacturing, labor-based economy, does not in fact result in the increased happiness of the many, the labouring poor. Here, Malthus challenges (and extends to its logical conclusion) Smith's benchmark claim of free-market capitalism that the pursuit of self-interest by consumers and producers results in a general increase in the public welfare, by suggesting that with conditions improving, population increases until the increased demand for jobs drives down wages.¹⁰

And, I argue, this is in part what Barbauld suggests in her poem *Eighteen Hundred and Eleven,* that while the "wealth" of a nation, the "freedom" of its individuals, may increase objectively, "the mass of misery grows" (320). Whatever the extent to which Barbauld was familiar with the thought of Malthus, this key narrative insight in the poem works along the same lines

as the distinction that Malthus makes regarding "self-interest," where he identifies man as a being not "wholly intellectual," but rather differently "compounded of a rational faculty and corporal propensities" (91). Malthus states that given man's identity as "compound being," his "corporal propensities" are likely to affect his "voluntary actions," to the extent that he may determine to "act contrary to" his "conviction as a rational being" (92):

> The cravings of hunger, the love of liquor, the desire of possessing a beautiful woman, will urge men to actions, of the fatal consequences of which, to the general interests of society, they are perfectly well convinced, even at the very time they commit them. Remove their bodily cravings, and they would not hesitate a moment in determining against such actions. Ask them their opinion of the same conduct in another person, and they would immediately reprobate it. But in their own case, and under all the circumstances of their situation with these bodily cravings, the decision of the compound being is different from the conviction of the rational being. . . . The first great awakeners of the mind seem to be the wants of the body. . . . They are the first stimulants that rouse the brain of infant man into sentient activity, and such seems to be the sluggishness of original matter that [these stimulants along are enough] to continue that activity which they first awakened.

> (XIII.92, 93; XVIII.128-29)

Here, Malthus argues against Smith that the pursuit of self-interest is no guarantee of an increase in public welfare, however much man may use his "rational faculty" to justify his "corporal propensities." Like Malthus, then, Barbauld encourages us to see beyond the enlightenment rhetoric of "rational" man—beyond, that is, his "Genius" of "lofty thought," and his "higher life" in "freedom"—to the corporal side of his "compound being" (Malthus), which manifests his materialist desire for wealth and conquest in his "deeds of blood" (Barbauld 326, 332, 32). With "grandeur's growth"—she reminds both contemporary and current advocates of the "golden tide of Commerce"—"the mass of misery grows" (320, 62).

In *Eighteen Hundred and Eleven,* Barbauld extends the Malthusian argument embracing its proto-Marxist elements, and yet criticizing its gendered, misogynist rhetoric. Where she exposes British nationalist rhetoric as explicitly gendered, reading the poem by way of Malthus helps us to see the rhetorical appropriation and exploitation of a feminine-gendered term like "freedom" by masculinist, expansionist interests. Where the poem's enlightenment rhetoric works to justify desire in the name of rationality, its form instances this process of justification: from the initial appearance of "freedom" (where the "Colossal power with overwhelming force / Bears down each fort of Freedom in its course" (7-8)), to its echo in the final lines of the poem (wherein

"Genius fans the noble strife, / And pours through feeble souls a higher life; / Shouts to the mingled tribes from sea to sea, / And swears—Thy world, Columbus, shall be free" (331-34)). In the narrative space between these instances, the trope evolves from signifying (feminine) chaste victim, to in the end suggesting a vehicle of (masculine) "conquesting desire," of hegemonic appropriation. And so what I see is that "Freedom's progress" in the narrative of *Eighteen Hundred and Eleven* ironically represents the masculine appropriation of a feminine allegorical figure; it is through this narrative appropriation that Barbauld exposes the gendered logic of hegemonic enlightenment rhetoric.

Notes

1. Julie Ellison, "The Politics of Fancy in the Age of Sensibility," in *Revisioning Romanticism: British Women Writers 1776-1837,* ed. Carol Shiner Wilson and Joel Haefner (Philadelphia: U of Pennsylvania P, 1994) 241.

2. Marlon B. Ross, "Configurations of Feminine Reform: The Woman Writer and the Tradition of Dissent," *Revisioning Romanticism: British Women Writers 1776-1837,* ed. Carol Shiner Wilson and Joel Haefner (Philadelphia: U of Pennsylvania P, 1994) 224.

3. Ross 105.

4. Anne K. Mellor, "The Female Poet and the Poetess: Two Traditions of British Women's Poetry, 1780-1830," *Studies in Romanticism* 36 (Summer 1997): 271.

5. Anna Letitia Barbauld, *Eighteen Hundred and Eleven, A Poem* [1812], in *The Poems of Anna Barbauld,* ed. William MacCarthy and Elizabeth Kraft (Athens: U of Georgia P, 1994) 152-61. Hereafter cited in the text by line reference only.

6. Using the same conjunction of light and reason, the poem later narrates a paradigmatic evolution of man as "human brute" who, "roused to better life, his sordid hut forsakes: He thinks, he reasons, glows with purer fires, / Feels finer wants, and burns with new desires" (219-22).

7. William Godwin, *An Enquiry Concerning Political Justice and Its Influence on General Virtue and Happiness,* 1793.

8. Thomas Robert Malthus, *An Essay on the Principle of Population, as It Affects the Future Improvement of Society: With Remarks on the Speculations of Mr. Godwin, M. Condorcet, and Other Writers* [1798], I.9, in *On Population: Thomas Robert Malthus,* ed. Gertrude Himmelfarb (New York: Modern Library, 1960) 3-150. Hereafter cited parenthetically in the text.

9. The notoriety of Malthus' *Essay* was said to have influenced Pitt to withdraw a Poor Bill he had previously sponsored, one which "would have made the relief allotment proportionate to the size of the family" (Gertrude Himmelfarb, introd., Thomas Malthus, *On Population* [xxiii]).

In fact, the reception of *1811* was not altogether positive: John Wilson Croker, an early reviewer, famously complains that he cannot "comprehend the meaning of all the verses which this fatidical spinster has drawn from her poetical distaff" (qtd. in William Keach, "A Regency Prophecy and the End of Anna Barbauld's Career," *Studies in Romanticism* 33 [Winter 1994]: 569). The reception of Malthus' *Essay* was even less receptive: William Cobbett addressed Malthus as "Parson," stating, "I have, during my life, detested many men; but never any one so much as you"; William Hazlitt attacked the *Essay* as a work, "in which the little, low, rankling malice of a parish-beadle, or the overseer of a workhouse is disguised in the garb of philosophy" (qtd. by Himmelfarb xxvi).

10. Adam Smith, *Inquiry into the Nature and Causes of the Wealth of Nations,* 1776.

Susan Rosenbaum (essay date fall 2001)

SOURCE: Rosenbaum, Susan. "'A Thing Unknown, Without a Name': Anna Laetitia Barbauld and the Illegible Signature." *Studies in Romanticism* 40, no. 3 (fall 2001): 369-99.

[*In the following essay, Rosenbaum dismisses assertions by some critics that Barbauld's poetry was shaped by the restrictive forces of contemporary social conventions, in particular the widespread notion of feminine identity as inherently restrained, modest, and unassertive. On the contrary, Rosenbaum argues, Barbauld's poetry represents a bold indictment of the political and economic constraints of her time and ultimately establishes a link between her private, domestic role as a woman and her public, expressive identity as an author.*]

1. INTRODUCTION

Although she was a well known and highly respected writer of poetry, children's literature, civil sermons, and critical prose, Anna Laetitia Barbauld (born Aikin, 1743-1825) was reluctant to view herself as a professional author. Most crucially, Barbauld did not depend on her writing for a livelihood, and emphasized the social and moral concerns shaping her forays into print. Her notion of poetic labor was forged not only in the culture of sensibility, but in the culture of religious dissent. The Aikins were active members of the non-conformist community located in Lancashire county; Barbauld's father, John Aikin, served as a tutor in divinity at Warrington Academy, and Barbauld was informally educated in this environment. In 1774 Anna Laetitia Aikin married Rochemont Barbauld, a graduate of Warrington and a dissenting minister. One of the most famous academies of its kind, Warrington served as an important center of dissenting thought in the late eighteenth century.[1] Joseph Priestley taught at Warrington from 1761 until 1767, and became close friends with the Aikins.

Barbauld's acquaintance with Priestley and his works purportedly inspired her to write her first poems.[2] Her initial readership was the dissenting community in which she lived; Barbauld circulated her poetry in manuscript to friends and to the students and tutors at Warrington. Through these channels, her fame spread, but Barbauld shunned publicity. In *A Legacy for Young Ladies,* she emphasized that women's role is "to be a wife, a mother, a mistress of a family. The knowledge belonging to these duties is your professional knowledge, the want of which nothing will excuse." Literary knowledge could be a "duty" for men, but for women it was to be used for "the purposes of adorning and improving the mind, of refining the sentiments, and supplying proper stores for conversation."[3] Accounts of Barbauld's literary career suggest that she had to be persuaded to publish her works at all. She published her first poems anonymously in 1772, in a volume of songs edited by her brother John, and in a volume of hymns edited by a tutor at Warrington, William Enfield. In response to "many demands" Barbauld prepared her first solo volume, *Poems,* which was published by Joseph Johnson in 1773 and printed by the Eyres press in Warrington. *Poems* went through three editions that year, reaching a fifth edition by 1776 and a sixth by 1792; an American edition was printed in 1820. Following *Poems,* Barbauld published *Epistle to William Wilberforce* [*Epistle to William Wilberforce, Esq., on the Rejection of the Bill for Abolishing the Slave Trade*] (1791) and *Eighteen Hundred and Eleven* (1812) with Joseph Johnson, and placed some additional poetry in magazines and anthologies.[4]

While Barbauld produced works in many genres, her total production as a poet was slight; the bulk of her poetry remained unpublished until after her death.[5] Even following the success of *Poems,* printed under her name, she continued to circulate work by manuscript, often preferring to send poems to friends rather than publish them. Similarly, anonymity was not simply a cloak Barbauld wore prior to securing a measure of literary fame, as was the norm with many women writers[6]; throughout the course of her career, Barbauld chose to publish

some of her poetry anonymously, to sign some poems "A Lady," or to use the initials A.L.B. or A.B. The poetic persona she cultivated was one of privacy, modesty, and restraint.

Such claims to privacy by eighteenth-century women writers were highly conventional, serving to display compliance with gendered codes of public decorum. Barbauld was certainly influenced by these codes, and scholars have tended to view her as conservative in her acceptance of imposed gendered roles and the doctrine of separate spheres. For instance, Carol Shiner Wilson notes the lack of conflict in Barbauld's poetry "between the needle of domesticity and the pen of artistic desire found in many women writers."[7] But recent work is beginning to suggest that representing her poetic labor as an extension of her private, domestic role did not simply signal Barbauld's acquiescence with gendered limits, but formed a complicated, albeit complicitous, critique of the political and economic systems that shaped her experience as a woman writer and religious dissenter.[8] Crucial to this revision, I will argue, is an understanding of how Barbauld's poetry was produced and circulated, knowledge that the scrupulous edition of Barbauld's poetry by McCarthy and Kraft has recently supplied.

This essay argues that Barbauld develops a lyric aesthetic based on the miniature object so as to textually and materially define a circulation distinct from the dominant, commercially controlled circuits of exchange. The miniaturist poem offers itself to a small, local audience through the conceit of the gift rather than the commodity. A key thread in the fabric of the literature of sentiment, miniaturist literature advertises itself as the product of feminine, domestic handicraft; in doing so, it appears to accept its "minor" status, its role as adornment, the themes of domestic life and moral virtues. While it is a literature defined by the limits of its thematic and formal reach, these limits also serve as the source of its power and critique: Barbauld inscribes her miniaturist poetry as the privileged unit of a representational and political economy opposed to capitalist expansion in its imperialist variety, and to its poetic counterpart, the expansive romantic self. At stake in her use of a miniaturist aesthetic is a model of poetic sincerity based not on autobiographical confession, but on anonymity and the concealment of the personal. Although she wrote and published alongside the first generation romantics, Barbauld—due to her use of Augustan diction and emphasis on the object world rather than on expressions of private feeling—has been seen as an anachronistic throwback to eighteenth-century neoclassical writers. An exploration of Barbauld's miniaturist aesthetic not only reveals that she was actively immersed in the cultural world of romanticism, but that her poetry charts an influential if little-recognized response to the marketing of poetic sincerity and the culture of literary celebrity.[9]

2. ANONYMITY AND LITERARY PROPERTY

Barbauld reflects on the limits and possibilities of the miniature as a model for female authorship in an early unpublished poem, **"An Inventory of the Furniture in Dr. Priestley's Study."**[10] This poem considers the scene of poetic production from an unnamed or anonymous narrator's perspective, placing perspective itself in question. What renders Barbauld's poem a miniaturist study is its concern with spatial perspective versus temporal narration: titled an "inventory," it advertises itself as the work of fancy versus imagination, as nothing more than the accumulation of visual, minute detail.[11] In overt theme and purpose the poem is domestic, its work comparable to the mental survey someone such as Priestley's wife or maid might perform as she glances in the study to check that everything is in its proper place.

Although an inventory would appear to have little political import, the narrator's description of Priestley's furniture belies this expectation. Priestley was one of the most well-known republican dissenters of the late eighteenth century. By describing the objects in his study, the narrator draws an implicit portrait of the man and his intellectual and political engagements, investing neutral objects with political meaning. Indeed, at stake in this poem about furniture is the relationship between possessions and their owners, property and authorship. The poem begins with a contrast between landed property and intellectual capital:

> A map of every country known,
> With not a foot of land his own.
> A list of folks that kicked a dust
> On this poor globe, from Ptol. the First;
> He hopes,—indeed it is but fair,—
> Some day to get a corner there.

(1-6, *Poems* [*The Poems of Anna Letitia Barbauld*] 38-39)

The narrator alludes to works that Priestley has authored—*The New Chart of History* (1769) and *The Chart of Biography* (1765)—and implies that these books are the only form of property available to him. Priestley's lack of material property and the unlikelihood that his name will pass into posterity, connotes the history of unequal treatment, specifically the deprivation of civil and political liberties, experienced by dissenters under British law.[12] This situation resonates doubly for Barbauld, who suffered exclusions not only as a dissenter but as a woman (Ross, "Configurations" ["Configurations of Feminine Reform"] 93).

Yet language, the narrator shows, is a medium able to subvert the exigencies of material circumstance:

> A group of all the British kings,
> Fair emblem! on a packthread swings
> The fathers, ranged in goodly row,
> A decent, venerable show,
> Writ a great while ago, they tell us,
> And many an inch o'ertop their fellows.

* * *

> The meek-robed lawyers, all in white;
> Pure as the lamb,—at least, to sight.

(7-16)

While the classics of religion and law lining Priestley's shelves indicate that he is a faithful English citizen, the narrator implies that appearances deceive, through her description of the spatial arrangement of these works. The fact that the British kings are "swinging on a packthread" connotes an image of the kings hanging by their necks, an "emblem" not of justice and order but of the glorious revolution and Priestley's republican politics (*Poems* 247). Similarly, by stating that the works of the church fathers make a "venerable show," and that the lawyers appear "pure as the lamb,—at least to sight," the narrator reveals the limits of the visible. In this manner she suggests that her project of visual description belies its manifest appearance, that the meaning of the inventory can be discerned not simply in the objects she catalogues, but in what she implies. More specifically, meaning accrues in her use and arrangement of Priestley's objects in the poem. The portrait of Priestley emerges through what remains invisible without the paintbrush of language: the history and use of his objects. Language itself, then, in its doubleness, its ability to refer to both what is visible and invisible, can evade the exigencies of the material, visible world, defying attempts to declare written texts as material forms of property.

The narrator develops an apt metaphor for language as a propertyless medium—electricity—as she inventories the tools of science that Priestley employs in his study:

> A shelf of bottles, jar and phial
> By which the rogues he can defy all,—
> All filled with lightning keen and genuine,
> And many a little imp he'll pen you in;
> Which, like le Sage's sprite, let out,
> Among the neighbours makes a rout;
> Brings down the lightning on their houses,
> And kills their geese, and frights their spouses.
> A rare thermometer, by which
> He settles, to the nicest pitch,
> The just degrees of heat, to raise
> Sermons, or politics, or plays.

(17-28)

Priestley wrote a *History of Electricity* in 1767; the "phial" or Leyden jar was used to store electricity, which when discharged "made a spark like lightning" (*Poems* 247). The narrator draws a parallel between writing and lightning through the use of a pun, that classic figure of doubleness: punning on the word "pen," she refers both to the electrical "imps" Priestley pens or cages in the jars or phials, and to the verbal "imps" he creates in his treatises. Like electricity, language is invisible until it is released from its "pen" and circulated; only at this point can it achieve contact, creating tangible sparks. Additionally, the allusion to "Le Sage's sprite" would resonate with a contemporary audience; it refers to *Le Diable Boiteux* by Rene Le Sage, in which "a student releases from a phial in a laboratory a spirit named Asmodeus, who creates a furor among the neighbors by lifting the roofs from their houses and revealing their private lives" (*Poems* 248). The narrator implies that Priestley's muse, like le Sage's sprite, aims to strike discord. On the other hand, Priestley was responding to a violent social conflict, a conflict which would eventually result in personal domestic havoc, the burning of his study and laboratory in the Birmingham riots of 1791.[13]

Through her alliance with the doubleness of language, the narrator distinguishes herself from Priestley, criticizing his incendiary form of writing. Although dissenters are "unfairly" barred from property, power, and civil liberties, the narrator presents Priestley's response to this, his agitation for reform, as no different in kind from the oppression he seeks to counter. His desire for a "corner" of the map renders his political "commerce" as corrupt as that of his enemies':

> Papers and books, a strange mixed olio,
> From shilling touch to pompous folio,
> Answer, remark, reply, rejoinder,
> Fresh from the mint, all stamped and coined here;
> Like new-made glass, set by to cool,
> Before it bears the workman's tool
> A blotted proof-sheet, wet from Bowling.
> —"How can a man his anger hold in?"—
> Forgotten rimes, and college themes,
> Worm-eaten plans, and embryo schemes;—
> A mass of heterogeneous matter,
> A chaos dark, nor land nor water;—
>
> (29-40)

Comparing the varieties of polemical treatises in Priestley's study ("answer, remark, reply, rejoinder") to freshly minted coins, the narrator points out the connections between financial and political commerce. In using such treatises, Priestley subjects his politics to the logic of the marketplace, to the competition, one-upmanship, and desire for property and power that fuels the proliferation of texts and commodities. More pointedly, the narrator suggests that Priestley is not simply a victim of the marketplace, but that the kind of polemical rhetoric he deploys drives the proliferation of print; the marketplace thrives on political division and strife, the distinctions between the "shilling touch" and "pompous folio," and between their authors. The image

of the blotted proof-sheet, spoiled by excess ink, implies—by its ambiguity or doubleness of reference—Priestley's culpability in this system. On one hand, the question "How can a man his anger hold in" could allude to Priestley's righteous anger at the printer, who is guilty of a mistake; Priestley is thus the victim, the purity of his motives "blotted" by the market. On the other hand, the cause for the excess ink may lie with Priestley, the printer producing in the blurred proof-sheet an accurate representation of the dissenter's angry polemics; when they are subsumed by anger, individual words and meanings lose distinction. From this perspective, Priestley's politics are smudged or corrupted by his method.

The imagery of violence and chaos resonates with what seems to be a subtext for the entire poem, Pope's *Dunciad,* his satire on the "dulness" and maliciousness of hack writers. Consider Pope's rendition of the goddess of dulness overlooking her works:

> Here she beholds the Chaos dark and deep,
> Where nameless somethings in their causes sleep,
> 'Till genial Jacob, or a warm Third-day
> Call forth each mass, a poem or a play.
> How Hints, like spawn, scarce quick in embryo lie,
> How new-born Nonsense first is taught to cry,
> Maggots half-form'd, in rhyme exactly meet,
> And learn to crawl upon poetic feet.
>
> (53-60)[14]

In Pope's vision of chaos, the literary market causes the proliferation of dulness; Martinus Scriblerus, Pope's editorial mouthpiece, tells us in his preface that "Paper also became so cheap, and printers so numerous, that a deluge of authors cover'd the land" (344). What results is reproduction run amok, with "Genial Jacob" (Jacob Tonson, a leading publisher) calling forth births before their time, producing deformities in a parody of divine procreation.[15]

Similarly, in Barbauld's poem, the narrator presents an image of hideous birth and deformity:

> New books, like new-born infants, stand,
> Waiting the printer's clothing hand;—
> Others a motley ragged brood,
> Their limbs unfashioned all, and rude,
> Like Cadmus' half-formed men appear;
> One rears a helm, one lifts a spear,
> And feet were lopped and fingers torn
> Before their fellow limbs were born;
> A leg began to kick and sprawl
> Before the head was seen at all,
> Which quiet as a mushroom lay
> Till crumbling hillocks gave it way;
> And all, like controversial writing,
> Were born with teeth and sprung up fighting.
>
> (41-54)

The reproduction of these texts involves both the author and the market, the newborns awaiting the "printer's clothing hand." Like Pope's "half-form'd maggots," these men/texts were born/printed too soon, their deformities indicative of what happens to political writing that conforms to the logic of the marketplace. The result is war without purpose or resolution, violence that breeds further violence. The narrator alludes to "Cadmus' half-formed men," an episode from Ovid's *Metamorphoses,* to flesh out this connection; Cadmus plants the teeth of a dragon, which are born "feet first, as armed men, who slay one another" (*Poems* 248). Through the grotesque image of half-birthed bodies violently attacking one another before they can even see one another, the narrator conveys what happens when men/texts are governed not by their "head" or reason, but by passion.[16] Clear "sides" are lacking in such battle, as are winners and losers: all become tools of a stronger force, the marketplace that feeds off their passion, turning severed limbs into so many coins.

The inventory thus leaves the domestic scene and enters the arena of politics and economy, blurring the distinction between Priestley's professional domain and the domestic domain of the narrator.[17] Priestley's study emerges as a landscape of failed warfare. Personification renders what was implicit—the narrator's perspective on Priestley—explicit; vision and the world of objects are openly subverted by the narrator's imagination and language.[18] Priestley himself takes shape, through his implication in his texts, as one of Cadmus' half-formed warriors. Revealing Priestley's deformities through the narrator's use of personification, Barbauld valorizes by contrast a form of literary production opposed to competition and attack (Ross, "Configurations" 104-5). In using language as a weapon Priestley achieved public notoriety, and a certain amount of celebrity; his name thus became a kind of property in the marketplace, an allegorical signifier or personification of the man. In contrast, it is significant that Barbauld does not name herself in the poem, resisting the assertion of an authorial "I" except through the mediation of Priestley's property. By resisting the creation of property in her name, Barbauld signals that she does not use language as a weapon, nor as a source of celebrity or professional profit.[19] Rather, her labor to make the implicit explicit suggests that she draws on the powers of language as a propertyless medium to make manifest or *expose* the hidden interests and deformities of power. Her inventory radiates outwards from furniture to suggest its embeddedness in questions of property, politics, and commerce. Breaking down public/private boundaries, she shows that the interiority of the self, like the bourgeois interior she inventories, is supported or framed by political and economic interests.

In this respect, Barbauld's critique of Priestley resembles her critiques of Coleridge, Southey, and female writers of sensibility such as Charlotte Smith, who chose to follow the melancholic muse.[20] In general, Barbauld portrays these poets' tendencies towards isolation and melancholy as self-indulgent, and their displays of emotion, like Priestley's displays of anger, as excessive. The charge of self-indulgence was tied to Barbauld's sense that in dwelling on private suffering, these poets overlooked or ignored others' feelings and perspectives. Moreover, private suffering fed the cause of celebrity in the marketplace; Barbauld implies that these poets exploited and even marketed private emotion. Thus Barbauld urges Coleridge (whom she met in 1797) to chase away "each spleen-fed fog." Melancholy had "pampered" him "with most unsubstantial food," rendering him indolent; she warns him to remain "on noble aims intent," to seek "fair exertion, for bright fame sustained" (**"To Mr. S. T. Coleridge"** 30, 36, 40, *Poems* 132-33). Fame was a noble goal only if sought "For friends, for country . . ." (41). While Barbauld shares with the poets of sensibility the delights of isolation and nature, she stresses that she seeks out these retreats not to dwell on her private pain, but to articulate divine presence: "If friendless, in a vale of tears I stray, / Where briars wound, and thorns perplex my way, / . . . / In every leaf that trembles to the breeze / I hear the voice of GOD among the trees; / With thee in shady solitudes I walk . . ." (**"An Address to the Deity"** 49-50, 61-63, *Poems* 5).

Barbauld transforms her exclusion from holding property, her position on the margins of circuits of political and economic exchange, into a moral advantage. A literary production involving slightness and anonymity signifies her distance from motives of profit, property, and celebrity. Namelessness signifies a form of self representation dedicated to ideals distinct from the marketplace, as is evident in the closing lines of **"Inventory"** [**"An Inventory of The Furniture in Dr. Priestley's Study,"**] in which Barbauld imagines the poem's reception:

> "But what is this," I hear you cry,
> "Which saucily provokes my eye?"—
> A thing unknown, without a name,
> Born of the air and doomed to flame.
>
> (55-58)

The poem could be interpreted on the visual level alone, as a "nameless" piece of trash to be thrown into the fireplace. Indeed, according to the logic of competition and celebrity, Barbauld's nameless poem would be "doomed to flame." Yet Barbauld's refusal to name "you" or "I" mars the visible surface of the poem, unsettling reference. The "thing unknown, without a name" could refer not only to Barbauld's poem, but to one of the political pamphlets lining the study; "Namelessness" might connote, as it does in Pope's lines ("Here she beholds the Chaos dark and deep, / Where nameless somethings in their causes sleep"), not anonymous texts, but texts churned out for the market, lacking distinction even when named.

In this manner Barbauld unsettles the significance of the name as a marker of property in the self. Another poem about Priestley, **"To Dr. Priestley. Dec. 29, 1792,"** written soon after the passage of the Royal Proclamation Against Seditious Writings and Publications (May 1792) and the Birmingham riots, evidences Barbauld's attempts to redefine the value of the name. She asks of Priestley: "Burns not thy cheek indignant, when thy name, / On which delighted science lov'd to dwell, / Becomes the bandied theme of hooting crowds?" (5-7; *Poems* 125). Priestley's name, due to his outspoken criticism of the church and his immersion in political pamphlet wars, oversignifies, as a political marker of republican dissent and as a target of "the slander of a passing age." His name is reduced to common currency, his works to "nameless somethings," "doomed to flame." Yet Barbauld argues that his name is owed a "debt of fame," which she assures him will be paid, "when thy name, to freedom's join'd, / Shall meet the thanks of a regenerate land" (20-21). Barbauld's poem works to change the valence of his name, to begin paying off that debt. Redefining the significance of the name, then, is connected to the goals of dissent, allied at this moment to the ideals of the French Revolution, which also spurred acts of re- naming—of the republic and its calendar.[21] Given the seditious writings act, Barbauld did not publish **"To Dr. Priestley,"** but circulated it privately to Priestley's supporters; however, as she noted in a letter to her son, "some of the ministers . . . got hold of & would print (it)."[22] The poem appeared in the *Morning Chronicle* on Jan. 8, 1793, unsigned.

Anonymity in this instance served as protection against political censorship and persecution, but this was not always Barbauld's motive in concealing her name; it is significant that she published both the *Epistle to Wilberforce* [*Epistle to William Wilberforce, Esq., on the Rejection of the Bill for Abolishing the Slave Trade*] in 1791, and *1811* under her own name, even though both treated political affairs. Moreover, given Barbauld's thematization of naming in her poetry and prose, and her resistance to representing herself in her poetry, we can infer that concealment of her signature was connected to her negotiation of literary commerce.

3. NAME DISGUISE AND THE RHETORIC OF SINCERITY

Conventions of name concealment—including anonyms, pseudonyms, initials, anagrams, and numerous variations on these practices—were ubiquitous in British newspapers, periodicals, and volumes of prose and poetry during the romantic period. Conventions of name disguise accompany the emergence of the newspaper and periodical in the seventeenth century, and this tradition continues until the latter half of the nineteenth century.[23] In many eighteenth-century periodicals, such as *The Tatler* (Isaac Bickerstaff), *The Spectator* (Mr.

Spectator), *The Gentleman's Magazine* (Sylvanus Urban), and *The Lady's Magazine* (Mrs. Stanhope), the editor assumed a name and persona which was used to unify the periodical (Shevelow 71). Regular feature writers as well as correspondents to newspapers and periodicals often employed assumed names. The Nichols File of *The Gentleman's Magazine* best exemplifies how widespread this practice was: this file contains a complete record of the magazine from 1731 to 1863, with over 13,000 attributions of authorship filled in by the Nichols family; this figure does not include the enormous number of articles that remain unidentified.[24] Mary Hiller estimates that between 1824 and 1900, 75% of articles published in monthlies and quarterlies were signed with anonyms or pseudonyms (124). Southey, Shelley, Byron, Mary Robinson, Jane Austen, Anna Seward, and Coleridge all used name disguises at some point in their careers, indicating the centrality of this practice.

The practice of name concealment began to decrease in the late 1850s and early 1860s. Although the *London Review* was founded in 1809 on the principle of signed articles, it failed after four issues (Hiller 124). *Macmillan's Magazine* began to use signatures in 1859, and new periodicals established in the 1860s and early 70s explicitly defined their editorial policy around the value of the signature.[25] Established periodicals soon followed suit. The periodical *The Nineteenth Century,* established in 1877, printed the names of its celebrated writers on its front cover, indicating the ascendancy of the signature (Hiller 126).

With this shift from name concealment to signature, name concealment became a matter of historical interest; dictionaries of anonyms, pseudonyms, and fictitious names began to appear in which scholars described this practice in its various forms, and revealed and catalogued the "true identities" of eighteenth- and nineteenth-century authors.[26] The first of these dictionaries was published in 1868 by Olphar Hamst, Esq. (an anagram for Ralph Thomas), *Handbook of Fictitious Names* (London, 1868); John Edward Haynes followed suit in 1882 with *Pseudonyms of Authors, Including Anonyms and Initialisms* (New York, 1882); and Samuel Halkett and John Laing in the 1880's, with *Dictionary of Anonymous and Pseudonymous English Literature.*[27]

The revelation of "true" authorship in these dictionaries was not a new practice, but was rather a formalization of the guesswork, gossip, and sharing of knowledge that had always accompanied use of name disguise in the public media. Penetrating authors' disguises had become a game-of-sorts, and their assumed names riddles to be solved (*Nichols File* 15, 19, Ezell 14); discussion of the identity of authors was a constant theme in eighteenth- and nineteenth-century correspondence

(Shattock 16, Hiller 126). As it turns out, assumed names were often "open secrets" within certain circles of readers (Shattock 15, Hiller 142, Ezell 18). Authors were identified by their distinctive style or subject matter. Also, authors sometimes revealed their identity to friends, or provided clues to their coterie through their choice of name disguise.[28] As Samuel Halkett stated in the preface to his dictionary, "varying degrees of concealment can be traced, ranging from a pseudonym which offers a complete disguise to one which hides nothing at all. An author may desire to remain unknown to the general public only, and may therefore adopt a pseudonym which is transparent to his friends . . ." (xii). For instance, while some authors completely obscured their names, using a series of asterisks and stars to mark their "signature," others simply used their initials or a variation thereof. Many authors used more than one assumed name; Richard Gough (1735-1809), who was the principal reviewer for the *Gentleman's Magazine* during the 1780s and 90s, used almost a hundred different signatures (*Nichols File* 10).

This brief history begs the obvious question: why were these practices of name disguise so pervasive, and why were they replaced by the explicit use of the signature in the late nineteenth century? An adequate answer would have to account for the great variety of contexts in which assumed names were used in the eighteenth and nineteenth centuries, clearly an enormous project. By way of beginning to approach this question, I will discuss a repeated concern of the literature about assumed names: defenses of name concealment and defenses of uses of the signature both relied on the rhetoric of sincerity. Periodicals that defended name disguise argued that it permitted sincere expression without fear of reprisal, while critics of name disguise argued that only when authors had to append their signatures and assume public responsibility for their statements, would they write honestly and ethically (Hiller 125, Shattock 16).

Sincerity is essential to the culture of sensibility, and by the late eighteenth century had become a dominant rhetoric of literature. By sincerity, I refer to the range of expressive gestures and conventions used by writers to mark the voice of the textual speaker as their own, including assertions of spontaneity, originality, artlessness, authenticity, and confessionalism. Logically, name disguise and textual claims to sincerity would seem to be at odds, but I propose that they are integrally connected. Judith Pascoe makes a similar argument in her recent work on romantic theatricality. In comparing Mary Robinson's use of multiple pseudonyms with Wordsworth's stable authorial voice, she argues that Wordsworth no less than Robinson "struck a pose, but his was that of the sincere rural dweller."[29] In other words, Wordsworth's sincerity was as much a performance as Robinson's, but where she embraced the the-

atricality of language and identity, he tried to repress it (Pascoe 242). Judith Pascoe, Catherine Gallagher and Mary Jacobus, among others, have persuasively connected the theatricality of self-representation to authors' negotiations of their reputations in the literary marketplace[30]; conversely, we might view the rhetoric of sincerity as emerging to mediate both the author's increasing dependence on the value of their "name" in the literary marketplace and changing conditions of literary property.

Following Pope's lawsuit against Curll in 1741, the Statute of Anne was used to provide an early form of copyright protection, signaling the writer's property in his/her name. A claim to a unique, recognizable identity began to prove crucial to the value of the literary work as a commodity in the marketplace.[31] But readerly anxiety about professional authorship accompanied this change; the possibility of making profits from a literary work spurred fears that the professional author was not to be trusted, mirroring larger uncertainties about transparency of motive in a burgeoning and competitive market economy.[32] At stake was the author's role in and influence on a social collectivity defined by the tension between moral conduct versus economic commerce; to cite Wordsworth, what values would bind together a social fabric "melted and reduced / To one identity by differences / that have no law, no meaning, and no end?"[33] Sincerity, then, was not a transparent rhetoric that professional commerce corrupted, but rather developed in tandem with it so as to mediate readerly distrust and anxiety. Built into sincerity was its opacity—the necessary possibility of disguise, artifice, and theatricality.

Name concealment conventions played a vital role in the production of authorial sincerity: the assumed name was the garb that clothed the poem as a printed commodity, and helped guide the public in translating the poetic text into the figure of the "sincere" poet. Barbauld is not a theatrical poet in the manner of a Byron, Mary Robinson, or Charles Baudelaire, who assume and take off numerous disguises to expose and critique the theatricality of sincerity itself, drawing attention to the role of the reader and market in producing the values through which the poet's performance is judged. However, Barbauld was certainly aware of the theatricality or "doubleness" of language, that language could be used to disguise identity and to deceive others as much as to illuminate or expose.[34] Like Wordsworth in his "Essays upon Epitaphs," Barbauld's textual strategy is to define a morally transparent language, a language resistant to its own potential for theatricality or "doubleness."

Her twist on the "autobiographical" poem—**"On a Lady's Writing"**—demonstrates this endeavor (*Poems* 70):

Her even lines her steady temper show;
Neat as her dress, and polish'd as her brow;
Strong as her judgment, easy as her air;
Correct though free, and regular though fair:
And these same graces o'er pen preside
That form her manners and her footsteps guide.

Barbauld stresses the transparency of writing, the correspondence between a lady's moral conduct and her signature. Rather than expressing sincerity in personal terms, Barbauld objectifies the signature, divesting it of particularity such that it comes to stand for all ladies, and perhaps for the common practice of signing a poem as "a lady." As in her **"Inventory"** poem, by resisting the assertion of subjectivity within the poem, Barbauld aligns herself with language itself, with the crisp, clear signature.

By blurring or obfuscating the particulars of her identity within her texts, a practice often corroborated by concealment of the name attached to the poem, Barbauld employs what we might call the "illegible signature." While Charlotte Smith sought to connect her poetic persona to her "real" suffering, which she described in the Prefaces to her poems so as to garner readerly sympathy and a measure of celebrity, Barbauld claims the sincerity of the lyric voice but resists readerly efforts to read her poems for clues to her life, for details which might identify her as a recognizable personality.[35] Although the illegible signature may seem to render Barbauld an abstract "type," her self-presentation in her poetry serves to assure her readers that her goal is to cleanse language of deception and ground it in morality, to make the invisible visible. This is to say that the "illegibility" of her signature is planned; her signature was supposed to be read, or legible, in certain ways but not in others. Rather than stating in her work, "I am speaking sincerely and these experiences are real," Barbauld suggests that true sincerity must be inferred, that it is inconsistent with such proclamations.[36]

Publishing poetry anonymously or by partially concealing her name with initials did not function simply as an erasure of self, but confirmed Barbauld's textual self-presentation. We can surmise that to readers Barbauld knew, or to readers familiar with Barbauld's work and style, her authorship of poems printed anonymously was an open secret. Although she participated in writerly commerce, Barbauld worked to articulate a "private" publicness, contingent on being recognized by a coterie of dissenting readers while remaining anonymous within the larger reading public. Hence name disguise served not simply as a form of feminine decorum or as protection against persecution, but also as a model for a kind of "sincere" authorship opposed to the conflation of naming and property, to the culture of celebrity. Ironically, the illegible signature—by sectioning off a realm of "privacy" that the reader cannot penetrate—guarantees the sincerity (or what Barbauld refers to as the visual and moral transparency) of language.

4. The Geography of the Gift

Thus we can conclude that the illegible signature within Barbauld's poetry is connected to how Barbauld viewed literary property, influencing how she published and circulated her work. In short, she devised strategies, both textual and material, for defining a poetic circulation distinct from, though often contained within, dominant circuits of exchange. This strategy helps to explain a central formal and thematic pattern in her poetry, related to the method she employs in **"Inventory"**: the presentation of the poem as a small object and the poet as its implicit observer, absorbed into the act of looking. More specifically, Barbauld presents many of her poems as written on, inscribed on, or placed alongside a domestic object, toy, or piece of furniture. This body of work includes **"Inscription for an Ice-House," "Inscribed on a Pair of Screens," "Lines placed over a chimney-piece," "Lines with a Wedding Present," "Lines written in a young lady's Album of different-coloured Paper," "Verses written in the leaves of an ivory Pocket-Book, presented to Master T(urner)," "Verses written on the Back of an old Visitation Copy of the Arms of Dr. Priestley's Family, with Proposals for a new Escutcheon," "Written on a Marble," "To a Lady, with some Painted Flowers," "To the Miss Websters, with Dr. Aikin's 'Wish,' which they expressed a desire to have a Copy of,"** and so forth. While the verse epistle was a common poetic form, Barbauld's variation on it—the poem not simply as letter but as small object or gift—asks us to evaluate this pattern in the context of her criticisms of literary property.

Certain of Barbauld's object poems, such as **"Written on a Marble,"** employ the trope of inscription, while other poems were literally inscribed on or in the objects mentioned. For example, consider the production of **"Verses written in the Leaves of an ivory Pocket-Book"**; William Turner writes that Barbauld visited his family, and "at the close of her visit, she presented to the writer of this paper, then a little boy between seven and eight years old, an ivory memorandum book, on the leaves of which, after she was gone, were found written the following lines" (*Poems* 235). Similarly, several poems, such as **"Lines with a Wedding Present,"** literally accompanied the gifts they name. Even poems not thematically presented as domestic objects or gifts were often treated as such. For instance, the story behind **"The Mouse's Petition,"** is that Priestley found the poem waiting for him one morning, twisted among the wires of the cage housing a mouse he was planning to use for his experiments on gases (*Poems* 244). One wonders whether Barbauld left **"Inventory"** for Priestley to find on the desk in his study.

In inscribing and circulating these poems as miniature objects, Barbauld establishes an economy of exchange based not on the commodity-for-sale, but on the gift.[37]

As Amanda Vickery argues, "home-made gifts were usually offered by women and were seen as time, labour and affection made concrete."[38] In this manner Barbauld defines her poetic labor as the consolidation of private, moral community, exploiting the association of women's writing with feminine handicrafts to distinguish her works from those sold for profit.[39] The emblem of private community was the home, and she presents several of her object poems as inscriptions on furniture or appliances in the home. For instance, **"Lines placed over a Chimney-Piece"** bless the fireplace and the home's spiritual warmth: "Love and Joy, and friendly mirth, / Shall bless this roof, these walls, this hearth" (13-14, *Poems* 98). These lines are meant to be part of the chimney they celebrate and bless. In the case of the object poems she chose not to publish, Barbauld's handwriting testified that her labor was of the hand—personal and artisanal rather than public and commercial.[40] But the logic remained the same in the case of the object poems she did print and publish: the trope of inscription on a gift evokes the labor of handwriting and the originary context of creation, resisting the status of the poem as a printed copy sold to an unnamed public. Thus Barbauld sought to transform exchange value to use value, resisting the alienation of her labor and the absorption of moral interests within economic commerce by inscribing her reader as receiver of a gift.

In many of these object poems Barbauld attempts to do more than give a gift, to establish a mode of circulation opposed to purely economic commerce; several poems criticize the connection between representation, property, and the economy of empire. In this sense Barbauld's gifts are instructional, seeking to elicit resistance as much as affective ties. **"Written on a Marble,"** an unpublished poem likely composed while the Barbaulds were teaching at the Palgrave School, uses the miniature object to juxtapose schoolboy scuffles and wars over empire (*Poems* 103):

> The world's something bigger,
> But just of this figure
> And speckled with mountains and seas;
> Your heroes are overgrown schoolboys
> Who scuffle for empires and toys,
> And kick the poor ball as they please.
> Now Caesar, now Pompey, gives law;
> And Pharsalia's plain,
> Though heaped with the slain,
> Was only a game at *taw.*

Although the poem is not literally written on a marble, by using the trope of inscription Barbauld makes a visual analogy between the small poem and its object, implying that her poem as material object is akin to the marble as object. Thus the poem is embedded in the second analogy at work, that between a game of taw and nations fighting over empire; though bigger, the world is "just of this figure," figure referring both to the marble and to the poem's figural representation of it. Barbauld's use of the "figure" of the marble serves to undercut and deflate the claims of size and power. Miniaturizing power—showing it to be motivated by schoolboy greed and competition—exposes the small, petty ambitions that underlie battles such as Pharsalia's plain. As in **"Inventory,"** her arrangement or juxtaposition of objects makes the invisible visible, enabling her to discuss objects in their circuits of exchange.

The connection between games at taw and wars for empire is more than figural, Barbauld implies. Toys were materially connected to empire; in the eighteenth century "children had become a trade, a field of commercial enterprise for the sharp-eyed entrepreneur."[41] John Brewer observes that "In 1730 there were no specialized toyshops of any kind, whereas by 1789 toyshops everywhere abounded, and by 1820 the trade in toys, as in children's literature, had become very large indeed" (Brewer 310). Not only did Britain's commercial growth and overseas trade influence the creation of new markets in "luxury" items such as children's toys, but the toys themselves often reflected national interests in growth and progress. For instance, popular toys often replicated, in miniature, machines such as printing presses and camera obscuras; also popular were toy soldiers and forts, and dolls' houses, toys that not only taught gender roles but which influenced attitudes towards the defense and value of property.

Barbauld, as an educator and writer of children's literature, actively contributed to this expanding market in children's education, welfare, and entertainment. But if children's toys often confirmed dominant values about property, Barbauld as educator sought to undo this link, to expose or denaturalize the connections between national interests and common objects. Thus, though **"Written on a Marble"** is on the one hand addressed to the adult reader potentially implicated in the engines of war and empire, it was also likely addressed to an audience whose conduct Barbauld held sway over: the boys she educated at the Palgrave school. Similarly, in **"The Baby-House,"** she presents the poem as a lesson given to a young girl, Agatha, about her toy's wider social and material significance. Barbauld exposes the values about property that the sale of dollhouses implicitly support; she warns Agatha, "think not . . . you own / That toy, a Baby-House, alone" (19-20, *Poems* 177-78). Barbauld then proceeds to supply examples of the real houses these baby-houses invoke:

> The peasant faints beneath his load,
> Nor tastes the grain his hands have sowed,
> While scarce a nation's wealth avails
> To raise thy Baby-house, Versailles.
> And Baby-houses oft appear
> On British ground, of prince or peer;
> Awhile their stately heads they raise,
> The' admiring traveller stops to gaze;

He looks again—where are they now?
Gone to the hammer or the plough;
Then trees, the pride of ages, fall,
And naked stands the pictured wall;
And treasured coins from distant lands
Must feel the touch of sordid hands;
And gems, of classic stores the boast,
Fall to the cry of—Who bids most?

(37-52)

In supplying this context, Barbauld implicates the doll-house in a system of class and national interests that sustains or replicates itself at the expense of nature ("trees, the pride of ages"), peasants, and unseen peoples from "distant lands." The "admiring traveller," like the innocent child playing with her toy, is unknowingly complicit in sustaining this system of class interests. In other words, by juxtaposing baby-houses with "something bigger, but just of this figure," Barbauld reveals that the idle games of children are connected to the "touch of sordid hands," the game of capital ("who bids most"). Barbauld's critique of property was certainly influenced by her gender; part of the project in her poems on the marble and dollhouse is an exposure of how everyday objects in their implication in a wider system of commerce and national interests support and sustain conventional gender roles. Joanna Baillie, a friend and protegé of Barbauld's, also exposes the connections between gender roles and commerce in her two object poems ("Lines to a Teapot" and "Lines to a Parrot"), which similarly supply the histories of these objects and their implication in circuits of exchange supporting empire and patriarchy.[42] Although Barbauld's "gifts" are implicated in the system of commerce and consumption, contributing to the penchant for collecting toys and other items, she attempts to reveal and resist this status.

Drawing "lines to" objects is a useful characterization of Barbauld's project; rather than simply describe objects, she maps what is implicit, the lines that radiate outwards from objects to their implication in commerce and politics. In a lecture to young ladies on the uses of history and geography, Barbauld makes explicit the connection between visual, spatial mapping and the representation of politics and power. Geography, she argues, is one of the "eyes of History," and thus the study of maps reveals more than meets the eye:

> . . . Thus geography, civil geography, would be seen to grow out of history; and the mere view of the map would suggest the political state of the world at any period.
>
> It would be a pleasing speculation to see how the arbitrary divisions of kingdoms and provinces vary and become obsolete, and large towns flourish and fall again into ruins; while the great natural features, the mountains, rivers, and seas remain unchanged, by whatever names we please to call them, whatever empire incloses them within its temporary boundaries.[43]

When one joins history to geography, the lines on maps appear as "temporary boundaries" that reflect the interests of empire and the state of politics; similarly, the names of "mountains, rivers, and seas" appear as "arbitrary" designations, symbols used to signify an ownership and control of land that is only temporary. From Barbauld's perspective, the claims to possession put forth by names and lines on maps are undermined by the fact of historical change (the rise and fall of regimes), and by the permanence of the "natural features" of the earth; human history is subsumed by the frame of natural history.

Barbauld's thoughts on geography clarify her use of mapping and description in her poetry; her own poetic miniatures, in supplying the history and contexts of geography (or the invisible frames supporting the visual, spatial world and its objects), seek to "unname" things, to resist the language, economy, and politics of property as practiced in late eighteenth-century England. The miniaturist text—that which explicitly presents itself as a slight, fanciful, visually detailed description—is thus peculiarly qualified to expose or sketch in the forces that spatialize and miniaturize it, that seek to limit its size and value. In Barbauld's hands, a map of the miniature becomes a history of the gigantic.

5. JUXTAPOSITION AND THE WORK OF TRANSLATION

What we are now in a position to see is that Barbauld's use of the trope of vision, her emphasis on accurate description, encodes a moral politics. Accuracy is the cornerstone of a miniaturist representation supposedly limited to the accumulation of tiny visual detail, yet which strays from this task to reveal "circumstance" as the unspoken or hidden interests of power. Through her absorption into seeing and the objects she describes, or what I have called the "illegible signature," Barbauld turns language outwards, focusing on how language mediates objects, perspective, and power. While the poet is the "seer" in these poems, sincerity functions not as evidence of the poet's autobiographical experience, but as an index of her ethical use of representation; sincerity in Barbauld's writings refers to the use of language with attention to its power to speak for, expose, or represent others, and conversely, the power to misrepresent and exploit suffering.

Barbauld clarifies the ethical aspects of sincerity in the tracts she wrote in the early 1790's for appointed fasts, **"Sins of Government, Sins of the Nation"** (1793) and **"Reasons for National Penitence"** (1794).[44] The tracts define their occasion as a communal reflection on sin, but merge religious and political conduct; as Barbauld states in **"National Penitence,"** "If we have committed any sins as a nation, we are called upon to confess them with sincere and unfeigned penitence. . . . We must resolve to turn from our evil conduct; and we must listen to a lesson of instruction, under the pressure of affliction. Unless we do this, the confession of our crimes will resemble the timid and superstitious devotion of savages" (**"National Penitence"** [**"Reasons for National Penitence"**] v). In asking for sincere confessions, Barbauld locates individual responsibility for national political conduct at the level of responsibility for language. She articulates a political economy of representation in which everyday language use contributes to the system of representative government. Simply put, individuals express political citizenship not through the exercise of the vote, but by using language sincerely, a moral practice open to all persons. Misrepresentation is thus an act of political violence, for it infringes on the political rights of others:

> If you slander a good man, you are answerable for all the violence of which that slander may be the remote cause; if you raise undue prejudices against any particular class or description of citizens, and they suffer through the bad passions your misrepresentations have worked up against them, you are answerable for the injury, though you have not wielded the bludgeon or applied the firebrand. . . .
>
> (**"Sins of Government"** [**"Sins of Government, Sins of the Nation"**] 409)

As political citizens, individuals must take responsibility for hypocrisy regarding national political conduct:

> . . . for we can not surely exclaim with sincerity, that we are fighting to restore order and authority to a country, if treasons and rebellions have been the fruit of our intrigues, and if anarchy and dissention have formed a part of our policy. We have looked "like the innocent flower," but we have really been "the serpent under it," if we have displayed, by this perverse and inconsistent conduct, our zeal for the blessings of peaceful and regular government.
>
> (**"Reasons for National Penitence"** xi)

More trenchantly, in both tracts Barbauld argues that insincere representation is used to justify the goal of national economic interests, regardless of who is oppressed or killed in this pursuit. She describes the ways in which the language of religion, the "blessing of God," is used to justify war and imperialism: ". . . we have calmly voted slaughter and merchandized destruction—so much blood and tears for so many rupees, or dollars, or ingots. Our wars have been wars of cool calculating interest, as free from hatred as from love of mankind . . ." (**"Sins of Government"** 401). Barbauld asks that individuals rewrite such prayers in "plain language," stripped of hypocrisy: "God of love . . . we beseech thee to assist us in the work of slaughter. Whatever mischief we do, we shall do it in thy name; we hope, therefore, thou wilt protect us in it" (403-4). What Barbauld calls for in the use of sincere representation is an act of *translation*:

> We should, therefore, do well to translate this word war into language more intelligible to us. When we pay our army and our navy estimates, let us set down—so much for killing, so much for maiming, so much for making widows and orphans, so much for bringing famine upon a district, so much for corrupting citizens and subjects into spies and traitors, so much for ruining industrious tradesmen and making bankrupts . . . so much for letting loose the daemons of fury rapine and lust within the fold of cultivated society, and giving to the brutal ferocity of the most ferocious, its full scope and range of invention.
>
> (**"Sins of Government"** 401)

Translation involves denaturalizing a word such as "war," translating its exchange value to use value, profits to human costs, coins into maimed bodies. It is the process Barbauld tries to elicit from readers of her object poems when she juxtaposes a decontextualized object with its history in economic and political affairs.

Translation works not through sympathetic identification, but through the juxtaposition of scale and perspective. Barbauld was well aware of the limits of sympathetic identification; the failure of sympathy to produce political change is the occasion of *Epistle to Wilberforce*, in which Barbauld comments: "The Preacher, Poet, Senator in vain / Has rattled in her sight the Negro's Chain," for Britain "knows and she persists—Still Afric bleeds, / Uncheck'd, the human traffic still proceeds" (3-4, 15-16, *Poems* 114-18). Emotional rhetoric is powerless against the desire for profit: "All, from conflicting ranks, of power possest, / To rouse, to melt, or to inform the breast. / Where seasoned tools of avarice prevail, / A Nation's eloquence, combined, must fail . . ." (23-26). Barbauld also thematizes the limits of her own power to effect change. In **"On Education,"** she points out these limits, arguing that "a fast, or a sermon, are prescriptions of very little efficacy" compared to the power of circumstance.[45]

Rather than ask for identification with the oppressed, Barbauld employs a literature of limits, one that exposes the gaps in and barriers to sympathetic identification, and the labor required to oppose "circumstance" and achieve shifts in power. The political labor she describes is by definition difficult and painstaking:

> We want principles, not to figure in a book of ethics, or to delight us with "grand and swelling sentiments"; but principles by which we may act and by which we may suffer. Principles of benevolence, to dispose us to real sacrifices; political principles, of practical utility; principles of religion, to comfort and support us under all the trying vicissitudes we see around us. . . . Principles, such as I have been recommending, are not the work of a day.
>
> (**"Sins of Government"** 411-12)

While sermons were well-suited to inspiring this labor, I want to conclude by suggesting that Barbauld's miniaturist poetry was also involved in the ethical project of translation and sincere language-use, but went about its task in a different manner. Rather than preach, her poetry instructs readers by stimulating their imagination and reasoning abilities. Play and pleasure are central to Barbauld's educational method and political aims, and this helps to explain the curious mixture of lightness and gravity in her poetry.[46] Barbauld in fact wrote many "puzzle" and "riddle" poems, aimed to teach children to sharpen their use of reason and imagination.[47] Her object poems are also puzzles of a sort; juxtapositions of scale ask the reader to consider spatial relationships and societal relationships, and to interrogate their own "frame" or perspective. Barbauld asks readers to leave their shoes not to stand in those of another, as in sympathetic identification, but momentarily to take the position of the map-maker, who looks down upon the world so as to ask how and why the map changes.

Barbauld articulates the importance and curious weight of her delicate labor at the end of **"Washing Day,"** a poem in which she compares the labor of writing with the female work of washing (*Poems* 133-35):

> At intervals my mother's voice was heard,
> Urging dispatch; briskly the work went on,
> All hands employed to wash, to rinse, to wring,
> To fold, and starch, and clap, and iron, and plait.
> Then would I sit me down, and ponder much
> Why washings were. Sometimes thro' hollow bole
> Of pipe amused we blew, and sent aloft
> The floating bubbles, little dreaming then
> To see, Mongolfier, thy silken ball
> Ride buoyant thro' the clouds—so near approach
> The sports of children and the toils of men.
> Earth, air, and sky, and ocean, hath its bubbles,
> And verse is one of them—this most of all.
>
> (74-86)

As Marlon Ross argues, "The disparity between the child's leisure, the capacity to sit and ponder, and the women's endless hard work . . . is akin to Wordsworth's sense that the hard work of building a nation is at odds with the idle pursuit of poetry. But whereas Wordsworth attempts to recuperate poeticizing as hard work . . . Barbauld is satisfied to let the disparity stand" (*Contours* [*The Contours of Masculine Desire*] 228). Even more pointedly, Barbauld implies that the hard work of nation-building is achieved through the idle pursuit of poetry. The juxtapositions in the poem—between the child's play and the women's work, between the child's bubble and Barbauld's verse, between the verse bubble and Montgolfier's balloon—ask the reader to make connections, to "ponder" how these disparate activities are mutually implicated, just as they are asked to ponder how a toy marble is implicated in the struggle for empire. Barbauld's labor, thematized in the poem ("then would I sit me down, and ponder much"), is to set up these juxtapositions and to inspire the reader to ponder them. And it is ultimately her labor

that connects the disparate activities in the poem: her verse bubble is connected to Montgolfier's balloon, the sports of children to the toils of men, in that both are the product of the flights of leisured imagination, of the power of the mind to make unexpected connections. Indeed, the way in which the poem spatially describes the child blowing bubbles implies that Montgolfier's balloon emerges from her pipe, or that the practice of imagination directly impacts scientific invention.[48] Although Barbauld's verse bubble is shaped by the limits of her domestic role, she shows that her verse bubble allows her to venture out of the domestic domain and to participate in and shape, however invisibly (i.e. through the nameless, propertyless medium of language) "the toils of men."

Like Montgolfier's balloon, Barbauld's verse bubble surveys the landscape from a superior vantage point, the mapmaker's perspective.[49] Yet Barbauld, by exposing the lines drawn from the tiny bubble to the balloon, from washing to nation-building, not only sees the map, but also sees backwards and forwards into history, sees that the names and boundaries distinguishing the sports of children from the toils of men are a product of circumstance that can change. As Elizabeth Bishop states in "The Map," "More delicate than the historians' are the map-makers' colors."[50] It is the delicacy of the mapmaker that permits Barbauld's confidence: that as a miniaturist who makes visible the vicissitudes of history, property and empire, her bubble of breath can perhaps escape the weight of circumstance:

> It is impossible to contemplate without a sentiment of reverence and enthusiasm, these venerable writings which have survived the wreck of empires; and, what is more, of languages; which have received the awful stamp of immortality, and are crowned with the applause of so many successive ages. It is wonderful that words should live so much longer than marble temples;—words, which at first are only uttered breath; and, when afterwards enshrined and fixed in a visible form by the admirable invention of writing, committed to such frail and perishable materials: yet the light paper bark floats down the stream of time, and lives through the storms which have sunk so many stronger built vessels.

("On the Classics," *A Legacy for Young Ladies* 31)

Notes

1. See Betsy Rodgers, *Georgian Chronicle: Mrs. Barbauld & Her Family* (London: Methuen, 1958) 33-63.

2. Priestley wrote in his memoirs that "Mrs Barbauld has told me that it was the perusal of some verses of mine that first induced her to write anything in verse. . . . Several of her first poems were written while she was in my house, on occasions that occurred while she was there." Cited in Rodgers,

Georgian Chronicle 57. See also "Introduction," *The Poems of Anna Laetitia Barbauld,* eds. William McCarthy and Elizabeth Kraft (Athens and London: U of Georgia P, 1994) xxix. Cited hereafter as *Poems.*

3. "Letter One," from "On the Uses of History," *A Legacy for Young Ladies, Consisting of Miscellaneous Pieces, in Prose and Verse, by the Late Mrs. Barbauld* (London: Longman et al, 1826; Providence, RI: Brown/NEH Women Writer's Project, 1993) 21.

4. All information on publication history comes from McCarthy and Kraft, "Introduction" and "Sources of the Poems," *Poems* (xxxi, xxxv-xxxvii, 356-63). In their Introduction, McCarthy and Kraft note that Barbauld's manuscripts reached a powerful literary audience, including William Woodfall, the first reviewer of the *Poems,* and Oliver Goldsmith. Lucy Aikin, Barbauld's niece who prepared the posthumous collection of Barbauld's poetry in 1825, wrote that it was only through Barbauld's brother's insistence that "her Poems were selected, revised, and arranged for publication" in 1773 (*Poems* xxx). The Eyres printing press was located in Warrington, and "became the foremost provincial press," printing many works of the dissenters (Rodgers 49).

5. *Poems* (1773) contained 33 poems, and Barbauld published 22 additional poems during her lifetime. Lucy Aikin published 52 poems in the collected *Works* (1825), claiming that they had been chosen by Barbauld (*Poems* xxxi). The 1993 collection includes 24 further poems, and McCarthy and Kraft speculate that many other poems have been lost (*Poems* xxxv).

6. Edward Jacobs argues that many women writers began their careers by publishing with circulating libraries, and that a disproportionate number of works published in this manner were anonymous. Typically, however, "once these authors made a name, they usually sold it to members of the established network of publishers against whom circulating libraries were trying to compete in the first place." Edward Jacobs, "Anonymous Signatures: Circulating Libraries, Conventionality, and the Production of Gothic Romances," *ELH* 62 (1995): 620.

7. Carol Shiner Wilson, "Lost Needles, Tangled Threads: Stitchery, Domesticity, and the Artistic Enterprise in Barbauld, Edgeworth, Taylor, and Lamb," *Re-Visioning Romanticism: British Women Writers, 1776-1837,* eds. Carol Shiner Wilson and Joel Haefner (Philadelphia: U of Pennsylvania P, 1994) 181. William McCarthy argues that recent commentators have found Barbauld and her poetry "disappointingly unfeminist." In doing so, they follow the lead of Mary Wollstonecraft in her caustic dismissal of Barbauld's poem "To a Lady, With Some Painted Flowers" in *Vindication* [*A Vindication of the Rights of Woman*]. See, "'We Hoped the *Woman* Was Going to Appear': Repression, Desire, and Gender in Anna Letitia Barbauld's Early Poems," *Romantic Women Writers: Voices and Counter-Voices,* eds. Paula R. Feldman and Theresa M. Kelley (Hanover: Associated UP of New England, 1995) 114-15.

8. McCarthy argues for a "feminist understanding of her need to idealize the female in the way she does" (115). Previous criticism, he asserts, overlooks the personal or biographical origins of Barbauld's poetry, which is often displaced or idealized. To read the poetry through the lens of biography is to materialize Barbauld's coded endorsements of female desire and pleasure. Isobel Armstrong reads Barbauld's "Inscription for an Ice-House" not as a minor poem, but as an engagement with Malthus, Adam Smith, Hume, and Burke. She also argues that the language of "emotion, affect, and feeling" does not simply signal entrapment by a culture that conflates female experience with bodily sensation, but functions as an analytical language, one concerned with the foundations of epistemology ("The Gush of the Feminine: How Can We Read Women's Poetry of the Romantic Period?" *Romantic Women Writers* 25). Marlon Ross re-evaluates Barbauld's poetry by arguing that we must approach women's political discourse of the early romantic period in the context of dissent. Ross asserts that to speak about politics as a woman was necessarily to occupy a position of dissent, to oppose the political establishment. Nor is it a coincidence, he points out, that many politicized women were religious nonconformists, given that dissent was a tradition that emphasized freedom of conscience and civil liberties. For the dissenting woman, isolation from political power was not simply a limit but an advantage, for it provided her with a political voice uncontaminated by "the corrupt interests of established power" (92); conformity to "feminine caution and decorous conduct" spelled not an absence of politics but a veiled, complicitous politics of dissent, one contingent on "feminine purity" as "political advantage" ("Configurations of Feminine Reform: The Woman Writer and the Tradition of Dissent," *Re-Visioning Romanticism* 92, 94).

9. In this respect Barbauld has much in common not only with Hannah More, but with Wollstonecraft and Jane Austen in their critiques of sensibility. In her use of the miniature object as the site of this critique of sensibility, Barbauld anticipates Austen

as what Poovey calls a "self-confident miniaturist." Austen described the canvas of her novels as "the little bit (two inches wide) of Ivory on which I work with so fine a Brush, as produces little effect after much labour." Labour, then, exists in inverse proportion to production. Mary Poovey, *The Proper Lady and the Woman Writer: Ideology as Style in the Works of Mary Wollstonecraft, Mary Shelley, and Jane Austen* (Chicago: U of Chicago P, 1984) 173.

10. McCarthy and Kraft state that this poem was perhaps written around 1771; however, given the discussion of flames and violence in the poem, and the references to Priestley's books and scientific instruments (Priestley's library and laboratory were burned in the Birmingham riots of 1792), I wonder whether the poem was perhaps written after the riots. If so, the "inventory" becomes a more explicitly ironic meditation on Priestley's politics and their relation to property. The poem was not published until after Barbauld's death, in the 1825 *Works*.

11. On the gendering of imagination and fancy as used by romantic poets, see Marlon Ross, *The Contours of Masculine Desire: Romanticism and the Rise of Women's Poetry* (NY, Oxford: Oxford UP, 1989) 155-86. See also Julie Ellison, "The Politics of Fancy in the Age of Sensibility," *Re-Visioning Romanticism* 228-55 and "'Nice Arts' and 'Potent Enginery': The Gendered Economy of Wordsworth's Fancy," *Centennial Review* 33 (1989): 441-67. On the gendering of the detail, see Naomi Schor, *Reading in Detail: Aesthetics and the Feminine* (NY, London: Routledge, 1987) 4, 20. Although she doesn't use the concept of the miniature, Judith Pascoe connects Charlotte Smith's interest in detailed botanical observation with a desire to expand the reach of her poetry beyond the domestic sphere. "Female Botanists and the Poetry of Charlotte Smith," *Re-Visioning Romanticism* 204-5. The best study of the miniature object and the ways in which writers represent it is Susan Stewart's chapter, "The Miniature," from *On Longing: Narratives of the Miniature, the Gigantic, the Souvenir, the Collection* (Durham: Duke UP, 1993) 37-69. Svetlana Alpers' discussion of seventeenth-century Dutch art, famous for its miniaturist visual detail, is also relevant to my discussion of Barbauld's visual tactics. The Dutch artist is characterized by absorption in what is seen, is defined by his "selflessness or anonymity." Alpers describes a painting of David Bailly, called "Still Life" (1651) in which the artist paints himself surrounded by a variety of objects; the method is that of the inventory or catalogue, the artist another "object" in this display. *The Art of*

Describing: Dutch Art in the Seventeenth Century (Chicago: U of Chicago P, 1983) xxi, 83, 106.

12. Specifically, the Corporation and Test acts required that anyone who held office in any Corporation, or who was elected to public or to military office, take the Sacrament according to the rites of the Church of England; these acts effectively barred dissenters from holding political office. Some dissenters, by pledging "occasional conformity," were elected to public office, but at the cost of their religious beliefs. Dissenters were also barred from the universities, hence the institution of academies such as Warrington. The Corporation and Test Acts were not repealed until 1828.

Most dissenters were involved in commerce or in the professions, but were not holders of landed property. Property in the eighteenth century was the most effective guarantee of political representation. As Linda Colley notes, "members of the landed elite made up over 75 percent of the Commons' membership as late as 1867." Peers were also usually "men with landed estates to their name." Moreover, "landed men virtually monopolised high office at the royal court and were massively over-represented in the upper ranks of the army and navy, in the diplomatic and colonial service, in the hierarchy of the Church of England and in the administration of justice," *Britons: Forging the Nation 1707-1837* (New Haven: Yale UP, 1992) 61.

Barbauld and Priestley were Unitarians, a sect that was "intellectual in their orientation, influenced by science and philosophy, and admiring analytic skills in their ministers." Unitarians were concentrated in Essex, Stoke Newington, and Birmingham. Leonore Davidoff and Catherine Hall suggest that this sect was unusually persecuted given their belief in the human nature of Jesus, *Family Fortunes: Men and Women of the English Middle Class, 1780-1850* (Chicago: U of Chicago P, 1987) 96-97.

13. The Birmingham Riot occurred on July 14-17, 1791. The homes of several Birmingham dissenters, including Priestley, were sacked and burned by a "church and king mob." The riot was ostensibly instigated by a public dinner held in Birmingham to celebrate Bastille Day. The mob ransacked two Unitarian meeting-houses and one baptist meeting house, released prisoners, and burned and looted shops and houses of dissenters including Priestley's home. E. P. Thompson suggests that while there was legitimate resentment against the wealth and reformist tactics of some dissenters, several Tory magistrates and clergy were certainly involved in organizing the riots. Apparently the magistrates directed the rioters to the unitarian

meeting houses and would not intervene nor prosecute those involved. Priestley himself printed evidence in support of this theory. E. P. Thompson, *The Making of the English Working Class,* 80-81, 85; R. B. Rose, "The Priestley Riots of 1791," *Past and Present* (Nov. 1960): 68-88.

14. *The Poems of Alexander Pope,* ed. John Butt (New Haven: Yale UP, 1963). Citations are to the *Dunciad* Variorum. McCarthy and Kraft suggest the *Dunciad* as a subtext for Barbauld's "Inventory" (*Poems* 248).

15. See Marlon Ross, "Authority and Authenticity: Scribbling Authors and the Genius of Print in Eighteenth-Century England," *The Construction of Authorship: Textual Appropriation in Law and Literature,* eds. Martha Woodmansee and Peter Jaszi (Durham: Duke UP, 1994) 231-57. Ross argues that "the only way Pope can assert the authority of the author is to denounce the constant usurpation of illegitimate authority by illegitimate heirs to the throne of poesy." Ross argues that Pope achieves this by over-naming: "He forces us to remember the names of those whom he wants forgotten, for those names become, in his authoritative rendering, exactly that: mere names, phantoms of voices, rather than real voices that can command our attention" (244-45).

16. Davidoff and Hall note that Unitarians "disliked the zeal and enthusiasm of the evangelicals, particularly the ways in which they relied on an appeal to emotion rather than reason . . ." (*Family Fortunes* 95).

17. Many professional men in market towns such as Birmingham practiced their profession at home, dedicating a room or rooms within the house to this purpose. Thus the house itself was divided into areas that were "public" and "private" (Davidoff and Hall, *Family Fortunes* 366).

18. Laura Mandell describes Barbauld's critical project as one of exposure and demystification in her excellent article on Barbauld's politics of personification. She states: "Disputing the imaginary 'nation' advanced by emerging bourgeois ideology, Barbauld uses personification to demystify its 'realist' discourse. Her political theories and poetry interrogate the fiction of a non-aesthetic, non-ideological truth" ("'Those Limbs Disjointed of Gigantic Power': Barbauld's Personifications and the (Mis)Attribution of Political Agency," *SiR* [*Studies in Romanticism*] 37 [Spring 1998]: 30).

19. Ann Taylor Gilbert, a dissenting poet also from the Suffolk/Norfolk region, wrote a poem titled "Remonstrance" which states: "our conquest is composed retreat; Concealment our renown."

Cited in Davidoff and Hall 457; originally published in J. Conder, ed. *Associate Minstrels* (1812). Barbauld states in a poem titled "To Mr. Barbauld, November 14, 1778": "Our bliss, all inward and our own, / Would only tarnished be, by being shown" (31-32; *Poems* 91-92). Air—related to the poetic breath—is what contaminates or tarnishes the privacy of their bliss; hence the poem which celebrates this bliss must itself avoid visibility.

20. Barbauld has several poems which address (and admonish) the melancholic poet more generally: "Autumn, a Fragment," "Verses Written in an Alcove," "Verses on Mrs. Rowe," and "An Address to the Deity." Catherine Moore notes that in Barbauld's criticism of female novelists, she prefers "sense to sensibility." "'Ladies . . . Taking the Pen in Hand': Mrs. Barbauld's Criticism of Eighteenth-Century Women Novelists," *Fetter'd or Free? British Women Novelists, 1670-1815,* eds. Mary Anne Schofield and Cecilia Macheski (Athens: Ohio UP, 1986) 392. "To Mr. S. T. Coleridge," was published anonymously in 1799 in the *Monthly Magazine.* A conjectural attribution in the Kraft and McCarthy volume suggests that Barbauld wrote a poem that rebukes Southey, published in the *Gentleman's Magazine* in 1799 and signed "a Lady." Significantly, Southey's attitude towards Barbauld became harsh after 1799 (*Poems* 333). Although many of the male romantics had met Barbauld, they were very critical of her. Southey was behind the *Quarterly* review of *1811,* a review so vicious that Barbauld did not publish again (Rodgers 140-42). Coleridge ridiculed Barbauld in his lectures on Shakespeare in 1808 (Rodgers 148). Wordsworth wrote that Barbauld "was spoiled as a poetess by being a dissenter," though Crabb Robinson reported that Wordsworth thought her the "first of our literary women" (Rodgers 149). Charles Lamb damned the "cursed Barbauld crew" in a letter to Coleridge, arguing that Barbauld's children's literature had replaced poetry with science. Rod McGillis, "That Great Writer in the English Language," *Children's Literature Association Quarterly* 13.4 (1988): 162-64.

21. The relationship between dissent and support for the French Revolution is a complex one. Davidoff and Hall argue that many dissenters originally supported the revolution, allying their own desire for civil liberties with those of the French. Anglicans feared this alliance, and viewed presbyterian principles as by definition republican. Following the Priestley riots of 1791, many dissenters retreated into social and political conservatism (*Family Fortunes* 96-97). On the significance of re-naming in the French Revolution see Mona Ozouf, "Revolutionary Calendar," *A Critical Dic-*

tionary of the French Revolution, eds. Francois Furet and Mona Ozouf, trans. Arthur Goldhammer (Cambridge: Harvard UP, 1989) 538-47.

22. Barbauld's letters at this time indicate her fear of persecution. To her son, Barbauld wrote that some of the ministers printed the lines to Dr. Priestley, but "of the Dialogue & fragment do not give any copies & do not read & show the Historical fragment, except to our particular friends, & return it to me when you have an opportunity because some things in it would appear too free if read to any but friends. Never within my memory, did public affairs occupy so large a space in the minds of every one, or give such scope to conjecture" (Rodgers 211).

23. Mary Ruth Hiller, "The Identification of Authors: The Great Victorian Enigma," *Victorian Periodicals: A Guide to Research,* eds. J. Don Vann and Rosemary T. Van Arsdel (NY: MLA [Modern Language Association], 1978) 124. Kathryn Shevelow, *Women and Print Culture: The Construction of Femininity in the Early Periodical* (London, NY: Routledge, 1989) 71-72.

24. James M. Kuist, ed. *The Nichols File of The Gentleman's Magazine: Attributions of Authorship and Other Documentation in Editorial Papers at the Folger Library* (Madison: U of Wisconsin P, 1982) vii, 18-20.

25. See Hiller 126; Kelly Mays, "The Disease of Reading and Victorian Periodicals," *Literature in the Marketplace: Nineteenth-Century British Publishing and Reading Practices,* eds. John O. Jordan and Robert L. Patten (Cambridge: Cambridge UP, 1995) 168; Joanne Shattock, *Politics and Reviewers: The Edinburgh and the Quarterly in the Early Victorian Age* (London, Leicester, NY: Leicester UP, 1989) 16.

26. John Edward Haynes lists the various types of fictitious names as pseudonyms, anonyms, anagrams (transposing letters of the name), phraseonyms (a phrase related to the subject matter), titlenyms (use of a title), and initialism (use of one or more initials, often in combination with dashes or stars). The reasons for using fictitious names that he lists include modesty, fear of personal injury, and desire to increase sales of a work by inspiring curiosity. John Edward Haynes, "Preface," *Pseudonyms of Authors, Including Anonyms and Initialism* (New York, 1882). Dr. James Kennedy also surveys the reasons for uses of fictitious names, citing timidity, diffidence, fear of consequences, and shame. Kennedy notes that the different kinds of name-disguises offer "varying degrees of concealment. . . . An author may desire to remain unknown to the general public only, and may therefore adopt a pseudonym which is transparent to his friends. . . ." The use of initials and dashes also falls under this category; friends of the author can easily recognize the true identity. While he notes that the number of authors who sign works with their initials is "very large," he does not speculate as to why this is the case. Dr. James Kennedy, ed. "Notes on Anonymity and Pseudonymity," *Dictionary of Anonymous and Pseudonymous English Literature, New and Enlarged Edition* (London: Oliver and Boyd, 1926).

27. Margaret Ezell, however, notes earlier studies of name disguise, including Vincent Placcius' *Theatrum Anonynorum et Pseudonymoron* (1674) and Adrien Baillet's *Auteurs déguisez* (1690). Margaret J. M. Ezell, "Reading Pseudonyms in Seventeenth-Century English Coterie Literature," *Essays in Literature* 21 (1994): 14. Ralph Thomas considers his work "the first of the kind, so far as we know, that has ever been attempted in the English language" (ix). Certainly the appearance of many such works in the late nineteenth century is significant, although earlier guides had appeared.

28. Margaret Ezell points out that pseudonyms often served not as protective masks, but as passwords to signal membership in an exclusive small group (18, 21).

29. Judith Pascoe, *Romantic Theatricality: Gender, Poetry, and Spectatorship* (Ithaca, London: Cornell UP, 1997) 178.

30. Catherine Gallagher, *Nobody's Story: The Vanishing Acts of Women Writers in the Marketplace, 1670-1820* (Berkeley: U of California P, 1995). Mary Jacobus, "Splitting the Race of Man in Twain: Prostitution, Personification, and *The Prelude,*" *Romanticism, Writing, and Difference: Essays on* The Prelude (Oxford: Clarendon, 1989) 260-36. Judith Pascoe, "Theatricality and the Literary Marketplace: Poetry Publication in the *Morning Post,*" *Romantic Theatricality* 163-83. Pascoe notes that Robinson as well as Coleridge and Southey at various times use anonyms, pseudonyms, or their proper names, without apparent rationale, signifying the blurring of the line between theatrical and authentic or natural modes of self-representation. Catherine Gallagher like Pascoe ascribes agency to women writers' uses of anonyms and fictional personae; she argues in her study of eighteenth-century women novelists that to go nameless was not to be a "nobody"; the anonym or the dash signifies "an outside where a referent too important to be named waits to be discovered" (213).

31. See Catherine Gallagher, *Nobody's Story* 155-56; Mark Rose, "The Author in Court: Pope v. Curll

(1741)," *The Construction of Authorship: Textual Appropriation in Law and Literature,* eds. Martha Woodmansee and Peter Jaszi (Durham: Duke UP, 1994) 211-29.

32. Esther Schor makes this argument in *Bearing the Dead: The British Culture of Mourning From the Enlightenment to Victoria* (Princeton: Princeton UP, 1994) 50-51.

33. William Wordsworth, *The Prelude 1799, 1805, 1850,* eds. Jonathan Wordsworth, M. H. Abrams, Stephen Gill (NY, London: Norton, 1979), Book 7, lines 703-5.

34. Barbauld lectures children on this very topic in "A Lecture on the Use of Words," stating that not only is lying wrong, but that they must strive to use language accurately; imprecision itself is a fault, "it hurts our sincerity" (*A Legacy for Young Ladies* 13).

35. See Sarah Zimmerman, "Charlotte Smith's Letters and the Practice of Self-Presentation," *Princeton University Library Chronicle* 53 (1991): 59.

36. I am grateful to Rei Terada for this suggestion. Barbauld's introduction to Smith's *The Old Manor House* in *The British Novelists* (1810) indicates that Barbauld conflates Smith's insistence on her sincerity with her tone of complaint: "her later publications would have been more pleasing, if the author, in the exertions of fancy, could have forgotten herself; but the asperity of invective and the querulousness of complaint too frequently cloud the happier exertions of her imagination" (*The British Novelists; with an Essay and Prefaces, Biographical and Critical,* vol. 36 [London 1810] viii).

37. Charles Rzepka argues that De Quincey presents his *Confessions* as a gift rather than as a commodity to mystify his status as a "writer for hire." His writings "are meant to be enjoyed by their recipients as offerings of affection, sympathy, and understanding, not as commodities alienable from the personality of their producer." The gift economy positions De Quincey "at the margins of the market economy" (*Sacramental Commodities: Gift, Text, and the Sublime in De Quincey* [Amherst: U of Massachusetts P, 1995] 17, 25). Similarly, E. P. Thompson's notion of "moral economy" is useful as a frame for understanding writers' attempts to establish a gift economy within the marketplace in the eighteenth century ("The Moral Economy of the English Crowd in the Eighteenth Century," *Customs in Common* [NY: The New P, 1993] 185-258).

38. Amanda Vickery, "Women and the World of Goods: A Lancashire Consumer and Her Posses-

sions, 1751-81," *Consumption and the World of Goods,* eds. John Brewer and Roy Porter (London and NY: Routledge, 1993) 286-87.

39. Simon Schaffer discusses Priestley's *History of Electricity,* noting that "Good marketing was a key to his literary career. So was political networking: the 'Society of Honest Whigs' at St. Paul's Coffee House helped him get access to metropolitan savants. His radical friends engineered election to the Royal Society in 1766 to help sales of the History. Priestley also formed a crucial connection with the great radical bookseller Joseph Johnson. . . . Priestley's highly successful work, which ran to three substantial editions in six years, was accompanied by a cheaper booklet for amateurs, designed effectively to compete with the handbooks of Martin and his colleagues," in "The Consuming Flame: Electrical Showmen and Tory Mystics in the World of Goods" (*Consumption and the World of Goods* 513).

40. Susan Stewart argues that the sign of the miniature is the hand; not only can miniatures be held in the hand, but they are often presented as handmade. She comments: "Whereas industrial labor is marked by the prevalence of repetition over skill and part over whole, the miniature object represents an antithetical mode of production: production by the hand, a production that is unique and authentic" (68). See also Alpers 72.

41. J. H. Plumb, "The New World of Children in Eighteenth-Century England," *The Birth of a Consumer Society: The Commercialization of Eighteenth-Century England,* eds. Neil McKendrick, John Brewer, J. H. Plumb (Bloomington: Indiana UP, 1982) 310.

42. Joanna Baillie, *Fugitive Verses* (London: Edward Moxon, 1840) 153-67. Baillie, however, addresses not the child but the collector, whose penchant for exotic items also sustained empire. Andrea Henderson argues that although Baillie attempts to oppose consumerism in the "Introductory Discourse" to her first volume of plays, this work is influenced by the logic of late-eighteenth-century consumerism in its emphasis on "the subtle and intellectual pleasures of collecting" ("Passion and Fashion in Joanna Baillie's 'Introductory Discourse,'" *PMLA* 112.2 [March 1997]: 199).

43. Anna Laetitia Barbauld, "Letter III" from "On the Uses of History," *A Legacy for Young Ladies* 50.

44. Anna Laetitia Barbauld, "Sins of Government, Sins of the Nation," *The Works with a Memoir by Lucy Aikin,* ed. Lucy Aikin, 2 vols. (London: Longman, 1825) 1.381-412. "Reasons for National Penitence" (London: G. G. and J. Robinson, 1794;

Providence, RI: Brown/NEH Women Writer's Project, 1993). Benjamin Flower printed extracts of "Sins of Government" on July 20, August 31, and October 4, 1793 in the *Cambridge Intelligencer.*

45. Anna Laetitia Barbauld "On Education," *The Works with a Memoir by Lucy Aikin* 1.320.

46. Isobel Armstrong writes that Barbauld "had perfected a language which combined gravitas with sensuous delicacy, magisterial weight with limber syntax." See, "Caterpillar on the Skin," *Times Literary Supplement,* 12 July 1996: 28.

47. Barbauld wrote a variety of puzzle poems, including "Enigma," "Logogriph," and at least six "riddle" poems. She states in "On Riddles," *A Legacy for Young Ladies*:

> Finding out riddles is the same kind of exercise to the mind which running and leaping and wrestling in sport are to the body. They are of no use in themselves,—they are not work but play; but they prepare the body, and make it alert and active for any thing it may be called to perform in labour or war. So does the finding of riddles, if they are good especially, give quickness of thought, and a facility of turning about a problem every way, and viewing it in every possible light.
>
> (15)

48. Barbauld was very interested in ballooning, and watched an exhibition in 1784. The Montgolfier brothers launched the first balloon in 1783 in France; the English believed that Priestley's discovery of oxygen was directly responsible for this invention (*Poems* 298).

49. For eighteenth-century illustrations of the view of earth from the perspective of a hot-air balloon, see Barbara Stafford, *Voyage Into Substance: Art, Science, Nature, and the Illustrated Travel Account, 1760-1840* (Cambridge: MIT [Massachusetts Institute of Technology] Press, 1984), especially Figures 100 and 155.

50. *The Complete Poems,* 1927-1979 (New York: Farrar, Straus and Giroux, 1979) 3.

Lisa Zunshine (essay date spring 2002)

SOURCE: Zunshine, Lisa. "Rhetoric, Cognition, and Ideology in A. L. Barbauld's *Hymns in Prose for Children*." *Poetics Today* 23, no. 1 (spring 2002): 123-39.

[*In the following essay, Zunshine offers a cognitive reading of Barbauld's* Hymns in Prose for Children, *focusing on Barbauld's ideological approach to instructing children.*]

Dr. Johnson did not approve of Anna Laetitia Barbauld's writings for children, less on account of his general dislike for people who wrote for "infants" than because he regretted her "voluntary descent from possible splendor to painful duty" (quoted in Ellis 1874: 75). As a well-educated, promising young author, she should have chosen a worthier field for her creative endeavors, or as Johnson put it after reading the 1779 installment of her *Lessons for Children*:[1]

> Miss Aikin [A. L. Barbauld's maiden name] was an instance of early cultivation, but in what did it terminate? In marrying a little Presbyterian parson, who keeps an infant boarding-school, so that all her employment now is "to suckle fools, and chronicle small beer." She tells the children, "This is a cat, and this is a dog, with four legs and a tail; see there! You are much better than a cat or a dog, for you can speak."
>
> (Quoted in Boswell 1971 [1934]: 408-9)

Johnson refers here to A. L. Aikin marrying in 1774 the Reverend Rochemont Barbauld and moving with him to a small Dissenting congregation at Palgrave (Suffolk), where they managed a boarding school for boys. He goes on to imagine his chagrin had his (hypothetical) daughter thought of marrying "such a fellow" after receiving "such an education." Miss Aikin's intellectually degrading marriage seems to account for her attenuated literary ambitions.

Several of Dr. Johnson's friends (including Charles Burney and his daughter Frances) considered this comment unjust. Barbauld herself seemed unperturbed by criticism and in 1781 published her next book dedicated to the religious education of young children, *Hymns in Prose for Children,* which contains passages much like those that had irked Dr. Johnson in her *Lessons* [*Lessons for Children*]. Referring to "young animals of every kind," she notes that they "may thank [God] in their hearts, but we can thank Him with our tongues; *we are better than they,* and can praise Him better" (Barbauld 1866 [1781] [*Hymns in Prose for Children*]: 9, emphasis added). The birds "can warble," she goes on, "and the young lambs can bleat, but we can open our lips in His praise, we can speak of all His goodness" (ibid.).

The observations on the hierarchy of living things (warbling and bleating beasts versus articulate humans) that Barbauld stubbornly made in book after book and that Dr. Johnson thought the epitome of triteness have become a subject of renewed critical attention in recent years. Far from dismissing such observations as a sad symptom of a writer's intellectual inertia, scholars of eighteenth-century culture increasingly view them as complexly implicated in what Isaac Kramnick (1983: 40) broadly characterizes as the period's project of "socializing" children to the ideological creed of bourgeois society.[2] Alan Richardson (1989) points out that the dialogic structure of *Hymns* [*Hymns in Prose for Chil-*

dren] and the fixed character of the provided answers, for example, "But who is the shepherd's Shepherd? who taketh care for him? . . . God is the shepherd's Shepherd . . . he taketh care for all," in fact align the book with eighteenth-century catechistic discourses (Barbauld **1866 [1781]**: 12). The catechistic teaching method, with its stress on the "mechanical production of set answers, obedient behavior within the educational setting, and (for the lower classes) passive literacy," engendered a system of education that remained a "means of maintaining class distinction rather than facilitating social mobility" (Richardson 1989: 853; 854-55). Indeed Barbauld's (**1866 [1781]**: 46, 48) elegant rhetorical closures neatly translate into the hegemonic ones: "The father, the mother, and the children make a family; the father is the master thereof. . . . Many towns, and a large extent of country, make a kingdom . . . a king is the ruler thereof."

One unexpected effect of situating Barbauld's *Hymns* within the eighteenth-century catechistic tradition is that it nudges scholars toward a fresh assessment of the rhetorical undercurrents of the deceptively smooth surface of Barbauld's narrative, an analysis that until recently seemed almost pointless. Barbauld's reliance on common biblical imagery prompted some critics to call her scriptural emblems "conventional, explicated, and as familiar as the iconography of the cross" (Summerfield 1984: 237). Coupled with what Dr. Johnson saw as a dumbed-down style of writing, the conventionality of Barbauld's iconography appeared to hold no surprises for students of eighteenth-century prose. I suggest, however, that the rhetorical appeal of *Hymns* resides not in the originality of its scriptural images (the originality that her intended three-to-five-year-old readers could hardly appreciate) but in the way Barbauld selects and juxtaposes the hymns, complementing and legitimatizing the ideological coercion implied by the book's catechistic structure. With its series of leading questions and undeviating answers, the catechism seems to circumscribe intellectual (and ultimately political) initiative, indeed, to *define* what constitutes an acceptable initiative. So does Barbauld's framing of particular biblical images, though in a much more subtle and practically imperceptible way. In what follows I argue that, by deploying a conceptual framework made available by recent theoretical breakthroughs in cognitive anthropology, we can get a more nuanced perspective of Barbauld's rhetorical engineering. I particularly consider the key message of the first part of her *Hymns*—"Man is made to praise the God who made him"—and examine possible cognitive underpinnings of such a functional approach to human beings (Barbauld **1866 [1781]**: 40).[3]

Before I proceed with my argument, however, I want to point out what, in my opinion, is at stake in investigating the cognitive aspects of the *Hymns.* It is my general contention that a cognitive approach can be useful in our analysis of ideologically charged cultural representations because part of the appeal of such representations comes from their ability to tap into certain cognitive contingencies that arise from the constant interplay between the human brain and its environment. As an effort to influence human beings, ideology will always be attuned to the intricacies of human cognition, and because of this the exploration of our cognitive makeup becomes increasingly important for scholars invested in cultural studies. Once literary critics, such as Richardson, have identified Barbauld's *Hymns* as participating in the eighteenth-century project of socializing children to their "proper" stations in life, we should move further and analyze the cognitive dimension of the ideological stance of her book.

Barbauld's (**1866 [1781]**: 1-3) book opens with the following paraphrase of the first chapter of Genesis:

> Come, let us praise God, for He is exceeding great. . . . He made all things; the sun to rule the day, the moon to shine by night. He made the great whale, and the elephant; and the little worm that crawleth on the ground. The little birds sing praises to God, when they warble sweetly in the green shade. The brooks and rivers praise God, when they murmur melodiously amongst the green pebbles. I will praise God with my voice; for I may praise Him, though I am but a little child.

The governing theme of God's relationship with his creatures is introduced in this opening: God is a maker, and the objects of his craftsmanship ("all things," including birds, brooks, and children) praise him in their various ways. The second hymn makes the same point. After a lively description of blooming flowers, fruit trees, and sporting animals (goslings, chickens, lambs, butterflies), we are told that all living creatures "thank Him that hath made them alive" (8). In the third hymn Barbauld depicts in turn a rose, a lion, and the sun and then turns again to him who "made" (a word repeated five times in the course of this 342-word hymn) the rose, the lion, and the sun and whose beauty, strength, and glory vastly supersedes theirs. **"Hymn Seven"** reiterates the theme of God the maker: "we can praise the great God who made us" (36); "we that are so young are but lately made alive" (37); "He fashioneth our tender limbs, and causes them to grow; He maketh us strong, and tall, and nimble" (38); and finally, the phrase I see as a leitmotiv of this cluster of hymns, "man is made to praise God who made him" (40).

Thus in the first seven hymns children are portrayed as engaged (or encouraged to engage) in only one activity, praying and thanking God for making them. God on the other hand is presented as a skillful craftsman responsible for producing a variety of living beings, including human children. Barbauld reiterates here the age-old paradigm describing the ideal relationship between God and his creatures. She echoes in particular John Milton's *Paradise Lost,* where Adam implores Eve to "ever praise him" that "made us" (Milton 1993 [1674]: 96-97) and where Satan, remembering the "heav'n's matchless King" who "created" him, admits God's "service" was not "hard":

> What could be less than to afford him praise,
> The easiest recompense, and pay him thanks,
> How due!

> (Milton 1993 [1674]: 86)

Because the formula "man is made to praise God who made him" had long become an ethical and theological commonplace, a further query into why Barbauld decided to adapt it for her book seems superfluous. Yet as Oliver Morton (1997: 102) points out, the project of cognitive science today bears out William James's observation that "it takes mind debauched by learning to carry the process of making the natural seem strange so far as to ask for the 'why' of any instinctive act." Indeed, prompted by the availability of suggestive empirical data provided by cognitive anthropologists, we can look anew into the rhetorical appeal of the old adage about God's creatures praising their maker for Barbauld's audience of three to five year olds untutored in biblical and Miltonic imagery. The basic assumption behind such an inquiry is that any "natural" or instinctively "true" or "unarguably" commonsensical notion is not just a cultural or social construction but also a cognitive construction in that it exploits in particularly felicitous ways certain contingencies of our evolved cognitive architecture.

The concept of a cognitively constructed cultural phenomenon highlights the absurdity of the charge of "biological determinism" sometimes leveled against cognitive science. Once we become aware of the fact that during its million-years-old evolutionary history our brain learned to privilege certain ways of processing information and interpreting its environment, we gain the new freedom of questioning some of our hitherto unquestionable assumptions and a new platform from which to interrogate venerable social institutions. Consequently if we want to understand the appeal that the juxtaposition of these two ideas—God "fashioneth" children; children ought to pray to Him—had for Barbauld when she was writing her *Hymns,* it is not enough to say that it was a respectable literary and theological notion well suited for the implicit catechizing structure of her book. We should also inquire into the cognitive foundations of such a juxtaposition, an inquiry made possible by a series of suggestive studies of categorization, particularly of our differentiation between natural kinds and artifacts.

Based on a series of experiments conducted by developmental psychologists and cognitive anthropologists,

Scott Atran (1990) posits that people tend to distinguish categorically natural kinds from artifacts and to perceive the former in terms of their undefinable "essences" and the latter in terms of their "functions."[4] For example, three-year-old children judge a skunk to be a skunk even when presented with it wearing a zebra "outfit." The skunk seems to retain that underlying "skunkness" that makes it different from other animals. A tiger without legs is still a tiger, not a new species of animal. A log, on the other hand, is not judged as having any specific quality of "logness" about it; in fact it seems to change its "identity" quite often. *Depending on its current function,* it can be perceived as firewood, a bench, or a battering ram.[5] A cup with a sawed-off bottom becomes a bracelet or a cookie cutter—nothing about it is perceived as intrinsically "cupful." Atran (1990: 63) argues that a "cross-cultural predisposition (and possibly innate predisposition) to think [about the organic world in terms of underlying essences] is perhaps partly accounted for in evolutionary terms by the empirical adequacy that presumption of essence afforded to human beings in dealing with a local biota [flora and fauna]." Such a presumption "underpins the taxonomic stability of organic phenomenal types despite variation among individual exemplars" (6). In other words, our Pleistocene ancestors could make certain inferences about every new (previously unencountered) organic specimen if they could recognize it as belonging to a certain taxonomic category. For example, it would make sense to be wary of any tiger, not just the one who ate your cousin yesterday, because it is in the "nature" of tigers to prey on humans. Further a tiger with three legs would still be perceived as a tiger, not a new three-legged species of animal with unknown properties, because it is in the "nature" of tigers to have four legs and the exception on hand testifies only to the peculiar personal history of this particular exemplar. Atran (ibid.) points out that "*all and only* living kinds are conceived as physical sorts whose intrinsic 'natures' are presumed, even if unknown," which means the set of inference procedures used to deal with living things is different from that for dealing with artifacts (emphasis added). This observation supports one of the most provocative assertions advanced by cognitive anthropologists today, namely that different cognitive domains have different architectures defined by their respective evolutionary histories. It is likely, for example, that the domain dedicated to processing information about living kinds is older than the domain that processes information about artifacts because of the phenomenal importance and variety of organic forms (as compared to artifacts) in early stages of human evolutionary history.[6]

Let me pause here and offer an important proviso about the described tendency to perceive living kinds in terms of their "essences." Atran and his colleagues make clear that such a tendency does not reflect the actual existence of any underlying essences.[7] What it reflects instead is the fact that for millions of years such "essentialism" might have served as a cognitive "shortcut" instrumental in helping our ancestors orient themselves amid the bewildering variety of natural kinds, including poisonous plants and predators. The ascription of imagined essences was useful for categorization and thus contributed to the survival of the human species. As such it was selected for in thousands of consecutive generations and became a part of our cognitive makeup. What it means is that it remains easy for us—though not at all necessary since nothing about it is "biologically determined"—to jump to essentialist conclusions when dealing with other human beings.[8] Understanding our evolutionary history can thus help demystify some of our less appealing psychological reactions and avoid the epistemological cul-de-sac of viewing them as wholly socially constructed or wholly "natural." In fact I believe that, if we want to challenge social institutions explicitly or implicitly upholding various forms of essentialism, we should investigate the ways the rhetorical practices of such institutions exploit this particular cognitive shortcut.

The proclivities to view natural kinds, such as animals and plants, as "having invisible essences that cause their perceptual attributes" (Cosmides and Tooby 1994: 101) and human-made artifacts in terms of their intended function represent only two examples of what cognitive psychologists and anthropologists, such as Atran, John Tooby and Leda Cosmides, Frank Keil, Dan Sperber, Pascal Boyer, Alan Leslie, and others, characterize as *domain-specific cognitive adaptations.* They suggest that such adaptations, that is, specialized information-processing cognitive mechanisms, evolved in response to the statistically stable features of problems faced by our hunter-gatherer ancestors during the Pleistocene era. As it is beyond the scope of this article to do justice to their arguments, I focus only on the points I find particularly illuminating for my present analysis of Barbauld's *Hymns.*

Cosmides and Tooby (1994: 87) point out that "for humans, the situations our ancestors encountered as Pleistocene hunter-gatherers define the array of adaptive problems our cognitive mechanisms were *designed* to solve, although these do not, of course, exhaust the range of problems they are *capable* of solving." To put it starkly, a domain-specific cognitive adaptation that may have evolved a million years ago in response to the necessity to quickly identify the predator today participates in enabling us to process such complex cultural representations as poems and chess problems. I use the word *participates* to emphasize the fact that cultural representations draw not on one but on several different cognitive domains, activating respective inferences associated with those domains. Barbauld's image of a child made to praise the God who created the child

is an example of such a domain-crossing representation as it mobilizes structural properties of at least two cognitive domains, the one evolved to process information about natural kinds and the one evolved to process information about artifacts. The child, a living being, is characterized as being "made," artifact-like, by the omnipotent craftsman. The effect of such characterization is that, because artifacts are typically viewed in terms of their intended functions, it becomes easier for readers to conceptualize the child as having a function—in this particular context the function of praying. Or to put it slightly differently, the importance and duty of praying are legitimized through the never explicitly articulated but nevertheless cognitively compelling appeal to structural properties *attributed* to "made" objects.

Cognitive scientists as well as literary scholars interested in cognitive approaches to culture offer several suggestive ways of theorizing our ability to process representations emerging at the intersection of several different conceptual domains, such as the one above. So Keil (1994: 252) thinks domain-specific cognitive mechanisms engage in "opportunistic" behavior, "constantly trying to find resonances with aspects of the real world structure. . . . Although [these domains] may have evolved in direct response to the pressing needs of being able to learn quickly about particular [environmental patterns], it may also be part of their nature to be constantly seeking out new resonances with other sets of phenomena, hence our tendencies (often through metaphor) to anthropomorphize computers, to see personality in fluid dynamic terms, or see design in randomness." In other words, think of the time you looked at the three roughly equidistant inkblots on a piece of paper and fancied you saw a face: two eyes and a nose. A cognitive anthropologist would argue that what is taking place at such moments is that a cognitive domain responsible for face recognition is reaching out and playing with its environment, checking if that random inky pattern can possibly satisfy the input conditions of the information (faces) this domain has evolved to process. Such a view agrees with Ellen Spolsky's (2001) notion of the "hard-wired" flexibility and creativity of human cognitive processes and allows us to consider a literary text as a complex amalgamation of ontological violations, a carefully organized body of adventuresome attempts to reach out and establish new connections between different conceptual domains.

An important question at this point is whether or not Barbauld's "domain-crossing" imagery somehow destabilizes our perception of ontological differences between natural kinds and artifacts. On the one hand, to answer the question in the affirmative would be to fall into the Piagetian trap of assuming that the child's cognitive architecture is homogenous across all cognitive domains and that the "differentiation or specialization of architecture is purely the result of psychological development and never initially its cause" (Leslie 1994: 122). According to this point of view, the peculiar crossing of domains observed in Barbauld's **Hymns,** that is, the conceptualization of living beings as artifacts with an emergent function of praying, could "confuse" the child audience as to the categorical alignment of human beings. In fact exactly the opposite is the case. As Atran (1990: 217) points out, symbolic speculation (e.g., assertions of animism) is never confused, even by preverbal children with "commonsense knowledge of matters of fact." If we adopt the cognitive anthropological perspective, we can say that Barbauld's domain-crossing attribution is rhetorically effective because the cognitive domain dealing with living beings is structurally distinct from that dealing with artifacts and both of these domains actively recruit information from their environment that supports their respective "preconceptions" about the world. For example, seeing a bird fly reinforces our "innate," for lack of a better word, expectation that living beings are self-propelling entities. A sight of a flying chair would be perceived as anomalous, that is, it would not be assimilated by the domains processing the information about artifacts and natural kinds as a matter of fact.

This view is supported by the fact that in spite of the presumed triteness of Barbauld's metaphor (i.e., children as artifacts) it remains a recognizable metaphor. No matter how frequently we encounter representations of "artificially" made human beings—in Barbauld's days such representations were provided by biblical and Miltonic discourses, to name a few—they still retain their shock value. This shock value is variously calibrated, depending on the cultural contexts in which those images appear, but the very fact that we never "get used" to them and continue to find their subject matter ontologically suggestive should give us some idea of the tenacity of the division between the cognitive domains that process information about natural kinds on the one hand and artifacts on the other.

Still, even if these images do not have the power to challenge our deep-seated perception of difference between natural kinds and artifacts as such, they can affect on other levels our conceptualization of represented specimens or groups of specimens. Coming back to Barbauld's image of children made to praise God who made them, outside of Barbauld's narrative, artifacts certainly remain inanimate objects that cannot praise God, and children remain living beings that cannot be characterized by a single unambiguous function. Nevertheless, however transitory in cognitive terms, the image of children made to serve certain functions still registers as an ideologically pregnant conceptual framework within which the objectification of human beings is a possibility.

Curiously the children in Barbauld's book pray to God because they are *able to do so* ("birds can warble, but we can open our lips in His praise"), *not* because prayer could procure them some benefits, for example, to make them stronger, happier, or more beloved in God's eyes. This turns out to be an important distinction for the following reason. Although the functional approach clearly appears to be more adequate when we deal with artifacts, certain properties of living things also invite functional explanations. The crucial difference between the kind of functional explanation applied to properties of living things and artifacts is, as Keil (1994: 237) points out, that the functional properties of living things have self-serving purposes ("rabbits have fluffy fur to keep themselves warm"), whereas the purposes for artifacts tend to be other-serving ("coats have fluffy polyester to keep people warm"). In other words, had Barbauld implied that children themselves benefit from praying, that their "function" of praying is *self-serving,* the emergent conceptualization of humans as "made [artifact-like] to pray" would have been compromised. This, however, never happens: children in her book pray because they "can," because they are "made" this way. The attribution of the "natural," unidimensional, unswerving function works particularly well in a text that seeks to develop children's knowledge of God within strictly defined limits, a part of the larger, class-informed social project of guiding and containing literacy.[9]

The questions raised by the analysis of Barbauld's seemingly straightforward didactic maneuver, the insistence that children are "made" to praise God who made them, are thus far from trivial. They alert us to the untold complexities of the interactions between our evolved cognitive architecture and cultural representations and in particular to the cognitive foundations of ideologically charged rhetoric. It has been my contention that, in the case of **Hymns,** the ontological ambiguity arising out of the conceptualization of children as artifacts (i.e., in terms of their function) resolves itself ideologically. In fact it can be said that a functional approach can be easily mobilized to support ideological agendas because an argument that begins with the premise that some groups of people (social classes, castes, sexes) were "made" to perform certain duties implicitly taps our cognitive proclivity to associate "made" objects with certain rigidly defined functions.[10]

On the other hand, the same functional approach can work to heighten psychological tension in narratives that lack the ideological transparency of the catechist. Consider, for example, the suggestiveness of Mary Shelley's *Frankenstein* (1818), which arises from the uncertainty of the ontological status of the Creature. Technically speaking he is an artifact, being literally "made" by Victor, and yet he remains functionless or unnaturally (humanly) multifunctional and thus threatening. By contrast, the figure of the Golem, yet another artificially produced creature, may be perceived as much less equivocal because it (mostly) sticks to its function of protecting the Jews of Prague and obediently exits when that function is fulfilled. By activating a host of conceptual inferences belonging to different cognitive domains, representations of artificially produced ("made") human beings present us with a cognitive challenge. We experience this challenge as an ambiguity, a creative opening, a promise of a potential that can be realized and interpreted differently depending on its specific cultural, ideological, and literary contexts.

Barbauld of course did not think in terms of natural kinds and artifacts when she wrote *Hymns.* For thousands of years writers and rhetoricians captivated the hearts and intellects of their audiences without the benefit of having cognitive scientists explain that what they do constitutes activating "domain-specific" inferences. These cognitive operations run on such a fundamental level as to be practically imperceptible; even today little is known about their exact workings. Moreover trying to explain the intended rhetorical impact of her writings, an author can develop an intuitively appealing and ideologically suitable "prototheory" of the child's cognitive development, and this theory could be based on assumptions that frequently run against those held by cognitive anthropologists today, which is largely the case with Barbauld.

Barbauld saw her *Hymns* as radically different from the "multitude of books professedly written for children" and yet "not adapted to the comprehension of a young child" (quoted in Ellis 1874: 101-2).[11] In the preface to her book, she obliquely criticizes her famous predecessor Isaac Watts, author of *Divine Songs for the Use of Children* (1715). Ironically Barbauld's (**1866 [1781]**: v) characterization of Watts's "Hymns for Children" seems to echo, in letter, not in spirit, Dr. Johnson's earlier regrets that she chose the "painful duty" of writing for infants over the "possible splendor" of addressing a more sophisticated adult audience. She writes that Watts "is deservedly honoured for the condescension of his Muse, which was very able to take a loftier flight" (v). At any rate, Barbauld concludes, poetry is wasted on young readers. It should not "be lowered to the capacities of children. . . . They should be kept from reading verse till they are able to relish good verse; for the very essence of poetry is an elevation in thought and style above the common standard; and if it wants this character, it wants all that renders it valuable" (v). Another problem plaguing contemporary literature for children is, in Barbauld's opinion, the unnecessary artfulness of story lines. She argues that a "connected story, however simple, is above [the] capacity . . . of a child from two to three years old" (quoted in Ellis 1874: 101-2) and only interferes with the grand project of impressing upon the child's mind the "full force of the idea of God" (Barbauld **1866 [1781]**: vi). It is much more beneficial, she contends, to connect "religion with a variety of sensible objects, with all that he sees, all he hears

. . . and thus, by deep, strong, and permanent associations, [lay] the best foundation for practical devotion in future life" (vi). And (mark this, Dr. Johnson!), "the task is humble, but not mean; for to lay the first stone of a noble building, and to plant the first idea in a human mind, can be no dishonor to any hand" (quoted in Ellis 1874: 101-2).

At first glance Barbauld's critique of competing books for children (those burdened with "connected stories" and/or poetry) seems rather conventional. As early as 1712, William Jole (quoted in Demers 1993: 38) complained in *The Father's Blessing Penn'd for the Instruction of His Children* about what he perceived as the weaknesses of contemporary literature for children:

> Of all the Books in print, I cannot find
> One Godly Book exactly to my mind,
> Meetly proportioned to Children's strength;
> Some are too short, but most do err in length.

As Patricia Demers (1993) notes in her analysis of moral and religious literature for children to 1850, the situation did not seem to improve much by the close of the eighteenth century. In 1795 Dorothy Kilner, in her *First Principles of Religion* . . . , lamented the fact that "in a cause of such infinite moment, as implanting the first principles of religion on the minds of infants, no age has yet exerted themselves, or fixed on any *rational* plan of instruction" (quoted in Demers 1993: 39 [italics mine]).[12] A "godly" book, a book that answered the needs of a cause of "such infinite moment," would be the one that could, in Lady Eleanor Fenn's words in 1783, "catch [children] gently" by adjusting to their conceptual level and rendering them more pliable for further indoctrination (ibid.). Such a book would work early to impress upon the children the importance of, in James Talbott's words of 1707, "Subjection to the Will of those that are more capable to govern and direct" them than the children themselves are, a fit preparation for future cheerful compliance with the will of their social betters (ibid.). Accordingly, when Barbauld censures the practice of presenting young children with literature presumably "above [their] capacity," she reacts against among other things the social irresponsibility of untoward educators. The author who chooses to cloud the child's mind with unnecessarily complicated notions instead of "catching" the child "gently" by tailoring the readings to the child's cognitive development, misses the precious opportunity to inaugurate the child's successful socialization to his or her station in life.

Apart from such political (and self-promotional) overtones, Barbauld's discussion of contemporary children's literature is interesting for its underlying assumptions about the cognitive capacities of very young children. Barbauld (**1866 [1781]**: vi) argues that the idea of God should be stripped of any extraneous embellishments and inculcated in the child's mind on the level of immediate perception so, at some point, the child "never remembers the time when he had no such idea." Each "sensible object, all that he sees, all he hears" should be conceptually mediated by religious thought and so thoroughly assimilated in the child's mind that he or she will "see the Creator in the visible appearances of all around him" (ibid.). The danger of course is that as a result "his religious ideas may be mixed with many improprieties" (ibid.). But with time "his correcter reason will refine [those] away," and the child will emerge awash in "that habitual piety, without which religion can scarcely regulate the conduct, and will never warm the heart" (ibid.). Even while her practical advice concerning the age at which the child should be exposed to religious ideas radically diverges from his, Barbauld seems to share John Locke's (1988 [1690]: 319) associationist premise developed in his *Essay concerning Human Understanding*: "Let custom from the very childhood have joined figure and shape to the idea of God, and what absurdities will that mind be liable to about the Deity!" Interestingly, Barbauld seems to assume that young children have no innate cognitive structures for concept formation. Thus catching the child at that tender age when the child is first ready to invest his or her mental representations of external objects with meaning, one can radically influence the structure of these representations, or, to use Barbauld's own words, "plant the first idea in a human mind."[13]

From the perspective of cognitive analysis, Barbauld in **Hymns** does the opposite of what she thinks she is doing. In her "Preface" and "Advertisement" she implicitly represents the child's mind as a blank slate liable to take in and to bear any inscriptions, however free-ranging and arbitrary, provided by the environment. At the same time one of the key "messages" of the first part of her book—children ought to pray to God because he made them—is grounded in our cognitive predisposition for conceptualizing living beings differently from artifacts. Barbauld's "message" makes sense on what we may call an intuitive level precisely because her young reader's mind is *not* a blank slate. It is rather an infinitely complex agglomeration of cognitive susceptibilities adapted in the process of human evolution to recognize and interpret (and, unavoidably, misinterpret) environmental stimuli according to the perceived properties of those stimuli. For example, when the properties of a given object (in **Hymns,** the child) seem to satisfy the input conditions of the domain of artifacts (the child was "made"), certain inferences associated with the domain of artifacts (e.g., "artifacts have functions") will be activated, and the reader will be favorably disposed to consider claims about the uniformly defined "function" of this object (here the function of praying).

Consequently it is unlikely that a child would be equally open to associate just about *any* "absurdity" with the "idea of God." Some "absurdities" will be more cognitively felicitous than others and thus will be remembered better and picked up by other members of a culture more readily. As cognitive scientists, such as Cosmides, Tooby, Boyer, and Sperber, suggest: "The assumption that mental representations with different content are equally easy to transmit is false. Representations whose content taps into a domain for which we have specialized mechanisms will be transmitted very differently than representations whose content does not tap into such a domain" (Cosmides and Tooby 1994: 108).[14] Independently from the writer's awareness of her or his own and the readers' fundamental cognitive processes, the writer has to mobilize our domain-specific cognitive architecture in the attempt to influence readers. The implicit appeal to evolved cognition thus emerges as one of the crucial elements of a rhetorically compelling and ideologically suggestive literary endeavor.

Notes

1. *Lessons for Children* came out in several installments: *Lessons for Children of Two to Three Years Old* and *Lessons for Children of Three Years Old* (1778), *Lessons for Children from Three to Four Years Old* (1779), *Lessons for Children* part 3 (1787), and *Lessons for Children* part 4 (1788).

2. See Alan Richardson 1994: 111 for a critique of Kramnick's vision of the *unified* bourgeois ideology.

3. By referring to cognitive anthropologists and psychologists as a cohesive group, I dramatically downplay of course the fact that scholars working in the field of cognitive studies represent a broad variety of paradigms and frequently disagree with each other.

4. See Frank Keil 1986, 1989, and 1994. Keil (1994: 247) suggests that "perhaps as early as the first year of life, children are able to adopt clear functional stances toward a variety of artifacts, where they clearly understand that various properties have purposes, and can invent new tools as well." As Atran (1990: 50) reports, in another series of "transformation" experiments conducted by developmental psychologists, even three year olds "tended not to admit costume change (e.g., putting a horse in a zebra outfit) as a change of identity." Atran (281) also mentions the findings of the study by Susan Gelman and Ellen Markman, in which four year olds "expected the 'kind' of thing something is—as indicated by being called 'bird,' 'fish,' 'squirrel,' etc.—to override misleading appearances in predicting the extension of its 'inherent' properties (e.g., what it eats, how it breathes,

whether it has eggs or seeds inside, the nature of its eyelids and feet, but *not,* e.g., how much it weighs, how fast it moves, whether it is visible at night, etc." See also Susan Carey and Elizabeth Spelke 1994.

5. Note that a log is a potentially ambiguous example. In its "former existence" (as an oak, for instance) it would be classified as an organic object and thus conceptualized in terms of its underlying essence rather than its function.

6. See Keil 1994: 251 for a discussion of cognitive foundations of our learning about functional objects.

7. The folk attribution of imagined essences should be distinguished of course from the fact that, as Leda Cosmides and John Tooby (1994: 101) point out, "the species-typical genetic endowments of species, and the common ancestry of larger taxa do cause an indefinitely large set of similarities to be shared among members of natural kind, as does a common chemical structure for different instances of a substance."

8. See, for example, Lawrence Hirschfeld (1994), who suggests that it may partially account for racism and other unappealing embodiments of essentialist thinking.

9. See Richardson 1989 and 1994.

10. Consider, for example, an argument advanced in a different context in a book by Deidre Shauna Lynch, *The Economy of Character: Novels, Market Culture, and the Business of Inner Meaning* (1998). Investigating the objectification of women in the increasingly commercialized world of the eighteenth-century novel, Lynch (1998: 166) uncovers the ideological implications of the reduction of people to "commodified still lifes."

11. I refer to the "Advertisement" for Barbauld's *Hymns* as it appeared in her 1777 letter to her brother John Aikin.

12. Compare Kilner's emphasis on the need for the "rational" plan for instruction with Barbauld's 1781 assertion that "among the books composed for some use of children, though there are many, and some on a very rational plan, which unfold the system and give a summary of the doctrines of religion, it would be difficult to find one calculated to assist them in the devotional part of it" (1866 [1781]: b).

13. We find various forms of the modern development of this theory in the work of Jerome S. Bruner, Jean Piaget, and L. Vygotsky. See Bruner et al. 1966; Inhelder and Piaget 1964; Vygotsky 1986.

14. See Sperber 1997 on the "epidemiology" of culture and Boyer 1996 on the transmission of religious beliefs.

References

Atran, Scott

1990 *Cognitive Foundations of Natural History: Toward an Anthropology of Science* (Cambridge: Cambridge University Press).

Barbauld, Anna Laetitia

1866 [1781] *Hymns in Prose for Children* (London: John Murray).

Boswell, James

1971 [1934] *Boswell's Life of Johnson,* edited by George Birkbeck Hill, D.C.L; rev. and enlarged ed., edited by L. F. Powell, vol. 2 (Oxford: Clarendon).

Boyer, Pascal

1996 *The Naturalness of Religious Ideas: A Cognitive Theory of Religion* (Berkeley: University of California Press).

Bruner, Jerome S., Rose R. Olver, and Patricia M. Greenfield et al.

1966 *Studies in Cognitive Growth: A Collaboration at the Center for Cognitive Studies* (New York: Wiley).

Carey, Susan, and Elizabeth Spelke

1994 "Domain-Specific Knowledge and Conceptual Change," in *Mapping the Mind: Domain Specificity in Cognition and Culture,* edited by Lawrence A. Hirschfeld and Susan A. Gelman, 169-200 (Cambridge: Cambridge University Press).

Cosmides, Leda, and John Tooby

1994 "Origins of Domain Specificity: The Evolution of Functional Organization," in *Mapping the Mind: Domain Specificity in Cognition and Culture,* edited by Lawrence A. Hirschfeld and Susan A. Gelman, 85-116 (Cambridge: Cambridge University Press).

Demers, Patricia

1993 *Heaven upon Earth: The Form of Moral and Religious Children's Literature, to 1850* (Knoxville: University of Tennessee Press).

Ellis, Grace A.

1874 *A Memoir of Mrs. Anna Laetitia Barbauld, with Many of Her Letters* (Boston: James R. Osgood and Co.).

Fenn, Eleanor

1783 *Cobwebs to Catch Flies; or, Dialogues in Short Sentences Adapted to Children from the Age of Three to Eight Years,* 2 vols. (London: J. Marshall).

Gelman, Susan, and Ellen Markman

1987 "Young Children's Inductions from Natural Kinds: The Role of Categories and Appearances," *Child Development* 58: 1532-41.

Hirschfeld, Lawrence A.

1994 "Is the Acquisition of Social Categories Based on Domain-Specific Competence or on Knowledge Transfer?" in *Mapping the Mind: Domain Specificity in Cognition and Culture,* edited by Lawrence A. Hirschfeld and Susan A. Gelman, 201-33 (Cambridge: Cambridge University Press).

Inhelder, B., and J. Piaget

1964 *The Early Growth of Logic in the Child,* translated by E. A. Lunzer and D. Papert (New York: Norton).

Jole, William

1712 *The Father's Blessing Penn'd for the Instruction of His Children* (London: G. Conyers).

Keil, Frank

1986 "The Acquisition of Natural Kinds and Artifact Terms," in *Conceptual Change,* edited by A. Marrar and W. Demopoulos, 133-53 (Norwood, NJ: Ablex Publishing Group).

1989 *Concepts, Kinds, and Cognitive Development* (Cambridge: MIT [Massachusetts Institute of Technology] Press).

1994 "The Birth and Nurturance of Concepts by Domains: The Origins of Concepts of Living Things," in *Mapping the Mind: Domain Specificity in Cognition and Culture,* edited by Lawrence A. Hirschfeld and Susan A. Gelman, 234-54 (Cambridge: Cambridge University Press).

Kilner, Dorothy

1795 *The First Principle of Religion, and the Existence of a Deity, Explained in a Series of Dialogues Adapted to the Capacity of the Infant Mind* (London: John Marshall).

Kramnick, Isaac

1983 "Children's Literature and Bourgeois Ideology: Observations on Culture and Industrial Capitalism in the Later Eighteenth Century," *Studies in Eighteenth-Century Culture* 12: 11-44.

Leslie, Alan M.

1994 "ToMM, ToBy, and Agency: Core Architecture and Domain Specificity," in *Mapping the Mind: Domain Specificity in Cognition and Culture,* edited by Lawrence A. Hirschfeld and Susan A. Gelman, 119-48 (Cambridge: Cambridge University Press).

Locke, John

1988 [1690] *An Essay concerning Human Understanding* (New York: Prometheus).

Lynch, Deidre Shauna

1998 *The Economy of Character: Novels, Market Culture, and the Business of Inner Meaning* (Chicago: University of Chicago Press).

Milton, John

1993 [1674] *Paradise Lost,* edited by Scott Elledge (New York: Norton).

Morton, Oliver

1997 "Doing What Comes Naturally," *New Yorker,* November 3, 102-7.

Richardson, Alan

1989 "The Politics of Childhood: Wordsworth, Blake, and Catechistic Method," *ELH* 56: 853-68.

1994 *Literature, Education, and Romanticism: Reading as Social Practice, 1780-1832* (Cambridge: Cambridge University Press).

Sperber, Dan

1997 *Explaining Culture: A Naturalistic Approach* (Oxford: Blackwell).

Spolsky, Ellen

2001 *Satisfying Scepticism: Embodied Knowledge in the Early Modern World* (Aldershot: Ashgate).

Summerfield, Geoffrey

1984 *Fantasy and Reason: Children's Literature in the Eighteenth Century* (London: Methuen and Co.).

Talbott, James

1811 [1707] *The Christian School-Master; or, The Duty of Those Who Are Employed in the Public Instruction of Children Especially in Charity Schools* (London: F. C. & J. Rivington).

Vygotsky, L.

1986 *Thought and Language,* translated by Alex Kozulin (Cambridge: MIT Press).

Robin DeRosa (essay date 2002)

SOURCE: DeRosa, Robin. "A Criticism of Contradiction: Anna Leticia Barbauld and the 'Problem' of Nineteenth-Century Women's Writing." In *Women as Sites of Culture: Women's Roles in Cultural Formation from the Renaissance to the Twentieth Century,* edited by Susan Shifrin, pp. 221-31. Burlington, Vt.: Ashgate Publishing Company, 2002.

[In the following essay, DeRosa examines questions of authenticity and female identity as they relate to Barbauld's works. In DeRosa's view, Barbauld's authority

as a writer resides in her subtle use of paradox and contradiction, through which she continually undermines traditional conceptions of womanhood and power.]

To the vast majority of both nineteenth- and twentieth-century literary critics, Anna Leticia Barbauld has not been woman enough. John Wilson Croker, famous for his skewering attack on *Eighteen Hundred and Eleven* in the Tory *Quarterly Review* in 1812, wrote, 'We had hoped . . . that the empire might have been saved without the interference of a lady-author . . . An irresistible impulse of public duty . . . [has] induced [Mrs. Barbauld] to dash down her shagreen spectacles and her knitting needles, and to sally forth.'[1] Barbauld was attacked for the 'traitorous' quality of the poem, as interpreted by many critics of the time who felt that it was akin to a crime against the nation to predict the fall of Britain, especially during the tenuous years of Napoleon's encroachment. But what Croker's criticism displays is the way that many critiques of Barbauld's material—especially her poetry—counted as her greatest crime her failure to uphold the appearance of the docile, domestic woman of the private home space. This, of course, is not particularly surprising, since women authors of the nineteenth century constantly found themselves at odds with social custom from the very first moments that they picked up their pens to write. What is interesting, and perhaps surprising, however, is the way that today's critics replicate the charge against Barbauld that she is not woman enough. In the last five years, since Barbauld has been 'recovered' and placed (tenuously) into the academy's revised Romantic canon, critics have found fault with her failure to stand up for women's rights in any kind of consistent or explicit way. This is, admittedly, an inversion of Croker's accusation against her, but nineteenth- and twentieth-century critics share an impulse to fix Barbauld on the political spectrum, and to somehow make her gender identity continuous and compatible with her written material.

No recent critics of whom I am aware have intended to belittle Barbauld and her work. In general, today's critics tend to want to 'rescue' Barbauld from her own conservatism, demonstrating how she should rightfully be recognized as one of the mothers of British Romanticism. But these accolades are tempered by a wistful disappointment that Barbauld could not quite live up to the image that critics currently create for women writers from the Wollstonecraftian era. Marlon Ross, in a chapter relevantly entitled 'The Birth of a Tradition: Making Cultural Space for Feminine Poetry,' writes, 'The limits of Barbauld's feminism are also the limits of her poetics. A woman who cannot grant women absolute equal rights with men also cannot grant them the right to write freely from the dictates of their own desire.'[2] Embedded in this critique is an assumption that desire is somehow outside political strictures, and that

women who do not transcend social boundaries around gender roles will not be able to write authentically. In the final sentences of a section on Wollstonecraft and Barbauld in *The Muses of Resistance*, Donna Landry praises Barbauld's recognition of the importance of women's work; but a moment later, she concludes, 'The boldness of such a recognition cannot be sustained. Barbauld's text remains marked by contradictions that she shares with other women writers.'[3] Here, the contradictions that mark the text (**'The Rights of Woman'**), even though they are understandable and explainable, are the endpoint of the discussion. William Keach, who has been instrumental in situating Barbauld in the revised Romantic canon, is sensitive to the precarious position of women writers during the period. Specifically, he is interested in what he calls the status of 'double dissent,' in which dissenting women such as Barbauld are encouraged to think of themselves as the spiritual equals of men within their religion, and yet are expected to subordinate themselves just the same to the men in their lives (fathers, brothers, ministers, etc.). Despite noting this complex positionality, Keach, like Ross, finds fault with Barbauld: 'The limits of Barbauld's position of "double dissent" are evident throughout **"The Right of Woman"** [*sic*]: her own active participation in the public sphere of political as well as literary discourse, based again and again on an appeal to "common" human nature and universal human rights, falters when faced with the prospect of breaking from middle-class norms of gender.'[4]

My intention is not to argue that Ross and Keach are uniformly wrong in their critique of Barbauld's complicated relationship to feminism, but I do think it important to consider the emphasis here. If so many critics are so keen to note the complex of competing personal and political circumstances that subsume the writing of women from the Romantic period, why are they not interested in reading that contradiction within women's texts? In other words, Ross and Keach attempt to resolve the paradox of the conservative woman writer by explaining away her traditional values as failures, limits, stumbles in her otherwise groundbreaking career. I do not want to dispute that gender inflects women's writing; quite conversely, I am suggesting that we must not be so quick to fix women such as Barbauld (and this paradigm could of course be extended to other women writers of the period such as Hannah More and Felicia Hemans) to particular points on any historical-political spectrum, but we must instead allow the contradictions in their lives and work to signify in new and sometimes unstable ways. In 'Women Readers, Women Writers,' Stuart Curran discusses nineteenth-century women writers who earned a good living from writing that extolled traditional values. 'Rather than see inconsistency, or worse, hypocrisy in such attitudes,' he writes, 'we should perhaps recognize the priority of the enveloping cultural contradictions within which these figures labored.'[5] Though many critics have delineated the qualities of these contradictions, none have extended these contradictions into a theory of reading that can offer productive interpretations of the works of these women writers. The aim of this essay is to use the self-contradiction inherent in the work of Anna Barbauld to sketch a new, nonjudgmental, complex vision of 'conservative' Romantic women writers.

Barbauld's essay **'Against Inconsistency in Our Expectations'** starts with a plea: 'As most of the unhappiness in the world arises rather from disappointed desires than from positive evil, it is of utmost consequence to attain just notions of the laws and order of the universe, that we may not vex ourselves with fruitless wishes, or give way to groundless and unreasonable discontent.'[6] This statement characterizes the Mrs. Barbauld that critics—of both the nineteenth and twentieth centuries—have known and loved to discuss: committed to order, to social position, to good cheer, to the idea that there are, in fact, 'just laws' which, when learned and memorized, can guide humanity on its course to heightened morality and civility. But a small contradiction, one that grows throughout the essay as a whole, begins to emerge. There is (mostly) no positive evil, and yet there are laws and order. This is a quintessentially Barbauldian maneuver, in which that which masks as the most fixed, stable, regulatory truth is in fact revealed to be fluctuating, man-made, temporal, etc. 'Consider this world as a great mart of commerce,' she writes, 'where . . . riches, ease, tranquility, fame, integrity, [and] knowledge' are our 'commodities.'[7] On the one hand, this certainly suggests an ordered world comprised of purchasable values, but on the other, it associates lofty, meritorious notions such as integrity and fame with products that can be acquired by essentially vulgar people. In fact, she suggests that a 'mean, dirty fellow' isn't unlikely to be wealthy: 'Not in the least. He made himself a mean, dirty fellow for that very end.'[8] But the essay isn't just a simple attack on the seedy ladder climbers in high society. It goes farther than that, suggesting that the premise that social laws derive from self-evident and organic truths belies the discontinuity between inner worth and outer worth, indeed between the inner and outer in general, underlying those very laws.

'Nature,' Barbauld writes, 'is much more frugal than to heap together all manner of shining qualities in one glaring mass. Like a judicious painter, she endeavors to preserve a certain unity of style and coloring in her pieces.'[9] Here, Nature exists through a metaphor in which she is compared to a human; the idea that the world is a man-made market economy and not a divinely inspired Pope-ian universe is strengthened. In addition, the equation of Nature and the 'judicious painter' de-naturalizes the natural itself, invoking not a spontaneous and wild divine energy but a cultured and cautious human artificer. 'There are combinations of moral qualities which never can take place but in idea,' Barbauld writes, suggesting that the urge to merge conflicting dreams can always only be literary (for what is an idea if it is not, like language, the sign or representation of a thing that is separate from itself?). But this is where she fully reveals her paradox. Though the thrust of the essay is undoubtedly conservative in that it does, on one level, provide a matrix upon which human beings can grid themselves into classes, occupations, genders, it also simultaneously reveals that grid to be artificial, culturally constructed, and enticingly transgressable.

In **'On Female Studies,'** an essay written as a series of letters to a young woman friend, Barbauld treads a thin line between an argument in favor of women's rationality, and one that supports the view of women as primarily sentimental creatures. 'From books, from conversation, from learned instructors,' she writes, 'she will gather the flower of every science; and her mind, in assimilating everything to itself, will adorn it with new graces.'[10] The flower-gathering metaphor would have struck a chord with her contemporaries, as botany was one of the few sciences in which women were encouraged to participate. And the diction of 'adorning' and 'grace' also suggests a female-appropriate activity, related to decorating, ornamentation, and holy virtue. But embedded in this traditional word choice is an untraditional message, for botany is *not* the science (or at least not the *only* science) being discussed here, nor is this a tract about women's dress or women's moral fiber. Instead, the diction cloaks a remarkable vision of female education. Indeed, the essay suggests that women, rational creatures, should have access to science, history, etc., but it also suggests that such subjects, when learned by women, will be fundamentally altered. On one level, this asserts that the truths of science are produced by the mind, and, more significantly, are malleable and impermanent (and in post-Enlightenment Britain, this would have been an unsettling claim from anyone, let alone a woman). On another level, it asserts that science is not an essentially masculine discipline, and that it can and will be feminized by women who study it. This does not necessarily endorse an essentializing concept of separate spheres; Barbauld's attention to the way that external truth and gendered disciplines are constructed by human minds instead suggests that such separate spheres are infinitely permeable, and anything but distinct.

In the conclusion to this essay, Barbauld again cloaks a potentially radical revisioning of 'truth,' 'gender,' and 'order' in traditional, conservative rhetoric. 'The modesty which prevents [the learned woman] from an unnecessary display of what she knows,' she writes, 'will cause it to be supposed that her knowledge is deeper than in reality it is: as when the landscape is seen through the veil of a mist, the bounds of the horizon are hid.'[11] For all of its self-contradictions, this is a nearly dizzying passage. The 'modesty' that prevents women from appearing too learned is partially the social stricture that quietly asserts that proper nineteenth-century women were not supposed to be well-educated in certain fields. And yet, Barbauld claims, by hiding her education, a woman can actually appear even more educated than she actually is, which certainly violates the limits and boundaries set up around women's proper fields of study (morality, *belles lettres,* botany, etc.). Barbauld demonstrates how women can use the very limits that bind them as the vehicles that carry them out of their feminine spheres. The veil of modesty is in this scenario that which fully unveils the woman as a scholar. In her study of Barbauld's poetry, Laura Mandell notes what she calls the 'contradictory potential' of Barbauld's use of personification, in that it can both 'serve and subvert ideological mystification.'[12] This is, I would argue, precisely the potential that characterizes her prose writing in general.

Though I have so far been primarily concerned with Barbauld's oft-ignored prose writings, the themes I am addressing can be found throughout her poetry as well. In **'To a Lady, with some painted Flowers,'** Barbauld confuses the natural and the artificial:

> Flowers to the fair: To you these flowers I bring,
> And strive to greet you with an earlier spring.
> Flowers sweet, and gay, and delicate like you;
> Emblems of innocence, and beauty too.[13]

As the title tells us, the flowers are painted, but this leaves much still to be determined. Is the narrator bringing a painting of flowers to a real lady, or is the lady part of the painting as well? The flowers are, like the lady, sweet, gay, and delicate, but could the 'too' in the third verse suggest that, *like the lady,* the flowers are *emblems* of beauty and innocence? The flowers, 'born for pleasure and delight alone,' are chillingly similar to the woman, as both emerge as representations for something else. 'Nor blush, my fair,' the poem concludes, 'to own you copy these; / Your best, your sweetest empire is to please.'[14] Here, the woman is a copy of the flowers, inverting the traditional metaphor that would place the flowers as vehicle to the woman's tenor. But as we know, the flowers themselves are copies of *real* flowers. In a sense, Barbauld jostles the very notion of priority or originality, opting instead to paint a world where artifice inhabits even the most natural of spaces: the woman's body and the poem. The flowers are called 'lovely without art,' which rings ironic for, of course, the flowers *are* art, that is, painted. If the poem reinscribes a feminine stereotype, all flowers, grace, and ornament, it also deconstructs such a stereotype by revealing its arti-

ficial core. The allusion to women's 'empire' in the final line catches the spirit of the Barbauldian paradox: through a self-conscious interrogation of the mechanisms that confine women to their feminine graces, women can become powerful. The paradox does not relieve women's oppression by inverting the male-female power differential, nor does it step outside of its confining culture; instead, it parodically plays with the constructedness of the social order, revealing its instability, its unnaturalness, and its arbitrary 'nature.'

This paradox seems particularly evident in **'The Rights of Woman,'** a poem that has troubled many twentieth-century feminists. It is most often read as an anti-Wollstonecraftian response to the woman question, and a pointed attack on Wollstonecraft herself, who had attacked **'To a Lady, with some painted Flowers'** in the *Vindication.* Though Wollstonecraft and Barbauld were noted allies on a number of political platforms, William McCarthy and Elizabeth Kraft have this to say about **'The Rights of Woman'**: 'It need not be read as representing ALB's [Anna Laetitia Barbauld's] considered judgment on women's rights; rather, it is an outburst of anger at Wollstonecraft.'[15] In order to preserve Barbauld's feminist potential, McCarthy and Kraft feel impelled to treat Barbauld's only poem which explicitly addresses women's rights as a mere 'outburst of anger' by an insulted lady. I cannot, of course, discount the possibility that Barbauld was peeved at Wollstonecraft, but I think it quite likely that there is more going on in this complicated poem. The poem certainly advocates that woman 'resume thy native empire o'er the breast,' suggesting that she is most adept at ruling the sentimental, emotional side of the world. And yet, the poem also constantly calls attention to how women achieve their femininity, their access to special emotional powers: not through a biological assignment of gendered characteristics but through an elaborate system of performance and ornamentation. 'Go forth arrayed in panoply divine,' Barbauld writes, 'That angel pureness which admits no stain.'[16] Is the pureness intrinsic to the woman, or has she arrayed herself in that, as well? And though the pureness *admits* of no stain, is this perhaps a cover for what is, underneath, slightly imperfect or marred? 'Gird thyself with grace,' the poem continues, again suggesting that the most natural of feminine qualities not only has to be put on, but that it must be put on like the armor of a knight. 'Thou mayest command, but never canst be free,' may suggest, as many readers understand, that women should abandon their unladylike quest for dominance and power, but it might also suggest that hierarchy in general always inscribes a binary opposition which holds captive both of its poles. As opposing elements in the poem are aligned (as in the girding of the grace), Barbauld melts the binaristic system itself; the loss of separate rights, while admittedly a potential setback for nineteenth-century women on the cusp of a major feminist uprising, is less a disappointing failure than a caution to feminists that demanding rights and demanding freedom are not, in fact, the same thing.

Even more popular than **'The Rights of Woman,'** **'Washing-Day'** is certainly the Barbauld poem which is most anthologized today. Critic Anne Mellor has suggested that Barbauld's celebration of the value of the quotidian, of daily domestic duties and social involvements, helped to turn British literature as a whole towards a national literary taste that favored domestic life and matrimonial happiness.[17] Though Mellor is passingly interested in what she calls Barbauld's 'study of narratology,' revealed in the poet's groundbreaking outlining of omniscient, first person, and epistolary styles, she does not significantly relate the celebration of the everyday with the self-conscious attention to style in Barbauld's texts. **'Washing-Day,'** I would argue, is as concerned with connecting the role of poetry to domestic labor as it is with investing washing day with epic importance. The poem's opening, which takes up the question of the poem's meter, claims that the gossipy domestic muses speak in 'slip-shod measure,' which belies the near-perfect iambic-pentameter of **'Washing-Day.'** This is the first quiet suggestion that this poem and its subject, while masking as the banal and the daily, are in fact worthy of the formal literary tradition that it is often said by critics to 'mock.' In fact, the poem enters into a complex dialectic; on the one hand, it mocks itself and its subject through hyperbolic comparisons (of a housewife on washing day and Guatzimozin roasting on burning coals), but on the other hand, its own form recalls the epic form of *Paradise Lost,* casting the washing day into a pre-eighteenth-century-epic context. In other words, it is impossible to know whether the form is ironic here, since its ironies are potentially relieved by the very form that creates them.

As the lonely male character wanders onto the scene of the poem, he receives a cold reception from both the washing and **'Washing-Day'**: 'Crossing lines / Shall mar thy musings, as the wet cold sheet / Flaps in thy face abrupt . . . / Looks, blank at best, and stinted courtesy shall he receive.'[18] The diction here ('lines,' 'sheet,' 'blank') refers *both* to the wash and to lines of poetry, written upon blank sheets, or written, as this poem is, in blank verse. The wash and the poem are both inaccessible to men, and they are positioned as an obstacle to his pure musings. I would suggest that this is a radical departure from what is conventionally called 'British Romanticism,' in that poetry is revealed not to be a connection to the inner landscape of man's mind or soul, but to the exterior world of object, of domestic labor. Lines cross and looks are blank; indeed the poem is confusing to the musing, self-indulgent mind. The poem only makes sense, is only readable, when the reader's identity is subsumed by the physical presence of the laundry. When the crossed lines are clotheslines and the blank looks are simple signs of the washers' annoyance, then the reader can avoid the insult of being slapped in the face, like the male character. That the male character is called 'thee' intensifies the poem's delicious game of cat and mouse with the reader; we must outwit the poem's interpellation in order to turn 'thee' and 'thy' into 'friend,' 'he,' and, finally, 'the unlucky guest.'

The final lines of the poem return again to the question of the connection between washing and the poem about washing: 'Then should I sit me down, and ponder much / Why washings were. Sometimes thro' hollow bole / Of pipe amused be blew, and sent aloft / The floating bubbles, little dreaming then / To see, Mongolfier, thy silken ball / Ride buoyant thro' the clouds—so near approach / The sports of children and the toils of men. / Earth, air, and sky, and ocean, hath its bubbles, / And verse is one of them—this most of all.'[19] Elizabeth Kraft argues that this finale demonstrates how the imagination can transcend the domestic context.[20] This seems likely, but I think it only part of the significance of these rich and complex lines. First of all, the young girl who witnesses the chaos of washing day becomes the grown-up narrator who remembers sitting down to ponder why washings were. This retrospective is set against the metaphor of Mongolfier's (for Montgolfier's) balloon, which can only be made by the elder of the two (yet single) narrative perspectives. What strikes me as compelling here is that the bubble precedes the balloon in the poem's narrative sequence, and that the balloon is cast as that which is like a bubble (it 'so near approach[es] / The sports of children'). A tension exists between the priority of the bubble and its attendant status as 'original' or 'ideal,' and the ensuing fruition of the bubble's potential in the rise of the silken ball. Barbauld disrupts the order between tenor and vehicle, pitting chronological time (the priority of the bubble) against human history (the triumph of the balloon). By taking the historical triumph of the balloon and casting it as an attempt to achieve a kind of bubble-hood, Barbauld disrupts rational conceptions of progress, associated here with both the science of aviation and the literary-esque 'dreaming' of the male muser, instead investing the original object with significance. Metaphors generally depend on a detachment from thing-ness, an imprecise discursive maneuver in which an original morphs into something else, while still retaining its own discrete identity. But Barbauld, by playing with the very concepts of priority, chronology, and progress changes metaphor from a move to the figurative into a move toward the literal.

By calling verse a 'bubble,' Barbauld does not mean that verse is frivolous or childish. Instead, I think she takes poetry itself and transforms it from a discourse on the egotistical sublime into an incarnation of the quotidian; this is not merely a shift in subject matter, but a formal, stylistic shift as well. For Barbauld, **'Washing-Day'** is a poem which thematizes its own struggle to transform parody and metaphor into both an inversion of meaning (washing is *not* being 'mocked' in this mock-heroic epic; bubbles do *not* strive to be balloons in this poem's comparison) and an investigation of poetry's forms and devices. In this sense, to say that **'Washing-Day'** is a poem about daily life is true, but we can also extend this argument, saying that the poem is about the quotidian quality of poetry itself. Consider, as well, that washing day is part of a domestic routine of maintaining order in the household, and yet, simultaneously, it is the day, as the poem demonstrates, during which that same household is thrust into chaos. The poem suggests that the very stuff of order, order itself, even, carries the seed of its own undoing. Barbauld has it both ways here, conforming to proper themes for women poets and strengthening the separate sphere that contains women's roles while also rebelling against these very themes and revealing the constructedness of the supposedly natural condition of gender.

Barbauld's ***Eighteen Hundred and Eleven,*** a poem for which she was attacked during her time because of its 'treasonous' overtones, makes a similar claim about order: 'Fairest flowers expand but to decay; / The worm is in thy core, thy glories pass away; / Arts, arms and wealth destroy the fruits they bring.'[21] The poem is concerned with Britain's corruption in the years of the Napoleonic wars, and Barbauld, who ultimately seems to end the poem by throwing in the towel on Britain and turning to America for regenerative hope, was condemned by period critics for injecting doubt into what was supposed to have been an era of seamless nationalism. But 'fairest flowers,' though here a clear allusion to Britain, might also be the ornaments and signs that define women in culture; Barbauld suggests that such trappings make women what they are, as well as ensure the ensuing demise of the same women. The worm in the core is both an allusion to Satan, merged as he is with Eve's purity, and masculinity, which as femininity's opposite is also inextricably part of the 'feminine's' definition. In other words, if we look at the poem in the context not of the Napoleonic wars but of Barbauld's literary works as a whole, we can trace the development of a paradox in which the status quo is revealed to be transient and corrupt even at the height of its invisibility or naturalness.

'Thy world, Columbus, shall be free,' the poem ends. But does this suggest that America will somehow be freed from the worm in the flower dilemma? Isn't America raised here as precisely the 'fairest flower?' It, too, will have its fall, as all systems must. Far from being a fatalist, though, Barbauld instead suggests that hope is possible and appropriate, for as systems fail, new opportunities arise which, though culturally pro-

duced and eminently fallible, can resituate the human mind into a context that feels freer and more comfortable. Critic Sarah Robbins, who writes on Barbauld's many children's tales, says of Barbauld's moralizing fables, 'Barbauld's texts assume that becoming cultured is essential to being truly human.'[22] Robbins characterizes becoming cultured as learning proper, civilized codes of behavior, but I would argue that for Barbauld, these kinds of efforts to mold the wild child into the perfect English citizen are, ironically, the kinds of efforts which characterize the human compulsion to control anxiety through the building of systems, orders, and identities. In this sense, then, culture and natural 'humanness' are opposites *and* inseparably continuous. 'America' is not a land apart from culture, but a symbol of the human compulsion to dismantle and rebuild temporal social orders.

In his article, 'We Hoped the *Woman* Was Going to Appear,' William McCarthy describes Barbauld's unhappiness with the status of women, suggesting that her use of idealization in her so-called 'pattern' poems (or 'character' poems) is her 'usual form of psychic defense—compensatory fantasy.'[23] This sets up Barbauld's view of gender as that which must be escaped—in a kind of delusional way—through poetry. I would argue that her fantasy does not compensate for a 'real,' unsolvable problem, but makes concrete interventions into the characterization of the 'real.' Just as she predicts the fall of her country in ***Eighteen Hundred and Eleven,*** Barbauld's texts envision the most solid of systems as deeply flawed already, and these flaws are illuminated, rather than eliminated, in her fantastic works. In 'Romanticism and the Colonization of the Feminine,' Alan Richardson notes the appropriation of a feminine sensibility by soul-searching male Romantic writers such as Wordsworth and Shelley. He wonders (somewhat facetiously, no doubt), 'Why didn't [women writers of the time] simply claim these characteristics as, after all, their own and become (or create) Romantic heroines in their own right?'[24] Anna Barbauld's texts offer a strong set of responses to such a question. First, her work takes issue with the 'after all,' since Barbauld more often than not challenges the naturalizing assumptions that comprise the foundation of separate spheres rhetoric. Second, her work is consistently occupied with the slippage, demonstrated here by Richardson, between the heroine/the story or poem and the writer/her textual production. Though Richardson seems unaware of the meatiness of this slip, Barbauld continually asks how her work is related to its repercussions in the real world. Today's critics have been quick to embrace Barbauld as a kind of missing link between Enlightenment rationality and Victorian self-improvement, and they have praised her, too, for her groundbreaking efforts in opening Romantic writing to the woman's voice. But in both cases, critics have tried to explain away her conservatism as a maternal relic of the good domestic teacher or as an odd, inexplicable accompaniment to her feminism. Instead, I think it time that we recognize that Barbauld herself was interested in the paradoxes which inhabit much of her work, and that she has thematized over and over again the tricky situation of speaking out against the master in the master's own language.

Notes

1. William McCarthy and Elizabeth Kraft, eds., *The Poems of Anna Leticia Barbauld* (Athens: The University of Georgia Press, 1994), 310.

2. Marlon Ross, *The Contours of Masculine Desire: Romanticism and the Rise of Women's Poetry* (New York: Oxford University Press, 1989), 217.

3. Donna Landry, *The Muses of Resistance: Laboring-Class Women's Poetry in Britain, 1739-1796* (Cambridge: Cambridge University Press, 1990), 273.

4. William Keach, 'Barbauld, Romanticism, and the Survival of Dissent,' in *Romanticism and Gender,* ed. Anne K. Mellor (New York: Routledge, 1993), 56.

5. Stuart Curran, 'Women readers, women writers,' in *The Cambridge Companion to British Romanticism,* ed. Stuart Curran. (Cambridge: Cambridge University Press, 1993), 190.

6. Grace A. Ellis, *A Selection from the Poems and Prose Writings of Mrs. Anna Læticia Barbauld* (Boston: James R. Osgood and Company, 1874), 234.

7. Ellis, 235-6.

8. Ellis, 238.

9. Ellis, 242.

10. Ellis, 286.

11. Ellis, 286-7.

12. Laura Mandell, '"Those Limbs Disjointed of Gigantic Power": Barbauld's Personifications and the (Mis)Attribution of Political Agency,' *Studies in Romanticism* 37, no. 4 (1998): 27-41.

13. McCarthy and Kraft, 77.

14. McCarthy and Kraft, 77.

15. McCarthy and Kraft, 289.

16. McCarthy and Kraft, 121.

17. Anne K. Mellor, 'A Criticism of Their Own: Romantic Women Literary Critics,' in *Questioning Romanticism,* ed. John Beer (Baltimore: The Johns Hopkins University Press, 1995) 32, 36.

18. McCarthy and Kraft, 134.

19. McCarthy and Kraft, 135.

20. Elizabeth Kraft, 'Anna Letitia Barbauld's "Washing-Day" and the Montgolfier Balloon,' *Literature & History* 4, no. 2 (1995): 33.

21. McCarthy and Kraft, 160.

22. Sarah Robbins, '*Lessons for Children* and Teaching Mothers: Mrs. Barbauld's Primer for the Textual Construction of Middle-Class Domestic Pedagogy,' *The Lion and the Unicorn* 17, no. 2 (1993): 139.

23. William McCarthy, 'We Hoped the *Woman* Was Going to Appear: Repression, Desire, and Gender in Anna Letitia Barbauld's Early Poems,' in *Romantic Women Writers: Voices and Countervoices,* eds. Paula R. Feldman and Theresa M. Kelly. (Hanover: University Press of New England, 1995), 134.

24. Alan Richardson, 'Romanticism and the Colonization of the Feminine,' in *Romanticism and Feminism,* ed. Anne K. Mellor. (Bloomington: Indiana University Press, 1988), 21.

William McCarthy and Elizabeth Kraft (essay date 2002)

SOURCE: McCarthy, William, and Elizabeth Kraft. Introduction to *Anna Letitia Barbauld: Selected Poetry and Prose,* edited by William McCarthy and Elizabeth Kraft, pp. 11-32. Peterborough, Ontario, Canada: Broadview Press Ltd., 2002.

[*In the following essay, McCarthy and Kraft consider Barbauld's reputation as an author during her lifetime, appraising her influence on the development of British Romantic literature in the early nineteenth century. The authors contend that Barbauld deserves an exhaustive critical reassessment by modern scholars, one stripped of the preconceived notions of gender and class that distorted earlier evaluations of her work.*]

If we could travel back to the year 1800 and ask who were the leading British writers of the day, the answer would not be William Wordsworth or Samuel Taylor Coleridge or William Blake. The answer instead would include, on anybody's short list, Anna Letitia Barbauld. Her début book, *Poems* (1773), had been greeted as an important event in the world of letters. "We congratulate the public on so great an accession to the literary world, as the genius and talents of Miss Aikin," wrote the *Monthly Review.* "We very seldom have an opportunity of bestowing praise with so much justice, and so much pleasure" ([Woodfall], p. 137). Mary Scott and David Garrick paid her tributes in verse; Elizabeth Montagu, "Queen of the Bluestockings," sought her acquaintance; and younger women, such as the future poet Mary Robinson, read her enthusiastically. The young Coleridge walked forty miles in order to meet Barbauld; the young Wordsworth imitated her in his early poems. In 1798 *The Lady's Monthly Museum* asserted Barbauld's poetic pre-eminence without reserve: her poems "are now in the possession of every person who has any pretensions to taste, and every library in the kingdom; and public suffrage has amply ratified their claim to distinction" (p. 173).

As a poet, Barbauld can claim to be considered a founder of British Romanticism. She was no less important—and, if anything, she exerted still greater influence—as an innovating writer for children. This part of her work originated in experimental teaching at the school she and her husband ran at Palgrave, in Suffolk, from 1774 to 1785. Her *Lessons for Children* and *Hymns in Prose for Children* profoundly affected infant pedagogy and the culture of childhood for a full century at least, both in England and the United States. *Lessons,* a reading primer, directly influenced the theories and practices of Maria Edgeworth and her father, and its impact on nineteenth-century readers is suggested by the fact that the poet Elizabeth Barrett Browning remembered *Lessons* so well that she could still quote its opening page at the age of thirty-nine (McCarthy, "Mother of All Discourses," p. 196). Our headnote to *Hymns in Prose* [*Hymns in Prose for Children*] attempts to sketch the even greater impact of *Hymns* on its readers. *Lessons* and *Hymns* were reprinted often during the nineteenth century.

Barbauld was also an admired essayist, regarded by her contemporaries as superior to Joseph Addison and nearly the equal of Samuel Johnson. In her essays she addressed leading issues of her time—ethics, esthetics, education, even political economy—on equal terms with writers such as David Hume and Edmund Burke. Both in verse and prose, she dared to engage in political debate, urging major concerns of her social group, middle-class Protestant Dissent. She stirred and shocked her contemporaries by her intense polemics in favor of religious liberty (*An Address to the Opposers of the Repeal of the Corporation and Test Acts*) and against the British government's entry into war with the French Republic (*Sins of Government, Sins of the Nation*). She vigorously condemned British participation in the international slave trade (*An Epistle to William Wilberforce* [*Epistle to William Wilberforce, Esq., on the Rejection of the Bill for Abolishing the Slave Trade*]), and her last publication, the poem *Eighteen Hundred and Eleven,* incurred obloquy and political defamation for protesting against the apparently unending and catastrophic war with France.

As if these achievements were not enough, Barbauld also performed with distinction as a literary critic. She

wrote the first biography of the novelist Samuel Richardson and edited the first collection of his letters; she produced a major body of commentary on the English novel and, like Samuel Johnson before her, lent her name and pen to a large-scale canon-making enterprise, *The British Novelists,* twenty-eight novelists gathered in fifty volumes.

Taken altogether, Barbauld's career can be described as that of a typical "person of letters"; she belongs to the first generation of professional women writers in England whose work was received with unqualified admiration. *The Lady's Monthly Museum* was one of many witnesses to Barbauld's leading rank among her peers: "This lady has been recognised for many years by the public . . . as one of its best benefactors, for contributing . . . very liberally both to instruct and reform the community. And we fondly trust, she will yet long continue to delight and cultivate the national taste, in the direction and improvement of which her labours have already been so singularly useful" (p. 170).

But Barbauld can also be characterized, in the phrase coined by Antonio Gramsci, as an "organic intellectual," an intellectual who articulates the issues of her own social class at a time when that class is asserting its claims to power and respect. Barbauld's class was the middle class, and she became an outstanding spokeswoman for it at its insurgent, liberal best. In what she liked to call the "middle station of life," she saw opportunities to create better, happier, and freer human beings than existing society allowed. To create a new kind of human being was the main conscious project of the Enlightenment; Jean-Jacques Rousseau's Émile, brought up to be ignorant of everything he has not personally experienced and to dismiss with contempt the "prejudices" of society, is the classic, but also the most extreme, product of that ambition. Barbauld, less ostentatious than Rousseau, and with a much more grounded sense of what can actually be done, never proclaimed herself an innovator. Nonetheless, as the Victorian feminist Clara Balfour perceived, Barbauld in her quiet way undertook nothing less than the reeducation of her society (*Working Women* [*Working Women of the Last Half Century*], p. 6).

DISSENT

Of defining importance for Barbauld's outlook and project was the fact that she was the daughter and grand-daughter of Presbyterian schoolmasters. Doctrinally, Presbyterianism originated as a Scottish version of Calvinism. As formulated in the Westminster Confession (1647), its creed declared the total sinfulness of human nature and the consequent impossibility of good thoughts or deeds without direct intervention by God. Human beings having, in Adam's disobedience, sinned against God, they deserved nothing but divine wrath and punishment; only free grace (not earned—earning it would be impossible—but given by God for His mysterious purposes) could save humans from damnation. It was believed that rather few would be saved, and they only by throwing themselves on the mercy of Jesus Christ (Mautner, "Introduction," p. 10).

During the eighteenth century many Presbyterians receded from these doctrines ("gloomy" doctrines, as the receders were apt to call them). Under the guidance of the Scottish ethical philosopher Francis Hutcheson (1694-1746), two or three generations of recovering Calvinists—among whom were Barbauld's parents and grandparents—learned to regard human beings as the fundamentally good creatures of a beneficent Creator, and to believe that humans could achieve salvation by loving God and (in practice, much the same thing) acting benevolently towards their fellow beings. Barbauld built this revised, optimistic faith into *Hymns in Prose for Children,* making it the first influential religious primer for children that offered a kindly and loving religion. In 1792 she summed up this benevolent faith in the eloquent closing pages of a pamphlet, *Remarks on Mr. Gilbert Wakefield's Enquiry into the Expediency and Propriety of Public or Social Worship*:

> When a good man . . . is about to resign his soul into the hands of his Maker, he ought to do it, not only with a reliance on his mercy, but his justice; a generous confidence and pious resignation should be blended in his deportment. It does not become him to pay the blasphemous homage of deprecating the wrath of God, when he ought to throw himself into the arms of his love. . . . The age which has demolished dungeons, rejected torture, and given so fair a prospect of abolishing the iniquity of the slave trade, cannot long retain among its articles of belief the gloomy perplexities of Calvinism, and the heart-withering perspective of cruel and never-ending punishments.

> (pp. 71-72, 75-76)

In the face of advancing Methodism, with its re-emphasis on Original Sin and human worthlessness, these sentiments were not just retrospective; they were again timely.[1] Doctrinally, Barbauld became—and remains today—an inspiring voice in behalf of the ideal of human self-respect.

Barbauld's co-religionists also adopted various opinions regarding the composition of the deity; instead of the orthodox Trinity (Father, Son—Jesus Christ—and Holy Ghost), they were inclined to regard God as a single being and Jesus as a created figure, perhaps divine or perhaps only an inspired human. There is little evidence that this particular issue mattered much to Barbauld; she wrote that "unity of *character* in what we adore, is much more essential than unity of person" (*Remarks* [*Remarks on Mr. Gilbert Wakefield's Enquiry into the Expediency and Propriety of Public or Social Wor-*

ship], pp. 70-71; our italics). She cared more about what she almost called God's personality than about the number of aspects to attribute to him. One of the leading arguments in her 1775 essay **"[Thoughts] on the Devotional Taste"** is that theological disputation about the nature of God chills religious emotion and withers the believer's sense of relation to God as to a person. Although by no means anti-intellectual (she despised the "noise and nonsense" of popular evangelicalism), Barbauld had more than sufficient exposure to theological discussion during the years when her father was tutor in Divinity at Warrington Academy, and she wanted a large counterbalance of devotional feeling and imagination.

Socially, the consequences of being Presbyterian depended on where in Britain one lived. Barbauld's Aikin ancestors, as long as they lived in Scotland, were members of the established (i.e. legally supported) Presbyterian Kirk. As soon as her grandfather emigrated to England, however, his Presbyterianism condemned him to minority status as a second-class citizen, a Dissenter from the Church of England. There was a long tradition, fading but not dead—and galvanized into disturbing life in the 1790s—of regarding Dissenters collectively as threats to the state because some of their sectarian ancestors in the mid-seventeenth century had led a revolution against Church and King. Hence, laws restricting their liberties and acting to their prejudice remained on the books. Dissenters could not serve in the military, accept an appointive office under the Crown, or hold elective municipal office unless they "conformed" to the Church of England by taking the sacrament there. They could not take degrees at Oxford or Cambridge without "subscribing" to—that is, swearing that they believed—the creed of the English Church, embodied in its Thirty-Nine Articles. They were obliged to pay tithes to support the Established Church even though they did not attend it. If they took positions as schoolmasters they were obliged (until 1779) to subscribe to parts of the Thirty-Nine Articles. Their churches—or chapels, as they were called—received no regular public support (unlike the Church of England, which owned a great deal of property and was publicly funded as well); Dissenting clergy had to live on the salaries voted them by their congregations. Many became schoolteachers in order to eke out their incomes.

The line of work most open to Dissenters was commerce; "we are a mercantile people," Barbauld remarked accurately in *An Address to the Opposers* [*An Address to the Opposers of the Repeal of the Corporation and Test Acts*] (p. 270 below). Whether they were shopkeepers, brewers, bankers, rich factory-owners or merchants who could afford to buy country houses, Dissenters regarded themselves as middle-class. They liked to think of the "middle station" (as the philosopher David Hume called it [*Selected Essays*, p. 6]) as especially favorable to virtue, both personal and political. Like other groups experienced in political subjection, they were sensitive to questions of political equity and personal rights. Joseph Priestley stated the connection succinctly in a 1774 *Address to Protestant Dissenters of all Denominations*: "*Religious liberty,* indeed, is the immediate ground on which you stand, but this cannot be maintained except upon the basis of *civil liberty*" (p. [3]). Thus, while the first demand of nearly all English Dissenters was an end to the laws that discriminated against them, many also sympathized with the American colonists in their complaints about being taxed without being represented in Parliament; most supported domestic efforts to reform Parliamentary representation by redistricting Britain; most supported abolition of the slave trade, and many became enthusiasts for the French Revolution and agitated against war with France. Political liberalism could be an act of Hutchesonian benevolence, too; one Dissenter in 1795 traced his partiality to the French Revolution directly back to his experience of hearing Francis Hutcheson's weekly lectures on Christianity. Hutcheson, he recalled, taught that Christianity was "the religion of Truth & Reason: wch can have no other enemies, but the irrational & the wicked. From this the transition to me seems natural & easy to the enlarged principles on wch the French Revolution was first founded" (Kenrick, Letter [Letter to Timothy Kenrick, 7 June 1795]). Anna Barbauld's political liberalism was that of her group. Her expressions of it, in *An Address to the Opposers of the Repeal of the Corporation and Test Acts* and *Sins of Government, Sins of the Nation,* were hers alone, matched in eloquence perhaps only by the very different writings of Tom Paine.

EDUCATION

Barbauld grew up surrounded by the boys at her father's school at Kibworth. At three and a half she acquired a brother, John, over whom she early attained to lifelong influence, and who encouraged her invaluably in her literary career. Her youthful surroundings accustomed her to dealing with boys; when she and Rochemont Barbauld opened Palgrave School in 1774, she must have felt quite at home.

Educating boys was attractive not only because it was familiar. It offered scope for Barbauld's "large ambitious wish" (to quote a phrase she used in writing of the Corsican patriot, Pascal Paoli ["**Corsica,**" l. 124]) to intervene in the making of her nation's political and ethical culture. She and her husband regarded education as a patriotic act, and an act of benevolence: "the true patriot," Rochemont wrote, ". . . will gladly undertake a task whereby he may so essentially contribute to the welfare of his country." At the same time, "a prominent feature of his character is love towards the rising generation."[2] In a patriarchy like eighteenth-century En-

gland, the best way to form (or reform) the culture would be to form the citizen, who by definition was male. At Palgrave School, Barbauld set herself to disseminating the culture of benevolence by forming boys into liberal citizens.

One way to describe Barbauld's project is to put it in terms of a text she almost certainly knew well, Francis Hutcheson's outline of "Our Duties toward Mankind" in his *Short Introduction to Moral Philosophy* (1747).[3] Hutcheson's starting-point, the epicenter of human relationships, is the nuclear family. From there, "benevolent affections" spread outward in an ever-widening circle of concern: to all who "are . . . bound by an intercourse of mutual offices," to "acquaintance and neighbours," to "all our Countrymen"; and further, "in men of reflection there is a more extensive good-will embracing all mankind, or all intelligent natures" (*Short Introduction*, p. 67). Barbauld illustrates Hutcheson's widening circle in **"Hymn VIII"** of *Hymns in Prose,* where she begins with a family of father, mother, and children, moves thence to their neighbors, then to the village in which they live, then to the kingdom, then to the world itself, and a vision of inclusiveness which we today would call "multi-cultural": "All are God's family . . . they pray to him in different languages, but he understandeth them all; he heareth them all; he taketh care of all." The next wave in Hutcheson's expanding circle is "a tender compassion toward any that are in distress, with a desire of succouring them" (p. 67); and in **"Hymn VIII"** there follows the address to the enslaved African, "Negro woman, who sittest pining in captivity. . . ."

Barbauld's two children's books, *Lessons for Children* and *Hymns in Prose for Children,* between them track Hutcheson's circle on a larger scale. The opening scene of *Lessons* presents Mother with her two-year-old son on her lap; she is about to induct him into the world of things and the symbols by which humans relate themselves to things and to other creatures. *Lessons* itself, through its four little volumes, performs that induction, leading the child to ever-widening horizons (informational and ethical horizons, and even geographical ones). Then *Hymns in Prose* leads the child reader, a bit older now, to the horizon of the divine. The mediator between child and world in *Lessons* is always Mother; in *Hymns* the mediator is not specifically identified, but the child who had just finished *Lessons* would probably assume the continuity of Mother into *Hymns*. Thus the two books themselves move outward, staging the family (in which, textually, Mother presides) as the place from which the world, and even the universe, is conceptually grasped.

It is even possible to conceive Barbauld's writing career itself in terms of Hutcheson's circle. She begins by constructing a self, an identity or range of possible identities which will embody a disposition capable of diffusing benevolent affection to friends and neighbors—and, not least, to herself. Her early poems may be seen as experiments in the making of such an identity—whether it be the carefree hedonist of **"The Invitation,"** the chastened stoic of **"Hymn to Content,"** or the severely powerful goddess Liberty in **"Corsica."** Publishing these explorations of potential selves, Barbauld incidentally became a model to her women readers, who, in the words of one of them, "feel thy feelings, glow with all thy fires, / Adopt thy thoughts, and pant with thy desires."[4]

Barbauld needed an identity which would be socially allowed to a woman and therefore realizable in action, but which would also make the most of what was socially allowed to woman: an identity which could be not merely realized, but made a stage from which to intervene in her culture. She could not be a doctor like her brother, but she could achieve comparable—indeed, greater—authority in a role to which women were increasingly being summoned: the role of Mother.[5] For Barbauld, motherhood was not a biological role (she never gave birth) but a social one: at Palgrave School she was surrogate mother to some 130 boys besides her adopted son (and actual nephew) Charles. In *Lessons* and *Hymns,* "Mrs. Barbauld" became surrogate mother to thousands of English, American, and even (via translations) European children for a full century.

From Mother through Teacher lay the road to Reformer. Barbauld's first abolitionist statement was the address to "Negro woman" in **"Hymn VIII"** of *Hymns in Prose.* When, after a nine-year hiatus, she reappeared in 1790 as a political writer (to the delight of her co-religionists and the dismay of Establishment people who had accepted her as a poet), Barbauld was simply diffusing her benevolence to, as it were, the next circle out. Her great pamphlets of the 1790s and her two great poems, *An Epistle to William Wilberforce* and *Eighteen Hundred and Eleven,* extend the horizon of Mother's concern to the ends—and the end—of the British Empire.

In the latter poem, Mother might be said to appear as Niobe weeping over her dead children. For, indeed, in some important respects Barbauld's project came to a tragic end. The pupils at her school, who were to be the "rising generation" of a politically reformed nation, were mostly kept out of power by a government which, by 1792, had dug in its heels against reform of any kind and, in 1793, entered upon a twenty-year-long world war against France, the war which *Eighteen Hundred and Eleven* deplores. The liberal values espoused by Barbauld and her group increasingly became suspect; she found herself disliked and even ridiculed by the younger generation whom we now know as "the Romantic Poets." One member of that generation, John Wilson Croker, has often been credited—if that is the

right word—with single-handedly ending her literary career; so abusive was his review of *Eighteen Hundred and Eleven* that it is said to have discouraged her from further efforts to publish.

In the longer run, however, liberal reform did achieve at least some success. The laws against Dissenters were repealed at last in 1828 and 1829. In 1807 Parliament consented to make illegal British participation in the slave trade; in 1834 it emancipated the slaves in the British colonies. Sadly, Barbauld did not live to see most of these achievements. But it is fitting, and she would have rejoiced to know, that the man who drafted the Reform Act of 1832—the act which, after fifty years' agitation for it, redistricted Great Britain to more truly represent the electorate in Parliament—was a man who, when a child, had been her pupil at Palgrave School, and who still, as an adult, remembered her maternal teaching with respect and affection.[6]

"Ingenuous"

The leading project conceived and attempted by the Enlightenment was nothing less than the reinvention of the human being. Hence, from John Locke through Jean-Jacques Rousseau and Maria Edgeworth (and a host of lesser figures), theorizing education stands among the foremost intellectual efforts of the century. Although, as we have remarked, Barbauld was more modest and much less rash than Rousseau, like him she envisions a human being uncorrupted by various social malpractices. Her favorite adjective to describe that person is "ingenuous."

Synonyms for "ingenuous" in Barbauld's sense of the word are "unadulterated," "fresh," "authentic." She seeks, both in herself and in others, to cultivate the disposition (which she assumes exists) to respond "naturally" to experience. The "natural" response is the response that has not been dulled by repetition, smothered by false cleverness, tutored into mere intellectuality, or perverted by self-interest. The ingenuous person responds to experience directly, without equivocation, evasion, self-doubt, or self-consciousness. The emotion is appropriate to the event and is uncluttered by second-guessing. And—in line with Hutchesonian ideas of human goodness—it is a generous, outgoing, sympathetic emotion. If an emotion of joy, it wants to communicate itself to other people, to be shared: "joy," she writes in *Remarks on . . . Social Worship,* "is too brilliant a thing to be confined within our own bosoms" (p. 19). If it is an emotion of sorrow, it wants at once to relieve the suffering to which it responds; it takes the form of Pity, which in Barbauld's allegory (pp. 207-09 below) is represented as the offspring of Sorrow and Love.

Ingenuousness is easily spoiled, however, by social practices which tend to produce shame. In **"Thoughts on the Devotional Taste,"** Barbauld invites us to "observe an ingenuous youth at a well-wrought tragedy. If all around him are moved, he suffers his tears to flow freely; but if a single eye meets him with a glance of contemptuous indifference, he can no longer enjoy his sorrow, he blushes at having wept, and in a moment his heart is shut up to every impression of tenderness" (p. 219 below). Barbauld, we may gather from this telling passage, was deeply sensitive to ridicule (no doubt because she was very good at ridicule herself) and understood its power to shrivel authentic emotion.

Ingenuousness is equally vulnerable to being deadened by habit. A close student of associationist psychology, Barbauld understood that habit has a contradictory character: on one hand, it builds lifelong patterns of response (and that is what she aims to do in **Hymns in Prose**), but on the other, it tends to enervate response by making stimuli overfamiliar. Thus she says to her co-religionists that devotional feeling is vitiated by their habit of theological discussion, which renders the terminology of religion so commonplace that religion loses its emotional force. Among her many reasons for hating war is the effect of war on human sensibility: it hardens human beings by inuring them to atrocities. Emotions themselves can be exhausted by repetition, especially if they have no outlet in action. Hence Barbauld's cool remarks about fictions which inspire pity; readers wear out their capacity for pity on imaginary figures instead of actively helping real-life unfortunates. (She was of course a great reader of novels herself, these views notwithstanding; and in 1810, introducing **The British Novelists,** she asserted with a challenging straightforwardness that she read them for pleasure. In 1810, owning up to *enjoying* novels—instead of pretending to read them for moral lessons—could also be an act of ingenuousness.)

Ingenuousness, as this example may suggest, is not a matter *purely* of emotion; to have social impact, it must inform the moral and intellectual person also. An honest heart sheds tears at the horrific narratives of slave-trading presented in Parliament by William Wilberforce and his allies (**Epistle to William Wilberforce,** l. 31); had there been more such hearts in Parliament, Barbauld implies, the British slave trade would have been ended in 1791. In its intellectual aspect, ingenuousness is simply intellectual honesty. Barbauld appeals to the ingenuousness (in this sense) of her Church-of-England readers when she tells them that unless they can accept the Thirty-Nine Articles in their *purest and simplest sense,* unsophisticated by clever interpretations designed to accommodate heterodox beliefs, they are deluding themselves about their allegiance (**Address to the Opposers,** p. 275 below). The intellectual and ethical aspects of ingenuousness coalesce in what Barbauld calls "the delicacy of conscience" (**Sins of Government** [**Sins of Government, Sins of the Nation**], p. 306 below) or, much the same thing, "the genuine, unperverted moral sense of mankind" (**Remarks on . . . Social Worship,** p. 73). A delicate (innocent, unequivocating—in short, *honest*) conscience is hurt by laws which require swearing solemn oaths on trivial occasions. An honest conscience cannot reconcile trafficking in human beings with claiming to be a Christian nation—or, indeed, implore the assistance of God in an effort to slaughter one's fellow humans. When invited to participate in such acts of ethical incoherence, an honest conscience responds, appropriately, with indignation.

In her writing Barbauld aims, among other things, to *model* the "natural" response to a stimulus. In her poetry, this will be better perceived if the poem is read aloud with attention to what she would have called "just" intonation: doing that, one finds oneself speaking "appropriately" in tones of affection, prayer, grief, or whatever. She grounds the "natural" response to stimuli in our physical makeup (the devotional taste, for example, is seated in the passions and "is in a great degree constitutional" [p. 211 [below]]); thus the physical action of uttering her poems puts us in touch with the "natural" responses which they encode. The greatest moments, perhaps, in Barbauld's political tracts are moments in which her rhetoric models for the reader the sound—indeed, the very rhythm—of moral indignation. To read such passages is to experience what moral indignation feels like, and to receive in that experience a lesson in political morality. In her writing Barbauld is thus always a teacher, always urging or modelling the appropriate response to events.

She was not just a "feeler," however. On the contrary, she values Enlightenment reason equally with feeling. (Contemporaries perceived this when they credited Barbauld, in gendered terms, with a "masculine" head and a "feminine" heart.[7]) In her early essays Barbauld uses reason to peel away false, confused responses to stimuli; to achieve clarity of understanding, which (she assumes) leads at once to honesty of feeling and thence to honesty of action. She hates false feeling and irrational displays of feeling (such as the "noise and nonsense" of evangelical religious meetings) and resents efforts to jerk her chain. The term to which she appeals here is "taste"; "taste" functions for her as the mediator between the reason which clarifies and the honest response which results from clarity. The fact that she values both reason and feeling equally will help to explain what might otherwise seem like a tendency in her writing to turn up on both sides of every issue: she is often trying to redress some imbalance between reason and feeling.

GENDER

When Barbauld's contemporaries praised her "masculine" head and "feminine" heart, they were acknowledging, in the only terms they seem to have had available, that her writings appeared to them to transcend—or better, to unite—qualities which they were accustomed to assigning exclusively to one or the other sex. They were saying that, contrary to custom, the fact of her being a woman did not seem to bear upon her performance as a writer—that her writings manifested, rather, something like a completed humanity.

The situation is really more complicated than that, both for her in her life and for us in our reading of her. Barbauld was brought up by a mother with very strict notions of gender propriety, and she chafed under the restraints imposed by her gender: being "feminine" was always difficult for her, at every level from the etiquette of body movement up to exclusion from the male professions.[8] (Her poem **"To Dr. Aikin on his Complaining that she neglected him"** evinces serious interest in medicine, and medical metaphors are rather common in her writing; perhaps she would have liked to be a doctor.) Reading her today, it is easy to see gender issues in her texts—especially her early poems, in which, as we have remarked, she explores or "tries on" a variety of possible female roles. Then too, modern readers of Barbauld have always had to deal with Mary Wollstonecraft's accusation, apropos Barbauld's poem **"To a Lady, with some painted Flowers,"** that she denigrated women by speaking of them in "the language of men"; and with Barbauld's reply to Wollstonecraft, **"The Rights of Woman,"** which has usually been taken—erroneously, we think—as a repudiation of Wollstonecraft's ideal of sexual equality.

That said, there is nevertheless value in trying to understand Barbauld as a "trans-gendered" writer. In her own life, she had no particular investment in being socially female; indeed, her essay on **"Fashion"** [**"Fashion, a Vision"**] displays a deep aversion to some aspects of that social condition—to the encumbrances of late-eighteenth-century female dress, and to the rituals by which active and agile girls are transformed into constricted, "marriageable" young ladies. Her early achievement of a lifelong authority over her brother gave her mediated access to the public sphere and confidence in managing younger men and boys, and thus, as we have seen, opportunity to intervene in public culture. Important as the social role of Mother was to her educational project, it was not her sole writing guise: when she intervened directly in politics, she did so as an apparently ungendered "Dissenter" and "Volunteer." In her capacity as a middle-class spokesperson she behaves simply as a "citizen" in the 1790s Revolutionary sense, and her contemporaries do not always perceive her as female. (One of them, William Keate, was horrified to learn that the *Address to the Opposers* was the work of a "female pen" [p. 262 below].)

Barbauld even found some advantage in women's exclusion from the technical knowledge necessary to the male professions. She had seen enough of the male display of technical learning in theology discussions at Warrington Academy to perceive how professional knowledge can deaden sensibility. Women, she believed—and in this she was Victorian ahead of her time—surpassed men in the capacity to feel, and in sensitivity to imaginative constructs like literature. They did so in part from "nature," but also for the very reason that they were "excused from all professional knowledge" (**"On Female Studies,"** p. 475 below) and thus preserved from the narrowing influence of specialization. As amateurs in literature and science, women would be better humanists than men.

To be sure, in her letters **"On Female Studies"** Barbauld works both sides of this street, asserting both that women have no profession and that their profession is motherhood and the management of the family. Since Barbauld herself was never a biological mother, and was by profession a writer, she has been accused by some latter-day feminists of imposing on other women a standard to which she did not hold herself.[9] But on this issue she is actually much closer to Wollstonecraft than has commonly been believed. (Wollstonecraft has sometimes been used, unjustly, as a stick to beat Barbauld with.) Both conceived of motherhood as a civic, or citizenly, role; as the role, par excellence, from which society would be reformed. Motherhood was a profession, but it also trumped all the mere professions because it was responsible for the fashioning not of doctors or theologians or politicians but of entire human beings. Motherhood was the matrix of any future society; a fully humanized mother—which is to say, an educated woman—would be what Barbauld, as we have seen, sought to be in her role as civic mother, a reformer. That is the role for which Victorian feminists such as Clara Balfour valued Barbauld.

Logically, the role would not even have to be filled by a biological woman: a person of either sex could act as a civic "mother" to the next generation, so long as that person's own humanity was fully realized. Barbauld herself seems never to have drawn this inference, although it is implicit in her actual performance as a (non-biological) mother and as a teacher, and in the fact that she and her husband conceived themselves to be engaged equally, at Palgrave School, in the same enterprise. (To a degree, their provinces within the school even overlapped: she taught reading and religion to the small children, but also geography and history to older pupils; her husband taught Latin and Greek of course, but she reports that he "delighted to entertain" young children [**"Memoir of the Rev. R. Barbauld,"** p. 708].) Barbauld always preferred an ideal of partnership between men and women to the thought of contention between them; that is part of the burden of her much-misunderstood poem, **"The Rights of Woman."** In the vocabulary of her time—a vocabulary which, we have seen, was applied to her by her admirers—she appears to have believed that "masculine" and "feminine" were two parts of a human whole.[10]

"MRS. BARBAULD"

Today Barbauld is regaining what we believe to be her rightful place in literature, but her recovery is a recent event. Thirty years ago, "Mrs. Barbauld" was known, when at all, only as an historical appendage to "more important" writers, a background figure in the contexts literary studies had created for her canonized contemporaries.

One of those contemporaries we have already noticed: Mary Wollstonecraft. In the books and articles of those few (but increasingly prominent) scholars who were working at that time in early women's writing, Barbauld appeared as a socially conservative foil for Wollstonecraft and other radical feminists.[11] We have suggested already that this representation was more caricature than portrait, that Barbauld's stance on questions about gender was more complicated than such a polemical depiction could acknowledge. But being painted an "anti-feminist" was probably not as damaging to Barbauld's literary reputation as another distortion was. It was her treatment as an aesthetically conservative foil for Samuel Taylor Coleridge that firmly relegated Barbauld to small print, as it were; as his canonical stature rose, her claim to serious attention fell.

Anecdotes associated with Coleridge are largely responsible for keeping Barbauld's presence alive in our cultural memory, but they do so by creating "Mrs. Barbauld"—a somewhat prissy representative of the "last age" with a ludicrous surname. The story associated with Coleridge's most popular poem provides a clear example of the way Barbauld was caricatured by literary history. Students introduced to the English literary canon in the 1960s and 1970s by the standard anthologies were likely to read in a prominent and lengthy footnote Barbauld's objection to *The Rime of the Ancient Mariner* on the grounds that it has no moral. They also read there Coleridge's zinger of a response: "I told her that in my own judgment the poem had too much."[12] Twentieth-century instructors drew on that exchange to illustrate the difference between "neoclassical didacticism" and "Romantic imaginative freedom," generally for the purpose of valorizing Romantic sensibility at the expense of eighteenth-century aesthetic standards (real or presumed). Rhetorically, Coleridge "wins" the exchange; and, historically, overt didacticism fell out of favor with poets and critics alike. The anecdote does not redound to Barbauld's credit.

Barbauld's actual historical impact on Blake, Wordsworth and Coleridge received no documentation in mid-twentieth-century anthologies; even as late as 1996

the *Norton Anthology of English Literature* situated her as a "minor" poet following the "Major Romantics."[13] Until then, she survived only in Coleridge's pithy refutation of her critical judgment. Seeing Barbauld through Coleridge's eyes in this way, however, actually inverts the power dynamic as it would have been experienced by the writers themselves. For, from Barbauld's perspective, Coleridge was a member of the "younger generation"; from his perspective, she was a member of the literary "establishment."

Aspects of Barbauld's anecdotal status in the annals of literary history are directly related to a generational struggle we have insufficiently imagined. We have convinced ourselves of the powerlessness of women in the "patriarchal past" to the degree that we sometimes fail to perceive the actual influence exerted by women writers of Barbauld's generation upon their contemporaries. By the time Wordsworth and Coleridge came on the literary scene, Barbauld occupied significant cultural space. The Coleridge anecdotes—both positive and negative—might be said to arise from a young man's effort to position himself in a world where she represented literary authority. The story of Coleridge's long walk to meet Barbauld confesses her preeminence; Coleridge's claim to have bested her on *The Rime of the Ancient Mariner* is an attempt to subvert her power. Other antagonistic efforts took the form of jokes about Barbauld's strange (i.e., "un-English") name, a name no one was sure—then or since—how to pronounce. (The consensus today seems to be that Anglicized "Barbold" was favored by her contemporaries, although her husband's family would have pronounced it, in French, "Barbo.") Thus Charles Lamb, the essayist, joked about her kinship to the "other bald lady," the novelist and dramatist Elizabeth Inchbald. These jokes survived the moment that occasioned them, and "Mrs. Barbauld" survived along with them, at least in name—or something like her name. But the quips, like the anecdotes, had the effect of positioning her outside the literary mainstream. These attempts to "kill the mother" did just that—metaphorically, anyway. For, although "Mrs. Barbauld" became part of our literary heritage, she did so by associations that discredited her even as they kept her name alive.

Of course, Barbauld's fate was not unique. In 1970, few women writers from the period 1660-1830 could claim canonical status. Aphra Behn had yet to enjoy the attention she now receives, though by 1973 her tale *Oroonoko* was available in a Norton paperback edition, and critical essays on her had begun to appear in learned journals. Frances (then "Fanny") Burney enjoyed similar quasi-canonical status. Still, neither Behn nor Burney could claim equality with Jane Austen, whose novels, with their formal and linguistic precision, responded well to New Critical readings. Austen's excellence was demonstrable by twentieth-century aesthetic standards;

the achievements of Behn and Burney somewhat less so. As for the host of female writers whose works seemed inextricably bound to the times in which they were produced, they remained the subjects of what we might term antiquarian or specialist interest. If they were anthologized, it was under the heading "minor poets" or "other writers," and most did not appear even there.

When the recovery of women writers of the past began in earnest in the 1980s, expressions of surprise at Barbauld's talent and achievement in light of her obscurity were common. Barbara Brandon Schnorrenberg called her "one of the most neglected writers of her day"—a judgment emphatically reiterated by Terry Castle in a review of Roger Lonsdale's collection of *Eighteenth-Century Women Poets*. Lonsdale himself articulated a more precise amazement: "[T]here is a striking confidence and authority in the **Poems** (1773) of Anna Aikin Barbauld. . . . There was no female precedent for the accomplishment of the blank verse in her **'Corsica'**" (p. xxxiii).

As these comments suggest, it is a cause for wonder that Anna Barbauld suffered such an eclipse. The reasons are matter for speculation. Did Coleridge and Lamb indeed write the script for Barbauld's reception by generations of readers and critics to come? Or were the jokes and anecdotes merely the symptoms of deeper ideological biases? Barbauld's gender was surely one reason she was relegated to the margins for so long. And perhaps she was less interesting to critics and literary historians than she might otherwise have been because she did not write novels or plays—both genres associated with women writers and readerships. It is possible too that her Dissenting background was also a factor—perhaps even the primary factor—in the diminishing of her literary reputation.

Whatever the reasons, as we begin to look anew at Barbauld's achievement, to replace "Mrs. Barbauld" with Anna Letitia Barbauld, we must make an effort to do so without the assumptions about gender, class and genre that have prejudiced judgment in the past. And we should also remember that Barbauld is neither the first nor the last writer to be reassessed in terms of cultural or aesthetic significance. The recovery of the Metaphysical Poets by T. S. Eliot and others springs to mind as an available example. But there is another, closer to home. It is not so long ago that Defoe scholars had to fight both aesthetic (formalist) and ideological (Anglican) prejudice as they argued for the foundational role of that author not only in the development of the novel as a genre but also in the articulation of modern values and habits of mind.[14] That battle is largely won, but as we try to understand the importance of Anna Letitia Barbauld to our thought, culture and literature, it is instructive to remember that the case had to be made

for other writers, male as well as female, whom we now regard as essential to our understanding of the field of literary studies, without whom we would consider ourselves and our discipline diminished. Barbauld's poems, essays and editorial achievements enriched the literary world of the late eighteenth and early nineteenth centuries. Her concerns remain pertinent at the juncture of the twentieth and the twenty-first centuries as we continue to fight oppression globally, as we struggle to maintain a sense of aesthetic pleasure in an increasingly technological world, as we confront the things that never change: birth, death, love, hope, loss, despair and faith. The following selections provide a glimpse into Barbauld's world, her historical moment; in doing so, they speak to us and future generations as well.

Notes

1. For the creed of the Methodist Countess of Huntingdon's "Connection" and a Methodist death-bed scene rather different from the scene Barbauld imagines, see *The Life and Times of Selina Countess of Huntingdon* (London, 1839), 2:440-43, 499.

2. Quoted in McCarthy, "Celebrated Academy," p. 295. A fine exposition of Barbauld's project for mediated intervention in her culture is Sarah Robbins, "'Women's Studies' Debates in Eighteenth-Century England: Mrs. Barbauld's Program for Feminine Learning and Maternal Pedagogy," *Michigan Feminist Studies,* 7 (1992-93): 53-81.

3. She mentions "Hutcheson's Ethics" approvingly in *Remarks on . . . Social Worship,* p. 70.

4. Mary Scott, *The Female Advocate* (1774), quoted in McCarthy, "'We Hoped the *Woman* Was Going to Appear,'" p. 114. McCarthy surveys the range of female identities explored by Barbauld in her early poems.

5. For a detailed, if somewhat negative, reading of roles associated with motherhood in eighteenth-century literature, see Toni Bowers, *The Politics of Motherhood: British Writing and Culture, 1680-1760* (Cambridge: Cambridge University Press, 1996). On Barbauld's interest in medicine, see below.

6. The man was Thomas Denman; see her poem, "Lines to be spoken by Thomas Denman," below, and its headnote.

7. Thus the anonymous author of *Jack and Martin: a Poetical Dialogue, on the Proposed Repeal of the Test-Act* (Hereford, 1790) credits Barbauld with "female Softness,—manly Sense" (p. 12). In 1826 the *Monthly Review* appreciated her "masculine understanding" and "truly feminine heart" (3rd series, 1:73). Henry Holland (1788-1873), who met Barbauld in his youth, admired her "masculine

understanding and gentle feminine character" (Holland, *Recollections of Past Life* [London, 1872], p. 12).

8. On Barbauld's discomfort with her social femininity, see the letter published by Lucy Aikin in 1825 ("Memoir," pp. xvii-xxiv); on Barbauld's strict upbringing, see LeBreton, *Memoir,* pp. 24-25.

9. See, for example, Marilyn Williamson, "Who's Afraid of Mrs. Barbauld? The Blue Stockings and Feminism," *International Journal of Women's Studies* 3 (1980):89-102.

10. A close reading of Barbauld's poem "Corsica" by Karen Hadley in a paper delivered at the Sixth Annual Conference on 18th- and 19th-Century British Women Writers (Davis, CA, 28 March 1997) argued persuasively that Barbauld's figure Liberty represents an androgynous ideal, neither merely feminine nor merely masculine.

11. In her introduction to the 1975 edition of Wollstonecraft's *Vindication of the Rights of Woman,* for example, Miriam Kramnick names Elizabeth Carter, Hester Thrale, Frances Burney, Hannah More, and Anna Barbauld as women who not only failed to "embrace [Wollstonecraft's] principles" but who were also "scrupulously careful to avoid any contamination by feminism" (p. 37). Kramnick finds Barbauld's refusal to support a plan for a "woman's college" particularly damning (pp. 37-38). On that issue, see McCarthy, "Why Anna Letitia Barbauld Refused to Head a Women's College: New Facts, New Story," forthcoming in *Nineteenth-Century Contexts* [23, no. 3 (2001)].

12. In the Oxford anthology, published in 1973, the footnote references the title of the poem; the Norton anthologies include the story in a note toward the end of the poem, referencing the mariner's summation of the meaning of his tale. The Norton retains the note in the 7th edition of the anthology, published in 2000.

13. Pamela Plimpton discusses the implications and distortions of this placement and selection in "Anna Letitia Barbauld: Editorial Agency and the Ideology of the Feminine." The latest edition of the anthology places Barbauld first in the volume and includes four poems: "To a Little Invisible Being," "A Summer Evening's Meditation," "Washing-Day," and "Life."

14. Defoe, like Barbauld, was a Protestant Dissenter, and he met with some of the same resistance she has encountered in terms of literary assessment. While he enjoyed a place in the canon of the English novel throughout the twentieth century, it was not until the 1960s that Defoe received attention as a serious artist as opposed to "intuitive genius" or "instinctive story-teller." During that decade, studies by Maximillian Novak, G. A. Starr, and J. Paul Hunter changed the conventional perception of Defoe.

Sources of the Texts

Barbauld, Anna Letitia. *An Address to the Opposers of the Repeal of the Corporation and Test Acts.* London: J. Johnson, 1790. Revised in second edition, 1790; third and fourth editions, 1790.

————. *Hymns in Prose for Children.* London: J. Johnson, 1781. Revised in "sixteenth" edition, 1814.

————. *Poems.* London: J. Johnson, 1773. Second and third (revised) editions, 1773; fourth edition, 1774; fifth edition, 1776-77; revised edition, 1792.

————. *The Works of Anna Laetitia Barbauld. With a Memoir by Lucy Aikin.* 2 vols. London: Longman, Hurst, Rees, Orme, Brown, and Green, 1825. ("Dialogue in the Shades.")

Bibliography

Aikin, Lucy. "Memoir." In *The Works of Anna Laetitia Barbauld.* 1: [v]-lxxii.

Balfour, Clara. *Working Women of the last Half Century: The Lesson of their Lives.* London: Cash, 1854.

[Barbauld, Anna Letitia]. "Memoir of the Rev. R. Barbauld." *Monthly Repository,* 3 (1808):706-09.

————. *Remarks on Mr. Gilbert Wakefield's Enquiry into the Expediency and Propriety of Public or Social Worship.* London: Johnson, 1792.

Hume, David. *Selected Essays.* Ed. Stephen Copley and Andrew Edgar. Oxford: Oxford University Press, 1993.

Hutcheson, Francis. *A Short Introduction to Moral Philosophy.* 1747. Reprint. Philadelphia: Crukshank, 1788.

Kenrick, Samuel. Letter to Timothy Kenrick, 7 June 1795. MS Sharpe 178/48, University College London, Library. Quoted by permission.

Lady's Monthly Museum, 1 (1798):169-79. "Mrs. Anna Letitia Barbauld."

LeBreton, Anna Letitia. *Memoir of Mrs. Barbauld.* London: Bell, 1874.

Lonsdale, Roger, ed. *Eighteenth-Century Women Poets: An Oxford Anthology.* Oxford: Oxford University Press, 1989.

McCarthy, William. "The Celebrated Academy at Palgrave: A Documentary History of Anna Letitia Barbauld's School." *The Age of Johnson,* 8 (1997): 279-392.

———. "Mother of All Discourses: Anna Barbauld's *Lessons for Children*." *Princeton University Library Chronicle,* 60 (1998-99): 196-219.

———. "'We Hoped the *Woman* Was Going to Appear': Desire, Repression, and Gender in Anna Barbauld's Early Poems." *Romantic Women Writers: Voices and Counter-Voices,* ed. Paula Feldman and Theresa Kelley. Hanover, NH: University Press of New England, 1995. 113-37.

Mautner, Thomas. "Introduction." *On Human Nature,* by Francis Hutcheson. Ed. Thomas Mautner. Cambridge: Cambridge University Press, 1993.

Plimpton, Pamela. "Anna Letitia Barbauld: Editorial Agency and the Ideology of the Feminine." Paper, Modern Language Association Annual Conference, Chicago, 28 Dec. 1995.

[Priestley, Joseph]. *Address to Protestant Dissenters of all Denominations, on the Approaching Election of Members of Parliament, with respect to the State of Public Liberty in General, and of American Affairs in Particular.* London: Johnson, 1774.

Schnorrenberg, Barbara Brandon. "Barbauld, Anna Laetitia." In *A Dictionary of British and American Women Writers 1660-1800.* Ed. Janet Todd. Totowa, NJ: Rowman and Littlefield, 1985.

Wollstonecraft, Mary. *A Vindication of the Rights of Woman.* Ed. Miriam Kramnick. New York: Penguin, 1975.

[Woodfall, William.] Review of Aikin's *Poems. Monthly Review,* 48 (1773): 54-59, 133-37.

Mary Ellen Bellanca (essay date fall 2003)

SOURCE: Bellanca, Mary Ellen. "Science, Animal Sympathy, and Anna Barbauld's 'The Mouse's Petition.'" *Eighteenth-Century Studies* 37, no. 1 (fall 2003): 47-67.

[*In the following essay, Bellanca analyzes Barbauld's poem against the backdrop of shifting public attitudes toward animal welfare in the eighteenth and nineteenth centuries.*]

> The immediate use of natural science is the power it gives us over nature.
>
> Joseph Priestley, *The History and Present State of Electricity*

> An infant may destroy life, but all the kings of the earth cannot restore it.
>
> Anna Barbauld and John Aikin,
> **"What Animals Are Made For"**

Mealtime in the household of Joseph Priestley could evidently be an unorthodox affair, punctuated by the introduction of newly caught animal specimens for his scientific experiments. As the natural philosopher's friend, Anna Letitia Aikin (later Barbauld) had occasion to observe this phenomenon first-hand. In 1771, in experiments that would lead to his discovery of oxygen, Priestley was using live mice to test the effects of mixing air with various gases. One evening when Barbauld was visiting, according to memoirist William Turner, "It happened that a captive [mouse] was brought in after supper, too late for any experiment to be made with it that night, and the servant was desired to set it by till next morning." Overnight, while Priestley may have contemplated the composition of air, Barbauld made a composition of her own: her poem **"The Mouse's Petition,"** which was found, Turner reports, "twisted among the wires of the cage" the next day when it "was brought in after breakfast." Cast in the mouse's voice, the poem makes an eloquent, if tongue-in-cheek, argument for the rodent's release:

> Oh! hear a pensive prisoner's prayer,
> For liberty that sighs;
> And never let thine heart be shut
> Against the wretch's cries.
>
>   * * *
>
> If e'er thy breast with freedom glow'd,
> And spurn'd a tyrant's chain,
> Let not thy strong oppressive force
> A free-born mouse detain.
>
>   ("Poem 19," lines 1-4, 9-12)[1]

According to Turner, the plea was so effective that Priestley let the mouse go.[2]

"The Mouse's Petition" struck a responsive chord as well with contemporary and later readers. It has been reprinted often, by admirers ranging from Mary Wollstonecraft to the World Wildlife Fund, and it may have influenced Robert Burns's "To a Mouse." The text was first published in Barbauld's *Poems* in 1773, entitled **"The Mouse's Petition, Found in the Trap where he had been Confined all Night"** and dedicated "To Doctor Priestley." Readers immediately seized upon it as an indictment of animal experimentation.[3] Barbauld disclaimed any intent of criticizing Priestley, but *her* critics saw the poem as a denunciation of "the cruelty practised by experimental philosophers, who seem to think the brute creation void of sensibility, or created only for them to torment."[4] By 1796, two years before *The Rime of the Ancient Mariner*—"the great English romantic poem about the consequences of mistreating the animal kingdom"—Samuel Taylor Coleridge could write, "thanks to Mrs. Barbauld, . . . it has become universally *fashionable* to teach lessons of compassion towards animals."[5]

Invoking liberty and decrying tyranny, **"The Mouse's Petition"** lends itself to interpretations in which the suppliant mouse, a mouthpiece for liberal reform, stands in for detained and oppressed humans. Marlon Ross, for example, asks whether it is "a political poem that uses the occasion of an 'imprisoned' mouse to satirize the 'enlighteners'" or "a political poem that . . . make[s] a serious petition for the rights of commoners."[6] The caged, trapped, or abused animal was admittedly a powerful image in print and iconography for various kinds of imprisonment, whether physical, psychological, or social. In a complex texture of reciprocal signification, one vulnerable group often pointed to another, so that slaves were represented as confined or exploited animals, women as slaves or as caged birds, pet animals as slaves. Opposition to injurious uses of nonhuman creatures, such as hunting, blood sports, and scientific experiments, increased in the 1770s alongside debates about slavery. Barbauld's **"Petition"** wields a rhetoric of sensibility that sought to change attitudes about inequality—and the potential violence of unequal power relations—in many forms: chattel slavery, incarceration, marriage, labor, and animal ownership.[7] In the 1790s, while publishing children's texts that promoted animal sympathy, Barbauld would mobilize what Moira Ferguson calls the century's "multilayered discourse on cruelty" to castigate the nation, in her *Epistle to William Wilberforce, [Epistle to William Wilberforce, Esq., on the Rejection of the Bill for Abolishing the Slave Trade]* for failing to halt the slave trade.[8]

In this essay, however, I focus on the more immediate and literal context of **"The Mouse's Petition"**—the use of living animals in scientific experiments, which by midcentury had emerged as a topic of public debate[9]—and on the role of science in Barbauld's work. Defenders of animal experiments maintained, in a rationale argued since antiquity, that nonhuman creatures exist to serve human needs and require no ethical consideration because they possess neither souls nor rational minds. But scientific, political, and social changes in the eighteenth century, including shifting constructions of human-animal relations, worked to undermine some ancient assumptions. Rapid discoveries of exotic species around the globe, including thousands of insects and microorganisms—to say nothing of extinct animals that no human had ever seen—challenged anthropocentric complacency. Extending sensibility's valorization of feeling, advocates for the "brute creation" promoted the new belief that animals experience sensation and can therefore suffer pain.[10] The first-person plea of Barbauld's mouse, who claims to have a "brother's soul" (line 34), gives voice to the concern with animal suffering and to a cultural "myth of kinship"[11] based on fellow-feeling.

"The Mouse's Petition" also provides an entry point for exploring late-century dynamics of science and gen-

der. As a young woman excluded from the fraternity of experimental natural philosophers, Barbauld commented on Priestley's work not in the laboratory or in scientific correspondence but in the domestic spaces of the dining room and the meal table. Working in a tradition of women's anthropomorphic writing about animals, Barbauld does "challenge the male universe exemplified by Priestley's scientific experiments," as Stuart Curran observes.[12] Yet the **"Petition"** does not simply inscribe a showdown between scientific patriarchy and feminine sensibility. Alongside the "universe" of experimental inquiry flourished another world of women's scientific learning. Barbauld, like Priestley, valued the advancement of scientific knowledge as well as the quality of "humanity" or compassion toward nonhuman animals. Nor was Priestley insensitive to animal welfare; as we shall see, his own writings betray an uneasiness about hurting weaker creatures in the pursuit of knowledge. Barbauld's works, in general, simultaneously promote science knowledge for women and men, reinforce cultural boundaries between the sexes' intellectual territories, and warn against the excessive ambition of male scientists. Her poetry both celebrates and critiques an Enlightenment science that increased the physical comfort of human beings yet destroyed animals for knowledge about their bodies, and opened intellectual avenues to women yet kept them well behind its frontiers of discovery.

As a crowded discursive space, then, the mousetrap imagined in Barbauld's poem captures a moment in a multivocal dialogue encompassing the poet, the natural philosopher, and the cultures of science and sensibility. The **"Petition"** embodies, but does not reconcile, tensions in both Barbauld's and Priestley's work between the desire for knowledge and misgivings about its ethical and humanitarian costs. In addition, the poem experiments with a motif that recurs subtly but persistently in Barbauld's work: the dangers inherent in the manipulation of nature by an increasingly technocratic world view.

SCIENCE FOR "BOTH SEXES," WOMEN'S "BOUNDED SPHERE"

Barbauld may be situated in the eighteenth-century culture of science in which women studied the natural world for "rational amusement" and personal improvement. Practitioners of traditional herbal healing, women also became enthusiastic "consumers of scientific knowledge" by reading books and by collecting and sketching plants and flowers. Some aristocratic women studied and patronized botany, entomology, and astronomy.[13] Barbauld's books for children exerted an important influence on younger writers such as Charlotte Smith, Priscilla Wakefield, and Sarah Trimmer, who earned public authority and success by popularizing scientific knowledge. As an author and educator, Barbauld encouraged "many young persons of both sexes" to study and appreciate the natural world.[14] At the same time, her career is emblematic of a "cultural paradox" in attitudes toward women's learning: general knowledge, including science knowledge, was approved, but "excessively" serious pursuits were ridiculed as pedantic and unfeminine.[15] Anticipating a backlash against female learnedness, Barbauld acceded—reluctantly, it may be—to the subordination of women's intellectual interests to their domestic vocation.

Learning about natural processes was, for Barbauld, not only desirable but imperative. At Warrington Academy, the Dissenting college founded by her father, the curriculum was "particularly strong in natural science."[16] There Barbauld became friends with Priestley, who was a tutor at the academy, and his wife, Mary Priestley, as well as Hester Chapone, an advocate of scientific knowledge for women.[17] Later, Barbauld's work as a collaborating writer and editor with her brother, John Aikin, a polymath with interests in medicine, natural philosophy, and chemistry, brought her into contact with current work in natural science.[18] At the Palgrave School, which she founded with her husband, Rochemont Barbauld, she instructed scores of boys, including Joseph Priestley Jr., about "the natural history of animals," reportedly in an engaging way.[19] Although Charles Lamb famously condemned the "cursed Barbauld crew" for "cramming" children with the "sore evil" of science, modern scholars have found that Barbauld's students enjoyed and fondly remembered her "imaginative and entertaining" teaching, especially in natural history.[20]

Like the works of Smith, Trimmer, and Wollstonecraft, Barbauld's books introduce readers to factual observation at an early age. Her *Lessons for Children* prompts youngsters to follow the stages of insect metamorphosis—"all the pretty butterflies that you see flying about were caterpillars once, and crawled on the ground"—and her instruction on animal habits and habitats fosters sympathy: "Here is a poor little snail crawling up the wall. Touch him with your little finger. Ah, the snail is crept into his shell. . . . Let him alone, and he will soon come out again."[21] Barbauld and Aikin's prose collection, *Evenings at Home: or, the Juvenile Budget Opened,* revels in the passionate, if relentlessly empirical, fascination with nature that characterizes many educational texts of the 1790s. Replete with facts about oaks, pines, grasses, "Leguminous Plants," and "Compound Flowers," the volume uses the popular form of the edifying adult-child dialogue to cultivate a sense of wonder.[22] In older students, including women, Barbauld urged reverence for nature as well as knowledge. In a series of letters to "Young Ladies" [*Legacy for Young Ladies*], she wrote: "The great laws of the universe, the nature and properties of those objects which surround us, it is unpardonable not to know: it is more unpardon-

able to know, and not to feel the mind struck with lively gratitude."[23] General science was a topic of lifelong learning: in 1800, attending a lecture at the Royal Institution, the poet was "much pleased to see a fashionable and very attentive audience, about one third ladies, assembled for the purposes of science and improvement."[24]

Barbauld's early poems dramatize interactions with nature that were culturally sanctioned for women. For **"To Mrs. P[riestley], with some Drawings of Birds and Insects,"** she consulted Thomas Pennant's *British Zoology*[25] and possibly her own observation. The poem acts out the naturalist's essential tasks, cataloguing and classifying behaviors and habitats of "various [bird] nations" (Poem 3, line 21). The poem also discusses bird migration, a topic of keen interest to eighteenth-century ornithologists:

> When winter bites upon the naked plain,
> Nor food nor shelter in the groves remain;
>
> * * *
>
> The congregated nations wing their way
> In dusky columns o'er the trackless sea.
>
> (lines 61-2, 65-6)[26]

In this portrait of the poet as a naturalist, Barbauld embraces nature study as a leisure activity to fill the "lonely hour" (line 121) and as a satisfying medium of female friendship.

However, her writings also propagate the view that men and women are not entitled to the same degree of learning about nature. **"To Dr. Aikin on his Complaining that she neglected him"** (Poem 7) describes Barbauld's experience with the sexes' divergent "paths." The poem recalls the interests and "sympathy" that she and her brother shared in their youth, until maturity sent them on different assignments: "Our path divides—to thee fair fate assign'd / The nobler labours of a manly mind" (lines 20, 50-1). In adulthood, the sister's scope is confined to "more humble works, and lower cares" (line 52). While John Aikin will garner acclaim for his medical work and his writing, Barbauld acknowledges her own "bounded sphere" (line 6). The poem's negatives suggest the self-restraint of desire: Barbauld will not "strive to soar too high, / Nor for the tree of knowledge vainly sigh"; rather, she will "Check the fond love of science and of fame, / A bright, but ah! a too devouring flame" (lines 56-9). In Harriet Guest's view, the poet "briefly . . . chafes" against the prescribed difference in life paths; William McCarthy goes further, arguing that these passages express Barbauld's "wistful enviousness" of Aikin's opportunities: the text "document[s] her resentment of woman's restricted fate [and] her imaginative resistance to that fate."[27]

Barbauld's "bounded sphere" limns the containment of women's intellectual aspirations in an era when, as Ann

B. Shteir has written, the "fear of female learnedness was a leitmotif" in texts about women and science, which often brandished the horrifying "specter" of over-educated spinsterhood.[28] Harriet Guest has documented the host of contradictory roles in which the "learned lady" could be cast: public spectacle, icon of British progressiveness, potential sexual scandal, imitator of male scholarly over-specialization.[29] Women's participation in "science culture" notwithstanding, the perceived benefits of formal scientific study were limited. Shteir notes that until well into the nineteenth century, women were "excluded from formal participation in the public institutions of . . . science. They could not be members of the Royal Society [which admitted Priestley] or the Linnean Society, could not attend meetings, read papers, or (with very rare exceptions) see their findings published in the journals of these societies."[30]

The disapproval that could shadow intellectual women helps to contextualize the much-debated letter of 1774 in which Barbauld declines an invitation to establish a young "ladies'" academy.[31] For women "to be taught in a regular systematic manner the various branches of science," she writes, would more likely produce "such characters as the '*Precieuses*' or the '*Femmes scavantes*' of Moliere, than good wives or agreeable companions." Advanced learning for women entails deception and risks public humiliation:

> Young ladies, who ought only to have such a general tincture of knowledge as to make them agreeable companions to a man of sense, and to enable them to find rational entertainment for a solitary hour, should gain these accomplishments in a more quiet and unobserved manner. . . . The thefts of knowledge in our sex are only connived at while carefully concealed, and if displayed, punished with disgrace.[32]

A woman's ultimate calling is the domestic sphere, which affords little room for intellectual pursuits:

> The line of separation between the studies of a young man and a young woman appears to me to be chiefly fixed by this,—that a woman is excused from all professional knowledge. . . . Women have but one [department in life], and all women have the same. . . . It is, to be a wife, a mother, a mistress of a family. The knowledge belonging to these duties is your professional knowledge, the want of which nothing will excuse.

Young women are also "excused" from hands-on scientific research: the most suitable lessons for them are those that "may be learnt at home without experiments or apparatus."[33]

These rules of engagement appear to govern **"The Invitation"** (Poem 4), a rural retreat poem written, like **"To Mrs. P,"** for an absent woman friend.[34] Early in the poem, the outdoors is a scene of female pleasures both

sensory and cerebral. Nature's energies are represented through feminine bird and plant imagery: "FLORA," deity of the botanical world, wields the spring's "transforming power," and "heav'n-born" science, a key attraction at Warrington, is also feminine, a proud, "ardent" eagle that can soar almost anywhere (lines 42, 98, 101). By the poem's end, however, the emphasis moves from the country's leisurely delights to the academic pursuits of Warrington's (male) inmates, which include zoology, botany, and entomology:

> Some [students] pensive creep along the shelly shore;
> Unfold the silky texture of a flower;
> With sharpen'd eyes [that is, microscopes] inspect an
>   hornet's sting,
> And all the wonders of an insect's wing.
> Some trace with curious search the hidden cause
> Of nature's changes, and her various laws;
> Untwist her beauteous web, disrobe her charms,
> And hunt her to her elemental forms.

> (lines 155-62)

Along with the poem's focus, power relations have radically shifted. When the school's formal studies enter the picture, feminine nature diminishes in strength. No longer a transformative force, "she" becomes passive and sexualized, acted upon rather than acting—even preyed upon. The earth makes herself available for the students' searching, inspection, and analysis, and she obligingly "opens all her secret springs" for the "inquiring youth" who would "hunt" and "disrobe" her (lines 97, 95).

The people who perform all this inspecting, tracing, and disrobing of nature are male. Some are laborers, the "sons of toil" who "scoop the hard bosom of the solid rock" to build the Duke of Bridgewater's canal. "Resistless" and patient, these men "compel the genius of th'unwilling flood" to make the river run where designing humans choose (lines 59-60, 61, 63). But the most important masculine players are Warrington's product, "MAN," the alumni who, "impell'd by some resistless force" like the canal builders, will assume important positions in trade and the professions (lines 153, 145). The triumphant power of science contrasts starkly with Barbauld's feminine "Muse," who appears at the poem's end: "Unequal far such bright designs to paint, / . . . My drooping Muse folds up her fluttering wing" (lines 185, 187).

"The Invitation" does not attack scientific activities or the exclusion of women from advanced formal study. On the contrary, the poet expresses pride in both the "little group" of students whom "their country calls" and the canal, which will foster "social plenty" (lines 135, 78). Barbauld's portrayal of feminine "Nature" suggests her immersion in a cultural language that subjects the feminine to a knowledge system used largely by men. As gender theorists have argued, the myth of nature as "Woman" both describes and fosters an agenda of mastery in Enlightenment science. The metaphor does not empower actual flesh-and-blood women but identifies them with passive, pliable "Nature" and empowers actual men to control both women and the material environment.[35] In **"The Invitation,"** women look on with awe as male scientists and engineers apply knowledge that has valued real-world consequences, using powers that surpass the "drooping," "fluttering" capability of the feminine.

The shifting borderlines in Barbauld's writings between insistence on knowledge for all and acceptance of feminine limitations exemplify her culture's ambiguities about nature, gender, and knowledge. Women could and did pursue natural history in its descriptive, aesthetic, and noninvasive modes; they became serious students of science, taught the young, and produced successful books for general readers. But women were not encouraged to become experimental or theoretical scientists, the producers and "shapers" of new knowledge.[36] Barbauld's very phrasing is suggestive: as she writes in *A Legacy for Young Ladies,* women were "excused" from the professions, but "nothing [would] excuse" them from their domestic duty. Harriet Guest suggests that the public/professional and private/domestic realms were more fluidly interactive than previously recognized, so that women's "exemption from [professional] productivity" may have been vital to their valued role of "civilizing" men.[37] Even so, Barbauld's language of offense and judgment, pardon and excuse hints that the stakes were high for the transgressively intellectual woman. The anecdote of the surreptitious deposit of her **"Petition"** in Priestley's mousetrap epitomizes women's need to maneuver around cultural proscriptions when they wanted to speak about science. Nonetheless, Barbauld's acquiescence to gender divisions in scientific study did not preclude criticism of one man's practice.

"So Much Mangled": Priestley and Vivisection

If Barbauld was an outsider to experimental science, she was an insider in the Priestleys' "social circle," whose "brightening influence raised [her] pensive mind" ([**"On Mrs. P[riestley]'s Leaving Warrington,"**] Poem 1, lines 41-2). Their home provided a safe environment for intellectual dialogue and broadened the young poet's horizons beyond the bounds prescribed by her parents.[38] By no means was **"The Mouse's Petition"** the only text in which she challenged Joseph Priestley; rather, it was one volley in an ongoing battle of wits between the friends about the pursuit of knowledge.

Their dialogue begins with Barbauld's reaction to Priestley's *History of the Present State of Electricity.* In the preface to the second edition, Priestley locates himself with other natural philosophers atop the mountain of knowledge: "To look down from the eminence, and to see, and compare all those gradual advances in the ascent, cannot but give the greatest pleasure to those who are seated on the eminence, and who feel all the advantages of their elevated situation." His agenda is ambitious, his claims for science sweeping: "The immediate use of natural science is the power it gives us over nature, by means of the knowledge we acquire of its laws; whereby human life is, in its present state, made more comfortable and happy. . . . And by these sciences also it is, that the views of the human mind itself are enlarged, and our common nature improved and ennobled."[39]

Barbauld's response is **"The Hill of Science: A Vision,"** a prose work published the same year as **"The Mouse's Petition."** In it she echoes Priestley's own phrasing while she rewrites the hill-of-science allegory to question the value of the "eminence" on which her friend is "seated." In Barbauld's text—part *Pilgrim's Progress,* part *Purgatorio*—a pilgrim-dreamer labors toward the mountaintop "temple of Truth." Barbauld's hill is noticeably messier than Priestley's, due to the "heaps of rubbish, [which] continually tumbled down from the higher parts of the mountain." Some climbers become "disgusted" and give up: "sitting down on some fragment of the rubbish, [they] harangued the multitude below with the greatest marks of importance and self-complacency." But Barbauld's protagonist is rescued by a sudden apparition: not Truth but the goddess Virtue, a "form of diviner features and a more benign radiance," who imperiously announces, "Science may raise you to eminence, but I alone can guide you to felicity!"[40] Barbauld's **"Hill of Science"** reads like a reminder to Priestley of his own assertion that the claims of "benevolence" and moral virtue supersede the pursuit of power over nature. As he had written, "The greatest, and noblest use of philosophical speculation is the discipline of the heart, and the opportunity it affords of inculcating benevolent and pious sentiments upon the mind. . . . The contemplation of the works of God should give a sublimity to [the philosopher's] virtue . . . and teach him to aspire to the moral perfections of the great author of all things."[41]

One realm in which virtue might cultivate a "discipline of the heart" was sympathy for animals. In parallel but not coincidental developments, experiments on animals had begun to attract criticism around midcentury, when the discourse of sensibility began to assert nonhuman creatures' capacity to suffer pain. The emphasis on animals' feeling departed from debates of previous eras, when condemnations of cruelty usually cited human-centered reasons such as animals' value as property or the belief that animal abusers would likely abuse humans as well.[42] In Barbauld's lifetime, while English culture remained strongly anthropocentric, animal "feeling"—a conflation of physical sensation and emotion—took on unprecedented importance.[43] More people insisted that to inflict needless suffering on animals was "wrong regardless of whether or not it [had] any human consequences." Like Tristram Shandy's uncle Toby, who spares a fly's life, sensitive persons decided that even unpopular creatures such as snakes, toads, and spiders deserve respect, and some expressed qualms about killing insects or catching mice in traps.[44]

Throughout Barbauld's writings, a menagerie of beset birds, cats, dogs, and other "small vulnerable animals" provides company for the furry captive of **"The Mouse's Petition."**[45] Barbauld and Aikin's *Evenings at Home* contains many pieces that imagine the world from animal characters' viewpoints. In **"The Transmigrations of Indur,"** for example, a kind man realizes his wish to become different animals with "rational souls" and memory, whereupon he experiences firsthand the dangers and predations of animal existence.[46] These stories clearly imply that living things exist for their own reasons, not merely for human exploitation. That message is propounded explicitly in the dialogue **"What Animals are Made For,"** in which a father exhorts his young daughter not to kill flies simply because she finds them annoying:

> [T]he Creator equally desires the happiness of all his creatures, and looks down with as much benignity upon these flies that are sporting around us, as upon ourselves. . . . We have a right to make a reasonable use of all animals for our advantage, and also to free ourselves from such as are hurtful to us. So far our superiority over them may fairly extend. But we should never abuse them for our mere amusement, nor take away their lives wantonly. . . . An infant may destroy life, but all the kings upon earth cannot restore it.[47]

If destroying flies was questionable, it is not surprising that disapproval attached to experiments on animals. Such experimentation had played a key role, since the Renaissance, in advancing knowledge about anatomy, physiology, and medicine. In the seventeenth century, vivisection—that is, dissection or other surgical procedures performed on living animals for research or teaching—had been involved in such fundamental discoveries as the "lacteals," or lymphatic system, and circulation of the blood. By the eighteenth century, animal experiments were generating controversy outside the scientific community. Defenders of vivisection argued that the knowledge gained was unavailable through other methods and that, as creatures without reason, animals could be treated as objects with no moral claim on humans.[48] In Jonathan Swift's satire of speculative science in *Gulliver's Travels,* indignities perpetrated on a dog serve to lambaste experimental practices as crude and preposterous, without necessarily implying sympathy for the dog. Other writers, more respectful of science in general, weighed the potential

benefits of research against its costs in harm to animals. The *Spectator* and the *Gentleman's Magazine* declared vivisection pointless and unnecessary as well as cruel, while Alexander Pope questioned the "right" to kill animals even for medical discoveries important to human health.[49] A particularly strong indictment appeared in Samuel Johnson's *Idler* in 1758. Although Johnson usually followed science with enthusiasm, in this essay he expressed "abhorrence" for "the inferiour professors of medical knowledge"—a "race of wretches," he declared, "whose favourite amusement is to nail dogs to tables and open them alive; to try how long life may be continued in various degrees of mutilation, or with the excision or laceration of the vital parts. . . . if the knowledge of physiology has been somewhat encreased, he surely buys knowledge dear, who learns the use of the lacteals at the expence of his humanity."[50]

The phrase "at the expence of humanity" must have resonated with Joseph Priestley, for it appeared some nine years later in his account of his own work. Priestley performed "a great number of experiments on animals," beginning with the research discussed in his *History of the Present State of Electricity*. These experiments earned him some distinction: according to Benjamin Franklin, "Animals larger and more difficult to kill, appear to have been killed by the doctor's Apparatus, than by any other before used."[51] But the *History* also betrays Priestley's ambivalence, even distaste, about this aspect of his work. Narrating his study of the physiological effects of lightning strikes, Priestley describes his subjection of a rat, a shrew, cats, and dogs to electric shock and the resulting "violent" convulsions and other disturbing effects. In one instance, to spare a cat so treated from a "lingering death," Priestley was moved to administer a "second stroke" to put the creature out of its misery. When he tried a larger shock on the head of a dog, "all his [the animal's] limbs were extended, he fell backwards, and lay without any motion, or sign of life, for about a minute." After half an hour of convulsions, the dog "kept discharging a great quantity of saliva; and there was also a great flux of rheum from his eyes, on which he kept putting his feet; though in other respects he lay perfectly listless." The dog survived in this condition until the next day, when Priestley "dispatched [him], by shooting him through the hinder part of his head."[52]

Priestley expresses explicit doubts about these methods in connection with the dramatic result of an experiment on a frog. He had dissected the frog's thorax to observe its heartbeat, then administered an electric shock: "Upon receiving the stroke, the lungs were instantly inflated; and, together with the other contents of the thorax, thrown quite out of the body." After some tentative movements, "at last the creature seemed as if it would have come to life, if it had not been so much mangled." In an uneasy echo of Johnson, Priestley concludes that "it is paying dear for philosophical discoveries, to purchase them at the expence of humanity."[53] Barbauld probably knew about these episodes from reading the *History,* if not from firsthand observation. At Warrington, Priestley performed his experiments in an outbuilding near his house; he welcomed witnesses, and it seems likely he would discuss his work with Barbauld and other friends. Even if Barbauld did not witness any experiments in person, she may have heard their audible results—such an explosion of mixed gases on one occasion that, according to Priestley, "burst a glass and had like to have done me a mischief."[54]

Mice entered Priestley's lab in the early 1770s when, undertaking the work that led to his isolation of oxygen, he sought "a farther insight into the constitution of the atmosphere."[55] Curious about the differences between ordinary and "noxious" air, Priestley determined that a "full-grown mouse" enclosed in a glass vessel of "common air" could survive for "about a quarter of an hour." He then placed mice in vessels of air mixed with various contaminants and observed the effects on their respiration, as well as the effects of their breathing on the contained air. In what vivisection opponents would doubtless call adding insult to injury, Priestley studied, among other things, the effects on live mice of breathing air that was "generated solely from putrefying mice, which I have been collecting some months, than which nothing can be more deadly."[56] It was while he was thus engaged that Barbauld placed her poem of animal advocacy in a mouse's cage, where it was discovered "after breakfast."

THE "FELLOWSHIP OF SENSE": "THE MOUSE'S PETITION"

Infiltrating the workspace of experiment via the domestic spaces of Priestley's home, **"The Mouse's Petition"** brings the cultures of science and sensibility into intimate proximity. Neither strictly public nor strictly private, Priestley's house-cum-laboratory may qualify as Harriet Guest's "third site" of social exchange, an arena where private interactions could incubate public virtues.[57] The mouse's postprandial plea is a compact rhetorical performance that deftly weaves a critique of Priestley's work with the playful wit of the light occasional poem and a web of allusion to the serious debate about animals. The poem deploys two culturally powerful apparatus, the language of feeling and anthropomorphic ventriloquism, to imagine a sentient but subject creature as an effective *speaking* subject.

To begin with the critique of vivisection, though the mouse's entrapment can certainly symbolize human bondage, its immediate poignancy arises from the literal details of Priestley's method. The mouse's sighing is not only a convention of sentimental literature; it also puns on the fact that the actual mouse may suffocate.

The captive's desire for "the vital air" (line 21) is thus quite literal as well. Further, its assertion that light and air are "common gifts" (line 24) plays on Priestley's references to "common air"—air both ordinary and meant to be shared by all:

> The chearful light, the vital air,
> Are blessings widely given;
> Let nature's commoners enjoy
> The common gifts of heaven.
>
> (lines 21-4)

The **"Petition"** takes advantage of the "overlapping rhetorical strategies" noted by Ann Van Sant in narratives of suffering and scientific accounts: like Priestley's experiment, Barbauld's poem "isolat[es] the creature and mak[es] it suffer."[58] The poet literalizes the conventional scene of sensibility in humanitarian and literary texts—the display and scrutiny of a representative feeling captive—to figure the distress of an actual flesh-and-blood victim.

Elaborating on Barbauld's warning that "Virtue" is more desirable than intellectual "eminence," the poem casts a dubious eye on the manipulation of weaker creatures. The mousetrap's "wiry grate" is associated with the "tyrant's chain," which Priestley ordinarily would "spurn," and with the traps of fate that threaten "men, like mice" (lines 6, 10, 48, 46). The mouse thus joins the dreamer of Barbauld's **"Hill of Science"** in raising moral rectitude above callous or soulless scientific achievement. In place of ambition, the **"Petition"**'s language of feeling seeks to ignite Priestley's sympathetic imagination: the mouse appeals not only to its captor's head but to his "breast" or heart, which the mouse implores him to open so he may open the trap (line 9). The "well taught philosophic mind" should be more, not less, compassionate to other creatures; indeed, it should feel "for all that lives" (lines 26, 28). The mouse's plea is concerned not so much with prospective bodily discomfort as with the painful emotions it already feels: "For here forlorn and sad I sit, / . . . And tremble at th' approaching morn, / Which brings impending fate" (lines 5, 7-8). The desired response is that modeled in Barbauld's later poem **"The Caterpillar,"** in which the speaker's recognition of her kinship with a "helpless thing" makes her "feel and clearly recognise / . . . [its] fellowship of sense with all that breathes" (Poem 133, lines 1, 25-7).

In this approach Barbauld allies herself with other writers, such as Anne Finch and Anna Seward, who imagined animal subjectivity in human terms. G. J. Barker-Benfield asserts that women writers in particular, who found themselves "vulnerable" and "dependent" in a culture dominated by men, "put themselves 'in the place' of animals" even more than they did that of poor people, prisoners, slaves, or other intended beneficiaries of reform.[59] Women's texts about animals, says Margaret Anne Doody, "mix humour and compassion with a strong sense of the immediate and physical as the speaker projects herself . . . into the being" of another creature.[60] In adopting the mouse's subject position, Barbauld's **"Petition"** anticipates her admonishment in *Hymns in Prose for Children* that humans must speak on behalf of "dumb" nature.[61]

In addition to its literary genealogy, the **"Petition"** is also descended from philosophical debates about humans' relationship with other creatures. From time to time in Western history, opponents of cruelty have countered the argument that animals lack mind or spirit by hypothesizing that they may have "rational souls"[62]—a notion that implies both reasoning power and the potential for an afterlife. In this vein, the mouse warns Priestley:

> If mind, as ancient sages taught,
> A never dying flame,
> Still shifts thro' matter's varying forms,
> In every form the same,
>
> Beware, lest in the worm you crush
> A brother's soul you find;
> And tremble lest thy luckless hand
> Dislodge a kindred mind.
>
> (lines 29-36)

A few commentators on animal welfare believed in the transmigration of souls, as did Priestley for a short time, and Barbauld's mouse craftily uses the scientist's former belief against him.[63] The animal may, after all, be a kindred spirit who shares the fellowship not only of "sense" or feeling but also that of mind.

The mouse draws on philosophical issues in other ways. It backs up its appeal to Priestley's sympathy with an argument older than the interest in animals' feelings: the consequences to humans of their own cruelty. The mouse wishes the scientist "health," "peace," and "heartfelt ease" if he spares its life (lines 42, 43). Conversely, and more ominously, it hints at what may happen if he does not: "when destruction lurks unseen, / Which men, like mice, may share," there may be no "kind angel" around to "break the hidden snare" for Priestley (lines 45-8). The poem thus affirms human-animal kinship with playful irony by reminding Priestley that what happens to the mouse can easily happen to the man.

RESISTING THE TECHNOLOGY OF ENTRAPMENT

The caged mouse is not the only natural entity in Barbauld's poems ensnared by human machinery. Other creatures, as well as energy bearing forces such as rivers and lightning, share the mouse's predicament, confined or channeled by technology. In **"To Mrs. P[riest-**
ley]," a pheasant caught in a "wiry net" feels "Oppress'd by bondage" and longs, like the mouse in its grate, for liberty (Poem 3, lines 51, 54). The prose poem **"Epitaph on a Goldfinch"** mourns a freedom-loving bird abducted by the "pitiless hands of a two-legged animal without feathers" and "confined in a grated prison." The goldfinch's repeated "petition for redress" goes disregarded until at last the bird dies.[64] In other poems, as in **"The Mouse's Petition,"** natural entities yearn for release from scientific gadgets wielded by Priestleyesque projectors.

Priestley's self-confessed "enthusiasm" for natural philosophy arose in part from his delight in "philosophical instruments." In the *History of Electricity* he recommends financing equipment purchases by spending less money on books, "which are generally read and laid aside, without yielding half the entertainment." Instruments provide "an endless fund of knowledge" and reveal nothing less than the "operations . . . of the God of nature himself, which are infinitely various. By the help of these machines, we are able to put an endless variety of things into an endless variety of situations." Nature does not always cooperate, however, and that recalcitrance creates a need for substantial resources, especially experimental apparatus: "Nature will not be put out of her way, and suffer her materials to be thrown into all the variety of situations, which philosophy requires, . . . without trouble and expence."[65]

In this struggle between the "requirements" of natural philosophy and a stubborn feminine nature, Barbauld's poems may be rooting for the latter. Several of them concern devices contrived to manipulate natural forces, but those devices dominate phenomena only for a time. In **"Inscription for an Ice-House,"** the season of winter is imprisoned by "man, the great magician," who molds the elements to his will and presses winter into the domestic service of preserving food (Poem 95, lines 4-5). The Montgolfier brothers' hot-air balloon, an exciting invention that appears in **"Washing-Day,"** enables men to harness warm air and elude gravity (Poem 102). **"An Inventory of the Furniture in Dr. Priestley's Study"** lists among the scientist's equipment Leyden jars containing electric charges (Poem 21, line 19). Like the icehouse, these devices are manmade, that is, specifically masculine; as Isobel Armstrong asserts, the phrase "man, the great magician" "surely [signifies] the masculine subject alone."[66] Like the "resistless" men who "control the genius of th'unwilling flood" in Barbauld's **"The Invitation,"** all these technologies of entrapment seek to appropriate the creatures and powers of (usually) feminine nature.

These poems share the ineradicable ambivalence of Barbauld's other texts about science. In general they approvingly treat inventions like the icehouse and the hot-air balloon as instruments of progress that will better the human condition. But the mastery that these technologies represent entails a price, the poems imply, in the uncertainty of what trapped phenomena, "oppress'd by bondage," may do. Winter is confined in the icehouse only temporarily and will inevitably escape "To rush in whirlwinds forth, and rule the year" (line 31). The hot-air balloon in **"Washing-Day"**—whose first, experimental passengers were three domestic animals[67]—could crash or go awry. The poem wryly deflates, as it were, the balloonists' triumph, an instance of "the toils of men" that resemble "the sports of children" (Poem 102, line 84). The lightning in Priestley's laboratory "phials" could wreak havoc in the neighborhood, like the exploding gases that once almost did him "a mischief." Like a rogue spirit, if released these electric charges could "Bring down the lightning on [the neighbors'] houses, / And kill their geese, and fright their spouses" ([**"An Inventory of the Furniture in Dr. Priestley's Study,"**] Poem 21, lines 16, 21, 23-4). In these texts, experimental gadgetry disrupts or threatens domestic tranquility and normalcy—such as the women's work in **"Washing-Day"**—as well as the lives of helpless creatures. Elaborating on the problematic entrapment in **"The Mouse's Petition,"** these images of incarcerated nature call into question a headlong optimism about aggressive technocracy—an optimism that, paradoxically, Barbauld was inclined to share.

BARBAULD'S DISCLAIMER AND THE "PETITION'S" RECEPTION

Although William Turner reports that the **"Petition"** moved Priestley to free one particular mouse, the philosopher continued to use mice in his work with gases until at least 1775 (then, citing imprecise results, he decided "not to make any more experiments with mice").[68] The reading public, in contrast, took the poem's antivivisection implications more to heart. At the same time, Barbauld's dialogue with critics further exposes unresolved conflicts in her attitudes. The *Critical Review,* treating the poem as an attack on Priestley, amended its subtitle to say sarcastically that the petition was found by "the *humane* Dr. P." (emphasis in original). Evidently familiar with Priestley's work on electricity, the reviewer misreported that the mouse had been caught "to be tortured by electrical experiments," not for experiments with gases. The writer went on to "commend the lady's humanity for endeavouring to extricate the little wretch from misery" and to "testify our abhorrence of the cruelty practised by experimental philosophers."[69] Similarly, *The Monthly Review* desired that **"The Mouse's Petition"** would "be of service to that gentleman [Priestley] as well as other *experimental* philosophers, who are not remarkable for their humanity to the poor harmless animals, that are so ill-fated as to fall in their way."[70] In later editions of her *Poems,* Barbauld distanced herself from faultfinding over Priestley's experiments. A note in the third, fourth, and fifth editions

reads, "The Author is concerned to find, that what was intended as the petition of mercy against justice, has been construed as the pleas of humanity against cruelty. She is certain that cruelty could never be apprehended from the Gentleman to whom this is addressed; and the poor animal would have suffered more as the victim of domestic economy, than of philosophical curiosity."[71]

Barbauld's backpedaling here is puzzling. Her implication that it was "justice" to experiment with the mouse undercuts the poem's message of sympathy. On the other hand, the poet may have been not merely "concerned" but horrified to see her good friend condemned in print as "not remarkable for [his] humanity." Her note may be a defense against such a perception as much as a disclaimer about the intent of the **"Petition."** (She may also be dryly hinting that animal sympathy, as a practical matter, has its limits: just as the mouse would have been killed as a pest, most people would not hesitate to exterminate vermin in their homes.) Decades later, after Barbauld's death, Turner's account of the poem's genesis reproduced her efforts at damage control, possibly out of loyalty to the Aikin circle. Like Barbauld, Turner represents Priestley's use of mice as unavoidable and treats their fate in the lab as relatively humane: "no more easy or unexceptionable way of making such experiments [on gases] could be devised, than the reserving of these little victims of domestic economy, which were thus at least as easily and as speedily put out of existence, as by any of the more usual modes."[72] For many other readers, **"The Mouse's Petition"** clearly asserts a humble creature's right to exist unmolested by human machinations. Possibly by way of Burns's "To a Mouse," variations on the phrase "men, like mice" have become shorthand, an equation representing humans' and other animals' shared vulnerability to the vicissitudes of an uncertain world.[73]

Barbauld's anxiety about the poem's reception speaks to the final irreconcilability of the tensions in her dialogue with Priestley. Knowledge is desirable, both writers agree, but the costs of knowledge—in animal suffering, in manipulation of nature, in "trouble and expence"—are high. Discovering "Truth" at the expense of compassion and "humanity" is a purchase disturbingly "dear," as Priestley had put it. In the end, **"The Mouse's Petition"** is neither a definitive pronouncement on animal experiments nor a broadside attack on science, but a nonce utterance provoked by a caged animal at Priestley's "hospitable board" (Poem 19, line 40). Mock-serious though its tone may be, this slight poem about a small mammal is a nexus of more epochal phenomena: experimental science, the culture of sensibility, advocacy for animals, and the gendered politics of knowledge. A sidelong subversion of Enlightenment technocracy, **"The Mouse's Petition"** is a scene of engagement among competing but interdependent discourses struggling to come to terms with the material world and with its meanings for thinking, feeling women and men.

Notes

1. William McCarthy and Elizabeth Kraft, eds., *The Poems of Anna Letitia Barbauld* (Athens, Ga.: Univ. of Georgia Press, 1994). Quotations of Barbauld's poems are from this edition, hereafter cited in text by poem number and line number. For the full text of "The Mouse's Petition," see appendix.

2. William Turner, "Mrs. Barbauld," *Newcastle Magazine*, n.s., 4 (1825): 184, qtd. in McCarthy and Kraft, *Poems,* 244. Turner, of Newcastle, was an early historian of Warrington Academy, an Aikin family acquaintance, and a collector of Anna Letitia's poems. See McCarthy and Kraft, *Poems,* 204, 377.

3. McCarthy and Kraft, *Poems,* 245.

4. Review of *Poems* [by Anna Letitia Aikin], *Critical Review* 35 (1773): 192-5.

5. Lawrence Buell, *The Environmental Imagination: Thoreau, Nature Writing, and the Formation of American Culture* (Cambridge: Cambridge Univ. Press, 1985), 185; Samuel Taylor Coleridge, *The Watchman,* ed. Lewis Patton, vol. 2 of *The Collected Works of Samuel Taylor Coleridge* (London: Routledge and Kegan Paul, 1970), 313.

6. Marlon B. Ross, "Configurations of Feminine Reform: The Woman Writer and the Tradition of Dissent," in Carol Shiner Wilson and Joel Haefner, eds., *Re-Visioning Romanticism: British Women Writers, 1776-1837* (Philadelphia: Univ. of Pennsylvania Press, 1994), 98-9.

7. Donna Landry, *The Invention of the Countryside: Hunting, Walking, and Ecology in English Literature, 1671-1831* (Basingstoke, U. K.: Palgrave, 2001), 8, 123-4.

8. Moira Ferguson, *Animal Advocacy and Englishwomen, 1780-1900: Patriots, Nation, and Empire* (Ann Arbor: Univ. of Michigan Press, 2001), 3-4. For more on anti-slavery rhetoric and representations of animals, see Markman Ellis, *The Politics of Sensibility: Race, Gender and Commerce in the Sentimental Novel (Cambridge: Cambridge Univ. Press, 1996),* 50-5. Barbauld's "Epistle to William Wilberforce, Esq. on the Rejection of the Bill for abolishing the Slave Trade" is number 87 in *Poems.*

9. Ferguson, *Animal Advocacy and Englishwomen,* 4.

10. Andreas-Holger Maehle and Ulrich Trohler, "Animal Experimentation from Antiquity to the End of the Eighteenth Century: Attitudes and Arguments," in Nicolaas A. Rupke, ed., *Vivisection in Historical Perspective* (London: Croom Helm, 1987), 30.

11. Keith Thomas, *Man and the Natural World: A History of the Modern Sensibility* (New York: Pantheon, 1983), 167-9, 175-6.

12. Stuart Curran, "Romantic Poetry: The I Altered," in *Romanticism and Feminism,* ed. Anne K. Mellor (Bloomington: Indiana Univ. Press, 1988), 197.

13. Ann B. Shteir, *Cultivating Women, Cultivating Science: Flora's Daughters and Botany in England, 1760 to 1860* (Baltimore: Johns Hopkins Univ. Press, 1996), 2. On women aristocrats and natural history, see Shteir, *Cultivating Women,* 47-50; and David E. Allen, *The Naturalist in Britain: A Social History* (London: Allen Lane, 1976), 28-9. For broader historical context on women and science, see Barbara T. Gates and Ann B. Shteir, eds., *Natural Eloquence: Women Reinscribe Science* (Madison: Univ. of Wisconsin Press, 1997), 5-7; and Londa Schiebinger, *The Mind Has No Sex? Women in the Origins of Modern Science* (Cambridge, Mass.: Harvard Univ. Press, 1989).

14. Lucy Aikin, preface to *A Legacy for Young Ladies, Consisting of Miscellaneous Pieces, in Prose and Verse, by the Late Mrs. Barbauld* (Boston: David, Reed, 1826), iv. On Barbauld's influence, see William McCarthy, "The Celebrated Academy at Palgrave: A Documentary History of Anna Letitia Barbauld's School," *Age of Johnson* 8 (1997): 280.

15. Gates and Shteir, *Natural Eloquence,* 7; Patricia Phillips, *The Scientific Lady: A Social History of Women's Scientific Interests 1520-1918* (London: Weidenfeld and Nicolson, 1990), 129-30.

16. McCarthy and Kraft, *Poems,* 227.

17. Lucy Aikin, *Memoir,* vol. 1 of *The Works of Anna Laetitia Barbauld. With a Memoir by Lucy Aikin,* 2 vols. (London: Longman, 1825), x-xi.

18. The Aikin circle was connected with the coterie of naturalist-writers that included Thomas Pennant and Gilbert White. John Aikin was a friend of Pennant, whose *British Zoology* Barbauld may have known; see McCarthy and Kraft, *Poems,* 334, 224. In 1795 Aikin edited a *Calendar of Nature* gleaned from White's naturalist's journals and *Natural History of Selborne,* and he brought out the book's second edition in 1802. These collaborations suggest that Barbauld had ample access to natural history knowledge.

19. Aikin, *Memoir,* xxv.

20. *Letters of Charles and Mary Lamb,* ed. Edwin W. Marrs Jr. (Ithaca: Cornell Univ. Press, 1975-78), 2:81-2; McCarthy, "Celebrated Academy at Palgrave," 313.

21. Barbauld, *Lessons for Children,* Part I (Charleston, S.C.: J. Hoff, 1807), 12, 10-11.

22. John Aikin and Anna Barbauld, *Evenings at Home; or, the Juvenile Budget Opened,* rev. and ed. Cecil Hartley (New York: Hurd and Houghton, 1864). See, for example, the dialogue "Eyes, and No Eyes; or, The Art of Seeing," 274-81. Barbauld's and Aikin's works also reproduce conservative expectations about the gendered pursuit of knowledge. Unlike the dialogues led by female mentors in the works of Trimmer, Wakefield, Wollstonecraft, and others, most of the natural history dialogues in *Evenings at Home* feature boy protagonists identifying specimens for adult male teachers. While girls are depicted studying gravity and the movements of the earth, equally often they learn lessons of moral virtue, including compassion for animals. Judging by Lucy Aikin's attributions, John Aikin probably wrote most of the natural history dialogues in *Evenings at Home*; see *Memoir,* xxxvi-xxvii. For more on dialogues and female teacher-mentors, see Gates and Shteir, *Natural Eloquence,* 7-12; Shteir, *Cultivating Women,* 81-103; Mitzi Myers, "Impeccable Governesses, Rational Dames, and Moral Mothers: Mary Wollstonecraft and the Female Tradition in Georgian Children's Books," *Children's Literature* 14 (1986): 31-59; and Greg Myers, "Science for Women and Children: The Dialogue of Popular Science in the Nineteenth Century," in John Christie and Sally Shuttleworth, eds., *Nature Transfigured: Science and Literature, 1700-1900* (Manchester: Manchester Univ. Press, 1989), 173-81.

23. Barbauld, *Legacy for Young Ladies,* 29.

24. Barbauld, letter printed in *Works,* 2:67.

25. McCarthy and Kraft, *Poems,* 244.

26. Charlotte Smith also discusses bird migration in her poetry; see, for example, "The wheat-ear," in *The Poems of Charlotte Smith,* ed. Stuart Curran (New York: Oxford Univ. Press, 1993), 194-6. Gilbert White was fascinated by the mystery of whether swallows migrate or hibernate.

27. Guest, "Eighteenth-Century Femininity: 'A Supposed Sexual Character,'" in Vivien Jones, ed., *Women and Literature in Britain, 1700-1800* (Cambridge: Cambridge Univ. Press, 2000), 53; McCarthy, "'We Hoped the *Woman* Was Going to Appear': Repression, Desire, and Gender in Anna Letitia Barbauld's Early Poems," in Paula R. Feldman and Theresa M. Kelley, eds., *Romantic Women Writers: Voices and Countervoices* (Hanover, N.H.: Univ. Press of New England, 1995), 116.

28. Shteir, *Cultivating Women,* 56.

29. Guest, *Small Change: Women, Learning, Patriotism, 1750-1810* (Chicago: Univ. of Chicago Press, 2000), 95-110.

30. Shteir, *Cultivating Women,* 37.

31. This letter has been a touchstone for critical debate about Barbauld and feminism. See Guest, "Eighteenth-Century Femininity"; McCarthy, "We Hoped"; and Daniel White, "The 'Joineriana': Anna Barbauld, the Aikin Family Circle, and the Dissenting Public Sphere," *Eighteenth-Century Studies* 32.4 (1999): 530-1. McCarthy, who is preparing a biography of Barbauld, maintains that her niece, Lucy Aikin, edited the letter in *Works* to make Barbauld appear safely conservative. He predicts that the letter, when seen in "full biographical context," will have a new import; see McCarthy, "A 'High-Minded Christian Lady': The Posthumous Reception of Anna Letitia Barbauld," in Harriet Kramer Linkin and Stephen C. Behrendt, eds., *Romanticism and Women Writers: Opening the Doors of Reception* (Lexington: Univ. of Kentucky Press, 1999), 189.

32. Aikin, *Memoir,* xvii-xviii.

33. Barbauld, *Legacy for Young Ladies,* 24-6. Of course, neither Priestley nor anyone else was a "professional" scientist in the eighteenth century. Barbauld is marking the difference between acquiring and producing knowledge; in addition, any avocation that would distract women from their domestic "professional knowledge" is problematic. Priestley's scientific work was not without difficulties; he labored constantly to get financing, equipment, and collegial support. His experiments were subject to criticism and sometimes ridicule, but he was not criticized for violating gender norms as an aspiring woman scientist would likely have been.

34. For an analysis of science and gender in this poem that overlaps with mine in some respects, see Penny Bradshaw, "Gendering the Enlightenment: Conflicting Images of Progress in the Poetry of Anna Letitia Barbauld," *Women's Writing* 5.3 (1998): 357-9.

35. Evelyn Fox Keller, *Reflections on Gender and Science* (New Haven: Yale Univ. Press, 1985), 64. Other key sources on "feminine" nature include Sherry B. Ortner, "Is Female to Male as Nature Is to Culture?" in Michelle Zimbalist Rosaldo and Louise Lamphere, eds., *Women, Culture, and Society* (Stanford: Stanford Univ. Press, 1974), 67-87; Carolyn Merchant, *The Death of Nature: Women, Ecology, and the Scientific Revolution* (San Francisco: Harper and Row, 1980); and Gillian Rose, *Feminism and Geography: The Limits of Geographical Knowledge* (Minneapolis: Minnesota Univ. Press, 1993).

36. Gates and Shteir, *Natural Eloquence,* 6. I borrow the distinction between "student of science" and

"scientist" from Trevor Levere, "Coleridge and the Sciences," in Andrew Cunningham and Nicholas Jardine, eds., *Romanticism and the Sciences* (Cambridge: Cambridge Univ. Press, 1990), 296.

37. Guest, *Small Change,* 238.

38. McCarthy, "We Hoped," 120-2.

39. Priestley, *The History of the Present State of Electricity, with Original Experiments,* 2nd ed. (London: J. Johnson and J. Payne, 1769), v, xviii, xvii.

40. "The Hill of Science: A Vision," in *Miscellaneous Pieces, in Prose,* by John Aikin and Anna Letitia Aikin [Barbauld] (London: J. Johnson, 1773), 31-4, 38. Lucy Aikin attributes authorship of "The Hill of Science" to Barbauld in *Memoir,* lxv.

41. Priestley, *History of Electricity,* xviii.

42. See John Passmore, "The Treatment of Animals," *Journal of the History of Ideas* 36.2 (1975): 201-2; Thomas, *Man and the Natural World,* 149-51, 154.

43. Ann Jessie Van Sant shows that sensibility, informed by traditional notions of emotion as "partly physical," collapsed the categories of physiological and psychological in its rhetoric of suffering. Language about emotion was "rephysicalized" and psychological experience "prominently located in the body"; see *Eighteenth-Century Sensibility and the Novel: The Senses in Social Context* (Cambridge: Cambridge Univ. Press, 1993), 93, 97. On sensibility and theories of the nervous system, see G. J. Barker-Benfield, *The Culture of Sensibility: Sex and Society in Eighteenth-Century Britain* (Chicago: Univ. of Chicago Press, 1992), 3-9.

44. Thomas, *Man and the Natural World,* 151. On the reluctance to destroy vermin, see Thomas, *Man and the Natural World,* 173, 176. For more background on the complexities of cultural attitudes toward animals, see Harriet Ritvo, "Learning from Animals: Natural History for Children in the Eighteenth and Nineteenth Centuries," *Children's Literature* 13 (1995): 72-93; Ritvo, *The Animal Estate: The English and Other Creatures in the Victorian Age* (Cambridge, Mass.: Harvard Univ. Press, 1997); and Landry, *Invention of the Countryside,* 7-9, 113-25.

45. Mitzi Myers, "Of Mice and Mothers: Mrs. Barbauld's 'New Walk' and Gendered Codes in Children's Literature," in Louise Wetherbee Phelps and Janet Emig, eds., *Feminine Principles and Women's Experience in American Composition and Rhetoric* (Pittsburgh: Univ. of Pittsburgh Press, 1995), 275. This article contains a useful discussion of "The Mouse's Petition" and of animals in Barbauld's works for children.

46. Aikin and Barbauld, *Evenings at Home* (1864 ed.), 114.

47. Aikin and Barbauld, *Evenings at Home; or, The Juvenile Budget Opened,* 2nd ed. (Philadelphia: A. Bartram, 1802), 2:103.

48. Maehle and Trohler, "Animal Experimentation," 14-20, 34-7. In the later nineteenth century, the term *vivisection* came to be used more broadly to denote any kind of experimentation, surgical or otherwise, on live animals.

49. See Maehle and Trohler, "Animal Experimentation," 28-32.

50. *The Yale Edition of the Works of Samuel Johnson,* vol. 2, ed. W. J. Bate, John M. Bullitt, and L. F. Powell (New Haven: Yale Univ. Press, 1963), 56. On Johnson and science, see Phillips, *The Scientific Lady,* 156-7.

51. Joseph Priestley, *Scientific Autobiography of Joseph Priestley,* ed. Robert E. Schofield (Cambridge, Mass.: Massachusetts Institute of Technology Press, 1966), 35. Franklin's remark appears in a paper of his that is printed in *Scientific Autobiography,* 67.

52. Priestley, *History of Electricity,* 618-20. The reference to "a lingering death" appears in Priestley's account of the same experiment in his *Scientific Autobiography,* 35.

53. Priestley, *History of Electricity,* 621-2.

54. Priestley, *Scientific Autobiography,* 65. On witnesses to Priestley's experiments, see *Scientific Autobiography,* 22, 32; on his setup at Warrington, see Betsy Rodgers, *Georgian Chronicle: Mrs. Barbauld and Her Family* (London: Methuen, 1958), 41.

55. Priestley, *Autobiography of Joseph Priestley,* ed. Jack Lindsay (Teaneck, N.J.: Associated Univ. Presses, 1970), 113-4.

56. Priestley, *Scientific Autobiography,* 88.

57. Guest, *Small Change,* 11-12.

58. Van Sant, *Eighteenth-Century Sensibility,* 30, 71.

59. Barker-Benfield, *Culture of Sensibility,* 234, 227, 231.

60. Doody, "Women Poets of the Eighteenth Century," in Vivien Jones, ed., *Women and Literature in Britain, 1700-1800* (Cambridge: Cambridge Univ. Press, 2000), 231.

61. *Hymns in Prose for Children* (London: J. Johnson, 1781), 10-11. Barbauld writes, "The birds can warble, and young lambs can bleat; but we can open our lips in [God's] praise, we can speak of all his goodness. Therefore we will thank him for ourselves, and we will thank him for those that cannot speak." For more on women writers and animal sympathy, see Barker-Benfield, *Culture of*

Sensibility, 232-6, and Mitzi Myers, "Impeccable Governesses" (see note 22), 43, 46-7.

62. Passmore, "Treatment of Animals," 197-8, 208.

63. On the concept of transmigration, see Thomas, *Man and the Natural World,* 138-41; on Priestley's beliefs, see McCarthy and Kraft, *Poems,* 246.

64. Barbauld, *Legacy for Young Ladies,* 105.

65. Priestley, *History of Electricity,* ix-x, xvi.

66. Isobel Armstrong, "The Gush of the Feminine: How Can We Read Women's Poetry of the Romantic Period?" in Paula R. Feldman and Theresa M. Kelley, eds., *Romantic Women Writers: Voices and Countervoices* (Hanover, N.H.: Univ. Press of New England, 1995), 14. I am indebted to this essay for calling my attention to gadgetry in other Barbauld texts. Armstrong notes that "Inscription for an Ice-House," while "not quite the first poem written to a refrigerator," is "certainly one of the earliest hymns to technology."

67. See Ann Messenger, *His and Hers: Essays in Restoration and Eighteenth-Century Literature* (Lexington: Univ. Press of Kentucky, 1986), 191.

68. Priestley, *The Discovery of Oxygen: Part 1* (Edinburgh: E. S. Livingstone, 1961), 18.

69. Review of *Poems* [by Anna Letitia Aikin], *Critical Review* 35 (1773): 193.

70. Review of *Poems* [by Anna Letitia Aikin], *Monthly Review* 48 (1773): 138, qtd. in McCarthy and Kraft, *Poems,* 245.

71. Qtd. in McCarthy and Kraft, *Poems,* 245.

72. Qtd. in McCarthy and Kraft, *Poems,* 245.

73. John Steinbeck's *Of Mice and Men* may be the most obvious example; WorldCat lists at least five nonfiction books about laboratory animals whose titles contain the words "mice and men."

John Mee (essay date 2003)

SOURCE: Mee, John. "Barbauld, Devotion, and the Woman Prophet." In *Romanticism, Enthusiasm, and Regulation: Poetics and the Policing of Culture in the Romantic Period,* pp. 173-213. Oxford: Oxford University Press, 2003.

[In the following excerpt, Mee discusses aspects of political, moral, and religious enthusiasm in Barbauld's writings. Mee argues that the vigor and forcefulness of Barbauld's style set her apart from most other women writers of her era.]

From the 1780s Barbauld often practised a less politely amiable idea of public discourse, one which sometimes made frequent use of prophetic language to break through 'plausive argument, the daring lye | The artful gloss' (*Epistle to Wilberforce* [*Epistle to William Wilberforce, Esq., on the Rejection of the Bill for Abolishing the Slave Trade*]: *BP* [*The Poems of Anna Letitia Barbauld*] 116, ll. 28-9). Barbauld's writing from this period insists that 'Truth is of a very intolerant spirit. She will not make any compromise with Error.'[1] Whereas candour had to make its compromise with Anglican manners in some of the earlier writing, now there is a much less conciliatory attitude. Barbauld's 'mental mode is that of intervention now rather than meditation'.[2]

Before looking at her writing from this period in more detail, however, we need to acknowledge that even in her first volume this strain had been a feature of her poetry. Any narrative of linear development from the amiability of the Warrington years to the radicalism of London threatens to blind us to the diversity of her poetry and the pressure that she continually put on the limits of sensibility. If there are hints of an extreme of unworlding in **'An Address to the Deity',** these are more pronounced in another of the poems in her 1773 volume **'A Summer Evening's Meditation'.** Her intentions in this respect are indicated to the reader by the epigraph from Young's *Night Thoughts*: '*One sun by day, by night ten thousand shine*' (*BP* 81). The epigraph effectively announces that the poem will 'launch into the trackless deeps of space' (*BP* 83, l. 82), and in doing so signals Barbauld's sense of equality with the male canon of poetic enthusiasm.[3] An even more obvious poetic influence on Barbauld's poem in this respect would have been Mark Akenside's *The Pleasures of Imagination,* edited by Barbauld two decades later, but published in a revised edition just before Barbauld's *Poems.*[4] Her critical essay on Akenside contrasted 'the deepest gloom' of Young's Calvinism with the more liberal sentiment to be found in *The Pleasures of Imagination*:

> The religion of the other, all at least that appears of it, and all indeed that could with propriety appear in such a Poem, is the purest Theism; liberal, cheerful, and sublime; or, if admitting any mixture, he seems inclined to tincture it with the mysticism of PLATO, and the gay fables of ancient mythology.[5]

Her own **'A Summer Evening's Meditation'** is full of Shaftesburian rapture—the rapture that Barbauld's essay on Akenside identified as a direct source for *Pleasures of Imagination*—at the limitlessness of creation, but in the process Barbauld discovers the God within:

> At this still hour the self-collected soul
> Turns inward, and beholds a stranger there
> Of high descent, and more than mortal rank;
> An embryo GOD; a spark of fire divine.
>
> (*BP* 82, ll. 53-6)

Again this would seem to echo Akenside's poeticization of Shaftesbury:

. . . we feel within ourselves
His energy divine: he tells the heart,
He meant, he made us to behold and love
What he beholds and loves, the general orb
Of life and being; to be great like him,
beneficent and active.[6]

The end of the Barbauld's poem does provide the standard disclaimer that acknowledges the impossibility of her encompassing the infinite perspective to which she aspires:

. . . Let me here
Content and grateful, wait th'appointed time
And ripen for the skies: the hour will come
When all these splendours bursting on my sight
Shall stand unveil'd, and to my ravish'd sense
Unlock the glories of the world unknown.

(*BP* 84, ll. 117-22)

But any understanding of these lines purely in terms of female modesty needs also to take into account the kinds of disavowal endemic in eighteenth-century poetic enthusiasm per se. Those found in Coleridge's 'Religious Musings' are a late example of this reflex in the elite poetics of unworlding. Male poets were thought to have the ability to express their enthusiasm without dissolving their selves, but had to demonstrate their discipline. The review of 'Religious Musings' written by Barbauld's brother credited Coleridge with managing this feat, but also reveals that such judgements were not unconditional. Given this disciplinary context, the sustained exploration of the imagination's yearning for 'solitudes of vast unpeopled space' (*BP* 83, l. 94) in Barbauld's poem is perhaps all the more remarkable, the concluding disavowal notwithstanding. However much the poetics of amiable sociability defines her poetry of this period, Barbauld did not forswear the attempt at the sublime of poetic enthusiasm. Indeed she was later bold enough to suggest that at least one male precursor had not always been sufficiently able to practise the ardour of enthusiasm that he preached. Barbauld claimed that most of Akenside's poem had the appearance 'of being laboured into excellence'. She preferred poetry that savoured more of 'being thrown off at once amidst the swell and fervency of a kindled imagination':[7]

IF the genius of AKENSIDE be to be estimated from this Poem, . . . it will be found to be lofty and elegant, chaste, classical, and correct: not marked with strong traits of originality, not ardent nor exuberant. His enthusiasm was rather of that kind which is kindled by reading and imbibing the spirit of authors, than by contemplating at first hand the works of nature.[8]

Whether she would have pressed this judgment in 1773 is a moot point, but poems such as **'A Summer Evening's Meditation'** are effectively an assertion of her ability to a stretch beyond Akenside and others in the school of Shaftesbury without annihilating the self. The *Westminster Magazine* similarly detected 'a masculine force in them which the most vigorous of our [male] poets has not excelled'. The judgment does not present her as a poet of delicate sensibility, but as someone capable of stretching the religious sublime to invigorating lengths.[9]

These matters are questions of degree. How far could enthusiasm be pushed before it came to be regarded as too vehement and entangled in the passions? Did self-annihilation offer an invigorating vision of Eternity or a terrifying prospect of dissolution? How far did the gender of the writers and the readers concerned influence these judgements? Barbauld affiliated herself in **'An Address to the Deity'** and **'A Summer Evening's Meditation'** with a poetics of unworlding that Akenside, Young, and others had learnt in part from Shaftesbury, but she granted her own enthusiasm more latitude than some of these male precursors, whom she judged neither sufficiently 'ardent nor exuberant'. Judgements by writers and critics about how far such enthusiasm could be taken varied according to a reading context that changed over the eighteenth century as well as in relation to the social and gendered identities of writers and readers. Possibly the rehabilitation of enthusiasm charted by Irlam had developed further towards a freedom about 'form-lessness' in the 1770s than it had for Akenside in the 1740s.[10] Even so there remained in play questions about how such enthusiasm could be regulated into properly aesthetic forms. Relatively speaking, religious reveries such as **'A Summer Evening's Meditation'** were capable of being conceived of as private, and so insulated from the infectious enthusiasm of the crowd. Self-annihilation could be risked in a sphere that limited the dispersal of the self. 'Meditation' could be seen as a key word in this respect, bringing Barbauld close to the Anglican perception that proper religious warmth was a matter of quiet devotion that shunned the crowd. The morals and manners movement that has been seen as comprising Dissenters such as Barbauld as well as Church of England evangelicals such as her sometime friend Hannah More always defined the difference between its religious feelings and the less regulated passions of the Methodists in terms of this kind of distinction.[11] Neither, for all their unworlding of experience, do **'An Address to the Deity'** or **'A Summer Evening's Meditation'** display the public disputatiousness that Barbauld found alarming in much of Priestley's religious writing. Nothing in them pushes Barbauld's affective religion close to the crowd. Yet even in her early poetry Barbauld sometimes did carry her enthusiasm over into public and political matters that pushed against the insulating walls of the private sphere.

'PATRIOT ENTHUSIASM'

If she was a follower of Akenside, his example was not limited to 'ideas of the fair and beautiful in morals and in taste, gathered from the writings of SHAFTESBURY, HUTCHINSON', but also what she saw as the poet's 'high sense of liberty'.[12] Akenside was a poet strongly identified with the patriot enthusiasm of the Whig tradition despised by Hume and Samuel Johnson. Johnson condemned Akenside's 'unnecessary and outrageous zeal for what he called and thought liberty'. Dissenters such as Andrew Kippis, another product of Doddridge's at Northampton, were much more likely to be attracted to what they saw as his 'most ardent spirit of liberty'.[13] Barbauld's poem **'Corsica'**, the poem that leads off her 1773 collection, articulates some of that spirit for the radical opposition of the 1760 and 1770s. The late 1760s saw a growing campaign of opposition to the government for its failure to live up to what were represented as the true Whig principles of liberty. The letters of 'Junius' in the *Public Advertiser* attacked the government for its use of bribery and corruption to manipulate Parliament, extolled the cause of John Wilkes, and took the part of the American colonies in their campaign against taxation without representation. Patriot opinion was also calling on the government to intervene on the side of the Corsicans, under General Pasquale Paoli, who were preparing to resist the invasion plans of their French overlords. Barbauld's poem is a contribution to this campaign written in the style of Akenside's patriot enthusiasm:

> What then should BRITONS feel? should they not catch
> The warm contagion of heroic ardour,
> And kindle at a fire so like their own?
>
> (*BP* 21, ll. 15-17)

No less than Akenside, Barbauld here makes 'raptur'd fancy' the basis of a poetics of liberty. Akenside understood his *Pleasures of Imagination* to work 'by exhibiting the most engaging prospects of nature, to enlarge and harmonize the imagination, and by that means insensibly dispose the minds of men to a similar taste and habit of thinking in religion, morals, and civil life'.[14] Barbauld encouraged a similar enthusiasm for virtue. Deeds such as Paoli's '. . . give mankind | A glimpse of higher natures' (*BP* 24, ll. 108-9). Such glimpses, Barbauld suggests, can encourage Britain to live up to its reputation as the home of liberty.

Her poem **'The Invitation'** is quite explicit about the role of enthusiasm in drawing the individual out of the private into the public sphere through the power of sympathetic identification:

> And fond enthusiastic thought, that feeds
> On pictur'd tales of vast heroic deeds;
> And quick affections, kindling into flame
> At virtue's, or their country's honour'd name.
>
> (*BP* 13, ll. 121-4)

Lucy Newlyn is surely right to suggest that from early on Barbauld proceeded on the assumption that 'few can reason, but all can feel'.[15] I do not wish to exaggerate the extent to which Barbauld stretched her idea of sympathy towards what her contemporaries would have re-

garded as a dangerous enthusiasm. Much of what she wrote even in this strain stays within the bounds of what was regarded as the poetics of the sublime, however open to contestation such boundaries were. Her poetic enthusiasm needs to be placed side by side with her strictures on Priestley's 'vigour'. One should also note that there are disavowals even in poems such as **'The Invitation'** when it comes to the specific possibility of a woman either sustaining 'patriot passion' (l. 167) or 'launch[ing] our souls into the bright unknown' (l. 182):

> Here cease my song, Such arduous themes require
> A master's pencil, and a poet's fire:
> Unequal far such bright designs to paint,
> Too weak her colours, and her lines too faint,
> My drooping Muse folds up her fluttering wing,
> And hides her head in the green lap of spring.
>
> (*BP* 15, ll. 83-8)

Even so, what Lucy Newlyn calls Barbauld's 'lively experimentation with contemporary male forms' often does push at the limits taken to regulate the poetics of enthusiasm, even for her male precursors such as Akenside, never mind what was thought to be possible for a woman writer to do in the genre.[16] The practice of her enthusiasm in such poems, as the *Westminster Magazine* saw it, exceeded her professions of female modesty.

Even those who admired the achievement of her 1773 volume sometimes registered a concern at the stretch and power of her imagination in such poems. The positive review she received for **Poems** from William Woodfall in the *Monthly* illustrates the gendered ambivalence towards her success. Woodfall was impressed with 'the smoothness and harmony' of her poetry; but the 'justness of thought, and vigour of imagination' he found 'extraordinary'.[17] His remarks pertain particularly to **'Corsica'**; a poem written in a strain of patriot enthusiasm that the second part of the review implied was more properly a masculine province. After the praise that takes up most of the first part of the review, Woodfall reveals the disappointment of his expectation that 'the *Woman* was going to appear':

> If she, as well as others of our female writers, has, in pursuing the road to fame, trod too much in the footsteps of the men, it has been owing, not to a want of education, but to a want of *proper* genius. If the amiable Writer of these poems had been educated more under the direction of a mother, than of a father: if she had taken her views of human life from among her female companions, and not altogether under the direction of men, either living or dead, we should have been as much enchanted with her feminine beauties, as we are now pleased and astonished by the strength of her imagination, the variety of her knowledge, and the goodness of her heart.[18]

Woodfall praises the volume as a whole, but admits his disappointment that there is not more of feminine softness in it. His opinion is not, however, reducible to a complaint at the lack of feeling as such. He is disappointed at the absence of *softer* emotions and the language of love associated with what he thinks of as female sensibility. What he finds extraordinarily present in their stead is the vigorous patriotism of **'Corsica'** and the religious sublime of poems such as **'An Address to the Deity'**: both genres that he assumes to be masculine. For all that he admires 'the variety of her knowledge, and the goodness of her heart', his comments on the 'proper genius' of women suggests a doubt over whether a woman writer is ever going to be truly capable of regulating such poetic enthusiasm. There are hints in this direction in the muted negative comments on **'Corsica'** in the first part of the review. Woodfall implies that ardour has overtaken judgement in the portrait of Paoli. He also registers pleasure bordering on relief at Barbauld's acknowledgement of disappointment ('the error of her zeal') in the additional lines added after Paoli's defeat at the Battle of Pontenuovo in June 1769:

> . . . Forgive the zeal
> That, too presumptuous, whisper'd better things
> And read the book of destiny amiss.
> Not with the purple colouring of success
> Is virtue best adorn'd: th'attempt is praise.
> There yet remains a freedom, nobler far
> Than kings or senates can destroy or give;
> Beyond the proud oppressor's cruel grasp
> Seated secure; uninjur'd; undestroy'd;
> Worthy of Gods: The freedom of the mind.
>
> (*BP* 26, ll. 192-201)

Written some time after the main part of the poem, these lines may simply express Barbauld's dismay at Paoli's eventual fate. She continues to zealously assert 'the freedom of the mind'. Yet Woodfall eagerly seizes on the lines as a welcome disavowal of public intentions and proof that her patriot enthusiasm was not taking her too far beyond the boundaries that circumscribed women writers.

Let me return now to Anne Janowitz's suggestion that Barbauld took on a new language of political intervention when she moved to London in the 1780s and mixed with the intellectual activists of the Joseph Johnson circle. Janowitz thinks of this transformation in terms of its use of a language of 'analysis' rather than of the 'manners' prized in the discourse of sensibility.[19] Barbauld's writing in pamphlets such as *An Address to the Opposers of the Repeal of the Corporation and Test Acts* (1790) and *Sins of Government, Sins of the Nation* (1793) certainly represents a direct intervention in politics, but whether or not this shift represents a movement to a language of 'analysis' is another matter. Not that I am suggesting that Barbauld was not perfectly capable of offering a cool analysis of the political situation in the early 1790s. Her intellectual acuity is be-

yond question; and plenty of it is on display in these pamphlets. What I want to guard against is any possibility of Janowitz's careful opposition between 'analysis' and 'manners' being reduced to one between 'reason' and 'feeling'. Barbauld's political writing of this period is nothing if not impassioned, and often takes on a tone of unapologetic patriot enthusiasm. Indeed, now this language seems more unbridled in its readiness to adopt a fully prophetic register and put aside the regulatory caution of much of her earlier writing. Whereas her 1775 essay had cautioned against excessive candour, now it seems Barbauld is unwilling to admit of any limit to the pursuit of truth: 'The spirit of Enquiry, like a severe and searching wind, penetrates every part of the great body politic; and whatever is unsound, whatever is infirm, shrinks at the visitation.'[20] *An Address to the Opposers* displays the millenarian confidence in the 'sure operation of increasing light and knowledge' that brought Burke's charge of enthusiasm down on the head of Richard Price.[21] The caution of Barbauld's earlier writing is thrown aside in favour of directly prophetic exhortation:

> Can ye not discern the signs of the times? The minds of men are in movement from the Borysthenes to the Atlantic. Agitated with new and strong emotions, they swell and heave beneath oppression, as the seas within the Polar Circle, when, at the approach of Spring, they grow impatient to burst their icy chains; when what, but an instant before, seemed so firm, spread for many a dreary league like a floor of solid marble, at once with a tremendous noise gives way . . . and the air resounds with the clash of floating fragments.[22]

If the 'floating fragments' of this passage were picked up in Coleridge's 'Kubla Khan', as they may well have been, it seems significant that he was to equivocate about taking the prophetic mantle that Barbauld seems to seize so confidently here. One of her opponents, William Keate, described the style of the pamphlet as 'very animated . . . ; but as the author did not allow himself time to cool, with great intemperance'. A sentence added to his critique recorded his shock to discover that language of such extravagance could have come from 'a female pen'.[23] *Sins of the Government, Sins of the Nation* for its part casts itself as a kind of jeremiad against the government's proclamation of a day of fasting in support of the war effort. Quite specifically Barbauld takes on the role of the prophet at the city gate who castigates God's people for back-sliding after the example of their rulers, and prophesies doom to the nation as a consequence. Such a confrontationally prophetic mode, especially when it was discovered that it came from the pen of a woman, was immediately seized on as proof of the enthusiasm of which Dissenters were always suspected. Barbauld's political writing of this period was easily satirized as the voice of the hysterical prophetess. Women, as I pointed out in my first chapter, were felt to have a biological disposition towards this species of enthusiasm. Barbauld's opponents quickly availed themselves of the association. Horace Walpole, for instance, who had been an admirer of her poetry, began to refer to her as 'Deborah Barbauld' in his letters, and identified her with the sectarian extremism of 'Presbytyrants'.[24] Soon afterwards he was refusing to read her work. Later he dismissed Barbauld and Helen Maria Williams as 'two prophetesses'.[25] *Sins of Government, Sins of the Nation* is written in a vigorous and prophetic style. When Barbauld translated Rousseau's idea of the general will into the language of the Bible in her pamphlet, the *British Critic* made the predictable reply in terms of Burke's over-determined redefinition of enthusiasm: 'The glorious effects of it are however displayed in a style of enthusiasm, which is rather forgetful of facts.'[26]

In her writing of this period, Barbauld often seems willing to grant an extended licence to the politics and poetics of affect that made it almost impossible for political opponents such as the *British Critic* to refrain from accusing her of enthusiasm. In poems such as **'To a Great Nation'** and *Epistle to Wilberforce* no less than the political pamphlets of this period, her own style is concerned not so much with control as provoking her readers into action. As with a great deal of other political writing from the first few years of the 1790s, the emphasis is a Blakean 'rouz[ing of] the faculties to act' ('To Dr Trusler, August 1799': E [*The Complete Poetry and Prose of William Blake*] 702). Of course, not all those in favour of political change agreed where the line between raising political consciousness and encouraging a dangerous enthusiasm was to be found. Barbauld's exchange with Gilbert Wakefield over the propriety of public worship, for instance, in some respects seems to mirror the disagreement between Godwin and Thelwall discussed in Chapter 2. Although writing in a religious rather than political context, Barbauld and Wakefield were equally as exercised as Godwin and Thelwall over the dividing line between democratic sympathies and the delirium of enthusiasm.[27] Wakefield had resigned from a position as an Anglican clergyman and taken up the post of Classics tutor at the Warrington Academy in 1779, but he refused to participate in the public forms of worship practised by the Dissenters there. Although it was dedicated to John Aikin, his *Enquiry into the Expediency and Propriety of Public or Social Worship* (1792) made it clear that he thought even liberal Dissenters still too prone to the enthusiasm of their seventeenth-century forebears. The *Enquiry* contrasted the simplicity of Christ's worship with the 'fervour' of 'all *methodists,* and most *dissenters*'.[28] At certain points in his argument Wakefield simply sounds like a radical Protestant bewailing the continuation of popish superstition in the reformed churches: '*Christians,* who pretend to a love of enquiry and a regard for the scriptures, might be ashamed to defend practices, which rest on no better authority, than the *Popish* trum-

pery of *traditionary* superstitions.' But he goes beyond this position in his fear that any kind of 'social worship' will infect the purity of prayer with the multitude's 'tumultuous murmurs'.[29] Barbauld's reply was predicated on a contrary view of the necessity and desirability of human sociability: 'prone as men are in every other circumstance to associate together, and communicate the electric fire of correspondent feelings', she found it strange that Wakefield should recommend 'unsocial reserve only where those interests are concerned which are confessedly the most important'.[30]

Her pamphlet is not unconcerned about the infectious nature of human sympathy running out of control. Indeed, her idea of public worship sometimes sounds as if its primary concern is containment: 'Public worship has this further advantage over private, that it is better secured against languor on one side, and enthusiasm on the other.' Public worship both encourages the ardour proper to such important matters and provides a crucible for it to be regulated into its proper shape. But at other points in her pamphlet, she seems willing to grant an almost limitless expansion to the ability of human beings to be moved by one another's feelings:

> The flame indeed may be kindled by silent musing; but when kindled it must infallibly spread. The devout heart, penetrated with large and affecting views of the immensity of the works of God, the harmony of his laws, and the extent of his beneficence, bursts into loud and vocal expressions of praise and adoration; and from a full and overflowing sensibility, seeks to expand itself to the utmost limits of creation. The mind is forcibly carried out of itself; and, embracing the whole circle of animated existence, calls on all above, around, below, to help to bear the burden of its gratitude. Joy is too brilliant a thing to be confined within our own bosoms; it burnishes all nature, and with its vivid colouring gives a kind of factitious life to objects without sense or motion.[31]

My next chapter will argue that Wordsworth's ability to impart such 'factitious life' was both a source of joy and anxiety to the poet. Here the concern about regulating such enthusiasm into appropriate limits present elsewhere in Barbauld's pamphlet and much of her other work seems to fall away. We have much more of Priestley's sense that excess of fervour is a better risk to take than indifference. To Wakefield passages of this tone and style only confirmed his sense that Dissent had not progressed beyond the enthusiasm of the seventeenth century. He was particularly sharp on Barbauld. Rounding impatiently on the idea of 'devotional taste,' as Priestley had done, Wakefield attacks her for promoting ideas of religion 'that savour of all that is visionary, fanatical, and superstitious'. Her attempts to distinguish between the feeling of sensibility and the passions of the crowd are dismissed. She is indicted among those who have 'transferred religion . . . from the *intellect* and *heart* to *fancy* and the *senses*'.[32] Her plea that the social affections be allowed into religious observance is dismissed as 'extravagant enthusiasm'. No less than the *British Critic,* whose politics he was deeply opposed to, Wakefield sees Barbauld's doctrines as undermining the rational basis of religion and playing to the unstable and evanescent emotions of the crowd: 'The flame of enthusiasm crackles loud, and blazes bright; but soon vanishes into air.'[33] Unlike Priestley, however, Wakefield seems not just opposed to Barbauld's aestheticization of religious feeling, but to the idea of any kind of affect being allowed a place in the context of religious worship. Wakefield may have been particularly dismissive of a female opponent, but in the next section of his pamphlet Priestley is accused of the same lapse:

> The *Doctor* like *Mrs. Barbauld,* entertains certain conceits of habitual devotion, which are, to my apprehension at least, romantic and mysterious; intoxicating vapours from the chasm of puritanical fanaticism.[34]

Wakefield admired Priestley's political and philosophical principles, but as with Godwin's commentary on Thelwall, where those principles were being promulgated on the basis of affect, they were deemed to be liable to transmutation into the mere enthusiasm of the crowd. Both Barbauld and Priestley, if in different ways and at different times, no less than Thelwall, were acutely aware of the dangers of ardour developing into enthusiasm, but their faith in sympathy meant that they could see enthusiasm as a lesser evil than the empty formality of superstition, whether of the Church or State. Wakefield was much less sure that there was any difference: they were both simply forms of unreason.

RETIRING FROM ENTHUSIASM?

The relative latitude that Barbauld gives the affections in the early 1790s might be seen as a specific product of the optimism of the early years of the revolutionary decade. By the mid-1790s many Dissenters had retreated from this confidence in the liberating potential of the social sympathies. Anne Janowitz has noted that some relaxed 'passionate radical and internationalist aim of *fraternité* . . . into a more local and familiar idea of friendship'.[35] Keach offers an even more negative account of a 'movement from enthusiastic assertiveness to pessimistic resignation'.[36] The parallel movement in Coleridge's poetry published in dissenting periodicals at the time has already been discussed, but the movement was neither universal nor unequivocal in those circles. Janowitz, for instance, usefully contrasts the responses of John Aikin and Gilbert Wakefield. Aikin wrote to Wakefield just after his release from prison in 1798 inviting him to abandon his political militancy in favour of a more restricted idea of sociability: 'Cease then, my Friend, thy generous hopeless aim . . . And in the soothing voice of friendship drown | The groans and shouts, and triumphs of the world.' Wakefield's reply refuses to back down from his defi-

ance of 'the grim visage of despotic power, | lawless, self-will'd, fierce, merciless, corrupt'.[37] One might be reminded of Judith Thompson's contrast between Coleridge and Thelwall. Certainly the discourse of retirement in the latter remains regretful and still oriented towards an eventual return to the public arena.[38] Barbauld herself comes close to the position of Thelwall. Her **'To Mr. S. T. Coleridge'** offers a direct reflection on the dangers of retirement in the context of the disillusionment of the late 1790s. Indeed we might see the poem as entering into a dialogue with Coleridge's 'Reflections on Having Left a Place of Retirement'.

Both Barbauld and Coleridge's poems were originally published in the *Monthly Magazine,* edited by Barbauld's brother John Aikin. Coleridge's poem, as we have seen, extols the engaged virtues of the prison reformer John Howard, but between its two early versions becomes increasingly equivocal about 'Entering into Active Life' (to use the phrase from the original title). Barbauld had praised Howard herself in **'Hymn: Ye are the Salt of the Earth,'** another poem originally published in the *Monthly.* The hymn represents the political activists of her time as latter-day prophets:

> Your's is the writing on the wall,
> That turns the tyrant pale.
>
> (*BP* 128, ll. 35-6)

Taken together these poems by Barbauld and Coleridge published in the *Monthly* ought to be seen as part of a debate within the dissenting community about the limits of their patriotic enthusiasm. Even several decades later, Barbauld's poetry could still be regarded by a relatively sympathetic reviewer as going too far in its ardour. Her poem **'To the Poor'** (129-30), for instance, inflected like her hymn with the language of biblical prophecy was chastised for precisely this failing in the *Literary Gazette*:

> Mrs. Barbauld's fiery democracy sometimes carried her almost the length of profanation; witness the following passage in Lines **'To the Poor'** which we do not quote, however, without giving their author credit for the utmost benevolence of heart and excellence of intention, though her patriotic enthusiasm ran away with her understanding and disqualified her judgment.[39]

Barbauld's poem to Coleridge administers a gentle chastisement of its own, but for quite different reasons. In place of the idea of enthusiasm as a paradigm-busting force that Barbauld came increasingly to share with Priestley, Coleridge is represented as someone whose imagination is tempted towards conformity and withdrawal.[40]

One might contrast Barbauld's attitude towards Coleridge with the changing nature of her view of Priestley during this period. What in the 1770s seem to have represented a rough and unmannerly enthusiasm in Priestley's zeal, by the 1790s is more often looked upon as a laudable commitment. Her sonnet **'To Dr. Priestley. Dec. 29, 1792'**, for instance, praises Priestley's 'ample stretch of thought' (**BP** 125, l. 15) that seems able to grasp 'future periods' (l. 16), whereas earlier she had represented such 'stretch' as threatening to snap even her elastic notion of sociability. A review of Priestley's character in 1803 suggested that she was weighing up the vicissitudes in her own response to the philosopher:

> One person . . . may be disposed to laugh at the Birmingham philosopher for the precipitous and unguarded manner in which he has thrown his opinions before the public; for the hearty good will with which he enters into the arena of controversy; for the amusing egotism of a heart that has nothing to hide; for the frankness with which he pours himself out before his readers . . . but there are others who will view with affectionate reverence, the child-like simplicity of an ingenuous. Penetrating, and philosophical spirit, the generous imprudence of an eager champion for truth, who follows her, regardless of consequences, in every track where he entertains the least hope of finding her; and the comparative indifference for personal considerations . . . which has made him neglect those guards and fences within which a more wary combatant would have intrenched himself.[41]

As the tone of the paragraph suggests, Barbauld's response at the time of writing, when Priestley was exiled in the United States, was more inclined to an 'affectionate reverence' for what she could forgive as a form of 'generous imprudence'. Faced with a political and religious establishment that seemed to be asserting the old hierarchies, to the point that they had driven Priestley from his home, Barbauld stresses the heroism of his enthusiasm. Writing in the 1770s, she had been able to imagine an accommodation of Dissent with the Church of England under the rubric of 'liberal sentiments', in 1803 the establishment was looking more and more like a tyranny that had to be opposed with honest indignation.

If Barbauld was forced more and more into retirement by the practical position of Dissenters in a hostile print culture (and, more specifically, the breaking up through death and imprisonment of the circle that surrounded the publisher Joseph Johnson), there is little sign that she either passively accepted this situation or transmuted it into a Romantic idea of a 'higher' freedom. *The Female Speaker* anthology brought out in 1811 may have stressed the importance of regulating the passions, but its inclusion of Shaftesbury's apostrophes kept alive the flame of patriot enthusiasm. One of her selections from Isaac Watts illustrates her continuing commitment to the politics of sympathy and society rather than any idea of retirement as a good in itself:

> Our souls may be serene in solitude, but not sparkling, though perhaps we are employed in reading the works of the brightest writers. Often has it happened, in free discourse, that new truths are strangely struck out, and the seeds of truth sparkle and blaze through the company, which in calm and silent reading would never have been excited.[42]

The year after she published *The Female Speaker,* Barbauld came before the public for one last time as a poet and patriot, but one adopting a more detached and disinterested voice than the 'sparkle and blaze' of patriot enthusiasm.

Barbauld's *Eighteen Hundred and Eleven* is a very slippery poem. Lucy Newlyn has spoken, for instance, of its 'generic unclassifiability'.[43] In terms of content, it offers a prophetic vision of the decline of the British Empire and the emigration of the spirit of liberty to America (an idea that had been current at least since the American War of Independence). Yet descriptions of the poem both now and in the responses of Barbauld's contemporaries often seem undecided as to whether it ought to be regarded as a prophecy or a satire. Croker's infamous attack on the poem, for instance, barely mentions its generic relation to prophecy, or, perhaps even more strangely, the known history of Barbauld's prophetic interventions in public debates in the 1790s. The more sympathetic *Monthly Review* did begin by nothing its prophetic content: 'By long prescriptive right, poets are prophets as well as satirists, and, while they lash the vices and follies of the present generation, can take a glance at futurity and announce things that will be "hereafter"'; but it is a comment about the casting of satire in terms of a prediction of the future, rather than the poem's style as such, and the review has little to say about the specific form of Barbauld's 'prophetic warnings'.[44] Perhaps one should not be surprised about the lack of serious comment on Barbauld's career as prophet, since the poem certainly has less of the spirit or style of Old Testament prophecies than her poetry or prose works of the early 1790s. Although at certain key points it personifies and addresses Britain and London as the Book of Jeremiah does Jerusalem, one could only very loosely describe the poem as a 'jeremiad'.[45] Most critics usually start by thinking of the poem in terms of Juvenalian satire. Reviews by Barbauld's contemporaries pointed out the parallels with Samuel Johnson's imitation of Juvenal's third satire in 'London'.[46] Certainly what Maggie Favretti calls the 'skilfully phrased heroic couplets' of Barbauld's poem do not suggest the irregularity and metaphorical obscurity strongly associated with biblical style (Blake's 'London' rather than Johnson's is a more obvious translation of Lowth's theories on prophetic poetry into contemporary poetic form).[47] Coleridge's 'Religious Musings' moves further in this direction than Barbauld's poem, although not without equivocations of its own. Both Coleridge and Barbauld offer an account of the progress of liberty and enlightenment in Britain. Both were oriented towards a politically reformist view of history, foregrounding names such as Milton and Priestley, a point that Barbauld's reviewers were quick to make. For the pre-millenialist vision of Coleridge's poem, these men appear as agents of a divine will working itself out in history (in 1795-6, of course, when 'Religious Musings' was written, it was easier to see history as the positive expression of divine will for a reform-minded Dissenter). No less than John Howard in Barbauld's hymn, they are latter-day prophets, but *Eighteen Hundred and Eleven* is much less biblical in its treatment of these heroes of reform than Coleridge's poem or Barbauld's own work from the 1790s. Barbauld stresses their 'Roman virtue' (*BP* 156, l. 148) rather than their patriot enthusiasm, that is, their disinterested concern for their country rather than their zeal. Patriot enthusiasm was strongly associated with Akenside's name when it came to poetry, and if her stately couplets do not call to mind a biblical style, nor do they seem influenced by the flexible blank verse of his 'heady blend of patriot zeal and poetic enthusiasm'.[48] Blank verse was associated with the poetics of religious and political liberty, liberated as it was, in Blake's words, from 'the modern bondage of Rhyming', and Barbauld had exploited the connection herself to considerable effect in poems such as '**Corsica**' and '**A Summer Evening's Meditation**'. For all that it is a vision of futurity, *Eighteen Hundred and Eleven* attempts little of the zeal of the former or the 'unworlding' effects of the latter. Its description of London in ruins does not attempt a vision from Eternity. There is a restraint and even a certain detachment for most of the poem that helps explain why some reviewers described it as a satire and stressed its coldness.

This point should not be exaggerated. Her poetry and prose over the previous decades had demonstrated that both the righteous indignation of prophetic register and the ardour of patriot enthusiasm were well within her grasp as a writer when she chose. There are points in *Eighteen Hundred and Eleven* where the rhythm does intensify and a more apocalyptic tone emerges:

> There walks a Spirit[49] o'er the peopled earth,
> Secret his progress is, unknown his birth;
> Moody and viewless as the changing wind,
> No force arrests his foot, no chains can bind.

(*BP* 158, ll. 215-18)

Yet I am not sure that much else in the poem represents Barbauld 'assuming the mantle of an Old Testament prophet'.[50] The powerful apostrophes and exhortations of her poetry and prose of the early 1790s quickly, as we have seen, provoked politically hostile reviewers to ridicule her as the histrionic figure of female prophecy. *Eighteen Hundred and Eleven* is more cautious in this regard than the prose of the 1790s. If Barbauld eschewed the rhetorical possibilities of prophecy and patriotic enthusiasm for the most part in her poem, however, she was not to escape censure for what was her most widely reviewed poem. Not surprisingly, the conservative press attacked Barbauld's poem as an act of literary treason at a time of war, but for the most part these reviewers did not chastise her as a 'Deborah', nor even as someone whose 'patriotic enthusiasm ran away with her understanding and disqualified her judgment'. Croker's infamous attack in the *Quarterly* stressed instead the coldness and regularity of her poem rather than its ardour.[51] The *Eclectic* suggested there was something unfeeling and 'unfilial' about such a poem at a time of war: 'It seems hardly possible that such a poem as this could have been produced, without the concurrence of a peculiarly frigid temperament,—with a system of speculative opinions which seem contrived to damp every glowing sentiment,—and the spirit of that political party, which cherishes no sympathy with the honour and happiness of England.'[52] These reviews perpetuate Burke's language in their representation of Unitarianism as a frozen zone. He had been able to conflate ideas of Dissent as simultaneously overly warm and too frigid. Although Barbauld was accused of too much warmth by political opponents both before and after 1812, it is the charge of frigidity that is the dominant target in the reviews of *Eighteen Hundred and Eleven*. In relation to Barbauld here the strategy suggests that she is unwomanly in her lack of specifically domestic feeling. The poem displayed a species of grandeur, suggested the *Eclectic*; 'it has a vigour and majesty', that potentially places it in the line of Akenside's patriotic enthusiasm, but uses the designation to reinforce its perception of the lack of feminine softness in the poem.[53] The criticism recalls Woodfall's discussion of '**Corsica**' and his concern that her poetry did not display the softer emotions. Croker's review deploys similar assumptions to more damagingly hostile effect.

One might say that *Eighteen Hundred and Eleven* was caught in the same discourse of sensibility—now turned to an explicitly conservative political agenda, as it had been in the hands of Burke—that she herself had sometimes expounded. Burke had suggested the self-sufficiency of dissenting controversialism was unfeeling in its disregard for tradition, manners, and the domestic ties. Reviewers of *Eighteen Hundred and Eleven* similarly disapprobated Barbauld for her privileging of speculative opinions and stoical disinterestedness over the ties of hearth and home at a time of war, and made it clear that this crime was particularly heinous for one of her sex. Yet they could scarcely attack this controlled and measured poem for what could be considered an unworldly ardour either of passion or speculation. Barbauld had eschewed the enthusiasm that she had shown herself capable of articulating in favour of a more subdued political intervention at a time of national despair. Righteous indignation, she may have judged, would have been inappropriate at such a juncture, and anyway would have enabled reviewers to parody her as the hysterical prophetess. As it was, Barbauld's very detachment seems to have been understood as a violation of the assumptions of gender in relation to genre. Maggie Favretti has put the matter adroitly: 'The very "distinterested" [*sic*] composure and vision necessary in a gentleman who could claim to interpret the "interests of Europe" was somehow threatening, emerging as it was from the pen of an old woman.'[54] Barbauld's detachment suggested that she had the elevated prospect that was seen to be the particular domain of the gentleman, and in the discourse of civic humanism the basis of his claim to be able to judge the best interests of his society. If during the eighteenth century there was a great deal of confusion about exactly who in a commercial society could claim this sort of disinterestedness, it was unlikely to be granted to a woman. Hannah More, as Favretti notes, had quite specifically pointed out that women did not have access to 'that wider range of distant prospects which he who stands on a loftier eminence commands'. Shaftesbury's great apostrophes to freedom are predicated on an access to this kind of prospect.[55] The supposed distinterestedness given concrete form by his position as an aristocratic landowner is the social guarantee that stands behind his enthusiasm; Shaftesbury's 'ascent' takes off from a prospect that he literally owns. His apostrophes were included in the *Female Speaker* anthology that was published just a year before *Eighteen Hundred and Eleven.* Barbauld's taste for them is reflected in her love of Akenside, but *Eighteen Hundred and Eleven* generally eschews such enthusiasm to emphasize instead the 'equal wide survey' that must precede it in classical republican thought. Even so, for Croker and Barbauld's other critics this measure of control was itself unnatural. It is as if Croker would have been happier to have encountered the more predictable stereotype of the hysterical prophetess. Joanna Southcott would have made an easy contemporary parallel for satire. Woodfall had suggested that the more rapturous poetry of **'Corsica'** ignored the fact that 'there is a sex in minds as well as in bodies . . . A woman is as perfect in her kind as a man: she appears inferior only when she quits her station, and aims at excellence out of her province.'[56] Whatever register such a political intervention adopted, enthusiastic or disinterested, it was going to be viewed as a crime against the sexed nature of writing.

Most contemporary criticism dealing with Barbauld has represented her as an advocate of female sensibility. Some critics have argued that this advocacy often pushes against ideas that excluded the affections from the public sphere. Judgements about these matters need to acknowledge that she was more than capable of the patriot zeal associated with Akenside, the religious sublime of Young, and the righteous indignation of biblical prophecy. All three kinds of writing were and perhaps still are associated with masculine 'vigour', but there is a danger that we essentialize such judgements if we persist in seeing Barbauld as primarily a creature of sensibility rather than someone also closely involved with the developing poetics of enthusiasm. Male writers could not simply assume their rights to the religious or political sublime; it was always haunted with the spectre of a degeneration into another kind of enthusiasm altogether. Barbauld's friend and colleague Joseph Priestley's prose was always subject to this criticism, but so also were poets such as Akenside when they were deemed not to have sufficiently regulated their ardour into proper poetic form. Such judgements about boundaries depended in part on who was doing the judging. Patriot zeal was always going to look like mere enthusiasm to someone such as Samuel Johnson, especially when expressed in the language of affect that Shaftesbury passed to Akenside. If the person being judged were a Dissenter, he was likely to be granted even less latitude; if the writer were a Dissenter and a woman, even less; but the catch for Barbauld was that regulation itself was often felt to be largely beyond a woman writer. Reviewers expected from women neither the vigour of enthusiasm nor the coolness of detachment, but a response that was feeling but submissive and 'melting'. 'Softness' rather than vigour or control were expected. One may praise Barbauld's ability to work within and challenge these expectations over a long and productive career, but ultimately she was caught in this trap. Even her own niece ended up having to present her as a champion of domestic virtues and children's literature. What the *Westminster Magazine* had once believed to be a genius exceeding 'the most vigorous of our poets' became 'a legacy for young ladies'. The latter was conceived of as a safe and innocuous haven from the kind of religious and political controversy that Barbauld had excelled at for several decades.[57]

Notes

1. *An Address to the Opposers of the Repeal of the Corporation and Test Acts,* 4th edn. (1790), 15.

2. Janowitz, 'Amiable and Radical Sociability', 73.

3. On Young and enthusiasm, see Shaun Irlam, *Elations: The Poetics of Enthusiasm in Eighteenth-Century Britain* (Stanford, Calif.: Stanford University Press, 1999), chs. 6 and 7.

4. Mark Akenside, *The Pleasures of Imagination,* ed. with a critical essay by Anna Letitia Barbauld ([London,] 1795). *Pleasures* had been published before her first volume of poems in *The Poems of Mark Akenside, M.D.* ([London,] 1772).

5. 'Essay on Akenside's Poem on the Pleasures of Imagination', in Akenside, *Pleasures of Imagination,* pp. i-xxxvi.

6. Akenside, *Pleasures of Imagination,* 119: iii. 624-9.

7. Barbauld, 'Essay on Akenside's Poem', p. xi.

8. Ibid., p. xxix.

9. See 'Observations on Female Literature', *Westminster Magazine,* 4 (1776), 283-5: 285.

10. See Irlam, *Elations,* 3, on formlessness, and Pat Rogers, 'Shaftesbury and the Aesthetics of Rhapsody', *British Journal of Aesthetics,* 12 (1972), 244-57, on Shaftesbury's influence on eighteenth-century ideas of organic form.

11. On More's admiration for Barbauld, see G. J. Barker-Benfield, *The Culture of Sensibility: Sex and Society in Eighteenth-Century Britain* (Chicago: University of Chicago Press, 1992), 264.

12. 'Essay on Akenside's Poem', pp. viii and xvi.

13. Both quoted in Meehan, *Liberty and Poetics,* 53.

14. Mark Akenside, 'The Design', in *Pleasures of Imagination,* pp. vii-viii.

15. 'On Romances: An Imitation', in *The Works of Anna Laetitia Barbauld. With a Memoir by Lucy Aikin,* 2 vols. (1825), ii. 172. See Newlyn, *Reading, Writing, and Romanticism,* 164.

16. Newlyn, *Reading, Writing, and Romanticism,* 157.

17. *Monthly Review,* 48 (1773), 54-9 and 133-7 (the review appeared in two sections): 54.

18. Ibid. 137.

19. Janowitz, 'Amiable and Radical Sociability', 62.

20. Barbauld, *Address to the Opposers,* 33.

21. Ibid. 31.

22. Ibid. 31-2.

23. William Keate, *A Free Examination of Dr. Price's and Dr. Priestley's Sermons* ([London,] 1790), 55 and 64. See the discussion of Keate's response in Janowitz, 'Amiable and Radical Sociability', 72-3.

24. 'To Hannah More, 29 September 1791', in *The Yale Edition of Horace Walpole's Correspondence,* ed. W. S. Lewis, 48 vols. (New Haven: Yale University Press, 1937-83), xxxi. 361-2.

25. 'To Mary Berry, 26 July 1791', ibid. xi. 320.

26. *British Critic,* 2 (1794), 81-5: 84.

27. In fact both Barbauld and Wakefield were deeply involved in political matters at this time. See Janowitz, 'Amiable and Radical Sociability', 75-6. Her reply to Wakefield explicitly drew analogies between social worship and political meetings. She described forms of religious worship as 'a virtual declaration of the rights of man', because 'invidious distinctions of wealth and titles are not admitted'. See Barbauld, *Works* [*The Works of Anna Letitia Barbauld*], ii. 448 and 446.

28. Wakefield, *An Enquiry into the Expediency and Propriety of Public or Social Worship* rev. edn. ([London,] 1792), 15 and 14.

29. Ibid. 18-19.

30. Barbauld, *Works,* ii. 419.

31. Ibid. 421 and 428.

32. *A General Reply to the Arguments against the Enquiry into Public Worship* (1792), 20-1.

33. Ibid. 21.

34. Ibid. 26.

35. Janowitz, 'Amiable and Radical Sociability', 77.

36. Keach, 'Barbauld, Romanticism and the Survival of Dissent', 56.

37. Quoted in Janowitz, 'Amiable and Radical Sociability', 77.

38. See the discussion of Thelwall and Coleridge's attitudes to retirement in the previous chapter.

39. *Literary Gazette,* 24 Sept. 1825, 611. The poem had been written in 1795, but was not published until 1825.

40. Lisa Vargo usefully situates Barbauld's poem as part of a debate about activism in Unitarian circles, but does not notice the background of the issue in Barbauld's relationship to Priestley. See 'The Case of Anna Laetitia Barbauld's "To Mr C(olerid)ge"', *Charles Lamb Bulletin,* 102 (1998), 55-63.

41. Barbauld's account was published in the *Norwich Iris,* 24 Dec. 1803. See *BP* 246.

42. See 'On Conversation from Watts', in *The Female Speaker,* 79-80.

43. Newly, *Reading, Writing, and Romanticism,* 168.

44. See *Monthly Review,* 67 (1812), 428-9. The more hostile *Anti-Jacobin Review,* 42 (1812), 209 also mentioned Barbauld's role as prophet, but only as a dismissive aside: 'Mrs B. is a prophet; and to prophets it is given to penetrate the veil of futurity'; it comments on her 'prediction of the decline of British commercial power'.

45. The description is Anne K. Mellor's, see her 'The Female Poet and the Poetess: Two Traditions of British Women's Poetry, 1780-1830', in Armstrong and Blain (eds.), *Women's Poetry in the Enlightenment,* 91.

46. Mellor makes this point, ibid. Comparison between Barbauld's poem was also made by contemporaries, see *Universal Magazine,* 17 (1812), 217.

47. Favretti, 'The Politics of Vision', 99.

48. Meehan, *Poetics of Liberty* [*Liberty and Poetics*], 54.

49. One might compare this line to Barbauld's description of a time when 'the genius of Philosophy begins walking abroad' in *Sins of the Government, Sins of the Nation*. The difference is the unequivocal prophetic mode of the latter passage (it comes directly after the exhortation of her readers to look at 'the signs of the times') compared to the more 'disinterested' mode of *Eighteen Hundred and Eleven*.

50. Mellor, 'The Female Poet', 92.

51. See the *Quarterly Review*, 7 (1812), 309-13.

52. *Eclectic Review*, 8 (1812), 474-8: 475.

53. Ibid. 478.

54. Favretti, 'The Politics of Vision', 108.

55. More's *Strictures on the Modern System of Education*, quoted ibid. 102. See John Barrell's work for the best exploration of how the aristocratic idea of disinterestedness evolved to meet the situation of a commercial society; for instance, *English Literature in History 1730-1780: 'An Equal Wide Survey'* (Hutchinson, 1983) and 'The Public Prospect and the Private View: The Politics of Taste in Eighteenth-Century Britain' in his *The Birth of Pandora and the Division of Knowledge* (Basingstoke: Macmillan, 1992). Favretti reads Barbauld's poem as a critique of the lack of genuine disinterested public spiritedness in such a society.

56. *Monthly Review*, 48 (1773), 137.

57. William Keach points out that the title of Lucy Aikin's anthology of Barbauld's writing, *A Legacy for Young Ladies*, had already become 'the most familiar way of representing her to early nineteenth-century readers', 'Barbauld, Romanticism and the Survival of Dissent', 45.

Select Bibliography

I. PRIMARY SOURCES

Place of publication London unless stated.

BARBAULD, ANNA LETITIA, *An Address to the Opposers of the Repeal of the Corporation and Test Acts*, 4th edn. (1790).

——*Sins of Government, Sins of the Nation; or, A Discourse for the Fast Appointed on April 19, 1793* (1793).

——'Essay on Akenside's Poem on the Pleasures of Imagination', in Mark Akenside, *The Pleasures of Imagination*, ed. Anna Letitia Barbauld (1795), pp. i-xxxvi.

——*The Female Speaker; or, Miscellaneous Pieces, in Prose and Verse, Selected from the Best Writers, and Adapted to the Use of Young Women* (1811).

——*The Works of Anna Laetitia Barbauld. With a Memoir by Lucy Aikin*, 2 vols. (1825).

——*The Poems of Anna Letitia Barbauld*, ed. William McCarthy and Elizabeth Kraft (Athens: University of Georgia Press, 1994).

II. SECONDARY SOURCES

FAVRETTI, MAGGIE, 'The Politics of Vision: Anna Barbauld's *Eighteen Hundred and Eleven*', in Isobel Armstrong and Virginia Blain (eds.), *Women's Poetry in the Enlightenment: The Making of a Canon, 1730-1820* (Basingstoke: Macmillan, 1999), 99-110.

IRLAM, SHAUN, *Elations: The Poetics of Enthusiasm in Eighteenth-Century Britain* (Stanford, Calif.: Stanford University Press, 1999).

JANOWITZ, ANNE, 'Amiable and Radical Sociability: Anna Barbauld's "Free Familiar Conversation"', in Gillian Russell and Clara Tuite (eds.), *Romantic Sociability: Social Networks and Literary Culture in Britain, 1770-1840* (Cambridge: Cambridge University Press, 2002), 62-81.

KEACH, WILLIAM, 'Barbauld, Romanticism and the Survival of Dissent', *Essays and Studies*, 51 (1998), 44-61.

MEEHAN, MICHAEL, *Liberty and Poetics in Eighteenth Century England* (Beckenham: Croom Helm, 1986).

MELLOR, ANNE K., 'The Female Poet and the Poetess: Two Traditions of British Women's Poetry, 1780-1830', in Isobel Armstrong and Virginia Blain (eds.), *Women's Poetry in the Enlightenment: The Making of a Canon, 1730-1820* (Macmillan, 1999), 81-98.

NEWLYN, LUCY, *Reading, Writing, and Romanticism: The Anxiety of Reception* (Oxford: Oxford University Press, 2000).

THOMPSON, JUDITH, 'An Autumnal Blast, a Killing Frost: Coleridge's Poetic Conversation with John Thelwall', *Studies in Romanticism*, 36 (1997), 427-56.

Alice G. Den Otter (essay date summer 2004)

SOURCE: Den Otter, Alice G. "Pests, Parasites, and Positionality: Anna Letitia Barbauld and 'The Caterpillar.'" *Studies in Romanticism* 43, no. 2 (summer 2004): 209-30.

[*In the following essay, Den Otter examines the political and moral undertones of Barbauld's poem "The Caterpillar."*]

Readers who were first Introduced to Anna Letitia Barbauld (1743-1825) as the prudish school matron who wrote prose hymns for children and complained that Samuel Taylor Coleridge's "Ancient Mariner" lacks a "moral"[1] may be surprised to find this same woman supporting the thieves who prey immorally upon the rich:

> When a rich West India fleet has sailed into the docks, and wealth is flowing in full tides into the crammed coffers of the merchant, can we greatly lament that a small portion of his immense property is by these means [fraud and thievery] diverted from its course, and finds its way to the habitations of penury?[2]

Responding to *A Treatise on the Police of the Metropolis* by Patrick Colquhoun (1796), Barbauld refuses to condemn the prowling poor who are "forever nibbling at our property," suggesting that such thieves should be seen, albeit in macrocosmic terms, as necessary to a balanced economy rather than as agents of injury or damage. "I would rather wish to consider them," she writes in her **"Thoughts on the Inequality of Conditions"** (1807), "as usefully employed in lessening the enormous inequality between the miserable beings who engage in them, and the great commercial speculators, in their way equally rapacious, against whom their frauds are exercised" (**S** [*Selected Poetry and Prose*] 352-353). Barbauld recognizes, in other words, that the rich merchants in their colonizing and slave trading practices have no more right to their property than do the prowlers, and she ponders why the legal system protects the rich while perpetuating hegemony over the poor (**S** 347). Although she focuses in other texts on chastising the exploitative tyrants (**"Corsica,"** *Epistle to Wilberforce* [*Epistle to William Wilberforce, Esq., on the Rejection of the Bill for Abolishing the Slave Trade*], *Sins of Government* [*Sins of the Government, Sins of the Nation*], etc.), she strives in her **"Thoughts"** essay to sympathize with those who plunder out of need rather than greed. And although she cautions, in her role as middle class educator, that "fraud and robbery are not right" and that individuals with "higher notions of virtue" are forbidden to steal, she nevertheless returns to the immense satisfaction she receives from contemplating this "providential" system of "imposition and peculation" whereby "property is drawn off and dispersed, which would otherwise stagnate" (**S** 354).

The ability to see the whole system in motion, to appreciate relations among individuals as functions of a larger communal process, and to recognize the relative ethics of leveling practices regardless of the questionable contents raises Barbauld above the petty realm of technical morality to which Coleridgean scholars have often condemned her.[3] Indeed, her "great acuteness" of mind—which Coleridge admired and even envied in the early years of their acquaintance[4]—gives her insight into the dependencies and counter-dependencies underlying various subject positions and leads her to reject a static social system. "I am apt to suspect that the greatest good done by the numerous societies for the reformation of manners," she writes, "is by bringing the poor in contact with the rich" (**"Thoughts"** [**"Thoughts on the Inequality of Conditions"**] **S** 355). Somehow she recognizes that the basis of morality is more corporeal than love or pity. First comes a contact, a face to face meeting, a bodily interrelation. Only then is there some hope that hierarchical oppression will be unsettled: "The distress which might languish at a distance, will be amply relieved if it comes near enough to affect the nerves" (**S** 351). And yet, at what point do prowlers come too close for comfort? At what point do the weak become the strong, the useless become the basis of meaningful relation? And at what point do the relative positions one plays become more significant than the contents one professes? This essay traces several of these issues in Barbauld's poem **"The Caterpillar,"** which struggles to articulate the interrelations between proprietor and prowler, privileged and unprivileged, victor and survivor, in conventional and yet potentially subversive ways. Touched by one caterpillar from her garden, the speaker considers her complex identification with and resistance to systems of power, engaging several discourses of biology, politics, and ethics, in a movement that does not end where it began. By the end, the reader is left to ponder the whole system of moral virtue: is it virtuous to protect pests and parasites as necessary parts of this system or is such protection merely an indulgent weakness of a virtuous mind?

Recent critical studies of Anna Letitia Barbauld have persuasively argued that much of her insight into communal ethics is due to her upbringing in a Unitarian home,[5] which necessitated a position of "double dissent."[6] This position involves allegiance to the nonconformist tradition of Dissent—promoting religious and political freedom and equality—but it also involves independence from restrictions of gender to which Dissenters still subscribed.[7] Indeed, double dissent helps to explain not only Barbauld's political agendas but also her otherness from male Romantic writers who periodically indulged in melancholic solipsism.[8] Despite the increasing suspicion towards Dissent in the early nineteenth century, she does not relinquish her drive toward equality and justice for all, although her insights and positions do not appear rigid or unchanging. Responding to varying historical stimuli, she shifts readily from subversive wit to sincere patriotism, from superficial pleasure to austere critique, or from skeptical hesitation to indulgent generosity. In the process, she engages the pests and parasites who haunt the borders of equality and threaten to overwhelm the virtuous sympathies of Dissent.

Barbauld's **"The Caterpillar"** was written several years after she was critically condemned in 1812 for publishing *Eighteen Hundred and Eleven,* a poetic castigation of British politics and society. By 1815,[9] Barbauld—age 72—had retreated from the public realm and was presenting herself as a tender-hearted and personable woman, an ethos that prevails throughout most of the caterpillar poem. Meanwhile, her fellow Britons had begun to soften towards Napoleon Bonaparte, who had dramatically returned from the Isle of Elba in March only to be defeated at the Battle of Waterloo in June. Seeming to echo this softening atmosphere, **"The Caterpillar"** moves from sympathy for a little insect to pity for a defeated enemy, employing a conventional analogy between garden pests and political adversaries.[10] But although the poem's kind sensibility brings a "fellowship of sense with all that breathes," the last lines suddenly announce that such sensibility is "not Virtue" (41; **P** [*The Poems of Anna Letitia Barbauld*] 173). It is as if Barbauld regains her public voice and wins the emotional acquiescence of her audience, only to challenge their morality from the inside out. More is at stake than caterpillars and defeated soldiers. Oscillating between pest control and playfulness, parasitism and pity, positionality and piety, Barbauld's poem generates a dynamic revision of interpersonal ethics that extends beyond the preservation of humanity to which *Eighteen Hundred and Eleven* appears to be dedicated and in the shadow of which **"The Caterpillar"** appears to crawl. To see the challenge in this oscillation and revisioning, we need to look at the poem from the beginning.

PESTS

The opening of Barbauld's **"The Caterpillar"** depicts a moth larva that crawls out of the speaker's clothing, down her arm, and onto her hand.[11] Unlike the stereotypical female such as "Little Miss Muffet" in the Victorian nursery rhyme, she is not frightened by the sudden proximity of a moving insect. Instead, she creates a relationship of trust with the creature, treating it as if it were an innocent child requiring her protection rather than a conventionally reviled pest. She is intrigued with the caterpillar's beauty and she promises not to kill it:

> No, helpless thing, I cannot harm thee now;
> Depart in peace, thy little life is safe;
> For I have scanned thy form with curious eye,
> Noted the silver line that streaks thy back,
> The azure and the orange that divide
> Thy velvet sides; thee, houseless wanderer
> My garment has enfolded, and my arm
> Felt the light pressure of thy hairy feet;
> Thou hast curled round my finger; from its tip,
> Precipitous descent! with stretched out neck,
> Bending thy head in airy vacancy,
> This way and that, inquiring, thou hast seemed
> To ask protection; now, I cannot kill thee.

(1-13; **P** 172-73)

The implication is that such a lovely creature is unable to fend for itself and certainly is not dangerous.

Unfortunately, though, the coloring of the caterpillar belies its seeming innocence. Barbauld does not identify the caterpillar she describes, but her description matches entomological illustrations and identifications of the European tent caterpillar, Order Lepidoptera, Family Lasiocampidae, Species Malacosoma Neustria, also known as the larva of the Lackey moth.[12] No other caterpillar quite matches "the silver line that streaks thy back, / The azure and the orange that divide / Thy velvet sides" (4-6). This caterpillar has a bright blue base, including its head, with orange (and sometimes black) stripes on both sides of a middle white line. Moreover, the skin is covered with reddish-brown hairs which are pleasant to touch, like velvet, unlike the Brown-tailed Moth larvae and other caterpillars whose hairs are irritants, causing severe rash. What an unsuspecting reader might not realize is that this beautiful Lackey caterpillar has the potential to be a severe pest, defoliating and disfiguring apple and other deciduous trees from April to June, and living until it is full-grown in a communal silken tent spun over leaves and twigs. Erasmus Darwin's *Economy of Vegetation* (1791) includes the tent caterpillar among pests to be removed from the garden, citing as main aggravation the "gluey thread" which the caterpillar spins.[13] Still, the greatest damage concerns the eating of leaves during a prolific season. Although each caterpillar eats only a small fraction of the available leaf tissue, a community of caterpillars can defoliate an entire tree.[14] Even those plants that are not totally infested are weakened by the pillage, making Samuel Johnson's etymology of "caterpillar" rather apt: "from *cates,* food, and *piller,* to rob; the animal that eats up the fruits of the earth."[15]

Barbauld's *Eighteen Hundred and Eleven* maligns a similar insect thief, an herbaceous worm that quickens the biological cycle of growth and decay for flowers and fruit. Eating from within the core, this worm metaphorically is strong enough to destroy a great nation:

> [. . .] fairest flowers expand but to decay;
> The worm is in thy core, thy glories pass away;
> Arts, arms and wealth destroy the fruits they bring;
> Commerce, like beauty, knows no second spring,

(*Eighteen* [*Eighteen Hundred and Eleven*]
313-316; **P** 160-61)

Because decay is inevitable, all growth by nature is "in vain," including the flourishing of oranges and olives, the raising of youths and virgins, and the dreams of fancy and imagination. Even "angel charities in vain oppose" this worm that grows in wealth at the expense of the poor (319). Its pillage is not an act of God, but of culture feeding upon nature, being composed of "Arts, arms, and wealth"—the very things that made Britain strong in the eighteenth century and protected it from France at the beginning of the nineteenth: technology, war, and capitalism. Barbauld's choice of metaphor indicates that all three elements are pests, ravaging the bounty, even the transplanted bounty, of nature in their advances of progress, power, and profit. This idea was not new: eighteenth-century conservatives had already warned against excessive advances in commerce and industrialism, advocating moderation instead. Barbauld's suggestion, though, is that these advances are morally doom-ridden, like a worm inviting "Famine," "Disease and Rapine" (15-16; **P** 152), the very fatalism of her suggestion being cause for alarm. Since industrial innovation, colonial expansion, and financial success were promoted with such optimism in the early nineteenth century, no wonder that conservative and liberal critics alike denounced the poem's meddling in politics and business, attacking Barbauld as if herself were the pest to be controlled (**P** 309-11).

In contrast to such doom, **"The Caterpillar"** appears to ignore the destructive nature of its subject. While the speaker in *Eighteen Hundred and Eleven* complains about crime, fraud, want, and woe resulting from the cultural worm, the speaker in **"The Caterpillar"** does not articulate the damages. In fact, she does not mention the caterpillar's robbery of her garden at all,[16] presenting the creature as part of a community that appears innocently passive: "folded in their silken webs they lay / Thriving and happy" (18-19; **P** 173). Lackey larvae do, indeed, bask in their tents in the sun, since sunshine heightens their body temperature, aiding their digestion and growth (Fitzgerald 32, 157-66). But Barbauld implies that such basking is all that they do. She makes a similar claim of innocence in her poem **"To Mrs. P[riestley], with some Drawings of Birds and Insects"** in which she depicts "the Insect race" as living a life of pleasure—"their task all play" (95; **P** 8). One would never guess that "the main task" of a caterpillar is to eat.[17]

As **"The Caterpillar"** progresses, it nevertheless becomes clear that Barbauld's speaker sometimes sees the thriving insects as pests to be destroyed. Perhaps it is simply the profusion of the creatures that arouses suspicion. Or, perhaps the speaker succumbs to agricultural propaganda, obediently acting upon entomological indications that butterflies and their larvae are relatively harmless, whereas "a great number of injurious species" are present among moths and their larvae, which are responsible for the defoliation of orchards, gardens, farms, and forests.[18] Linnaeus in 1750 notes that "a few little nocturnal moths can cause the loveliest orchards where neither labor nor money had been spared and which usually produce hundreds of tons of fruit to yield now no more than 100 apples or pears."[19] As the agricultural revolution advanced, increasing soil productivity, the necessity for eliminating hindrances to profit likewise increased. The London Aurelian Society was formed in 1801 not only to encourage standard classification of insect collections, but also "to point out to the public

the readiest and most desirable methods of destroying such as possess properties that are inimical to the welfare of mankind,"[20] thus making insecticide sound morally justified. The recommended pest control was a combination of mechanical and chemical methods, removing and destroying all caterpillars in sight and poisoning the rest with any toxic materials at hand, including "strong soapsuds, potash water, whitewash plus glue, whale oil soap plus Peruvian guano, and solutions of whale oil soap" (Dethier 108). In Barbauld's poem, the eradication of caterpillars is a completed action, meticulously directed against the whole Lackey community:

> Yet I have sworn perdition to thy race,
> And recent from the slaughter am I come
> Of tribes and embryo nations: I have sought
> With sharpened eye and persecuting zeal,
> Where, folded in their silken webs they lay
> Thriving and happy; swept them from the tree
> And crushed whole families beneath my foot;
> Or, sudden, poured on their devoted heads
> The vials of destruction. This I've done
> Nor felt the touch of pity.
>
> (14-23; **P** 173)

The speaker's lack of reference to any motives for killing and her reported lack of pity for the victims suggests that the pest control has been ideologically programmed to be common sense. Of course one must destroy unprofitable creatures that inhabit human terrain. That, after all, is sound anthrocentric husbandry: remove the worm, cut off the infested branch, and kill the caterpillars.

Nevertheless, the violence of the speaker's actions invites scrutiny since the exaggerated "perdition" and "slaughter" appear to indite not only the gardener, but also the agricultural scientists who have advocated such drastic measures. In her youth, Barbauld observed the work of natural historians whom she met while her father taught at the Dissenting Academy in Warrington. In a 1760s poem called **"The Invitation: To Miss B . . . ,"** Barbauld describes those who study nature and experiment upon it:

> Some pensive creep along the shelly shore;
> Unfold the silky texture of a flower;
> With sharpen'd eyes inspect an hornet's sting,
> And all the wonders of an insect's wing.
> Some trace with curious search the hidden cause
> Of nature's changes, and her various laws;
> Untwist her beauteous web, disrobe her charms,
> And hunt her to her elemental forms.
>
> (155-62; **P** 14)

Although Barbauld does not voice overt disapproval in this poem, her verb choices nevertheless are troubling. "Untwist," "disrobe," and "hunt" suggest discomfort with the "meddling intellect" that William Wordsworth descries in "The Tables Turned"—"We murder to dissect."[21] Indeed, the words "curious" and "sharpened eye" reappear in **"The Caterpillar"** in a destructive context, turning common sense into "persecuting zeal." Pest control begins to appear like a slaughter of innocents that lacks motive or rationality.

The persecution, of course, is recounted in light of the one surviving caterpillar with which the poem begins, enhancing the speaker's former guilt so as to highlight her current generosity to this little pest. The tone almost implies a self-parody, using what William Keach calls "the deceptively familiar key of quasi-comic sentimentality" ("Barbauld" ["Barbauld, Romanticism and the Survival of Dissent"] 50). Yet, the speaker is not as obviously playful as in Barbauld's earlier **"Mouse's Petition"** (composed 1771) or in Burns's "To A Mouse" (composed 1785), both of which make teasing comments about the insignificance of the little creature's thieving. In **"The Caterpillar,"** the speaker seems to ignore any warrant for destruction, using the vocabulary of Romantic individuality to explain why she is making an exception for this particular being:

> but when thou,
> A single wretch, escaped the general doom,
> Making me feel and clearly recognise
> Thine individual existence, life,
> And fellowship of sense with all that breathes,
> Present'st thyself before me, I relent,
> And cannot hurt thy weakness.
>
> (23-29; **P** 173)

Other caterpillars might have escaped as well, flinging themselves out of sight on silken threads, only to return when the danger is past. But Barbauld's speaker does not consider that possibility. Nor does she consider that only one pair of moths is required to lay fertilized eggs on a leaf and enable a new colony of caterpillars to emerge the following spring. Instead she ponders her own resistance to completing the extermination, noting three times that she cannot kill this individual survivor: "I cannot harm thee" (1); "I cannot kill thee" (13); "I relent, / And cannot hurt thy weakness" (28-29). Somehow the caterpillar has shifted position from a pest, ruining the garden, to a parasite, a poor prowler who feeds on the sympathy of the speaker and profits from her generosity.

PARASITES

[*A Dictionary of the English Language*]

Samuel Johnson's *Dictionary* in 1755 defines "parasite" as "one that frequents rich tables, and earns his welcome by flattery." This definition was already present in ancient Greek and Roman cultures,[22] remaining the sole meaning until the late seventeenth century, when the word began to expand, via the adjective "parasitic," into the biological realm. By the early eighteenth century, Chambers' *Cyclopedia* (1727-1741) was using "parasite" to describe a type of plant that relied upon another plant for sustenance or support, such as "moss, lichens, and mistletoe,"[23] although the social definition continued to predominate. Not until 1826 was the noun used by Kirby and Spence's manual on entomology to refer to animals who "live in or upon another organism" (*OED*), the definition most commonly associated with parasites today. This etymological development is well summarized by Michel Serres, who recognizes a continuity in conception: "The intuition of the parasitologist makes him import a common relation of social manners to the habits of little animals."[24] According to Serres, all parasites share the same systemic function: interrupting a normal flow (of food, of life, of power) and feeding upon the diverted energy (8). This interruptive function, as we shall see, operates subtextually in Barbauld's **"The Caterpillar,"** giving the poem several parasitical dimensions.

The speaker's reason for saving the caterpillar is not that she forgives or suddenly appreciates the creature's foraging in her garden, but that its colorful beauty and charm interrupt her desire to kill it. She is seduced by its endearing movements upon her hand and interprets its gestures as communication, a request for asylum by a "houseless wanderer" (6), an uninvited guest, a social parasite. To kill such a creature would be contrary to codes of hospitality, as Barbauld argued wittily almost forty-five years earlier in **"The Mouse's Petition"**: "Beware, lest in the worm you crush / A brother's soul you find" (33-34; **P** 37). Of course, in **"The Caterpillar,"** the wariness is somewhat slow in being realized. "Whole families" of caterpillars are crushed mercilessly before the speaker finds a "brother's soul" for whom she feels a sense of responsibility. But this one survivor stops her, flattering her with its seemingly playful attention and vulnerable trust. Indeed, it appears to her as a kindred spirit, an individual worthy of respect, someone who makes her "feel and clearly recognize / Thine individual existence, life, / And fellowship of sense with all that breathes" (25-27). And so she allows the little parasite to remain on her property, eat from her trees, and interrupt the quality of her fruit.

The traditional problem with social parasites, of course, is that they interrupt not only a host's planned activities and food rations but also the reciprocity of regular gift exchange.[25] Although they certainly accept gifts such as food, shelter, clothing, or money from the host, they drain the host of resources by giving nothing in return. Or, more precisely, what they give in return for substantial gifts are insubstantial transiencies: entertainment, praise, perhaps even—as is the case in Barbauld's **"Caterpillar"**—"fellowship of sense" (27). Clearly, from a materialist perspective, parasites appear to give less than they receive. As Serres notes, the exchange is uneven—"voice for matter, (hot) air for solid, superstructure for infrastructure" (35)—allowing some parasites to grow rich from the material profit they thus accrue. No wonder that they are frequently mentioned in literature with contempt. Shakespeare's *Timon of Athens,* for example, curses the "smooth, detested parasites, / Courteous destroyers, affable wolves, meek bears" who do not return Timon's gifts when he is in need (III.vi.92-95). Similar disgust ensues in Thomas Paine's 1791 *Rights of Man,* where the French Revolution is hailed as the only way to cleanse "the Augean stable of parasites and plunderers."[26] Barbauld herself shows disrespect for parasites in her essay **"Against Inconsistency in Our Expectations."** Suggesting that one must adjust expectations to suit one's manner of living, she notes that anyone who expects to receive unearned dignities and preferments must give up scruples and "be a slave-merchant, a parasite, or—what you please" (S 231). That she would group the parasite with the slave-merchant, when she detests slavery, suggests she finds parasites despicable too.

Still, as we have seen with the West India fleets, Barbauld is able to condemn a thieving activity while appreciating its leveling role in a hierarchical economy. In **"The Caterpillar,"** the speaker fights the plunder of her harvest while appreciating the individual caterpillar's ability to "mak[e]" her "feel and clearly recognize" that she is not the only living being in her garden (25-27). Indeed, she seems to consider this heightened awareness a suitable exchange for the caterpillar's eating, suggesting that parasites might not disrupt gift exchange so much as alter the dynamics of the relationship. J. Hillis Miller makes a similar point with respect to literary parasitism, arguing that the parasite not only "block[s] the endless chain of giving" but also "keeps the chain open, undecidable."[27] A lack of reciprocity on one level is thus an opening for fresh connections on another, inspiring more giving, more "fellowship of sense with all that breathes" (**"Caterpillar"** 27). Perhaps on this other level the parasite even enables the host to give the "pure gift" that Jacques Derrida considers to be "impossible": the gift that is given without any expectation of return.[28]

Barbauld's speaker certainly appears to expect nothing from the caterpillar to whom she gives hospitality, acting as if she has already received sufficient spiritual sustenance from its beauty and innocent individuality. Yet, it is odd that she expresses her own gift in negative terms: rather than offering food or shelter like a proper host, she merely says she "cannot" harm, kill, or hurt this one member of the tribe whom she has tried to exterminate. Burns's "To a Mouse," written fourteen years after Barbauld's caterpillar poem, enacts similar destruction and salvation, without expecting any return for generosity. But Burns's speaker at least refrains from killing in the first place, apologizing for ruining the mouse's nest, expressing sorrow at the human breach of

"Nature's social union" and offering words of comfort to the frightened "little beastie."[29] Barbauld's speaker in **"The Caterpillar"** does none of this. If, as David Perkins points out, Burns's words are patronizing and self-serving, ultimately bestowing more sympathy on the speaker than on the mouse,[30] then how much more so are the words of Barbauld's speaker. She admits she killed the caterpillar's family without a "touch of pity," but instead of expressing remorse, she merely allows the individual who has attracted her admiration to leave unharmed. She neither promises future protection nor revises her stance on pest control, as her earlier mouse-speaker requests and as Burns's speaker appears to do. No wonder she expects no return. Even her gift of life is really no more than non-death—letting live what was already alive—the type of hollow gift that an opportunistic parasite would tend to give.[31] Could it be, as Serres notes so frequently in response to La Fontaine's parables, that "the feast changes hosts, and the guest changes roles" (62)?

Setting aside the possibility that Barbauld's speaker may just be following the burlesque conventions of eighteenth-century addresses to animals (e.g. Thomas Gray's "Ode on the Death of a Favourite Cat," or Robert Fergusson's "The Sow of Feeling"), we might note that she does use rhetorical skill to bend circumstances in her favor, much like a social parasite would tend to do. First she delights the audience with the caterpillar, following Sir Philip Sidney's insight that delight "gives so sweet a prospect into the way, as will entice any [one] to enter into it."[32] Then she flatters us with her trust—using an intimate first person singular rather than personified collectives[33]—and endears us with her vulnerability—confessing her pity, her violence, and her hesitation—thus creating an ethos that far exceeds the cold contempt of the speaker in *Eighteen Hundred and Eleven.* Unlike the Cassandra-like prophet crying from the margins unwelcome and unheard, the speaker in **"The Caterpillar"** actively participates in her subject, enacting a middle-class gardener protecting her property, shifting to compassion, and sharing her profitable experience with others like herself. This active participation is a key component of her appeal, forming a common ground with the middle-class reader and inducing a willingness to be persuaded, for surely we can trust a speaker who is moved by beauty and lets a creature live.

At the same time, however, **"The Caterpillar"**'s establishment of a participatory ethos is more parasitical than the cynical and defeatist observations with which the speaker in *Eighteen Hundred and Eleven* interrupts liberal expectations of egalitarian or patriotic sentiment. Exploiting the caterpillar narrative, Barbauld deftly reverses her public image of political pest-controller by appearing to be gentle and maternal, thus preparing her audience, through a kind of narrative appetizer, for what we shall see is a more subtle tirade against the vanity of British sympathies. When the poem abandons the caterpillar two thirds of the way, never mentioning it again, it appears that the narrative has less to do with the colorful, helpless larva than with the speaker's moral agenda. Why else would topic and tone shift so abruptly: "I relent / And cannot hurt thy weakness. So the storm / Of horrid war, o'erwhelming cities, fields, / And peaceful villages, rolls dreadful on" (28-31; **P** 173)? The caterpillar appears to bear no significance in itself, serving merely as pleasurable food for thought, a metaphorical device for the speaker to discuss the vices and virtues of slaughter and salvation.

When a second narrative appears, echoing the caterpillar episode but making no explicit connection other than the word "So," the speaker becomes omniscient, validating her earlier pest control by analogy to war which, despite being "horrid" and "dreadful," translates murder into "triumphant" victory and the killer into an empathetic "hero":

> So the storm
> Of horrid war, o'erwhelming cities, fields,
> And peaceful villages, rolls dreadful on:
> The victor shouts triumphant; he enjoys
> The roar of cannon and the clang of arms,
> And urges, by no soft relentings stopped,
> The work of death and carnage. Yet should one,
> A single sufferer from the field escaped,
> Panting and pale, and bleeding at his feet,
> Lift his imploring eyes,—the hero weeps;
> He is grown human, and capricious Pity,
> Which would not stir for thousands, melts for one
> With sympathy spontaneous.
>
> (29-41; **P** 173)

The parallelism with the speaker's pity for the caterpillar is obvious, although the aesthetic qualities of the "single sufferer" are eclipsed by his piteous state and the heroism of the victor. Clearly the sympathetic act is the focal point of the tale, depicting a typical Romantic valorization of the individual and the softening of the hero's heart. Barbauld's own distaste for war, announced so severely in *Eighteen Hundred and Eleven*, surges momentarily in lines 29-31, only to be ameliorated by this act of forgiveness between hero and enemy. The wonder is that a hard soldier can "grow[] human" and feel "sympathy spontaneous," despite his usual "work of death and carnage."

But there is a barbed ending, interrupting one's pleasure in the act of rescue, by suggesting that gardener and war hero have capitulated to the weakness of sensibility:

> —'Tis not Virtue,
> Yet 'tis the weakness of a virtuous mind.
>
> (41-42; **P** 173)

Instantly the heroism is deflated. The hero is no longer a virtuous savior but a gullible innocent who has been flattered into letting down his or her defenses. That is how Prussia viewed Britain's refusal to execute Napoleon Bonaparte at the Battle of Waterloo, acquiescing to the Duke of Wellington's letter of remonstrance only "from esteem for the Duke and English weakness."[34] The saved enemy suddenly resumes pest status as potential destroyer, like the Trojan Horse, waiting to be accepted into the inner sanctum in order to wreak havoc. Virtue, presumably, would have acted on principle: an enemy is an enemy; a friend is a friend. The weaker mind, however, is overcome by excessive sensibility. As Barbauld notes in her earlier poem **"A Character,"** what prevents one from being fully virtuous is "sensibility too finely wrought, / Too quickly roused, too exquisite for peace, / Too deeply thoughtful for unmingled ease" (14-16; **P** 69). Excess sensibility is too responsive to changing circumstance, whereas Virtue remains constant. Thus it is not Virtue to make exceptions for one "single sufferer," although the intent may be virtuous.

Through this ending, which undercuts the romance of salvation, the speaker in **"The Caterpillar"** reveals her ultimate position of power. She no longer plays the kind gardener who, like the humane victor on the battlefield, acts out the contents of hospitality while giving the audience pleasure. Instead, she shifts to a higher moral ground, pronouncing judgment upon the producer of pleasurable sensibility and implying that both her involvement in the caterpillar narrative and her telling of the war narrative were mere rhetorical performances, designed to win assent from the audience so as to reinstate her political voice of righteous prophecy. Having related the pleasures of moral narratives, she now forces her audience to reconsider those pleasures. First she entices sympathy, then she subverts it, making "Virtue" itself an unfamiliar entity that relies on her rhetorical position for affirmation or disavowal. If only one understood her position, one could elude the "weakness of a virtuous mind." Thus she feeds on the comforts of the status quo, like a parasite who swallows up her audience's pleasures while making them dependent on her for moral enlightenment.

POSITIONALITY

Barbauld often startles the reader with such barbed endings, popping the mock-heroic bubbles of **"Washing Day"** with the off-hand remark that "verse is one of them [the bubbles]—this most of all" (86; **P** 135), snagging her exaggerated call to arms in **"The Rights of Woman"** with the warning that "separate rights are lost in mutual love" (32; **P** 122), and halting her praise of **"a Lady with Some Painted Flowers"** with what could be either a compliment or an insult: "Your best, your sweetest empire is to please" (18; **P** 77). Such powerful conclusions lift Barbauld's poems beyond the positions of sensibility and sentiment with which her culture was saturated. As Isobel Armstrong points out, Barbauld assists in "getting away from the gush of the feminine regarded simply as a consent to nonrational and emotional experience."[35] Indeed, Barbauld does not occupy any simple position, often analyzing complex situations first one way, then another and leaving ambiguities for the reader to resolve.

The mobility of such shifting positions nevertheless requires attention, especially since the abrupt ending of **"The Caterpillar"** seems to undermine an admirable sympathy for "all that breathe." The whole poem seems to encourage a Romantic position of respect and pity for individuals who normally would be despised, only to conclude, without apparent justification, that such affect is "not Virtue," despite its virtuous intent. Perhaps William Wordsworth's reference to Barbauld as an "old snake" twice in a May 1812 letter[36] is not surprising, since her poetic habit does seem to imply a forked tongue. Praising an experience at one moment and then undermining it decisively at another appears to indicate duplicity rather than virtuous consistency. And yet, as Michel Serres notes with regard to La Fontaine's parables, characters who are most duplicitous are also those who increase the complexity of relations and excite system awareness since they are concerned not so much with the contents of isolated meals or fixed ideas as with the interconnections, the interplay of positions that enable further advantageous movement. According to Serres, "that is the meaning of the prefix *para-* in the word *parasite*: it is on the side, next to, shifted; it is not on the thing, but on its relation. It has relations, as they say, and makes a system of them. It is always mediate and never immediate" (38). Thus, Barbauld's shifting positions might, in fact, enable movement and communal responsibility, forcing us into reevaluation of what sympathy, pity, and even Virtue really entail.

Beyond this spur to activity, though, shifting positions might also be reactive, revealing sites of resistance to a repressive situation. Although Barbauld is vocal enough in critiquing plans and activities that threaten the public good, she seems hesitant to defend herself personally from attack, as if to do so would be to grant too much credibility to her opponents and too much importance to her own self image. Unable to object openly, perhaps because of her gendered position, Barbauld writes poems that mimic (with varying degrees of satire) the perspectives she finds problematic, only to undercut them with swift bursts of wit that contain enough ambiguity to be retractable if required. Such is the case with **"The Rights of Woman"** which responds to Wollstonecraft's condemnation of **"To a Lady."** And such is the case with **"The Caterpillar,"** which I would argue responds to the condemnation Barbauld received by John Wilson Croker in June 1812 for her poem *Eighteen Hundred and Eleven.*[37] Told to "desist from satire" so as to spare

"both the victims and heroes of her political prejudices," Barbauld's public response was silence, as recommended by her best friend Maria Edgeworth: "silent contempt is the best answer."[38] If, as Josephine McDonagh suggests, gender bias was at stake in the negative onslaught, then this response too was gendered, being a woman's only respectable response.[39] Her shifting positionality, then, was her only remaining means of resistance, intervening in politics subversively, parasitically, so as to provoke revolutionary change.

"The Caterpillar," written four years later than the doomed poem, manages to insert a judgment about British sensibility that suggests Barbauld was by no means ready to recant. To a certain extent, **"The Caterpillar"**'s speaker does resume her domestic duty, superintending the garden nursery and using physical means to bring pests under control. But the whole poem resists traditional superintendence. The "intervention of a lady-author" returns, the very first word of the poem breaking silence with a "No" that establishes a refusal to follow expected behavior. Appearing to be in mid-conversation with a "helpless thing," the speaker almost repeats the "no" when rephrasing her initial "No . . . I cannot harm thee" into "now, I cannot kill thee" (13), swerving only slightly to reduce the fuzzy impression that she is apologizing to the creature for being unable to end its life. The most powerful site of resistance, though, is the ambiguous pronoun reference at the end: "'Tis [It is] not Virtue." Here, I think, is where **"The Caterpillar"** makes an intriguing rebuttal, subtly suggesting that the sympathies and caprices of the nineteenth-century middle-class audience lack Virtue, despite virtuous intentions. Because the pronoun is ambiguous, the suggestion slides away from counter-attack, opening to interpretation various positional possibilities.

If "'Tis" refers to "sympathy," which is the last noun preceding the pronoun, then the declaration "'Tis not Virtue, / Yet 'tis the weakness of a virtuous mind" appears to echo Bernard Mandeville's caution against pity in his *Fable of the Bees; or, Private Vices, Public Benefits*:

> Pity, tho' it is the most gentle and the least mischievous of all our Passions, is yet as much a Frailty of our Nature, as Anger, Pride, or Fear. The weakest Minds have generally the greatest Share of it, for which Reason none are more Compassionate than Women and Children. It must be own'd, that of all our Weaknesses it is the most amiable, and bears the greatest Resemblance to Virtue; nay, without a considerable mixture of it the Society could hardly subsist: But as it is an impulse of Nature, that consults neither the publick Interest nor our own Reason, it may produce Evil as well as Good.[40]

Noting that pity has contributed to various corruptions, such as unchastity and bribery, Mandeville argues that it must be tempered with an awareness of the public good before it is to be commended. Pity, regarded in isolation, can lead one astray. Nevertheless, Mandeville is the first to suggest that private weaknesses and even vices could contribute to social good. Thievery, for example, is seen as increasing business for locksmiths and bailiffs as well as bringing more wealth into circulation. This is the premise to which Barbauld alludes in her essay on the **"Thoughts on the Inequality of Conditions"** in which she argues that the prevention of "lower orders from preying upon the property of the higher[] would be a curse and not a blessing" (**S** 352). Indeed, she suggests that the "divine government" permits some vices in order to maintain a balanced universe. "We send the cat after the rat, and the bailiffs after the rogue," she writes, "but nature intended all should live" (**S** 353).

We need to remember, of course, that Barbauld's **"Caterpillar"** poem appears a century after Mandeville, a century during which the concept of virtue shifted as commercial society gained prominence. According to J. G. A. Pocock, traditional masculine virtues of autonomy, rationality, and security were overthrown by commitments to the "soft, civilizing, and feminizing" virtues of sociability, sentimentality, and interdependence.[41] Sympathy toward merchants and peddlers and politeness toward clients enhanced trade while purchases of delicate commodities, such as poetry, proved the customer to have refined taste and artistic sensibility. Within such a context, sympathy imaginatively contributed to a union with nature while practically contributing to a continual flow of commerce. Still, the same sensibility encouraged by consumer capitalism could lead to what Erasmus Darwin calls "Sympathia Aliena," one of the "Diseases of Volition" listed in the medical section of his 1794-1796 *Zoonomia*. Darwin describes this disease as an excess of sympathy, warning that it can lead to self-annihilation:

> This sympathy, with all sensitive beings, has been carried so far by some individuals, and even by whole tribes, as the Gentoos, as not only to restrain them from killing animals for their support, but even to induce them to permit insects to prey upon their bodies.[42]

Although sympathy might enable commerce, some self-interest is yet required for self-preservation, requiring rational virtues of discrimination rather than sympathy. That, at least, is Barbauld's position in her earlier political tract, ***An Address to the Opposers of the Repeal of the Corporation and Test Acts*** (1790), in which she boldly recommends fighting evil with the dispatch of sound husbandry: "Whatever is loose must be shaken, whatever is corrupted must be lopped away; whatever is not built on the broad basis of public utility must be thrown to the ground" (**S** 277). This excision of corruption is precisely the type of utilitarian action with which the speaker of **"The Caterpillar"** destroys the Lackey community, an act that is neither condemned nor validated by the end of the poem.

An alternative reading of the ambiguous "'Tis" leads to a more modulated position that is equally plausible. Instead of referring to "sympathy," it could refer to "capricious Pity"—which is, after all, the subject of the previous sentence. In this case, the speaker might not be questioning the virtue of pitying per se but rather the caprice by which it is offered only to certain kinds of individuals. "Capricious Pity," operating on whim or caprice, "would not stir for thousands" but "melts for one," an idiosyncratic melting that is not Virtue—capital V—unless extended from the one to the many. As Barbauld's 1771 **"Mouse's Petition"** argues, "The well taught philosophic mind / To *all* compassion gives; / Casts round the world an equal eye, / And feels for *all* that lives" (25-28; **P** 36; my emphasis). Isolated and selective excesses of pity are not desirable, especially when the majority are threatened by war, poverty, and woe. Mary Wollstonecraft's *Vindication of the Rights of Woman* appears to support such a position, specifically criticizing uneducated and irrational women for engaging in capricious pity "just as the whim of the moment directs,"[43] rather than extending generosity with equal fairness. Indeed, Wollstonecraft's complaint is that such women often show an excessive kindness to animals, gushing about the pathos of nature, while treating servants and children with contempt:

> The lady who sheds tears for the bird starved in a snare [. . .] will nevertheless, keep her coachman and horses whole hours waiting for her, when the sharp frost bites, or the rain beats against the well-closed windows which do not admit a breath of air to tell her how roughly the wind blows about. And she who takes her dogs to bed, and nurses them with a parade of sensibility, when sick, will suffer her children to grow up crooked in a nursery.
>
> (172-73)

Barbauld condemns similar caprices of sensibility in her essay **"An Inquiry into those Kinds of Distress which Excite Agreeable Sensations,"** suggesting that sympathy with the eccentric victims of Romance leaves "hardly any pity to spare for the common accidents of life" (**S** 207). Once again here is a demand for a more universal ethics. It is not Virtue to feel sympathy for one individual if one kills "without a touch of pity" an entire community.

There is yet one other possibility as antecedent for the reference of "'Tis" in **"The Caterpillar."** Since there are two dashes in the final sentence, the intervening words about the hero's sympathy might be read as a removable insertion, so that the words after the second dash actually refer to the defeated soldier before the first: "Yet should one, / A single sufferer from the field escaped, / Panting and pale, and bleeding at his feet, / Lift his imploring eyes,—[. . .]—'Tis not Virtue, / Yet 'tis the weakness of a virtuous mind" (35-42; **P** 173). Here Virtue would stand beyond self-preservation. The sufferer's pathetic supplication, regardless of the virtues of humility and suffering, is not Virtue, but weakness. Virtue would not beg for relief, like a helpless parasite, but would bear suffering with soldierly courage and fortitude. As Barbauld notes in **"An Inquiry into those Kinds of Distress which Excite Agreeable Sensations,"** "Virtue has a kind of self-sufficiency; it stands upon its own basis, and cannot be injured by any violence" (**S** 204). Adding "helplessness and imperfection" to a character, such as the sufferer's "escape" from the field of battle, might arouse "tenderness or familiar love," but it nevertheless detracts from a fully heroic stance (**S** 204). Virtue requires unalloyed strength, which sentimentally virtuous minds are too weak to accomplish. The problem with this last possibility, nevertheless, is that Barbauld praises tenderness and love in many of her works, suggesting that cold "Virtue" is not necessarily the ultimate ideal. For example, her 1795 poem **"To the Poor"** angrily mocks sermons preached to the hungry and oppressed during war time, exaggerating the advocacy of virtuous stoicism: "Bear, bear thy wrongs, fulfil thy destined hour, / Bend thy meek neck beneath the foot of power!" (11-12; **P** 129). Surely stoic Virtue on the part of victims enables exploitation to continue, a situation that Barbauld consistently opposes in her discussions of social responsibility.

Rather than resolve the ambiguity of the ending to **"The Caterpillar,"** we might consider seeing all three possibilities as strands of a very complex positionality. The speaker plays between different positions, each of which is supportable by other works, but none of which is rigid or definitive, making Virtue multidimensional and even seemingly contradictory at times. Whereas *Eighteen Hundred and Eleven* presents a single moral position, castigating a "profound disorder" (McDonagh 75) in society and politics, **"The Caterpillar"** presents a relative ethics that shifts as circumstances shift, presenting an assumed order that nevertheless is disjunctive, disrupting conventional analogies and comfortable sensibilities with a subversive style and an abrupt conclusion that provokes serious thought. Indeed, Barbauld's positionality encourages varying affinities, engaging and yet intervening in Romantic sensibility, supporting the prowling poor and yet forcing readers to rethink the ideological implications of sympathy and pity. These affinities are not exactly the same as double dissent, although the quest for equality, so central to nonconformist dissenters and disadvantaged women, certainly is crucial to Barbauld's varying voices. By remaining unfixed, however, Barbauld addresses both the dangers and the values of pests and parasites, adopting and then jarring ethical considerations so that thought is opened toward wider flows of animate relations. This is not weakness but a Virtue.

Notes

1. Samuel Taylor Coleridge reports Barbauld's complaint in a March 1832 entry of his *Table Talk*, ed. C. Woodring, 2 vols. (Princeton: Princeton UP, 1990) 1: 272-73: "Mrs. Barbauld once told me that she admired the Ancient Mariner very much, but that there were two faults in it: it was improbable, and had no moral. As for the probability, I

owned that that might admit some question but as to the want of a moral, I told her that in my own judgment the poem had too much; and that the only, or chief fault, if I might say so, was the obtrusion of the moral sentiment so openly on the reader as a principle or cause of action in a work of pure imagination." For detailed discussions of this episode, see Deirdre Coleman, "The Unitarian Rationalist and the 'Winged Spider': Anna Letitia Barbauld and Samuel Taylor Coleridge," *Imperfect Apprehensions: Essays in English Literature in Honour of G. A. Wilkes,* ed. Geoffrey Little (Sydney, AU: Challis, 1996) 148-63 and Lisa Vargo, "The Case of Anna Laetitia Barbauld's 'To Mr C[oleridge],'" *Charles Lamb Bulletin* 102 (April 1998): 55-63. Vargo particularly cautions readers not to continue reading Barbauld as a footnote to Coleridge.

2. Anna Letitia Barbauld, "Thoughts on the Inequality of Conditions," *Selected Poetry and Prose,* ed. William McCarthy and Elizabeth Kraft (Orchard Park, NY: Broadview P, 2002) 353. Subsequent citations from this edition appear parenthetically in the text as S followed by page number.

3. William McCarthy and Elizabeth Kraft note the marginalization in their introduction to *The Poems of Anna Letitia Barbauld* (Athens, GA: U of Georgia P, 1994) xxxv. Subsequent citations from this edition appear parenthetically in the text as P followed by page number.

4. Coleridge, in *Collected Letters of Samuel Taylor Coleridge,* ed. E. L. Griggs (Oxford: Clarendon, 1956) 1.578, ends a letter to John Prior Estlin on March 1, 1800, with the following postscript: "The more I see of Mrs Barbauld the more I admire her—that wonderful *Propriety* of Mind!—She has great *acuteness,* very great—yet how steadily she keeps it within the bounds of practical Reason. This I almost envy as well as admire."

5. Mitzi Myers, "Of Mice and Mothers," *Feminine Principles and Women's Experience in American Composition and Rhetoric,* ed. Louise Wetherbee Phelps and Janet Emig (Pittsburgh: U of Pittsburgh P, 1995) 259.

6. Marlon Ross, "Configurations of Feminine Reform," *Re-visioning Romanticism,* ed. Carol Shiner Wilson and Joel Haefner (College Park: U of Pennsylvania P, 1994) 93.

7. William Keach, "Barbauld, Romanticism and the Survival of Dissent," *Romanticism and Gender,* ed. Anne Janowitz (London: Brewer, 1998) 49-50.

8. Laura Mandell, "Transcending Misogyny: Anna Letitia Barbauld Writes Her Way Out," *Misogynous Economies: The Business of Literature in Eighteenth-Century Britain* (Lexington: U of Kentucky P, 1999) 130.

9. Editors William McCarthy and Elizabeth Kraft use the fairly chronological arrangement of Lucy Aiken's edition of *The Works of Anna Letitia Barbauld. With a Memoir,* 2 vols. (London: Longman, Hurt, Rees, Orme, Brown, & Green, 1825; further referenced as W with volume and page) to suggest that "The Caterpillar" was composed around 1816 (P 322). However, several factors suggest 1815 might be a more likely date. First of all, Barbauld was not actively composing in 1816, according to her letter on August 23rd to Maria Edgeworth, which appears in *Memoir of Mrs. Barbauld including Letters and Notices of Her Family and Friends,* ed. Anna Letitia Le Breton (London: George Bell, 1874) 164: "Writing anything I have not felt equal to [thanks to ill health], and reading has at times been a task to me, but at present I feel better." Secondly, as Jonathan Bate has pointed out in "Living with the Weather," *SiR* [*Studies in Romanticism*] 35.3 (1996): 431-40, the summer of 1816 was the "year without a summer," with below average temperatures, minimal sunshine, and abundant rainfall from April onwards. It is unlikely that caterpillars were abundant that year (or the following, which was similarly cool), since cold, inclement weather is unfavorable to their growth. See Terrence D. Fitzgerald, *The Tent Caterpillars* (Ithaca: Cornell UP, 1995) 212-15. Thirdly, the poem mentions that "horrid war [. . ./ . . .] rolls dreadful on" (30-31), implying that Britain is still at war, which no longer was true in 1816. Nor was it true in June 1814, when Barbauld wrote to Mrs. Fletcher about the peace of Paris and Napoleon Bonaparte's abdication, calling the latter a tyrannical "despot" (W 2: 140). The most feasible alternative would be June 1815, after Napoleon had dramatically returned from the Isle of Elba in March. Although Napoleon requested peace with Britain, and although many of the British believed Britain should make peace with him, Parliament nevertheless voted in favor of renewed warfare. By June 1815, the war resumed its ferocity, both French and British commanders appearing to "enjoy / The roar of cannon and the clang of arms" ("The Caterpillar" 32-33). By the time Napoleon surrendered to the British in July, after his defeat at Waterloo on June 18, caterpillar season was over.

10. As my colleague Mike Richardson has pointed out, this convention was particularly active in the Renaissance. Stephen Gosson's *The Shoole* [*sic*] *of Abuse,* which prompted Sir Philip Sidney's *Defence of Poetry* in the sixteenth century, includes the following subtitle: *Conteining a Plesaunt Invective against Poets, Pipers, Plaiers, Iesters, and Such Like Caterpillers of a Commonwealth* (London: Thomas Woodcocke, 1579). Similarly, gardeners in William Shakespeare's *Richard* II (III.iv.46-47) grumble about keeping the royal grounds in perfect order when the whole country is like a ruined garden "Swarming with caterpillars." Indeed, "caterpillar" is defined figuratively by the *Oxford English Dictionary* as "a rapacious person, one who preys upon society." Shakespeare references are from *The Complete Works,* ed. Arthur Henry Bullen (Oxford: Shakespeare Head P, 1904) and will henceforth appear parenthetically in the text in the following format: act, scene, line.

11. McCarthy and Kraft mention an anonymous poem from 1804 entitled "The Caterpillar" in which the speaker argues that the caterpillar on a lady's gown has a soul. McCarthy and Kraft add "We do not know whether ALB [Anna Laetitia Barbauld] had seen this poem" (P 322).

12. Jim Porter, *The Colour Identification Guide to Caterpillars of the British Isles* (London: Viking, 1997) 21, 81; W. J. Stokoe, *The Caterpillars of British Moths,* ed. G. H. T. Stovin (London: Warne, 1948) 92-93.

13. Erasmus Darwin, *The Economy of Vegetation,* part 1 of *The Botanic Garden; A Poem in Two Parts* (London: Johnson, 1791) 201: 494.

14. Although Priscilla Wakefield's *Introduction to the Natural History and Classification of Insects* (London, 1816) does not mention European tent caterpillars or Lackey moths per se, she does note that some caterpillars can be "so numerous, as to cause great destruction to the verdure of the country" (86).

15. Samuel Johnson, *A Dictionary of the English Language* (1755; rpt. New York: AMS, 1967). Further references appear in the text. Note that the *Oxford English Dictionary* offers an alternative possible source from OF [Old French] *chatepelose,* literally "hairy or downy cat."

16. Nor do most entomological publications from the period. For example, Moses Harris' *English Lepidoptera: Or, The Aurelian's Pocket Companion* (1775; rpt. Hampton, Middlesex: Classey, 1969) includes the food of various caterpillars (including the Lackey) since they tend to be specialist eaters and are most easily found on their preferred plants. But Harris does not condemn their eating or suggest any pest control.

17. Bernhard Grzimek et al, eds., *Grzimek's Animal Life Encyclopedia, Vol. 2: Insects* (New York: Van Nostrand Reinhold, 1975) 321.

18. Ralph Howard Davidson and Leonard Marion Peairs, *Insect Pests of Farm, Garden, and Orchard,* 6th ed. (New York: John Wiley, 1966) 37.

19. Linnaeus (Carl Linne), as quoted by V. G. Dethier, *Man's Plague? Insects and Agriculture* (Princeton, NJ: Darwin P, 1976) 57.

20. Proceedings of the London Aurelian Society, quoted by L. O. Howard, *A History of Applied Entomology* (Washington: Smithsonian Institution, 1930) 217.

21. William Wordsworth, "The Tables Turned," *Selected Poems and Prefaces,* ed. Jack Stillinger (Boston: Houghton Mifflin, 1965) 107, lines 26, 28.

22. Cynthia Damon indicates in her book *The Mask of the Parasite: A Pathology of Roman Patronage* (Ann Arbor: U of Michigan P, 1997) that Greek parasites tended to arrive at rich homes without an invitation, being obsessed by the desire for free food, whereas their Roman counterparts were often patronized by their hosts and perceived by observers as opportunistic dependents who claimed to earn their food through various entertainments and obsequious services. The Roman model persisted well into the Romantic era, enabling Mary Wollstonecraft's 1790 *Vindication of the Rights of Man,* in *Political Writings,* ed. Janet Todd (Toronto: U of Toronto P, 1993) to use "parasites" to describe "men of some abilities [who] play on the follies of the rich" (24).

23. Chambers, *Cyclopedia* (1727-1741), as cited by the *Oxford English Dictionary.* Further citations from the dictionary appear parenthetically in the text as *OED.*

24. Michel Serres, *The Parasite,* trans. Lawrence R. Schehr (Baltimore: Johns Hopkins UP, 1982) 7. Further references appear parenthetically in the text. Serres also notes a third type of "parasite" that is present as a noun in French, but appears only adjectivally in English: the acoustical parasite, also known as static, the noise that distorts meaning and interferes in the normal transmission of sound (8). One *Oxford English Dictionary* definition of "parasitic" is "unwanted subsidiary phenomena and effects."

25. Marcel Mauss, *The Gift: Forms and Functions of Exchange in Archaic Societies,* trans. Ian Cunnison (New York: Norton, 1967), describes gift exchange as an obligatory and ongoing back-and-forth pattern of social relations involving gifts, return-gifts, counter-return gifts, ad infinitum. Each return gift must be of equal or slightly greater value than the gift previously received so as to preserve social respect and to encourage further gift giving.

26. Thomas Paine, *The Rights of Man* (1791; rpt. New York: Doubleday, 1989) 283.

27. J. Hillis Miller, "The Critic as Host," *Critical Inquiry* 3.3 (1977): 446, 444. Miller defends deconstructive literary critics from accusations of parasitism upon a text by arguing that critics are not parasites but hosts who give meaning to the text. It is the text which is parasitically dependent upon intertexts and interpretations for meaning.

28. Jacques Derrida, *The Gift of Death,* trans. David Willis (Chicago: U of Chicago P, 1995) 112.

29. Robert Burns, "To a Mouse," *The Longman Anthology of British Literature,* vol. 2A, ed. Susan Wolfson and Peter Manning (New York: Longman, 1999), lines 8, 1; page 302.

30. David Perkins, "Human Mouseness: Burns and Compassion for Animals," *Texas Studies in Literature and Language* 42.1 (2000): 9, 12-13.

31. Serres notes that parasites use language so skillfully that they can make even non-events, such as the averting of disaster, appear to be gifts: "You [the vulnerable host] live with no other need, and suddenly, someone [the parasite] claims to have saved your country, protected your class, your interests, your family, and your table. And you have to pay him for that [. . .]" (22).

32. Sir Philip Sidney, *A Defence of Poetry,* ed. Jan Van Dorsten (1966; rpt. Oxford: Oxford UP, 1978) 144.

33. Laura Mandell, "'Those Limbs Disjointed of Gigantic Power': Barbauld's Personifications and the (Mis)Attribution of Political Agency," *SiR* 37 (1998): 27-41, suggests that Barbauld typically employs personification and demystification of abstractions in her poetry.

34. David Hamilton-Williams, *The Fall of Napoleon* (New York: Wiley, 1994) 255. Napoleon's life was spared several times during and after the Battle of Waterloo on June 18, 1815. Ironically the motive for such kindness might not have been sympathy so much as an attempt on Wellington's part to redeem his character, having been reproached by Parliament for signing the allied declaration against Napoleon (Hamilton-Williams 254).

35. Isobel Armstrong, "The Gush of the Feminine: How Can We Read Women's Poetry of the Romantic Period?" *Romantic Women Writers: Voices and Counter Voices,* ed. Paula R. Feldman and Theresa M. Kelley (Hanover, NH: UP of New England, 1995) 15.

36. William Wordsworth, *The Letters of William and Dorothy Wordsworth,* vol. 8, ed. Alan G. Hill (Oxford: Clarendon, 1993) 72, 79. Wordsworth's distrust of Barbauld was partly based upon the mistaken assumption that she was the nasty reviewer of Charles Lamb's *John Woodvil* (Vargo 56), and partly a response to her poetic editions of Akenside, Collins, and others in which she forestalled "natural feeling and judgment" through

misconceived prefaces (William Wordsworth, *The Critical Opinions of William Wordsworth*, ed. Markham L. Peacock [Baltimore: Johns Hopkins UP, 1950] 181). As Laura Mandell points out, Wordsworth shared with Coleridge and Lamb an increasing dislike for "the cursed Barbauld crew" (Lamb, qtd. in Mandell, "Transcending" 129).

37. John Wilson Croker, "Review of *Eighteen Hundred and Eleven*," *Quarterly Review* 7 (1812), argues that Barbauld has "miserably mistaken both her powers and her duty, in exchanging the birchen for the satiric rod, and abandoning the superintendance [*sic*] of the 'ovilia' of the nursery, to wage war on the 'reluctantes dracones,' statesmen, and warriors, whose misdoings have aroused her indignant muse." Repeatedly sending Barbauld back to the domestic realm, Croker expresses dismay at this "intervention of a lady-author," suggesting that "the interests of Europe and of humanity" would be better served by her silence.

38. Edgeworth, in Le Breton 157. Most of the twenty poems Barbauld wrote after 1812 remained unpublished until her death in 1825. William Keach, "A Regency Prophecy and the End of Anna Barbauld's Career," *SiR* 33 (1994): 571, notes that Croker's criticism effectively ended Barbauld's publishing endeavours: "A prolific and influential literary career came to an end."

39. Josephine McDonagh, "Barbauld's Domestic Economy," *Romanticism and Gender* 63-64.

40. Bernard Mandeville, *The Fable of the Bees; or Private Vices, Public Benefits* (1712); rpt. *Eighteenth-Century English Literature*, ed. Geoffrey Tillotson et al (New York: Harcourt, Brace & World, 1969) 277.

41. J. G. A. Pocock, *Virtue, Commerce, and History: Essays on Political Thought and History, Chiefly in the Eighteenth Century* (Cambridge: Cambridge UP, 1985) 253.

42. Erasmus Darwin, *Zoonomia*, 2 vols. (1794-1796; rpt. New York: AMS P, 1974) 2: 384.

43. Mary Wollstonecraft, *Vindication of the Rights of Woman*, ed. Carol Poston, 2nd ed. (New York: Norton, 1988) 48.

FURTHER READING

Biographies

LeBreton, Anna Letitia. *Memoir of Mrs. Barbauld Including Letters and Notices of Her Family and Friends.* London: G. Bell and Sons, 1874, 236 p.

Offers personal recollections of Barbauld, written by her great niece.

Rogers, Betsy. *Georgian Chronicle: Mrs. Barbauld & Her Family.* London: Methuen, 1958, 29 p.

Evaluates Barbauld's life and career against the backdrop of her family history.

Wakefield, Dick. *Anna Laetitia Barbauld.* London: Centaur, 2001, 113 p.

Appraises Barbauld's life and career, arguing that she played a central role in the leading political and literary movements of her era.

Criticism

Bordo, Haley. "Reinvoking the 'Domestic Muse': Anna Laetitia Barbauld and the Performance of Genre." *European Romantic Review* 11, no. 2 (spring 2000): 186-96.

Examines the relationship between Barbauld's use of mock-epic literary conventions and her attitude toward traditional gender roles in the poem "Washing-Day," drawing on the theories of Judith Butler.

Bradshaw, Penny. "Gendering the Enlightenment: Conflicting Images of Progress in the Poetry of Anna Lætitia Barbauld." *Women's Writing* 5, no. 3 (1998): 353-71.

Examines Barbauld's attitudes toward technology, social reform, and gender issues through a reading of her poetry.

———. "The Limits of Barbauld's Feminism: Re-Reading 'The Rights of Woman.'" *European Romantic Review* 15, no. 1 (winter 2005): 23-37.

Analyzes Barbauld's explorations of gender politics in the poem.

Burns, Nicholas. "'Thy World, Columbus!': Barbauld and Global Space, 1803, *1811*, 1812, 2003." *European Romantic Review* 16, no. 5 (December 2005): 545-62.

Highlights foreshadowings of modern globalization in Barbauld's poem *Eighteen Hundred and Eleven*.

Davies, Kate. "A Moral Purchase: Femininity, Commerce, and Abolition, 1788-1792." In *Women, Writing and the Public Sphere, 1700-1830,* edited by Elizabeth Eger, Charlotte Grant, and Clíona Ó Gallchoir, pp. 133-59. Cambridge: Cambridge University Press, 2001.

Compares depictions of the slave trade in the writings of Barbauld and Hannah More.

Jones, Robert. "What Then Should Britons Feel? Anna Laetitia Barbauld and the Plight of the Corsicans." *Women's Writing* 9, no. 2 (2002): 285-303.

Discusses Barbauld's representation of the Corsican struggle for independence in her 1768 poem "Corsica," comparing her portrayal of the country with that of James Boswell in *An Account of Corsica* (1768).

Keach, William. "Barbauld, Romanticism, and the Survival of Dissent." *Essays and Studies* 51 (1998): 44-61.
Examines issues of dissent and religious freedom in Barbauld's political poetry.

Keane, Angela. "The Market, the Public and the Female Author: Anna Laetitia Barbauld's Gift Economy." *Romanticism: The Journal of Romantic Culture and Criticism* 8, no. 2 (2002): 161-78.
Considers economic and gender issues as they relate to the publication of Barbauld's writings.

Levine, William. "The Eighteenth-Century Jeremiad and Progress-Piece Traditions in Anna Barbauld's *Eighteen Hundred and Eleven.*" *Women's Writing* 12, no. 2 (2005): 177-86.
Analyzes Barbauld's use of an anachronistic verse style in the poem as a means of protest against the imperialist, male-oriented literary models of her age.

Mahon, Penny. "In Sermon and Story: Contrasting Anti-War Rhetoric in the Work of Anna Barbauld and Amelia Opie." *Women's Writing* 7, no. 1 (2000): 23-38.
Discovers similar pacifist elements in the two authors' works.

McCarthy, William. "A 'High-Minded Christian Lady': The Posthumous Reception of Anna Letitia Barbauld." In *Romanticism and Women Poets: Opening the Doors of Reception,* edited by Harriet Kramer Linkin and Stephen C. Behrendt, pp. 165-91. Lexington: University Press of Kentucky, 1999.
Surveys critical writings devoted to Barbauld's work.

———. "Mother of All Discourses: Anna Barbauld's *Lessons for Children.*" In *Culturing the Child, 1690-1914: Essays in Memory of Mitzi Myers,* edited by Donelle Ruwe, pp. 85-111. Lanham, Md.: Scarecrow Press, Inc., 2005.

Examines Barbauld's radical view of motherhood in her writings for children.

Moore, Catherine E. "'Ladies . . . Taking the Pen in Hand': Mrs. Barbauld's Criticism of Eighteenth-Century Women Novelists." In *Fetter'd or Free? British Women Novelists, 1670-1815,* edited by Mary Anne Schofield and Cecelia Macheski, pp. 383-97. Athens: Ohio University Press, 1986.
Analyzes Barbauld's critical writings while discussing her views on the role of women in the development of the novel form in England.

Pickering, Samuel F. "Mrs. Barbauld's Hymns in Prose: 'An Air-Blown Particle' of Romanticism?" *Southern Humanities Review* 9 (1975): 259-68.
Relates romantic elements in Barbauld's hymns to the writings of William Wordsworth.

Rogers, Katharine M. "Anna Barbauld's Criticism of Fiction—Johnsonian Mode, Female Vision." *Studies in Eighteenth-Century Culture* 21 (1991): 27-41.
Compares Barbauld's approach to literary criticism with that of Samuel Johnson, while analyzing the feminist qualities of her critical writings.

Vargo, Lisa. "The Aikins and the Godwins: Notions of Conflict and Stoicism in Anna Barbauld and Mary Shelley." *Romanticism: The Journal of Romantic Culture and Criticism* 11, no. 1 (2005): 84-98.
Evaluates representations of the relationship between politics, family, and gender in Barbauld's 1773 essay "Against Inconsistency in Our Expectations" and Mary Shelley's novel *Lodore* (1835).

White, Daniel E. "The 'Joineriana': Anna Barbauld, the Aikin Family Circle, and the Dissenting Public Sphere." *Eighteenth-Century Studies* 32, no. 4 (summer 1999): 511-33.
Examines Barbauld's years at Warrington Academy, analyzing the relationship between her involvement with the Dissenting movement and the development of her early verse.

Additional coverage of Barbauld's life and career is contained in the following sources published by Thomson Gale: *Dictionary of Literary Biography,* **Vols. 107, 109, 142, 158;** *Literature Resource Center;* *Nineteenth-Century Literature Criticism,* **Vol. 50; and** *Reference Guide to English Literature,* **Ed. 2.**

Madame Bovary

Gustave Flaubert

French novelist, playwright, short story writer, essayist, and letter writer.

The following entry presents criticism of Flaubert's 1857 novel *Madame Bovary*. For additional discussion of the novel, see *NCLC*, Volumes 10 and 66; for discussion of *L'Éducation sentimentale* (1869; *Sentimental Education*), see *NCLC*, Volumes 19 and 179; for discussion of *Salammbô* (1862), see *NCLC*, Volume 135; for information on Flaubert's complete career, see *NCLC*, Volumes 2 and 62.

INTRODUCTION

Most scholars regard Gustave Flaubert's *Madame Bovary* (1857) as a seminal work in the history of the modern novel. The narrative chronicles the life and death of Emma Bovary, a discontented wife and mother whose extramarital affairs ultimately lead to her undoing. An in-depth examination of thwarted desire, the novel paints a tragic portrait of a woman whose ideal of happiness becomes gradually suffocated, both by the weakness of her own character and by the repressive moral standards of her age. At the same time, the book levels a scathing attack on nineteenth-century bourgeois values, exposing what Flaubert perceived to be the self-righteousness and crassness of middle-class society. The work shocked contemporary readers, both in the ferocity of its satire and in its rigorously objective, unornamented prose style. The novel also earned unwelcome notoriety for Flaubert, who found himself on trial for obscenity shortly after the book's publication. He was eventually acquitted. In spite of its inauspicious beginnings, *Madame Bovary* soon garnered recognition from serious critics and authors as a major novel; today it is widely acknowledged as a foundational work of modern literature. The book's profound exploration of human psychology was revolutionary for its time, and Flaubert's highly exact, meticulous style greatly influenced the prose of later writers Guy de Maupassant, Joseph Conrad, and Emile Zola, among numerous others.

PLOT AND MAJOR CHARACTERS

Madame Bovary opens in the city of Rouen on the day that Charles Bovary, a shy, clumsy boy of fifteen, appears for his first day in a new school. The anonymous narrator, who is one of the students, describes the new boy's arrival in a detached, matter-of-fact tone, remarking only that Charles comes from a small town in the country, and that his ill-fitting clothes and uncouth manner suggest that he has limited means. As the book delves deeper into Bovary's background, it describes his parents' loveless marriage, his mother's uncompromising ambition for her son, and his own personal struggles to overcome his awkwardness and gain acceptance among his peers. Although an unremarkable student, Bovary works diligently, eventually passing his medical examinations and becoming a doctor in the small town of Tostes. Through his mother's scheming he enters into an undesirable marriage with a wealthy widow several years older than he. His wife's frail health and bitter attitude quickly drain Bovary's strength, and he becomes miserable.

Bovary's outlook changes dramatically when he meets Emma Rouault, the young daughter of a wealthy patient. Infatuated with Emma's beauty and innocence, Bovary begins to devise pretexts for visiting her house as often as possible, eventually arousing his wife's jealousy. When his wife suddenly falls ill and dies, Bovary begins making more frequent social calls to the Rouault house, engaging the young Emma in conversation. Although hesitant at first, she gradually divulges more and more about her life: she attended a convent school as a girl, and she is an avid reader of romance novels, which have largely shaped her unrealistic notions of love and marriage. The love-struck Charles soon proposes to Emma, and the two are married in a lavish ceremony.

Once the couple settles into their married routine, however, Flaubert begins to probe the deep discontent within Emma's character. Bored with the slow pace and uneventfulness of country life, Emma reads constantly, once again seeking escape in romantic novels. Her dissatisfaction reaches its peak after she attends a gala ball at a wealthy neighbor's estate. The contrast between the elegance of the party and the banality of her everyday life wounds Emma's pride, and she begins to act out against her husband. The ball proves pivotal in the evolution of Emma's character, as she now finds it impossible to tolerate what she perceives as the stasis and mediocrity of her life with Charles. Emma's growing unhappiness also exacts a toll on her physical health, especially after she becomes pregnant. Alarmed by his wife's sudden deterioration, Charles decides that she needs a change of scenery, and they move to the town of Yonville-l'Abbaye.

In Yonville-l'Abbaye, Emma gives birth to a daughter, Berthe. Although Emma adores the little girl at first, she soon becomes discontented with motherhood, and she grows increasingly depressed. During this time Charles and Emma become acquainted with their neighbor, the self-absorbed and insufferable town pharmacist, Homais. The presence of Homais in their lives only makes Emma's frustration more acute; his long-winded, pompous speeches render her increasingly desperate for more stimulating company. She soon befriends Léon, a young law clerk. Emma and Léon have a great deal in common; they both feel stifled by the moral and cultural backwardness of provincial society, and they both seek distraction in literature. In spite of her powerful affection for Léon, however, Emma is ill-prepared to act on her feelings; after Léon declares his love for her, Emma abruptly withdraws with a mixture of shame, confusion, and guilt. Suddenly resolved to become a dutiful, respectable wife, she throws herself into her household duties, while the disconsolate Léon leaves for Paris.

Soon after Léon departs from Yonville-l'Abbaye, Emma makes the acquaintance of a wealthy bachelor, Rodolphe. A notorious philanderer, Rodolphe resolves to conquer the bored young housewife; he declares his love for her and soon, during a horseback riding outing in the local forest, manages to seduce her, initiating a passionate affair. Although she wants to maintain the affair's secrecy, Emma becomes increasingly brazen in her behavior, arousing the suspicions of her neighbors. She also begins to act with greater hostility toward her husband, although he remains blind to her infidelities. The tension in their relationship becomes even more pronounced after Charles botches an operation on a club-footed man, resulting in the amputation of the patient's leg. Bovary's reputation as a doctor suffers irreparable damage, and Emma's disgust with his failings becomes acute. She plunges more deeply into her relationship with Rodolphe, borrowing money from the unscrupulous moneylender Lheureux in order to buy her lover expensive gifts. As her love for Rodolphe becomes more intense, she hatches a scheme to run away with him, to which he initially agrees. In truth, however, Rodolphe has become bored with Emma, and he decides against making the trip, effectively terminating the affair. The distraught Emma becomes gravely ill, and the cost of treating her plunges her husband even further into debt.

Soon after Emma's recovery, Charles takes her to the opera in Rouen in the hopes of raising her spirits. By chance, she encounters Léon at the opera. The romantic spark between them is quickly rekindled, and they embark on a love affair. Emma begins making frequent trips to the city, borrowing more and more money from Lheureux in order to pay for travel and fashionable clothes. In spite of the ardor with which they thrust themselves into the affair, Emma and Léon grow weary of each other before long and are unable to mask their mutual disgust. By this point, however, Emma's tragic course has become irreversible. As she becomes increasingly bored in her affair with Léon, she begins to spend more extravagantly, borrowing from Lheureux at increasingly exorbitant interest rates. When Lheureux threatens to begin confiscating Charles Bovary's property, Emma is in danger of being exposed. In a final, desperate attempt to escape financial ruin, she seeks financial help from Rodolphe, even offering to leave her husband. Rodolphe dismisses her proposition, however; in anguish, she swallows a large dose of arsenic and dies.

Although Charles idealizes his dead wife at first, he soon discovers love letters among her possessions, and her infidelities are exposed. Heartbroken, he dies a short time later. At the novel's conclusion, the orphaned Berthe becomes the charge of Bovary's elderly aunt, who sends the girl to work in a cotton mill.

MAJOR THEMES

At its core, many scholars have suggested, *Madame Bovary* is an indictment of the materialism and superficiality of the bourgeoisie. Flaubert's disdain for middle-class mediocrity, and for the stifling effects of this mediocrity on the individual, is felt throughout the novel: in his depictions of the crassness and ignorance of Emma's desires, in his portrait of Charles Bovary's slavish devotion to his unfaithful wife, and in the crude, selfish, and ultimately commonplace pursuits of the novel's minor characters. Flaubert's portrayal of Emma epitomizes the powerlessness of the individual within the framework of an oppressive social hierarchy. Although the author's assessment of her character is largely unsympathetic, he is not entirely merciless toward her. Roland Champagne describes Emma's inability to achieve contentment as "incompetence" while also arguing that her yearnings are thwarted by the "mismatch of bourgeois expectations and Charles Bovary." Throughout the narrative, external forces—rigid social customs, as well as the duplicity of scheming individuals—clearly exert a powerful influence on the actions of Flaubert's protagonist, rendering her virtually helpless to enact any of her life's goals, vague and uncertain as they may be. In the end, Emma emerges as much a victim of circumstance as she is the architect of her own downfall.

Flaubert offers a different perspective on bourgeois vulgarity in his depiction of Emma's husband, Charles. Charles has no discernible personal ambitions; he is a doctor almost by accident. The entire focus of his energy revolves around his wife's happiness, although he remains ignorant of her desires until after her death. By concentrating on the banal aspects of Charles's character, scholars argue, Flaubert transforms him into a representative figure within nineteenth-century bourgeois society: he is the complacent, ineffectual professional. In various ways, the other residents of Yonville-l'Abbaye also exhibit this general sense of debased, weakened individuality. Homais, in spite of his self-aggrandizing rhetoric, demonstrates little competence as a man of medicine; the remorseless Rodolphe seeks only to satisfy his own vanity, willfully unaware of the deep anguish that ultimately drives his former lover to suicide. Even Léon, in spite of his thoughtful, passionate nature, ultimately reveals himself as weak, failing twice to act decisively on his love for Emma. These are the types of people Flaubert chose as the prime representatives of French society in the mid-nineteenth century.

CRITICAL RECEPTION

Although *Madame Bovary* caused a minor scandal when it first appeared in 1857, with a number of readers expressing outrage over the novel's alleged immorality, it also elicited high praise from serious literary reviewers. Early critics, notably Charles Baudelaire, expressed admiration for the novel's emotional and psychological depth, as well as for its innovative prose technique. Henry James, in his influential study *French Poets and Novelists* (1888), described the novel as a landmark of literary realism, even as he identified what he perceived as the work's imaginative failings. Over the years, a number of other critics and scholars have explored the question of realism with respect to Flaubert. Writing in the *Bookman* in 1895, Harry Thurston Peck outlined the distinction between Flaubert's brand of realism, which he described as primarily rooted in metaphor, and the more directly descriptive naturalism of such authors as Emile Zola. In the mid-twentieth century, scholars began to pay closer attention to the link between Flaubert's technique and the novel's symbolic framework and central themes. In *The Perpetual Orgy*, Mario Vargas Llosa uses the term "protoplasmic narrator" to describe the breadth of Flaubert's narrative point of view, arguing that this approach lends the work its psychological depth. Over the years, the relationship between language and meaning in *Madame Bovary* has been analyzed by numerous scholars, among them William A. Johnsen, who examined the modern elements in Flaubert's prose style; Mary Donaldson-Evans, who discussed the metaphorical significance of medical terminology in the novel; and Naomi Schor, who evaluated Flaubert's narrative strategies within the context of the linguistic theories of Jacques Derrida, Giles Deleuze, and Roland Barthes. Since the 1990s, a number of influential feminist readings of the novel have emerged. Patricia McEachern has suggested that Emma's character exhibits signs of an eating disorder, while George Smith has critiqued what he views as Flaubert's misogynistic depiction of his protagonist. In a 2002 essay Roland Champagne evaluated the relationship between Emma's mistreatment of her own body and her perverse conception of womanhood.

PRINCIPAL WORKS

Madame Bovary: moeurs de province [*Madame Bovary: A Tale of Provincial Life*] (novel) 1857
Salammbô (novel) 1862
L'Education sentimentale, histoire d'un jeune homme. 2 vols. [*Sentimental Education: A Young Man's History*] (novel) 1869
Le Candidat, comédie en 4 actes [*The Candidate: A Humorous Political Drama in Four Acts*] (play) 1874
La Tentation de Saint Antoine [*The Temptation of Saint Anthony*] (novel) 1874
Trois contes [*Three Tales*] (short stories) 1877
Bouvard et Pécuchet [*Bouvard and Pécuchet*] (novel) 1881
Œuvres complètes. 8 vols. (novels, short stories, plays, travel essays, and prose) 1885
Correspondance. 4 vols. (letters) 1887-93
Les Mémoires d'un fou (novel) 1901
Notes inédites de Flaubert (prose) 1910
Œuvres de jeunesse inédites (prose) 1910
Théâtre: Le Candidat, Le Château des coeurs, Le Sexe faible (plays) 1910
Dictionnaire des idées reçues [*Flaubert's Dictionary of Accepted Ideas*; *A Dictionary of Platitudes*] (prose) 1913
Voyages. 2 vols. (prose) 1948
Carnets de travail (prose) 1988

*Comprised of the stories "Un Coeur simple," "La Légende de Saint Julien l'Hospitalier," and "Hérodias."

CRITICISM

Atlantic Monthly (essay date November 1891)

SOURCE: "Two French Men of Letters." *Atlantic Monthly* 68, no. 404 (November 1891): 695-701.

[*In the following excerpt, the author discusses Flaubert's attitude toward literary realism as it relates to the composition of* Madame Bovary. *The reviewer contends that Flaubert's realism derives from the honest expression of his imagination rather than from a meticulous reproduction of external phenomena.*]

[Flaubert's] convictions remained to the last romantic, or he thought they did; it was a part of his loyalty to cling to the old enthusiasms, a part of his suffering and acuteness of indignation to wage war against the stupidity of commonplace and the hideousness of fact.

"They think me in love with the real, whereas I execrate it; it is out of hatred of realism that I have undertaken this novel. But I have no less detestation for the false idealism by which we are fooled in these days. . . . I beg, however, that you will not judge me by this book. La Bovary [*Madame Bovary*] has been for me a matter of deliberate choice, a set theme. All that I love is not there. I will give you in a little while something more elevated, in a more appropriate setting." This is to a lady, and may be taken partly as a gracious way of putting things. But to one of his critics he writes in the same tone: "Do you believe that this ignoble reality, the reproduction of which disgusts you, does not turn my stomach as well as yours? If you knew me better, you would know that I execrate every-day life. I have always kept away from it personally as much as I could. But æsthetically I wanted this once, and only this once, to go to the bottom of it. Accordingly I went at the thing in an heroic manner,—I mean in a minute one,—accepting everything, saying everything, painting everything; which is an ambitious way of expressing it." And later, to the same correspondent, in a tone which would contradict his apparent disavowal of *Madame Bovary,* but confirms the real tenor of his testimony to its reality: "You attack details; you should take exception to the whole. The brutal element is ingrained, and not on the surface. We cannot whiten negroes, and we cannot alter the blood of a book; all that can be done is to impoverish it."

This is coming very near to the kernel of the matter. The blood of a book is not a deliberate infusion; the author who writes a great work in opposition to his theory is not concealing, but declaring, the true color of his conception of life. It is not necessary, in order to be a realist, to love "ignoble realities;" it is a matter of truth, not of sentiment; and the feeling which penetrates to a sense of something higher behind the ignoble reality is to be valued only as it brings more and truer tones into the picture. The truth of *Madame Bovary* has stamped its impress deeply into literature, and the word "realism" would have to be widely diverted from its simple and spontaneous meaning to exclude such a work from its category. When Flaubert speaks of art as "thought in form made concrete, a feeling of *violent* nature, and arrived at its highest term of idealism in expression," he touches the point at which the two words "idealism" and "realism" join. His confidences in regard to the dif-

ficulty of composition show that his constant care was to write close to his thought; to make form and expression, as he himself says, "like body and soul." It is a suggestive circumstance in this matter of realism that two of its greatest masters should in different ways have denied or deserted its standard. Flaubert, after writing *Madame Bovary* "out of hatred of reality," sought refuge in history and the past to avoid another picture of the actual life of his day; and Tolstóy, after seeing with such clearness of vision in *Anna Karénin* the good and the ignoble at once, has hidden his head in the sand of a fatalistic religion. Is the perception of every-day truth as fatal to its prophets as are the visions of poetry to the bard "blasted with excess of light"?

Harry Thurston Peck (essay date October 1895)

SOURCE: Peck, Harry Thurston. "The First of the Realists." *Bookman* 2, no. 2 (October 1895): 130-33.

[*In the following excerpts, Peck evaluates Flaubert's role in the development of French realism. Peck elucidates the distinction between realism and naturalism, arguing that Flaubert's compact, restrained prose style is what lends* Madame Bovary *its subtle metaphorical power.*]

Historically, of course, realism in literature is generally traced back to Rousseau, who in his *Confessions* furnished a suggestion and an example of the tremendous force that exists in naked veracity; and the application of this idea to fiction-writing is to be found primarily in the novels of Marie-Henri Beyle (Stendhal) and of Balzac; but even in Balzac the realism is often in abeyance and the work is coloured by the glow of a great and flaming imagination which throws upon the screen figures larger than life itself, with a splendid yet too romantic exaggeration of every trait of character, so that Baudelaire complains of Balzac that in his pages every one, down to the very scullions, have genius. It is, therefore, in Flaubert, rather than in any of his predecessors, that we are to find the fruition and perfection of the realistic theory; while the influence of his personal association, as well as of his published work, directed the early labours of Turgenieff, Daudet, Maupassant, and Émile Zola. . . .

[H]is first and greatest work, *Madame Bovary,* was not published until 1857, when the author was in his thirty-seventh year.

This wonderful novel was brought forth with great travail and mental anguish. To write was indescribably difficult to Flaubert, who, like Balzac, tortured himself in his devotion to style, writing, rewriting, excising, waiting hours for just the right word to come to him, and often at the last ruthlessly cutting out paragraphs that had cost him a week's incessant toil. In eight days of endless labour, so he tells a friend, he had finished only two pages; and the agony of creation was intense. Clothed in a dressing-gown of extraordinary pattern, he would rise at four and work till ten, snarling like a wild beast over his desk, groaning, chanting each phrase as he finished it, and sometimes, when just the right phrase seemed hopelessly beyond his grasp, bursting into howls of despair, with floods of passionate tears. But the great reward came to him at last. Published in the *Revue de Paris,* and then in a book, *Madame Bovary* became the sensation of the year. It was, as a critic has said, not a realistic novel; it was, rather, realism itself. The vividness and truth of its every character, the compact and muscular form in which it is cast, the absolute perfection of its style, all raised it to the rank of a classic from the moment of its completion. . . .

Madame Bovary is a very striking illustration of the difference between true realism and the excesses of the naturalistic school. Everywhere Flaubert is reticent and self-restrained. Take the famous scene where Emma drives about Rouen with Léon Dupuis in the closed cab—a paragraph suppressed on the original appearance of the story in the *Revue de Paris*—and consider how a naturalistic novelist like Zola would have treated the same incident. Instead of a paragraph we should have had a chapter, and what a reeking, unsavoury, unspeakable chapter it would have been! Moreover, Flaubert's merits are seen just as truly in his treatment of the characters and events that are subordinate to his central theme. All his provincials—Charles, the immortal Homais, the crafty peddler Lheureux, the gentleman-farmer Boulanger, the country notabilities at the agricultural show—all these and a score of others are sketched with a wealth of incident fully equal to Balzac's, and a fidelity beyond even that of the French Shakespeare. In every portion of this epoch-making work Flaubert is seen to be absolutely apart from the writers who have abused and corrupted the example of their great master, and who, as has been strikingly said, see only the beast in man, and view humanity as "a swarming, huddled mass of growling creatures, each hounded on by his own foul appetites of greed and lust."

Robert Wooster Stallman (essay date January 1949)

SOURCE: Stallman, Robert Wooster. "Flaubert's *Madame Bovary.*" *College English* 10, no. 4 (January 1949): 195-203.

[*In the following essay, Stallman examines Flaubert's use of irony in the novel.*]

Flaubert and Henry James, among the moderns, are the great masters of ironic contemplation. Irony is a fundamental in the architectonics of *Madame Bovary.* Emma Bovary is Flaubert's name for the ironic chain of contradictory feelings and moods, the conflicting attitudes, that he has imposed upon her. Emma makes the most of her opportunities for romance, but her opportunities need not necessarily have appeared in the shape of Rodolphe or Léon; as Percy Lubbock says, she would have found others if these had not been at hand.

> None of the events really matter for their own sake; they might have happened differently, not one of them is indispensable as it is. . . . The *events,* therefore, Emma's excursions to Rouen, her forest-rides, her one or two memorable adventures in the world—all these are only Flaubert's way of telling his subject, of making it count to the eye. They are not in themselves what he has to say, they simply illustrate it.[1]

Emma is not a unified creation. Flaubert sacrifices her for the thesis that she represents. Her plight applies to human beings everywhere and always, the romantic pursuit of happiness being a permanent part of our nature. In the passion-pinched multitudes who crowd our movie-palaces, Emma has her present-day counterparts—the movie-screen fulfilling for them all the impossible passions which Emma Bovary failed to obtain. Flaubert's theme, namely, that the quest for happiness cannot be realized in the world of everyday experience, is a theme of universal validity. Our world, no less than Emma Bovary's, is split by the same tragic disparity between inner dream and external reality. We, too, are betrayed by reality at every turn.

Flaubert's achievement is, by common consent, an achievement in technique. His originality is the method he has engineered, and it is by way of these technical innovations that his kinship with Henry James and Joseph Conrad is to be defined. It is Flaubert's method of ironic or indirect description that places him foremost among technical innovators. The opening passage to chapter vii of Part I, for instance, aptly illustrates his technical dexterity. Observe how he analyzes Emma's mood or emotion:

> She thought, sometimes, that, after all, this was the happiest time of her life—the honeymoon, as people called it. To taste the full sweetness of it, it would have been necessary doubtless to fly to those lands with sonorous names where the days after marriage are full of laziness most suave. In post-chaises behind blue silken curtains to ride slowly up steep roads, listening to the song of the postilion re-echoed by the mountains, along with the bells of goats and the muffled sound of a waterfall; at sunset on the shores of gulfs to breathe in the perfume of lemon trees; then in the evening on the villa-terraces above, hand in hand to look at the stars, making plans for the future. It seemed to her that certain places on earth must bring happiness, as a plant peculiar to the soil, and that cannot thrive elsewhere. Why could not she lean over balconies in Swiss châlets, or enshrine her melancholy in a Scotch cottage, with a husband dressed in a black velvet coat with long tails and thin shoes, a pointed hat and frills?[2]

Emma's mood is developed and defines itself (from ex-altation as symbolized in "honeymoon," to nostalgic longing, shifting to sadness) by means of a series of images which are the formula for the particular emotion. At the key-word "honeymoon," which connotes for Emma a vague feeling of happiness, her awareness of the actual world ends and her reverie begins. Flaubert's summoning-up of a complex of feelings by a set of images is the method of Conrad in *The Heart of Darkness,* the atmosphere in that story being engendered by a structure of sense-impressions which objectify the atmosphere and evoke it. The blue-silken curtains of Emma's post-chaise, like the drawn blinds of Léon's cab (in Part III, chap. i), are supposed to conceal an enactment of pent-up passion, but ironically the concealed exotic passion is celebrated without any lover—only by the lonely woman inside. The coach is empty! Emma is again without a lover in that Scotch cottage, wherein she enshrines her melancholy. The man inside, the husband "in a pointed hat and frills," is not physically present at all. This void is filled by Emma's own impassionate visions. As when she later writes love letters to Léon:

> But whilst she wrote, it was another man she saw, a phantom fashioned out of her most ardent memories, of her finest reading, her strongest lusts, and at last he became so real, so tangible, that she palpitated wondering, without, however, the power to imagine him clearly, so lost was he, like a god, beneath the abundance of his attributes. He dwelt in that azure land where silk ladders hang from balconies under the breath of flowers, in the light of the moon. She felt him near her; he was coming, and would carry her right away in a kiss.
>
> [Part III, chap. vi, p. 332]

These journeys in quest of "a profound felicity" form the crux of Emma's experiences. Her dream states are inevitably followed by fits of depression ("these transports of vague love wearied her more than great debauchery").

> She was constantly promising herself a profound felicity on her next journey. Then she confessed to herself that she felt nothing extraordinary. This disappointment quickly gave way to a new hope, and Emma returned to him more inflamed, more eager than ever. She undressed brutally, tearing off the thin laces of her corset that nestled around her hips like a gliding snake. She went on tiptoe, barefooted, to see once more that the door was closed, then pale, serious, and, without speaking, with one movement, she threw herself upon his breast with a long shudder.
>
> [Part III, chap. vi, pp. 323-24]

Here again, as similarly in the imagined experience of her honeymoon, the mood of anticipated joy is canceled out by an impression of emptiness.

All Emma's romantic moods of illusory happiness crumble in countermoods of despair. The whole novel is constructed of a series of built-up moods—feelings of *"felicity, passion, rapture"*—which collapse in negative states of disillusioning reality. The contrast centering in the opposition between romantic aspiration or illusion *and* reality is Flaubert's primary structural device. This two-part pattern of ironic contrasts defines the structural formula of *Madame Bovary.*

I. ILLUSION VERSUS REALITY

The aspect of illusion has its chief symbolization in Emma and Léon. She awakens in him a thousand desires, and he, in turn, stirs in her the same visionary feelings. This romantic affinity is the sole bond between them.

> Love, she thought, must come suddenly, with great outbursts and lightnings,—a hurricane of the skies, which falls upon life, revolutionises it, roots up the will like a leaf, and sweeps the whole heart into the abyss. She did not know that on the terrace of houses it makes lakes when the pipes are choked, and she would thus have remained in her security when she suddenly discovered a rent in the wall of it.
>
> [Part I, chap. iv, p. 117]

Her whole life is a constant discovering of "a rent in the wall" of her reverie-world. It is always being built up in the future or in the past. What happiness she had had in her childhood! As for Charles, the dull plodding country doctor, though he is the coin of commonplace reality, one side of him is minted of illusion—he, too, has naïve dreams which are doomed to disappointment. He has grandiose notions of himself as a master-surgeon, he has fireside reveries, and he has romantic ideas about funerals. The Emma that he worships, idol-like, does not exist. He makes a shrine of her memoried image:

> To please her, as if she were still living, he adopted her predilections, her ideas; he bought patent leather boots and took to wearing white cravats. He put cosmetics on his moustache, and, like her, signed notes of hand. She corrupted him from beyond the grave.
>
> [Part III, chap. xi, p. 372]

Nor is Homais, the apothecary, without illusions—namely, his faith in Progress, a faith which he shared with his century. And, finally, there are the illusions of the bourgeois (their faith in religion, science, government), which are summed up for them in the speech of the councillor at the *comices agricoles* (Part II, chap. viii).

II. REALITY VERSUS ILLUSION

The antiromantic is represented by Rodolphe, the cynical squire and coarse adulterer, and by Lheureux, the dry-goods merchant and money-lender, who plies Emma with gifts for her lover on credit. They exploit Emma's romantic malady for their own ends.

Rodolphe's strategy for winning Emma is by professing himself to be the exponent of a New Morality, one that is absolute and eternal. He pitches his pretended moral code to the same idealistic plane as that of Emma's romantic dreams.

> "But one must," said Emma, "to some extent bow to the opinion of the world and accept its moral code."
>
> "Ah! but there are two," he replied. "The small, the conventional, that of men, that which constantly changes. . . . But the other, the eternal, that is about us and above, like the landscape that surrounds us, and the blue heavens that give us light."
>
> [Part II, chap. viii, p. 167]

The morality of common man is but a conspiracy by which society traps and persecutes Pure Love. The moral code of Rodolphe is the code of the gods.

> She noticed in his eyes small golden lines radiating from black pupils; she even smelt the perfume of the pomade that made his hair glossy. Then a faintness came over her; she recalled the Viscount who had waltzed with her at Vaubyessard, and his beard exhaled like this hair an odour of vanilla and citron, and mechanically she half-closed her eyes the better to breathe it in.
>
> [Part II, chap. viii, p. 167]

Rodolphe's sham vision, Flaubert is hinting, has a certain odor about it. And Emma, how readily she transfers her intoxication from the perfume of Rodolphe's sentiments to the perfume of his pomade! As for the self-indulgent Vaubyessards, their moral fiber is quite as slippery as Rodolphe's perfumed pomade. Flaubert's commentary on them figures through his image of the imbecilic old Duke de Laverdière—that mocking piece of grim reality to which Emma is perversely blind. His physical decay symbolizes moral disintegration. But Emma, knowing what a dashing figure he had cut before the Revolution, gazes on him in reverent fascination: "He had lived at court and slept in the bed of queens!" The description of the patricians assembled at the Comte de Vaubyessard's ball is a picture in scale-model of the French aristocratic world. Here is Flaubert's style at its best:

> Their clothes, better made, seemed of finer cloth, and their hair, brought forward in curls towards the temples, glossy with more delicate pomades. They had the complexion of wealth—that clear complexion that is heightened by the pallor of porcelain, the shimmer of satin, the veneer of old furniture, and that an ordered regimen of exquisite nurture maintains at its best. Their necks moved easily in their low cravats, their long whiskers fell over their turned-down collars, they wiped their lips upon handkerchiefs with embroidered initials that gave forth a subtle perfume. Those who were beginning to grow old had an air of youth, while there was something mature in the faces of the young. In their unconcerned looks was the calm of passions daily sati-

ated, and through all their gentleness of manner pierced that peculiar brutality, the result of a command of half-easy things, in which force is exercised and vanity amused—the management of thoroughbred horses and a society of loose women.

> [Part I, chap. viii, pp. 52-58]

This dramatized picture embodies Flaubert's criticism of French aristocratic society. The images—"pallor of porcelain," "veneer of old furniture," "their necks moved easily in their low cravats," "a command of half-easy things . . . the management of thoroughbred horses and a society of loose women"—the images at once describe and satirically appraise. They are images telling of pride and elegance but also of decadence, telling of dignity and power but also of sterility and corruption. They hint at the doom of France's ruling class.

As in the scene of the patricians, so in the scene at the opera (Part II, chap. xv) and in the scene of the *comices agricoles* (Part II, chap. viii) a dramatized picture is presented as symbol. These pictured impressions are images of reality charged with meaning. An image of reality is turned to symbol—a clock, a whip, a piano, a cactus plant, or a hat. Crass reality is represented in the loathsomely disfigured blind beggar, the vendor of romantic song. He, too, exploits deluded dreamers. He mocks them with his ditty of constant love:

> To speak to you he threw back his head with an idiotic laugh, then his bluish eyeballs, rolling constantly, at temples beat against the edges of the open wound. He sang a little song as he followed the carriages—
>
> > "Maids in the warmth of a summer day
> > Dream of love, and of love alway."
>
> And all the rest was about birds and sunshine and green leaves.
>
> [Part III, chap. v, p. 307]

When he intrudes again, chanting beneath the window of Emma's deathroom, his song, now a death-song, coincides with Emma's death-rattle:

> "The blind man!" she cried. And Emma began to laugh, an atrocious, frantic, despairing laugh, thinking she saw the hideous face of the poor wretch that stood out against the eternal night like a menace.
>
> > "The wind is strong this summer day,
> > Her petticoat has flown away."
>
> She fell back upon the mattress in a convulsion. They all drew near. She was dead.
>
> [Part III, chap. viii, pp. 371-72]

Blind and with time's clattering stick, he is Reality personified as the Eternal Menace. For Emma he is a bitterer poisoner than arsenic. Other symbols for the same mocking intent are the apricots, the token of bitter reality (Part II, chap. xii); the whip (Part II, chap. xii); and the clock (Part III, chap. v). At the opera, transported from dull life into a fantasy world of intoxicated passion, Emma measures her own personal plight against the fortunes of Lucie de Lammermoor—

> The voice of the prima donna seemed to her to be but echoes of her conscience, and this illusion that charmed her as some very thing of her own life. But no one on earth had loved her with such love. . . .
>
> Oh, why had not she, like this woman, resisted, implored? She, on the contrary, had been joyous, without seeing the abyss into which she was throwing herself. Ah! if in the freshness of her beauty, before the soiling of marriage and the disillusions of adultery, she could have anchored her life upon some great, strong heart, then virtue, tenderness, voluptuousness, and duty blending, she would never have fallen from so high a happiness. . . .
>
> . . . and, drawn towards this man by the illusion of the character, she tried to imagine to herself his life—that life resonant, extraordinary, splendid, and that might have been hers if fate had willed it. . . . She longed to run to his arms, to take refuge in his strength, as in the incarnation of love itself, and to say to him, to cry out, "Take me away! carry me with you! let us go! Thine! thine! all my ardour and all my dreams!"
>
> The curtain fell.
>
> [Part II, chap xv, pp. 257, 258, 259]

This unreal world is as hostile to Emma as is the real (but seemingly unreal) world from which she has momentarily escaped. Like the falling curtain, reality intrudes to mock Emma's tragic plight. Like the gas-filled air of the theater, reality suffocates her aspirations and dreams. Emma can neither adapt herself to the world of commonplace experience nor create as compensation an inner world of her own.

Her attempts to construct a substitute world fail her again and again. Having embalmed her love for Rodolphe, she addresses the Lord—addresses the Lord, as she kneels on her Gothic *prie-dieu,* in "the same suave words that she had murmured formerly to her lover in the outpourings of adultery. It was to make faith come; but no delights descended from the heavens, and she arose with tired limbs and with a vague feeling of a gigantic dupery" (Part II, chap. xiv). This identification of religion with love is a recurrent ironic motif. It is worked out thus: The cathedral, which Emma in a last vain pretense of purity selects for her clandestine tryst with Léon, is identified as "a huge boudoir spread around her"—the arches bending down to gather the confession of her angel-like love (Part III, chap i). In this metaphor of church as boudoir, the values inherent in the one object are equated with the values in the other (both parts of the comparison are stated). At the climax of Emma's liaison with Rodolphe, we are given this image of Emma: "One would have thought that an artist apt in conception had arranged the curls of hair upon her neck; they fell in a thick mass, negligently, and with the changing chances of their adultery, that unbound them every day" (Part II, chap. xii). The mass of loosened hair symbolizes her moral decline (only one part of the comparison is given, the visual image). Her external perfections ("Her voice now took more mellow inflections, her figure also") are an ironic contrast to her spiritual disorder. We are told that Emma "found again in adultery all the platitudes of marriage." And we may add: all the platitudes of religion. The platitudes of religion are symbolized in the holy water which Monsieur Bournisien sprinkles around Emma's death-room. For Monsieur Bournisien the holy water purifies. For Homais, it contaminates. He resprinkles the room with chlorine. The church, represented by the Abbé, has failed Emma in her quest for a faith. Religion succors her not a whit more than do her dreams of a requited love. Both are, for her, coined of the same debased quality. It was the Abbé's indifference to her plight (in the scene where she goes to him for help: Part II, chap. vi)—in a word, it was the inability of the church to provide a prop—that precipitated Emma's moral disintegration. That prop removed, "She revelled in all the evil ironies of triumphant adultery."

The blueprint upon which Flaubert pins Emma is tool-marked with ironies that doom her from the start. A passionate, overimaginative Emma is paired with a complacent, unimaginative Charles; each is the other's diametrical opposite. That Charles, the personification of humdrum commonplace reality, will be totally incapable of resolving the problem of their contrary natures is foreshadowed in the opening description of the schoolboy's oval, whalebone-stiffened hat: "It was one of those headgears of composite order, in which we can find traces of the bearskin, shako, billycock hat, sealskin cap, and cotton nightcap; one of those poor things, in fine, whose dumb ugliness has depths of expression, like an imbecile's face" (Part I, chap. i). The ridiculous hat foretells the pathetic man that the young Charles will become.[3] That his marriage will turn to ash is signified by Emma's act of throwing her wedding bouquet into the fire: "It flared up more quickly than dry straw. Then it was like a red bush in the cinders, slowly devoured. She watched it burn. The little pasteboard berries burst, the wire twisted, the gold lace melted; and the shrivelled paper corollas, fluttering like black butterflies at the back of the stove, at last flew up the chimney" (Part I, chap. ix). "Ah! my poor dreams," she might be saying as she watches them shrivel. Their collapse is foreshadowed in this image of melted gold lace, twisted wire, and burst pasteboard berries and corollas.

Of all Flaubert's innumerable technical devices, the one that has had perhaps the greatest influence is the device of the double mood. A built-up flight from reality collapses in a brutal fact, noble emotions are canceled out by juxtaposed ignoble ones, grandiloquent sentiments are knocked sideways by mocking intrusions. The outstanding occasion is the famous scene at the Comices Agricoles (where Rodolphe first courts Emma). The speech of the councillor is geared with the conversation of the lovers. His platitudes about progress, patriotism, and love are synchronized with Rodolphe's platitudes about the new morality and the eternity of his passion for Emma. The two alternating attitudes answer each other and cancel out each other's values. After the speech, prizes are awarded to deserving farmers, and here the irony reaches its culminating pitch in the intensified counterpointing of the following double talk:

> And he seized her hand: she did not withdraw it.
>
> "For good farming generally!" cried the president.

Which is to suggest that the romantic courtship of Rodolphe and Emma amounts to no more than animal breeding.

> "Just now, for example, when I went to your house."
>
> "To Monsieur Bizat of Quincampoix."
>
> "Did I know I should accompany you?"
>
> "Seventy francs."

Which is the price of a courtesan's favors.

> "A hundred times I wished to go; and I followed you—I remained."
>
> "Manures!"

That Rodolphe could not tear himself away from her is derisively mocked by the shout of "Manures!" And his promise—

> And I shall remain to-night, to-morrow, all other days, all my life!

is jeered at again: for this faithful lover, a gold medal!

> "To Monsieur Caron of Argueil, a gold medal!"
>
> "For I have never in the society of any other person found so complete a charm."
>
> "To Monsieur Bain of Givry-Saint-Martin."
>
> "And I shall carry away with me the remembrance of you!"
>
> "For a merino ram!"

The "merino ram" figures for Rodolphe's bestial lusts. Observe the brutal mockery in the last of these retorts:

> "But you will forget me; I shall pass away like a shadow."
>
> "To Monsieur Belot of Notre-Dame."

> "Oh, no! I shall be something in your thought, in your life, shall I not?"
>
> "Porcine race; prizes—equal; to Messrs. Lehérissé and Cullembourg, sixty francs!"
>
> [Part II, chap. viii, pp. 171-72]

They are pigs, the pair of them.[4]

The words "merino ram," "manures," and "porcine race" reduce the lovers to that level. They are a savage commentary on Rodolphe's vows of eternal fidelity. But it is not alone these lovers who are being satirized (as Mr. Turnell notes), it is the whole basis of love. Furthermore, Flaubert is attacking not only sexual passion but the French agricultural class as well:

> The meeting was over, the crowd dispersed, and now that the speeches had been read, each one fell back into his place again, and everything into the old grooves; the masters bullied the servants, and these struck the animals, indolent victors, going back to the stalls, a green crown on their horns.

As for Rodolphe's hypocrisy, his eternity of passion soon turns into "the eternal monotony of passion," Emma being for him no different from any of his other mistresses. His hypocrisy is symbolized by the manufactured tear he fakes upon his *lettre de rupture,* his former love letters providing him with the required dose of inspiration for this one (Part II, chap. xiii).

We might characterize the entire novel, in its architectonics of conflicting attitudes, as a two-part house or duplex. It is a house divided into an upstairs of moral conventions—it is filled with tawdry illusions and images of felicity, passion, rapture—and a nihilistic cellar loaded with symbols of disintegration, with moods of ennui, chagrin, *tristesse.* Flaubert's fundamental nihilism, which denies all values, is at odds with the conventional morality supporting these very values, namely, those of love, morality, religion, science. The word "adultery," which is constantly spoken by the tenants upstairs, has no meaning in the scheme of things down below. As spectators, we do not feel with the emotions of Emma against the emotions of Rodolphe, but rather we feel emotion *at* Emma herself. She is the tenant, who suffers most from the moral confusion in this duplex structure of the novel. Emma, the hungry soul whose life is "but one long tissue of lies," inhabits both parts of the house. She is constantly shifting about, now upstairs (the muddled romantic) and now downstairs (the hardened realist). An instance of this last phase is occasioned when Emma returns to Rodolphe in a desperate attempt to borrow from him the money her creditors demand (one of the best scenes in the book). This is a different Emma from the self-deluding dreamer. Here is the hardened realist:

> "But when one is so poor one doesn't have silver on the butt of one's gun. One doesn't buy a clock inlaid with tortoiseshell," she went on, pointing to a buhl

timepiece, "nor silver-gilt whistles for one's whips," and she touched them, "nor charms for one's watch. Oh, he wants for nothing! even to a liqueur-stand in his room! For you love yourself; you live well. You have a château, farms, woods; you go hunting; you travel to Paris. Why, if it were but that," she cried, taking up two studs from the mantelpiece, "but the least of these trifles, one can get money for them. Oh, I do not want them; keep them!"

And she threw the two links away from her, their gold chain breaking as it struck against the wall.

[Part III, chap. viii, p. 356]

The voice is masculine, the tone brittle in its sneer.

In Flaubert's works, plot is subsidiary to the analysis of psychological motives and processes. The analysis of Emma's spiritual disintegration ends in a negation of all spiritual values. *Madame Bovary* has been called an onslaught on the foundations of human relationships and on human nature itself. It is not this nihilism that damns the book, however. Nor does the burden of "immorality," for which Flaubert was charged and prosecuted in 1857. The basis for critical censure lies in the ambivalence of attitudes which conflict and cancel out each other.[5] Nevertheless, *Madame Bovary,* even with its many defects, survives all criticism. And then there is that perfect short story **"A Simple Heart."**[6] These two works represent Flaubert's outstanding achievement. There is also the extrinsic one of his immense influence on the development of the novel. Certainly, all this is achievement enough for a location of his genius (as by John Middleton Murry) among "the greatest heroes in the second rank of letters." At least that!

Notes

This essay, part of a textbook ("The Art of Modern Fiction," to be published in 1949), aims to provide the student with an introductory analysis of the novel. For further analyses see R. P. Blackmur's "Notes on Four Categories in Criticism" (explicates Emma's cordial glass as image, Part I, chap. iii), *Sewanee Review,* Vol. LIV (autumn, 1946); Percy Lubbock's *Craft of Fiction* (1921); Allen Tate's "Techniques of Fiction" (explicates Binet's lathe as symbol), in *Forms of Modern Fiction* (1948); and especially Martin Turnell's "Flaubert," *Scrutiny,* Vol. XIII (autumn, 1945; spring, 1946). There is an excellent critical redaction, a scale-model of the novel, by Richard Penny, in *Studies in Nineteenth Century Literature.* See also Joseph Frank's "Spatial Form in Modern Literature" (explicates the *comices agricoles* scene), *Sewanee Review,* LIII (spring, 1945), 230 ff.

1. Lubbock, *op. cit.,* p. 82.

2. The text used is the "Modern Library" edition [(New York: 1957)], p. 46.

3. The critics who have found it a fault that the novel opens and closes with Bovary have not taken into

account the use to which he is put. The novel opens with Bovary because he is to function in terms of symbolic foreshadowing. Mr. Somerset Maugham thinks it was Flaubert's purpose "to enclose the story of Emma within the story of her husband as you enclose a painting in a frame. He must have felt that so he rounded off his narrative and gave it the unity of a work of art" (*Atlantic Monthly,* CLXXX [November, 1947], 139).

4. This scene illustrates, as Frank demonstrates, the spatial form of the modern novel. Flaubert himself hinted at its space-time logic when, in a letter, he commented on this scene: "Everything should sound simultaneously; one should hear the bellowing of the cattle, the whispering of the lovers and the rhetoric of the officials all at the same time" (see Frank's analysis and also Albert Thibaudet's *Gustave Flaubert, 1821-1880* [Paris, 1922]).

5. As Turnell says, the critic is faced with the problem of deciding "what value should be attached to Flaubert's pessimism, whether it is a mature conception of life or an immature cynicism which is masquerading as mature vision."

6. In his distinguished introduction to *Three Tales* (New Directions, 1944), Harry Levin points out that "A Simple Heart" is a sequel to *Madame Bovary,* "more particularly to the episode at the agricultural show, where Catherine Leroux, a single heroic figure in a crowd of *mufles,* had been cited for half a century of servitude."

Louise Dauner (essay date April 1956)

SOURCE: Dauner, Louise. "Poetic Symbolism in *Madame Bovary*." *South Atlantic Quarterly* 55, no. 2 (April 1956): 207-20.

[*In the following essay, Dauner discusses the ways in which physical description evokes emotion in the novel. Dauner argues that Flaubert's attention to the symbolic aspects of everyday life lends the work its poetic quality.*]

April 15, 1857, *Madame Bovary* was published in book form after a mutilated version, begun in October, 1856, in the *Revue de Paris,* had culminated in prosecution of the managing editor of the review, of Flaubert, and of the printer. Although the court decided that the book was not irreligious and immoral, and it was an undoubted financial success, *Madame Bovary* received few favorable contemporary reviews; many, indeed, found it "utterly immoral and irreligious"; almost all found it shocking in its "brutality"; and the review written by Duranty, the editor of *Realisme,* noted an excessive and indiscriminating use of detail, "neither emotion nor feeling nor life in this novel," a style "never personal," a method "always physical description, never impression"; in brief, a book in which "all interest is lacking." Even Saint-Beuve, who wrote admiringly of the style and of many pictorial scenes, submitted as a main reproach that "there is no goodness in the book. Not a character represents it."

But time sometimes laughs at critics; today, nearly one hundred years later, it has neatly reversed these verdicts. Mr. Percy Lubbock finds **Madame Bovary** "perpetually the novel of all novels which the criticism of fiction can not overlook; as soon as ever we speak of the principles of the art, we must be prepared to engage with Flaubert." Mr. Allen Tate says in an essay on the techniques of fiction, "Gustave Flaubert created the modern novel"; and "it has been through Flaubert that the novel has at last caught up with poetry." Analyzing the scene in which Emma, after her receipt of Rudolphe's letter, runs into the attic, where in agitation and growing hysteria she hears the turning lathe of Binet, Mr. Tate finds in the lathe the tool by which "Flaubert gives us a direct impression of Emma's sensation at a particular moment . . . and thus by rendering audible to us what Emma alone could hear he charged the entire scene with actuality."

These insights by modern critics provide an ironically amusing counterpoint to Duranty's criticism of 1857, along with the suggestion that through this rendering of the impression, this charging of the scene with actuality, Flaubert approaches the realm of poetry. Taking off from this point, we may suggest another method by which **Madame Bovary** comes to us as poem.

Granted that **Madame Bovary** is among the most "perfect" of novels, as a work of self-conscious art it delights us by its masterly management of point of view, its pervasive, sustained irony, its sharp, objective characterization, its dramatic presentation of realistic detail and setting to the point where, as Mr. Lubbock has observed, Yonville acting upon Emma is "as essential as she is herself" and like a character in a dramatic cast. Everything in this novel is deliberate. "It is difficult for me to imagine," wrote Flaubert in a letter in 1853, "that I will ever write anything more carefully calculated."

In addition to all this, one of the major achievements of this novel lies in its superb use of symbolism. Here too the novel moves into the realm of poetry; for poetry, as indirect statement, must depend largely upon the use of symbols, and much of the aesthetic and even moral interest of **Madame Bovary** lies in the symbols: those elements in the narrative which communicate so richly values over and above their literal meanings.

Speaking generally, Flaubert's symbolism in **Madame Bovary** functions much like that of a poet such as Rob-

ert Frost: It is not an esoteric, personal symbolism, like, for instance, Mr. Eliot's, but a symbolism which is literally rooted in the nature of things. As in Frost's poetry, one need never read for any meaning beyond the literal. An adequate unit of meaning will still be apprehensible, for the symbol is always a natural part of or element in the given situation or instance. Yet, to comprehend and use the symbols is enormously to enrich the aesthetic and even moral values of the novel and to walk simultaneously on two levels, as though one maintained a delicate balance both on the earth of the commonsense literal and in the air of the poetic, which is an integral part of the experience that poetry gives us.

Among "major" symbols, those which reappear with either a consistent or thickened meaning in different parts of the narrative, selected somewhat arbitrarily, are the symbol of the garden, interpreted semantically, and in associations of time, place, mood, and even produce (Rudolphe's gifts of fruit); the symbol of water, as it is associated here with rivers, pools, boats; the lathe of Binet; and the blind beggar. From those "minor" symbols which appear only briefly, but significantly, may be mentioned the whip, the stag head, the fireworks, and the arsenic.

The garden is probably the dominant symbol of the novel, considering the number of times it appears and its richness of connotation. It appears four times in Part I, the Tostes section of Emma's life. We note it for the first time when Emma is making a bride's inventory of the house to which Charles has brought her. One of her first acts as mistress of the house is to have seats made around the sundial in the garden, an act which suggests not only her energy and initiative (and perhaps her ambition to eradicate as much of the first wife as she can, and to impress Charles with her domestic competence) but also her incipient romanticism. A little later, when she has realized the wide discrepancy between her idealized vision of Romance and the routine of marriage to a man who eats largely of boiled beef and onions, then goes to bed, lies on his back, and snores, she repairs to the garden by moonlight and, reciting passionate rhymes and singing melancholy adagios, tries to make herself in love with him. In both instances the garden functions as a character symbol, suggesting her ambition and her bourgeois romanticism.

At Vaubyessard, at the ball, she glances out the window which opens upon the garden, where she sees "the faces of peasants pressed against the window looking in at them." Then she remembers her father, his farm, herself as she skimmed the cream off the milk pans in the dairy. From the garden the memory-association rises of a past as remote from her present as her actual present is remote from this single night of wealth and society. All that is real and good in Emma lies in this recalled vision of her early life, as all that is to be artificial and corrupt is also at the very moment implicitly there. For this night, Flaubert tells us, "made a hole in her life . . . in its friction against wealth something had come over it that could not be effaced." After the details fade, the occasion still remains for her as a long regret. Here, then, the garden poses a kind of antiphony in time and character, embracing past, present, and, by implication, future; suggesting Emma as presently at the still point of her turning world: not as she was, nor yet as she will be.

The final garden appearance in Tostes is a pure mood mirror. It is winter; no birds are to be heard; all seems asleep. The vine is like a great sick serpent, and the plaster curé has lost his right foot. All is dormant and depressing. Here the garden is the objective correlative of Emma's disgruntled, self-pitying disillusionment in her marriage.

In Part I, as Mr. R. P. Blackmur points out, Flaubert has "surrounded a possibility" with anecdote, comment, scenes, and images. Whatever Emma is we do not as yet know. But in the rest of the novel "the sequence begins to discover a direction"—Bovarysme—"an habitual, an infatuated practise of regarding . . . the world as other than it is; it is an attempt to find in the world what is not there." It is for Emma a tragic and fatal attempt. Much of the fatality is psychically contiguous with the garden or actually enacted within its physical bounds. Since the stage lights of the novel will gradually darken into the blackness of Emma's horrible and pitiful death, we may rightfully expect some correlation between the tonal symbolism of the garden and the denoument; and when we inquire briefly into the semantics of the word "garden," an inquiry not necessary in the "lighter" first part of the novel, this is exactly what we find.

In Indo-European languages the basic meaning of "garden" is an enclosure devoted to the cultivation of useful plants. As such, it implies several associated ideas: first, fertility, or productivity, which easily expands into the garden as symbolic of love or sex. So it often appears in Oriental literature. Then there is the concept of the garden as representing a deliberate, planned order with regard to what is to grow there; and we vision Emma's garden as a typical French or English formal garden, with its sand and grass, its plaster statue, and the bench in the arbor. This concept of formal order may be expanded into an idea of social and moral order, which is created or destroyed, depending upon the ethical sensibility of the human being. Of course there are also two obvious religious connotations, that of the Garden of Eden, in which was enacted the mythic Fall of man from the state of innocence, and the Garden of Gethsemane, the scene of Christ's betrayal. These connotations are richly and variously present in the symbolic gardens of *Madame Bovary.*

In the later fulfilment of Emma's destiny the garden appears, with light or dramatic importance, in at least seven instances. Emma's single taste of "high life" having created in her such a malaise that her bad health persuades Charles to move to Yonville, she meets there Leon, the young clerk at the notary's. They are immediately attracted to each other by their mutual boredom, romantic "delicacies," interests in "art," and the world of society and drama represented for them by Paris. It is not long before Leon accompanies Emma on a walk to see her infant, who has been put out to nurse. As they slowly return to Yonville, Emma, still frail and easily fatigued, takes Leon's arm.

They pass by the walls of gardens, where "wallflowers had sprung up between the bricks, and with the tip of her open sunshade Madame Bovary, as she passed, made some of their faded flowers crumble into a yellow dust, or a spray of overhanging honeysuckle and clematis caught in its fringe and dangled for a moment over the silk." They speak inconsequentially; "yet their eyes were full of more serious speech, and while they forced themselves to find trivial phrases, they felt the same languor stealing over them both."

Now this is the 1850's, and Freud has not yet made his suggestive interpretations of sex symbolism; nevertheless, we must trust to the accuracy of the creative intuition. In these quick objective details and in Emma's casually deliberate violation of the wallflowers with the tip of her sunshade, Flaubert has employed a sharp symbolic "touch" that immediately crystallizes the implicit sexual tone which underlies both the concept of the garden and the tension of the walk, and which also foreshadows Emma's affair with Leon. Indeed, as yet, she is herself a kind of "wallflower"—emotionally untouched; we remember that marriage makes no difference at all in her; it is Charles who is noticeably changed after his wedding-night. And the honeysuckle and clematis, with their sensuous sweetness and frail clinging insistence, suggest some of the very qualities which Emma's false perspective attributes to romantic love. The symbolic detail is quick and transient, but highly valuable for both the emotional tone of the scene and for later developments in the narrative.

After Leon's departure for Rouen, Emma's melancholy revives her memories of their togetherness, of the happy afternoons they had spent at the end of the garden as he sat reading aloud to her, and "the reverie which we give to all things that will not return" mingles with her self-reproach for not having allowed herself to love him. Again the garden acts, now as the physical stimulus which recreates the emotion. Later, after her seduction by Leon, and when he comes to Yonville to see her, it is behind the garden that she meets him, as previously she had so often met Rudolphe.

The garden is the necessary and literal stage for Emma's affair with Rudolphe. The fissure in the garden wall becomes the "post-box" for their daily love notes. And all through the winter, three or four times a week, it is here that they hold their trysts.

An associated symbol, the fruit which Rudolphe often sends to Emma, should be mentioned here. Often a love letter from Rudolphe is hidden in the bottom of the basket, and it is thus in a basket of apricots that he conveys to her the letter with which he finally breaks the relationship. Not only are the apricots symbolically suggestive of the primarily sexual nature of their relationship, but the psychological association of the fruit with the fruit of the Garden of Eden, which brought to man his tragic and sinful knowledge, comes at once to mind to underscore Emma's fall from grace. And Emma's ultimate realization of Rudolphe's insincerity is like a flaming sword—not angelic but demonic—which slashes into the very core of her consciousness.

After her ensuing collapse and long illness, her first walk is around the garden. It is October, and the sand of the paths disappears beneath the dead leaves. Charles guides her into the arbor to the garden seat, but she is made giddy by the invoked memory of her past affair, and from that evening her illness recommences with more complex symptoms. Now she develops an antipathy for the garden, keeps the blinds of the house down on that side, and the next spring, in a sort of psychic vengeance, has it ploughed up from end to end. In these moments, the garden functions quite simply as a symbol of mood and memory.

In the days which are tending toward Emma's growing desperation under the pressures of Lheureux, Charles walks alone in the garden or tries to teach the child, Berthe, to read there. Now, choked with long weeds, it reflects their mutual depressions. After Emma's death, it is here that we find Charles, "a long-bearded, shabbily-clothed, wild man, who wept aloud as he walked up and down"; and it is here that he sits in benumbed grief; and finally, it is here, on the seat in the arbor, that he dies, holding in his hand the long strand of hair which Homais had cut off for him as Emma lay in her casket.

Thus the garden functions as a poetic symbol in a variety of ways: Moving from the lighter tone of a character symbol and an emotional backdrop, it assumes the darker qualities that foreshadow Emma's increasing involvements. It repeatedly carries the sexual connotation and so becomes a thematic symbol. With its connotation of betrayal it underscores Emma's betrayals of Charles, which are also betrayals of social and moral order. As such, it assumes an ethical and even mythic

significance. Finally, at Charles's death it is pervaded with a tone of tragic irony. In possessing all of these values, it acts exactly as does any appropriate poetic symbol.

Perhaps the next most apparent symbol is that of water. Again, classic and modern interpretations come immediately to mind: Freud's version of water as a female sex symbol, Jung's interpretation of water as symbolizing the Collective Unconscious, Thale's definition of it as the source of all life. Recurring to Emma's first walk with Leon, we note that they return to Yonville by the river. "It flowed noiselessly, swift, and cold to the eyes; long, thin grasses huddled together in it as the current drove them, and spread themselves upon the limpid water like streaming hair." In one spot, where the ground is muddy, they have to cross on large stones placed in the mud. "She often stopped a moment to look where to place her foot, and tottering on the stone that shook, her arms outstretched, her form bent forward with a look of indecision, she would laugh, afraid of falling into the puddles of water." The sexual implication is insistent in the flowing water and the grasses like streaming hair; and Emma's crossing of the muddy spot and her physical unbalance delicately highlight her psychic and moral indecision.

Water provides the symbolic background for her seduction by Rudolphe. "He drew her farther on to a small pool where duckweeds made a greenness on the water. Faded waterlilies lay motionless between the reeds." When she visits Rudolphe in the early morning, she has to go by the walls alongside of the river. The bank is slippery—like her own moral position now—and in order not to fall, she catches hold of the tufts of faded wallflowers (and again we note the "matching" of the wallflowers to her emotional and moral state). On her return home her shoes are often muddied, again a highly suggestive detail.

The three-day "honeymoon" with Leon was spent at the Hôtel-de-Boulogne on the harbor. In the evening they took a covered boat to one of the islands, and when they returned at night "the boat glided along the shores of the islands. They sat at the bottom, both hidden by the shade, in silence. The square oars rang in the iron thwarts, and, in the stillness, seemed to mark time, like the beating of a metronome, while at the stern the rudder that trailed behind never ceased its gentle splash against the water." It is all here, scarcely requiring comment: The gentle caress of the gliding water, the boat itself with its darkness and silent secret intensity, and the sense of escape from time and place, all adding up literally to the consummation of their mutual desire and symbolically to an emphasis upon the completely sensual. The boat is especially suggestive, its darkness and interiority giving it appropriately a uterine symbolism.

Water, by association, appears in the description of the hotel room where Emma and Leon hold their trysts, where the bed is "in the shape of a boat," and the chimney holds two pink shells "in which one hears the murmur of the sea." One may note in passing other sexual symbols that describe the room, the "bell-shaped bedside," the curtain rods ending in arrows, and the great balls of the andirons. And the description of the cab in which Emma's seduction by Leon occurs as "with blinds drawn . . . shut more closely than a tomb, and tossing about like a vessel" is strongly and cumulatively female in its symbolism.

Emma's last tryst with Rudolphe before their intended elopement occurs in the moonlight beside the river. Perhaps it is not excessive to note also that it is Charles's errand to get Emma barley-water at the theatre at Rouen that occasions the encounter which reintroduces Leon into Emma's life.

Thus, throughout, the water symbolism serves a thematic function in that its strong sexual connotation reminds us of the sexual drive of the novel, which, as Blackmur has said, "is the shape of a life which is the shape of a woman which is the shape of a desire."

We come now to the symbol which seems to have made the sharpest impression on critics, though it has been studied not as "symbol" but as an instrument employed in a special literary technique, the lathe of Binet. When Emma has received Rudolphe's shattering letter and has gone up into the attic, the sharpest of her various sense impressions, of heat, the glare of light, the awareness of height, is the humming sound of the turning lathe. Her emotional confusion becomes a physical vertigo. "It seemed to her that the ground of the oscillating square went up the walls, and that the floor dipped on end like a tossing boat." As she stands at the open window, the humming of the lathe, "like an angry voice," calls to her to throw herself on the paving-stones below. But here the lathe is more than merely a sense stimulus. It is an extraordinarily fine symbol for her volcanically crumbling mental world, for the crazy spinning of her distracted thoughts. She is hysterical; literally, at the moment, schizophrenic, both a self that wills destruction and a self that, the next moment, nearly faints with terror at the nearness of her escape.

Later, when she has been served the notice of the distraint, she goes to try to borrow money from Binet, who is working over his wood . . . "the white dust was flying from his tools . . . the two wheels were turning, droning. . . ." This is a characteristic activity for Binet; but for the reader, the reappearance of the turning wheels instantly recalls the attic scene and so produces not only a cause-and-effect connection but also a kind of Greek inevitability; for Emma's compulsion to elude the monotony and emptiness of her life has caused her illicit passions, which cause her mad extravagances and deceptions, which cause her death.

Still a third time the lathe functions, when, hardly knowing what she is doing, she leaves Binet, who has rejected her plea, and finds herself at Nurse Rollet's. As she throws herself, sobbing and nearly hysterical, on the bed, Nurse Rollet, not knowing what to do for her, withdraws to her spinning-wheel and begins spinning flax. Emma fancies that what she hears is Binet's lathe and begs her to stop. If we allow the lathe to act now as a cumulative symbol, it will again recall to us the invitation to suicide that Emma first heard in it. So carefully is every detail in this novel laid, we may suspect that, consciously or not, Emma too heard in Nurse Rollet's spinning-wheel an echo of the same insidious suggestion. At any rate, it is only a little later, after her humiliating and fruitless visit to Rudolphe, that she carries out the psychic suggestion of the humming voice. In all of these scenes, the lathe has been effectively employed as a symbol of her mental convulsion. It is purely a psychological and emotional symbol.

The fourth major symbol to be treated here, and surely one of the most memorable in the novel, is that of the blind beggar. Flaubert does not shirk a single one of the revolting details:

> A mass of rags covered his shoulders, and an old staved-in hat . . . hid his face; but when he took it off he discovered in the place of eyelids empty and bloody orbits. The flesh hung in red shreds, and there flowed from it liquids that congealed into green scales down to the nose, whose black nostrils sniffed convulsively. To speak to you he threw back his head with an idiotic laugh; then his bluish eyeballs, rolling constantly, towards the temples beat against the edge of the open wound. He sang a little song as he followed the carriages—
>
> > Maids in the warmth of a summer day
> > Dream of love, and of love alway.

Sometimes he suddenly appears behind Emma; he particularly appears after her trysts in Rouen with Leon and on the Sunday when she has gone frantically to Rouen to try to raise money, when she tries to induce Leon to steal to get her money—perhaps the most overt revelation of her moral deterioration. Finally, almost melodramatically, in her dying moments she hears his song, and, thinking she sees the hideous face of the poor wretch "standing out against the eternal night," she laughs "an atrocious, frantic, despairing laugh" and falls back in her death convulsion.

In his diseased and idiotic being the blind man is a brutal, violent, unforgettable symbol of Emma's moral and spiritual corruption, which is the corruption of beauty. Perhaps the most painful item is that of his eyes. This, too, is significant. For it is in Emma's eyes that much of her beauty has lain. Charles' first awareness of it lies here. "Her real beauty was in her eyes. Altho brown, they seemed black because of the lashes, and her look came at you frankly, with a candid boldness." After her seduction by Rudolphe, she marvels at her face in the mirror. "Never had her eyes been so large, so black, of so profound a depth." During the affair, when her beauty seems to blossom in full plenitude, "her eyelids seemed chiselled expressly for her long amorous looks, in which the pupil disappeared." And Charles thinks her then "delicious and quite irresistible" and is himself, and always, and with an almost Grecian tragic irony, "blind." In her final appeal to Rudolphe, when he has drawn her on his knees before his refusal to help her, "she was charming to see, with her eyes, in which trembled a tear, like the rain of a storm in a blue calyx."

The song of the blind beggar, in its ironic contrast, has a Shakespearean overtone; one thinks of the mad song of Ophelia, though what is poignantly pathetic there becomes horrible here. But the song connection with Emma is notable, for Emma's "theme-song" too is love, which, like the blind man's idiocy, tends at last to mania.

Thus the blind beggar becomes a pure character-symbol, focusing for us in his tormented and foully diseased body the tormented and diseased spirit of Emma, who failed because she, too, was "blind." Nowhere does *Madame Bovary,* "the book which is moral—ultramoral," as Flaubert wrote of it, speak more powerfully of the eternal corruption that may reside in the spirit of man and of woman than in this symbolic figure.

Considering now the minor symbols, let us look briefly at two which relate to Rudolphe. Early in the affair with him, Emma has ordered from Lheureux a riding whip to give to Rudolphe. When the next day Lheureux calls upon her with a bill, which she is unable to pay, and says that he will be forced to take back the goods, he also says that he will ask Charles to return the whip to him. On Emma's emphatic protests, he immediately senses that she is carrying on an intrigue, and this is the first hold which Lheureux gains over Emma. From now on, and increasingly, he literally holds a "whip hand" over her. It is also of interest that Charles's first inflammatory contact with Emma occurs when, concluding his first visit to her father, he looks for his whip, which has fallen to the floor and which both stoop to recover. During this gesture his breast brushes against Emma's back. "She drew herself up, scarlet, and looked at him over her shoulder as she handed him his whip." The whip functions as one of the many intricate strands which integrate the plot. Also, in both instances, it suggests itself appropriately as a masculine symbol.

The other "Rudolphe-symbol" is that of the stag head, which hangs over Rudolphe's bureau. He sits directly beneath it when he writes his letter of rejection to Emma. It has a triple value. First, it is the stag head with the horns, the traditional folk symbol for the cuckold which Rudolphe has made Charles. Then Rudolphe too is pre-eminently the male animal: He knows nothing of love, only of lust. Emma is a pretty mistress, who ministers to his male ego and his sensuality, a pleasing toy for him to enjoy and corrupt; but he has no intention of eloping with her or of becoming involved in any serious, responsible relationship. Rudolphe came, saw Emma, conquered—and departed; and Emma too is a trophy, a sign of pursuit and capture. The stag head, as trophy, is a souvenir, like the contents of Rudolphe's biscuit box, his mementos of past conquests: Emma's handkerchief and miniature and letters, other women's bouquets, garters, pins, light and dark hair, all are jumbled indiscriminately together. Typical sensualist that he is, Rudolphe often remembers nothing at all of the givers and dismisses them all and the experiences they represent with the bored epitaph, "What a lot of rubbish!" "For pleasures, like school boys in a school courtyard, had so trampled upon his heart that no green thing grew there, and that which passed through it, more heedless than children, did not even, like them, leave a name carved on the wall." Thus the stag head is a fitting and concentrated symbol of the character of the man who had captured it—the hunter of both animals and women.

A poetic symbol with "recall" value like the lathe is that of the fireworks. Rudolphe's mental seduction of Emma can be timed rather sharply to the day of the agricultural show. They have walked and sat together during the speeches and awards, after which he has escorted Emma home. In the evening, he sees her again during the fireworks, and as she watches the luminous rays of the rockets, so Rudolphe watches her.

The fireworks, which may well connote the emotional state of Rudolphe and Emma at this time, also carry an implication of the nature of the affair itself, with its explosive, luminous quality for Emma, and its transience and black extinction. Again, when Rudolphe has refused to lend her the money, and she has left him, the fireworks appear as a brilliant visual and psychological metaphor. As Emma leaves Rudolphe's chateau, she is lost in stupor; though her blood is roaring through her veins, the earth seems to her as the breaking waves of the sea, and "everything in her head, of memories, ideas, went off at once like a thousand pieces of fireworks." Suddenly it seems to her that fiery spheres are exploding in the air "like fulminating balls when they strike," and are whirling, whirling. . . . The madness that is coming upon her is actualized by the kinesthetic power of the images, and the whirling of the mental fireballs again recalls to us Binet's lathe. It is in this state of mental turmoil, which she feels as "an ecstasy of heroism," that she goes directly to the druggist's shop to get the arsenic.

The arsenic, like the blind beggar, is a brutal symbol. Its first manifestation is the bitter taste which awakens her out of her sleep. Then, a terrible thirst, choking, vomiting, and an icy cold that creeps from her feet to her head. And then the real agony begins. As the poison works, her beauty literally disappears. Her lips are drawn, her limbs convulsed, and her body is covered with brown spots.

As the poison destroys her body and corrupts her beauty, so have her adolescent romanticism, her false vision, her sensual lust, and her dishonesty poisoned and destroyed her spirit. Even some of the symptoms, the bitterness, the thirst, became metaphorical of her embittered spirit and her driving thirst for the passion that she conceives to be romance. As the poison only slowly achieves its final effect, we are reminded of Emma's slow inevitable descent into the immorality of which her suffering and death are now the inevitable end. So the extreme unction administered to Emma by the priest summarizes the sins of this perennial romancer: "first, upon the eyes, that had so coveted all worldly pomp; then upon the nostrils, that had been greedy of the warm breeze and amorous odours; then upon the mouth, that had uttered lies, that had curled with pride and cried out in lewdness; then upon the hands that had delighted in sensual touches; and finally upon the soles of the feet, so swift of yore, when she was running to satisfy her desires, and that would now walk no more." As though not content with its living torment, the effect of the poison lingers after Emma's death. As the women raise her head to place upon it a wreath, a black liquid issues from her mouth to the hazard of her wedding dress—a powerfully ironic touch, for the wedding dress is all that remains of the Emma whom Charles had married and adored.

Horrible as is the nature of her death, perhaps no other means of suicide would have been as appropriately, even as profoundly, impressive; for the poison's dissolution of her body and her beauty is a visible manifestation of the spiritual corruption that follows upon her frantic seeking for romance and self-fulfilment. The irony is that these are legitimate quests, and we all live in hope of achieving them. But Emma, shallow, weak, immature, selfish, made them direct ends or goals, never realizing that they can exist probably only as by-products of mature acceptance and responsibility and disinterestedness. Thus the arsenic functions, like the blind man, as an objective correlative, and its tone is ironic: in its "reversal" of life, love, and beauty, it correlates with Emma's reversal of values; for even when she sometimes appears to act morally, she acts for the wrong reasons; and she never recognizes "first things," nor learns to put them first.

It is not the purpose of this study to evaluate the "morality" of *Madame Bovary,* the ultimate significance of its ethical comment upon human life. And certainly

Flaubert is no Dostoevsky and offers here no redemptive formula or hope for the Emmas of the world. Yet the book does possess a morality of its own—the kind of morality that Henry James, for instance, recognized as the goodness, the trueness, that inheres in the aesthetic object. In this sense, which is the Greek sense, the Good, the True, the Beautiful do tend to merge, and Beauty is Truth, Truth, Beauty. Flaubert was enough of a classicist and student of Greek literature to have absorbed a good deal of this attitude. Thus, in so far as *Madame Bovary* achieves a near-perfection of technical and artistic value, it creates its own intrinsic aesthetic morality. The thing of beauty *is* a joy forever, and one of the enduring delights of this novel lies here; and this "here" means the exquisitely chiselled structure, which includes the symbolic usage.

The symbols, then, are "naturals," real elements, always in the objective situation. But they also exist, as we have seen, for varied values: as character definers, as foreshadowers of events, as mood and objective correlatives, as theme-intensifiers, and as tonal devices, especially for irony. These values would seem to place *Madam Bovary* on one more level within the realm of poetry; so the ethical energy of its theme is even more effectively communicated through the moving power of its aesthetic.

Note

All quotations from the novel are from Charles I. Weir, Jr's. edition, published by Rinehart & Co., 1948.

Margaret Tillett (essay date 1961)

SOURCE: Tillett, Margaret. "On Reading *Madame Bovary.*" In *Madame Bovary and the Critics: A Collection of Essays,* edited by B. F. Bart, pp. 1-25. New York: New York University Press, 1966.

[*In the following essay, originally published by Oxford University Press in* On Reading Flaubert *in 1961, Tillett offers an in-depth analysis of the novel's narrative technique and major themes. Tillett asserts that, in spite of* Madame Bovary's *reputation as a landmark work of French realism, traditional oppositions between Romanticism and realism do not apply to the book; rather, a tension between art and bourgeois materialism lies at the novel's core. In Tillett's view, the power of* Madame Bovary *ultimately resides in the dense, multilayered quality of Flaubert's prose style.*]

The most famous of Flaubert's works, published in 1857, has now weathered over a century of praise and blame. It is difficult to imagine that more could be discovered about the origins and composition of any work of fiction, than has been discovered about *Madame Bovary.* But if it were possible to forget all the mass of information that now exists about the book, to imagine a state of not knowing of Flaubert's correspondence, or the story of his life, or that he ever said "*Madame Bovary,* c'est moi"—to imagine that one simply possessed the last edition corrected by him in his lifetime, without any notes or comments—in fact, that one was reading it as he meant it to be read, and as most people probably do read it for the first time—what impression would it give?

An impression of power, authority perhaps, of being the work of a writer free of any affectations or pettinesses. The famous "realism" has of course lost its edge by now; it seems improbable that the most memorable aspects of *Madame Bovary,* for a reader familiar with the novels and plays of the 1940's and 1950's, would be the description of the results of the bungled operation on the club-foot of Hippolyte the ostler, or the love-scenes between Emma and Léon, or even certain details of the death of Emma. Artists of great sincerity and integrity, in Flaubert's time, were never entirely free from the desire to *épater le bourgeois*; the same is certainly true for present-day artists, but the *bourgeois* has become infinitely more difficult to *épater* [startle]. To read the speeches for the accusation and the defence in the notorious trial of Flaubert for "outrage to public morals" is to enter another, perhaps wryly amusing, world. No; the story is certainly firmly anchored in the human "real" of a certain time and place—here, the province of Normandy towards the end of the July monarchy—and the subtitle, *Moeurs de Province,* suggests that this is important; but it is not all-important. The great thing in *Madame Bovary* is the impression it gives of the continual vibration of an acute sensitivity held in control, an instrument finely tuned, giving a true note. The main character lives as a series of recognizable moods conveyed with remarkable feeling and power; in these the universality of the work lies. Emma Bovary is a Romantic, and the Romantic outlook on life as it appears here, caricatured by Flaubert, is immediately recognizable to everyone, to those who suppose that it is a symptom of adolescence and must be outgrown, and to those who know, as Flaubert himself did, that at its best it is admirable, the only defence against insidious soul-destroying materialism. There is no real opposition between Romantic and Realist; the great adversary is the Materialist, the anti-poet.[1] Unfortunately Romanticism is all too often represented in life by such as poor Emma Bovary, shoddily pursuing a shoddy ideal, a piece of imitation jewellery if ever there was one. This bastard Romanticism is what Flaubert is satirizing in *Madame Bovary.* Emma, possessing beauty and some intelligence, lacks one quality which is essential to the genuine Romantic—warmth of heart, which her creator did

possess and which he endeavoured to conceal from his readers. Emma's capricious acts of material "generosity" have little significance:

> *. . . elle jetait parfois aux pauvres toutes les pièces blanches de sa bourse, quoiqu'elle ne fût guère tendre cependant, ni facilement accessible à l'émotion d'autrui, comme la plupart des gens issus de campagnards, qui gardent toujours à l'âme quelque chose de la callosité des mains paternelles.[2]*

> [. . . sometimes she would toss all the silver in her purse to the poor, although she was not really of a tender disposition nor easily moved by the plight of others; she was, rather, like most country folk, whose souls always retain something of the callouses on the hands of their ancestors.]

And in fact she is completely selfish. Another of the worst tendencies of the Romantic disposition—the tendency to self-dramatization—is very marked in her. But she has such intelligence and taste that she adapts herself easily to the society of the aristocracy, at La Vaubyessard. The picture of Emma at the ball, dancing with a vicomte, is the one that has to be constantly called to mind if the full measure of her increasing misery and degradation is to be brought home, and if the reader is to feel for her any sympathy at all. Flaubert therefore recalls it, with delicate touches, throughout the book, the last reminder of it coming towards the end, when she is in Rouen making a desperate attempt to find money to pay her debts:

> *Elle s'arrêta pour laisser passer un cheval noir, piaffant dans les brancards d'un tilbury que conduisait un gentleman en fourrure de zibeline. Qui était-ce donc? Elle le connaissait. . . . La voiture s'élança et disparut.*

> *Mais c'était lui, le Vicomte!*[3]

> [She paused to let a tilbury pass, its black horse prancing between the shafts as a sable-clad gentleman drove it. Who could he be? She knew him. . . . The carriage leaped forward and disappeared.

> But, it was the Viscount!]

In the first chapters, Flaubert is mainly concerned with Charles, and with Emma only as she appears to others. His first analysis of Emma is in Chapter 6 of Part I (the dramatic technique of the delayed emergence of the principal character is one that rarely fails in its effect) and here he shows the disastrous results of an upbringing in which every hazard increased an already excessive tendency to sentimentality. By the time she left her convent school, she was corrupted by the nonsense of popular pseudo-Romantic literature and art, but remained hard and independent:

> *Cet esprit, positif au milieu de ses enthousiasmes, qui avait aimé l'église pour ses fleurs, la musique pour les paroles des romances, et la littérature pour ses excita-*

*tions passionnelles, s'insurgeait devant les mystères de
la foi, de même qu'elle s'irritait davantage contre la
discipline, qui était quelque chose d'antipathique à sa
constitution.*[4]

[Her mind and spirit, very practical even in the midst
of her enthusiasms, which had loved the church for its
flowers, music for the words of the romances, and literature for the excitement of its love stories, revolted in
the presence of the mysteries of the Christian faith,
much as she became irritated with its discipline, which
was contrary to her nature.]

There is something in the character of Emma which
condemns her to be second-rate, in spite of all her
struggles; and at the end of Chapter 6 it is perfectly
clear that if she had all the good fortune in the world,
second-rate as a human being she would be condemned
to remain. Thus early in the book the reader finds himself involved in a series of speculations about human
nature and destiny that are never openly suggested by
Flaubert, and realizes that this is a writer who will actually put into words only about one-fifth of what he has
to say.

It is Flaubert's own sensibility that gives to this record
of Emma's life and emotions its passages of great
beauty, its moments of tension and tragedy, but also its
humour. Flaubert's inarticulate sexton Lestiboudois,
ringing the Angelus at his own convenience and growing potatoes in a corner of the cemetery, would not be
much out of place in the churchyard at Elsinore; and
there are many other memorable personalities and situations sketched lightly but ineffaceably on the memory
so that the overall impression of *Madame Bovary* is not
completely tragic: the *pompiers* and the *garde nationale*
at the agricultural show; Charles at the opera; the loquacious guide at the cathedral baulked of his prey; Homais whenever he speaks; and the Homais family, large
and small, all enveloped to the chins in white aprons,
making jam. Flaubert really had a Shakespearean sense
of the ways of interrupting tension and tragedy by humour—in both cases it is sometimes embarrassingly
tasteless, but more often its nature and position in the
work are instinctively right. Flaubert was a lifelong student and devotee of the works of Shakespeare; but of
Thomas Hardy, who also knew how to create over-
whelmingly the sense of a mood, and to lighten a predominantly sombre view of life with flashes of humour,
he had certainly never heard. Hardy's *The Return of the
Native,* published in 1878, two years before Flaubert's
death, has certain similarities with *Madame Bovary*; it
is set in an English province in the same decade; in
both works the tragedy is relieved by humour all provided by provincials and rustics; in both the landscape,
constantly presented to the reader in all its aspects, influences the characters; in both a sense of driving fatality hangs over the main characters; in both the heroine
is a young woman far superior in intelligence and sensibility to her acquaintances, ambitious, sighing for life in

Paris, suffering from frustration, unwisely married,
driven by despair to death. Eustacia Vye is of the same
race as Emma Bovary, a dramatizer of self:

> To be loved to madness—such was her great desire.
> Love was to her the one cordial which could drive
> away the eating loneliness of her days. And she seemed
> to long for the abstraction called passionate love more
> than for any particular lover.[5]

An exact description of the desire of Emma Bovary.
Eustacia too plans to run away with her "Rodolphe,"
Damon Wildeve, whose character recalls to a certain
extent that of Emma's first lover. Eustacia's husband is
the *Native* of the title, unlike Charles Bovary in everything but failure to understand his wife—a hypersensi-
tive, intelligent only son, without worldly ambition.
Eustacia's mother-in-law is not merely a source of exasperation to her, but the unwitting cause of the tragic
situation that drives the girl to despair. The strongest resemblance between the books is not so much in details
of the plots as in the fact that the two novels cover the
same gamut of moods with the same intensity. But the
approaches of the two authors to their subjects are so
very different that a consideration of each may illumine
the other.

Hardy is no more given to moral judgments than Flaubert; but he is on the side of his characters. Flaubert
himself is the satirist of human weakness. For Hardy,
the satirist is the one to whom he refers as the "Supreme Power" or, in *Tess,* as the "President of the Im-
mortals."

> To Eustacia the situation seemed such a mockery of
> her hopes that death appeared the only door of relief if
> the satire of Heaven should go much further.[6]

Her beauty and distinction are such that:

> The gloomy corner into which accident as much as in-
> discretion had brought this woman might have led even
> a moderate partisan to feel that she had cogent reasons
> for asking the Supreme Power by what right a being of
> such exquisite finish had been placed in circumstances
> calculated to make of her charms a curse rather than a
> blessing.[7]

The "satire of Heaven" is illustrated by the small coincidences and accidents and misunderstandings that give
rise to the tragedy, and even more by the tragedy implicit in the clash of the characters themselves. Eustacia's husband Clym Yeobright is presented fairly, his
weakness and strangeness revealed, but also his capacity for love and self-torment. Charles, the husband of
Emma, is seen from an angle that ensures that the predominant image of him shall be the most grotesque
possible. His unshakeable devotion to the unworthy
Emma is simply made to appear as one example of his
lack of intelligence. In Hardy's more charitable view

such devotion would create in Charles not, indeed, intelligence, but a kind of sixth sense, an intuition, and would certainly not make him more obtuse than ever. Hardy's humble lovers, aware of their inferiority, all have this delicacy of perception that contrasts movingly with their unpolished speech and plainly furnished minds. But the whole emotional power of Flaubert's work is concentrated in one character, minutely analyzed, one fundamentally incapable of loving, but always pursuing a false image of love; Hardy's power is diffused among several characters, all loving in different ways, each way as true as the others. Eustacia and Clym; Wildeve; the gentle Thomasin, Clym's cousin; Mrs. Yeobright his mother; the strange wanderer Venn, Thomasin's self-effacing lover; even Charley, a slightly older and bolder "Justin"—all love more or less deeply according to their natures, some happily, some unhappily, and each for a time holds the centre of the stage. This spreading of interest among the characters may be why *The Return of the Native* lacks some of the force and cohesion of *Madame Bovary.* Emma is never for a moment out of sight. Eustacia too would have been worth this riveted attention; as it is, her character tends to be partly imagined and completed by the reader. Her end comes too soon, but the ultimate degradation of Emma is unimaginable for her. Her death is an interruption—Emma's a conclusion. One thing Flaubert did with all his main characters was to follow them relentlessly to the end of their story—they might continue to live at the end of the book, as Frédéric Moreau does in *L'Education sentimentale,* but nevertheless they have reached the limits of their destiny as human beings.

Flaubert penetrates in two brilliant paragraphs to the core of Emma's despair as she leaves Rodolphe's house for the last time, describes in detail her death from poisoning, her funeral, its aftermath. At Eustacia's death all is darkness and confusion, and her final thoughts are not revealed. Hardy says quietly:—"She had used to think of the heath alone as an uncongenial spot to be in: she felt it now of the whole world."[8] And of Eustacia dead:

> They stood silently looking upon Eustacia, who, as she lay there still in death, eclipsed all her living phases. Pallor did not include all the quality of her complexion, which seemed more than whiteness; it was almost light. The expression of her finely carved mouth was pleasant, as if a sense of dignity had just compelled her to leave off speaking. Eternal rigidity had seized upon it in a momentary transition between fervour and resignation. Her black hair was looser now than either of them had ever seen it before, and surrounded her brow like a forest. The stateliness of look which had been almost too marked for a dweller in a country domicile had at last found an artistically happy background.[9]

That is all. But brooding over the whole work, and all Hardy's work, is the question that Flaubert never asks—of the meaning of human suffering and destiny.

The whole force of Flaubert's work is that in spite of his detachment, his sarcasm, his levity, his apparent denial of souls to his characters, his readers are prompted to ask the question themselves.

In both works the secondary characters emphasize the isolation and superiority of the main one. But Hardy's are rather Shakespearean rustics set down on Egdon Heath in the nineteenth century. Flaubert's, as his subtitle suggests, are essentially of the nineteenth century, destined to represent the creeping tide of bourgeois smugness and complacency, the prosaic materialism that Flaubert saw overwhelming poetry, the triumph of the anti-poet Homais and all his kind. Hardy, though he movingly depicts a vanished rural England, is really more concerned with the human lot in general than with the human beings of one period. But the place, the scene, has greater importance than the period.

The attitudes of the two writers towards places seem at first radically different. Hardy's description of Egdon Heath in *The Return of the Native,* his loving and accurate record of the Dorset of the past, are part of his enduring fame. Flaubert in *Madame Bovary* seems to love Normandy no more than he does its inhabitants; yet for most lovers of Normandy the province is unforgettably evoked in his book. A series of brief studies of outline, colour and sound runs through the whole work—short passages, recording the passing of the seasons with their subdued northern tones. On Charles's first visit to the Roualt farm:

> La pluie ne tombait plus; le jour commençait à venir, et, sur les branches des pommiers sans feuilles, des oiseaux se tenaient immobiles, hérissant leurs petites plumes au vent froid du matin. La plate campagne s'étalait à perte de vue, et les bouquets d'arbres autour des fermes faisaient, à intervalles éloignés, des taches d'un violet noir sur cette grande surface grise, qui se perdait à l'horizon dans le ton morne du ciel. . . .[10]

> [The rain had stopped; day was breaking, and on the leafless branches of the apple trees birds perched motionless, fluffing out their little feathers in the morning chill. The flat countryside stretched as far as the eye could see, and the clusters of trees about the farmhouses dotted here and there seemed like splotches of black and purple against this great grey surface, which disappeared at the horizon into the dull tone of the sky. . . .]

As in all Flaubert's writing, the effect is conveyed as much by the sounds as by the sense of the words—here by three or four low-pitched recurring vowels. Each one of the other descriptions rings equally true. Flaubert is not a regional novelist, and scenery takes second place; the most important territories are in the minds of his characters. But for many readers the place and climate are among the strongest memories of *Madame Bovary.*

Toutes sortes de bruits joyeux emplissaient l'horizon: le claquement d'une charrette roulant au loin dans les ornières, le cri d'un coq qui se répétait ou la galopade d'un poulain que l'on voyait s'enfuir sous les pommiers. Le ciel pur était tacheté de nuages roses; des lumignons bleuâtres se rabattaient sur les chaumières couvertes d'iris; Charles, en passant, reconnaissait les cours. . . .[11]

[All sorts of joyous sounds filled the scene: the clattering of a wagon as it rolled along a distant rut, the repeated crowing of a cock, or the galloping of a foal disappearing through the apple trees. The clear sky was spotted with pink clouds; a bluish glow spread down over the cottages surrounded with iris; Charles recognized the farmyards as he passed them. . . .]

At the beginning of *The Return of the Native* the description of Egdon Heath sets the tone of the whole book, and Egdon is itself an essential part of the story. It gives a sense of dignity and timelessness which contributes much to the greatness of the novel. Flaubert allows himself no such aid as this long, meditative initial description; his picture of Yonville and its surroundings at the beginning of Part II is deliberately prosaic. But one of the usual effects of his shorter descriptions is to give glimpses of the vast, which set in perspective his human beings and their little interests; as for example the passage in Chapter 7 of Part I, quoted by Saint-Beuve and by many critics since:

Il arrivait parfois des rafales de vent, brises de la mer qui, roulant d'un bond sur tout le plateau du pays de Caux, apportaient, jusqu'au loin dans les champs, une fraîcheur salée. Les joncs sifflaient à ras de terre, et les feuilles des hêtres bruissaient en un frisson rapide, tandis que les cimes, se balançant toujours, continuaient leur grand murmure. . . .[12]

[There were occasional gusts of wind, breezes from the sea which in a single rush would reach the Caux region and even bring the cool smell of salt way out into the fields. The reeds whistled as they bent to earth, and the leaves of the beeches trembled and rustled, while their tops, endlessly swaying, kept up their strong murmuring. . . .]

Which for the sound and rhythm of the lines can be remembered like poetry. By such lines, at fairly long intervals, Flaubert maintains his contact with the universal. In his work no less than in Hardy's the setting is of immense importance. And in most enduring works of fiction there is surely an association of moments of keen psychological observation with memorable places—a coincidence of experience and surroundings that creates the "atmosphere" of the book and makes it remain alive when the physical attributes of the characters, and the story itself, have become blurred in the memory. The important thing is the impression of true human experience given by the novel, and the most intense moments of that experience are associated usually with places. These places the reader himself creates in

his imagination with the guidance of the writer, and they become familiar territory. When this happens, and they are associated with feelings recognizably real and profound, the novel endures, whatever its defects may be. The story may be a tissue of improbabilities, the dialogue often absurd, the characters odd—as they are for example in *Jane Eyre*—but the emotions are real, and so are Thornfield and Hay Lane, and the country round Whitcross, and Moor House. In *The Return of the Native* certain accidents and coincidences strain credulity at times, the characterization is uneven—but the emotional force of the book, inseparable from the vast sweep of Egdon, is deep and true. In **Madame Bovary** it is not a case of improbability or oddity—on the contrary the story is banal and the characters depressingly mediocre—but this matters less than it might because La Vaubyessard, Tostes, the house at Yonville and the room in Rouen are bound up with universal and most powerfully evoked emotions of ecstasy, despair, and fear. And in passing it may be said that it is essential that all these places should remain in the imagination—the spell is broken if one is confronted with some actual village or house said to be the scene of an event in fiction. Any reader's imaginary Yonville is nearer to the truth of **Madame Bovary** than the actual village of Ry, for long generally accepted as the model for Flaubert's Yonville.[13] And Hardy's Wessex too, though it is so graphically described, is to some extent a realm of the imagination.[14]

The great difference between Hardy's treatment of Eustacia's story and Flaubert's treatment of Emma's lies, however, less in the approach of each writer to the characters and scenes than in the way each constructs his work. By comparison with Flaubert's, Hardy's novel is shapeless, largely because of the device which he so constantly uses in his works, of taking one character a certain way, and then running back to see what another has been doing in the meantime. Flaubert avoids such awkwardness of construction by never leaving his main character. But his great originality lies in his having given to the form or *outline* an importance comparable with the importance of the form—symphonic, fugal, rhapsodic—in a musical composition. To carry the musical analogy too far would be ridiculous; but the fact remains that for certain readers the form of Flaubert's works gives a pleasure rather like that given by form in music. In **Madame Bovary,** the construction of the three sections, the placing of the *Comices Agricoles* scene, the final sentences of the chapters like strong chords, the variations in tempo and key, and many other features, indicate that Flaubert was a writer whose work literally took shape,[15] and that in his hands the novel assumed the dignity of a work of art.

Hardy, at the end of *The Return of the Native,*[16] admits that he substituted a banal ending for the one that would have been aesthetically fitting. The last short section,

Aftercourses, interesting as it may be, is artistically superfluous and out of key. This truckling to public taste is absolutely unimaginable in Flaubert. The chapters that follow the death of Emma are essential, for her influence prevails after her death—in the lives of Charles, dying of despair in poverty and degradation, and the wretched little orphan Berthe, sent at the age of six or seven to earn her living in a factory; while the main point of the book comes with the final irony of the triumph of Homais, smug, pompous high priest of the cult of material progress which was already widespread in Flaubert's time and has since come to extend its senseless tyranny over most of the world.

The book is tragic, in spite of the levity with which Flaubert often treats his characters; and part of the tragedy lies in the mediocrity of these characters, all dimly aware of some sublime notion of Love, Duty, Renown, Joy, towards which they strive as towards remote mountain peaks. Certain chapters in the book seem to emphasize this aspect of the tragedy, turning the reader's attention from a particular to a general dilemma; making him see beyond Emma and her affairs other human beings fruitlessly longing for greatness, falling short in some way. The first of these chapters is Chapter 9 of Part I, one of the most brilliant of Flaubert's analyses of Emma's moods; the second, the *Comices Agricoles* scene, Chapter 8 of Part II; and the third, the very brief Chapter 3 of Part III, the "honeymoon" of Emma and Léon at Rouen.

In Chapter 9 Emma is living on the memory of the ball at La Vaubyessard. On the way home she and Charles had picked up a cigar-case dropped by one of a party of horsemen, and she imagines that it belongs to the Vicomte with whom she danced. She thinks of his life in Paris, and wonders about the city. And at this point Flaubert widens the horizon so that for a moment Emma is almost lost in a universal mood of longing and exile:

> *La nuit, quand les mareyeurs, dans leurs charrettes, passaient sous ses fenêtres en chantant* la Marjolaine, *elle s'éveillait; et, écoutant le bruit des roues ferrées qui, à la sortie du pays, s'amortissait vite sur la terre:*
>
> *—Ils y seront demain! se disait-elle.*
>
> *Et elle les suivait dans sa pensée, montant et descendant les côtes, traversant les villages, filant sur la grande route à la clarté des étoiles. Au bout d'une distance indéterminée, il se trouvait toujours une place confuse où expirait son rêve.*[17]

[At night when the fish vendors would pass beneath her windows with their wagons singing *la Marjolaine*, she would waken and listen to the noise of the wheels with their iron rims which would be muffled as they left the village and reached the softer ground:

"They will be there tomorrow!" she would say to herself.

And in her mind's eye she would follow them up hill and down dale, through the villages and moving along the open ground beneath the clear stars. After an indeterminate distance, there would always be a confused region in which her dream would expire.]

On a map of Paris she traces imaginary walks; buys a subscription to a Paris paper; reads novels whose scene is Paris, and reads at meals; dreams of the Vicomte:

> *Mais le cercle dont il était le centre peu à peu s'élargit autour de lui, et cette auréole qu'il avait, s'écartant de sa figure, s'étala plus loin, pour illuminer d'autres rêves.*[18]

[But the circle of which he was the center grew little by little around him, and the halo which he had, moving out from his face, spread out further and illuminated other dreams.]

Then follows the famous passage beginning:

> *Paris, plus vaste que l'Océan, miroitait donc aux yeux d'Emma dans une atmosphère vermeille.*

[Paris, wider than the ocean, glittered before Emma's eyes in a rosy haze.]

Impossible here not to recall Balzac (whose books Emma has been reading) and the beautiful lines from the opening pages of *Le Père Goriot*:

> *Mais Paris est un véritable océan. Jetez-y la sonde, vous n'en connaîtrez jamais la profondeur. Parcourez-le, décrivez-le? quelque soin que vous mettiez à le parcourir, à le décrire; quelque nombreux et intéressés que soient les explorateurs de cette mer, il s'y rencontrera toujours un lieu vierge, un antre inconnu, des fleurs, des perles, des monstres, quelque chose d'inouï, oublié par les plongeurs littéraires.*

[But Paris is a real ocean. No matter where you take your sounding, you will never learn its depth. Travel about it, describe it? No matter how carefully you travel over it and describe it, no matter how many and how careful explorations you make of this sea, there will always remain an unexplored spot, an unknown cavern, flowers, pearls, monsters, something unheard of, forgotten by the literary divers.]

In fact the picture of Paris which forms in Emma's imagination is obviously derived from the *Comédie Humaine*.

The falseness of her view of her own situation is stressed, with great shrewdness:

> *Tout ce qui l'entourait immédiatement, campagne ennuyeuse, petits bourgeois imbéciles, médiocrité de l'existence, lui semblait une exception dans le monde, un hasard particulier où elle se trouvait prise, tandis qu'au-delà s'étendait à perte de vue l'immense pays des félicités et des passions.*[19]

[Everything that hemmed her in, the boring countryside, the idiotic petty bourgeois, the mediocrity of her life, seemed to her an exception in the world, a special piece of misfortune in which she was trapped, while out beyond as far as the eye could see there stretched the immense land of felicity and passion.]

Emma, perpetually contrasting her actual surroundings with the ideal ones of her imagination, tries to introduce into her life some of the elegance of which she has read. And she fritters away her time:

> *Elle souhaitait à la fois mourir et habiter Paris.*[20]

[She longed both to die and to live in Paris.]

The complete contrast of Charles's life with hers is forcefully made—his hard work, his delight in Emma, who contemptuously watches him as he dozes after dinner, and grows more and more irritated with his coarse manners. She waits endlessly for something to happen.

> *Comme les matelots en détresse, elle promenait sur la solitude de sa vie des yeux désespérés, cherchant au loin quelque voile blanche dans les brumes de l'horizon.*[21]

[Like sailors in distress, she looked about over the solitude of her life with despairing eyes, seeking somewhere in the distance a white sail amidst the mists of the horizon.]

One recalls Baudelaire's "matelots oubliés dans une île," and the other exiles of *Le Cygne*.

Behind the half-humourous manner in which Flaubert depicts Emma's suffering, there is a profound seriousness. The tragic exhaustion of energy in futile longings, the sickness of heart, are poignantly conveyed. There is no invitation from La Vaubyessard that year:

> *L'avenir était un corridor tout noir, et qui avait au fond sa porte bien fermée.*[22]

[The future was a black corridor with the door at the end shut tight.]

She becomes more and more idle and languid. At this point Flaubert concentrates the whole mood he is depicting into two sounds—the cracked note of the church bell, and the howling of a dog:

> *Au loin, parfois, un chien hurlait: et la cloche, à temps égaux, continuait sa sonnerie monotone qui se perdait dans la campagne.*[23]

[In the distance, at intervals, a dog would howl: and with even beat, the bell kept up its monotonous tolling which disappeared out over the countryside.]

It is evident by now that the magic of the chapter lies in the way in which, from point to point, Flaubert places an image of infinite distance, emphasizing Emma's longing for escape; and at the same time constantly brings her back to consciousness of her real surroundings in the village of Tostes, where the same things happen at the same time every day. The climax of this long investigation of her *ennui* comes with the description of the itinerant organ-grinder with his puppets performing a dance in a miniature ball-room. This passage is one of the most Flaubertian in the book, because it so clearly reveals the essential quality of the writer—his extreme sensitivity to shades of feeling, his imagination and carefully controlled sympathy, his power of making the apparently straightforward description of something unremarkable contain whole worlds of meaning and suggest long trains of thought. Any commentary on a passage of this sort tends to be a blundering intrusion. All that is needed is to listen to Flaubert, intently.[24]

From this point onwards the movement of the chapter gains speed, with the self-abandon of Emma to her misery, and her reckless display of it to her father, and to her mother-in-law; the actual physical illness caused by her unhappiness; and Charles's decision to move for her sake away from Tostes. The detailed description of her destruction of her wedding-bouquet,[25] which she discovered by chance in a drawer, suggests three things particularly—the fixed abstracted gaze of the habitual day-dreamer ("Elle le regarda brûler," etc. [She watched it burn . . .]): the end of an unhappy phase of her marriage (the hope of departure from Tostes marks the beginning of a reawakening interest in life); but also the "Pourquoi, mon Dieu, me suis-je mariée?" [Heavens, why did I get married?] of an earlier chapter[26]—the first words spoken by Emma in the book.

The *Comices Agricoles* scene is a masterpiece of technique. Innumerable critics have commented on the effects of contrast, the dry humour, the passages of description, notably of the charming appearance of Emma, the field of the show, the old servant receiving her medal, the dignitaries on the platform; and the skilfully prepared climax when, at the prize-giving ceremony, Emma with Rodolphe in the town-hall sees in a kind of dream her past life, and unknowingly, an indication of what is to come as she watches in the distance the old coach l'Hirondelle "qui descendait lentement la côte des Leux, en traînant après soi un long panache de poussière"[27] [which came slowly down the Leux hill dragging a long plume of dust behind itself]—the coach which is afterwards to play so great a part in her rendezvous with Léon at Rouen.

Flaubert has in fact assembled in this chapter all his chief characters; even Léon, who is not at Yonville, is present at one time in Emma's thoughts. The construction of the chapter has an orderliness, a rhythmic movement of its own which command the admiration of the reader. But here the author's style is satirical. Humanity in the mass is repellent to him, and this is obvious from certain comments:

> *Tous ces gens-là se ressemblaient;*[28] . . . *toutes les bouches de la multitude se tenaient ouvertes, comme pour boire ses paroles;*[29] . . . *ces bourgeois épanouis.*[30]

[All these people looked alike; . . . every mouth in the crowd was open, as if to drink in his words; . . . these complacent bourgeois.]

The visiting councillor's speech is a collection of pompous platitudes; the banquet at the close of the festivities, too crowded; the fireworks, damp; Homais's account of the proceedings, written for the *Fanal de Rouen,* frankly ridiculous in its exaggeration. The official banalities of the main speech are equalled by the Romantic ones of the conversation of Emma and Rodolphe. In fact, in this assembly of characters, not one is portrayed as a likeable human being; that is to say, not one of the recurring characters. The two who receive sympathetic treatment from Flaubert do not appear elsewhere in the book; they are the old farm-servant Catherine Leroux, and the youngest son of the mayor, in national guard uniform with a helmet much too large:

Il souriait là-dessous avec une douceur tout enfantine, et sa petite figure pâle, où des gouttes ruisselaient, avait une expression de jouissance, d'accablement et de sommeil.[31]

[He was smiling beneath it with childish gentleness, and his pale little face covered with drops of perspiration showed his delight, his fatigue, and his drowsiness.]

But such moments of gentleness are rare. At the close of this chapter more than at any other point in the book, perhaps, the reader may find himself longing for a character with some depth and goodness. As Sainte-Beuve wrote when first reviewing the book: "Pourquoi n'avoir pas mis là un seul personnage qui soit de nature à consoler, à reposer le lecteur par un bon spectacle, ne pas lui avoir ménagé un seul ami? . . ."[32] [Why did the author not include a single character who could console the reader and give him some respite by his goodness; why not have allowed the reader at least one friend?] and Matthew Arnold, a few years later: ". . . not a personage in the book to rejoice or console us; the springs of freshness and feeling are not there to create such personages. . . ."[33] Obviously the lack of sympathetic principal characters is a strange feature of the book, and one is tempted to wonder whether, if Flaubert had developed differently the character of Charles, he would have given greater force to the tragedy of *Madame Bovary.* But such speculations are part of the pleasure of reading Flaubert; he was obviously quite capable of doing things that he did not choose to do, and that his critics have often considered he should have done. In *Madame Bovary* the two minor characters of the boy Justin and the child Berthe are created with delicacy and compassion. Any minor character is a potential major one, and if he had chosen to make either of them the central figure of a novel, would his attitude towards them have changed? Would his sad and indignant view of humanity have ensured that any major character should be at worst completely selfish and at best rather

ludicrous? Perhaps. And yet the curious thing about the *Comices* scene is that behind all the pretentiousness and shallowness and hypocrisy occupying the front of the stage, there is a hint of a world of innocence and enjoyment—the *sourire de béatitude* of Catherine Leroux on many other faces. And there is too, all around crowded Yonville, the peaceful sunlit countryside. Flaubert, writing of this chapter when he was completing it, said: "C'est un dur endroit, j'y ai *tous* mes [sic] personnages de mon livre en action et en dialogue . . . et par là-dessus un grand paysage qui les enveloppe. Mais, si je réussis, ce sera bien symphonique."[34] [It is a difficult passage. I've included all my characters moving about and talking . . . and over against it all a great countryside which envelops them all. But if I can succeed in it, it will be quite symphonic.] One of the delights of analyzing this chapter is to try to see how he has managed to convey the impression of this surrounding countryside without ever describing or even mentioning any aspect of it. And for those readers who were immediately aware of the "symphonic effect" of the chapter, and for whom a later reading of his letters simply confirmed that this was the effect he had been aiming at, the *Comices Agricoles* scene will always be one of the major pleasures of literature.

Chapter 3 of Part III is as brief as the *Comices* scene is long; the most important feature of it is that it evokes for a moment an image of beauty and innocence, bringing home all the more painfully the second-rateness and sordidness of the situation of Emma and Léon. Here is the passage in which Flaubert achieves this curious effect (they are returning by boat from an island where they have dined. Emma is singing):

Sa voix harmonieuse et faible se perdait sur les flots; et le vent emportait les roulades que Léon écoutait passer, comme des battements d'ailes, autour de lui.

Elle se tenait en face, appuyée contre la cloison de la chaloupe, où la lune entrait par un des volets ouverts. Sa robe noire, dont les draperies s'élargissaient en éventail, l'amincissait, la rendait plus grande. Elle avait la tête levée, les mains jointes, et les deux yeux vers le ciel. Parfois l'ombre des saules la cachait en entier, puis elle réapparaissait tout à coup, comme une vision, dans la lumière de la lune.[35]

[Her voice, harmonious and soft, disappeared over the waves; and the wind carried off the roulades which Léon heard pass about him like the beating of wings.

She sat across from him leaning against the bulkhead, into which the moonlight entered through an open shutter. Her black dress, its folds spreading fanlike about her, made her seem slimmer and taller. Her head was raised, her hands joined and she looked upward toward the sky. Sometimes the shadow of a willow would hide her entirely, then she would suddenly reappear, like a vision, in the moonlight.]

Then Flaubert shatters the image, as though throwing a stone into calm water, by the boatman's reference to a lively party he took out the other day, of which the gayest member, according to his description, could have been no other than the faithless Rodolphe. We return to the little intrigues of Emma's real life. And though we realize that throughout the chapter Emma is seen by the romantic Léon who is in turn observed by a sardonic Flaubert, the impression of a momentary glimpse of something pure, remains.

The famous chapter in which Flaubert describes at length the death of Emma from arsenic poisoning has many features more interesting than the medical detail so carefully collected by the author. For example, Emma's last meeting with Rodolphe: it is made perfectly clear at the end that her impulse to kill herself comes from a sense of betrayal in love, and betrayal by Rodolphe—not from the more immediate disasters, her disappointment with Léon and her desperate financial situation:

> *. . . elle ne se rappelait point la cause de son horrible état, c'est-à-dire la question d'argent. Elle ne souffrait que de son amour, se sentait son âme l'abandonner par ce souvenir, comme les blessés, en agonisant, sentent l'existence qui s'en va par leur plaie qui saigne.*[36]

> [. . . she did not remember the reason for her horrible predicament, that is, the problem of money. She was suffering only in her love and could feel her soul slipping away from her through this memory, as men dying of their wounds feel their life escaping through their bleeding gashes.]

It is almost as though Flaubert were suggesting that Emma had indeed loved Rodolphe profoundly. It is notable that her mental state as she leaves La Huchette for the last time is similar to the one she experienced after Rodolphe first abandoned her. On that occasion, her wild flight to the top of the house, to the empty attics, almost ends in suicide as she leans dizzily out of the window. This time the wild flight is repeated:

> *Puis, dans un transport d'héroïsme qui la rendait presque joyeuse, elle descendit la côte en courant, traversa la planche aux vaches, le sentier, l'allée, les halles, et arriva devant la boutique du pharmacien.*[37]

> [Then, in a sort of heroic ecstasy which made her feel almost joyful, she ran down the slope, crossed the cattle bridge, followed the path and the walk, passed by the marketplace, and ended before the pharmacist's shop.]

But even the great dramatic exit from life is bungled and turns into a sordid, lengthy physical agony.

Another interesting feature of this scene is the sudden appearance, carefully engineered by Flaubert, probably with symbolical intent, of the blind beggar with his hideously diseased face and his bawdy little song. That this unfortunate, whom Emma had so often seen as she returned from Rouen, should appear in Yonville to consult Homais at the very moment of her death is scarcely credible; but it is a coincidence of which one can imagine Hardy approving. For him, the most hideous of earthly realities forming the last image in the mind of one who could not bear very much reality, would be an example of the endlessly inventive cruelty of Heaven. For Flaubert, the horrible apparition signifies more probably the embodiment of Emma's degradation. Flaubert is concerned, too, with departing in a startling way from the conventional, sentimental idea of the death-scene with repentance and consoling foretastes of bliss. But on the whole the introduction of the beggar gives a touch of Romantic melodrama which weakens the end of the scene.

But perhaps the most important thing of all in this chapter is the character of Dr. Larivière, the famous doctor from Rouen. Important because here at last is the "personage . . . to rejoice and console us" supposed by Matthew Arnold not to exist in the book. This is a human being after Flaubert's own heart, and he does not conceal his admiration. Certainly the description of Dr. Larivière occupies only one paragraph, and his visit to Yonville a couple of pages—but as the whole is quintessential Flaubert, the character assumes great dramatic importance. For Larivière stands out in complete contrast to all the other characters in the book.

> *Dédaigneux des croix, des titres et des académies, hospitalier, libéral, paternel avec les pauvres et pratiquant la vertu sans y croire, il eût presque passé pour un saint si la finesse de son esprit ne l'eût fait craindre comme un démon. Son regard, plus tranchant que ses bistouris, vous descendait droit dans l'âme et désarticulait tout mensonge à travers les allégations et les pudeurs.*[38]

> [Scorning medals, titles, and academies, hospitable, generous, fatherly with the poor and practicing virtue without believing in it, he would almost have passed for a saint, had not the keenness of his wit made him feared as a demon. His eye, sharper than his scalpel, cut through to one's soul and laid bare all the lies beneath the claims and fears.]

But he is not too hardened by experience to shed a tear at the despair of Charles. Most critics have commented on this fine description, usually to point out that it was Flaubert's tribute to his father;[39] but the importance of the paragraph in the book can scarcely be over-stressed. It simply sets the whole of the rest in perspective—all the pettiness and stupidity, the hysteria and incompetence, the false emotion and unworthy ambition. It suggests the exacting standard by which Flaubert was inclined to measure other human beings, himself included, and their actions. By writing in this way of Larivière, Flaubert balances his picture of provincial life, for Larivière is a provincial too. The fact that Flaubert could bring so vividly to life, in so short a space, this vital and dominating character suggests that it was with deliberate intent that he turned his gaze upon failures and nonentities and the pathetic or ludicrous weaknesses of human beings, and composed almost entirely in the minor key. Larivière, after all, is an example of the triumph of the good; he occupies a position of importance and is revered and loved.

But the apotheosis of Homais closes the book. "Il vient de recevoir la croix d'honneur." [He has just been made a member of the Legion of Honor.] There he stands, perpetuated by this perfect tense, eternally pleased with himself. Emma and Charles are dead, Berthe condemned to a probably brief life of hardship; but the chemist's family is "florissante et hilare" [flourishing and joyful].

> *Napoléon l'aidait au laboratoire, Athalie lui brodait un bonnet grec, Irma découpait des rondelles de papier pour couvrir les confitures, et Franklin récitait tout d'une haleine la table de Pythagore.*[40]

> [Napoleon helped him in the laboratory, Athalie embroidered his caps for him, Irma cut out round pieces of paper to cover the jam pots, and Franklin recited the Pythagorean table all in one breath.]

It is perhaps more disturbing than amusing to imagine what Homais's descendants might be like today, if they inherited his character. But let us hope that by some irony of fate the family produced a poet—indifferent to wealth, reputation or "progress," devoting his whole life to the creation of something with no material value at all. But Flaubert was aware of the growing power of the Homais breed; his Homais is too intelligent and enterprising, and above all loquacious, not to be a prominent member of society. Flaubert speaks of "la profondeur de son intelligence et la scélératesse de sa vanité"[41] [his profound intelligence and his criminal vanity], and in fact the two characteristics not infrequently produce a public figure full of sound and fury. Homais, the little tutelary genius of bustling busybodies, with his Gradgrindish passion for collecting and disseminating Facts, would have gloried in the sound, which since the invention of wireless is one of the inescapable conditions of social life, of the human voice perpetually imparting information. But ". . . fermons notre porte, montons au plus haut de notre tour d'ivoire, sur la dernière marche, le plus près du ciel. Il y fait froid quelquefois, n'est-ce pas? Mais qu'importe? On voit les étoiles briller clair et l'on n'entend plus les dindons"[42] [. . . let us lock our doors and climb to the top of our ivory tower, on the last step, as near to heaven as we can reach. It is sometimes cold up there, you know. But what does it matter; you can see the stars shining clearly and you no longer have to listen to the turkeys] wrote Flaubert while he was composing **Madame Bovary.** And Flaubert from the top of his ivory tower could see more than Homais and his kind ever dreamed existed. ". . . tous mes personnages . . . et par là-dessus un grand paysage qui les enveloppe" [all my characters . . . and over against it all a great countryside which envelops them all].

The words which have seemed to me to come nearest to explaining the peculiar charm of this inexhaustible novel are Coleridge's words about the "power of poetry"; which is, he said, "by a single word, perhaps, to instil that energy into the mind, which compels the imagination to produce the picture."[43] This art of filling a small number of words with great significance, this compulsive power over the imagination of his reader, is remarkably developed in Flaubert's case. And again, if one tries to pay tribute to the form of the work, the aspect of it that had so much significance for Flaubert, and which he so much desired should be understood—what would please him more than to say that he had ". . . the sense of musical delight, with the power of producing it"[44] which Coleridge said is a gift of imagination?

Notes

1. Flaubert uses the expression "anti-poète" in a letter. *Correspondance,* III [*Oeuvres complètes de Gustave Flaubert* (Paris: L. Conrad, 1910-1930], 141.

2. [*Madame Bovary* in *Oeuvres complètes de Gustave Flaubert* (Paris: L. Conrad, 1910-1930),] Pt. 1, Ch. ix, p. 92.

3. Pt. 3, Ch. vii, p. 412.

4. P. 54.

5. Thomas Hardy, *The Return of the Native* (London: Macmillan Co., 1954), Ch. vii, p. 79.

6. [Hardy,] Book 4, Ch. iii, p. 303.

7. *Ibid.*

8. Book 5, Ch. vii, p. 414.

9. Book 5, Ch. ix, p. 446.

10. [Flaubert] Part I, Ch. ii, p. 16.

11. Part 3, Ch. x, p. 466.

12. P. 63.

13. Or Neufchâtel-en-Bray, or more recently Forges-les-Eaux. See René Herval, *Les Véritables Origines de "Madame Bovary"* (Paris: Librairie A. G. Nizet, 1957).

14. In the 1912 preface to *The Woodlanders,* Hardy says of the hamlet of "Little Hintock"—"To oblige readers I once spent several hours on a bicycle . . . in a serious attempt to discover the real spot."

15. For a remark on the point where the actual division into chapters took place, see "*Madame Bovary* (nouvelle version précédée des scénarios inédits)," J. Pommier and G. Leleu (Paris, José Corti, 1959), p. xvii.

16. The writer may state here that the original conception of the story did not design a marriage be-

tween Thomasin and Venn. . . . But certain circumstances of serial publication led to a change
of intent. Readers can therefore choose between
the endings, and those with an austere artistic code
can assume the more consistent conclusion to be
the true one. (*Aftercourses,* footnote to Ch. iii.)

17. P. 80.

18. P. 81.

19. P. 82.

20. P. 84.

21. P. 87.

22. P. 87.

23. P. 88.

24. P. 90.

25. P. 94.

26. Ch. vii, p. 62.

27. Part 2, Ch. viii, p. 204.

28. P. 195.

29. P. 202.

30. P. 207.

31. P. 202.

32. *Les Grands Ecrivains Français,* par Sainte-Beuve.
    XIXe Siècle. Les Romanciers. (Paris: Garnier,
    1927), II, 181.

33. Matthew Arnold, *Essays in Criticism* (2nd Series)
    (London: Macmillan Co., 1915), *Count Leo Tols-
    toi,* p. 276.

34. To Louise Colet, September 7, 1853, *Correspon-
    dance,* III, 335.

35. Pp. 354-55.

36. Part 3, Ch. vii, p. 432.

37. Pp. 432-33.

38. Part 3, Ch. vi, p. 441.

39. In any case certain details of the description, nota-
    bly the reference to Larivière's hands, would sug-
    gest that this was a portrait from the life.

40. Part 3, Ch. xi, p. 477.

41. P. 473.

42. To Louise Colet, November 22, 1852, *Correspon-
    dance,* III, 54.

43. *Coleridge's Shakespearean Criticism,* ed. T. M.
    Rayson (London: Constable, 1903), II, 174.

44. *Biographia Literaria* [(1817)], XV.

Harry Levin (essay date 1963)

SOURCE: Levin, Harry. "The Female Quixote." In *The
Gates of Horn: A Study of Five French Realists,* pp.
246-69. New York: Oxford University Press, 1963.

[*In the following essay, Levin examines the interplay of
ideal and reality in the novel.*]

As if to put the finishing touches on Flaubert's self-
portrait of the artist as a saint, Anatole France likened
him to the gigantic and unswerving figure of Saint
Christopher, painfully leaning upon an uprooted oak,
and stoutly bearing French literature from the romantic
to the naturalistic bank of the stream.[1] The quarrel between his two selves—or, perhaps more precisely, the
adaptation of temperament to discipline—fitted him
uniquely for that mission. His youth, as he recalled it,
seemed like some flamboyant cathedral, interposing its
stained-glass windows between him and the world.[2] The
fact that his native habitat had been a hospital, in all actuality, sanctioned his later efforts to attain a clinical
view. This did not entail a rejection of poetry, since he
maintained that disillusion was a hundred times more
poetic than illusion.[3] The best way of detaching the one
from the other was that which he had learned from our
classic source; and to it, to *Don Quixote,* he attributed
his artistic origins.[4] To it he returned again and again,
smitten with its Spanish malady, savoring its gay melancholy, praising its "perpetual fusion of illusion and
reality."[5] The generous streak of quixotry in his own nature did not go unremarked by such friends as Alphonse
Daudet.[6] Critics have not been remiss in underlining the
close analogy between his masterwork and that of Cervantes. Surveying the state of the novel in 1876, an article by Emile Montégut made Flaubert blush by commenting: "Just as Cervantes dealt the death-blow to the
chivalric mania with the very weapons of chivalry, so
with the very devices of the romantic school Gustave
Flaubert has demolished the false ideal that it brought
into the world."[7] The doughty deed would not have
been committed, in either of these cases, if the time had
not conjoined with the talent. Shortly before 1843, in
reviewing a play by Scribe, the prophetic Søren Kierkegaard had paused for a footnote to wonder: "It is
remarkable that the whole of European literature lacks a
feminine counterpart to *Don Quixote.* May not the time
for this be coming, may not the continent of sentimentality yet be discovered?"[8]

Heroines were certainly not lacking, and their scope
had somewhat widened since the eighteenth century.
Marriage was not so much their happy ending as it was
the precondition of their unhappiness and an incentive
to their emancipation. Delphine or Corinne, the *femme
fatale* of Madame de Staël, was presented as the feminine counterpart—and, consequently, the moral superior—to the *homme fatal* of Byron and Chateaubriand.

The trousers, the cigars, and the masculine pseudonym of George Sand were the badges of an upsurging feminism, which met with its travesty in the transvestism of Théophile Gautier's *Mademoiselle de Maupin.* Emerging from the domestic incompatibilities of her *Indiana,* George Sand lived through the adventurous passions of her subsequent protagonists, stopping just short of *Lélia*'s unhappy denouement. Her whole-hearted involvement in her heroine fostered a special empathy with her feminine readers. Transported from their everyday lives to her romanticized sphere, they could view themselves in the role of *la femme incomprise,* the unappreciated wife, the misunderstood woman. That vogue had its *cause célèbre* in 1840, when the pampered and well-connected Madame Lafarge was tried and found guilty of poisoning her vulgar provincial husband. Her defense and her memoirs, clearly nourished by sentimental fiction, gained devout support among the public, and were read by Flaubert on the advice of Louise Colet. They moved such moralists as Alfred Nettement to suggest that the veritable poison must have been an immoral novel.[9] A prize-winning discourse by Menche de Loisne extended this logic by accusing Eugène Sue of fomenting the revolution of 1848.[10] The February uprising was also described by Saint-Marc Girardin as "a scene from *Les Mystères de Paris.*"[11] The Second Empire, with its tighter controls and its philistine party-lines, made such reactions official; while Flaubert was completing **Madame Bovary,** the Academy of Moral and Political Sciences was calling for an inquiry into the demoralizing influence of the *roman-feuilleton.*[12] The incidence of adultery is not subject to computation; but crimes of passion seemed to be breaking out more and more shockingly; while the suicide rate more than tripled during the years between 1830 and 1880 in France.[13] How much had literature done to spread the moral contagion?

Flaubert's novel, though it won no prizes, could have been construed as another inquest into this critical problem. His persistent theme, according to Paul Bourget, was the hazard of thought; the reading habit itself was his principle of social disequilibrium; and Bourget retrospectively endeavored to summon Flaubert as a witness for his own anti-intellectualism.[14] On his side Bourget could indeed count the elder Madame Bovary, who seeks to cancel her daughter-in-law's subscription to a circulating library, denouncing the librarian as a poisoner.[15] She is volubly seconded by the opinionated M. Homais in Flaubert's original manuscript, wherein the book trade is similarly denounced by a reactionary aristocrat.[16] But these denunciations were retrenched, and the denouncers were never Flaubert's spokesmen. Bad novels merely reflected that narcissistic indulgence which occupied him more seriously as a target. To set forth what Kierkegaard had spied out, to invade the continent of sentimentality, to create a female Quixote—mock-romantic where Cervantes had been mock-he-

roic—was a man's job. Jane Austen might have done it, but not George Sand, whose *Elle et lui* was reversed when Alfred de Musset retold their romance in *Lui et elle.* The act of detachment had to be incisive and virile, the gesture of a crusty bachelor interrupting the banns to point out the impediments. The first word of the title proclaims a change of status: instead of *La Princesse* or *La Religieuse,* plain *Madame* without the ennobling *de.* Housewives had rarely played title-roles before, except in the raffish tales of Paul de Kock; Balzac's *Madame Firmiani* stresses its heroine's misalliance; and *Madame Angot,* the revolutionary operetta, is about a parvenu fishwife. Madame Bovary! the appellative warns us that our heroine is married, and to a bourgeois—a premise not for romance, but for complications, if she happens to be romance-minded. The latent romanticist within Flaubert had been suppressed when Maxime Du Camp and Louis Bouilhet had advised him to burn the original draft of his **Tentation de saint Antoine.**[17] These friends had advised him to discipline himself by taking up a modern subject, something down to earth, such middle-class stuff as Balzac had just been handling in *Les Parents pauvres.*

Bouilhet, who had studied medicine under Flaubert's father, proposed the local and recent case of another former student. In 1848 at the town of Ry, the second wife of a Dr. Delamare, after a series of adulteries and extravagances, was rumored to have poisoned herself and precipitated her husband's suicide, leaving an orphan daughter. Flaubert acknowledged this suggestion, and the years of critical midwifery that supported it, when he dedicated **Madame Bovary** to Bouilhet.[18] To Du Camp, we are informed by the latter, Flaubert's acknowledgments were appropriately medical: "I was ridden by the cancer of lyricism, and you operated; it was just in time, but I cried out in pain."[19] Part of the cure was their Mediterranean voyage, which left Flaubert bored with the exotic and homesick for the commonplace. From a French hotel-keeper in Cairo, a M. Bouvaret, he picked up a name for his bovine country doctor: *forum bovarium* is a cattle-market.[20] Among his **Notes de voyage** he jotted down an occasional reflection upon his future theme: "The poetry of the adulterous wife is only true to the extent that she is at liberty in the midst of fatality."[21] To the heroine of George Sand, resisting the prose of her environment, such poetry may be subjectively true. But to the extent that she is caught in the network of objective circumstance, that free will is subjected to determining necessity, the truth about her is bound to be unpoetic; what seems beautiful must prove false. To the extent that her intimate fantasies are exposed by the light of external realities, that sense undercuts sensibility, Flaubert's treatment is like that of other realists. But where the fantasy of *Don Quixote* took on the guise of a vanishing heroism, which the heroine did not jeopardize with her presence, the feminine outlook of **Madame Bovary** is consistently belied by its masculine characters. Where romance, to Cervantes, signified knightly adventure, to Flaubert—more narrowly and intensively—it signifies passionate love. The means of exposure, which put Cervantes' realism on a solid and genial basis, was an appeal to the common sense of the bourgeoisie. That would have been, for Flaubert, almost as delusive and fantastic as romanticism itself. Hence he often seems to have taken the realistic method and turned it inside out. "Realism seems to us with *Madame Bovary* to have said its last word," commented Henry James, with a sigh of somewhat premature relief.[22]

In sharpest contradistinction to Don Quixote, whose vagaries were intellectual, Emma Bovary's are emotional.[23] Hence they are counterweighted by no earthbound Sancho Panza, but by the intellectually pretentious M. Homais. The comic relief that he injects into Emma's tragedy is later to be elaborated into the unrelieved comedy of *Bouvard et Pécuchet.* Because it is herself that she misconceives, where Don Quixote's misconception of actuality could be corrected by reference to his fellow men, she remains incorrigibly tragic. This paranoiac attitude of Emma's, this self-hallucination induced by overreading, this "habit of conceiving ourselves otherwise than as we are," is so epidemic that Jules de Gaultier could diagnose the weakness of the modern mind as *Bovarysme.*[24] The vicarious lives that film stars lead for shop-girls, the fictive euphoria that slogans promise and advertisements promote, the imaginary flourishes that supplement and garnish daily existence for all of us, are equally Bovaristic. If to Bovarize is simply to daydream, as everyone does to a greater or lesser extent, the criterion is not how much we do so, but whether our daydreams are egoistic like Emma's or altruistic like Don Quixote's. Every epoch depends upon some verbal medium for its conception of itself: on printed words and private fictions, if not on public rituals and collective myths. The trouble came when, instead of the imitation of Christ or the veneration of Mary, readers practised the emulation of Rastignac or the cult of Lélia. Yet, whatever their models, they were romanticizing a reality which would otherwise have been formless and colorless; for when nature has established norms of conduct, art is called upon to publicize them. "There are people who would not fall in love if they had never heard of love," said La Rochefoucauld. Denis de Rougemont has tried to substantiate that epigram by arguing that the erotic motive was superimposed upon the West through medieval romance.[25] Paolo might never have loved Francesca, in Dante's memorable episode, had not the book of Galeotto acted as a go-between.

But the writer, if not the reader, cannot afford to be swept off his feet by emotions involved in a given story. Thus Flaubert, in his first *Education sentimentale,* describes the youthful reading of his poet, Jules:

He reread *René* and *Werther,* those books of disgust with life; he reread Byron and dreamed of the solitude of his great-souled heroes; but too much of his admiration was based on personal sympathy, which has nothing in common with the disinterested admiration of the true artist. The last word in this kind of criticism, its most inane expression, is supplied to us every day by a number of worthy gentlemen and charming ladies interested in literature, who disapprove of this character because he is cruel, of that situation because it is equivocal and rather smutty—discovering, in the last analysis, that in the place of such a person they would not have done the same thing, without understanding the necessary laws that preside over a work of art, or the logical deductions that follow from an idea.[26]

It follows that Emma Bovary and her censors, though their ethics differed, shared the same esthetic approach. Jules on the other hand would learn, as did Flaubert, to differentiate a work of art from its subject-matter and the artist from his protagonist. The anecdote of Cervantes on his deathbed, identifying himself with his hero, has its much quoted Flaubertian parallel: *Madame Bovary c'est moi.*[27] But this equivocal statement was not so much a confession as a cautious disclaimer of certain resemblances which Madame Delamare's neighbors, without indulging in unwarranted gossip, might have suspected. In so far as Flaubert lived the part, as any novelist enters into his fully realized characterizations, it was a *tour de force* of female impersonation. The identification was not nearly so close as it had been with Saint-Antoine or would become with Frédéric Moreau. It is true that, on summer days, he worked in the arbor where he stages trysts between Emma and Rodolphe; that the cigar-case, the seal inscribed *Amor nel cor,*[28] and other relics actually commemorate his own affair with Louise Colet; that Louise may well have suggested aspects of Emma, and Emma's lovers and husband may have embodied aspects of Gustave. But the very first premise of the book was the suppression of his own personality,[29] and his later pronouncements adhere with stiffening conviction to the principle of *ne s'écrire.* Empathy is seasoned with antipathy whenever he writes about Emma to Louise; he repeatedly complains that the bourgeois vulgarity of his material disgusts and nauseates him.[30] He would much prefer to write a book without a subject; or rather, he would like to abolish the transitions and obstacles between thought and expression; and he prophesies that literary convention, like the Marxian concept of the state, will some day wither away.[31]

Flaubert had chosen the legend of *La Tentation de saint Antoine* in accordance with his personal predilections. Baudelaire, who preferred the more imaginative work, explained *Madame Bovary* as a sort of wager. "The budding novelist found himself facing an absolutely worn-out society—worse than worn-out, brutal and greedy, fearing nothing but fiction and loving nothing but property."[32] Deliberately choosing the drabbest setting, the pettiest characters, the most familiar plot, he undertook to create a masterpiece out of them, to turn their shapeless ugliness into formal beauty. He did not quite succeed in assimilating the psychology of his heroine, in the opinion of Baudelaire: "Madame Bovary has remained a man." Now it may be—in fact, it would be Dorothy Richardson's hypothesis—that no masculine novelist can ever quite penetrate the feminine mentality. Nevertheless, as Matthew Arnold perceived, Tolstoy's portrayal of Anna Karenina could be more warmly sympathetic than the "petrified feeling" that went into Flaubert's portraiture.[33] Insofar as he attached his narration to his heroine, Flaubert was detaching himself from those whom she repudiated and from those who repudiated her. Thereby he ostensibly gave up, to the indignation of his critics, the moralistic prerogatives of the narrator. He replaced sentiment, so Brunetière charged, with sensation.[34] He developed the technical device that handbooks term point of view by adapting the rhythms of his style to the movement of his character's thoughts. By limiting what has more precisely been termed the center of consciousness to the orbit of a single character—and, with Henry James, a peculiarly limited character—purists could intensify the focus of the novel still further. Nonetheless **Madame Bovary** begins, as if with a prologue, in the first person; then it switches from an anonymous classmate, of whom we learn no more than that, to Charles Bovary; through Charles's eyes we first glimpse Emma's fingernails, and gradually experience his delayed reaction; thereafter the action is mainly, though by no means exclusively, circumscribed within her range of perception.[35] But toward the end the perspective opens up and detaches itself from Emma more and more; her pantomime interview with the tax-collector is reported as witnessed by a chorus of townswomen; and Flaubert's account of her funeral terminates with the various night-thoughts of the men who have loved her.

And there are such moments as when, having escorted his lovers into a curtained cab, Flaubert draws back a tactful distance and projects a rapid sequence of long-range shots, so that—instead of witnessing their embrace—we participate in a tour of the city of Rouen, prolonged and accelerated to a metaphorical climax. The invisible omnipresence that stage-manages these arrangements is normally expressed by *on,* initially by *nous,* but never by *je.* The author's commentary is to be inferred from his almost cinematographic manipulation of detail: the close-up of a religious statuette, for example, which falls from the moving-wagon into fragments on the road between Tostes and Yonville. Such comment is transposed to a scientific key when, after the unsuccessful operation, Emma slams the door on Charles and breaks his barometer. Henceforth the incongruous memento of his failure is the patent-leather shoe affixed to the artificial limb of his patient, the no longer clubfooted stableboy. A silly cap which characterizes Charles on his first appearance, a pocket-knife which betokens his coarseness in Emma's eyes—nothing is mentioned that does not help to carry the total burden of significance. Hence every object becomes, in its way, a symbol; the novelist seeks the right thing, as well as the right word; and things are attributes which define their owners, properties which expedite the stage-business.[36] Charles's first marriage is tellingly summed up by a bouquet of withered orange blossoms in a glass jar, while a handsome cigar-case retains the aroma of fashionable masculinity that Emma has inhaled at the ball. Such effects are governed by a rigorous process of selection, far removed from the all-inclusive collection by which Balzac accumulated background. The atmosphere, for Flaubert, is the story; the province is both his setting and his subject—the colorlessness of local color. The midland that he depicts is a bastard territory, somewhere along the borders of Normandy, Picardy, and Ile-de-France, where the speech has no accent, the landscape no character, the soil no richness.[37] Even the cheese thereabouts is lacking in savor. Everything seems, like Charles's conversation, "as flat as a sidewalk."[38]

To render flatness flatly, however, is to risk the stalemate that confronted Pope when he tried to excoriate dullness without becoming dull. Flaubert, deploying his full stylistic resources, relieves the ennui by colorful allusion and invidious comparison. What is literally boring he renders metaphorically interesting. The river quarter of Rouen, at first sight, is "a small, ignoble Venice."[39] The names of famous surgeons are mock-heroically sounded in connection with Charles's professional activities. Similes, ironically beautiful, frequently serve to underline ugly realities: thus the pimples on the face of his first wife had "budded like a springtime."[40] Occasionally Flaubert seems to set thousands of miles between himself and the situation at hand, as when—with the anthropological objectivity he had shown at his niece's baptism—he notes the similarity between a statue of the Virgin in the village church and an idol from the Sandwich Islands.[41] The gap between the heroine and her chronicler opens wide with a Shakespearean simile, linking her amorous intoxication to the butt of Malmsey in which the Duke of Clarence was drowned.[42] Despite Flaubert's more usual closeness to his dramatis personae, he austerely dissociates himself from their subjective opinions, and italicizes certain expressions which their lack of fastidiousness has forced him to cite. He manages to approximate their points of view, while retaining the detachment of the third person and avoiding the formality of indirect discourse, through his mastery of *le style indirect libre.*[43] Though this term seems to have no English equivalent, it denotes the kind of grammatical figuration, the modulation of tenses, the dropping of pronominal antecedents, and the resulting internalization of narrative which, thanks primarily to Flaubert, are now employed in most of our novels and short stories.

> She gave up music. Why play? Who would listen?[44]
>
> * * *
>
> What sunny days they had had! What fine afternoons, alone in the shade at the depth of the garden![45]
>
> * * *
>
> Never before had he come across such grace of speech, such good taste in attire, such supple, dovelike poses. He admired the exaltation of her spirit and the lace of her petticoat.[46]

Through the first two quotations we catch the lilt of Emma's internal monologue. In the third, for a sentence, the voice of Léon echoes the naïveté of her previous responses to Rodolphe, and then yields to the voice of Flaubert, with a clear-cut dissociation which makes manifest Léon's confusion. Meaningful juxtaposition is Flaubert's signature, where Balzac's was miscellaneous accretion. Where Balzac's descriptions were like introductory stage-directions, Flaubert introduces objects as they swim into the ken of his personages. His personages, since they are the fluid receptacles of sense-impressions, are much less numerous than the sharply moulded types from the Balzacian mint. In the English novelist's sense, says Elizabeth Bowen, Emma is not a character at all: "She consists in sentiments and sensations, in moments for their own sake."[47] Flaubert's technique of characterization, as he formulated it to Taine, was "not to individualize a generality, like Hugo or Schiller, but to generalize a particularity, like Goethe or Shakespeare."[48]

He forwarded this large intention by deciding to portray a particular individual who also happened to be a universal type—who, as he put it, suffered and wept in twenty French villages.[49] She had actually existed in the ill-fated Madame Delamare;[50] and, as Zola remarked, her sisters went on existing throughout France.[51] Even while Flaubert was writing his novel, her misadventures were being enacted by the wife of his friend, the sculptor Pradier; and some of Louise Pradier's confidences became Emma Bovary's indiscretions.[52] Strangely enough, the latter's fate was to be paralleled by that of the novel's first English translator, Karl Marx's daughter, Eleanor Marx-Aveling. American readers recognize Emma's kinship with Carol Kennicott, the capricious wife of Sinclair Lewis' country doctor in *Main Street,* and are struck by recurring features of small-town subsistence which abridge the spatial and temporal intervals between Gopher Prairie and Yonville-l'Abbaye. Flaubert's preoccupation with his heroine's environment is emphasized by his subtitle, **Moeurs de province**—how far a cry from the sympathetic overview that subtitles *Middlemarch, A Study of Provincial Life!*

His social observation, which of course is more precise and analytic than Balzac's, concentrates upon a much smaller terrain and thoroughly exhausts it. His fiction starts from, and returns to, fact; when in a newspaper he came across the very phrase that he had put into his imaginary orator's mouth, he congratulated himself that literature was being reduced to an exact science at last.[53] When **Madame Bovary** appeared, it was saluted by the magazine *Réalisme* as "a literary application of the calculus of probabilities."[54] Though that is a far cry from any classical doctrine of probability, it looks beyond mere particularizing toward some meaningful pattern into which all the particulars must fit, a result which is predictable from the data, the logical deductions that follow from an idea. The concrete details that Flaubert selects, we have noticed, are always typical and often symbolic. We notice too his tendency to multiply the specific instance into a generalization. In his treatment of crowds, at the wedding or the exhibition, traits which were individually observed are collectively stated. Similarly, the plural is applied to immediate experiences which have become habitual, as in this summary of the doctor's routine:

> He ate omelets on farmhouse tables, poked his arm into damp beds, felt the warm spurts of blood-letting in his face, listened for death-rattles, examined basins, turned over a good deal of dirty linen; but every evening he found a blazing fire, a laid-out table, comfortable chairs, and a well-dressed wife, so charming and sweet-smelling that it was hard to say whence the odor came, or whether her skin were not perfuming her chemise.[55]

The second half of this highly Flaubertian sentence brings us home to Emma, balances the attractions of her day against the revulsions of Charles's, and registers the incompatibility of their respective ways of life. A sequence of vividly physical manifestations, ranging through the clinical toward the sensual, unfolds itself for us just as it did for Charles. Strain is compensated by relaxation; pain and suffering give place to comfort and well-being; but, contrasted with the grim concreteness of his own sensations and the tangible solidity of his cases, there is something elusive and possibly deceptive in the person of Emma, which is vaguely hinted by her ambiguous perfume. More commonly we see the uxorious husband, from her vantage-point, as the thick-skinned personification of plodding mediocrity: the medical man well suited to the village of Tostes, whose competence is strained by the town of Yonville. From his earliest entrance into the schoolroom, he falters between the comic and the pathetic; his solitary youth and loveless first marriage prepare him for the ungrateful role of the cuckold; on his visit to the chateau he seems indeed to be playing the bourgeois gentleman. His very schoolmates have found him too unromantic, yet his love is the most devoted that Emma finds—as Flaubert expressly states in his work-sheets, adding: "This must be made very clear."[56] His own devotion to his motherless niece is doubtless reflected in Charles's tenderness toward his daughter, Berthe. In the final retrospect—the analogue of that weary reunion which rounds out *L'Education sentimentale*—Charles, over a bottle of beer with his wife's lover, Rodolphe, forgives him and blames the whole affair on "fatality."[57] Rodolphe, though he has blamed fatality in his farewell letter to Emma,[58] was scarcely a fatalist when he took the initiative; while Emma has enjoyed, as long as it lasted, the poetic illusion of liberty. Now that it has yielded to necessity, and the probable has become the inevitable, Charles is left to bear—and it kills him—the unpoetic truth.

The issue is poised between his materialistic plane, which is vulgar but real, and her ideal of refinement, which is illusory. "Charles' conjugal night: plans for his career. his child. Emma: dreams of travel. the lover. villa on the shore. until dawn . . ."[59] This bare notation was expanded by Flaubert into two of his most luminous pages—pages which reveal not only the nocturnal reveries of the doctor and his wife, her Italianate fancies and his Norman calculations, but the conflict within Flaubert's dual personality between lyricism and criticism—or, to use his synonym for the latter, "anatomy." To anatomize Emma's imagination is succinctly to recapitulate the romantic movement itself, moving from the primitive idyll of *Paul et Virginie* through the polychromatic mysticism of Chateaubriand's *Génie du Christianisme* toward the vicarious passions of George Sand and Balzac. Emma's sentimental education, accompanied by the excitations of music and perfumed by the incense of religiosity, is traced back to the convent where she has been schooled. From the drab milieu she has known as a farmer's daughter, her extracurricular reading conjures up the allurements of escape: steeds and guitars, balconies and fountains, medieval and Oriental vistas. Dreaming between the lines, she loses her identity in the heroines of the novels she peruses, the mistresses to whom verses are inscribed, the models in the fashion magazines. The ball at the Château de Vaubyessard lends a touch of reality to her fictious world, which Flaubert likened—in a discarded metaphor—to "a drop of wine in a glass of water."[60] When she discovers a kindred soul in the young law-clerk Léon, the only person in the community who seems comparably sensitive to boredom and yearning and the arts, their friendship is "a continual traffic in books and romances."[61] And when a neighboring landowner, the sportsman-philanderer Rodolphe, assists her to fulfill her sexual desires, fantasy and actuality seem to merge in the realization: "I have a lover!"[62]

But adultery ends by reasserting "the platitudes of marriage,"[63] and neither condition teaches Emma the meaning of "the words that looked so fine in books: 'felicity,' 'passion,' and 'intoxication.'"[64] Here, more explicitly than in *Don Quixote* itself, language is of the essence; the basic misunderstanding, since it is verbal, is regulated by the flow and ebb of Flaubert's prose; and his rhetoric is constantly expanding into purple passages which are trenchantly deflated by his irony. The ensuing style, he feared, might read like "Balzac chateaubrianisé."[65] Yet if that compound means eloquent banality rather than banal eloquence, it is not too inept a summation of what Flaubert attempted and achieved; and those literary auspices are not inappropriate for the incongruity between Emma's high-flown sentiments and Charles's pedestrian bumblings. If we ever forgot that the book was about an ill-matched pair, we should be reminded by the way that sentences double back upon themselves and episodes are paired off against one another. The two turning-points of the first part, the fourth and eighth chapters, frame a significant contrast between the peasantry and the aristocracy. The garish colors of the rustic wedding, the raw haircuts of the farmers, the lengthened communion-dresses of the girls, the boisterous jokes and substantial viands in the manner of Brueghel, are pointedly offset by the grand entertainment at the chateau, where the stately dancers display "the complexion of wealth, that fair complexion which is enhanced by the pallor of porcelain, the shimmer of satin, the veneer of fine furniture."[66] In the second part a similar pairing occurs, which even more fatally brings out the variance between Charles and Emma: the operation versus the opera. On the one hand his surgical incompetence, the gangrenescent cripple, and the amputated foot are portents of Emma's relapse. On the other the romantic libretto from Scott, *Lucia di Lammermoor,* the swaggering tenor Lagardy as Edgar, and the coruscating spectacle would corrupt purer souls than hers; we may recall Natasha in *War and Peace.* Overwhelmed by "Edgar Lagardy,"[67] Emma becomes, in effect, Lucia Bovary.

The two antithetical strains are juxtaposed in the central chapters of the book, where the agricultural exhibition takes place in the public square while Rodolphe flirts with Emma in the privacy of the deserted neo-Greek town hall. His amorous pleas are counterpointed by the bureaucratic platitudes of the political orators outside; a prize for the highest quality of manure is awarded at the delicate moment when he grasps her hand; the bifurcation is so thoroughgoing that the National Guard and the fire brigade refuse to march together; and the series of anticlimaxes culminates when nightfall brings a fizzle of dampened fireworks. Now Flaubert built up this scene by writing out continuous speeches for both sets of characters, which he thereupon broke down and rearranged within the larger framework of the situation.[68] By such means he caught that interplay of cross-purposes which is increasingly stressed through the third and last part, above all in the cathedral and at the deathbed. He told Louise Colet that the method of *Madame Bovary* would be biographical rather than dramatic,[69] yet biography seems to branch out into drama at all the crucial stages of Emma's career; and these, in turn, furnish the novel with its six or eight major scenes—several of which are overtly theatrical or, at any rate, ceremonial. Their relation to the rest of the book, and to his ambivalent purpose, may be gathered from his further remark that "dialogue should be written in the style of comedy, narrative in the style of epic."[70] Mock-epic would probably be a more accurate classification of Flaubert's tone, as differentiated from the various inflections he reproduces, and softened by lyrical interludes when he is Emma. The many contrasting strands of discourse are so closely interwoven that the texture is uniformly rich, although it varies from one chapter to the next. Each of them advances the narrative a single step, scores a new point and captures another mood, much as a well-turned short story does in the hands of Flaubert's innumerable emulators.

The chapter, as Flaubert utilizes it, is in itself a distinctive literary genre. Its opening is ordinarily a straightforward designation of time or place. Its conclusion habitually imposes some striking effect: a pertinent image, an epigrammatic twist, a rhetorical question, a poignant afterthought. "She had loved him after all."[71] The succession of episodes, like the articulation of a rosary, shapes the continuity of the work. The three-part structure allows the novelist, with a classicism seldom encountered in novels, to give his conception a beginning, a middle, and an end: to study first the conditions of Emma's marriage, then her Platonic romance and her carnal affair, and finally the train of consequences that leads to her death. Different leading men play opposite her, so to speak, in these three successive parts: Charles in the first, Rodolphe in the second, Léon in the third. The setting broadens with her aspirations, starting from the narrowest horizon, Tostes, proceeding to the main locale, Yonville, and ultimately reaching the provincial capital, Rouen. Not that she wished to stop there. "She wanted simultaneously to die and to live in Paris,"[72] Flaubert apprises us in a characteristic zeugma, and he seems to have toyed with the notion of granting her that double-barreled wish. But he wisely decided to confine her to the province, reserving his study of the metropolis for the fortunes of Frédéric Moreau. The chronology of *Madame Bovary,* which spans the decade from 1837 to 1847, roughly corresponds with the period of *L'Education sentimentale,* stopping just short of the mid-century crisis. Each of its subdivisions, conforming to a rough but Dantesque symmetry, covers slightly more than three years. The crucial season would seem to be the autumn of 1843, when Rodolphe fails to elope with Emma and she is plunged into brain fever. Up to that stage, with manic fervor, her illusions mount; after that, with steady disillusionment, she sinks toward her last depression. The dating coincides, more or less, with Flaubert's failure to pass his examinations, and with the neurotic crisis of his personal career.

Between the autumn of 1851 and the spring of 1856 his concentrated labor was the writing of *Madame Bovary.* For those who hold—with André Gide—that the gestation of art is more interesting than the finished product, no record could be more fascinating than Flaubert's correspondence during those four years and a half. The parallel lives of the author and the heroine, daily, weekly, monthly, yearly, charge the novel with their emotional tension. Imaginative effort was reinforced by documentation when Flaubert sought the proper shading for Emma's hallucinations by immersing himself in *Keepsakes* and other feminine periodicals.[73] By plying his brother with queries about surgery and toxicology, he filled in the peculiar symptoms his outline required: "Agony precise medical details 'on the morning of the twenty-third she had vomiting spells again . . .'"[74] He familiarized himself with the children of his brain by drawing a map of Yonville and keeping files on its citizens.[75] He controlled his plot—or should we say he calculated his probabilities?—by carefully drafting and firmly reworking scenarios. The embryonic material for his novel comprised some 3600 pages of manuscript.[76] The demiurgic function of reducing that mass to its present form might be compared to the cutting of a film; and, rather than speak of Flaubert's "composition" in the pictorial sense, we might refer, in kinetic terms, to montage. To watch him arranging his artful juxtapositions, or highlighting one detail and discarding another, is a lesson in artistic economy. To trace his revision of a single passage, sometimes through as many as twelve versions, is the hopeful stylist's *gradus ad Parnassum.* It is therefore a boon to students of literature that Flaubert's drafts and variants have been gathered and printed. But to reincorporate them into a composite text of *Madame Bovary,* interpolating what he excised, reamplifying what he condensed, and thereby undoing much of what he so purposefully did—as has been done in the so-called *Nouvelle version*—is a doubtful service to his intentions. Flaubert might have preferred Bowdlerization.

He did protest against expurgations when the novel was serially published in the *Revue de Paris*; but Du Camp and his editors had not expurgated enough to appease the prudery of the imperial police; and Flaubert, together with the publisher and the printer, was prosecuted for outraging civic and religious morality. The outrage, so the prosecution alleged, was worse than pornography; it was blasphemy.[77] Flaubert's offense was less a concern with sex than an attempt to link sex with religion. It mattered little that the linkage had been effected on the naïve level of Emma's confused motivation, or that his analysis could be corroborated, by such sympathetic clerics as Bishop Dupanloup,[78] from their first-hand remembrance of country confessionals. The ruse of citing passages out of context figured heavily in the trial, and the government staked much of its case on the passage where Emma receives extreme unction. It was a precarious example, since by definition that sacrament hovers ambiguously between the worlds of sense and spirit: shift the emphasis, as Joyce does in *Finnegans Wake,*[79] and it becomes an apology for the flesh. Flaubert's defense, by warily refusing to admit the ambiguity, was able to claim the support of orthodox sanctions, along with the precedent of such diverse French writers as Bossuet and Sainte-Beuve. It argued that *Madame Bovary* as a whole, far from tempting its readers to sensualism, offered them an edifying object-lesson. Considerable stress was laid *ad hominem* on the bourgeois respectability of the Flaubert family. Won by such arguments, the judge acquitted Flaubert and his accomplices, with a parting disquisition on taste and a fatherly warning against "a realism which would be the negation of the beautiful and the good."[80] Six months later, when *Les Fleurs du mal* was condemned, Flaubert must have wondered whether he or Baudelaire was the victim of judicial error. Meanwhile, in April 1857, when *Madame Bovary* came out as a book, its intrinsic ironies were enhanced by a preliminary dedication to Flaubert's lawyer and an appended transcript of the court proceedings.

Great books have their proverbial fates, among which banning and burning may not be the hardest, since these involve downright conflicts of principle. It may be harder for the serious artist, be he Flaubert or Joyce, to emerge from the cloud of censorship into the glare of scandalous success. The public reception of Flaubert's first book, at all events, hardened those equivocal attitudes which had been poured into it. To avoid the accusation of immorality, he was pushed into the embarrassing position of a moralist. If the novel was not pornographic, it must be didactic—or had he stopped beating his wife? Taine spins an amusing anecdote of an English project to translate and circulate *Madame Bovary* as a Methodist tract, subtitled *The Consequences of Misbehavior.*[81] The respectable Lamartine, cited on Flaubert's behalf, declared that Emma's sins were too severely expiated.[82] Why need Flaubert have been so much less merciful than Jesus was toward the woman taken in adultery? Partly because he was not exemplifying justice, partly because he may have been punishing himself, but mainly because her infractions of the seventh commandment were the incidental and ineffectual expression of an all-pervasive state of mind: Bovarism. Her nemesis, as Albert Thibaudet shrewdly perceived,[83] is not a love affair but a business matter: her debt to the usurious merchant, Lheureux. When the bailiffs move in to attach the property, their inventory becomes a kind of autopsy. The household disintegrates before our eyes, as its component items are ticked off, and we think of the auction in *L'Education sentimentale.* This empty outcome, by the Flaubertian rule of opposites, is a sequel to the agricultural exhibition, where rural prosperity smugly dispenses its awards. And the lonely figure of Charles, left to brood among unpaid bills and faded love-letters, has been foreshadowed by Père Rouault after Emma's wedding, "as sad as an unfurnished house."[84]

The vacuum her absence creates for her father and husband echoes the hollowness of her own misapplied affections. Rodolphe's gallantry, after meeting her desires halfway, proves to be no more than a cynical technique of seduction. Léon's sentimentalism is quite sincere, until she seduces him, and then it vanishes like growing pains. "Every notary bears within him the ruins of a poet."[85] Consequently, amid the most prosaic circumstances, there will still be some spark of poetry, and in Yonville-l'Abbaye it is Emma Bovary. It is not, alas, the Princesse de Clèves; nor could that model of all the compunctions have flourished there; for her delicacy presupposes reciprocal comportment on the part of others. Emma's dreams are destined, at the touch of reality, to wither into lies. Is that a critique of her or of reality? If she suffers for her mistakes, shall we infer that those who prosper are being rewarded for their merits? If we cannot, we can hardly assume—with the novel's courtroom apologists—that it preaches a self-evident moral. If it were a play, our reactions would be clearer; we are more accustomed to facing her plight in the theater; we disapprove of Hedda Gabler's intrigues and pity the wistful Katerina in Ostrovsky's *Storm.* Though she possesses the qualities of both those heroines, Emma is essentially a novelistic creation, set forth in all her internal complexities. Entrammelled by them, we cannot pretend to judge her, any more than we can judge ourselves. But, guided by Flaubert, perhaps we can understand her: *Madame Bovary c'est nous.* With her we look down from the town hall upon the exposition, a sordid rustic backdrop for Rodolphe's welcome advances. Again, at her rendezvous with Léon, the lovers occupy the foreground; but this time it is the massive cathedral of Rouen that looks down upon them; and its sculptured warriors and stained-glass saints, too hastily passed by, are the mute upholders of higher standards than those which Emma and Léon are engaged in flouting. "Leave by the north portico, at any rate," the verger shouts after them, baffled by their indifference to Gothic antiquities, "and see the Resurrection, the Last Judgment, Paradise, King David, and the Condemned in Hellfire!"[86]

The heavy judgment that Flaubert suspends, and which we too withhold, is implicit in this hurried exclamation. It affects the lovers as little as the extinct abbey affects Yonville, in whose name alone it survives. Yet oblique reference accomplishes what overt preaching would not, and those neglected works of art bear an ethical purport. The category of *moraliste,* which is so much more comprehensive with the French than with us, given its condensation of morals and manners, still applied to Flaubert *malgré lui.* Whereas he seemed immoral to those who confused him with his characters, and seems amoral to those who take at face value an aloofness which is his mask for strong emotions, he protested too much when he claimed to be impersonal. If he deserves Maupassant's adjective "impassive,"[87] it is because all passion has crystallized beneath the lucent surfaces of his prose. He is not above making sententious and aphoristic pronouncements upon the behavior of his characters: "A request for money is the most chilling and blighting of all the winds that blow against love."[88] Nor does he shrink from stigmatizing Emma's acts as phases of "corruption"[89] and even "prostitution."[90] More positively he betrays his sympathy, when it seems most needed, by the adjective *pauvre*. The crippled groom is a "poor devil,"[91] and so is the blind man; the luckless Charles is "poor boy,"[92] and the gestures of Emma's agony are made by "her poor hands."[93] The word regains its economic overtones, and Flaubert's tone is uniquely humanitarian, when he pauses before the "poor garments"[94] of Catherine Leroux. The hands of this aged peasant woman, in definitive contrast to Emma, are deformed with toil. On the platform "before those expansive bourgeois," personifying "half a century of servitude," her mute and ascetic presence strikes the single note of genuine dignity amid the pomposities and hypocrisies of the agricultural exhibition. Flaubert deliberately classifies her with the attendant livestock, for whose impassivity he reserves his compassion. His irony intervenes to measure her reward, twenty-five francs for a lifetime of service, against two pigs which have just gained prizes of sixty francs apiece. An earlier and crueller twist, which Flaubert finally left out, pictures her deaf apprehension lest the judges accuse her of stealing the twenty-five francs.[95]

Here is Flaubert's response to those who criticize **Madame Bovary** for its apparent lack of positive values. The human qualities he really admired, the stoic virtues of patience, devotion, work, are not less admirable when they go unrewarded. His careful portrait of Catherine Leroux—together with many landscapes, small and subdued, of his fog-tinted Normandy—belongs with the canvases then being painted by Courbet at Ornans and Millet at Barbizon.[96] Peasant faces, though never conspicuous, are always in the background; they watch Emma through the broken windowpanes of the chateau.[97] Animals, too, are sentient characters: her mysterious greyhound, Djali, is almost a demonic familiar, which has its opposite number in the goat Djala,[98] the mascot of *Notre-Dame de Paris*. The people that Flaubert treats sympathetically are life's victims like the club-footed Hippolyte, those whom Hugo would name *Les Misérables* and Dostoevsky *The Insulted and the Injured*. Surely the kindest person in the story is the druggist's errand-boy, Justin, whose dumb affection is the unwitting instrument of Emma's death, and whose illicit reading-matter is her ironic epitaph: a book entitled *Conjugal Love*.[99] The meek do not inherit Flaubert's earth; the good, by definition, are the ones that suffer; and the unhappy ending, for poor little innocent Berthe,

is grim child-labor in a textile factory. The most downtrodden creature of all, the dog-like Blind Man, is linked by a grotesque affinity with Emma herself. Envisaging him as a "monster,"[100] a *memento mori,* an incarnation of fleshly frailty, Flaubert had originally planned to make him armless and legless rather than visionless; and he pointedly accentuated Emma's disillusion by the swish of the driver's whip that knocks the helpless beggar off the coach. This is coincident with the critical stroke that once laid Flaubert prostrate on a muddy Norman road. His blind man dogs his heroine's missteps to her very deathbed, with a terrible mimicry which is not unworthy of King Lear's fool; and there his unseasonable song, a lyric from Restif de la Bretonne[101] about young girls' dreams of love, finds its long awaited echo of relevance. Emma's eyes open to a recognition scene "like a person waking from a dream,"[102] like Don Quixote when death restores his aberrant sense of reality.

The counterpoint set up in the cathedral attains its fullest resolution—far from the rented room at the Hôtel-de-Boulogne—in Emma's bedchamber. There priestly rites alleviate clinical symptoms; the unction allays the poison; and, taking formal leave of her five senses one by one, Flaubert breaks off his prolonged sequence of associations between sacred and profane love. In so far as orchestration is based on arrangement rather than statement, Flaubert's can best be appreciated by comparing this episode with a remotely analogous one from *The Old Curiosity Shop,* the famous sermon on the reiterated text: "Dear, gentle, patient, noble Nell was dead." Flaubert, who evokes what Dickens invokes and elaborates what the Englishman simplifies, dismisses his heroine more abruptly and absolutely: "She no longer existed."[103] Thereafter Emma's death-watch unites "in the same human weakness"[104] Father Bournisien, with his holy water, and M. Homais, with his bottle of chlorine. Since religion is served by the priest as inadequately as science is by the pharmacist, it is not surprising that neither force has operated benignly on Emma's existence, or that the antagonists—as Bournisien predicts—"may end by understanding one another." Homais, the eternal quacksalver, is a would-be writer as well as a pseudo-scientist, who practises the up-to-date art of journalism and is most adept at self-advertisement. Because his shop is the source of Emma's arsenic, he is an unconscious accomplice in her suicide; and he instigates the ill-advised surgery that poisons Hippolyte's leg and blackens Charles's reputation. When his own prescription, the antiphlogistic pomade, fails to cure the Blind Man's scrofula, it is typical of him to add insult to injury, persecuting his patient while continuing to pose as the benefactor of mankind. M. Homais is definitively shown up by the retarded arrival of Dr. Larivière, just as the introduction of Catherine Leroux is a standing rebuke to Emma's course of conduct. Hereupon, Flaubert, inspired by memories of his father, dedicates a strongly affirmative paragraph to the understanding physician, who pursues the compassionate calling of medicine as religiously as a medieval saint. But the doctor is no god-in-the-machine, and it is too late for an antidote. With a tear he discerns the prognosis at once and with a farewell pun he diagnoses the complaint of Homais. His difficulty is not *le sang* but *le sens*[105]—neither anemia nor hypertension, nor indeed that lack of sense from which poor Emma suffered, but insensibility, the defect of her quality.

What is worse, the disease is contagious. With the rare exception of the stranger Larivière, and the dubious hope of agreement between the cleric and the anticlerical, nobody in Yonville seems to understand anybody else. And though collective misunderstanding is comic, failure to be understood is a personal tragedy. Though Emma, misunderstood by her husband and lovers and neighbors, misunderstands them and herself as well, at least she harbors a feeling of something missed; whereas the distinguishing mark of Homais is the bland assurance that he never misses anything. His Voltairean incantations, his hymns to progress, his faith in railroads and rubber, his fads and statistics, his optimism—a hundred years later—may seem as far-fetched as Emma's delusions of grandeur. His clichés, embedded like fossils in his newspaper articles, Flaubert was momentarily tempted to say, "would enable some future Cuvier of the moral sciences to reconstruct clearly all the ineptitude of the nineteenth-century middle class, if that race were not indestructible."[106] Of that hardy breed M. Homais survives as our prime specimen. Neither a creation nor a discovery, he represents the fine flower of the species that pervaded the *Comédie humaine,* the ripe perfection of the philosophy whose accredited spokesman was M. Prudhomme. This was enthusiastically attested when Prudhomme's creator and actor, Henry Monnier, sought permission to dramatize and enact Homais.[107] The latter is more successful in attaining their common ambition, the decoration of the Legion of Honor; while his predecessor, M. Prudhomme, must content himself, when the curtain falls, with "a decorated son-in-law."[108] The curtain-line of their spiritual relative, that famous father-in-law, M. Poirier,[109] is his resolve to be "peer of France in 'forty-eight," an aspiration which has meanwhile been thwarted by the revolution of that date. But the unabashed Homais goes from strength to strength; the Empire will shower its accolades upon him and his brethren; and the dazzling glimpse of him in his hydroelectric undervest is a virtual apotheosis.

When he equipped his personage with a motto, "Il faut marcher avec son siècle!,"[110] Flaubert may have remembered his newly decorated friend, Maxime Du Camp, whose *Chants modernes* were prefaced by a Whitmanesque declaration: "Tout marche, tout grandit, tout s'augmente autour de nous . . ."[111] Those reverberations stridently blended with the journalistic watchword of Saint-Marc Girardin, "Il faut marcher, marcher toujours . . ."[112] Any endeavor which aims to keep in step with one's century, as Flaubert realized better than most of his contemporaries, is bound to be outdistanced in the long run. He took the province for his ground because it was an available microcosm, because it exaggerated the ordinary, because its dearth of color sharpened its outlines; but he did not assume that provinciality was confined to the hinterland or, for that matter, to any territory. M. Homais is historically, rather than geographically, provincial. The habit of equating one's age with the apogee of civilization, one's town with the hub of the universe, one's horizons with the limits of human awareness, is paradoxically widespread: it is just what Russian novelists were attacking as *poshlost,* or self-satisfied mediocrity. It is what stands between Emma Bovary and the all-too-easily-satisfied citizens of Yonville. Her capacity for dissatisfaction, had she been a man and a genius, might have led to Rimbaldian adventures or Baudelairean visions: "Anywhere out of the world." As things stand, her retribution is a triumph for the community, a vindication of the bourgeoisie. Flaubert, who does not always conceal his tenderness toward those who suffer, not infrequently reveals his bitterness toward those whose kingdom is of this world. We cannot sympathize with the prosperous Homais as we could with Balzac's bankrupt César Birotteau; and, unlike his prototypes on the comic stage, Flaubert's druggist is not just a harmless busybody, a well-meaning figure of fun; he is the formidable embodiment of a deeply satirical perception which was adumbrated in Le Garçon and eventuates in ***Bouvard et Pécuchet.*** His Bovarism would be more illusive than Emma's, if the modern epoch did not conspire to support his bumptious ideology and to repay his flatteries with its honors. His *boutonnière,* like the one conferred on Tolstoy's Russian guardsman, symbolizes more than Napoleon intended—and less. For the symbol is an empty ornament, the badge of society's approval is meaningless, when it goes unsupported by reality.

What, then, is real? Not the mean guerdon awarded to Catherine Leroux, but the lifelong service that earned it so many times over. And what is realism? Not the pathology of Emma's case, but the diagnostic insight of Larivière. Charles Bovary, for all his shortcomings, remains the great doctor's disciple, and retains the peasant virtues of his own patients; he is led astray by other motives than his own, by sentimentalism through Emma and pretentiousness through Homais. As the thrice-injured party, conjugally betrayed, professionally humiliated, financially ruined, Dr. Bovary is the neglected protagonist. If Emma is a victim of the situation, he is her victim, and her revenge against the situation is to undermine his way of life. The depths of his ignominy can be gauged by the idealized achievements of Dr. Benassis in Balzac's *Médecin de campagne.* Flaubert's ideal, though it is more dishonored than observed, fortifies him against those negative values which triumph in his book, and rises to an unwonted pitch of affirmation with the character-sketch of Dr. Larivière: his disinterested skill, his paternal majesty, his kindness to the poor, his scorn for all decorations, his ability to see through falsehood. His most revealing epithet is *hospitalier*,[113] since it connotes not only hospitality but Flaubert's birthplace, his father's hospital at Rouen, and also the stained-glass figure of Saint Julian the Hospitaller, whom the verger of the cathedral pointed out in an earlier draft,[114] and who would later be Flaubert's knightly hero. The hospital and the cathedral: such, in retrospect, are the substance and the form of **Madame Bovary.** The attitude that embraces the distance between them, that comprehends both the painful actualities and the grandiose aspirations, and that can therefore make each paragraph comment dynamically upon itself, is Flaubertian irony. Irony dominates life, so Flaubert asserted by precept and example.[115] So it does, particularly for those who are occupied with art as well as life, and unflinchingly face the problems of their interrelationship. Hence the irony of ironies: a novel which is at once cautionary and exemplary, a warning against other novels and a model for other novelists, the classic demonstration of what literature gives and what literature takes.

Notes

The notes that follow [. . .] simply indicate the bibliographical references in their most compact form. It will be seen that most of the quotations or citations have been directly translated or paraphrased from the original French. The place of publication for books, unless it is stated otherwise, is Paris. The publishers of the editions chiefly used are Le Divan for Stendhal, Conard for Balzac and Flaubert, Fasquelle (Bernouard) for Zola, and Gallimard (Pléiade) for Proust. It has seemed more convenient to cite chapters or section headings rather than pages, in referring to certain standard works which have been frequently and variously reprinted.

1. Anatole France/*La Vie littéraire* (1895), III, 303.

2. some flamboyant cathedral/*Correspondance* [(1926-33)], III, 130.

3. more poetic than illusion/*Ibid.,* I, 163.

4. his artistic origins/*Ibid.,* II, 442.

5. "perpetual fusion of illusion and reality."/*Ibid.,* III, 53.

6. Alphonse Daudet/*Oeuvres complètes* (1930), XII, p. 79.

7. Emile Montégut/*Dramaturges et romanciers* (1890), p. 262; cf. *Correspondance*, VII, 369.

8. Søren Kierkegaard/*Either/Or,* tr. D. F. and L. M. Swenson (Princeton, 1944), I, 210; cf. Maurice

Bardon, "*Don Quixote* et le roman réaliste français," *Revue de littérature comparée* (January, 1936), XVI, 78.

9. Alfred Nettement/*Etudes critiques sur le feuilleton-roman* (1845), I, 355.

10. A prize-winning discourse/Charles Menche de Loisne, *L'Influence de la littérature française de 1830 à 1850 sur l'esprit et les moeurs* (1852), p. 318.

11. "a scene from *Les Mystères de Paris*."/L. W. Wylie, *Saint-Marc Girardin, Bourgeois* (Syracuse, 1947), p. 100.

12. influence of the *roman-feuilleton*/[Pierre] Martino, *Le Roman réaliste* [*Sous le Second empire* (1930)], p. 97.

13. the suicide rate/Louis Proal, *Le Crime et le suicide passionels* (1900), p. 309.

14. Paul Bourget/*Essais de psychologie contemporaine* (1893), I, 148f.

15. denouncing the librarian/*Madame Bovary* (1921), p. 175.

16. original manuscript/*Madame Bovary: nouvelle version,* ed. Jean Pommier and Gabrielle Leleu (1949), pp. 211, 327 [hereafter, *Nouvelle version*].

17. Maxime Du Camp and Louis Bouilhet/Du Camp [*Souvenirs littéraires* (1883)], I, 437.

18. critical midwifery/*Correspondance,* VI, p. 102.

19. ". . . I cried out in pain."/*Madame Bovary,* p. 483.

20. M. Bouvaret/*Voyages,* ed. René Dumesnil (1948), pp. 44, 591; *Correspondance,* VI, p. 107; cf. A. M. Gossez, "Homais et Bovary, hommes politiques," *Mercure de France* (July 16, 1911), XCII, 282.

21. "in the midst of fatality"/*Notes de voyages* (1910), I, 60.

22. Henry James/*French Poets and Novelists* [(London, 1878)], p. 258.

23. contradistinction to Don Quixote/See Helmut Hatzfeld, "*Don Quijote* und *Madame Bovary*," *Idealistische Philologie* (April, 1927), III, 55ff.

24. Jules de Gaultier/*Le Bovarysme* (1902), p. 13; cf. Dr. Genil Perrin and Madeleine Lebreuil, "Don Quichotte paranoiaque et le bovarysme de don Quichotte," *Mercure de France* (September 15, 1935), CCLXII, 45ff.

25. Denis de Rougemont/*L'Amour et l'occident* (1939).

26. "He reread *René* . . ."/*Oeuvres de jeunesse [inédites* (1910)], III, 143.

27. *Madame Bovary c'est moi*/René Dumesnil, *La Vocation de Flaubert* (1961), pp. 222ff.

28. *Amor nel cor*/*Madame Bovary*, p. 264.

29. suppression of his own personality/*Correspondance*, IV, 164; II, 361.

30. the bourgeois vulgarity of his material/*Ibid.*, III, 276, 339.

31. will some day wither away/*Ibid.*, II, 345.

32. [Charles] Baudelaire/*Oeuvres*, [ed. Y. G. Le Dantec (1935),] II, 444.

33. Matthew Arnold/*Essays in Criticism* (London, 1896), II, 276.

34. [Ferdinand] Brunetière/*Le Roman naturaliste* [(1883)], p. 156.

35. her range of perception/See B. F. Bart, "Aesthetic Distance in *Madame Bovary*," *PMLA* (December, 1954), LXIX, 1112ff.

36. things are attributes/See H. A. Stein, *Die Gegenstandswelt im Werke Flauberts* (Blescherode-am-Harz, 1938), pp. 68, 32.

37. the soil no richness/*Madame Bovary*, p. 96.

38. "as flat as a sidewalk."/*Ibid.*, p. 57.

39. "a small, ignoble Venice."/*Ibid.*, p. 11.

40. "budded like a springtime."/*Ibid.*, p. 13.

41. the Sandwich Islands/*Ibid.*, p. 98.

42. the butt of Malmsey/*Ibid.*, p. 266.

43. *le style indirect libre*/See Marguérite Lips, *Le Style indirect libre* (Geneva, 1926), p. 186.

44. "She gave up music . . ."/*Madame Bovary*, p. 88.

45. "What sunny days they had had!"/*Ibid.*, p. 172.

46. "Never before . . ."/*Ibid.*, p. 367.

47. Elizabeth Bowen/*Collected Impressions* (London, 1950), p. 25.

48. technique of characterization/*H. A. Taine: sa vie et sa correspondance* (1904), II, 232.

49. twenty French villages/*Correspondance*, III, 291.

50. Madame Delamare/See René Herval, *Les Véritables Origines de "Madame Bovary"* (1957); René Vérard, *Epilogue de "L'Affaire Bovary": La Victoire de Ry* (Rouen, 1959).

51. [Emile] Zola/*Romanciers naturalistes* [(1925)], p. 119.

52. Louise Pradier's confidences/See Gabrielle Leleu and Jean Pommier, "Du nouveau sur *Madame Bovary*," *Revue d'histoire littéraire de la France* (July-September, 1947), XLVII, 216ff; cf. René Dumesnil, "La véritable Madame Bovary," *Mercure de France* (November 1, 1948), CCCIV, 431ff.

53. an exact science/*Ibid.*, III, 285.

54. *Réalisme*/Martino, *Le Roman réaliste*, p. 93.

55. "He ate omelets . . ."/*Madame Bovary*, p. 84.

56. "This must be made very clear."/*Nouvelle version*, p. 84.

57. "fatality."/*Madame Bovary*, p. 480.

58. farewell letter to Emma/*Ibid.*, p. 281.

59. "Charles' conjugal night . . ."/*Nouvelle version*, p. 94.

60. "a drop of wine . . ."/*Ibid.*, p. 224.

61. "a continual traffic . . ."/*Madame Bovary*, p. 137.

62. "I have a lover!"/*Ibid.*, p. 225.

63. "the platitudes of marriage"/*Ibid.*, p. 401.

64. "the words that looked so fine . . ."/*Ibid.*, p. 47.

65. "Balzac chateaubrianisé."/*Correspondance*, II, 316.

66. "the complexion of wealth . . ."/*Madame Bovary*, p. 71.

67. "Edgar Lagardy,"/See Léon Bopp, *Commentaire sur Madame Bovary* (Neuchâtel, 1951), p. 348.

68. . . . both sets of characters/*Madame Bovary: ébauches et fragments inédits*, ed. Gabrielle Leleu (1936), I, 562ff.

69. biographical rather than dramatic/*Correspondance*, III, 247.

70. "dialogue should be written . . ."/*Ibid.*, III, 359.

71. "She had loved him after all."/*Madame Bovary*, p. 26.

72. "She wanted simultaneously . . ."/*Ibid.*, p. 84.

73. *Keepsakes*/*Nouvelle version*, p. 43.

74. "Agony precise medical details . . ."/*Ibid.*, p. 32.

75. a map of Yonville/See Ernest Bovet, "Le Réalisme de Flaubert," *Revue d'histoire littéraire de la France* (January-March, 1911), XVIII, 14.

76. some 3600 pages of manuscript/*Nouvelle version*, p. v.

77. worse than pornography/*Madame Bovary*, p. 562; cf. Alexander Zévaès, *Les Procès littéraires au dix-neuvième siècle* (1924), pp. 71ff.

78. Bishop Dupanloup/Goncourt, *Journal* [(1888)], II, 1089.

79. Joyce/*Finnegans Wake* (New York, 1939), p. 349.

80. "a realism which would be the negation . . ."/*Madame Bovary*, p. 629.

81. Taine/*Vie et opinions de M. Fréderic-Thomas Graindorge* (1870), p. 185.

82. Lamartine/*Madame Bovary*, p. 587.

83. Albert Thibaudet/*Gustave Flaubert* [(1935)], p. 96.

84. "as sad as an unfurnished house."/*Madame Bovary*, p. 42.

85. "Every notary . . ."/*Ibid.*, p. 401.

86. "Leave by the north portico . . ."/*Ibid.*, p. 336.

87. "impassive,"/*Ibid.*, p. 542.

88. "A request for money . . ."/*Ibid.*, p. 429.

89. "corruption"/*Ibid.*, p. 384.

90. "prostitution."/*Ibid.*, p. 425.

91. "poor devil,"/*Ibid.*, p. 250, 369.

92. "poor boy,"/*Ibid.*, p. 291.

93. "her poor hands."/*Ibid.*, p. 446.

94. "poor garments"/*Ibid.*, pp. 208ff.

95. stealing the twenty-five francs/*Nouvelle version*, p. 367.

96. Courbet/See Louis Hourticq, *La Vie des images* (1927), p. 211; H. A. Hatzfeld, *Literature through Art* (New York, 1952), pp. 167ff.

97. the broken window-panes of the chateau/*Madame Bovary*, p. 72.

98. the goat Djala/See L. P. Shanks, *Flaubert's Youth* (Baltimore, 1927), p. 43.

99. *Conjugal Love*/Madame Bovary, p. 344.

100. "monster,"/*Nouvelle version*, p. xxx.

101. Restif de la Bretonne/*Ibid.*, p. 124.

102. "like a person waking from a dream,"/*Madame Bovary*, p. 447.

103. "She no longer existed."/*Ibid.*, p. 449.

104. "in the same human weakness"/*Ibid.*, pp. 458, 460.

105. not *le sang* but *le sens*/*Ibid.*, p. 445.

106. some future Cuvier/[*Madame Bovary*:] *Ebauches et fragments inédits,* II, 576.

107. Henry Monnier/[René] Dumesnil, *Gustave Flaubert* [: *son hérédité, son milieu, sa méthode* (1905)], p. 233.

108. "a decorated son-in-law."/*Nouvelle version*, p. 111n.

109. M. Poirier/Emile Augier et Jules Sandeau, *Le Gendre de Monsieur Poirier* [(1864)], IV, iv.

110. "Il faut marcher avec son siècle!"/*Madame Bovary*, p. 102.

111. Maxime Du Camp/See E. M. Grant, *French Poetry and Modern Industry* (Cambridge, Mass., 1927), p. 86.

112. journalistic watchword/Wylie, *Saint-Marc Girardin*, p. 154.

113. *hospitalier*/Madame Bovary, p. 441.

114. an earlier draft/*Nouvelle version*, p. 497.

115. Irony dominates life/*Correspondance*, II, 407.

John Hagan (essay date spring 1969)

SOURCE: Hagan, John. "Une Ruse de Style: A Pattern of Allusion in *Madame Bovary*." *Studies in the Novel* 1, no. 1 (spring 1969): 6-16.

[*In the following essay, Hagan assesses the influence of Dante's* Inferno *on the style and structure of* Madame Bovary. *Hagan argues that the character of the Blind Beggar serves as a symbol of eternal damnation in Flaubert's novel.*]

So much recent critical attention has been directed to the structural correspondences, "counterpoint," leitmotifs, and symbolic patterns of *Madame Bovary* that we have been able to see more clearly than ever before how completely it anticipated some of the most important novelistic "innovations" of the early twentieth century.[1] The remarkably close kinship between these techniques of Flaubert's masterpiece and those, for example, of Joyce's *Portrait of the Artist* is now patent. The danger, obviously, of pursuing this line of investigation is that it can easily result in an ever more humorless search for tenuous and arbitrary subtleties of form which will gradually warp the book out of recognition. But at the risk of falling into this very trap, I should like to suggest that there is still one highly important complex of motifs in the novel whose nature and significance have apparently been overlooked. To understand it will, among other things, provide a key to the meaning of the famous Blind Beggar of Part III, who has been so often praised or condemned by Flaubert's commentators, but so rarely interpreted. A number of the ingredients of this complex, or the passages in which they appear, have been extensively noticed before, of course, but always in isolation, never as part of a larger design. It is this design which must be made clear.

A favorite critical exhibit has always been the black and white "papillons" (appearing respectively at the very end of Part I and near the beginning of Part III) to which Flaubert ironically compares the charred paper petals of Emma's wedding bouquet and the scraps of her letter of refusal to Léon. Georges Poulet has also explored at length what he calls the "circular character of Flaubert's representation of reality,"[2] and has cited as a conspicuous example of this another well-known passage—that near the end of Part I, chapter 7, in which Emma's straying thoughts are compared to the circular movements of her greyhound running about the fields. But no critic seems to have shown either how Flaubert brings the butterfly and the circle motifs into conjunction, or how he unites both with still a third motif, that of the wind.[3] Only when we see the butterfly, circle, and wind images as part of a single system of references can Flaubert's full symbolic intent be grasped. Poulet is certainly right in maintaining that Flaubert's use of circles is sometimes a way of suggesting Emma's sense of her constricted existence,[4] and he may even be right in maintaining that it "is a new way of presenting the relations between the mind and all surrounding reality," so that "human consciousness shows itself as it is, as a sort of core, around which sensations, thoughts and memories move in a perceptible space," expanding or contracting according to circumstance.[5] But the moment we place the circle imagery in relation to that of the butterflies and the wind—as Flaubert himself does—we become aware of still another dimension of meaning, which depends not on any correspondence between circular movement and the presumed operations of consciousness, but on the kind of submerged literary allusion we have come to expect in modern fiction and poetry.

In analyzing Flaubert's description of Emma's greyhound, Poulet actually obscures the image relations I have mentioned by quoting from only one of the novel's early drafts: "Her thoughts, aimless at first, were wandering at random, like the handsome greyhound who, unleashed, was running round and round in the field, chasing a rat in a furrow, or bringing himself to a stop in order to nibble the poppies."[6] The final version of this passage is strikingly different: Flaubert not only somewhat compresses it, but he introduces the motif of the butterflies for the first time, and in such a way as to link it very closely with that of the circle: "Sa pensée, sans but d'abord, vagabondait au hasard, comme sa levrette, qui faisait des cercles dans la campagne, jappait après les papillons jaunes, donnait la chasse aux

musaraignes ou mordillait les coquelicots sur le bord d'une pièce de blé."[7]

Only a few paragraphs later the initial statement of the thematic pattern is then completed by the introduction of the wind motif. Flaubert tells us that on some of these occasions when Emma and her dog wandered outside the village

> il arrivait . . . des rafales de vent, brises de la mer qui, roulant d'un bond sur tout le plateau du pays de Caux, apportaient, jusqu'au loin dans les champs, une fraîcheur salée. Les joncs sifflaient à ras de terre, et les feuilles de hêtres bruissaient en un frisson rapide, tandis que les cimes, se balançant toujours, continuaient leur grand murmure. Emma serrait son châle contre ses épaules et se levait . . . une peur la prenait, elle appelait Djali [the dog], s'en retournait vite à Tostes par la grande route, s'affaissait dans un fauteuil, et de toute la soirée ne parlait pas.
>
> (p. 63)

No doubt the main reason Emma is terrified on occasions like this is that the wind mirrors her unconscious impulse to rebel—an impulse which can manifest itself at this point only to the extent of impelling her along the highway out of the constricting town. But if we watch its development in conjunction with the other two images, the wind will acquire an even broader and richer connotation.

It is brought into association next, we observe, with the circle during the ball at Vaubyessard in Part I, chapter 8. First, the circle alone is used to describe the movements of Emma and the vicomte during the momentous waltz, whose memory will become a key factor in her subsequent corruption:

> Ils commencèrent lentement, puis allèrent plus vite. Ils tournaient: tout tournait autour d'eux, les lampes, les meubles, les lambris, et le parquet, comme un disque sur un pivot . . . d'un mouvement plus rapide, le vicomte, l'entraînant, disparut avec elle jusqu'au bout de la galerie, où, haletante, elle faillit tomber, et, un instant, s'appuya la tête sur sa poitrine. Et puis, tournant toujours, mais plus doucement, il la reconduisit à sa place . . .
>
> (pp. 73-74)

Even here there is a suggestion of the wind in the dancers' intoxicated "whirling," but metaphor becomes fact only a few paragraphs later, when Emma, having retired with Charles to their bedroom in the chateau, leans out the window, and while the music of the waltz "bourdonnait encore ses oreilles," breathes "le vent humide qui lui rafraîchissait les paupières" (p. 74).

With the famous passage on the burning of the wedding bouquet at the end of chapter 9 there is a reappearance of the butterfly motif: "les corolles de papier, racornies, se balançant le long de la plaque comme des papillons noirs, enfin s'envolerènt par la cheminée" (p. 94). The wind also is implied here, but its next explicit appearance is again in connection with the circle. As Emma listens to Rodolphe's lovemaking and watches the Agricultural Fair from the window of the town hall in Part II, chapter 8, she remembers the ball which took place in the corresponding chapter of Part I, and her mind becomes momentarily confused:

> il lui sembla qu'elle tournait encore dans la valse, sous le feu des lustres, au bras du vicomte, et que Léon n'était pas loin, qu'll allait venir . . . et cependant elle sentait toujours la tete de Rodolphe à côté d'elle. La douceur de cette sensation pénétrait ainsi ses désirs d'autrefois, et comme des grains de sable sous un coup de vent, ils tourbillonnaient dans la bouffée subtile du parfum qui répandait sur son âme.
>
> (p. 204)

Then, only a few moments later, at the very instant Rodolphe's passionate declarations are reaching a climax, the wind is reunited with the butterfly motif, and the permutations of the images are thus mathematically completed:

> "Oh! merci! Vous ne me repoussez pas! Vous êtes bonne! Vous comprenez que je suis à vous! Laissez que je vous voie, que je vous contemple!"
>
> Un coup de vent qui arriva par les fenêtres fronça le tapis de la table, et, sur la place, en bas, tous les grands bonnets des paysanes se soulevèrent, comme des ailes de papillons blancs qui s'agitent.
>
> (p. 207)

If we look closely at the context of all of these passages, we will see that they have been meticulously associated by Flaubert with each of the three main phases of Emma's emotional life which have developed up to this point: the emergence of her marital discontent, the frustration caused by the temporary loss of Léon, and the beginning of her passion for Rodolphe. This pattern continues to the end. Appearing either separately or linked, the wind, butterfly, and circle motifs consistently chart the tragic remainder of Emma's career of adultery. When she dashes across the meadows in the first flush of her passion for her early-morning rendezvous in Rodolphe's chateau, for example, "son foulard, noué sur sa tête, s'agitait au vent dans les herbages . . ." (p. 227). When she suffers the shock of Rodolphe's letter of rejection, Binet's lathe—appropriately turning out napkin rings—whirls and whirs with agonizing stridency (pp. 284-85). When she and Léon meet in the Rouen cathedral, the verger calls their attention to "un grand cercle de pavés noirs . . . la circonférence de la belle cloche d'Amboise" (p. 333). When she at last surrenders to Léon, the cab in which they are riding whirls them in circles around the city, and the fragments of *her* letter of rejection, caught and scattered by

the wind, "s'abattirent plus loin, comme des papillons blancs, sur un champ de tréfles rouges tout en fleur" (p. 338). When she later waits in vain for Léon to rescue her from her desperate money entanglements, she is tortured by the sound of mère Rollet's spinning wheel, thinking it is Binet's lathe again (p. 423), and "elle se mit à faire des tours de promenade dans le jardin, pas à pas" (p. 425). Finally, when Rodolphe also betrays her and she rushes from his chateau for the last time, determined upon suicide, she stumbles "contre les tas de feuilles mortes que le vent dispersait" (p. 431).

That there is a deliberate pattern here—a delicate network of structurally pertinent images—would thus seem indisputable. But what does this pattern signify? Was Flaubert's choice of these particular images rather than others to mark off the crucial phases of the action a merely arbitrary one, or were they chosen because he wanted them to carry some special implication? Once the question is posed, the answer presents itself so readily that it seems only to state the obvious. Flaubert has his eye on the most famous section of Dante's *Inferno*—Canto V, where in the Second Circle of Hell are condemned the archetypal carnal sinners, Paolo and Francesca. As a woman led into adultery by the reading of romantically erotic literature, Francesca is, of course, Emma Bovary's classic prototype. Even her celebrated remark, "Nessun maggior dolore / Che ricordarsi del tempo felice / Ne la miseria" (11. 121-23), has its counterpart in Emma's obsessive nostalgia for the convent which exacerbates her present sufferings by appearing regularly in chapter 6 of each of the novel's three Parts (pp. 54, 153-54, 392). The meaning of the image pattern I have been describing therefore becomes clear at once: it derives exactly from the manner of the Dantean lovers' punishment, which is, of course, to be blown in eternal circles around their sphere of Hell by fierce winds symbolic of their uncontrolled passion.

> Io venni in luogo d'ogni luce muto,
>   Che mugghia come fa mar per tempesta,
>   Se da contrari venti è combattuto.
> La bufera infernal, che mai non resta,
>   Mena li spirti con la sua rapina;
>   Voltando e percotendo li molesta.
> Quando giungon davanti a la ruina,
>   Quivi le strida, il compianto, il lamento;
>   Bestemmian quivi la virtù divina.
> Intesi ch'a così fatto tormento
>   Enno dannati i peccator carnali,
>   Che la ragion sommettono al talento
>
> (11. 28-39)

> Di qua, di là, di giù, di su li mena;
>   Nulla speranza li conforta mai,
>   Non che di posa, ma di minor pena
>
> (11. 43-45)

There are, it is true, no "butterflies" in this section of Dante's Hell, but there is an equivalent of them. Emphatically, on three occasions, to suggest the affinity between his carnal lovers and sub-human creatures of mere instinct, Dante compares the situation and behavior of the sufferers to those of birds.

> E come li stornei ne portan l'ali
> > Nel freddo tempo, a schiera larga e piena,
> > Così quel fiato li spiriti mali (11. 40-43)
> E come i gru van cantando lor lai,
> > Faccendo in aere di sè lunga riga,
> > Così vidi venir, traendo guai, (11. 46-48)
> Quali colombe dal disio chiamate,
> > Con l'ali alzate e ferme, al dolce nido
> > Vegnon per l'aere dal voler portate,
> Cotali uscir de la schiera ov' è Dido,
> > A noi venendo per l'aere maligno . . .
>
> (11. 82-86)[8]

These similarities between Flaubert's imagery and Dante's are, I submit, too complete and striking to be merely coincidental. Flaubert, of course, is not suggesting by these parallels that the "sins" of Emma and Francesca are identical in their source and nature, or that these characters are to be judged in the same way; the literary correspondences do not imply ethical ones. Obviously, there is a universe of difference between Flaubert's interpretation of Emma's adultery and Dante's of Francesca's. By placing Emma in the perspective of Dante's world of discourse, the parallelism serves in large part to make clear this very difference between a traditionally religious view of life and a nineteenth-century Naturalistic one. Emma's "damnation" is, in effect, her life here and now. As Alfred G. Engstrom has shown, Flaubert employs a similar strategy to focus a difference in interpretation when he implicitly compares Emma at the moment of her seduction by Rodolphe to Dido at the moment of her seduction by Aeneas.[9] Moreover, the result in both cases is an irony which works ambiguously in two ways at once—to diminish Emma in the manner of the mock-heroic, and to enlarge her by inviting a comparison between her and such a distinguished literary ancestry. This double view, reinforced of course by many other details in the novel, is of the very essence of our response to her character and fate, which moves back and forth throughout between scorn and tragic sympathy.

As far as I know, Flaubert never testified explicitly that he had ever been particularly interested in the Paolo and Francesca story, but we know from a letter of May 8-9, 1852, to Louise Colet, that he did read the whole of the *Inferno* in a French translation at an early stage of the composition of **Madame Bovary** ("J'ai lu dernièrement tout l'*Enfer* de Dante (en français)"),[10] and that, while he had serious reservations about Dante's art,[11] he was unquestionably impressed by it, at least in part: "Cela a de grandes allures. . . . Un souffle immense par moments."[12] Was one of these great moments Canto V? It would be nice to have conclusive proof

that it was! But we do know from a later reference in the correspondence with Louise Colet how forcibly at least some of Dante's imagery could fasten itself in his memory. Trying in a letter of August 14, 1853, to describe the depression caused him by a visit to Trouville, he compares his feelings to the punishment meted out in Canto XXIII of the *Inferno* to the hypocrites: "La chape de plomb que le Dante promet aux hypocrites n'est rien en comparaison de la lourdeur qui me pèse alors sur le crâne."[13] Is it not reasonable to suppose that if Flaubert remembered this passage, he also remembered the imagery connected with Paolo and Francesca, whose story was so much more strikingly akin to the novel which he was writing at this very time?

Indeed, the probability of this is greatly increased by strong evidence of Dante's influence elsewhere in the novel itself. For instance, just before Emma and Léon go whirling off in the cab where she is to surrender again to her carnal passion, the verger who has been showing them the historical sights of the Rouen cathedral enjoins them to drive past the north door, and in doing so unwittingly utters what amounts to a resoundingly Dantesque warning: "'Sortez du moins par le portail du nord . . . pour voir la *Résurrection*, le *Jugement dernier*, le *Paradis*, le *Roi David*, et les *Réprouvés* dans les flammes d'enfer'" (p. 336). Dantean influence also helps explain at this point a curious feature of the novel's structure. Although the cab ride takes place in Rouen at the end of Part III, chapter 1, the city itself is not described until chapter 5, after Emma and Léon's affair has fully developed. The reason for this becomes apparent as soon as we perceive that Flaubert wants us to recognize the city as a miniature Inferno, and that he knows we can do this only after we have first seen the lovers completely "damning" themselves. Only when thus alerted can we grasp the significance of the fact that the approach to the city is a *descent,* and see the symbolic appropriateness of the fog, the smoke, the roar of the foundries played off ominously against the pealing church bells, the leafless trees, and—once again—the gusts of wind.

> Descendant tout en amphithéâtre et noyée dans le brouillard, elle s'élargissait au delà des ponts, confusément. La pleine campagne remontait ensuite d'un mouvement monotone, jusqu'à toucher au loin la base indécise du ciel pâle. Ainsi vu d'en haut, le paysage tout entier avait l'air immobile comme une peinture; les navires à l'ancre se tassaient dans un coin; le fleuve arrondissait sa courbe au pied des collines vertes, et les îles, de forme oblongue, semblaient sur l'eau de grands poissons noirs arrêtés. Les cheminées des usines poussaient d'immenses panaches bruns qui s'envolaient par le bout. On entendait le ronflement des fonderies avec le carillon clair des églises qui se dressaient dans la brume. Les arbres des boulevards, sans feuilles, faisaient des broussailles violettes au milieu des maisons, et les toits, tout reluisants de pluie, miroitaient inégalement, selon la hauteur des quartiers. Parfois un coup de

vent emportait les nuages vers la côte Sainte-Catherine, comme des flots aériens qui se brisaient en silence contre une falaise.

(pp. 363-64)

The Inferno-like character of this scene is further established if we see it in relation to its structural counterpart in Part II, chapter 9—namely, the description of Yonville as seen by Emma when she stands with Rodolphe on the hill overlooking the town on the day of her first seduction.

> On était aux premiers jours d'octobre. Il y avait du brouillard sur la campagne. Des vapeurs s' allongeaient à l'horizon, entre le contours des collines; et d'autres, se déchirant, montaient, se perdaient. Quelquefois, dans un écartement des nuées, sous un rayon de soleil, on apercevait au loin les toits d'Yonville, avec les jardins au bord de l'eau, les cours, les murs, et le clocher de l'église. Emma fermait à demi les paupières pour reconnaître sa maison, et jamais ce pauvre village où elle vivait le lui avait semblé si petit. De la hauteur où ils étaient, toute la vallée paraissait un immense lac pâle, s'évaporant à l'air. Les massifs d'arbres, de place en place, saillissaient comme des rochers Noirs; et les hautes lignes des peupliers, qui dépassaient la brume, figuraient des grèves que le vent remuait.

(pp. 219-20)

In this passage Yonville is Rouen's antithesis—a place of innocence and marital fidelity which Emma is about to leave behind forever; a Garden of Eden, in a sense, whose abandonment will lead inevitably to her later descent into the abyss. A certain wistfulness in Emma's attitude implied here as she pauses to look back and searches vainly for her house obscured by the mists makes us keenly aware of the affinity between her later reckless eagerness to plunge into Rouen and that appalling hardness of heart which drives the typically Dantean sinner to his hideous damnation.

> Quelque chose de vertigineux se dégageait pour elle de ces existences amassées, et son coeur s'en gonflait abondamment comme si les cent vingt mille âmes qui palpitaient là lui eussent envoyé toutes à la fois la vapeur des passions qu'elle leur supposait. Son amour s'agrandissait devant l'espace, et s'emplissait de tumulte aux boudonnements vagues qui montaient. Elle le reversait au dehors, sur les places, sur les promenades, sur les rues, et la vieille cité normande s'étalait à ses yeux comme une capitale démesurée, comme une Babylone ou elle entrait. Elle se penchait des deux mains par le vasistas, en humant la brise; les trois chevaux galopaient, les pierres grinçaient dans la boue, la diligence se balançait, et Hivert, de loin, hélait les carrioles sur la route . . .

(pp. 364-65)

Emma, of course, is not alone in this infernal coach. As she returns at night from her rendezvous in "Babylon," her fellow travellers too are cast in Dantesque perspective and chiaroscuro.

> Puis les voyageurs de l'*Hirondelle* finissaient par s'endormir, les uns la bouche ouverte, les autres le menton baissé s'appuyant sur l'épaule de leur voisin, ou bien le bras passé, dans la courroie, tout en oscillant régulièrement au branle de la voiture; et le reflet de la lanterne qui se balançait en dehors, sur la croupe des limoniers, pénétrant dans l'intérieur par les rideaux de calicot chocolat, posait des ombres sanguinolentes sur tous ces individus immobiles.

(pp. 370-71)

The expressions and postures of the sleepers, played upon by the "ombres sanguinolentes," are symbolically those of the dead and damned, whom Emma herself is at least metaphorically aware that she is about to join: "Emma, ivre de tristesse, grelottait sous ses vêtements, et se sentait de plus en plus froid aux pieds, avec la mort dans l'âme" (p. 371). Indeed, two chapters later, when another carriage, apparently driven by the vicomte, whirls heedlessly past her as she is departing from Rouen and her lover for the last time, she is filled with such an overpowering sense of everything abandoning her that "elle se sentait perdue, roulant au hasard dans des abîmes indéfinissables" (p. 413). The image of the abyss appears later too when she is parting for the last time from Rodolphe: "Alors sa situation, telle qu'un abîme, se représenta" (p. 432); and in actions which ironically parallel her original descents into Rouen, "elle haletait à se rompre la poitrine. Puis, dans un transport d'héroïsme qui la rendait presque joyeuse, elle descendit la côte en courant" and goes to her death (p. 432).

Only if we accept the Dantean overtones of such passages, I submit, are we able to appreciate the full implications of Flaubert's language—of his impassioned search for "le mot juste"—and his famous "ruses de style." The "Dantesque symmetry" of the novel to which Harry Levin casually refers[14] is no mere arbitrary embellishment, but a working out on the structural level of an elaborate system of references which constitute a great part of the novel's very texture of thought and feeling. And here at last in these references do we also have, I believe, a clue to the elusive significance of the terrible Blind Beggar who haunts the novel from his first appearance in Part III, chapter 5, to the time of Emma's death.

As a merely "realistic" figure, l'Aveugle will not work at all, of course. He seems to exist on an imaginative plane quite distinct from that occupied by the other characters in the novel. But the critics have not been able to agree on what he signifies. Alfred G. Engstrom, for instance, suggests that he is a symbol of death—of Atropos, the Third Fate, who cuts the thread of life.[15] Martin Turnell maintains that he might be the Devil.[16] Both of these interpretations seem too subjective. If we follow up the implications of the Dantean references, however, an answer more consistent with the main drift of Flaubert's imagination readily appears. Looming up before Emma on the slope that leads downward into the Babylon-city, assaulting her sight and hearing with his hideously diseased features and his bawdy song which, significantly, "descendait au fond de l'âme comme un tourbillon dans un abîme, et l'emportait parmi les espaces d'une mélancolie sans bornes" (p. 370), and finally appearing at the very moment of her death to terrify her with the prospect of seeing his face before her forever "dans les ténèbres éternelles" (p. 449), the Blind Beggar is nothing less than a creature out of the *Inferno* itself—a damned sinner who serves as a metaphor of the damnation which Emma has made of her own life. To be sure, there is nothing to relate him specifically to Emma's own circle of Hell—that of Paolo and Francesca. Rather, the nature of his affliction ("La chair s'effiloquait par lambeaux rouges; et il en coulait des liquides qui se figeaient en gales vertes jusqu'au nez, dont les narines noires reniflaient convulsivement" (p. 369) and the purpose of his bawdy song (to entice to lust) might point to Circle Eight, where the flatterers are punished by being immersed in excrement (Canto XVIII, 11. 106-14) and the falsifiers by having their bodies covered with great sores from head to foot (Canto XXIX, 11. 73-75). But we need not look in Flaubert for any allegory as exact as Dante's. What he is striving for is simply a massive poetic suggestiveness which will reinforce and bring to climactic focus all the Dantesque elements of language and structure which have been subterraneously shaping the novel from the start. The Blind Beggar gives these elements their synthesis. To nothing in the novel is a musical analogy more appropriate: he is the grand final theme in which all the motifs we have been examining culminate *brilliantly*.

Notes

1. Interesting recent studies along these lines include the following: D. L. Demorest, *L'expression figurée dans l'oeuvre de Flaubert* (Paris, 1931), pp. 454-74; Alfred G. Engstrom, "Flaubert's Correspondence and the Ironic and Symbolic Structure of *Madame Bovary*," *Studies in Philology*, XLVI (1949), 470-95; Georges Poulet, "The Circle and the Center: Reality and *Madame Bovary*," *Western Review*, XIX (Summer 1955), 245-60; Martin Turnell, "*Madame Bovary*," *Sewanee Review*, LXV (1957), 531-50; Jean Rousset, *Forme et Signification, essais sur les structures littéraires de Corneille à Claudel* (Paris, 1962), pp. 109-33; William Bysshe Stein, "*Madame Bovary* and Cupid Unmasked," *Sewanee Review*, LXXIII (1965), 197-209.

2. Poulet, p. 248.

3. John C. Lapp, "Art and Hallucination in Flaubert," *French Studies*, X (1956), 322-44, discusses the wind imagery in the novel, but only very briefly and only as a reflection of Flaubert's convulsive seizures.

4. Poulet, p. 251.

5. *Ibid.,* p. 259.

6. *Ibid.,* p. 249.

7. *Madame Bovary* (*Oeuvres Complètes de Gustave Flaubert*. Paris, 1930), pp. 61-62. Hereafter all references to this text will appear in parentheses after the citations.

8. Flaubert's debt to this passage may also be seen, perhaps, in his otherwise curious choice of the name "Hirondelle"—i.e., swallow—for the name of the old coach which takes Emma to and from her assignations with Léon in Rouen.

9. "Virgil, Ovid, and the Cry of Fate in *Madame Bovary*," *Philological Quarterly*, XXXVII (1958), 125.

10. *Correspondance* (*Oeuvres Complètes de Gustave Flaubert. Nouvelle Edition Augmentée. Deuxième Série*, 1847-52. (Paris, 1926), p. 408.

11. *Ibid.* ("Cette oeuvre a été faite pour un temps et non pour tous les temps"). Cf. a letter of March 31, 1853, to the same correspondent, in which Flaubert declares that "La Fontaine vivre tout autant que le Dante" (*Ibid., Troisième Série*, 1852-54, p. 150).

12. *Deuxième Série*, p. 408. Cf. a letter of April 9, 1851, to Louis Bouilhet, in which Flaubert refers in passing to Dante, along with Goethe and Shakespeare, when trying to describe the powerful impression made on him by Michelangelo's *Last Judgment* (*Ibid.*, p. 305).

13. *Troisième Série*, p. 290.

14. *The Gates of Horn* (New York, 1963), p. 260.

15. "Flaubert's Correspondence and the Ironic and Symbolic Structure of *Madame Bovary*," pp. 493-94.

16. "*Madame Bovary*," p. 546.

Eugene Hollahan (essay date January 1973)

SOURCE: Hollahan, Eugene. "Irruption of Nothing: Sleep and Freedom in *Madame Bovary*." *Studies in Philology* 70, no. 1 (January 1973): 92-107.

[*In the following essay, Hollahan analyzes the symbolic relationship between sleep and freedom in the novel. According to Hollahan, sleep represents conditions of calm, stability, and order, while freedom embodies forces of innovation and change. Hollahan argues that the tension between these two states lies at the heart of Emma Bovary's struggle to find romance in a complacent, indifferent society.]*

Among the stunning artistic effects of **Madame Bovary** is the introduction, orchestration, and resolution of a complex major motif constituted in part by frequent repetition of a pair of polarized terms—sleep and freedom. The sleep motif is introduced in the opening scene, in the classroom to which young Charles Bovary is brought by the headmaster, and it is concluded only on the final page of the book with the closing reference to the material and social success of Homais the apothecary, one of several characters linked with and characterized in part by complacent drowsiness and sleep. Throughout the story in scattered and various contexts, the words for *sleep, sleeping,* and *asleep* occur fifty-four times, with the words for *nap, dozing* and related words also appearing in other contexts. The strong overall effect of these regularly recurrent words is reinforced by specific occurrences on thirty-six occasions of the word for *bed,* as well as additional references to cradles and so forth. All of these specific verbal repetitions call attention to the presence and importance in plot and theme of sleep and sleepiness, a dominant note in mood and atmosphere as well as in much of the characterization. Contrasted with this tonal sleepiness that earmarks the society Flaubert describes in **Madame Bovary** is a febrile desire for wakeful, unrestricted freedom that agitates and destroys the main character Emma Bovary. On ten occasions attention is called to her throbbing desire for freedom by use of the words for *free* and *freedom,* so that the device of verbal repetition also underscores the freedom motif as it appears in character and action. A corollary use of verbal repetition is the textural presence on fifty-five occasions of the word for *window,* with windows being the device by which Flaubert and Emma establish a direct linkage between the sleepiness that is found primarily indoors in the houses of Tostes and Yonville, and the freedom that seems to Emma to lie somewhere vaguely out of doors. Thus a verbal pattern of *sleep-window-freedom* establishes a motif that, in interaction with plot, character, setting, conflict, mood, and atmosphere, invests the novel with much of its imaginative power as well as its structural unity and thematic significance. In brief, Emma wishes to escape from the sleepy, limited world of mediocrity to which she is condemned by her life with Charles Bovary; she hopes to find freedom in the seemingly more active, varied world that she thinks she has discovered during her many lonely hours spent gazing longingly from her window. However, instead of achieving a romantic escape or "eruption" from drowsy loneliness, she finds only her death, which is ironically shown as an "irruption of nothingness" (*survenue du néant*), a breaking-in of nihilistic blankness upon her

chaotic self rather than a breaking-out into romantic deliverance as she had expected. The chief irony of the story, then, is that in her quest for freedom from sleepiness she finds only death, which is presented as being nothing more than another kind of sleep.

* * *

Texturally, **Madame Bovary** is thick with specific verbal references to the motif of sleep. Nearly every character is shown at some time as he lies asleep, a significant difference being that the agitated main character, Emma, is said only twice to be sleeping, once literally in Part II and once metaphorically as she lies dead in Part III. Specific references to sleep occur throughout the book, both the opening and closing scenes being marked directly or indirectly by the sleep motif, and sleepiness is one of the main aspects of characterization as well as of mood and atmosphere. On the first page, as the headmaster brings the gawky Charles Bovary into the classroom, the unidentified narrator mentions that some of the boys had been slumbering, a characteristic trait of Flaubert's personages in this book.[1] The motif is repeated in the description of Charles's cynical father who sleeps late and lazily dozes in the kitchen (5-7). Charles himself is often shown sleeping or dozing, once when both he and the priest-tutor fall asleep during Charles's lessons (8-9). Charles is also said to sleep soundly in the *lycée* dormitory (9), and much later he is said to be drowsy with fatigue when he is called to Les Bertaux to attend Emma's father for a broken leg, as he rides along thinking about his present wife Heloise lying asleep at home (16-7). Significantly, when he has met and been charmed by young Emma Rouault, he has difficulty sleeping (31), one of the author's variations on the sleep motif being that an emotionally-aroused person does not wish to sleep but rather to savor consciousness and wakeful desire, an assumption to be abundantly illustrated in Emma herself. When Charles and Emma marry, adult guests and children attending the wedding feast fall asleep in their chairs (39-40), suggesting the soporific temper of provincial social life. Also, once Charles is married he quickly falls into a domestic routine that includes falling asleep the moment his back touches the sheets (59), denoting the somnolence of their married sexual life. Even at the exciting ball at La Vaubyessard, Charles is half-asleep, and he falls asleep quickly after the ball is over (73-5). Near the end of Part I, Charles's characterization is presented primarily in terms of sleepy insensitivity to his wife's unhappiness, as for example when he habitually falls asleep over his medical journal *La Ruche Médicale* (85). As the bored Emma waits impatiently for something exciting to happen in her life, and immediately before Charles decides to move to Yonville-L'Abbaye for her health, Flaubert provides a striking image of winter nature, an image that epitomizes the sleep motif as it has been presented in these early episodes: everything seemed to be sleeping:

> Les jours qu'il faisant beau, elle descendait dans le jardin. La rosée avait laissé sur les choux des guipures d'argent avec de longs fils clairs qui s'éntendaient de l'un à l'autre. On n'entendait pas d'oiseaux, tout semblait dormir, l'espalier couvert de paille et la vigne comme un grand serpent malade sous le chaperon du mur, où l'on voyait, en s'approchant, se traîner des cloportes a pattes nombreuses. Dans les sapinettes, près de la haie, le curé en tricorne qui lisait son bréviaire avait perdu le peid droit, et même le plâtre, s'écaillant à la gelée, avait fait des gales blanches sur sa figure.
>
> (89)

Dormant winter nature is in this scene an effectively clarifying image of the drowsy mediocrity of Emma's environment, as well as of her own unawakened desire for freedom and stimulation; this winter image suggests an oblique rebuke of both Emma and her static society in that, much later, nature awakes to spring fullness, ironically on the day of her funeral (466).

Emma wishes to escape from her comatose emotional surroundings, but moving to Yonville in Part II does not provide her with an escape from a sleepy atmosphere, for the opening description of the town concludes with the image of Yonville as a lazy town which lay by the banks of the Rieule like a cowherd drowsing in a noonday nap (97). The indoors of houses, too, are linked again with sleepiness, as the billiard table at the Lion d'Or is said to serve as a bed during the hunting season, sleeping as many as six men at one time (102-3). Predictably, the habitually torpid Charles is sleeping in the carriage that first brings them to Yonville (109), and during their first meal at the Lion d'Or, when Emma and Leon are getting acquainted, Mme. Lefrançois the innkeeper sleeps by the fire (116), as if representing the unalert, indolent local citizenry who do nothing to prevent Emma's tragedy. The total first impression the reader receives of Yonville is that the town is literally and figuratively asleep (117), even though Emma herself rather desperately refuses to see at first this significant similarity between Yonville and her former home at Tostes.

Numerous references to sleep occur throughout Part II, involving a wider assortment of characters. Charles continues to sleep inordinately, napping sluggishly as he waits for patients in his consulting room (121); baby Berthe is asleep when Emma and Leon visit Mme. Rollet the wet nurse upon Emma's first daring excursion out of the sleepy respectable town (128); Mme. Rollet herself, seeking money and pity, complains that she falls asleep from fatigue (129); Homais' children fall asleep on chairs and have to be put bodily to bed (136); Homais and Charles fall asleep after their domino games, thus leaving the frustrated Emma and Leon opportunity to become more deeply involved in romantic intrigue (137). Also, a kind of implicit provincial social philosophy indirectly stresses a connection between bourgeois mediocrity and bourgeois sleepiness as the prefectural councilor Lieuvain, who delivers a trite speech at the Agriculture Show, directly declares that current prosperous, peaceful times allow citizens a good night's sleep (197). Many subsequent references reinforce this general idea, as Mme. Homais inertly thinks of sleep after the fireworks at the Agriculture Show (212), Rodolphe is shown to be languidly sleeping at La Huchette when the sleepless Emma goes to see him in the early morning (227-8), Charles sleeps while Emma keeps her rendezvous with Rodolphe in the arbor (234), and, in one of his fatuous articles, Homais naively accords the highest praise to scientists who make the supreme sacrifice of going without sleep in order to benefit mankind (247). Moreover, the stupefied Charles continues to sleep ignorantly beside the wakeful Emma, who is restlessly plotting a runaway escape with Rodolphe (271); ironically, Rodolphe sends Emma a letter in which he refuses to leave with her, and then he sleeps a late, untroubled sleep the next day, oblivious to the torture he has caused his jilted lover (283). A touch of comic irony is added to the motif when, at the end of Part II, as Emma is in Rouen with Charles attending the opera, Charles suggests that she remain in town by herself so as to be able to attend the opera again with Leon, genially telling the hesitant Emma, in effect, to "sleep on" the idea (318).

Specific verbal references to sleep in Part III broaden and deepen the motif. When Emma returns from her sexual holidays in Rouen, other passengers in the Hirondelle fall asleep (370), leaving only the depraved, confused adventuress awake. In addition, Emma's nagging about her domestic unhappiness forces Charles to sleep in the attic (399). Also, Mme. Homais informs the great Dr. Larivière that she worries about her husband's worsening habit of falling asleep after dinner (445). After Emma's death, the anguished, perplexed Charles stays resolutely awake for a time but eventually falls asleep when he is exhausted (453). And, in a significant scene where the author contrasts mysterious human experiences such as death with the superficialities of reason and religion, Homais and Abbé Bournisien, the argumentative pair of watchers at Emma's wake, both fall asleep after being worn out with watching and disputing; only Charles's horrified scream at seeing Emma's dead face is able to wake the two sleepers (458-9). Near the end of the book, some of the tying up of loose plot strands includes mentioning that, whereas Emma's grieving father left Charles's house because he could not sleep in the house where she had died, Rodolphe and Leon, who both exploited Emma's pitiful unhappiness, continue to sleep peacefully. Moreover, Emma's frustrated young admirer Justin is unable to sleep, as he is shown kneeling on her grave, weeping and sobbing (469).

Of special interest is the way the author presents his main character in relation to the sleep motif which dominates the lives of most of the important minor characters. The predominant fact is that Emma rarely sleeps, or is at least rarely shown sleeping, and thus she stands directly in contrast with nearly everyone else in Tostes and Yonville, in whose benumbed routines sleep is a major factor, even an addiction. Not until nearly one-third of the way into the story is Emma said to sleep, and then only after lying awake for hours enjoying the thought that Leon loves her (143). Again, she pretends to sleep when she is actually planning to run away with Rodolphe, lying awake dreaming dreams of pleasure and freedom (271), as usual not falling asleep until dawn. A poignant episode showing her asleep occurs when she suffers brain fever and sleeps fitfully (288), and in her guilty worry about the whereabouts of Rodolphe's fateful letter which precipitated her fever, she sleeps a troubled sleep (290). The crucial point in Emma's attitude toward sleep, which initially represents to her the dull frustration of life with Charles, comes when she is totally bored with Leon and oppressed by financial worry: hence, she wishes for death or a state of continual sleep, the two being equivalent in her mind (402), thus pointing explicitly toward the climactic episode when she dies horribly of arsenic poisoning. After this point, the exhausted young woman is shown progressively more stupefied with fatigue, as when she returns from her regular Thursdays in Rouen paralyzed with tiredness (415). Gradually she slips into a drowsiness like the one from which she has spent her energies fleeing, and this aspect of the sleep motif is resolved ironically when the dead Emma is shown in her coffin, being watched over by the dozing Homais and Bournisien, while the narrator says that now Emma had finally become like everyone else, sharing a common human weakness (*la même faiblesse humaine*).

> M. Bournisien, plus robuste, continua quelque temps à remuer tout bas les lèvres, puis, insensiblement, il baissa le menton, lâcha son gros livre noir et se mit à ronfler.
>
> Ils étaient en face l'un de l'autre, le ventre en avant, la figure bouffie, l'air renfrogné, après tant de désaccord se rencontrant enfin dans la même faiblesse humaine; et ils ne bougeaient pas plus que le cadavre à côté d'eux qui avait l'air de dormir.
>
> (458)

The death of her body follows the death of her questing spiritual yearning for freedom, and she has found in deathly sleep the only freedom she was ever likely to experience.

Less frequent than the numerous references to sleep but sufficiently effective as a contrast with sleep in terms of Emma's motivation are specific references to freedom, nearly all of them linked with Emma herself. Initially the word for *free* occurs in connection with Emma when Flaubert's heroine, disappointed with giving birth to a daughter, wishes instead it had been a son, since a male child could grow up to be free—free to range the world, taste forbidden passions, and so forth (123). Thus, she implicitly links her desire for freedom with those dark elements in her mentality that yield to excesses, substitute gratifications, and, in general, to sensuality. A second occurrence of the word for *free* is in the scene in the woods when Emma first yields sexually to Rodolphe's experienced importunity and to her own private wishes, first making a half-hearted attempt to free herself from his grasp but finally giving in (223). That her quest for freedom will end badly is again suggested when, after receiving a letter from her father which precipitates her remorseful desire to break off with Rodolphe and become a dutiful wife again, she wistfully remembers her girlhood, when she had been happy, hopeful, and free (239). Further hint that she will only misuse any freedom she attains occurs when the narrator says that the bored, depraved Emma, having recommenced the liaison with Rodolphe, loses all sense of self-restraint, and her glances grew bolder and her language freer (266). The logical, inevitable outcome of her hysterical attempt to seize freedom is suggested when Rodolphe informs her that he will not run away with her, and Emma stands at the attic window holding his letter, tempted to jump, and telling herself that she is free to act (285). Also, the moral debasement resulting from her misguided efforts to achieve freedom is revealed explicitly when she objects to the suspicious Charles that she would not feel free to go to her piano lessons with Mlle. Lempereur if he becomes upset whenever she fails to return on time (383); in effect, Emma herself perverts her ideal of freedom by directly employing it as part of her own excuse for her sins, and the narrator notes that she then makes free use of her husband's stupid permissiveness. The final occurrence of the word in connection with Emma's experience is in the final scene with Rodolphe when she begs for money and is refused, Emma rebuking the hard-hearted Rodolphe for rejecting her despite his being rich, happy, and free (431), in a scene that, as will be shown, is the culminating event of the main plot of the novel. Obviously, the unrecognized goal of Emma's quest all along has been the triple coffin to which she is finally confined, an enclosing image that directly contradicts the freedom she had sought and one which logically epitomizes the bondage (236) and slavery (265) which have been hinted at throughout the story. Massive reinforcement of this confinement motif, the ironic reversal of the freedom motif, is introduced by the image of the asylum to which the Blind Beggar is forcibly confined at the wishes of the vindictive conformist Homais (474). Thus, in her deathly sleep Emma has really found her way to a condition comparable to the drowsiness from which she had originally wished to escape. The great subtle point of Emma's experience has been that, the more strenuously she moved toward imagined freedom such as she thought she had seen through her window, the more she moved into the condition of deep sleep from which she hoped she was fleeing.

Simply and plausibly, the windows which are mentioned variously more than sixty times are Flaubert's and Emma's device for mediating between her sleepy domestic world with its tonal drowsy mediocrity and the seemingly more alert, active world outside with its imagined, wished-for stimulation. Many episodes in Emma's own personal experience are linked with windows, her initial characteristic stance being to stand at the window with her head leaning wistfully against the pane (21). After she is married to Charles, and while she still imagines that she can love him, she usually watches from a window as he leaves on his rounds (46), additionally revealing her temporary satisfaction by closing the window after he leaves, as if to shut out the outside world. Soon, however, as she becomes vaguely discontent, she yearns for freedom, associating it with romantic chatelaines leaning engagingly out of charming casement windows (51). After the exciting ball at La Vaubyessard, a new characteristic stance appears in her own behavior as she herself leans out of the upstairs bedroom window to prolong the illusion of freedom created by the lavish dinner and dancing (74). Later, she is twice stimulated by hearing secular music through the window, once when nocturnal fishmongers pass by singing *La Marjolaine* (80) and once again when a hurdy-gurdy plays sentimental tunes (90), both occasions provoking her to think of the great inaccessible world and the bitterness of her life. During the period of emotional transition, she responds to Charles's clumsiness by leaning out of the window to cool and calm herself (86), the act of opening a window becoming a sign of her capriciousness and restlessness (92).

That her compulsive window-watching will not be lessened by moving to Yonville is made clear when she first enters her new bedroom and looks hopefully out at the misty meadow surrounding the sleepy town (117). Also, after she becomes mildly interested in the seemingly sensitive Leon, she catches glimpses of him from her parlour window and then deliberately watches him go about his business in Yonville (134). As the pair develop a deeper interest in each other, they flirt while standing at the flower pots they have installed in their facing windows (137-8). Even so, the window, which has become such a devilish instrument for Emma, can still be a potential agent for good, as one day she hears through a window the Angelus being played at church (153), and then she goes there hopefully to secure ad-

vice from Abbé Bournisien, only to return disappointed from her interview with the priest. Her disappointment deepens when Leon leaves Yonville, finding her, when he comes to say goodbye, leaning dejectedly against a window pane once more (166). The closing of this episode in her experience is marked by the falling of her window curtain, which Leon sees drop as he crosses the street.

However, windows continue to be important in Emma's attempt to escape the sleepy life in which she feels trapped, as she first espies Rodolphe Boulanger through the window when he brings his servant to Dr. Bovary to be bled (176-7). Also, in one of the most famous and important episodes in the book, she and Rodolphe watch the Agriculture Show from the second floor window of the town hall (196-210), and after she has commenced the sexual affair with Rodolphe, a serious change occurs in the tone of the narrative as Emma now finds herself outside of, rather than inside, the windows and fearful of being seen by the respectable people (229). The sinister change in Emma's character is reflected in the references to the windows, as the previously innocent use to which Emma put windows gives way to her using them to signal her lover (267). The potential self-destructiveness latent in the misuse of perspectives provided by windows is emphasized when Emma, having received the jilting letter from Rodolphe, stands at the attic window and contemplates a suicidal jump (285). At the end of this long episode with Rodolphe, another serious alteration occurs in her life and behavior as a result of the brain fever and its attendant psychological trauma, but an almost smooth transition is effected into the next episode by Emma's being shown during her convalescence seated at a window looking out (294). Effective also in showing the compulsive repetitiveness in her window-gazing, as well as showing the stimulating dramatic appeal of window-gazing, is the theatre box from which she gazes enthralled at the opera *Lucie de Lammermoor* (310-1), this theatre box being a surrogate for, and epitome of, all the windows through which she yearningly looks out in hope of liberation.

In Part III, up to the very end of her story, Emma is repeatedly shown at windows in significant functional scenes. As she waits for the morning coach which will take her to a rendezvous in Rouen with Leon, she gazes nervously from her window at the sleeping town (362); in Rouen, anticipating her sinful pleasures, she greedily leans out the carriage window and breathes deeply (364); while waiting impatiently for Leon, who has been detained at lunch by the insistently cheerful Homais, she leans impatiently against the windowpane of her hotel room (386), as she had characteristically done in the beginning of her disillusionment. Finally, and as if in retribution for her misuse of the enlarged vistas provided by windows, her actual suicide is linked with a window image. After being rejected again by Rodolphe, she runs hysterically to Homais' house and knocks at the kitchen window to attract Justin's attention, thereby getting into the house where she fatally eats arsenic poison (433-4). In general, one can say that at almost every step in Emma's progressive dissolution, her disposition and actions are presented in relation to actual windows and metaphoric windows which mediate, hopefully at first and then tragically, between the world of sleep and the world of freedom.

Experiences of other characters in **Madame Bovary** are also presented in relation to windows, thus reinforcing the motif as it appears in the experience of Flaubert's main character. In some instances, the windows mentioned in connection with these other characters are merely instances of the windows which customarily take the place of city boulevards and theatres in provincial life; at other times, they take on some of the sinister or other thematic aspects of the windows linked with Emma herself. Charles, for example, is early shown leaning quiescently out the window to escape briefly from the difficult studies of medical school (11). Also, after the death of his first wife Heloise, he stays awake for one of the few nights of his life, leaning out the window, staring in the direction of Les Bertaux (31). Moreover, after he has married Emma, who seems to be taking over control of his life, his glum mother regards his new married happiness like a man looking through a window at revelers in his own house (60). Other characters, such as Binet and Mme. Tuvache, are shown at times near or looking out of windows, as for example when Mme. Tuvache sees Emma going out alone and conventionally disapproves (127). The flattering Leon tells Emma upon the resumption of their flirtation that he formerly watched her longingly from his window (325), and his open hotel-room window in Rouen suggests the joyful freedom he feels while anticipating the rich sexual license he hopes to enjoy with Emma, a richness implied by polished silver shining in a jeweler's street display window that he passes on his way to meet her (329-30). Most suggestive, however, of all the windows associated with other minor characters is the carriage window at which the hideous Blind Beggar first appears on the road to Rouen (370) and the window of Emma's deathbed room, outside of which the Beggar appears again at the moment of her death (449), both window images reinforcing the latent horror suggested earlier by the gargoyle windows of Parvis Notre-Dame (335). Final scenes showing windows used thematically appear when the desolate, widowed Charles leans dejectedly out of the window of his home (453) and when the townspeople safely watch Emma's funeral from their windows (465). In general, then, but with signal differences, minor characters are presented in scenes employing the window image in various ways that create ironic and pathetic relations with Emma's own experience.[2]

* * *

As much as Flaubert's thematic substance and resonance derive from his careful awareness and employment of the social conventions of the provincial society in Tostes and Yonville-L'Abbaye, Emma's initially innocent fondness for going out for walks, accompanied or alone, particularly the latter, serves as a structural device for the main plot, giving the novel an effective plot unity. Put simply, the idea is that the freedom which Emma imagines she sees through the window, she wishes to obtain by pursuing it, literally by walking out of the house to get it. Emma's propensity for walking out alone, so obviously linked to the massive emotional experience which constitutes the heart of the novel, is made apparent early in her marriage when she is just becoming disillusioned with the lethargic Charles, wondering why she ever married him, and finding some slight consolation in taking solitary walks to the avenue of beeches at Bonneville, accompanied only by her pet Italian greyhound (61). This dangerous habit which leaves her prey to demoralizing solitude and its inevitable self-pity unregulated by social considerations is again revealed when she first arrives at Yonville-L'Abbaye, where she had hoped to make a fresh start, as she inquires of Leon during the first evening meal at the Lion d'Or whether the unpromising neighborhood has at least some pleasant walks (112). In combination with the large developments in characterization, setting, mood, and atmosphere, these two details establishing Emma's habit of going for walks make possible for the author the creation of a unifying main plot consisting of a clear representative event, defining event, functional halfway point, crisis, culminating event, and climax.

By the time the author is ready to initiate the main plot, it seems abundantly clear that the theme will evolve from one or more of the possible orchestrations of the sleep-freedom motif, the passive windows through which Emma longingly gazes at the imagined freedom of the inaccessible great world outside giving way, perhaps necessarily, to actual outdoor excursions, mostly unsanctioned, by Flaubert's young heroine. The representative event in which the author's thematic intention first seems to be implied occurs not long after the couple has arrived in Yonville. Emma, who had had for a month the stimulating company of Charles's cynical, dubious father, decides impulsively and unwisely one day after the elder Bovary's departure that she must see her baby Berthe who is being kept at the wet nurse's house, and she follows this impulsive decision with a quick walking trip to Mme. Rollet's house (125-6). As she walks through the town at high noon, the houses are shuttered close as custom dictates, and Emma meets Leon and persuades him to walk with her to the wet nurse's house, a daring action on Emma's part which intensifies the developing emotional attachment between her and Leon and which brings her under the disapproving scrutiny of the townspeople, particularly Mme. Tuvache, who declares privately that Madame Bovary was risking her reputation. Linking up logically with this representative event is the defining event occurring in Chapter 9 of Part II, when Emma, having commenced her sexual liaison with Rodolphe Boulanger, decides, again impulsively, to visit her lover at his home in La Huchette, running through the damp morning grass to arrive breathless and aroused for a session of lovemaking (226-8). On this occasion her foolhardiness is perhaps even more apparent, even the grateful Rodolphe warning her that she was risking her reputation. A significant moment in the plot development is reached at the halfway point of the story, when Emma, prompted to remorse for her sins by the pathetic letter from her father, resolves to reform, stop seeing Rodolphe, and try to love Charles once more. The opportunity for her to find the dull Charles lovable again comes in the treacherous guise of his operation on Hippolyte's clubfoot, and Emma is fully aware that this will be her last chance to retrace her steps and regain at least a semblance of virtue and wifeliness (240). But with the hideous failure of the operation, Emma feels deeper revulsion towards Charles. With whatever slight virtue she retains crumbling before her shame and humiliation, she turns automatically and vindictively again to sin; adultery triumphs over virtue, and Emma revels in the sordid prospects before her (256-8). Her return to Rodolphe sets the direction for the rest of the novel, pointing toward the crisis in the plot when she will have to make one final decision.

The crisis is prepared for at the end of Part II, when having been deserted by Rodolphe, and having suffered brain fever, experienced an intense if short-lived religious vision, and languished in a lengthy convalescence, Emma has agreed to attend the opera in Rouen with Charles (305); becoming enthralled by, and emotionally involved with, the suffering heroine in *Lucie de Lammermoor,* she is emboldened when she sees Leon again after a three-year absence. The crisis itself is the implied moment when Emma decides against her better judgement, but fully in accord with her frustrated sensual desires, that she will remain in Rouen without Charles, ostensibly to attend the opera again in the ingratiating company of Leon. Her going alone to meet Leon at the church is a heightened equivalent of her earlier impulsive decisions in the representative event and defining event when she also went out alone seeking freedom. Even at the moment of her yielding to the desire to be with Leon (321), she herself is aware of the foolishness of her self-indulgence, but she does not back away from her choice, and, after this crucial decision and consequential action, she becomes steadily more sexually depraved, debt-ridden, and mentally disordered. The culminating event which completes this pattern of linked significant actions on the part of the main character is one last example of Emma's habit of

going out alone despite social disapproval in her attempt to find freedom in the form of forbidden pleasures. When her enormous debts finally bring about a court action against her, she hysterically runs out to several persons, seeking a loan of money to pay at least part of her indebtedness, first asking Leon, then Notary Guillamin, then Binet, followed by a pointless visit to Mme. Rollet, and finally, in the culminating event itself, running to La Huchette to plead with her former lover Rodolphe, whom she has not seen for three years. In stooping to this desperate action, she herself is unaware that she is prostituting her last bit of integrity (425). Rodolphe's refusal or inability to aid her is simply the last of many rejections she has experienced in her quest for freedom. Moreover, at the climax of the novel, her horrible death from arsenic poisoning, the cumulative impact of all these disappointed gestures at freedom forces on the reader the conclusion that confining death as represented physically by the coffin, and elsewhere throughout the novel by the recurring presence of the gravedigger Lestiboudois, was in fact the only kind of freedom or fate that ever was possible for Emma. A conclusion to this series of events involving Emma's walking out of her house is reached at the last rites, administered by Abbé Bournisien, when her feet that had swiftly hastened her to slake her lust for freedom are anointed along with her sinful human eyes, nostrils, mouth, and hands (446-7). Taken as a whole, the events analyzed here unify and structure the plot of the novel, evolving as they do from the essential trait of the heroine, reflecting the dominant trait of her society, and showing the author's conclusions in his effort at delineating the tensions between the initial polarities of the innate desire for sleep and the innate desire for freedom, ending with Emma's final exposure to nothingness.[3]

In conclusion, it seems hardly possible to overestimate the importance of the sleep-freedom motif to Flaubert's purpose in **Madame Bovary.** It is one of the most satisfying and significant artistic elements in this fine realistic novel. As a recurrent motif, pervasive throughout the text, it carries into the story many concepts of importance in the orchestration of Flaubert's philosophic theme. For example, as has been illustrated, the setting is presented as alternately dormant and agitated, as in winter and spring. The characters are presented either as inert and sluggish or, in the case of the revelers at La Vaubyessard or the debauchees at Rouen, as singularly active, even feverishly active. Emma herself is the one character who seriously attempts to exchange sleepiness for freedom, and hence she serves tragically as the main character. Abstractly, sleep represents in this novel complacency, stability, calm, tradition, and order, whereas freedom is allied with change, excitement, innovation, and disruption. Finally, the esthetic and psychological tensions created by Emma Bovary's pitiful plight as she bounces back and forth between sleep and freedom seem to generate the main theme of *Madame Bovary*; if one makes the most of potential symbolic implications of individual words and phrases in their natural conjunction with the obvious plot structure, the theme is the hazard of man's desire and quest for freedom. The overall rhythmic flow created by texture and action gives the novel its primary coherence, with the central conception being Emma's romantic gestures at escape from sleepy, insidious materialism. From dream to dream, from sorrow to sorrow, Emma ruminates her unhappiness, finding the cause in the dormant tenor of her drowsy society. Perhaps as much as any other motif in this richly-varied book, the sleep-window-freedom pattern as it governs character, texture, and structure gives the novel its most pleasing intrinsic form, as well as conveying the author's pessimistic view of human destiny.

Notes

1. As the clumsy boy Charles is immediately made an object of ridicule by the other boys, the author thus introduces the minor motif of the scapegoat, a fact of importance since it foreshadows the treatment Emma receives from the citizens of Yonville-L'Abbaye. This psychological phenomenon of the unifying social function and value of the scapegoat is more fully developed in another novel, William Golding's *Lord of the Flies*. See Eugene Hollahan, "Running in Circles: A Major Motif in *Lord of the Flies*," *Studies in the Novel*, II (1970), 22-30, which additionally illustrates the textural-structural methodology employed here. Page references in the present essay are to Gustave Flaubert, *Madame Bovary: Moeurs de Province, Oeuvres Complètes de Gustave Flaubert* (Paris, 1930), VII.

2. Jean Rousset notes some of Flaubert's many windows in *Madame Bovary*, providing a detailed technical analysis of "Windows and the Plunging View," concluding that windows and plunging perspectives are "neuralgic points" in the narrative. Jean Rousset, "*Madame Bovary* or The Book About Nothing," in Raymond Giraud, *Flaubert: A Collection of Critical Essays* (Englewood Cliffs, 1954), p. 126.

3. Two other critics have noticed the general tonal force of the sense of nothingness in *Madame Bovary*. In a famous passage in *Mimesis*, Eric Auerbach clarifies the importance for literature of Flaubert's discovery of the "unconcrete despair" of many human lives: "Nothing happens, but that nothing has become a heavy, oppressive, threatening something. How he accomplishes this we have already seen; he organizes into compact and unequivocal discourse the confused impressions of discomfort which arise in Emma at the sight of

the room, the meal, her husband. Elsewhere too he seldom narrates events which carry the action quickly forward; in a series of pure pictures—pictures transforming the nothingness of uniform days into an oppressive condition of repugnance, boredom, false hopes, paralyzing disappointments, and piteous fears—a gray and random human destiny moves toward its end." (Eric Auerbach, *Mimesis: The Representation of Reality in Western Literature,* tr. Willard Trask [Princeton, 1953,] ch. XVIII.) In addition, Robert M. Adams notes that in Flaubert's books the sense of nothingness is constant and is always a social phenomenon. Robert M. Adams, *Nil: Episodes in the Literary Conquest of Void in the Nineteenth Century* (Oxford University Press, 1966), pp. 69-73.

Robert W. Greene (essay date winter 1978)

SOURCE: Greene, Robert W. "Clichés, Moral Censure, and Heroism in Flaubert's *Madame Bovary*." *Symposium* 32, no. 4 (winter 1978): 289-302.

[*In the following essay, Greene examines the link between linguistic eloquence and self-awareness in the novel's central characters. According to Greene, Flaubert employs clichés liberally throughout the work as a means of confining Emma Bovary to a state of moral, intellectual, and emotional stagnation. Greene argues that Emma's attempts to escape this cliché-ridden milieu, while hopeless and frantic, ultimately make her a heroic figure.*]

In French fiction, characters who possess little or no critical self-consciousness regarding the language they use and whose speech or writing, virtually as a consequence of their naïveté in this area, is but a stream of platitudes, often bear the brunt of satire or moral censure in the novels in which they appear. Surely the most memorable embodiment in all of French fiction of mindless clichés wedded to ethical imbecility is Homais, the smug, ruthless pharmacist in *Madame Bovary*. The druggist's moral callousness is rendered time and again by his linguistic obtuseness, his blatant insensitivity to his own total imprisonment in clichés. Homais, however, is not the only example of linguistic "stupidity" in *Madame Bovary*. Nor is he alone in exhibiting a corresponding tone-deafness in the verbal and ethical realms. In fact, one would be hard put to find a single character in Flaubert's masterpiece, except possibly Emma herself, whose state of inner decay or grace (as the case may be) is not indicated quite accurately by his or her degree of awareness, visceral or otherwise, of the problematic and inherently controlling nature of all utterance.

I propose to elucidate the various forms that this correlation or proportion assumes in Madame Bovary, as well as the patterns of meaning that are traced by these forms when they are considered in their ensemble. In so doing, I hope particularly to adduce new reasons for viewing Emma's increasingly frantic behavior in an entirely positive, even heroic light,[1] and as perhaps emblematic of Flaubert's own gallant efforts to expose once and for all the prematurely conclusive, hence disastrously reductive effect of all clichés.

Flaubert's interest in clichés asserted itself early and stayed with him till the end of his days. Moreover, if anything, it seems to have grown more insistent with the passing years, for almost everywhere in the posthumously published *Bouvard et Pécuchet* and *Le Dictionnaire des Idées reçues* one finds evidence of a profound fascination with clichés—clichés of language, of thought, and of behavior. These works also make plain their author's disgust with humanity's blindness to, and meanness of spirit because of, the tangle of bromides in which it is caught. But a full quarter of a century before writing *Bouvard et Pécuchet,* Flaubert was already drawn irresistibly to the cliché, as an inspection of the variorum edition of *Madame Bovary* reveals; many of the passages cut from the novel in the course of its laborious composition are the hackneyed obiter dicta of Bovary *père* and Homais.[2] A decade earlier still, Flaubert's obsessive concern with the paralyzing incrustations of verbal habit shows in his letters, where he frequently juggles a variety of conventionalized voices (a trait of his that has become particularly apparent since the publication of Volume I of the unexpurgated *Correspondance*). For example, in a letter to Ernest Chevalier written in July 1844, when Flaubert was only twenty-two years old, the tone shifts abruptly from award-ceremony speechifying to classic schoolboy obscenity, with the letter's signatory, Flaubert himself, obviously in command of both voices, as well as of the shifts between them.[3]

As a stylistic device in Flaubert's fiction, coupling of discordant voices or codes, so as to display the conventional, banal and manipulative aspects of all discourse, attains grotesquely dramatic form in the celebrated *comices agricoles* section of *Madame Bovary.* Rodolphe seeks to seduce Emma with a string of romantic clichés. By way of counterpoint, congratulatory bombast accompanying the distribution of prizes wafts up to the lovers from the square below their window, sporadically interrupting and, for the reader, thoroughly deflating Rodolphe's ardent jargon. Unlike the rhetorical situation of the letter, however, now of course it is not a signature but the stark interweaving of conflicting yet oddly complementary recitations that betrays the presence of an ironic viewer or narrator.[4]

In the present context, the character of Rodolphe is especially intriguing because he virtually alone in the novel appreciates the power that accrues to those who can wield clichés effectively. Not only does he figure

out quickly that in order to win Emma he has only to babble sentimental phrases evocative of romantic literature, he also knows, linguistically speaking, exactly how to break off with her. Accordingly, he composes his farewell letter in the most cynical manner imaginable, selecting and weighing his words always with an eye to their impact on Emma. "Voilà un mot qui fait toujours de l'effet" (p. 281), he says to himself contentedly after writing several lines reminiscent of Chateaubriand. On the other hand, if Rodolphe is capable of exploiting the persuasive resources of speech and writing, when he listens to Emma's passionate murmurings he completely assimilates her words and feelings to those of previous mistresses, unable to perceive "la dissemblance des sentiments sous la parité des expressions" (p. 265). Significantly, it is Rodolphe's lack of discriminating sense in this regard that moves Flaubert, usually discreet, to stretch his marvelously elastic *style indirect libre* beyond its breaking point and intrude directly upon his story with the rueful (and now famous) observation that "la parole humaine est comme un chaudron fêlé où nous battons des mélodies à faire danser les ours, quand on voudrait attendrir les étoiles" (p. 265). Whether or not the conceptual model for language involved here (that of a deep, rich vein of feeling pre-existing and surpassing in value a thin, monotonous trickle of words) is consistent with the theory of language implied in Flaubert's canon as a whole or even in *Madame Bovary,*[5] the passages quoted, which decry the discrepancy that must forever separate intention from expression, call attention to the limitations and, by extension, the problematical nature of language. These passages also make it abundantly clear that while Rodolphe can skillfully arrange readymade phrases for a specific purpose, he can neither devise fresh formulations nor conceive of the possibility that fresh feelings may lie behind worn-out expressions. So although he is endowed with a kind of animal cunning for mining the formulaic basis of discourse, he has no capacity at all for enriching *la langue* with his *parole,* or, what is more important, for reflecting upon the problematics of language. Any metalinguistic commentary in the text is attributable not to him but to an occasionally intrusive narrator, a barely disguised spokesman for Flaubert himself. Rodolphe is thus a technician of words without a theory of language.

Emma's other lover, Léon, lacks Rodolphe's deliberate if casual flair for using language as an instrument of power. That Léon should also be less sympathetic to the reader than Rodolphe seems no accident, given the system of correlative values set up in *Madame Bovary.* Both lovers eventually abandon Emma, but Léon's conduct in this regard seems more reprehensible than Rodolphe's. The reason this is so relates to Léon's naïveté regarding his own linguistic practice and to his bad faith as a rising, career-minded bourgeois. Appropriately enough, the most successful career trajectories in the novel are traced by Homais ("Il vient de recevoir la croix d'honneur" [p. 481]) and Léon ("mariage de M. Léon Dupuis . . . notaire à Yvetot, avec Mlle Léocadie Leboeuf, de Bondeville" [p. 471]). Not counting Emma, these characters also happen to be the most thoroughly dominated by the verbal equivalent of received ideas, the stereotyped pronouncements of dead idols (Voltaire and Walter Scott, respectively). Hence this equation: In *Madame Bovary,* those characters who are most eager to achieve social and professional respectability are precisely those least conscious of their own patterns of speech and writing, least aware of the second-hand nature of their every utterance. Flaubert's scorn for linguistic "bêtise" is thus inextricably bound up with his hatred for everything bourgeois.

Léon's career, paradigmatically middleclass, steadily ascends along the terraced path of carefully planned stages. It is thus a kind of cliché in itself and at the same time an ideal foil for Charles Bovary's equally ineluctable, step-by-step decline into failure. From his first encounter with Emma until the end of their affair, Léon's conduct is one of utter bad faith in that his every action ultimately is subsumed by his bourgeois calling. Upon meeting, Emma and Léon immediately engage in what may be called a romantic duet, spontaneous, unreflected on the part of both. But we must distinguish between these two examples of unpremeditated behavior. Emma is doomed, driven by keepsake-fueled dreams to spend and expend her life searching out people and situations to match her fantasies. Léon, by contrast, bourgeois to the core, incapable of excess or of losing sight of his future, will never allow his romantic yearnings to deflect him for long from his well-plotted course to the notaryship of Yvetot. Thus when on that first evening at the Lion d'or he says to Emma, "Oh! j'adore la mer" (p. 112), he is in an important sense indulging in both deception and self-deception. For, as his subsequent behavior indicates, he simply does not feel the insatiable hunger for a transcendant ideal that such an avowal suggests to Emma. He has by no stretch of the imagination been touched to the very marrow of his being by his reading in romantic literature as Emma has been by hers.

Léon's reasons for breaking off with Emma are even more revealing of his archetypically bourgeois nature. Pressed by his employer, Maître Dubocage, with arguments like "une telle intrigue nuirait plus tard à son établissement" (p. 400), Léon resolves to stop seeing Emma. With disheartening ease, he then encapsulates the liaison, transforming it into an episode, a phase in the Rouen stage of his career, the fling that precedes and perhaps even facilitates settling down to the serious business of establishing himself as a notary. He sheds his romanticism as if it were an outmoded suit of clothes and turns his searing love affair with Emma into the cliché of a young man on the rise sowing his wild oats:

> D'ailleurs, il allait devenir premier clerc: c'était le moment d'être sérieux. Aussi renonçait-il à la flûte, aux sentiments exaltés, à l'imagination: car tout bourgeois, dans l'échauffement de sa jeunesse, ne fût-ce qu'un jour, une minute, s'est cru capable d'immenses passions, de hautes entreprises. Le plus médiocre libertin a rêvé des sultanes; chaque notaire porte en soi les débris d'un poète.

> (pp. 400-401)

This powerful if indirect indictment of Léon's middle-class spinelessness is almost obscured by the apparently harsher and certainly more explicit censure reserved for Homais. The most treacherous character in the novel, Homais hides his various betrayals (of Charles Bovary, probably of Bovary's predecessor, definitely of his three successors, of the blind beggar, of Hippolyte, of Justin) behind a barrage of Enlightenment commonplaces. Now since language itself betrays, by distorting the feelings it is supposed to convey—"D'ailleurs, la parole est un laminoir qui allonge toujours les sentiments" (p. 324), the narrator observes—any user of language who fails to acknowledge this problem is also a traitor. All the more despicable, therefore, is the individual who, like Homais, acts as if the problems posed by language did not even exist and who has, moreover, like the pharmacist, "toujours des expressions congruentes à toutes les circonstances imaginables" (p. 187).

But it is in his exploration of Homais's relationship with the priest Bournisien that Flaubert renders his harshest judgment of Homais, as well as of the traditional values and institutions in nineteenth-century French society that conspire to stifle the threat to the established order of things represented by Emma's life and death. Throughout most of the novel—that is, until Emma's wake—Homais and Bournisien are depicted as unyielding adversaries, ideological enemies to the death. Together they constitute a variation on the theme of the perennial tug-of-war in France between *curé* and *instituteur.* As such, they symbolize the rival claims of France's Christian and republican heritage, warring historical currents which between them, according to the conventional wisdom, define or specify what France is and which, though inimical, join in common cause during her hour of need. It is this entire, quasi-sacred, semi-official myth of France that Flaubert explodes at Emma's wake.

After alternately arguing and dozing through the night while waking Emma's corpse, priest and druggist share an early morning repast:

> Ils managèrent et trinquèrent, tout en ricanant un peu sans savoir pourquoi, excités par cette gaieté vague qui nous prend après des séances de tristesse; et, au dernier petit verre, le prêtre dit au pharmacien, tout en lui frappant sur l'épaule:

> "Nous finirons par nous entendre!"

> (p. 460)

This final *entente cordiale* can hardly surprise us since in the course of the night the two men have drawn upon analogous platitudes and have performed parallel rituals to the end of reintegrating Emma's anarchic spirit into the orderly ethos of Yonville: e. g., "M. Bournisien aspergeait la chambre d'eau bénite et Homais jetait un peu de chlore par terre" (p. 460). The divine and the secular powers, church and state (Homais, after all, will soon be inducted into the Legion of Honor), relying on catechistic, scientistic, right-thinking responses, come together to paper over the abyss that Emma's suicide has opened up. The climactic complicity in repression of these high-minded opponents turns a vital polarity into a pious fraud, a cliché of the lowest sort.

Both of these eventually friendly enemies have a share in Emma's downfall. Although collaborating with Homais at the time of Emma's death, Bournisien seems considerably less wicked than the druggist. For one thing, he lacks Homais's hypocrisy and calculating ambition. On the other hand, vis-à-vis Emma, Bournisien is probably no less guilty than Homais; like the druggist, he is totally deaf to the tired, cliché-ridden quality of his every utterance, and hence unaware of his own destructive effect on the novel's main character. Ironically, Homais, who considers himself a latter-day *philosophe,* sounds and, in his articles, writes like Pangloss. His speech, sprinkled like Pangloss' with many an inappropriate "*car,*" gravitates constantly toward pastiche without his being aware of it. Instead of emulating Voltaire's, his prose is an amalgam of irrelevant erudition, humorlessness and pomposity, and thus constitutes an unintentional caricature of his model's writings. A wall of verbiage, buttressed by his secret desire to subvert Charles Bovary's medical practice, stands between Homais and Emma.

Bournisien shuts Emma out even more effectively than Homais does. When she goes to the priest to seek his counsel, he forecloses on the intent of her initial stammerings before she has a chance to explain herself. He begins by quoting Saint Paul ("Enfin, que voulez-vous! nous sommes nés pour souffrir, comme dit Saint Paul" [p. 156]) and ends a few minutes later by rushing into the church to conduct a catechism class for the children of the parish. As Emma starts walking back home she hears "la grosse voix du curé, la voix claire des gamins" intoning:

> —Etes-vous chrétien?
>
> —Oui, je suis chrétien.
>
> —Qu'est-ce qu'un chrétien?
>
> —C'est celui qui, étant baptisé . . . , baptisé . . . , baptisé.
>
> (p. 159)

The familiar question-and-answer dialogue fades, marking the real close of Emma's fruitless encounter with the priest, who now has come to stand for the alien codes surrounding her. The witless, repetitive exercise turns into an undifferentiated buzz of words that underscores Emma's isolation in the universe of discourse. She is a prisoner in solitary confinement, a victim of meaningless or misleading formulas, whether from sacred or profane texts. Like Binet's droning lathe, which endlessly grinds out the same round napkin holders, the inhabitants of Emma's world, of Yonville and her readings, spew forth the same phrases over and over again. They gradually choke her soul with unrelievedly trite expressions just as Binet slowly fills up his house with uniform ciphers of wood.

The ultimate source of Emma's tragic situation involves the common denominator of these stifling formulas. Emma lives, suffers, and dies alone because she inhabits a universe of discourse that is not of her making and that, with killing consequences, denies her reality. This universe comes exclusively from the literature of authority and romance, essentially male-created and biased in favor of men, the literature of patriarchy: the catechism ("Elle . . . comprenait bien le catéchisme, et c'est elle qui répondait toujours à M. le vicaire, dans les questions difficiles" [pp. 48-49]) and *Paul et Virginie, Le Génie du christianisme,* Walter Scott, Lamartine, and their imitators, all assigning women roles of passivity and dependence in relation to men. If both sexes in Flaubert's novel are prisoners of clichés, men, who constitute a kind of steward or trustee class vis-à-vis language, are at least able to change codes more or less at will (witness Léon, Rodolphe, Homais who, rabid Republican though he may pretend to be, does not shrink from adopting royalist diction to obtain the Legion of Honor, or Charles who after Emma's death acquires her romantic lexicon). Not even that rather dubious option is available to Emma, who, as a woman, is a mere receptacle for language with no distance at all from her patterns of speech and writing. Moreover, she identifies completely with the heroines she encounters in her reading or at the theater. When she attends a performance of *Lucia di Lammermoor* (based on a Walter Scott novel), for example, "la voix de la chanteuse ne lui semblait que le retentissement de sa conscience" (p. 311).

At some level of her consciousness, however, Emma grasps all this and knows that if she is to gain control of her destiny she will have to "become" a man.[6] Indications of her instinctual knowledge of this imperative occur throughout the novel, starting with her first appearance in the text. Charles has been called to the Rouault farm to tend to the old peasant's broken leg. The grown daughter, Emma, mistress of the house since her mother's death, is shown to be totally inept at "womanly" skills and unusually bold, almost "unladylike" in her way of looking at people. As for her appearance, she wears, "comme un homme, passé entre deux boutons de son corsage, un lorgnon d'écaille" (pp.

20-21). Later in the novel, just before Emma meets Rodolphe, the phrase "comme un homme" is used again: "elle se fait une raie sur le côté de la tête et roula ses cheveux en dessous, comme un homme" (p. 174). Significantly, the three words are now followed immediately in the text by remarks showing that Emma, in an almost conscious effort to emancipate herself, to rid herself of her convent-bred, quintessentially female persona, tries to break out of both her monolingualism and her reading diet of keepsake literature: "Elle voulut apprendre l'italien: elle acheta des dictionnaires, une grammaire, une provision de papier blanc. Elle essaya des lectures sérieuses, de l'histoire et de la philosophie" (p. 174). She soon abandons these projects of course and thus fails in her attempt to escape her femaleness through new words. The theme of repressed desire to change into a man is subtly reprised a few pages further on, when Emma and Rodolphe meet for the first time. He marvels at the fact that she has never fainted at the sight of blood or on any other occasion (unlike young Justin, Homais's apprentice, who has just swooned while watching Charles bleed one of Rodolphe's servants). "C'est extraordinaire pour une dame" (p. 180), Rodolphe exclaims.

The dominant role Emma assumes in her relations with Charles and later with Léon is even more suggestive of her aspirations to masculinity. In both relationships, she flouts conventions and reverses time-honored hierarchies. On the morning after her wedding night with Charles, "c'est lui plutôt que l'on eût pris pour la vierge de la veille, tandis que la mariée ne laissait rien découvrir où l'on pût deviner quelque chose" (p. 41). As for Léon, "il ne discutait pas ses idées; il acceptait tous ses goûts; il devenait sa maîtresse plutôt qu'elle n'était la sienne" (pp. 383-84). With Léon especially, Emma's passion takes on the character of an increasingly urgent need to transcend the fleeting pleasures of carnal love for some higher, more permanent realm of feeling: "D'où venait . . . cette insuffisance de la vie, cette pourriture instantanée des choses où elle s'appuyait?. . . . Chaque sourire cachait un bâillement d'ennui, chaque joie une malédiction, tout plaisir son dégoût, et les meilleurs baisers ne vous laissaient sur la lèvre qu'une irréalisable envie d'une volupté plus haute" (pp. 392-93). It need hardly be stressed that such spiritual questing is, in romantic literature at least, the natural occupation not of heroines but of heroes.

Emma's profound dissatisfaction with her lot as a woman finds most direct expression during her pregnancy when she daydreams of having a son:

> Elle souhaitait un fils; il serait fort et brun, et s'appellerait Georges; et cette idée d'avoir pour enfant un mâle était comme la revanche en espoir de toutes ses impuissances passées. Un homme, au moins, est libre; il peut parcourir les passions et les pays, traverser les obstacles, mordre aux bonheurs les plus lointains.

> Mais une femme est empêchée continuellement. Inerte et flexible à la fois, elle a contre elle les mollesses de la chair avec les dépendances de la loi. Sa volonté, comme le voile de son chapeau retenu par un cordon, palpite à tous les vents, il y a toujours quelque désir qui entraîne, quelque convenance qui retient.

> (p. 123)

This passage reveals, besides Emma's obvious projection of herself into her hoped-for son's future life, the implicit comparison between what her life actually is—hopeless straining against unbreakable chains—and what she imagines it would be, were she a man—soaring above and beyond all bonds and bounds. Thus her so-called *bovarysme,* her constant wish to be other than what she is, in the final analysis comes down to a diffuse but consuming desire on her part to be a man. And she is drawn to the masculine state because she sees man as living free while she, a mere woman, languishes in a prison of physical weakness, laws and conventions. To the reader, however, the walls of Emma's prison are the clichés of patriarchy imprinted on her psyche long before her marriage and pregnancy. By the cruellest of ironies, her unconscious aspirations toward "maleness" merely underscore the extent to which she has been taken in by these clichés.

In a broader perspective, in the novel seen as a whole, these clichés, with their drowning effect on Emma, are but so much derisive flotsam on a male-created sea of complacency, poltroonery and misogyny. Throughout **Madame Bovary,** maleness is systematically linked with evil. Rodolphe, craven exploiter of women, is introduced as "de tempérament brutal et d'intelligence perspicace, ayant d'ailleurs beaucoup fréquenté les femmes et s'y connaissant bien" (p. 181). When he faces Emma for the first time since sending her the farewell letter some three years before, he is presented as but an example of the general condition of male cowardice: "depuis trois ans, Rodolphe l'avait soigneusement évitée, par suite de cette lâcheté naturelle qui caractérise le sexe fort" (p. 428). Elsewhere in the novel the association of maleness and moral weakness lies just below the surface. To appreciate how pervasive this association is, one has only to consider the minor male characters: e. g., smug, robot-like Binet, sly, rapacious Lheureux, conspiratorial, sexually importuning Guillaumin; even the good surgeon Larivière, eager to be gone from Yonville before Emma dies, is concerned most of all for his reputation. As early as the Vaubyessard ball there is already the hint that men constitute an arrogantly cruel caste:

> Quelques hommes (une quinzaine) de vingt-cinq à quarante ans, disséminés parmi les danseurs ou causant à l'entrée des portes, se distinguaient de la foule par un air de famille, quelles que fussent leurs différences d'âge, de toilette ou de figure. . . . Dans leurs regards indifférents flottait la quiétude des passions journelle-

ment assouvies; et, à travers leurs manières douces, perçait cette brutalité particulière, que communique la domination des choses à demi faciles, dans lesquelles la force s'exerce et où la vanité s'amuse, le maniement des chevaux de race et la société des femmes perdues.

(pp. 70-71)

The defects of the important male characters are more glaring still. When Léon evades helping Emma, who is on the brink of financial ruin, she shouts at him: "Quel lâche tu fais!" (p. 411) and the reader can only agree. When Charles, knowing all now, expresses no anger at Rodolphe during a chance encounter, Rodolphe finds him "bien débonnaire pour un homme dans sa situation, comique même, et un peu vil" (p. 480). Again the reader must agree. Among his other faults, Homais is a misogynist. This becomes clear the day he spends in Rouen with Léon: "Homais se délectait. Quoiqu'il se grisât de luxe encore plus que de bonne chère, le vin de Pomard, cependant, lui excitait un peu les facultés, et, lorsque apparut l'omelette au rhum, il exposa sur les femmes des théories immorales" (p. 387). But Homais is hardly exceptional in this regard, for an ambience of misogyny permeates Emma's world and becomes almost palpable at the moment of her death. Then, as throughout her life, the parameters of her consciousness are defined by a combination of sacred and profane texts, scripts that ratify Emma's sense of herself as a sensual, fallen woman, a transgressor of patriarchal laws and thus a validation of misogynistic clichés. The last words she hears are the prayers of the priest performing the final cleansing sacrament of extreme unction, and moments later, the vaguely salacious ditty of the blind beggar. Recognizing the beggar's song, Emma sits bolt upright on her death bed, cries "L'Aveugle!" and with her very last breath laughs "d'un rire atroce, frénétique, désespéré" (p. 449). For the first time, all the words of the song are given:

> Souvent la chaleur d'un beau jour
> Fait rêver fillette à l'amour,
> Pour amasser diligemment
> Les épis que la faux moissonne,
> Ma Nanette va s'inclinant
> Vers le sillon qui nous les donne,
> Il souffla bien fort ce jour-là,
> Et le jupon court s'envola!

(pp. 448-49)

A typical specimen of misogynistic paraliterature, the song, sprung full-blown from the anti-female *gaulois* strain in French culture, articulates the classic male fantasy of the lustful maiden. Emma thus gives up the ghost in a crossfire of religious and secular clichés that reiterate her sins and inadequacies. But in her final seconds of life, she achieves a kind of moral superiority over her destiny (which, in her case at least, is obviously a function of her anatomy). She resists the reductionism of patriarchy by laughing sardonically, hysteri-

cally, as if acknowledging the horrible appropriateness of the ditty's serving as her viaticum. In the end, the grace of ironic vision saves her, or comes as close to doing so as is required by the demands of heroism in literature.

For Emma is indeed the central, heroic figure in *Madame Bovary.* Her ever restless spirit glows brilliantly against the pale wall of self-satisfaction formed by her fellow Yonvillais.[7] In an important sense, moreover, Emma's fate engages that of all women. Thus Baudelaire, more misogynist than not, was more justified than he could possibly have realized when predicting "toutes les femmes *intellectuelles* lui [à Flaubert] sauront gré d'avoir élevé la femelle à une si haute puissance."[8] For whatever her victory, Emma, although herself unaware of it, wins on behalf of all those—especially women—who have been crushed by the oppressive, foreclosing verbal fossils they unwittingly have internalized.

And the closer Emma approaches total ruin, the more panache she acquires, as if readying herself for that final, ironic "rire atroce, frénétique, désespéré." Just after Léon has refused her financial help, she encounters the blind beggar while waiting for the coach to take her back to Yonville: "Emma, prise de dégoût, lui envoya, pardessus l'épaule, une pièce de cinq francs. C'était toute sa fortune. Il lui semblait beau de la jeter ainsi" (p. 415). When later that same day Guillaumin attempts to take sexual advantage of her monetary disadvantage, Emma leaves the notary's house hissing: "Vous profitez impudemment de ma détresse, monsieur! Je suis à plaindre, pas à vendre" (pp. 419-20). Her plea for aid rejected finally by Rodolphe, she recovers her pride by declaiming: "Mais, moi, je t'aurais tout donné, j'aurais tout vendu, j'aurais travaillé de mes mains, j'aurais mendié sur les routes, pour un sourire, pour un regard, pour t'entendre dire: 'Merci'" (pp. 430-31). Still later, more exalted than defeated by her hopeless situation, she chooses to rush headlong to meet her doom rather than merely await it passively. If formerly she played at romantic heroism, she now embraces her fatal role entirely, "presque joyeuse" in her decision to ingest the arsenic she knows Homais keeps locked in his shop: "Alors sa situation, telle qu'un abîme, se représenta. Elle haletait à se rompre la poitrine. Puis, dans un transport d'héroïsme qui la rendait presque joyeuse, elle descendit la côte en courant, traversa la planche aux vaches, le sentier, l'allée, les halles, et arriva devant la boutique de pharmacien" (pp. 432-33). Once again, of course, she will be cheated by the discrepancy that separates the reality of her life from the clichés of her reading, and she will not die peacefully in her sleep, as she had been led to expect she would, but slowly and in excruciating pain. Nevertheless, her flailing courage and perverse dignity carry her through it all and these qualities set her apart from everyone else in the novel.

In yet another of the cruel ironies abounding in *Madame Bovary*, Justin, who worships Emma, is the one who gives her access to the arsenic. But when he sees her eating the poison (instead of simply taking some to kill rats, her declared purpose in asking for it), Justin cries out "Arrêtez!" (p. 434) and unsuccessfully tries to stop her. Justin's shouted command in this circumstance is one of his extremely rare utterances in the novel. Most of the time by far he stays in the background, a shadowy, silent, nearly aphasic figure of pubescent longing. He is in love with Emma, but his is the unnoticed, inarticulate attachment of the early adolescent to the mature woman.

Like that other mooning adolescent, Chérubin in *Le Mariage de Figaro,* Justin is fascinated by everything about the object of his adoration, including articles of her clothing. And as with Chérubin, whose part is traditionally played by a woman, there is a considerable amount of indeterminacy in Justin's sexuality (in variation on the theme of shifting sexuality introduced by Emma). For example, when the apprentice pharmacist faints "like a woman" at the sight of blood, Homais, his employer and master, chastizes him: "il faudra pourtant garder son sangfroid, raisonner, se montrer homme . . . !" (p. 179). But Justin will never "se montrer homme" just as he will almost never speak, since to be a man in *Madame Bovary* means to speak with ease, and to speak with ease is to utter patriarchal clichés and in so doing join Emma's oppressors.

On the night following her burial, Justin's infinite grief at her lonely graveside equals Emma's immeasurable discontent in life: "Sur la fosse, entre les sapins, un enfant pleurait agenouillé, et sa poitrine, brisée par les sanglots, haletait dans l'ombre, sous la pression d'un regret immense, plus doux que la lune et plus insondable que la nuit" (p. 469). Clearly, as Leo Bersani has pointed out, "Flaubert reserves his deepest sympathy for the dumb."[9] Justin's immense, unspoken love for Emma is that of a child, a speechless Chérubin, a diffident male still uncompromised by the language of men.

Paradoxically enough, Justin's polar opposite in the novel is his official mentor Homais. Where the former is virtually mute, filled with loving care and as much female as male, the latter—glibness itself—is heartlessly competitive and a complete misogynist to boot. As the epitome of such middleclass vices in *Madame Bovary,* Homais resembles the Garçon, that mythical, collective creation of Flaubert's childhood friends, his sister Caroline and himself. (Flaubert noted the resemblance between the Garçon and Homais at least once.[10]) But the Garçon is both the outrageously boorish bourgeois and the merciless critic of everything bourgeois.[11] He has a capacity for savage, lucid laughter totally lacking in Homais. A sense of irony and the power of self-criticism are in fact precisely the qualities most conspicuously absent in the pharmacist. Homais is easily as crudely male as the Garçon (and in the present context Flaubert's fixation on *that* name for brutishness incarnate hardly seems fortuitous), the druggist is certainly as thick and as vain and as fluent in clichés as the mythical figure. But, because he is unconscious and thus uncritical of himself, Homais remains an incomplete Garçon. The Garçon's other, better half in *Madame Bovary,* the source of frenzied, self-mocking laughter in the novel, of "un rire atroce, frénétique, désespéré," is, at least for one crucial moment, Emma.

Emma, in turn, emerges as Flaubert's most fully elaborated surrogate in his lifelong, epic struggle to escape the prison-house of clichés. Long before *Bouvard et Pécuchet* and *Le Dictionnaire des Idées reçues* saw print, *Madame Bovary,* through the tragedy of its main character, dramatized Flaubert's abiding conviction that humanity's fatal flaw lay in its implacable need to utter definitive statements, to formulate conclusions. ("L'ineptie consiste à vouloir conclure," he once wrote to Louis Bouilhet.[12]) Flaubert's usual disdain for linguistic "bêtise" notwithstanding, Emma's absolute deafness to her own voice denies the correlation that everywhere else in *Madame Bovary* keys such obtuseness into moral turpitude. But her very insensibility to herself speaking and writing, combined with her flagrant transgression of the novel's basic "law" in this regard, should alert us to Emma's special, symbolic function for Flaubert. Her plight as victim obliged to make do with clichés, with expressions that guarantee intelligibility but that oppress her, constitutes an early, transmuted, yet recognizable tableau of Flaubert's enduring dilemma as a writer. Perfect verbal transparency, epitomized by the cliché, was, he always knew, at once his highest aspiration and his nemesis. Here, perhaps, we are approaching the ultimate significance of "Madame Bovary, c'est moi."

Notes

1. What might be called the "heroic" tradition in criticism on *Madame Bovary* dates back to Baudelaire's seminal essay-review first published in 1857; see Charles Baudelaire, *Œuvres complètes,* Y. G. Le Dantec, ed., "Bibliothèque de la Pléiade" (Paris: Gallimard, 1954), pp. 1003-13. Twentieth-century developments within this critical tradition would include (for example): Albert Thibaudet, *Gustave Flaubert* (Paris: Gallimard, [1935], 1963), esp. pp. 92-122 in the 1963 edition; Harry Levin, *The Gates of Horn: A Study of Five French Realists* (New York: Oxford University Press, 1963), pp. 246-69; Victor Brombert, *The Novels of Flaubert: A Study of Themes and Techniques* (Princeton, N.J.: Princeton University Press, 1966), pp. 37-91; Dennis Porter, "Gustave Flaubert's Middle-Class Tragedy," *Forum for Modern Language Studies,* 23 (January 1977), 59-69.

2. See Gustave Flaubert, *Madame Bovary, nouvelle version précédée des scénarios inédits,* Jean Pommier, Gabrielle Leleu, eds. (Paris: Corti, 1949). For a brief but suggestive characterization of the excisions that Flaubert made in his manuscript while preparing it for publication, see John Porter Houston, *Fictional Technique in France, 1802-1927* (Baton Rouge, La.: Louisiana State University Press, 1972), pp. 71-72.

3. Gustave Flaubert, *Correspondance, I (janvier 1830 à avril 1851),* Jean Bruneau, ed., "Bibliothèque de la Pléiade" (Paris: Gallimard, 1973), pp. 211-12.

4. Gustave Flaubert, *Madame Bovary: Mœurs de Province,* Vol. VIII of *Œuvres complètes* (Paris: Louis Conard, 1910), pp. 197-210. Subsequent parenthetical page references are to this edition.

5. The proposition that Flaubert's own theory of language is indeed reflected in his narrator's statement concerning "la parole humaine" finds support in Leo Bersani's assertion that "Flaubert had an almost Platonic view of reality. He speaks in his correspondence as if subjects existed somewhere outside of language, and the exhausting labor to which he condemned himself was to find the expressions which would merely convert reality, without changing its nature, into language." See Gustave Flaubert, *Madame Bovary,* tr. Lowell Bair, Leo Bersani, ed. (New York: Bantam Books, 1972), p. xvi.

6. Emma's "virile" propensities were first noted by Baudelaire. In *The Novels of Flaubert,* pp. 88-89, Victor Brombert reviews Baudelaire's main points and then offers some suggestive observations of his own. In developing my approach to Emma's "masculinity," I have greatly benefited from Brombert's insights into this matter, even if I eventually diverge from them rather considerably.

7. As Harry Levin has put it: "Her capacity for dissatisfaction, had she been a man and a genius, might have led to Rimbaldian adventures or Baudelairian visions: 'Anywhere out of the world,'" (p. 168).

8. Baudelaire, *Œuvres complètes,* p. 1010.

9. Leo Bersani, *Balzac to Beckett: Center and Circumference in French Fiction* (New York: Oxford University Press, 1970), p. 170.

10. "Le personnage ridicule de mon roman est un voltairien, philosophe matérialiste (comme le Garçon!)." Quoted from an unpublished letter in the "Préface" to Gustave Flaubert, *Madame Bovary,* Jacques Suffel, ed. (Paris: Garnier-Flammarion, 1966), p. 18.

11. See, for example, Jean Bruneau, *Les Débuts littéraires de Gustave Flaubert (1831-1845)* (Paris: Armand Colin, 1962), pp. 150-60; Jean-Paul Sartre, *L'Idiot de la famille,* II (Paris: Gallimard, 1971), pp. 1214-31, *passim*; Jonathan Culler, *Flaubert: The Uses of Uncertainty* (Ithaca, N.Y.: Cornell University Press, 1974), pp. 161-65.

12. Charles Carlut, *La Correspondance de Flaubert: étude et répertoire critique* (Columbus, Ohio: Ohio State University Press, 1968), p. 599.

Eugene F. Gray (essay date spring-summer 1978)

SOURCE: Gray, Eugene F. "Emma by Twilight: Flawed Perception in *Madame Bovary.*" *Nineteenth-Century French Studies* 6, nos. 3 and 4 (spring-summer 1978): 231-40.

[*In the following essay, Gray analyzes Flaubert's use of description in the novel, focusing on the relationship between Emma's character and images of evening and darkness. Gray argues that the shadows that surround Emma throughout the work symbolize her spiritual blindness.*]

The effectiveness of Gustave Flaubert's use of description has long been a subject of discussion among critics, whose reactions have ranged from the open admiration of Zola to the sharp (and unfair) criticism of Duranty. The former proposed Flaubert as a model for emulation,[1] while the latter saw in *Madame Bovary,* for example, only the "obstination de la description."[2]

For the most part neither the early admirers nor the early critics of Flaubert's style seemed to understand the function of description in his works. Only Maupassant, having learned his own technique from the master himself, seems to have completely grasped the significance of Flaubert's practice. He and Flaubert both were "illusionnistes,"[3] bending every effort to communicate the illusion of reality, i.e. a vision or impression which the reader will apprehend as real, rather than attempting to reproduce Reality itself, something impossible to encompass within a finite art form.

Presenting the illusion of reality implies presenting reality as experienced by a sentient being, fixed in time and space and limited in his perceptions. In much of Flaubert's fiction, the sentient being is represented by a character or a narrator who observes the action. Descriptive details thus become an integral part of the narrative and of character portrayal and form an aspect of point of view. The character's development is studied through his perceptions of and reactions to reality; the narrator's voice serves to render these reactions and perceptions in words.

Scenes containing descriptive details presented from the point of view either of a character or of an immanent narrator abound in *Madame Bovary.* In the opening scene the narrator is himself a member of Charles's class. The initial description of Yonville in Chapter One of Part Two is given from the moving vantage point of a traveler passing through the town. A large part of the *Comices agricoles* (Chapter Eight of Part Two) is presented from Emma's point of view as she watches the scene with Rodolphe from a window in the town hall. (This scene is of course made more complex by Flaubert's ironic juxtaposition of details.) The spectator, Emma, is stationary, but the focus changes as she receives impressions from Rodolphe, from the officials' platform, and from the stagecoach on the horizon. These three scenes illustrate three variants of what might be called cinematographic technique: fixed camera-fixed focus, fixed camera-changing focus, moving camera-changing focus.

The presentation of sense impressions as experienced by characters in the novel or by an immanent narrator, the central concept of "illusionnisme," implies that ambient conditions affecting the characters' perceptions will usually be mentioned in descriptive passages. Such conditions may result from the character's position in space (e.g. Emma's position at the window of the town hall during the *Comices agricoles*. Such spatial effects are common in Flaubert's works). But because of Flaubert's acute visual sense ("Je sais voir et voir comme voient les myopes, jusque dans les pores des choses, parce qu'ils se fourrent le nez dessus"),[4] his descriptions infallibly include a reference to conditions which might affect the characters' visual perception, and especially to the illumination of the scene.

Flaubert's early critics were often content to point out the pictorial, Parnassian qualities of his descriptions, especially the play of light. Commenting on the well-known descriptive passage with which Flaubert opens the third chapter of **Salammbô**. Gustave Lanson wrote: "C'est la lumière qui est l'objet de sa [Flaubert's] description, qui en fait l'unité. . . . La plume a voulu être, ici, un pinceau."[5] As early as 1880 Brunetière drew attention to a number of Flaubert's more striking descriptive passages, showing that Flaubert's practice was to mention those aspects of a scene which reflected or refracted the incident light. This technique Brunetière characterized as a "procédé de peintre."[6] Remarks comparing Flaubert's descriptions to paintings have formed a leitmotiv of Flaubert criticism ever since. Flaubert himself had used the same analogy; composing **Madame Bovary,** he wrote, was "peindre couleur sur couleur et sans tons tranchés."[7]

More recent critics have attempted to trace the development of Flaubert's techniques of rendering light. Benjamin Bart has shown how much Flaubert's interest in light and color was stimulated by his trip to the Near East in 1849-1851.[8] Certainly Flaubert's remark. "Axiome: c'est le ciel qui fait le paysage,"[9] shows that by this time (1850) he was fully conscious of the influence of light upon one's perceptions. But the following passage from the first **Education sentimentale** suggests that even before his major voyages, Flaubert had begun to develop an interest in describing the effects of light: "Un grand rayon de soleil, entré par un trou de la muraille, traversait en diagonale tout le théâtre, une poussière dorée et remuante montait en tressaillant dans cette ligne droite, un quinquet de la rampe, frappé par lui, brillait et éclairait, comme allumé."[10] Although other interesting examples of descriptions of the effects of light can be found during this same period, descriptive passages written during and after Flaubert's voyage to the Near East are more frequent and of better quality.[11]

The use of lighting in the descriptive passages of **Madame Bovary** is thus the result of several years' apprenticeship on Flaubert's part, deriving from the lessons learned in writing **Par les champs et par les grèves** and especially the notes which he made of his trip to the Near East [**Notes de Voyage**]. Despite the severe limitations resulting from the choice of the Norman countryside as a setting for the novel and of the *couleur cloporte* of the fictional landscape, Flaubert's skill in rendering nuances of light is readily apparent to the attentive reader. His goal, as he later wrote to Sainte-Beuve (**Correspondance,** V, 60-61), was to make his descriptions contribute to the development of character and action.

Flaubert's aim is especially well carried out in the presentation of Emma. She is often described from a particular vantage point in space (the same holds true for other characters as well), and the details of the descriptions depend upon ambient lighting conditions. Emma's eyes, for example, are "noirs à l'ombre et bleu foncé au grand jour."[12] Moreover, one particular aspect of lighting, dim or attenuated, seems to be preferred. Emma, in accord with her Romantic character, moves in and prefers a crepuscular atmosphere.

The reader's first glimpse of Emma is from Charles's point of view. Charles Bovary has set out before dawn at the urgent request of Emma's father. Preoccupied with thoughts of the broken leg which he will soon have to set, Charles, only half-awake, does not take much notice of Emma as she comes to the door to greet him. This fact, coupled with the extremely dim light of early morning, accounts for Emma's brief, anonymous presentation: "Une jeune femme, en robe de mérinos bleu garnie de trois volants, vint sur le seuil de la maison pour recevoir M. Bovary" (p. 15).

Once inside the Rouault kitchen, where a fire is burning in the fireplace, Charles notices those objects which are highlighted by the firelight: the breakfast bowls, clothes hung up to dry, and especially the polished kitchen utensils hanging on the wall, "où miroitait inégalement la flamme claire du foyer, jointe aux premières lueurs du soleil arrivant par les carreaux" (p. 15). While materials for setting Rouault's leg are being prepared, Charles notices a few details of Emma's person, such as "la blancheur de ses ongles" (p. 16), where the nominal expression emphasizes the impression, and her eyes: "quoiqu'ils fussent bruns, ils semblaient noirs à cause des cils" (p. 16). The conditions surrounding this first meeting are not such as to allow Charles and Emma to perceive one another clearly.

Charles returns frequently to the Rouault farm, more frequently than is required by the condition of his patient. Flaubert uses the iterative aspect to describe several of these visits, for which Charles arises and leaves early. One particular visit introduces a corollary to the crepuscular motif under consideration: the use of attenuated light sources, representing Emma's flight from strong, direct light. The incident light of this brief scene, sunlight, is quite strong, but Emma protects herself from it by means of a parasol, so that Charles sees her in filtered light. The play of sunlight produces a somewhat surreal effect: "L'ombrelle, de soie gorge-de-pigeon, que traversait le soleil, éclairait de reflects mobiles la peau blanche de sa figure" (p. 19). The result is a distorted visual impression of Emma's face.

In the next substantial scene containing both Charles and Emma, Charles perceives her once again under less than ideal conditions. The scene takes place in the kitchen of the Rouault farm with the shutters closed, so that Charles at first does not perceive Emma, but notices the play of light on objects in the room:

> Par les fentes du bois, le soleil allongeait sur les pavés de grandes raies minces qui se brisaient à l'angle des meubles et tremblaient au plafond. Des mouches, sur la table, montaient le long des verres qui avaient servi, et bourdonnaient en se noyant au fond, dans le cidre resté. Le jour qui descendait par la cheminée, veloutant la suie de plaque, bleuissait un peu les cendres froides
>
> (p. 23)

Flaubert's method is clear. The reader does not learn whether Emma is in the room until the more striking details of the scene have been noted: the rays of light, which produce a definite directional effect, the buzzing flies in the partially empty glass of cider, even the light scattered from the ashes. As in the scene depicting Emma's and Charles's first encounter (supra p. 234), which was illuminated by weak sunlight and firelight, Flaubert posits two sources of light (from the chimney and through the shutters), and mixes them. The mixing of different types of light and of different sense impressions is found quite often in Flaubert's descriptions. As in the passage quoted from the first **Education senti-mentale** (supra p. 233). Flaubert has used the dynamic technique of following a light ray.

Charles and Emma therefore meet and become acquainted with each other in scenes which are poorly illuminated. It has been said that "Charles 'sees' Emma . . . but is constitutionally unable to *understand* her,"[13] but the dim lighting in which Emma is presented makes it doubtful that Charles ever really sees her at all (and more importantly, the same holds true for Emma's perception of Charles). He receives conflicting impressions of Emma, varying according to ambient conditions, which he is unable to integrate into a veridical, coherent whole, for each impression erases the previous one: "Mais jamais il [Charles] ne put la voir en sa pensée, différemment qu'il ne l'avait vue la première fois, ou telle qu'il venait de la quitter tout à l'heure" (p. 24). Only his initial impression, the most incomplete and rapid of all, is stronger than the others. Charles's view of Emma is limited forever.

The illumination of the scenes in which Emma's point of view predominates (that is, beginning with Chapter Six) often produces the same shadowy, crepuscular atmosphere as noted in the scenes studied above. These crepuscular scenes, too numerous to be listed exhaustively here, frequently occur at key points in the action of the novel.

One of the most important of these scenes is the ball at the Château de la Vaubyessard. Charles and Emma arrive at the château "à la nuit tombante, comme on commençait à allumer les lampions dans le parc" (p. 48). Emma, like so many heroes and heroines of Romance before her, has reached the outer confines of a magical new world. As she enters the dining room, "Emma se sentit . . . enveloppée par un air chaud, mélange du parfum des fleurs et du beau linge, du fumet des viandes et de l'odeur des truffes" (p. 49)—she is now completely immersed in this new world. The artificial lighting in the dining room contributes to the fairy-tale atmosphere: "Les bougies des candélabres allongeaient des flammes sur les cloches d'argent; les cristaux à facettes, couverts d'une buée mate, se renvoyaient des rayons pâles" (p. 49). Notice that Flaubert's technique of mixing sensations and different degrees of sensation has been carried to a high degree here, and serves to underscore the intensity of Emma's experience. Not only is there a mixture of olfactory, tactile and visual sensations, but the light rays, already weak as they emanate from the candles, become progressively weaker as they are reflected from the silver dish covers and refracted from the vapor-covered crystal.

The next substantial scene of the novel is in Yonville, at the *Lion d'Or*. Emma and Charles arrive after nightfall. Emma goes straight to the fireplace in the kitchen, where "du bout de ses deux doigts elle prit sa robe à la hauteur du genou, et, l'ayant ainsi remontée jusqu'aux chevilles, elle tendit à la flamme, par-dessus le gigot qui tournait, son pied chaussé d'une bottine noire" (p.

81). Léon Bopp found this pose to be "singulière,"[14] but Flaubert, by placing Emma in this situation, is able to make use of the play of light. Bathed in a "lumière crue" (p. 81), and covered by "une grande couleur rouge" (p. 81) (notice the nominal structure here), which changes in synchronization with the wind coming through the half-open door, Emma is observed by Léon. Flaubert has repeated the conditions of dim and distorting illumination which obtained during Charles's and Emma's first meeting. Léon's initial impression of Emma is as limited as was Charles's.

Another important scene in which the crepuscular motif is at least partially present in Rodolphe's seduction of Emma. Although Emma's and Rodolphe's excursion begins at noon (p. 161), the countryside is covered with fog, so that "toute la vallée paraissait un immense lac pâle" (p. 162), while under the pine trees "une lumière brune circulait" (p. 163). (Bopp, p. 248, criticized this last detail.) Similarly Emma's face, covered by a veil, appears "dans une transparence bleuâtre, comme si elle eût nagé sous des flots d'azur" (p. 164), so that her perception of the surroundings is distorted. At the point where Emma yields, "les ombres du soir descendaient" (p. 165).

The clandestine meetings between Emma and Rodolphe at first take place in his château in early morning (as did Charles's first visit to the Rouault farm), later mainly at night. When Rodolphe decides to end the affair, he sends Emma a farewell letter about mid-afternoon and passes through Yonville that same evening in his tilbury. Emma faints after recognizing the lights of Rodolphe's carriage as it passes in the dark.

Emma's accidental meeting with Léon takes place in the evening at the theater. Once again, as with the Vaubyessard ball, Emma is exposed to a magical world, the world of Walter Scott, but this time she is purely a spectator, and after the intermission her attention is easily distracted by Léon's presence. Their first meeting alone takes place in Emma's hotel room, from five until after eight o'clock in the evening. Finally, Emma obtains the arsenic in the evening as the Homais family is tranquilly having supper. After the poison has begun to take effect, we read that "une confusion de crépuscule s'abattait en sa pensée" (p. 324).

The preceding examples, although selective, show the consistency of Flaubert's practice. In addition he himself eliminated from the published edition many similar passages, several of which have been restored in the edition prepared by Jean Pommier and Gabrielle Leleu.[15]

Flaubert's predilection for crepuscular settings has led him to depict situations which, strictly speaking, are improbable or unbelievable, for he prolonged artificially certain episodes so that they would conclude in twilight. Léon Bopp has drawn attention to two such scenes. One of them is Emma's and Léon's mock-epic ride in the hackney cab, its shades tightly drawn, lasting from around noon until six o'clock in the evening. "Les deux amants ont passé quelque cinq à six heures dans leur fiacre fermé, aux heures les plus chaudes de la plus chaude saison. Si donc le cocher, sur son siège, a 'presque' pleuré de soif, eux aussi, dans leur carriole surchauffée par le soleil, durent être bien altérés" (Bopp, p. 387). Moreover, by prolonging the lovers' ride until six o'clock, Flaubert caused Emma to miss the stagecoach, which normally left Rouen at three o'clock and arrived in Yonville at six o'clock. On this occasion, although Hivert waited for Emma for 53 minutes, it is hard to accept the fact that she could return to the hotel, pack her bag, pay her bill, rent a carriage and still catch the *Hirondelle* before it reached Yonville (cf. Bopp, p. 387).

An analogous problem occurs in the scene where Emma obtains the arsenic. It is about seven o'clock in the evening. "Peut-être un critique vétilleux ferait-il remarquer ici qu'on n'a point l'impression que quelque quatre heures se soient écoulées depuis l'instant où la mère Rollet indiquait à Emma qu'il était presque trois heures" (Bopp, p. 492). A similar improbability was pointed out by Ernest Bovet.[16] He estimates that Emma, on the day she received Rodolphe's farewell letter, spent four hours in the attic. The amount of text devoted to this scene does not make it apparent that her stay in the attic was so prolonged.

Flaubert's predilection for shadowy settings in *Madame Bovary,* a predilection which greatly increases the improbability of some situations, indicates that his conception of Emma includes as an essential component the crepuscular decor.[17] Emma is in fact a creature of darkness, most active at night and shunning the bright light of day. She would have been married at midnight by torchlight but for her father's veto (p. 27). In the convent and after her marriage to Charles, especially during periods of depression, Emma spends long hours in her room, curtains drawn, sometimes reading until dawn (pp. 40, 107, 128, 294-95). Bright light makes her blink, and on one occasion, a visit to the wet-nurse with Léon, the heat of midday causes her to feel weak (p. 93). Her clandestine meetings with Léon generally occur in a hotel room with curtains drawn. Flaubert's stated aim of depicting character through description indicates that Emma's preference for shadowy dimly-lit settings is suggestive of her temperament.

More generally, however, the crepuscular motif illustrates Emma's most serious shortcoming, one which is shared by Charles Bovary and by many of Flaubert's other principal characters, namely lack of vision. Emma is condemned to view the world through the *verres de couleur*[18] of the stereotyped novels and engravings which she favors and of her own Romantic temperament. The allegorical figure of the blind beggar (who was originally to be a *cul-de-jatte,* cf. Pommier and Leleu [**Madame Bovary, Nouvelle version précédée des scénarios inédits**], p. 106), whatever else he may represent, symbolizes Emma's moral and spiritual blindness. Not once, except perhaps on her deathbed as she gazes for the last time into her mirror, does Emma fully perceive her situation. Thus, as sightless as the blind beggar who importuned her on the outskirts of Rouen (and whom the author, for esthetic reasons, contrived to be present at her death), Emma may be viewed as a victim of her own flawed perception.

Notes

1. Emile Zola, "Du roman," *Œuvres complètes,* ed. Henri Mitterand (Paris: Cercle du Livre Précieux, 1966-69), X, 1301.

2. Louis-Emile-Edmond Duranty, *Le Réalisme,* 15 mars 1857 (rpt. Paris: L'Arche du Livre, 1970), p. 79.

3. Term coined by Guy de Maupassant in the preface to *Pierre et Jean, Œuvres complètes* (Paris: Conard, 1930), XXI, xv.

4. *Correspondance* (Paris: Conard, 1926-33), II, 343.

5. Gustave Lanson, *L'Art de la prose* (Paris: Fayard, n.d.), pp. 278-79.

6. Ferdinand Brunetière, "Gustave Flaubert," *Revue des Deux Mondes* (15 juin, 1880), p. 831.

7. *Correspondance,* III, 86. The question of Flaubert's relationship to painting is not limited to the style of his landscape descriptions. Jean Seznec has shown to what extent Flaubert was stimulated by paintings and engravings in "Flaubert and the Graphic Arts," *Journal of the Warburg and Courtauld Institutes,* VIII (1945), pp. 175-190.

8. Benjamin F. Bart, *Flaubert's Landscape Descriptions* (Ann Arbor: University of Michigan Press, 1956), pp. 8-9.

9. *Notes de voyages* (Paris: Conard, 1910), II, 19. Quoted by Bart, p. 8.

10. *Œuvres de jeunesse* (Paris: Conard, 1910), III, 67. Two other examples of the play of light in this novel were noted by D. L. Demorest, *L'Expression figurée et symbolique dans l'œuvre de Gustave Flaubert* (Paris: Presses Modernes, 1931), p. 214.

11. Demorest reached a similar conclusion based on a study of Flaubert's imagery, pp. 617-618.

12. *Madame Bovary,* ed. Cl. Gothot-Mersch (Paris: Garnier, 1971), p. 34. Unless otherwise indicated all further references to the novel will be to this edition.

13. Victor Brombert, *The Novels of Flaubert* (Princeton: Princeton University Press, 1966), p. 42.

14. Léon Bopp, *Commentaire sur "Madame Bovary"* (Neuchâtel: A la Baconnière, 1951), p. 137.

15. *Madame Bovary, Nouvelle version précédée des scénarios inédits,* ed. Jean Pommier and Gabrielle Leleu (Paris: José Corti, 1949), pp. 157, 165, 188, 216, 379, 532, 537 for example).

16. Ernest Bovet, "Le Réalisme de Flaubert," *Revue d'Histoire Littéraire de la France,* 18 (1911), p. 25.

17. Emma is not the only heroine whom Flaubert portrayed in this manner; cf. the initial portrait of Marie in *Novembre* (*Œuvres de jeunesse,* II, 198), or portraits of Madame Renaud in the first *Education sentimentale* (*Œuvres de jeunesse,* III, 80) and of Marie Arnoux in the *Education sentimentale* of 1869 (Conard edition of the *Œuvres complètes* [Paris, 1936], XI, 65), but only in *Madame Bovary* does the crepuscular setting reach such a high degree of consistency.

18. One of the longer finished passages omitted from the published version of the novel depicts Emma, the morning after the Vaubyessard ball, looking at the landscape through colored pieces of glass (see Pommier and Leleu, p. 216). Flaubert had used similar imagery in the *Mémoires d'un fou*: "Chacun de nous a un prisme à travers lequel il aperçoit le monde" (*Œuvres de jeunesse,* I, 530) and in a letter to Miss Leroyer de Chantepie in 1857: "La philosophie telle qu'on la fait et la religion telle qu'elle subsiste sont des verres de couleurs qui empêchent de voir clair" (*Correspondance,* IV, 243-44). The image was not new in Flaubert's time, see Marmontel's article "Vérité relative" in his *Elément de littérature*: "L'habitude, le préjugé, l'opinion sont autant de verres diversement colorés, à travers lesquels chacun de nous voit les objets," in *Œuvres complètes* (1818-1820, repr. Geneva: Slatkine, 1968), V, 260.

William A. Johnsen (essay date May 1979)

SOURCE: Johnsen, William A. "*Madame Bovary*: Romanticism, Modernism, and Bourgeois Style." *Modern Language News* 94, no. 4 (May 1979): 843-50.

[*In the following essay, Johnsen discusses qualities of modernity in the novel's prose style. Johnsen argues that Flaubert's style derived from the bourgeois sensibility that formed his cultural milieu, even as it strove to rebel against the provincial, limiting forces of this same sensibility.*]

The strident opposition to Romanticism of such Modernists as Eliot and Hulme has not dissuaded critics like Frank Kermode, Robert Langbaum, and more recently, Walter Ong, from discerning Modernism's kinship to Romanticism, from discovering the origins of Modernism at the beginning of the nineteenth century. Ong argues that Romanticism and Modernism reflect a major shift in consciousness: a conservative society which can only preserve what it knows by oral and manuscript tradition, gradually transforms into a modern society secure enough in what it knows to seek new forms of knowledge. This shift is made possible by the improvement of technology for information storage, retrieval, and dissemination. Yet Ong's hypothesis cannot plumb the recesses of Flaubert's darker understanding of the modern technological age emerging before him, in which bourgeois entrepreneurs now will mass produce and distribute exotic experiences for a clientele which imagines that its romanticism is anti-bourgeois, and in which novelist entrepreneurs will disseminate realistic fictions to an audience which imagines its scrupulous objectivity protects it from a romanticism it has outgrown.

Everyone knows the story of how Flaubert came to write *Madame Bovary.* After listening to him read *La Tentation* [*La Tentation de Sainte Antoine*], du Camp and Bouilhet insisted that he must curb his lyricism. If Romanticism was once an escape from bourgeois mediocrity, it was now obsolete, as repetitious and banal as the imbecility it fled from. *Madame Bovary* was the stern antidote prescribed by his friends; the narrator is a recently disabused romantic who now maturely regards a romanticism at one with bourgeois stupidity. But Flaubert already knew, as the first generation romantics had come to realize, that Romanticism was by now out-of-date; thousands of bourgeois were bored with emotions they had never felt. Flaubert was trying to go beyond Romanticism in *La Tentation,* but du Camp shrewdly writes: "sous prétexte de pousser le romantique à outrance, Flaubert, sans qu'il s'en doutât, retournait en arrière, revenait à l'abbé Raynal, à Marmontel, à Bitaubé même, et tombait dans la diffusion."[1] The promise of Modernism is to place oneself beyond the anxiety of belatedness (*pace* Harold Bloom). But Flaubert's attempt to go beyond the derivative romanticism of others only exposes, once again, his kinship to the bourgeois. Bourgeois style is the attempt to mask one's belatedness by slavishly imitating or competing with the modernity of others who are themselves masking their anxiety by compulsively rehearsing their antipathy to the bourgeois. By fulfilling his worst fears of self-exposure, du Camp and Bouilhet help Flaubert, in *Madame Bovary,* to render the bourgeois and the antipathy to the bourgeois as a single phenomenon endlessly repeated, to reveal Modernism as bourgeois style.[2]

My discussion of the bourgeois devaluation of symbols consciously parallels Siegfried Giedion's analysis of Empire Style in *Mechanization Takes Command.*[3] Napoleon, whom Giedion calls the first self-made man of the nineteenth century, encouraged the two Paris designers, Percier and Fontaine, to create a style for France that would at once gain respect for Napoleon's imperial aspirations, and compensate for his common origin. Empire Style randomly plundered other cultures for symbols of authority and juxtaposed them in a single object without regard for the radical difference of their original contexts. The development of mass production and distribution allowed these objects to be reproduced and marketed cheaply until, by Flaubert's time, France had been flooded with devalued symbols. The aristocratic forms of pre-revolutionary France, as well as pseudo-relics of Egypt and ancient Greece, emerge as bourgeois commodities now available to anyone.

The special enterprise of the nineteenth-century bourgeois becomes the devaluing and merchandizing of symbols. By purchasing symbols divorced from their original contexts, the bourgeois escape their belatedness by experiencing vicariously the aristocratic signifieds of Greece and Egypt. But these objects fail to sustain the climate of nobility they promise, and are quickly discarded for newer objects, each new purchase inspiring a greater desire and a greater disappointment. The emptiness of the signifiers increases the desire for a more substantial experience, but it is a substantiality only a voyeur would desire. To a voyeur, vicarious experience looks substantial (or, as we shall see, realistic) because it is empty. The Erysicthonic appetite for new experiences is the classic double bind that nourishes the compulsive accumulating and discarding of symbolic objects in modern society.[4]

The world of *Madame Bovary* is glutted with commercially devalued symbols like Charles' hat.[5] One thinks immediately of the scratched dinner plates which set forth the story of Mademoiselle de la Vallière (48), or the wedding cake which the *new* Yvetot confectioner, anxious to impress potential customers, creates for Emma; a temple on the bottom, a dungeon in the middle layer, and a green field on top. Or even the Yonville town hall, directly influenced by Empire Style ("construite *sur les dessins d'un architecte de Paris*"— 99, Flaubert's italics), with its incredible melange of incompatible architectural motifs.

These irrational objects promise to realize for their owners the excitement that romantic literature can only describe as someone else's. But the novels that Emma reads are something more than a wholesale catalogue for bourgeois commodities. Romantic literature specializes in uncommon experience designed to relieve boredom; eventually, the genre of romantic literature becomes like an overflowing warehouse where the stock gets confused (52-53). The lending library exacerbates the chimerical by flooding consciousness with contradictory images whose only relation is that they are uncommon, anti-bourgeois, that is to say, romantic. These images follow one another in such profusion that, "à la fois," they merge into one entity. The country that Emma desires as an alternative to *petits bourgeois imbéciles* exists as a single landscape only as a bourgeois commodity.

In their first conversation Emma and Léon enthusiastically confirm the convenience, the accessibility of experience packaged in books.

> On ne songe à rien, continuait-il, les heures passent. On se promène immobile dans des pays que l'on croit voir, et votre pensée, s'enlaçant à la fiction, se joue dans le détail ou poursuit le contour des aventures. Elle se mêle aux personnages; il semble que c'est vous qui palpitez sous leurs costumes.
>
> (114-15)

Romantic literature teaches how to desire as well as what to desire. Léon describes to Emma the meditative position that frees the soul to travel to the country of romance. By renouncing physical involvement, the reader can experience romance vicariously, and engage the sympathetic companionship of a character who is in fact the reader himself returning from the far side of the fiction. Reading romantic literature is the exemplary spiritual exercize in bourgeois culture.

The structure of romantic desire creates the illusion of a painting in linear perspective, which tells the viewer where he stands, and invites the imagination to leave the body to travel into the painting towards the vanishing point along the path of his gaze. Emma follows the path to the vanishing point (Paris) *in her thoughts,* but in the end her dreams are never realized. "Au bout d'une distance indéterminée, il se trouvait toujours une place confuse où expirait son rêve" (80).

We, however, examine Emma's naiveté from a sophisticated point of view we share with (or copy from) the narrator: we know *le genre* of vicarious experience, we know better than to try to eat the grapes off the canvas. We know that romanticism fails to escape bourgeois mediocrity because romanticism is itself a bourgeois commodity appropriate for a later stage of bourgeois consciousness.

> D'ailleurs, il [Léon] allait devenir premier clerc: c'était le moment d'être sérieux. Aussi renonçait-il à la flûte, aux sentiments exaltés, à l'imagination:—car tout bourgeois, dans l'échauffement de sa jeunesse, ne fût-ce qu'un jour, une minute, s'est cru capable d'immense passions, de hautes entreprises. Le plus médiocre libertin a rêvé des sultanes; chaque notaire porte en soi les débris d'un poète.
>
> (400-401)

The narrator's generalizing tone shares with a like-minded reader his assumption that he is articulating wisdom all mature men have learned. Ultimately one must recognize that desire is not fulfilled in this world. But the ultimate bourgeois folly is to imagine that one has finally outgrown an emotionally and financially extravagant compulsion for exotic experiences. Mature realism is only the bourgeois screen for voyeuristic self-titillation. Each renunciation prepares for a fiercer abandonment.

Let us consider the sequence of events by which Emma comes to understand her love for Léon in Chapter 5, Part II. She is interrupted from her meditation by Lheureux, who attempts to sell her some exotic merchandise. She ultimately refuses to buy anything, but Lheureux is not fooled. She is only crediting her account with virtue she can spend again later. ("Comme j'ai été sage! se disait-elle en songeant aux écharpes"—46). Her rejection of Léon's intimacy likewise increases her desires and his also. Repression is more erotically ennervating than satisfaction.

> par ce renoncement, il la plaçait en des conditions extraordinaires. Elle se dégagea, pour lui, des qualités charnelles dont il n'avait rien à obtenir; et elle alla, dans son coeur, montant toujours et s'en détachant à la manière magnifique d'une apothéose qui s'envole.
>
> (148)

The narrator, older than Léon, understands the pleasure of thwarted passion. Isolation is the proper environment for relationships informed by the standards of vicarious experience. The narrator scrupulously accentuates the serenity of Léon's renunciation, as opposed to the dangerous unrest of Emma's self-inflicted privation (149-50). The ascetic air of self-denial ("Je suis vertueuse") which wins the esteem of the bourgeois cannot assuage Emma's frustration. The profusion of commodities in the marketplace revealed by Lheureux, like the countless romantic novels in the lending libraries, display all that Emma has foregone through a wisdom later regretted as timidity. The frustrations of flesh, money, and passion confound themselves because they obey the same law of desire: the new technology celebrates its power by exaggerating and manipulating to an intolerable degree the disparity between the depiction of the wealth of others and the comparative impoverishment of the self. The romantic novel is the microcosm of the bourgeois marketplace. Customers must be made to feel that they cannot escape boredom by standing pat with what they already have; only new purchases can avail them of the more exciting lives of others. Aristocratic forms which can only be delivered by divorcing them from their original contexts are engaged vicariously by a self denying its own context. The novel (and the marketplace) arrange an engagement of empty signifiers organized by a voyeur's conception of a future world of pure signifieds.[6]

The relationship of passion, material possessions, and sexual love is continuous. Emma compensates for resisting Léon by reversing the scruples of domestic virtue with which she confounded him.

> Une femme qui s'était imposé de si grands sacrifices pouvait bien se passer des fantaisies. Elle s'acheta un prie-Dieu gothique, elle dépensa en un mois pour quatorze francs de citrons à se nettoyer les ongles; elle écrivit à Rouen, afin d'avoir une robe en cachemire bleu; elle choisit chez Lheureux la plus belle de ses écharpes; elle se la nouait à la taille par-dessus sa robe de chambre; et, les volets fermés, avec un livre à la main, elle restait étendue sur un canapé, dans cet accoutrement.
>
> (173)

Emma finally buys Lheureux's best scarf, but it will end up in the closet with all her other *fantaisies,* devalued symbols which cannot deliver what they promise. Emma wants to appropriate the ascetic nobility of intellectual self-discipline to confer dignity on her sexual repression. The bourgeois marketplace creates a climate of expectations that reduces history and philosophy to commodities which, as commodities, can only disappoint their customers. This, in turn, increases their appetite for future satisfaction, like a gambler trying to break a losing streak by doubling his bet. One begins to feel the menacing pertinence of the councillor's description of the new age at the agricultural fair: "partout fleurissent le commerce et les arts; partout des voies nouvelles de communication, comme autant d'artères nouvelles dans le corps de l'Etat, y établissent des rapports nouveaux" (198).

With the instincts of a merchant like Lheureux, Rodolphe seduces Emma by offering to break the relentless cycle of promise and disappointment in which Emma and Léon have acquiesced. Rodolphe promises to realize in her world the vicarious experience of romantic reading (198-99). Predictably, Rodolphe knows the *fantaisies et folies* of the women he seduces, but he also knows the structure of romantic desire. He paints her past disappointment and hopes for future bliss, as she does, in linear perspective. He knows that romantics derive their dreams from books, then attempt to fulfill them in action. Like Paolo and Francesca, they dream (read), act, then read again, "tour à tour." Emma regards him as the successful *voyageur* who has gone down the dark corridor, opened the door to the light, and returned. He subtly identifies himself as the companion of her dreams who resides at the horizon. He encourages her, like the heroes of her books and dreams, to experience vicariously his success in passing beyond the vanishing point of romantic desire.

Emma chooses to believe what Rodolphe only pantomimes. Emma repeatedly abandons the fixed point of view of bourgeois desire. While watching the intense passion depicted in the stage production of Scott's *Lucy of Lammermoor,* Emma considers, then rejects, the safety of the emotional detachment characteristic of Rodolphe, Léon, and the narrator.

> Mais ce bonheur-là, sans doute, était un mensonge imaginé pour le désespoir de tout désir. Elle connaissait à présent la petitesse des passions que l'art exagérait. S'efforçant donc d'en détourner sa pensée, Emma voulait ne plus voir dans cette reproduction de ses douleurs qu'une fantaisie plastique bonne à amuser les yeux et même elle souriait intérieurement d'une pitié dédaigneuse quand, au fond du théâtre, sous la portière de velours, un homme apparut en manteau noir.
>
> (312)

Emma is creating a pose for her own protection. She would think of the *bonheur* of romance as destructive of desire because she wants to see herself as mature and realistic, beyond desire, beyond the optical illusion of romance. Disdain would protect her from her suicidal desire for the same passion as others seem to experience. But realistic detachment is useless when Lagardy, as Edgar, appears on stage.

> Il devait avoir, pensait-elle, un intarissable amour, pour en déverser sur la foule à si larges effluves. Toutes ses velléités de dénigrement s'évanouissaient sous la poésie du rôle qui l'envahissait, et, entraînée vers l'homme par l'illusion du personnage, elle tâcha de se figurer sa vie, cette vie retentissante, extraordinaire, splendide, et qu'elle aurait pu mener, cependant, si le hasard l'avait voulu.
>
> (313)

This is what Léon, Rodolphe, and the narrator are protecting themselves from, by convincing themselves that they have exhausted romanticism. They have completed their sentimental education, experienced the last new wave, everything from here on is boring but safe. Not the bourgeois boredom that romanticism rejects, but the wise ennui of mature realism that has outgrown romanticism. Like Léon, Rodolphe becomes immune to the lure of experiences with Emma that seem to him monotonous repetitions of what he has already known.

> Il s'était tant de fois entendu dire ces choses, qu'elles n'avaient pour lui rien d'original. Emma ressemblait à toutes les maîtresses; et le charme de la nouveauté, peu à peu tombant comme un vêtement, laissait voir à nu l'éternelle monotonie de la passion, qui a toujours les mêmes formes et le même langage. . . . Mais, avec cette supériorité de critique appartenant à celui qui, dans n'importe quel engagement, se tient en arrière, Rodolphe aperçut en cet amour d'autres jouissances à exploiter.
>
> (265)

We recognize again the bourgeois confounding of flesh, money, and passion. Emma is judged as a commodity whose *nouveauté* has diminished, in a sexual metaphor of slackening passion which echoes Rodolphe's initial fantasy of exploiting Emma after their first meeting: "il revoyait Emma dans la salle, habillée comme il l'avait vue, et il la déshabillait" (181). Rodolphe survives disappointment, minimizes risk, through emotional detachment: he knew he wouldn't be happy with her anyway. But this narrator who convinces us he has fitted the precise word to each occasion, who treats cliches with disdainful italics, suddenly unmasks himself, relinquishes his protective distance from Emma, and speaks with fierce eloquence of the degrading standards of originality and novelty. We compare, in the brilliant turn occasioned by the paragraph following ("Mais, avec cette supériorité . . ."), the hysterical, dangerous (where can it lead except madness?) sympathy of the narrator, and the ruthless objectivity of Rodolphe. The universal compulsion for new experiences has trapped the narrator between cruel indifference and suicidal empathy. It is in this context of a recently completed decision to be vulnerable no more, that we must regard the objectivity of the narrator's presentation of the triumph of Homais and Lheureux.

Homais' initial appearance in the novel clarifies the already initiated movement of a tradition-bound society disappearing before a modern society addicted to novelty. "Tout est changé! Il faut marcher avec son siècle!" (102). Homais advises Madame Lefrançois how to profit commercially from the lust for new experiences: get rid of the old pool table for a new one in the contemporary style, and set up a benefit for the independence of Poland. Madame Lefrançois is scandalized: people will continue to come to the *Lion d'Or* because they always have and, as for the pool table, it sleeps six and is also useful for folding clothes on. For Madame, *le billard* signifies (without rupture) that solid four-footed useful object in her front room, but for Homais it appropriates by association the romantic symbols of Paris fashion. By the end of the novel, Homais' prophecy of competition from across the street is fulfilled. Lheureux takes over the *café français*, renames it *les favorites du commerce* (!), and threatens to lure away the picturesque Hivert.

Homais knows how to take advantage of the devaluation of symbols during the reign of *le roi bourgeois*: signifiers now float free of signifieds, and derive their intelligibility from other families of empty signifiers. His greatest triumph is to arrange around himself, by his own journalism (the *voies nouvelles de communication* of the councillor's speech), a kindred diction powerful enough to attract, by sympathy, the *croix d'honneur*.

The narrator is trapped between a suicidal romanticism and an inhuman realism. He cannot allow himself to feel the plight of Emma and Charles, lest he become abused like they do. To protect himself from Rodolphe, he must become like Rodolphe, and betray Emma; to protect himself from Homais, he must, like Homais, regard style, the art of signifying, as the absolute manner of seeing things, and regard what he writes about as nothing.

Notes

1. *Souvenirs littéraires de Maxime du Camp* (Paris: Hachette, 1962), p. 109.

2. I have previously discussed Modernism as a system of futile oppositions in "Toward a Redefinition of Modernism," *Boundary 2,* II, 3 (Spring 1974), 539-56.

3. (New York: W. W. Norton & Co., 1969), pp. 329-44. I am indebted to Richard Wasson's use of this book in "'Like a burnished throne': T. S. Eliot and the Demonism of Technology," *The Centennial Review,* XVII, 3 (Summer 1969), pp. 302-16.

4. Du Camp, having reached "maturity," observed the failure of desire in the more "naive" Flaubert the way the narrator of *Madame Bovary* observes Emma.

> Je m'attendais, de la part de Gustave, à une explosion d'enthousiasme: il n'en fut rien; cette autorisation qu'il désirait avec une intensité douloureuse, lui causa une sorte d'accablement dont je fus stupéfait. On eût dit qu'il y avait chez lui une détente subite d'aspiration et que son projet n'avait plus de prix du moment que l'exécution en devenait certaine. Cette observation, que je faisais pour la première fois, m'affligea; j'eus lieu de la renouveler souvent, car le rêve le satisfaisait bien plus que la réalité. Il désirait les choses avec une ardeur qui allait jusqu'à la souffrance, se désolait de ne les pouvoir obtenir, maudissait la destinée, nous prenait à témoin de son infortune, et dès qu'il était mis en possession de l'objet de ses convoitises, se trouvait déçu et s'en occupait à peine. "Plus grands yeux que grand ventre," disait ma grand-mère, qui le connaissait bien.

5. Where Charles is introduced as "un nouveau habillé en bourgeois" (p. 23).

6. Jonathan Culler, in *Flaubert. The Uses of Uncertainty* (London: Paul Elek, 1974), characterizes Flaubert as a forerunner of modern semiology, who discovered the stupidity of signs, the absolute difference between signifier and signified. Culler discusses Charles' hat, for example, as an overabundance of signs that defies integration or recuperation (p. 91). Culler is surely right to sense the intimacy of Flaubert's thought to modern semiology, but Foucault's analysis of madness offers here a suggestive analogy. Should we work backwards to discover in Flaubert an anticipation of

what we already know, or might we discover in Flaubert's work the origin of modern semiology in bourgeois culture?

D. A. Williams (essay date March 1980)

SOURCE: Williams, D. A. "The Role of Binet in *Madame Bovary*." *Romanic Review* 71, no. 2 (March 1980): 149-66.

[*In the following essay, Williams challenges mainstream critical assertions that the character of Binet plays an insignificant role in the novel. Williams contends that, in his role as a craftsman, Binet serves as the embodiment of Flaubert's profound doubts and fears as an artist.*]

It might be thought that everything worth saying about **Madame Bovary** has now been said. There are, however, aspects of this endlessly suggestive work which have not received the attention they deserve. Of the minor characters, the Blind Man has been singled out for detailed analysis,[1] whilst Binet, the tax-official with the mania for the lathe, has been largely neglected. He is, of course, mentioned in various studies of the novel,[2] but usually only to be dismissed as the embodiment of bourgeois mediocrity. This neglect is not altogether surprising, for Binet is a decidedly unappealing character, apparently lacking in depth, whose inclusion in the novel is something of a mystery. Yet, as this article will try to show, Binet is a profoundly significant figure and not just a typical representative of the provincial bourgeoisie. Flaubert has, in fact, used a minor and rebarbative figure to raise—discreetly and obliquely—fundamental issues relating to the nature of art and life. Out of a kind of aesthetic embarrassment, he has selected the most insignificant and unpromising character in order to present some of his deepest fears and doubts. This alone makes it worth the reader's overcoming the initial response of distaste which Binet customarily provokes.

Madame Bovary was essentially, in Flaubert's view, 'une biographie plutôt qu'une péripétie développée'.[3] But, although the main emphasis undoubtedly falls on the psychological development of Emma, the claim implicit in the subtitle, **Mœurs de Province,** obliges Flaubert to depict the life of provincial society in considerable detail. The two elements are most successfully combined when socially representative characters are shown to have a direct psychological impact upon the heroine. Thus, at various points, Homais, Bournisien and Lheureux influence, usually adversely, the way Emma develops, propelling her along a course which culminates in suicide. Emma's egocentric nature and the furtive nature of her adulterous experiences restrict her contact with many of the inhabitants of Yonville, however, with the result that it is not always possible for minor characters to have a direct effect upon the heroine. But even where there appears to be little direct influence, a character may take on symbolic overtones and thereby ensure that it is not without relevance to the heroine's predicament. Flaubert makes his characters earn their keep; if they are to lodge in the novel, they must have either a psychological or a symbolic value.

The exploitation of characters within the economy of the novel is rich and varied but it is constantly and carefully regulated by the same underlying principle. As early as the first **Éducation sentimentale** Flaubert was aware of the way in which contrasting characters are mutually supportive: 'le caractère de Jules n'est lumineux qu'à cause d'Henry. Un des personnages isolé serait faible'.[4] In the process of differentiation, the device which is most frequently used is that of antithesis. The important point about this device is that, since it establishes an axis of comparison, it links the elements it puts in opposition to each other, fulfilling both a structural and a psychological function. Flaubert rarely thinks of characters as isolated units, but in conjunction with a succession of partners, each of which differs in some definite respect. Thus, Binet is paired at different points not only with Léon who is romantically-minded, unpunctual and voluble where he is pedestrian, punctual and taciturn, but also with Homais, Guillaumin and Emma herself.[5]

Oppositions may link Binet with other elements in the text but they do not determine the manner of his insertion into the narrative or the amount of attention devoted to him. The presentation of Binet is, in fact, extremely varied; even such an apparently unimportant character benefits from the diversity of narrative techniques at Flaubert's disposal. Binet is established firmly in the reader's mind in the opening scene of Part II (pp. 393-416)[6] throughout which, typically and comically, his lips remain sealed. This taciturnity means that he cannot reveal himself through what he says like Homais and Léon, obliging Flaubert to present him either through the eyes of other characters or omnisciently. Both these methods are combined in a pleasingly symmetrical pattern. First Binet is characterized by Madame Lefrançois ('son pareil n'existe pas sur la terre pour l'exactitude') and her forecast that he will enter on the dot of six is promptly confirmed ('Six heures sonnèrent. Binet entra.'). This brief action is followed by an extended omniscient description of Binet's physical and moral characteristics in which Flaubert follows a traditional pattern (the 'portrait'). Then there is another description of the way Binet behaves, emphasizing his taciturnity and once again Binet is seen through the eyes of Homais and Madame Lefrançois. This skillful combination of different methods of presentation ensures that Binet remains in the background, subordinated to the characters through whose eyes he is for most of the time seen but also that his moral and physical contours are not blurred.

The next reference to Binet is brief (p. 415). The contrast between the romantic activity of Emma and Léon, tending their hanging gardens, and the pedestrian activity of Binet, working at his lathe, allows the important motif of the whirring of the lathe to be introduced and thereby prepares for the scene in which Emma first attempts suicide. Binet is now presented through anonymous provincial eyes ('on voyait'); from this viewpoint there is something aberrant about his dedication to his lathe. Although he has now been transferred to his natural habitat (his attic), the sound of the lathe 'qui s'entendait jusqu'au *Lion d'or*' preserves an important auditory link with the inn where he is soon to be coopted into the role of reluctant confident to the lovesick Léon (p. 416). The choice of Binet for this role is both comical and perverse, as Flaubert hints in a *scénario*: 'faire servir Binet à être le confident de Léon—mais Binet ne répond pas'.[7] Léon is tiresomely talkative ('il vous entretenait sans cesse de ses charmes et de son esprit') but the task of silencing the garrulous clerk falls appropriately on the surly, anti-social tax-official, whose first spoken words, ironically, disclaim any interest in the heroine ('Que m'importe à moi, puisque je ne suis pas de sa société!'), emphasizing the gap separating the two characters, a gap which will not be bridged as long as Emma is involved with Léon.

When he next appears (p. 432), Binet at first seems as lacking in curiosity in Léon as he had been in Emma, refusing to discuss his affairs with Madame Lefrançois who is as poor as Léon at assessing who is likely to lend a sympathetic ear. But, despite his uncommunicative reaction, Binet is puzzled by Léon's uneasiness and is prompted to give him comically inappropriate advice ('Moi, à votre place, j'aurais un tour!') and to express a mixture of disdain and smugness in the chin-stroking that is one of his characteristics. In earlier versions, he proceeds to berate modern youth, a development which was finally omitted, though at a late stage,[8] probably because it detracted from the impression of surly taciturnity Flaubert wished to create. Although he is presented in an unsympathetic light, on account of the direct access given to his inner feeling ('Son camarade, toutefois, lui paraissait fort singulier'), Binet becomes momentarily more familiar to the reader, though he is immediately distanced by the use of dialogue and by being seen from outside.

At the agricultural fair Binet, like other characters, has a field day. In his capacity as captain of the local fire-brigade, he is in charge of the guard of honour and supervises the firework display, discharging his duties with a comic 'raideur de mécanique':[9] 'sanglé dans sa tunique, il avait le buste si raide et immobile, que toute la partie vitale de sa personne semblait être descendue dans ses jambes' (p. 445). Deference to military values also impairs his vision for he now wears his visor pulled down: 'Il entendait peut-être, mais ne devait rien apercevoir à cause de la visière de son casque qui lui descendait sur le nez' (p. 458). Both the presenting of arms (p. 453) and the firework display (p. 460) turn out to be comic disasters but, like the rest of Yonville, Binet is impervious to failure.

Up to this point there has been no direct contact between Binet and Emma with the result that Binet is introduced almost incidentally. He figures more prominently, however, soon after the relationship with Rodolphe has begun; Emma at first savours adultery 'sans remords, sans inquiétude, sans trouble' (p. 474) but experiences the second of these emotions when she is startled out of her wits by Binet, who jumps up out of his hiding-place one early morning as she is returning from a visit to Rodolphe (pp. 476-7). Since, in shooting from dry land, he is committing a minor illegality, Binet mirrors as well as exacerbating Emma's anxiety. Having previously been a purely comic figure, Binet now assumes—in Emma's eyes at least—a more threatening aspect. Emma lies badly about her movements and betrays herself by suddenly taking leave of an uncharacteristically talkative Binet with an abrupt 'bonsoir' even though it is still morning. Emma has the impression that Binet is a sinister, revengeful figure who wishes to hound her down later that evening, which is spent with Homais from who Binet requires various articles for his equipment. The litany of Binet's requests provokes mounting unease in Emma, as dangerous substances like vitriol are demanded, but the reader is left in some doubt about the objective likelihood of Binet's deliberately seeking to taunt her, since, though she does not realize it, he has no more desire than she has to publicize his early morning activities. In an earlier version, her fears are, in fact, shown to be ill-founded when it becomes clear that Binet does not have Emma in mind when he makes reference to those who welcome damp weather ('Car pour les biens de la terre, c'est fort heureux!').[10] Even in the final version there is a distinct possibility that Emma is comically wide of the mark in attributing to Binet the necessary subtlety to make veiled hints about her behaviour. Ill-founded or not, however, Emma's reaction puts her relationship with Rodolphe on a new, less carefree footing. Unwittingly Binet has been the occasion of Emma's entering a more secretive phase.

The next reference to Binet is brief (p. 485). His voice is added to the general conspiracy to persuade Charles to perform the club-foot operation. The atypical nature of this intervention is stressed ('Binet, qui ne se mêlait jamais des affaires d'autrui'); though he is the opposite of the meddling Homais, Binet, too, on this occasion, connives to bring about a disastrous venture which is to leave Emma completely disillusioned with Charles and totally dependent upon Rodolphe.

It is not, therefore, entirely inappropriate that Binet, through the intermediary of his lathe, should have a part to play in her first suicide attempt (p. 513). Emma has received the letter from Rodolphe and rushes to the attic where she hears the strident sound of the lathe, which, in her confused state of mind, seems 'comme une voix furieuse qui l'appelait'. In an earlier version it is not just the sound of the lathe which is distorted; Emma has the same strange visual experience as Jules in the first *Éducation sentimentale*,[11] involving the sudden magnification of a distant object:

> le profil de Binet en casquette, qui passait alors à la lucarne, lui parut tout rapproché d'elle, à deux pas et monstrueux comme à travers la lentille d'un phare.[12]

The hallucinated quality of her perception at moments of great stress has led critics to interpret her reaction to the sound of the lathe as a 'purely psychological notation'.[13] Refracted through the distorting lens of Emma's consciousness, Binet takes on a nightmarish quality.

There is, however, a brief moment during Emma's convalescence (p. 524) when he is seen in a less garish light. Binet's appearance at this juncture is somewhat gratuitous. Charles and Emma, in company with Homais and Bournisien, are in the habit of drinking cider in the arbour and Binet is close by, trying to catch crayfish in the river. In an earlier version his presence is even more unaccountable for the noise of the bottles being opened frightens the crayfish away. Was there nowhere else he could have gone fishing? The weakness of the motivation is further emphasized by the use of the iterative imperfect, implying that his presence is habitual.[14] It is difficult for the reader to accept that he would repeatedly risk losing his prey or be repeatedly invited to open cider bottles, particularly as he bungles the operation.[15] The inclusion of Binet does, however, allow the idea of his being a hunter to be stressed and at the same time cuts him down to size. And once again he is indirectly instrumental in Emma's embarking upon a course which proves disastrous, for in talking, however tiresomely, about the theatre, he helps to persuade her to go to the Rouen opera-house where she will meet Léon.

Binet does not appear in Part III until Emma is driven by her financial position to seek aid from him (pp. 604-5). Her choice of Binet is in some ways surprising. Unlike Guillaumin, who, Emma is informed, harbours a secret affection for her, Binet has never shown the slightest interest in her. Whilst the visit to Guillaumin is described omnisciently, the visit to Binet is seen through the eyes of two women, Madame Tuvache and Madame Caron; shorn of normal verbal accompaniment, the movements of Emma and Binet appear absurd. Although the two women are comically ill-equipped to divine what is happening ('Elle le prie pour obtenir un retard à ses contributions'), it soon becomes apparent to even their sluggish minds that Emma is making shameful advances and that Binet, as is only to be expected of a brave soldier, is rejecting them, a hypothesis which is finally confirmed by the first words which can be clearly heard, 'Madame! y pensez-vous!'. The main function of this scene does not lie in its demonstration that Emma is ready to prostitute herself—this is the point made in the following visit to Rodolphe. Nor is the unlikely encounter engineered simply in order to bring home the telling contrast between a woman at her wits' end and a man who has, in Alison Fairlie's words, 'found the mediocre man's solution: unthinking absorption in an unambitious task'.[16] What we are told exceeds what is necessary for such a contrast. In a long paragraph in which the limitations of witness technique are ignored, Flaubert describes the apotheosis of Binet as manic craftsman, for he is on the verge of completing a strange and intricate wood carving. Binet's activity now reaches a rhythmic climax as the dust comes flying off his lathe and the wheels whir ferociously round and round. Bliss such as that of Binet is relatively rare in the uncomfortable world of *Madame Bovary* and the reader begins to suspect that he does not truely belong to that world. Flaubert at this crucial juncture has chosen to project a profoundly parodic image of the artist at work, catapulting a minor and apparently insignificant character into an astonishing *mise en abyme* which allows him to convey a piercing insight into the element of inevitable cruelty at the heart of literary creation.

The final references to Binet are less important. When Emma returns to La Mère Rollet (p. 605) she confuses the sound of the nurse's spinning wheel with that of the lathe. Lastly, Binet is one of several villagers who seek free advice from Larivière (p. 620), complaining of sudden pangs of hunger. Neither of these details is devoid of suggestive overtones but clearly Binet's moment of glory is over. Binet is destined finally to assume a position of total detachment; he fails to attend Emma's funeral (p. 635) and, pursuing his solitary hobby into the night (p. 643), appears totally oblivious to Charles's suffering.

This brief analysis of Binet's role in the plot reveals that he makes a limited number of appearances and that these often coincide with important stages in Emma's development, giving him an unexpected weight and importance. Binet's final significance—social, psychological and, in particular, symbolic—does not, however, derive solely from his role in the 'chronological' chain of events but also emerges from his place in 'analogical' patterns linking characters and events.[17] Binet's inferior position in Yonville society is questionably established by Homais: 'C'est qu'il y a bien de la différence, voyez-vous, entre quelqu'un qui a reçu de l'éducation et un ancien carabinier qui est percepteur!' (p. 393). Binet, himself, takes a different view, refusing to allow the pharmacist to blind him with scientific terminology, just as Bournisien refuses to surrender to his anti-clerical arguments. Despite his lack of education, Binet occupies a comfortable niche in provincial society. His professional duties, compared to those of Charles or Homais, seem particularly undemanding; indeed, he is not once shown exercising these duties and seems to enjoy unlimited leisure in which to pursue his solitary hobby.[18] Nor is his lack of social graces as big a disadvantage as Homais claims (p. 394), for Binet is the most contented character in the book, completely at ease in his anti-social way of life. Binet does not withdraw completely from society, however, nor does he consistently shun the public gaze. He requires the company of the impractical Leon in order to confirm his sense of his own superiority and the military virtues which he incarnates require the collective approval of Yonville society at the agricultural fair. And even if he spends most of his time shut up in his attic, he at first relishes Emma's presence in the inner sanctum since she can undertake a review of his prodigious output.

Binet's psychological significance is neither complex nor elusive. There is something almost too obvious about his character which leads Flaubert to make the strange claim in an earlier version that 'avant de voir l'extérieur de cet homme, il semblait que l'on en vit d'abord le dedans'.[19] Binet's inner self, like the internal organs of a jelly-fish, is immediately apparent. In his case, since nothing is hidden, the scalpel can be put aside. In a similar fashion the 'intérieur' in which he works, his 'atelier', is unscreened, open to the public gaze. But, whilst anyone can perceive Binet, Binet himself perceives little, either literally on account of the visor which impedes his vision or figuratively on account of his lack of interest in other human beings. Ultimately the psychological penury of Binet is a function of his lack of perception, for to perceive in the Flaubertian scheme of things is potentially enriching, since it involves the self's receiving or ingesting some aspect of the external world.

The corollary of Binet's lack of interest in the outer world is an inward-looking, self-protective, highly constricted personality type,[20] manifesting itself in several ways. Binet's neat appearance, punctuality and regular habits all point to a desire to hold himself in check whilst his tight-fistedness and hoarding of serviette rings reflect a compulsive urge to retain. The panoply of practical skills which Binet displays all result from the desire to control and dominate, whether it be the pieces of wood he turns into serviette rings, the various forms of wild life he pursues or the cider which threatens to shoot out of the bottle. Binet refuses anything which might disturb his inner peace; he is a 'célibataire sans passions', wedded to his lathe whose mechanical rotations are totally predictable and which, for him, has almost become human (on one occasion he tells Homais that 'il allait revoir son tour').

As is often the case in *Madame Bovary* inner and outer correspond. The outward manifestations of Binet's constricted personality are the tight-fitting clothes which enclose his skinny frame, the meticulously kept beard which 'contournant la mâchoire, encadrait comme la bordure d'une plate-bande sa longue figure terne' and, most comically, the helmet which compresses his skull-bones. In the system of facial types,[21] Binet's 'longue figure terne' connotes persistence and mediocrity, his small eyes, like those of Lheureux, indifference to others, his flattened forehead limited intellect, whilst his 'profil maigre' and his 'corps maigre' suggest a passionless way of life and his characteristic chin-stroking is the emblem of his inward-looking, self-regarding outlook.

Binet derives much of his psychological significance from his place within a pervasive pattern of constriction. His ready acceptance of a narrow, limited way of life recalls that of Charles. One of the comparisons used to describe his tight-fitting uniform—'plus étroitement et mieux qu'un baudet dans son harnais'[22] echoes the image used to describe the way Charles 'accomplissait sa petite tâche quotidienne à la manière du cheval de manège, qui tourne en place les yeux bandés, ignorant de la besogne qu'il broie' (p. 333) and contrasts with the one used to describe Emma's behaviour in the convent: 'elle fit comme les chevaux que l'on tire par la bride: elle s'arrêta court et le mors lui sortit des dents' (p. 361). Binet and Charles are both opposed to Emma, having come to terms with the constrictions of provincial life and gladly welcoming confinement within a narrow orbit. Emma, on the other hand, feels trapped in her 'maison trop étroite' (p. 424) and finally breaks explosively out of the restricted framework within which she lives. Again there is a contrast with Binet, apparent in another of the earlier images associated with Binet's uniform: 'mieux qu'une andouille sous les ficelles qui la compriment' which recalls the image of 'le vin d'une bouteille dont les ficelles sont coupées' used to evoke Emma's outpouring of repressed energy in adultery.[23] The contrast between active striving and passive acceptance also comes out in the two comparisons to fish; Emma 'bâille après l'amour, comme une carpe après l'eau sur une table de cuisine' (p. 444) whilst Binet 'restait là comme une alose, sans dire un mot' (p. 394). Binet does break out of confinement on one occasion, jumping out of the barrel in which he is hiding like a Jack-in-a-box but this is not a real escape and when Emma departs we are told that 'il rentra dans son tonneau'. Ironically, beneath the contrast there is a similarity between Binet and Emma since Emma, having broken out of the restricted framework of her previous life in her relationship with Rodolphe, gravitates to enclosed space in her relationship with Léon[24] and is even, at one point, compared to 'le duc de Clarence dans son tonneau de malvoisie' (p. 500). Contrasting patterns of expansion and constriction allow Flaubert to create a strong opposition between life in death and death in life: Binet survives but in such restricted conditions that he can scarcely be said to live whilst the price Emma pays for living (i.e. escaping from confinement) is a death which is both figurative (drowning in water, trapped in the coffin-like 'fiacre') and literal (enclosed in her coffin).

Although not without social and psychological significance, Binet's real fascination lies in the way he is both recalcitrant and amenable to symbolic interpretation. The tax-official is an 'homme muet', his taciturnity seeming almost to betoken a refusal to assume symbolic meanings, a perverse, reader-frustrating a-symbolism. But a kind of seepage of repressed symbolic meaning occurs as a result of Flaubert's decision to allow the lathe to speak on Binet's behalf. Whilst Binet's lips are tightly sealed, his beloved instrument emits a continuous, almost irrepressible sound which figures prominently in the extraordinarily dense pattern of sound pervading the novel. The exact significance of the 'ronflement' is not easy to pin down; however, it is pregnant with a meaning whose delivery threatens to be protracted.

Flaubert was well aware of the capacity of certain sounds to invite and frustrate interpretation; in the first *Éducation sentimentale* he makes the strange mangy dog tantalize Jules much as it tantalizes the reader:

> Jules tâchait de découvrir une différence quelconque dans la monotonie de ces sons furieux, plaintifs et frénétiques tout ensemble; il s'efforçait de les deviner et saisir la pensée, la chose, le pronostic, le récit ou la plainte qu'ils voulaient exprimer, mais son oreille n'entendait que les mêmes vibrations presque continues, stridentes, toutes pareilles, qui se prolongeaient les unes après les autres.[25]

The same basic human need to impose meaning on the blank, uncomprehending surface of the world is illustrated in Emma's readiness to connect the sound of the lathe with an external and malevolent force driving her to her doom. The sound produced by the lathe is an extreme example of an undifferentiated external reality; Emma's attempts at symbolic differentiation are viewed in an ironic light.

This is not to say, however, that it is not possible to ascribe to the sound of the lathe an appropriate meaning. The reader of *Madame Bovary* is in a privileged position, confronted not with the disorder of reality like Emma, but with 'du réel écrit',[26] with reality which has been subjected remorselessly to a process of aesthetic patterning, or more specifically with a pattern of inter-related sounds which generate symbolic harmonies out of range of the heroine's hearing. The whirring of the lathe has a central place in a carefully graduated sequence of disturbing sounds which mark critical points in Emma's development. The initial description of the whirring as 'monotone' is an index of the humdrum round of provincial life which is destined to prove increasingly irksome to Emma. In the first suicide attempt, the whirring becomes more strident—'il partit d'un étage inférieur une sorte de ronflement à modulations stridentes'. It now seems unrelenting, almost human to Emma's troubled mind: 'le ronflement du tour ne discontinuait pas, comme une voix furieuse qui l'appelait'. There is a short distance between the innocuous and the ominous; the 'répétition continuelle' to which human activity can be reduced,[27] may contain in its serial continuity elements which totalize the horrifyingly grotesque nature of endless repetition. When it is heard for the last time ('les deux roues tournaient, ronflaient'), the sound of the lathe seems to have lost some of its stridency mainly because it is no longer described from Emma's point of view but the power it continues to exert over her is suggested in the next scene where, confusing the sound of the lathe with that of La Mère Rollet's spinning wheel, she implores her to stop.

The reader's reaction to the descriptions of the sound of the lathe is conditioned by the generalized use of the words 'ronfler' and 'ronflement' to evoke somnolence and mental confusion,[28] and, more directly, by the contrast between the continuous whirring which forms the groundswell or base accompaniment to Emma's life and a series of sounds which pierce the silence such as the 'cri rauque et doux des corbeaux' and the 'cri vague et prolongé' (pp. 470 and 472), heard in the wood, or the 'hurlement' emitted by the Blind Man. Both types of sound are submitted to a process of distortion; just as the mechanical sound of the lathe is perceived as a voice calling out, human sounds are artificially prolonged to the point of sounding inhuman, as if to blur the distinction between continuous and instantaneous sound.[29] Numerous links[30] allow these various sounds to be read as a series of variation on a theme. As Kirton points out 'the perceptive consciousness of Emma, periodically [. . .] reconstitutes itself, each time finding a basic sameness in its condition as well as an increasingly clear definition of its negative aspects'.[31] Whilst the basic sameness of Emma's condition is evoked by the monotonous repetition of certain sounds, the clarification of its negative aspects results from their progressive defamiliarization, achieved largely through a systematic manipulation of the spatial relations between perceived sound and perceiving consciousness. At first, potentially disturbing sounds are located in the distance and have an uncertain bearing on Emma's predicament but gradually they come closer and assume an inescapable relevance to her position. The vertiginous, nightmarish quality of several of these sounds is accentuated by further modifications of spatial relations. In the first suicide attempt, the sound of the lathe comes from a new quarter, from below, and seems to draw her downward, whilst the Blind Man's voice, though close to Emma in the coach, 'avait quelque chose de lointain qui bouleversait Emma' (p. 569).

The intensification of the sound pattern creates the impression that Emma is undergoing a kind of auditory persecution. Even if due allowance is made for the distorting effect of her consciousness, it still seems as if she is being pursued or hounded down by certain sounds. The idea of pursuit is not confined to the sound of the lathe, however, but is persistently associated with Binet who, comically but appropriately, is a 'chasseur' and afflicted with sudden pangs of hunger. The halfsuppressed truth about Binet is that he is after Emma's blood. On one occasion he actually aims his rifle at her (p. 476) but he is usually shown pursuing various forms of life with which Emma is metaphorically and metonymically linked. The earlier version contains two suggestive references to escaping prey:

Alors une compagnie d'oiseaux qui s'enfuyaient lui passa près des épaules avec un long bruit d'ailes, et en claquant du bec dans le brouillard[32]

* * *

Les écrevisses s'enfuyaient à grands coups de leurs pinces, pour se tapir dans la vase[33]

The descriptions follow the two occasions when Emma has escaped a premature death, the first when Binet himself had almost shot her, the second when she had almost committed suicide. Emma's fear of 'cet imbécile à carnassière' (p. 477) is not totally unjustified.

It has been argued that Binet can be regarded as a modern equivalent of Lachesis, the second of the three Fates.[34] But if he pursues Emma throughout the novel, it is not so much in order to point to the working of an external fatality but more as a result of Flaubert's desire to state within the work itself the cardinal importance of the artist himself in determining the fate of the heroine. Although he had come to believe that there was no justification for writing a novel about an artist,[35] he nonetheless continued to introduce artist-figures into his work, though usually under the cover of intense, selfprotective parody. Binet is Flaubert's most profound and self-critical picture of the artist at work.

In Binet Flaubert has projected in a mercilessly parodic form the life he claimed the artist should adopt. Binet's misanthropy, his solitary way of life, the apparent penury of his existence are all consistent with the image of bear-like recluse cultivated by Flaubert in his *Correspondance*.[36] More importantly, through Binet Flaubert is developing an alternative definition of the artist who is now presented as first and foremost a craftsman rather than a visionary. The artist, Flaubert is suggesting, is not to be regarded as an olympian figure, a thinker cut off from humanity in his ivory tower, but as an ordinary mortal, an artisan, almost a public spectacle in his provincial attic. The image of craftsman is rich in implications, shifting the emphasis from what the artist is to what he does. Binet himself is an insignificant figure, comfortably installed within the provincial community whose stability he in no way threatens.[37] What is significant about Binet is his devotion to his lathe, the continuity of his effort, the hard work of which he is capable. Not that Flaubert's vision of the artist as craftsman is euphoric. The products of Binet's lathe are devoid of any use or value. They serve no purpose whatsoever. For Binet work has become obsessive, an end in itself, the symptom of some profound disturbance, a self-justifying activity, divorced from any human concern. The artist may no longer live in glorious isolation; he has not become any the more human.

Flaubert's assimilation of the artist to a craftsman allows him to articulate a despairing vision of the worthlessness of his own activity. He once declared, in one of his blacker moods, that he saw the future in terms of 'une masse de papier blanc qu'il faut couvrir de noir, uniquement pour ne pas crever d'ennui, et comme on a un tour dans son grenier quand on habite la campagne'.[38] For Flaubert the lathe epitomizes bourgeois resourcefulness, a suspect self-sufficiency, the attempt to stave off an anguished awareness of the purposelessness of life by plunging oneself into a kind of mechanical nirvana.[39] The analogy between Binet and the artist is, therefore, deliberately derogatory and self-critical and allows serious reservations about artistic activity to be made. Binet, we are told, hoards his serviette rings 'avec la jalousie d'un artiste et l'égoisme d'un bourgeois'; artist and bourgeois both suffer from the same vice of possessiveness, comically amassing the worthless products of their own misplaced ingenuity. The mechanical, repetitive activity of Binet is disturbingly reminiscent of that of the writer who equally obsessively polishes his periods and rounds off his paragraphs[40] and, more comically, with his pen taking the place of the gouger, experiences the same refined sexual pleasure in putting the finishing touches to his work as is most clearly evoked in an earlier version:

il écartait les narines, il tendait sa prunelle, l'âme passée tout entière dans le bout de son doigt qui, appuyé sur la gouge suivait d'un mouvement délicat le buis en rotation.[41]

Binet is as pleased as Punch (whom he resembles in aggressiveness), totally unaware of the futility of his own endeavours. He is on the verge of completing his imitation of 'une de ces ivoireries indescriptibles, composées de croissants, de sphères creusées les unes dans les autres, le tout droit comme un obélisque et ne servant à rien'. It is a grotesque, non-figurative monstrosity, an example of complexity for complexity's sake, expressing Flaubert's deepest fears about his own artistic ingenuity. Like Binet, he himself is on the verge of completing his task but he may have achieved no more with words than Binet with wood. All the complex patterns, the network of interlocking symbols, the structural intricacies contrived with such effort may be part of a total creation as sterile as Binet's wood carving, equally devoid of any meaningful correspondence with anything outside itself.[42]

It is no accident that Binet should be on the verge of completing his *magnum opus* at the very moment when Emma is being driven to suicide. Flaubert expresses through Binet his awareness of a purely artistic necessity shaping Emma's life. It has been argued that the freedom of fictional characters is always severely restricted, if not negated, by the exigencies of novelistic discourse; in his analysis of Balzac's story, Sarrasine, Barthes points out that '*Sarrasine est contraint par le discours* d'aller au rendez-vous avec la Zambinella: la liberté du personnage est dominée par l'instinct de conservation du discours'.[43] In ***Madame Bovary*** there is a particularly powerful retroactive determinism at work; the completion of the novel necessitates the suicide of Emma.[44] Such is Flaubert's self-consciousness in writing ***Madame Bovary,*** however, that he cannot refrain from obliquely indicating the tyranny of story, as Bonnefis has pointed out: 'Il arrive [. . .] que l'histoire, par une sorte de regard intérieur projeté sur sa nature et sa constitution, renvoie, sans renoncer à sa finalité, l'image de l'impérieux déterminisme qu'elle exerce'.[45] The character who most clearly embodies this retroactive determinism is not Homais, as has been claimed,[46] but Binet whose latent revengeful attitude and offensive weapons (sabre, rifle, gouger) acquire a special significance. The final picture of Binet's wrapt immersion in his model-making allows Flaubert to denounce his own cruelty in putting the heroine to death for the sake of something of questionable value. The contrast between Binet's calm smugness and Emma's intense anguish enacts a devaluation of art in the face of life. The artist is placed in the same category as the vapid aristocrats of la Vaubyessard; the pleasure he has in overcoming the 'difficulté facile' of his work compares with the 'brutalité' they manifest in 'la domination de choses à demi faciles' (p. 372). It is Emma, however, who has to pay the price for Binet's easy artistic fulfilment; the monotonous humming of the lathe—the necessary concomitant of artistic creation—symbolizes 'la contrainte implacable du discours'[47] which drives Emma through various stages of frustration to suicide. Flaubert's *mea culpa* locates true authenticity beyond art. It also has the paradoxical effect of deepening the illusion of the heroine's independent existence, since what on one level is recognized to be an abstract fictional construct (the 'character' of Emma) is on a deeper level pitied as if it were human.

Although writer and heroine are related to each other as hunter and quarry, there are strong similarities between their respective activity and achievement. Multiple parallels between writing and living exist since both are shown to be shaped by the same underlying rhythms and movements. The circular pattern of much of Emma's experience[48] is duplicated in the rotation of the wheels of the lathe which in turn is associated with the production of well-turned sentences. In both cases, the repetition of circular movement produces a monotonous continuity, expressed in the 'ronflement' of the lathe, which symbolizes both the basic sameness underlying the apparent diversity of Emma's experience and the homogeneous stylistic substance to which Flaubert reduces the diversity of the real, what Proust described as Flaubert's 'trottoir roulant [. . .] au défilement continu, monotone, indéfini'.[49] It was always important for Flaubert that well-turned pages or paragraphs should run into each other, producing an impression of fluidity: 'Chaque paragraphe est bon en soi, il y a des pages, j'en suis sûr, parfaites. [. . .] C'est une série de paragraphes bien tournés, arrêtés, et qui ne dévalent pas les uns sur les autres'.[50] Continuity is not the final goal, however; indeed one critic has suggested that 'dans le système flaubertien le continu définit le degré extrême de la non-valeur'.[51] Just as circular movement should give rise to an impression of linear continuity, so continuity ideally should produce a kind of totality, a complex, two-dimensional surface or 'assemblage'. The ideal lived achievement for Emma is symbolized in the intricate interwoven pattern of the cigar case which is the result of continuous devotion:

> Un souffle d'amour avait passé parmi les mailles du canevas; chaque coup d'aiguille avait fixé là une espérance ou un souvenir, et tous ces fils de soie entrelacés n'étaient que la continuité de la même passion silencieuse.
>
> (p. 377)

Needless to say, her own life falls short of this ideal, degenerating into an 'assemblage de mensonges, où elle enveloppait son amour comme dans des voiles, pour le cacher' (p. 572). Likewise for Flaubert a novel should aspire, by virtue of 'la précision des assemblages, le poli de la surface, l'harmonie de l'ensemble' to the same effect of complete unity as he detected in the Walls of the Acropolis but he fears that in practice he may have achieved something as gratuitously intricate and over-organized as Binet's 'assemblage de sphères et de croissants'.

The underlying parallels between writing and living are possibly what accounts for the name given to the tax-official. It has been suggested that Binet brings to mind the verb 'bobiner', to reel or wind,[52] but the more obvious association is with 'biner' which comes via the Provençal 'binar' from the vulgar latin 'binare', to do something twice. In modern French 'biner' has two meanings; 'donner une seconde façon aux terres, aux vignes' and 'célébrer deux or trois messes le même jour à deux endroits différents'. Appropriately enough the name Binet is used for two characters in ***Madame Bovary.*** Acting in accordance with the first meaning of the word, Monsieur Binet of Quincampoix wins a prize for his excellent cultivation of the land (p. 461). The tax-official, however, is equally well-named since his destiny, like that of the artist, is to double, duplicate and repeat. Binet is afflicted with the comic and compulsive binarism which constitutes the worst possible kind of order in Flaubert's eyes.[53] His lathe has two wheels which turn together and his well polished boots have 'deux renflements parallèles, à cause de la saillie des orteils' which, in addition to repeating each other, almost succeed in duplicating phonetically the 'ronflement' of the lathe. Binet also repeats himself, fighting at Bautzen and Lutzen (p. 605), refusing to listen to either Léon or Madame Lefrançois, hunting both wild ducks and crayfish and producing innumerable identical serviette rings. He also mirrors the behaviour of other character, in particular that of Emma. When he goes out hunting he experiences an 'inquiétude' akin to that of Emma when he surprises her, resulting in both cases from the breaking of a law or convention. When Emma visits Binet at the end of the novel he is scandalized by her advances, blushes and recoils just as she has done in her previous visit to Guillaumin.[54] Binet also doubles for the absent author and at the end of the novel is duplicating in wood the type of carving usually found in ivory, as if to imply that the novelist always copies a copy and can never be truly original but must always repeat, in an imperfect medium, something that is already given.[55]

Flaubert's true confession is not to be found in the ***Correspondance*** but in ***Madame Bovary*** itself, despite all that Flaubert said about the need to be impersonal. But the intensity of the confessional urge in Flaubert is matched by the intensity of the urge to disparage, producing a comic portrait of the artist as a craftsman. As is often the case in Flaubert, idiocy and insight are difficult to disentangle;[56] some of Flaubert's most persistent doubts and profound intuitions are expressed through the most grotesque character in the book and the lathe, that emblem of bourgeois mediocrity, emits a series of auditory clues about the monotony of life and literature. Flaubert's picture of the artist at work is not in the least self-indulgent or self-approbatory; Binet toils over the lathe for long hours but he is smug, oblivious to others, blood-thirsty and lacking in perception. In an age of mass-produced objects, his activity has become anachronistic; the fruits of his labour therefore simply accumulate and all he can create is a monument to stupidity. In addition to acting as a useful corrective to inflated views of the artist's importance, Flaubert's bleak and stringent self-portraiture in ***Madame Bovary*** sustains a central paradox: Flaubert enhances the aesthetic achievement of his work by refusing to celebrate it in his work.

Notes

1. Cf. P. M. Wetherill, '*Madame Bovary*'s Blind Man', *The Romanic Review,* lxi (1970), 35-42 and M. Sachs, 'The Role of the Blind Beggar in *Madame Bovary*', *Symposium,* xxii (1968), 72-80.

2. The fullest analysis can be found in L. Bopp, *Commentaire sur Madame Bovary,* La Baconnière, 1951.

3. *Correspondance,* Conard, Paris: (1926-37), iii. 247.

4. *Correspondance,* ii. 343.

5. The *scénarios,* published in *Madame Bovary, Nouvelle version* (ed. J. Pommier and G. Leleu), Corti, Paris, 1949, contain abundant evidence of Flaubert's quest for clear differentiation. Cf. 'Entrée de Mr le curé. [. . .] la différencier de celle de Binet qui est attendue', XXIX, p. 60 and 'Trois visites bien distinctes. L'heureux.—BRUTAL [. . .] Mr Guillaumin—FROID, POLI. Binet.—SCANDALISE', LV, p. 104. C. Gothot-Mersch (*La Genèse de Madame Bovary,* Corti, Paris: 1966, p. 266) has commented on the use of binary groups as 'un procédé d'invention et un schéma structurel'.

6. All page references are to the Pléiade edition of *Madame Bovary, Œuvres de Flaubert,* Paris, 1951.

7. *Madame Bovary, Nouvelle version,* XXX, p. 61.

8. From the copyist's manuscript. Cf. *Madame Bovary* (ed. C. Gothot-Mersch), Garnier, Paris, 1971, p. 393.

9. Cf. H. Bergson, *Le Rire, Œuvres,* Pléiade, Paris, 1959, p. 391; 'Ce qu'il y a de risible [. . .], c'est une certaine raideur de mécanique là où l'on voudrait trouver la souplesse attentive et la vivante flexibilité d'une personne'.

10. *Madame Bovary Nouvelle version,* p. 391.

11. Cf. *Œuvres complètes,* Seuil, Paris, 1964, i. 313: 'Il y avait sur la gauche un petit taillis, d'où étaient sorties ces deux formes vagues, qui touchaient en ce moment au marchepied de la calèche; je crus voir du bleu et quelque chose de flottant comme une robe. Et puis, tous les objets grandirent et je les vis nettement'.

12. *Madame Bovary, Nouvelle version,* p. 444.

13. Wetherill, art. cit., p. 40.

14. *Madame Bovary, Nouvelle version*, p. 462.

15. Cf. R. Huss, 'Some Anomalous Uses of the Imperfect and the Status of Action in Flaubert', *French Studies*, xxxi (1977), p. 145 for a discussion of the use of the imperfect 'to describe events which are so detached and clearly delineated as to be experienced by the reader as unique'.

16. *Flaubert: Madame Bovary*, Arnold, London, 1962, p. 34.

17. The distinction between chronological and analogical relationships is made in A. Fairlie, 'Some Patterns of Suggestion in *L'Éducation sentimentale*', *Australian Journal of French Studies*, vi (1969), p. 275.

18. Cf. Bopp's comment (op. cit., p. 109) that Binet 'semble être un percepteur qui ne perçoit pas grand-chose, un fonctionnaire qui, en dépit d'une certaine ponctualité, fonctionne peu'.

19. *Madame Bovary, Nouvelle version*, p. 215.

20. He is almost a textbook illustration of the personality type analyzed by Freud in 'Character and Anal Eroticism' in *The Complete Psychological Works of Sigmund Freud*, The Hogarth Press, London, 1959, ix. 169-75.

21. Cf. C. Gothot-Mersch, 'La Description des visages dans *Madame Bovary*', *Littérature*, 15. 1974, 17-26.

22. *Madame Bovary, Nouvelle version*, p. 336.

23. *Madame Bovary, Nouvelle version*, p. 382.

24. Cf. S. Hasumi, 'Ambivalence flaubertienne de l'ouvert et du clos', *Cahiers de l'association internationale des études francaises*, 1971, p. 267: 'Sa vie ne sera qu'une tentative perpétuelle vers des espaces fermés'.

25. *Œuvres complètes*, i. 353.

26. *Correspondance*, iii. 268.

27. *Correspondance*, iii. 331: 'notre activité n'est qu'une répétition continuelle, quelque diversifiée qu'elle ait l'air'.

28. Somnolence is endemic in *Madame Bovary*; 'ronflement' is used to express mental confusion on p. 346: 'quelque chose de monotone comme le ronflement d'une toupie bourdonnait à ses oreilles'.

29. Cf. 'une voix qui se traînait' (p. 472) and 'sa voix, faible d'abord et vagissante, devenait aiguë. Elle se traînait dans la nuit comme l'indistincte lamentation d'une vague détresse' (p. 569).

30. A common element is harshness, frequently denoted by the adjective 'rauque'; cf. 'le cri *rauque* et doux des corbeaux' (p. 470), 'et une voix s'éleva, une voix *rauque*, qui chantait' (p. 623) and the earlier version, 'le bruit du tour avec des ronflements plus *rauques* et plus pleins ne discontinuait pas' (*Madame Bovary, Nouvelle version*, p. 444).

31. 'Flaubert's Use of Sound in *Madame Bovary*', *Forum for Modern Language Studies*, xi (1975), p. 43.

32. *Madame Bovary, Nouvelle version*, p. 389.

33. *Madame Bovary, Nouvelle version*, p. 462.

34. A. G. Engstrom, *Darkness and Light*, Mississippi Romance Monographs, 1975, p. 57. Some of the echoes detected by Engstrom are questionable. Binet is not shown making use of his measuring rod and his complaint about pangs of hunger refers to something habitual not to a state immediately prior to Emma's death. The most suggestive detail discussed by Engstrom is that of the white dust which flies off the lathe and reappears on Emma's eyelids (p. 627) but this might be interpreted differently if Binet is regarded as an artist-figure.

35. Cf. *Correspondance*, ii. 379: 'Pourquoi prendre l'éternelle figure *insipide* du poète qui, plus elle sera ressemblante au type, plus elle se rapprochera d'une abstraction, c'est-à-dire de quelque chose d'anti-artistique'. Cf. also V. Brombert's comment ('La Première *Éducation Sentimentale*', *Europe*, Sept-Nov., 1969, p. 30): 'Dans la perspective flaubertienne l'artiste-héros s'avère impossible. Pour qui maintient comme credo que les grands maîtres de l'art mettent au rebut leurs personnalités, le seul acte héroïque possible est une abdication, un sacrifice qui ne saurait même pas devenir un thème tragique'.

36. Cf. 'Fais comme moi: romps avec l'extérieur; vis comme un ours, un ours blanc' (i. 192); 'Je suis ours et veux rester ours dans ma tanière, dans mon antre, dans ma peau, dans ma vieille peau d'ours, bien tranquille et loin du bourgeois et des bourgeoises' (*Correspondance, Supplément*, Paris: Conard, 1954, i. 39).

37. Cf. R. Barthes, *Le Degré zéro de l'écriture*, Seuil, Paris: 1953, p. 54: 'L'écriture artisanale, placée à l'intérieur du patrimoine bourgeois, ne dérange aucun ordre; privé d'autres combats, l'écrivain possède une passion qui suffit à le justifier: l'enfantement de la forme'.

38. *Correspondance*, vi. 378.

39. The *Dictionnaire des idées reçues* contains the following entry: 'Tour: Indispensable à avoir dans son grenier, à la campagne pr. les jours de pluie'.

40. Cf. C. Duchet, 'Roman et objets: l'exemple de *Madame Bovary*', *Europe*, Sept-Nov., 1969, p. 177: 'l'écrivain est l'artisan qui tourne sa phrase et arrondit ses périodes, comme Binet ses ronds de serviette'. For further discussion of the writer as artisan cf. C. Burgelin, 'La Flaubertolâtrie', *Littérature*, 15, 1974, 5-16.

41. *Madame Bovary, Nouvelle version* p. 588.

42. If the wood carving represents one extreme—formalism unchecked by mimetic intent—the toy village described in an earlier version (*Madame Bovary, Nouvelle version*, p. 458) represents another equally unacceptable extreme, that of naive mimeticism unimpeded by considerations of form.

43. *S/Z*, Seuil, Paris, 1970, p. 141. Also cf. J. Culler, *Structuralist Poetics*, Routledge and Kegan Paul, London, 1975, p. 209: 'Plot is subject to teleological determination: certain things happen in order that the *récit* may develop as it does'.

44. J. Neefs, *Madame Bovary de Flaubert*, Hachette, Paris, 1972, p. 58: 'Le déterminisme rétrograde qui fonctionne dans tout récit est ici particulièrement puissant et signifiant. Par la "précision des assemblages et la rareté des éléments", par la certitude des indices, l'histoire de Charles et le passage d'Emma sont happés par leur fin'.

45. P. Bonnefis, 'Récit et histoire dans *Madame Bovary*', *La Nouvelle critique*, 1968, Linguistique et critique, p. 159. By 'histoire' Bonnefis means what Barthes means by 'discours'.

46. Neefs, op. cit., p. 59: 'Homais est délégué dans la fiction à chaque bifurcation narrative, figure de l'aveuglement postée en chaque lieu cardinal, fatalité narrative, véritable porte-malheur'.

47. Barthes, *S/Z*, p. 142.

48. Cf. G. Poulet *Les Métamorphoses du cercle*, Plon, Paris, 1961, pp. 370-96.

49. *Chroniques*, Gallimard, Paris, 1927, p. 194.

50. *Correspondance*, iii. 92.

51. P. Bonnefis, art. cit., p. 159.

52. Engstrom, op. cit., p. 54.

53. J. Culler, *Flaubert: The Uses of Uncertainty*, Paul Elek, London, 1974, p. 171.

54. Cf. 'Un flot de pourpre monta vite au visage de Madame Bovary. Elle se recula d'un air terrible, en s'écriant [. . .]' (p. 602) and 'Binet était rouge jusqu'aux oreilles [. . .] tout à coup, comme à la vue d'un serpent, il se recula bien loin en s'écriant [. . .]' (p. 605).

55. This sense of the derivative nature of literary discourse finally reaches panic proportions in *Bouvard et Pécuchet*, Cf. Huss, art, cit., p. 146 and Note 30.

56. Cf. *Correspondance*, iv. 53: 'La bêtise n'est pas d'un côté et l'esprit de l'autre. C'est comme le vice et la vertu, malin qui les distingue'.

Naomi Schor (essay date 1980)

SOURCE: Schor, Naomi. "For a Restricted Thematics: Writing, Speech, and Difference in *Madame Bovary*." In *The Future of Difference*, edited by Hester Eisenstein and Alice Jardine, pp. 167-92; translated by Harriet Stone. Boston: G. K. Hall & Co., 1980.

[*In the following essay, Schor offers a multilayered analysis of Flaubert's use of language in the novel.*]

It is time to say out loud what has been whispered for some time: thematic criticism, which was given a first-class funeral a few years ago, is not dead. Like a repressed desire that insists on returning to consciousness, like a guilty pleasure that resists all threat of castration, thematic criticism is coming out from the shadows. This new thematic criticism is not, however, a nostalgic textual practice, a "retro" criticism, a regression to the styles (of reading) of the 1950s. Just as hyperrealism in painting is a return to the figurative passed through a minimalist grid, neothematism is a thematism passed through the filter of structuralist criticism. One could even argue that a certain structuralism, namely structural semantics, was in fact never anything but recuperation of thematism, a structuralist neothematism.

But it is not our purpose to study the persistence of thematics; the point is not, within the narrow framework of our study, to anticipate a history of contemporary criticism which is yet to be written. Rather it is a question of opening an inquiry into the continuity that links thematics, structural semantics, and even "poststructuralism." This very undertaking, this implicit valorization of continuity, is precisely what to our eyes constitutes thematics' characteristic, distinctive feature: I shall term thematic all textual practices that suffer from what might be called, in the manner of Bachelard, an Ariadne complex, all readings that cling to the Ariadne's thread ("fil conducteur"), whether it be the "synonymic chains"[1] of Barthes, the "chain of supplements"[2] of Derrida, or the "series"[3] of Deleuze. Be it vertical, horizontal, or transversal, the Ariadne's thread haunts the texts of Barthes, Derrida, and Deleuze, not in the typically structuralist form—that is, metalinguistic—of the Greimasian isotope, but in a poetic form: the thread ("fil") has become an extended metaphor. As Deleuze's "spider web,"[4] Barthes's "braid,"[5] and Derrida's "texture"[6] indicate, the relationship between the "textual" and the "textile"[7] is on its way to becoming one of the obsessive metaphors of current criticism. How are we to explain this obsession common to thinkers otherwise so different? One seductive hypothesis is that they all draw from the same source, namely Proust's metaphoric repertory. The following quotations from Richard (on Proust), Derrida (on Plato), and Barthes (on the pleasure of the text) substantiate this notion:

> Thematization thus clearly resembles weaving. The interweaving of all thematic series assumes in the Proustian daydream the form of a net in which the matter of the work is caught, or that of a network, both innervational and cybernetic, that enables us to circulate in it from link to link, knot to knot, "star" to "star" with the utmost freedom; because "between the least significant point in our past and all the others there exists a rich network of memories offering a plethora of communications."[8]

* * *

> The dissimulation of the woven texture can in any case take centuries to undo its web: a web that envelops a web, undoing the web for centuries; reconstituting it too as an organism, indefinitely regenerating its own tissue behind the cutting trace, the decision of each reading. There is always a surprise in store for the anatomy or physiology of a critique that might think it had mastered the game, surveyed all the threads at once, a critique that deludes itself too, in wanting to look at the text without touching it, without laying a hand on the "object," without risking—which is the sole chance of entering into the game by getting a few fingers caught—the addition of some new thread. Adding, here, is nothing other than giving to read. One must manage to think this out: that it is not a question of embroidering upon a text, unless one considers that to know how to embroider is still to take heed to follow the given thread. That is, if you follow me, the hidden thread.[9]

While taking the opposite view from Derrida insofar as hidden meaning is concerned, Barthes adopts his textile metaphor; Derrida's *istos* becomes Barthes's *hyphos*:

> *Text* means *Tissue*; but whereas hitherto we have always taken this tissue as a product, a ready-made veil, behind which lies, more or less hidden, meaning (truth), we are now emphasizing, in the tissue, the generative idea that the text is made, is worked out in a perpetual interweaving; lost in this tissue—this texture—the subject makes himself, like a spider dissolving in the constructive secretions of its web. Were we fond of neologism, we might define the theory of the text as an *hyphology* (*hyphos* is the tissue and the spider's web).[10]

The metaphors that these authors weave again and again are extremely significant, since according to Freud the only contribution of women "to the discoveries and inventions in the history of civilization" is a "technique," "that of plaiting and weaving."[11] The thread unraveled by Ariadne, cut by the Fates, woven by Penelope, is a peculiarly feminine attribute, a metonym for femininity. There is thus cause to speculate about the relations (necessarily hypothetical at the current stage of our knowledge) between a thematic reading and a feminine reading, by which I certainly do not mean that reading practiced uniquely by women. If my hypothesis concerning the femininity of thematism were justified, this would explain its culpabilization on the one hand and, paradoxically, its masculine recuperation on the other. This hypothesis presupposes a question: does reading have a sex? And this question in turn brings up another: does writing have a sex? It is, as we will attempt to demonstrate, precisely this question of the sex of writing that underlies *Madame Bovary.* We can no longer read *Madame Bovary* outside of the "sexual problematic"[12] that Sartre analyzed in its author, but we must no longer separate the sexual problematic from the scriptural problematic, as did Baudelaire, who was the first to qualify Emma Bovary as a "strange androgynous creature."[13]

Let us note at the close, in order to weave the many threads of our introduction, that there exists in *Madame Bovary* the description of an object which can be readily inscribed in the line of thought that we have just evoked. I am referring to the green silk cigar-case that Charles picks up when leaving la Vaubyessard and that Emma so preciously keeps. Read, or reread, in light of the preceding remarks, this passage seems to assume a new meaning: the green silk cigar-case becomes the emblem of the imbrication of weaving, the text, and femininity. *Madame Bovary* thus contains not only an objective correlative of its production, but a protocol for its interpretation as well:

> It had been embroidered on some rosewood frame, a pretty piece of furniture, hidden from all eyes, that had occupied many hours, and over which had fallen the soft curls of the pensive worker. A breath of love had passed over the stitches on the canvas; each prick of the needle had fixed there a hope or a memory, and all those interwoven threads of silk were but the continued extension of the same silent passion.[14]

To conclude these prolegomena, I would like to put to the test a new thematics that I propose to call a "restricted thematics" because, if the definition of the field of possible themes must henceforth answer to the call for literary specificity, the reciprocal play of speech and writing will replace the time/space paradigm privileged since Proust, with speech occupying the field of time, and writing inscribed in that of space. Unlike the "general" thematic reading which always tends toward "an infinite reading" (Richard, op. cit., p. 8), which exists, that is, in an anamorphous relationship with the text, restricted thematics would be the equivalent of an anastomosis, sectioning the text in order to bring together binary opposites (on the semantic plane), doubles (on the actantial plane), and repeated sequences (on the evenemential plane).

> *En somme, cette femme est vraiment grande, elle est surtout pitoyable, et malgré la dureté systématique de l'auteur, qui a fait tous ses efforts pour être absent de*

son oeuvre et pour jouer la fonction d'un monteur de marionnettes, toutes les femmes intellectuelles lui sauront gré d'avoir élevé la femelle à une si haute puissance, si loin de l'animal pur et si près de l'homme idéal. . . .

Baudelaire

As a starting-point for our reflection, let us recall René Girard's statement concerning Flaubert's "grotesque antithesis":

As Flaubert's novelistic genius ripens his oppositions become more futile; the identity of the contraries is drawn more clearly.[15]

If—as we are firmly convinced—this breakdown of opposites is manifest at all levels of the Flaubertian text and along its entire diachronic course, how does it apply to the writing/speech opposition, explicitly thematized by Flaubert in *Sentimental Education,* during a conversation between Frédéric and Madame Arnoux: "She admired orators; he preferred a writer's fame."[16]. Does this orators/writers opposition also participate in the obsessional tyranny of the identity of the contraries, in this system of growing in-differentiation?

The speech axis permits a first division of the characters in *Madame Bovary* into two large categories: those who are adept at speaking, such as Rodolphe and Homais, and those who are not, such as Charles and Emma. But the insufficiency of this first distribution is instantly apparent since certain characters adept at speaking are not good listeners. The speech axis must be subordinated to the communication axis, a bipolar axis with at one end an encoder/emitter, at the other a decoder/receiver. Depending on whether or not a character exhibits the aptitudes for encoding and decoding, we can forsee four combinations:

(1) encoding + (2) encoding − (3) encoding + (4) encoding −
    decoding +   decoding −   decoding −   decoding +

If we examine the characters named above[17] in light of these *roles,* certain aspects of the speech problematic in *Madame Bovary* emerge.

From his first appearance, Charles reveals himself to be an impotent speaker:

The new boy then took a supreme resolution, opened an inordinately large mouth, and shouted at the top of his voice as if calling someone, the word "Charbovari."

(p. 3)

Incapable of articulating the syllables of his name, Charles can but repeat the words of others:

Charles's conversation was commonplace as a street pavement, and every one's ideas trooped through it in their everyday garb, without exciting emotion, laughter, or thought.

(p. 29)

What distinguishes Charles's conversation from that of the glib speaker is not so much its painful banality, but its neutrality. His is an inefficient speech, lacking resonance, a speech in which nothing is transmitted from the enunciator to his interlocutor. Nevertheless, it must be noted that this "zero" on the encoding plane will have a great word, his last:

He even made a phrase ("un grand mot"), the only one he'd ever made:

"Fate willed it this way."

(pp. 254-55)

The effect of this grandiloquent sentence is, however, doubly subverted by its receptor, Rodolphe:

Rodolphe, who had been the agent of this fate, thought him very meek for a man in his situation, comic even and slightly despicable.

(loc. cit.)

First irony: the receptor is, in fact, the encoder. It is Rodolphe who was the first to put the word "fate" into circulation in the novel when he composed his letter breaking with Emma:

Why were you so beautiful? Is it my fault? God, no! only fate is to blame!

"That's a word that always helps," he said to himself.

(p. 146)

And Charles reads this letter (pp. 249-50). As we will see below, once launched, this word will continually reappear. In using it in talking to Rodolphe, Charles only completes the series, closes the circuit: Rodolphe → Emma → Charles → Rodolphe. Second irony: the original encoder (the "voluntary deceiver"[18], presents himself as judge and condemns his imitator (his involuntary dupe). Flaubert thus puts the parrot and the hypocrite back to back.

With Charles the inability to encode goes along with an inability to decode which makes him unable to understand Emma. For Emma, speaking to Charles is a last resort:

At other times, she told him what she had been reading, some passage in a novel, a new play, or an anecdote from high society found in a newspaper story; for, after all, Charles was someone to talk to, an ever-open ear, an ever-ready approbation. She even confided many a thing to her greyhound! She would have done so to the logs in the fireplace or to the pendulum of the clock.

(p. 44)

Charles's qualifications as a listener are minimal; they can be reduced to the possession of an ear and the promise of his ever-identical reaction. The equivalence established among Charles, the greyhound, the logs, and the pendulum says a great deal about his inability to de-code, for the progression from the animate to the inani-mate, the choice of the logs and the pendulum in the domestic code, with their semes of hardness (hence the figurative meaning of "bûche" [log]: "stupid person") and mechanicity, confirms Charles's nullity: he actual-izes combination #2, which is doubly negative.

Initially, Rodolphe seems gifted with all the faculties that Charles lacks. This is not to say that his discourse is more "original" then Charles's, but that he draws from the same dictionary of received ideas as Emma: he speaks her language. The juxtaposition in the oft-commented-upon chapter of the agricultural fair of Ro-dolphe's conventional seduction of Emma and the func-tionaries' set speech serves only to underscore the parallelism of the two discourses: opposed on the spa-tial (vertical) axis, Rodolphe and the two orators echo each other on the speech axis, as the intersection of the two discourses indicates. The only difference between Rodolphe's speech and that of Charles is that Rodol-phe's acts upon Emma; it evokes dreams, it becomes action, love.

A clever encoder, Rodolphe is also a cunning decoder of corporeal semiology; he is a diagnostician of great talent:

> Monsieur Rodolphe Boulanger was thirty-four; he com-bined brutality of temperament with a shrewd judg-ment, having had much experience with women and being something of a connoisseur. This one had seemed pretty to him; so he kept dreaming about her and her husband.
>
> "I think he is very stupid. She must be tired of him, no doubt. *He has dirty nails, and hasn't shaved for three days.*"

(p. 93, emphasis mine)

But it is precisely that which enables him to decode this *clue,* namely his experience, that prevents him from de-coding Emma's oral messages. Having spent his life re-peating, indeed perfecting, an invariable scenario whose only variant is the partner, Rodolphe cannot go beyond clichés, ready-made formulas. Everything happens as if Rodolphe's decoding mechanism were programmed to function only with information that has already been re-ceived. We find in Rodolphe the same "linguistic deaf-ness"[19] that Genette analyzes in certain Proustian char-acters who, he remarks, only hear what they can or want to hear, that is, in the extreme, what they can or want to say. Rodolphe's decoding of Charles's speech (see above) exemplifies this form of listening by projec-tion. Emma's case is, however, far more complex:

> He had so often heard these things said that they did not strike *him* as original. Emma was like all his mis-tresses; and the charm of novelty, gradually falling away like a garment, laid bare the eternal monotony of

passion, that has always the same shape and the same language. He was unable to see, this man so full of ex-perience, the variety of feelings hidden within the same expressions. Since libertine or venal lips had murmured similar phrases, he only faintly believed in the candor of Emma's; he thought one should be aware of exag-gerated declarations which only serve to cloak a tepid love; *as though* the abundance of one's soul did not sometimes overflow with empty metaphors, since no one ever has been able to give the exact measure of his needs, his concepts, or his sorrows. The human tongue is like a cracked cauldron on which we beat out the tunes to set a bear dancing when we would make the stars weep with our melodies.

(p. 138, emphasis mine)

The increased intervention of the narrator from the "him" of disassociation (indirect intervention) to the "as though" of judgment (direct intervention) translates the importance that Flaubert attaches to this passage, in which he puts forth his speech problematic. In effect, this passage does no more than reiterate an invariant opposition: unique feelings versus common speech. In other words: how does one communicate difference by means of sameness, how does one give an individual charge to words used by all? With Flaubert the renewal of the cliché is not so much a matter of style as meta-physics, for, on a purely linguistic plane, there is in his work as a constant inspiration by the cliché, an aspira-tion by the received idea. Thus in *Sentimental Educa-tion* the cliché favors more than it prevents the commu-nication of passionate feelings: "He . . . poured out his love more freely through the medium of commonplaces" (p. 197). But what the cliché cannot communicate is unicity. Two presuppositions underlie this passage: first, there is a "dissimilarity of feelings," original feelings, unique essence; second, in an ideal system of speech there is a total adequation of the word and the psychic signified. Flaubert's oral ideal is, to use Genette's ex-pression, nothing but a new "avatar of cratylism,"[20] which is hardly surprising in this avowed Platonist.

Madame Bovary tests the romantic notions of excep-tionality and ineffability, for the destiny of the romantic hero is bound up with a theory of speech.[21] The "double intervention"[22] noted above translates the doubling of the narrative sequence; we could adopt here the writer/ novelist distinction proposed by Marcel Muller to ac-count for two of the seven voices in *Remembrance of Things Past,*[23] attributing to the "writer" Rodolphe's point of view, and to the "novelist" Emma's. To assign Rodolphe's decoding a minus sign—Rodolphe would actualize combination #3—amounts to espousing the cause of the novelist, who supports Emma's essential superiority/difference, betrayed not only by the inferior-ity of those who surround her, but also by speech, which is not up to her level. René Girard, it should be noted here, adopts the point of view of the writer, indirectly justifying Rodolphe: "the opposition between Emma and Charles, and between Emma and the citizens of Yonville is essential only in Emma's mind."[24]

If, however, we follow the thread of the thematic paradigm speech/writing, we find that the structuring opposition of the novel is neither Emma versus Rodolphe nor Emma versus Charles (nor is it the commonplace of traditional criticism, Homais versus Bournisien); the privileged doublet is none other than Emma versus Homais, a fundamental opposition half-expressed, half-concealed by their names, which should be read "Femm(a) versus Hom(ais)"—*Femme* (Woman) versus *Homme* (Man). This reading consists of remedying Emma's lack by restoring her truncated "F" to her, and of cutting off Homais's supplement by putting his adjunctive suffix in parentheses. How can one fail to see in the operations to which Flaubert subjected the terms of sexual opposition to generate the characters' names, the equivalent of castration on the plane of the signifier? We could thus term the castration axis the arch-axis, the principal axis that subordinates all the other semantic axes of the novel.

Opposed to Emma's inability to find the words necessary to express her thoughts (one of the corollaries of the cratylian theory being that thoughts/feelings *precede* speech), is the always reiterated adequation of the pharmacist's thoughts and words:

> Perhaps she would have liked to confide all these things to some one. But how tell an undefinable uneasiness, changing as the clouds, unstable as the winds? Words failed her and, by the same token, the opportunity, the courage.
>
> (p. 29)

> "What a dreadful catastrophe!" exclaimed the pharmacist, who always found expressions that filled all imaginable circumstances.
>
> (p. 96)

Emma's incapacity, let us note, is intermittent; her cyclothymia is also a pathology of speech:

> On certain days she chattered with feverish profusion, and this overexcitement was suddenly followed by a state of torpor, in which she remained without speaking, without moving.
>
> (p. 48)

This alternate encoding can be represented as follows:

Emma: encoding + / -

Nevertheless, on the speech-encoding plane, Homais is the undisputed winner. Of all the characters in the novel, he is the only one to work tirelessly at his expression. For him talking is both a delight (*jouissance*) (". . . for the pharmacist much enjoyed pronouncing the word 'doctor,' as if addressing another by it reflected on himself some of the grandeur of the title" [p. 120]), and an art ("Homais had meditated at length over his speech; he had rounded, polished it, given it the proper cadence; it was a masterpiece of prudence and transitions, of subtle turns and delicacy . . ." [p. 181]). Unlike Rodolphe, Homais does not speak a stilted language, but takes pleasure in hearing and reproducing new thoughts, stylish expressions. Thus we see him, in the course of a conversation with Léon, reveal his extraordinary mimetic gifts, speaking "Parislang":

> . . . he even used slang to impress [. . .] the "bourgeois," saying "flip," "cool," "sweet," "neat-o," and "I must break it up," for "I must leave."
>
> (p. 202)

If Rodolphe is a smooth talker, if he dexterously manages the code of the vile seducer, Homais has a gift for *languages* (Latin, English, slang) that he handles with the love of a savant, an expert in transcoding.

But if on the communication axis Homais wins out over Emma, who, it must be remembered, does not shine as a decoder, allowing herself to be easily duped by the clichés that Rodolphe reels off to her both before and after their affair ("It was the first time that Emma had heard such words addressed to her, and her pride unfolded languidly in the warmth of this language, like someone stretching in a hot bath" [p. 112]; "She yielded to his words . . ." [p. 226]), when one turns to that delayed communication, writing, the balance of forces is equalized. Certain readers, unaware of Emma's scriptural activities, will perhaps be surprised at this affirmation. It is, however, in the area of writing that the Emma/Homais rivalry turns out to be the most violent; it is to the extent that they practice two different forms of writing that their sexual opposition becomes significant. The medal that motivates Homais and whose reception closes the novel—"He has just been given the cross of the Legion of Honor" (p. 255)—is destined to crown his writings, which are numerous. He is the classic pedant scribbler, having published "'at my expense, numerous works of public usefulness, such as' (and he recalled his pamphlet entitled, *On Cider, Its Manufacture and Effects,* besides observations on the wooly aphis that he had sent to the Academy; his volume of statistics, and down to his pharmaceutical thesis)" (p. 253). Compared to this journalistic logorrhea, what has Emma published? Nothing, but she does write. What, to my knowledge, has escaped critical notice is the thematic and structural relationship between **Madame Bovary** and the first **Education** [**Sentimental Education**]: the Emma/Homais couple is a new avatar of the Jules/Henry couple. Even those who have taken literally the famous exclamation *"Madame Bovary, c'est moi"* have bypassed the essential, the too-evident, in their concern for the anecdotal similarities between Emma and Gustave. Emma is also the portrait of an artist, but of the artist as a young woman, and it is this difference, this bold representation of the writer as a woman which disconcerts, which misleads, and which, for these reasons, must be examined.

Emma's search for love's passion is doubly motivated by literature. First there is "external mediation,"[25] the desire to transform the (dead) letters that she has read into lived experience, to coincide with literary models:

> And Emma tried to find out what one meant exactly in life by the words *bliss, passion, ecstasy,* that had seemed to her so beautiful in books.
>
> (p. 24)

When she becomes Rodolphe's mistress, this much longed-for identification seems to be realized; Emma progresses from the passive status of a reader to the active status of a heroine:

> Then she recalled the heroines of the books that she had read. . . . She became herself, as it were, an actual part of these lyrical imaginings; at long last, as she saw herself among those lovers she had so envied, she fulfilled the love-dream of her youth.
>
> (p. 117)

Finally, with Léon she attains her goal: from a heroine-for-herself she is transformed into a heroine-for-others: "She was the mistress of all the novels, the heroine of all the dramas, the vague 'she' of all the volumes of verse" (p. 192).

But this first love-letters link conceals another of prime importance to our study: Emma seeks a lover not only to become a novelistic character, but especially to become an author. When, in the early stage of her marriage, Emma settles in to wait for "something to happen," she outfits herself in advance with a writer's tools:

> She had bought herself a blotter, writing-case, penholder, and envelopes although *she had no one to write to.* . . .
>
> (p. 43, emphasis mine)

What Emma lacks is not a lover, but a receiver ("destinaire"), and what she desires through this receiver-pretext for writing is literary fame. To convince oneself of this, one need only compare the above quotation with another seemingly innocent remark which follows one page later. Emma wants Charles to become a great doctor because:

> She would have wished this name of Bovary, which was hers, to be illustrious, to see it displayed at the booksellers', repeated in the newspapers, known to all France.
>
> (p. 44)

By bringing together these two segments of the same sentence, of the same phantasm, we witness the emergence of Emma's profound ambition: to be a famous novelist. Why then is this wish expressed on the one hand by an intermediary, projected onto Charles, and on the other hand occulted by the separation of the means (writing instruments) from the end (to be famous)? This repression, this censure, results from Emma's sex. What she envies in a man is not so much the possibility of traveling, but the possibility of writing; what she lacks in order to write are neither words nor pen, but a phallus.

Imbued with eighteenth-century literature, Emma cannot conceive of a literary production other than a novel by letters, and the taking of a lover is the necessary condition for this form of writing. Once she becomes Rodolphe's mistress, Emma begins her epistolary novel. Rodolphe serves as both her initiator and her receiver:

> From that day on they wrote to one another regularly every evening. Emma placed her letter at the end of the garden, by the river, in a crack of the wall. Rodolphe came to fetch it, and put another in its place that she always accused of being too short.
>
> (p. 117)

This little game of hide-and-seek inaugurates Emma's apprenticeship, which will go through three stages, the first of which is marked by the persistence of the illusion of communication. Rather than renounce this illusion, Emma brings to correspondence all those desires unsatisfied by conversation, continuing to valorize *exchange,* clinging to the double role of sender/receiver that defines the interlocutor. Thus Emma complains of the brevity of Rodolphe's letters; thus she demands verses from Léon:

> She asked him for some verses—some verses "for herself," a "love poem" in honor of her.
>
> (p. 201)

If initially Emma writes to receive letters, to take pleasure in the communication forbidden, impossible on the speech plane, writing subsequently becomes the adjuvant of a "waning passion" in the manner of an aphrodisiac:

> . . . in the letters that Emma wrote him she spoke of flowers, poetry, the moon and the stars, naive resources of a waning passion striving to keep itself alive by all external aids.
>
> (p. 205)

It is only during the third stage when the receiver-lover has been demystified, unmasked as the double of her husband—"Emma found again in adultery all the platitudes of marriage" (p. 211; an excellent example of the identity of opposites!)—that Emma must yield to the evidence: she no longer loves Léon, but she continues more and more to love to write. It is only at this stage that Emma fully assumes her role as writer:

> She blamed Léon for her disappointed hopes, as if he had betrayed her. . . .
>
> She none the less went on writing him love letters in keeping with the notion that a woman must write to her lover.
>
> But while writing to him, it was another man she saw, a phantom fashioned out of her most ardent memories, of her favorite books, her strongest desires, and at last he became so real, so tangible, that her heart beat wildly in awe and admiration, though unable to see him distinctly, for, like a god, he was hidden beneath the abundance of his attributes. . . . She felt him near her; he was coming and would ravish her entire being in a kiss. Then she would fall back to earth again shattered; for these vague ecstasies of imaginary love would exhaust her more than the wildest orgies.
>
> (pp. 211-12)

The "but" signals the passage from one stage to another, the final subordination of love to writing, the metamorphosis of writing dictated by conventions into writing that flows from the heart. The latter writing is diametrically opposed to conversation-communication in that it presupposes the absence of a receiver, compensates for a lack, thereby embracing emptiness. As Freud demonstrates in *The Poet and Daydreaming,* the fictive character, like this composite being who is sketched by Emma's pen, is the product of all the unsatisfied desires of its creator. Transcoded into psychoanalytic terminology, the "phantom" that Emma perceives is a phantasm. Moreover, writing, such as Emma practices it (such as Flaubert practiced it), is a solitary pleasure: the phantasmic scene is seduction. The pleasure that Emma experiences in rewriting Léon, in giving herself a lover three times hyperbolic, is intensely erotic.

To write is to leave the prey for the shadow, and, in the end, writing is to become the shadow itself: the author-phantom must succeed the character-phantom. Thus, just before swallowing the arsenic, Emma appears to Justin "majestic as a phantom" (p. 229). The apprenticeship of the heroine-artist can lead only to death, but to an exemplary death, because suicide generates language. In the novel to die a natural death (*belle mort*) is to commit suicide, because suicide is the very act that links the coming to writing with the renunciation of life. Like Madame de Tourvel, like Julie, Emma does not die without having written a last letter: "She sat down at her writing-table and wrote a letter, which she sealed slowly, adding the date and the hour" (p. 230). Of this letter we know only the first words: "'Let no one be blamed . . .'" (p. 231). The fragmentary state of this letter is highly significant, because the gap created

by the ellipsis leaves forever unanswered the essential question: in this ultimate letter, *ultima verba,* does Emma complete the final stages of her apprenticeship, does she succeed in inventing for herself a writing that goes beyond clichés, beyond the romantic lies that they carry with them? The first words are only a (negative) repetition of Rodolphe's words, tending to invalidate any hypothesis of last-minute literary conversion. This letter immediately evokes the imitative circuit. If, in the letter that Charles composes right after Emma's death, we find both thematic (novelistic ideas) and stylistic (use of the imperative: "'Let no one try to overrule me'") echoes of Emma's previous letters, we are struck, too, by the firmness of expression resulting from a very bold use of asyndeton. In fact, one could cite this passage as an example of the Flaubertian enunciation which, according to Barthes's formula, is seized by "a generalized asyndeton"[26]:

> I wish her to be buried in her wedding dress, with white shoes, and a wreath. Her hair is to be spread out over her shoulders. Three coffins, one oak, one mahogany, one of lead. Let no one try to overrule me; I shall have the strength to resist him. She is to be covered with a large piece of green velvet. This is my wish; see that it is done.
>
> (p. 239)

Is this writing a personal find of Charles's, whose writing up to this point vied in ineptitude with his speech (note the fifteen drafts that he writes to have Dr. Larivière come *before* Emma's death), or can one see in it the pale reflection, traces of Emma's last letter?

In the Flaubertian novelistic universe, in which substitution chains organize the narrative, nothing is less evident than the principles of closure that govern this neurotic serialization. Since in Emma's mind the Viscount = Léon = Rodolphe (p. 106), what prevents her from continuing indefinitely this substitution of one lover for another? In theory the series is open-ended; the resources of a substantial rhetoric and logic are inexhaustible.[27] In effect, Emma's death is not synchronic with the exhaustion of the narrative because, after her death, she is replaced by other characters: formerly the *subject* of substitution, she becomes its *object.* Thus Félicité, her maid, wears her dresses: "[she] was about her former mistress's height and often, on seeing her from behind, Charles thought she had come back . . ." (p. 249); and Charles begins to imitate her:

> To please her, as if she were still living, he adopted her taste, her ideas; he bought patent leather boots and took to wearing white cravats. He waxed his moustache and, just like her, signed promissory notes.
>
> (p. 250)

But, on the actantial plane, on the plane of the novel's structuring opposition, Emma/Homais, Emma is succeeded by the blind man, a Beckettian character whose *symbolic* value has for a long time preoccupied the critics[28] and whose function still remains to be pinpointed. According to our reading, his function is above all heuristic: whereas the opposition between Emma and Homais is implicit, concealed by anagrams, that between the blind man and Homais is explicit, manifest on the evenemential plane.

The blind man's doubling of Emma is prepared a long time in advance: from his first appearance the blind man finds in Emma a listener; his melancholic song evokes an echo in Emma's mind (p. 193); later she gives him her last five-franc coin (see in this scene the opposition: Emma's excessive generosity versus Homais's excessive greed; by her *gift,* Emma is united with the blind man against Homais [p. 219]). Finally, on her deathbed, Emma hears the blind man, believes she sees him, and pronounces her last words: "'The blind man!'" (p. 238). The seme common to Emma and the blind man is monstrosity, physical in the one, moral in the other. It is precisely the blind man's monstrosity that brings upon him Homais's hostility: Homais would like to cure the blind man, that is, reduce his difference, "normalize" him. The blind man/Homais sequence only repeats the clubfoot/Homais sequence; in both cases the science preached by the pharmacist is never anything but the means of replacing heterogeneity with homogeneity, thereby earning the gratitude and esteem of his clients. Nevertheless, unlike the crippled clubfoot, the blind-man-ever-blind flouts Homais, publicly exhibiting the wounds that the pharmacist's recommendations and pomades could not cure. Homais, unable to silence this embarrassing witness to the inefficacy of his speech, begins to pursue him through writing; a fierce fight ensues between the garrulous blind man and the prolix pharmacist:

> He managed so well that the fellow was locked up. But he was released. He began again, and so did Homais. It was a struggle. Homais won out, for his foe was condemned to lifelong confinement in an asylum.
>
> (p. 251)

The superimposition of the Emma/Homais // blind man/ Homais rivalries reveal within writing the same opposition that we detected above at the center of speech: efficacy versus inefficacy. We can thus posit the following equivalence:

$$\frac{\text{Efficacy}}{\text{Inefficacy}} \simeq \frac{\text{Rodolphe's speech}}{\text{Charles's speech}} \simeq \frac{\text{Homais's writing}}{\text{Emma's writing}}$$

While Emma's writing remains, so to speak, a dead letter, transforming nothing, producing no impact on the external world, Homais's writing is able to exile if not kill, and becomes a means of social advancement.

Moreover, this superimposition permits the disengagement of an attribute, an invariant qualification of the *victim*: the victim, woman or blind man, is a being who lacks an essential organ, in fact, as Freud repeats at several points, the same organ, since according to his theory blindness = castration. The victim's final failure is inscribed in his/her body; Emma's monstrosity is physical as much as it is moral. The blind man's doubling of Emma punctuates the text, assures it readability: woman, this "defective" monster ("*monstre à la manque*"), is the privileged figure of the writer, and especially of the writer Flaubert, a "failed girl" ("*fille manquée*") according to Sartre's thesis. It would, moreover, be easy to demonstrate that Emma's writing apprenticeship is consistent with an attempt to change sex, to reverse castration. The refusal of femininity, the temptation of virility, are not given once and for all from the beginning; before going that route, Emma will try to follow the path of integration, to accept the feminine destiny that Freud charts for the "normal" woman: marriage and maternity. But, just as marriage ends in failure, Charles being unable to succeed *in Emma's place,* motherhood ends in disappointment: George, the phantasmic phallic-son, turns out to be only Berthe, a child worthy of Charles. Thus, much before Freud, Flaubert well understood that in order for maternity to fully satisfy penis-envy, the child must be male (which would condemn over half of all women to inevitable neurosis):

> She hopes for a son; he would be strong and dark; she would call him George; and this idea of having a male child was like an expected revenge for all her impotence of the past. A man, at least, is free; he can explore all passions and all countries, overcome obstacles, taste of the most distant pleasures. But a woman is always hampered. Being inert as well as pliable, she has against her the weakness of the flesh and the inequity of the law. . . .
>
> She gave birth on a Sunday at about six o'clock, as the sun was rising.
>
> "It's a girl!" said Charles.
>
> She turned her head away and fainted.
>
> (p. 63)

Unable to obtain a phallus by "phallic proxy,"[29] Emma seeks to satisfy her desire to change sex through transvestism. Partial at the beginning of the novel, the disguise is completed just before Emma's death:

> Like a man, she wore a tortoise-shell eyeglass thrust between two buttons of her blouse.
>
> (pp. 11 12)

> . . . she parted [her hair] on one side and rolled it under, like a man's.
>
> (p. 89)

"[How could] I go riding without proper clothes?"

"You must order a riding outfit," he answered.

The riding habit ["amazone"] decided her.

(p. 113)

On that day of Mid-Lent she did not return to Yonville; that evening she went to a masked ball. She wore velvet breeches, red stockings, a peruke, and a three-cornered hat cocked over one ear.

(p. 212)

But, as Sartre demonstrates, for Flaubert sexuality belongs to the realm of the imagination; disguise is, then, only an *analogon* of Emma's imaginary sex. In the last analysis, it is only on the imaginary plane, i.e., on the plane of the role *played* in the couple, that Emma's growing virility asserts itself. The order of her affairs, Rodolphe before Léon, thus assumes its meaning: whereas in her relationship with Rodolphe Emma plays the female role, traditionally passive, in her relationship with Léon the roles are reversed: ". . . he was becoming her mistress rather than she his" (p. 201).

It is not by chance that the writing apprenticeship and the "virility apprenticeship," if I may call it that, follow paths which ultimately converge at the time of Emma's affair with Léon, for their affair marks the triumph of the imaginary over the real, this being the precondition of all writing. If, insofar as the effect *on* the real is concerned, Homais's writing surpasses Emma's, considered in terms of the "reality effect," it is without any doubt Emma's (Flaubert's) writing that surpasses Homais's, for the "reality effect" can only be achieved through a total renunciation of any real satisfaction, can only be the just reward of sublimation, i.e., castration. For Flaubert writing thus has a sex, the sex of an assumed lack, the feminine sex.

* * *

It would seem, however, that all these oppositions are outweighed by Flaubert's radical distrust of language in general, a distrust evident in Emma's most bitter discovery, namely that ". . . everything was a lie" (p. 206). For the Flaubert of **Madame Bovary** language is constantly undermined by its potential for lying, lying in the largest sense of the term, including hyperbole as well as the willful distortion of facts, and mystified idealization as well as cynical reductionism. The generalization of lying erases both the differences between forms of writing and the differences between writing and speech. Emma's letters and Homais's published pieces thus participate in the same "a-mimesis": both he and she depart from reality, embellishing facts, adjusting them to their needs. They "invent"—"Then Homais invented incidents" (p. 251). On the other hand, Emma's idealization—"irrealization," Sartre would say—of

Léon on paper is only the resumption, the materialization of the oral self-idealization of the two lovers that occurs on the occasion of their reunion in Rouen:

. . . this was how they would have wished it to be, *each setting up an ideal* to which they were now trying to adapt their past life. Besides, *speech is like a rolling machine that always stretches the sentiment it expresses.*

(p. 169, emphasis mine)

Things would be too simple if there were not at least one exception to the rule; hence old Roualt appears to escape the treason of language. His annual letter enjoys a harmony both metaphoric (letter = writer) and metonymic (letter = reality contiguous to the writer). The hiatus between writer, words, and things is here reduced to a minimum. In fact, in the Flaubertian system the opposite of lying is not telling the truth, but immediacy, because the least distance between the sender and the receiver, the writing subject and the Other, as well as that between man and Things, opens a gap through which lies penetrate:

She held the coarse paper in her fingers for some minutes. A continuous stream of spelling mistakes ran through the letter, and Emma followed the kindly thought that cackled right through it like a hen half hidden in a hedge of thorns. The writing had been dried with ashes from the earth, for a little grey powder slipped from the letter on her dress, and she almost thought she saw her father bending over the hearth to take up the tongs.

(p. 124)

Examined more closely, this model of paternal writing is in fact threatened from all sides. In spite of the spelling mistakes and the "intradiagetic"[30] metaphor which guarantee the writer's adherence to words and things, the gap is there, manifest in the form of a lack: thought is compared to a "half hidden" hen. Adherence is thus only partial, and if this letter conveys writing-matter (letter + ashes), it is the matter itself that represents "the price to be paid": the symbolic Father is the dead Father.

Two consequences follow from this. First, for the characters who, unlike old Roualt, maintain relations with the world that are strongly mediated by written as well as spoken language, such as Emma, there is only one way in which to enjoy immediacy, and that is to step outside language. The two great erotic scenes of the novel link bliss (*jouissance*), plenitude, with the suspension of all linguistic communication. The initiation by Rodolphe culminates in one of the great Flaubertian silences, to borrow another expression from Genette[31]:

Silence was everywhere. . . . Then far away, beyond the wood, on the other hills, she heard a vague, prolonged cry, a voice which lingered, and in silence she heard it mingling like music with the last pulsations of her throbbing nerves.

(p. 116)

If in this scene the spoken word is supplanted by a non-articulated, a-semantic cry, in the coach scene the written word is torn to shreds, reduced to insignificance:

> One time, around noon, in the open country, . . . a bare hand appeared under the yellow canvas curtain, and threw out *some scraps of paper that scattered* in the wind, alighting further off like white butterflies on a field of red clover all in bloom.
>
> (p. 177, emphasis mine)

The euphoric form of the letter is thus the sperm-letter: in *Madame Bovary,* as in *The Temptation of Saint Anthony,* happiness is "being matter."

But if fictional characters, these "paper beings," find their happiness beyond or without language, what of the writer who is condemned to work in an articulate and signifying language? The writer cannot be for Flaubert but a pursuer of lies, making do for want of something better, with available means, i.e., language, language which is always both judge and plaintiff, source of lies and condemner of lies, poison and antidote, *pharmakon.* There is in *Madame Bovary* a character who appears to fulfill this prophylactic function. It is, as if by chance, a doctor, Doctor Larivière, a character with quasi-divine attributes: "The apparition of a god would not have caused more commotion" (p. 233).[32] Note in what terms Flaubert describes his diagnostic gifts:

> His glance, more penetrating than his scalpels, looked straight into your soul, and would *detect any lie,* regardless how well hidden.
>
> (p. 234, emphasis mine)

These are exactly the same terms that Flaubert uses to define his stylistic ideal when, in a letter to Louise Colet contemporary with the writing of *Madame Bovary,* he criticizes Lamartine for not having "this medical view of life, this view of Truth."[33] Truth, it must be remembered, is for Flaubert a matter of style. To be true, the writer need only substitute for the doctor's look the equivalent instrument in his art, i.e., his style:

> a style . . . precise like scientific language . . . a style that would penetrate into ideas like the probe of a stylet.
>
> (loc. cit.)

The structural homology of the two sentences in question, with, on the one hand, the scalpel-glance which "looked straight into your soul," and on the other the "stylet-style" which "penetrates into ideas," underscores the identity of scriptural approach and surgical procedure. There is nothing less passive, less feminine, than the relationship with language known as "les affres du style" (pains of style): the reader of the correspondence concerning *Madame Bovary* cannot but be impressed with the aggressive and even sadistic relationship of Flaubert with the sentences and paragraphs of his novel that he sets about dissecting, unscrewing, undoing, unwriting, to use expressions found throughout his letters.[34] To convey the inarticulate, one must disarticulate. As Sartre observes, "style is the silence of discourse, the silence in discourse, the imaginary and secret end of the written word."[35]

Flaubert's stylistic ideal completes his writing ideal; if Flaubert's writing refers to what one might call, playing a bit on Kristeva's terms, a "gyno-text," then his style aspires to a "phallo-text," a masculine "pheno-text":

> I love above all else nervous, substantial, clear sentences with flexed muscles and a rugged complexion: I like male, not female, sentences. . . .[36]

In the last analysis the "bizarre androgyn" is neither Flaubert (Sartre) nor Emma (Baudelaire), but the book, locus of the confrontation, as well as the interpenetration of *animus* and *anima,* of the masculine and the feminine.

By definition a *restricted* thematic study cannot claim to be all-encompassing. We are thus able to take note of a final demarcation separating the new thematic criticism from the old: concerned with thematic structure or, better still, structuring themes, new criticism must not go beyond the framework of the individual novel (poem, drama). (This does not, of course, exclude intertextual allusions and references.) Defining the corpus in this manner, restricted thematics reintroduces a diachronic dimension into the always synchronic or a-chronic apprehension of traditional thematic criticism, thereby substituting "a new hermeneutic, one that is syntagmatic, or metonymic" for "the classical hermeneutic that was paradigmatic (or metaphoric)."[37] As we have observed, the writer/speech paradigm overdetermines not only the actantial distribution of characters but also the consecutive progression of the narrative sequences. I mean *overdetermine* because a thematic approach cannot by itself account for the multiple functioning of a text, but, given its "intent," one cannot really do without it.

POSTSCRIPT

To publish a (brand-new) translation of a not so recent (1976) article as a record of my workshop is to perpetrate a sort of hoax, though perhaps a necessary one: short of a verbatim transcription, there exists no acceptable and, above all, accurate mimesis of such an eminently oral event. I did not read this article at the workshop (though I did draw very heavily on it); indeed, I did not read from any prepared text; rather I spoke (or as one malcontent would have it, "lectured"!) from a couple of pages of notes. Were I to publish these notes, they would surely be even less intelligible than an unedited transcript of the proceedings, so in order to enter into the record a halfway faithful account of what actually happened, I have in effect prepared a third text, based on my notes, a tape of the session (graciously provided by the Barnard Women's Center), and my own recollections. Adherence to some unwritten code of academic ethics is not, however, my prime reason for adding this postscript; I simply wish to indicate how in the context of the conference—its agenda and its proceedings—points merely alluded to in the article were amplified, and how in the course of the workshop other points were raised.

As announced in the short description of the workshop I had prepared for prospective participants, my intention was "to explore the complex ramifications of Flaubert's well-known but little understood exclamation: 'Madame Bovary is me.'" The question I wanted to raise was: what happens when a male author identifies with his female protagonist to the point of fusion or *con*fusion? I call this mysterious creative process *female im-personation*. Obviously this process is at work in all male-authored gyneco-centric literature, but there is some justification for granting **Madame Bovary** paradigmatic status, for, as Mary McCarthy notes in her "foreword" to the Signet edition, "there is hardly a page in the novel that he [Flaubert] had not 'lived,' and he constantly drew on his own feelings to render Emma's. All novelists do this, but Flaubert went beyond the call of duty. Madame Bovary was not Flaubert, certainly; yet he became Madame Bovary. . . ."[38]

Now what further makes **Madame Bovary** a privileged example of female im-personation is the fact that this paper sex-change operation is singularly complicated, a great deal more so than I had suggested in my article, where I make some glancing allusions to Baudelaire and Sartre before going on to discuss how the anxiety of sexual difference informs the structure of the novel, pitting as it does a male and a female writing principle against each other. In the context of this conference, the sources of this anxiety in Flaubert's autobiography seemed to me to require a great deal more attention. Two critical texts would provide a common ground for discussion: Baudelaire's still pertinent essay on **Madame Bovary,** wherein the question of Emma's sex is raised for the first time, and Sartre's monumental biography of Flaubert, wherein for the first time the question of Flaubert's sexuality is raised. The anxiety of difference which pervades **Madame Bovary** draws its affective resonance from Flaubert's own complex sexual organization.

Using xeroxed handouts of pages drawn from Baudelaire's essay, we focused on the following passage in which the poet-critic is explaining how Flaubert succeeded against all odds in transforming a trivial subject (provincial adultery) into a great work of art: the process described amounts to a form of symbolic castration.

To accomplish the tour de force in its entirety the author had only to divest himself (as much as possible) of his sex and to become a woman. The result is a marvel; in spite of all his zeal as an actor, he could not keep from infusing virile blood into the veins of his creation, and Madame Bovary, in what is the most forceful, most ambitious, and also most contemplative in her nature, has remained a man. Just as Pallas Athena sprang full armed from the head of Zeus, so this strange androgynous creature has kept all the attraction of a virile soul in a charming feminine body.[39]

Reduced somewhat schematically, for Baudelaire: male author + female protagonist = androgyn. Now two interdependent and obviously questionable assumptions ground this formulation: one, "man" is a monolithic being; two, man is superior to woman. Thus, both here and in a subsequent passage, where Baudelaire goes on to detail Emma's masculine traits, all her positively valorized attributes are ascribed to her vestigial virility. Perhaps Baudelaire's most telling gesture is his inclusion of hysteria among Emma's "masculine" virtues; indeed—and this reveals the locus of Baudelaire's own identification with Flaubert's heroine—he sees in her an image of "the hysterical poet" (146).

Baudelaire's text elicited several comments from the participants, relating to the etymology and symptomatology of hysteria, and its possible motivation of the name of Bovary, which, as one astute participant pointed out, contained the word ovary. It was only later, after the workshop was over, that I realized that the (B)ovary hypothesis did not work quite as well in the original French, for Bovary does not rhyme with *ovaire,* though they do, of course, share the same stem. In retrospect, I'm glad I didn't think of this objection on the spot. The intervention was important not for its ultimate validity or contribution to Flaubert studies—which, by the way, do feature far wilder onomastic fantasies—but for its contribution to the *working* of the workshop. It was a welcome sign of the participants' willingness to join in some of the wordplay I had put on the board. (It also provided comic relief!)

From Baudelaire we shifted to Sartre. Here I restricted myself to the not so modest task of presenting in hopelessly simplified form Sartre's remarkable analysis of Flaubert's "*sexual problematic.*"[40] (I was fortunate enough to have among the participants a woman who was writing her thesis on *L'Idiot de la famille* and was thus able to help me in my presentation.) According to Sartre, when Flaubert looks at himself in the mirror, "his initial impulse is to see himself as a woman" (693). This observation should not, however, be taken to mean that Flaubert is a homosexual, or at any rate a male homosexual; rather, Sartre argues, Flaubert's sexuality is passive, and because he (Flaubert) associates passivity with femininity, he wishes to play the feminine role in his sexual fantasies and encounters. In other words—

Flaubert's own—he is a "lesbian." Here Sartre makes a useful and important distinction between the homosexual and the *perverse*: "by this word I mean to designate any erotic attitude in which there is derealization *in the second power*" (694). This is precisely what occurs during Emma's love affair with Léon. But before we get to Sartre's reading of those scenes, we must consider another useful distinction he introduces, the one between androgyny and hermaphroditism. For him, as for Baudelaire, Emma is an androgyn, but his constituent equation is radically different: "Emma is androgynous: in the arms of Rodolphe—a real man . . .—she swoons. . . . When she goes to make love with Léon, it is she who is the hunter" (710).

This alternatively active and passive sexual behavior does not, in Sartre's vocabulary, qualify as perverse; what is perverse and, by the same token, anxiety-producing are the erotic games Emma and Léon play, enacting their fantasies in fear and trembling. Perversion, Sartre insists, is not linked to specific sexual practices—one can be perverse while making love in the orthodox missionary position. Perversion is a pathology of the imaginary. When Emma and Léon make love, they form a doubly hermaphroditic couple, for each partner is endowed with a real (biological) sex and an "unreal" (imaginary)) one: "What Léon is after in Emma is the satisfaction of what has become *his vice,* the desire to imagine that he is a woman being caressed by a woman. Emma too is worried: through the role she is playing, that she cannot help but play, it would seem that she perceives the unreal threat of a permanent sex change" (711). What is of particular interest to us in Sartre's analysis is the connection he makes between perversion and anxiety, which is, in this instance, an anxiety of difference. To follow his immensely subtle and persuasive reading is to see how the novel moves ineluctably toward the collapse of sexual differences. The event that comes closest to this final catastrophe is the masked ball, which is presented as the ultimate degradation, for on that occasion masquerade is inseparably linked to slumming, which is to say, a breakdown of class difference.

The question of the breakdown of difference elicited a fair amount of discussion. One participant felt very strongly that Emma had been "sold the American dream," and suffered the fate of a *déclassée,* excluded from the predominant discourse. Others pointed out other instances of collapsing differences in the novel: see, for example, the celebrated Chapter VIII, with its description of the Agricultural Show. Viewed in my perspective, this strictly local event can be seen as a re-enactment of the Carnaval, with its ritual suspension of all structuring differences, as well, of course, as their ultimate restoration. The masked ball appears then to be a degraded repetition—a pleonasm, for in Flaubert, as Sartre points out, repetition always implies degrada-

tion—of the central, euphoric version of the festival. Similarly, Flaubert's disquieting use of syllepsis—as in, "At one and the same time she wanted to die and to live in Paris" (77)—could be taken to figure that breakdown of difference.

In lieu of a conclusion, I shared with the participants in the workshop an inchoate insight that had come to me as I listened to Audre Lorde make prose sing. I began to rethink Emma's deathbed scene, and her famous, enigmatic last cry: "'The blind man!'" (302). In my article I stress the negative attributes common to both Emma and the beggar, in particular their "castration." Now I wonder if I had not overlooked, in an act of critical deafness, their obvious *positive* link: a certain relationship to music. The blind beggar is after all also a singer, and throughout the novel Emma's quest is set to music: in the convent, at her wedding, at home (her piano), in Tostes (the organ-grinder), at la Vaubyessard, at the opera in Rouen, throughout the novel there is an insistent musical accompaniment to the heroine's life, a melodic subtext, as it were. What is significant, then, in the beggar's song are not the words, but the music. If, as had been suggested, Emma is denied access to the predominant discourse, she enjoys privileged access to that preverbal, preoedipal register that Julia Kristeva has retrieved from beneath the symbolic: the pulsating, rhythmic semiotic.[41] Somehow, in the course of the conference, my topic had changed from the anxiety to the joy of difference.

Notes

1. Roland Barthes, *S/Z,* tr. Richard Miller (New York: Hill and Wang, 1974), p. 93.

2. Jacques Derrida, *Of Grammatology,* trans. Gayatri Chakravorty Spivak (Baltimore: The John Hopkins University Press, 1976), p. 152.

3. Gilles Deleuze, *Proust et les signes* (Paris: P.U.F., 1971); *Logiques du sens* (Paris: 10/18, 1973). (All translations unless otherwise indicated are those of the translator of this article—trans.)

4. Deleuze, "Table ronde," in *Cahiers Marcel Proust* 7 (1975): 91.

5. Barthes, op. cit., p. 160.

6. Derrida, *La dissémination* (Paris: Seuil, 1972), p. 71 (translation mine—N.S.).

7. Derrida, *La dissémination,* p. 73.

8. Jean-Pierre Richard, *Proust et le monde sensible* (Paris: Seuil, 1974), p. 221.

9. Derrida, *La dissémination,* pp. 71-72; my thanks to Barbara Johnson for allowing me the use of this paragraph from her translation (Jacques Derrida, *Dissémination* [Chicago: Univ. of Chicago Press, forthcoming in 1981]).

10. Barthes, *The Pleasure of the Text,* tr. Richard Miller (New York: Hill and Wang, 1975), p. 64.

11. Sigmund Freud, "Femininity," *New Introductory Lectures on Psychoanalysis,* tr. James Strachey (New York: Norton, 1961), p. 132.

12. Jean-Paul Sartre, *L'Idiot de la famille,* I (Paris: Gallimard, 1971), p. 703.

13. Charles Baudelaire, *Ouevres complètes* (Paris: Pléiade, 1961), p. 652.

14. Gustave Flaubert, *Madame Bovary,* tr. Paul de Man (New York: Norton, 1965), pp. 40-41. (All page numbers refer to this edition.) Cf. Claude Duchet, "Romans et Objets: L'Exemple de *Madame Bovary,*" *Europe* 485-87 (Sept.-Nov. 1969): 172-201. To Duchet's remarks about the cigar-case I would add only the following: if in the last chapter of the first part of the novel the cigar-case is opposed to the wedding bouquet, in the novel in general it is opposed not to a manifest, but to a virtual object. In effect, the textile activity of the aristocratic Penelope who wove the luxury object is opposed to that of the proletarianized Penelope, Berthe, who, it must be remembered, ends up in a "cotton-mill" (p. 255). Thus Flaubert privileges weaving both as a model of textual production and as a means of closure; the Bovarys' decline and Emma's failure translate into the transformation of the silk thread into the cotton thread, i.e., into the degradation—the "Manchesterization," as Duchet would say—of the Ariadne's thread.

15. Rene Girard, *Deceit, Desire & the Novel,* tr. Yvonne Freccero (Baltimore: Johns Hopkins Univ. Press, 1965), p. 152.

16. Flaubert, *Sentimental Education,* tr. Robert Baldick (London: Penguin, 1978), pp. 92-93. Cf. in *Madame Bovary* this bit of dialogue between Emma and Léon: "'That is why,' he said, 'I especially love the poets. I think verse is more tender than prose, and that it makes one weep more easily.' 'Still in the long-run it is tiring,' continued Emma, 'and now, on the contrary, I have come to love stories that rush breathlessly along, that frighten one'" (p. 59). This superimposition valorizes the invariant relationship which in Flaubert subordinates the speech/writing, poetry/prose paradigms to the man/woman paradigm, enabling us to establish the following equivalency:

$$\frac{\text{woman}}{\text{man}} \simeq \frac{\text{orators}}{\text{writers}} \simeq \frac{\text{prose}}{\text{poetry}}$$

Moreover, this first conversation retroactively announces their sexual relationships: Emma's masculinity versus Léon's femininity. The genres have a sex and each sex selects, prefers the complementary or supplementary genre-sex. We will return to this notion below.

17. This "survey"—partial but motivated—obviously cannot account for all the oral manifestations in the text. Among the main characters, Léon's omission is particularly conspicuous. Let us state briefly that the relations of Léon and Emma are marked by the seal of silence; either they do not talk to each other, or their words are not recounted: "Had they nothing else to say to one another? Yet their eyes were full of more serious speech, and while they forced themselves to find trivial phrases, they felt the same languor stealing over them both; it was like the deep, continuous murmur of the soul dominating that of their voices" (p. 68). "She did not speak; he was silent, captivated by her silence, as he would have been by her speech" (p. 75). ". . . Then they talked in low tones, and their conversation seemed the sweeter to them because it was unheard" (p. 71). All this will culminate in the coach scene. Léon is shy, and shyness is the degree-zero of speaking.

18. Claude Bremond, *Logique du récit* (Paris: Seuil, 1973), p. 263.

19. Gerard Genette, "Proust et le langage indirect," *Figures II* (Paris: Seuil, 1969), p. 228.

20. Genette, *Poétique* 11 (1972): 367-94; 15 (1973): 113-33; 15 (1973): pp. 265-91.

21. Hence the numerous similarities between the speech problematic in Flaubert and Constant, cf. Tzvetan Todorov, "La Parole selon Constant," *Poétique de la prose* (Paris: Seuil, 1971), pp. 100-17.

22. Victor Brombert, *Flaubert par lui-meme* (Paris: Seuil, 1971), p. 59.

23. Marcel Muller, *Les Voix narratives dans la Recherche du temps perdu* (Geneve: Droz, 1965), pp. 8, 91-175. The question of Flaubertian *irony* (or in other words, of point of view) must be raised here, a question which creates what Barthes terms "a salutary discomfort of writing . . . for the very being of writing . . . is to keep the question *Who is speaking?* from ever being answered" (Barthes, *S/Z,* p. 140).

24. Girard, p. 149. Does the problematic case of Rodolphe require the insertion of a new combination, a combination between types 1 and 3: encoding +, decoding +/-?

25. Girard, p. 9 and passim.

26. Barthes, *The Pleasure of the Text,* p. 9.

27. See Raymond Debray-Genette, "Les Figures du récit dans *Un coeur simple,*" *Poétique* 3 (1970).

28. For a discussion of the diverse symbolic readings of the blind man see P. M. Wetherill, "*Madam Bovary*'s Blind Man: Symbolism in Flaubert," *Romantic Review* 61:1 (1970).

29. Luce Irigaray, *Speculum de l'autre femme* (Paris: Editions de Minuit, 1974), p. 106.

30. See Genette, *Figures III* (Paris: Seuil, 1972), pp. 236-41, and Jacques Neefs, "La figuration réaliste," *Poétique* 16 (1973): 472.

31. See Genette, "Silences de Flaubert," *Figures* (Paris: Seuil, 1966), pp. 223-43.

32. For a magnificent demystification of this entire passage the reader should consult Sartre, op. cit., pp. 454-61.

33. Flaubert, *Extraits de la correspondance,* ed. Geneviève Bollème (Paris: Seuil, 1963), p. 71.

34. See Barthes, "Flaubert et la phrase," *Nouveaux essais critiques* (Paris: Seuil, 1972), p. 141.

35. Sartre, *L'Idiot de la famille,* II, p. 1618.

36. Flaubert, *Extrait de la correspondance,* p. 30.

37. Genette, "Table ronde," in *Cahiers Marcel Proust,* pp. 91-92.

38. Mary McCarthy, "Foreword," in Gustave Flaubert, *Madame Bovary,* tr. Mildred Marmur (New York: New American Library, 1964), p. x. Any subsequent references to the novel will be to this edition.

39. Charles Baudelaire, *Baudelaire as a Literary Critic,* tr. Lois B. Hyslop and Francis E. Hyslop, Jr. (University Park: Pennsylvania State Univ. Press, 1964), pp. 143-44.

40. Sartre, *L'Idiot de la famille,* I, p. 703. All translations are mine; the emphases are Sartre's. All subsequent page references will be included in the text.

41. Julia Kristeva, *La révolution du langage poétique* (Paris: Seuil, 1974), pp. 17-100 and passim.

Phillip A. Duncan (essay date winter-spring 1985)

SOURCE: Duncan, Phillip A. "Symbolic Green and Satanic Presence in *Madame Bovary*." *Nineteenth-Century French Studies* 13, nos. 2 and 3 (winter-spring 1985): 99-104.

[*In the following essay, Duncan analyzes the metaphorical significance of the color green in the novel.*]

The colors of *Madame Bovary* are neutral or veiled, with little exception. We might expect this of a landscape softened by the hazes of Norman waters. And, a novel in which depression and ennui are central naturally supports its psychological wasteland with what is chromatically insipid and sad. Only two colors are relatively emphatic: blue and green. The former occurs repeatedly as a sign of happiness or promised happiness and especially at those moments when Emma dreams of escape to rare and idyllic places where love blooms eternally. Green signals, in a sense, the other face of the coin. It occurs, occasionally, in its pejorative form "verdâtre," to reinforce the dreary social ambiance or, more generously, in other contexts as a sexual and/or Satanic allusion.

Green has always been the inevitable sign of springtime and fertility. It was thought, for example, that the Nile turned green before the fecundating inundations of spring. It is a short step from natural fertility to human sexuality and love. In Rome, green was the color usually worn by courtesans. The association of the color with eroticism continues into French and other continental cultures.[1] A familiar illustration is that of Henry IV who became "le vert galant" because of his multiple affairs.

In Flaubert's novel, indications of green in nature are associated with the arousal of sexual desire in Emma. After Emma's disappointing marriage and the move to Yonville she meets a compatible spirit in Léon. One day she and Léon are returning from a visit to the cottage where a nurse is keeping her infant daughter. As they pass through the fields Emma is charmed by her companion and her emotional and almost physical abandonment is stated in nature: "de grandes herbes minces s'y courbaient ensemble, selon le courant qui les poussait, et comme des chevelures vertes abandonnées s'étalaient dans sa limpidité."[2] The undulant grasses express visually Emma's sensuous surrender. The metaphoric evocation to loosened "green hair" is an unmistakable erotic reference inviting the reader to recall an earlier scene in which Emma's hair with its "mouvement ondé vers les tempes" (p. 339) communicates to Charles her sensual nature.

Leon is still too unformed to guide this platonic idyll to adultery before he moves away to Rouen. As for Emma, she has become susceptible to dalliance. She meets Rodolphe and in the course of the "comices agricoles" she yields to verbal seduction. As Rodolphe speaks she enters again one of those moments of longing in which her physical being seems to dissolve and she senses a boundless exhilaration. Intoxicated by her desire, "elle ouvrit les narines à plusieurs reprises, fortement pour aspirer la fraîcheur des lierres autour des chapiteaux" (p. 459). Here twining vegetation (implicitly green) is an emblem of Emma's sexual vulnerability. Rodolphe pursues his strategy of seduction. One day when he and Emma have dismounted from horseback in the countryside Rodolphe speaks of his love and, "il l'entraîna plus loin, autour d'un petit étang, où des lentilles d'eau faisaient une verdure sur les ondes" (p. 472). The verdant duckweed swaying in the water repeats the anticipated sexual motif.

Emma's health fails when Rodolphe abandons her. At a moment of crisis she asks for communion and again experiences that illusion of the disintegration of formal matter and the coincident release and expansion of her spirit. It seems to her, says Flaubert, that her being, rising toward God, is going to be annihilated in love like burning incense that dissipates in vapor. But her response during this phenomenon remains curiously erotic. When the crucifix is presented she advances her lips to accept the body of the Savior "en défaillant d'une joie céleste" (p. 520). At this moment she thinks that she perceives Heaven itself and God the Father "au milieu des saints tenant des palmes vertes" (p. 520). The waving of the green palm leaves relates this scene to the previous scenes of sexual seduction.

To complete Emma's convalescence, Charles takes her to the opera in Rouen where she finds Léon again. When Léon appears and takes her hand she feels once more an attraction that she has not felt "depuis ce soir de printemps où il pleuvait sur les feuilles vertes, quand ils se dirent adieu, debout au bord de la fenêtre" (p. 533)—trembling green vegetation at a moment of desire unfulfilled and regretted. The window serves to concretize her illusion of the opportunity of expansion and escape.

Later, when Léon has succeeded in luring Emma into a substitute bedroom, a closed carriage, for a frenetic gallop around Rouen, they pass, at one point, behind some hospital gardens, "le long d'une terrasse toute verdie par des lierres" (p. 548). Once more sinuous, vining plants are a concrete metaphor of sexual desire. At every point in the narrative where Emma succumbs to her passion, green, swaying plants are code-objects of her corruption; and only at such moments do these vegetal references appear.

This fluid, verdant movement is surely related in the author's psyche to the insinuating serpent of the Garden of Eden which is often green in European painting. The serpent is, of course, the agent of erotic temptation and the alter ego of the ultimate Tempter, himself frequently represented as clad in green. There is an old pan-European folk belief that strangers wearing green are to be avoided—they may be disguised demons of sexuality who will lead the innocent to doom in the forest. D. P. Cassel refers to encounters with Satan clothed in green in the legends of two dozen different German-speaking regions of central Europe.[3] Louis Réau, in his exhaustive search of Christian iconography, identifies green (and red) as "la couleur de Satan."[4] He adds that red and green are associated with the Devil ". . . le vert parce que c'est la couleur du serpent et le symbole

du mal."[5] Thus, the trace of green leads from springtime vegetation to the presence of Satan, the Tempter.

In Flaubert's novel a stranger "wearing green" appears at Emma's door, bearing a green box in the "lumière verdâtre du crépuscule" (p. 137). The apparition of Lheureux is an eruption of the occult in the dismal stagnation of provincial life. Already weary of her marriage to Charles, Emma has just become aware of her infatuation with Léon. She had fallen asleep the evening before "remplie d'un enchantement nouveau" (p. 418). Thirsting always for what nature and her social circumstances deny her, she is now mentally prepared for "sin." The following day, as Lheureux arrives, night is falling—an uneasy and appropriate moment of transition that suggests the passage of her spirit from the relative innocence and clarity of her youth to darkness of soul. Lheureux is the emblem and the catalyst of transition. While he is exemplary of a social species and has a significant function in the narrative—to expedite Emma's inevitable destruction—he is also the personification of Temptation and Evil.

Lheureux is a man without clear origins and the only outsider in the Norman community of *Madame Bovary.* He is Gascon, dark, from another world. "Né Gascon, mais devenu Normand, il doublait sa faconde méridionale de cautèle cauchoise." (pp. 418-19) In the opinion of Léon Bopp, "s'il fallait en croire la réputation des Gascons et des Normands, cette seule phrase suffirait à nous laisser prévoir ce qu'on peut attendre du bonhomme, à nous prévenir contre lui."[6] Lheureux's back is always half-bent, serpentine, in a posture of one offering gratification—at a price to be reckoned later. Possessed of a "figure grasse, molle, sans barbe" (p. 418), he comes to entice Emma with scintillating bagatelles from his green box. He reminds us of Gogol's demonic Chichikov, another plump and glossy interloper.

Chichikov, the collector of dead souls, arrives in the town of N with a traveling chest which the author describes in unnecessarily meticulous detail. Vladimir Nabokov warns us that this "is not a box at all but a circle in hell. . . ."[7] He notes particularly the compartment with little troughs for pens, sealing wax and such instruments that are used for collecting dead souls, along with the space for paper—"paper being the Devil's main medium of intercourse" (pp. 90-91). For Mr. Chichikov is the Devil on his way through the countryside suborning souls. There is in the box, also, a small secret drawer for money: "This could be slipped out inconspicuously from the side of the chest (Chichikov's heart)" (p. 92). Paper, pens, and money are the tools of the Devil. An especial talent of Flaubert's Devil is accounting: "il faisait, de tête, des calculs compliqués, à effrayer Binet lui-même" (p. 419). And it is by the agency of financial records and legal papers that he dooms the unwary. At the end of all the enumerated exotica of Lheureux's box its real significance surfaces in the ominous: "quatre coquetiers en coco, ciselés à jour par des forçats" (p. 419).—"forçats" in some circle of Lheureux's hell, laboring to trap still other minions for his keep. Nabokov perceives Chichikov's traveling chest as a projection of his "soul"; so is the box of Lheureux.

Lheureux, it has been pointed out,[8] links together the themes of adultery and usury in Flaubert's novel. His first convocation seems to endorse Emma's tentative seduction by the "refined" and Romantic Léon, and his green box is a cornucopia of frivolous rarities which solicit Emma's sexual and esthetic cravings and invite her to excess. Emma's aspiration to perfect love (mired in lust) and her desire for rich and beautiful surroundings damn her. Lheureux stimulates both "sins."

After the usurer's first apparition, he returns on the scene again at a second critical moment of Emma's moral devolution. Lheureux insinuates himself into the company of Rodolphe and Emma (wearing a green hat) as they enter the "comices agricoles" as though to encourage, symbolically, Emma's fall. Rodolphe succeeds in ridding the couple of his fawning and unwelcome presence. Later, when Emma has become the mistress of Rodolphe, she charges Lheureux with providing a handsome whip as a gift for her lover. When Lheureux threatens to "la redemander à Monsieur" (p. 498) for lack of payment, Emma loses her composure. She cannot permit Lheureux to approach her husband on the matter and thus reveal the liaison. Lheureux then knows that he has her trapped. He provides the accoutrement necessary for her anticipated flight from Yonville with Rodolphe. Lheureux's next important encounter with Emma comes soon after her assignation (her first) with Léon in the fiacre in Rouen. He suggests that she obtain power of attorney to settle the estate of Charles' father which gives her the excuse she needs to consult Léon in Rouen. From this point Emma's encounters with Lheureux become increasingly bitter and the merchant's demands for payment become increasingly insistent until he finally condemns her to financial ruin.

Lheureux's function in the action of the novel is to incite Emma to overextend herself financially and even compromise herself sexually. "En intervenant toujours aux moments où l'héroïne s'engage plus avant dans sa passion coupable," notes a recent critic, "et en lui permettant d'assouvir ses convoitises, luxe et voluptés mêlés, il la précipite aussi toujours plus vite à la ruine, et à la mort."[8] In what D. A. Williams calls the "mythology of Emma,"[9] Lheureux is the incarnation of Satan the Tempter. The agency by which he entraps the soul of Emma is matter—the raptures of (relative) luxury and the ecstasies of the body. This perception of Lheureux is related to the reader's understanding of the blind beggar. The latter appears to be emblematic of the human condition and an alternate manifestation of Emma. His body is corrupted by disease—a projection of Emma's moral decay and possession by Evil through the flesh. At the same time, Emma's aspiration to refinement and happiness in love, no matter how vulgarly exhibited, represents incipient spiritualization, while the blind beggar possesses his incorruptible song. Flaubert confirms the beggar's polarity by the ambiguous color of his eyes. They are described on the one hand as "bluish"—the chromatic cypher for Emma's longed-for and idealized state of romantic fulfillment. They are also perceived as "greenish"—tinctured by Satan—sign of man's concession to Evil which is translated in the beggar's disfigurement. From the beggar's eyes "il coulait des liquides qui se figeaient en gales vertes jusqu'au nez" (p. 291), a purulent transposition of the undulant vegetation which accompanied the stages of Emma's erotic corruption.

Green is one of the two poles of the color symbolism of **Madame Bovary.** If blue suffuses Emma's vision of a paradise of love, it is green that marks the way to perdition. And, her Satanic nemesis is the predatory Lheureux who first materializes at her door in an aura of green. Lheureux immolates Emma, as he has père Tellier before her, and then turns to others in his pursuit of "dead souls." He facilitates the progress of the tragedy and he illustrates a certain professional type in a novel that intends, in part, to document social life in the countryside. But, like Homais, Binet,[10] and the beggar,[11] he also incarnates a supranatural presence in Flaubert's allegory of the spirit enthralled in flesh.

Notes

1. These examples of the role of green in Mediterranean cultures have been borrowed from Vernon Chamberlin's "Symbolic Green: A Time-honored Characterizing Device in Spanish Literature," *Hispania,* 51 (1968), 29-30.

2. Gustave Flaubert, *Madame Bovary,* 2 vols. Texte établi et annoté par A. Thibaudet et R. Dumesnil (Paris: Editions Gallimard [Bibliothèque de la Pléiade], 1951), I, 411. Subsequent references are to this edition and are incorporated in the text.

3. D. P. Cassel, *Der grüne Papagei. Eine Symbolik des Grün* (Berlin: R. Schaeffer, 1888), pp. 43-48.

4. Louis Réau, *Iconographie de l'art chrétien,* 3 vols. (Paris: Presses Universitaires de France, 1955-59), I, 73.

5. Réau, *Iconographie,* II, 69.

6. Léon Bopp, *Commentaire sur "Madame Bovary"* (Neuchâtel: A la Braconnière, 1951), p. 173.

7. Vladimir Nabokov, *Nikolai Gogol* (Norfolk: New Direction Books, 1944), p. 90.

8. Guy Riegert, *Flaubert, "Madame Bovary"* (Paris: Hatier, 1971), p. 41.

9. D. A. Williams, "The Role of Binet in *Madame Bovary,*" *The Romanic Review,* 71 (1980), 149.

10. Williams, "The Role of Binet," pp. 149-66.

11. See Murray Sachs, "The Role of the Blind Beggar in *Madame Bovary,*" *Symposium,* 22 (1968), 72-80 and P. M. Wetherill, "*Madame Bovary*'s Blind Man," *The Romanic Review,* 61 (1970), 34-42.

Mary Donaldson-Evans (essay date spring 1990)

SOURCE: Donaldson-Evans, Mary. "A Pox on Love: Diagnosing *Madame Bovary*'s Blind Beggar." *Symposium* 44, no. 1 (spring 1990): 15-27.

[*In the following essay, Donaldson-Evans examines the relationship between Flaubert's prose style and his use of medical metaphors in the novel. Donaldson-Evans suggests that the beggar's illness symbolizes Flaubert's disenchantment with the power of language.*]

Medical readings of Flaubert's famous novel [*Madame Bovary*] are not in short supply;[1] nor are studies focusing on the function and symbolism of the blind beggar.[2] Oddly enough, however, the graphic details of the beggar's condition and the peculiarities of Homais's suggested therapies have never come under close scrutiny, despite the large amount of attention accorded to the novel's other medically inspired descriptions (Emma's hysteria, her poisoning, the clubfoot operation). Yet scholars have clearly been troubled by the grotesque nature of the ailment, and William Paulson goes so far as to suggest that we cannot piece together the seemingly disparate elements in the description unless we place it in the context of "prior discursive and textual treatment of the blind."[3] Flaubert, clearly, had departed from the Romantic tradition that equated loss of sight with wisdom, a tradition that produced such inspirational figures as old Chactas. Nevertheless, most critics agree that Emma's encounter with this hideous figure is a "recognition scene" of sorts and is associated with insight. Variously interpreted as a symbol for reality, nemesis, conscience, "the hound of fate," love in a bourgeois culture, the beggar is routinely reduced to his two most salient characteristics: his blindness and his general repulsiveness. With few exceptions, he is just as routinely ignored by recent scholars, who, in a deconstructionist mode, focus their attention on Flaubert's undoing of the realist enterprise, his subversive use of language.[4]

Flaubert's preoccupation with language is well known, as is his penchant for the medical metaphor. In this study, I propose to demonstrate that the two phenomena are closely related, and that they come together in the figure of the blind beggar. My evidence will be both textual and extratextual: I will attempt, first, to pinpoint the beggar's position in the complex network of relationships connecting the characters. Following that, I will use the correspondence, biographical and historical data, nineteenth-century medical writings and literary antecedents in an effort to diagnose his illness. Finally, I hope to show how the creation of this complex character is consistent with Flaubert's linguistic project.

To date, those who have focused on the beggar's role have placed the emphasis on his singularity; they have tended to assume that he is, in his striking monstrosity, *original.* In fact, a close examination of the passages in which he is described reveals him to be nothing more than a composite of characters and characteristics presented earlier. Thus, his physical blindness recalls the metaphorical blindness of Emma, Homais and Charles (to name but three of Flaubert's characters who are blinded by one form or another of *bêtise*). As the recipient of Emma's last five-franc coin, he is the degraded replacement of Léon and Rodolphe, who had been the beneficiaries of her sexual and economic *largesse.* As a living spectacle of disease, he becomes the incarnation of Emma's moral corruption. He is, finally, a social outcast and a mental deficient, and as such, the hyperbolic counterpart of the isolated schoolboy, Charles, whose lack of intelligence is affirmed throughout the novel.

In addition to setting up conspicuous parallels between the beggar and the novel's protagonists, the text also undercuts the notion of the former's originality by establishing precedents for nearly all of his activities. He is identified by his begging and the evocative quality of his music with the organ grinder, by his fall from a moving vehicle and his skin condition with Charles's flaking plaster curate, by his role as Homais's victim with Hippolyte, by his grotesque mime with the novel's dogs, by his position as the last male for whom Emma spares a thought with the novel's lovers, real and imagined. From the bungling health officer who makes her his wife to the crucified Christ on whom she bestows her last kiss, Emma's quest for the Incarnation of Love, for the real-life equivalent of dashing heroes encountered in her reading of eighteenth-century sentimental literature, ends with the beggar, recalling perhaps Candide's search for happiness that had ended in the company of a toothless and repulsive Cunégonde. Desire gives way to disgust, and the euphoria that Emma experiences when she believes she has found, in "l'Homme-Dieu,"[5] the Lover of her dreams, is replaced by a more sobering recognition: Love's last incarnation assumes the shape of the Beast of Concupiscence.[6] Emma's final convulsion, as she sees the face of the beggar rising before her in the eternal darkness of death, is a hideous mockery of the convulsions that precede the "petite mort" of sexual intercourse.

To reach this savagely cruel climax, the narrative has led us (and Emma) through numerous "false incarnations," of which the most obvious ones are Charles, Rodolphe and Léon. As we have seen, the beggar's links to these characters are solid and highly visible. But if we continue to peel back the layers of the text, we can also uncover links of a different sort connecting him with other men who awaken a certain prurient curiosity in Emma but with whom sexual contact remains metaphorical. To take but two examples, the Duc de Laverdière and Edgar Lagardy appear, economically speaking, antithetical to the downtrodden vagrant, but they in fact prefigure him in numerous ways. The signifiers of decrepitude that characterize the debauched old aristocrat (his red-rimmed eyes, his deafness, his "lèvres pendantes" (46) from which fall drops of sauce, his childlike dependence upon others to help him eat) will be transformed and pressed into service to describe the beggar's condition. And the agent of this transformation is disease: The infirmity is now blindness, resulting not from a natural decline in faculties brought on by age (as was Laverdière's hearing loss), but rather from a nonspecific illness. The same may be said of the other characteristics: from red-rimmed eyes to bloody orbits, pendulous lips to skin hanging in shreds, dripping sauce to oozing sores, the mechanism of the transformation is identical. The aristocrats had seemed to Emma paragons of health and virility, and indeed, when confronted with the duke, she sees not the pathetic old man he has become, but the dashing lover he was. In a serial substitution typical of this narrative,[7] the old aristocrat is replaced by a younger version of himself, the viscount, who is in turn replaced as an object of Emma's interest by Rodolphe, himself finally replaced by Christ in a short-lived renewal of religious fervor. And then the cycle begins again with the opera singer, Lagardy, occupying a position parallel to that of Laverdière as unseeing object of Emma's contemplation, who serves as catalyst for her dreams of love. Like the Duc de Laverdière, Lagardy captivates Emma's imagination by his reputation as a capricious womanizer. However, as an itinerant performer, one who literally "sings for his supper" and whose song can be interpreted as a *mise en abyme* of Emma's story, he also anticipates the beggar.[8] Again, the gulf that separates these characters appears at first unbridgeable—the healthy complexion ("une de ces pâleurs splendides" [208]) and mellifluous voice of the former versus the skin eruptions and alternately thin and raucous voice of the latter—until a juxtaposition of the two passages reveals startling similarities. And, as was the case with the Laverdière/beggar doubling, the latter appears as a debased version of the former. To the languorous rolling of Lagardy's eyes corresponds the beggar's flickering pupils; to the former's tale of the tragic romance corresponds the latter's bawdy song; to the pathos of Lagardy's gestures of despair corresponds the beggar's "comédie" (278),[9] which has been interpreted as a lewd mime of copulation.[10] The description of Lagardy's performance also has strong sexual over-

tones, from its allusion to the singer's "bel organe" (208) and the orgasmic cry uttered by Emma, "qui se confondait avec la vibration des derniers accords" (209) to the phallic "épée nue" (210) brandished by Lagardy and Emma's reflection that the tenor must have an inexhaustible love, "pour en déverser sur la foule à de si larges effluves" (210). This reflection is followed by her fantasy of traveling to the theatres of Europe with Lagardy, waiting backstage like a modern-day "groupie" to gather, "béante, les expansions de cette âme qui n'aurait chanté que pour elle seule" (211). When the curtain falls, she sinks back into her seat, palpitating, exhausted.

The sexual innuendos of this passage are, of course, not gratuitous. I suggest that the opera scene, which marks a kind of *prise de conscience* for Emma in which she becomes—at least for a moment—painfully aware of the deceptive nature of art, functions also as a transformation of her *mal romantique.*[11] Thereafter, her "illness" takes on a more explicitly erotic cast. She is dominated, not by melancholy, but by a new kind of depraved sensuality. No longer credulous, as she had been with Rodolphe, she seeks in her relationship with Léon (who replaces Lagardy) not the ineffable pleasure of romantic love but the more earthy thrills of carnal possession.[12]

Enter the beggar: If the opera had stirred in Emma bitter memories of her wedding day when, on a small path in the middle of a wheat field, she had walked slowly toward the church, "sans s'apercevoir de l'abîme où elle se précipitait" (209-10), the beggar's song offers a less romanced version of her downfall. Here, the agricultural metaphor serves to tie together two of the novel's most important thematic strands, Eros and Thanatos. Virginal and unsuspecting on her wedding day, stooping only to pick thistles from her trailing wedding dress, Emma is transformed in the course of the narrative (and by the beggar's song) into a loose woman whose provocative posture and short skirt signal her sexual *disponibilité,*[13] while by her diligent gathering of the phallic sheafs of wheat she is hastening her own demise, harvesting the products of the Grim Reaper. From this perspective, the *abîme* she had failed to see on her wedding day is an anatomical image, a trite little furrow in her (sexual) garden.

Early in the novel, Emma had dreamed of finding a real-life referent for words encountered in her reading, *ivresse, félicité, passion.* The beggar is blind, diseased and imbecilic, the cruelly grotesque incarnation of a related trio: *amour aveugle, amour-maladie, amour fou.* As such, he serves as a monstrous cliché, the ironic conclusion to Emma's quest. However, when his symptoms are examined more closely, in the light of the medical understanding of Flaubert's time, we begin to see the outlines of an even more cynical picture. Flaubert himself points the way for us to proceed in his allusion to that famous reference tool, the *Dictionnaire des sciences médicales*. In the novel, the multivolume work decorates Charles's bookshelves, its pages uncut. Let's cut the pages and see what light it can shed on the novel.

The medical dictionary distinguishes between two types of feminine pathologies of love, *l'érotomanie* "qui n'est que la mélancolie produite par un amour malheureux, dont rien ne peut distraire" (226) and *la nymphomanie,* "fureur utérine ou métromanie . . . maladie hideuse qui transforme une femme, jusque-là pudique, en une bacchante effrénée."[14] It is my contention that Emma's novelistic progress takes her from the first to the second, from *le mal romantique* to what one could term *le mal vénérien*. I shall not linger on a discussion of the psychological foundation for such a transition, because the studies devoted to Emma's hysteria are numerous enough. Rather, I will focus on the physical representation of her degradation, the beggar, whose condition was meant to evoke the awful specter of venereal disease.

Perhaps the most significant feature of the lengthy first paragraph devoted to this nameless character (one of the few in the novel) is that it does not contain a specific reference to his blindness, although subsequent to Emma's diagnosis (for the passage in which the word *aveugle* first appears is rendered in indirect free style), the narrative will privilege the epithet *aveugle* over all others. The alert reader is given the information necessary to diagnose his condition even before the text has done so in the allusion to his cane, the orbital motion of his head, and the constant movement of his cloudy pupils. But there are other, more anomalous features: His eyelids are atrophied, his corneas blood-injected. Facial skin hangs in shreds around the eyes, mirroring the ragged clothing covering his shoulders, and a pus-like liquid oozes from the diseased flesh as far as the outer edge of his convulsively sniffing nostrils. When he speaks, he throws back his head with a "rire idiot" (291), and his voice has a peculiar quality, "faible d'abord, et vagissante." Medically, this is a complex picture, and the blindness appears to be no more than one symptom among many of a systemic disease affecting not only the eyes, but other organs—the skin, the brain, the larynx—as well. Generations of literary critics have mocked Homais's attempts to cure the beggar with a diet and ointments, but no one, to my knowledge, has reflected on the fact that for the pharmacist, the diagnosis is not amaurosis (simple blindness), but scrofula. In the nineteenth century, this term was an all-purpose designation for skin pathologies of uncertain origin and presenting somewhat varied characteristics. *Le Dictionnaire des Sciences médicales* appears to confirm Homais's diagnosis listing, among the symptoms of scrofula, cutaneous eruptions of various forms, especially on the head, inflammation of organs that contain many glands, such as the eyes, tumors that develop on the eyelids, a secretion of mucus from the eyes. Advanced scrofula is sometimes characterized by cretinism. At first, the beggar's condition appears to conform to this description.

But what of his blindness? Even in its most advanced stages, scrofula alone was not believed to lead to sight loss. Furthermore, the campaign that Homais wages against the beggar after his failure to cure him is based upon the assumption of contagion: scrofula was not considered contagious. Moreover, scrofula, although of long duration and improperly understood, was considered curable. Flaubert's correspondence with Bouilhet leaves no doubt but that he intended the beggar's illness to be regarded as incurable. And finally, the scrofulitic's characteristic cough was missing from Flaubert's description. Such a departure from clinical accuracy was clearly not typical of Flaubert. How and why did it come about?

The fact that Flaubert sought the help of his friend and medical consultant, Louis Bouilhet, for the beggar's symptoms is well known. The correspondence between the two men on this subject bears witness to the difficulty that he had in the creation of this character, originally intended as a legless cripple. Bouilhet dissuaded him from making his beggar a *cul-de-jatte,* a figure that Hugo had already used, and suggested instead "un grand gaillard avec un chancre sous le nez, ou bien un individu avec un moignon nu ou sanguinolent." Before writing his passage, Flaubert sought further suggestions ("Faut-il que mon homme ait une dartre au visage, des yeux rouges, une bosse, un nez de moins? que ce soit un idiot ou un bancal?") Interestingly, Bouilhet's response is unknown, although Benjamin Bart believes that "its tenor can be inferred, as the final form of the Blind Man is an amalgam."[15] If Bart is right (and I believe he is), then Flaubert's choice of details testifies less to his concern for referential accuracy in portraying a specific illness than to his desire to evoke a certain etiological category. My belief is that the beggar is a medical composite, a "living" counterpart to that often-cited composite object at the other end of the text, Charles's cap, which with its disparate assemblage of forms and fabrics, was an insignia of its owner's stupidity, its "laideur muette [ayant] des profondeurs d'expression comme le visage d'un imbécile" (4). In the same way, the diseased and filthy beggar, with his mime and song, and above all his peculiar collection of medical symptoms, was meant to evoke a specifically sexual pathology. Many of his symptoms—the loss of the eyelids, the ophthalmia, the strange alteration of the voice, the skin eruptions—were associated just as readily with syphilis or gonorrhea as with scrofula, and the distinction between these illnesses was often blurred. Although syphilis had not yet been clinically proven to be a cause of blindness (the syphilis virus was not to be isolated until 1905), it and gonorrhea (more commonly known at the time as blennorhagie) were associated with various ophthalmic conditions, some grave enough to lead to complete loss of eyesight.[16] The description of gonorrheal ophthalmia features a pronounced redness of the eye, herniation of the eyelid, and a secretion that is described as follows by Larousse: "C'est un muco-pus d'abord sanguinolent et liquide qui s'épaissit, devient verdâtre et absolument semblable à l'humeur blénnor-rhagique."[17] The condition, which when untreated leads quickly to blindness, could well have been Flaubert's inspiration for the description of the beggar. Further-more, skin pathologies, especially those that featured various types of eruptions, were widely associated with sexually transmitted diseases in the nineteenth century, as the alliance of the two medical specialities, derma-tology and venerealogy, shows.[18] Scrofula itself was as-sociated with venereal disease, and the *Dictionnaire des sciences médicales* lists, among its numerous predispos-ing causes, "la syphilis des parents . . . l'exercice pré-maturé des parties sexuelles, la masturbation, la syphi-lis."

The next question, of course, is why Flaubert would have brought to Emma's bedside a sordid victim of ve-nereal disease. Aside from the obvious symbolic impor-tance of such a figure, the extra-textual motivation was no doubt strong indeed. Venereal disease caused a gen-eralized anxiety in nineteenth-century France, some-what akin to the pathological fear of AIDS of today. According to Theodore Zeldin, 180 books were pub-lished on syphilis alone between 1840 and 1875, and he does not include in that figure "obscure theses, innu-merable articles, works on other sexual illnesses, and the vast literature on female diseases."[19] Zeldin points to the immense popularity of a treatise on diseases of the sexual organs, marketed for "men of the world," which sold 7,000 copies each year between 1853 and 1862. The remarkable success of Debay's well-known *Hy-giène et Physiologie du Mariage* (172 editions between 1848 and 1883) also suggests a preoccupation with the physical elements of human sexuality and the related topics of disease and dysfunction, although it did not include a section of syphilis. Zeldin puts it very aptly:

> It did not take Freud to make the French worry about sex. On the contrary, it might be argued that they be-came interested in obscure, unconscious and invisible sexual problems only when their directly physical troubles in this connection ceased to be overwhelming.
>
> (867)

The vulgarization of medical knowledge that later in the century led to a truly medical view of reality, had already begun in Flaubert's time. Although he was later to poke fun at his compatriots' phobia,[20] he had reason to share their concern. Biographers agree that in 1850, while traveling in the Middle East, Flaubert contracted syphilis. A letter to Bouilhet dated 14 November 1850 offers compelling evidence: "Il faut que tu saches, mon cher Monsieur, que j'ai gobé à Beyrouth sept chancres, lesquels ont fini par se réunir en deux, puis en un. En-fin, cela s'est guerry."[21] Flaubert's optimism was short-lived. A month later he was again suffering from syphi-lis' characteristic skin lesions. In accordance with its standard clinical development, the skin condition was followed first by impotence and hair loss, then by the secondary effects of the mercury treatment, swelling of the tongue, and tooth loss. His physical appearance was repulsive, and although the symptoms clearly differed from those of the blind beggar, the evidence that Flaub-ert intended his character to be suffering from a related venereal infection is overwhelming. The fact that the passage describing the purulent flow of mucus from the beggar's eyes was suppressed by *La Revue de Paris* lends weight to this hypothesis.[22]

In 1836, with the publication of his influential *De la prostitution dans la ville de Paris,* Parent-Duchâtelet had performed a veritable autopsy of what has become known as the "oldest profession in the world." His study included a discussion of the link between prostitution and venereal disease and a proposal for hygienic re-forms to solve what was rapidly becoming a national health problem. In his chronicle of a woman's down-fall, Flaubert had seen fit to end his heroine's amorous odyssey on a particularly somber note by making her attempt (unsuccessfully) to prostitute herself. After evoking the economic debasement of love, one is not surprised that he would turn to that other scourge of sexual exchange, the "poison" that his contemporaries feared more than any other—venereal disease.[23]

The reduction of love to a hideous pathological condi-tion spread by genital contact recalls the famous scene from *Candide* in which the still-innocent hero meets his tutor after several months' separation. When asked about the deplorable state of his health (for Pangloss has been transformed by syphilis), the tutor replies: "C'est l'amour; l'amour, le consolateur du genre hu-main, le conservateur de l'univers, l'âme de tous les êtres sensibles, le tendre amour."[24] *Le Pere Goriot,* Balzac's literary portrayal of the destruction of love by Restoration society, had featured a similar image in a crumbling, flaking statue of "l'Amour" that graces the courtyard of the Maison Vauquer: "A voir le vernis écaillé qui la couvre, les amateurs de symboles y dé-couvriraient, peut-être un mythe de l'amour parisien qu'on guérit à quelques pas de là."[25] The reference is to the Capucins Hospital (also known as l'hôpital des Vénériens). Onto the base of the statue are inscribed the following words from Voltaire: "Qui que tu sois, voici ton maître: Il l'est, le fut, ou le doit être."

Considered in the light of these two antecedents, Flaub-ert's arresting personification of love's pathology may seem less than original. This patent lack of originality may be the most important feature of this ambiguous creation. If the beggar is, on the one hand, a composite, the grotesque fusion of characters and images met not only by Emma within the novelistic space, but by the reader in prior texts, then he becomes a perfect figure for the déjà-vu/déjà-lu experience that so distressed his creator. Furthermore, his scabrous exhibitionism and his salacious song solidify his identification with sexuality and with the most banal aspects of this universal preoccupation. Nor is it an accident that the words to the beggar's song are borrowed from a story by Rétif de la Bretonne, that eighteenth-century profligate who was known as "le Voltaire des femmes de chambre." Rétif, who had himself died of syphilis, was known for his inordinate appetite for a dazzling array of sexual perversions, and the titillating details of his erotic exploits had only recently come to light.[26] Flaubert himself, no doubt influenced by the medical environment of his childhood, had elected a clinical perspective in recounting his tale of an adulterous woman. Yet, for all of its realistic detail, **Madame Bovary** is but a variant on the age-old tale of the fatal consequences of feminine lust, figured so succinctly by the agricultural metaphor of Rétif's ditty. In one way or another, all of "Emma's men" have sown their oats: It is in gathering the product of this activity, in the harvest, that Emma marches steadily towards the tomb (*le sillon*).

I alluded earlier to the sexual connotations of the word *sillon*. The fact that this term was also a common item in the lexicon of dermatologists, used to describe certain forms of skin lesions, may not be coincidental. This brings us back to the specific nature of the beggar's condition and to his relationship with Homais.[27]

The incarnation of *bêtise* and blind faith in what have been called the nineteenth century's twin deities, Science and Progress, Flaubert's pharmacist is also the most ardent Voltairian in the novel, pompously citing the Enlightenment *philosophe* at every opportunity. However, his utopian ideals put him quite at odds with his spiritual "mentor" and his own naiveté (symbolized perhaps by the fact that the first letters of his children's names spell *naif*) lead him to misread and misunderstand Voltaire, so that for the reader, he is associated less with the *philosophe* author than with the protagonist of his best-known narrative. It is thus a sneering indictment of the pharmacist's stupidity that, while for Emma the beggar is clearly a devastating reminder of something incurably horrendous (whether it be her own corruption or that of love), the opportunistic Homais decides to cure him. As earlier in the novel with Emma, his diagnosis is simplistic, for he is as incapable of distinguishing between invisible cause and visible symptom as Emma had been of separating reality from illusion. Furthermore, by attributing to his pharmacist the arrogant conviction that he can cure a blind man infected with what he believes to be scrofula, Flaubert is

setting up a double contrast, burlesque in nature, between Homais and Christ, who cured the blind with his spittle, and between him and French kings from Louis IX to Charles X, who performed ritualistic cures of scrofula merely by touching the afflicted.[28] Homais is neither Christ nor King, and his proposed remedy is as foolish as his diagnosis. Aside from the inappropriate prescription of a diet high in meat, beer and wine to an alcoholic beggar who lives on scraps,[29] the antiinflammatory ointment would treat the external symptoms only, but not the cause of the beggar's "horrible infirmité" (to borrow Homais's words). Statistics cited by contemporary medical studies testify to the poor results attained by such ointments which, significantly, had attained a certain notoriety as a widely prescribed but ultimately useless treatment for venereal disease. An experiment involving 10,000 syphilitics conducted in 1833 had proven its inefficacy.[30] Even if we accept as accurate Homais's diagnosis of scrofula (rather difficult to do in view of the text's insistence on his incompetence as a diagnostician), the smug complacency with which he promises to heal the beggar must have appeared ludicrous given the mystery in which the disease and its etiology were shrouded. During Flaubert's time, a wide array of skin ailments, routinely diagnosed as scrofula, was subjected to a vast range of remedies, prompting the author of the *scrofules* entry in the *Dictionnaire des sciences médicales* to write, after listing numerous remedies, one as useless as the other, "si le lecteur n'est pas las de lire, je me lasse d'écrire un pareil farrago, monument hideux de l'empirisme le plus rebutant" (402).

The failure of Homais's treatment is visible testimony to his quackery, making of the beggar an *enseigne* in a way the pharmacist never intended, his blood-red eyes and oozing green pus a derisive complement to the ostentatious red-and-green display of the pharmacy's *devanture*. And just as he had represented for Emma the last in several Incarnations of Love, the beggar stands at the end of a series for Homais as well. A potential obstacle to the pharmacist's social ascension and a threat to his reputation, he is the Incarnation of Disease, the eloquent emblem of the dishonesty of medicine's brash promises, as promoted by the most notorious of its (illegal) practitioners, the country pharmacist.

What then does he represent for the reader? A monstrous incarnation of concupiscence and disease, Flaubert's beggar simultaneously exposes the charlatanism of the novel's archetypal bourgeois and serves as mime, repeating by gestures and words (the words of *another*) the tale of Emma's demise. Functionally, he may thus be identified with Flaubert, who chose to tell Emma's tale (and in so doing to mock the bourgeoisie), in the borrowed language of the cliché.

The notion of *cliché* brings me to a final point. The beggar is in a way a living indictment of banality, himself a composite figure, a *lieu commun* who exposes through his morbidity, his poverty and his vulgarity the meaningless clichés of sentimental and scientific discourse. The fact that his symptoms may point to venereal disease, that category of illness particularly common among the literati and which accounted for one of the nineteenth century's most pervasive phobias,[31] solidifies his link to banality. As Huysmans's decadent hero Des Esseintes was to say later in the century, "Tout n'est que syphilis." But the beggar's symptoms may also be said to symbolize the monstrous petrification of language. Victor Brombert, noting "a great deal of oozing, dripping and melting in Flaubert's fictional world,"[32] expressed his belief that Flaubert used liquid imagery to convey a sense of boredom and despair. The observation is all the more pertinent when one realizes that this flow of fluids generally follows some kind of tumescence, whether it be the gush of blood and pus from Hippolyte's tumefied leg, the rush of sentimental clichés from Rodolphe's lips, or the grandiloquent flow of scientific commonplaces from Homais's pen. In this light, the mucus that oozes from the swollen membranes of the beggar's unseeing eyes is doubly significant. In the first place, the mucus becomes the perfect figure for love, cynically reduced to the tumescence and detumescence of coitus. But the mucus also becomes Flaubert's most eloquent metaphor for language, conceived as the ludicrous result of a pathological swelling, a putrid seepage, destined to congeal in the repulsive form of the *lieu commun*.[33]

Notes

1. See, for example, Eugene Gray, "The Clinical View of Life: Gustave Flaubert's *Madame Bovary*," in *Medicine and Literature,* ed. Enid Rhodes Peschel (New York: Neale Watson Academic Pub., 1980) 81-87; Douglas Siler, "La Mort d'Emma Bovary: sources médicales," *Revue d'Histoire Littéraire de la France* 81 (1981): 719-746; Lawrence Rothfield, "From Semiotic to Discursive Intertextuality: The Case of *Madame Bovary*," *Novel* (Fall 1985): 57-81; Maryline Lukacher, "Flaubert's Pharmacy," *Nineteenth-Century French Studies* 14 (1985-86): 37-50; Hela Michot-Dietrich, "Homais, Homeopathy, and *Madame Bovary*," *Stanford French Review* 11 (1987): 313-321.

2. Among these, the most relevant are by Max Aprile, "L'Aveugle et sa signification dans *Madame Bovary*," *Revue d'Histoire Littéraire de la France* 76 (1976): 385-392; Nicolae Babuts, "Flaubert: Meaning and Counter-meaning," *Symposium* 40 (Winter 1986-87): 247-58; Alfred Engstrom, "Flaubert's Correspondence and the Ironic and Symbolic Structure of *Madame Bovary*," *Studies in Philology,* July, 1949: 471-495; Murray Sachs, "The Role of the Blind Beggar in *Madame Bovary*," *Symposium* 22 (Spring 1968): 72-80;

William Bysshe Stein, "*Madame Bovary* and Cupid Unmasked," *Sewanee Review* 73 (1965): 108-209; P. M. Wetherill, "*Madame Bovary*'s Blind Man: Symbolism in Flaubert," *Romanic Review* 61 (1970): 35-42; Michael V. Williams, "The Hound of Fate in *Madame Bovary*," *College Literature* 1 (Winter, 1987): 54-61.

3. *Enlightenment, Romanticism and the Blind in France* (Princeton University Press, 1987) 206.

4. Exceptions among recent scholars are those who are preoccupied with the role of speech vs. writing in the novel. Naomi Schor ascribes to the blind man the heuristic function of doubling Emma as a structural opposite of Homais ("For a Restricted Thematics: Writing, Speech and Difference in *Madame Bovary*," *Modern Critical Interpretations,* ed. Harold Bloom [New York: Chelsea House], 1988, 61-81); for Gerald Prince, the blind man, like the numerous other characters who tell "bad stories" is punished by his creator, for whom the only "good story" is one that is written. ("Madame Bovary et le thème du récit," Paper delivered at the 14th annual Colloquium in Nineteenth-Century French Studies, University of Michigan, October, 1988).

5. Gustave Flaubert, *Madame Bovary* (Paris: Garnier, 1961) 301. All further references to the novel, given in the text of the article, will be from this edition.

6. In this interpretation, I am following the lead of William Bysshe Stein (*op. cit.*) who, tracing through the novel the iconographic representations of Love, has seen in the beggar a debased Cupid.

7. Naomi Schor (among others) has seen the importance of this structural device. For her, "substitution chains organize the narrative" (*op. cit.,* 74).

8. For an analysis of the way in which the opera doubles the novel, see Lukacher's article. Another provocative reading of the opera scene is to be found in Nathaniel Wing's *Limits of Narrative* (New York: Cambridge University Press 1986).

9. An earlier version of the novel had attributed to him a "geste obscène." Furthermore, a ms. variant offers additional proof that the beggar was to be seen as a debased Lagardy, because Flaubert originally intended to have his travelers discuss the beggar's mimetic talents, after which Homais was to express the opinion that "si cet homme avait reçu dans sa jeunesse de l'éducation, il serait maintenant à briller sur les théâtres de Paris." (Jean Pommier et Gabrielle Leleu, *Madame Bovary,* Nouvelle Version précédée des scénarios inédits [Paris: Corti, 1949] 581).

10. See Victor Brombert, *The Novels of Flaubert* (Princeton: Princeton University Press, 1966) 75.

11. Eric Gans (*Madame Bovary: The End of Romance,* New York: Twayne, 1989) also sees this scene as pivotal, but in his interpretation, the transformation is in Emma's newfound attachment to the artist (as opposed to the illusions of art).

12. There is considerable textual support for this assertion. Léon himself becomes aware of a transformation: "Il ne savait pas quelle réaction de tout son être la poussait davantage à se précipiter sur les jouissances de la vie. Elle devenait irritable, gourmande et voluptueuse . . ." (299). See also 305, 310, 318, and *passim.*

13. See Michael Riffaterre, "Flaubert's Presuppositions," *Diacritics* 11 (1981): 2-11.

14. Paris: Panckoucke, 1821. From the entry entitled "La Femme."

15. "Louis Bouilhet, Flaubert's 'accoucheur,'" *Symposium* 17 (Fall 1963): 188.

16. See Edward Hocken, *Practical Treatise on Ophthalmic Medicine* (London: Samuel Highly, 1844).

17. See "La Blennorhagie" in P. Larousse, *Grand Dictionnaire Universel* [Paris 1866-90], II, 817.

18. The appearance of the first scientific periodical devoted exclusively to these specialties, the *Annales des maladies de la peau et de la syphilis,* founded and edited by the famous syphilologist, Pierre Louis Alphée Cazenave, dates from 1843; other periodicals followed later in the century (e.g., *Journal des maladies cutanées et syphilitiques, Bulletin de la société française de dermatologie et de syphiligraphie*). See John Crissey and Lawrence Parish, *The Dermatology and Syphililogy of the Nineteenth Century* (New York: Praeger, 1981) for a thorough treatment of the topic.

19. Theodore Zeldin, *France 1848-1945: Intellect, Taste and Anxiety,* II (Oxford: Clarendon Press, 1977) 867.

20. Of syphilis, he wrote in *Le Dictionnaire des idées reçues* "*Plus ou moins tout le monde en est affecté.*"

21. Quoted in Jacques-Louis Douchin, *La Vie érotique de Flaubert,* (Paris: Pauvert, 1984) 118.

22. Although the journal that serialized Flaubert's novel excised passages for a variety of reasons and without explanation, the editors were particularly sensitive to those descriptions that might attract the attention of censors, and in view of the fact that they left intact the graphic account of Hippolyte's gangrene, it is reasonable to assume that their objection to the description of the beggar's eyes was founded on "moral" issues.

23. My use of the word *poison* is not gratuitous: In fact, syphilis in particular was repeatedly referred to as a poison in the medical literature of the period.

24. Voltaire, *Candide* (Oxford: Basil Blackwell, 1966) 8. It may be of some relevance that Flaubert, whose admiration for Voltaire was boundless, claimed to have read *Candide* twenty times. *Madame Bovary* contains more references to Voltaire than to any other author (7 mentions).

25. Honoré de Balzac, *Le Père Goriot* (Paris: Garnier-Flammarion, 1966). For an excellent analysis of the centrality of this icon in Balzac's novel, see Allan Pasco, "Image Structure in *Le Père Goriot,*" *French Forum* 7 (1982): 224-34.

26. Two biographies of Rétif were published in the early 1850's, one authored by Gérard de Nerval, the other by Charles Monselet.

27. Murray Sachs has warned against interpretations of the beggar's role that fail to take into account episodes subsequent to Emma's death. His own reading, which emphasizes the divergent reactions of Emma and Homais to the beggar, is particularly insightful and provocative. My interpretation, although not in conflict with his, adopts a different angle of vision.

28. See Roderick E. McGrew, "King's Touch" in *Encyclopedia of Medical History,* (London: MacMillan, 1985) 159-160.

29. Standard practice at the time was to tailor the prescription to the economic status of the patient. See Jacques Léonard, *La Vie Quotidienne du médecin de province au XIXe siècle* (Paris: Hachette, 1977) 73-75.

30. See A. Bertherand, *Précis des maladies vénériennes* (Paris: Baillière, 1852). Hocken (*op. cit.*) states that mild gonorrhoeal conjunctivitis yields readily to an antiphlogistic treatment, but that the remedy is not effective for more severe forms of the illness.

31. See Roger Williams, *The Horror of Life* (Chicago: University of Chicago Press, 1980) and Patrick Lasowski, *Syphilis: Essai sur la littérature française du xixe siècle* (Paris: Gallimard, 1982) for two very different treatments of the links between syphilis and literature in 19th-century France.

32. "The Tragedy of Dreams," in *Modern Critical Interpretations: Madame Bovary,* ed. Harold Bloom (New York: Chelsea House, 1988) 18.

33. The initial idea for this article came from one of my students at the University of Delaware, Nina

Chang, to whom I offer thanks here. I also thank Dr. Richard Jahnle, my own ophthalmologist, and Dr. William Tasman, Ophthalmologist-in-Chief at Wills Eye Hospital, Philadelphia, PA, for their gracious assistance. Both physicians agreed that venereal disease would have been a likely diagnosis.

Lawrence Birken (essay date April 1992)

SOURCE: Birken, Lawrence. "Madame Bovary and the Dissolution of Bourgeois Sexuality." *Journal of the History of Sexuality* 2, no. 4 (April 1992): 609-20.

[*In the following essay, Birken evaluates Emma Bovary's character within the context of nineteenth-century theories of psychology. Birken challenges critics who describe Emma as a narcissist, suggesting that such a label conceals more profound issues concerning her sexuality. According to Birken, Emma's transgressions, rather than representing pathological behavior, in fact symbolize a radical undermining of the bourgeois social order.*]

It is widely conceded that Gustave Flaubert's **Madame Bovary** represents an important turning point in western culture. In a recent study, for example, Eric Gans noted that the work was a "watershed in the history of the novel," thus constituting a "major transformation in both content and form."[1] Condemned as subversive and even obscene when published in 1856, **Madame Bovary** continues to fascinate critics, many of whom regard it as an adumbration of the androgynous world of late twentieth-century consumer culture. In this context, many of these critics have attacked Emma Bovary, the novel's protagonist, as excessively "narcissistic" and thus infantile. Indeed, in his *Culture of Narcissism*, Christopher Lasch went so far as to disparage Emma as the "prototypical consumer of mass culture."[2] But the use of the psychoanalytic concept of narcissism to stigmatize Emma Bovary merely covers up her real crime of challenging the middle-class sexual order.

To better understand how the stigma of narcissism has helped to preserve that order, it is necessary to recognize that the modern concept was constructed by sexologists in the last decade of the nineteenth century. At a time when the cultural assumptions of the bourgeois epoch were under increasing assault, the emerging science of sex codified these assumptions in what appeared to be an eternal law of desire. Sexologists advanced an evolutionary theory that explained self-love as the remnant of an earlier phase of asexual reproduction in which the love for the other necessary for sexual reproduction had not yet appeared. Because it was one of the givens of evolutionary theory that females differentiated

less from this asexual phase than did males, it made sense to assume that women retained a larger component of self-love. Moreover, the simple empirical investigation of the contours of middle-class life familiar to sexologists seemed to support the notion that women were more self-absorbed and vain than were men. In 1896, the American psychologist Colin Scott thus described a "primary law of courtship" in which "the male is physically active, but non-reflective, the female passive, but imaginatively attentive to the states of the excited male." Scott's work suggested that woman normally sees herself through the eyes of man, thus desiring herself because she desires only what her man desires. Around this time, Havelock Ellis wrote of a "tendency which is sometimes found, more especially perhaps in women, for the sexual emotions to be absorbed, and often entirely lost in self-admiration."[3] In 1899, the German psychiatrist Paul Näcke coined the term "Narcismus." It was within this context that Freud developed his conception of narcissism during the years from 1910 to 1914. In the latter year, Freud actually published his epochal paper "On Narcissism: An Introduction." In that piece, Freud reinforced the tendency to associate narcissism with femininity, although in a more subtle way than did his precursors. "On Narcissism" actually portrays the self as the original focus of desire, a focus displaced to external sexual objects only by the exigencies of reality. The first duality is thus that between a focus on the self and a focus on external objects. Within this theoretical framework, Freud was able to distinguish between two ways of choosing objects in the external world, a "narcissistic" object-choice based on the original self-love and an "anaclitic" object-choice modeled on the more advanced love for the "mother or her substitute." Of course, Freud believed that "complete object-love of the anaclitic type is, properly speaking, characteristic of the man," while women (and children) tend to make a more narcissistic object-choice.[4]

Nevertheless, the sexologists in general and Freud in particular were in some ways ambivalent toward the middle-class life their theories ostensibly supported. Not only was psychoanalysis based on a Darwinism that subtly subverted the bourgeois sexual order by postulating a hermaphroditic ancestry for humankind, but Freud himself was aware of the tragic implications of that order which, however well based on natural sexual difference it claimed to be, could not take into consideration the individual sexualities of all who lived within it. While some writers such as Herbert Marcuse and Daniel Yankelovich have accentuated this radical or pluralistic side of psychoanalysis in order to justify the dissolution of bourgeois society, defenders of that society have tended to exaggerate the conservative side of Freud's work. Freud himself, in the wake of the Darwinian hypothesis of humanity's androgynous ancestry, could hypothesize that people were at base transsexual, polymorphous, and narcissistic even if he did stigmatize these characteristics as primitive in the adult. By diluting the idea of an original (if primitive) narcissism as a positive force and instead treating it as a deficit, critics like Lasch are in effect reviving the elements of a pre-Darwinian world view. This squares with their very clear interest in conserving the middle-class ideology of sexual difference by portraying it as eternal and natural.[5]

In reality, it appears that an ideology of sexual difference was associated with the ascendancy of the bourgeoisie in western Europe after the middle of the eighteenth century. Recent historiography suggests that western societies were at one time less concerned with sexual inequality than with political inequality. Up to the French Revolution, the argument goes, the cultures of the west had institutionalized the old Indo-European division of society into three orders or "estates," the first devoted to prayer, the second to war, and the third to the creation of wealth. The primacy of this "asymmetrical" distinction between clergy, knights, and commonality was registered in the way in which gender was encased within order. Consequently, an aristocratic woman possessed the potential to exercise political power not necessarily available to bourgeois men. And while asymmetrical sexual functions existed within each order, the inequality between orders possessed such greater significance that it made possible the potent royal mistresses, regents, and female saints preeminent in early modern history.[6]

In the context of this argument, a case can be made that the domestication of the aristocracy, culminating in what Nobert Elias has called the court society, helped to erode sexual distinctions among the clerical and lay elite. Certainly, the emergence of the modern state was bound up with the disintegration of the old religious and military functions and the consequent reduction of aristocrats to courtiers and eventually mere ornaments in the royal household. In baroque courts modeled on the French, both sexes engaged in affairs, took lovers, dressed in beautiful clothes, and displayed a conspicuous vanity. But in the course of the eighteenth century, the emergence of a "bourgeois" critique of the Old Regime was accompanied by a radical reorganization of baroque social and psychosexual categories. Enlightenment thinkers, such as Rousseau, wrote as if the emancipation of the male population and the consequent establishment of a natural society practically demanded deemancipation of the female population. In particular, the enfranchisement of the middle-class male appeared to require the disenfranchisement of the aristocratic female whose power was so emblematic of the Old Regime and its caste system. Thus, for Rousseau the establishment of a universal citizenship among males was accompanied by the foundation of a "natural" sexuality in which the distinctions between the sexes were accentuated and women were effectively excluded from the realm of citizenship; if it was man's right to be a citizen, it was woman's duty to nurture citizens.[7]

What happened—in France rather quickly after 1789, though elsewhere in Europe in a more leisurely fashion—was a radical restructuring of gender. Society thus was reorganized so that all men theoretically stood within the polity, while women were gathered from the various orders, lumped together, and expelled from that polity. As Traian Stoianovich has noted, the tripartite order of clergy/nobility/commonality simply gave way to a new, two-part male/female order.[8] Consequently, a chasm opened between the male and the female, between the public and the private, between the political and the personal, and between the state and the family. In this context, the distinction between the sexes was actually accentuated, now appearing in sharp relief against the universal equality ascribed to all males. The "embourgeoisement" of political discourse was thus accompanied by an increasing recognition of sexual dimorphism. Writers such as the revolutionary orator Joseph Barnave seemed to treat liberty as a natural characteristic of the male. Indeed, Barnave believed that "in a nation long nurtured in liberty the citizens have acquired a manly and vigorous character." Eighteenth-century writers thus contrasted the masculine west with an effeminate East where men were made passive and weak by submitting to absolute rule. Against this background, the baroque itself may have appeared increasingly "Oriental" and the old court society increasingly like those Eastern despotisms that made men effeminate by denying them their natural liberties.[9]

Evidence for what Stoianovich has identified as a profound "virilization" of western culture after the French Revolution appears on several levels. For example, the way in which the emerging middle-class culture took its stand against the comparatively androgynous baroque is exemplified by the increasing dichotomization of dress. In his study of the history of fashion, René Konig noted how the bourgeois male broke with the court by dressing in cheerless dark clothes. It was as if, in the course of the nineteenth century, the very idea of fashion was relegated to the newly constituted feminine domain while bourgeois men purged themselves of what appeared to be the effeminate manners of the aristocracy. Amplified by that "revolutionary asceticism," which linked republicanism to masculinity, "men's fashions, apart from a few minor changes, crystallized into a kind of permanent form."[10]

At the same time, the banishing of masculine fashion was accompanied by the decline of male nudity in the arts. In nineteenth-century painting, the uncovering of women went hand in hand with the covering-up of men. It was as if the biblical taboo against looking at the nudity of the father (Gen. [Genesis] 9: 22-27) was extended to the whole male sex within the bourgeois order. The Enlightenment thus did not so much abolish political asymmetry in favor of liberty and equality as it made sexual asymmetry the new form of political caste, so that sex (and in this way eventually race) became the ideological limit of democracy. We need not embrace the Marxism of art critic John Berger to agree with him that the association of nudity with femininity was a historical phenomenon somehow connected with the emergence of a middle-class order. Writers such as Kenneth Clark have long noted that during the late eighteenth and early nineteenth centuries, female nudity increasingly eclipsed male nudity in western painting. In describing that painting, Berger affirmed that "men look at women" while "women watch themselves being looked at," thus underscoring the ultimately historical character of Scott's primary law of courtship as well as Freud's conception of narcissism. The decline of masculine fashion and nudity toward the end of the eighteenth century suggests a repudiation of the values of court society. Male fashion may have withered when the objectification of the male came to be associated with the hated Old Regime, male nudity when the bourgeois began to insist that he could no longer be an object of aristocratic rule.[11]

Bourgeois society was thus bedeviled by a profound contradiction. Identifying itself with universal freedom and liberty, the bourgeois world actually depended on the limitation of freedom and liberty implicit in sexual dichotomization in order to reproduce itself. But just as baroque society had created the conditions for its own disintegration and thus the emergence of a middle-class order, so the very successes of the bourgeois world paved the way for its dissolution. In the second half of the nineteenth century, the growth of science and industry, as well as the growing participation of women in the political world, pointed toward the erosion of the middle-class sexual order. By the middle of the nineteenth century, there may have been a growing sense of the artificiality of sexual distinctions that had once seemed natural. Within this context, a realistic portrayal of middle-class society might even seem offensive to a middle-class public. One of the earliest artists to use realism and irony in this way was Edouard Manet. In his controversial *Déjeuner sur l'herbe,* painted in the same era that ***Madame Bovary*** was written, two fully clothed and well-dressed men lunch in bucolic surroundings with a nude young woman. In the background there is a second young woman, dressed in a light, nearly translucent garment. On the one hand, Manet's painting is almost surrealistic in the sense that it portrays a scene that was not likely to occur in well-mannered French society (at least in the open). On the other hand, the piece is utterly realistic in portraying the power relationships implicit in the bourgeois sexual order. In the foreground group of three figures, the juxtaposition of clothed men with the unclothed woman reveals the *po-*

litical asymmetry of the sexes later codified by Freud in "On Narcissism"; woman's possession of a body deprives her of the world while man's possession of the world deprives him of a body. By contrasting unclothed woman with clothed man in the same picture, Manet shockingly portrays the internal contradictions of middle-class sexuality.[12]

But what is merely implicit in Manet's work Flaubert makes explicit. If the former delineates the contradictions of bourgeois sex in all starkness, the latter not only depicts these contradictions but introduces as his protagonist a woman who actively (if unsuccessfully) seeks to resolve them. In Flaubert's most famous novel, Charles Bovary, a rather mediocre and physically unimpressive country doctor, marries the beautiful and refined Emma Rouault. By the middle-class standards of the time, Charles is a good husband, and he has made a good marriage. Far from abusing his wife, he idolizes her with boundless and heartwrenching tenderness. Far from denying her, he showers her with all the material goods and benefits his hard-earned income can provide. In every sense Charles appears to love his wife selflessly, "overvaluing" her.[13]

Emma, by contrast, appears predictably vain and self-absorbed. She merely tolerates her husband, her indifference seemingly growing in proportion to his love for her; she is possessed of "a kind of icy charm." She ignores her own daughter, hardly even thinking of her. Taken as a whole, Emma appears to exemplify those beautiful, narcissistic women who, Freud tells us, "have the greatest fascination for men" precisely because they are indifferent to them.[14]

On the surface, then, the Bovary household is a textbook example of the sexual dimorphism later delineated in "On Narcissism." Yet a deeper analysis reveals that Emma is hardly one of those women who wish to be loved rather than to love. On the contrary, Emma is completely loved and yet remains completely unhappy. Dissatisfied with a husband who only looks at her and never at himself, she wants a husband at whom she can look back. But it is precisely this wish that cannot be accommodated within the bourgeois sexual order. For Charles is the kind of mediocre but hardworking man who epitomizes that order. Such a petit bourgeois citizen was hardly supposed to be attractive. Charles, Flaubert reminds us, was dull, sluggish, unimaginative, boorish, disheveled, inclined to corpulence, and none of these qualities improve with age. We thus hear that his "trousers were too tight for him round his stomach" and that "his puffy cheeks seemed to be pushing his eyes, which had always been small, right up into his temples." Now, this is not the grandiose ugliness of the aristocratic epoch but the mediocre dumpiness of a France whose smallholders had been multiplied into the millions by the Revolution. This unattractiveness is the result of a process that, in only a few generations, has transformed a nation of revolutionary ascetics into a complacent petit bourgeoisie. In emphasizing Charles's unattractiveness, Flaubert is also indicting a whole mode of life.[15]

But it is not merely that Charles is unattractive; it is that he cannot imagine being attractive. Within the horizon of bourgeois values, Emma cannot complain. Indeed, her problem can barely be put into words.[16] And to whom, within the compass of respectable society, could she complain? Could she say that her husband was dull and unattractive when the very nature of bourgeois society conspired to render men so? It is of course all too easy to say that Emma was simply the victim of her own objectless discontent or that she was a woman who did not like the limitations of being a woman. But these limitations, after all, were imposed by the logic of history, not nature. It was bourgeois society that had banished women from politics. Men, with a monopoly of political power, could look at women. Women, dismissed from politics, could not look back. In this sense narcissism was merely the compensation for the powerless, the hunger for attention taking the place of ambition. So Freud himself concedes that "women, especially if they grow up with good looks, develop a certain self-contentment which compensates them for the social restrictions that are imposed on them in their choice of an object."[17]

But it is precisely the case that Emma is *not* possessed of this self-contentment. It is not that she is too narcissistic but that she is not narcissistic enough, not that she is too vain but that she is not vain enough to simply absorb the affection and admiration of a husband who looks only at her and not at himself. Because her desire for a self-aware and even self-absorbed husband cannot be accommodated within the bourgeois sexual order, Emma turns to fantasy and eventually adultery. That order has purged adult men not only of vanity, but of the sensuality that vanity stimulates. Neither the druggist Homais nor the moneylender Lheureux, the two pillars of the local petit bourgeoisie, possess the slightest residue of sensuality. They are complacent men of commerce. In Emma's world the qualities she wishes to find in a man are relegated to the world of women, children, and the immature. Thus her attentions turn to Léon, the exception who proves the rule. Flaubert accordingly emphasizes Léon's androgynous characteristics, noting that his "nails were longer than was customary at Yonville" and that he possessed "an exquisite candour in his bearing" as well as "long, fine, curving lashes" and a "smooth cheek," the marks of undifferentiated youth. And it is that very youth, embodied in his charming "timidity," that compels Emma to look back at him and to take him in hand, making it impossible for her to be merely the object of *his* desire.[18]

But Léon's immaturity underscores the ultimate inability of Emma to satisfy her desires within the framework of the bourgeois epoch. It is perhaps for this very reason that she longs for those earlier ages in which, among the aristocracy at least, certain women had the power to look at men, and certain men enjoyed being looked at. If past epochs are the stuff that dreams are made of, Emma seeks out the remnants of those epochs in order to realize her dreams. It is at the ball at La Vaubyessard that she first comes into physical contact with the past—if only in an attenuated form. A once-in-a-lifetime event, the ball becomes for Emma a peak experience that serves as the standard against which all future happiness must be measured. Surrounded by what in reality are the ghosts of a dead social order, Emma nevertheless experiences the waking dream of La Vaubyessard as more real than bourgeois reality. It is a dream saturated with desire, in which the bourgeois Charles is completely out of place. Emma refuses to dance with her husband, ostensibly because "it's not quite the thing for a doctor to dance," but she appears more than willing to dance with the dandified young men whose "handkerchiefs . . . were embroidered with large monograms and emitted a delicious scent."[19]

Emma is in fact drawn to the sleek, catlike remnants of the aristocracy. She is mesmerized by the dandies, relics of the past who preserve the aristocratic ethos in an increasingly middle-class world. Above all, the dandy retains the androgynous character of court society and consequently rejects the bourgeois differentiation of the sexes. Emma is attracted to the "gentleman" Rudolphe Boulanger "of La Huchette," a vain and insensitive man who affects the manners and eccentricities of the aristocracy. If Charles is kind but unattractive, then Rudolphe is unkind but seductive, with his "curl of black hair, that figure at once so strong and so elegant." Here is a man—and not merely a boy—at whom Emma can look back. Of course, even the real aristocrats that Emma meets at La Vaubyessard are only remnants of what was once a ruling class, and Rudolphe is only a pseudoaristocrat. Nevertheless, at the margin of the bourgeois world, among the dandies and the pseudoaristocrats who affect a dandified air in order to convince the world that they are aristocrats, Emma seems to find some kind of ideal.[20]

If Emma's rejection of Charles represents a refusal to be limited to the feminine sphere that bourgeois society has assigned her, her choice of lovers represents an almost conscious appropriation of the rights of the masculine sphere. Thus, she moves toward an androgynous state. But Emma's androgyny signals her inability to reconcile her desires to the highly differentiated sexual order instituted by the triumphant bourgeoisie in the years following the French Revolution. Emma repudiates this sexual differentiation by demanding the right to love others like a man, as well as herself like a woman. But the only models available to her were models rooted in a baroque past, in which the court and the salon were the focus of a male-female intimacy and community of interests alien to the highly polarized world of the nineteenth-century middle-class sexual order. Emma was obliged to live in this past, haunted by the ghosts of a vanished civilization.[21]

It is thus ironic that in the fullness of time Emma Bovary appears something like a visionary and that her fundamentally reactionary attitudes now seem revolutionary. But as the nineteenth-century bourgeois culture has given way to twentieth-century mass society, women have reentered the public sphere in greater numbers than ever before. In the century since the death of Flaubert, the two-function male/female order, which had ousted the tripartite system of the baroque, has given rise to what in effect is a single-function culture united under the sign of consumption. But when women enter the public sphere, they appear to gain the right to look at men as men have looked at women. Men, in other words, may be becoming more self-conscious of their bodies even as women are becoming more conscious of their ambitions, so that the two sexes converge. Can we not then speak of the reappearance of certain elements of the baroque, albeit on a much vaster scale worthy of the enormous wealth that makes mass culture possible? No longer confined to court or salon, this new baroque permeates the societies of the west, although it is most dramatically evident in the nightclubs and bars that dot our erotic landscape. In a more subtle way, the twentieth century has led at least in the west to what French writer Guy Hocquenghem refers to as the imminent "sexualization of the world" that "corresponds to the dissolution of the human [or bourgeois]." The disintegration of classic bourgeois society registers itself in the adoption of an increasingly flamboyant style of dress by males and females alike and in a greater awareness of sexual ambiguity. Indeed, the availability of sex-change surgery suggests that sex itself has come to be a matter of individual choice. Within this context, there has been a restoration of a community of interests between the sexes often missing from the nineteenth-century world. But it is precisely this affinity between Baroque and mass cultures that helps to explain why Flaubert's reactionary challenge to the bourgeois sexual order could adumbrate a genuinely revolutionary dissolution of that order; baroque culture and mass culture are equally opposed to the system of values underpinning bourgeois sex.[22]

The argument elaborated above suggests that the defense of those values by writers on both the Left and the Right rests on shaky ground. If the middle classes of nineteenth-century France and a few other western nations accentuated sexual distinction to an unusual degree, then critical theory is wrong to make use of a theoretical apparatus such as psychoanalysis, which takes these unusual conditions as typical and natural. Even if psychoanalysis marked a partial emancipation from bourgeois conditions, it preserved and naturalized a whole set of middle-class assumptions about sexual life. Chief among these was the postulation of a fundamental asymmetry between the sexes, which encased women in a double-bind from which they could not escape. This sexual asymmetry loosely equated androgyny, femininity, and narcissism in a way that closed off any options for transgressing the gendered spheres in an acceptable (that is, healthy) way. Thus a normal woman was passive and narcissistic, but a women who rebelled against her sexual role moved toward an androgyny that was also narcissistic. Exploiting these theoretical difficulties in Freud's original work, a plethora of cultural conservatives have purged that work of any revolutionary content and turned it into a mere defense for a dying middle class. Thus, the idea of narcissism very likely may go the way of the earlier concept of degeneration, which even in Havelock Ellis's era was beginning "to disappear from scientific terminology, to become a mere term of literary and journalistic abuse."[23] This abuse is heightened by the tendency of cultural conservatives to conflate the Freudian notions of the primitive and the pathological. When Freud stigmatized deviations from bourgeois sex as "primitive," he did not see them as necessarily "pathological." Instead, he believed that illness arose from the conflict between the non-bourgeois desires he considered primitive and the bourgeois society. Modern psychoanalysis, however, apparently regards sexual deviations from the bourgeois order as pathological in themselves, just as it regards nonbourgeois societies as nonviable in themselves, abandoning the original Freudian dialectic between individuals and the society in which they live. In this way, a parochial set of nineteenth-century standards are preserved into our age under the guise of science.

In this context the alleged narcissism of Emma Bovary becomes politically significant. On the one hand, when Giles Mitchell argues in the pages of *American Imago* that Emma's narcissism is a morbid condition that leads to the "death she has always carried in her beautiful body," he is in effect equating the dissolution of bourgeois sexuality with the disintegration of life itself. On the other hand, when Christopher Lasch presents Emma as the forerunner of today's well-adjusted consumer, he is equating the nonbourgeois values of mass culture with the destruction of all culture. In this sense, Emma is the embodiment of all women whose transgression of the limits of gender threatens to disintegrate the sexual order that cultural conservatives—and perhaps secretly all of us—equate with life itself.[24]

Notes

1. See Eric Gans, *Madame Bovary: The End of Romance* (Boston, 1989), p. 6.

2. Christopher Lasch, *The Culture of Narcissism: American Life in an Age of Diminishing Expectations* (New York, 1979), pp. 95, 152; and see Dominick LaCapra, *"Madame Bovary" on Trial* (Ithaca, NY, 1982).

3. Colin Scott, "Sex and Art," *American Journal of Psychology* 7 (January 1896): 207; Havelock Ellis, "Auto-Erotism: A Psychological Study," *Alienist and Neurologist* 19 (January 1898): 280.

4. Sigmund Freud, "On Narcissism: An Introduction," *The Complete Psychological Works of Sigmund Freud* (London, 1957), 14:73-102.

5. In addition to Lasch, see Joel Kovel, *The Age of Desire: Reflections of a Radical Psychologist* (New York, 1981); Alexander Lowen, *Narcissism: Denial of the True Self* (New York, 1983); Daniel Yankelovich, *New Rules: Searching for Fulfillment in a World Turned Upside-Down* (New York, 1981); Herbert Marcuse, *Eros and Civilization* (Boston, 1966). The narcissism debate is well handled in Stephanie Engel, "Femininity as Tragedy: Re-examining the 'New Narcissism,'" *Socialist Review* 10 (September-October 1980): 77-104; and in Janice Doane and Devon Hodges, *Nostalgia and Sexual Difference: The Resistance to Contemporary Feminism* (New York, 1987). For my own views on this important subject, see Lawrence Birken, "The Sexual Counterrevolution: A Critique of Cultural Conservativism," *Social Research* 53 (Spring 1986): 3-22.

6. The ideas in this paragraph are discussed at length in Traian Stoianovich, "Gender and Family: Myths, Models, and Ideologies," *History Teacher* 15 (November 1981): 67-117.

7. For more on the bifurcated model of society that prevailed between 1750 and 1900, see Lorenne Clark and Linda Lange, eds., *The Sexism of Social and Political Theory* (Toronto, 1979); and more recently, Linda Nicholson, *Gender and History* (New York, 1986); and Joan Landes, *Women and the Public Sphere in the Age of the French Revolution* (Ithaca, NY, 1988).

8. See Stoianovich, pp. 67-80.

9. See Immanuel Chill, ed., *Power, Property, and History: Barnave's "Introduction to the French Revolution" and Other Writings* (New York, 1971), p. 141.

10. René Konig, *A la Mode: On the Social Psychology of Fashion* (New York, 1973), pp. 154-64.

11. See John Berger, *Ways of Seeing* (New York, 1985), p. 47; Edward Lucie-Smith, ed., *The Male Nude: A Modern View; An Exhibition Organized by François de Loueville* (New York, 1985), preface; Donald Lowe, *History of Bourgeois Perception* (Chicago, 1982), pp. 97, 100-105.

12. Robert Ray, *Manet* (New York, 1986), pp. 22-23, 49.

13. See Gustave Flaubert, *Madame Bovary* (New York, 1981), pp. 47, 62-63.

14. Ibid., pp. 62-63, 80, and the "icy charm" reference on p. 120; compare to Freud, pp. 89-90.

15. Flaubert, pp. 62, 75.

16. Ibid., p. 53.

17. Freud, pp. 88-89.

18. Flaubert, pp. 107, 248.

19. Ibid., p. 64.

20. Ibid., p. 199.

21. For another analysis of Madame Bovary as a woman in conflict with her age, see E. J. Sabiston, "The Prison of Womanhood," *Comparative Literature* 25 (1973): 335-51.

22. Guy Hocquenghem, *Homosexual Desire* (London, 1978), p. 131.

23. For the original reference, see Havelock Ellis and J. A. Symonds, *Sexual Inversion* (London, 1897; rpt. New York, 1975), p. 137.

24. See Giles Mitchell, "Flaubert's *Emma Bovary*: Narcissism and Suicide," *American Imago* 44 (Summer 1988): 124; the way in which the dissolution of bourgeois sexuality is often equated with the disintegration of life itself is further explored in Lawrence Birken, *Consuming Desire: Sexual Science and the Emergence of a Culture of Abundance, 1871-1914* (Ithaca, NY, 1988).

Paul Andrew Tipper (essay date 1995)

SOURCE: Tipper, Paul Andrew. "*Madame Bovary* and the Bitter-Sweet Taste of Romance." *Orbis Litterarum* 50, no. 4 (1995): 207-13.

[*In the following essay, Tipper analyzes the symbolic relationship between sugar and arsenic in the novel.*]

Flaubert's **Madame Bovary** has an impressive metaphorical density where apparently neutral signifiers constitute either some echo of something already read or point to similar allusions in the text yet to be read. It is a novel in which text and subtext dovetail to produce both a realistic surface of denotation bearing on a knowable fictional universe and a symbolic network of connotation, the latter comprising, as Rosemary Lloyd has noted, 'one of the central structuring devices in *Madame Bovary*'.[1] My aim in this study is to analyse one of the novel's aesthetic structuring devices, hitherto unexplored: the motif of sweetness, both literal and figurative, its function being to underscore the text's central thematics—the discrepancy between illusion and reality and the lethal dangers inherent in (con)fusing the two.

By way of an introduction to what will be predominantly a stylistic analysis of sugar references, I refer readers to the *Concordances to 'Madame Bovary,'*[2] where key-word-in-context data may be obtained at a glance. In addition to the novel's twelve explicit references to *sucre*,[3] one might include the novel's sprinkling of references to *dust*. *Poudre* occurs eight times;[4] this signifier is potentially bivalent inasmuch as it can refer periphrastically to both sugar and arsenic. Indeed, three specific references to *white dust* in the novel actually collapse the sugar/poison opposition, where two normally antithetical referents are suggestively rendered by two identical signifiers.[5] My aim here, however, is not to embark upon an analysis of dust. The study of *dust/powder* and its sinister symbolic function in the novel has already been undertaken by D. T. Shukis who affirms that 'the dust sprinkled liberally through the pages of the novel foreshadows the death of its heroine and heightens the sense of tragic inevitability in the novel.'[6]

The thesis of this particular analysis will derive much of its validity from the impact made by the two strategically positioned references to a metonym of sugar and a metonym of poison which occur in Part I, chapter 8 and Part III, chapter 8 respectively, so generating a compass of symmetry, classical in its sweep, within the parameters of which is enacted Emma's drama. This drama marks a relentless shift of focus from attachment to illusion to the death of all illusions, as the sweet turns sour, as illusion is destroyed by the real. The first of the two notations, bearing on the sweet, is so worded as to generate a mordant irony, for the perspective is Emma's and flawed: 'Le sucre en poudre même lui parut plus blanc et plus fin qu'ailleurs' (p. 51). Emma's chronic tendency to hyperbolize experience is much in evidence, her appropriation of experience being somewhat romanticized simply because she has been invited to an aristocratic ball at *la Vaubyessard* where for once in her life she can enjoy the luxury of white sugar and the luxury of playing the part of a Romantic heroine in the arms of the waltzing *Vicomte* (p. 54). Momentarily, the illusion of bliss has been realized; her *ennui* now dissipated, she no longer yearns for an *ailleurs*. *La Vaubyessard* is her own *ailleurs* and it is therefore in the logical order of things that the white, finely granulated sugar should be of a better quality than the sugar to be found elsewhere. Emma marvels at it, imbibing the ambient luxury with all the sensuality she can muster, eyes half-closed. But such dreams are fragile and

fleeting. Once the ball is over, the pleasure subsides and the memory of the events fades fast in Emma's mind, showing it up to be what it always was—pure illusion: '. . . elle faisait des efforts pour prolonger l'illusion de cette vie luxueuse . . .' (p. 55).

The grim counterpart to this idealized figural perspective occurs at the moment of suicide as Emma crams arsenic into her mouth. Margaret Lowe has commented on the ironic kinship between the sugar at the ball and this white poison powder at the end of the novel: 'The dazzling white sugar at *La Vaubyessard* will be balanced by the white powder of the arsenic which kills Emma (an equivalence between sugar and poison is established throughout the book and in the rough drafts Emma actually eats the arsenic "à même comme du sucre").'[7] This is the only observation the scope of her study will allow, but Lowe has sensitized readers to a polarity of signification, which 'is precisely Flaubert's essential method for conveying irony.'[8] This method, clearly, is one which carries an ironizing intent activated by a dual-level discourse: Emma's signifying system standing in dichotomous relation to the text's signifying system. What Emma had ingested and taken to be a mirror of the real as a girl—romanticized literature in the form of *keepsakes*—, is an illusion corroborated by the apparent sweet beauty of dream-come-true made available to her at the ball with its glamorized powdered white sugar. However, Emma's romanticized perspective is undermined at her suicide when the beauty of illusion is devalorized as the nourishing turns noxious, as Emma comes to see that the sweet signifiers of literary romance are all lies and deception.

The dangers inherent in establishing a plausible link between literal sugar and metaphorical sugar references in the novel are evident; it may appear aberrant to attempt a textual correlation of *sucre* references with, say, the references to *keepsakes*. Emma's romances are metaphorically sweet in that they invite participation in a dream-world which is seen to be preferable to an unpalatable reality. However, this fact alone is not sufficient to justify a correlation between sugar and literature. What *does* justify such a correlation is the suggestive way in which the text plays on a romance-sugar nexus and a romance-poison nexus, the former corresponding to dream, the latter to reality. If the reader accepts the bivalence of *dust/powder* notations in the novel, then the correlation is justifiable and the symphonic reverberations allowing of such a link are clearly audible. For example, the sweet illusions Emma has preserved in adulthood are entertained as a direct result of misreading literature: '. . . Emma se graissa donc les mains à cette poussière des vieux cabinets de lecture' (p. 38). The discourse is morally loaded, implicit criticism coming directly from the narrator's emotive use of a conventionally-established symbol of negativity and undoing—*dust*. The narratorial perspective reiterates the textual idiolect making up the *plan du réel* in the novel; the following subtextual message is articulated: misreading may lead to ruin if one's outlook is Romantic.

References to sugar exist in explicit and elliptical forms in *Madame Bovary.* The novel's references to explicit sugars generate an allusiveness, the impact of which varies according to the contexts in which they appear.[9] Then there are references to *metaphorical sugars,* the source of Emma's problems: *keepsakes* with their accompanying tinsel images; pulp romances and all the wildly exaggerated fictions they contain. Such works of popular art provide Emma with a burst of spiritual and emotional sustenance. But just as the ingestion of real sugar provides a peak of active potential followed by a trough, so the ingestion of romance holds the promise of potential fulfilment, only to be followed by demoralization as a jejune reality supersedes the dream.

Whenever Emma's illusions are fuelled, she is metonymically linked with either literal or metaphorical sugar. But just as all roads lead to Rome, so all superficially sweet references lead inexorably to the bitter sugar/poison which is the *poudre blanche* agent of death. This is the trajectory Emma's life must follow, a path symbolically reiterated by sugar turned poison, white powder appealing turned white powder appalling. A literal sugar notation marking a high point in Emma's life appears at the bloodletting where her dreams seem once more about to come true. Justin faints at the sight of blood spurting; Emma sets about reviving him by dissolving sugar in water: '. . . elle faisait fondre des morceaux de sucre' (p. 132). At this precise juncture Rodolphe vows to seduce a receptive Emma. He succeeds and Emma swoons in sexual pleasure in the forest (like the *femmes étalées* figuring in those *keepsakes,* p. 39) and is wooed by his meretricious displays of chivalric romance. Compellingly, during one of her matutinal trysts at his residence, a bedside prop is *sugar*: '. . . une grosse pipe qui était sur la table de nuit, parmi des citrons et des morceaux de sucre' (p. 169).

If the sweet taste of illusion is experienced during the high points of Emma's existence, then the bitter taste of reality is in her mouth whenever she is forced to confront her *real* situation. The association of *sucre* on seven occasions with Homais—emblem of realism *par excellence*—bolsters the sugar/poison correlation, for Homais's store is the repository of both sugar and arsenic. Emma's euphoria following an adulterous assignation with Rodolphe, for example, is dampened when she is reminded of the harsh reality of her status as wife. She has to cope with her husband's distress on learning of the sudden death of his father and it is in Homais's shop that she learns the news. Once again, the descriptive backdrop includes a reference to sugar: 'sucre râpé, du sucre en morceaux' (p. 252). But Emma's metonymical relation to sugar is contaminated by

poison as she is no longer able to avoid the practicalities of everyday living and it is on this same occasion that she discovers the location of the *poudre blanche* with which she will end her life some seventy pages later. The suggestive link here between sugar and poison is obliquely rehearsed on an earlier occasion in Homais's shop. Binet is looking to buy a substance to clean the rust from his guns and requests some 'acide de sucre' (p. 171). The referent, denoted by an oxymoronic signifier, is sweet and sour. Moreover, his *truthful* explanation for wishing to make this purchase provides a pre-echo of Emma's *mendacious* justification for *her* later purchase of the arsenic which she maintains is to kill rats (p. 320).

The suggestivity of the definitive version of *Madame Bovary* is explicit statement in the rough drafts to the novel. On page 187 of the Nouvelle version of *Madame Bovary,*[10] is a reference to an explicit metonymic link between sugar and romance. Sickly-sweet fictions would be smuggled into the convent by an indulgent old lady: 'C'était la confidante, elle vous faisait des petites commissions en cachette, vous achetait des tablettes de chocolat, et vous prêtait des livres amusants en cachette.' If the old lady purveys elliptical sugar and fiction in the earlier versions of this episode, contrasting with the supply of fiction only in the definitive version (p. 38), then a sugar/romance nexus must be *inferred* as Flaubert's characteristic method of oblique suggestion achieves perfection in the final, polished version. This presupposition assists the reader in his making sense, for example, of Bournisien's advice following Rodolphe's brutal severing of relations with Emma. She, in desperation, turns to the priest for guidance and his dismissive prescription underscores his insensitivity to the real needs of the soul. Bournisien, assuming Emma's listlessness to be due to poor digestion, recommends that she drink a glass of sugar and water: 'Il faut rentrer chez vous . . . boire . . . un verre d'eau fraîche avec de la cassonade' (pp. 116-7). At this moment in time it is the sugar of illusion that Emma needs to fuel the spirit and not literal sugar to feed the body. Ironically, when Emma *is* in need of real nourishment to energize her, the inept priest this time recommends a diet of literature of a sickly-sweet nature; Emma should borrow 'des espèces de romans à cartonnage rose et à style douceâtre' (p. 219). The priest's advice becomes invested with a compelling figurative breadth when the reader recalls the vituperations of Madame Bovary *mère* against third-rate literature. She upheld then that the unscrupulous bookseller was a supplier of toxic reading matter and ought to be apprehended for his immoral activities: 'N'aurait-on pas le droit d'avertir la police, si le libraire persistait quand même dans son métier d'empoisonneur' (pp. 129-30). Charles's mother knows that the metaphorical sugar of romance can be toxic when it feeds the illusions of a woman with ideas above her station. Moreover, this woman happens to be a spendthrift—a further manifestation of a rejection of the real—and squanders money on *sugar,* much to the consternation of Bovary *mère* (p. 44). Might one not affirm with a degree of certainty that the bookseller, Boulard, has his counterpart in Homais? He, too, purveys poison and fiction, for in addition to selling sugar and arsenic, he sells the story of Emma's suicide in the *Fanal de Rouen,* a written prevarication conflating arsenic and sugar (p. 334), a miniaturized emblem of Emma's indefatigable conflation of life and art.

The detail of Emma's ingestion of arsenic 'comme du sucre'[11] has been excised from the final version, but the suggestiveness inherent in the comparison with eating sugar at the moment of her chosen means of suicide is consistent with Emma's illusory belief that her death will be a romantic and painless passage into oblivion: 'Je vais m'endormir et tout sera fini!' (p. 322). The cruel irony of this belief is that her agony and death are in reality a far cry from the dignified languishing that is the yearned-for romantic exit from life. And there is an even deeper irony insofar as that agony stands in metonymical relation to *sugar.* Priest and pharmacist look helplessly on as Larivière attempts to work his magic and save Emma. The surgeon drinks coffee, purveyed and sweetened by Homais (p. 329). Just as the realist Homais's insidious rise parallels the romantic Emma's pathetic decline, so his verbal ennobling of the sugar—he refers to it in Latin—parallels *her* private ennobling of it at *la Vaubyessard.* Emma's miserable life comes to a close and the sweet confectionery of *la Vaubyessard* reveals its true colour—the deathly, ghastly white of vacuous illusion. The sweetness of the ice-cream that Emma had eaten there (p. 53) is perniciously transformed into the bitter taste of the sugar-poison as she expires: 'Cet affreux goût d'encre continuait' (p. 322). The taste of the poison is the taste of ink, is the taste of *the* ink used to write the fictions that Emma took to be the real thing. And it is the taste of the ink that Flaubert used to compose **Madame Bovary,** the ink he used first to create, then to destroy, an incompetent reader of fiction. *Caveat lector.*

As Thierry Ferraro has observed, **Madame Bovary,** too, may be a noxious commodity in the wrong hands: '. . . les romans de Flaubert ne sont pas à mettre entre toutes les mains.'[12]

This article has investigated and analysed one of the many symbolic paradigms in **Madame Bovary.** The differing textual ploys whereby sugar and poison are conflated only to be dichotomized, the sweet and the bitter conjoined only to be divorced, corresponds to the hiatus between dream and real, between Emma's foolish fusion of dream and reality and the textual corrective to that foolishness. References to sugar, literal and figurative, constitute a leitmotif in **Madame Bovary** which at once furnishes a metacommentary on Emma's delu-

sional *Weltanschauung* enacted on *le plan de l'imaginaire,* while enriching the text's aesthetic infrastructure with a bitter-sweet pattern of suggestion that is a salutary lesson to us all.

Notes

1. Rosemary Lloyd, *Madame Bovary,* Unwin Hyman, London, 1990, p. 65.

2. *A Concordance to Flaubert's 'Madame Bovary',* 2 vols., Carlut, Dubé, Dugan, Garland Publishing inc, New York, 1978.

3. The edition referred to is *Madame Bovary,* édition de Claudine Gothot-Mersch, Garnier, Paris, 1971. See pp. 44, 51, 61, 92, 132, 169, 171, 252, 329, 334.

4. See pp. 51, 114, 149, 156, 163, 193, 253, 321.

5. On one occasion *poudre* denotes sugar (p. 51) and on two occasions it denotes arsenic (pp. 253, 321).

6. David T. Shukis, 'The Dusty World of *Madame Bovary*', in: *Nineteenth Century French Studies,* 7, nos 3 & 4 (spring-summer 1979), 213-219, p. 214.

7. Margaret Lowe, *Towards the real Flaubert: A Study of 'Madame Bovary,'* Clarendon Press, Oxford, 1984, p. 48.

8. *Ibid.,* p. 48.

9. Some references to *sucre* will become invested with a heavier load of symbolic signification than others, according to context. For example, the seven references to *sucre* standing in metonymical relation to Homais render themselves available for figurative charging, since he is the common element in the sugar-poison dichotomy (pp. 92, 171, 252, 329, 334). All of these references are also in metonymical relation to Emma, so completing the circuit.

10. *Madame Bovary,* Nouvelle version précédé des scénarios inédits. Présentation par Jean Pommier et Gabrielle Leuleu, José Corti, Paris, 1949.

11. *Madame Bovary,* Nouvelle version, *op. cit.,* p. 599.

12. Thierry Ferraro, *Flaubert,* Marabout, 1992, p. 18.

Patricia A. McEachern (essay date spring 1997)

SOURCE: McEachern, Patricia A. "True Lies: Fasting for Force or Fashion in *Madame Bovary?*" *Romance Notes* 37, no. 3 (spring 1997): 289-98.

[*In the following essay, McEachern discusses depictions of the female body in the novel. According to McEachern, Emma's compulsion to starve herself parallels the psychological motivations associated with eating disorders.*]

Success for the nineteenth-century woman necessitates marrying well: she has no good economic or social alternative. Her body is her sole source of power. She must remain svelte, yet maintain the curves necessary to attract: hence, for women, body-size is closely tied to economic security. To manipulate the body she must manipulate her appetite. An eating disorder is sometimes the unfortunate result that occurs when a woman who succeeds in controlling her body begins to use that control to seek the personal power she is otherwise lacking. In this paper, I shall analyze how Emma Bovary uses what Lilian R. Furst calls "disorderly eating" to gain control over her life by manipulating her body (153).

Through much medical and psychological research carried out in the twentieth century, it has become clear that the anorectic's concern about weight is a superficial symptom of a more serious problem. For the anorectic, the act of controlling her food intake serves as a proxy for governing all other aspects of her life. A lack of a sense of autonomy and effectiveness combined with certain personality traits and other environmental factors provide fertile ground for the development of an eating disorder. The anorectic's obsessive drive to emaciate herself is, in fact, a form of nonverbal discourse. This will become evident in my analysis of *Madame Bovary.* Emma desperately and quietly seizes power and control in one of the few ways she sees available: control of her body. For Emma, the grasp for power through fasting is not always a conscious decision, however, as she begins to lose weight, she discovers, for the first time, an addictive attraction to the ability to control one "small" area of her life. Emma fights against her powerlessness through the symbolic language of self-starvation.

Emma fits the profile of a woman with an eating disorder in a number of ways. For example, at times she engages in bizarre eating habits such as drinking great quantities of vinegar or nothing but tea all day. In addition, most anorectics are perfectionists and in the nineteenth century they attempted to be the "angel in the house." At one point, Emma plays at perfection as a means of manipulation. Later, after her long illness, her interest in becoming pure and ethereal is more sincere. Anorectics often confess dissatisfaction with society's expectations of their role as women and occasionally express a desire to be a man. Baudelaire was the first to perceive Emma's "virility." In an 1857 review of *Madame Bovary* published in *L'Artiste,* he states that Flaubert

n'a pas pu ne pas infuser un sang viril dans les veines de sa créature, et que madame Bovary, pour ce qu'il y a en elle de plus énergique et de plus ambitieux, et aussi de plus rêveur, madame Bovary est restée un

homme. Comme la Pallas armée, sortie du cerveau de Zeus, ce bizarre androgyne a gardé toutes les séductions d'une âme virile dans un charmant corps féminin.

(480)

Emma rebelliously adopts masculine clothing and at one point even goes so far as to smoke in public, a singularly masculine prerogative.

Because Emma has so few options available to her and so little control over her life, an eating disorder appears to be a partial solution to her frustration and a temporary means of manipulating Charles. Her husband's lack of success becomes hers as well. While Charles is satisfied with his simple life, Emma is not and she has no control over her situation. The sense of control Emma lacks is eventually provided by the control she seizes over her body through fasting.

The preoccupation with food and eating in *Madame Bovary* has already been established. In "The Power of the Powerless," for example, Lilian R. Furst points out that descriptions of Emma's environment during adolescence and marriage are permeated with food and food-related imagery. While those around her use food as a source of pleasure and security, Emma handles food in a much more complex fashion (157-159). She learns to control her eating as a method of dealing with frustrations and manipulating others. Emma's refusal of food, as well as her choices of food are simultaneously highly individualistic and classically anorexic: she exploits her refusal to eat in imaginative and psychologically complex ways. Refusing food becomes a symbolic means of repudiating her station and role in life, a very effective method of controlling Charles, and a means of appearing to conform to social expectations (after the death of Charles' father, for example) so as to be able to better control her social situation at a later date.

Emma's preference for exotic and refined dishes which is epitomized by the culinary extravaganza at the chateau at La Vaubyessard is more than just the representation of romantic excess and a reflection of her belief that she is a superior being who has somehow wound up in the wrong place. A repast is saturated with meaning for Emma. It serves as a metaphor either for her actual station in life, as represented by the onion soup Charles slurps at dinner time, or the position in society she is convinced should, by all rights, be hers, as represented by the lavish dinner served at La Vaubyessard. Roland Barthes observes that

When he buys an item of food, consumes it, or serves it, modern man does not manipulate a simple object in a purely transitive fashion; this item of food sums up and transmits a situation; it constitutes an information; it signifies. That is to say that it is not just an indicator of a set of more or less conscious motivations, but that it is a real sign, perhaps the functional unit of a system of communication.

(50)

Barthes continues: "One could say that an entire 'world' (social environment) is present in and signified by food" (54). Emma Bovary is especially sensitive to the "world" that food and food consumption signifies for her.

The banquet at La Vaubyessard becomes not only a sensual experience, but more importantly it serves as a brief entrée into the lifestyle for which Emma hungers. The meal of "grenades," "ananas," "potages à la bisque et au lait d'amandes, des puddings à la Trafalger" serves as a symbol for all that is noble, "ladylike," delicate and refined; that is, everything she yearns to be.[1] Emma mistakenly associates the anemic paleness of the guests with a diet that to her bespeaks a superior lifestyle: "Ils avaient le teint de la richesse, ce teint blanc que rehaussent la pâleur des porcelaines, les moires du satin, le vernis des beaux meubles, et qu'entretient dans sa santé un régime discret de nourritures exquises" (591). Her preference for "ladylike" and refined dishes is quite typical of the "fasting girls" of the nineteenth century who were said to have had "ethereal appetites" and who presumed that their delicate constitutions could only digest such dainty morsels as a "bit of wedding cake" or a "wren's leg on toast" (Brumberg 172). Anorectics make what would seem to others to be unusual food choices for both psychological and physiological reasons which to them appear quite sound.

On some level, Emma understands that she is "ineffective" before her marriage, still, she thinks of herself as being in a kind of holding pattern.[2] She must accept this period of waiting before a man arrives through whom she expects to fill her life with meaning.[3] Because she is so willing to live through a man and she believes that she can actually become effective by living vicariously, her disillusionment is that much greater when she gradually discovers that marriage is far from fulfilling her expectations. Her feeling of ineffectiveness intensifies as she begins to understand that she is henceforth blocked from seeking the kind of relationship she is convinced could bring her happiness.

As Emma's disappointment with her marriage grows, she gradually begins to experience what Flaubert describes as a "détachement intérieur," (588) yet even while she is intensely depressed, she attempts to control her environment and compensate for her unhappiness by being a perfect wife. She prepares special meals, offering guests delicacies garnished in imaginative ways. Furthermore, she manages Charles accounts for him efficiently and graciously. In spite of the fact that Emma is terribly despondent and lonely, Charles perceives his wife as being perfectly contented: "Il la croyait heureuse; et elle lui en voulait de ce calme si bien assis, de cette pesanteur sereine, du bonheur même qu'elle lui donnait" (588). In fact, most families of anorectics insist that everything in the family is fine. Citing Hilde

Bruch: "Most parents emphasized the stability, if not the happiness, of their homes. Only intensive therapeutic work revealed the distortions and tensions underlying this facade of normality" (81). She goes on to explain that

> The parents emphasized the normality of their family life, with repeated statements that 'nothing was wrong,' sometimes with frantic stress on 'happiness,' directly denying the desperate illness of one member. Often they emphasized the superiority of the now sick child over his siblings.
>
> (82)

The exceptional efforts Emma makes to discharge her duties as a perfect wife exhibit just such "superiority." This attempt at perfection in the restricted scope of possibilities available to her is a struggle for control that she will soon replace by the manipulation of her own body and its physiological needs.

Flaubert emphasizes Emma's loneliness and her increasing sense of isolation. Bruch speaks of this very sensation that Emma undergoes which is so common to anorectics:

> There are . . . many references to extreme isolation and loneliness, a feeling of being excluded from all real life. 'I am completely isolated, I sit like in a glass sphere. I see other people through a glass wall, their voices penetrate to me. I long for being in real contact with them. I try but they don't hear me.'
>
> (221)

Emma's intense loneliness is juxtaposed against Charles' infuriating contentment at table: "Il mangeait le reste du miroton, épluchait son fromage, croquait une pomme, vidait sa carafe, puis s'allait mettre au lit, se couchait sur le dos et ronflait" (588). Emma perceives Charles' comfortable sense of satisfaction (a satisfaction she herself has created), as well as his total inability to recognize what is happening to her, and she resents it.

There are early indications of Emma reducing her food intake and using mealtime to make a passive-aggressive statement about her dissatisfaction after the couple returns from La Vaubyessard. "A table même, elle apportait son livre, et elle tournait les feuillets, pendant que Charles mangeait en lui parlant" (594). She reads while Charles eats, making no pretense of listening to his conversation. Although Flaubert does not explicitly maintain that Emma is not eating, the fact that he mentions Charles eating and Emma reading, is evidence that this is, indeed, the case. Flaubert employs the imperfect tense to convey the repetitive nature of the scene, consequently we understand that if Emma is not yet skipping meals, she is cutting down on a regular basis. That Flaubert does not draw attention to this fact by having Charles comment on it is interesting inasmuch as this is precisely what happens in families when the anorexic behavior begins. The condition usually goes unnoticed in the beginning stages and even if an anorectic becomes emaciated families often remain in denial to a great extent.

Because Emma deems the food one eats and the way one consumes it to be a sign of one's social standing, Charles' offensive table manners epitomize both the lifestyle she abhors and her utter inability to change it. Food, in other words, functions here as the sign of social position, of which bad table manners is the signifier and powerlessness is the signified. To cite Barthes:

> Food serves as a sign not only for themes, but also for situations; and this, all told, means for a way of life that is emphasized, much more than expressed, by it. To eat is a behavior that develops beyond its own ends, replacing, summing up, and signalizing other behaviors, and it is precisely for these reasons that it is a sign.
>
> (57)

Mealtimes are replete with meaning for Emma, as is illustrated by the following well-known passage.

> Mais c'était surtout aux heures des repas qu'elle n'en pouvait plus, dans cette petite salle au rez-de-chaussée avec le poêle qui fumait, la porte qui criait, les murs qui suintaient, les pavés humides; toute l'amertume de l'existence lui semblait servie sur son assiette, et à la fumée du bouilli, il montait du fond de son âme comme d'autres bouffées d'affadissement. Charles était long à manger; elle grignotait quelques noisettes, ou bien, appuyée du coude, s'amusait, avec la pointe de son couteau, à faire des raies sur la toile cirée.
>
> (596)

In his famous analysis of this passage, Erich Auerbach describes this paragraph as "the climax of the portrayal of her despair" (483).

> The husband, unconcernedly eating, becomes ludicrous and almost ghastly; when Emma looks at him and sees him sitting there eating, he becomes the actual cause of the "elle n'en pouvait plus"; because everything else that arouses her desperation—the gloomy room, the commonplace food, the lack of a tablecloth, the hopelessness of it all—appears to her, and through her to the reader also, as something that is connected with him, that emanates from him, and that would be entirely different if he were different from what he is.
>
> (Auerbach 484)

In a form of private protest, Emma's behavior becomes decisively more anorexic in a variety of ways, for example, she merely picks at a few hazelnuts while Charles continues to stuff himself. Significantly, her resentment of Charles is most evident at table, where her

powerlessness is so habitually underscored. In addition, she, who had always been extremely meticulous about her appearance, now begins to go days without getting dressed.

During the period when the eating disorder becomes entrenched, anorectics often become intensely moody and combative. They frequently choose to drink and eat things that to most people would seem bizarre or unappetizing, such as large quantities of vinegar or mustard, or they limit themselves to one or two foods. Emma is no exception: "Emma devenait difficile, capricieuse. Elle se commandait des plats pour elle, n'y touchait point, un jour ne buvait que du lait pur, et, le lendemain, des tasses de thé à la douzaine. Souvent, elle s'obstinait à ne pas sortir, puis, elle suffoquait, ouvrait les fenêtres, s'habillait en robe légère" (596). It is at this time that she begins to suffer from heart palpitations and she is described as becoming quite pale, both of which are evidence of the disorder as well. When Charles suggests that if her health does not improve soon he will have to seriously consider establishing his practice elsewhere, Emma consciously realizes the manipulative power fasting can afford her: "Dès lors, elle but du vinaigre pour se faire maigrir, contracta une petite toux sèche et perdit complètement l'appétit" (597). Once Emma recognizes that she can control Charles completely simply by depriving herself of food, she does not hesitate to employ this new technique.

Emma is acutely aware of the limitations imposed on her because of her gender. This is no where made more evident than it is by her reaction to the birth of her child:

> Elle souhaitait un fils; il serait fort et brun, et s'appellerait Georges; et *cette idée d'avoir pour enfant un mâle était comme la revanche en espoir de toutes ses impuissances passées.* Un homme, au moins, est libre; il peut parcourir les passions et les pays, traverser les obstacles, mordre aux bonheurs les plus lointain. Mais une femme est empêchée continuellement. Inerte et flexible à la fois, elle a contre elle les mollesses de la chair avec les dépendances de la loi. Sa volonté, comme le voile de son chapeau retenu par un cordon, palpite à tous les vents, il y a toujours quelque désir qui entraîne, quelque convenance qui retient.
>
> —C'est une fille! dit Charles.
>
> Elle tourna la tête et s'évanouit.
>
> (604, emphasis mine)

Womanhood denotes powerlessness to Emma. Although anorectics almost universally experience a need for self-empowerment, they do not all recognize that this motivates their behavior. Emma's acute consciousness of her own impotence is eloquently expressed in the preceding passage. In her view, to be a man is to be free and to be a woman is to be trapped. Had she given birth to a son she could have perhaps enjoyed his freedom vicariously. Emma's perception of men as free and women as imprisoned is taken up again when Rodolphe attempts to seduce her at the agricultural fair. She tells him: "Vous n'êtes guère à plaindre. Vous êtes libre" (621) and she refers to women as "nous autres pauvres femmes!" (622). Later, she will tell Léon that he cannot possibly understand the limitations her gender imposes: "car, vous n'êtes pas une femme, vous" (653). Woman is controlled by the law and by the "weaknesses of the flesh." Emma cannot control the law, but she can and will control her own flesh.

Emma does make occasional attempts at playing the role of the ideal mother and wife: "Elle déclarait adorer les enfants; c'était sa consolation, sa joie, sa folie, et elle accompagnait ses caresses d'expansions lyriques" (610). She endeavors to project an image of the ideal woman, that is, the proverbial "angel of the house." Her socialization makes it inevitable that she correctly discern what an ideal woman is (i.e., someone who sacrifices herself for others). During one of these periods when Emma attempts to be the perfect wife, Flaubert laconically mentions: "Emma maigrit, ses joues pâlirent, sa figure s'allongea" (610). Emma plays the role of perfect mother, but it does not fulfill her. Berthe is merely a prop for Emma's theatrical performance: try as she may, maternal instincts come to Emma only sporadically. The more she denies herself in her effort to succeed at fulfilling society's expectations, the more she suffers from "nerves." "Elle restait brisée, haletante, inerte, sanglotant à voix basse et avec des larmes qui coulaient" (611). It is only after her marriage that this nervous condition begins; that is, only when she comes to the realization that this is the best her life will ever be and that she does not have the power to change her circumstances.

Because Emma defines her happiness and success through the accomplishments or actions of a man, Charles' hideous and tragic failure resulting from the botched operation he performs on poor Hippolyte is the final straw for her. Her fate and her identity are inextricably bound to that of a man who is a failure. His inadequacy sullies her because being a wife is her profession. She feels a double sting because she had denied the extent of Charles' mediocrity to herself. "Emma, en face de lui, le regardait; elle ne partageait pas son humiliation, elle en éprouvait une autre: c'était de s'être imaginé qu'un pareil homme pût valoir quelque chose, comme si vingt fois déjà elle n'avait pas suffisamment aperçu sa médiocrité" (637). She has made what she perceives as great sacrifices for Charles in the only sphere in which she has the opportunity to act. Now she resents him for not being worthy of her efforts to be the ideal wife. Her sacrifices were for naught.

Emma's final act of self-destruction occasions an act of exaggerated consumption. In Emma's explanation to Justin of why she needs the arsenic that she will swallow greedily in the manner of a desperate bulimic: "Elle prétendit avoir besoin de tuer les rats qui l'empêchaient de dormir" (680), she quite possibly discloses more truth than she herself realizes. We are left to wonder if the rats are but a metaphor for the limitations in her life, the lack of control that provokes her constant state of anxiety and restlessness.

The socially accepted view of women's fragility in the nineteenth century actually predisposed them to be likely victims of the debilitating condition of an eating disorder. When one adds to this ideal of frailty the addictive sense of power that often accompanies anorexia, one can understand why this disorder sometimes appears to a woman to be a solution to a problem she cannot define and often does not know she has: her own sense of powerlessness. This paper is intended to provide an analysis of some of the literary manifestations of anorexia nervosa in **Madame Bovary** in the hope of contributing to the understanding of a fascinating, albeit self-destructive, struggle for self-empowerment.

Notes

1. Flaubert, Gustave, *Madame Bovary* (Paris: Editions du Seuil, 1964) 591. All subsequent references are to this edition.

2. Anorectics almost universally report experiencing what Hilde Bruch describes as "an all-pervasive, paralyzing sense of ineffectiveness" that leads to the pseudo-solution of an eating disorder (3).

3. "Pas d'existence individuelle pour la jeune fille, en tutelle chez ses parents, elle attend le mari. Un seul devoir alors absorbe pour elle tous les autres: la plupart des autres même n'existant qu'en vue de lui: la jeune fille doit se conserver vierge pour l'homme qui l'épousera" (Pelletier 1).

Works Cited

Auerbach, Erich. *Mimesis: The Representation of Reality in Western Literature.* Trans. Willard R. Trask. Princeton: Princeton UP, 1953.

Barthes, Roland. "Toward a Psychology of Contemporary Food Consumption." *European Diets from Preindustrial to Modern Times.* Eds. Elborg and Robert Forster. New York: Harper, 1975.

Baudelaire, Charles. *"Madame Bovary." Baudelaire: Oeuvres complètes.* Ed. Michel Jamet. Paris: Editions Robert Lafont, 1980.

Bruch, Hilde, M.D. *Eating Disorders: Obesity, Anorexia Nervosa, and the Person Within.* New York: Basic, 1973.

Brumberg, Joan Jacobs. *Fasting Girls: The History of Anorexia Nervosa.* New York: NAL, 1988.

Flaubert, Gustave. *Madame Bovary.* Vol. 1 of *Oeuvres complètes.* Paris: Editions du Seuil, 1964.

Furst, Lilian R., and Peter W. Graham, eds. "The Power of the Powerless: A Trio of Nineteenth-Century French Disorderly Eaters." *Disorderly Eaters: Texts in Self-Empowerment.* University Park: Pennsylvania State UP, 1992.

Pelletier, Madeleine. *L'Emancipation sexuelle de la femme.* Paris: M. Giard et E. Brière, 1911.

Elissa Marder (essay date fall 1997)

SOURCE: Marder, Elissa. "Trauma, Addiction, and Temporal Bulimia in *Madame Bovary.*" *Diacritics* 27, no. 3 (fall 1997): 49-64.

[*In the following essay, Marder examines Emma Bovary's despairing relationship to time in the novel. Describing Emma's condition as a "temporal disorder," Marder suggests that her failure to achieve happiness lies in a fundamental disconnect between the language of romantic ideals and the language of life.*]

> Lisez, et ne rêvez pas. Plongez-vous dans de longues études. Il n'y a de continuellement bon que l'habitude d'un travail entêté. Il s'en dégage un opium qui engourdit l'âme [Read and do not dream. The only thing that is continually good is the habit of stubborn work. It emits an opium that numbs the soul].
>
> —Gustave Flaubert to Louise Colet

> *Madame Bovary* I daresay is about bad drugs.
>
> —Avital Ronell, *Crack Wars*

If Flaubert's **Madame Bovary** remains so timely, it is because its heroine, Emma, suffers from the quintessential malady of modernity, the inability to incorporate time into experience. Emma's missed encounter with her own life, her inability to "get a life," as we say now in America, renders her our contemporary in the strangest sense of the word. She is our contemporary not because we live in the same time but because her failure to live in time has come to define our own. Paradoxically, Emma Bovary has been so well preserved (she is, in some sense, "more alive" now than ever) because she incarnates and inaugurates a modernity that can be defined by the erosion of the possibility of living in time. In Flaubert's minute and meticulous descriptions of the particular temporal disorders that afflict Emma (as we shall see, she can neither bear witness to an event nor remember one, she can neither live in the present nor project a future, she is incessantly subject to bouts of involuntary forgetting even as she is preoccu-

pied by obsessive rites of recollection, she attempts simultaneously to conjure up time and to stop it), we can read the prophetic traces of a depiction of the temporal structure of the many forms of trauma and addiction that have come to define contemporary American culture.

But before turning to Flaubert's prescient and powerful analysis of how Emma Bovary suffers from a "temporal disorder," let us take a brief look at how the notions of trauma and addiction have been described in a contemporary analysis of modern culture. In his recent book *On Flirtation*, the British child psychoanalyst Adam Phillips redescribes ordinary neurosis as a traumatic response to an inability to live in time. He writes:

> People come to psychoanalysis when there is something they cannot forget, something they cannot stop telling themselves, often by their actions, about their lives. And these dismaying repetitions—this unconscious limiting or coercion of the repertoire of life stories—create the illusion of time having stopped (or rather, people believe—behave as if they have stopped time). In our repetitions we seem to be staying away from the future, keeping it at bay.
>
> [153]

Phillips goes on to explain that "[f]or Freud these repetitions are the consequence of a failure to remember. . . . Whatever cannot be transformed, psychically processed, reiterates itself. A trauma is whatever there is in a person's experience that resists useful redescription. Traumas, like beliefs, are ways of stopping time" [153-54]. Phillips's argument rings with a seductive simplicity: neurosis is defined as a temporal disorder, and the contemporary psychoanalytic "cure" does nothing less than promise time. It presumably offers the subject the option of accepting the contingencies of living in time over the pleasure and pain that attend the attempt to stop it.

Nonetheless, Phillips's claim, that contemporary neurosis can be expressed as an attempt to stop time, should perhaps make us pause. Stopping time, in the time of Balzac, Gautier, Baudelaire, and Flaubert, was once conceived of as part of the privileged domain reserved for art and the artist. We might have naively assumed that in the realm of the "real world," for "real people" time remains an implacable fact of life. The task of falling out of time, after all, would seem to necessitate either an accident of enormous magnitude (a trauma in the traditional sense) or the reliance upon an external substance—hashish, opium, alcohol, or cocaine—one of those mind-altering substances that so preoccupied the nineteenth-century advocates of *paradis artificiels*. So what is surprising and particularly suggestive about Phillips's observations is not that the ordinary neurotic *fails* to stop time, but rather that he or she *succeeds* so well. This dubious "success" is incontestably well documented in the realm of American popular culture, where—in television talk shows, sitcoms, tabloids, self-help books, and twelve-step programs as well as on the dwindling couches of analysts, who have, for the most part, been replaced by millions of prescriptions for Prozac and Zoloft—trauma and its uncanny other, addiction, are visibly the most emblematic and paradoxically *popular* illnesses of our time.

Phillips's invocation of the notion of "trauma" in the context of everyday pathologies only further complicates the problem. When he writes, rather casually, that "traumas, like beliefs, are ways of stopping time," what has happened to our implicit understanding of what trauma is and how it occurs? Trauma is more or less classically understood as a response to an event so extraordinary that, in the language of the American Psychiatric Institute (cited by Cathy Caruth in her introduction to *Trauma: Explorations in Memory*), it is "outside the range of usual human experience" [3]. Because the event is so threatening (it often occurs in the case of near-death encounters) and because the experience cannot be assimilated, the event is mechanically reproduced as recollection bereft of memory. As Caruth writes, "[t]he pathology consists, rather, solely in the *structure of experience* or reception: the event is not assimilated or experienced fully at the time, but only belatedly, in its repeated *possession* of the one who experiences it. To be traumatized is precisely to be possessed by an image or event" [4-5]. Because this atemporal "possession" prevents the traumatized subject from experiencing (in the sense of assimilating) the precipitating event, that nonevent comes to organize a systematic disruption of many, if not all, other life experiences. We could argue that in the uncontrollable and often unmanageable repetitions of the traumatic event, the subject's inability both to forget and to remember the event is lived as if time itself had become a persecutory enemy, an overwhelming other.

But if the subject of "trauma" is, as we have said, "possessed" by time, what is the temporal status of the addicted subject? How and why can trauma and addiction be read as uncanny inversions of a similar temporal disorder? In both cases, certainly, the subject appears to be "possessed" and is apparently condemned to acts of compulsive repetition unto death in either literal or symbolic ways. But where the traumatic subject is seemingly dominated by an inability to forget, the addicted subject seems driven by a strange, compulsive *need* to forget. If trauma can be understood as the attempt to survive an inassimilable encounter with "near-death," the structure of addiction emerges as a strange kind of "near-life" experience. Where the traumatized subject cannot get away from the voice of time, the addicted subject seemingly cannot find a place *in* it. Time, for the addict, is not figured as an anthropomorphized persecutory other—but rather appears almost like something that happens elsewhere, to other people. The time of addiction is a time, like trauma, "outside the range of usual human experience," but in the case of addiction, the subject appears to be exiled from time rather than possessed by it.

The temporal coincidence of the appearance of *Madame Bovary* with that of *Les fleurs du mal* leads one to ask about the historical status of this failure of experience. The traumatized voice of a subject "possessed" by time echoes through many of Baudelaire's poems, but the most explicit example of traumatic paranoid possession can be found in "L'horloge." In "L'horloge," the poet conjures up a demonic figure of time in the opening first line, "Horloge, Dieu Sinistre" ("Clock, Sinister God"), and immediately loses control over his own voice. The voice of the clock usurps that of the poet and then repeats the command "souviens-toi" ("remember") again and again in increasingly mechanized tones until it condemns the poet to death in the last line. But where Baudelaire's work might be dominated by the figure of trauma (even though it is he and not Flaubert who put addiction at the center of his concerns), it is in Flaubert's novel that we find—in place of the druglike flowers of evil, with their lure of opiate aroma—the full-blown structure of an addiction with no point of return. By insisting upon the effects of this addicted temporality, I hope to explain why, as any reader of *Madame Bovary* knows, Emma never had a life to lose.[1]

Flaubert's *Madame Bovary* is perhaps one of the most eloquent analyses of the temporal pathology of the language of everyday life available to us. Long before Marcel Proust dramatized the problem of time through the figures of *memoire volontaire* and *involontaire,* Emma Bovary struggled against the demon of involuntary forgetting. If Proust must be seen as the indelible archivist of the telling of the modern subject's narration of his relationship to lost time, Flaubert can be read as the scribe, the copyist, of the modern subject's non-narratable relation to wasted time. But unlike Proust's narrator, Flaubert's Emma Bovary cannot seek lost time; instead, as the novel explicitly demonstrates, she is in search of time itself, in the form of an event. Unable to isolate anything in her "daily life" that she can grasp in the form of an "event," she turns to fiction. While virtually all readers and critics of *Madame Bovary* (beginning, of course, with the legal, political, and cultural institutions that saw fit to put the book on trial) would agree with Michael Riffaterre's observation that "*Madame Bovary* is a fiction about the dangers of fiction" [183], critics have widely divergent ways of interpreting the causes and consequences of Emma's reading habit.[2] Reading Emma's reading habits is a favorite activity of *Bovary*'s [*Madame Bovary*'s] critics, many of whom seem to be vaguely reassured by the notion that Emma's misfortunes and suffering can in large part be attributed to her unhealthy and ultimately misguided dependency on works of fiction. This tendency is exemplified by Victor Brombert's claim that "Emma's flaw is that she uses art to feed her dreams, instead of placing her dreams in the service of art" [113]. Such a reading implies that Emma's suffering stems from the fact that she is a bad reader of the relationship between art and life.[3] By turning briefly to the first passage in the text that introduces *Madame Bovary*'s reader to Emma as reader, I would like to suggest that if one too quickly concludes that Emma is simply a bad reader, Flaubert's reader risks glossing over the complexity of his idiomatic and highly disturbing articulation of how time and experience can become unhinged in both life and art. In the concluding paragraph of chapter 5, part 1, Flaubert writes:

> Avant qu'elle se mariât, elle avait cru avoir de l'amour; mais le bonheur qui aurait dû résulter de cet amour n'étant pas venu, il fallut qu'elle se fût trompée, songeait-elle. Et Emma cherchait à savoir ce que l'on entendait au juste dans la vie par des mots de *félicité*, de *passion*, et d'*ivresse*, qui lui avaient paru si beaux dans les livres.
>
> [69]

> Before marriage she thought herself in love; but since the happiness that should have followed failed to come, she must, she thought, have been mistaken. And Emma tried to find out what one meant exactly in life by the words *bliss, passion, ecstasy*, that had seemed to her so beautiful in books.
>
> [24]

The obvious irony of this passage derives from the fact that Emma resolves the discrepancy between her lived experience of love and her reading knowledge of love by concluding that the error lies not in her books but in her life. Such a reading only confirms two common characterizations of Emma Bovary: at worst, she is a foolish, provincial woman who deludes herself with romantic fantasies, and at best she is a pathetic travesty of an artist because she tragically misrecognizes the proper hierarchy between "Art" and "Life." Both of these interpretations are certainly textually justified and are supported and seemingly solicited by Flaubert's explicitly contemptuous descriptions of Emma in the correspondence as well as his implicit critique of Emma throughout the text of *Madame Bovary*. Furthermore, in the passage itself Flaubert seemingly establishes a distance between the voice of narrative authority and Emma's faulty reasoning by adding the telltale attribution "songeait-elle" to Emma's conclusion that she has been mistaken about life: "il fallut qu'elle se fût trompée, songeait-elle." The phrase "songeait-elle" underscores the notion that even when engaging in the act of facing the barren reality of her life, Emma can do nothing other than dream.

Presumably bereft of any form of experience other than those received from books, Emma can only perceive

that she has not yet had an event by comparing the lexicon of her life with that of the novels she has read. The word that trips her up is, not surprisingly, "amour." What is surprising is that Emma's difficulty reconciling the difference between book-love and her lived experience emerges not in relation to the word's meaning or definition, but rather in relation to its temporal effects and narrative function. Novel reading has taught Emma that "amour" ought to announce an inaugural event that propels a life into a durable and continued state of "bonheur" ("happiness"). Hence one knows that one has "possessed love" ("avoir de l'amour") only when that love produces an event that guarantees temporal continuity in the form of "bonheur." The disappointing revelations occasioned by Emma's marriage are consequently multiple: in the first place, the marriage cannot function as an event in itself because it does not occur at the properly eventful hour of midnight: "Emma eût, au contraire, désiré se marier à minuit" [59]; ("Emma would, on the contrary, have preferred to have a midnight wedding" [18]). Next, the marriage fails to produce the anticipated state of happiness, and finally, and perhaps most important, these first two failures force her to acknowledge that she has been jilted by an "event" at the altar of time. The temporal finality and precision of the words "le bonheur qui aurait dû résulter de cet amour n'étant pas venu" almost anthropomorphizes "bonheur" into the missing bridegroom, whose absence at the wedding necessarily obliterates the meaning and the function of the event. Instead of enabling her to begin an eventful life by establishing a bridge between the world of fiction and the language of life, the word "love" opens up an irrevocable abyss between the formlessness of lived time and the experience of narrative meaning provided by fiction. The fissure between the fictional temporality of the word "love" and its seemingly absent corresponding referent in the real world functions rhetorically like a catachresis, a figural term that has no literal meaning. As we shall see in greater depth later on, the appearance of the word "amour" in *Madame Bovary* is always hyperinvested in strange ways and almost always signals the presence of a temporal disorder.[4] In this passage, once Emma recognizes the disconnection between the word "amour" and its fictional referent, she learns that any and all words could potentially become meaningless in the language of life: "Et Emma cherchait à savoir ce que l'on entendait au juste *dans la vie* par des mots de *félicité*, de *passion* et d'*ivresse* . . ." [my emphasis].

When, however, this passage is read in the context of Flaubert's presentation of Emma's so-called life, it takes on additional resonances. Let us begin by recalling that according to the narrative structure of the novel, Emma, unlike Charles, never had any "real life experiences" onto which fantasy or fictional events were grafted. Whereas the narrative of *Madame Bovary* begins with the fabulous scene of Charles Bovary's primal traumatic schoolroom humiliation through "decapitation" (the loss of his beloved and monstrous "casquette") and traces the subsequent vicissitudes of his daily life (ranging from Charles's mediocre study habits to the events that culminate in his first marriage), the narrative of Emma's "life" prior to her encounter with Charles emerges only after it becomes clear in the above passage that her marriage has failed to constitute the inaugural event of her life. Immediately after this discovery, chapter 6 begins with the recitation of Emma's reading history ("Elle avait lu *Paul et Virginie* et elle avait rêvé la maisonette de bambous . . ." [70] / "She had read 'Paul and Virginia,' and she had dreamed of the little bamboo-house . . ." [24]), which introduces, supplements, and ultimately supplants the subsequent narration of her past lived life story: "lorsqu'elle eut treize ans, son père l'amena lui-même à la ville pour la mettre au couvent" [70] ("When she was thirteen, her father himself took her to the convent" [25]). In other words, Emma's substitution of literature for life cannot merely be read as a character flaw since, at the level of the novel's narrative, Flaubert presents her life as if it were actually produced by her readings rather than as a series of lived experiences. Like Emma herself, who apparently has no access to her life that has not been mediated by a prior fictional referent, *Bovary*'s reader is given no access to Emma's "life" that has not already been presented as a fictional production. Paradoxically, however, in the very moment in the text when Emma discovers that her marriage has failed to inaugurate her life, at the level of the novel, Emma's disappointment in her marriage initiates the moment when the fictional life of the character known as Emma Bovary is truly born. Prior to this moment, as critics have often observed, the narrative voice displays Emma as a specular object of Charles's gaze, seen almost entirely through his eyes.[5] It is only after Emma literally becomes "Madame Bovary" and realizes that her newly acquired identity has nonetheless failed to provide her with a life that her thoughts and feelings begin to permeate the *style indirect libre* of the authorial voice.

Thus, from the outset of the novel, the subjective presence of the character "Madame Bovary" is animated by and depends upon her alienation from her experience of life. For this reason, rather than reading Emma's recourse to fiction as a cause of her future misfortunes, I prefer to read Emma's reading as the first significant manifestation of her temporal disorder—the fact that her life seemingly unfolds in a temporal void.[6] Therefore, while it is indisputable that Emma displays a naive belief that literature can be directly transformed into life, it is nonetheless quite possible that through her very inability to read her life, Emma provides Flaubert's reader with the novel's most rigorous and lucid embodiment of how time can be severed from experience in modern life. By starting from the assumption that Flaubert's oft-cited utterance "Madame Bovary,

c'est moi" should be read quite literally, I hope to resist the temptation to read Emma's plight as either pathetic or tragic in order to uncover critical traces of the history of the modern subject.

Emma's gradual discovery that her life consists of a monotonous temporal vacuum motivates her growing dependency on fictional models of temporal structures. Her most significant early abuse of fiction occurs in the wake of her mother's death. Because the temporal void in which she exists prevents her from being able to sustain the experience in time or to secure its meaning by placing it within a meaningful temporal context, she attempts to compensate for the temporal insufficiency of the literal death by using literary devices to enhance and prolong the experience. Although the actual death fails to constitute a "natural" event for Emma, she welcomes the very idea of death as a potentially fortuitous cure for her timelessness. By applying the basic tenets of romantic aesthetic ideology onto the material fact of her mother's death, she fabricates the following fiction of the future: she anticipates an experience of durable, melancholic inconsolability that culminates in a productive projection of her own future death so that she might ultimately experience a dramatic, spiritual literary rebirth.

> Quand sa mère mourut, elle pleura beaucoup les premiers jours. Elle se fit faire un tableau funèbre avec les cheveux de la défunte, et, dans une lettre qu'elle envoyait aux Bertaux, toute pleine de réflexions tristes sur la vie, elle demandait qu'on l'ensevelît plus tard dans le même tombeau. Le bonhomme la crut malade et vint la voir. Emma fut intérieurement satisfaite de se sentir arrivée du premier coup à ce rare idéal des existences pâles, où ne parviennent jamais les coeurs médiocres. Elle se laissa donc glisser dans les méandres lamartiniens, écouta les harpes sur les lacs, tous les chants des cygnes mourants. . . .
>
> [73]

> When her mother died she cried much the first few days. She had a funeral picture made with hair of the deceased, and, in a letter sent to the Bertaux full of sad reflections on life, she asked to be buried later in the same grave. The old man thought she must be ill, and came to see her. Emma was secretly pleased that she had reached at a first attempt the rare ideal of delicate lives, never attained by mediocre hearts. She let herself meander along with Lamartine, listened to harps on lakes, to all the songs of dying swans. . . .
>
> [27-28]

However, as the conclusion of the passage demonstrates, Emma never achieves the state of anticipated inconsolability that she had hoped would serve as incontestable proof of an indelible memory. Despite all the excessive gestures that she performs in order to preserve it, her mother's memory quickly evaporates. And even Emma is disillusioned by how her romantic theories of death fail to endure the test of practical application and hence cannot be considered particularly useful. Much to her dismay and confusion, she discovers that Death offers no greater chance of a future than life does. Her fantasy of a new life, a life renewed by literary tropes of rebirth, is reduced to the vapidity of received ideas. Emma's factory of literary cliches not only fails to supply her with an experience of a lived event that endures, but also hastens the demise of this experience through empty repetition:

> Elle s'en ennuya, n'en voulut point convenir, continua par habitude, ensuite par vanité, et fut enfin surprise de se sentir apaisée, et sans plus de tristesse au coeur que de rides sur son front.
>
> [74]

> She soon grew bored but wouldn't admit it, continued from habit first, then out of vanity, and at last was surprised to feel herself consoled, and with no more sadness at heart than wrinkles on her brow.
>
> [28, trans. modified]

But in order to appreciate the gravity of this passage and to understand the textual ramifications of its twisted logic, we must take a closer look at the mother/daughter relationship depicted in it. In the first place, we are compelled to observe that this is virtually the only moment in *Madame Bovary* where Emma makes any reference to the mother.[7] Moreover, the missing mother becomes the site of a disruption of moral, psychological, and temporal categories. It appears that this mother exists only through her death: by dying she offers Emma a pretext for the activity of mourning and a promise of rebirth. In a perverse reversal of the natural tropes of maternity, when Emma asks to be buried with her mother in the same grave, the figure of the womb is replaced by that of the tomb in her fantasy of rebirth. But although Flaubert's transvaluation of the maternal function is announced through the substitution of figures of death for figures of life, what is at stake is not simply a confusion of life and death.

This dead mother appears as the first unmistakable annunciation of the activities of involuntary forgetting, mechanical repetition, and failed mourning that pervade the text of *Madame Bovary.* Unlike Charles's mother or Emma's father, the figure of Emma's mother never attains the status of a psychological character; she appears only to disappear, and this disappearance becomes remarkable precisely because it leaves no mark. The only "surprise" that this terminal nonevent can elicit is the surprise of nothingness itself. Flaubert circumscribes the surprising emptiness of this voided experience through an analogy between two unwritten texts: the absence of sadness in Emma's heart is strikingly compared to the absence of wrinkles on her forehead. The missing wrinkles prove that time remains unwritten

there: "Elle . . . fut enfin surprise de se sentir apaisée, et sans plus de tristesse au coeur que de rides sur son front." The ironic analogy between Emma's absent affect and her unmarked forehead reiterates that the mother's death fails as event because it cannot mark the passage of time. It comes as no surprise, therefore, that even in her death, Emma's mother cannot give her life because she cannot give her time.

Although she never reappears in the novel, Emma's dead mother is perhaps the most opaque and unreadable figure in the entire text of *Madame Bovary.*[8] This figure becomes unreadable in part because she is barely written—existing only as the void that serves as the apparent origin of all future nonevents, including, of course, Emma's warped nonmaternal relation to her own daughter, Berthe. But if one is tempted (as I am partially suggesting here) to read the failed mourning of the dead mother as the first and most extreme example of the many temporal dysfunctions that permeate this novel, it is no less important to insist that the textual meaning and function of this dead mother cannot simply be read through classical psychological or psychoanalytic paradigms. Flaubert hardly seems to be suggesting that Emma's problems can in any way be attributed to a lack of maternal care. He does, however, seem to place Emma, and the entire world of *Madame Bovary,* in a realm where mothers no longer guarantee the existence of a state of nature. Flaubert's maternal function connotes neither an inviolable, preverbal natural bond between mother and child nor a natural temporal frame in which birth and death constitute events and childbearing insures that generations progress forward naturally through time.

Emma's attempts to mourn the mother's death are doomed to repeat the very formlessness of this maternal nonevent. Although she anticipates that the death will be accompanied by feelings of "sadness," Emma soon finds herself in a state of disconnected boredom ("elle s'ennuya"). In *Crack Wars,* Avital Ronell reminds us that nineteenth-century boredom, like melancholia, is mourning's dysfunctional evil twin. She goes on to argue that when failed mourning passes as boredom, the cultural site formerly assigned to death becomes occupied by addictive structures that often manifest themselves through drug dependency. Ronell writes:

> As symptom, boredom is co-originary with melancholia. It pervades everything, and cannot be simply said to erupt. Nor does it desist of its own. It is prior to signification, yet it appears to be a commentary on life; it is, at least for Emma, the place of her deepest struggle. . . . Boredom, with its temporal slowdown and edge of anguish, is also an authentic mode of being-in-the-world. . . . Emma's boredom appears to exhaust a certain reserve before it has been tapped. It is a companion to loss, but raised on tranquilizers. In *Madame Bovary,* boredom opens up a listening to disap-

pearance, fabricating a society's holding pattern over the death that traverses us. . . . This forms the threshold through which the existence of Emma Bovary is made to pass, a zone of experience that conspires with "nothing at all," the extenuation of the subject. Something like an ontology of boredom announces its necessity here. We are reminded that for Baudelaire and Gautier, Flaubert's contemporaries and acquaintances, this experience of nothing is at times laced with drugs.

[119-20]

The link that Ronell suggests between boredom, failed mourning, and the structure of addiction is borne out by the conclusion of the passage: Emma's boredom transforms subjective mourning rituals into an empty habit ("habitude"). This alienated mechanical repetition ultimately degenerates into an eviscerated narcissism, "vanité," before fading away completely.

Although the legacy of the mother's death lies precisely in the fact that she passes away outside the passage of time and without leaving a trace, the aftermath of this maternal disappearance seemingly produces a temporal void in Emma which she attempts to counteract by searching for an event. Having no access to the experience of an event in her life, she turns to fiction in order to learn how to manufacture one. Her readings dispense fictive highs, which she confuses with lived events. The passions she feels when reading stimulate her desire to reproduce in life the excitations simulated by fiction. Because Emma's literary taste for the generic tropes of Romantic fiction teaches her that events (like the "coup de foudre" that heralds love) occur both instantaneously and by chance, she attempts to apply the laws of fiction to life by waiting for an eventful surprise in the form of love or adventure. But since the laws of fiction, unlike life, systematically guarantee the arrival of unanticipated events, Emma's readings place her in a peculiar historical and philosophical predicament: how can one anticipate the arrival of an event which must be, by definition, both surprising and instantaneous?

In the following passage, which comes from the last chapter of part 1, as Emma waits impatiently for the arrival of a hypothetical event that presumably would transform her empty existence into the experience of a real life, she begins to realize, with increasing desperation, that she has not been invited to the dance of Life. Flaubert writes:

Au fond de son âme, cependant, elle attendait un événement . . . chaque matin, à son réveil, elle l'espérait pour la journée et elle écoutait tous les bruits, se levait en sursaut, s'étonnait qu'il ne vînt pas; puis, au coucher du soleil, toujours plus triste, désirait être au lendemain. . . . Dès le commencement de juillet, elle compta sur ses doigts combien de semaines lui restaient pour arriver au mois d'octobre, pensant que le marquis d'Andervilliers, peut-être, donnerait encore un bal à la Vaubyessard. Mais tout septembre s'écoula sans lettres

ni visites. Après l'ennui de cette déception, son coeur, de nouveau, resta vide, et alors la série des mêmes journées recommença.

Elles allaient donc maintenant se suivre ainsi à la file, toujour pareille, innombrables, et n'apportant rien! Les autres existences, si plates qu'elles fussent, avaient du moins la chance d'un événement. Une aventure amenait parfois des péripéties à l'infini, et le décor changeait. Mais pour elle, rien n'arrivait. Dieu l'avait voulu! L'avenir était un corridor tout noir, et qui avait au fond sa porte bien fermée.

[96]

All the while, however, she was waiting in her heart for an event. Each morning, as she awoke, she hoped it would come that day; she listened to every sound, sprang up with a start, was surprised that it did not come; then at sunset, always more saddened, she wished that it would already be tomorrow. . . . From the beginning of July she counted off on her fingers how many weeks there were to get to October, thinking that perhaps the Marquis d'Andervilliers would give another ball at Vaubyessard. But all September passed without letters or visits. After the shock of this disappointment her heart once again remained empty, and then the same series of identical days started all over again. So now they would keep following one another, always the same, innumerably, and bringing nothing. Other existences, however flat, had at least the chance of an event. One adventure sometimes brought with it infinite consequences and the scenery changed. But for her, nothing happened. God had willed it so! The future was a dark corridor, with its door at the end well locked up.

[44-45, trans. modified][9]

In the opening lines of this passage, it appears to Emma (and the reader) almost as if it is an "accident"—an event of some sort—that has interfered with the arrival of *her* anticipated event: "chaque matin, à son réveil, elle l'espérait pour la journée et elle écoutait tous les bruits, se levait en sursaut, s'étonnait qu'il ne vînt pas. . . ." The text begins by suggesting that it is the absence of an event that impedes Emma's ability to live life daily and concludes with the more disturbing notion that it is her inability to gain access to the temporal unit "day" that renders any potential future event impossible. For Emma, time cannot be measured; it flows away in smaller and smaller doses. Initially week by week, then day by day, and ultimately drop by drop, it becomes clear that the problem here is not with an event that has stopped time, but rather with a figure of time that cannot assimilate an event.

At first, Emma counts *on* time by attempting to count it, literally, in the weeks that she counts off on her fingers. But in order even to be able to count time—to represent time in meaningful units—Emma must be able to rely on the hope that the only event that has ever had any lasting meaning for her, the ball at Vaubyessard, could be repeatable. The ironic futility of this hope is extremely complex and ultimately fatal; the event of the ball cannot be repeated as lived experience for Emma in part because her presence at it was entirely determined by chance. The invitation to the ball depends on the convergence of an inimitable series of chance occurrences: the marquis happened to develop an abscess in his mouth just prior to the ball; the cherries happened to be bad at Vaubyessard and good at the Bovary's farm that year, and when the marquis wants some cherries, he catches sight of Emma and whimsically decides to invite the couple to the ball. It is only by accident, therefore, that Emma goes to the ball in the first place, and once she gets there she is more an alienated and dizzied spectator at the event than a participant in it.

Perhaps because the ball at Vaubyessard appears to correspond, almost uncannily, to the expectations she receives from fiction, it is virtually the only incident in the text of **Madame Bovary** that even remotely functions like a life event for Emma. Moreover, unlike the failed event of her mother's death, which loses all reality, provides neither continuity nor consistency, and evaporates from her memory without leaving a trace, the ball remains the only occurrence in her life that she doesn't inadvertently forget. Everything and everyone else, all other presences and absences are subject to erosion and are effaced.

Functioning as the singular and traumatic temporal point of reference for Emma, the ball tantalizes her into temporary hopefulness by providing her with a powerful if illusory repository into which she tries to insert her own experiences. Upon leaving the ball, Emma seizes the viscount's lost cigar-case (which Charles had picked up) in order to sustain and preserve her memory of the event. Emma treats the cigar-case as if this thing could somehow objectify lost time—as if this object were uniquely endowed with the capacity to conserve time by giving it a physical form. As receptacle, this object seems to incarnate formally the very thing missing from her life: a temporal lost object, a representational container capable of incorporating time. After the scene at the ball until the end of part 1, the cigar-case functions as a kind of sacred relic that promises that the life she witnessed at the ball will be hers in an imaginary afterlife. But in the pages directly preceding her discovery that she will never again be invited to the ball, the cigar-case no longer functions as a reliable container for memories of an imaginary future. Bereft of an external temporal object that could contain time for her, Emma now attempts to incorporate time with her body, by counting it on her fingers. But we understand that this attempt has failed when Flaubert writes, in the middle of the passage of "lost days" quoted above, that "tout septembre s'écoula sans lettres ni visites." The verb "s'écoula" reiterates the notion everywhere present in the text of **Madame Bovary** that time is made of fluids (water, sweat, blood, saliva) that flow away drop by drop. Thus when the month of September "drips away," time dissolves and, like drops of rain, slips through Emma's fingers instead of being counted on them. After this line, time becomes irrevocably detached from both her experience and her body.

Emma's fall out of time is depicted as a fall from grace. When she is not invited to return to the ball, Emma's faith in the redemptive temporality of an event is shattered. And, as Flaubert rather rigorously demonstrates, to lose faith in time's capacity to contain an event is tantamount to losing faith in God, life, and the future. The future becomes lost, and the past is unattainable. From the moment (which is not a moment) when days lose their numerability, Emma's days are effectively numbered. At first she encounters her days as if they are traumatic "shocks" ("elle écoutait tous les bruits, se levait en sursaut, s'étonnait qu'il ne vînt pas") and then falls out of them before they are over: "puis, au coucher du soleil, toujours plus triste, désirait être au lendemain." By the end of the passage, the unit of time normally called "day" has become entirely meaningless. In this context, the Alcoholics Anonymous refrain "one day at a time" rings like a perverse inverted echo of Emma's malady and reminds us, once again, how addiction can be read through its temporal disorders. For the alcoholic, the phrase "one day at a time" functions in a dual fashion—it both reminds the addict that time *exists* and attempts to allow him or her a way of breaking time down into meaningful units. But unlike the alcoholic, not only is there no twelve-step program to address Emma's predicament, but the fluid substance that she abuses is not alcohol but time itself. Through the representations of time as well as the verbal time (tenses) of representation in the above passage, we can already read Emma's free-fall into the addictive temporality that leads inevitably to her death and dissolution.

Emma's exposure to the corrosive fluidity of time in the passage of "lost days" reminds us that Flaubert uses the rhythmic sound of water dripping "goutte par goutte" ("drop by drop") as the novel's temporal measure from the famous moment that melting snow first falls on Emma's umbrella during her early courtship with Charles:

> L'ombrelle, de soie gorge-de-pigeon, que traversait le soleil, éclairait de reflets mobiles la peau blanche de sa figure. Elle souriait là-dessous à la chaleur tiède; et on entendait les gouttes d'eau, une à une, tomber sur la moire tendue.
>
> [51]

> The parasol, made of an iridescent silk that let the sunlight sift through, colored the white skin of her face with shifting reflections. Beneath it, she smiled at the gentle warmth; and one heard the drops of water, one by one, fall on the taut silk.
>
> [13, trans. modified]

But by the time we reach the passage of lost days, Emma's body is no longer granted the symbolic protection implied by the presence of a parasol. From this point on, when water falls, drop by drop, it gradually eats away at Emma's capacity either to conserve time or to be protected from its erosion.[10] Although I do not have the time to develop this point here, I would like to point out that this liquefied time seeps into the very foundations of the novel. At every structural and metaphorical level, *Madame Bovary* relies heavily upon architectural figures. The novel's narrative is constructed on a foundation of literal or metaphorical edifices (from the bizarre "pièces montées" of Charles's hat and the infamous wedding cake to the elaborate structural blueprints that accompany most of the descriptions of houses, churches, statuettes, and factories) that become inundated by the increasingly corrosive presence of watery time.

But the beginning of Emma's ultimate dissolution can be traced in her inability to metabolize time through her body. In the verbal vertigos of the passage of lost days, we can already read the first unmistakable signs of what will later blossom into a full-blown addiction—an addiction that I am choosing to call "temporal bulimia." There is a direct correlation between Emma's anorectic refusal to eat and her numerous bulimic attempts to devour time. Unlike Charles, who consumes time as effectively as he eats dinner ("[il] s'en allait, ruminant son bonheur, comme ceux qui mâchent encore, après dîner, le goût des truffes qu'ils digèrent" [68] / "[he] . . . went on, re-chewing his happiness, like those who after dinner taste again the truffles which they are digesting" [24]), Emma rejects food and tries to eat time instead. At the moment when she is planning to run away with Rodolphe, for example, Flaubert writes: "elle vivait comme perdue dans la dégustation anticipée de son bonheur prochain" [222] ("she was living as if lost in the anticipated taste of her future happiness" [my trans.]). But Emma never manages to digest the taste of the "future happiness" that tantalizes her. She vacillates between failed attempts to preserve time, bitter attempts to consume it, and falls into despairing acts of abjecting it.

In the context of this discussion, one might even go so far as to say that Emma is as unable to digest her own death as she is to swallow her future happiness or to assimilate her experiences into the corpus of a "life."[11] As *Bovary*'s readers know well, Emma tries to kill herself by literally stuffing her face with poison: "[Elle] . . . saisit le bocal bleu, en arracha le bouchon, y fourra sa main, et, la retirant pleine d'une poudre blanche, elle se mit à manger à même" ("[She] . . . seized the blue jar, tore out the cork, plunged in her hand, and withdrawing it full of white powder, she ate it greedily" [229]). As several critics have observed, Emma's attempt to swallow her own death constitutes the final term in a long series of attempted auto-ingestions and self-incorporations [see Tanner; Richard; Ronell]. Philippe Bonnefis has pointed out that while the curious expression "elle se mit à manger à même" is almost grammatically meaningless, the words "à même" function as a homophonic reversal of Emma's name and thus indicate that in the act of eating the poison, she effectively eats her own name.[12] As such, Emma feeds herself with herself in a final attempt to provide herself with a body capable of containing and retaining her experience. It is not clear whether to read this ultimate auto-cannibalistic act as Emma's attempt to feed her death with her life or as an attempt to feed her life with her death. The terrible irony of the gesture is, of course, that both acts are indistinguishable and that they both fail. Emma's death is not more containable than her life was; the suicide scene (if it actually deserves the name) is flooded with vomit. Although Emma's agony consists of constant vomiting, she manages to retain just enough poison in order to live and not quite enough in order to die convincingly.

Let us recall that Emma's vomit continues to flow even after she is dead. Although Emma presumably "dies" at the end of part 3, chapter 8, the most infamous instance of her suicidal vomit occurs posthumously. In chapter 9, Emma's body spews streams of black liquid: "il fallut soulever un peu la tête, et alors un flot de liquides noirs sortit, comme un vomissement, de sa bouche" [349] ("They had to raise the head a little, and a rush of black liquid poured from her mouth, as if she were vomiting" [242]). This powerful and strange image raises several questions concerning the fate of Emma Bovary and the text in which she is written. In the first place, it would seem that Emma's body refuses to acknowledge the moment of her own death; paradoxically, her body vomits her death instead of "living" it. The temporal disjunction between the fact of her subjective death and her body's sustained mechanical expulsive activity only repeats in death the many prior instances of failed events Emma experiences in her life. Furthermore, the black liquid that oozes out of Emma's lifeless body seems to transform the death scene into a parodic inversion of a birth scene. But instead of the formless "afterbirth" that accompanies the birth of a child, Emma's posthumous peristalsis appears almost as a figure of a kind of "after-death." Here, if we recall Emma's attempts to give herself a life by confusing her own rebirth with her mother's death, we discover that Emma has no greater access to her own death than she had to her own life.

Although critics have interpreted the black liquid that flows from Emma's mouth as a figure for a writer's ink, the association between posthumous vomit and ink renders the figure even more difficult to read.[13] In other words, who is writing this scene and whose failure to live, die, or write is being expressed in it? If we follow the path indicated by feminist readings by Naomi Schor and Janet Beizer, we might conclude that Flaubert needs to abject his feminine identification with Emma by perversely transforming the formless, ineffectual vomit of her lifeless body into the formal ink of his style [see Schor; Beizer]. And although such a reading is both possible and plausible, I would like to suggest that in this monstrous moment, which couples a disgusting image of lifeless bodily expulsion with a distorted image of literary production, the corrosive liquid temporality of Emma Bovary's "life" seeps into Flaubert's narrative voice through his *style indirect libre.*

For in much the same way as Emma Bovary fails to transform her life or death into an event, the narrative voice of **Madame Bovary** displays the same strange temporal uncertainty about whether a life can be lived, whether a death constitutes an event, and whether the act of writing is an addictive response to a temporal disorder that manifests itself through failed mourning. Throughout the corpus of **Madame Bovary,** we find that the bodies that cannot digest time end up by being consumed by it. As we have seen, although Emma's life was eaten by the time she couldn't contain, her body suffers an even more horrifying fate. It vomits its own death, and corrodes the lives of the surviving characters. Emma's death leaks into Charles's life; he attempts to contain her death by ordaining that she be buried in three coffins; he attempts to mourn Emma by liquidating his remaining funds in order to adorn his own body with the clothes that might have pleased her. In short, as the narrative voice makes clear, "elle le corrompait par dela le tombeau" [360] ("She corrupted him from beyond the grave" [250]). But Charles's memory, in spite of his all-consuming efforts to commemorate Emma, is ultimately subjected to the corrosive force of involuntary forgetting: "une chose étrange, c'est que Bovary, tout en pensant à Emma continuellement, l'oubliait; et il se désespérait à sentir cette image lui échapper de la mémoire au milieu des efforts qu'il faisait pour la retenir" [363] ("A strange thing was happening to Bovary; while continually thinking of Emma, he was nevertheless forgetting her. He grew desperate as he felt this image fading from his memory in spite of all efforts to retain it" [252]). Thus Emma's posthumous existence produces in Charles the same strange combination of simultaneous preservation and erosion that permeated her living existence. Flaubert describes this uncanny temporal dysfunction in one of the most significant and signatory abject images in the entire novel. In part 2, chapter 1, Flaubert's narrative voice shifts abruptly to the present tense:

> Depuis les événements que l'on va raconter, rien, en effet, n'a changé à Yonville . . . les foetus du pharmacien, comme des paquets d'amadou blanc, se pourrissent de plus en plus dans leur alcool bourbeux, et, au-dessus de la grande porte de l'auberge, le vieux lion d'or, déteint pas les pluies, montre toujours aux passants sa frisure de caniche.

[108]

> Since the events about to be narrated, nothing in fact has changed at Yonville . . . the spongy white lumps, the pharmacist's foetuses, rot more and more in their cloudy alcohol, and above the big door of the inn the old golden lion, faded by rain, still shows passers-by its poodle mane.

[51-52]

This is one of the rare moments (perhaps unique) in **Madame Bovary** where Flaubert links a future tense ("que l'on va raconter") to a past tense ("n'a changé") through a present tense ("se pourrissent"). But the temporal perversity of this passage undermines the apparent normality of its verbal structure: all of these verb tenses depict actions that take place outside of time and that refer to the monstrous nonactivities of aborted nonsubjects. Paradoxically, the very action described is one of a stasis (preservation) that is nonetheless engaged in a nonending process of erosion and decomposition. Moreover, this description of the impact of time on the fetuses in the bottles encapsulates, in miniature, the temporal structure of Emma Bovary's "life." Emma's access to "life" is as stillborn and continuously eroded as that of the bottled babies. And, just as Homais's fetuses go on marinating in their bottles long after the events recounted in the text of **Madame Bovary** have occurred, Emma's body floats in that fluid, bitter, viscous narrative substance that has been aptly called Flaubert's *free indirect style.* But that name is far too proper, too antiseptic, for the phenomenon it purports to describe. One must not forget that when Flaubert describes Homais's fetuses in their bizarre state of suspended petrification and erosion, he addresses us—his readers—directly in the narrative voice of our own time. In the strange reflexive present of the verb "se pourrissent," Flaubert announces a temporal structure of addiction that exceeds the confines of the literature of the nineteenth century and seeps into the experience of modern life. Like Emma Bovary, and Homais's fetuses, addicted culture is fermented by a corrosive past that is strangely preserved without being remembered. Whether or not Flaubert ever actually said, "Madame Bovary, c'est moi," we should recall that from the novel's enigmatic first word, "nous," it is certain that Flaubert was always already writing to and about us.

Notes

1. The problem of drugs and addiction in *Madame Bovary* was first raised by Avital Ronell in *Crack Wars.* My analysis supports most of her conclusions, but is more focused on the relationship between time and addiction.

2. Riffaterre's actual argument is far more complicated. He shows that the act of reading functions

as a metaphorical hinge between Romantic definitions of women and the overdetermined presuppositions of the word "adultery." He writes:

> Nothing could be clearer: one word's ultimate presupposition, its etymology, entails the whole fictional text. . . . The adulteress either commits suicide or sinks into prostitution. As for the first metaphorical step, I might call it fictional without any play on words, since the errant wife is stepping out of bounds when she secretly indulges in the reading of scandalous novels and in a daydreaming identification with the women who slink about the never-neverland of wish-fulfillment.

[182-83]

3. The implications of this claim would be that Emma is Flaubert's mirror image—where he understands that Life should be put in the service of Art, she, by contrast, is unable to convert her life into Art. It is interesting to observe that in this context, feminist critics such as Naomi Schor and Janet Beizer establish a dichotomy between Flaubert and Emma Bovary similar to that espoused by more traditional critics like Victor Brombert. Of course, the feminist critics diverge with traditional readings about the *cause* of the inverted identification between Emma and Flaubert. I am deeply indebted to both Naomi Schor's "For a Restricted Thematics: Writing, Speech and Difference in *Madame Bovary*" and Janet Beizer's chapters on Flaubert and Louise Colet in her recent book *Ventriloquized Bodies: Narratives of Hysteria in Nineteenth-Century France*. Beizer offers a brilliant and persuasive account of how Flaubert hystericizes Emma Bovary in an attempt to purge himself and his text of femininity.

4. I am planning to show that love becomes the privileged figure of temporal erosion in *Madame Bovary* in a forthcoming book chapter entitled "Eros, Erosion: Sentimental Liquidations in *Madame Bovary*." Both Jean-Pierre Richard and Tony Tanner pursue the implications of liquidating love.

5. See Jean Rousset, "*Madame Bovary*." More recently, Peter Brooks discusses how Emma Bovary's body is systematically inserted into a visual field in "The Body in the Field of Vision."

6. Here I diverge from Jonathan Culler's oft-cited remark in *Flaubert: The Uses of Uncertainty*: "If there is anything that justifies our finding the novel limited and tendentious it is the seriousness with which Emma's corruption is attributed to novels and romances" [146].

7. Emma does evoke her dead mother fleetingly twice: while courting Charles [56] and in the early days of her affair with Rodolphe [198].

8. Curiously, the absence of this figure has rarely been addressed in the critical literature. One no-table exception is Dominick LaCapra's suggestive remarks in *Madame Bovary on Trial*. LaCapra observes that "[e]qually significant for the rupture of the generational cycle is the fact that Emma's mother is dead as the story opens, and she does not seem to play a significant part in Emma's life" [181]. It is surprising to note in this context that although Avital Ronell brilliantly identifies the presence of a "toxic maternal" in *Madame Bovary,* she focuses more on Emma's toxic effect on her daughter rather than on the toxic effect of her own mother's absence [see *Crack Wars*]. Likewise, Janet Beizer stresses the importance of the repression of motherhood in the novel from the perspective of Emma as mother rather than as daughter. I think LaCapra is correct in seeing the mother's death as a temporal, generational rupture. As he puts it, "[e]conomically as well as socially, Emma has no productive or reproductive function" [181].

9. I am fascinated by the fact that there are several glaring mistranslations in this particular passage in Paul de Man's otherwise remarkable translation of *Madame Bovary*. For example, he translates "l'ennui" as "shock" and "innombrables" as "immovable." These "mistranslations" seem to be the result of an interpretative move rather than simple "errors." More precisely, it seems plausible that if de Man were reading Flaubert through Walter Benjamin's writings on Baudelaire, he might have been compelled to stress the paralytic, traumatic nature of time in his translation. Of course, it could also have been a simple mistake.

10. For extremely useful discussions of the importance of fluids in *Madame Bovary* see Jean-Pierre Richard and Janet Beizer. I particularly admire Beizer's conclusion to her chapter "Writing with a Vengeance": "He chose his poison: it was water. Playing with madness like Mithridates with poison, he volatized the water, the emotional effusion, the rush of ink, the romantic flow. Poisoning himself gently in measured doses, he turned liquid to vapor and cured his style; he vaporized hysteria and hysterized the text" [166].

11. As Jean-Pierre Richard puts it: ". . . c'est l'un des aspects de la maladie bovaryste que ce manque fondamental de *retenue*. . . . Emma se jette goulûment sur toutes les proies: en voulant tout immédiatement consommer, elle ne peut rien retenir. Tout l'abandonne, et ses expériences l'appauvrissent au lieu de l'enrichir" [142] ("This fundamental lack of *reserve* is one of the traits of the Bovary illness. . . . Emma pounces greedily on her prey: but by wanting to consume everything immediately, she can retain nothing. Every-

thing abandons her, and her experiences impoverish her instead of enriching her" [my trans.]).

12. Philippe Bonnefis made this observation in a conversation with me.

13. See, for example, Nathaniel Wing, who writes: "Throughout the novel desire, narrative and writing in general produce corrosive effects. These are figured most directly and powerfully, perhaps, during Emma's agony, with the likening of the taste of poison to the taste of ink, and later in the same sequence when the narrator describes a certain black fluid oozing from Emma's mouth" [133].

Works Cited

Baudelaire, Charles. "L'horloge." *Les fleurs du mal. Oeuvres complètes.* Ed. Claude Pichois. Paris: Gallimard, 1975. 1: 81.

Beizer, Janet. *Ventriloquized Bodies: Narratives of Hysteria in Nineteenth-Century France.* Ithaca: Cornell UP, 1994.

Brombert, Victor. "Flaubert and the Status of the Subject." *Flaubert and Postmodernism.* Ed. Naomi Schor and Henry Majewski. Omaha: U of Nebraska P, 1984. 100-15.

Brooks, Peter. "The Body in the Field of Vision." *Body Work: Objects of Desire in Modern Narrative.* Cambridge: Harvard UP, 1993. 88-122.

Caruth, Cathy. Introduction. *Trauma: Explorations in Memory.* Baltimore: Johns Hopkins UP, 1995. 3-12.

Culler, Jonathan. *Flaubert: The Uses of Uncertainty.* Ithaca: Cornell UP, 1974.

Flaubert, Gustave. *Madame Bovary.* Ed. Jacques Suffel. Paris: Garnier-Flammarion, 1979. Trans. of *Madame Bovary.* Trans. and ed. Paul de Man. New York: Norton, 1965.

LaCapra, Dominick. *Madame Bovary on Trial.* Ithaca: Cornell UP, 1982.

Phillips, Adam. *On Flirtation: Essays on the Uncommitted Life.* Cambridge: Harvard UP, 1994.

Richard, Jean-Pierre. *Littérature et sensation: Stendhal, Flaubert.* Paris: Seuil, 1954. 135-252.

Riffaterre, Michael. "Flaubert's Presuppositions." *Flaubert and Postmodernism.* Ed. Naomi Schor and Henry Majewski. Omaha: U of Nebraska P, 1984. 177-91.

Rousset, Jean. "Madame Bovary ou le livre sur rien." *Forme et signification: Essais sur les structures littéraires de Corneille à Claudel.* Paris: José Corti, 1984. 109-33.

Ronell, Avital. *Crack Wars: Literature, Addiction, Mania.* Lincoln: U of Nebraska P, 1992.

Schor, Naomi. "For a Restricted Thematics: Writing, Speech and Difference in *Madame Bovary.*" *Breaking the Chain: Women, Theory, and French Realist Fiction.* New York: Columbia UP, 1985. 3-28.

Tanner, Tony. *Adultery in the Novel: Contract and Transgression.* Baltimore: Johns Hopkins UP, 1979.

Wing, Nathaniel. "Emma's Stories: Narrative, Repetition and Desire in *Madame Bovary.*" *Emma Bovary.* Ed. Harold Bloom. New York: Chelsea House, 1994. 133-64.

Roy Chandler Caldwell, Jr. (essay date January 2000)

SOURCE: Caldwell, Roy Chandler, Jr. "Madame Bovary's Last Laugh." *French Forum* 25, no. 1 (January 2000): 55-74.

[*In the following essay, Caldwell analyzes the thematic relationship between laughter and death in the novel.*]

> Mieux est de ris que de larmes escrire Par ce que rire est le propre de l'homme.
>
> Rabelais

> Death is inseparable from laughter.
>
> Bakhtin

The sequence of events [in *Madame Bovary*] leading to Madame Bovary's death begins with a night of pleasure. At a masked ball in Rouen Emma "sauta toute la nuit, au son furieux des trombones."[1] The next day she returns home to discover Lheureux's treachery. Her house will be seized; she must have money. The furious trombones seem to accompany her accelerating course as she races from man to man—from Léon to Maître Guillaumin to Binet to Rodolphe—in an attempt to raise money: all in vain. Finally, she sees a way out in the arsenic of Homais's pharmacy. Home now, she enjoys at last a moment of calm, and falls victim to what will not be the last of the series of illusions that has been her life: "Ah! c'est bien peu de chose, la mort! pensait-elle; je vais dormir et tout sera fini!" (391). Soon the frightful anguish begins: the violent wracking of Emma's body, accompanied by Charles's sobs and lamentations. Doctors arrive, but Emma is beyond hope. The priest Bournisien offers the solace of religion. Emma, "saisie de joie, avec des visions de béatitude éternelle" (399), stretches her neck, fastens her lips to the crucifix, and plants there "le plus grand baiser d'amour qu'elle eût jamais donné" (399).

After a less than exemplary life, Emma now appears to be dying correctly; anointed, absolved, wept over, attended by husband, doctor, priest, politician, she appears at last submissive, ready to play her role in the deathbed script written for her by men. Not quite yet, for the other Emma now returns; she asks for her mirror, contemplates her dying face, sheds tears, sighs, then falls back on the pillow. After the lull induced by crucifix and mirror, the tempo quickens as Emma hurtles toward death. Flaubert the good doctor's son now spares us none of the grisly clinical detail: the breast heaves; the tongue lolls out of the mouth; the eyes roll and darken. Crescendo with accelerando: as the death rattle mounts, the priest rushes his prayers to the accompaniment of Bovary's stifled sobs. All is building to its proper ritual end.

Suddenly the spell is broken. Outside the room another player makes an unexpected entrance. The deathbed scene hangs suspended as the principals hear heavy boots on the sidewalk, the rattle of a stick, then a rough voice breaking into song:

> Souvent la chaleur d'un beau jour
> Fait rêver fillette à l'amour

Emma jerks up in bed, like, Flaubert tells us in a curious metaphor which has anticipated her death and then revived her, "un cadavre que l'on galvanise." We never know if she has recognized already her nemesis from the Rouen road by his boots, his stick, or the first two verses of this song she knows well and will soon know better. At any rate, she listens longer before identifying him:

> Pour amasser diligemment
> Les épis que la faux moissonne,
> Ma Nannette va s'inclinant
> Vers le sillon qui les donne.

"L'aveugle!" she cries. And now something extraordinary happens. Emma begins to laugh. "Et Emma se mit à rire, d'un rire atroce, frénétique, désespéré, croyant voir la face hideuse du misérable, qui se dressait dans les ténèbres éternelles comme un épouvantement." This deathbed scene has come undone. The principal player has shamefully forgotten her role. The wild laughter continues as the blind beggar concludes his song:

> Il souffla bien fort ce jour-là,
> Et le jupon court s'enleva!

The convulsion of laughter becomes, or was, the convulsion of death. She falls back on her bed, and when the others approach, Emma exists no longer (400-01).

Debts, lovers, poison, extreme unction, the mirror, the blind beggar and his song: the elements of this sequence have been amply discussed by criticism. The final scene has been generally read as the final assault by Flaubert's brutal irony on Emma's illusions—in this case, her last-minute religious conversion. The blind man has re-

ceived especial attention. This poor wretch, whose rotting face is an emblem of the realist impulses within the novel, has dogged the young woman's steps through her last adultery; his song offers a symbolic commentary on her life.[2]

The final act in the drama, however, has been curiously neglected by criticism. Emma dies laughing, in the literal sense of the term. When critics have addressed this laughter, they have given it but cursory treatment. Michael Riffaterre calls it a bitter laugh that comes from a sudden knowledge of her fall. Stephen Heath sees it expressing "the atrocious farce of existence." Similarly, Victor Brombert calls it a "sinister laugh," which "does not bespeak the peace of a soul about to be released from human bondage," a laugh which, Brombert continues, "sounds much rather like a Satanic expression of scorn in the face of life's ultimate absurdity, death."[3]

In my reading of the novel I had always taken more or less this position: Emma's last laugh was mad, bitter, nihilistic. And yet something in this reading did not fully suffice; something in that laugh spilled over my interpretation of it and kept on haunting me. Over the years I have accumulated other laughs where I detected an echo of Emma's: the jest of a condemned man who slips mounting a scaffold, the laughter of Jelly Roll Morton's *Hyena Stomp,* the three-minute laugh from a record entitled *How to Belly Dance for Your Husband* in Godard's *La Femme mariée,* the joke-before-dying of the *Phantom of the Opera,* all Nana's laughing through Zola's novel, Casanova's and Diderot's *Neveu*'s laughter, the laughter Clamance hears crossing bridges in Paris, the creole laughter of resistance in Raphaël Confiant, even the laughter of the gods in Homer.

How are we to interpret this dying laugh, Emma's last conscious act? Flaubert's text calls it "un rire atroce, frénétique, désespéré," to be sure, but these qualifications do not exhaust its meaning. Two codes clash here: the gestures of despair/the forms of laughter. Emma might have died otherwise desperately than with a laugh; she might have wailed, wept, cried, cursed, shrieked. Her desperate laugh remains a laugh nonetheless, and thus belongs to the semantic field comprised of other forms of laughter, within the novel and without. I propose here an interrogation of Madame Bovary's last laugh. I plan to read several theories of laughter, and to examine the laughter elsewhere in *Madame Bovary.* I want to know what Emma finds suddenly so humorous as she dies, what she is laughing at, and who, if anyone, is laughing with her.

* * *

Trailing this elusive laughter brought me first to Henri Bergson's well-known study *Le Rire: essai sur la signification du comique.* Here Bergson defines the comic as the mechanical stamped on the human, rigidity in conflict with life itself: "Les attitudes, gestes et mouvements du corps humain sont risibles dans l'exacte mesure où ce corps nous fait penser à une simple mécanique."[4] While this conception of laughter may describe the novel's opening laugh—that of the schoolboys as they watch Charbovari's comic pantomime of stand-up, sit-down, drop-the-cap, it hardly seems apt to explain Emma's dying laughter. It is she laughing not we readers, and where could she see the mechanical except in her own "galvanized" jerking upright? Certainly her vision of the beggar's hideous face would represent not the mechanical but rather the human, all-too-human. Further aspects of Bergson's notion of laughter likewise appear too narrow to encompass Emma's laugh. For him, laughter is always a social phenomenon: "On ne goûterait pas le comique si on se sentait isolé. Il semble que le rire ait besoin d'un écho. . . . Notre rire est toujours le rire d'un groupe" (4-5). But Emma's laugh has no echo except her own fatal convulsion; she laughs all alone. For Bergson, laughter inevitably contains malice, "un petit fond de méchanceté"; in it "la nature a utilisé le mal en vue du bien" (151, 152). Laughter is thus a social corrective: "Est comique le personnage qui suit automatiquement son chemin sans se soucier de prendre contact avec les autres. Le rire est là pour corriger sa distraction et pour le tirer de son rêve" (102). And: "[Le rire] a pour fonction d'intimider en humiliant" (152). But Emma's laugh could not be intimidating or humiliating, nor does it function as a social corrective. This laugh seems directed at no one; for, at the threshold of death, Emma finds herself at last positioned altogether outside society, free of its constraints.

In his historical overview of laughter, Mikhail Bakhtin observes that in the seventeenth and eighteenth centuries laughter lost its universal character, and became "a light amusement or a form of salutary social punishment of corrupt and low persons."[5] Voltaire reads Rabelais as "naked and straight satire"; for Enlightenment thought anchored in reason, Bakhtin writes, "the gay, century-old laughter becomes something despicable" (117). The decline of laughter continued into the grave nineteenth century when the "strict and scientific" seriousness (present since the Renaissance) became an ever more important element in established belief systems (123). Laughter becomes nasty, suspect—and not only in *Le Rire*. Another nineteenth-century writer echoes Bergson's condemnatory tone in his discussion of laughter. In *De l'essence du rire*, first published in 1855, Baudelaire begins his discussion of laughter with a characteristically splenetic description:

> Le rire vient de l'idée de sa propre supériorité. . . .
> Remarquez que le rire est une des expressions les plus
> fréquentes de la folie. . . . J'ai dit qu'il y avait
> symptôme de faiblesse dans le rire; et, en effet, quel

signe plus marquant de débilité qu'une convulsion nerveuse, un spasme involontaire comparable à l'éternuement, et causé par la vue du malheur d'autrui?[6]

Baudelaire begins by defining laughter as a form of mockery, as Bergson would do afterwards: laughter arises from a feeling of superiority. But Baudelaire departs from the ratiocentric notions inherited from the preceding century and develops a theory broader than Bergson's would be. Baudelaire distinguishes two antithetical strains of laughter: first, the *comique significatif,* a social, mocking comic which closely resembles Bergsonian laughter; the second, the *grotesque,* or *comique absolu,* expresses not the laugher's feeling of superiority over other people in a social context, but the idea of superiority over nature. Baudelaire privileges this second sort of laughter: "Le rire causé par le grotesque a en soi quelque chose de profond, d'axiomatique et de primitif qui se rapproche beaucoup plus de la vie innocente et de la joie absolue que le rire causé par le comique de mœurs" (375). Baudelaire concludes that in France, "pays de pensée et de démonstration claires, où l'art vise naturellement et directement l'utilité," the comic tends to be *significatif* rather than *absolu*; the French are lacking "la prodigieuse bonne humeur poétique" necessary for the grotesque, he claims (375).

Emma's sudden explosion of laughter would be just the sort of confirmation of the *comique absolu* Baudelaire stipulates ("Il n'y a qu'une vérification du grotesque, c'est le rire, et le rire subit" [375]). Emma's last laugh is *subit* and has certainly been called grotesque, but no one, to my knowledge, has linked it with "la vie innocente" or "une joie absolue." Indeed, the term *grotesque* is almost a commonplace in criticism of the deathbed scene. Already the figure of the blind beggar prompts such an interpretation. His first appearance on the road to Rouen strongly images the terror and repulsiveness associated with the grotesque:

> Il y avait dans la côte un pauvre diable vagabondant
> avec son bâton, tout au milieu des diligences. Un amas
> de guenilles lui recouvrait les épaules, et un vieux castor
> défoncé, s'arrondissant en cuvette, lui cachait la figure; mais, quand il le retirait, il découvrait, à la place
> des paupières, deux orbites béantes tout ensanglantées.
> La chair s'effiloquait par lambeaux rouges; et il en coulait des liquides qui se figeaient en gales vertes jusqu'au
> nez, dont les narines noires reniflaient convulsivement.
> Pour vous parler, il se renversait la tête avec un rire
> idiot; alors ses prunelles bleuâtres, roulant d'un mouvement continu, allaient se cogner vers les tempes, sur le
> bord de la plaie vive.

> (340)

Another of Flaubert's celebrated composite descriptions, this passage may be, as Tanner suggests of Charles's *casquette, "lisible* but not *visible."*[7] The lurid colors of the decaying flesh would represent the grotesque as elaborated by Hugo in the "Préface" to *Crom-*

well: in the vicinity of the ugly (as Aristotle had situated it),[8] at the opposite pole of the sublime; the deformed, the ridiculously distorted, the monstrously horrible, pointing to an inhuman, nocturnal, and abysmal realm.[9] But there is a further play in Flaubert's description which suggests another dimension of the grotesque. The open wounds, the blackness of the nostrils, the gaping eye sockets—all these details obscenely reveal the insides of the body.[10] I should say too that the *aveugle*'s description prefigures the deathbed scene through several motifs: both eyes are rolling; the convulsive movements of the beggar's black nostrils announce Emma's final convulsion; and the *rire idiot* closes this passage as the *rire frénétique* closes her life.

Two conflicting notions of the grotesque clash in the deathbed scene, and lead toward different interpretations of Emma's final laugh. For Wolfgang Kayser the grotesque is "a play with the absurd," or the suddenly "estranged world."[11] The grotesque undercuts the categories we apply to our world view, Kayser claims; it "consists in an unimpassioned view of life on earth as an empty, meaningless puppet play or a caricatural marionette play" (186). For the deathbed scene this notion of the grotesque would produce an interpretation aligned with those of Riffaterre, Heath, and Brombert I cited above. The beggar's song brings the deathbed ritual crashing down, by provoking in Emma a final, cynical recognition that behind the elaborate illusion dubbed life rests the abyss she sees imaged in the beggar's empty sockets. But this interpretation does not exhaust the meaning of the scene. For the rotting flesh of the blind man's eyes open another realm of possibilities, I believe. The strongly imaged putrefaction announces the hideousness of the physical changes which will, after several days, spill black liquid from the corpse's mouth. The erasure of the limits between Emma's body and the world begins already.

The focus on Emma's body, the physical changes it undergoes before and after her death, leads to the second theory of the grotesque, a theory developed by Bakhtin in his book on Rabelais. Readers are doubtless surprised to see Bakhtin invoked here, for the affirmation of the corporeal which permeates all the Russian's thought seems at odds with the spirit of Flaubert, who everywhere says no to nature. A reading, perhaps perverse, of *Madame Bovary* through Bakhtin's theory is authorized, I believe, by the coincidence within the deathbed scene of the two elements which form the axes of Bakhtin's theory: the grotesque and laughter. Indeed, Charles Bernheimer has already suggested the pertinence of Bakhtin for reading Flaubert: "Flaubert's project may be viewed as an attempt to preserve the comic dynamics of what Mikhail Bakhtin has called carnivalized literature while emptying carnival of its

life-affirming dimension."[12] Keeping Bernheimer's qualification in mind, I would like to examine Bakhtin to find what his theory may yield for Emma's last laugh.

Unlike Kayser, Bakhtin situates the grotesque squarely in the realm of the corporeal. The three main acts of the "grotesque body," he writes, are "sexual intercourse, death throes (in their comic presentation—hanging tongue, expressionless, popping eyes, suffocation, death rattle) and the act of birth" (353). In *Madame Bovary,* of course, we never see Emma engaged in sexual intercourse; Flaubert has arranged a set of artful dodges to cover the transgressive act.[13] Nor is the scene of childbirth rendered in any physical detail (although its cruel timing, I would argue, does produce a decidedly comic effect). The deathbed scene indeed contains all the "comic" realist elements listed by Bakhtin, but none provokes laughter. The essential principle of grotesque realism, Bakhtin writes, is degradation, that is, "the lowering of all that is high, spiritual, abstract; it is a transfer to the material level, to the sphere of earth and body in their indissoluble unity" (119-20). The transfer of Emma's body to the material level occurs only in the novel's final scene. Before this moment the young woman's body rarely appears. Tanner remarks that what we see of her is not her body but the series of elaborate costumes she wears (269). For Peter Brooks, too, Emma's body is absent in the text. "Emma as an object of the gaze and of desire is repeatedly 'metonymized,' fragmented into a set of accessory details rather than achieving coherence as either object or subject," he writes. In other realist novelists (Dickens, Balzac) description functions as synecdoche: "details are always legible as signs of the whole."[14] Not in Flaubert, Brooks contends, where no whole ever forms: "Flaubert tends to suggest that there is no essence, no coherent substance, no real object of desire, behind or beyond the phenomenal surface. . . . Emma has no body—of her own. Her body is the social and phantasmatic construction of the men who look at her," he concludes.[15] At her death her body does appear at last, but her final degradation would not represent the affirmation of "the reproductive lower stratum," the level of the "fruitful earth and the womb," Bakhtin celebrates (21). In this Flaubert belongs to his age. In the nineteenth century, Bakhtin observes, "the ever unfinished nature of the body was hidden, kept secret: conception, pregnancy, childbirth, death throes, were almost never shown. . . . The accent was placed on the completed self-sufficient individuality of the given body" (29). Philippe Perrot's remarks on the general direction of nineteenth-century re-fashioning of the female body are also pertinent here:

> Travail incessant de la culture sur la nature, action continue du corps idéal sur le corps réel, confrontation canonique poussant aux déformations les plus violentes (comme les constrictions du corset) ou aux réformations les plus insidieuses (comme l'ascèse du régime alimentaire): il s'agit toujours d'arracher à l'humaine

apparence sa trop humaine apparence, de la socialiser en la dénaturant, de la sublimer en la cultivant, de la pétrir afin d'en détourner le seul destin biologique, d'en faire, aussi, un instrument symbolique.[16]

Indeed, in spite of his opposition to his time and his class, Flaubert seems fully engaged in this project. Emma's body must be separated from the rest of the world. An individuated bourgeois body, "a closed, completed unit," it never becomes the collective grotesque body transgressing its own limits and symbolizing growth and renewal (Bakhtin 26).

If Bakhtin's theory of the grotesque has limited value for a reading of Emma's deathbed scene, his theory of laughter will prove more productive. Bakhtin develops his notion of laughter within an historical framework. The phenomenon of laughter, he demonstrates, has possessed and been assigned different meanings at different cultural moments. A major reinterpretation of laughter's role in human affairs occurred during the seventeenth century: laughter became only mockery—that is, a demonstration of superiority, a form of social corrective—just the type of laughter Bergson theorized in *Le Rire*.[17] Before this, in the Middle Ages and again, in modified form, during the Renaissance, laughter still possessed "a relatively whole character," and was "related to the entire living process." In it could be heard the celebration of the grotesque body, "the triumphal tones of birth and renewal" (64). This was the laughter of popular festivals, especially of carnival. Bakhtin describes carnival laughter thus:

> First of all, it is a festive laughter. Therefore, it is not an individual reaction to some isolated "comic" event. Carnival laughter is the laughter of all the people. Second, it is universal in scope; it is directed at all and everyone, including the carnival's participants. The entire world is seen in its droll aspect, in its gay relativity. Third, this laughter is ambivalent: it is gay, triumphant, and at the same time mocking, deriding. It asserts and denies, it buries and revives.
>
> (11-12)

Carnival laughter has an important ideological dimension, as well. Bakhtin cites Alexander Herzen: "laughter contains something revolutionary. . . . Voltaire's laughter was more destructive than Rousseau's weeping" (92). Unlike official festivals of church and state, carnival effected and celebrated "temporary liberation from the prevailing truth and from the established order; it marked the suspension of all hierarchical rank, privileges, norms, and prohibitions" (10). Official thought of the Middle Ages (like that of the nineteenth century) admitted truth only through the serious, and denied laughter any philosophical value. But carnival laughter, Bakhtin claims, effectively constructed a counterworld complete with its own truths; in affirming the human and the material against the abstract law of order, it became an instrument of resistance:

> It was the victory of laughter over fear that most impressed medieval man. It was not only a victory over mystic terror of God, but also a victory over the awe inspired by the forces of nature, and most of all over the oppressions and guilt related to all that was consecrated and forbidden. . . . It was the defeat of authoritarian commandments and prohibitions, of death and punishment after death, hell and all that is more terrifying than the earth itself. Through this victory laughter clarified man's consciousness and gave him a new outlook on life. This truth was ephemeral; it was followed by the fears and oppressions of everyday life, but from these brief moments another unofficial truth emerged, a truth about the world and man which prepared the new Renaissance consciousness.
>
> (90-91)

For this revolutionary new consciousness (exemplified by Rabelais), laughter had a deep philosophical value; it permitted access to certain truths, certain aspects of the world that serious perspectives could not reach.[18]

In Emma's dying laugh I admit hearing echoes of the liberatory, anti-dogmatic, resistant, philosophical laughter of Bakhtin. Her laugh expresses a recognition, the passage from ignorance to knowledge, a sudden understanding of something which had been previously hidden. As Wilda Anderson writes in her book on *Le Neveu de Rameau*: "Laughter occurs at the exact moment when what had previously been experienced as dissonant is suddenly transformed into a new harmonic relationship. . . . Laughter is the physical expression of the pleasure felt; it is the psychological manifestation of a gestalt switch, and thus a passionate form of knowledge."[19] Emma dies laughing in a spasm of pleasure precipitated by the unexpected knowledge she has acquired in dying. If her story represents a form of tragedy, as some critics have suggested, would it not be precisely in these terms: at the moment of dying she recognizes truth, but too late?[20]

* * *

Before discussing in greater depth just what truth Emma recognizes as she dies, I should like to shift my approach from theory to text. Although Emma's dying laugh is indeed the last laugh within *Madame Bovary,* it is by no means the only one. From its opening scene in the schoolroom the text assembles a series of laughs, which receive different meanings from the contexts in which they occur. Across these differences, however, one may make a general assessment of how laughter is used in *Madame Bovary,* where it appears, and what it means. To know fully Emma's final laugh, one must know better all the adjacent laughter of which it partakes.

I have already commented that the schoolboy laughter at Charles Bovary coincides with Bergson's conception of laughter as a form of social corrective, and as the mechanical imposed on the human. The famous first-person plural voice employed during this scene functions, as Lilian Furst points out, to forge an identification between us readers and the schoolboys.[21] Their laughter becomes our laughter. As he must write, Charles *is* ridiculous, and he remains so as long as we do not begin to pity him.[22] Charles's ridiculousness will continue to elicit the laughter of mockery through the novel. At medical school the students laugh at his accents and his clothes (93); Canivet laughs in scorn when he sees the results of Charles's surgery to correct Hippolyte's clubfoot (249). Charles recognizes his own ridiculousness and fears the laughter of others. In a strangely ironic and premonitory passage he imagines the scope of his future notoriety: "on allait rire, au contraire, clabauder! Cela se répandrait jusqu'à Forges! jusqu'à Neufchâtel! jusqu'à Rouen! partout!" (252). Now our laughter has become multiple: at Charles's exaggerated sense of his own importance (as if Rouen cares about this insignificant country doctor); at the small scope of his world (Rouen seems to be his horizon); but also, metaleptically, at the justness of his remarks (they are laughing at him everywhere). Everyone around him is laughing, except, sadly, his wife. In the passage where Emma articulates her dissatisfaction with marriage, absence of mirth figures prominently: "La conversation de Charles était plate comme un trottoir de rue, et les idées de tout le monde y défilaient, dans leur costume ordinaire, sans exciter d'émotion, de rire ou de rêverie" (101).

Who laughs in *Madame Bovary*? Emma laughs almost from the first moment we see her, and she laughs with her lovers—I will discuss this presently. But there is much other laughter. Emma hears Berthe laughing (240), a laughter associated with innocence and domestic bliss, rare in the novel. Félicité laughs at Justin's naivete (256). The laughter of Bournisien, the priest with grease stains on his cassock, is "épais" (178), and "opaque" (286)—degenerate descendant of Bakhtinian grotesque laughter. The innkeeper Madame Lefrançois laughs till she cries when she hears the "farces" her customers recount (140); here, too, one may find vestiges of the laughter, popular and festive, Bakhtin finds in Rabelais. Emma's father laughs "doucement" when he speaks with Charles (84). But Homais does not laugh, nor does Charles's mother. And Binet, mirror of his age, sits silently "comme une alose, sans dire un mot" even when all around him are laughing (140). Charles, who incites laughter, laughs himself only once in the novel. Sitting with Rouault after the death of his first wife, "Charles se surprit à rire; mais le souvenir de sa femme, lui revenant tout à coup, l'assombrit" (80). We know that Charles's affection for his first wife was not particularly deep. His arrested laughter can only signify that he has forgotten then suddenly recalled that

his social role demands he present the appearance of the grieving widower: another of the *idées reçues* which govern all his life.

This episode exposes one of the principal thematic functions of laughter in *Madame Bovary*. Again and again, laughter signifies the pleasurable recognition of a momentary breach in social decorum. Emma laughs when she takes her scandalous walks in the company of Léon (160), laughs at the *Commices agricoles* when Rodolphe abruptly dismisses the bothersome Homais (202), and again when Madame Bovary *mère* reproaches her for allowing Félicité to receive gentlemen callers at the Bovarys' backdoor (260). Emma takes pleasure from being scandalous. From her first appearance in the novel her laughter reveals her propensity to risk violating social convention. At her father's farmhouse Emma laughs when she offers to drink with Charles, and again, in a description with a high erotic charge, as she drinks: "la tête en arrière, les lèvres avancées, le cou tendu, elle riait de ne rien sentir, tandis que le bout de sa langue, passant entre ses dents fines, léchait à petits coups le fond du verre" (81). This is no Bergsonian laughter, no laughter which represses eccentricity, which serves as social corrective by inspiring fear in the object of ridicule (Bergson 15). This laughter dismisses society. Emma laughs when she senses herself suddenly outside the small world which holds her imprisoned. Furthermore, she associates laughter with life elsewhere. On the road from La Vaubyssard, cigar-smoking *cavaliers* laugh as they pass the Bovary's plodding cart (115). One of them surely drops the green cigar-case which will set her dreaming of Parisian life. "Dans les cabinets de restaurants où l'on soupe après minuit riait, à la clarté des bougies, la foule bigarrée des gens de lettres et des actrices" (119). In this vision converge themes of social marginalization, of literature (*gens de lettres*), of free eroticism (*actrices*), with a *bande sonore* in which one again hears the echoes of Bakhtinian/Rabelaisian festive laughter. Léon's own dreams of escape and the Parisian *demimonde* contain a similar laughter: "Paris alors agita pour lui, dans le lointain, la fanfare des bals masqués avec le rire de ses grisettes" (183). Laughter celebrates the flaunting of taboos; it acknowledges transgression.

This laughter receives its full charge in *Madame Bovary* when it coalesces with eroticism. Already in her first, repressed, passion for Léon, laughter represented the space of the couple's intimacy (171), but not until she meets the perpetually laughing Rodolphe does the association of eroticism and transgression become fully realized.[23] Although his first seduction of her requires solemnity, soon laughter accompanies their erotic activity. When she visits him mornings at his house, "Rodolphe, en riant, l'attirait à lui et il la pressait sur son cœur" (231). Later, this laughter will be transformed. When she presses him ("Nous irons vivre ailleurs"), he gives her the slip with a laugh: "Tu es folle, vraiment! dit-il en riant. Est-ce possible?" (255). Shortly afterward he laughs away the claims of love once again: "Crois-tu m'avoir pris vierge? exclamait-il en riant" (259). Laughter has knotted the erotic bond; now it unknots. Laughter seems to represent the breaking of routine; it precipitates, or announces change; it emboldens one to believe change may occur.

This erotic, liberatory, transgressive laughter is heard throughout Emma's adultery with Léon. On the eve of her ride in the *fiacre* Léon kisses her neck, and she reacts with "de petits rires sonores" (310); in *sonores* we hear all her pleasure. Soon, during their regular trysts in the hotel room with the ship-shaped bed, after the initial words and caresses, "ils se regardaient face à face, avec des rires de volupté et des appellations de tendresse" (337). And, in an image linking themes of eroticism, festivity, transgression, excess, exuberant joy, "elle riait d'un rire sonore et libertin quand la mousse du vin de Champagne débordait du verre léger sur les bagues de ses doigts" (337-38). But as the dénouement approaches, laughter changes key. When Charles's mother demands the return of the *procuration,* Emma's laugh prefigures the desperation and frenzy of her dying laugh: "Emma se mit à rire d'un rire strident, éclatant, continu: elle avait une attaque de nerfs" (348). When Charles, the good husband, intervenes, opposing his mother, Emma returns to Rouen, where she laughs with her lover at having escaped, at having won: "Quel débordement, le jeudi d'après, à l'hôtel, dans leur chambre, avec Léon! Elle rit, pleura, chanta, dansa, fit monter des sorbets, voulut fumer des cigarettes, lui parut extravagante, mais adorable, superbe" (349). Already here we see the gathering patterns of fate and the psychological changes in Emma. She no longer restrains her laughter; her resistance to the bourgeois world will break out into overt opposition. To be sure, during other moments of her affair with Léon the two are not laughing. An iterative scene from the final days catches Emma swinging wildly between hope and despair: "Elle se déshabillait brutalement, arrachant le lacet mince de son corset, qui sifflait autour de ses hanches comme une couleuvre qui glisse"; then "pâle, sans parler, sérieuse, elle s'abattait contre sa poitrine avec un long soupir" (356-57). No laughter appears as the scene continues: "Cependant, il y avait sur ce front couvert de gouttes froides, sur ces lèvres balbutiantes, dans ses prunelles égarées, dans l'étreinte de ses bras, quelque chose d'extrême, de vague et de lugubre, qui semblait à Léon se glisser entre eux, subtilement, comme pour les séparer" (356). (Although this passage partially masks what it recounts, it represents in microscopic corporeal detail a moment of erotic activity.) The overflowing champagne becomes an image of her laughter during this time. Now she flaunts convention openly, jumping for joy all night long to the sound of furious trombones. Her laughter has become the expression of an excess of energy, a gratuitous and wasteful expense of vital force, a boastful and excessive celebration of life. Although I cannot go so far as to claim hearing in this laugh any affirmation of life, I will say that I detect in it the prodigality, the monstrosity, and the resistance of Bakhtinian laughter.[24]

* * *

Emma's dying laugh reverberates with strains from all her other laughter through the novel. It is mocking, scandalous, transgressive, erotic, voluptuous, resistant. But in a less general way, the last laugh represents a response to the set of particular circumstances around her death. Something there makes her laugh. I claimed above that this laugh expresses the pleasure of a sudden acquisition of knowledge. What might be this new understanding Emma acquires on her deathbed?

Let me begin by backing up to an earlier moment of the deathbed scene. Just before the final agony, Emma isolates herself from the ritual in which she plays the principal role: she asks for her mirror, and gazes at herself a long while. In this moment appears the trace of an earlier mirror-scene: after her first tryst with Rodolphe, she returns home, catches sight of herself in the mirror, is astonished at the transformation of her face. "J'ai un amant! un amant!" (229), she says. (Beside the mirror another motif links the scenes of adultery and her dying: her big eyes. After her ride with Rodolphe, Emma observes her own face: "elle s'étonna de son visage. Jamais elle n'avait eu les yeux si grands, si noirs, ni d'une telle profondeur" [229]. At her deathbed it is Berthe who remarks Emma's eyes: "Oh, comme tu as de grands yeux, maman!" [393].) Although we have no access to her thoughts on the deathbed, I suggest that she would be addressing herself in similar terms in this mirror. At both moments the mirror triggers a kind of dramatic narcissism; seeing herself from the outside as it were, Emma is able suddenly to envision herself *within* the scene playing itself around her. Both the role of adulteress and expiring heroine appeal to her romantic sensibility forged, as we know, in the heat of excessive novel-reading. Emma reckons herself in a "privileged condition," playing a dramatic role in a scenario from beyond the social quotidian (Brombert 83).

Here I find a strain of Bergsonian laughter which indeed pertains to the moment and movement of Emma's last laugh. The ceremonial side of social life contains a "comique latent," Bergson writes, "lequel n'attendra qu'une occasion pour éclater au grand jour" (34-35). As clothing is to the individual body, ceremonies are to the social body: both owe their gravity to their identification with what they cover; both too lose this gravity as soon as they are detached from what they hide. A ceremony thus becomes comic when our attention focuses on its *ritual* aspects, when we neglect its content and see only its form. The stiffness, rigidity of all ceremony suggests an image of a mechanical form superimposed on life (Bergson 35). When the blind beggar's song breaks the spell of the deathbed ceremony, Emma explodes into laughter at seeing the series of empty gestures and speech which are enclosing and staging her death. She laughs, I believe, at those around her, the pillars of the social order who must banish the scandalousness of death from the moment of dying, thereby affirming and confirming the social order; and she laughs at herself, for this time she has taken on a role not of her own choosing but imposed on her by all the Charles, Bournisiens, and Homais.[25]

But Emma's laugh represents another recognition as well. Bergson writes that a situation is always comic "quand elle appartient en même temps à deux séries d'événements absolument indépendantes, et qu'elle peut s'interpréter à la fois dans deux sens tout différents" (73-74). On her deathbed Emma perceives herself in one series of events: the dying woman. With the beggar's trespass on the scene arrives a cluster of associations belonging to another series. The beggar represents for Emma her weekly trips to Rouen where she spent afternoons laughing with her lover. In her vision of the blind man's hideous face, Emma perceives that her death belongs also to a series of erotic events. Flaubert reinforces this recognition by Emma through a subtle control of narrative material. Until this moment the text had withheld the complete lyrics to the beggar's song. During her trips to Rouen, while she sat dreaming of love, Emma had always mistaken the lyrics. She had heard the first verses correctly ("Souvent la chaleur d'un beau jour / Fait rêver fillette à l'amour"), but the rest was transformed in her imagination: "Et il y avait dans tout le reste des oiseaux, du soleil et du feuillage" (340). (These motifs, incidentally—the *oiseaux, soleil, feuillage*—figure prominently in the scene of her first adultery, the afternoon ride with Rodolphe.) Dying, Emma no longer dreams, and she catches the song's true words for the first time:

> Pour amasser diligemment
> Les épis que la faux moissonne,
> Ma Nannette va s'inclinant
> Vers le sillon qui les donne
> Il souffla bien fort ce jour-là,
> Et le jupon court s'enleva!

The scythe and the skirt, carried off by a gust: in the song, as in the deathbed scene itself, elements of eros and thanatos cross.

Georges Bataille cites Sade: "There is no better way to know death than to link it with some licentious image."[26] The beggar's song and Emma's recognition of its meaning are doubled in the deathbed scene by the pattern of erotic activity which has traversed it. Emma's panting accelerates, accompanied by Charles's

sobbing and Bournisien's intonations in a dead language. I recall that her ribs are shaken by "un souffle furieux"; this word *furieux* echoes the sound of the trombones at the masked ball in Rouen, but also her second adulterous ride, this one with Léon in the *fiacre,* where the coachman hears a voice from inside crying "furieusement" (317) for him to keep going, where after a long day rolling through the suburbs the same coachman wonders: "quelle fureur de la locomotion poussait ces individus à ne vouloir point s'arrêter" (317). On her deathbed, the rhythm of Emma's breathing accelerates until the beggar's song brings her to climax: she jolts upright, her nostrils flared, her hair undone. If orgasm is *la petite mort,* would death not be *le grand orgasme*?

So Emma dies laughing, recognizing in a flash that her dreams of love have always been dreams of death. Her laugh is erotic, and thus it retains the resistant, transgressive force of her earlier laughter. As I suggested earlier, at the end Emma laughs at herself and the deathbed ritual in which she plays a part. But she is laughing too at the other players in the ceremony: at Homais, Bournisien, Canivet, and at Charles. Naomi Schor reads Flaubert's famous exclamation ("Madame Bovary, c'est moi") literally. She identifies the heroine's aspirations with the novelist's: "Emma seeks a lover not only to become a novelistic character, but especially to become an author" (16). I would extend this identification of author and heroine to the dying laugh, with all its ironic and oppositional power. For an instant "the fog in Emma's head" clears, and she recognizes the pattern of her life.[27] For an instant her laugh is Flaubert's, and ours, for throughout the novel he and we have laughed at the pettiness of all these characters who surround her.

To be sure, Flaubert's qualification of Emma's laugh as "atroce, frénétique, désespéré" (400) might seem to argue against my fundamentally positive reading of it. I would counter by asking: in a text using skillfully the tactics of uncertainty, are we sure whose voice speaks to qualify Emma's laugh in this way? Is it Flaubert, or the other actors of the deathbed scene, for whom we suspect such a laugh could only be atrocious, frenetic, desperate? Even if we deny the possibility that the passage is riddled with irony, and hear only the voice of authority, must we not recognize that Flaubert, like his characters, was a creature of his age? Reading Bakhtin reveals that laughter too has a history. In the nineteenth century it may not have been possible, even for a Flaubert, to conceive laughter other than through the dominant values of rationalism and scientific seriousness. Today, after Bakhtin, after Nietzsche, after Freud, after Breton, after Derrida, laughter has regained something of the value it held for Rabelais.

Flaubert wrote his heroine a laughing death, and with a laugh a grotesque death becomes sublime. Nothing in Emma Bovary's life became her like the leaving it.

Notes

1. Gustave Flaubert, *Madame Bovary* (Paris: Garnier-Flammarion, 1986) 365.

2. Jean Starobinski, "L'Échelle des températures: lecture du corps dans *Madame Bovary*," in *Travail de Flaubert,* ed. Gérard Genette and Tzvetan Todorov (Paris: Seuil, 1983), interprets the *aveugle* as "la face hideuse du réel en excès" (61). Other critics, however, find that the theatricality of the blind man's appearance threatens to disrupt the realist code within the novel. Jonathan Culler, *Flaubert: The Uses of Uncertainty* (Ithaca: Cornell UP, 1985), comments: "The irony of the Blind Man's appearance at three crucial moments of Emma's life and the implicit commentary provided by his songs and actions gives a metaphorical neatness to her fate" (187). For a discussion of the blind beggar within the context of nineteenth-century medicine, see Mary Donaldson-Evans, "A Pox on Love: Diagnosing Madame Bovary's Beggar" *Symposium* 44:1 (Spring 1990) 15-27. Michel Riffaterre, "Flaubert's Presuppositions," in *Critical Essays on Gustave Flaubert,* ed. Laurence M. Porter (Boston: Hall, 1986), sees in the beggar's song "a metaphor of Emma's degradation: a sexual one and therefore most apt" (84).

3. Riffaterre 84-85; Stephen Heath, *Gustave Flaubert: Madame Bovary* (Cambridge: Cambridge UP, 1992) 109; Victor Brombert, *The Novels of Flaubert: A Study of Theme and Technique* (Princeton: Princeton UP, 1966) 75.

4. Henri Bergson, *Le Rire: essai sur la signification du comique* (Paris: Quadrige/PUF, 1940) 22-23.

5. Mikhail Bakhtin, *Rabelais and his World,* trans. Hélène Iswolsky (Bloomington: Indiana UP, 1984) 67.

6. Charles Baudelaire, *De l'essence du rire: et généralement du comique dans les arts plastiques,* in *Œuvres complètes,* ed. Marcel A. Ruff (Paris: Seuil, 1968) 372.

7. Tony Tanner, *Adultery in the Novel: Contract and Transgression* (Baltimore: Johns Hopkins UP, 1979) 238.

8. Aristotle, *On Poetry and Style,* trans. G. M. A. Grube (Indianapolis: Liberal Arts P, 1958), calls the ludicrous "a species of ugliness," and "a sort of flaw and painfulness which is not painful or injurious" (10).

9. Victor Hugo, "Préface," *Cromwell,* in *Théâtre complet* (Paris: Gallimard, 1953) 409-54.

10. The play of hiding and revealing in this passage recalls Roland Barthes's definition of the erotic. The locus of the erotic is not, he argues, the fully uncovered sex, but "là où le vêtement baille"—"la mise en scène d'une apparition-disparition": for example, the thin strip of skin glimpsed between glove and sleeve. *Le Plaisir du texte* (Paris: Seuil, 1973) 19-20.

11. Wolfgang Kayser, *The Grotesque in Art and Literature,* trans. Ulrich Weisstein (Bloomington: Indiana UP, 1963) 187, 184.

12. Charles Bernheimer, *Flaubert and Kafka: Studies in Psychopoetic Structure* (New Haven and London: Yale UP, 1982) 126.

13. Tanner attributes this tactic not to any bourgeois prudishness on Flaubert's part, but sees it rather as an essential strategy of the nineteenth-century novel of adultery. He writes: "The invisible, inaudible deed becomes a silence and an absence in the text that gradually spreads, effectively negating what is made audible and present" (13). The invisibility of the adulterous act corresponds to the gap within the social structure produced by adultery, he concludes.

14. Peter Brooks, *Body Work: Objects of Desire in Modern Narrative* (Cambridge: Harvard UP, 1993) 92.

15. Brooks 95. Starobinski takes a different approach to Emma's body. For him it becomes the site of an "expérience cénesthétique," a series of "perceptions corporelles" quite rare in literature before Flaubert. Starobinski opens his discussion by analyzing a scene where Emma, sewing in her father's kitchen, presses her cool palm against her hot face: "ce n'est pas la première fois, dans le récit, qu'Emma est figurée, dans le geste d'un contact avec son propre corps, suscitant ou s'efforçant de modifier elle-même sa sensibilité" (48). For Starobinski Emma's body assumes a different importance than it would take in a Bakhtinian perspective.

16. Philippe Perrot, *Le Corps féminin* (Paris: Seuil, 1984) 8.

17. Dragon Kujundzic, "Laughter as Otherness in Bakhtin and Derrida," *Discours Social* 3: 1-2 (Spring-Summer 1990): 291, finds the Western origins of the denunciation of laughter in Plato, long before the seventeenth century, or the official culture of the Middle Ages. Plato would banish laughter from the Republic: "If anyone represents men of worth as overpowered by laughter we must not accept it, much less of gods" (*Republic*, III, 388e); "laughter is the opposite of logos and self knowledge" (*Philebus*, 48c and on); "reason restrains the comic out of fear" (*Republic*, X, 606c).

18. Bakhtin 66. David Patterson, "Laughter and the Alterity of Truth in Bakhtin's Aesthetics," *Dis-*

cours Social 3: 1-2 (Spring-Summer 1990): 295, celebrates the liberatory and revelatory power of Bakhtinian laughter: "laughter is a moment of the unveiling of what is forever hidden from discourse; it is the peal of silence that announces the void which haunts creation; and it is a portal through which the ineffable truth may enter the event of creation. If the truth sets us free, laughter frees the truth; for truth cannot happen in the absence of freedom."

19. Wilda Anderson, *Diderot's Dream* (Baltimore and London: Johns Hopkins UP, 1990) 245.

20. For interpretations of Emma as a tragic figure, I cite Erich Auerbach, *Mimesis: The Representation of Reality in Western Literature,* trans. Willard R. Trask (Princeton: Princeton UP, 1968) 490 ("Very often the reader is moved by [Emma's] fate in a way that appears very like tragic pity"); and Michael Issacharoff, "Unwrapping the Comic," in *Approaches to Teaching Flaubert's* Madame Bovary, ed. Laurence M. Porter and Eugene F. Gray (New York: Modern Language Association of America, 1995) 77 ("the tone of *Madame Bovary* prefigures, in many ways, Eugène Ionesco's notion of tragic farce").

21. Lilian R. Furst, *Fictions of Romantic Irony* (Cambridge: Harvard UP, 1984) 69-71.

22. Bergson signals the *insensibilité* which accompanies laughter. He writes: "Le rire n'a pas de plus grand ennemi que l'émotion" (3).

23. My reading here coincides with Naomi Schor, *Breaking the Chain: Women, Theory, and French Realist Fiction* (New York: Columbia UP, 1985), who observes that "the binding of female energy is one of (if not) the enabling condition of the forward movement of the classical text" (xi). For Mario Vargas-Llosa, *The Perpetual Orgy: Flaubert and Madame Bovary,* trans. Helen Lane (New York: Farrar, Strauss, and Giroux, 1986), this repression is not confined to female sexuality: "The ambitions that lead Emma into sin and death are precisely those that Western religion and morality have most savagely combatted throughout history" (13).

24. Perrot links the nineteenth-century denaturing of the female body with the ideology of the rising bourgeoisie. For this class, "la saleté, son cycle et son parcours vont évoquer la fuite du temps (décomposition de la mort), l'énergie dilapidée (fermentation 'pour rien'), l'obstacle au rendement (l'encrassement de la 'machine'), la dépense improductive" (26). Emma's prodigality derides the ideology of her class.

25. Balzac's *Lys dans la vallée* (Paris: Garnier-Flammarion, 1972) provides an example of the successfully executed deathbed ritual. Just before her death, Madame de Mortsauf confesses the terrible desire which has consumed her, and attempts to seduce her horrified lover, Félix de Vandenesse. The latent erotic elements of Madame Bovary's deathbed scene are overt here. Madame de Mortsauf's grotesque dance of death has shattered the thin layer of convention which keeps social life ordered. How can the social order be confirmed after such a breach, after its tenets have been revealed as lies? The doctors and spiritual advisors prepare Madame de Mortsauf's final scene with a large dose of opium which cancels her body and (re)converts her into pure spirit. Madame de Mortsauf now reappears as she was of old: serene, selfless, saintly, with her eyes fixed on "les joies célestes de la terre promise" (276). Her deathbed scene then becomes a model of how nineteenth-century woman should die.

26. Georges Bataille, *Erotism: Death and Sensuality,* trans. Mary Dalwood (San Francisco: City Lights, 1986) 11.

27. Early in the novel Félicité describes the symptoms of a young woman she had known: "Son mal . . . était une manière de brouillard qu'elle avait dans la tête" (74). Tanner adopts this formula to describe Emma's state of confusion at the end of her life.

Susanna Lee (essay date winter 2001)

SOURCE: Lee, Susanna. "Flaubert's *Blague Supérieure*: The Secular World of *Madame Bovary*." *Symposium* 54, no. 4 (winter 2001): 203-17.

[*In the following essay, Lee discusses Flaubert's ironic attitude toward God in the novel. In Lee's view, Flaubert deliberately undermines any possibility of redemption or transcendence for Emma through his systematic critique of religious institutions and practices.*]

Flaubert often used the figures of a natural scientist or an unconcerned God as models for his authorial mode in **Madame Bovary**.[1] Following him, critics such as Pierre Bourdieu and Jonathan Culler have used those figures in writing about the novel's narrative indeterminacies. For them as for Flaubert, the absence of God and the rise of science signify the denial of a last word, a negation of transcendence and determination. In a similar critical vein, Richard Terdiman, Ross Chambers, and Nathaniel Wing describe the novel in terms of a modern meaninglessness, of a nineteenth-century crisis. In this article, I argue that God's absence or indifference is more than a metaphor for a narrative mode; it is a foundational event in **Madame Bovary,** the explicit reason for Emma's contaminated existence. The atmosphere of hopelessness in the novel is specifically connected to the systematic denial of God and, what is more, to the seamless replacement of God with the dispassionate and secular author.

During the writing of *Madame Bovary,* Flaubert turned to natural science as a model for narrative disengagement. In an 1853 letter to Louise Colet, he writes: "C'est là ce qu'ont de beau les sciences naturelles: elles ne veulent rien prouver. . . . Il faut traiter les hommes comme des mastodontes et des crocodiles. Est-ce qu'on s'emporte à propos de la corne des uns et de la mâchoire des autres? Montrez-les, empaillez-les, bocalisez-les, voilà tout, mais les apprécier, non" ([*Correspondance*] 154). It is around the time that Flaubert writes this letter that European science does in fact begin to treat humans like mastodons or crocodiles. The human organism is studied as the product of the metamorphosis of species, and that metamorphosis as the enactment of natural forces. Species are described without emotions, as the scientist remains personally uninvolved with the object of study. For Flaubert, particularly in *Madame Bovary,* the scientist's indifference becomes the foundation for a narrative mode. Emma is a natural phenomenon to be documented, an organism to be considered. In an earlier letter to Louise Colet, Flaubert described such detachment in other terms: "Quand est-ce qu'on écrira les faits au point de vue d'une *blague supérieure,* c'est-à-dire comme le bon Dieu les voit, d'en haut?" (37). In this proposition, the dispassionate glance of the scientist becomes the derisive regard of God. On the one hand, the *blague supérieure* refers to what God discerns on earth—chaos, perhaps, grandiose dreams, mindless insistence on *idées reçues.* But the *blague* is also to be found in the regard itself, in the concept of God as satirical spectator. The very idea that God regards the earthly scene with detached amusement is perceived as a joke, and a rather troubling one. For rather than a spiritual presence and a structuring force, God comes to stand for uninterested contempt, absence, and distance—for the sense that the connection of God to the world has come undone.

When Flaubert introduces the *blague supérieure,* God's detached vision is primarily a metaphor for narration: the author wants to write as God sees. God becomes a figure for the obscure, ironic, and contemptuous author, a connection underscored in Flaubert's famous statement that "l'auteur, dans son œuvre, doit être comme Dieu dans l'univers, présent partout, et visible nulle part" (61). The obscure and distant nature of God, it seems, is really a way to handle problems of narrative situation, authority, and determinacy. For instance, Pierre Bourdieu writes: "It is here, in this narrative with no beyond, in the irreconcilable diversity of its perspectives, in the universe from which the author has deleted himself but remains, like Spinoza's god, immanent and co-extensive with his creation—it is here that we find Flaubert's point of view" (211). The diversity of narrative perspectives finds a metaphor in Spinoza's god. For Jonathan Culler, the metaphoric God is more demonic than Spinozan but remains the figure of a particular narrative mode: "It is not so much God's objectivity Flaubert desires as his absence: the world will be totalized in a negative fashion, its order shown to be that of an ironic joke. . . . Flaubert's *blague supérieure* should have a thoroughly demoralizing effect which men would take as a correlate of their objective condition" (79). In this statement, as in Flaubert's own declaration about God in the universe, the remoteness of God becomes a metaphor for the absence of a dependable narrative source or point of view. The reader is to be demoralized, as if confronted with a malicious and vaporous God. But in *Madame Bovary,* God's absence and negativity are more than metaphors, for as Flaubert's *blague supérieure,* the novel produces a radical and disorienting shift in the concept of God. *Madame Bovary*'s writing coincides with a significant period of spiritual and philosophical transition in Western Europe from a religious to a secular culture. The novel is a document of that transition and a deliberate enactment of it. Flaubert, with the detachment and entitlement of the natural scientist, cheerfully seats himself in the place that God has abandoned, creating a bleak and triumphant portrait of the modern secular world.

The nineteenth-century transition to secularity, as a continuation of the eighteenth-century transition, is not accomplished through a direct assault on the idea of transcendent structure but rather through the conceptual construction of a reasonable and harmonic world without transcendence. In one sense, this replacement is theoretical, an intellectual modification. Nonetheless, it produces a considerable mutation in the philosophical and spiritual atmosphere, which is much addressed in the literature of the nineteenth century. J. Hillis Miller describes the mutation in his introduction to *The Disappearance of God*:

> The lines of connection between us and God have broken down, or God himself has slipped away from the places where he used to be. He no longer inheres in the world as the force binding together all men and all things. Only if God would return or if we could somehow reach him might our broken world be unified again. But . . . there seems to be no way to re-establish connection.
>
> (2)

Miller's comment and my reading do not refer to God in a particular theological context, but rather to a transcendent and immanent being that animates and orders the world. In Miller's account, the subtle elimination of a sense of order and presence, the disconnection of the world from God, is a disorienting philosophical and ontological phenomenon. The disorientation, spiritual in nature, is a substantial thematic presence in *Madame Bovary* and a crucial element in Flaubert's narrative project. However, whereas Miller's poets lament the decline of God, Flaubert documents it, encourages it, then revels in it and in the problems it produces. This is the foundation of the *blague supérieure*: a modern historical phenomenon presented as a sign of emptiness and hopelessness. At the same time, it becomes an occasion for narrative manipulation by the ironic and secular author. Miller finds that the disappearance of God has eradicated a "force binding together all men and all things." But in *Madame Bovary,* the secular structure of the narrative is an ironic order that binds together all things in an atmosphere of secular homelessness and derision.

One way that Flaubert connects his barren world to the disconnection from God is the ridicule of the spiritual. Some of the novel's most dismal moments are, significantly, those that represent religious enthusiasm and the desire for spiritual connection. Emma, for instance, has three experiences with religion: her education at the convent in Rouen, the consultation with Bournisien, and the months of piety after Rodolphe's abandonment. In Rouen at the age of thirteen, as numerous critics have commented, Emma finds sensual pleasures, but not God: "Cet esprit, positif au milieu de ses enthousiasmes, s'insurgeait devant les mystères de la foi, de même qu'elle s'irritait contre la discipline, qui était quelque chose d'antipathique à sa constitution" (69). Although the "enthusiasms" are meant to be religious in nature, and although the very word (God within) implies a religious experience, no such experience takes place. It is not God who is within, just Emma. So it is that Emma "au milieu de ses enthousiasmes" is closed to religion and faith—a closure that will stand as the foundation for subsequent spiritual failures.

Emma's later spiritual failures occur because she cannot reach outside herself. But this first episode's focus on the mind and its limitation within fantasies at first reads not as a *blague,* but as a natural modern fact. Georges Poulet writes:

> Pour la première fois, dans le domaine du roman, la conscience humaine apparaît telle qu'elle est, comme un centre toujours reconstitué, autour duquel se poursuit indéfiniment le vol convergent ou divergent des sensations et des souvenirs. Et pour la première fois aussi . . . le roman arrive à exprimer ce qu'on peut appeler la densité ou l'épaisseur de la substance humaine. Épaisseur qui peut être celle qui se forme à partir du centre de la conscience s'épandant dans toutes les directions. . . .
>
> (391)

In the natural world, Poulet states, the mind "radiates" out to what is around it. "S'épandant dans toutes les directions" implies the mind's vast and perhaps boundless domain, its extension into and onto the surrounding world. So it is for Emma in Rouen. But it is worth noting that this extension, while celebrating the range and centrality of the mind, stands to eliminate God and the notion of the outside. When every circumstance is described through the radiating mind, then there is no space for an "outside." There is no space for God and transcendence, because the mind incorporates God, as it were, and so eliminates the vast transcendent outsideness of the idea. J. P. Richard discerned the same absorption in Emma's memories: "Les états de confusion de la rêverie permettaient à ces ailleurs de devenir des ici: mais on peut difficilement nommer phénomène de mémoire cette invasion molle par laquelle le passé revient inonder le présent. Il y est annulé, non possedé" (158-59). This elimination of a transcendent *ailleurs* (and of a past) is explicitly an effect of the secular world: everything is here, must be here, since there is no beyond. As Georg Lukács puts it: "The individual is no longer significant as the carrier of transcendent worlds. . . . He now carries his value exclusively within himself; indeed, the values of being seem to draw the justification of their validity only from the fact of having been subjectively experienced, from their significance to the individual's soul" (117). And then, to explain this phenomenon: "The individual, the vehicle of the utopian challenge to reality, was crushed by the brute force of reality; here, defeat is the precondition of subjectivity" (117). In Lukács's interpretation, consciousness (subjectivity) eclipses the external world because that world recedes or becomes inaccessible. It is no longer a home; the "brute force of reality" acts on the human soul without comforting or strengthening it. The radiating mind, in this interpretation, is reacting to the world's emptiness, building its home, compensating for a transcendence that is no more or that sustains no more. The problem in *Madame Bovary,* though, is that Emma neither wants nor is able to "carry value exclusively within herself." As Emma becomes an adult, she dreams of "transcendent worlds." The radiation of her consciousness becomes a dismal reminder of the departure of transcendence, of the "outside" that the narrator steadily eliminates.

When Emma is a young woman in the convent, her resistance to religion can be read as adolescent impatience and self-absorption. As a married adult in Tostes and Yonville, she is no longer content to remain "au milieu de ses enthousiasmes." She wants to see spiritual fantasies actuated, to have words (and ideas) "represent an attainable object" (72), as Nathanial Wing puts it.[2] But the narrative denies this dream, rendering the outside, and in particular the spiritual outside, more and more inaccessible. Emma's first religious episode in Yonville begins at her window, as she hears the *Angelus*: "Alors un attendrissement la saisit: elle se sentit molle et tout abandonnée comme un duvet d'oiseau qui tournoie dans la tempête; et ce fut sans en avoir conscience qu'elle s'achemina vers l'eglise, disposée à n'importe quelle dévotion, pourvu qu'elle y courbât son âme et que l'existence entière y disparut" (156-57). The desired spiritual experience in this episode is one of nothingness—of the disappearance of existence. As she leans out the window, into the vast outside, she prepares for this obliteration. But the nothingness that Emma finds is of another sort. Rather than a sublime state of spiritual calm, nothingness becomes the simple absence of incident and meaning. She pursues religion in the hope that "l'existence entière y disparut," but she finds no "there" to enact or generate this disappearance. Instead of transcendence, Emma comes to the "brute (and secular) force of reality" and of Flaubert's *blague supérieure.*

The episode starts as Emma "entendit tout à coup sonner *l'Angelus.*" But as she nears the church and passes Lestiboudois, the latter "pour ne pas rogner la journée, préférait interrompre sa besogne, puis la reprendre, si bien qu'il tintait *l'Angelus* selon sa commodité" (157). The ringing bells, then the convent memories, the inspiration to devotion, the trip to the church—these incidents come about because of Lestiboudois's mundane human convenience. Further on, the narrator notes: "D'ailleurs, la sonnerie, faite plus tôt, avertissait les gamins de l'heure du catéchisme" (157). The *Angelus* is explicitly not for Emma but for the children who distract Bournisien from her during the consultation. Indeed, when Emma arrives at the church, it has faded: "Le bourdonnement de la cloche diminuait avec les oscillations de la grosse corde qui, tombant des hauteurs du clocher, traînait à terre par le bout" (157).

As the ringing fades, each sound becomes fainter than the one before, until at last no sound can be heard. This diminution is emblematic of the gradual fading of religion from the world of the novel, of Emma's inclination to a God that is no more, that means no more. The studied contamination of Emma's spiritual pursuit continues in the church. As Emma comes to the house of God, she finds only human banalities and cacophonies. Shouting children, rattling marbles, Bournisien's stupid chatter—these are the realities that substitute for God. And these, ironically, were the same sort of realities that pushed Emma to turn to the church in the first place. Flaubert's *blague supérieure* insists that Emma's interest in religion bring her to the very terrestrial banalities that she had wanted, through religion, to escape. God has departed: what remains are the empty ceremonies and discourses of an obsolete cultural delusion.

The scene of Emma coming to the church as the *Angelus* fades out is symbolic of the fading of religion in the novel. But this is not the first faded *Angelus* that we encounter. The first is found in the description of Charles's lessons: "C'était aux moments perdus qu'elles se donnaient . . . ou bien le curé envoyait chercher son élève après *l'Angelus,* quand il n'avait pas à sortir" (29). These recitations take place when the *Angelus* is over—when the religious moment has symbolically ended and God has departed. Significantly, neither Charles's education nor Emma's spiritual pursuits, coming in the wake of the faded *Angelus,* are suited to the modern world. The novel creates, in a sense, an aftermath, a residue of religion. What becomes of religion and the spiritual pursuit when God has departed? What becomes of meaning? The response to these questions is found in the mechanism of repetition that Flaubert uses to disclose and undermine bourgeois cultural and religious discourse and to contaminate the episodes of spiritual enthusiasm.

Ross Chambers writes of Emma: "She seems not to realize that in trying to escape banality and in searching for something 'new' she is only condemning herself to an existence of repetitions" (176). The repetitions become degradations, and the initial substance is either eliminated or degraded in turn. So it is with the *Angelus*: the ringing of the bell is a repetition, as are the various instances of ringing, and religious rituals in general. Charles's education, for instance (which, as Chambers observes, constitutes the novel's initial and foundational repetitions), is also performed "dans la sacristie, debout, à la hâte, entre un baptême et un enterrement" (29). This symbolic space of a life becomes, for the priest who performs those ceremonies on a regular basis and for Charles, who stands between them, a space between and among repetitions. Existence itself, connected symbolically to these religious ceremonies, is reduced to empty routine, to "moments perdus," as is the *Angelus* for Lestiboudois and the fact of spiritual consultation for Bournisien. This repetition continues as the children chant at Emma's departure: "Qu'est-ce qu'un chrétien? C'est celui qui, étant baptisé . . . , baptisé . . . , baptisé . . ." (161). This ceremony, and the idea of new life and new naming that it signifies, becomes a repeated word that fades as Emma returns home. The reiteration of sounds without meaning, of ceremonies without substance, of devotions without object, becomes in this episode the substance of religion.

The degradation that Chambers finds in repetition is enacted here as the reduction of religion to a series of emptied discourses that function in turn as emblems of disconnection from God. The author uses his literary arsenal to undermine God and the dream of spiritual solace, as the mechanism of repetition indicates the gradual replacement of spiritual substance with the secular author's deliberate narratological machinations. After the consultation, Emma returns to her house, doomed by the experience to more of the initial frustration of the "inside." The brute force of reality has acted and won. But that brute force is again confronted, and the futile episode repeated, for despite the sense that God is inaccessible, what Poulet named "la conscience humaine telle qu'elle est" is nonetheless unable to tolerate God's absence. The *blague supérieure,* the disconnection of God from human experience, also produces Emma's blindness to, and incapacity to cope with, that disconnection. Lukács's idea of the character who "carries his value exclusively within himself" cannot come to be for Emma, who pursues a transcendence that Flaubert steadily erases.

The second time that Emma turns to religion is after Rodolphe has abandoned her; she becomes ill and believes the end is near: "À mesure que l'on faisait dans sa chambre les préparatifs pour le sacrement, que l'on disposait en autel la commode encombrée de sirops et que Félicité semait par terre des fleurs de dahlia, Emma sentait quelque chose de fort passant sur elle, qui la débarrassait de ses douleurs, de toute perception, de tout sentiment" (278-79). In this episode, as in the former, the words that describe the spiritual moment are the same words that doom and ridicule it. The moment opens promisingly, with a "quelque chose de fort" that seems to come upon Emma—to come from outside rather than within her. But this sense of an outside is undone in the next sentence: "il lui sembla que son être, montant vers Dieu, allait s'anéantir dans cet amour comme un encens allumé qui se dissipe en vapeur." The "il lui sembla" contradicts the "débarrassement de toute perception" and so undermines the eclipsing power of "quelque chose de fort." Again, the void that Emma dreams of becomes one of meaninglessness and sameness.

One of the most conspicuous elements in this religious episode is the failure of prayer. Emma attempts prayer again and again: "Quand elle se mettait à genoux sur son prie-Dieu gothique, elle adressait au Seigneur les mêmes paroles de suavité qu'elle murmurait jadis à son amant, dans les épanchements de l'adultère. C'était pour faire venir la croyance, mais aucune délectation ne descendait des cieux" (281). Her reiterated prayers do not produce a connection with God. In a sense, the failure can be said to come from Emma's superficiality, from her complete absence of faith, understanding, and patience, and from her use of adulterous discourse in petitions to God. But let us consider it further. Emma has said the same words to Rodolphe, who has heard them from other women, who have read them in books and said them to other men. But what is scandalous in this instance is not the fact of repetition, but the transposition from an adulterous to a pious discursive domain. In fact, it is not at all unusual for prayers to be repetitions of words said by others. In this domain, repetition in word and action is in some sense expected.

Richard Terdiman describes Flaubertian repetition in terms of re-citation, a mechanism that discloses the emptiness in ideological discourse: "It appears that the discourse of ideology traverses entire social networks without the slightest alteration. In effect it desubjectifies the subjects who only imagine that they are speaking it" (210). Any articulation, then, risks becoming an unconscious or automatic "performance" of bourgeois discourse, an ironic (re)production of a ubiquitous but plastic social order. Prayers, as repetitious as any other discourse and in a sense more so, are nonetheless meant to produce a distinct and authentic spiritual connection. They are, paradoxically, repetitions of authenticity, of subjective and objective force—the sort of repetitions that Lawrence Schehr reads as emblems of "home, a state of repetition and reinscription, something that Flaubert seeks endlessly to avoid, since repetition implies ground and the crisis that he is eternally inscribing refuses both this ground and its safety" (234). And of course, Flaubert does eliminate this ground. Sacred repetition becomes empty repetition, and the objective force of prayer is denied. The dream of a spiritual experience is degraded, reduced to meaningless cultural routines, futile mental performances. Rather than participating in an authentic spiritual dialogue, the person who prays in Flaubert's world, desubjectified or not, is simply carrying out the sort of delusion of connection that plagues Emma both in religion and in her romances.

Wing comments that "desire, when associated with the nouns which serve as its signifier, can only remain virtual, a possibility forever suspended. When it is articulated as the narrative of fulfilled pleasure, however, desire is linked inevitably with the alienating repetitions of the stereotype" (49). When it comes to God and religion, the desire for spiritual recompense is meant to be suspended. Unlike the desire for love or money, it is not meant to be made substance, to be put to the test in some concrete sense. Emma's failure to be content with that suspension, the fact that her desire for God is no different than her desire for new clothes, must therefore produce frustration. But the reduction of religion to useless repetitions implies that that suspension is itself misleading. What is suspended, it seems, is mere emptiness: there is nothing within it, nothing to hope for, no hereafter to aspire to. This emptiness is demonstrated again and again in Emma's material desires, and it promises to be demonstrated again in the spiritual, as Emma's prayers become "alienating repetitions" of a cultural *blague,* a vacuous and futile routine.

When Emma's desires for a spiritual connection are derailed, when God is denied, what Miller named the "force binding together all men and all things" is eliminated, creating, for Emma and the reader, an unpleasant limbo. For, although religion has become empty and meaningless, the secular world in ***Madame Bovary*** is no more promising. Flaubert's repetition and desubjectification, while undermining religion, also undermine what Lukács called the "subjective experience." Singular experiences and identities, the substance of secular value, are in **Madame Bovary** not so singular and not so valuable. Because re-citation desubjectifies not just speech and writing but thought and experience, the inner life of the individual, which proposes to act as a repository of meaning and value, is unable to do so. The transition from the religious to the secular becomes a demoralizing limbo, a suspension between the obsolescence of God and the incoherence of the secular world.

Important to the *blague supérieure* is the sense that although religion has become vacuous, no other source for meaning and substance and promise is possible. What remains in the aftermath of religion in Flaubert's representation is the mundane and invariable fact of the world as it is. One of the reasons that this banality reads as both demoralizing and natural is that the sociological and cultural transition from religion to nonreligion was in the 1850s a phenomenon in process. Flaubert enacted this transition by performing and mocking the important elements in it: the gradual disconnection from God, the decline of the spiritual pursuit, the rise of bourgeois materialism. His demoralizing performance was then able to read as historical realism, as a document of the world as it was.

Another element in this nineteenth-century transition, manipulated and made sinister in the novel, is the rise of the natural sciences. As demonstrated in his 1853 letter to Louise Colet, Flaubert embraced that rise—not for the understanding it contributed, but for the dreams and grandiosities that it eliminated. The substitution of natural principles for the Supreme Architect became another element to represent and ridicule, another element of the *blague supérieure*.

Science in the 1850s is for the most part detached from religion: it concentrates not on the machinations of an ordering God but on the function of natural principles. Flaubert uses this replacement both as a model for his detached narration and as an important ironic component in his *blague supérieure*. For in this novel, the transition from religion to science is more about detriment than about advancement. Instead of bringing an increase in empirical understanding, the transition simply eliminates sentiment and possibilities. The elimination is represented in the novel through various means. Perhaps foremost among them is the scientific flattening of religious discourse, which connects the decline of meaning to the substitution of science for religion.

One such instance is in the episode of the *comices agricoles*. Here, Rodolphe's declarations to Emma are replete with the melodious words of sacred order. A few examples: "Les âmes se réuniront, s'aimeront, parce que la fatalité l'exige" (200); "Pourquoi nous sommes-nous connus? Quel hasard l'a voulu?" (202); "Je ne sais quelle force encore m'a poussé vers vous! Car on ne lutte pas contre le Ciel!" (211). And again, in the letter

that ends their romance: "Est-ce ma faute? O mon Dieu! Non, non, n'en accusez que la fatalité!" (266). These words read as ironic and vacuous, be it because *fatalité* is a "serious" word that Rodolphe parodies or because Flaubert intends it as a meaningless sound. In either case, Rodolphe's *fatalité* is empty of meaning, turned into what Terdiman named a re-citation. And once emptied, it remains so. The word is never "restored" to a loftier meaning, nor can it evoke, except negatively or ironically, a nobler world. *Fatalité* is bound to, and can never be greater than, the discourse that articulates it. God, then, the God of *fatalité,* is imperceptibly but definitively drained from the word—diminished, limited, as it were, to the insincere dimensions of Rodolphe's discourse.

Albert Thibaudet describes Emma's romances this way: "Les deux hommes [Rodolphe et Léon] ne sont que le mâle sous une loupe d'entomologiste. Le mâle la veut, la cherche . . . elle resiste, mais quelque chose en elle comme en nous sait de science certaine qu'elle va à une sorte de trappe noire . . ." (110) Thibaudet reads the characters as insects of a sort, bound to natural characteristics. The comment is of interest because the detached meticulousness that it discerns in Flaubert's descriptions is also present within Rodolphe's conversation. Thibaudet notes, for instance, that Rodolphe's first perception of Emma is impersonal: "On voudrait habiter la ville, danser la polka tous les soirs! Pauvre petite femme! ça baille après l'amour, comme une carpe après l'eau sur une table de cuisine. Avec trois mots de galanterie, cela vous adorerait, j'en suis sûr! . . . Oui, mais comment s'en débarrasser ensuite?" (180). But what is noteworthy is that Rodolphe's detachment, like Flaubert's, comes from a natural scientist's perception. "Comme une carpe après l'eau" is a zoological comparison; "avec trois mots" and "on voudrait habiter la ville" are schematic descriptions of nutrition and habitat. One can detect a medical quality in Rodolphe's scrutiny. As he is "sous la loupe" of Flaubert, so Emma is "sous la loupe" of Rodolphe. And as Flaubert's "loupe" is his means to manipulate and contaminate the hand of God, so Rodolphe's "loupe" is his means to manipulate and contaminate that hand within the Flaubertian world. Rodolphe's seduction of Emma suggests that a scientific detachment and a disinterested manipulation of divine rhetoric are the keys to success. But that detachment, of course, comes at the price of sentiment and substance. Science has come to replace religion, and the "loupe" to replace the soul.

Emma, however, does not grasp this substitution, and it is her blindness that enables the *blague supérieure*. The emptiness in Rodolphe's words is demoralizing not because it obstructs Emma's seduction, but because it does not. She does not understand that the transition from a religious to a nonreligious world, from sacred orchestrations to natural realities, has changed the nature of discourse. In a secular world run on natural principles, the word *fatalité* is not meant to actually indicate the hand of God. Or rather, the concepts of *fatalité* and of the hand of God do not, in themselves, explain or lend substance to anything. *Fatalité* can be a metaphor for spirit, force, or for natural principles, but it is a metaphor only, a verbal decoration. Scientists understand this limitation. In scientific discourse of the late 1850s, the "hand of God" comes increasingly to mean simply "realities at work." When the zoologist Richard Owens lectured in 1858 about natural selection as "the axiom of the continuous operation of creative power, or of the ordained becoming of living things," he added: "Always, also, it may be well to bear in mind that by the word 'creation' the zoologist means 'a process he knows not what.'"[3] Claude Bernard writes: "Pour agir, il faut être matérialiste, car on n'agit pas sur autre chose que la matière. Pour comprendre, penser et croire, il faut être spiritualiste, car la matière elle-même n'explique rien. Autrement dit, pour agir il faut être empirique. Pour comprendre, il faut être théoricien" (82). To be a "théoricien" is to discern contexts and patterns. To be a "spiritualiste" is to discern in those contexts and patterns a sort of atmosphere that can then be rendered in poetic words and used to adorn the empirical facts.

Such decoration is not uncommon in nineteenth-century scientific writing. One instance of it appears in an 1852 treatise on natural selection by the botanist Charles Naudin: "Puissance mystérieuse, indéterminée, fatalité pour les uns; pour les autres, volonté providentielle, dont l'action incessante sur les êtres vivants détermine, à toutes les époques de l'existence du monde, la forme, le volume, et la durée de chacun d'eux, en raison de sa destinée dans l'ordre des choses dont il fait partie."[4] The verbal emblems of sacred order are used to ornament the phenomenon of natural selection. That phenomenon would remain with or without the words. *Fatalité* does not lend the plants any substance or interest that they do not already have. It does not change the nature or origin of the selection process. What is ironic in *Madame Bovary* is that *fatalité* does not so much ornament the seduction as construct it. A disingenuous Rodolphe pronounces *fatalité* and Emma is seduced, animated by Flaubert's ironic hand. As Rodolphe says, "Voilà un mot qui fait toujours de l'effet" (266). Rather than a "laminoir qui allonge les sentiments," the word in this instance replaces sentiment. The blatant emptiness in *fatalité* indicates that ironic replacement, that seduction *ex nihilo,* that seamless substitution of the hand of the author for the hand of God.

Here, the transition from religion to science is connected with a subtle drain of meaning from the word. But in other moments, the transition is made even more dismal, as science becomes a repository for the absurd and the useless. Such uselessness is particularly evident in moments of medical distress—ironically, the arena to which science proposes to bring wisdom and solace. In the episode of Hippolyte's operation, for instance, Homais writes his article: "Ce que le fanatisme autrefois promettait à ses élus, la science maintenant l'accomplit pour tous les hommes!" (238) The idea of religious men and women as the "élus du fanatisme" deprecates religion and prepares the space for a more modern substitute: Homais proposes science. But because Homais is the author and Charles the proposed *savant,* the replacement is less than promising. Indeed, the failure of the operation indicates the failure of the substitution: science is to be as absurd and problematic as the religion that it replaces. This sentence and the episode that contains it in effect close both doors. Progression and regression are equally impossible. For the patient, for instance, when science fails, a return to religion ("fanatisme") has already been undermined: "la religion pas plus que la chirurgie ne paraissait le secourir" (241). As Julien Barnes writes, "Flaubert does not believe in progress" (213). His nonbelief is significant, for *Madame Bovary* is born of a historical moment in which progress is considered extremely important. Religion has faded; something, one imagines, must replace it. But Charles, Emma, and the people of Yonville are in a sort of philosophical and spiritual limbo, without the solace of religion and without the foundations and capacities of science. In Flaubert's transition to science, much has been lost and nothing gained.

The advent of science becomes a glum *blague* once again on Emma's deathbed. When the doctor Larivière arrives at the house, we read, "l'apparition d'un dieu n'eût pas causé plus d'émoi" (406). The surgeon has replaced God as the force of salvation. And yet he can do nothing for Emma; he turns around and goes to lunch with Homais. Science, in the end, is useless. Indeed, every declaration about its virtues comes from the bombastic pharmacist or from M. Guillaumin, who comments to Charles that because "un homme de science ne peut s'embarrasser aux détails pratiques de la vie," a power of attorney for Emma is indispensable (354). Science is brought into *Madame Bovary* not as an admirable explanatory and diagnostic instrument, but as an emblem of modern emptiness and inadequacy. It is represented not for what it contributes but for what it eliminates, not for what it can do but for what it cannot.

Science, in the novel, does not produce the "binding force" that Miller wrote about. Instead, the "binding force" becomes the form of the narrative. The inaccessibility of God in *Madame Bovary* comes out as a palpable narrative manipulation, a deliberate *blague* on the foolish believer. The hand of the author denies the hand of God and, in an ironic sense, simultaneously substitutes for it. This substitution of the author for God connects the modern elimination of God to narrative authority and to the very fact or form of the novel. This connection, visible in Flaubert's contamination of Emma's spiritual moments, is present, as we saw, in his use of repetition and emptied discourse.

The *blague supérieure* in **Madame Bovary** comes not only from the steady elimination of God from Emma's world, from the demoralizing vacuum that is left in God's wake, but from the sense that it is the human author who produces, orchestrates, and revels in that vacuum. The author's contamination of and substitution for God is enacted through narrative mechanisms such as repetition and, as we shall see, religious symbolism. But before we turn to this mechanism, let us consider how Flaubert's narrative indeterminacies contribute to the atmosphere of secular incoherence. Culler notes the uncertainties and the dissolutions of meaning in Flaubert's prose. Wing finds that "the story of the delusions of stories is not outside the delusions it re-cites" and that "narrative performance," the Flaubertian "solution, consistently raises questions about the authority of narrators" (76). Schehr reads in these raised questions a deliberate destabilization, an enactment of a crisis.[5] The narrative indeterminacies in Flaubert's novel and the crisis in representation can be interpreted as performances or enactments of the novel's uncertain secular circumstances. The disconnection from God in **Madame Bovary** is not what it was for Miller's Victorian poets, a *fait accompli* to be mourned. In Flaubert's novel, that disconnection is manifested as an abstract unpleasantness, a problematic sense of absence—more a threatening uneasiness than a solid cultural fact. The questions about narrative authority and crises in representation contribute to and delineate the bleak ontological atmosphere of the secular world. The repetitions, uncertainties, and empty discourses in the novel act as predictions or enactments of what becomes of meaning in a world without God. More (or less) than realism, then, the novel is a particular sort of performance, a sinister production and document of a historical and spiritual phenomenon.

Madame Bovary, as I have pointed out, does not so much mourn the disconnection from God as generate and revel in it, using it as the foundation for a *blague supérieure.* The decline of God is in direct proportion to the ascendance of the author, who eliminates and then cheerfully replaces the hand of God. That replacement is to be found in the narrative mechanisms of repetition and empty discourse that structure Emma's spiritual failures. It is also to be found in Flaubert's manipulation of religious emblems and allegories—a manipulation that not only plots the gradual decline of God but discloses the deliberate pleasure and power that Flaubert finds in it.

Emma's second religious episode, as we have seen, is initiated with religious emblems. The ritualistic preparations for communion, such as the constructed altar and the petals on the floor, are the reason and inspiration for Emma's spiritual anticipation. As words motivate Emma in Rodolphe's seduction, so emblems motivate her in this sequence. And as the religious episode continues, so does Emma's enthusiasm for religious emblems: "Elle voulut devenir une sainte. Elle acheta des chapelets, elle porta des amulettes; elle souhaitait avoir dans sa chambre, au chevet de sa couche, un reliquaire enchâssé d'émeraudes, pour le baiser tous les soirs" (280). The emblems, though, as various critics have noted, do not produce the desired spiritual experience. Instead, they result in an absence of meaning, or a dead space where meaning should be. Each symbol is a negative reminder, vacuous and flat. And each ritual honors the spiritual solace that Emma is denied—signifies, that is, the denial of meaning.

The pursuit of religion through its emblems and rituals is exaggerated and made ridiculous in the novel, but that is not so unusual. In a dialogue on religion, Schopenhauer writes about symbols and symbolism:

> Religion is truth allegorically and mythically expressed, and so rendered attainable and digestible by mankind in general. Mankind could not possibly take it pure and unmixed, just as we can't breathe pure oxygen; we require an addition of four times its bulk in nitrogen. In plain language, the profound meaning, the high aim of life, can only be unfolded and presented to the masses symbolically, because they are incapable of grasping it in its true signification.
>
> (16)

In this interpretation, the symbolic can and sometimes must be the receptacle for meaning. The symbolic (attendance at church, prayer, or simply the concept of God) is the conduit to the "high aim of life," as nitrogen is the conduit to breathable air. Flaubert turns the road into a dead end. The symbolic does not "mean," or it means only negatively. The symbolic register has been deactivated, underscoring the ridicule of the spiritual pursuit. But to understand this deactivation as a fundamental aspect of Flaubert's *blague,* as the narrator's displacement of the hand of God, we consider religious emblems as presented in the rest of the novel.

As a convent girl, Emma eats from a scratched dish: "Les explications légendaires, coupées çà et là par l'égratignure des couteaux, glorifiaient toutes la religion . . ." (64). On the road to Yonville, the plaster priest statue, already chipped, "tombant de la charette à un cahot trop fort, s'était écrasé en mille morceaux sur le pavé de Quincampoix!" (129). And, again, the *Angelus* "diminuait avec les oscillations" as Emma comes to the Yonville church. Religious emblems, in the hands of the narrator, literally come apart, fade out, and are obscured. A similar contamination is visited on religious sacraments: at Emma's tumultuous wedding, "les herbes rudes avec les petits dards des chardons" attach to the dress (54). At Berthe's baptism, Charles's father dumps champagne on the child's head (132).

The disintegration of these emblems and sacraments is concrete and progressive. And unlike the rosaries and the altar in Emma's room, these emblems have a symbolic value in the narrative. Victor Brombert reads this value as moral or ethical: "At times, the symbolic detail serves as an ironic punctuation, as it almost graphically plots the stages of a moral evolution. . . . The gradual destruction of the ecclesiastical figure [the priest statue] parallels the gradual disintegration of their marriage" (18). The literal destruction of religious symbols, as Brombert reads it, traces Emma's ethical decline. But it also traces the destruction or dismantling of the symbolic register, reflecting and enacting the continuous unavailability of religious experience and of what Schopenhauer named "the high aim of life." Flaubert's *blague supérieure* here undoes the religious emblems that Emma embraces and turns them into ironic emblems of narrative authority. Their destruction acts on and within the story to "graphically plot" Emma's spiritual failure. God then becomes an ironic mechanism in the hands of Flaubert, a narrative instrument of deception and manipulation.

The elimination of God in **Madame Bovary** is enacted with subtle deliberation. And yet, most ironically, this elimination appears natural and realistic. Natural principles in the 1850s come to replace God, though Emma does not understand this modern transition. The absence of transcendence and the emptiness of metaphors and emblems are in some sense facts of the modern world. In the voice of the natural scientist, and with ironic delectation, Flaubert uses that emptiness to represent Emma as a sort of unadapted organism—the unselected. Emma's interest in God and her dreams about transcendence make her unable to flourish in Flaubert's secular world, which in its turn seems like a modern fact, a natural if unfortunate condition. A scientist does not mourn and ruminate on what an unadapted animal could have become in other circumstances or what could be done to protect it from the world, and Flaubert does not mourn in **Madame Bovary.** The narration does not resonate with what could have been, had circumstances been different, because circumstances are relentlessly and resolutely not different. Flaubert stands as scientist and as ordering God, as author and documentor of the *blague supérieure*, which celebrates the eradication of God at the hand of narrative authority—the hand that contaminates, parodies, and in the end substitutes for the hand of God.

Notes

1. Flaubert, *Correspondance* 1852, 37, 61; 1853. 154.

2. See also Bersani: "Nothing is meant by these words (*félicité, passion ivresse*) in life; they 'mean' only verbally, and especially in books. . . . The gap between an excessively signifying imagi-

nation and an insignificant world occasionally produces attacks of acute anxiety in Emma" (33).

3. Richard Owens, "Address to the British Association on the Nature of Limbs," cited in Darwin, *The Origin of Species,* 58.

4. Charles Naudin's article on evolution appeared first in the *Revue Horticole,* 1852; cited in Darwin, *The Origin of Species,* 61.

5. "The decentering of the Flaubertian narrative . . . figures both the crisis at work in the act of inscription and the paradox that produces this crisis: the inscribed event must constatively or performatively occur somewhere. Yet Flaubert elects to remove this somewhere, a removal that itself marks the permanent crisis in representation" (224).

Works Cited

Barnes, Julien. *Flaubert's Parrot.* New York: Knopf, 1985.

Bernard, Claude. *Philosophie.* Paris: Hatier-Boivin, 1954.

Bersani, Leo. "Flaubert and Emma Bovary: The Hazards of Literary Fusion." *Flaubert's* Madame Bovary. Ed. Harold Bloom. New York: Chelsea House, 1988.

Bourdieu, Pierre. *The Field of Cultural Production.* New York: Columbia UP, 1993.

Brombert, Victor H. *The Novels of Flaubert.* Princeton: Princeton UP, 1966.

Culler, Jonathan. *Flaubert: The Uses of Uncertainty.* Ithaca: Cornell UP, 1974.

Darwin, Charles. *The Origin of Species.* London: Penguin, 1968.

Flaubert, Gustave. *Correspondance.* Paris: Conard, 1926-33.

———. *Madame Bovary.* Paris: Gallimard, 1972.

Lukács, Georg. *The Theory of the Novel.* Trans. Anna Bostock. Cambridge: MIT Press, 1971.

Miller, J. Hillis. *The Disappearance of God.* Cambridge: Harvard UP, 1963.

Poulet, Georges. *Les Métamorphoses du Cercle.* Paris: Plon, 1961.

Richard, Jean-Pierre. *Littérature et Sensation.* Paris: Editions du Seuil, 1954.

Schehr, Lawrence. *Rendering French Realism.* Stanford: Stanford UP, 1997.

Schopenhauer, Arthur. *Religion: A Dialogue.* Trans. T. Bailey Saunders. London: Swan Sonnenschein, 1899.

Terdiman, Richard. *Discourse/Counter-Discourse.* Ithaca: Cornell UP, 1985.

Thibaudet, Albert. *Gustave Flaubert.* Paris: Editions Gallimard, 1935.

Wing, Nathaniel. *The Limits of Narrative.* Cambridge: Cambridge UP, 1986.

Roland A. Champagne (essay date 2002)

SOURCE: Champagne, Roland A. "Emma's Incompetence as Madame Bovary." *Orbis Litterarum* 57, no. 2 (2002): 103-19.

[*In the following essay, Champagne examines Emma Bovary's struggle to liberate herself from the societal constraints imposed on her by marriage. Drawing on the theories of French sociologist Pierre Bourdieu, Champagne outlines two opposing conditions for Emma: the habitus, in which her role as bourgeois wife is defined; and the hexis, characterized by her identification with her physical self. According to Champagne, while Emma succeeds throughout the novel in finding freedom in her body, her death—and subsequent burial in her wedding dress, according to custom—ultimately imprisons her within the confines of a bourgeois conception of womanhood.*]

Pierre Bourdieu's social science orientation for the habitus and the hexis enables us to provide a relational model for situating the literary events of ***Madame Bovary.*** Emma's incompetence at being a wife according to the bourgeois habitus allows her to expand her competence as a woman by following the hexis of her female body. This struggle between hexis and habitus in Emma moves through five stages. First of all, her education in the convent provides her with the habitus of what a bourgeois wife should be and the separation of a woman's dreams from the reality of a housewife's tasks. Secondly, as a young married woman, Emma's suffering allows her to experience her individual opposition to the asphyxiation of marriage relative to the freedom of her womanhood. Thirdly, through language, Emma begins to externalize her struggle and in the fourth stage of her evolution to break the rules of the habitus. Finally, in the fifth stage, Emma chooses the competence of her hexis by appropriating her own space in dying. Nevertheless, the habitus reigns as Emma is buried in her wedding dress as if to enshrine in the code of marriage, and thus to disguise, the incompetence of her life.

Flaubert's work has been elaborated sociologically as a well-structured aesthetic ensemble by Pierre Bourdieu. Flaubert's ***Madame Bovary*** (1857), strangely enough, was not the focus of Bourdieu's attention even though the novel can be profitably read through what he identifies as 'living socially . . . inserted into the network of relationships . . . which are recalled through the form of . . . controls and constraints' ([*Les Règles de l'art*] 1992, 53). One of Flaubert's contemporaries, Barbey D'Aurevilly, stated in 1865 that the central crisis for such controls and constraints occurred at the Vaubyessard ball where 'the world outside enters in the heart of ***Madame Bovary*** never to leave' (['M. Gustave Flaubert'] 1865, 53). However, with Bourdieu's theory of the hexis/habitus as a methodological guide, this crisis can be identified much earlier in Emma's life, that is, during her formative years in the convent. While the hexis is a physical orientation of the body in a cultural setting, the habitus is a cultural disposition learned through social encoding. These terms can be helpful in reading Emma Rouault's conflicted identity as Madame Bovary.[1] The habitus of what it means to be a married woman sets up what she is going to reject with the hexis of her body. The finger-pricking episodes, taken together as a hexis, prepare the reader for the violent confrontation of Emma Rouault with the bourgeois expectations, that is the habitus, of what it means to be a wife. In her case, she is destined to be a bourgeois accomplice to Charles Bovary's incompetence at finding his place among others. Emma effectively manifests her own incompetence at being the husband's deferential handmaiden with the requisite properly wifely demeanor while seeking her competence as a woman in a role other than bourgeois wife.

Emma ironically foreshadows her incompetence at a wife's work by pricking her finger while doing needlework during the widower Charles Bovary's visit to her father's farm. This single act of pricking her finger points to her incompetence at a married woman's work, in this case thread and needle. The violent nature of the act underscores her rejection of the expected skills of a bourgeois wife. Within Pierre Bourdieu's social science orientation, he has adapted the word 'hexis' to mean 'a certain durable organization of one's body and of its deployment in the world' (Thompson 13). In Emma Rouault's context, the 'hexis' becomes a concept opposed to the 'habitus,' the expectations of society as appropriated by an individual. Emma's context is the bourgeois, capitalist society examined by Flaubert, the novelist whose role has been described as 'a disseminator of the already said, a transcriber of the codes of social discourse' (Ramazani 11). Curiously, after her marriage to Charles, Emma pricks her finger once again, this time with the flowers from her wedding bouquet shortly before disposing of them in anger about her marriage into the fireplace. This occurs prior to moving from Tostes to Yonville-l'Abbaye, a move that surely signifies, as Paula Roberts notes in her study of space in ***Madame Bovary,*** that married life is abandoned (['L'Espace dans *Madame Bovary*'] 1994, 2). Emma just cannot seem to do the tasks asked of a married woman, in this case handling flowers, without drawing her own blood. Even when Homais asks her, upon her arrival in Yonville, whether she will do the wifely thing and tend a garden, she shrugs it off as being of no personal interest to her.

Bourdieu's methodological process reveals the links and the breakdowns in the communication of wifely expectations to Emma. His sociological model is instructive about the struggle at the core of Emma's personality. He insists that his model represents modern science's 'relational' (1992, 255), rather than structuralist, way of thinking and thus enables us to see ourselves through relationships. As opposed to the structuralist or static analytical categories that would portray Emma as the unfaithful spouse, for example, Bourdieu's habitus offers the possibility of understanding the evolution, struggle, growth, and behavior modification in the character of Emma from her girlhood as Emma Rouault to her married identity as Madame Bovary. In addition, the play between habitus and hexis allows the reader to appreciate the struggle in her character as part of the contiguous changes in society around her. Gossip and reputation-formation influence the limited space within which Emma can work out her identity relative to her habitus. While Sartre notes that Flaubert was subject to an 'idiosyncratic habitus with a specific kind of interiorization' ([*L'Idiot de la famille*] 1972, 55), we could say the same thing about Flaubert's creation, Emma Rouault: that is, she is subject to an individual's wrestling with the expectations of what a wife should be. Indeed, Bourdieu's method helps us to understand a schizophrenic personality that society created through its inculcation of habitus within Emma. In effect, Flaubert's literary model shows us that 'Emma experiences everything twice, first in exalted and then in degraded form' (Beizer 144). The terms of hexis and habitus become especially useful for their oppositional roles in Emma, although Bourdieu did not necessarily invent them as such. They do present the relational conflict that subtends the psychological crisis for Emma as delineated recently by Susanna Lee: 'Emma's later spiritual failures occur because she cannot reach outside herself' ([*'Flaubert's blague supérieure'*] 2001, 205). The internal struggle between the habitus and he hexis focalizes this incompetence.

Emma effectively models the disjunction of personality that the habitus of society has produced within many of us. Her waltzing with the Vicomte at the Vaubyessard ball recurred many times with Léon and Rodolphe (Roberts 5) and was predicted once she pricked her fingers with the reality of her incompetence as a wife. Her waltzing represents her choice of partners in life and the rhythm that she wanted for herself. The hexis of her bodily disposition in the dance with multiple partners effectively creates a space in which she can express her identity separately from what the habitus of marriage disposes her to be. As Stephen Heath reminds us, this experience provides the principal disjunction of the

novel: 'Emma becomes the heroine she wants to be, finds herself in the novels of adultery she has read, but that heroine, these novels, do not correspond to any reality of things' ([*Gustave Flaubert*] 1992, 83). This makes the mirrors she uses all the more ironic for her. The lack of correspondence between the hexis and habitus in her life makes her unable to see herself as others, especially we readers, do. Five steps lead us to the conclusion that Emma breaks with the bourgeois expectations for a spouse and becomes incompetent at meeting these standards while seeking alternate roles for herself as a woman. First of all, the habitus of the French culture's understanding of wifely behavior meets with a mismatch in Emma's education during her formative years. Secondly, Emma's suffering is a key to her awareness of a problem in her adaptation to the habitus. Thirdly, language is 'cultural capital' (Harker 43) according to Bourdieu and thus the instrument by which the habitus activates its rules determining the nature of her marriage to Charles. Thus, Emma's language is a key to examining the role of habitus in her behavior. Fourthly, breaking the rules becomes the basis for her to invent her own womanly code in contradistinction to the habitus. Lastly, Emma's incompetence is modeling behavior[2] for a generative scheme leading to the conquest of the smile whereby she acknowledges her release from imprisonment in the habitus of a married woman.

I. THE HABITUS AS CULTURAL UNDERSTANDING

The habitus is a social disposition learned through formal and family education. Emma acquired competing versions of the habitus through her convent education and subsequent life on her father's farm. The problem is that the opposition between these two becomes stark in the hexis of her initial finger prick, suggesting her incompetence with needlework. On the one hand, she received a mystical idea of the religious union with Christ from the priest's sermons in the convent: 'Les comparaisons de fiancé, d'époux, d'amant céleste et de mariage éternel qui reviennent dans les sermons lui soulevaient au fond de l'âme des douceurs inattendues' (Flaubert [*Madame Bovary*] 37)[3] [The comparisons of fiancé, of husband, and of heavenly lover with an eternal marriage which recur in the sermons stirred up an unexpected mellowness in the depths of her soul]. On the one hand, this promised satisfaction in the depths of her soul sets up Emma's transcendental attitude toward society's expectations of a wife. On the other hand, the habitus—that is the dispositions of an individual which, as Charles Taylor describes it, 'encodes a certain cultural understanding' (Taylor 58)—of what is expected of a bourgeois wife is assimilated internally, though not thoroughly, into Emma Rouault the woman. Her father's farm provides this cultural context, wherein her father observes that 'elle a trop d'esprit pour la culture' (25) [she is too independent for farm-work]. She nervously bites her lips, suggesting her discomfort with the prospect of spending the rest of her life in the service of her father on his farm. Meanwhile, Charles's first wife, Héloïse, ironically fantasizes about Emma's 'belle éducation' (19) with the supposedly sophisticated sewing skills and acquired refinements. And yet these are not the qualities that attract Emma to Charles. Her white nails and the direct gaze of her brown eyes are the ordinary features that appeal to this ordinary man.

The mismatch of bourgeois expectations and Charles Bovary provides the setting for Emma's own incompetence. While his classmates had the practice ('nous avions l'habitude' 4) of brashly throwing their caps on the floor, Charles could not manage to pay attention to them and instead held his cap shyly on his knee in direct contradiction to his father's ambition for him: 'avoir du toupet, un homme réussit toujours dans le monde' (8) [with audacity a man always succeeds in the world]. Charles shows himself to be especially incompetent in living up to his father's masculine, athletic model of 'l'idéal viril de l'enfance . . . à la spartiate' (7) [the Spartan, virile ideal for childhood]. Michael Riffaterre tells us that society and Charles's father would like Charles to be more than he ever proves himself to be: 'Charles does have what it takes to keep his female satisfied, if only she would give him a chance' (['Flaubert's Presuppositions'] 1981, 81). His chance is imbedded in the bourgeois values instilled in him. For example, when he first arrives at *les Bertaux*, the Rouault farm, Charles judges it to be acceptable in appearance ('une ferme de bonne apparence' 15). Judging by appearances, constituting a veil that Emma does not respect, Charles is comfortably drawn into the farmhouse where a great hearth fire awaits. These bourgeois trappings were conducive to his adopting the role of gallantry in order to court the waiting 'Mademoiselle Emma.' And then Emma pricks her finger during one of Charles's first visits.

Her awkwardness in needlework is not unrelated to the myrtle wreaths she shows Charles in her bedroom. Those wooden, and therefore artificial, myrtle wreaths were bourgeois awards given to her for her academic success. It is ironic that she brings Charles into her bedroom to show him how scholarly she had been, while we learn later that the authorities of the convent were happy to see her leave because she did not care for religious mysteries and 'elle s'irritait davantage contre la discipline, qui était quelque chose d'antipathique à sa constitution' (41) [she was even more annoyed with discipline, which was something contrary to her constitution]. She was an independent thinker who resisted the strictures of discipline and dogma that imposed control over the youth in the convent by channeling their thinking. After all, Bourdieu tells us that 'children are inducted into a culture, are taught the meanings which constitute it, partly through the inculcation of the ap-

propriate habitus' (Taylor 58). Yet Emma resisted the complete 'inculcation.' Her struggles with what society expected of her began when she challenged the ways of the convent schooling she received.

II. EMMA'S SUFFERING

Emma distinguishes her kind of suffering. Léon, Rodolphe, and Charles all acknowledge suffering as part of their daily lives. Her suffering, however, is claustrophobic. During the ball at Vaubryessard, she tells Charles to stay in one place for fear of being mocked by others for not knowing how to conduct himself, in this case, how to dance. Her admonition of 'reste à ta place' (51) [stay in your position] does not hold for her. She refuses to be limited by the habitus. When she tells the local parish priest, Bournisien, that she is suffering, he just shrugs her off by encouraging her to do her duty and to accept suffering as a common condition: 'nous sommes nés pour souffrir, comme dit saint Paul' (115) [we were born to suffer, in St. Paul's words].

Society's habitus thus views suffering as a condition of belonging to the group and accepting its rules. For example, Charles as husband agreeably watches Emma (90) sew while Léon the outsider to the marriage takes exception to Emma's needlework. As Léon observes her sewing, he notices that 'les doigts d'Emma semblaient s'y écorcher par le bout' (108) [the ends of Emma's fingers seemed to be chafed from it]. Léon does not see Emma as his wife and instead understands that this work wears away at her body. Once again the hexis of her body is communicating the unfitness of wifely decorum. Emma's body reflects Bourdieu's view of the hexis: 'the body is the site of incorporated history' (Thompson 13). Flaubert's story unravels this history as Emma bites her lips until they bleed (122), thus showing her anguish at not being content with her disposition toward 'un gouffre vague' (112) [an anonymous abyss] that she admits to Félicité as having consciously recognized only after her marriage. In this state of emotional upheaval, Emma flouts the social codes, as when she publicly parades her friendship with Léon to go see her child, who was living with Mme Rollet the wet-nurse, only to have the mayor's wife spread the rumor that 'madame Bovary se compromettait' (94) [Madame Bovary was compromising herself].

Emma thus begins to be openly hostile to the habitus. A key to reading her open hostility is what she wears one day when Charles is courting her at her father's farmhouse: 'Elle portrait, comme un homme, passé entre deux butons de son corsage, un lorgnon d'écaille' (17) [Like a man, she wore between the buttonholes of her blouse, a turtle-shell pince-nez]. Charles Baudelaire, Flaubert's contemporary and acquaintance, picked up on this association and remarked that Emma embodies 'virile virtues' ([*Oeuvres complètes*] 1975, 82) such as the spirit of domination that sparks her to unravel the rules of the habitus. When she was pregnant, she hoped for a boy and fainted after the baby's birth when she was told that the baby was a girl. She herself was thus perpetuating the female habitus by bringing yet another female body into the world to be controlled by society's expectations. And yet she is determined to drive a wedge between the habitus of her role as wife and her female desire: 'it is as if Emma knows, in the depths of her seething heart, that the most essential component of her whole enterprise is the desire which animates her female body' (Maraini 94). The suffering entails the difference between that desire and dispositions toward roles that trap the desire within her body, as provided by the habitus.

III. Language as the Cultural Capital of the Habitus

Pierre Bourdieu's research indicates that language contains what he calls, after a Marxian fashion, 'the cultural capital of the habitus' (Harker 43). By 'capital', he means the currency of exchange that attributes value to a cultural commodity. Language achieves this status obviously for Flaubert who, as is well known, invested considerable effort in his search for *le mot juste*. His character Emma is not as articulate as he was. Indeed, Flaubert's narrative voice approaches Emma's frustration with language in the famous passage: '. . . la parole humaine est comme un chaudron fêlé où nous battons des mélodies à faire danser les ours, quand on voudrait attendrir les étoiles' (196) [. . . human speech is like a cracked cauldron on which we play tunes to make bears dance when what is desired is to touch the stars]. Emma's situation, during her initial attraction de Léon, is associated with such anguish at the lack of the right words: 'Alors, les appétits de la chair, les convoitises d'argent et les mélancolies de la passion, tout se confondit dans la même souffrance' (111) [Thus the appetites of the flesh, the lust for money, and the sad moments of passion, all of these were confounded in the same suffering]. Bourdieu notes that the mixture of lexical fields is no accident. In this case, Flaubert's expressions, 'the appetites of the flesh' and 'the lust for money,' are sensual inter-penetrations of the melancholy state of Emma's desire when confronted with the habitus of the *moeurs de province,* the 'bourgeois manners' that are the subtitle of **Madame Bovary.**

What is not so obvious is Emma's investment in language. Stratton Buck notes that '. . . Emma's tragedy stems in part from her inability to find words adequate to her feelings or her needs . . .' ([*Gustave Flaubert*] 1966, 71-72). Her inarticulate nature brings her close to Flaubert's own fascination with the crucial importance of words. Even Flaubert's distant narrator acknowledges the problem: 'mais comment dire un insaisissable malaise' (42) [but how do you express an elusive dis-

comfort]. When Emma blurts out to Father Bournisien the words *je souffre*, she effectively situates her opposition to the habitus of language by not adapting words appropriate to her role as the doctor's wife. She should be adopting the vocabulary of duty according to Father Bournisien who, ironically as Emma's *directeur de conscience,* is also suffering from his own inability to control the local brats disturbing the peace around his church. Meanwhile, Emma cannot adequately communicate the details of her own suffering to those around her. During her boating escapade with Leon, he asks if she is suffering. She cannot find the precise cause of her anguish except to say that it is probably just an evening chill in the air.

The crucial identification of suffering with choking brings Emma to a realization of her imprisonment by the habitus. Her linking of 'je souffre' [I am suffering] and 'j'étouffe' [I am choking] leads her to have the windows opened in order to breathe fresh air. This is a key investment in the cultural capital of language because of her words bridge suffering and space. At the ball, she used the French word *place* to tell Charles to keep his relative position. When the Bovarys move to Yonville, Emma brags to Homais that she enjoys changing places ('j'aime à changer de place' 82). Relative to others in her society, ruled by the habitus and the dispositions it gives them, Emma would have her husband retain his bourgeois status while she is anxious to change the disposition of 'wife' which is choking her.

The windows motif especially underscores Emma's investment in the cultural capital of language. Let us take two of the many commentators on the role of windows in this novel. Jean Rousset reminds us that 'the window combines open and enclosed space, represents an obstacle as well an escape, a sheltering room as well as an area of endless expansion, a circumscribed infinity' (['An Aspect of Flaubert's Technique'] 1965, 67). Paula Roberts observes that the window is literally a means for Emma to look outside as if she did not belong to the internal enclosure of the windows (Roberts 5). This play of inside/outside is also functioning within Emma's limited use of language as metaphorical windows expressing the simultaneous transparency and frustrations of her desire. The transparency entails the ability of her dreams to transcend the enclosures offered by the limited dispositions of the habitus of wife for Emma. She can literally see beyond the windows, for example toward Léon strolling freely outside marriage or Rodolphe fleeing the responsibility of a married woman with a child. She thus seeks association with the freedoms of both Léon and Rodolphe, only to find that they cannot provide the space she needs. She is metaphorically enclosed by her financial dependence on her husband Charles and thus precluded from making decisions that allow her to leave her role as wife. The windows of her home entrap Emma with her few words, those acceptable for the limited dispositions that the habitus of wife provides, for example as a devoted mother to Berthe or as a faithful, deferential partner to Charles. Emma refuses these dispositions of the habitus of bourgeois wife while concomitantly being incapable of finding the words for what lies outside the windows. In the village of Tostes, she was almost agoraphobic and then claustrophobic as she struggled with the habitus and the hexis: 'Souvent, elle s'obstinait à ne pas sortir, puis elle suffoquait, ouvrait les fenêtres, s'habillait en robe légère' (68) [Often, she would stubbornly stay inside, then she was suffocating, opened the windows, and was scantily clad]. Upon finally speaking the words *j'étouffe,* she subsequently realizes that her concomitant salvation involves opening windows. On her deathbed, she requests that the windows be opened for there, too, she was suffocating from the ideologies of this life.

In examining language as the cultural capital of habitus, we must recall, with Jonathan Culler, that a novel such as *Madame Bovary* is 'writing, not a world' ([*Flaubert*] 1974, 230). As such the story of Emma Rouault is the stuff of written language especially that provided by Flaubert who, to repeat the insight into his role as a novelist, is 'a disseminator of the already said, a transcriber of the codes of social discourse' (Ramazani 114). His words fix Emma in the habitus of language encoded in narrative and direct irony both toward her and toward the habitus as Flaubert sets up the expectations of bourgeois society against the desire of the individual. Here, narratology instructs us in how language becomes the cultural capital of the past and how that past fixes Emma's fate. Gerald Prince's narratological study of *Madame Bovary* notes the preponderance of flashbacks to flash-forwards in the structure of the novel: 'If flashbacks are more numerous (about forty), their most important function is to present the characters' antecedents . . .' (['A Narratological Approach to *Madame Bovary*'] 1995, 88-89). Hence, in Emma's early years, especially those before her marriage, the repetitive dispositions of habitus through language began to appear. As Bourdieu remarks, 'the habitus . . . tends to reproduce the conditions of its own production by producing . . . objectively coherent strategies which are also systematically characteristic of a kind of reproduction' ([*La Noblesse d'Etat*] 1989, 387 [my trans.]). These 'strategies' entail how language incorporates the rules of marriage. Emma cannot have access to words that are not allowed within the household of a socially sanctioned marriage. This is her reticence, the nothing, that is at the center of *Madame Bovary.* Her lack of the exact words to express her desires sets up Flaubert's insight about the deepest desire of the writer-artist: to appear to treat one subject and to actually treat a totally different one (Sartre 20). Rather than to speak about Emma, Flaubert is actually speaking about the lack of ties between her and society, the nothing condemning her before her life began.

Returning to the issue of her financial dependence on Charles, Emma's wifely language cannot incorporate her personal financial accounting. Her debts are her husband's debts. She brought no financial resources into their marriage. She had few household skills and was thus of little value to her father on the farm. M. Rouault reasoned that a doctor as a prospective son-in-law meant that there would be little bickering over Emma's lack of a dowry. Then there was Charles's own misjudgment not only about M. Rouault's wealth, which had likewise been foreshadowed by Charles's mistake about the dowry in his first marriage to Héloïse, but also about Emma's physical beauty. Neither attribute was enough to provide capital for the success of the marriage between Charles and Emma. Her body, which obsessed Charles during their courtship, ironically houses the desires that challenge the habitus of wifely language through the hexis of her womanly behavior writ larger. That hexis began to be expressed through the finger pricks in her needlework and from the wedding bouquet. Her corporal dispositions continue to struggle with the habitus so that she could no longer endure the boredom of Charles's meager conversational abilities. The reader can almost hear her sigh in exasperation as she struggles with the repetitive behavior of her husband, such as his embrace coming home from work. Emma is thus primed to follow her hexis and to reject the habitus of being a wife.

IV. Breaking the Rules

Emma is not altogether without power as a spouse. She manipulates the code of a woman's cultivation to her benefit. A wife is supposed to be the hostess to the family's guests. In nineteenth-century France, the skill of piano-playing was part of how a well-educated wife was expected to entertain in the drawing room. Homais, as the mainstay of bourgeois values in Yonville, advises Charles to support the idea because it promotes the habitus of the maternal role of the wife as the educator of her child and promises a rewarding financial investment. Lucette Czyba reminds us that the socio-economic status of women thus influences their adaptation of the habitus of wife as mother ([*Mythes et idéologie de la femme dans les romans de Flaubert*] 1983, 56). Men likewise reinforce the linkage keeping the wife in her place within this socio-economic niche, that is, subservient to male dominance. As the proponent of the bourgeois habitus to Charles in Yonville, Homais therefore encourages the musical lessons because Charles wins twice: '. . . en engageant Madame à étudier, vous économisez pour plus tard sur l'éducation musicale de votre enfant' (266) [. . . by involving your wife in these studies, you invest in the musical education of your child]. Her piano lessons, under the guise of the town doctor's pretensions to culture and the promise of hospitality through the financial support of his wife's entertainment and education potential, are manipulated to give her excuses to go to Rouen to meet her lover, the new and exciting Léon who had traveled away from Yonville to Paris with all its pretenses at cultivation. Emma thus plays on the margins of respectability as a wife to seek her personal desires. The habitus of wifely comportment is thus compromised by the hexis of womanly desire. As such, Emma breaks the rules of being deferential to her husband and being a faithful spouse. She is in control of her actions after having learned to be unfaithful with Rodolphe. With the new and exciting Léon, Emma does the seducing and arranging the lovers' rendezvous. She thus enacts the fantasies derived from the novels and romances she read during her convent education.

And yet Emma needs to distance herself from the habitus of her marriage not only by going away in trysts but by displacing herself away from her husband permanently. She pleads with Rodolphe—'Emmène-moi, emmène-moi' (198) [Take me away, take me away]—as if he were a chevalier who could whisk her away on his noble steed. Here again the habitus intervenes. This time it is the guilt of mother-love assimilated from the habitus that conditions Emma to propose that she take Berthe with her as she and Rodolphe plan to leave Yonville. Rodolphe is not so comfortable with that part of the agreement. Let us remember here that it was with another man, Léon, when Emma first 'compromised' her reputation by bringing him along to see her child. Another disjunction, a sign of the opposition of her bodily hexis to the habitus that informs her that, she must stay in her marriage, occurs in her fainting spells—a Romantic device that in Emma expresses the disparity between her desires and the expectations of society's laws symbolized by her marriage to Charles (Chambers 159). After receiving Rodolphe's letter, Emma faints, as she did upon hearing the news that her child was a girl. Her bodily hexis could not bear to promote the habitus to yet another woman. In fact, as Louise Kaplan argues, 'With these feminine frivolities [such as her fainting spells], she masks her dominating spirit, her desire to penetrate the veil of illusion' (1991, 236). Emma's aspirations as a woman again and again are not synchronized with the rules of what a woman can be according to the habitus of the wife. Instead, she breaks the rules but cannot exit the entrapping habitus despite her fainting routine.

Emma's illness after the departure of Rodolphe exemplifies the struggle between the hexis and the habitus. In today's terms, we would say that there is a psychosomatic effect of Emma's desire on her body's dispositions. The bower in the Bovary garden is a revealing symbol of the protective role of the habitus. This bower is literally a decorative structure offering shade and a place for climbing plants and flowers. Through her destruction of her bridal flowers in Tostes and her rejection of Homais's appeal to her gardening talents when she first arrived in Yonville, Emma rejected her wifely duty to work with flowers. Yet the bower was a constructed place among flowers, almost an inverted womblike shape that provides shelter from the sun and harsh light, where Emma was courted by the young Léon and was attracted by his promise of cultivation outside of marriage. After Rodolphe's letter, Charles escorts her, during her illness, to the bower. Emma is strident in her rejection of that place—'Oh! Non, pas là, pas là!' (215) [Oh no, not there, not there!]—as if the bower reminded her of the false hope that another could save her from her fate as a wife. This same bower will shelter Charles after Emma's death, when Charles himself experiences the suffocation of the habitus regarding marriage and its social dispositions.

Emma maintains a non-wifely deferential behavior toward her husband until the end. Her behavior can be characterized as 'virile' insofar as she does not acquiesce to the habitus of how a woman in marriage should act and instead 'strains against ever-narrowing spaces throughout her life' (Tipper 375). The habitus effectively reduces her space as a woman while she struggles to find her own in which prodigality reigns. She ignores the expectation that a bourgeois wife defer to the financial solvency of her husband, the wage-earner of the family. She tosses her last five-franc coin to the blind beggar as the ultimate act of defiance toward a habitus disposing her to be concerned, as a responsible wife, with protecting the solvency of her household. Emma's lack of deference for the inferior position of the bourgeois wife to her husband explodes the financial predicament of a wife dependent upon her husband's income in a capitalist environment. While Homais lauds Charles's opportunity to save money by sending Emma off to Rouen for piano lessons, Emma in fact uses this occasion as a subterfuge for her prodigality. When her careless financial ways finally lead to jeopardizing Charles's estate, she must ironically appeal yet again to the habitus of men as the financial resource for women. Prostitution is constantly implied when Emma goes to the lawyer Guillaume, to Léon, and to Rodolphe for income to alleviate the financial quandary she has incurred for her marriage. Her integrity, the hexis of her body, must be sacrificed for the survival of the habitus.

Her only viable space is the literary one created by Flaubert because there the life she wanted to promote in the son she never had can be asserted in the martyrdom of her suicide. She must die because she cannot live within the space that the habitus had prepared for her. Even her death is a struggle because she imagined for herself the facile death of the heroines in her romances. Instead, her body once again communicates the hexis of opposition to the habitus that had prepared her for a very different death. Bourdieu's explanation of the habitus is insightful: 'Bref, l'habitus est le principe de la structuration sociale de l'existence temporelle, de toutes les anticipations et les présuppositions à travers lesquelles nous construisons pratiquement le sens du monde, c'est-à-dire sa signification, mais aussi, inséparablement, son orientation vers l'*à-venir*' (1992, 450) [Simply put, the habitus is the principle of the social structuring of temporal existence, of all the anticipations and the presuppositions through which we practically make sense of the world, that is, its meaning, but also, inseparably, its orientation toward *what is to come*]. Making 'sense of the world' in which she found herself is the real rub for Emma and the reason why the hexis of her woman's body is opposed to the habitus of society's dispositions for a wife. Emma's whole life was thus planned by the structuring of her education as a woman and as a wife. The expectations of being woman and wife were incompatible in Emma. Her death was written in that incompatibility. But there is more. Emma is also a model as a literary product in which we can examine the interests of the habitus because, as Bourdieu tells us, 'the fact that the literary or artistic production appears as disinterested . . . does not mean that it is' (Thompson 16). So let us examine the nature of the interests in Emma's story.

V. EMMA'S MODELING BEHAVIOR

The benefit of the literary modeling of Emma is that we can see and examine both sides of the divide. Once Emma and Rodolphe begin their liaison, she looks at herself in the mirror and exclaims, almost ecstatically: 'J'ai un amant! un amant!' (167) [I have a lover, a lover!]. She does not see the woman who transgresses her expectations of fidelity as a wife. She is said to have found 'dans l'adultère toutes les platitudes du mariage' (296) [in adultery all the platitudes of marriage]. Curiously, her mirror gives her a view of her otherness to the habitus of a married woman. This mirror-image of her otherness prefigures the one she uses on her deathbed when she is also listening to the blind beggar, that haunting character she encountered in Rouen who recalls the mythological figure of Tiresias, the blind seer who is reputed to have had a bisexual identity. Tiresias incarnates a mythological bonding of masculine and feminine as well as the linking of past and future to contrast with Emma's own life that constantly vacillates between these poles. While she is sometimes deferentially feminine in the early stages of her liaison with Rodolphe and assertively masculine in her sexual relationship with Léon, she finds calmness in reflecting upon her past within the walls of the convent and consolation in the possibility that Rodolphe will take her away to some ideal future life over there. Emma's future had already been inscribed in the habitus of marriage she had read about and learned in the convent. Even Rodolphe is part of that socially inscribed hope that heterosexuality builds into the male as the harbinger of hope and deliverance from women's responsibility for their own destiny. Bourdieu reminds us that the habitus entails 'the near-perfect anticipation of the future inscribed in all the concrete configurations . . .' ([*The Logic of Practice*] 1990, 66).

None of these configurations lasts for Emma, however, as we readers learn. She is instead perpetually anguished by the present-day habitus of marriage whose dispositions leave her reflecting upon 'd'où venait cette insuffisance de la vie . . .' (289) [where does this lack in life originate]. Only as she gazes upon herself in a handheld mirror on a deathbed does she finally listen to and imagine a face-to-face confrontation with the blind beggar/Tiresias who sings about love and the attractions between the sexes. Curiously, it is then that Emma appears almost mystically transported beyond the habitus. The explosive confrontation between Emma and her other produces this bizarre laughter just prior to her death, so that we could agree that 'Emma laughs when she senses herself suddenly outside the world which holds her imprisoned' (Cladwell 66). The beggar leads her to this awareness that there is an outside, an other to the habitus that held her captive. Even after her death, Charles sees to it that she is buried in her wedding dress, slippers and crown. The habitus of marriage reigns over the hexis of her body despite her momentary glimpse of transcendence.

Emma's modeling behavior also entails an ironic justification of the habitus. Her struggle with her learned dispositions in marriage and her discontent keeps her life and her narrative energized. Despite Emma's fragmented relationship with the habitus, never totally assimilated by and often fragmented, characteristics that are after all part of the experience of modernity, we reaffirm with Bourdieu '. . . the strategies intended simply to neutralize the action of time and ensure the continuity of interpersonal relations, making continuity out of discontinuity' (1990, 107). Of course, time and marriage must continue after Emma. A recent sequel to ***Madame Bovary,*** a novel entitled *La Fille d'Emma* (Buffard 2001), shows that the pattern exemplified in the character of Emma continues despite her death. Flaubert's novel thus models what Bourdieu calls for in the method of habitus as 'an acquired system of generative schemes' (1990, 55). This all began with Emma's pricking her finger while doing needlework, the hexis in the habitus, Flaubert's way of criticizing the very system which educates us about being who we are.

Notes

1. Her married name in the title of the novel conveys her disappearance even before the reader learns about Emma Rouault: '. . . the title designates her role as a married woman in a world of rigid restraints, impassible barriers, and impossible divorce' (Berg and Martin 31).

2. Emma's hexis provides modeling behavior in contradistinction to 'the model of the happy nuclear

family, as promulgated by the *Code Napoléon*' (Orr 27). Louise Kaplan reminds us that '. . . Emma's adulterous passions and neglect of her motherly duties mark her as a threat, a subversive force, an underminer of the structures of the bourgeois family' ([*Female Perversions*] 1991, 202).

3. Henceforth, page numbers following the French text will refer to this edition of *Madame Bovary.*

Works Consulted

Baudelaire, Charles. 1975. *Oeuvres complètes,* v. 2. Ed. Claude Pichois. Paris: Gallimard.

Beizer, Janet. 1993. *Ventriloquized Bodies: Narratives of Hysteria in Nineteenth-Century France.* Ithaca: Cornell University Press.

Berg, William J. and Laurey K. Martin. 1997. *Gustave Flaubert.* New York: Twayne.

Bourdieu, Pierre. 1989. *La Noblesse d'Etat: Grandes Ecoles et Esprit de Corps.* Paris: Minuit.

———1990. *The Logic of Practice.* Tr. Richard Nice. Stanford: Stanford University Press.

———1991. *Language and Symbolic Power.* Trs. Gino Raymond and Matthew Adamson. Cambridge [Ma.]: Harvard University Press.

———1992. *Les Règles de l'art: Genèse et structure du champ littéraire.* Paris: Seuil. Tr. Susan Emmanuel as *The Rules of Art: Genesis and Structure of the Literary Field.* Stanford: Stanford University Press, 1995.

Buck, Stratton. 1966. *Gustave Flaubert.* Boston: Twayne.

Buffard, Claude-Henri. 2001. *La Fille d'Emma.* Paris: Grasset.

Cladwell, Jr., Ray Chandler. 2000. 'Madame Bovary's Last Laugh.' *French Forum,* XXV, No. 1 (January), 55-74.

Chambers, Ross. 1988. 'Vapeurs d'Emma, vertige du texte: *Madame Bovary* et la mélancolie.' In Michael Guggenheim, ed. *Women in French Literature.* Saratoga [Ca.]: Anma Libri, pp. 157-167.

Culler, Jonathan. 1974. *Flaubert: the Uses of Certainty.* Ithaca: Cornell University Press.

Czyba, Lucette. 1983. *Mythes et idéologie de la femme dans les romans de Flaubert.* Lyon: Presses Universitaires de Lyon.

D'Aurevilly, Barbey. 1865. 'M. Gustave Flaubert.' Tr. Robert Steele. Reprinted in Laurence M. Porter, ed. *Critical Essays on Gustave Flaubert.* Boston: G. K. Hall, 1986, pp. 50-57.

Elias, Norbert. 1983. *The Court Society.* Tr. Edmund Jephcott. New York: Pantheon.

Flaubert, Gustave. 1971. *Madame Bovary.* Ed. Claudine Gothot-Mersch. Paris: Garnier Frères.

Harker, Richard, Cheleen Mahan and Chris Wilkes, eds. 1990. *An Introduction to the Works of Pierre Bourdieu: The Practice of Theory.* New York: St. Martin's Press.

Heath, Stephen. 1992. *Gustave Flaubert: Madame Bovary.* Cambridge: Cambridge University Press.

Kaplan, Louise B. 1991. *Female Perversions.* New York: Doubleday.

Lee, Susanna. 2001. 'Flaubert's *blague supérieure*: The Secular World of *Madame Bovary.*' *Symposium,* CIV, No. 4 (Winter), 203-217.

Maraini, Dacia. 1998. *Searching for Emma: Gustave Flaubert and* Madame Bovary. Tr. Vincent J. Bertolini. Chicago: University of Chicago Press.

McEachern, Patricia A. 1997. 'True Lies: Fasting for Force or Fashion in *Madame Bovary.*' *Romance Notes,* XXXVII, No. 3 (Spring), 289-298.

Orr, Mary. 2000. *Flaubert: Writing the Masculine.* Oxford: Oxford University Press.

Prince, Gerald. 1995. 'A Narratological Approach to *Madame Bovary.*' In Laurence M. Porter and Eugene F. Gray, eds. *Approaches to Teaching Flaubert's Madame Bovary.* New York: Modern Language Association, pp. 84-89.

Ramazani, Vaheed K. 1988. *The Free Indirect Mode: Flaubert and the Poetics of Irony.* Charlottesville: University of Virginia Press.

Riffaterre, Michael. 1981. 'Flaubert's Presuppositions.' Reprinted in Laurence M. Porter, ed. *Critical Essays on Gustave Flaubert.* Boston: G. K. Hall, 1986, pp. 76-86.

Roberts, Paula. 1994. 'L'Espace dans *Madame Bovary.*' *Chimères,* XXI, No. 2 (Fall), 1-12.

Rousset, Jean. 1965. 'An Aspect of Flaubert's Technique: Point of View.' Tr. Paul de Man. Reprinted in Laurence M. Porter, ed. *Critical Essays on Gustave Flaubert.* Boston: G. K. Hall, 1986, pp. 58-75.

Sartre, Jean-Paul. 1972. *L'Idiot de la famille,* v. 2: *Gustave Flaubert de 1821 à 1857.* Paris: Gallimard.

Taylor, Charles. 1993. 'To Follow a Rule. . . .' In Craig Calhoun, Edward Li Puma, and Moishe Postone, eds. *Bourdieu: Critical Perspectives.* Chicago: University of Chicago Press, pp. 45-60.

Thompson, John B. 1991. Introduction to Pierre Bourdieu. *Language and Symbolic Power.* Trs. Gino Raymond and Matthew Adamson. Cambridge [Ma.]: Harvard University Press.

Tipper, Paul Andrew. 1999. 'Emma's Feet in Clay.' *The Modern Language Review,* XCIV (April), 366-376.

Malcolm Bowie (essay date 2004)

SOURCE: Bowie, Malcolm. Introduction to *Madame Bovary: Provincial Manners,* translated by Margaret Mauldon, pp. vii-xx. Oxford: Oxford University Press, 2004.

[In the following essay, Bowie offers an overview of the novel's characters and major themes. Bowie suggests that the work's modernity lies in Flaubert's recognition throughout the narrative of the inherently transitory, arbitrary power of language.]

I

Flaubert's approval rating among his fellow writers has always been exceptionally high, and for many of them *Madame Bovary* (1857) has been a particular object of veneration. 'It has a perfection that not only stamps it, but that makes it stand almost alone,' wrote Henry James in 1902; 'it holds itself with such a supreme unapproachable assurance as both excites and defies judgment.' Nearly twenty years later, Proust pointed to the 'grammatical beauty' of Flaubert's style in *Madame Bovary* and elsewhere, and to the new vision of the world, comparable to the philosophy of Immanuel Kant, that Flaubert had achieved by way of an artfully reinvented imperfect tense. Vladimir Nabokov, lecturing to students at Wellesley College in Massachusetts in the immediate aftermath of the Second World War, picked up the refrain, and performed a dazzling close analysis of the novel. 'Stylistically it is prose doing what poetry is supposed to do,' he announced, before setting out to expose the compressed layers of poetic implication that Flaubert had packed into his most celebrated work. For well over a century, this approving chorus has sounded internationally, and brought together a range of otherwise dissimilar critical voices.

Great writers cannot be expected to approve unreservedly of their predecessors' efforts, however, for each has his own slant of vision to find, and his own battery of stylistic effects to nurture and perfect. Emma Bovary, for James, was a limited 'reflector and register' of the real world, and suffered from the selfsame poverty of consciousness that his own heroines were uniformly spared. Proust was rude about Flaubert's style, finding in it something of the moving pavement and the mechanical digger, and he entertained a further subversive thought: perhaps Flaubert was a great writer who had schooled himself out of writing well. Even Nabokov, the most admiring of these three witnesses to Flaubert's genius, spends a delicious page itemizing the avoidable implausibilities that the master had incorporated into his text. What all Flaubert's fellow professionals agree on, despite their reservations, is that *Madame Bovary* marks a moment of decisive discontinuity in the history of the European novel, and that prose fiction produced in its wake, and under the influence of Flaubert's singular style, could move in directions that were quite new.

In part, the surprise that Flaubert sprang on the first readers of *Madame Bovary,* and that many readers coming to him for the first time at the beginning of the twenty-first century are still likely to experience, has to do with the banality of his subject matter and the relentless microscopic vision that he brought to bear on it. Emma and her provincial neighbours are little in moral stature, limited in intelligence, stunted in their ambitions, sordid in their private thoughts, and ridiculous in their public prating and posturing. Around his centrally placed married couple, locked into their miseries, Flaubert has laid out a gallery of unedifying stereotypes: Homais the self-seeking pharmacist, who represents secularism and republican virtue at their lowest ebb; Bournisien the fleshly priest, much given to empty ecclesiastical exhortation; Rodolphe the well-to-do landowner and full-time rake. No trade or profession escapes Flaubert's derision. No individual represents true decency. How can a serious novel, a work of high art, be made from material of this kind? And how can an artistic project aiming so low be sustained over hundreds of pages? These are genuine sources of puzzlement, and even when Flaubert's astonishing ironic gift has been recognized many readers are likely to find themselves wondering how it was ever possible to expend so much irony on targets such as these. With undimmed malice, Flaubert has Bournisien and Homais watch over Emma's corpse at the end of the novel, one of them sprinkling her room with holy water and the other with chlorine. This double gibe, although delivered in exquisite symmetrical syntax, surely comes too late in the day, and after too many sallies of the same sort.

If we follow various of the tourist trails through modern Normandy, looking out for the legacies of Emma, Charles, Homais, and Bournisien as we go, we are likely to be confirmed in the view that Flaubert has misjudged the task of the novelist and the wishes of his audience. The secluded world of Yonville-l'Abbaye and its surrounding hamlets exists to this day. The river Andelle still flows, and sudden vistas still guide the eye across the fields to an isolated church or chateau. The modern Ry, with its long main street, prides itself on being the prototype for Flaubert's imaginary village, and reminders of the novel, down to its tiniest descriptive phrases, are everywhere in the locality: the grey-white cliffs in the area are streaked with brick-red, as described at the beginning of Part II, and flowers grow on the roofs of thatched cottages, exactly as Flaubert specifies towards the end of the book (p. 301). For the modern visitor, as for Emma herself, the metropolis of Rouen is at once nearby and as remote from this quiet rural landscape as Jerusalem or Constantinople. Finding the topography of the novel still largely intact, preserved in a green museum just north of the N31, those who worry about such things are likely to begin worrying all over again about realism in fiction. Surely novelists of note must have better things to do with their time than to tell their readers what they already know, or can easily discover elsewhere. If one is going to map the contours of *la France profonde,* or trace out the flat expanses of an average bourgeois marriage or adulterous affair, one needs the leaven of metaphor, or ideas, or speculative adventure. The writing must crackle with invention at some level. One cannot just preside, poker-faced, over the everyday world, setting it down as a procession of precisely observed details, and expect one's reader to stay the course.

Flaubert certainly wanted to create a first impression of himself as the author of a guileless guidebook to a region and its manners. The flat, deadpan tone mattered to him, and he returned to it at intervals throughout the work. But other impressions are soon superimposed on this one. The miracle of Flaubert's writing is in the stealth with which he adjusts its focus from one word to the next, or from sentence to sentence. Proust's excavating machine is often to be heard in the background, and there are entire paragraphs of **Madame Bovary** that seem to be made of constricted telegrammatic utterances placed end to end, but even here the enumeration of details has a living pulse to it:

> As there were not enough stable boys to unharness all the horses, the gentlemen rolled up their sleeves and got down to it themselves. Depending on their social position, they wore dress coats, frock coats, jackets both short and long: good-quality dress coats, treated with great respect by the entire family, and brought out of the wardrobe only on solemn occasions; frock coats with voluminous tails that flapped in the breeze, cylindrical collars, and big pockets like miniature sacks; jackets of coarse cloth, generally worn with a brass-banded peaked cap; very short-skirted jackets with, at the back, two buttons close together like a pair of eyes, and tails that might have been hacked straight from a single piece of cloth with a carpenter's hatchet.

> (pp. 25-6)

These are the male guests arriving for the wedding of Emma and Charles, or rather this is their attire come loose from their bodies and recorded as a series of shapes and sociological meanings. On the one hand, the narrator seems to be having fun at the expense of his country folk, and to be suggesting, by way of a determined transfer of attention from persons to clothing, that local festivities of this kind are nothing but show and pantomime: all right if you live in a village, as Ger-

trude Stein once remarked, but if not, not. Failures of dress sense have been sorted into a jeering catalogue by one who clearly knows better about such matters than his Norman neighbours. On the other hand, however, something more akin to a musical exposition is also going on in this paragraph. There are three thematic kernels—dress coats, frock coats, and jackets—and each of them is no sooner stated than subjected to an elaborate process of variation. Flaubert's prose speaks of an ordinary world that is becoming fantastical even as each separate notation is set down: these country-dwellers are beginning to flap like birds and to grow eyes in the back of their jackets. And it speaks, too, of a playful, self-delighting intelligence at work upon whatever undistinguished fragments of the real world it finds to hand.

It will be plain to many readers of **Madame Bovary,** from its first page onwards, that this is a novel in which something strange and undeclared is going on, and that Flaubert has other than 'realist' designs upon us. Charles's famous cap—'Ovoid in shape, its curves enlarged with whalebone, it began with three circular sausage-shaped layers'—is already much more than a preliminary indicator of its owner's character. To be sure this exercise in ponderous description does tell us about the clumsiness and ill-fittingness of Charles himself, but it introduces us at the same time to another major tendency of Flaubert's imagination, by which he devalues and simultaneously revalorizes the objects that fall beneath his gaze. The cap is a concoction and a contraption, a bundle of heterogeneous components, yet at the same time it resembles a complex measuring device, a theodolite or an astrolabe perhaps, designed for use in two or more dimensions at once. In its concoctedness it resembles a work of art, and in its intersecting planes and conjoined materials it resembles an instrument of intellectual enquiry. This strange, stranded piece of headgear is a warning of excitements and provocations to come, and the first in a long Flaubertian series of uncanny, proto-surrealist assemblages.

By far the commonest, and most acclaimed, device used by Flaubert to float his own and his reader's attention between incompatible value-systems is the one known to critics of the novel as 'free indirect style'. This is a familiar enough feature of many literary works, and of everyday conversation for that matter, but Flaubert uses it with a persistence and range of implication that are quite new. Sometimes it simply involves a momentary discord, a single word that switches us from an impersonal to a personal viewpoint: 'And her husband, knowing that she enjoyed going for drives, found a second-hand gig which, once it was fitted with new lamps and splash-boards of quilted leather, looked almost like a tilbury' (p. 31). The conveyance named at the end of this sentence takes us from a no-nonsense narrative viewpoint, in which the refurbishment of shabby vehicles can be mentioned without shame, to the very heart of Emma's impatient aspirations. A tilbury, even an approximate one, would mark the beginning of an upward gradient in Emma's social life.

More telling, however, are those extended passages in which two systems seem to be cross-hatched, or in which two ways of looking at the world each provide the other with a distorting gravitational field. In this slightly later account of Emma's fantasies in full self-dramatizing swing, for example, narrator and character enter into a rapturous dialogue. Emma is already making damaging comparisons between her own marriage-partner and those that others are likely to have found for themselves:

> For indeed not all husbands were like this one. He might have been handsome, witty, distinguished, attractive, as were no doubt the men her old school friends from the convent had married. What must they be doing now? In the city, with the noises of the streets, the hum of the theatres, and the bright lights of the balls, they were leading lives where the heart had space to expand, the senses to blossom. But her life was as cold as an attic with a skylight facing north, and boredom, like a silent spider, was weaving its web in every shadowy recess of her heart.
>
> (p. 41)

This is an impulsive interior monologue, a moving picture of daydreaming as it happens, and at first the narrator's voice edits it only lightly. Emma speaks for herself, and is discreetly nudged from time to time towards symmetry in her phrasing or precision in her diction. But in the last sentence there is a change of gear. The narrator both wants and does not want to share her view of things. The meagre skylight, the northern prospect, and the busy spider are borrowed from Emma's favourite adolescent reading. They are literary hand-me-downs, the prefabricated parts of a Gothic stage-set. Yet *ennui*, that special, virulent sub-species of boredom, was a badge of honour for certain of Flaubert's poetic contemporaries, and for the novelist himself at times. Baudelaire praised its repulsiveness highly, and imagined with relish a hideous population of spiders at work in the bored individual's brain. Emma, using her own version of the image, has become a woman of her time, and a poet of sorts. Her still adolescent habits of imagination have brought her into radical company, and the commentator who seemed to despise her a moment ago has suddenly found in her a soul-mate, and a fellow devotee of extreme emotional states.

There is, then, a counter-current of poetic suggestion running through Flaubert's portrait of the Normandy landscape and its desperate middle-class inhabitants. On the face of it everything in the human realm is flat and drab, and the beauties of nature can do little to enliven or elevate the minimal life-stories that unfold here. Yet the voice of the narrator, as it shrinks and then suddenly expands its range of sympathies, proves to be a very unreliable guide to this supposedly worthless rural scene. That voice absorbs and re-inflects other people's points of view, and in so doing becomes mobile and accommodating. 'What will he do next?', the reader begins to ask of this capricious narrator. There can be no real doubt, for example, that Rodolphe, the first lover Emma finds outside her marriage to Charles Bovary, is a cad and a boor, and the following passage certainly begins by emphasizing his lack of discrimination. Rodolphe is reacting to Emma's declarations of love and admiration, all of which he has heard before, from earlier mistresses:

> He could not see—this man of such broad experience—the difference of feeling, beneath the similarity of expression. Because wanton or venal lips had murmured the same words to him, he only half believed in the sincerity of those he was hearing now; to a large extent they should be disregarded, he believed, because such exaggerated language must surely mask commonplace feelings: as if the soul in its fullness did not sometimes overflow into the most barren metaphors, since no one can ever tell the precise measure of his own needs, of his own ideas, of his own pain, and human language is like a cracked kettledrum on which we beat out tunes for bears to dance to, when what we long to do is make music that will move the stars to pity.
>
> (p. 170)

With the words 'as if the soul in its fullness' a halt is called to the flow of Rodolphe's self-justifying reverie on the language of lovers. The narrator takes Rodolphe's views seriously, thinks of them indeed as a fledgling philosophy of language, and enters into debate with them. Even a scoundrel may be worth arguing with. The narrator corrects an imperceptive character, and offers a superior philosophical basis for any future enquiry into amorous speech. The arbitrariness of the verbal sign, much discussed in modern linguistic theory, is already here, as is the importance of considering context in seeking to understand any communicative act. A hinge in the middle of the paragraph thus connects the views of a cad with a fine tragic insight into the limitations of human language. Abruptly, in the last sentence, a universal sorrow and rage sing out, and mere Rodolphe has acted as the pretext for their song.

Flaubert clearly enjoys the company of fools, and beats the drum with relish for his dancing bears. But there is much more to the design of the book, and to the virtuosity of its execution, than these singular moments of collusion between a storyteller and his cast of characters. Such moments are distributed throughout the novel and together create a pattern of long-range echoes and refrains, but much of the internal architecture of Flaubert's narrative involves a smaller and more elastic series of supporting struts. For many readers of the text in its original French the first inkling of this quality will come not from large movements of recurrence, but from the fall of sounds and phrases within individual sentences. Flaubert has a predilection for things, actions, or attributes that come at him in threes, and the shoes worn by the young Charles Bovary on the first page of the novel—'heavy, badly shined, and studded with nails'—offer a foretaste of countless formulations of the same threefold kind. He also enjoys assonance, alliteration, rhyme, and near-rhyme, and these features can descend as a seemingly gratuitous sound-texture upon any incidental observation: 'L'air, passant par le dessous de la porte, poussait un peu de poussière sur les dalles' ('A draught of air from under the door stirred a little dust on the flagstones', p. 22). On occasion the triadic obsession and the sound-play coincide to produce a bizarre effect of motiveless emphasis: 'Un peu plus bas, cependant, on était rafraîchi par un courant d'air glacial qui sentait le suif, le cuir et l'huile' ('But just a little further away, refreshing gusts of chilly air smelling of tallow, leather, and oil could be felt', p. 196). Emma is about to see Donizetti's *Lucia di Lammermoor* for the first time, and the air of Rouen is already alive with a premonition of tunes and harmonies. In both these cases, it is the silent air that suddenly breaks into sound inside the Flaubert sentence, but any neutral or characterless medium can be turned into sensory stuff in the same way. At this local level, the novelist's self-appointed task is clearly that of bringing ordinary things together into an enchanted interlace. Even agriculture can be musicalized by verbal art: Emma's father, visiting the young couple at their first home together, talks insistently of 'veaux, vaches, volailles' ('calves, cows, poultry', p. 60).

The web of connections operating on a larger scale between the separate phases of Flaubert's plot is the novel's most extraordinary feature. Moreover, one of these combined patterns of sound and sense comes close to offering Flaubert's own commentary on his narrative technique. It concerns the passage of meaning across space and time, and the waning of meaning that sets in as the novel moves towards its bleak denouement. The key terms in the miniature lexicon concerned are 'loin', 'lointain', 'éloigner', 'vague', and, bringing with them a further series of events that unfold in empty air, 'vibration' and its synonyms. This language of distance and remoteness, of far horizons and reverberating sound, cuts across the exact technical languages—of farming, pharmacy, medicine, and commerce—that Flaubert also exploits exhaustively. Flaubert's dry-goods store of useful objects has a current of vagueness and inscrutability running through it.

II

Emma Bovary is one of European literature's most celebrated dreamers and fantasists, and she is introduced to us as a specialist in long perspectives that end mist-

ily. In Part I of the novel, this note is struck often, and with no more than a tinge of disapproval on the narrator's part. Looking into the distance may, after all, be the sign of a forward-flung creative mind at work:

> And in her thoughts she followed them, up and down the hills, through the villages, racing along the highway by the light of the stars. Then, always, after an indeterminate distance, things became a blur, and her dream died away.
>
> (p. 52)

> But, very gradually, the circle whose centre he was grew larger round him, and that halo he wore shifted away from him, to shine its radiance on other dreams.
>
> (p. 52)

> They lived on a higher plane than other people, somewhere sublime between heaven and earth, among the storm clouds. As for the rest of the world, it was lost in shadows, it was nowhere, it seemed not to exist. Indeed, the closer things were to Emma, the more her thoughts avoided them.
>
> (p. 53)

In the first of these extracts, Emma is imagining the travels of a fish-vendor's cart, in the second remembering the mysterious Vicomte with whom she had danced at the ball of La Vaubyessard, and in the third dreaming of superior people at large. But in all three cases, her mind, for all its lack of self-aware analytic power, is presented as an active force. It builds possible worlds. It projects itself into realizable futures. And even when a blur sets in and dreams die away, Emma is in good company—that of all strenuous thinkers who have had exactly this sensation of an intellectual limit being reached.

Flaubert's heroine is soon to be firmly censured for her distance-seeking habits of mind and for the cult of vagueness that they seem to foster, and her error is linked with the misuse of the printed word. Léon, a clerk who has a serious passion for prose fiction, has just praised books for the fantasies they encourage, and for the passions they allow readers to savour at second hand:

> 'That's true! That's true!' [she said.]
>
> 'Have you ever had the experience', Léon continued, 'of finding, in a book, some vague idea you've had, some shadowy image from the depths of your being (*de loin*), which now seems to express perfectly your most subtle feelings?'
>
> 'Yes, I have,' she replied.
>
> (p. 75)

Passages of this kind are theatricalized exercises in literary criticism and have two principal targets: literary authors who promote either sentimentality or mental slackness generally, and readers who do not know how to read. Flaubert assails both groups with acerbity and irrepressible comic invention. If Emma had read better books, and read them better, he seems to imply, she would not now be in her advanced delusional state. Second-rate books have rotted her judgement, and undermined her survival instinct. If only she had been able to keep a clear eye on things close at hand—been more of a realist, as one might say—she could have achieved intellectual coherence, self-control, and a worthwhile role in the community.

Yet Flaubert's criticism of poor reading habits does not in fact take him very far in this direction. His tenderness towards Emma is intense, and all the more moving for having no loose sentiment in it. The plain facts of her case are what matters, and the material medium in which her life is led. And this is where resonance and reverberation enter his drama, offering their own view of distance, disappearance, and the ending of the human life-span. Bells ring often in *Madame Bovary.* Their sound carries over long distances, and expires slowly. They join forces with other resonating chambers, manmade and natural, to create an animated acoustic picture:

> She sank into that kind of brooding which comes when you lose something for ever, that lassitude you feel after every irreversible event, that pain you suffer when a habitual movement is interrupted, when a long-sustained vibration is suddenly broken off.
>
> (p. 110)

> Then she heard, in the distance, from the other side of the wood, on those other hills, a vague, long-drawn-out cry, a voice that seemed to linger in the air, and she listened to it in silence, as it blended like a melody with the last vibrations of her tingling nerves.
>
> (p. 143)

> The chill of the night spurred them to more passionate embraces; the sighs on their lips seemed to them more ardent; their eyes, dimly seen, seemed to them larger, and, in the silence, low-spoken words dropped into their hearts with a crystalline ring, echoing there with an ever-growing resonance (*en vibrations multipliées*).
>
> (p. 150)

These are all sexual as well as sonorous vibrations: the first passage refers to Léon's departure from Yonville, and to the state of semi-arousal that his presence had recently provoked in Emma; the second and third concern her lovemaking with Rodolphe, and its afterglow of sympathetic sound-echoes from the natural world around them. But in all such cases Flaubert's scientific reminder is clear: the human organism vibrates, for its nerve-structure ordains that it should, and that quality of rhythm or periodicity inside the individual connects him or her to the larger process of nature. This imagery

is perhaps closer to Franz Anton Mesmer's recently fashionable doctrine of universal 'animal magnetism' than to the latest physiological discoveries of Flaubert's own day, but its force is of an entirely this-worldly kind: humans are excitable organisms, however much they try to spiritualize and etherealize themselves, and it is in the nature of things that such entities should come into being, flourish for a while, and then cease to be. Vibrations in due course stop. Bells fall silent. At the hands of nature, or by their own hand, people die.

If Emma behaves self-defeatingly in her choice of reading matter, therefore, and is rather contemptible in her taste for far-off things, she is altogether admirable in her creaturely self-assertion. She is a sexual being, a vibratory power-source, and seeks to fill the empty space of reverie with the spasms and transports of her own desire. She is a fully sentient everywoman and everyman, and, while bringing a characteristic touch of stage-management to her own dying, understands her own mortality as part of the natural order:

> They were behind her forever, thought Emma, all the betrayals, the infamies, and the myriad cravings that had tormented her. She did not hate anyone, now; a twilight confusion was settling over her thoughts, and, of all the world's sounds, Emma heard only the intermittent sobbing of that poor man, soft and faint, like the fading echo of an ever-more distant symphony.
>
> (p. 283)

Flaubert is closer here to sentimentality than anywhere else in the novel, and these sentences, read in isolation, may seem to offer a coyly consoling view of death. Occupying their proper place in the elaboration of the text, however, they bring Flaubert's natural history of human feeling to a cogent culminating point. Emma is dying, Charles is lost in grief, and the sounds of nature are continuing to vibrate around them. Her extinction has been many times foretold in the sound-world of the novel, and the 'intermittent sobbing' of Charles and its gradual falling away into silence are the last premonition of what is soon to occur. Just as the sound of a struck chord decays, or as biological processes reach their term, so Emma dies. An 'ever-more distant symphony' connects her not only to the noise of nature but to the cadenced prose and the acoustic artifice of her creator.

III

Flaubert became famous in his lifetime for the supposed extreme cruelty with which he described his heroine's downfall and death. He was depicted in a cartoon of the day as a bloodstained surgeon, triumphantly butchering his own fictional creature. And those commentators on the novel who dwell at length on Flaubert's irony have tended in their own quieter way to suggest that the art of dissection is his main business.

Madness is everywhere, they point out, from the preposterous forenames of the Homais offspring to the three coffins, one inside the next, in which Emma Bovary is eventually laid to rest. Irony is the instrument—by turns lancet, scalpel, and surgical saw—by means of which the intricate anatomy of human folly is exposed to view. Such an account of the novel's tone and manner does fit certain of the textual facts rather well, and we would not be reading it with the imaginative absorption it demands if we did not sometimes find ourselves wincing, cringing, or laughing aloud at the performance. But the emotional texture of Flaubert's book is much richer than this suggests, even in its bravura pieces for the ironic imagination.

The following, for example, is one such piece, in which Emma dreams of eloping with Rodolphe to the sun-drenched south:

> Often, from a mountaintop, they'd catch a sudden glimpse of a magnificent city with domes, and bridges, and ships, and forests of lemon trees and cathedrals of white marble, whose slender steeples were capped by storks' nests. Their carriage had slowed to walking pace because of the enormous flagstones; the ground was strewn with bouquets of flowers that women in red bodices held up to you as you passed by. You could hear the ringing of bells and the whinnying of mules, blending with the murmur of guitars and the sound of fountains, the moisture from which, carried on the breeze, was cooling pyramids of fruit heaped below pale statues that smiled through the flying spray. And then, one evening, they'd come to a fishing village, where brown nets lay drying in the wind along the cliff and in front of the cottages. This was where they'd stop and make their home: they'd live in a low, flat-roofed house shaded by a palm tree, in the shelter of a bay, by the sea. They'd ride in gondolas, they'd laze in swaying hammocks, and their life would be free and flowing like their silken garments, warm and star-studded like the soft night skies they'd gaze at.
>
> (p. 174)

At one level this is a simple caricature of the Mediterranean landscape as seen by residents of the chilly north. In a succession of tiny snapshots Flaubert seems to acquire clairvoyant knowledge of the modern tourist industry, complete with its package holidays and gleaming brochures, and Emma's *vita nuova* proves to be wondrously tawdry and novelettish. The syntax in which the whole survey is conducted is enumerative rather than hierarchical, as befits the continuous gliding of desire from one fantasy gratification to the next. All of us who have taken lazy journeys south stand accused by those fishing nets, gondolas, and hammocks.

Yet this is also a portrait of fiction being born, and Flaubert is too self-conscious an artist to miss the points of comparison between his own calling as a novelist and the plot-making in which Emma indulges. The story she tells herself has an abrupt beginning, an eventful middle, and a reposeful end; it has protagonists and minor characters; it has adventure, surprises, and colourful incidents, and edges the interwoven human sense-fields towards a dizzying neurological overload. The occupants of the ever-changing scene are magically attuned to the sounds and rhythms of nature.

The echoes that pass between Flaubert's own performance as a writer and the doomed self-inventions of his protagonist are such as to make Henry James's talk of Emma's 'poverty of consciousness' seem, for a great critic, oddly wide of the mark. If we imagine that consciousness isolated for a moment from the feints and ruses of Flaubert's literary style, it proves to be an unusual, multiform thing: Emma, after all, is a person who can desire at one and the same time, and with no sense of contradiction, to die and to move to Paris (p. 54). But as soon as we put this active changeable mind back into the force field of Flaubert's writing, matters become altogether more complex. The 'grammatical beauty' that Proust described, and the poetry that Nabokov found in Flaubert's prose, create diffraction patterns across the textual surface of the book, and these patterns, in their turn, create a continuous lattice of cross-references between the novelist at work and the life led by his principal character. At the risk of making a grave category mistake, we could say that Emma and Flaubert share a mind, and an art, and that their joint consciousness suffers not at all from poverty.

Madame Bovary contains countless comments on stylistic questions, and many implicit comparisons between the style of the novel we are reading and the verbal habits, many of them objectionable, of its characters. Homais, for example, holds up a mirror to his creator while preparing to break the news to Emma of her father-in-law's death: 'He had pondered over what to say, making his phraseology more orotund, more polished, and more harmonious; it was a masterpiece of prudence, judicious transitions, subtle wording, and delicacy' (p. 222). For a moment, Flaubert's own meticulous craftsmanship is in the dock, charged with hypocrisy and bad faith. Yet the complicity between Emma and Flaubert is much more intimate and revealing than passing self-commentaries of this kind. Emma, as we have noted, is alert to echoes and resonances in the world around her, and is presented as a fragile and destructible component of the natural order. Flaubert's writing, beyond the apparent dryness of its many clipped formulations, becomes an echo-chamber in its own right. Assonance, alliteration, rhyme, the syntactic mirroring of sentence in sentence, and the long-distance play between images all combine to produce the sympathetic word-web in which Emma is enfolded. When it comes to the originality of Flaubert's narrative technique these patterns of repetition and recall deserve particular mention, for they not only connect phase to phase within an unfolding tragic tale but they give narrative itself a role in Flaubert's natural history of the human imagination: we live our creaturely lives in the sentences we place end to end, and in the stories we wish them to tell. We live at the mercy of the fictions we ourselves create.

For many critics and historians of French literature, Flaubert is by far the most modern of the great nineteenth-century novelists, and it is easy to see why. While being an originator of 'realism' in prose fiction, and one of its touchstones, he also looks beyond the realist dispensation, and rejoins the playful, self-reflexive tradition of Cervantes, Rabelais, and Sterne. What makes his writing in **Madame Bovary** distinctively modern, however, rather than the simple continuation of an earlier self-conscious literary manner, is the extreme vulnerability that Flaubert ascribes to writers in the exercise of their craft. They live with the arbitrariness of language, and make it their own. The wordscapes they create for themselves are porous and transitory. The sounds they make reverberate in the empty air. Small wonder, therefore, that Flaubert should have felt so close to his chronically deluded heroine, and that his best-known remark about her should have been 'Madame Bovary, c'est moi!'

FURTHER READING

Criticism

Bart, B. F. Madame Bovary *and the Critics,* edited by B. F. Bart. New York: New York University Press, 1966, 197 p.

    Offers a range of critical interpretations of the novel.

Bell, Sheila. "'Un pauvre diable': The Blind Beggar in *Madame Bovary.*" In *Studies in French Fiction in Honour of Vivienne Milne,* edited by Robert Gibson, pp. 25-42. London: Grant & Cutler, 1988.

    Examines Flaubert's use of irony in depicting the character of the blind beggar.

Brombert, Victor. "*Madame Bovary*: The Tragedy of Dreams." In *The Novels of Flaubert: A Study of Themes and Techniques,* pp. 37-91. Princeton: Princeton University Press, 1966.

    Analyzes the relationship between comedy, irony, and tragedy in the novel.

Brooks, Marilyn, and Nicola Watson. "*Madame Bovary*: A Novel about Nothing." In *The Nineteenth-Century Novel: Identities,* edited by Dennis Walder, pp. 9-28. London: Routledge, 2001.

Discusses Flaubert's explorations of adultery, suicide, and ennui in the novel.

Busi, Frederick. "Flaubert's Use of Saints' Names in *Madame Bovary.*" *Nineteenth-Century French Studies* 19, no. 1 (fall 1990): 95-109.

    Explores the influence of religion and mysticism on Flaubert's conception of the novel's central themes.

Gans, Eric. Madame Bovary: *The End of Romance.* Boston: Twayne Publishers, 1989, 138 p.

    Examines the underlying sense of disillusionment that characterizes the novel.

Heath, Dan. *Gustave Flaubert:* Madame Bovary. Cambridge: Cambridge University Press, 1992, 157 p.

    Investigates the historical and cultural context surrounding the novel's composition while evaluating the work's structure, narrative technique, and major themes.

Ippolito, Christophe. "Flaubert's Pearl Necklace: Weaving a Garland of Images in the Reader's Memory." *Symposium* 54, no. 3 (fall 2000): 168-87.

    Discusses the metaphorical relationship between women and flowers in *Madame Bovary.*

Lambros, Anna V. *Culture and the Literary Text: The Case of Flaubert's* Madame Bovary. New York: Peter Lang, 1996, 85 p.

    Studies the novel's cultural, social, and historical contexts.

Maraini, Dacia. *Searching for Emma: Gustave Flaubert and* Madame Bovary, translated by Vincent J. Bertolini. Chicago: University of Chicago Press, 1998, 156 p.

    Analyzes the contradictory, ambivalent relationship between Flaubert and his heroine, combining an indepth reading of the novel with a close examination of the author's correspondence.

Meyer, Priscilla. "*Anna Karenina*: Tolstoy's Polemic with *Madame Bovary.*" *Russian Review* 54, no. 2 (spring 1995): 243-59.

    Compares the two authors' attitudes toward their fictional heroines and toward the moral implications of adultery.

Orr, Mary. Madame Bovary: *Representations of the Masculine.* Bern: Peter Lang, 1999, 228 p.

    Examines questions of gender, sexuality, and manhood in *Madame Bovary* through an analysis of the novel's male characters.

Paskow, Jacqueline Merriam. "Rethinking Madame Bovary's Motives for Committing Suicide." *Modern Language Review* 100, no. 2 (spring 2005): 323-39.

Analyzes Flaubert's depiction of suicide in the novel.

Petruso, Thomas S. "*Madame Bovary* in the Consumer Society." *Qui Parle: Literature, Philosophy, Visual Arts, History* 1, no. 1 (fall 1985): 46-59.

Explores the relationship between self-deception, alienation, and consumerism in *Madame Bovary* through an analysis of the writings of Georges Perec and Jean Baudrillard.

Porter, Dennis. "*Madame Bovary* and the Question of Pleasure." In *Flaubert and Postmodernism,* edited by Naomi Schor and Henry F. Majewski, pp. 116-38. Lincoln: University of Nebraska Press, 1984.

Analyzes the novel's language and themes as they relate to the reader's experience of engaging with the text.

Porter, Lawrence M., and Eugene F. Gray, eds. *Approaches to Teaching* Madame Bovary. New York: The Modern Language Association of America, 1995, 167 p.

Includes essays devoted to exploring diverse critical approaches to the work.

Raitt, Alan. *The Originality of* Madame Bovary. Oxford: Peter Lang, 2002, 150 p.

Assesses the novel's innovative qualities, paying particular attention to Flaubert's unique approach to structure, point of view, and language.

Rothfield, Lawrence. "From Semiotic to Discursive Intertextuality: The Case of *Madame Bovary.*" *Novel: A Forum on Fiction* 19, no. 1 (fall 1985): 57-81.

Offers a semiotic interpretation of the novel, focusing on Flaubert's depiction of adultery.

Tipper, Paul Andrew. "Emma's Feet on Clay: The Ironies of Romanticized Location in *Madame Bovary.*" *Modern Language Review* 94, no. 2 (spring 1999): 366-76.

Discusses Flaubert's ironic use of place names in the novel.

Additional coverage of Flaubert's life and career is contained in the following sources published by Thomson Gale: *Dictionary of Literary Biography,* **Vols. 119, 301;** *DISCovering Authors;* *DISCovering Authors: British Edition;* *DISCovering Authors: Canadian Edition;* *DISCovering Authors Modules: Most-studied Authors* **and** *Novelists;* *DISCovering Authors 3.0;* *European Writers,* **Vol. 7;** *Exploring Short Stories;* *Guide to French Literature,* **Vol. 1789 to the Present;** *Literature and Its Times,* **Vol. 2;** *Literary Movements for Students,* **Vol. 1;** *Literature Resource Center;* *Nineteenth-Century Literature Criticism,* **Vols. 2, 10, 19, 62, 66, 135, 179;** *Novels for Students,* **Vol. 14;** *Reference Guide to Short Fiction,* **Ed. 2;** *Reference Guide to World Literature,* **Eds. 2, 3;** *Short Stories for Students,* **Vol. 6;** *Short Story Criticism,* **Vols. 11, 60;** *Twayne's World Authors;* **and** *World Literature Criticism,* **Vol. 2.**

Wilhelm Hauff
1802-1827

German novelist and short story writer.

The following entry presents an overview of Hauff's life and works.

INTRODUCTION

Wilhelm Hauff was a popular early-nineteenth-century German fiction writer. Although he died when he was only twenty-four, he cultivated a sizable readership during his brief career, producing several popular novels, story and fairy tale collections, and novellas. As scholar Erich P. Hofacker Jr. has observed, his works bear the imprint of such contemporaries as E. T. A. Hoffmann and Ludwig Tieck, particularly in his use of fantastical, sometimes grotesque characterizations, as well as in his explorations of traditional German fairy tale motifs. In the eyes of many commentators, including early twentieth-century critics like Garrett W. Thompson, Clarence Willis Eastman, and W. H. Carruth, among Hauff's most important influences was Sir Walter Scott, whose fiction provided the impetus for his best-known work, the novel *Lichtenstein* (1826). Although he was a mainstream writer and generally adhered to the popular conventions of his day, Hauff did introduce a number of important new elements to early-nineteenth-century German literature. According to Thompson, *Lichtenstein* represents a significant milestone in the emergence of the German historical romance, notably in its detailed depictions of landscapes and local customs. Hauff's fairy tales helped redefine the genre; as Maureen Thum has argued, while Hauff's tales contained traditional qualities of fantasy and magic, they also introduced a new focus on psychological and moral issues, making them important early examples of German literary realism. Hauff's work remained popular for decades after his death; many of his stories and novellas were translated into English, and a number of nineteenth-century commentators extolled his fiction as an important precursor of the realist school. Hauff's literary reputation has faded over time, however, and most modern literary scholars regard him as a decidedly minor writer.

BIOGRAPHICAL INFORMATION

Wilhelm Hauff was born on November 29, 1802, in the Swabian city of Stuttgart. He was the second son of August Friedrich Hauff, a government minister, and Hedwig Wilhelmine Elsässer Hauff. In 1806 the family moved to Tübingen, where Hauff's father was appointed secretary for the royal court of appeals. Three years later, following the death of his father, Hauff moved with his mother, older brother, and two younger sisters into the home of his maternal grandparents. Hauff found solace in his grandfather's vast library, devouring the novels of Friedrich de la Motte Fouqué, Henry Fielding, Tobias Smollett, and Christian August Vulpius, among others. In 1817 Hauff moved to a monastery in Blaubeuren, where he studied theology. According to Hofacker, the secluded, quiet life of the cloister proved ill-suited for the gregarious young man, and Hauff later characterized his three years at Blaubeuren as unhappy ones.

In 1820 Hauff enrolled in the Tübinger Stift, a distinguished Protestant theological university that counted among its graduates Johannes Kepler, Georg Hegel, Friedrich Hölderlin, and Friedrich Schelling. Hauff thrived at the college; he became a member of the Feuerreiter, a fraternity dedicated to radical political causes, and he began to write poetry, composing numerous satirical and patriotic verses commemorating Napoleon's defeat at Waterloo. He also edited *Kriegs- und Volks-Lieder* (which may be translated as "War and Folk Songs"). During his student years, Hauff traveled on a university-sponsored trip along the Rhine River, his first journey outside of his native Swabia. These experiences later formed the basis of his *Mittheilungen aus den Memoiren des Satan* (1826-27; *Memoirs of Beelzebub*, 1846).

Although he earned his doctorate in theology in 1824, Hauff expressed little interest in joining the clergy. Upon leaving school, he found work as a private tutor in the home of Ernst Eugen, a high-ranking official in the Württemberg War Ministry. According to Hofacker, the aristocratic, cultured atmosphere of the Eugen household ignited Hauff's literary imagination, and over the next year and a half, he produced much of his best literary work, including the satirical novel *Der Mann im Mond oder Der Zug des Herzens ist des Schicksals Stimme* (1825), a parody of the sentimental novels of Karl Heun; the historical novel *Lichtenstein*; *Mittheilungen aus den Memoiren des Satan*; and *Das Bild des Kaisers* (1828), a novella inspired by an excursion with the Eugen family along the Neckar River. Hauff also wrote many of his best fairy tales during this period, stories he would later include in his acclaimed "Maerchenalmanache," or fairy tale almanacs; and he became a regular contributor of book reviews and essays to various literary journals.

By the spring of 1826, Hauff had established himself as one of Germany's most promising young authors. Hoping to gather more experience for his writing, he left his job with Eugen and embarked on an extended journey through France, the Netherlands, and northern Germany. In December of that year, he returned to Stuttgart, where he soon became editor of the journal *Morgenblatt*. In February 1827, he married his cousin, Luise Hauff. Throughout this period, he continued to produce a high volume of new work, in spite of deteriorating health. By the fall of 1827, Hauff had discovered that he suffered from a severe nervous condition; in October he stopped eating, and within weeks he was bedridden with a form of encephalitis. A program of bloodletting accelerated his decline, and he died on November 18, 1827.

MAJOR WORKS

Hauff produced an impressive body of work before his untimely death at the age of twenty-four. Most scholars agree that, of all of Hauff's writings, the historical novel *Lichtenstein* remains his crowning achievement. Influenced to a large degree by the works of Sir Walter Scott, *Lichtenstein* represents Hauff's attempt to create a mythology surrounding the formation of the Germanic state of Württemberg. The narrative invents a fictional portrait of Ulrich, Herzog von Württemberg, a sixteenth-century German duke. While the real-life Ulrich was a notoriously violent and unjust ruler, Hauff's Ulrich emerges as a national hero whose political astuteness and moral righteousness helps guide the German people into the modern age. In this respect, scholars have argued, the novel embodies many of the debates surrounding nationalism and the formation of a unified state that dominated German intellectual circles in the early nineteenth century. Hauff's speculations on the possibilities of political reform struck a chord with German readers of the period, particularly in the aftermath of the Napoleonic wars.

Hauff's fairly tales also brought him widespread popularity. A selection of Hauff's best tales first appeared in his two "Maerchenalmanache": the *Maerchenalmanach für Söhne und Töchter gebildeter Stände auf das Jahr 1827* (1827) and the *Maerchenalmanach für Söhne und Töchter gebildeter Stände auf das Jahr 1828* (1828). Scholars have found the tales innovative in their emphasis on real, as opposed to fantastical, solutions to their characters' problems. In arguably his best-known tale, "Der Zwerg Nase" ("Longnose the Dwarf"), Hauff tells the story of a young boy, Jacob, who is transformed into a hideous dwarf by a witch. The tale is striking both for its complex portrayal of adolescence and for its refusal to depict Jacob's plight in sentimental terms. Hauff's novellas failed to garner the same general acclaim as his fairy tales, but a few of them remain noteworthy. Among the most important are *Das Bild des Kaisers, Jud Süss* (1827), and *Phantasien im Bremer Ratskeller* (1827). Like his fairy tales, Hauff's novellas are characterized by their mixing of fantastical and realistic elements.

During his lifetime, Hauff also earned widespread fame as a satirist. His first published work, the satirical novel *Der Mann im Mond oder Der Zug des Herzens ist des Schicksals Stimme,* caused a sensation in literary circles when it first appeared in 1825. The book parodies the work of popular sentimental novelist Karl Heun, who published under the name of H. Clauren. Hauff used the same pseudonym for his satire and employed many of the same clichéd literary conventions that characterized Heun's novels, notably his reliance on melodramatic plot devices and one-dimensional characterizations. Ironically, Hauff's novel came to be regarded as a prime example of literary kitsch later in the nineteenth century. In his *Mittheilungen aus den Memoiren des Satan,* Hauff focuses his satirical eye on the proliferation of memoirists in the 1820s. Written from multiple points of view, the work parodies nationalism, academic pedantry, and the character of Satan himself, whom Hauff portrays as a frustrated, world-weary artist.

CRITICAL RECEPTION

Although his work enjoyed considerable popular and critical acclaim in the nineteenth century, Hauff remains relatively unknown to modern readers. In the late-nineteenth and early-twentieth centuries, a number of scholars, among them Clarence Willis Eastman, H. W. Carruth, and Garrett W. Thompson, published influential articles examining the relationship between Hauff's fiction and the historical novels of Sir Walter Scott. Since that time, however, very few critical studies of Hauff's writings have appeared. The 1990s did witness a small revival of interest in Hauff's work. Maureen Thum analyzed the subversive elements in Hauff's historical romances, examining the works within the context of Mikhail Bakhtin's theories of carnivalized discourse. Jefferson S. Chase and Irving Massey have critiqued Hauff's portrayals of Jewish characters in the novella *Jud Süss,* while David Blamires has studied the symbolic uses of deformity in Hauff's fairy tales.

PRINCIPAL WORKS

Der Mann im Mond oder Der Zug des Herzens ist des Schicksals Stimme [as H. Clauren] (novel) 1825

Die Bettlerin vom Pont des Arts [*The True Lover's Fortune; or, The Beggar of the Pont des Arts*] (novella) 1826; published in journal *Morgenblatt*

Lichtenstein: Romantische Sage aus der würtembergischen Geschichte. 3 vols. [*The Banished: A Swabian Historical Tale*] (novel) 1826

Mittheilungen aus den Memoiren des Satan. 2 vols. [*Memoirs of Beelzebub*] (novel) 1826-27

Jud Süss [*The Jew Suss: A Tale of Stutgard, in 1737*] (novella) 1827; published in journal *Morgenblatt*

Maerchenalmanach für Söhne und Töchter gebildeter Stände auf das Jahr 1827 [editor and contributor] (short stories) 1827

Phantasien im Bremer Ratskeller: Ein Herbstgeschenk für Freunde des Weines [*The Wine-Ghosts of Bremen*] (novella) 1827

Das Bild des Kaisers (novella) 1828; published in *Taschenbuch für Damen: Auf das Jahr 1828*

Maerchenalmanach für Söhne und Töchter gebildeter Stände auf das Jahr 1828 [editor and contributor] (short stories) 1828

Novellen. 3 vols. (novellas) 1828

Sämtliche Schriften. 36 vols. (novels, novellas, and short stories) 1830

Select Popular Tales: From the German (short stories) 1845

The Caravan: A Collection of Popular Tales (short stories) 1850

Arabian Days' Entertainments (short stories) 1858

Little Mook, and Other Fairy Tales (short stories) 1881; also published as *Longnose the Dwarf and Other Fairy Tales*, 1903

Tales of the Caravan, Inn, and Palace (short stories) 1881

Sämtliche Märchen (short stories) 1986

CRITICISM

Charles B. Goold (essay date 1896)

SOURCE: Goold, Charles B. Introduction to *Tales from Hauff*, pp. v-xii. Boston: Ginn & Company, Publishers, 1896.

[*In the following excerpt, Goold asserts that Hauff's best stories compare favorably with the tales of Hans Christian Andersen and the Brothers Grimm.*]

In 1825, [Hauff] began to publish, under the title of **Märchen-Almanach,** a collection of stories with the recital of which he had previously entertained his pupils of the baron's household. The publication of these stories was continued during the two following years. The general plan of each of the series is the same,—a main narrative interwoven with various tales related by the chief characters. The first of these groups of stories is entitled **Die Karawane**; the second, **Der Sheik von Alessandria**; the third, **Das Wirtshaus im Spessart.** These tales are in many respects the most characteristic of Hauff's writings, and upon them his reputation largely rests. They are the offspring of a poetic and healthy imagination, and are clothed in an attractive literary dress. The plot, while neither original nor deep, reaches a natural and effective climax. The characters are clearly drawn; the sentiment is clean and wholesome. Taken as a whole the stories will compare favorably with those of Andersen and Grimm.

Meanwhile Hauff had also successfully tried his hand at other types of literary composition. His **Mitteilungen aus den Memoiren des Satans, Der Mann im Mond** [**Der Mann im Mond oder Der Zug des Herzens ist des Schicksals Stimme**], and **Lichtenstein** were all written while their author was a member of the von Hügel household. Of these productions the most elaborate is **Lichtenstein,** an historical romance, in which may be seen traces of the influence of Scott. Though written in an incredibly short space of time, and therefore not without marks of hasty composition, it won for its author favorable comment, and greatly added to his growing popularity.

Garrett W. Thompson (essay date 1911)

SOURCE: Thompson, Garrett W. "Wilhelm Hauff's Specific Relation to Walter Scott." *Publications of the Modern Language Association of America* 26 (n.s. 19), no. 4 (1911): 549-92.

[*In the following excerpts, Thompson outlines the numerous parallels between Hauff's* Lichtenstein *and the novels of Sir Walter Scott. According to Thompson, Hauff borrowed almost all of his character types, narrative techniques, and themes from Scott's writings.*]

I Introduction

In 1899 Dr. C. W. Eastman read a paper before the Modern Language Association, in which he maintained that of all Scott's novels *Ivanhoe* served Hauff most completely as the source of his historical romance, **Lichtenstein.** In 1903 this claim was disputed by Dr. W. H. Carruth, who thro the same channel advanced his reasons for believing that *Waverley* and not *Ivanhoe* was the model in question. A year later Max Schuster in a monograph[1] discussed Hauff's relation to his historical sources; and almost simultaneously the whole problem of his historical and literary dependence was treated by Max Drescher.[2] Incisive and scholarly as these inquiries are, it has seemed to us in the light of our own studies that one phase of the matter still offered opportunity for further investigation. The evidence of Hauff's attitude toward Walter Scott is by no means meagre or indirect; and we have never been able to persuade ourselves that this specific relation has been adequately determined. In any case it is insufficient merely to ask whether *Waverley* or *Ivanhoe* was the prototype, or, as Drescher did, arbitrarily to choose only six of Scott's novels for comparison. The situation demanded rather a most careful study of all the works to which Hauff had access, and an equally careful analysis of the evidence thus obtained.

We know from Hauff's own statements that he definitely decided to write an historical novel and carried the idea about in his mind for some time; that Scott's immense popularity in German revealed to him how and in what form he could best please the reading public; that Walter Scott was the only model he ever had definitely in mind. We know furthermore that his acquaintance with the latter's works and technique was intimate. As he himself says: "Freilich kamen mir bei diesen Gedanken noch allerlei Zweifel. Ich müsste die Werke dieses grossen Meisters nicht nur lesen, sondern auch studiren, um sie zu meinem Zweck zu benützen."[3] As the result of this conviction he analysed critically twelve of Scott's novels in his *Studien* and makes elsewhere special mention of *Quentin Durward*. Ernst Müller (*Euphorion*, 4, 319) says of him: "Es steht fest, dass er Scott zum Vorbild hat in *Lichtenstein*." When we consider in addition that during Hauff's literary activity Scott wielded a most intensive and extensive influence in Germany; that Hauff openly admired and avowed him as a master novelist, pays a glowing tribute to him in the introduction to *Lichtenstein* and defends him against German criticism; when we consider also that his studies of Scott immediately preceded the composition of *Lichtenstein,* we are prepared to find a close relationship between the two authors, and indeed a much closer relationship than has hitherto been asseverated. . . .

IV Hauff's Historical Sources

As the actual historical materials of *Lichtenstein* could not have been drawn from the Waverley series, they do not belong to our present inquiry. His fidelity to his own sources has been investigated by Max Schuster, as we have already pointed out. He discusses how far Hauff followed fact and fiction, and ascribes the deviations from historical record to ignorance and a superficial attitude on the author's part. He says: "Wo er (Hauff) am schroffsten der geschichtlichen Wirklichkeit widerspricht, in der Darstellung des Huttenschen Falls und der Schlacht bei Türkheim, tat er es in gutem Glauben an die Richtigkeit seiner Auffassung. Was ihm anzuwerfen ist, ist nicht so wohl eine unerlaubte Willkür, eine Misshandlung der ihm bewussten, his-

torischen Tatsachen, sondern der Mangel an gründlicherem Eindringen in die geschichtlichen Voraussetzungen und Entwickelungen, das ihn zu einer tieferen Auffassung vom Charakter seines Helden hätte führen können."[4] Drescher finds Hauff historically correct in his general purpose and explains discrepancies as well as inaccuracies by the great haste in which the novel was written. This historical material Hauff gives partly as supplementary data in the form of notes and annotations, partly as narrative with maximum brevity, partly by word of mouth, partly in actual scenes. So little of it enters into the novel itself that we shall consider it in connection with the nature and structure of the plot.

V The Characters

When Hauff had consulted his historical and legendary sources, the problem of using these materials, combining them with his own inventions was no small one. He must have asked himself three questions: What characters should he select? How should he construct his plot with reference to them? How should this structure be filled in with such situations and embellishments as would enhance the attractiveness of the novel as a work of literary art?

As characters who carry on the action we have Georg von Sturmfeder, the hero; a prince, Duke Ulrich von Württemberg; a baron, Herr von Lichtenstein, devoted to the Duke; a heroine, Marie, the Baron's daughter; a secondary lady, Bertha von Besserer; a secondary baron, Dietrich von Kraft, who loves Bertha; an unprincipled counselor, Ambrosius Volland; two generals, Georg von Frondsberg and Truchsess Waldburg, the former of whom befriends, the latter dislikes, the hero; a peasant-guide, Pfeiffer von Hardt, with wife and daughter (Bärbele). The Duke, the Counselor, and the two Generals are historical, the others fictitious. As the remaining characters, tho many of them are historical, have no organic connection with the plot, they do not claim our attention. The two Generals were officers in the Swabian army which opposed the Duke of Württemberg in 1519; as, however, they receive no characterisation at the hands of their biographers, Hauff's treatment of them in relation to his hero-plot is an invention. The physical deformity, the caricature and ridiculous aspect which Hauff assigns to Volland are likewise unconfirmed by the latter's biographers. The Chancellor took office after the Armer Konrad rebellion; he accompanied the Duke on both exiles, but was not responsible for the abrogation of the Tübingen Compact, so that here again Hauff took liberties with historical facts in the interest of his plot. His carefully detailed explanation of his purpose to present the Duke's character in a subdued light prepares us for the variations which we actually find, and obviates the necessity of seeking reasons for the freedom which Hauff's own view-point justifies. He states that doubtless public opinion was too much influenced against Ulrich by the prejudicial bitterness of Ulrich von Hutten, who attacked him with great vigor; that he (Hauff) in all his investigations had not found one writer who condemned the Duke entirely; that the latter was affected by bad influences and environment: that his youth and indiscretions were against him; that the harshness of his character was offset by his more elevated traits, by his strength of soul and his indomitable courage. Pfaff also says: "Über seine Denk- und Gemütsart haben Mit- und Nachwelt gar verschiedene Urteile gefällt, man hat ihn bald zu schlimm, bald zu gut geschildert."[5]

If, then, Hauff emphasizes the Don Juan and chivalrous aspects of Ulrich's character, ascribing his cruelty and unwise statesmanship to evil influences, his procedure is sufficiently motivated to escape the charge of having trifled with his sources.

The Scottian hero is prevailingly a young man, poor, of good birth, who, being uncertain as to his future, seeks and wins fortune thro the aid of a prince. In his *Studien* Hauff strongly defends this wavering type of hero. He says: "Wirft man aber die Frage auf, was ist höher im Roman, das Leben des Helden oder die Personen und Gegenstände, mit welchen letzterer in Berührung kommt, so ist es offenbar das letztere. Fragt man aber, zu was dann noch ein solcher Nichtheld, wenn die objective Darstellung der mannigfachen Erscheinungen des Lebens die Hauptsache im Roman ausmacht? man kann antworten, der Held . . . muss den Faden der Erzählung, an welchen sich einzelne Begebenheiten und Erscheinungen anreihen, abgeben. . . . Im Helden des Romans liegt der Spiegel, welcher uns die Gegenstände, denen er begegnet, klar zeigt." Among the hero types of his native literature Hauff found the wandering artist, the roaming adventurer, the subjective dreamer. Of these he says: "Man wollte unter Roman nicht mehr die Lebensbegebenheiten des Helden verstehen, sondern die Aufstellung und Entwickelung der menschlichen Ansicht über Kunst oder sonst ein Thema des geistigen Lebens, die sogenannte Geschichte war Nebensache."[6] Against this form of novel he further declares himself: "Der Roman war auch in der That ursprünglich nichts anders als getreuer Bericht über das Stillleben und die Handlungen des Helden. Die Wahrheit lag nicht im getreuen Bericht, sondern in Aufstellung der Motive zu Handlungen, in Darstellung seiner Gefühle. Diese Darstellung der Gefühle des Helden fordert aber eine genaue Darstellung der Gegenstände und Aussendinge die den Helden afficiren."[7] When we realize that Hauff expresses himself thus in defense of Scott's and in exposition of his own type of hero, and finds such a hero developed in sixteen of the Waverley novels which he read, there is every indication of a close relationship between the two authors.

Hauff's acquaintance with Scott's characters was intimate. In his *Studien* he reviews in detail fifty-six of them and accords several others an intelligent word of comment. His general judgment, if favorable, is that they are natural; if unfavorable, that they are merely sketched and therefore undeveloped. He bestows most attention upon *The Antiquary, Waverley, Ochiltree,* and *Mannering* in the order named. The characters which impressed him most are MacIvor, the Antiquary, Ochiltree, Elspeth, Rassleigh and Robin, Mary Stuart (in particular), John and Richard, Elisabeth and Varney. He regards *Rob Roy* as Scott's best novel on account of its vivid pictures and deep characters (Rassleigh, Diana, etc.); he extols *Old Mortality* for its great objectivity and fine gradation of character-types.

It is significant also that Hauff uses in *Lichtenstein* precisely those characters which are most common and most frequently recurrent in the Scottian technique. In inventing Herr von Lichtenstein as baron, Bertha as secondary lady, Dietrich von Kraft as secondary baron, Pfeiffer von Hardt as peasant-guide, etc., Hauff considered them, not as individuals capable of psychological differentiation, but as types whose functions were necessary to the evolution of the plot. The relation was everything, the name nothing. We have already seen how Hauff in the case of his historical characters made such arbitrary modifications as would best suit his purposes; it is evident, then, that he did not aim at accurate delineation of historical character. In the use of such compromises and the adoption of Scottian types he clearly worked in the interests of his plot, and that, too, of a plot in which fiction predominated. As to the origin of these created types Hofmann[8] suggests that Herr von Lichtenstein and Frondsberg were modeled after Hauff's grandfather, and George Sturmfeder after Hauff himself; that Marie's prototype was to be found in his own bride and also in his elder sister; that his grandfather's housekeeper was reflected in Marie's maid, Rosa, the peasant's wife, and Kraft's *Haushälterin*; that the peasant's daughter resembled Hauff's younger sister in *naïveté*. We present our own view later.

VI THE PLOT STRUCTURE OF *LICHTENSTEIN*

In his *Studien* Hauff insists that the novel, as offspring of the epic, must concern itself with the external fortunes of the hero; that these must have an organic nexus and unity; that they follow the law of an inner truth; that they offer not allegorical representations but a poetical picture of real life. He furthermore maintains that Scott's novels reveal the power of simple truth. "Welcher Dichter gibt wohl ein besseres Zeugnis dafür dass der Zauber der schlichten Wahrheit der grösste sei als Walter Scott?"[9] "In him," continues Hauff, "the unusual, the accidental, the irrelevant are absent, and the action follows the natural law of logic. The characters are true to themselves and our interest lies in knowing what they will and must do, while our suspense is maintained not by crass effects and exaggerations but by truly dramatic scenes and situations."[10] Following these Scottian principles of realism and organic unity, Hauff developed a fictitious plot in which the hero's career is the central action. The Duke figures historically in the occupation of Stuttgart and the battle of Türkheim, but here, as in all other scenes, his services are subordinated to the interests of the hero. In the hero plot the element of love is conspicuously predominant and the organic necessity of this relation converges every other issue toward the destiny of the lovers. Of the 36 chapters of *Lichtenstein,* 29 are devoted to the love-interest; of all the principal scenes of the novel only one does not concern itself with this interest—that which describes the organization of the Duke's forces for the seizure of Stuttgart; of all the festivities which attended the occupation of Stuttgart, George's wedding is the only one which Hauff describes in detail, 22 pages being devoted to it and five lines to a mere notice that the other events occurred; even in the naturally solemn scene where Schweinsberg reports the fall of Tübingen, Ulrich's greatest stronghold, and the latter stands on the brink of utter ruin—a scene where the hero's love-interest would seem to have no legitimate place—it reaches on the contrary its critical stage when the Duke in person urges Marie's father to ratify her union with George and demands in a decidedly bantering manner a kiss from the bride, which was to be delivered on her wedding day in Stuttgart.

Hauff wrote the love relation of *Lichtenstein* from his own heart. He was sentimental by nature, much given to *Schwärmerei* and susceptible to feminine charms; he had a strong youthful passion for his little neighbor Amalia, and in 1823 met his cousin Louise, whom he afterward married. From this very happy association arose many love lyrics (*Stille Liebe, Sehnsucht, Ihr Auge,* etc.), and during the three years which elapsed between the beginning of this love and the publication of *Lichtenstein* he passed thro the whole intense experience of engagement and separation, acquiring thus naturally a personal preparation for at least one portion of the task before him. As he essayed to develop an historical romance, he found himself at once familiar with the love relation of the hero and heroine, and, drawing readily from his own life, he followed the line of least resistance, gave unconscious predominance to this motive, and then, not without skill, wove the residue of his material about the one relation he most clearly understood. Moreover, the atmosphere of the love interest is thoroughly modern; its language and vocabulary are expressed in the plain, earnest, straight-forward manner of the 19th century; it is set forth in an unromantic zeal which reflects Hauff's own feelings rather than the mode of 1519; it contains an emphasized sentimentality which too greatly humanizes and therefore modernizes the lovers of a romantic novel of the 16th century; it describes the physical, not the intellectual and spiritual aspects of love; it involves quarrels, misunderstandings,

and reconciliations which are often juvenile in their *naïveté* and mark the course of unsophisticated affection rather than the dignified procedure of a formal work of literature. Numerous instances of this over-emphasis will be found in our discussion under "Diction." Its motive can be found only in the conclusion that Hauff wrote the major part of *Lichtenstein* from his own experience and therefore gave the prince-interest a minor place as well as importance in the evolution of the plot. And, indeed, in his *Studien* he calls attention to the fact that the prince is purposely subordinated to the hero in both *Waverley* and *Rob Roy*; he censures the *Abbot* on the other hand for undue prominence of the prince idea,—facts which also would seem to indicate Hauff's disproportionate valuation of heroes and princes. Of Scottian influence in the treatment of the love relation there can be no question. As to German sources, Drescher says: "Hauff arbeitet in der Darstellung des liebenden Paars Georg und Maria völlig selbständig."[11]

In comparison with the Waverley novels we shall now consider the plot arrangement of *Lichtenstein,* the motives which operate within the action, and the movements which are necessitated by the character relations. The Prince enters comparatively late into the action and at a time when the hero interest needs his assistance, as in thirteen of Scott's novels; the Prince aids the hero, prevailingly in the love interest, as in thirteen of Scott; the hero enters the action at the outset, being lukewarm toward the political side to which he is attached, and as the plot advances he leaves his first allegiance, joining the Prince, whose waning cause promotes the success of the hero's love interest and political fortunes, as in seven of Scott (in two the political sides are reversed); the Prince is dispossessed and seeks restoration without results, as in eight of Scott (in one the Prince regains the throne); the heroine and her father operate on the Prince's side, as in ten of Scott; the love of the hero and heroine antedates the beginning of the story, as in six of Scott; the Prince enters actively and extensively into the plot, i. e., into the fortunes of the hero, as in seven of Scott; the love interest dominates the initial scene of the book; a long separation of the lovers ensues followed by a reunion, which, tho clouded by its own uncertainties and the Prince's misfortunes leads to the ultimate happiness of the couple, as in six of Scott (and with modifications in others); a secondary lady serves the heroine's interests particularly in love, as in twelve of Scott; a baron related to the heroine by active participation in the plot welds the mutual interests of the hero, heroine, and Prince, as in fifteen of Scott; a peasant-guide operates widely and effects even more directly the organic unity of these same three interests, as in twelve of Scott; the peasant is aided by a wife, as in four of Scott; he is also assisted by a daughter, as in eight of Scott; an evil counselor acts against the hero and to the ultimate disadvantage of the Prince as in eleven of Scott; the hero is befriended (saved) by persons of the other side as in sixteen of Scott; the hero befriends (saves) persons of the other side, as in nine of Scott; a battle is used to decide the Prince's fate as in twelve of Scott.

The foregoing comparisons include not only the whole plot arrangement of *Lichtenstein* but also all the movements and character relations by which the action is carried on. We have already shown that the four historical characters are modified to fit Hauff's fictitious plot; that the invented personages conform in their functions accurately to Scottian types; that the hero interest and (in him) the love element preponderate. The comprehensiveness of the above analogies makes it clear that inside the plot the distribution of the action, interplay of motives, the relationships of the characters, the general scheme of development are duplicated manifold in the Waverley series.

VII ANALOGOUS SCENES, EVENTS, AND SITUATIONS WHICH FILL IN THE PLOT

When Hauff had determined the nature and scope of his plot and the general movements by which the action was to be carried on, it became necessary for him to fill in the structure with such concrete material as would vivify this plot and enhance the attractiveness of its content. To this end he was obliged to borrow or invent many scenes, events, and situations, and to adorn the intercourse of his characters by such devices as would make them not only real but interesting. That in so doing he leaned most heavily on Scott the accompanying evidence will show. In comparing the Waverley novels and *Lichtenstein* we find a total of 748 analogies, all of which are close, many striking, and none far-fetched. Taking into account those which are duplicated in the Scottian works themselves, we still have 453 as common to the two authors. As far as any single novel is concerned, *Quentin Durward* has the largest number of analogies, 98, the next being *Old Mortality* with 83. As it would be impossible to present this voluminous evidence in detail, the following examples will illustrate the nature and scope of imitation: Prison cell with haunted associations (murder, etc.); hero and prince meet in a cave; banquet with quarrel scene affecting the hero; ball where hero and heroine meet and have important interview; hero attacked, wounded, and healed in a cottage by women in 8 days; military procession viewed by hero and heroine; castle burns in sight of hero and prince; duel fought by the hero thro jealousy and stopped by the peasant-guide; a disguised spy on the prince's side passes thro the enemy's lines to friends in a stronghold to secure information; a high personage's garb assumed by a friend to effect the former's escape; escape of high personage by plunging into the water; messages sent in poetic or metaphorical form from heroine to hero; secondary lady brings about a meeting of the hero and heroine, cleverly keeping away her own lover, whose presence is necessary to effect the meeting; a high personage visits the heroine's father's

castle by night under mysterious circumstances which arouse jealousy in the hero, and anger, because the heroine refuses to divulge the secret; the hero saves the life of a hostile officer and is himself rescued in a similar manner. It is impossible in a mere citation to reproduce the striking correspondence of the majority of these situations; still, the few quoted above and the really astonishing total will further attest how completely Hauff absorbed the subject matter of the Waverley novels. . . .

VIII GENERAL CHARACTERISTICS

There are many general characteristics common to the practice of the two authors which, taken in connection with the inner analogies already noted, reveal how closely Hauff followed his master in all that pertained to the making of an historical novel. We give them in the accompanying list.

(1) Introductions which give the historical setting in condensed form, into which also the personal note of the author enters in explanation, self-defense, etc. (2) Poetical captions for the chapters, the poems being taken mostly from the past. (3) Explanatory footnotes. (4) Historical annotations at the end of parts. (5) Division into parts. (6) Use of dialect. (7) Inlaid poems. (8) Latin quotations. (9) Proverbs put into mouths of characters. (10) Use of oaths in the name of saints, St. Hubertus employed by both. (11) Breaks in the story to "bring up" different lines of development. (12) Breaks in the action caused by the use and discussion of general truths at the beginning of chapters (common in both). (13) Events carried over to the next chapter by such words as: "We will describe in the following chapter, etc." (rarer in Hauff). (14) Reference to "In those days" and "now." (15) Both authors' descriptions made in the order of the plot evolution and therefore organic in their relation to the whole. (16) Both employ group scenes; and Scott's favorite use of dialog and situations where two are involved is also found in Hauff. (17) Authors' reflections avoided. (18) Absence of subjectivity very characteristic. (19) Reader addressed, as: "Gentle reader," "geneigter Leser," etc. (20) Reference to old customs in comparison with modern usage. (21) Reference to sources as authority for facts for which the writers assumed no personal responsibility. (22) Scott in *Waverley* gives dates and sequences, "In the memorable year 1715," "Arrival of summer," etc.; Hauff follows this method in *Lichtenstein.* (23) Names of persons suited to their characters and occupations (Sturmfeder, Dryasdust, Mailsetter, etc.). (24) In expressing the vernacular of the common people Hauff maintains the natural and wholesome level of Scott as against the lower standard of his German contemporaries. (25) Both authors fond of describing characters and revealing their identity later with the words: "For it was he," "For the reader will recognize," etc. (26) Both give to certain persons a characteristic and recurrent form of expression. Lady Margaret (*Old Mortality*) refers persistently

to a former visit of the King, and Hauff's Rosalie speaks habitually in proverbs. (27) Scott frequently closes chapters with a situation which leads into the next chapter, with such expressions as: "The door opened and," etc. This occurs once in *Lichtenstein.* (28) Both remark frequently on the general nature of love and jealousy, as applicable to the hero and less directly to the heroine. (29) Soliloquy rare in both authors. (30) Reports and stories narrated by persons often interrupted by hearers. (31) Both authors use approximately the same number of chapters in each part. (32) Both use the form of dream which is interrupted by and ends in realities, where real persons are involved. (33) Both use the epic form of dialog, and avoid the dramatic method whereby (as in the case of many of the German *Ritter- und Räuberromane,* taken as they were from corresponding stage literature) designations of the speakers, asides, stage directions, etc., appeared in the novels. (39) Both refer informally to the "Chronicles." (35) Both defend their Prince in the introduction. (36) Both use poetry as an organic part of paragraphs (once in *Lichtenstein*). (37) Mysterious past of persons told late in the story. (38) Cults introduced and discussed (Dancing in Hauff, Euphuism and Astrology in Scott). (39) Curses used, many from foreign languages in corrupted form. (40) Latin expressions used by characters as an organic part of their statements (common in Scott). (41) "Jacta est(o) alea" used by both authors, once in English by Scott (*The Pirates*). (42) Both use such self-inclusive expressions as: "we," "let us," etc. (43) Personal references rare in both authors. (44) Both employ a clearing up which acquaints the reader with the fate or fortune of the principal characters. (45) Poetic quotations woven into the grammatical construction of the narrative (once in Hauff, common in Scott). (46) General truths common in both authors. (47) French expressions, few in Hauff, copious in Scott. (48) Influence of verses and songs a marked characteristic of both authors. (49) Both make objective presentation, not psychological analysis, of the characters. (50) Both agree in making disguises, changes of garb, attacks, and travels an organic part of the plot. (51) In both authors the element of fidelity in the peasant-guide is a peculiar characteristic. (52) Scott's simplicity of plot and method was not merely shared by Hauff, but in his *Studien* the latter cites *Waverley* as a proof that simplicity is the greatest art. Heinrich Heine also characterizes the form of *Waverley* as incomparable in simplicity.[12] (53) Both authors refer at the beginning of the chapter to the sentiment of the poetical caption. (54) Hero's nationality recognized by his dialect. (55) Both assemble the characters in a scene at the close of the story. (56) Both authors (Scott in most cases) possessed the great advantage of having traversed the geographical area of their stories and being thus personally familiar with the types, scenes, and nature of what they were attempting to describe. (57) In his *Studien* Hauff justifies the criticism that Scott often ends his novels too abruptly. But he imitates him also in this respect. After the defeat and escape of the Duke, the characters are assembled and then hurried from the

stage of action quite as suddenly as Scott would have done under similar circumstances. (58) In *Lichtenstein* Hauff drops the moralizing and particularly the satirical elements which are characteristic of his other works, and substitutes a plainly realistic mode of treatment. This substitution could take place only under strong influences, for it is radical, and no such influences were at hand in German literature. They must be Scottian. (59) Both set forth historical truth. It is true that Hauff gives more exact and numerous dates and a closer nexus of events, while Scott makes chronological skips which seem to argue for a looser historical causality. But Scott covers larger areas and develops so many lines of action,—while Hauff's plot and action are strikingly simple,—that after all the apparent difference is one of extent and not intent. Hauff states specifically that Scott's truth is that of presenting a faithful picture of the times and avows his own purpose to offer the same sort of pictures to his readers. (60) The national and patriotic element is very strong in both authors. Scott, and Hauff in imitation of him, showed that national character, national dialect, national characteristics could be a major element in the interest of fiction and not implements of burlesque and interlude as the stage had made them. (61) Scott (and herein he influenced Hauff) added to the gallery of imaginary personages more and greater figures than anyone except Shakespeare. He gave a complete *milieu* of landscape and interior setting such as not even Shakespeare could do with the limitations of the stage. He showed the possibilities of novels different from the ones he wrote. He lifted a class of literature from a condition half-despised, poorly-explored, popular in a bad sense, to repute and profit. He infused into it the tradition of moral and intellectual growth, health, manliness, truth and honor, freedom and courtesy. (62) Objective truth and realism very characteristic of both authors. (63) The "kulturgeschichtliche" element so brilliantly developed in Scott is reflected with fainter hue in Hauff, tho here also the latter stands in conscious relation to his master. Drescher speaks thus of Hauff's efforts: "Zusammenfassend lässt sich über die kulturgeschichtlichen Elemente im *Lichtenstein* sagen, dass Hauff hierfür zwar keine besonders tiefen Studien angestellt hat, dass es ihm aber dank seines Gedächtnisses, seiner scharfen Beobachtungsgabe und seines historischen Sinnes gelungen ist, das entsprechende Zeitkolorit zu wahren."[13]

X The Influence of Other Sources

The objection could easily be urged against the foregoing discussion that, dealing as it does only with Scottian sources, it might readily be invalidated by proving the existence and operation of German influences, to which Hauff would naturally be more inclined to yield. It is precisely the absence of such influences that adds value to our findings, as we shall endeavor to make clear.

The Storm and Stress movement was powerful in its endorsement and exercise of "Kraftgenialität" and equally powerful in its plea for individual liberty. Its literary horrors were excrescences, as its enthusiasm was the effervescence, of an idea which took deep hold on the German heart. Not only is there no trace of this movement in *Lichtenstein,* but Hauff in his *Studien* condemns Scott in several instances for representing the horrible to such a degree that it becomes repellent.

Of pseudo-Storm and Stress writers Drescher thus speaks: "Die Werke von Vulpius, Cramer und Spiess bilden insofern eine zusammengehörige Gruppe, als bei ihnen von einer eigentlichen Tendenz gar keine Rede sein kann . . . Völliger Mangel an wirklich innerer Empfindung, der durch Anwendung sich beständig steigernder Übertreibungen nur mühsam verdeckt wird, und das Gefühl des Erborgten, des gesucht Effectvollen, des gewaltsam Anempfundenen, das jeden Leser dabei erfasst, lässt uns derartige Machtwerke neben den mit lebendigem Blute geschriebenen Erzeugnissen des wirklichen Sturmes und Dranges als unwürdig verurteilen."[14] We know, moreover, that he was familiar with Fouqué, Hildebrand, and Van der Velde; in fact, he himself states that by his eleventh year he had read the greater part of the "Ritter und Räuberromane" of the Fatherland, which could scarcely fail to give direction to his boyish fancy. And yet these tales of horror eventually faded from his imagination and never entered as active influences into his literary technique, as can be amply proved by his own assertions in his *Studies of the Waverley Novels,* where, for instance, he condemns *Ivanhoe* for its analogy to the "Ritterromane der verflossenen Dezennien."

With reference to the handling of historical material by Cramer, Spiess, and Vulpius, Drescher says that "Hauff mit dieser gewissenlosen Art der Benutzung geschichtlichen Stoffes nichts gemein hat . . ."[15] When, moreover, Brandes calls Fouqué's knights "stuffed-out pieces of armor," and Julian Schmid vouches for the absence of color; when Drescher affirms that Hildebrand's historical personages serve only as a background to give "a sort of historical justification" to the cruelties of raging peasants; when, too, Hauff in his introduction to *Lichtenstein* declares his specific intention to stand, as Scott did, on historical ground, it seems impossible that he should have used or even considered such German sources.

The national and patriotic elements of Hauff's novel are unopposedly relegated to Scottian influence. The bitter complaint which Hauff lodges against his nation for its ignorance of and apathy toward things German would in itself prove that no German model stood before him in these respects. In matters of general historical tendency also Hauff is admitted to have used Scott more than any other author.

For the organic plot unity of *Lichtenstein* no one has claimed to find a German prototype. We again quote from Drescher: "Über die Compositionstechnik der deutschen Vorbilder Hauffs lässt sich etwas Anerkennendes nicht sagen . . . Solche Werke bestehen aus einer Unsumme von Episoden, die kaleidoskopartig ohne Rücksicht auf Haupt- oder Nebenhandlung aneinander bereiht vor dem Auge des Lesers vorüberziehen und bei dem objectiven, denkenden Beurteiler keinen andern Eindruck als den der Unwahrscheinlichkeit hinterlassen. Die Menge der Episoden erfordert eine entsprechend grosse Zahl von Personen, deren Aufgabe lediglich darin besteht, neue Konflikte zu ermöglichen."[16] Scott, too, introduces many persons into his novels, but he endeavors thereby not to create unrelated episodes but rather to enlarge and animate scenes which in themselves are organically connected with the plot. We have already shown Hauff's relation to the plot technique of the Waverley series.

Commenting on the manner in which German writers of Hauff's day handled the historical content of their novels Drescher says: "In der Verwendung des kulturgeschichtlichen Materials kann sich quantitativ keiner der deutschen Schriftsteller auch nur im entferntesten mit Scott messen. . . . In viel wirksamerer, die betreffenden Zeitverhältnisse wirklich umfassender Weise benützt . . . Scott das kulturhistorische Material. . . . Wie sehr Hauff auch diese Seite des englischen Meisters gewürdigt hat, mögen einige Stellen aus den Studien zeigen."[17] Hauff's own statements in this connection are conclusive: "Scott reflektirt als Historiker, indem er uns das ganze Bild einer Zeit . . . im Romane darstellt. . . . Die Ausmalung übertrifft beinahe an Interesse die Charactere."

We regard it as significant that Hauff uses satire and romantic tendencies in his other works and yet develops *Lichtenstein* in a serious and realistic tone. He does not show the pessimism and elegiac mood of the romantic writers, and in a letter to Herlossohn denies allegiance to any school, adding also: "Ich bin weder gegoethet noch getieckt." His eclectic attitude toward authors in general and his conspicuous departure from characteristic methods would obviously indicate that he consciously adopted a new technique in the case of *Lichtenstein,* and in the light of our accumulated evidence we ascribe this new *modus operandi* to the influence of Walter Scott.

Hauff's independent method of developing the love interest has already been discussed. In his native literature the love treatment prevailingly involved numerous pairs of lovers, countless love adventures of the same lover, and a spirit of fickleness which must have outraged Hauff's sense of sincerity and devotion. Says Drescher: "Keiner der älteren deutschen Autoren vermag nämlich ein einzelnes Liebesverhältnis so wirkingsvoll auszugestalten, dass es dauerndes Interesse zu erwecken und die Spannung des Lesers bis zu Ende wachzuerhalten imstande ist.[18] . . . Hauff arbeitet in der Darstellung des liebenden Paares Georg und Marie völlig selbständig."[19]

As proof that Hauff did not find among the German writers satisfactory ideas for the delineation of his characters, we quote from Drescher and refer our readers to conclusions which we already stated in this discussion. Drescher says in part: "Bei der Mehrzahl der deutschen Romanschreiber wäre es verlorene Mühe, nach einer auch nur einigermassen künstlerischen, beabsichtigten Charakterdarstellung forschen zu wollen; haben sie es doch meist kaum zu Ansätzen einer solchen gebracht. Alle Helden der Ritterromane, gleichviel ob Ritter oder Knappe, Herr oder Knecht, sind fast durchgängig nach ein und derselben Schablone behandelt; alle erweisen sich als tapfer, stark, furchtlos, unbändig im Zorn, als Freunde des Kampfes und des Humpens, etc."[20] Scott's own sense of the importance of clear characterization is too well known to English readers to require at this point any special emphasis. And Hauff's unbounded admiration of this power in his master, together with its effect on his actual methods, indicates beyond a doubt the source from which he drew his knowledge and valuation of clear character-sketching.

As more general points of deviation from German methods, we cite the fact that he avoids those episodes which militate so constantly in German literature against the maintenance of plot unity; that the subjectivity so peculiar to German novelistic technique is entirely absent in *Lichtenstein*; that in comparison with Hauff's well-motived travel technique with its relevant description of persons and places, the German modus of his day is unnatural, due to the authors' ignorance of the localities traversed by the characters, due also to the paucity of descriptive material as well as characteristic features and details which would make such scenes more concrete; that the writers of the "Ritter- und Räuberromane" (as these novels sprang from the "Ritter- und Räuberdramen") retained much of the stage technique, as: the development of dialog with stage directions in parentheses, the marginal designation of the persons speaking ("he," "she," "all," etc.). Both Scott and Hauff confined themselves to the epic, not the dramatic form, of development.

In his sketch, **Die Bücher und die Lesewelt,** Hauff states that prior to his adoption of Scott as model he had no one in mind whom he could definitely choose for that purpose. He then enumerates the reasons which determined his choice,—a circumstance which argues strongly against the possibility of other sources.

But we find that the strongest proof for Hauff's independence of German influence lies in his allegiance to the Scottian ideal of realism. As Mielke says: "Walter Scott showed the historian that history is not an accumulation of abstract ideas, but the same fulness of events that the historian meets in his own time; he taught the novelist that his characters must not be mere reflections of his thoughts, but differentiated by dress and occupation as well as by peculiarity of speech and manner of thinking; and as he recognized truth to be the real literary end, he sought his models not in higher circles of society where form takes the place of naturalness, but among the lower classes where he found sound happiness, humorous peculiarities and the homely sentiments which gave reality to his novels."[21] And, too, Hauff's own words (quoted elsewhere also) betray how deeply he felt the inner value of Scott's realism: "Welcher Dichter gibt wohl ein besseres Zeugnis dafür, dass der Zauber der schlichten Wahrheit der grösste sei, als Walter Scott?"[22]

XI CONCLUSION

We find, then, that the central point of *Lichtenstein* is the love interest of the hero and heroine; that this, as well as the unadorned style of the novel, we must regard as elements in which the influence of Walter Scott is not apparent; that the plot in its historical and fictitious aspects is entirely subordinated to the love interest; that the technique of this plot in its character types, action, arrangement, and general movement is unvaryingly Scottian; that the few historical events which Hauff might have borrowed from his historical sources are blended so thoroughly with Scottian methods and duplicated so often in the Waverley series that they can be referred with no small probability to English influence; that *The Abbot* is the most obvious single model of *Lichtenstein.* From his original purpose of writing an historical romance Hauff was swerved by the realism of his own love experience; unless this fact is given full weight, the correct emphasis and meaning of *Lichtenstein* cannot be determined. How heavily he leaned on Scott for the form and filling of his novel needs no final recapitulation; the detailed findings require no closing emphasis; we therefore leave the evidence to find its way to the judgment of those into whose hands this paper may have the good fortune to fall.

Notes

1. *Der geschichtliche kern von Hauffs* Lichtenstein [(1904)].

2. *Die Quellen zu Hauffs* Lichtenstein [(1904)].

3. *Die Bücher und die Lesewelt.*

4. P. 61.

5. Pfaff, *Gesch. Württembergs,* I, 386.

6. *Studien.*

7. *Ibid.*

8. [Hans Hofmann,] *Wilhelm Hauff* [Eschborn: Verlag D. Klotz, 1902], p. 77.

9. *Studien.*

10. *Ibid.*

11. P. 136.

12. *Kritik einer Biographie* von Th. Reynold (Nov., 1841).

13. P. 48.

14. P. 61.

15. P. 66.

16. P. 81.

17. P. 96 seq.

18. P. 134.

19. P. 136.

20. P. 104.

21. P. 92.

22. *Studien.*

Maureen Thum (essay date 1996)

SOURCE: Thum, Maureen. "Re-Visioning Historical Romance: Carnivalesque Discourse in Wilhelm Hauff's *Jud Süß*." In *Neus zu Altem: Novellen der Vergangenheit und der Gegenwart,* pp. 25-42. München: Wilhelm Fink Verlag, 1996.

[*In the following essay, Thum argues against prevailing critical assessments of* Jud Süß *as a "failed historical romance," contending that the work in fact represents a "deconstructed historical romance," one in which Hauff subverts traditional narrative devices while exposing the religious and racial prejudices of the petty bourgeois.*]

Wie pries ich mich glücklich, in einem Land zu wohnen . . . wo man . . . Satire versteht und zu würdigen weiß. (Hauff [*Sämtliche Werke in drei Bänden*] 1: 488)

While critics admit that Wilhelm Hauff's writings are illuminated by the occasional flash of talent and perhaps even of genius, they have dismissed most of his works out of hand as the hackwork of a dilettant and philistine whose mental horizon is restricted by the normative attitudes and prejudices of the petty bourgeois.[1] Hauff's 1827 novella *Jud Süß* is a case in point. Following the lead of Albert Mannheimer—who saw the work as a failed historical romance in which the author privileges the perspective of the (good, heroic, much suffering) bourgeois protagonists and attempts to justify the judicial murder of the (evil, corrupt, Jewish) antago-

nist, Joseph Oppenheimer—critics have described the novella as a hastily executed, essentially flawed work, with a strong ethnocentric—if not anti-semitic—bias.[2]

Novelist Lion Feuchtwanger refers to the work as "naively anti-semitic" (Gerber 282), linking the novella to an entire tradition of anti-semitic narratives, histories, parodies, and diatribes which, from 1737 onward, had accrued about the figure of Joseph Oppenheimer, the Jewish finance minister of Carl Alexander, Duke of Württemberg from 1733 to 1737.[3] Feuchtwanger's assessment of Hauff's novella as an antisemitic work has remained essentially unchallenged, despite the reservations expressed by Otto Hinz and Barbara Gerber.[4] If accurate, Feuchtwanger's reading would corroborate the almost universally held critical view that Hauff's works are limited by the narrow, prejudicial perspective of the petty bourgeois.

Jud Süß, however, is not a failed—i.e. imperfectly crafted—historical romance, as Mannheimer and Hinz have suggested. Nor is it an anti-semitic work reaffirming the ethnocentric bias and racial hatred of Hauff's sources. On the contrary, *Jud Süß* is a carnivalized or deconstructed historical romance. In the initial chapters of the novella, the author appears to reproduce the fixed generic codes and the correspondingly normative mindsets of popular and trivialized historical romance[5] and to establish a clearly ethnocentric bias that corroborates the ethnic slur of the novella's title. In subsequent chapters, however, he dismantles the clichés of popular romance and questions the normative assumptions underlying fixed, mechanically reproduced generic codes. In these chapters Hauff uses a strategy of carnivalesque reversals and unmaskings in order to expose the racial and religious prejudice of the bourgeois protagonists and to shed critical light on the vicious mechanisms of communal scapegoating. In Hauff's text, the citizens of Württemberg kill Joseph Oppenheimer in order to uphold the fiction of an orderly, harmonious society and the conventionally sanctioned image of their deceased leader.[6] Despite revisionist claims of heroism, by the conclusion of the novella none of the characters remains uncompromised or uncorrupted—except perhaps a single figure invented by Hauff: Lea Oppenheimer, who does not belong to this society. The response of this ethnic outsider to an inhuman and inhumane social system that transforms potentially good and charitable human beings into corrupt, cowardly, and even brutal individuals, is unambiguous rejection. Lea commits suicide, a gesture that indicts a society which not only countenances, but requires injustice and hypocrisy to preserve the illusion of a continued, harmonious status quo.[7]

One of Hauff's key narratorial strategies is the carnivalesque reversal. It is no accident that the novella begins with the word "Karneval," and that the initial chapters, more than a third of the narrative, are set during the carnival celebration of 1737. The carnival refers not only to the actual historical festival but also signals the carnivalesque in a wider, Bakhtinian sense. For Bakhtin, the carnival or the carnivalistic spirit in literature is expressed in the depiction of a world turned upside down, a world in which traditional social structures, established orthodoxies, and cultural norms are questioned and subverted. The often darkly—even sardonically—comic inversions of authority characteristic of the pre-lenten Carnival are staged in literary texts as the symbolic questioning of fixed social hierarchies and the hypothetical disruption of normative codes.

Central to the carnival is the masquerade. Donning a mask signals the adoption of an alternative identity and thus the blurring of normative social and cultural distinctions. Masquerade permits the individual to cross traditional barriers and to transgress inherited patterns of thought and language. In Hauff's novella, the masquerade plays a significant role, and the continued maskings and unmaskings in the text are a key to the author's carnivalesque strategy of reversal and inversion. In the initial chapters, almost all of the main characters are masked, and each of the masks signals to the reader a typical or stereotypical role which the character might be expected to play within the tale. However, as the narrative proceeds, the masks are removed, revealing a very different, unexpected identity and role that stands in ironic contrast to the earlier, assumed identity. These initial masks are central to the strategy of ironic unmasking and reversal that follows.

Gustav Lanbek, the young bourgeois actuary, and Lea Oppenheimer, Joseph's sister, wear similar masks, suggesting their expected roles as Romantic hero and heroine. Both are dressed in oriental garb. When the narrator introduces Gustav as a mysterious, handsome figure, "einen schlanken, schöngewachsenen Mann, der, als Sarazene gekleidet, sich durch die einfache Pracht seines Kostüms, wie durch Gang und Haltung vor gemeineren Masken auszeichnete" (477), the reader recognizes what was, by 1827, a literary cliché: the noble and often oriental(ized) hero.[8] Enmeshed as he is in mystery and intrigue, filled with vaguely (and anachronistically) Byronic longings, and secretly in love with Lea, the beautiful "Orientalin," Gustav appears to be playing a typical, if not stereotypical role. Even when he removes the mask, he seems a young man in charge, a man who is knowledgeable, purposeful, and strong: "Eine kühn gebogene Nase und dunkle, tiefblaue Augen gaben seinem Gesicht einen Ausdruck von unternehmender Kraft und einen tiefen Ernst" (479). Only his softly colored hair modifies the initial impression of strength.

Arrested during the carnival and confronted by the feared Joseph Oppenheimer, Gustav answers readily and courageously, apparently defying the power of the tyrant. However, the mask of the hero is rapidly stripped away, for despite his courageous mien and his desire to abandon cultural norms, Gustav remains the product of his conditioning. He so fears the censure of respectable society and the wrath of his authoritarian father that he is willing to disavow his secret and forbidden love for Lea even before that love is tested. Almost without a struggle, his romantic longings, like his fantasies of transgressing cultural and religious barriers, are sacrificed to the middle-class codes of behavior with which he is imbued. Lea, Gustav's romance counterpart, appears in equally stereotypical guise as "die Orientalin," attracting all eyes as she appears at the side of her brother during the carnival, "eine schlanke, zartgebaute Dame . . . in ein mit Gold und Steinen überladenes Kostüm gekleidet" (475). As the mysterious "Orientalin," a figure recurrent as a motif throughout romance and Romantic literature, she symbolizes the exotic and the erotic. The crowd of curious onlookers equate her identity with her costume and context, casting her in the role of *femme fatale* and fallen woman and assuming that she is not the sister but the mistress of Oppenheimer. She appears to them as the quintessential object of desire, devoid of autonomy or identity.[9]

When she lays aside "die lästige Larve," a very different identity comes to light. For Gustav, however, her human face is still obscured by the stereotypical images he projects upon her. He sees her both as romanticized fantasy of exotic womanhood, "eine solche Täuschung . . . wie sie die ergriffene Phantasie der Reisenden bei ihrer Heimkehr malte" (485), and as "das süße Geschöpf," "ein Kind," to be patronized as an innocent who knows nothing of the world and nothing of her position in Württemberg. He cannot imagine a mind behind those beautiful and exotic features. Though Gustav briefly wonders whether he should enlighten her: "Sollte er mit einem Mal den arglosen Wahn dieses liebenswürdigen Geschöpfs zerstören?" (484), that fleeting thought is never carried out. Ironically, as the reader soon discovers, Gustav is no less ignorant of social, cultural, and political realities, than Lea herself.

Lea resists the labels—"die Orientalin," "die Charmante," "das süße Geschöpf," or simply "die Jüdin"—which others use to define her identity, and her words demonstrate the inadequacy and erroneousness of such fixed images as an accurate reflection of her identity. Hauff has endowed her with an eloquent voice and with a consciousness, intelligence, and depth of passion that allow her to cross the boundaries set by ethnocentric discourse. Her voice suggests an alternative perspective which often conflicts with that of Gustav, the young bourgeois. Neither Gustav Lanbek nor Lea Oppenheimer fulfill the expected roles of romance hero and heroine initially signalled by their masks. Indeed, the expected scenarios and established patterns of romance narratives serve as a backdrop against which their aborted relationship is delineated in sharp, ironic contrast.

"Der alte Lanbek," the venerable *Landschaftskonsulent* who plays a leading role in the assembly, also sports a false identity for the carnival. "Die klaren grauen Augen," "der feste Schritt," and "seine volle sonore Stimme" (500) seem to corroborate the image of strength and purposefulness for the man Gustav sees as "der Allgewaltige" (490). Nevertheless, appearing in rustic garb and speaking ostensibly in the voice of the "people" and in the interests of the *Landvolk,* Lanbek stages a traditional, vituperatively anti-semitic "Bauerngespräch," during which he targets Joseph Oppenheimer as a power-hungry villain and as the incarnation of an alien evil that has intruded their formerly harmonious realm.[10] When Oppenheimer later reveals to an astonished Gustav that this hate-filled provocateur is his own father, the younger Lanbek has great difficulty in recognizing him: "Mein Vater ist ein ruhiger, gesetzter Mann, und sein Charakter, sein Amt, seine Jahre verbieten ihm das Publikum auf einem Maskenball zu amüsieren" (495). The stark contrast between Old Lanbek's patriarchal persona and his carnival mask, however, is no anomaly; rather it prefigures the later roles played by good, venerable, and well-intentioned human beings, who at the conclusion of the narrative engage in a communal act of ritualized violence. In donning the peasant mask, Old Lanbek also seeks to express symbolically his much vaunted altruistic devotion to the common good, but his concern for the common welfare of the people is subsequently revealed as a mask for the narrowly conceived economic and political self-interest of an egotistical bourgeois.

Joseph Oppenheimer is one of the few figures who appear unmasked in the initial scenes: his mask is carelessly attached to his hat, his real face revealed to the onlookers. Yet the absence of the mask is as telling as the disguises assumed by other characters. As the reader discovers, Oppenheimer, the human being, is masked as "Jud Süß," the stereotype of the court Jew, a communally accepted identity. The term "Jud Süß" with its intentional ethnic slur recurs with motif-like regularity throughout the novella—not as an unwitting revelation of Hauff's anti-semitism, but as the author's attempt to demonstrate the bigotry of the various characters who use this epithet. Indeed the stereotype of the court Jew is subverted and questioned throughout the subsequent narrative. Like his sister Lea, Joseph Oppenheimer is endowed with a clear and articulate voice that consistently, if implicitly, provides an alternative perspective. His voice, too, contradicts and casts doubt upon the validity of the prejudicial bourgeois perspective.

The "mask" of Carl Alexander, Duke of Württemberg, is disclosed to the reader only toward the conclusion of the narrative. Hauff, unlike his sources who depict the Duke at the center of the carnival festivities, has moved Carl Alexander completely off the stage, placing in the ruler's stead Oppenheimer as the *Glanzpunkt* of the festival and as the Carnival King who is subsequently to be uncrowned.[11] The carnival scenes thus serve to stage the bourgeois view of Oppenheimer as the autonomous and all-powerful courtier who has horribly deceived a good, brave, heroic, but distant ruler. Only later does the reader discover that Carl Alexander has all along been party to, if not mastermind of, the machinations and powerplays attributed to Oppenheimer. Indeed, the Duke has used Oppenheimer effectively as a cover for his own questionable money-making schemes and as camouflage for his bid to overthrow the assembly and arrogate the traditional rights of the *Landschaft*. Thus Oppenheimer, the "Court Jew," is actually the mask used by Carl Alexander to hide his nefarious activities from his subjects. The Duke has consciously exploited Oppenheimer, knowing that the latter, as ethnic outsider, would draw automatically the blame and thus serve as a scapegoat for the Duke.

The narrator, too, is "masked" in the opening chapters, appearing disguised as a bourgeois who privileges the perspective of the two middle-class protagonists. In subsequent chapters, however, the mask slips aside to reveal a critic rather than a supporter of the bourgeois protagonists. By the conclusion of the narrative, the mask has fallen, disclosing a persona not unlike the speaker in Jonathan Swift's "A Modest Proposal." In an acerbic and grimly ironic coda, the double-voiced narrator reveals that what parades as "justice" is in reality judicial murder. Joseph Oppenheimer is convicted and hanged—not because of personal "crimes" he has committed, but because he alone, as the ethnic outsider, is held responsible for the machinations of others and thus becomes the communal scapegoat.

Hauff carries out the carnivalesque overturning of normative views with a circumspection and indirection attributable in no small part to the strict censorship laws and sanctions enforced in the Duchy of Württemberg in the 1820s.[12] In a series of telling scenes, the authority and credibility of the bourgeois stance are implicitly called into question, its perspective shown to be narrow and egotistical. Gustav, the erstwhile Romantic hero, is unmasked as an anti-hero who betrays Lea out of fear of public censure, engages in double dealing with his father, and is less concerned with probity than with a facade of respectability.

Like Gustav, Old Lanbek is also unmasked in a series of compromising scenes that reveal him to be a scheming, mendacious, authoritarian, and bigoted man, who is subject to uncontrolled rage when his authority is questioned. The *Landschaftskonsulent*'s vaunted political far-sightedness is revealed to be nothing less than political myopia. He seriously miscalculates the role of the Duke and his complicity in the schemes blamed on Oppenheimer, and only a fortuitous accident—the Duke's sudden death—allows Old Lanbek and his fellow conspirators to escape possible charges of treason and to rewrite history, casting themselves in the role of heroes.

Even before he has shed his oriental costume, Gustav's mask as Romantic hero is removed. Over a period of several months, Gustav has courted Joseph Oppenheimer's sister, and Oppenheimer, who has recognized Gustav's father in the vituperative peasant from the carnival and who clearly wishes to avert an open rebellion, arrests Gustav, thinking him to be party to the conspiracy. When Oppenheimer confronts Gustav as to his intentions concerning Lea, the young actuary sees himself as courageously defying the fearsome tyrant. The defiant stance, however, barely conceals the young man's frightened betrayal of the woman he loves, as Gustav avoids the question of marriage. Oppenheimer offers his intended brother-in-law a promotion to the lucrative position of *Expeditionsrat,* a promotion that, as Gustav well knows, would allow him to skip no fewer than "vier Stufen, durch welche man sich sonst lange und mühevoll schleppte" (497). The promotion—invented by Hauff—plays a significant role throughout the narrative, as a touchstone for the probity of various characters.[13] It is not the fact that the promotion is undeserved, but the fear of public censure that causes Gustav to recoil in horror: "es war der schreckliche Gedanke, vor der Welt für einen Günstling dieses Mannes zu gelten, vor seinem Vater, vor allen guten Männern gebrandmarkt zu werden" (497). However, as the reader soon realizes, if Gustav can escape censure and keep his reputation intact, both he and his father are quite willing to keep the promotion, whether deserved or not.

Gustav now lies to Oppenheimer and to himself, claiming he had never entertained thoughts of marriage, had never loved Lea. For the first time, the narrator distances himself unambiguously from Gustav's perspective, exposing the young man's prejudice and fear of public censure: "so groß war die Furcht vor Schande, so tief eingewurzelt damals noch die Vorurteile gegen jene unglücklichen Kinder Abrahams, das sie sogar seine zärtlichen Gefühle für die schöne Tochter Israels in diesem schrecklichen Augenblick übermannten" (497-98). Gustav now resorts to legalistic double talk to extricate himself from what he has suddenly recognized to be a compromising situation:

> "Herr Minister," sprach er zögernd, "Lea kann keinen wärmeren Freund als mich haben; aber ich fürchte, daß Sie dieses Gefühl falsch deuten, mit einem anderen verwechseln, das—ich möchte nicht das Sie mich falsch verstehen, und Lea wird Ihnen nie gesagt haben, daß ich jemals davon gesprochen hätte. . . ."
>
> (498)

Gustav seeks to picture Oppenheimer as the infamous "Jud Süß," his father's arch enemy and an evil tyrant. He sees Oppenheimer as making improper claims on a young bourgeois official who bravely defies him by refusing to marry the Finance Director's sister in return for a bribe. The words of Joseph Oppenheimer, however, contradict Gustav's self-serving interpretation of the encounter and reveal a very different picture: he is an angry brother, whose sister has been courted by a young man who has no intention of marrying her, simply because she is Jewish, and who wishes to hide the troubling knowledge of his prejudice and fear from both Oppenheimer and himself. Gustav does not defy the tyrant but raises only legalistic objections, and Oppenheimer reacts with understandable anger, pointing to the painful truth that Gustav refuses to countenance: "War etwa meine Schwester gut genug dazu, Eure müßigen Stunden auszufüllen, zur Gattin aber wollt Ihr sie nicht? Wehe Euch, wenn Ihr so dächtet . . ." (498).

Gustav sees a villain, acting autonomously, without Carl Alexander's knowledge or consent; Oppenheimer's words reveal a man who knows that the Duke holds the power in the Duchy, and who recognizes that in the Duke's eyes, "Rebell ist jeder, der nur dem Land und nicht dem Herzog dient" (495). Oppenheimer is neither an autonomous actor in the political and economic game nor the enemy of the people as perceived by the bourgeois protagonists. Rather, he is the instrument of, and cover for, the machinations of Carl Alexander who has engaged him for this very purpose. Only the Duke's sudden death reveals Oppenheimer's precariousness and his vulnerability as the ethnic outsider, caught between the claims of the rising bourgeoisie, anxious to protect their social, political, and economic rights, and the counterclaims of an absolutist ruler, who with Oppenheimer as his camouflage seeks to buttress an already anachronistic system of government.

This initial encounter between Gustav and Oppenheimer is a paradigm for subsequent scenes in which Gustav's bourgeois stance is further undermined. When he appears before his father the next morning wearing the borrowed jacket of his military friend von Blankenburg, Gustav is once again in disguise, adopting now the borrowed role of the heroic *Krieger* who has defied the tyrant in his very lair. The assumed identity of the jaunty and undaunted warrior is as much at odds with Gustav's subsequent behavior as was the Oriental mask of the carnival. Too fearful of Old Lanbek's wrath to confess his forbidden relationship with Lea, Gustav has concocted a lie to explain the arrest and the sudden promotion to *Expeditionsrat.* Gustav's double dealing in this scene is no less damaging than his earlier betrayal of Lea.

Old Lanbek also appears in a dubious light during this compromising scene. His response to Gustav's promotion demonstrates that his overt altruism and patriotic devotion to the common good conceal quite different motives: economic self-interest and the drive to preserve and strengthen his social and economic position. Thus instead of rejecting the promotion as unethical, he devises a scheme not only to foil the machinations he attributes to Oppenheimer, but also to keep his son's promotion and good name: "noch weiß ich, gottlob, ein Mittel, uns das Vertrauen der Besseren zu erhalten, und du—wirst und bleibst Expeditionsrat!" (503). The scene concludes with a telling exchange in which Gustav expresses no concern about the questionable ethical implications of accepting the promotion to high public office, but questions instead whether it might harm his reputation. "Aber Vater!" he exclaims, when his father persists in the argument, "Ihr Ruf ist felsenfest, aber der meinige?" (504).

As Gustav's identity recedes behind the mask of his social and economic role, Lea's identity is revealed. Her clear articulate voice, like that of her brother, resists the stereotypes and labels others project upon her. During a brief encounter in the garden, while Gustav addresses her as "Kind" and lies to her about his absence, the sudden color rising to her cheeks indicates her quick understanding of the lie. This is no girl, "das jetzt lächelnd, träumend, sorglos wie ein Kind an einem furchtbaren Abgrund sich Blumen zu seinem Kranze pflückte" (513), as Gustav attempts to tell himself. Her words demonstrate an understanding of which Gustav is incapable. She comments, astutely, on the Catholic-Protestant conflict: "Ich bin nur froh, daß du nicht Katholik bist, da wäre es nicht möglich, aber ihr Protestanten habt ja kein kirchliches Oberhaupt und seid doch eigentlich so gut Ketzer wie wir Juden" (512). This comment, informed by Enlightenment wit and cultural relativism reminiscent of Montesquieu and Voltaire, scandalizes Gustav. Her assessment of Gustav's angry response is equally astute: "Ach, geh doch! . . . Daß ich es wagte, mein verhaßtes Volk neben euch zu stellen, bringt dich auf" (513). Her words reveal a clear-eyed understanding of her position and constitute as well a refusal to be patronized by a man who represents the mainstream mindset. As the narrative proceeds, the reader discovers that Lea is as passionate, charitable, and steadfast as she is intelligent. In a novella where there are neither real heroes nor real villains, she is the most sympathetic of all the characters.

A subsequent scene allows the bourgeois conspiracy to be seen from an unusual and ironic perspective. The gathering of the military and Church leaders in the Lanbek home is observed from an upstairs *Rumpelkammer* by Gustav's two sisters, Hedwig and Käthchen, who have been excluded from the proceedings and banished to their rooms. Käthchen's naive comments, while she watches through a vent in the ceiling, unintentionally provide ironic commentary on the real motives of the conspirators. Rather than a band of men in their self-

appointed roles as fearless heroes, Käthchen sees "gefährliche Männer," who have come together "wie beim Karneval" (519). As her words suggest, the carnival has now extended to include the entire duchy. Masked in their assumed identities, the various players act out a series of assumed roles in this dangerous and dehumanizing game. Hauff allows Käthchen's summary of the planned overthrow of Oppenheimer—"Denke nur . . . der Süß will uns katholisch machen und die Landschaft umstürzen, da verlöre der Vater und alle anderen verlören ihre Stellen" (520)—to reveal the real motives for the plot: the desire of the conspirators to secure their economic and social positions.

The unmasking of the Duke, like the unmasking of the conspirators, is accomplished by implication rather than by overt statement. The bourgeois are convinced that their ruler is distant, and heroic, and that the bid to usurp the powers of the *Landschaft*, like the rumored Catholic takeover, has been orchestrated entirely by Oppenheimer. The incongruity of the idea that a Jewish financier who, in the words of Käthchen, "will uns katholisch machen," somehow escapes them. The Duke, however, is not distant and deceived but an active participant. A single, key piece of information provides the unobtrusive, yet damning evidence of his complicity. The Duke's planned journey to Kehl has been publicized to such an extent that Obrist von Röder, one of the conspirators, sees it as a ploy: "Ich fürchte die ganze Fahrt ist nur Maske" (509). Von Röder suspects that the Duke might use the much publicized journey to hide the fact that he is actually at home, directing the overthrow of the *Landschaft*. This, indeed, proves to be the case.

On the night when the Duke is ostensibly absent, von Röder arrests Oppenheimer according to plan. He informs a worried Gustav that they need not fear repercussions from the Duke, for the latter has died, suddenly and unexpectedly of a stroke. To Gustav's question: "War er in Kehl?" (530)—in other words, was the Duke *really* absent—Obrist von Röder replies, with sadness: "Er ist in Ludwigsburg . . . gestorben" (530). In other words, he was *not* absent, and yes, he *was* implicated in the plot to overthrow the *Landschaft*. Gustav's response is telling: "Wie, in Ludwigsburg. . . . Oh, ewige Vorsicht!" (530). Divine intervention has indeed saved the conspirators, for in Hauff's re-visioning of history, Old Lanbek and the bourgeois faction would themselves have quite probably been arrested for treason—for blocking the Duke's own machinations in the name of the Duke—had the Duke not fortuitously died.

With full knowledge that Oppenheimer was the wrong target, the former conspirators and rebels—now heroes—arrest the finance minister. He is tried, convicted, and murdered in order to protect, simultaneously with their economic interests, their images as heroic, far-sighted men and in order to uphold unblemished the equally false, heroic image of the deceased Duke. Gustav, who retains his position as *Expeditionsrat,* is appointed to head the commission charged with prosecuting the Finance Director. Despite a sense of justice and humanity, Gustav carries out the commission's anti-semitic intent, even after he discovers the injustice of prosecuting only Oppenheimer, having learned that not only the Duke but at least four other men were implicated in the plot to overthrow the *Landschaft.* The young Lanbek "mit edlem Unwillen" presents the case to the commission, but the commission has no desire to prosecute any one other than Oppenheimer, since, as the narrator comments, "ihn der allgemeine Haß als den Schuldigsten bezeichnete" (533).

In the role of judge, Gustav now visits Oppenheimer in his dungeon cell, reversing the roles of the earlier prison scene. Gustav is not an evil man:

> das Herz des jungen Mannes war zu groß, als daß es hätte freudig pochen sollen, als er zum ersten Mal als Richter in den Kerker des Mannes trat, der jetzt entblösst von aller irdischen Herrlichkeit, angetan mit zerlumpten Kleidern, bleich, verwildert sich langsam an seinen rasselnden Ketten aufrichtete.
>
> (533)

Once again Oppenheimer resists Gustav's attempt to interpret his behavior as crass and self-serving. Oppenheimer asks for nothing for himself, only for pity for his sister: "als man in meinem Hause versiegelte, haben sie die rohen Menschen auf die Straße gestoßen" (533). Oppenheimer bitterly adopts the stance of his captors—"sie war ja eine Jüdin und verdiente also kein Mitleid"—but concludes with the plea: "sie hat nichts als das Kleid, das sie trug, als man sie von der Schwelle stieß—geben Sie ihr aus Barmherzigkeit ein Almosen" (533). While Gustav attempts to dismiss the plea as a mendacious ploy to elicit pity, the reader discovers that Oppenheimer's request is genuine. Lea has refused to accept the money secured outside the duchy, believing it tainted by the crimes of which Oppenheimer is accused.

Lea's powerful and eloquent voice overshadows that of Gustav in their final encounter; his lame excuses appear all the more paltry in the face of her resigned and bitter insight. During this painful and unsettling scene, Gustav's slavish adherence to conditioned responses reveals the potential inhumanity of normative codes. Lea pleads for mercy for her brother, whom Gustav can save from hanging by suppressing a single piece of evidence, a letter, which he alone possesses and which he alone has seen. Gustav's response to the woman he once loved—and perhaps still loves—is formal distance, interspersed incongruously with intimations of their former intimacy, as he alternately addresses her as

"Sie" and "du." He refuses to suppress the letter, not because it would violate his code of ethics to do so, but because it could compromise his facade of respectability with the very men who, as Gustav well knows, are intent on carrying through an act of injustice: "Nein—nein—es ist nicht möglich," he explains, "Sieh, Lea, mein Leben möchte ich hingeben, um deine Ruhe zu erkaufen, aber meine Ehre! Gott! meinen guten Namen! Es ist nicht möglich" (535). His words fail to mask the reality: to maintain his "good name" and his "honor"—i.e., his standing among the members of his social class—Gustav is prepared to act dishonorably, providing the final evidence that he knows will allow the commission to proceed "legally" with the killing.

Lea's quiet and despairing assent, as Gustav dismisses her with an almost ludicrously insufficient "ich will gewiß das Meinige tun" and "Gott weiß, daß ich nicht anders konnte," speaks more eloquently than would blame or angry protest (536). When he requests forgiveness for the act of betrayal he is about to commit, her final, brief response—"Ich habe nichts zu vergeben"—suggests her resigned recognition that normative social and cultural codes are too powerful for an ordinary and unheroic individual to transgress voluntarily, even in the name of compassion or justice (536). Her parting comment cuts with a double edge: "Möge der Gott meiner Väter dich so glücklich machen, wie es dein reiches Herz verdient" (537). Lea's suicide, reported as if in passing, and Gustav's failure ever to smile again, bear mute witness to Lea's despair and Gustav's belated recognition of his betrayal of others—and himself. The narrator, speaking from a distance which has now obscured these all but forgotten events, reports: "Man sagt, er habe nie wieder gelächelt . . . die Sage ging damals, daß er nur einmal und ein unglückliches Mädchen geliebt habe, das ihren Tod im Neckar freiwillig fand" (538). Continuing, the narrator relates: "Mein Großvater pflegte von ihm zu sagen: 'Er war einer von jenen Menschen, die, wenn sie einmal recht unglücklich gewesen sind, sich nicht mehr an das Glück gewöhnen mögen'" (538). Lea's parting phrase has become Gustav's curse.

The narrator, whose voice shifts throughout the novella, now adopts a double-voiced stance, in which his overt message is contradicted by an implied one. The trial itself, like the brutality of the judicial murder and the desecration of Oppenheimer's body, are passed over laconically, in a sentence or two, as possibly "tiring" to the reader: since the outcome is a foregone conclusion, and its predetermined course so predictable, relating it would be redundant. The narrator appears to accept the version of the events favorable to the town's citizenry, even as his words implicitly condemn the brutality of the communal act of violence, the sacrifice of the interloper with which the "carnival" of this text culminates:

Sie hingen ihn an einen ungeheuren Galgen von Eisen in einem eisernen Käficht auf. Im Dekret des Herzog Administrator hieß es: "Ihme zu wohlverdienter Straff, jedermänniglich aber zum abscheulichen Exempel." Beides, die Art, wie dieser unglückliche Mann mit Württemberg verfahren konnte, und seine Strafe, sind gleich auffallend und unbegreiflich zu einer Zeit, wo man schon längst die Anfänge der Zivilisation und Aufklärung hinter sich gelassen. . . .

(537)

The ostensible justification that the narrator appears to offer—reported in the words of men who lived at this time—is actually a tacit admission of communal guilt. The author's distance from this judgment, refracted through the voice of his fictive narrator, is revealed in the telling use of the verb "scheint." The carefully placed "scheint" puts into question the validity of an argument the narrator purports to find adequate and neutralizes the initial subjunctive "wäre":

Man *wäre* versucht, das damalige Württemberg der schmächlichsten Barbarei anzuklagen, wenn nicht ein Umstand einträte, den Männer, die zu jener Zeit gelebt haben, oft wiederholen, und der, wenn er auch nicht die Tat entschuldigt, doch ihre Notwendigkeit darzutun *scheint*. "Er mußte," sagen sie, "nicht sowohl für seine eigenen schweren Verbrechen als für die Schandtaten und Pläne mächtiger Männer am Galgen sterben."

Verwandtschaften, Ansehen, heimliche Verprechungen retteten die andern, den Juden—konnte und mochte niemand retten. . . .

(537; emphases mine)

Furthermore, since the "justification" offered for the judicial murder is clearly insufficient, the accusation of barbarism, which appears to be cast in the subjunctive mode of doubt, remains essentially unchallenged.

The final judgment, fully exculpating Oppenheimer, is attributed by the narrator—in a further ironic reversal—to Old Lanbek himself, who has recognized the erroneousness of his earlier assessment of Oppenheimer's role. Lanbek has not merely modified his earlier stance, he has reversed it: "so schrieb man, wie sich der alte Landschaftskonsulent Lanbek ausdrückte, 'was die übrigen verzehrt hatten, auf *seine* Zeche'" (537). It is a final judgment that has proven to be historically accurate.

Neither a failed historical romance nor an anti-Jewish document, Hauff's re-visioning of the Oppenheimer affair presents a narratorially sophisticated dismantling of the process of communal scapegoating. Astonishingly, Hauff's poetic "falsification" of historical narratives has produced an interpretation not unlike that of more recent historians of this period who have attempted to reconstruct the event based on sources and documents not available to Hauff. Like Hauff, in his fictive re-visioning of the event, they perceive the violence perpetrated on the Jewish financier not solely in terms of a racial ha-

tred which can be isolated as the single deciding factor. Instead, they see it as a communal act—a socially sanctioned killing—perpetrated at least in part as the result of highly complex, intersecting social, political, cultural and psychological factors that twentieth-century historians are still attempting to understand fully and to interpret in narratives divested of their ethnocentric bias.[14]

Notes

1. The few critics who acknowledge Hauff as a literary figure have given him at best brief, and for the most part negative mention. In the short "Nachwort" to the 1970 edition of Hauff's collected works [*Sämtliche Werke in drei Bänden*], Helmut Koopmann states a critical consensus when he comments, "im allgemeinen hat die Literaturgeschichte ihre Akten geschlossen, und das Urteil, das sie gefällt hat, ist so beschaffen, daß es eine ernsthafte Beschäftigung mit Hauff im Grunde genommen verbietet" (491).

   Otto Hinz, who recapitulates and expands upon earlier negative critical commentaries, sees *Jud Süß,* like Hauff's other novellas, as evidence of what is worst in the work of a talented hackwriter: "Nirgendwo sonst in Hauffs Werk tritt der Widerspruch zwischen seinem erzählerischen Können und den destruktiven Bedingungen hektischer Auftragschreiberei deutlicher zutage" (60). See also Barbara Gerber's brief summary of dismissive criticism designating Hauff—erroneously to my mind—as a minor Biedermeier figure (534, n3). Egon Schwarz, who makes the case—albeit with reservations—for a reassessment of two of Hauff's *Kunstmärchen,* is one of the few critics to contest the above consensus.

2. Mannheimer sees Hauff as adopting, unquestioningly and even naively, the perspective of Karl Pfaff's 1820 *Geschichte Württembergs*. Pfaff exculpates the citizens of Württemberg, and their heroic if distant leader, Duke Carl Alexander, and blames the Duke's corrupt ministers, particularly Joseph Oppenheimer (34). Mannheimer concludes, "So suchen Hauff und Pfaff den an Süss Oppenheimer begangenen Justizmord zu entschuldigen" (51).

3. As Mannheimer indicates, no fewer than three other Jewish financiers during this period had entered upon a similar career, and suffered a similar fate after the death of their aristocratic patrons (3-4). Oppenheimer, who was routinely designated by the ethnic slur, "Jud Süss," became an emblematic figure, the epitome of the "Court Jew." In eighteenth- and early nineteenth-century writings, Oppenheimer was recast in the role of villain and power hungry manipulator whose corruption brought about his richly deserved fall (Gerber 282).

4. Gerber sees the anti-semitic reading as reductionist, since it omits key elements of the novella: "Um Hauff's Novelle in dieser Weise beanspruchen zu können, mußte man sie rigoros auf eine antisemitische Lesart einebnen . . ." (534, n2). Hinz sees the novella as an unsuccessful attempt, "bei unverhohlener Sympathie für die Sache der rechtschaffenen Bürger, allen Exponenten der streitenden Parteien gerecht zu werden" (61). Hinz notes briefly that Hauff's figure is "weit entfernt von dem dämonischen Popanz" portrayed in the early pamphlet literature (61). Neither Hinz nor Gerber move beyond the brief comments, cited above, to explore the questions their observations raise.

5. Hauff astutely dismantles these normative codes and their corresponding mindsets in his 1826 "Kontroverspredigt."

6. Hauff uses a similar technique of dismantling ethnic stereotypes and revealing the mechanisms of communal scapegoating in his *Kunstmärchen,* "Abner, der Jude der Nichts gesehen hat." Critics have argued that the Frankfurt chapter in Hauff's *Mittheilung aus den Memoiren des Satan* (1825-26) demonstrates Hauff's anti-semitic stance, which is then reiterated in *Jud Süß* (1827). Although the speaker in the earlier Rabelaisian work is Satan, and although the Christian Church is equally travestied in the final grotesque scene of Satan's memoirs, the Frankfurt chapter has a distinctly ethnocentric bias and alienating tone that cannot be simply dismissed as the distortions of an unreliable narrator with whom Hauff did not necessarily agree. I wish to argue that Hauff's later works represent an altered perspective. Even Mannheimer, who sees Hauff as reiterating Pfaff's ethnocentric bias in *Jud Süß,* notes the marked difference between the depiction of the Jewish community in the earlier work and the portrait of Oppenheimer and his sister in the later novella, one of the last works completed before Hauff's death in 1827. The later novella is not an isolated case. In two cycles of *Kunstmärchen* which appeared in 1826 and posthumously in 1827, Hauff repeatedly portrays figures stigmatized and outcast by a normative community. These works prefigure the dismantling of ethnocentrism in the later novella, and suggest that the earlier work is not to be taken as an unequivocal sign for Hauff's ethnocentrism. Hauff not only alters his perspective in the later novella, but like Old Lanbek at the end of *Jud Süß,* he reverses his initial position.

7. Only Joseph Oppenheimer and Carl Alexander are based on actual historical figures. All of the other characters except for one or two military leaders, who make a cameo appearances, are Hauff's inventions. The positive figure of Lea—not present in the anti-semitic pamphlet literature—may have been drawn from a number of possible sources, including Lessing's *Nathan der Weise,* Sir Walter Scott's *Ivanhoe,* and a philosemitic work entitled *Der neue Weiberfeind und die schöne Jüdin* (Wien, 1773; see Mannheimer 66). Lea represents a remarkable alteration in a different sense as well, since she takes the place occupied by the figure of Henriette Fischerin, Oppenheimer's mistress in much of the pamphlet literature. As Mannheimer comments, "Die Maitressen des Juden werden in allen Flugschriften erwähnt" (57). In Hauff's novella, Oppenheimer's mistress is never mentioned, except by indirect reference to the Finance Minister's soirées. The sympathetic figure of Lea who accompanies her brother, who loves him, who pleads his case and who mourns for him, replaces Oppenheimer's mistress(es) found in Hauff's sources. This radical substitution and its concomitant reversal of values and expectations provides a telling commentary on Hauff's re-visioning of previous anti-semitic narratives.

8. Hauff, himself, portrayed such a figure, the Robber Orbasan, in his *Kunstmärchen* cycle *Die Karawane.* Hauff described trivialized versions of this stereotypical figure with acerbic wit in his "Kontroverspredigt" (1826).

9. Hauff similarly decried such stereotypes in his "Kontroverspredigt": "Die Dame des Stückes ist und bleibt immer dasselbe Holz- und Gliederpüppchen, die nach Verhältnissen kostümiert wird" (I: 804).

10. See Mannheimer's discussion of the "Bauerngespräche," focusing on the Oppenheimer affair (26-27).

11. See Mannheimer. While Oppenheimer was a merely a peripheral figure according to the sources describing the carnival, Carl Alexander, by contrast, was the central figure (Mannheimer 21-22).

12. Hauff had first-hand knowledge of the enforcement of censorship in the Duchy of Württemberg after the Vienna Congress (1814-15) and the Karlsbad Decrees of 1819, which had imposed rigid censorship on publications, restricted freedom of speech, and ordered the dismissal of all teachers who undermined public order or questioned existing political institutions (Reinhardt 467). Hauff's father had been arrested because of his republican sympathies. Held for a year without trial, he was finally released, his health broken (Pfäfflin 8). A distant cousin had undergone a similar experience. Released in 1825, he died shortly thereafter (Hofmann 39).

13. Mannheimer finds a possible source for the invented promotion in Karl Pfaff, who describes

"die Versuche Montmartins, den Landschaftskonsulenten Moser durch allerlei Gnadenbezeugungen für die Absichten der Wilkürherrschaft Karl Eugens zu gewinnen" (30). Montmartin gave a lucrative position to Moser's son-in-law, but the old man remained "unbeweglich" (31). In Hauff's account, the response of Old Lanbek is at best equivocal, encouraging his son to keep the promotion, while simultaneously working out a scheme to uphold the mendacious image of their integrity and probity.

14. Gerber's extensive study of the Oppenheimer affair has provided us with carefully researched picture of the actual historical events leading to the arrest, trial and hanging of Joseph Oppenheimer, as well as an overview of the extensive literature dealing with this historical event. See also Marquardt's account (184-96).

Works Cited

Bakhtin, Mikhail M. "Discourse in the Novel." *The Dialogic Imagination. Four Essays by M. M. Bakhtin.* Ed. Michael Holquist. Trans. Caryl Emerson and Michael Holquist. Austin: U of Texas P, 1981. 259-422.

————. *Problems of Dostoevsky's Poetics.* Ed. and Trans. Caryl Emerson. Minneapolis: U. of Minnesota P, 1984.

Gerber, Barbara. *Jud Süß, Aufstieg und Fall im frühen 18. Jahrhundert: Ein Beitrag zur historischen Antisemitismus- und Rezeptionsforschung.* Hamburg: Hans Christians, 1990.

Hauff, Wilhelm. *Jud Süß. Sämtliche Werke in drei Bänden.* Vol 2. Munich: Winkler, 1970. [1970a]

————. "Kontrovers-Predigt über H. Clauren und der Mann im Monde." *Sämtliche Werke in drei Bänden.* Vol. 1. Munich: Winkler, 1970. 794-824. [1970b]

Hinz, Ottmar. *Wilhelm Hauff: Mit Selbstzeugnissen und Bilddokumenten.* Hamburg: Rowohlt, 1989.

Hofmann, Hans. *Wilhelm Hauff: Eine nach neuen Quellen bearbeitete Darstellung seines Werdeganges.* Frankfurt a. M.: Diesterweg, 1902.

Koopman, Helmut, "Nachwort." Wilhelm Hauff. *Sämtliche Werke in 3 Bänden.* Vol. 3. Munich: Winkler, 1970a., *491-510.*

Mannheimer, Albert. *Die Quellen zu Hauffs Jud Süß.* Diss. Giessen: Münchow'sche Hofund Universitäts-Druckerei, 1909.

Marquardt, Ernst. *Geschichte Württembergs.* Stuttgart: Metzler, 1961.

Pfäfflin, Friedrich. *Wilhelm Hauff, der Verfasser des Lichtenstein: Chronik seines Lebens und Werkes.* Stuttgart: Fleischhauer und Spohn, 1981.

Pfaff, Karl. *Geschichte Württembergs.* 2 vols. Reutlingen: J. J. Macken, 1820.

Reinhardt, Kurt F. *Germany: 2000 Years: The Second Empire and the Weimar Republic.* Vol 2. New York: Frederick Ungar, 1962.

Schwarz, Egon. "Wilhelm Hauff, 'Der Zwerge Nase,' 'Das kalte Herz' und andere Erzählungen (1826/27)." *Romane und Erzählungen zwischen Romantik und Realismus.* Ed. Paul Michael Lützeler. Stuttgart: Reclam, 1983. 117-35.

Maureen Thum (essay date 1997)

SOURCE: Thum, Maureen. "Misreading the Cross-Writer: The Case of Wilhelm Hauff's *Dwarf Long Nose.*" *Children's Literature* 25 (1997): 1-23.

[*In the following essay, Thum evaluates Hauff's efforts to write for both children and adults in his fairy tales.*]

> The grotesque . . . discloses the potential of an entirely different world, of another order, of another way of life. It leads men out of the confines of the apparent (false) unity of the indisputable and stable.
>
> M. M. Bakhtin (*Rabelais* [Rabelais and His World],
> 48)

In their appeal to a dual audience, the literary fairy tales of Wilhelm Hauff (1802-27) epitomize the problematic nature of cross-writing. Hauff's three cycles of literary fairy tales, ***The Caravan*** (1826), ***The Sheik of Alexandria and His Slaves*** (1827), and ***The Inn in Spessart*** (1828, posthumously published), are directed at two seemingly disparate but by no means mutually exclusive readerships: an overt audience of bourgeois children, the "sons and daughters of the educated classes" (Hinz 112) to whom Hauff dedicated the three fairy-tale "almanacs,"[1] and an implied audience of aesthetically and politically sophisticated adults, whom he expected to be alert to his strategies of ironic reversal and indirection.

In the history of the *Kunstmärchen*, Hauff has been seen as an unusual and even a puzzling case. Insufficiently known to English-speaking readers, Hauff's tales, from the time of their publication, have nonetheless enjoyed an unabated popularity in German-speaking countries, where they continue to rank just behind the *Children and House Tales* of the Brothers Grimm (Klotz 210).[2] German critics have taken at face value Hauff's dedication of the tales to the offspring of the educated classes, as well as his claim, made in a letter to his publisher, that the tales are exclusively aimed at an audience of "girls or boys from twelve to fifteen years of age" (Pfäfflein 15). They have therefore dismissed Hauff's tales as inconsequential children's fantasies, ascribing his "juvenile popularity" (Koopmann 491) and "puzzling" success to his production of a presumably superficial and inferior product designed to cater to the tastes of an uncritical and aesthetically naive audience.[3]

In rejecting the tales as puerile fantasies, Hauff's German critics have disregarded the satirical and subversive intent expressed in the poignant allegory **"Fairy Tale as Almanac,"** which Hauff deliberately placed at the beginning of *The Caravan,* the first of his three cycles. They have thus greatly underestimated the author's craft—and his craftiness—as a cross-writer who wishes both to explore and to test the shifting relation between the child and the adult reader.

Hauff assumes the role of children's author precisely because it allows him to question the norms that an audience of children—prospective adults—are expected to adopt in order to fit into the world of their elders. During a period when severe sanctions were imposed on those who transgressed strictly enforced censorship laws, donning the mask of the children's writer allowed Hauff to conceal his critical stance from adult view, and thus to evade the vigilance of censors. Disguised as a writer for "mere" children, he could undercut the contemporary status quo with relative impunity.[4]

Still, precisely because Hauff's tales consciously transgress generational boundaries by engaging the child on one level while undertaking an ironic and satirical dismantling of societal norms on another, critics have been at a loss to categorize his works either as children's or as adult literature. Dismissing Hauff's tales as inferior "juvenile" fare, commentators have failed to look beyond their seemingly conventional and innocuous surface.

Thus, the German editors of two relatively recent scholarly editions of Hauff's collected works, published in 1962 and 1970, have characterized Hauff's writings as the productions of a hack writer whose mental horizon was circumscribed by the petty bourgeois prejudices of a literary and cultural philistinism. In full agreement, Volker Klotz, a respected German literary critic, sums up the prevailing consensus when he professes to be dismayed by Hauff's failure to vanish from the literary and popular scene. "Nowhere else in the history of the literary fairy tale," states Klotz, has such "dubious literary quality" been accompanied by such "an immense and continuous popularity among the reading public" (210).[5]

Viewing Hauff's literary fairy tales from the perspective of literary cross-writing, however, can provide a far clearer understanding of the author's intentionally ambiguous authorial stance. Neither a second-rate "children's" author nor a petty bourgeois ideologue, Hauff provides in his tales an astute, highly sophisticated exploration of that uncertain area between seemingly antithetical poles of experience: the area of wonder, of free-floating potentialities and magical intercessions associated with the child's "unreal" world of fantasy, and the area of social realities, psychological restrictions, and responsibilities so often identified with the "real" world of the adult. Indeed, Hauff repeatedly blurs the binary oppositions on which his contemporaries based their constructions of identity; thus he can be said to "hover," much like William Blake, between the opposed "states of perception" that the English poet had "labelled innocence and experience" (Knoepflmacher 497).

Hauff's novella-length tale *Dwarf Long Nose* is a case in point. In *Dwarf Long Nose,* Hauff deliberately enlists a juvenile protagonist in order to chart the ambiguous territory of a consciousness suspended between the world of the child and that of the adult. In its exploration of this in-between state, Hauff's tale furnishes a perfect example of Knoepflmacher's notion that the boundaries between a literature directed toward the child and that intended for the adult are uncertain at best—if indeed such clear lines of demarcation are at all discernible.

Dwarf Long Nose first appeared in Hauff's second cycle, *The Sheik of Alexandria and His Slaves,* but it has, at least in part due to its novella-like length, been frequently issued by itself. Much reprinted, the tale is as familiar to German speakers as are *Alice in Wonderland* and *The Wind in the Willows* to a British audience, or *Little Women* and *Huckleberry Finn* to Americans. English-speaking readers, however, may only know Doris Orgel's 1960 translation of *Dwarf Long Nose,* a book noteworthy not so much for Orgel's misleading and in some areas mistranslated rendition of Hauff's text as for Maurice Sendak's rich and highly suggestive illustrations, which are faithful to Hauff's own mockery of "pretension and stiffness" (Lanes 61). Indeed, Sendak's graphic interpretation of Hauff's text not only surpasses Orgel's translation, but also reveals that his understanding of this highly complex, multilayered work goes far beyond that of his academic critics, who have persistently overlooked the story's subtle, playful (and often acerbic) subversions.

In *Dwarf Long Nose,* Wilhelm Hauff conceals his subversive intentions beneath the deceptively benign surface of a conventional text. Camouflage is crucial to his concealments. The narrator first appears to establish a conventional portrait of a seemingly harmonious society and to rely, uncritically, on an entire repertoire of ostensibly familiar folk- and fairy-tale motifs and stereotypes. But Hauff soon upsets the expectations of his readers. He violates the generic codes he had seemed to invoke at the outset of his tale by engaging in a steady process of unmasking and ironic reversal. By the conclusion of the narrative, the conventional fairy-tale images and the petty-bourgeois idyll seemingly endorsed in the initial scenes have been dismantled and radically turned on their heads. The narrator thus destabilizes fixed views of identity, undercuts traditionalist codes, and exposes the underlying injuriousness of what had appeared on the surface to be an idealized portrait of community life.

The tale opens with what seems to be a typical fairy-tale scenario. Jacob, a good little boy who appears to embody all the proper social virtues, confronts a hoarse-voiced Herb Fairy, who ostensibly displays the malignancy of the stereotypical "wicked witch." Overly trustful, Jacob appears to fall victim to this bizarre stranger: he finds himself imprisoned for seven years in her enchanted house, where, transformed into a squirrel, he undergoes an apprenticeship as kitchen helper and chef. Released after his captivity, he is again transformed, this time into an ugly dwarf. As Jacob now discovers, he has acquired all the deformities he had formerly derided in the Wise Herb Fairy when she had first appeared on the marketplace seven years before. When he returns home, he is cruelly repudiated by his parents and by his entire community, none of whom can recognize the abducted boy.

Only by falling back on the culinary skills he acquired in the house of the Wise Herb Fairy can this creature—no longer called Jacob, but now known only as Dwarf Long Nose—find a place in a society that spurns misfits. He enters the service of a demanding duke and rises to the position of master chef, becoming a figure of widespread renown. But his career as court cook turns out to be precarious. On a whim of the finicky and capricious duke, Dwarf Long Nose is sentenced to death for "bad cooking." Aided by the extensive herbal lore of another outsider, an enchanted goose called Mimi, whom he had saved from the butcher's block, Dwarf Long Nose manages to recover his normal shape and to slip secretly out of the palace, leaving pandemonium in his wake. After the couple returns to her father's house, Mimi, too, is restored to her normal state.

Hauff's conclusion appears to present the conventional return to harmony and order, the expected happy ending of fairy-tale lore. Richly rewarded by Mimi's father, the sorcerer Weathergoat, Jacob returns home. Now joyfully recognized and received by the parents who had rejected him in his previous incarnation, Jacob sets up shop with the money from Weathergoat. As an adult, Jacob forsakes the fantasy world of his childhood and settles for the peaceful yet colorless realities of a petty bourgeois existence.

Pointing to its concluding return to "normalcy," critics have argued that *Dwarf Long Nose* is nothing more than a conventional children's tale. It is dominated, they contend, by a didactic author who promulgates a narrowly philistine mindset. If Hauff allows his child readers to indulge briefly in escapist fantasizing, he does so only in order to teach them that fantasy has no ultimate place in the adult bourgeois world he presumably endorses.[6]

Such a reading underestimates Hauff's relation to both his child and his adult readers. Restricted by harsh censorship laws that forbade any form of social or political criticism, Hauff was forced to resort to subterfuge: he concealed his subversive intentions beneath the seemingly innocuous cloak of fairy tales for children. A careful attention to the cues Hauff implants in his text reveals that he has no intention of indoctrinating the "sons and daughters of the educated classes" with bourgeois values. Instead, he values them as potential future allies. Like Jacob in the story, they are to be wrested away from a smug conformity; yet, unlike Jacob, who forgets his magical apprenticeship, they may remember after becoming adults their tutelage as momentary outsiders.

Hauff provides an important cue to his intentions in **"Fairy Tale as Almanac,"** the brief prologue to his first cycle of tales. He adumbrates his strategies of subversion and dissent in this brief, parable-like narrative in which Fairy Tale reports to her mother, Queen Fantasy, that her lot on earth has become increasingly difficult. As Fairy Tale explains, "intelligent guards" at the gates of the city—that is, of society—have barred her entrance. The guards are unequivocally censors whose "sharp eyes" and "sharp pens" (Hauff, *Sämtliche Werke* [*Sämtliche Werke in drei Bänden*], 2:8-10), probe into "everything" that comes from the realm of Queen Fantasy. As Fairy Tale plaintively explains, "If someone arrives who does not share their opinions, they raise a great clamour or murder him, or slander him . . . so that nobody believes what he says" (Hauff [*Sämtliche Werke*], 2:8). On the advice of Queen Fantasy, Fairy Tale resorts to a ruse to gain entrance into the city. Masked by the fabulous cloak of the fairy-tale almanac (the title that Hauff gave each of his cycles), she lulls the guards to sleep with her magical images. She then steps over their prone bodies and slips through the gate unobserved, aided by a friendly and enlightened adult who comments acerbically, pointing to the sleeping guards, "Your beautiful things mean nothing to them. Come quickly through the gate; then they will have no idea you are in the country, and you can continue your way undisturbed and unnoticed" (2:11). The kindly man takes Fairy Tale to his own children, and shelters her secretly in his house. Accessible to all the other children in the neighborhood, she can now carry out her forbidden activities undetected (2:11).

Hauff's parable not only indicates the subversive potential of his fantasies for the young, but also acknowledges his authorial strategies of concealment. In order to challenge the status quo, Hauff must, like Fairy Tale, slip past the censors, whether these are the real censors in the Duchy of Württemberg, where Hauff resided, or the internalized censors within the minds of his German readers. Internalized censors are, as Hauff implicitly recognizes, far more widespread and pernicious than those of any enforcement agency; they stir up prejudices that stifle any alternative, dissenting view of the world. **"Fairy Tale as Almanac,"** appearing in a prominent position as the preface to the first fairy-tale cycle, indicates that Hauff's dedication to the "sons and daughters of the educated classes," so carefully foregrounded on the frontispiece of the three fairy-tale "almanacs," acts as a screen for his desire to appeal to a far more diverse alliance between children and enlightened adults—here represented as coauditors of Fairy Tale—than critics have allowed.

As **"Fairy Tale as Almanac"** suggests, Hauff's narratives for children are characterized by a dialogic interplay between two implied audiences. *Dwarf Long Nose* is no exception. As a reader of this tale, the child is invited to empathize with the story's marginalized boy protagonist and to share the metamorphic process Jacob undergoes when he is transformed into a grotesque dwarf. Compelled to view the familiar world from Jacob's estranged perspective, the child adopts a potentially critical view. The adult, too, participates in a process of defamiliarization, yet is more likely than the child to engage the text intellectually and analytically. The adult reader is thus invited not only to partake of Jacob's alienation, but also to observe the dialogic process itself and thus to go beyond the child reader, who might welcome Jacob's final return to normalcy. The adult, by contrast, is encouraged, by concealed authorial cues, to decode Hauff's sharp critique of communal prejudice and stereotyping.

As part of his cross-writing strategy, then, Hauff has created a double-voiced text in the sense understood by Bakhtin: his carnivalized discourse "serves two speakers at the same time and expresses simultaneously two different intentions" ("Discourse" ["Discourse in the Novel"], 324). Yet these "intentions" also overlap, for the "two voices" in the text, like Hauff's two kinds of readers, cross each other and are "dialogically interrelated" (324).[7] Cross-writing thus invites cross-reading.

II

As Hauff's parable suggests, a careful reading of *Dwarf Long Nose* as a double-voiced text reveals that the author, like Fairy Tale, has taken pains to lull the censors to sleep before slipping past them with the aid of the child and the enlightened adult reader. The opening scene—the ostensible encounter between a "witch" and her "victim"—is paradigmatic of the author's consistent strategies of carnival unmasking and ironic reversal throughout the tale. The narrator first establishes a deceptively "normal" and conventional textual surface that relies on conventional images; he then proceeds to undermine these images. In the dismantling process, he unmasks himself as a subversive writer who challenges rather than reinforces the contemporary status quo.

In the initial pages of the tale, the narrator takes pains to depict a conventional petty-bourgeois idyll peopled by what appear to be stereotypical fairy-tale figures. The shoemaker, his wife, and their son Jacob form a small, modest family resembling the virtuous poor depicted in such tales as the Grimms' "The Shoemaker and the Elves." These are generally good, kind people who, as the reader expects, are bound to be rewarded for their charitable behavior.[8] Jacob, in particular, seems to be cast as an ideal, universally pleasing child. Kind, polite, hard-working, and obedient, he helps his mother at the marketplace, calling out her wares with his clear voice, attracting customers by his beauty, and earning large tips from the wealthy market patrons whose purchases he helps to carry.

The harmony of this scene appears to be disrupted by the arrival of an intruder, an old woman who has all the characteristics associated with the stereotypical wicked witch: "She looked rather ragged and tattered, had a small, sharp face with deep lines from old age, red eyes and a bent and pointed nose reaching down toward her chin. She walked, leaning on a long stick; and yet it was impossible to say how she moved, for she limped and slid and swayed" (Hauff, **"Zwerg Nase,"** *Sämmtliche Werke,* 2:113). The arrival of this ungainly stranger not only proves threatening to the burghers of the small town, but also shows its self-complacent ethos to be a total fraud. Jacob is now unmasked as being less innocent or childlike than the reader had expected. Conversely, the old woman, whom Jacob assumes to be a wicked witch, will reveal her true identity as the Wise Herbalist, or the Wise Herb Fairy, whose role is—as her name suggests—therapeutic rather than malevolent.

Jacob's response to the repulsive, hoarse-voiced old woman provides the first clear signal that all is not right in this harmonious world. The good, polite, kind child, habitually praised by his mother's clients for his pleasing and tractable manners, suddenly shouts at the old woman and derides her seemingly bizarre appearance: "Look here, you are a shameless old woman," he cries. "First you shove your horrible brown fingers into the beautiful herbs, then you squeeze them and hold them up to your long nose, so that anyone who sees wouldn't want to buy them any more" (2:113).

Jacob's anger and revulsion at first seem understandable to a reader, whether child or adult, who has been schooled in the ways of wicked witches, and who is therefore familiar with the drastic measures to which fairy-tale characters resort in order to banish or to destroy such undesirables. Only in retrospect, when the reader is led to question the stereotypically malignant image the old woman seems to represent, does the boy's indignant response appear out of place, going far beyond the apparent cause: the rude handling of market wares by a thoughtless customer. His knee-jerk response reflects the distrust and communal hatred of the outsider—a hatred that Jacob himself is forced to experience when he reappears in the marketplace as a grotesque dwarf whom the townsfolk no longer recognize as one of their own.

Symptomatic of his mindset, the boy does not recoil from making a thinly veiled threat to decapitate the old woman: "Don't wag your head so horribly back and forth. Your neck is as thin as a cabbage stem," he shouts, "It could easily break off and fall into the basket" (2:114). These expressions of communal hatred are all the more disturbing because Hauff has placed them in the mouth of an ostensibly innocent, spontaneously kind, and enviably comely boy. Equally if not more disturbing than his ghoulish comment is Jacob's final taunt, a rhetorical question indicating that the old woman's death would be at most an economic inconvenience, because it would frighten away the other customers: "And who would want to buy anything from us then?" (2:114).

Jacob's angry and rude outburst demonstrates that he has already been shaped by the narrow outlook of the provincial society whose material values he so unthinkingly espouses. Like a ventriloquist's puppet, Jacob utters words that are not his own. Because the old woman deviates from his society's norms, Jacob feels justified in attacking her as someone unprotected by the codes and courtesies extended to those accepted as fellow human beings. He also knows that everyone in the marketplace, including his mother, shares this view of the outsider. Indeed, Jacob's mother implicitly validates her son's statements by demanding that the woman either buy or leave: "If you want to buy something, make it quick. You are frightening away my other customers" (2:114). Only later when Jacob returns to the marketplace as an ugly dwarf does the pain inflicted by such conditioned responses fully come to light. Only then will Jacob be forced to the excruciating recognition that his community's hatred of Otherness applies even to one who can prove, like Jacob, that he was formerly one of its "normal" members.

In this process of unmasking and reversal, Hauff assigns the role of catalyst to the Herb Fairy. She wears a conventional mask herself and thus allows not only Jacob, but also Hauff's readers, to misread her as a stereotypical witch. Previous critics, taking the mask at face value, have seen the Herb Fairy with Jacob's prejudiced eyes. Doris Orgel goes so far as to reinforce the stereotype by substituting the misogynist label of "old hag" for Hauff's more neutral term "old woman" ("altes Weib") throughout much of her 1960 translation. She even adds the adjective "wicked," which is pointedly absent from the German text (Orgel 28).[9]

Yet the old woman is neither a witch nor a symbol of evil. Instead, this seemingly grotesque figure allows Hauff to expose the hostility toward aberrant behavior shown by the virtuous citizens of a community ready to malign all strangers as diabolical outsiders. Her malevolence is revealed to be an identity imposed on her by a community that projects its superstitious dread of the unknown on the grotesque stranger. Hauff implants sufficient authorial hints to challenge this arbitrary superimposition. Her actual name, "die Fee Kräuterweis"—literally "Wise Herb Fairy" or "Wise Fairy"—does not betoken the evil and destructiveness of a demonic figure, as Doris Orgel's translation suggests (Orgel omits the word "wise" from her name). Rather, the name suggests her mastery of herbal lore. The narrator thus signals that the Wise Herb Fairy is a figure in the tradition of the female healer, a tradition epitomized in German culture by the well known and much revered medieval mystic and intellectual Hildegard von Bingen.[10]

Contrary to the impression created by Orgel's translation, the narrator does not reinforce misogynistic stereotypes; instead, he eschews antifeminist labels, consistently avoiding such charged words as "Hexe" (witch), "Unholdin" (crone), or "Scheusal" (hag). This intentional avoidance signals the narrator's dissociation from those characters in the tale who call her "böse" (evil), a word that appears only twice in the text, and in a context that challenges its applicability.[11] Furthermore, by casting the Wise Herbalist as a fay (from the Latin *fata*, or "fate"), Hauff converts this misunderstood creature into one of those "goddesses of destiny" so prevalent in Continental folklore (Harf-Lancner 13). Far from exerting a malign influence, the Wise Herb Fairy is a severe female mentor or "mentoria" who initiates a therapy designed to "cure" Jacob of his blindness, a disability caused by his adoption of his elders' narrowly restrictive and prejudicial views.[12]

Just as the Herb Fairy defies antifeminist stereotypes of the diabolical old hag, so is her domain anything but conventional. Her enchanted house bears little resemblance to the expected evil witch's house familiar to readers of "Hänsel and Gretel." On the contrary, her dwelling is a transformative site—an extraordinary, magical realm of fluidity and mind-altering dreams. There, after drinking a fragrant broth she prepares for him, Jacob falls asleep and experiences the equivalent of a dream vision. Traditionally, dream visions have been portrayed as spiritual quests that often bring about a radical change in the perspective of the dreamer. As

Bahktin has noted, the dream world suspends the rules and values governing ordinary reality and prepares the way for the dreamer's new vision of the world (*Problems* [*Problems of Dostoevsky's Poetics*], 147).

Jacob's dream vision not only alters his original fix on the world, but also leads the reader to question a status quo to which the sleeper can no longer return. Awakened, Jacob epitomizes the solitary, insightful, and talented outsider who sees his society with alien eyes; in short, he is analogous to the writer or artist who views his society through defamiliarizing lenses. Hauff has the Wise Herb Fairy initiate Jacob into secrets known only to the greatest of chefs, so that he becomes an expert in his culinary "art." (The narrator repeatedly uses the word "Kunst"—art—to refer to Jacob's newly won skills.) Hauff thus relies on a metaphor for the writer that he also employed in his "adult" prose.[13] That Jacob is being trained as an "artist" is soon corroborated by his need to cater to the tastes of his patron, the local duke. Both the talented master chef and the talented writer must equally draw on their imaginative capacities to appeal—as Hauff emphasizes in his satire **"Books and the World of Readers"**—to the finicky taste of spoiled and pampered consumers. Furthermore, Jacob as master-chef must operate under prohibitions similar to those that an absolutist regime places on the creative artist.

In this context, the Wise Herb Fairy may be seen as a rather unconventional muse. Sendak's representation of her as she hovers over a fragrant broth—the source of Jacob's dream-vision—catches the anomaly of this figure. Ugly and homely the Herb Fairy may be, but in Sendak's rendering, she appears as big-bosomed, maternal, and smiling (Orgel 12).[14] She is Jacob's new "mother" and teacher, and her enchantments and chastisements facilitate Jacob's radically altered view of his former world.

Although a child reader may not respond analytically or intellectually to Hauff's strategies of unmasking and reversal, he or she cannot avoid participating in the changes *Dwarf Long Nose* dramatizes. Seeing the world anew through the eyes of Jacob—renamed Dwarf Long Nose—the child reader responds with a shared sense of precariousness and an equally strong desire for reempowerment. Parental rejection and fear of abandonment, so real to the child, are offset by the text's reassurance that the ugly dwarf who no longer resembles Jacob has nonetheless acquired skills and insights that make him unique. But in depicting Jacob's plight, Hauff's text also is unsparing. Thus, although a child may not remember or know what the word "prejudice" means, he or she cannot but respond viscerally to the experience of a boy who weeps bitterly when his father treats him as an imposter and whips him out of the shop and down the street, shouting invectives and showering blows on his humped shoulders.

If the child's perceptions of the normal and normative world are disturbed by such a scene, then Hauff has achieved his purpose: to provide an alternative view of reality informed by greater tolerance, enlightenment, and understanding. I have at least anecdotal evidence from two German-speaking readers who remember their childhood reading and rereading *Dwarf Long Nose* with startling clarity and vividness. Upon hearing the present interpretation, one of them stated, "I like to flatter myself that even as a child I perceived the concealed critique, and that I took it with me from the text." The other reader remembered that Jacob's final recovery of his former shape and identity, though satisfying, failed to offset the empathy he had felt for the ostracized and lonely dwarf.

III

Although the Herb Fairy ostensibly disappears from view in the next phase of Hauff's narrative, her attributes are retained by Jacob, who has now assumed her identity as a deformed, yet knowing, outsider. Child and adult, Self and Other are telescoped in this hunched, neckless figure. Dwarf Long Nose, no longer "little Jacob," is a hybrid figure caught in a liminal zone between a childhood he has already abandoned and an adulthood he has not yet reached. Dwarf Long Nose epitomizes Bakhtin's description of the grotesque as "a phenomenon in transformation" and "an as yet unfinished metamorphosis of death and birth, growth and becoming" (*Rabelais,* 24), which is quite different from the "ready-made completed being" (25) associated with traditional views of how identity is fashioned.

When Jacob emerges from his period of enchantment and reenters the everyday world, his age, like his identity, has become indeterminate. Although trapped in the body of a grotesque adult, he is still mentally a young boy of eight or twelve years old—Hauff gives conflicting ages, thus further blurring the time frame—who believes he left the marketplace just a few hours earlier.[15] Seven years have elapsed in the ordinary world; nevertheless, only a single afternoon appears to have passed during his dream vision. Jacob is chronologically fifteen (or nineteen?) years old, but having experienced no maturation from childhood to adulthood, he is mentally still a "child."

Jacob remains childlike in another sense as well. As an eight- or twelve-year-old boy in the marketplace, Jacob was already formed as a carefully conditioned adult. With all his preconceptions and prejudices fully developed, he was Bakhtin's "ready-made, completed being." Now, however, in the body of a grotesque adult, he finds that his former "grown-up" prejudices no longer fit an estranging universe. He has thus been "reborn" and must start over again by reliving a childhood based on different premises and assumptions. He must return to the position of a naive, unformed infant who has been "birthed" after a gestation period of seven years by an ancient and aged, yet wise, Herb Fairy. Hauff refers, if obliquely, to a relatively well-known European carnival figure: that of the pregnant and laughing "old hag" who "combines a senile, decaying and deformed flesh with the flesh of new life, conceived but as yet unformed" (Bakhtin, *Rabelais*, 25-26). (Unlike the traditional carnival figure, however, the Wise Herb Fairy is no hag, and she is far from senile.) Dwarf Long Nose, the child produced by this bizarre pregnancy, is a similarly anomalous figure. He combines the features of age and youth in a single grotesque being who is nonetheless neither child nor adult; and, by the same token, he crosses genders with the wise old woman whose powerful phallic nose he has inherited.[16] He is thus neither male nor female. Finally, as a figure with whom the reader empathizes and identifies, but who is nonetheless trapped in a deformed body, he is neither Self nor Other.

When the boy reenters the ordinary world, he still believes himself to be unchanged. Ironically, as the narrator's comments stress, he still tries to view the world and his place in it from his accustomed perspective. Very rapidly, however, his former view must give way to an unfamiliar and estranged outlook. Bakhtin refers to such shifts in perspective as "experimental fantasticality" and argues that such a disjunctive point of view permits the writer to depict "a radical change in the scale of the observed phenomena of life" (*Problems*, 116). In *Dwarf Long Nose,* the misshapen dwarf is forced to shed both his former values and his former view of himself, a drastic alteration in which the reader is invited to participate.

In order to elicit a visceral response from the (perhaps unwilling) reader, Hauff charts Jacob's gradual process of discovery and enlightenment in chilling detail. As he runs through the streets, hurrying back to the marketplace and to his mother, the former Jacob is hampered by gathering crowds who are shouting, "Hey look at the ugly dwarf. . . . Hey, look what a long nose he has, and see how his head sticks down in his shoulders, and his ugly brown hands" (Hauff, *Sämtliche Werke*, 2:119). Assuming that these exclamations are directed at some passing freak, Jacob is filled with curiosity. Only his haste prevents him from joining the crush of curious onlookers: "On any other day he would have run along with them, since he had loved to see giants or dwarfs all his life" (2:119). Unaware as yet that *he* is the misshapen outcast who will later be known by the metonymic name of "Nose," he still regards himself as a comfortable member of a majority who regards such freaks as a source of "innocent" entertainment.

When he at last looks into a mirror and sees the grotesque object he has become, Jacob experiences an estrangement from his own body and from his former hold on the world: in this depiction of doubled consciousness, symbolized by Jacob as he observes his altered image, the Self has literally become the Other. In the bizarre body reflected before him, he immediately recognizes an exaggeration of the old woman's features, and he remembers how, while still a comfortable member of the normal world, he had spurned and insulted her:

> His eyes had become small, like the eyes of a pig. His nose was monstrous, and hung down over his mouth and chin; his neck seemed to have been removed altogether, since his head was stuck deep into his shoulders. He could move it to the right and left only with great pain. His body was still the same size as it was seven years before, when he was twelve years old. But, while other children grow taller from the age of twelve to twenty, he had grown wider. His back and chest were buckled outward, and gave the appearance of a small over-stuffed sack. This heavy trunk sat upon two weak and spindly legs, which appeared incapable of carrying their burden. But his arms, which hung down his body, were all the larger for that; as large as the arms of a big, strong man. His hands were coarse and brownish-yellow, his fingers long and spidery. If he stretched them out, he could touch the floor without bending over.
>
> (2:123)

His Kafkaesque sense of self-estrangement brings about a radical shift in Jacob's view of himself and his place in the world. He suddenly feels older and "wiser," and, when he thinks of the old woman in the marketplace, he understands how and why this transformation has occurred.

The reader, whether experientially as a child, or experientially *and* analytically as an adult, can now see clearly the formerly idyllic, harmonious, petty bourgeois social order through the dwarf's defamiliarizing eyes. The small community of women in the market square is no longer friendly and welcoming, but hostile, angry, and vituperative. Jacob discovers that his grotesque appearance automatically excludes him from their society. His mother, Hanna, showers him with imprecations, just as Jacob had insulted the old woman seven years before. Calling him a "Missgeburt" (literally a misbirth, or a child born monstrously deformed), Hanna cries out, "What do you want from me, you ugly dwarf?" and orders him, "Get out of here!" (2:119). Soon Jacob's father, as noted, does not limit his response to verbal abuse.

Jacob's transformation allows Hauff to expand his critical scope by including an entire German duchy. Abandoned, rejected, and destitute, Jacob applies at the court of the local duke for the position of cook. His elevation to master chef, however, only underscores the continued precariousness of his position. Like a writer, this kitchen-artist must uneasily navigate between two seemingly separate worlds—a world of fantasy and imagination associated with the child, and a world of economic necessity and political machinations associated with the adult. Upon first entering the palace, Jacob is invited to become the duke's personal "pet" or "court dwarf," a position he proudly refuses because it does not allow him to exercise his genius in the art of cooking. As soon as Jacob is hired, the duke confers a new name upon what is now his creature by calling him "Zwerg Nase," which may be translated either as "Dwarf Nose" or simply, "Nose." The label not only signals the fact that Jacob is known only as an appendage to his own grotesque body; it also indicates Jacob's formal loss of individual identity and dignity. As a servant whose sole purpose is to cater to the sovereign's palate and submit to his lord's mindless whims, he exists only as an extension of the ducal will. Only as long as he can provide new recipes to enhance the duke's already bloated self-image is this kitchen-artist treated well. In one of Sendak's most memorable illustrations (Orgel 43), Dwarf Long Nose is seated, dog-like, his mouth open, as the duke feeds him morsels from the table—a privilege, the narrator notes sarcastically, that Jacob "knew well how to treasure" (2:130).

The satirical portrait of petty German princes during the early decades of the nineteenth century is unmistakable. In its precariousness and short duration, as well as its threatened outcome, Jacob's career parallels that of many a court favorite in eighteenth-century German duchies. Whether chef, financier, or court writer, the court favorite frequently rose only to suffer an abrupt fall.[17] Thus, after two years of faithful and impeccable service, Dwarf Long Nose is set an impossible task. The duke demands that he prepare a pâté whose secret ingredients are known only to a visiting prince whom the duke wishes to impress. When Jacob presents the dish, the visitor smiles "scornfully and secretively" as he tastes it, then pushes it away. Even though only a single ingredient has been omitted, the visitor claims that the savory dish is an unequivocal failure. Infuriated that his creature has punctured his self-image, the duke immediately withdraws his former praise: "You dog of a dwarf," he shouts, castigating his former favorite: "How dare you do this to your master?" (Hauff, *Sämtliche Werke,* 2:134). In punishment for the dwarf's "bad cooking" the duke threatens to "hack off his great head" (2:134). Threatened with death, Jacob falls on his knees and pleads, movingly, that the visiting prince reveal the secret ingredient: "Don't let me die for a handful of meat and flour" (2:135). His poignant plea indicates the absurdity of a political structure in which human life is worth nothing in the face of a princeling's most trivial and capricious whims.

Satirizing the numerous internecine and territorial squabbles among the dukes and princelings who competed for power and prestige throughout eighteenth-century Germany, Hauff depicts the bad cooking incident as triggering a war. The narrator wraps up the incident with playful yet pointed irony: "The Herb War," as it was named, was finally brought to an end by the "Peace of Pâté," so designated in the "annals of history" because during the feast celebrating their reconciliation the prince's chef prepares the pâté that Jacob had earlier failed to produce for the duke (2:137-38). The narrator's final comment, "Thus the tiniest causes often lead to great effects" (2:138) intentionally echoes, albeit more playfully and far less savagely, Voltaire's satirical lampoons in *Candide* against the misunderstood application of cause and effect. The intertextual echo, one of many references to Voltaire in Hauff's tales, points implicitly to Hauff's own covert satirical stance.

The conclusion of the Jacob and Mimi tale represents a complete anticlimax. When the two former outcasts escape and regain their normal shapes, the reader, schooled in fairy-tale paradigms, may well expect them to marry and live happily ever after. But they do not. The anticipated ending is aborted; Jacob returns home without Mimi. Seemingly forgetting his fantastic adventures as Dwarf Long Nose, Jacob opens up a little shop in his hometown and becomes old, respected, and prosperous—the epitome of a satisfied, upright, industrious, and colorless burgher. His previous years of suffering and rejection have left no trace on the tranquil surface of small-town existence.

But Hauff's ostensibly happy ending by no means signifies the author's resigned acquiescence to petty bourgeois values, as critics have contended (Schwarz 130; Klotz 210). Instead, it marks the last ironic reversal in this carnivalized tale. The intentionally abrupt and ironic ending suggests that the problems raised in the narrative have merely been set aside, not resolved. Again, Maurice Sendak's illustration catches the overlay of irony and whimsy that characterizes the final, folksy picture of Jacob as a happy burgher, smoking his pipe at the window of his shop and smiling contentedly (Orgel 63).

Wilhelm Hauff's *Dwarf Long Nose* exemplifies the difficulties encountered in the reception of cross-writing, as well as the transgressive potential of such writing. Misread as second-rate children's writing, Hauff's fairy-tale cycles have yet to be fully recognized by an academic and critical audience, and they have yet to be translated adequately into a modern English version that would include not only the tales themselves, but also the stories in which they are framed. Reading Hauff's tales without the frame stories is a little like reading Chaucer's *Canterbury Tales* without the General Prologue or the Head Links to each of the tales. Although the novella-length *Dwarf Long Nose* can certainly be read in its own right as a consummately crafted and multilayered work, a great deal of the wider context is necessarily lost in the absence of the frame tales.

Hauff's indirections as a children's author have unfortunately played into the prejudices of those who tend to segregate children's literature from "serious" adult literature. Thus, critics have regarded *Dwarf Long Nose* with the same condescension and distrust met by the aberrant Jacob/Dwarf Nose in the tale itself. Forced to disguise his voice and to conceal his subversive and dissenting stance beneath an innocuous mask, Hauff creates unusual barriers for any reader who approaches his texts with the preconceived notion that children's literature is neither worthy of nor susceptible to the careful analysis automatically granted to "adult" texts. Thus since the initial publication of his *Kunstmärchen* Hauff's artful mask has remained, for many readers, firmly in place; the signposts that mark the author's ironic strategies have yet to be noticed.

In making the case for a rereading of *Dwarf Long Nose,* I also wish to argue for a thorough reassessment of Hauff's other literary fairy tales. Modern readers who enter into Hauff's imaginative realm find his dual appeal to child and adult to be as resonant as is his attack on the mechanisms of stereotyping. They will appreciate him as did those initial readers, who—before the long critical silence and his subsequent rejection by academic scholars—had hailed him as a genius whose tales rival those of Brentano, E. T. A. Hoffmann, and Tieck.[18]

Notes

1. All translations of the German texts are my own. The citations from "Zwerg Nase" follow the text of *Sämtliche Werke.*

2. Hauff was a younger contemporary of the Grimm brothers. Although his literary and editorial activities spanned a mere three years, he was extraordinarily productive. Just ten months after becoming editor of J. F. Cotta's *Morgenblatt,* he died on November 18, 1827, at age twenty-four. His works, which were for the most part written and published between 1826 and 1827, demonstrate a remarkable variety and range. They include extensive journal entries, parodies, poems, sketches, a two-part satirical novel, half a dozen novellas, a historical romance in the manner of Sir Walter Scott, as well as three cycles of novella-length literary fairy tales. See Hinz (1989), Pfäfflein (1981), Beckmann (1976), and Hofmann (1902).

3. For Koopmann, "the history of literature has closed its files" on Hauff and has forbidden "any serious consideration of his works" (491).

4. During the post-Napoleonic restoration of absolutist forms of government in German-speaking countries, the Vienna Congress (1814-15) and the Karlsbad Decrees (1819) radically curtailed freedom of speech, imposed rigid censorship on publication, and ordered the dismissal of all teachers who undermined public order or who questioned the reestablishment of an absolutist status quo (Reinhardt 467). Although Wilhelm I of Württemberg, the duchy where Hauff resided, was among the less despotic of the absolutist petty princes, he often silenced critics by resorting to imprisonment without trial (Elias 312-13). Hauff's father and a cousin, Friedrich Hauff, were both victims of repressive measures. Imprisoned without trial, Hauff's father never recovered from the experience (Pfäfflein 8), whereas Hauff's cousin died shortly after being released, his health impaired by the imprisonment (Hofmann 39). Hauff, who was forced to rewrite his novella *Jew Süss* numerous times to escape censorship, thus had first-hand knowledge of the censors' destructive power.

5. Thus, for example, Fritz Martini dismisses Hauff as a "fabulizing improvisor" (535) whose work is marred by a narrow, petty bourgeois mindset. Egon Schwarz's astute discussion of *Dwarf Long Nose* grants Hauff some sharp flashes of irony but fails to recognize them as part of a sustained critical stance (130).

6. See Klotz, who argues that Hauff stifles fantasy with convention. According to Klotz, Hauff "draws on essential forms of the literary fairy tale and folk tale" but "weakens" and "strangles them, or wastes their former poetic energy" (210).

7. For certain aspects of the present study, I have adopted Bakhtin's concept of the multivoiced (carnivalized) text as opposed to the univocal (authoritarian, monologic) text, particularly as set forth in his *Problems of Dostoevsky's Poetics* and *Rabelais and His World.* For Bakhtin, multivocal literature expresses subversions akin to the questioning spirit of the European pre-Lenten Carnival, during which conventional and authoritarian structures are overturned through "a temporary suspension of all hierarchic distinctions and barriers among men and of certain norms and prohibitions of usual life" (*Rabelais,* 15). Unlike Bakhtin, however, I argue that such reversals are not necessarily free-floating and temporary phenomena. They are not confined to a carnival "time-out," which some anthropologists argue is merely a venting mechanism that permits authorities to stabilize and reaffirm the status quo (Davis 131-50). Instead, such dismantlings may lead—as historian Natalie Zemon Davis and medievalist Susan Crane argue—to a permanent state of questioning and

subversion, if not an outright revolt against an authoritarian and unjust status quo (Crane 129-30; Davis 131-50).

8. Also known as "The Elves," the tale concerns a poor but charitable and virtuous cobbler and his wife who are aided by elves. After the couple returns the favor, the elves depart. Nevertheless, business continues to improve: "as long as the shoemaker lived, all went well with him, and all his efforts prospered" (Grimm 198; Pantheon ed.).

9. Although this is the *only* area where Orgel consistently mistranslates the original text, it is a significant error because her mistranslation inserts antifeminist labels absent in the German text and thus "corrects" Hauff's text by reinstating the binaries—Good Mother versus Wicked Stepmother; Good versus Evil; Self versus Other—that Hauff set out to abolish.

10. The medieval abbess Hildegard von Bingen not only produced poetry and music, but also authored scientific treatises, including a learned lexicon of herbs in which she explained the curative properties of numerous medicinal plants used in the abbey infirmary and provided them with their vernacular German names.

11. The townspeople, scarcely credible witnesses, refer to the Herb Fairy as "evil," as will Jacob—after he first discovers his grotesque transformation, but before his adoption of a radically altered mindset.

12. I have adopted this term from Mitzi Myers's telling discussion of female guides or "mentoria" (31-59).

13. In a short story "Books and the World of Readers," Hauff refers to the writer who must cater to a mass audience of consumers as a "chef" who is required to "prepare something tasty" in a vain attempt to please the "spoiled palates" of a fickle reading public (Hauff, *Romane*, [*Märchen, Gedichte*,] 730).

14. She thus resembles the buxom Jewish mother Sendak later memorialized by reproducing a photograph of Sadie (Sarah) Sendak holding little Maurice within the Blakean panorama he created for Randall Jarrell's *Fly by Night* (1976). His mother, he told Selma Lanes, had a "gruff, abrupt manner," and hence may well have been associated in his mind with Hauff's uncouth nurturer (Lanes 18).

15. Hauff mentions Jacob's age on two different occasions. In the initial scenes, when the boy meets the Herb Fairy, he is eight years old (2:112). Later the narrator depicts Jacob as remembering that he was twelve (2:123) when these events took place. Doris Orgel, interpreting Hauff's intentional blurring of chronological time as an "error" on the part of the writer, "corrects" the age to twelve. Compare Orgel, who states that Jacob was "rather tall for his twelve years" (3) to Hauff's original: "for a boy aged eight, he was already quite big" (2:112).

16. In his discussion of "antique and medieval grotesque," Bakhtin notes the repeated and intentional association of the nose with the phallus throughout the carnival tradition (*Rabelais*, 87). Hauff clearly refers to this familiar linkage in his depiction of Dwarf Long Nose as crossing age and gender barriers.

17. See, for example, Barbara Gerber's discussion of Jewish financiers who rose to power in German duchies and who, after supplying money for the coffers of various dukes and princes, suffered a fall from favor and public approbation, often as the scapegoats for their masters' misdeeds. Hauff's novella *Jew Süss* demonstrates how one of these figures, Joseph Süss Oppenheimer, was scapegoated and judicially murdered. See my article on Hauff's dismantling of stereotypes in *Jew Süss* (Thum, "Re-Visioning [Historical Romance]"). Although he is not an ethnic outsider, Dwarf Long Nose is a grotesque Other who enjoys a parallel rise and fall when he is unfairly blamed for something he could not possibly have known about or have corrected.

18. Unlike Brentano, whose anti-Semitic stereotypes are so prominent in his story "Gockel, Hinkel and Gackeleia" (in which Jewish engravers are the villains), Hauff identifies with the superior yet maligned outcast both in *Dwarf Long Nose* and in a tale from the same collection entitled "Abner, The Jew Who Saw Nothing." It is surely no accident that the two tales should have appeared back to back as companion pieces in *The Sheik of Alexandria and His Slaves*. In "Abner, The Jew Who Saw Nothing" Hauff uses a tale from Voltaire's *Zadig* as the point of departure for his own demonstration of the mechanisms of stereotyping. Hardly the "naive" anti-Semite that Leon Feuchtwanger took him to be (quoted in Gerber 282), Hauff attacked not only Jews but also Christians and Christianity in his *Memoirs of Satan*, a two-part Rabelaisian satire. But if his heavy-handed Jewish caricatures—put in the mouth of Satan—are undeniably alienating to a twentieth-century reader, Hauff's subsequent works demonstrate a radical distancing from such Jewish stereotypes. In *Jew Süss*, he not only dismantles stereotypes and demonstrates the perniciousness of scapegoating, but also expresses his philo-Semitism by por-

traying Lea Oppenheimer, Joseph Oppenheimer's sister, unequivocally as the most intelligent, charitable, and heroic figure in the entire novella (see Thum, "Re-Visioning").

Works Cited

Bakhtin, Mikhail M. "Discourse in the Novel." *The Dialogic Imagination: Four Essays by M. M. Bakhtin.* Ed. Michael Holquist. Trans. Caryl Emerson and Michael Holquist. Austin: University of Texas Press, 1981. 259-422.

———. *Problems of Dostoevsky's Poetics.* Ed. and trans. Caryl Emerson. Minneapolis: University of Minnesota Press, 1984.

———. *Rabelais and His World.* Trans. Helene Iswolsky. Bloomington: Indiana University Press, 1984.

Beckmann, Sabine. *Wilhelm Hauff: Seine Märchenalmanache als zyklische Kompositionen.* Bonn: Bouvier Verlag, 1976.

Clark, Katerina, and Michael Holquist. *Mikhail Bakhtin.* Cambridge, Mass.: Harvard University Press, 1984.

Crane, Susan. *Gender and Romance in Chaucer's "Canterbury Tales."* Princeton, N.J.: Princeton University Press, 1994.

Davis, Natalie Zemon. *Society and Culture in Early Modern France.* Stanford, Calif.: Stanford University Press, 1965.

Elias, Otto Heinrich. "König Wilhelm I (1816-64)." In *900 Jahre Haus Württemberg,* ed. Robert Uhland. Stuttgart: Verlag W. Kohlhammer, 1985.

Gerber, Barbara. *Jud Süss, Aufstieg und Fall im frühen 18. Jahrhundert: Ein Beitrag zur Historischen Antisemitismus-und Rezeptionsforschung.* Hamburg: Hans Christians Verlag, 1990.

Grimm, Wilhelm, and Jacob Grimm, eds. *The Complete Grimms' Fairy Tales.* Trans. Margaret Hunt and James Stern. New York: Pantheon, 1944 and 1972.

———. *Kinder und Hausmärchen: Ausgabe letzter Hand mit den Originalanmerkungen der Brüder Grimm.* 3 vols. Ed. Heinz Rölleke. Stuttgart: Philipp Reclam, 1980.

Harf-Lancner, Laurence. *Les Fées au moyen âge.* Geneva: Editions Slatkine, 1984.

Hauff, Wilhelm. "Die Bücher und die Lesewelt." *Romane, Märchen, Gedichte.* Vol. 2 of *Wilhelm Hauff: Werke.* 2 vols. Stuttgart: J. B. Cotta, 1962. 727-43.

———. *Dwarf Long Nose.* Trans. Doris Orgel. Illus. Maurice Sendak. New York: Random House, 1960.

———. "Zwerg Nase." *Sämtliche Werke in drei Bänden.* Vol. 2. Munich: Winkler-Verlag, 1970.

———. *Tales by Wilhelm Hauff.* Trans. S. Mendel. 1890. Freeport, N.Y.: Books for Libraries, 1970.

Hinz, Ottmar. *Wilhelm Hauff: Mit Selbstzeugnissen und Bilddokumenten.* Hamburg: Rowohlt Taschenbuchverlag, 1989.

Hofmann, Hans. *Wilhelm Hauff: Eine nach neuen Quellen bearbeitete Darstellung seines Werdeganges.* Frankfurt a. M.: Moritz Dieterweg, 1902.

Klotz, Volker. *Das europäische Kunstmärchen.* Stuttgart: J. B. Metzler, 1985.

Knoepflmacher, U. C. "The Balancing of Child and Adult: An Approach to Victorian Fantasies for Children." *Nineteenth-Century Fiction* 37.4 (Mar. 1983): 497-530.

Koopman, Helmut. "Nachwort" (Afterword). In Hauff, *Sämmtliche Werke in drei Bänden.* Vol. 3. 491-510.

Lanes, Selma G. *The Art of Maurice Sendak.* New York: Harry N. Abrams, 1980.

Martini, Fritz. "Wilhelm Hauff," in *Deutsche Dichter der Romantik.* Ed. Benno von Wiese. Berlin: Erich Schmidt Verlag, 1983. 532-62.

Myers, Mitzi. "Impeccable Governesses, Rational Dames, and Moral Mothers: Mary Wollstonecraft and the Female Tradition in Georgian Children's Literature." *Children's Literature* 14 (1986): 31-59.

Orgel, Doris, trans. *Dwarf Long Nose* by Wilhelm Hauff. Illus. Maurice Sendak. New York: Random House, 1960.

Pfäfflein, Friedrich. *Wilhelm Hauff, der Verfasser des Lichtenstein: Chronik seines Lebens und Werkes.* Stuttgart: Fleischhauer und Spohn, 1981.

Reinhardt, Kurt F. *Germany: 2,000 Years. The Second Empire and the Weimar Republic.* Vol. 2 of 2 vols. New York: Frederick Ungar, 1962.

Schwarz, Egon. "Wilhelm Hauff, 'Der Zwerg Nase,' 'Das Kalte Herz' und andere Erzählungen (1826-27)." *Romane und Erzählungen zwischen Romantik und Realismus.* Ed. Paul Michael Lützeler. Stuttgart: Philipp Reclam, 1983. 117-35.

Thum, Maureen. "Kunstmärchen or Menippean Satire? Wilhelm Hauff's 'Abner der Jude, der nichts gesehen hat.'" Paper presented at the Kentucky Foreign Language Conference, Lexington, 23 Apr. 1993.

———. "Re-Visioning Historical Romance: Carnivalesque Discourse in Wilhelm Hauff's *Jud Süss.*" In *Neues zu Altem: Novellen der Vergangenheit und der Gegenwart.* Houston German Studies. Ed. Sabine Cramer and Gertrud Pickar. Frankfurt a. M.: Peter Lang, 1995.

Jefferson S. Chase (essay date July 1998)

SOURCE: Chase, Jefferson S. "The Wandering Court Jew and the Hand of God: Wilhelm Hauff's *Jud Süss* as Historical Fiction." *Modern Language Review* 93, no. 3 (July 1998): 724-40.

[*In the following essay, Chase examines the tension between themes of tolerance and prejudice in Hauff's* Jud Süss. *Chase concludes that the novella represents a work of "unacceptable historical fiction."*]

Though rarely read today, Wilhelm Hauff's *Jud Süß* is a watershed work in German cultural history. Published in July 1827 in Cotta's *Morgenblatt für gebildete Stände,* where Hauff himself worked as editor, the novella established the story of Josef Süss-Oppenheimer, financial advisor and general factotum under Duke Karl Alexander of Württemberg (1733-37), as legitimate literary and historical subject-matter. In the course of the next 150 years, some 100 to 200 literary works[1] were to retell the tale of Süss-Oppenheimer's mercurial rise from the Heidelberg ghetto and spectacular 1738 execution, after a notoriously unfair trial, for the crimes of extortion, office-selling, defamation of the monarchy, and high treason. Addressing a number of nineteenth-century social issues, especially those of Jewish emancipation and mainstream integration, this life story would prove extremely malleable. Almost by turns, the Süß figure was to emerge in successive retellings of the narrative as both a hero and a villain. Lion Feuchtwanger's novel *Jud Süß* of 1925, which makes the protagonist a hero for his refusal to convert to Christianity, would represent the apotheosis of the 'pro-Süß' tendency. The corresponding racist depth would come a scant fifteen years thereafter with Veit Harlan's now notorious film of the same title, where Süß appears as a scheming coward. Hauff's novella prefigures both the would-be philo-Semitic and anti-Semitic treatments of the Süss-Oppenheimer story and, as such, rehearses the entangled logic of emancipation and chauvinism so prominent in the German nineteenth century.[2] This article examines how the two sides of *Jud Süß* fit together.

The most immediate impression is that they do not. From the novella's first pages, a radical disjunction makes itself felt between the levels of *discours* and *histoire,*[3] between the narrator's constant, passionately advanced rhetoric of tolerance and a plot line in which the removal of the corrupt finance minister, and indeed of the Jews as a people, is crucial to the survival of the native community. The discrepancy manifests Hauff's dual aims for his narrative: his open fictionalization of the Süss-Oppenheimer story and his ambition of capturing the true essence of actual events from the past. In constructing his plot, he borrows liberally from literary models such as Walter Scott and avails himself of a range of what we today might consider crass anti-Jewish stereotypes.[4] Yet he is also concerned with maintaining the empirical authority of the historical record. Through his narrator, Hauff often draws attention to source material, even on those occasions when it seemingly contradicts the main thrust of his own narrative. The result is a work that says one thing and does another. To make sense of such a text, it is necessary to examine Hauff's strategies for transforming Süss-Oppenheimer into *Jud Süß,* especially his conscious deviations from the available historical record.[5] These moments of authorial intervention provide a record of Hauff's own attitudes and desires *vis-à-vis* history, suggesting why he chose to tell his story as he did. Moreover, investigating them allows us today to comment on a number of crucial issues in German Studies. *Jud Süß* is a very good place to start looking at, among other things, the parallel construction of minority and majority identity, the evolution of stereotypes over time, and the relation of both to standards of coherence for literary and historical narratives.

Any investigation into strategies of fictionalizing history involves reconstructing audience response, a rather frustrating enterprise for a story that appeared in serial form and did not attract a neat corpus of reviews. None the less, there can be little doubt that Hauff was a major writer and that the novella exercised an influence on generations of readers. At the tender age of twenty-five, the author of *Jud Süß* had become the literary editor of the most prestigious belletristic journal of the time and had already acquired a reputation as a German Walter Scott. Gervinus mentions him in the same sentence as Goethe, Tieck, Kleist, and Hoffmann, while Heinrich Laube writes in 1839 of Hauff's being extraordinarily popular with his contemporary readers.[6] *Jud Süß,* in particular, although its reception seems to have been swallowed up to some extent by public reaction to Hauff's sudden death shortly after its publication, enjoyed lasting currency in German culture. It was reprinted in numerous Cotta editions of Hauff's works and was selected for the Reclam Universal Library series some fifty years later. It was still in print around the turn of the century. What debate there is within the nineteenth-century reception revolves exclusively around literary reputation, some critics praising Hauff as a talent cut down tragically early in life, others dismissing him as an inferior imitator with a dubious style. No one seems to have questioned the basic legitimacy of a Scottian view of local history, nor was any doubt cast on whether Hauff himself had got past events right. The various aspects of this fundamental underlying consensus between author and public need to be made explicit, and the consensus itself critically scrutinized.

It would, of course, require a general reconstruction of literary standards and expectations to settle the issue of *Jud Süß*'s adherence and/or challenge to its audience's

Erwartungshorizont, something obviously beyond the scope of a single journal article. However, the discrepancies between Hauff's text and his sources can be analysed against the general backdrop of the time. By reading *Jud Süß* in this way, some preliminary conclusions can be reached about why the Süss-Oppenheimer story might have struck such a chord with both author and readers.

The deviations fall into a variety of categories. Some reflect received attitudes towards Jews and Jewishness; others would seem to be motivated by aesthetic considerations; still others address what are explicitly identified within the story itself as demands of historical necessity. This spectrum of authorial interventions mirrors the complex and varied levels on which historical fiction in general can be seen to function. Although the constellation may appear quite strange to today's eyes, *Jud Süß* represents (1) a report on a past incident, with authorial imagination being used to fill in source gaps and present events in readable form; (2) a literary work using detail from the past in order to enliven a literary story line; (3) a political allegory in which nineteenth-century reality is projected onto an eighteenth-century 'screen';[7] (4) an instance of self-conscious myth-construction and proto-nationalistic 'invention of tradition' along the lines argued for by a number of recent social theorists.[8] It is especially the last of these categories that can provide a clue as to how to understand *Jud Süß*'s dual promotion of tolerance and chauvinism. If we acknowledge Hauff's concern with inventing a piece of history to unite himself and his audience in a collective viewpoint, then the theme of social integration would subsume the enlightened narrator's carefully maintained distance from the crass Jew-hatred of earlier native society. From this vantage-point, *Jud Süß* can be seen to serve the pernicious function of advancing an essentially anti-Semitic narrative of history under cover of the ideal of a general brotherhood of man.

The idea of historical fiction being not only an ideological screen but a self-transfigurative myth points to the importance of perceived social necessity as a source of urgency in the narrative. By setting instances of conscious fictionalization in *Jud Süß* against the general social backdrop, especially the dramatic social changes and political crises of Hauff's world, we begin to see what might have made this version of the Süss-Oppenheimer story seem plausible and desirable to both author and public. Such speculations are important, because they address aspects of reflexive change within Hauff's work. With *Jud Süß*, Hauff was not only rewriting history with the help of certain received stereotypes (the Court Jew, the Beautiful Jewess, and the Wandering Jew), he was changing them, disembedding them from a world dominated by religion and specific late feudal forms of state, translating them into a secu-

lar and popular-authoritarian context.[9] It was a new conglomerate image, the image of the Wandering Court Jew, that *Morgenblatt* readers consumed in July 1827 and was to fascinate the imaginations of generations thereafter. The contradictions within this image, as indeed within *Jud Süß in toto,* were accepted because they were deemed historically necessary, and not surprisingly historical necessity emerges as one the novella's most prominent themes. A close reading of *Jud Süß,* followed by a discussion of its social context, will illustrate this point.

Since the novella falls outside the current literary canon, any reading of it probably must begin with a plot summary. As we join the story, the scheming Süß has been granted immunity from criminal prosecution in reward for various services performed on the crown's behalf. These have included the imposition of back-breaking taxes upon the local populace, which have not only increased the financial advisor's personal wealth but have allowed the military-minded Karl Alexander to maintain an exorbitantly large standing army. The first scene takes place at a Fasching-style masquerade party, given by Süß to celebrate his own birthday and to raise money. There, a group of disgruntled local élites costumed as peasants accuses him of conspiring to ruin the duchy financially and subjugate it to the domination of troops from Catholic Würzburg. While remaining loyal to the Duke, this group, led by the council leader Lanbek, will meet shortly thereafter to plan a rebellion to oust the financial advisor. The matter is complicated by the romantic involvement of Councillor Lanbek's son Gustav with Süß's beautiful sister Lea, a relationship Lanbek junior has been concealing from his traditional father. Süß then identifies the councillor as his masked verbal adversary at the ball, whereupon, in an attempt to connect himself and his line with one of the most respected local families, he tries to blackmail Gustav into marrying Lea. Acting on the advice of his father and other members of the anti-Süß party, Gustav accepts a government position and tolerates Süß's overtures. Not having the heart to reject Lea outright, he comes close to falling out with his own family after his attraction to her becomes known, only just managing to convince his father that the relationship has been nothing more than an indiscreet flirtation. Meanwhile, as the fateful night of planned rebellion arrives, events come to a unexpectedly sudden head in the form of a stroke that strikes down Karl Alexander and leaves Süß unprotected against popular anger. Süß tries to flee Stuttgart but is captured and, after a sensational trial with Gustav acting as prosecutor, executed. He is hanged from a giant iron gallows, in a cage suspended above the market place, where his body is left on display. Lea is last seen by the River Neckar and is presumed to have committed suicide.

Hauff did not have as much information about the historical Süss-Oppenheimer as we do today. None the less, he had no shortage of material upon which to draw. From 1737 onward, the Süss-Oppenheimer story had exerted a considerable fascination upon the public imagination, and a constant stream of Süss-related material had appeared in the intervening century between the execution and Hauff's novella. These encompassed pamphlets, flyers, and etchings, and the financial advisor also provided the subject-matter for countless verses and songs (Gerber, pp. 17-34; also her facsimile reproductions, pp. i-xiv). Hauff also seems to have relied on the recollections of his own grandfather, who had been Süss-Oppenheimer's next-door neighbour in real life and may have served as the model for the elder Lanbek character. While by no means yielding an objective or even internally consistent story of Süss's ultimately unhappy court tenure, this corpus of 'Sussiana' introduced some basic outlines for the narrative and the main themes that would interest both Hauff and later retellers of the story: those of social mobility, organized crime, bureaucratization and absolutist extension of the state, decay of religious barriers, and, of course, tensions between German and Jewish identities (Gerber, pp. 34-51, 147-269). In other words, the available source material provided ample compost for the twenty-five-year-old Wilhelm Hauff's imagination, as he attempted to make sense of a piece of local history whose brutality seemingly challenged many of his own sensibilities and values.

Although he stuck to the basic outlines of local history and biography, Hauff was clearly uninterested in either comprehensiveness or meticulous accuracy to the historical record.[10] He shows, for instance, a marked preference for fictional over real-life characters. Only two of the novella's characters were based on actual historical people: Süss-Oppenheimer himself and the capturing officer Erhard von Röder. Gustav has no known historical model, Lea was based on Rebecca from Scott's *Ivanhoe,* and indeed the whole Lea—Gustav plot strand was the stock literary one of forbidden love. All the other historical figures Hauff would have known from his sources, most conspicuously the head of state, Duke Karl Alexander, are depicted *in absentia,* if at all. The move away from historical persons towards fictional characters had a range of implications and possible motivations, which I shall discuss towards the end of this article. For the time being, however, I concentrate on the significance of Hauff's narrative strategy within the novella itself.

The immediate effect of omitting historical figures such as Karl Alexander was to focus attention, positive and negative, upon Süss. At several points, usually moments of narratorial *discours,* this fictionalization strategy allows critical comments to be made about the brutality and prejudice of the past. Towards the end of the story,[11]

the narrator even admits that Süss was unlikely to have been the main culprit behind the misdeeds of Karl Alexander's court: according to 'die, die zu jener Zeit gelebt haben', readers are told, Süss was executed not just for his own grave offences but 'für die Schandtaten und Pläne mächtiger Männer'. Such moments are, however, at odds with the rest of the novella, which depicts Süß as an Iago-like strategist, the real power behind a repressive, immoral, and turncoat régime. It is the financial advisor alone whom readers experience profiting from the brutal taxes in Württemberg, misusing his office for sexual purposes, and plotting to call in foreign troops to crush the native rebellion and make the populace become Catholic. Especially the last of these plot strands represents a clear and conscious authorial deviation from source material,[12] since the pro-Catholic faction in the Duke's court was generally believed to have been spearheaded by Franz Josef von Remchingen, one of Karl Alexander's leading generals, who is mentioned in the novella but who does not actually appear as a character. Moreover, Karl Alexander himself was a Catholic convert, a detail Hauff entirely neglects. The incongruity invites the question: how could such a story have been published by an ambitious and well-respected author in the most prestigious literary journal of the day? The answer lies in the thematic significance carried by Jewishness, specifically in a number of contemporary stereotypes within the novella, which give it coherence and persuasive force.

In the first place, Hauff's fictional world clearly draws upon the stereotype of the Court Jew, the image of the ambitious and resentful parvenu who, having cleverly mastered Gentile language, appearance, and customs, insinuates himself into power and secretly runs the government.[13] The first scene, that of the costume ball, immediately establishes Süß's function as such. By the end of the very first paragraph (p. 474), before we readers have even seen the man himself, the narrator has informed us that the 'misery and poverty' endemic in Württemberg are the result of the 'systematic and calculated interventions of an all-powerful minister'. Rumour has it that he keeps a number of mistresses, that he has passed over better-qualified men in handing out political offices to lackeys and highest bidders, and that the populace fears reprisals for the merest hint of opposition. Further on, we are told that it is the Duke's preoccupation with military matters that has allowed a cabal of 'Juden und Judenchristen' to seize the reins of power. The finance minister's role as Court Jew is also clearly indicated in Hauff's initial external description of him (p. 481). Although Süß's facial features seem 'well and nobly formed' and blessed with 'something imposing' (positive attributes crucial to the Court Jew's ability to penetrate the highest echelons of Gentile society) the protagonist Gustav Lanbek also finds himself alienated by the 'hostile and repulsive' furrows between the finance minister's eyebrows, the malicious expression of his mouth, and the 'truly horrible' forced laughter with which he accompanies a card game. This description is repeated nearly verbatim later on in the text (pp. 493-94).

The dichotomy between the externally impressive but internally corrupt Court Jew and the guileless native society he inhabits is reinforced through a pair of comments made under protection of carnival prerogative, or *Maskenfreiheit*, by guests at the ball. In response to an attempt by Süß at jovial camaraderie, the elder Lanbek, costumed as a peasant, levels a telling accusation. Hauff writes: "'Gott bewahre mich, daß ich Euer Freund sei, Herr Süß', erwiderte der Bauer. "Wär ich Euer Freund, so ginge ich wohl nicht in dem schlechten Rock und durchlöcherten Hut; Ihr macht ja Eure Freunde reich!'" (p. 482). In a similar vein, another unidentified guest, seeing a beautiful young woman on Süß's arm, remarks:

> Aus unserer Bekanntschaft [. . .] aus unsern Kreisen kann sie nicht sein, denn wenn es auch wahr ist, was man flüstert, daß schon mancher elende Kerl von einem Vater seine Tochter mit einer Bittschrift zum Juden schickte, so laut läßt keiner seine Schande werden, daß er sein liebliches Kind mit dieser Mazette auf den Ball schickt.

> (p. 476)

With good reason, this scene was replicated in the Nazi film about Süss-Oppenheimer (Tegel, *Jew Süß*, pp. 19-20). The setting of the masquerade ball not only serves the important practical function of allowing politically oppressed natives to speak their minds openly. It also has the symbolic connotation of people's true feelings and identities being concealed under social masks. That being the case, the choice of the peasant as counter-figure to the Court Jew can hardly be accidental. The peasant's connection with land reminds readers that Süß is legally a *Schutzbürger*, who must be specially invited onto Württemberg soil by the Duke, and the associated idea of food-growing points up the fact that the financial advisor himself does not produce anything, but lives off others' labour. In a few broad descriptive strokes, then, a dichotic spectrum of reference is established between the parasitic Court Jew and a native figure associated with land and *Heimat*. If there is any irony, it is that the peasant in this case is actually a fake. Yet irony was probably not the intended effect, since the first scene functions as a dress rehearsal for the anti-Süß rebellion to come. Indeed, such transformational role-playing emerges as a primary narrative thrust within the novella.

The symbolic importance of dress rehearsing becomes most obvious in connection with the novella's protagonist, Gustav Lanbek, who, in order to meet Lea during the ball, exchanges his original peasant costume for that of a Saracen. Gustav, of course, also must choose between fidelity to the 'peasant' world of native society and his personal attraction to the foreign Jewess. As the presence of such obvious symbolism would suggest, the figure of protagonist represents another primary locus of Hauff's fictionalizing the historical record. If the negative aspects of Karl Alexander's régime are displaced onto a scapegoated Süß, the office of representing healthy native society is transferred from the realm of putative fact into that of fiction via Gustav Lanbek. Indeed, within the novella as a whole, the story of the political rebellion takes a back seat to that of Gustav's inner conflicts and their eventual resolution. The contours of this plot line, with all its paradigmatic significance, are determined by two further stereotypes: that of the Beautiful Jewess and a collective variation of the Ahasverus or Wandering Jew legend.

I begin with Lea as Beautiful Jewess.[14] Hauff copied the figure from Scott's Rebecca, so blatantly, in fact, that one wonders whether the original audience might not have read many of the passages featuring Süß's fictional sister as direct literary citations. Like Rebecca, Lea is a positive character, depicted as both a vision of loveliness and a noble martyr who voluntarily renounces her claims on the protagonist. On the subject of her beauty Hauff is tellingly specific. Introducing her to his readers, he goes out of his way to engineer a situation, in the form of a missing mirror, that allows an extended description of Lea's appearance:

> Entzückt und mit leuchtenden Blicken betrachtete der junge Mann das schöne Mädchen. Man konnte ihr Gesicht die Vollendung orientalischer Züge nennen. Dieses Ebenmaß in den feingeschnittenen Zügen, diese wundervollen dunklen Augen, beschattet von langen seidenen Wimpern, diese kühn gewölbten, glänzendschwarzen Brauen und die dunkeln Locken, die in so angenehmem Kontrast um die weiße Stirne und den schönen Hals fielen und den Vereinigungspunkt dieser lieblichen Züge, zarte rote Lippen und die zierlichsten weißen Zähne noch mehr hervorhoben; der Turban der sich durch ihre Locken schlang, die reichen Perlen, die den Hals umspielten, das reizende und doch so züchtige Kostüm einer türkischen Dame—sie wirkten, verbunden mit diesen Zügen, eine solche Täuschung, daß der junge Mann eine jener herrlichen Erscheinungen zu sehen glaubte, wie sie Tasso beschreibt, wie sie die ergriffene Phantasie der Reisenden bei ihrer Heimkehr malte.

> (p. 485)

The figure of Lea has often been read as a sign of Hauff's ambiguous attitudes towards Jewishness: in fact Nazi writers, who originally used Hauff's novella as the basis for Veit Harlan's film, found the character too attractive and sympathetic for their purposes and had to rework the script (see Tegel, *Jew Süß*, pp. 19-20. Their scruples were justified, since for most of the story Lea appears as either a naively innocent child or a tragic heroine nobly accepting a terrible fate. None the less, as a comparison with Scott illustrates,[15] there are ambiguous undertones in Hauff's depiction of Lea, and she will ultimately play a negative role in the Gustav Lanbek plot line. Even in Hauff's initial description, flattering as that might seem, Lea's beauty indicates her basic foreignness: she represents the ultimate expression of the Orient and is seen dressed up in exotic gear. The same was, of course, the case in Scott. Unlike Scott, however, Hauff identifies uncanniness as the essence of Oriental beauty and depicts Lea's effect on Gustav as unnatural and unsettling. Rather than inspiring him, she, like the apparitions in Tasso's *Gerusalemme liberata,* puts her admirer under a magic spell.[16] Significantly, the corresponding passage in Scott features no such comparison: Hauff's deviation from his source (here fictional) again reveals his own authorial agenda.

Such a discrepancy might be dismissed as an aberration, were it not emblematic of the novella as a whole on the level of *histoire.* With her familial feelings for her brother and her unwillingness at the novella's end to condemn Gustav for his actions, also details taken from Scott, Lea emerges by the end of the story as a martyr, as a tragic heroine. None the less, Lea's influence on Gustav, from the vantage-point of the fictional native community and, I would argue, the novella itself, remains negative. This is made clear at an important juncture in the plot. Believing Gustav to have agreed to her brother's proposed *alliance,* she recites what she thinks to be the history of the engagement with surprising and otherwise unfamiliar flippancy:

> Du hast bei meinem Bruder um mich angehalten, und er sagte dir zu, im Fall ich wollte, und der Herzog durch ein Reskript das Hindernis wegen der Religion zwischen uns aufhöbe. Ich bin nur froh, daß Du nicht Katholik bist, da wäre es unmöglich, aber ihr Protestanten habt ja kein kirchliches Oberhaupt und seid doch eigentlich so gut Ketzer wie wir Juden.
>
> (p. 512)

Here the mask, as it were, slips from the Beautiful Jewess's face. This statement not only touches upon the sore point of religion, being made in the context of a Württemberg dominated by a 'strict and often ascetic' Protestantism (p. 474), but establishes a point of comparison between Lea and Süß. Both see native religion as a hindrance to be surmounted or, where possible, eradicated. Lea begins to attract sympathy again only after she has affirmed the impossibility of her attraction to Gustav and acknowledged the necessity of Jewish—Gentile apartheid. She cannot do this, however, until she has witnessed the destruction of her own family because of her brother's own ambitious disregard for traditional ethnic and religious boundaries. Thus, in the end, Hauff's positive depiction of Lea is outweighed by the price he forces her to pay. The same is most decidedly not the case for Scott's Rebecca, who remains pious and is not punished as drastically as Lea for diverting the hero from his appointed course. Nowhere is the distance between Hauff and Scott on the level of *histoire* more stark than in the fact that Rebecca and Isaac are allowed to seek exile, while Süß is condemned legally (Lea, narratively) to death.

Hauff's divergence from his model Scott reflects their differing views of history, and these in turn are conditioned by the metaphysical significance Jewishness possesses for the former but not the latter. Seen from the perspective of the Lanbeks, the Beautiful Jewess Lea represents no less of a threat to the welfare of the native community than her brother the Court Jew. In fact, Lea's beauty gives rise to a central thematic dichotomy between erotic desire and duty to family. Mistakenly believing that Gustav intends to sacrifice family interests to his passion for Lea, the elder Lanbek berates him as a 'Judas' and a 'patricide' (p. 514). Though the narrator distances himself on various occasions from the councillor's naked Jew-hatred, the author Hauff none the less allows the plot to endorse and enforce a stricture against intermarriage. Describing Gustav early on in the novella, Hauff writes:

> Er dachte an seinen stolzen Vater, an seine angesehene Familie, und so groß war die Furcht vor Schande, so tief eingewurzelt damals noch die Vorurteile gegen jene unglücklichen Kinder Abrahams, daß sie sogar seine zärtlichen Gefühle für die schöne Tochter Israels in diesem schrecklichen Augenblick übermannten.
>
> (pp. 497-98)

This passage typifies Hauff's ambivalence towards Jewishness, his vacillations between sympathy and repulsion, patronage and fear. On the surface, the narrator speaks the language of assimilation, describing anti-Semitic beliefs as 'the deeply rooted prejudices of those days' and Gustav's resolve to abandon Lea as a 'terrible moment'. Yet the context in which such humanistic sentiments occur pits them against a higher moral imperative, loyalty to one's own kind. The protagonist's sympathy with Lea is a positive quality, attesting to the kindness of his heart; yet in the course of the story he will have to overcome these feelings in order to avoid harming his own family. This act will be made easier because his attraction to Lea is seen not as love but an uncanny bewitchment.

The narrator's tendency to drift into collective terms such as 'the children of Abraham' in his depiction of Gustav's decision is anything but arbitrary. The rhetorical shift signals the presence of the third stereotype, the collectivized Ahasverus myth, the idea that the Jews as a people, because of some innate predatory viciousness, are fated to eternal homelessness.[17] This is precisely the idea invoked by the narrator as the ultimate justification for Gustav's abandoning Lea and her plight. Characteristically waffling, Hauff writes:

Er teilte zwar alle strengen religiösen Ansichten seiner Zeit, aber er schauderte über dem Fluch, der einen heimatlosen Menschenstamm bis ins tausendste Glied verfolgte und jeden mit ins Verderben zu ziehen schien, der sich auch den Edelsten unter ihnen auf die natürlichste Weise näherte. Er fand zwar keine Entschuldigung für sich selbst und seine verbotene Neigung zu einem Mädchen, das nicht seinen Glauben teilte, aber er gewann einigen Trost, indem er sein eigenes Schicksal einer höheren Fügung unterordnete.

(p. 517)

Gustav's abandonment of Lea is necessary so that he will not connect his family with the fate of social ostracization and homelessness, conceived both prosaically, as the potential social consequences of a mixed marriage, and fantastically, as an actual curse upon Jews collectively. Although his role in Süß's execution and Lea's suicide will rob him of his *joie de vivre* (readers are told he never smiled again (p. 538)), Gustav's action is the only one that will leave his conscience at rest, that will expiate the sin of his attraction to the foreign object of desire. 'Everyone' who comes into contact with Jews is dragged down, subjected to their own tragic destiny. If Gustav's people and Lea's are incompatible on such an absolute, essential, cosmic level, separation cannot be avoided. Even Lea's alabaster skin, otherwise a sign of beauty, ultimately comes to symbolize her destiny as a member of a tribe condemned to roam the earth like ghosts (p. 534). In the end, the Beautiful Jewess, too, reverts to the Wandering Jew.

The novella as a whole thus condemns the idea of intermarriage no less stringently, indeed far more so, than the elder Lanbek does. Here again, a comparison with Scott illuminates the chauvinistic thrust of Hauff's narrative. Scott, too, invokes the idea of the Jews as the people of Ahasverus in order to justify the separation of Rebecca and Ivanhoe. Yet because Isaac is not the villain of *Ivanhoe,* Scott's fictional universe remains far more open to potential reconciliation between Jews and Gentiles than Hauff's. The end of *Ivanhoe* depicts unfounded Gentile prejudice as the main factor condemning Jews to a perennial state of homelessness. Hauff, on the other hand, summons up the spectre of the Wandering Jew specifically to tip the balance between Gustav's conflicting desires and loyalties, his fear of shaming his family and his humane impulses, so that the protagonist can arrive at what is, from the perspective of the native community, the proper action against a serious threat. In the cyclical economy of Hauff's symbolism, the collective homelessness of the Jews provides a potential explanation for the crooked financial advisor's unethical and destructive behaviour: he does indeed turn out to be an angel of wrath, as Lea's governess calls him (p. 487), punishing the enemy 'Nazarenes'. In turn, the finance minister's underlying hatred of and malevolence towards native society condemns him and his kind to further homelessness. The cycle, as far as Hauff allows us to see, cannot be broken.

Thus, however much the narrator may frown upon the crass prejudices of 'those days', the novella as a whole does little to discredit them. On the contrary, anti-Jewish prejudice is transferred into a new political and mythological context, in which Gustav rejects Jewishness not just as Christian, but as a family member, patriot, and representative citizen. The ultimate problem with Süß from the novella's perspective is not that he is a typical Court Jew but that he is a Wandering Court Jew whose very destiny precludes assimilation into mainstream native society. The question then arises: what made such a combination and transformation of images plausible and/or desirable? For we must assume that *Jud Süß,* the first of what would turn out to be a century and a half of Süss-Oppenheimer narratives, possessed significant appeal for its audience. Readers may not have agreed with the novella's every detail (they may in fact not have regarded it as a masterpiece) but the villainous figure of Süß made a deep cultural impression. The reasons why need to be better understood.

In order to explain how Hauff was able to exploit the three stereotypes discussed and arrange the Süß-Lea-Gustav relationship so as simultaneously to justify and bemoan an act of anti-Semitic scapegoating, potential sources of persuasive force for the narrative have to be identified. Two likely places to look for them are in the realms of contemporary expectations for a range of discourse. The figure of *Jud Süß,* I would suggest, was successful because it served to construct desirable literary and historical narratives and thereby conformed to at least two types of perceived necessity. Although a full discussion of the audience's *Erwartungshorizont,* as pointed out earlier, is beyond the scope of the present article, by examining areas of external reference within the text it is possible to identify potential sources of persuasive force and appreciate better the power of the Wandering Court Jew figure. In a story where the necessity of historical events emerges as such a predominant theme, it should come as no surprise that the narrative tries to anchor itself in familiar literary forms and recent history.

I begin with a few points of literary reference. As the first part of this article has argued, Hauff's concentration of various plot and thematic elements in the figure of Süß represents one of his main authorial interventions, one with dramatic implications for the ultimate significance of the work on the level of *histoire.* Yet this intervention can also be understood as an aesthetic decision, taken to foster the consumability of the novella as a work of literature. By setting up Süß as sole villain and concocting the complementary Gustav-Lea plot strand, Hauff is able to arrange events efficiently and give his narrative a relative unity of place and time: the *erzählte Zeit* is a single month, the *Erzählzeit* only three days. Dramatic unity is, of course, almost a cliché of classicist aesthetics, and in the heavily classicist

1820s, Hauff's ability to construct a 'unified' plot no doubt contributed to the perceived literary quality of his work. Indeed, Hauff's depiction of Süß as a villain can itself be considered a literary gesture, since fictional works tend to be structured around binary oppositions, of which heroes and villains are a prominent form. Süß emerges from Hauff's depiction not only as a scapegoat but as a recognizably literary figure comparable to Iago, Edmund, or, of course, Shylock himself. Hauff's running imitation (if not plagiarism) of Scott, too, emphasizes the text's 'literariness'. Since Scott was arguably the most widely read novelist in early-nineteenth-century Germany, with *Ivanhoe* in particular as a great favourite with the rapidly expanding German readership, there is no reason to believe that the case was different in Hauff's time. My contention, then, is twofold: that ***Jud Süß***'s resemblance to novels such as *Ivanhoe* is likely to have enhanced its literary reputation and that the aesthetic aura enjoyed by Hauff's novella would have served to promote the persuasiveness of the stereotypical Süß figure. Neither argument implies that objective measures can be found for literary quality or that aesthetic effect can be separated from the stereotypes invoked during the narrative. On the contrary, the point is that literary criteria and stereotypes are inextricably intertwined, since the persuasive power of 'fixed' images greatly influences what is considered valid literary discourse, and *vice versa*.

Other perhaps even more important instances of extratextual reference can be identified in the realm of history. Numerous parallels exist between the eighteenth-century events and milieu depicted and the historical circumstances of the post-Napoleonic Württemberg in which Hauff wrote. The most basic of these is the situation of a native populace being ruled by a foreign power, which threatened to eradicate tradition. Similar issues of religion were involved: the French were, of course, Catholic, and Napoleon had swept aside traditional religious segregation in one fell swoop by emancipating German Jews from legal restrictions on trade and domicile. So, too, were questions of power and sexuality: as Heine's *Buch Le Grand* tells us, French troops took liberties similar to those of which Süß is accused. A third point of comparison resides in the hardship supposedly suffered by the native populace under Süß's rule and the series of agricultural crises that buffeted Southern Germany in the late 1810s. In an almost eerie parallel, these crises also resulted in a violent act of anti-Jewish scapegoating, the notorious Hep-Hep riots of 1819.[18] More specifically, several telling similarities can be identified between Karl Alexander and the nineteenth-century King Friedrich of Württemberg. Both stood accused of selling out native interests to foreigners, either by calling for foreign troops (in Karl Alexander's case) or by actually concluding an alliance with a conquering power (in Friedrich's). Moreover, both men's reigns raised broad issues of political

legitimacy and authority. In respective efforts to make their own power absolute, both Friedrich and Karl Alexander tried to force through changes in government that would have dismantled the Württemberg Diet and curtailed traditional prerogatives of the estates.[19] Not surprisingly, the speeches of the Lanbek party in the novella echo the post-war calls of native élites (for example, Ludwig Uhland) for the restoration of the Swabian *gutes altes Recht*.[20] Even Karl Alexander's sudden death, which functions in the narrative as a *deus ex machina* intervention allowing the Lanbek party to triumph over Süß, found a striking parallel in King Friedrich's unexpected passing on 30 October 1816. The point is not to explain every detail of Hauff's work in terms of exact political allegory but to draw attention to perceived historical similarity as a force guiding the plot. It is hard to imagine the original audience in 1827 reading the novella without thinking of recent history and drawing conclusions to reflect their own experience. After all, historical allegory as a means of depicting the Napoleonic experience was hardly unknown in German literature: Grillparzer's transparently allegorical drama *König Ottokars Glück und Ende* was first performed in 1825. Indeed, despite Hauff's omission of the ruling family from the novella's action, ***Jud Süß*** itself was considered a politically sensitive work at the time of its publication, passing the censors only after several cuts had been made.[21] An interpretation of the novella as a veiled statement about Württemberg's experience under Napoleon fits in well with Hauff's stated views in the rest of his work: in 1824 he published a number of **'War and Folk Songs'** commemorating German military successes in the previous decade (see **Werke** [*Sämtliche Werke*], III, 341-70), and his final novella, ***Das Bild des Kaisers,*** revolves around the post-Napoleonic division in German society between the despot's admirers and detractors. As will emerge shortly, the use of the seemingly anachronistic term 'German' for Hauff's subject-matter is entirely advised.

By acknowledging the historical allegory within ***Jud Süß,*** it is possible to identify a nativist-nationalist rationale behind Hauff's central narrative decision to refocus attention away from Karl Alexander onto Süß. The powerful negative connotations of the Jewish stereotypes divert culpability from the native monarch, taking King Friedrich, as it were, out of the nineteenth-century question. This displacement of blame suggests that despite considerable private-citizen hostility towards the German princes in the wake of the Napoleonic wars, both author and readers were still anxious to identify with native political figures. By transferring reader opprobrium from native ruler(s) to the stereotyped foreigner within, Hauff's novella serves to suppress the deep conflicts between monarchy and populace, characteristic of both centuries. Tragic though it might appear from the narrator's humanistic perspective, the exclusion of the Jew and Jewishness allows a temporarily stable image of native society to coalesce, whereby the rift between princes and populace can be seen as the result of foreign treachery. Native Württemberg emerges new and improved: the reputation(s) of the selfish native monarch(s) are rehabilitated, and the activism engendered by the unpleasant experience with Süß will presumably guard against similar crisis in the future. The only cost in the mythological economy is the ostracization of the outsiders.

In this light, **Jud Süß**'s central act of fictionalization may look like a textbook example of compensatory stereotyping, which, in many respects, it is. Yet Hauff's arrangement and omission of figures in the novella does not, as the psychological model of stereotyping would have it, happen unconsciously. On the contrary, Hauff demonstrates a clear awareness of the distortion involved in blaming Süß alone for the economic, political, and religious crises of the day. As previously mentioned (see again **Werke,** II, 537), the narrator openly acknowledges that Süß was effectively scapegoated and even goes on to question whether the finance minister's execution possessed sufficient power as a symbolic act to heal the wounds resulting from the crisis of state under Karl Alexander. Even-handed as that sentiment might sound, this statement again tips the author's hand as to his possible agenda, revealing his intense concern with social stability. Stability represents nothing less than a historical *sine qua non* for the existence of native society and will ultimately be used to justify Süß-Oppenheimer's brutal execution. The ground for such an idea is carefully laid throughout the text, starting with the repeated invocations of immutable fate. Gustav, we should remember, consoles himself for his role in Lea's suicide 'by subsuming his own fate under a higher destiny' (p. 517). This view is later directly endorsed by the narrator, who summarizes the import of the Süß execution in these terms:

> Es gibt im Leben einzelner Staaten Momente, wo der aufmerksame Beschauer noch nach einem Jahrhundert sagen wird, gerade hier mußte eine Krise eintreten, ein oder zwei Jahre nachher wären dieselben Umstände nicht mehr von derselben Wirkung gewesen. Es ist dann dem endlichen Geist nicht mehr möglich, eine solche Fügung der Dinge sich hinwegzudenken, und aus der unendlichen Reihe von möglichen Folgen diejenigen aneinanderzuknüpfen, die ein ebenso notwendig verkettetes Ganze bilden als ein verflossenes Jahrhundert mit allen seinen historischen Wahrheiten. Hier zeigte sich der *Finger Gottes,* pflegt man zu sagen, wenn man auf solche wichtige Augenblicke im Leben eines Staates stößt.

(p. 521)

The notion of the Süss-Oppenheimer execution as a crossroads in the life of the Württemberg state serves not only to underscore the foresight of the rebels but to contextualize the scapegoating of the Jewish finance minister as an unavoidable evil along the way towards promoting the welfare of the native community. Without the execution, the Württemberg known by Hauff and the original audience would not exist. By extension, this *de facto* historical necessity (the hand of God intervening in human destiny) also serves to justify Hauff's own narrative making a villain and a scapegoat out of Süß. Even if the novella admittedly distorts specific aspects of the historical record, readers are given a persuasive reason, that of maintaining the illusion of broad native solidarity against foreign incursions, to accept Hauff's version of history

In this regard, too, the story's paradigmatic, representative ambitions, focused on its hero, become fully apparent. The stock plot line of forbidden love between Gustav and Lea emerges as an instrumental device, on the one hand lending an aesthetic desirability to the historical fiction, and on the other serving both to highlight the idea that in moments of epochal crisis individual feelings must be sacrificed for the public welfare and to set up Gustav as a tragic hero worthy of admiration. Not only must Gustav renounce Lea; he himself has to prosecute Süß and bring about his destruction, after refusing a request by Lea to withhold a crucial piece of evidence. It is as though Hauff were making things as difficult as possible for his hero in order to stress the absolute nature of the dichotomy between exotic fascination and proper dedication to native welfare. Complementing this moral lesson, the rebellion plot line stages a subtle shift in representative authority from the ruling monarchy to the private citizenry. As well as obscuring the responsibility of the head of state for political corruption, the omission of Karl Alexander/Friedrich from the native-foreign equation also opens up the political stage to new actors. The novella can thus be read as a story of how the native hero emerges from his private existence in order to rescue his culture from a pernicious foreign influence, tacitly asserting his own representative identification with the public sphere itself in the process. Significantly, this progression never involves direct rebellion against traditional political authorities: the Lanbek party never aims to overthrow Karl Alexander but seeks merely to correct a source of excess within his government, of which the ruler is thought to be inadequately aware. None the less, the idea that representative citizens possess both the right and the duty to intervene in the development of their culture, regardless of whether it expresses itself as direct political rebellion, entails a transfer of authority of the most fundamental kind, one whose effects are often more decisive than political revolution.[22] If we assume that the activism of a private citizen such as Gustav Lanbek would have appealed to the 'educated classes' who were the *Morgenblatt*'s target audience and were becoming increasingly influential in German society, we can glimpse yet another powerful source of historical urgency for the Wandering Court Jew stereotype.

These two seemingly contradictory sources of perceived necessity, the conservative conceit of preserving 'native' society against foreign encroachment and the modernizing transfer of representative cultural authority to private citizens, are united in the concept of the nation. Although on the surface Hauff might seem to be concerned with just Württemberg and not, in any explicit sense, with Germany, the native society he depicts ultimately emerges on a national scale. Here again, it is useful to look at Hauff's biography and his other writing. He was a *Burschenschaftler,* like Gustav Lanbek in the novella, and a supporter of the Jahnian *Turnerbewegung*: his previously mentioned collection of **'War and Folk Songs'** included titles such as **"Turnerlust"** and **"Bundeslied"**. Commensurate with such beliefs, a recurring theme in his narrative work as a whole is the need for Germans of various regions to put aside provincial animosities and come together in a single community. *Das Bild des Kaisers* also revolves in part around the conflicts between Swabians and Prussians, in which the latter's separatist mentality comes in for repeated criticism (***Werke,*** II, 642, 645, 657-60). In **"O Deutschland, Deutschland"**, Hauff has one of the protagonists intone 'da sieht man, wie der Elend aus deiner eigenen Zersplitterung hervorgeht!' (II, 660).

Although the nationalist theme is not explicitly sounded in *Jud Süß*, the narrative does invite such an interpretation. The connection between Hauff's *großdeutsch* views and the novella is made manifest in the fact that Gustav Lanbek, like his creator, is a fraternity member, which implicitly aligns the native community with nationalistic aims and values. Moreover, the story of popular native rebellion in Württemberg lends itself to transposition onto a national scale. The Court Jew stereotype, after all, was common property among German speakers, thanks to shared aspects of history in the states where they lived. The basic plot of *Jud Süß* could have been easily transferred to Bavaria, Prussia, perhaps even Austria: there is no reason the depiction of the native community would change radically in a similar story set in Munich, Berlin, or Vienna. The Wandering Jew stereotype also has a national dimension. Since Jews as the collectivized people of Ahasverus are assumed to exist discrete from those around them, Swabians cannot be considered their proper antithesis. The equation, as it were, is unbalanced. The more symmetrical opposite number to the Wandering Court Jew would be the locally rooted German.

Perhaps the best indication that the presence of the Jew is meant to serve the function of national integration is Hauff's use of Süß as scapegoat for perhaps the most important difference threatening to divide Germans: that between the Protestant and Catholic religions. For all that the novella treats the Protestant—Catholic rivalry, the true conflict ultimately crystallizes as one between natives and Jews: astonishingly, the plan to make Würt-

temberg Catholic is primarily depicted not as a Jesuit plot on the part of Würzburg but as another of the Court Jew's schemes for increasing his own power. The disjuncture between 'native' and Jewish values not only obscures but subsumes the conflict between Catholic and Protestants. Thus, although Hauff does not draw explicitly nationalistic conclusions, he does depict the necessity for broad solidarity against 'foreign' threat, allowing for audience identification across region and confession. 'Germans' of various persuasions could unite in their 'not-Jewishness'.

Given the obvious appeal of nationalist modes of thinking in the wake of Napoleon, the integrative, teleological thrust of *Jud Süß* was clearly another factor encouraging its audience to accept Hauff's version of events. People tend to like narratives that tell them that they themselves and their way of life, their imagined past and culture, exist by divine ordinance. The performative power of the novella can perhaps be sensed here, a good place for this discussion to conclude. Intentionally or not, all High German literature of this period had nationalist implications. Written in the standard idiom, published in a journal of national scope, and consumed by an audience from Baden to Berlin, *Jud Süß* was no exception. The reading of *Jud Süß* by its original audience was itself a national event and Hauff's fiction was an artefact of the very proto-nationalistic identity it depicted. Not surprisingly, then, despite some critics' reservations about its literary quality, the novella found its way into the canon, and was reissued and anthologized throughout the nineteenth century. Even after it receded into obscurity, Hauff's recreation of the Süss-Oppenheimer story continued to echo within German culture. Both the Feuchtwanger novel and the Nazi film version of *Jud Süß* were influenced by the novella in a number of ways, from their adoption of the original overall 'romance vs. politics' narrative structure to the endorsement or rejection of specific details of the original work. Hauff's work established the image of the Jew Süß as a part of history in the public imagination. Precisely how to tell the story around this figure continued to concern authors of the most wildly divergent political views up to and through the Weimar and Nazi years. Even today, the question is still debated among scholars of the historical Süss-Oppenheimer and the various fictional versions of his life story.

This is not a question we today, with our rather reductive metaphors of national, ethnic, and other 'identity', are especially well equipped to answer. Were Hauff's novella to be rescued from the margins of literary history, it is not even clear how present-day readers should approach the narrative and its conflicting yet deeply connected messages of tolerance and chauvinism. Embedded within the context both of German resistance to French hegemony and of German discrimination against a subordinate and disadvantaged internal minority, ***Jud***

Süß challenges our criteria for politically acceptable literature. Must we not accept the novella, despite its use of anti-Jewish stereotypes, as Hauff's attempt to articulate an identity for himself and those he considered his people? And must we not also reject the story he told about the past, all narratorial protestations of tolerance notwithstanding, as pernicious, exclusionary, all-too-open to racist interpretation? I am more inclined to criticize *Jud Süß* as an example of unacceptable historical fiction than praise its tolerant side, but I would not pretend to be able to resolve the most basic issue of the Wandering Court Jew.[23]

Notes

1. The statistic comes from Friedrich Knilli, quoted in Frank Dietschreit, *Lion Feuchtwanger* (Stuttgart: Metzler, 1988), p. 102. See also Barbara Gerber, *Jud Süß: Aufstieg und Fall im frühen 18. Jahrhundert* (Hamburg: Christians, 1990), pp. 18, 282-86.

2. Critical interpretations of *Jud Süß* are rare. Those scattered discussions of the novella that do exist appear largely in works about the later versions of the story. These are split almost evenly along the question of whether the novella is anti-Semitic or not. A positive view of Hauff's work as first and foremost criticizing Süss-Oppenheimer's execution and promoting tolerance predominates, understandably, among those scholars who come to Hauff via the Nazi film *Jud Süß*: see Dorothea Hollstein's 'Dreimal *Jud Süß*: Zeugnisse "schmählichster Barbarei"—Hauffs Novelle, Feuchtwangers Roman und Harlans Film in vergleichender Betrachtung', *Der Deutschunterricht*, 3 (1985), 42-54. Similar conclusions are reached by the media historian Susan Tegel: see her *Jew Süss* (Trowbridge: Flicks Books, 1996) and 'Veit Harlan and the Origins of *Jud Süß*, 1838-9: Opportunism in the Creation of Nazi Anti-Semitic Film Propaganda', *Historical Journal for Film, Radio and Television*, 16 (1996), 515-31. Scholars who come to Hauff by some other route (for example, via Feuchtwanger) tend to be considerably harsher on Hauff: see Dietschreit, p. 99, and Florian Krobb, *Die schöne Jüdin: Jüdische Frauengestalten in der deutschsprachigen Erzählliteratur vom 17. Jahrhundert bis zum ersten Weltkreig* (Tübingen: Niemeyer, 1993), pp. 123-28.

3. My use of these terms follows that of Emile Benveniste. According to Benveniste, *discours* is formed by those elements of the text that refer or draw attention to the act of enunciation and the situation of telling. *Histoire*, on the other hand, is understood as the act of advancing one or more storyline(s), whereby the narrator tends to recede into the background. For a discussion of these ideas, see Lionel Gossman, *Between History and Literature* (Cambridge, MA: Harvard University Press, 1990), pp. 242-43.

4. My use of the term 'stereotype' conforms to its everyday meanings. A good definitional starting-point for these is Sander Gilman, who defines stereotypes as the reduction of the world, and especially other people, to a single characteristic or set of characteristics, tending toward absolute positive or negative value (*Difference and Pathology: Stereotypes of Sexuality, Race and Madness* (Ithaca, NY: Cornell University Press, 1985), esp. pp. 16-21). Stereotyping, as Gilman rightly points out, need not be seen as pathological; it represents a normal part of adult perception, a necessary simplification mechanism allowing individuals to deal with a bewildering variety of sensory information. My analysis differs from the psychological sort, however, in its concern for the historical and social aspects of stereotyping, for the stereotype as image received under certain unique conditions in time and space. One major task of my article is to describe how such 'fixed' images evolve in specific ways over time: Gilman's assertion that they are 'protean' seems to me unsatisfactory. Furthermore, as will emerge in the course of my reading of Hauff, this article aims to acknowledge the self-consciousness with which users often apply stereotypical images and to avoid treating them as ideologically blinkered victims of some essential psychic inability to cope with the world's complexity. Perhaps the most challenging aspect of analysing stereotypes is to understand their use by individuals who know in some sense that they are crassly simplifying their reality.

5. This task is made relatively easy by a number of detailed works about the historical Süss-Oppenheimer and later fictional treatments. On the historical figure, the major works are Selma Stern, *Jud Süss: Ein Beitrag zur deutschen und zur jüdischen Geschichte* (Berlin: Akademie, 1929); Curt Elwenspoeck, *Jud Süß Oppenheimer: Der große Finanzier und galante Abenteuerer des 18. Jahrhunderts* (Stuttgart: Süddeutsches Verlagshaus, 1926); Manfred Zimmermann, *Josef Süss-Oppenheimer, ein Finanzmann des 18. Jahrhunderts* (Stuttgart: Rieger, 1874). Though old, all are excellent empirical sources. My essay follows Stern's and Zimmermann's spelling of the name with the double 's' to distinguish the figure as he appears in the historical record, however 'fictional' that might be, from self-understood fictional depictions. On the various legends that sprang up around Süss-Oppenheimer in the nearly one hundred years between his execution and Hauff's novella, my source is Gerber (see note 1). On the question of literary models for the novella itself,

see Albert Mannheimer, *Die Quellen zu Hauffs Jud Süß* (Giessen: Kindt, 1909). My reconstruction of Hauff's fictionalization strategies draws upon all these works.

6. See G. G. Gervinus, *Geschichte der deutschen Dichtung,* 6 vols (Leipzig: Engelmann, 1853), v, 634, and Heinrich Laube, *Geschichte der deutschen Literatur,* 6 vols (Stuttgart: Hallberger, 1839), v, 145.

7. These categories expand on Harry E. Shaw's distinctions between various functions of history in historical fiction (*Forms of Historical Fiction: Sir Walter Scott and his Successors* (Ithaca, NY: Cornell University Press, 1983), pp. 51-149). The first three items in my list roughly correspond to Shaw's ideas of 'history as pastoral', 'history as drama', and 'history as subject', and I take the screen metaphor directly from him. The fourth category is my own.

8. The phrase is, of course, adopted from *The Invention of Tradition,* ed. by Eric J. Hobsbawm and Terence Ranger (London: Canto, 1983). See especially Hobsbawm's introduction, pp. 1-15. Though it certainly occurs in other contexts as well, the process can be seen as part of a larger imagination of national community, such as that described by Benedict Anderson in *Imagined Communities* (London: Verso, 1983). The nationalist implications of Hauff's *Jud Süß* will be discussed in detail at the end of my article.

9. A number of scholars from various disciplines have advanced the thesis of a basic discontinuity in the history of anti-Jewish sentiment. Earlier hostility, it is argued, centres on religion and socio-economic circumstances and at least in theory allows for the possibility of Jewish integration through conversion. A contrast is then drawn with later anti-Semitism, which posits an irremediable Jewish essence or identity as a people and in the course of the nineteenth century begins to shade over into pseudo-scientific racism. See Helmut Berding, *Moderner Antisemitismus in Deutschland* (Frankfurt a.M.: Suhrkamp, 1988), pp. 7-84; Paul L. Rose, *Revolutionary Anti-Semitism in Germany from Kant to Wagner* (Princeton, NJ: Princeton University Press, 1990), pp. 3-22; Reinhard Rürup, *Emanzipation und Antisemitismus* (Göttingen: Vandenhoeck & Ruprecht, 1975), pp. 95-108; Gavin Langmuir, *History, Religion and Antisemitism* (London: Tauris, 1990), pp. 275-305.

10. On Hauff's use of sources, see Mannheimer, pp. 75-81.

11. There is no definitive historical-critical edition of Hauff. All citations refer to W. Hauff, *Jud Süss,* in *Sämtliche Werke,* ed. by Sybille von Steinsdorff, 3 vols (Munich: Winkler, 1970), II, 476-538 (p. 537).

12. A joke made by one of the costumed natives, which elicits a violent response from Süß, unambiguously suggests that the finance minister is the mastermind of the Catholic plot (*Jud Süß,* p. 483).

13. On the Court Jew stereotype in society, see Gerber, pp. 51-99; Leon Poliakov, *The History of Anti-Semitism,* 3 vols (London: Elek, 1965), III, 229-34. For a discussion of corresponding images in world literature, see *Juden und Judentum in der Literatur,* ed. by Herbert A. Strauss and Christhard Hoffmann (Munich: dtv, 1985), pp. 106-210; *Conditio Judaica: Judentum, Antisemitismus und deutschsprachige Literatur vom 18. Jahrhundert bis zum Ersten Weltkrieg,* 2 vols, ed. by Hans Otto Horch and Horst Denkler (Tübingen: Niemeyer, 1989), I, 131-99; II, 35-168.

14. The best source on the Beautiful Jewess stereotype is the entire volume by Krobb cited above. He makes many of the same points about the ambiguity of the Lea figure as I do. See also Strauss, pp. 111-21; Poliakov, III, 326.

15. For purposes of comparison and contrast, it is worth quoting Scott's initial description of Rebecca in *Ivanhoe,* which bears a hardly accidental resemblance to the Hauff passage introducing Lea: 'The figure of Rebecca might indeed have compared with the proudest beauties of England, even though it had been judged by as shrewd a connoisseur as Prince John. Her form was exquisitely symmetrical, and was shown to advantage by a sort of Eastern dress, which she wore according to the fashion of the females of her nation. Her turban of yellow silk suited well with the darkness of her complexion. The brilliancy of her eyes, the superb arch of her eyebrows, her well-formed aquiline nose, her teeth as white as pearl, and the profusion of her sable tresses, which, each, arranged in its own little spiral of twisted curls, fell down upon as much of a lovely neck and bosom as a simarre of the richest Persian silk, exhibiting flowers in their natural colours embossed upon a purple ground, permitted to be visible—all these constituted a combination of loveliness, which yielded not to the most beautiful of the maidens who surrounded her' (*Ivanhoe,* ed. by Ian Duncan (Oxford: Oxford University Press, 1996), pp. 93-94).

16. The unhealthy strangeness of Gustav's attraction to the Beautiful Jewess is re-emphasized on several occasions in the story: for example, when Hauff writes of the 'Einfluß jenes wunderbaren Zaubers, der sich aus Rahels Tagen unter den Töchtern Israels erhalten haben soll' (p. 511).

17. According to popular Christian mythology, dating in this form back to the beginning of the seventeenth century, Ahasverus was a cobbler condemned to walk the earth for ever after displaying a lack of sympathy toward Christ on His march to Calvary. Extended to the group, the Wandering Jew stereotype defines historical homelessness as an instance of divine retribution visited upon the Jews as a people. On the legend, see Gregory K. Anderson, *The Legend of the Wandering Jew* (Providence, RI: Brown University Press, 1965), esp. pp. 174-242; Poliakov, III, 349-64; Rose, pp. 23-43. The list is by no means exhaustive. As a literary motif, the Wandering Jew was very much in fashion around the time of *Jud Süß*'s composition. On this topic, see Horch and Denkler, II, 53.

18. For a historical overview of the period, see Thomas Nipperdey, *Deutsche Geschichte 1800-66* (Munich: Beck, 1985), especially his discussion of agricultural crises of the 1810s and the Hep-Hep riots (pp. 249-50). For a general picture of economic conditions, see also James J. Sheehan, *German History 1770-1866* (Oxford: Oxford University Press, 1989), pp. 451-523.

19. See *Jud Süß,* p. 507. One point of anachronism in the narrative is Hauff's equation of the Swabian *gutes altes Recht,* a kind of protocol setting out the prerogatives of the monarchy and the estates, with a full blown constitution or *Verfassung.* In reality no such constitution existed in either eighteenth-century or nineteenth-century Württemberg, so that Hauff's depiction of the situation might be read as a frustrated democrat's wishful thinking.

20. A quotation from Uhland serves as the epigraph for *Jud Süß* (p. 474).

21. In a letter to his publisher, Johann Friedrich Cotta, of 19 June 1827 Hauff wrote of *Jud Süß*: 'Ich habe versucht ein möglichst lebendiges Bild jener für unser Vaterland so verhängnisvollen Zeit zu geben ohne jedoch irgend ein Interesse gegenwärtig lebender, hoher o. niederer Personen zu verletzen' (*Briefe an Cotta,* 3 vols, ed. by Maria Fehling and Herbert Schiller (Stuttgart: Cotta, 1927), II, 460. Strategically, the disclaimer about the interest of living parties excluded the recently deceased King Friedrich.

22. This reading of the Gustav figure draws heavily upon Jürgen Habermas's claims about the 'literary' versus the 'political' public sphere, put forth in his account of the 'private' family sphere and the rise of eighteenth-century salon culture (*Strukturwandel der Öffentlichkeit,* revised edn (Frankfurt a.M.: Suhrkamp, 1990), esp. pp. 116-21). As I argue shortly, a parallel claim can be made about the political import of *Jud Süß* itself as the work of the 'private' citizen Wilhelm Hauff.

23. I gratefully acknowledge the contribution of Steve Giles in formulating the arguments in this article.

David Blamires (essay date December 2002)

SOURCE: Blamires, David. "The Meaning of Disfigurement in Wilhelm Hauff's *Dwarf Nose." Children's Literature in Education* 33, no. 4 (December 2002): 297-307.

[*In the following essay, Blamires analyzes the symbolic function of deformity in the tale.*]

Wilhelm Hauff (1802-1827) was a younger contemporary of Jacob and Wilhelm Grimm. Born in Stuttgart in 1802 and educated at the University of Tübingen, he was tutor to the children of Baron von Hügel before embarking on a full-time literary career. This was tragically cut off in 1827, a few days short of his twenty-fifth birthday when he died of typhoid. Although by then Hauff had written enough to fill half a dozen volumes in a modern edition, he is known today principally for his fairytales. These appeared in the form of almanacs or keepsakes in three volumes: *Die Karawane* (*The Caravan,* 1825), *Der Scheik von Alessandria und seine Sklaven* (*The Sheik of Alexandria and His Slaves,* 1826), and *Das Wirtshaus im Spessart* (*The Inn in the Spessart,* 1827). These collections have been constantly reprinted in Germany, and individual tales are often issued separately. D. Maureen Thum asserts in Zipes's *Oxford Companion to Fairy Tales* that there are very few translations of Hauff into English, but this is untrue. There were around 25 translations of one or more of Hauff's tales between 1844 and World War I, and there have been several more since then. Individual tales frequently crop up also in general collections of fairytales.

Hauff differs from the Grimms in being a creator of fairytales, not a collector. For plots and individual motifs he drew on both literary and folktale sources, but his tales are still very much his own. They are literary works rather than printed forms of orally current material. In this respect, Hauff has more in common with Andersen than with the Grimms and Ludwig Bechstein, the other extremely popular editor of German fairytales in the middle of the nineteenth century.

The tale that I want to consider more fully here is one of Hauff's most popular inventions. *Zwerg Nase* (*Dwarf Nose*) was included in the second almanac, *Der Scheik von Alessandria und seine Sklaven,* and it is accessible in three recent English separate editions. It was translated by Doris Orgel as *Dwarf Long-Nose* and illustrated by Maurice Sendak in an edition published in New York by Random House in 1960. A British edition was published by The Bodley Head in 1979. A different translation by Anthea Bell appeared as *Dwarf Nose* with illustrations by Lisbeth Zwerger in 1994 (North-South Books). A third edition, entitled *Little Long-Nose,* based on translations by Jean Rosemary Edwards and Percy E. Pinkerton and illustrated by Laura Stoddart, was published by Walker Books in 1997. All three books are extremely attractive in presentation.

The protagonist of *Dwarf Nose* is a 12-year-old boy called Jacob, who is abducted by a nasty old woman and bewitched into slavery as a squirrel for seven years. During this time he learns how to cook. He subsequently escapes after smelling a mysterious herb that causes him to sneeze, but finds himself now to have the shape of an ugly dwarf with a long nose. He does not realize how much time has passed and, on making contact again with his mother and father, is not recognized by either of them, but rejected as a charlatan. Eventually he is able to trade on the skills he has learnt with the old woman and becomes a cook in the duke's household. On one of his shopping expeditions he buys a goose, which turns out to be Mimi, daughter of the enchanter Wetterbock, whom a wicked fairy has transformed into a goose.

Meanwhile, Dwarf Nose has achieved fame through his culinary skills and is challenged by one of the duke's guests to produce a *pâté souzeraine,* something he has never heard of before. Mimi helps him to find the necessary secret ingredient, the herb Niesmitlust (Sneeze-with-pleasure), which he realizes is the same herb that had released him earlier from his squirrel shape in the hateful old woman's house. He eats the herb and now turns into a handsome young man. He and Mimi escape from the duke's palace. Jacob takes Mimi back to her father, who disenchants her and rewards Jacob with sufficient gifts to buy a shop and become rich and happy. Jacob does not marry Mimi, but returns to his parents (though he must now be about twenty-two years old).

Unlike most traditional fairytales, *Dwarf Nose* does not end with a radical transformation of the hero's situation. It concludes merely with a heightened version of his status at the beginning of the tale. Jacob was the son of a shoemaker father and a market stallholder mother; now he has money for a shop of his own. The relative status of rich aristocracy and ordinary working person remains intact. There is no revolution, no breaking through class barriers, only a modest improvement in material welfare. Yet Jacob has suffered a great deal to reach this position, and we must ask ourselves why.

It is hard to see him as needing to be taught a lesson, since at his mother's market stall he does no more than scold the horrid old woman for handling and sniffing at the vegetables in such a way as to make other customers unwilling to buy them. Jacob acts in what he believes to be his mother's interests, since she is too anxious to say anything herself. He is not disobedient or careless like, say, the hero of *Jack and the Beanstalk.* He does not like the old woman's nasty brown fingers or her long nose and is fearful that her wobbly head might fall off into the basket of cabbages. Is his behaviour to be regarded as impudent and therefore meriting punishment? If so, the punishment seems excessive for conduct motivated purely out of concern for his mother's welfare. Readers of the story are much more likely to identify with Jacob's action and think it justified, since everything about the old woman is repulsive and described in negative terms. Jacob is surely an innocent victim, not a naughty boy who deserves to be taught a lesson.

Jacob's new life marks a huge change in his circumstances and takes place under the rubric of fear. He is scared of the ugly old woman and fears that her neck, which is as thin as a cabbage stalk, might break and cause her head to fall into the vegetable basket. He is disgusted by her nasty brown fingers and her long nose. Half crying, he is compelled by his mother to help the old woman carry her vegetables home. The old woman asks for help and promises to pay for it, so Jacob's mother orders him to go. With this act he is thrown out of the comfort and security of the family nest. Although he does not know it, he is beginning the transition from poverty to affluence, for although the old woman's house looks small and dilapidated from the outside, inside it is all splendour. Stranger still, the old woman has a multitude of guinea pigs and squirrels as servants scurrying at her beck and call. She makes a soup for Jacob, ostensibly before he returns home, and it is better than any he has tasted before, sweet and sour at the same time and very strong. The guinea pigs burn Arabian incense, and in its smell he falls asleep and experiences the subsequent time as if in a dream. His clothes are removed and in their place he gets a squirrel skin. He remains human on the inside, but outwardly he becomes an animal and is treated like one.

Jacob's dream lasts seven years. During this time he is employed in a variety of domestic tasks. The first year is occupied with shoe-cleaning, which he has already been used to in his father's house. In the second year the task changes to the strange one of collecting and sieving specks of dust caught in the sun (*Sonnenstäubchen*) in order to make bread for his toothless mistress. In the third year he has to collect drinking water for her with hazelnut shells from the dew on roses. After this he is transferred to cleaning the glass floors in the house. Only after this, in the fourth year, is he promoted to being kitchen boy, and ultimately he becomes the first pastry cook. At the end of seven years the old woman orders him to pluck and roast a chicken while she goes out and to have it ready on her return. Whilst collecting herbs for the stuffing, Jacob catches sight of a cupboard that he has previously not noticed. The door is half open, and he is now ready for what he discovers. Inside he finds herbs that smell strongly like the soup he had been given by the old woman on his arrival in the house. The stalks and leaves are bluish green, the flower a bright red edged with yellow. The smell causes him to sneeze, and he wakes out of his dream thinking he has simply been asleep for a short while after eating the soup. He feels somewhat stiff and keeps bumping into the wall and furniture, but then leaves the house.

Jacob's seven years in the old woman's house correspond to an apprenticeship. The period of training that he undergoes and the consequent separation from his parents that he suffers reflect, in fairytale terms, what must have been in Hauff's time a common experience for children put into service or apprenticeship and thus severed from their families. The disagreeable old woman is a projection of all the fears that this kind of training must have held for children. She is the embodiment of the arbitrary power of the employer. She buys six heads of cabbage from Jacob's mother, but by the time they are in her house they have changed horrifyingly into human heads. In some way they symbolize the dislocation of mind and body that Jacob is about to experience. When the old woman first appears in the story, she is described in terms that immediately identify her as a witch:

> . . . an old woman approached; she was ragged and in tatters, had a small, thin face wrinkled with aged, red eyes, and a pointed, hooked nose which came down almost to her chin. She leaned on a long cane, and it was a wonder that she could walk at all, for she limped and slipped and wobbled; it was as if she had wheels in her legs, and would keel over at any moment, with her pointed nose hitting the pavement.

> (Orgel [**Dwarf Long-Nose**], 1979, p. 4)

This pattern is set in 'Jorinde und Joringel,' a story that the Grimms took from Heinrich Jung-Stilling's autobiography of 1777:

> Nun war die Sonne unter: die Eule flog in einen Strauch, und gleich darauf kam eine alte krumme Frau aus diesem hervor, gelb und mager, große rothe Augen, krumme Nase, die mit der Spitze ans Kinn reichte.

> (KHM [*Kinder- und Hausmärchen*], 1812/1986, p. 330)[1]

> (Now the sun had set: the owl flew into a bush, and immediately afterwards a bent old woman came out of it, yellow and scrawny, with large red eyes and a crooked nose whose tip reached to her chin.)

The detail of the wobbly head seems to come from 'Hänsel und Gretel' (KHM, 1812/1986, 55). There appears to be no parallel for the witch's wobbling gait as though she were on wheels. It is not until Jacob has reverted to human shape that the old crone is further identified: a 90-year-old woman in the town supposes she could have been the wicked fairy Kräuterweis (the name means 'herb-wise'), who visits the town once every 50 years to buy all kinds of things.

But what of Jacob? It seems appropriate enough that he is turned into the shape of a squirrel, since squirrels, constantly jumping around and running up and down trees, provide an apt image of the harassed, hurrying life of a domestic servant. The *Handwörterbuch des deutschen Aberglaubens* (II, p. 658)[2] tells us that squirrels are supposed to be bewitched human beings, and they suffer from epilepsy. However, Hauff may conceivably have had in mind the role of the squirrel in the old Scandinavian cosmogony, for with Yggdrasill, the World Ash, whose branches reach to heaven and whose roots stretch down to the Underworld, the squirrel takes messages running up and down between the two. Together with its fellow animal, the guinea pig, the squirrel is an animal that human beings are generally fond of, so the fact that Jacob is transformed into one is not as disquieting as it would be with certain other creatures such as the rat.

During his period in the witch's strange dwelling Jacob's life is not his own, but he receives a training that will later serve him in good stead. When, however, he reverts to human shape after seven years, it is a shape quite different from what he had as a 12-year-old boy. It takes some time for him to become aware of how changed he is. Only when both his mother and his father fail to recognize him and reject him as their son, regarding him as a charlatan, does he realize that he is a changed person. When he first makes his way back to his home and hears people everywhere shouting "Ugly dwarf!" he thinks there must be a dwarf in the vicinity, but he does not realize that he himself is the object of their derision.

Jacob's dissociated consciousness arises from the changes that have taken place in his body over the seven-year period of adolescence. Although he is now 19, his body is the stunted size of a 12-year-old's. He has not grown vertically, but rather horizontally, and his body is deformed:

> His eyes had become small, like a pig's, his nose was enormous, hanging down over his mouth and chin, and the neck seemed to have disappeared altogether; for his head stuck deep down in his shoulders, and only with the greatest pains could he move it right and left . . . his back and chest were widely distended and looked like a small but heavily filled sack. This thick trunk was supported by small, weak legs which didn't seem up to their burden; all the larger were the arms hanging from the body, as large as those of a well grown man. His hands were coarse and brownish-yellow, his fingers

long and spider-like, and when he stretched them to their full length he could reach down to the floor without bending. That is what he looked like—little Jacob had turned into a misshapen dwarf.

(**Orgel**, 1979, pp. 26-27)

It is significant that his body now incorporates features that come from the witch's physiognomy, as well as those of a 12-year-old boy, whose upward growth has been impeded.

However, the feature that is given the most prominence in all of Jacob's disfigurement is his nose. Significantly, it is Jacob's father who first draws his attention to it and suggests, smilingly, that he might get a leather case for it. Up to this point Jacob has been unaware of its size and only now discovers, by feeling it, that it is "thick and a good two hand-lengths long" (**Orgel**, 1979, p. 24). When he actually sees himself in the barber Urban's mirror, tears come into his eyes, and he understands why his mother was unable to recognize him. Jacob does not take up his father's suggestion of covering his nose with a leather case, but it is clear that his father is either embarrassed or otherwise disconcerted at this prominent feature of Jacob's appearance. Although the nose is the organ of smell and is important in the story for Jacob's success in the art of cooking, its disproportionate size and Jacob's father's suggestion that it should be covered up suggest that it serves as a displacement for the penis. The penis grows considerably with the onset of puberty, and in erection it is of course much bigger still. The process of adolescent growth and the development of adult sexual characteristics are often unsettling experiences for a boy, and what happens with Jacob is an extreme and exaggerated example of it. After his long period of enchantment at the hands of the witch, Jacob has wanted to return to his parents, but finds himself rejected, unrecognized, and inhabiting a body that is mocked by other people and that he himself finds difficulty in accepting as his own. In the witch's house he had companionship with the other animals, but needed ultimately to escape the negative mother figure that the witch represents. Now he has to work out his own salvation independently.

It is virtually impossible for us to know whether Hauff, in 1826, would consciously have made the equation of nose with penis, but it is possible. The *Handwörterbuch des deutschen Aberglaubens* (VI, 969-79) notes: "Big, shapeless noses are popularly called cucumbers and the penis is compared with them. Whoever has such a one 'hasn't gone short when noses were given out.'" Given that reference works of this kind, particularly those concerned with folklore, tend to reproduce historical material, we can fairly safely assume that this note will apply to the nineteenth century in general. Furthermore, Freud's *The Interpretation of Dreams* (1899/1991) states simply: 'Comparisons between nose and penis are com-

mon, and the similarity is made more complete by the presence of hair in both places' (pp. 509-510). Perhaps there are caricatures or comic verses extant that would document the equation at an earlier date.

There are other instances of exaggeratedly large noses in literary sources, but they do not appear to have sexual significance. Hans Sachs in his carnival play *Der doctor mit der grosen nasen* (*The Doctor with the Big Nose*, 1559) uses the large nose to satirize the pretentiousness of the eponymous doctor. His source was Johannes Pauli's *Schimpf und Ernst* (*Comedy and Seriousness*), an extremely popular collection of moral and comic tales that went into forty-nine editions between 1555 and 1597. The *Handwörterbuch des deutschen Aberglaubens* (VI, 969-79) confirms this particular view of the large nose in noting that "Der großmächtige / dickprächtige / langstrekkende / weitschmekkende Nasen Monarch: Mit seiner hochansehenlichen / breitberühmten naseweisen / vielnutzbaren Grossen Nasen" (the most mighty, splendiferous, far stretching, far smelling nose monarch with his most impressive, widely famed, know-all, most useful big nose) is much mocked in literary works and broadsheets of the sixteenth century.

However, during the period of Hauff's lifetime we have another instance of a long nose in the Grimms' tale *Die lange Nase* (*The Long Nose*), which was included only in the 1815 volume of the first edition and replaced by *Der Krautesel* (*The Donkey Cabbages*) from the second edition onward. The story focusses on three discharged soldiers who gain three magic gifts from a dwarf and lose them through the trickery of a princess. One of them then by chance discovers a tree with apples that cause whoever eats them to grow an immensely long nose. Next to this tree grows another with apples that cause the long nose to fall off. Through them the soldiers regain their magic gifts. When the first soldier eats the first apple, his nose grows so long that he cannot stand up; it continues to grow through the length of the forest and sixty miles further. The exaggeratedly long nose is the reward and sign of folly. The story is a version of the folktale *The Three Magic Objects and the Wonderful Fruits* (Aarne and Thompson, 1973, no. 566), in which more commonly the wonderful fruit causes the eater to grow horns. This is, of course, a common symbol for being cuckolded, so the sexual implication is clear. Whether the Grimms and their contemporary readers understood the hyperbolically long nose in a sexual sense we do not know. *Die lange Nase* was removed from the main text of the KHM after the first edition and a summary placed among the notes instead. The modern reader may well interpret the long nose in a priapic sense.

Back now to ***Dwarf Nose***. It is the training as a cook in the witch's house that provides Jacob with the means to progress. Despite being laughed at for his appearance, he gains a post in the duke's household as a cook—not as the ducal dwarf or fool that his grotesque appearance would perhaps have entitled him to. His skill eventually elicits admiration from the kitchen staff, the duke himself, and the people who see him making purchases at the market. After nearly two years he accidentally finds that one of the three geese he has purchased is Mimi, the bewitched daughter of the wizard Wetterbock. When Jacob faces his supreme test—the creation of the *pâté souzeraine*—it is Mimi who leads him to where he can pick the herb Niesmitlust that is its defining ingredient. The name Niesmitlust is perhaps another sexual allusion, this time to ejaculation and orgasm, that is, to sexual maturity. The herb, the same as that which disenchanted him from his squirrel shape, grows beneath chestnut trees. The location is significant, for the horse-chestnut was commonly carried in the trouser pocket as an amulet, protecting one against a whole slew of ailments from rheumatism, gout and apoplexy to rashes, erysipelas, fever, giddiness, toothache and haemorrhoids (*Handwörterbuch des deutschen Aberglaubens*, VII, 790-91). Niesmitlust, however, is not a botanically attested herb, but its occurrence in the vicinity of chestnut trees perhaps provides some hint of its extraordinary power. In Hauff's story it is sufficient to transform Jacob from a long-nosed dwarf into a tall and handsome young man, whose first reaction is to fold his hands and pray in thankfulness.

Jacob recognizes his debt to Mimi, with whom he escapes from the duke's palace, and takes her to her father, who disenchants her and provides Jacob with gifts that enable him to return home, be accepted, and reunited with his parents and buy a shop, which leads him to become rich and happy. If this story had followed the usual fairytale pattern, Jacob and Mimi would have married, and Jacob would have become a prince, but Hauff avoided the themes of sexual romance and marriage in all his fairytales, so the ending focusses solely on Jacob's material welfare on achieving adulthood. Mimi remains merely an episode in Jacob's extraordinary life.

Compared with a typical fairytale of the Grimms, **Dwarf Nose** is obviously much more complex. As Jacob makes the painful transition from carefree boyhood to successful, independent adulthood, his adolescence is depicted in two parts rather than one, first as an animal, then as a dwarf. The popularity of the tale over nearly two hundred years points to Hauff's success in depicting the traumas of adolescence in a convincing and gripping way. The disjunction between Jacob's feelings about himself and the reality of his distorted body reflects not only the physical changes that take place in adolescence but also the emotional ones. Of course one does not have to interpret the long nose as a displacement for the penis, but their visual similarity and the father's suggestion that the nose should be covered do point in that

direction. When Adam and Eve became aware of their nakedness after eating the fruit of the tree of the knowledge of good and evil, they made coverings to hide their sexual parts. Jacob does not do this, perhaps because he is still innocent, but his father's reaction is analogous to that of Adam. When Jacob is finally transformed, he must be about 21, the age of maturity. His adult life (not part of the fairytale) has yet to begin.

A version of this article was given as a paper at the British IBBY Conference in November 2001 at the University of Surrey Roehampton.

Notes

1. References to the first edition of the *Kinder- und Hausmärchen* (KHM) (1812-15) are to the two-volume reprint edited by Heinz Rölleke (Göttingen: Vandenhoeck & Ruprecht, 1986).

2. References are to volume and page.

References

Aarne, Antti, and Thompson, Stith, *The Types of the Folktale*, second revision. Helsinki: Suomalainen Tiedeakatemia, 1973.

Bächthold-Stäubli, Hanns, *Handwörterbuch des deutschen Aberglaubens*. Berlin and Leipzig, 1929-42.

Freud, Sigmund, *The Interpretation of Dreams*, translated by James Strachey. London: Penguin, 1991.

Grimm, Jacob, and Grimm, Wilhelm, *Kinder- und Hausmärchen. Vergrößerter Nachdruck der zweibändigen Erstausgabe von 1812 und 1815*, Heinz Rölleke, ed. Göttingen: Vandenhoeck & Ruprecht, 1986.

Hauff, Wilhelm, *Dwarf Long-Nose*. Translated by Doris Orgel. Illustrated by Maurice Sendak. London, Sydney, Toronto: The Bodley Head, 1979.

Hauff, Wilhelm, *Dwarf Nose*. Translated by Anthea Bell. Illustrated by Lisbeth Zwerger. New York and London: North-South Books, 1994.

Hauff, Wilhelm, *Little Long-Nose*, based on translations by Jean Rosemary Edwards and Percy E. Pinkerton. Illustrated by Laura Stoddart. London, Boston, Sydney: Walker Books, 1997.

Zipes, Jack, ed., *The Oxford Companion to Fairy Tales*. Oxford and New York: Oxford University Press, 2000, 229-30.

FURTHER READING

Criticism

Brenner, C. D. "The Influence of Cooper's *The Spy* on Hauff's *Lichtenstein*." *Modern Language Notes* 30, no. 7 (November 1915): 207-10.

Outlines the similarities between the two novels, focusing on Hauff's reliance on Cooper's hero, Harvey Birch, in creating the character of Pfeifer von Hardt.

Carruth, W. H. "The Relation of Hauff's *Lichtenstein* to Scott's *Waverley*." *PMLA* 18, no. 4 (1903): 513-25.
Provides an exhaustive analysis of Scott's influence on Hauff's novel, arguing that, contrary to the assertions of other scholars, the work owes a far greater debt to *Waverley* than to *Ivanhoe*.

Eastman, Clarence Willis. "Wilhelm Hauff's *Lichtenstein*." In *American Germanica,* vol. 3: 1900, pp. 386-92. New York: MacMillan, 1901.
Argues that Hauff based his novel primarily on Scott's *Ivanhoe*.

Hofacker, Erich P., Jr. "Wilhelm Hauff." In *German Writers in the Age of Goethe, 1789-1832,* edited by James N. Hardin and Christoph E. Schweitzer, pp. 120-27. Detroit: Gale Research, 1989.
Provides a general overview of Hauff's life and works, evaluating his influence on the development of German literary realism.

Kontje, Todd. "Male Fantasies, Female Readers: Fictions of the Nation in the Early Restoration." *German Quarterly* 68, no. 2 (spring 1995): 131-46.
Explores the aesthetic, commercial, and nationalistic concerns of Hauff's novella *Die letzten Ritter von Marienburg.*

Massey, Irving. "*Jud Süß*: Stereotype and Guilt." In *Philo-Semitism in Nineteenth-Century Literature,* pp. 63-6. Tübingen, Germany: Max Niemeyer Verlag, 2000.
Examines charges of anti-Semitism directed toward *Jud Süß* while evaluating Hauff's depictions of Jews in the story.

Additional coverage of Hauff's life and career is contained in the following sources published by Thomson Gale: *Dictionary of Literary Biography,* **Vol. 90;** *Literature Resource Center*; **and** *Supernatural Fiction Writers,* **Vol. 1.**

How to Use This Index

The main references

> **Calvino, Italo**
> 1923-1985 .... **CLC 5, 8, 11, 22, 33, 39,**
> **73; SSC 3, 48**

list all author entries in the following Thomson Gale Literary Criticism series:

AAL = *Asian American Literature*
BG = *The Beat Generation: A Gale Critical Companion*
BLC = *Black Literature Criticism*
BLCS = *Black Literature Criticism Supplement*
CLC = *Contemporary Literary Criticism*
CLR = *Children's Literature Review*
CMLC = *Classical and Medieval Literature Criticism*
DC = *Drama Criticism*
FL = *Feminism in Literature: A Gale Critical Companion*
GL = *Gothic Literature: A Gale Critical Companion*
HLC = *Hispanic Literature Criticism*
HLCS = *Hispanic Literature Criticism Supplement*
HR = *Harlem Renaissance: A Gale Critical Companion*
LC = *Literature Criticism from 1400 to 1800*
NCLC = *Nineteenth-Century Literature Criticism*
NNAL = *Native North American Literature*
PC = *Poetry Criticism*
SSC = *Short Story Criticism*
TCLC = *Twentieth-Century Literary Criticism*
WLC = *World Literature Criticism, 1500 to the Present*
WLCS = *World Literature Criticism Supplement*

The cross-references

> See also CA 85-88, 116; CANR 23, 61;
> DAM NOV; DLB 196; EW 13; MTCW 1, 2;
> RGSF 2; RGWL 2; SFW 4; SSFS 12

list all author entries in the following Thomson Gale biographical and literary sources:

AAYA = *Authors & Artists for Young Adults*
AFAW = *African American Writers*
AFW = *African Writers*
AITN = *Authors in the News*
AMW = *American Writers*
AMWR = *American Writers Retrospective Supplement*
AMWS = *American Writers Supplement*
ANW = *American Nature Writers*
AW = *Ancient Writers*
BEST = *Bestsellers*
BPFB = *Beacham's Encyclopedia of Popular Fiction: Biography and Resources*
BRW = *British Writers*
BRWS = *British Writers Supplement*
BW = *Black Writers*
BYA = *Beacham's Guide to Literature for Young Adults*
CA = *Contemporary Authors*
CAAS = *Contemporary Authors Autobiography Series*
CABS = *Contemporary Authors Bibliographical Series*
CAD = *Contemporary American Dramatists*
CANR = *Contemporary Authors New Revision Series*
CAP = *Contemporary Authors Permanent Series*
CBD = *Contemporary British Dramatists*
CCA = *Contemporary Canadian Authors*
CD = *Contemporary Dramatists*
CDALB = *Concise Dictionary of American Literary Biography*

CDALBS = *Concise Dictionary of American Literary Biography Supplement*
CDBLB = *Concise Dictionary of British Literary Biography*
CMW = *St. James Guide to Crime & Mystery Writers*
CN = *Contemporary Novelists*
CP = *Contemporary Poets*
CPW = *Contemporary Popular Writers*
CSW = *Contemporary Southern Writers*
CWD = *Contemporary Women Dramatists*
CWP = *Contemporary Women Poets*
CWRI = *St. James Guide to Children's Writers*
CWW = *Contemporary World Writers*
DA = *DISCovering Authors*
DA3 = *DISCovering Authors 3.0*
DAB = *DISCovering Authors: British Edition*
DAC = *DISCovering Authors: Canadian Edition*
DAM = *DISCovering Authors: Modules*
   DRAM: *Dramatists Module;* **MST:** *Most-studied Authors Module;*
   MULT: *Multicultural Authors Module;* **NOV:** *Novelists Module;*
   POET: *Poets Module;* **POP:** *Popular Fiction and Genre Authors Module*
DFS = *Drama for Students*
DLB = *Dictionary of Literary Biography*
DLBD = *Dictionary of Literary Biography Documentary Series*
DLBY = *Dictionary of Literary Biography Yearbook*
DNFS = *Literature of Developing Nations for Students*
EFS = *Epics for Students*
EXPN = *Exploring Novels*
EXPP = *Exploring Poetry*
EXPS = *Exploring Short Stories*
EW = *European Writers*
FANT = *St. James Guide to Fantasy Writers*
FW = *Feminist Writers*
GFL = *Guide to French Literature,* Beginnings to 1789, 1798 to the Present
GLL = *Gay and Lesbian Literature*
HGG = *St. James Guide to Horror, Ghost & Gothic Writers*
HW = *Hispanic Writers*
IDFW = *International Dictionary of Films and Filmmakers: Writers and Production Artists*
IDTP = *International Dictionary of Theatre: Playwrights*
LAIT = *Literature and Its Times*
LAW = *Latin American Writers*
JRDA = *Junior DISCovering Authors*
MAICYA = *Major Authors and Illustrators for Children and Young Adults*
MAICYAS = *Major Authors and Illustrators for Children and Young Adults Supplement*
MAWW = *Modern American Women Writers*
MJW = *Modern Japanese Writers*
MTCW = *Major 20th-Century Writers*
NCFS = *Nonfiction Classics for Students*
NFS = *Novels for Students*
PAB = *Poets: American and British*
PFS = *Poetry for Students*
RGAL = *Reference Guide to American Literature*
RGEL = *Reference Guide to English Literature*
RGSF = *Reference Guide to Short Fiction*
RGWL = *Reference Guide to World Literature*
RHW = *Twentieth-Century Romance and Historical Writers*
SAAS = *Something about the Author Autobiography Series*
SATA = *Something about the Author*
SFW = *St. James Guide to Science Fiction Writers*
SSFS = *Short Stories for Students*
TCWW = *Twentieth-Century Western Writers*
WLIT = *World Literature and Its Times*
WP = *World Poets*
YABC = *Yesterday's Authors of Books for Children*
YAW = *St. James Guide to Young Adult Writers*

Literary Criticism Series
Cumulative Author Index

Aeschylus 525(?)B.C.-456(?)B.C. .. **CMLC 11, 51; DC 8; WLCS**
See also AW 1; CDWLB 1; DA; DAB; DAC; DAM DRAM, MST; DFS 5, 10; DLB 176; LMFS 1; RGWL 2, 3; TWA; WLIT 8

Aesop 620(?)B.C.-560(?)B.C. .... **CMLC 24**
See also CLR 14; MAICYA 1, 2; SATA 64

Affable Hawk
See MacCarthy, Sir (Charles Otto) Desmond

Africa, Ben
See Bosman, Herman Charles

Afton, Effie
See Harper, Frances Ellen Watkins

Agapida, Fray Antonio
See Irving, Washington

Agee, James (Rufus) 1909-1955 ...... **TCLC 1, 19, 180**
See also AAYA 44; AITN 1; AMW; CA 148; CAAE 108; CANR 131; CDALB 1941-1968; DAM NOV; DLB 2, 26, 152; DLBY 1989; EWL 3; LAIT 3; LATS 1:2; MAL 5; MTCW 2; MTFW 2005; NFS 22; RGAL 4; TUS

A Gentlewoman in New England
See Bradstreet, Anne

A Gentlewoman in Those Parts
See Bradstreet, Anne

Aghill, Gordon
See Silverberg, Robert

Agnon, S(hmuel) Y(osef Halevi) 1888-1970 .... **CLC 4, 8, 14; SSC 30; TCLC 151**
See also CA 17-18; CAAS 25-28R; CANR 60, 102; CAP 2; DLB 329; EWL 3; MTCW 1, 2; RGHL; RGSF 2; RGWL 2, 3; WLIT 6

Agrippa von Nettesheim, Henry Cornelius 1486-1535 .... **LC 27**

Aguilera Malta, Demetrio 1909-1981 .... **HLCS 1**
See also CA 124; CAAE 111; CANR 87; DAM MULT, NOV; DLB 145; EWL 3; HW 1; RGWL 3

Agustini, Delmira 1886-1914 .... **HLCS 1**
See also CA 166; DLB 290; HW 1, 2; LAW

Aherne, Owen
See Cassill, R(onald) V(erlin)

Ai 1947- .... **CLC 4, 14, 69; PC 72**
See also CA 85-88; 13; CANR 70; CP 6, 7; DLB 120; PFS 16

Aickman, Robert (Fordyce) 1914-1981 .... **CLC 57**
See also CA 5-8R; CANR 3, 72, 100; DLB 261; HGG; SUFW 1, 2

Aidoo, (Christina) Ama Ata 1942- .... **BLCS; CLC 177**
See also AFW; BW 1; CA 101; CANR 62, 144; CD 5, 6; CDWLB 3; CN 6, 7; CWD; CWP; DLB 117; DNFS 1, 2; EWL 3; FW; WLIT 2

Aiken, Conrad (Potter) 1889-1973 .... **CLC 1, 3, 5, 10, 52; PC 26; SSC 9**
See also AMW; CA 5-8R; CAAS 45-48; CANR 4, 60; CDALB 1929-1941; CN 1; CP 1; DAM NOV, POET; DLB 9, 45, 102; EWL 3; EXPS; HGG; MAL 5; MTCW 1, 2; MTFW 2005; PFS 24; RGAL 4; RGSF 2; SATA 3, 30; SSFS 8; TUS

Aiken, Joan (Delano) 1924-2004 ...... **CLC 35**
See also AAYA 1, 25; CA 182; 9-12R, 182; CAAS 223; CANR 4, 23, 34, 64, 121; CLR 1, 19, 90; DLB 161; FANT; HGG; JRDA; MAICYA 1, 2; MTCW 1; RHW; SAAS 1; SATA 2, 30, 73; SATA-Essay 109; SATA-Obit 152; SUFW 2; WYA; YAW

Ainsworth, William Harrison 1805-1882 .... **NCLC 13**
See also DLB 21; HGG; RGEL 2; SATA 24; SUFW 1

Aitmatov, Chingiz (Torekulovich) 1928- .... **CLC 71**
See Aytmatov, Chingiz
See also CA 103; CANR 38; CWW 2; DLB 302; MTCW 1; RGSF 2; SATA 56

Akers, Floyd
See Baum, L(yman) Frank

Akhmadulina, Bella Akhatovna 1937- .... **CLC 53; PC 43**
See also CA 65-68; CWP; CWW 2; DAM POET; EWL 3

Akhmatova, Anna 1888-1966 ..... **CLC 11, 25, 64, 126; PC 2, 55**
See also CA 19-20; CAAS 25-28R; CANR 35; CAP 1; DA3; DAM POET; DLB 295; EW 10; EWL 3; FL 1:5; MTCW 1, 2; PFS 18; RGWL 2, 3

Aksakov, Sergei Timofeevich 1791-1859 .... **NCLC 2, 181**
See also DLB 198

Aksenov, Vasilii (Pavlovich)
See Aksyonov, Vassily (Pavlovich)
See also CWW 2

Aksenov, Vassily
See Aksyonov, Vassily (Pavlovich)

Akst, Daniel 1956- .... **CLC 109**
See also CA 161; CANR 110

Aksyonov, Vassily (Pavlovich) 1932- .... **CLC 22, 37, 101**
See Aksenov, Vasilii (Pavlovich)
See also CA 53-56; CANR 12, 48, 77; DLB 302; EWL 3

Akutagawa Ryunosuke 1892-1927 ... **SSC 44; TCLC 16**
See also CA 154; CAAE 117; DLB 180; EWL 3; MJW; RGSF 2; RGWL 2, 3

Alabaster, William 1568-1640 .... **LC 90**
See also DLB 132; RGEL 2

Alain 1868-1951 .... **TCLC 41**
See also CA 163; EWL 3; GFL 1789 to the Present

Alain de Lille c. 1116-c. 1203 .... **CMLC 53**
See also DLB 208

Alain-Fournier .... **TCLC 6**
See Fournier, Henri-Alban
See also DLB 65; EWL 3; GFL 1789 to the Present; RGWL 2, 3

Al-Amin, Jamil Abdullah 1943- .... **BLC 1**
See also BW 1, 3; CA 125; CAAE 112; CANR 82; DAM MULT

Alanus de Insluis
See Alain de Lille

Alarcon, Pedro Antonio de 1833-1891 .... **NCLC 1; SSC 64**

Alas (y Urena), Leopoldo (Enrique Garcia) 1852-1901 .... **TCLC 29**
See also CA 131; CAAE 113; HW 1; RGSF 2

Albee, Edward (III) 1928- ..... **CLC 1, 2, 3, 5, 9, 11, 13, 25, 53, 86, 113; DC 11; WLC 1**
See also AAYA 51; AITN 1; AMW; CA 5-8R; CABS 3; CAD; CANR 8, 54, 74, 124; CD 5, 6; CDALB 1941-1968; DA; DA3; DAB; DAC; DAM DRAM, MST; DFS 2, 3, 8, 10, 13, 14; DLB 7, 266; EWL 3; INT CANR-8; LAIT 4; LMFS 2; MAL 5; MTCW 1, 2; MTFW 2005; RGAL 4; TUS

Alberti (Merello), Rafael
See Alberti, Rafael
See also CWW 2

Alberti, Rafael 1902-1999 .... **CLC 7**
See Alberti (Merello), Rafael
See also CA 85-88; CAAS 185; CANR 81; DLB 108; EWL 3; HW 2; RGWL 2, 3

Albert the Great 1193(?)-1280 ...... **CMLC 16**
See also DLB 115

Alcaeus c. 620B.C.- .... **CMLC 65**
See also DLB 176

Alcala-Galiano, Juan Valera y
See Valera y Alcala-Galiano, Juan

Alcayaga, Lucila Godoy
See Godoy Alcayaga, Lucila

Alciato, Andrea 1492-1550 .... **LC 116**

Alcott, Amos Bronson 1799-1888 ... **NCLC 1, 167**
See also DLB 1, 223

Alcott, Louisa May 1832-1888 . **NCLC 6, 58, 83; SSC 27, 98; WLC 1**
See also AAYA 20; AMWS 1; BPFB 1; BYA 2; CDALB 1865-1917; CLR 1, 38, 109; DA; DA3; DAB; DAC; DAM MST, NOV; DLB 1, 42, 79, 223, 239, 242; DLBD 14; FL 1:2; FW; JRDA; LAIT 2; MAICYA 1, 2; NFS 12; RGAL 4; SATA 100; TUS; WCH; WYA; YABC 1; YAW

Alcuin c. 730-804 .... **CMLC 69**
See also DLB 148

Aldanov, M. A.
See Aldanov, Mark (Alexandrovich)

Aldanov, Mark (Alexandrovich) 1886-1957 .... **TCLC 23**
See also CA 181; CAAE 118; DLB 317

Aldhelm c. 639-709 .... **CMLC 90**

Aldington, Richard 1892-1962 .... **CLC 49**
See also CA 85-88; CANR 45; DLB 20, 36, 100, 149; LMFS 2; RGEL 2

Aldiss, Brian W. 1925- .. **CLC 5, 14, 40; SSC 36**
See also AAYA 42; CA 190; 5-8R, 190; 2; CANR 5, 28, 64, 121; CN 1, 2, 3, 4, 5, 6, 7; DAM NOV; DLB 14, 261, 271; MTCW 1, 2; MTFW 2005; SATA 34; SCFW 1, 2; SFW 4

Aldrich, Bess Streeter 1881-1954 .... **TCLC 125**
See also CLR 70; TCWW 2

Alegria, Claribel
See Alegria, Claribel
See also CWW 2; DLB 145, 283

Alegria, Claribel 1924- .... **CLC 75; HLCS 1; PC 26**
See Alegria, Claribel
See also CA 131; 15; CANR 66, 94, 134; DAM MULT; EWL 3; HW 1; MTCW 2; MTFW 2005; PFS 21

Alegria, Fernando 1918-2005 .... **CLC 57**
See also CA 9-12R; CANR 5, 32, 72; EWL 3; HW 1, 2

Aleixandre, Vicente 1898-1984 .... **HLCS 1; TCLC 113**
See also CANR 81; DLB 108, 329; EWL 3; HW 2; MTCW 1, 2; RGWL 2, 3

Alekseev, Konstantin Sergeivich
See Stanislavsky, Constantin

Alekseyer, Konstantin Sergeyevich
See Stanislavsky, Constantin

Aleman, Mateo 1547-1615(?) .... **LC 81**

Alencar, Jose de 1829-1877 .... **NCLC 157**
See also DLB 307; LAW; WLIT 1

Alencon, Marguerite d'
See de Navarre, Marguerite

Alepoudelis, Odysseus
See Elytis, Odysseus
See also CWW 2

Aleshkovsky, Joseph 1929-
See Aleshkovsky, Yuz
See also CA 128; CAAE 121

Aleshkovsky, Yuz .... **CLC 44**
See Aleshkovsky, Joseph
See also DLB 317

Alexander, Lloyd 1924-2007 .... **CLC 35**
See also AAYA 1, 27; BPFB 1; BYA 5, 6,
7, 9, 10, 11; CA 1-4R; CANR 1, 24, 38,
55, 113; CLR 1, 5, 48; CWRI 5; DLB 52;
FANT; JRDA; MAICYA 1, 2; MAICYAS
1; MTCW 1; SAAS 19; SATA 3, 49, 81,
129, 135; SUFW; TUS; WYA; YAW

Alexander, Lloyd Chudley
See Alexander, Lloyd

Alexander, Meena 1951- .... **CLC 121**
See also CA 115; CANR 38, 70, 146; CP 5,
6, 7; CWP; DLB 323; FW

Alexander, Samuel 1859-1938 .... **TCLC 77**

Alexeiev, Konstantin
See Stanislavsky, Constantin

Alexeyev, Constantin Sergeivich
See Stanislavsky, Constantin

Alexeyev, Konstantin Sergeyevich
See Stanislavsky, Constantin

Alexie, Sherman 1966- .... **CLC 96, 154;**
NNAL; PC 53
See also AAYA 28; BYA 15; CA 138;
CANR 65, 95, 133; CN 7; DA3; DAM
MULT; DLB 175, 206, 278; LATS 1:2;
MTCW 2; MTFW 2005; NFS 17; SSFS
18

al-Farabi 870(?)-950 .... **CMLC 58**
See also DLB 115

Alfau, Felipe 1902-1999 .... **CLC 66**
See also CA 137

Alfieri, Vittorio 1749-1803 .... **NCLC 101**
See also EW 4; RGWL 2, 3; WLIT 7

Alfonso X 1221-1284 .... **CMLC 78**

Alfred, Jean Gaston
See Ponge, Francis

Alger, Horatio, Jr. 1832-1899 .... **NCLC 8, 83**
See also CLR 87; DLB 42; LAIT 2; RGAL
4; SATA 16; TUS

Al-Ghazali, Muhammad ibn Muhammad
1058-1111 .... **CMLC 50**
See also DLB 115

Algren, Nelson 1909-1981 ..... **CLC 4, 10, 33;**
SSC 33
See also AMWS 9; BPFB 1; CA 13-16R;
CAAS 103; CANR 20, 61; CDALB 1941-
1968; CN 1, 2; DLB 9; DLBY 1981,
1982, 2000; EWL 3; MAL 5; MTCW 1,
2; MTFW 2005; RGAL 4; RGSF 2

al-Hariri, al-Qasim ibn 'Ali Abu
Muhammad al-Basri
1054-1122 .... **CMLC 63**
See also RGWL 3

Ali, Ahmed 1908-1998 .... **CLC 69**
See also CA 25-28R; CANR 15, 34; CN 1,
2, 3, 4, 5; DLB 323; EWL 3

Ali, Tariq 1943- .... **CLC 173**
See also CA 25-28R; CANR 10, 99, 161

Alighieri, Dante
See Dante
See also WLIT 7

al-Kindi, Abu Yusuf Ya'qub ibn Ishaq c.
801-c. 873 .... **CMLC 80**

Allan, John B.
See Westlake, Donald E.

Allan, Sidney
See Hartmann, Sadakichi

Allan, Sydney
See Hartmann, Sadakichi

Allard, Janet .... **CLC 59**

Allen, Edward 1948- .... **CLC 59**

Allen, Fred 1894-1956 .... **TCLC 87**

Allen, Paula Gunn 1939- .... **CLC 84, 202;**
NNAL
See also AMWS 4; CA 143; CAAE 112;
CANR 63, 130; CWP; DA3; DAM
MULT; DLB 175; FW; MTCW 2; MTFW
2005; RGAL 4; TCWW 2

Allen, Roland
See Ayckbourn, Alan

Allen, Sarah A.
See Hopkins, Pauline Elizabeth

Allen, Sidney H.
See Hartmann, Sadakichi

Allen, Woody 1935- .... **CLC 16, 52, 195**
See also AAYA 10, 51; AMWS 15; CA 33-
36R; CANR 27, 38, 63, 128; DAM POP;
DLB 44; MTCW 1; SSFS 21

Allende, Isabel 1942- ... **CLC 39, 57, 97, 170;**
HLC 1; SSC 65; WLCS
See also AAYA 18, 70; CA 130; CAAE 125;
CANR 51, 74, 129; CDWLB 3; CLR 99;
CWW 2; DA3; DAM MULT, NOV; DLB
145; DNFS 1; EWL 3; FL 1:5; FW; HW
1, 2; INT CA-130; LAIT 5; LAWS 1;
LMFS 2; MTCW 1, 2; MTFW 2005;
NCFS 1; NFS 6, 18; RGSF 2; RGWL 3;
SATA 163; SSFS 11, 16; WLIT 1

Alleyn, Ellen
See Rossetti, Christina

Alleyne, Carla D. .... **CLC 65**

Allingham, Margery (Louise)
1904-1966 .... **CLC 19**
See also CA 5-8R; CAAS 25-28R; CANR
4, 58; CMW 4; DLB 77; MSW; MTCW
1, 2

Allingham, William 1824-1889 ...... **NCLC 25**
See also DLB 35; RGEL 2

Allison, Dorothy E. 1949- .... **CLC 78, 153**
See also AAYA 53; CA 140; CANR 66, 107;
CN 7; CSW; DA3; FW; MTCW 2; MTFW
2005; NFS 11; RGAL 4

Alloula, Malek .... **CLC 65**

Allston, Washington 1779-1843 .... **NCLC 2**
See also DLB 1, 235

Almedingen, E. M. .... **CLC 12**
See Almedingen, Martha Edith von
See also SATA 3

Almedingen, Martha Edith von 1898-1971
See Almedingen, E. M.
See also CA 1-4R; CANR 1

Almodovar, Pedro 1949(?)- .... **CLC 114, 229;**
HLCS 1
See also CA 133; CANR 72, 151; HW 2

Almqvist, Carl Jonas Love
1793-1866 .... **NCLC 42**

al-Mutanabbi, Ahmad ibn al-Husayn Abu
al-Tayyib al-Jufi al-Kindi
915-965 .... **CMLC 66**
See Mutanabbi, Al-
See also RGWL 3

Alonso, Damaso 1898-1990 .... **CLC 14**
See also CA 131; CAAE 110; CAAS 130;
CANR 72; DLB 108; EWL 3; HW 1, 2

Alov
See Gogol, Nikolai (Vasilyevich)

al'Sadaawi, Nawal
See El Saadawi, Nawal
See also FW

al-Shaykh, Hanan 1945- .... **CLC 218**
See Shaykh, al- Hanan
See also CA 135; CANR 111; WLIT 6

Al Siddik
See Rolfe, Frederick (William Serafino Aus-
tin Lewis Mary)
See also GLL 1; RGEL 2

Alta 1942- .... **CLC 19**
See also CA 57-60

Alter, Robert B. 1935- .... **CLC 34**
See also CA 49-52; CANR 1, 47, 100, 160

Alter, Robert Bernard
See Alter, Robert B.

Alther, Lisa 1944- .... **CLC 7, 41**
See also BPFB 1; CA 65-68; 30; CANR 12,
30, 51; CN 4, 5, 6, 7; CSW; GLL 2;
MTCW 1

Althusser, L.
See Althusser, Louis

Althusser, Louis 1918-1990 .... **CLC 106**
See also CA 131; CAAS 132; CANR 102;
DLB 242

Altman, Robert 1925-2006 .... **CLC 16, 116**
See also CA 73-76; CAAS 254; CANR 43

Alurista .... **HLCS 1; PC 34**
See Urista (Heredia), Alberto (Baltazar)
See also CA 45-48R; DLB 82; LLW

Alvarez, A. 1929- .... **CLC 5, 13**
See also CA 1-4R; CANR 3, 33, 63, 101,
134; CN 3, 4, 5, 6; CP 1, 2, 3, 4, 5, 6, 7;
DLB 14, 40; MTFW 2005

Alvarez, Alejandro Rodriguez 1903-1965
See Casona, Alejandro
See also CA 131; CAAS 93-96; HW 1

Alvarez, Julia 1950- .... **CLC 93; HLCS 1**
See also AAYA 25; AMWS 7; CA 147;
CANR 69, 101, 133; DA3; DLB 282;
LATS 1:2; LLW; MTCW 2; MTFW 2005;
NFS 5, 9; SATA 129; WLIT 1

Alvaro, Corrado 1896-1956 .... **TCLC 60**
See also CA 163; DLB 264; EWL 3

Amado, Jorge 1912-2001 ... **CLC 13, 40, 106,**
232; HLC 1
See also CA 77-80; CAAS 201; CANR 35,
74, 135; CWW 2; DAM MULT, NOV;
DLB 113, 307; EWL 3; HW 2; LAW;
LAWS 1; MTCW 1, 2; MTFW 2005;
RGWL 2, 3; TWA; WLIT 1

Ambler, Eric 1909-1998 .... **CLC 4, 6, 9**
See also BRWS 4; CA 9-12R; CAAS 171;
CANR 7, 38, 74; CMW 4; CN 1, 2, 3, 4,
5, 6; DLB 77; MSW; MTCW 1, 2; TEA

Ambrose, Stephen E. 1936-2002 .... **CLC 145**
See also AAYA 44; CA 1-4R; CAAS 209;
CANR 3, 43, 57, 83, 105; MTFW 2005;
NCFS 2; SATA 40, 138

Amichai, Yehuda 1924-2000 .. **CLC 9, 22, 57,**
116; PC 38
See also CA 85-88; CAAS 189; CANR 46,
60, 99, 132; CWW 2; EWL 3; MTCW 1,
2; MTFW 2005; PFS 24; RGHL; WLIT 6

Amichai, Yehudah
See Amichai, Yehuda

Amiel, Henri Frederic 1821-1881 .... **NCLC 4**
See also DLB 217

Amis, Kingsley 1922-1995 . **CLC 1, 2, 3, 5, 8,**
13, 40, 44, 129
See also AITN 2; BPFB 1; BRWS 2; CA
9-12R; CAAS 150; CANR 8, 28, 54; CD-
BLB 1945-1960; CN 1, 2, 3, 4, 5, 6; CP
1, 2, 3, 4; DA; DA3; DAB; DAC; DAM
MST, NOV; DLB 15, 27, 100, 139, 326;
DLBY 1996; EWL 3; HGG; INT
CANR-8; MTCW 1, 2; MTFW 2005;
RGEL 2; RGSF 2; SFW 4

Amis, Martin 1949- ... **CLC 4, 9, 38, 62, 101,**
213
See also BEST 90:3; BRWS 4; CA 65-68;
CANR 8, 27, 54, 73, 95, 132; CN 5, 6, 7;
DA3; DLB 14, 194; EWL 3; INT CANR-
27; MTCW 2; MTFW 2005

Ammianus Marcellinus c. 330-c.
395 .... **CMLC 60**
See also AW 2; DLB 211

Ammons, A.R. 1926-2001 .. **CLC 2, 3, 5, 8, 9,**
25, 57, 108; PC 16
See also AITN 1; AMWS 7; CA 9-12R;
CAAS 193; CANR 6, 36, 51, 73, 107,
156; CP 1, 2, 3, 4, 5, 6, 7; CSW; DAM
POET; DLB 5, 165; EWL 3; MAL 5;
MTCW 1, 2; PFS 19; RGAL 4; TCLE 1:1

Ammons, Archie Randolph
See Ammons, A.R.
Amo, Tauraatua i
See Adams, Henry (Brooks)
Amory, Thomas 1691(?)-1788 .... **LC 48**
See also DLB 39
Anand, Mulk Raj 1905-2004 ..... **CLC 23, 93, 237**
See also CA 65-68; CAAS 231; CANR 32, 64; CN 1, 2, 3, 4, 5, 6, 7; DAM NOV; DLB 323; EWL 3; MTCW 1, 2; MTFW 2005; RGSF 2
Anatol
See Schnitzler, Arthur
Anaximander c. 611B.C.-c. 546B.C. .... **CMLC 22**
Anaya, Rudolfo A. 1937- .... **CLC 23, 148; HLC 1**
See also AAYA 20; BYA 13; CA 45-48; 4; CANR 1, 32, 51, 124; CN 4, 5, 6, 7; DAM MULT, NOV; DLB 82, 206, 278; HW 1; LAIT 4; LLW; MAL 5; MTCW 1, 2; MTFW 2005; NFS 12; RGAL 4; RGSF 2; TCWW 2; WLIT 1
Andersen, Hans Christian 1805-1875 .... **NCLC 7, 79; SSC 6, 56; WLC 1**
See also AAYA 57; CLR 6, 113; DA; DA3; DAB; DAC; DAM MST, POP; EW 6; MAICYA 1, 2; RGSF 2; RGWL 2, 3; SATA 100; TWA; WCH; YABC 1
Anderson, C. Farley
See Mencken, H(enry) L(ouis); Nathan, George Jean
Anderson, Jessica (Margaret) Queale 1916- .... **CLC 37**
See also CA 9-12R; CANR 4, 62; CN 4, 5, 6, 7; DLB 325
Anderson, Jon (Victor) 1940- .... **CLC 9**
See also CA 25-28R; CANR 20; CP 1, 3, 4, 5; DAM POET
Anderson, Lindsay (Gordon) 1923-1994 .... **CLC 20**
See also CA 128; CAAE 125; CAAS 146; CANR 77
Anderson, Maxwell 1888-1959 .... **TCLC 2, 144**
See also CA 152; CAAE 105; DAM DRAM; DFS 16, 20; DLB 7, 228; MAL 5; MTCW 2; MTFW 2005; RGAL 4
Anderson, Poul 1926-2001 .... **CLC 15**
See also AAYA 5, 34; BPFB 1; BYA 6, 8, 9; CA 181; 1-4R, 181; 2; CAAS 199; CANR 2, 15, 34, 64, 110; CLR 58; DLB 8; FANT; INT CANR-15; MTCW 1, 2; MTFW 2005; SATA 90; SATA-Brief 39; SATA-Essay 106; SCFW 1, 2; SFW 4; SUFW 1, 2
Anderson, Robert (Woodruff) 1917- .... **CLC 23**
See also AITN 1; CA 21-24R; CANR 32; CD 6; DAM DRAM; DLB 7; LAIT 5
Anderson, Roberta Joan
See Mitchell, Joni
Anderson, Sherwood 1876-1941 ... **SSC 1, 46, 91; TCLC 1, 10, 24, 123; WLC 1**
See also AAYA 30; AMW; AMWC 2; BPFB 1; CAAE 104; CA 121; CANR 61; CDALB 1917-1929; DA; DA3; DAB; DAC; DAM MST, NOV; DLB 4, 9, 86; DLBD 1; EWL 3; EXPS; GLL 2; MAL 5; MTCW 1, 2; MTFW 2005; NFS 4; RGAL 4; RGSF 2; SSFS 4, 10, 11; TUS
Anderson, Wes 1969- .... **CLC 227**
See also CA 214
Andier, Pierre
See Desnos, Robert
Andouard
See Giraudoux, Jean(-Hippolyte)

Andrade, Carlos Drummond de ..... **CLC 18**
See Drummond de Andrade, Carlos
See also EWL 3; RGWL 2, 3
Andrade, Mario de .... **TCLC 43**
See de Andrade, Mario
See also DLB 307; EWL 3; LAW; RGWL 2, 3; WLIT 1
Andreae, Johann V(alentin) 1586-1654 .... **LC 32**
See also DLB 164
Andreas Capellanus fl. c. 1185- .... **CMLC 45**
See also DLB 208
Andreas-Salome, Lou 1861-1937 ... **TCLC 56**
See also CA 178; DLB 66
Andreev, Leonid
See Andreyev, Leonid (Nikolaevich)
See also DLB 295; EWL 3
Andress, Lesley
See Sanders, Lawrence
Andrewes, Lancelot 1555-1626 .... **LC 5**
See also DLB 151, 172
Andrews, Cicily Fairfield
See West, Rebecca
Andrews, Elton V.
See Pohl, Frederik
Andrews, Peter
See Soderbergh, Steven
Andreyev, Leonid (Nikolaevich) 1871-1919 .... **TCLC 3**
See Andreev, Leonid
See also CA 185; CAAE 104
Andric, Ivo 1892-1975 .... **CLC 8; SSC 36; TCLC 135**
See also CA 81-84; CAAS 57-60; CANR 43, 60; CDWLB 4; DLB 147, 329; EW 11; EWL 3; MTCW 1; RGSF 2; RGWL 2, 3
Androvar
See Prado (Calvo), Pedro
Angela of Foligno 1248(?)-1309 .... **CMLC 76**
Angelique, Pierre
See Bataille, Georges
Angell, Roger 1920- .... **CLC 26**
See also CA 57-60; CANR 13, 44, 70, 144; DLB 171, 185
Angelou, Maya 1928- ... **BLC 1; CLC 12, 35, 64, 77, 155; PC 32; WLCS**
See also AAYA 7, 20; AMWS 4; BPFB 1; BW 2, 3; BYA 2; CA 65-68; CANR 19, 42, 65, 111, 133; CDALBS; CLR 53; CP 4, 5, 6, 7; CPW; CSW; CWP; DA; DA3; DAB; DAC; DAM MST, MULT, POET, POP; DLB 38; EWL 3; EXPN; EXPP; FL 1:5; LAIT 4; MAICYA 2; MAICYAS 1; MAL 5; MBL; MTCW 1, 2; MTFW 2005; NCFS 2; NFS 2; PFS 2, 3; RGAL 4; SATA 49, 136; TCLE 1:1; WYA; YAW
Angouleme, Marguerite d'
See de Navarre, Marguerite
Anna Comnena 1083-1153 .... **CMLC 25**
Annensky, Innokentii Fedorovich
See Annensky, Innokenty (Fyodorovich)
See also DLB 295
Annensky, Innokenty (Fyodorovich) 1856-1909 .... **TCLC 14**
See also CA 155; CAAE 110; EWL 3
Annunzio, Gabriele d'
See D'Annunzio, Gabriele
Anodos
See Coleridge, Mary E(lizabeth)
Anon, Charles Robert
See Pessoa, Fernando (Antonio Nogueira)
Anouilh, Jean 1910-1987 ..... **CLC 1, 3, 8, 13, 40, 50; DC 8, 21**
See also AAYA 67; CA 17-20R; CAAS 123; CANR 32; DAM DRAM; DFS 9, 10, 19; DLB 321; EW 13; EWL 3; GFL 1789 to the Present; MTCW 1, 2; MTFW 2005; RGWL 2, 3; TWA

Anselm of Canterbury 1033(?)-1109 .... **CMLC 67**
See also DLB 115
Anthony, Florence
See Ai
Anthony, John
See Ciardi, John (Anthony)
Anthony, Peter
See Shaffer, Anthony; Shaffer, Peter
Anthony, Piers 1934- .... **CLC 35**
See also AAYA 11, 48; BYA 7; CA 200; 200; CANR 28, 56, 73, 102, 133; CLR 118; CPW; DAM POP; DLB 8; FANT; MAICYA 2; MAICYAS 1; MTCW 1, 2; MTFW 2005; SAAS 22; SATA 84, 129; SATA-Essay 129; SFW 4; SUFW 1, 2; YAW
Anthony, Susan B(rownell) 1820-1906 .... **TCLC 84**
See also CA 211; FW
Antiphon c. 480B.C.-c. 411B.C. .... **CMLC 55**
Antoine, Marc
See Proust, (Valentin-Louis-George-Eugene) Marcel
Antoninus, Brother
See Everson, William (Oliver)
See also CP 1
Antonioni, Michelangelo 1912- .... **CLC 20, 144**
See also CA 73-76; CANR 45, 77
Antschel, Paul 1920-1970
See Celan, Paul
See also CA 85-88; CANR 33, 61; MTCW 1; PFS 21
Anwar, Chairil 1922-1949 .... **TCLC 22**
See Chairil Anwar
See also CA 219; CAAE 121; RGWL 3
Anzaldua, Gloria (Evanjelina) 1942-2004 .... **CLC 200; HLCS 1**
See also CA 175; CAAS 227; CSW; CWP; DLB 122; FW; LLW; RGAL 4; SATA-Obit 154
Apess, William 1798-1839(?) .... **NCLC 73; NNAL**
See also DAM MULT; DLB 175, 243
Apollinaire, Guillaume 1880-1918 .... **PC 7; TCLC 3, 8, 51**
See Kostrowitzki, Wilhelm Apollinaris de
See also CA 152; DAM POET; DLB 258, 321; EW 9; EWL 3; GFL 1789 to the Present; MTCW 2; PFS 24; RGWL 2, 3; TWA; WP
Apollonius of Rhodes
See Apollonius Rhodius
See also AW 1; RGWL 2, 3
Apollonius Rhodius c. 300B.C.-c. 220B.C. .... **CMLC 28**
See Apollonius of Rhodes
See also DLB 176
Appelfeld, Aharon 1932- ... **CLC 23, 47; SSC 42**
See also CA 133; CAAE 112; CANR 86, 160; CWW 2; DLB 299; EWL 3; RGHL; RGSF 2; WLIT 6
Appelfeld, Aron
See Appelfeld, Aharon
Apple, Max (Isaac) 1941- .... **CLC 9, 33; SSC 50**
See also CA 81-84; CANR 19, 54; DLB 130
Appleman, Philip (Dean) 1926- .... **CLC 51**
See also CA 13-16R; 18; CANR 6, 29, 56
Appleton, Lawrence
See Lovecraft, H. P.
Apteryx
See Eliot, T(homas) S(tearns)

Barnes, Jim 1933- .... **NNAL**
See also CA 175; 108, 175; 28; DLB 175

Barnes, Julian 1946- .... **CLC 42, 141**
See also BRWS 4; CA 102; CANR 19, 54, 115, 137; CN 4, 5, 6, 7; DAB; DLB 194; DLBY 1993; EWL 3; MTCW 2; MTFW 2005; SSFS 24

Barnes, Julian Patrick
See Barnes, Julian

Barnes, Peter 1931-2004 .... **CLC 5, 56**
See also CA 65-68; 12; CAAS 230; CANR 33, 34, 64, 113; CBD; CD 5, 6; DFS 6; DLB 13, 233; MTCW 1

Barnes, William 1801-1886 .... **NCLC 75**
See also DLB 32

Baroja, Pio 1872-1956 .... **HLC 1; TCLC 8**
See also CA 247; CAAE 104; EW 9

Baroja y Nessi, Pio
See Baroja, Pio

Baron, David
See Pinter, Harold

Baron Corvo
See Rolfe, Frederick (William Serafino Austin Lewis Mary)

Barondess, Sue K(aufman)
1926-1977 .... **CLC 8**
See Kaufman, Sue
See also CA 1-4R; CAAS 69-72; CANR 1

Baron de Teive
See Pessoa, Fernando (Antonio Nogueira)

Baroness Von S.
See Zangwill, Israel

Barres, (Auguste-)Maurice
1862-1923 .... **TCLC 47**
See also CA 164; DLB 123; GFL 1789 to the Present

Barreto, Afonso Henrique de Lima
See Lima Barreto, Afonso Henrique de

Barrett, Andrea 1954- .... **CLC 150**
See also CA 156; CANR 92; CN 7; DLB 335; SSFS 24

Barrett, Michele .... **CLC 65**

Barrett, (Roger) Syd 1946-2006 .... **CLC 35**

Barrett, William (Christopher)
1913-1992 .... **CLC 27**
See also CA 13-16R; CAAS 139; CANR 11, 67; INT CANR-11

Barrett Browning, Elizabeth
1806-1861 ...... **NCLC 1, 16, 61, 66, 170; PC 6, 62; WLC 1**
See also AAYA 63; BRW 4; CDBLB 1832-1890; DA; DA3; DAB; DAC; DAM MST, POET; DLB 32, 199; EXPP; FL 1:2; PAB; PFS 2, 16, 23; TEA; WLIT 4; WP

Barrie, J(ames) M(atthew)
1860-1937 .... **TCLC 2, 164**
See also BRWS 3; BYA 4, 5; CA 136; CAAE 104; CANR 77; CDBLB 1890-1914; CLR 16; CWRI 5; DA3; DAB; DAM DRAM; DFS 7; DLB 10, 141, 156; EWL 3; FANT; MAICYA 1, 2; MTCW 2; MTFW 2005; SATA 100; SUFW; WCH; WLIT 4; YABC 1

Barrington, Michael
See Moorcock, Michael

Barrol, Grady
See Bograd, Larry

Barry, Mike
See Malzberg, Barry N(athaniel)

Barry, Philip 1896-1949 .... **TCLC 11**
See also CA 199; CAAE 109; DFS 9; DLB 7, 228; MAL 5; RGAL 4

Bart, Andre Schwarz
See Schwarz-Bart, Andre

Barth, John (Simmons) 1930- ... **CLC 1, 2, 3, 5, 7, 9, 10, 14, 27, 51, 89, 214; SSC 10, 89**
See also AITN 1, 2; AMW; BPFB 1; CA 1-4R; CABS 1; CANR 5, 23, 49, 64, 113; CN 1, 2, 3, 4, 5, 6, 7; DAM NOV; DLB 2, 227; EWL 3; FANT; MAL 5; MTCW 1; RGAL 4; RGSF 2; RHW; SSFS 6; TUS

Barthelme, Donald 1931-1989 ... **CLC 1, 2, 3, 5, 6, 8, 13, 23, 46, 59, 115; SSC 2, 55**
See also AMWS 4; BPFB 1; CA 21-24R; CAAS 129; CANR 20, 58; CN 1, 2, 3, 4; DA3; DAM NOV; DLB 2, 234; DLBY 1980, 1989; EWL 3; FANT; LMFS 2; MAL 5; MTCW 1, 2; MTFW 2005; RGAL 4; RGSF 2; SATA 7; SATA-Obit 62; SSFS 17

Barthelme, Frederick 1943- ...... **CLC 36, 117**
See also AMWS 11; CA 122; CAAE 114; CANR 77; CN 4, 5, 6, 7; CSW; DLB 244; DLBY 1985; EWL 3; INT CA-122

Barthes, Roland (Gerard)
1915-1980 .... **CLC 24, 83; TCLC 135**
See also CA 130; CAAS 97-100; CANR 66; DLB 296; EW 13; EWL 3; GFL 1789 to the Present; MTCW 1, 2; TWA

Bartram, William 1739-1823 .... **NCLC 145**
See also ANW; DLB 37

Barzun, Jacques (Martin) 1907- ..... **CLC 51, 145**
See also CA 61-64; CANR 22, 95

Bashevis, Isaac
See Singer, Isaac Bashevis

Bashevis, Yitskhok
See Singer, Isaac Bashevis

Bashkirtseff, Marie 1859-1884 .... **NCLC 27**

Basho, Matsuo
See Matsuo Basho
See also RGWL 2, 3; WP

Basil of Caesaria c. 330-379 .... **CMLC 35**

Basket, Raney
See Edgerton, Clyde (Carlyle)

Bass, Kingsley B., Jr.
See Bullins, Ed

Bass, Rick 1958- .... **CLC 79, 143; SSC 60**
See also AMWS 16; ANW; CA 126; CANR 53, 93, 145; CSW; DLB 212, 275

Bassani, Giorgio 1916-2000 .... **CLC 9**
See also CA 65-68; CAAS 190; CANR 33; CWW 2; DLB 128, 177, 299; EWL 3; MTCW 1; RGHL; RGWL 2, 3

Bastian, Ann .... **CLC 70**

Bastos, Augusto Roa
See Roa Bastos, Augusto

Bataille, Georges 1897-1962 .... **CLC 29; TCLC 155**
See also CA 101; CAAS 89-92; EWL 3

Bates, H(erbert) E(rnest)
1905-1974 .... **CLC 46; SSC 10**
See also CA 93-96; CAAS 45-48; CANR 34; CN 1; DA3; DAB; DAM POP; DLB 162, 191; EWL 3; EXPS; MTCW 1, 2; RGSF 2; SSFS 7

Bauchart
See Camus, Albert

Baudelaire, Charles 1821-1867 . **NCLC 6, 29, 55, 155; PC 1; SSC 18; WLC 1**
See also DA; DA3; DAB; DAC; DAM MST, POET; DLB 217; EW 7; GFL 1789 to the Present; LMFS 2; PFS 21; RGWL 2, 3; TWA

Baudouin, Marcel
See Peguy, Charles (Pierre)

Baudouin, Pierre
See Peguy, Charles (Pierre)

Baudrillard, Jean 1929-2007 .... **CLC 60**
See also CA 252; CAAS 258; DLB 296

Baum, L(yman) Frank 1856-1919 .. **TCLC 7, 132**
See also AAYA 46; BYA 16; CA 133; CAAE 108; CLR 15, 107; CWRI 5; DLB 22; FANT; JRDA; MAICYA 1, 2; MTCW 1, 2; NFS 13; RGAL 4; SATA 18, 100; WCH

Baum, Louis F.
See Baum, L(yman) Frank

Baumbach, Jonathan 1933- .... **CLC 6, 23**
See also CA 13-16R; 5; CANR 12, 66, 140; CN 3, 4, 5, 6, 7; DLBY 1980; INT CANR-12; MTCW 1

Bausch, Richard (Carl) 1945- .... **CLC 51**
See also AMWS 7; CA 101; 14; CANR 43, 61, 87; CN 7; CSW; DLB 130; MAL 5

Baxter, Charles 1947- .... **CLC 45, 78**
See also CA 57-60; CANR 40, 64, 104, 133; CPW; DAM POP; DLB 130; MAL 5; MTCW 2; MTFW 2005; TCLE 1:1

Baxter, George Owen
See Faust, Frederick (Schiller)

Baxter, James K(eir) 1926-1972 .... **CLC 14**
See also CA 77-80; CP 1; EWL 3

Baxter, John
See Hunt, E. Howard

Bayer, Sylvia
See Glassco, John

Bayle, Pierre 1647-1706 .... **LC 126**
See also DLB 268, 313; GFL Beginnings to 1789

Baynton, Barbara 1857-1929 .... **TCLC 57**
See also DLB 230; RGSF 2

Beagle, Peter S. 1939- .... **CLC 7, 104**
See also AAYA 47; BPFB 1; BYA 9, 10, 16; CA 9-12R; CANR 4, 51, 73, 110; DA3; DLBY 1980; FANT; INT CANR-4; MTCW 2; MTFW 2005; SATA 60, 130; SUFW 1, 2; YAW

Beagle, Peter Soyer
See Beagle, Peter S.

Bean, Normal
See Burroughs, Edgar Rice

Beard, Charles A(ustin)
1874-1948 .... **TCLC 15**
See also CA 189; CAAE 115; DLB 17; SATA 18

Beardsley, Aubrey 1872-1898 .... **NCLC 6**

Beattie, Ann 1947- ..... **CLC 8, 13, 18, 40, 63, 146; SSC 11**
See also AMWS 5; BEST 90:2; BPFB 1; CA 81-84; CANR 53, 73, 128; CN 4, 5, 6, 7; CPW; DA3; DAM NOV, POP; DLB 218, 278; DLBY 1982; EWL 3; MAL 5; MTCW 1, 2; MTFW 2005; RGAL 4; RGSF 2; SSFS 9; TUS

Beattie, James 1735-1803 .... **NCLC 25**
See also DLB 109

Beauchamp, Kathleen Mansfield 1888-1923
See Mansfield, Katherine
See also CA 134; CAAE 104; DA; DA3; DAC; DAM MST; MTCW 2; TEA

Beaumarchais, Pierre-Augustin Caron de
1732-1799 .... **DC 4; LC 61**
See also DAM DRAM; DFS 14, 16; DLB 313; EW 4; GFL Beginnings to 1789; RGWL 2, 3

Beaumont, Francis 1584(?)-1616 .. **DC 6; LC 33**
See also BRW 2; CDBLB Before 1660; DLB 58; TEA

Beauvoir, Simone de 1908-1986 .... **CLC 1, 2, 4, 8, 14, 31, 44, 50, 71, 124; SSC 35; WLC 1**
See also BPFB 1; CA 9-12R; CAAS 118; CANR 28, 61; DA; DA3; DAB; DAC; DAM MST, NOV; DLB 72; DLBY 1986;

Bessie, Alvah 1904-1985 .... **CLC 23**
  See also CA 5-8R; CAAS 116; CANR 2,
  80; DLB 26

Bestuzhev, Aleksandr Aleksandrovich
  1797-1837 .... **NCLC 131**
  See also DLB 198

Bethlen, T. D.
  See Silverberg, Robert

Beti, Mongo .... **BLC 1; CLC 27**
  See Biyidi, Alexandre
  See also AFW; CANR 79; DAM MULT;
  EWL 3; WLIT 2

Betjeman, John 1906-1984 ...... **CLC 2, 6, 10,**
  34, 43; PC 75
  See also BRW 7; CA 9-12R; CAAS 112;
  CANR 33, 56; CDBLB 1945-1960; CP 1,
  2, 3; DA3; DAB; DAM MST, POET;
  DLB 20; DLBY 1984; EWL 3; MTCW 1,
  2

Bettelheim, Bruno 1903-1990 .... **CLC 79;**
  TCLC 143
  See also CA 81-84; CAAS 131; CANR 23,
  61; DA3; MTCW 1, 2; RGHL

Betti, Ugo 1892-1953 .... **TCLC 5**
  See also CA 155; CAAE 104; EWL 3;
  RGWL 2, 3

Betts, Doris (Waugh) 1932- ..... **CLC 3, 6, 28;**
  SSC 45
  See also CA 13-16R; CANR 9, 66, 77; CN
  6, 7; CSW; DLB 218; DLBY 1982; INT
  CANR-9; RGAL 4

Bevan, Alistair
  See Roberts, Keith (John Kingston)

Bey, Pilaff
  See Douglas, (George) Norman

Bialik, Chaim Nachman
  1873-1934 .... **TCLC 25**
  See Bialik, Hayyim Nahman
  See also CA 170; EWL 3

Bialik, Hayyim Nahman
  See Bialik, Chaim Nachman
  See also WLIT 6

Bickerstaff, Isaac
  See Swift, Jonathan

Bidart, Frank 1939- .... **CLC 33**
  See also AMWS 15; CA 140; CANR 106;
  CP 5, 6, 7

Bienek, Horst 1930- .... **CLC 7, 11**
  See also CA 73-76; DLB 75

Bierce, Ambrose (Gwinett)
  1842-1914(?) ..... **SSC 9, 72; TCLC 1, 7,**
  44; WLC 1
  See also AAYA 55; AMW; BYA 11; CA
  139; CAAE 104; CANR 78; CDALB
  1865-1917; DA; DA3; DAC; DAM MST;
  DLB 11, 12, 23, 71, 74, 186; EWL 3;
  EXPS; HGG; LAIT 2; MAL 5; RGAL 4;
  RGSF 2; SSFS 9; SUFW 1

Biggers, Earl Derr 1884-1933 .... **TCLC 65**
  See also CA 153; CAAE 108; DLB 306

Billiken, Bud
  See Motley, Willard (Francis)

Billings, Josh
  See Shaw, Henry Wheeler

Billington, (Lady) Rachel (Mary)
  1942- .... **CLC 43**
  See also AITN 2; CA 33-36R; CANR 44;
  CN 4, 5, 6, 7

Binchy, Maeve 1940- .... **CLC 153**
  See also BEST 90:1; BPFB 1; CA 134;
  CAAE 127; CANR 50, 96, 134; CN 5, 6,
  7; CPW; DA3; DAM POP; DLB 319; INT
  CANR-134; MTCW 2; MTFW 2005; RHW

Binyon, T(imothy) J(ohn)
  1936-2004 .... **CLC 34**
  See also CA 111; CAAS 232; CANR 28,
  140

Bion 335B.C.-245B.C. .... **CMLC 39**

Bioy Casares, Adolfo 1914-1999 ... **CLC 4, 8,**
  13, 88; HLC 1; SSC 17, 102
  See Casares, Adolfo Bioy; Miranda, Javier;
  Sacastru, Martin
  See also CA 29-32R; CAAS 177; CANR
  19, 43, 66; CWW 2; DAM MULT; DLB
  113; EWL 3; HW 1, 2; LAW; MTCW 1,
  2; MTFW 2005

Birch, Allison .... **CLC 65**

Bird, Cordwainer
  See Ellison, Harlan

Bird, Robert Montgomery
  1806-1854 .... **NCLC 1**
  See also DLB 202; RGAL 4

Birkerts, Sven 1951- .... **CLC 116**
  See also CA 176; 133, 176; 29; CAAE 128;
  CANR 151; INT CA-133

Birney, (Alfred) Earle 1904-1995 .. **CLC 1, 4,**
  6, 11; PC 52
  See also CA 1-4R; CANR 5, 20; CN 1, 2,
  3, 4; CP 1, 2, 3, 4, 5, 6; DAC; DAM MST,
  POET; DLB 88; MTCW 1; PFS 8; RGEL
  2

Biruni, al 973-1048(?) .... **CMLC 28**

Bishop, Elizabeth 1911-1979 ..... **CLC 1, 4, 9,**
  13, 15, 32; PC 3, 34; TCLC 121
  See also AMWR 2; AMWS 1; CA 5-8R;
  CAAS 89-92; CABS 2; CANR 26, 61,
  108; CDALB 1968-1988; CP 1, 2, 3; DA;
  DA3; DAC; DAM MST, POET; DLB 5,
  169; EWL 3; GLL 2; MAL 5; MBL;
  MTCW 1, 2; PAB; PFS 6, 12; RGAL 4;
  SATA-Obit 24; TUS; WP

Bishop, John 1935- .... **CLC 10**
  See also CA 105

Bishop, John Peale 1892-1944 ..... **TCLC 103**
  See also CA 155; CAAE 107; DLB 4, 9,
  45; MAL 5; RGAL 4

Bissett, Bill 1939- .... **CLC 18; PC 14**
  See also CA 69-72; 19; CANR 15; CCA 1;
  CP 1, 2, 3, 4, 5, 6, 7; DLB 53; MTCW 1

Bissoondath, Neil (Devindra)
  1955- .... **CLC 120**
  See also CA 136; CANR 123; CN 6, 7;
  DAC

Bitov, Andrei (Georgievich) 1937- ... **CLC 57**
  See also CA 142; DLB 302

Biyidi, Alexandre 1932-
  See Beti, Mongo
  See also BW 1, 3; CA 124; CAAE 114;
  CANR 81; DA3; MTCW 1, 2

Bjarme, Brynjolf
  See Ibsen, Henrik (Johan)

Bjoernson, Bjoernstjerne (Martinius)
  1832-1910 .... **TCLC 7, 37**
  See also CAAE 104

Black, Benjamin
  See Banville, John

Black, Robert
  See Holdstock, Robert

Blackburn, Paul 1926-1971 .... **CLC 9, 43**
  See also BG 1:2; CA 81-84; CAAS 33-36R;
  CANR 34; CP 1; DLB 16; DLBY 1981

Black Elk 1863-1950 .... **NNAL; TCLC 33**
  See also CA 144; DAM MULT; MTCW 2;
  MTFW 2005; WP

Black Hawk 1767-1838 .... **NNAL**

Black Hobart
  See Sanders, (James) Ed(ward)

Blacklin, Malcolm
  See Chambers, Aidan

Blackmore, R(ichard) D(oddridge)
  1825-1900 .... **TCLC 27**
  See also CAAE 120; DLB 18; RGEL 2

Blackmur, R(ichard) P(almer)
  1904-1965 .... **CLC 2, 24**
  See also AMWS 2; CA 11-12; CAAS 25-
  28R; CANR 71; CAP 1; DLB 63; EWL
  3; MAL 5

Black Tarantula
  See Acker, Kathy

Blackwood, Algernon (Henry)
  1869-1951 .... **TCLC 5**
  See also CA 150; CAAE 105; DLB 153,
  156, 178; HGG; SUFW 1

Blackwood, Caroline (Maureen)
  1931-1996 .... **CLC 6, 9, 100**
  See also BRWS 9; CA 85-88; CAAS 151;
  CANR 32, 61, 65; CN 3, 4, 5, 6; DLB 14,
  207; HGG; MTCW 1

Blade, Alexander
  See Hamilton, Edmond; Silverberg, Robert

Blaga, Lucian 1895-1961 .... **CLC 75**
  See also CA 157; DLB 220; EWL 3

Blair, Eric (Arthur) 1903-1950 .... **TCLC 123**
  See Orwell, George
  See also CA 132; CAAE 104; DA; DA3;
  DAB; DAC; DAM MST, NOV; MTCW
  1, 2; MTFW 2005; SATA 29

Blair, Hugh 1718-1800 .... **NCLC 75**

Blais, Marie-Claire 1939- .... **CLC 2, 4, 6, 13,**
  22
  See also CA 21-24R; 4; CANR 38, 75, 93;
  CWW 2; DAC; DAM MST; DLB 53;
  EWL 3; FW; MTCW 1, 2; MTFW 2005;
  TWA

Blaise, Clark 1940- .... **CLC 29**
  See also AITN 2; CA 231; 53-56, 231; 3;
  CANR 5, 66, 106; CN 4, 5, 6, 7; DLB 53;
  RGSF 2

Blake, Fairley
  See De Voto, Bernard (Augustine)

Blake, Nicholas
  See Day Lewis, C(ecil)
  See also DLB 77; MSW

Blake, Sterling
  See Benford, Gregory

Blake, William 1757-1827 . **NCLC 13, 37, 57,**
  127, 173; PC 12, 63; WLC 1
  See also AAYA 47; BRW 3; BRWR 1; CD-
  BLB 1789-1832; CLR 52; DA; DA3;
  DAB; DAC; DAM MST, POET; DLB 93,
  163; EXPP; LATS 1:1; LMFS 1; MAI-
  CYA 1, 2; PAB; PFS 2, 12, 24; SATA 30;
  TEA; WCH; WLIT 3; WP

Blanchot, Maurice 1907-2003 .... **CLC 135**
  See also CA 144; CAAE 117; CAAS 213;
  CANR 138; DLB 72, 296; EWL 3

Blasco Ibanez, Vicente 1867-1928 . **TCLC 12**
  See Ibanez, Vicente Blasco
  See also BPFB 1; CA 131; CAAE 110;
  CANR 81; DA3; DAM NOV; EW 8;
  EWL 3; HW 1, 2; MTCW 1

Blatty, William Peter 1928- .... **CLC 2**
  See also CA 5-8R; CANR 9, 124; DAM
  POP; HGG

Bleeck, Oliver
  See Thomas, Ross (Elmore)

Blessing, Lee (Knowlton) 1949- .... **CLC 54**
  See also CA 236; CAD; CD 5, 6; DFS 23

Blight, Rose
  See Greer, Germaine

Blish, James (Benjamin) 1921-1975 . **CLC 14**
  See also BPFB 1; CA 1-4R; CAAS 57-60;
  CANR 3; CN 2; DLB 8; MTCW 1; SATA
  66; SCFW 1, 2; SFW 4

Bliss, Frederick
  See Card, Orson Scott

Bliss, Gillian
  See Paton Walsh, Jill

Bliss, Reginald
  See Wells, H(erbert) G(eorge)

Blixen, Karen (Christentze Dinesen)
  1885-1962
  See Dinesen, Isak
  See also CA 25-28; CANR 22, 50; CAP 2;
  DA3; DLB 214; LMFS 1; MTCW 1, 2;
  SATA 44; SSFS 20

Bloch, Robert (Albert) 1917-1994 .... **CLC 33**
See also AAYA 29; CA 179; 5-8R, 179; 20;
CAAS 146; CANR 5, 78; DA3; DLB 44;
HGG; INT CANR-5; MTCW 2; SATA 12;
SATA-Obit 82; SFW 4; SUFW 1, 2

Blok, Alexander (Alexandrovich)
1880-1921 .... **PC 21; TCLC 5**
See also CA 183; CAAE 104; DLB 295;
EW 9; EWL 3; LMFS 2; RGWL 2, 3

Blom, Jan
See Breytenbach, Breyten

Bloom, Harold 1930- .... **CLC 24, 103, 221**
See also CA 13-16R; CANR 39, 75, 92,
133; DLB 67; EWL 3; MTCW 2; MTFW
2005; RGAL 4

Bloomfield, Aurelius
See Bourne, Randolph S(illiman)

Bloomfield, Robert 1766-1823 ..... **NCLC 145**
See also DLB 93

Blount, Roy (Alton), Jr. 1941- .... **CLC 38**
See also CA 53-56; CANR 10, 28, 61, 125;
CSW; INT CANR-28; MTCW 1, 2;
MTFW 2005

Blowsnake, Sam 1875-(?) .... **NNAL**

Bloy, Leon 1846-1917 .... **TCLC 22**
See also CA 183; CAAE 121; DLB 123;
GFL 1789 to the Present

Blue Cloud, Peter (Aroniawenrate)
1933- .... **NNAL**
See also CA 117; CANR 40; DAM MULT

Bluggage, Oranthy
See Alcott, Louisa May

Blume, Judy (Sussman) 1938- .... **CLC 12, 30**
See also AAYA 3, 26; BYA 1, 8, 12; CA 29-
32R; CANR 13, 37, 66, 124; CLR 2, 15,
69; CPW; DA3; DAM NOV, POP; DLB
52; JRDA; MAICYA 1, 2; MAICYAS 1;
MTCW 1, 2; MTFW 2005; NFS 24;
SATA 2, 31, 79, 142; WYA; YAW

Blunden, Edmund (Charles)
1896-1974 .... **CLC 2, 56; PC 66**
See also BRW 6; BRWS 11; CA 17-18;
CAAS 45-48; CANR 54; CAP 2; CP 1, 2;
DLB 20, 100, 155; MTCW 1; PAB

Bly, Robert (Elwood) 1926- .... **CLC 1, 2, 5,
10, 15, 38, 128; PC 39**
See also AMWS 4; CA 5-8R; CANR 41,
73, 125; CP 1, 2, 3, 4, 5, 6, 7; DA3; DAM
POET; DLB 5; EWL 3; MAL 5; MTCW
1, 2; MTFW 2005; PFS 6, 17; RGAL 4

Boas, Franz 1858-1942 .... **TCLC 56**
See also CA 181; CAAE 115

Bobette
See Simenon, Georges (Jacques Christian)

Boccaccio, Giovanni 1313-1375 ... **CMLC 13,
57; SSC 10, 87**
See also EW 2; RGSF 2; RGWL 2, 3; TWA;
WLIT 7

Bochco, Steven 1943- .... **CLC 35**
See also AAYA 11, 71; CA 138; CAAE 124

Bode, Sigmund
See O'Doherty, Brian

Bodel, Jean 1167(?)-1210 .... **CMLC 28**

Bodenheim, Maxwell 1892-1954 .... **TCLC 44**
See also CA 187; CAAE 110; DLB 9, 45;
MAL 5; RGAL 4

Bodenheimer, Maxwell
See Bodenheim, Maxwell

Bodker, Cecil 1927-
See Bodker, Cecil

Bodker, Cecil 1927- .... **CLC 21**
See also CA 73-76; CANR 13, 44, 111;
CLR 23; MAICYA 1, 2; SATA 14, 133

Boell, Heinrich (Theodor)
1917-1985 ..... **CLC 2, 3, 6, 9, 11, 15, 27,
32, 72; SSC 23; WLC 1**
See Boll, Heinrich (Theodor)
See also CA 21-24R; CAAS 116; CANR
24; DA; DA3; DAB; DAC; DAM MST,
NOV; DLB 69; DLBY 1985; MTCW 1,
2; MTFW 2005; SSFS 20; TWA

Boerne, Alfred
See Doeblin, Alfred

Boethius c. 480-c. 524 .... **CMLC 15**
See also DLB 115; RGWL 2, 3; WLIT 8

Boff, Leonardo (Genezio Darci)
1938- .... **CLC 70; HLC 1**
See also CA 150; DAM MULT; HW 2

Bogan, Louise 1897-1970 .... **CLC 4, 39, 46,
93; PC 12**
See also AMWS 3; CA 73-76; CAAS 25-
28R; CANR 33, 82; CP 1; DAM POET;
DLB 45, 169; EWL 3; MAL 5; MBL;
MTCW 1, 2; PFS 21; RGAL 4

Bogarde, Dirk
See Van Den Bogarde, Derek Jules Gaspard
Ulric Niven
See also DLB 14

Bogosian, Eric 1953- .... **CLC 45, 141**
See also CA 138; CAD; CANR 102, 148;
CD 5, 6

Bograd, Larry 1953- .... **CLC 35**
See also CA 93-96; CANR 57; SAAS 21;
SATA 33, 89; WYA

Boiardo, Matteo Maria 1441-1494 .... **LC 6**

Boileau-Despreaux, Nicolas 1636-1711 . **LC 3**
See also DLB 268; EW 3; GFL Beginnings
to 1789; RGWL 2, 3

Boissard, Maurice
See Leautaud, Paul

Bojer, Johan 1872-1959 .... **TCLC 64**
See also CA 189; EWL 3

Bok, Edward W(illiam)
1863-1930 .... **TCLC 101**
See also CA 217; DLB 91; DLBD 16

Boker, George Henry 1823-1890 . **NCLC 125**
See also RGAL 4

Boland, Eavan 1944- ... **CLC 40, 67, 113; PC
58**
See also BRWS 5; CA 207; 143, 207;
CANR 61; CP 1, 6, 7; CWP; DAM POET;
DLB 40; FW; MTCW 2; MTFW 2005;
PFS 12, 22

Boll, Heinrich (Theodor) .... **TCLC 185**
See Boell, Heinrich (Theodor)
See also BPFB 1; CDWLB 2; DLB 329;
EW 13; EWL 3; RGHL; RGSF 2; RGWL
2, 3

Bolt, Lee
See Faust, Frederick (Schiller)

Bolt, Robert (Oxton) 1924-1995 ...... **CLC 14;
TCLC 175**
See also CA 17-20R; CAAS 147; CANR
35, 67; CBD; DAM DRAM; DFS 2; DLB
13, 233; EWL 3; LAIT 1; MTCW 1

Bombal, Maria Luisa 1910-1980 .... **HLCS 1;
SSC 37**
See also CA 127; CANR 72; EWL 3; HW
1; LAW; RGSF 2

Bombet, Louis-Alexandre-Cesar
See Stendhal

Bomkauf
See Kaufman, Bob (Garnell)

Bonaventura .... **NCLC 35**
See also DLB 90

Bonaventure 1217(?)-1274 .... **CMLC 79**
See also DLB 115; LMFS 1

Bond, Edward 1934- .... **CLC 4, 6, 13, 23**
See also AAYA 50; BRWS 1; CA 25-28R;
CANR 38, 67, 106; CBD; CD 5, 6; DAM
DRAM; DFS 3, 8; DLB 13, 310; EWL 3;
MTCW 1

Bonham, Frank 1914-1989 .... **CLC 12**
See also AAYA 1, 70; BYA 1, 3; CA 9-12R;
CANR 4, 36; JRDA; MAICYA 1, 2;
SAAS 3; SATA 1, 49; SATA-Obit 62;
TCWW 1, 2; YAW

Bonnefoy, Yves 1923- . **CLC 9, 15, 58; PC 58**
See also CA 85-88; CANR 33, 75, 97, 136;
CWW 2; DAM MST, POET; DLB 258;
EWL 3; GFL 1789 to the Present; MTCW
1, 2; MTFW 2005

Bonner, Marita . **HR 1:2; PC 72; TCLC 179**
See Occomy, Marita (Odette) Bonner

Bonnin, Gertrude 1876-1938 .... **NNAL**
See Zitkala-Sa
See also CA 150; DAM MULT

Bontemps, Arna(ud Wendell)
1902-1973 .. **BLC 1; CLC 1, 18; HR 1:2**
See also BW 1; CA 1-4R; CAAS 41-44R;
CANR 4, 35; CLR 6; CP 1; CWRI 5;
DA3; DAM MULT, NOV, POET; DLB
48, 51; JRDA; MAICYA 1, 2; MAL 5;
MTCW 1, 2; SATA 2, 44; SATA-Obit 24;
WCH; WP

Boot, William
See Stoppard, Tom

Booth, Martin 1944-2004 .... **CLC 13**
See also CA 188; 93-96, 188; 2; CAAS 223;
CANR 92; CP 1, 2, 3, 4

Booth, Philip 1925-2007 .... **CLC 23**
See also CA 5-8R; CANR 5, 88; CP 1, 2, 3,
4, 5, 6, 7; DLBY 1982

Booth, Wayne C. 1921-2005 .... **CLC 24**
See also CA 1-4R; 5; CAAS 244; CANR 3,
43, 117; DLB 67

Booth, Wayne Clayson
See Booth, Wayne C.

Borchert, Wolfgang 1921-1947 .... **TCLC 5**
See also CA 188; CAAE 104; DLB 69, 124;
EWL 3

Borel, Petrus 1809-1859 .... **NCLC 41**
See also DLB 119; GFL 1789 to the Present

Borges, Jorge Luis 1899-1986 ... **CLC 1, 2, 3,
4, 6, 8, 9, 10, 13, 19, 44, 48, 83; HLC 1;
PC 22, 32; SSC 4, 41, 100; TCLC 109;
WLC 1**
See also AAYA 26; BPFB 1; CA 21-24R;
CANR 19, 33, 75, 105, 133; CDWLB 3;
DA; DA3; DAB; DAC; DAM MST,
MULT; DLB 113, 283; DLBY 1986;
DNFS 1, 2; EWL 3; HW 1, 2; LAW;
LMFS 2; MSW; MTCW 1, 2; MTFW
2005; RGHL; RGSF 2; RGWL 2, 3; SFW
4; SSFS 17; TWA; WLIT 1

Borowski, Tadeusz 1922-1951 .... **SSC 48;
TCLC 9**
See also CA 154; CAAE 106; CDWLB 4;
DLB 215; EWL 3; RGHL; RGSF 2;
RGWL 3; SSFS 13

Borrow, George (Henry)
1803-1881 .... **NCLC 9**
See also BRWS 12; DLB 21, 55, 166

Bosch (Gavino), Juan 1909-2001 ..... **HLCS 1**
See also CA 151; CAAS 204; DAM MST,
MULT; DLB 145; HW 1, 2

Bosman, Herman Charles
1905-1951 .... **TCLC 49**
See Malan, Herman
See also CA 160; DLB 225; RGSF 2

Bosschere, Jean de 1878(?)-1953 ... **TCLC 19**
See also CA 186; CAAE 115

Boswell, James 1740-1795 ... **LC 4, 50; WLC
1**
See also BRW 3; CDBLB 1660-1789; DA;
DAB; DAC; DAM MST; DLB 104, 142;
TEA; WLIT 3

Bottomley, Gordon 1874-1948 ..... **TCLC 107**
See also CA 192; CAAE 120; DLB 10

Bottoms, David 1949- .... **CLC 53**
See also CA 105; CANR 22; CSW; DLB
120; DLBY 1983

Boucicault, Dion 1820-1890 .... **NCLC 41**

Boucolon, Maryse
See Conde, Maryse

Bourdieu, Pierre 1930-2002 .... **CLC 198**
See also CA 130; CAAS 204

Bourget, Paul (Charles Joseph)
1852-1935 .... **TCLC 12**
See also CA 196; CAAE 107; DLB 123;
GFL 1789 to the Present

Bourjaily, Vance (Nye) 1922- .... **CLC 8, 62**
See also CA 1-4R; 1; CANR 2, 72; CN 1,
2, 3, 4, 5, 6, 7; DLB 2, 143; MAL 5

Bourne, Randolph S(illiman)
1886-1918 .... **TCLC 16**
See also AMW; CA 155; CAAE 117; DLB
63; MAL 5

Bova, Ben 1932- .... **CLC 45**
See also AAYA 16; CA 5-8R; 18; CANR
11, 56, 94, 111, 157; CLR 3, 96; DLBY
1981; INT CANR-11; MAICYA 1, 2;
MTCW 1; SATA 6, 68, 133; SFW 4

Bova, Benjamin William
See Bova, Ben

Bowen, Elizabeth (Dorothea Cole)
1899-1973 . **CLC 1, 3, 6, 11, 15, 22, 118;**
SSC 3, 28, 66; TCLC 148
See also BRWS 2; CA 17-18; CAAS 41-
44R; CANR 35, 105; CAP 2; CDBLB
1945-1960; CN 1; DA3; DAM NOV;
DLB 15, 162; EWL 3; EXPS; FW; HGG;
MTCW 1, 2; MTFW 2005; NFS 13;
RGSF 2; SSFS 5, 22; SUFW 1; TEA;
WLIT 4

Bowering, George 1935- .... **CLC 15, 47**
See also CA 21-24R; 16; CANR 10; CN 7;
CP 1, 2, 3, 4, 5, 6, 7; DLB 53

Bowering, Marilyn R(uthe) 1949- .... **CLC 32**
See also CA 101; CANR 49; CP 4, 5, 6, 7;
CWP; DLB 334

Bowers, Edgar 1924-2000 .... **CLC 9**
See also CA 5-8R; CAAS 188; CANR 24;
CP 1, 2, 3, 4, 5, 6, 7; CSW; DLB 5

Bowers, Mrs. J. Milton 1842-1914
See Bierce, Ambrose (Gwinett)

Bowie, David .... **CLC 17**
See Jones, David Robert

Bowles, Jane (Sydney) 1917-1973 ..... **CLC 3,**
68
See Bowles, Jane Auer
See also CA 19-20; CAAS 41-44R; CAP 2;
CN 1; MAL 5

Bowles, Jane Auer
See Bowles, Jane (Sydney)
See also EWL 3

Bowles, Paul 1910-1999 ..... **CLC 1, 2, 19, 53;**
SSC 3, 98
See also AMWS 4; CA 1-4R; 1; CAAS 186;
CANR 1, 19, 50, 75; CN 1, 2, 3, 4, 5, 6;
DA3; DLB 5, 6, 218; EWL 3; MAL 5;
MTCW 1, 2; MTFW 2005; RGAL 4;
SSFS 17

Bowles, William Lisle 1762-1850 . **NCLC 103**
See also DLB 93

Box, Edgar
See Vidal, Gore
See also GLL 1

Boyd, James 1888-1944 .... **TCLC 115**
See also CA 186; DLB 9; DLBD 16; RGAL
4; RHW

Boyd, Nancy
See Millay, Edna St. Vincent
See also GLL 1

Boyd, Thomas (Alexander)
1898-1935 .... **TCLC 111**
See also CA 183; CAAE 111; DLB 9;
DLBD 16, 316

Boyd, William (Andrew Murray)
1952- .... **CLC 28, 53, 70**
See also CA 120; CAAE 114; CANR 51,
71, 131; CN 4, 5, 6, 7; DLB 231

Boyesen, Hjalmar Hjorth
1848-1895 .... **NCLC 135**
See also DLB 12, 71; DLBD 13; RGAL 4

Boyle, Kay 1902-1992 .... **CLC 1, 5, 19, 58,**
121; SSC 5, 102
See also CA 13-16R; 1; CAAS 140; CANR
29, 61, 110; CN 1, 2, 3, 4, 5; CP 1, 2, 3,
4, 5; DLB 4, 9, 48, 86; DLBY 1993; EWL
3; MAL 5; MTCW 1, 2; MTFW 2005;
RGAL 4; RGSF 2; SSFS 10, 13, 14

Boyle, Mark
See Kienzle, William X.

Boyle, Patrick 1905-1982 .... **CLC 19**
See also CA 127

Boyle, T. C.
See Boyle, T. Coraghessan
See also AMWS 8

Boyle, T. Coraghessan 1948- ..... **CLC 36, 55,**
90; SSC 16
See Boyle, T. C.
See also AAYA 47; BEST 90:4; BPFB 1;
CA 120; CANR 44, 76, 89, 132; CN 6, 7;
CPW; DA3; DAM POP; DLB 218, 278;
DLBY 1986; EWL 3; MAL 5; MTCW 2;
MTFW 2005; SSFS 13, 19

Boz
See Dickens, Charles (John Huffam)

Brackenridge, Hugh Henry
1748-1816 .... **NCLC 7**
See also DLB 11, 37; RGAL 4

Bradbury, Edward P.
See Moorcock, Michael
See also MTCW 2

Bradbury, Malcolm (Stanley)
1932-2000 .... **CLC 32, 61**
See also CA 1-4R; CANR 1, 33, 91, 98,
137; CN 1, 2, 3, 4, 5, 6, 7; CP 1; DA3;
DAM NOV; DLB 14, 207; EWL 3;
MTCW 1, 2; MTFW 2005

Bradbury, Ray 1920- .. **CLC 1, 3, 10, 15, 42,**
98, 235; SSC 29, 53; WLC 1
See also AAYA 15; AITN 1, 2; AMWS 4;
BPFB 1; BYA 4, 5, 11; CA 1-4R; CANR
2, 30, 75, 125; CDALB 1968-1988; CN
1, 2, 3, 4, 5, 6, 7; CPW; DA; DA3; DAB;
DAC; DAM MST, NOV, POP; DLB 2, 8;
EXPN; EXPS; HGG; LAIT 3, 5; LATS
1:2; LMFS 2; MAL 5; MTCW 1, 2;
MTFW 2005; NFS 1, 22; RGAL 4; RGSF
2; SATA 11, 64, 123; SCFW 1, 2; SFW 4;
SSFS 1, 20; SUFW 1, 2; TUS; YAW

Braddon, Mary Elizabeth
1837-1915 .... **TCLC 111**
See also BRWS 8; CA 179; CAAE 108;
CMW 4; DLB 18, 70, 156; HGG

Bradfield, Scott 1955- .... **SSC 65**
See also CA 147; CANR 90; HGG; SUFW
2

Bradfield, Scott Michael
See Bradfield, Scott

Bradford, Gamaliel 1863-1932 .... **TCLC 36**
See also CA 160; DLB 17

Bradford, William 1590-1657 .... **LC 64**
See also DLB 24, 30; RGAL 4

Bradley, David (Henry), Jr. 1950- .... **BLC 1;**
CLC 23, 118
See also BW 1, 3; CA 104; CANR 26, 81;
CN 4, 5, 6, 7; DAM MULT; DLB 33

Bradley, John Ed 1958- .... **CLC 55**
See also CA 139; CANR 99; CN 6, 7; CSW

Bradley, John Edmund, Jr.
See Bradley, John Ed

Bradley, Marion Zimmer
1930-1999 .... **CLC 30**
See Chapman, Lee; Dexter, John; Gardner,
Miriam; Ives, Morgan; Rivers, Elfrida
See also AAYA 40; BPFB 1; CA 57-60; 10;
CAAS 185; CANR 7, 31, 51, 75, 107;
CPW; DA3; DAM POP; DLB 8; FANT;

FW; MTCW 1, 2; MTFW 2005; SATA 90,
139; SATA-Obit 116; SFW 4; SUFW 2;
YAW

Bradshaw, John 1933- .... **CLC 70**
See also CA 138; CANR 61

Bradstreet, Anne 1612(?)-1672 .... **LC 4, 30,**
130; PC 10
See also AMWS 1; CDALB 1640-1865;
DA; DA3; DAC; DAM MST, POET; DLB
24; EXPP; FW; PFS 6; RGAL 4; TUS;
WP

Brady, Joan 1939- .... **CLC 86**
See also CA 141

Bragg, Melvyn 1939- .... **CLC 10**
See also BEST 89:3; CA 57-60; CANR 10,
48, 89, 158; CN 1, 2, 3, 4, 5, 6, 7; DLB
14, 271; RHW

Brahe, Tycho 1546-1601 .... **LC 45**
See also DLB 300

Braine, John (Gerard) 1922-1986 . **CLC 1, 3,**
41
See also CA 1-4R; CAAS 120; CANR 1,
33; CDBLB 1945-1960; CN 1, 2, 3, 4;
DLB 15; DLBY 1986; EWL 3; MTCW 1

Braithwaite, William Stanley (Beaumont)
1878-1962 .... **BLC 1; HR 1:2; PC 52**
See also BW 1; CA 125; DAM MULT; DLB
50, 54; MAL 5

Bramah, Ernest 1868-1942 .... **TCLC 72**
See also CA 156; CMW 4; DLB 70; FANT

Brammer, Billy Lee
See Brammer, William

Brammer, William 1929-1978 .... **CLC 31**
See also CA 235; CAAS 77-80

Brancati, Vitaliano 1907-1954 .... **TCLC 12**
See also CAAE 109; DLB 264; EWL 3

Brancato, Robin F(idler) 1936- .... **CLC 35**
See also AAYA 9, 68; BYA 6; CA 69-72;
CANR 11, 45; CLR 32; JRDA; MAICYA
2; MAICYAS 1; SAAS 9; SATA 97;
WYA; YAW

Brand, Dionne 1953- .... **CLC 192**
See also BW 2; CA 143; CANR 143; CWP;
DLB 334

Brand, Max
See Faust, Frederick (Schiller)
See also BPFB 1; TCWW 1, 2

Brand, Millen 1906-1980 .... **CLC 7**
See also CA 21-24R; CAAS 97-100; CANR
72

Branden, Barbara .... **CLC 44**
See also CA 148

Brandes, Georg (Morris Cohen)
1842-1927 .... **TCLC 10**
See also CA 189; CAAE 105; DLB 300

Brandys, Kazimierz 1916-2000 .... **CLC 62**
See also CA 239; EWL 3

Branley, Franklyn M(ansfield)
1915-2002 .... **CLC 21**
See also CA 33-36R; CAAS 207; CANR
14, 39; CLR 13; MAICYA 1, 2; SAAS
16; SATA 4, 68, 136

Brant, Beth (E.) 1941- .... **NNAL**
See also CA 144; FW

Brant, Sebastian 1457-1521 .... **LC 112**
See also DLB 179; RGWL 2, 3

Brathwaite, Edward Kamau
1930- .... **BLCS; CLC 11; PC 56**
See also BRWS 12; BW 2, 3; CA 25-28R;
CANR 11, 26, 47, 107; CDWLB 3; CP 1,
2, 3, 4, 5, 6, 7; DAM POET; DLB 125;
EWL 3

Brathwaite, Kamau
See Brathwaite, Edward Kamau

Brautigan, Richard (Gary)
1935-1984 .... **CLC 1, 3, 5, 9, 12, 34, 42;
TCLC 133**
See also BPFB 1; CA 53-56; CAAS 113;
CANR 34; CN 1, 2, 3; CP 1, 2, 3, 4; DA3;
DAM NOV; DLB 2, 5, 206; DLBY 1980,
1984; FANT; MAL 5; MTCW 1; RGAL
4; SATA 56

Brave Bird, Mary .... **NNAL**
See Crow Dog, Mary

Braverman, Kate 1950- .... **CLC 67**
See also CA 89-92; CANR 141; DLB 335

Brecht, (Eugen) Bertolt (Friedrich)
1898-1956 ..... **DC 3; TCLC 1, 6, 13, 35,
169; WLC 1**
See also CA 133; CAAE 104; CANR 62;
CDWLB 2; DA; DA3; DAB; DAC; DAM
DRAM, MST; DFS 4, 5, 9; DLB 56, 124;
EW 11; EWL 3; IDTP; MTCW 1, 2;
MTFW 2005; RGHL; RGWL 2, 3; TWA

Brecht, Eugen Berthold Friedrich
See Brecht, (Eugen) Bertolt (Friedrich)

Bremer, Fredrika 1801-1865 .... **NCLC 11**
See also DLB 254

Brennan, Christopher John
1870-1932 .... **TCLC 17**
See also CA 188; CAAE 117; DLB 230;
EWL 3

Brennan, Maeve 1917-1993 ... **CLC 5; TCLC
124**
See also CA 81-84; CANR 72, 100

Brenner, Jozef 1887-1919
See Csath, Geza
See also CA 240

Brent, Linda
See Jacobs, Harriet A(nn)

Brentano, Clemens (Maria)
1778-1842 .... **NCLC 1**
See also DLB 90; RGWL 2, 3

Brent of Bin Bin
See Franklin, (Stella Maria Sarah) Miles
(Lampe)

Brenton, Howard 1942- .... **CLC 31**
See also CA 69-72; CANR 33, 67; CBD;
CD 5, 6; DLB 13; MTCW 1

Breslin, James 1930-
See Breslin, Jimmy
See also CA 73-76; CANR 31, 75, 139;
DAM NOV; MTCW 1, 2; MTFW 2005

Breslin, Jimmy .... **CLC 4, 43**
See Breslin, James
See also AITN 1; DLB 185; MTCW 2

Bresson, Robert 1901(?)-1999 .... **CLC 16**
See also CA 110; CAAS 187; CANR 49

Breton, Andre 1896-1966 .. **CLC 2, 9, 15, 54;
PC 15**
See also CA 19-20; CAAS 25-28R; CANR
40, 60; CAP 2; DLB 65, 258; EW 11;
EWL 3; GFL 1789 to the Present; LMFS
2; MTCW 1, 2; MTFW 2005; RGWL 2,
3; TWA; WP

Breton, Nicholas c. 1554-c. 1626 .... **LC 133**
See also DLB 136

Breytenbach, Breyten 1939(?)- .. **CLC 23, 37,
126**
See also CA 129; CAAE 113; CANR 61,
122; CWW 2; DAM POET; DLB 225;
EWL 3

Bridgers, Sue Ellen 1942- .... **CLC 26**
See also AAYA 8, 49; BYA 7, 8; CA 65-68;
CANR 11, 36; CLR 18; DLB 52; JRDA;
MAICYA 1, 2; SAAS 1; SATA 22, 90;
SATA-Essay 109; WYA; YAW

Bridges, Robert (Seymour)
1844-1930 .... **PC 28; TCLC 1**
See also BRW 6; CA 152; CAAE 104; CD-
BLB 1890-1914; DAM POET; DLB 19,
98

Bridie, James .... **TCLC 3**
See Mavor, Osborne Henry
See also DLB 10; EWL 3

Brin, David 1950- .... **CLC 34**
See also AAYA 21; CA 102; CANR 24, 70,
125, 127; INT CANR-24; SATA 65;
SCFW 2; SFW 4

Brink, Andre 1935- .... **CLC 18, 36, 106**
See also AFW; BRWS 6; CA 104; CANR
39, 62, 109, 133; CN 4, 5, 6, 7; DLB 225;
EWL 3; INT CA-103; LATS 1:2; MTCW
1, 2; MTFW 2005; WLIT 2

Brinsmead, H. F.
See Brinsmead, H(esba) F(ay)

Brinsmead, H. F(ay)
See Brinsmead, H(esba) F(ay)

Brinsmead, H(esba) F(ay) 1922- ...... **CLC 21**
See also CA 21-24R; CANR 10; CLR 47;
CWRI 5; MAICYA 1, 2; SAAS 5; SATA
18, 78

Brittain, Vera (Mary) 1893(?)-1970 . **CLC 23**
See also BRWS 10; CA 13-16; CAAS 25-
28R; CANR 58; CAP 1; DLB 191; FW;
MTCW 1, 2

Broch, Hermann 1886-1951 .... **TCLC 20**
See also CA 211; CAAE 117; CDWLB 2;
DLB 85, 124; EW 10; EWL 3; RGWL 2,
3

Brock, Rose
See Hansen, Joseph
See also GLL 1

Brod, Max 1884-1968 .... **TCLC 115**
See also CA 5-8R; CAAS 25-28R; CANR
7; DLB 81; EWL 3

Brodkey, Harold (Roy) 1930-1996 .. **CLC 56;
TCLC 123**
See also CA 111; CAAS 151; CANR 71;
CN 4, 5, 6; DLB 130

Brodsky, Iosif Alexandrovich 1940-1996
See Brodsky, Joseph
See also AITN 1; CA 41-44R; CAAS 151;
CANR 37, 106; DA3; DAM POET;
MTCW 1, 2; MTFW 2005; RGWL 2, 3

Brodsky, Joseph . **CLC 4, 6, 13, 36, 100; PC
9**
See Brodsky, Iosif Alexandrovich
See also AAYA 71; AMWS 8; CWW 2;
DLB 285, 329; EWL 3; MTCW 1

Brodsky, Michael 1948- .... **CLC 19**
See also CA 102; CANR 18, 41, 58, 147;
DLB 244

Brodsky, Michael Mark
See Brodsky, Michael

Brodzki, Bella .... **CLC 65**

Brome, Richard 1590(?)-1652 .... **LC 61**
See also BRWS 10; DLB 58

Bromell, Henry 1947- .... **CLC 5**
See also CA 53-56; CANR 9, 115, 116

Bromfield, Louis (Brucker)
1896-1956 .... **TCLC 11**
See also CA 155; CAAE 107; DLB 4, 9,
86; RGAL 4; RHW

Broner, E(sther) M(asserman)
1930- .... **CLC 19**
See also CA 17-20R; CANR 8, 25, 72; CN
4, 5, 6; DLB 28

Bronk, William (M.) 1918-1999 .... **CLC 10**
See also CA 89-92; CAAS 177; CANR 23;
CP 3, 4, 5, 6, 7; DLB 165

Bronstein, Lev Davidovich
See Trotsky, Leon

Bronte, Anne
See Bronte, Anne

Bronte, Anne 1820-1849 ..... **NCLC 4, 71, 102**
See also BRW 5; BRWR 1; DA3; DLB 21,
199; TEA

Bronte, (Patrick) Branwell
1817-1848 .... **NCLC 109**

Bronte, Charlotte
See Bronte, Charlotte

Bronte, Charlotte 1816-1855 ...... **NCLC 3, 8,
33, 58, 105, 155; WLC 1**
See also AAYA 17; BRW 5; BRWC 2;
BRWR 1; BYA 2; CDBLB 1832-1890;
DA; DA3; DAB; DAC; DAM MST, NOV;
DLB 21, 159, 199; EXPN; FL 1:2; GL 2;
LAIT 2; NFS 4; TEA; WLIT 4

Bronte, Emily
See Bronte, Emily (Jane)

Bronte, Emily (Jane) 1818-1848 ... **NCLC 16,
35, 165; PC 8; WLC 1**
See also AAYA 17; BPFB 1; BRW 5;
BRWC 1; BRWR 1; BYA 3; CDBLB
1832-1890; DA; DA3; DAB; DAC; DAM
MST, NOV, POET; DLB 21, 32, 199;
EXPN; FL 1:2; GL 2; LAIT 1; TEA;
WLIT 3

Brontes
See Bronte, Anne; Bronte, Charlotte; Bronte,
Emily (Jane)

Brooke, Frances 1724-1789 .... **LC 6, 48**
See also DLB 39, 99

Brooke, Henry 1703(?)-1783 .... **LC 1**
See also DLB 39

Brooke, Rupert (Chawner)
1887-1915 .. **PC 24; TCLC 2, 7; WLC 1**
See also BRWS 3; CA 132; CAAE 104;
CANR 61; CDBLB 1914-1945; DA;
DAB; DAC; DAM MST, POET; DLB 19,
216; EXPP; GLL 2; MTCW 1, 2; MTFW
2005; PFS 7; TEA

Brooke-Haven, P.
See Wodehouse, P(elham) G(renville)

Brooke-Rose, Christine 1926(?)- ..... **CLC 40,
184**
See also BRWS 4; CA 13-16R; CANR 58,
118; CN 1, 2, 3, 4, 5, 6, 7; DLB 14, 231;
EWL 3; SFW 4

Brookner, Anita 1928- . **CLC 32, 34, 51, 136,
237**
See also BRWS 4; CA 120; CAAE 114;
CANR 37, 56, 87, 130; CN 4, 5, 6, 7;
CPW; DA3; DAM POP; DLB 194,
326; DLBY 1987; EWL 3; MTCW 1, 2;
MTFW 2005; NFS 23; TEA

Brooks, Cleanth 1906-1994 . **CLC 24, 86, 110**
See also AMWS 14; CA 17-20R; CAAS
145; CANR 33, 35; CSW; DLB 63; DLBY
1994; EWL 3; INT CANR-35; MAL 5;
MTCW 1, 2; MTFW 2005

Brooks, George
See Baum, L(yman) Frank

Brooks, Gwendolyn 1917-2000 .... **BLC 1;
CLC 1, 2, 4, 5, 15, 49, 125; PC 7;
WLC 1**
See also AAYA 20; AFAW 1, 2; AITN 1;
AMWS 3; BW 2, 3; CA 1-4R; CAAS 190;
CANR 1, 27, 52, 75, 132; CDALB 1941-
1968; CLR 27; CP 1, 2, 3, 4, 5, 6, 7;
CWP; DA; DA3; DAC; DAM MST,
MULT, POET; DLB 5, 76, 165; EWL 3;
EXPP; FL 1:5; MAL 5; MBL; MTCW 1,
2; MTFW 2005; PFS 1, 2, 4, 6; RGAL 4;
SATA 6; SATA-Obit 123; TUS; WP

Brooks, Mel 1926-
See Kaminsky, Melvin
See also CA 65-68; CANR 16; DFS 21

Brooks, Peter (Preston) 1938- .... **CLC 34**
See also CA 45-48; CANR 1, 107

Brooks, Van Wyck 1886-1963 .... **CLC 29**
See also AMW; CA 1-4R; CANR 6; DLB
45, 63, 103; MAL 5; TUS

Brophy, Brigid (Antonia)
1929-1995 .... **CLC 6, 11, 29, 105**
See also CA 5-8R; 4; CAAS 149; CANR
25, 53; CBD; CN 1, 2, 3, 4, 5, 6; CWD;
DA3; DLB 14, 271; EWL 3; MTCW 1, 2

Brosman, Catharine Savage 1934- ..... **CLC 9**
See also CA 61-64; CANR 21, 46, 149
Brossard, Nicole 1943- .... **CLC 115, 169**
See also CA 122; 16; CANR 140; CCA 1;
CWP; CWW 2; DLB 53; EWL 3; FW;
GLL 2; RGWL 3
Brother Antoninus
See Everson, William (Oliver)
Brothers Grimm
See Grimm, Jacob Ludwig Karl; Grimm,
Wilhelm Karl
The Brothers Quay
See Quay, Stephen; Quay, Timothy
Broughton, T(homas) Alan 1936- ..... **CLC 19**
See also CA 45-48; CANR 2, 23, 48, 111
Broumas, Olga 1949- .... **CLC 10, 73**
See also CA 85-88; CANR 20, 69, 110; CP
5, 6, 7; CWP; GLL 2
Broun, Heywood 1888-1939 .... **TCLC 104**
See also DLB 29, 171
Brown, Alan 1950- .... **CLC 99**
See also CA 156
Brown, Charles Brockden
1771-1810 .... **NCLC 22, 74, 122**
See also AMWS 1; CDALB 1640-1865;
DLB 37, 59, 73; FW; GL 2; HGG; LMFS
1; RGAL 4; TUS
Brown, Christy 1932-1981 .... **CLC 63**
See also BYA 13; CA 105; CAAS 104;
CANR 72; DLB 14
Brown, Claude 1937-2002 ... **BLC 1; CLC 30**
See also AAYA 7; BW 1, 3; CA 73-76;
CAAS 205; CANR 81; DAM MULT
Brown, Dan 1964- .... **CLC 209**
See also AAYA 55; CA 217; MTFW 2005
Brown, Dee 1908-2002 .... **CLC 18, 47**
See also AAYA 30; CA 13-16R; 6; CAAS
212; CANR 11, 45, 60, 150; CPW; CSW;
DA3; DAM POP; DLBY 1980; LAIT 2;
MTCW 1, 2; MTFW 2005; NCFS 5;
SATA 5, 110; SATA-Obit 141; TCWW 1,
2
Brown, Dee Alexander
See Brown, Dee
Brown, George
See Wertmueller, Lina
Brown, George Douglas
1869-1902 .... **TCLC 28**
See Douglas, George
See also CA 162
Brown, George Mackay 1921-1996 ... **CLC 5,**
48, 100
See also BRWS 6; CA 21-24R; 6; CAAS
151; CANR 12, 37, 67; CN 1, 2, 3, 4, 5,
6; CP 1, 2, 3, 4, 5, 6; DLB 14, 27, 139,
271; MTCW 1; RGSF 2; SATA 35
Brown, Larry 1951-2004 .... **CLC 73**
See also CA 134; CAAE 130; CAAS 233;
CANR 117, 145; CSW; DLB 234; INT
CA-134
Brown, Moses
See Barrett, William (Christopher)
Brown, Rita Mae 1944- .... **CLC 18, 43, 79**
See also BPFB 1; CA 45-48; CANR 2, 11,
35, 62, 95, 138; CN 5, 6, 7; CPW; CSW;
DA3; DAM NOV, POP; FW; INT CANR-
11; MAL 5; MTCW 1, 2; MTFW 2005;
NFS 9; RGAL 4; TUS
Brown, Roderick (Langmere) Haig-
See Haig-Brown, Roderick (Langmere)
Brown, Rosellen 1939- .... **CLC 32, 170**
See also CA 77-80; 10; CANR 14, 44, 98;
CN 6, 7
Brown, Sterling Allen 1901-1989 ...... **BLC 1;**
CLC 1, 23, 59; HR 1:2; PC 55
See also AFAW 1, 2; BW 1, 3; CA 85-88;
CAAS 127; CANR 26; CP 3, 4; DA3;
DAM MULT, POET; DLB 48, 51, 63;
MAL 5; MTCW 1, 2; MTFW 2005;
RGAL 4; WP

Brown, Will
See Ainsworth, William Harrison
Brown, William Hill 1765-1793 .... **LC 93**
See also DLB 37
Brown, William Larry
See Brown, Larry
Brown, William Wells 1815-1884 ...... **BLC 1;**
DC 1; NCLC 2, 89
See also DAM MULT; DLB 3, 50, 183,
248; RGAL 4
Browne, (Clyde) Jackson 1948(?)- ... **CLC 21**
See also CA 120
Browne, Sir Thomas 1605-1682 .... **LC 111**
See also BRW 2; DLB 151
Browning, Robert 1812-1889 . **NCLC 19, 79;**
PC 2, 61; WLCS
See also BRW 4; BRWC 2; BRWR 2; CD-
BLB 1832-1890; CLR 97; DA; DA3;
DAB; DAC; DAM MST, POET; DLB 32,
163; EXPP; LATS 1:1; PAB; PFS 1, 15;
RGEL 2; TEA; WLIT 4; WP; YABC 1
Browning, Tod 1882-1962 .... **CLC 16**
See also CA 141; CAAS 117
Brownmiller, Susan 1935- .... **CLC 159**
See also CA 103; CANR 35, 75, 137; DAM
NOV; FW; MTCW 1, 2; MTFW 2005
Brownson, Orestes Augustus
1803-1876 .... **NCLC 50**
See also DLB 1, 59, 73, 243
Bruccoli, Matthew J(oseph) 1931- ... **CLC 34**
See also CA 9-12R; CANR 7, 87; DLB 103
Bruce, Lenny .... **CLC 21**
See Schneider, Leonard Alfred
Bruchac, Joseph 1942- .... **NNAL**
See also AAYA 19; CA 256; 33-36R, 256;
CANR 13, 47, 75, 94, 137, 161; CLR 46;
CWRI 5; DAM MULT; JRDA; MAICYA
2; MAICYAS 1; MTCW 2; MTFW 2005;
SATA 42, 89, 131, 176; SATA-Essay 176
Bruin, John
See Brutus, Dennis
Brulard, Henri
See Stendhal
Brulls, Christian
See Simenon, Georges (Jacques Christian)
Brunetto Latini c. 1220-1294 .... **CMLC 73**
Brunner, John (Kilian Houston)
1934-1995 .... **CLC 8, 10**
See also CA 1-4R; 8; CAAS 149; CANR 2,
37; CPW; DAM POP; DLB 261; MTCW
1, 2; SCFW 1, 2; SFW 4
Bruno, Giordano 1548-1600 .... **LC 27**
See also RGWL 2, 3
Brutus, Dennis 1924- ... **BLC 1; CLC 43; PC**
24
See also AFW; BW 2, 3; CA 49-52; 14;
CANR 2, 27, 42, 81; CDWLB 3; CP 1, 2,
3, 4, 5, 6, 7; DAM MULT, POET; DLB
117, 225; EWL 3
Bryan, C(ourtlandt) D(ixon) B(arnes)
1936- .... **CLC 29**
See also CA 73-76; CANR 13, 68; DLB
185; INT CANR-13
Bryan, Michael
See Moore, Brian
See also CCA 1
Bryan, William Jennings
1860-1925 .... **TCLC 99**
See also DLB 303
Bryant, William Cullen 1794-1878 . **NCLC 6,**
46; PC 20
See also AMWS 1; CDALB 1640-1865;
DA; DAB; DAC; DAM MST, POET;
DLB 3, 43, 59, 189, 250; EXPP; PAB;
RGAL 4; TUS
Bryusov, Valery Yakovlevich
1873-1924 .... **TCLC 10**
See also CA 155; CAAE 107; EWL 3; SFW
4

Buchan, John 1875-1940 .... **TCLC 41**
See also CA 145; CAAE 108; CMW 4;
DAB; DAM POP; DLB 34, 70, 156;
HGG; MSW; MTCW 2; RGEL 2; RHW;
YABC 2
Buchanan, George 1506-1582 .... **LC 4**
See also DLB 132
Buchanan, Robert 1841-1901 .... **TCLC 107**
See also CA 179; DLB 18, 35
Buchheim, Lothar-Guenther
1918-2007 .... **CLC 6**
See also CA 85-88; CAAS 257
Buchner, (Karl) Georg
1813-1837 .... **NCLC 26, 146**
See also CDWLB 2; DLB 133; EW 6;
RGSF 2; RGWL 2, 3; TWA
Buchwald, Art 1925-2007 .... **CLC 33**
See also AITN 1; CA 5-8R; CAAS 256;
CANR 21, 67, 107; MTCW 1, 2; SATA
10
Buchwald, Arthur
See Buchwald, Art
Buck, Pearl S(ydenstricker)
1892-1973 .... **CLC 7, 11, 18, 127**
See also AAYA 42; AITN 1; AMWS 2;
BPFB 1; CA 1-4R; CAAS 41-44R; CANR
1, 34; CDALBS; CN 1; DA; DA3; DAB;
DAC; DAM MST, NOV; DLB 9, 102,
329; EWL 3; LAIT 3; MAL 5; MTCW 1,
2; MTFW 2005; NFS 25; RGAL 4; RHW;
SATA 1, 25; TUS
Buckler, Ernest 1908-1984 .... **CLC 13**
See also CA 11-12; CAAS 114; CAP 1;
CCA 1; CN 1, 2, 3; DAC; DAM MST;
DLB 68; SATA 47
Buckley, Christopher 1952- .... **CLC 165**
See also CA 139; CANR 119
Buckley, Christopher Taylor
See Buckley, Christopher
Buckley, Vincent (Thomas)
1925-1988 .... **CLC 57**
See also CA 101; CP 1, 2, 3, 4; DLB 289
Buckley, William F., Jr. 1925- ..... **CLC 7, 18,**
37
See also AITN 1; BPFB 1; CA 1-4R; CANR
1, 24, 53, 93, 133; CMW 4; CPW; DA3;
DAM POP; DLB 137; DLBY 1980; INT
CANR-24; MTCW 1, 2; MTFW 2005;
TUS
Buechner, Frederick 1926- ..... **CLC 2, 4, 6, 9**
See also AMWS 12; BPFB 1; CA 13-16R;
CANR 11, 39, 64, 114, 138; CN 1, 2, 3,
4, 5, 6, 7; DAM NOV; DLBY 1980; INT
CANR-11; MAL 5; MTCW 1, 2; MTFW
2005; TCLE 1:1
Buell, John (Edward) 1927- .... **CLC 10**
See also CA 1-4R; CANR 71; DLB 53
Buero Vallejo, Antonio 1916-2000 ... **CLC 15,**
46, 139, 226; DC 18
See also CA 106; CAAS 189; CANR 24,
49, 75; CWW 2; DFS 11; EWL 3; HW 1;
MTCW 1, 2
Bufalino, Gesualdo 1920-1996 .... **CLC 74**
See also CA 209; CWW 2; DLB 196
Bugayev, Boris Nikolayevich
1880-1934 .... **PC 11; TCLC 7**
See Bely, Andrey; Belyi, Andrei
See also CA 165; CAAE 104; MTCW 2;
MTFW 2005
Bukowski, Charles 1920-1994 ... **CLC 2, 5, 9,**
41, 82, 108; PC 18; SSC 45
See also CA 17-20R; CAAS 144; CANR
40, 62, 105; CN 4, 5; CP 1, 2, 3, 4, 5;
CPW; DA3; DAM NOV, POET; DLB 5,
130, 169; EWL 3; MAL 5; MTCW 1, 2;
MTFW 2005

Cobalt, Martin
See Mayne, William (James Carter)

Cobb, Irvin S(hrewsbury)
1876-1944 .... TCLC 77
See also CA 175; DLB 11, 25, 86

Cobbett, William 1763-1835 .... NCLC 49
See also DLB 43, 107, 158; RGEL 2

Coburn, D(onald) L(ee) 1938- .... CLC 10
See also CA 89-92; DFS 23

Cocteau, Jean 1889-1963 ... CLC 1, 8, 15, 16,
43; DC 17; TCLC 119; WLC 2
See also AAYA 74; CA 25-28; CANR 40;
CAP 2; DA; DA3; DAB; DAC; DAM
DRAM, MST, NOV; DFS 24; DLB 65,
258, 321; EW 10; EWL 3; GFL 1789 to
the Present; MTCW 1, 2; RGWL 2, 3;
TWA

Cocteau, Jean Maurice Eugene Clement
See Cocteau, Jean

Codrescu, Andrei 1946- .... CLC 46, 121
See also CA 33-36R; 19; CANR 13, 34, 53,
76, 125; CN 7; DA3; DAM POET; MAL
5; MTCW 2; MTFW 2005

Coe, Max
See Bourne, Randolph S(illiman)

Coe, Tucker
See Westlake, Donald E.

Coen, Ethan 1958- .... CLC 108
See also AAYA 54; CA 126; CANR 85

Coen, Joel 1955- .... CLC 108
See also AAYA 54; CA 126; CANR 119

The Coen Brothers
See Coen, Ethan; Coen, Joel

Coetzee, J.M. 1940- ...... CLC 23, 33, 66, 117,
161, 162
See also AAYA 37; AFW; BRWS 6; CA 77-
80; CANR 41, 54, 74, 114, 133; CN 4, 5,
6, 7; DA3; DAM NOV; DLB 225, 326,
329; EWL 3; LMFS 2; MTCW 1, 2;
MTFW 2005; NFS 21; WLIT 2; WWE 1

Coetzee, John Maxwell
See Coetzee, J.M.

Coffey, Brian
See Koontz, Dean R.

Coffin, Robert P(eter) Tristram
1892-1955 .... TCLC 95
See also CA 169; CAAE 123; DLB 45

Cohan, George M. 1878-1942 ...... TCLC 60
See also CA 157; DLB 249; RGAL 4

Cohan, George Michael
See Cohan, George M.

Cohen, Arthur A(llen) 1928-1986 ...... CLC 7,
31
See also CA 1-4R; CAAS 120; CANR 1,
17, 42; DLB 28; RGHL

Cohen, Leonard 1934- .... CLC 3, 38
See also CA 21-24R; CANR 14, 69; CN 1,
2, 3, 4, 5, 6; CP 1, 2, 3, 4, 5, 6, 7; DAC;
DAM MST; DLB 53; EWL 3; MTCW 1

Cohen, Leonard Norman
See Cohen, Leonard

Cohen, Matt(hew) 1942-1999 .... CLC 19
See also CA 61-64; 18; CAAS 187; CANR
40; CN 1, 2, 3, 4, 5, 6; DAC; DLB 53

Cohen-Solal, Annie 1948- .... CLC 50
See also CA 239

Colegate, Isabel 1931- .... CLC 36
See also CA 17-20R; CANR 8, 22, 74; CN
4, 5, 6, 7; DLB 14, 231; INT CANR-22;
MTCW 1

Coleman, Emmett
See Reed, Ishmael

Coleridge, Hartley 1796-1849 .... NCLC 90
See also DLB 96

Coleridge, M. E.
See Coleridge, Mary E(lizabeth)

Coleridge, Mary E(lizabeth)
1861-1907 .... TCLC 73
See also CA 166; CAAE 116; DLB 19, 98

Coleridge, Samuel Taylor
1772-1834 .... NCLC 9, 54, 99, 111, 177;
PC 11, 39, 67; WLC 2
See also AAYA 66; BRW 4; BRWR 2; BYA
4; CDBLB 1789-1832; DA; DA3; DAB;
DAC; DAM MST, POET; DLB 93, 107;
EXPP; LATS 1:1; LMFS 1; PAB; PFS 4,
5; RGEL 2; TEA; WLIT 3; WP

Coleridge, Sara 1802-1852 .... NCLC 31
See also DLB 199

Coles, Don 1928- .... CLC 46
See also CA 115; CANR 38; CP 5, 6, 7

Coles, Robert (Martin) 1929- .... CLC 108
See also CA 45-48; CANR 3, 32, 66, 70,
135; INT CANR-32; SATA 23

Colette, (Sidonie-Gabrielle)
1873-1954 .. SSC 10, 93; TCLC 1, 5, 16
See Willy, Colette
See also CA 131; CAAE 104; DA3; DAM
NOV; DLB 65; EW 9; EWL 3; GFL 1789
to the Present; MTCW 1, 2; MTFW 2005;
RGWL 2, 3; TWA

Collett, (Jacobine) Camilla (Wergeland)
1813-1895 .... NCLC 22

Collier, Christopher 1930- .... CLC 30
See also AAYA 13; BYA 2; CA 33-36R;
CANR 13, 33, 102; JRDA; MAICYA 1,
2; SATA 16, 70; WYA; YAW 1

Collier, James Lincoln 1928- .... CLC 30
See also AAYA 13; BYA 2; CA 9-12R;
CANR 4, 33, 60, 102; CLR 3; DAM POP;
JRDA; MAICYA 1, 2; SAAS 21; SATA 8,
70, 166; WYA; YAW 1

Collier, Jeremy 1650-1726 .... LC 6
See also DLB 336

Collier, John 1901-1980 . SSC 19; TCLC 127
See also CA 65-68; CAAS 97-100; CANR
10; CN 1, 2; DLB 77, 255; FANT; SUFW
1

Collier, Mary 1690-1762 .... LC 86
See also DLB 95

Collingwood, R(obin) G(eorge)
1889(?)-1943 .... TCLC 67
See also CA 155; CAAE 117; DLB 262

Collins, Billy 1941- .... PC 68
See also AAYA 64; CA 151; CANR 92; CP
7; MTFW 2005; PFS 18

Collins, Hunt
See Hunter, Evan

Collins, Linda 1931- .... CLC 44
See also CA 125

Collins, Tom
See Furphy, Joseph
See also RGEL 2

Collins, (William) Wilkie
1824-1889 .... NCLC 1, 18, 93; SSC 93
See also BRWS 6; CDBLB 1832-1890;
CMW 4; DLB 18, 70, 159; GL 2; MSW;
RGEL 2; RGSF 2; SUFW 1; WLIT 4

Collins, William 1721-1759 ...... LC 4, 40; PC
72
See also BRW 3; DAM POET; DLB 109;
RGEL 2

Collodi, Carlo .... NCLC 54
See Lorenzini, Carlo
See also CLR 5, 120; WCH; WLIT 7

Colman, George
See Glassco, John

Colman, George, the Elder
1732-1794 .... LC 98
See also RGEL 2

Colonna, Vittoria 1492-1547 .... LC 71
See also RGWL 2, 3

Colt, Winchester Remington
See Hubbard, L. Ron

Colter, Cyrus J. 1910-2002 .... CLC 58
See also BW 1; CA 65-68; CAAS 205;
CANR 10, 66; CN 2, 3, 4, 5, 6; DLB 33

Colton, James
See Hansen, Joseph
See also GLL 1

Colum, Padraic 1881-1972 .... CLC 28
See also BYA 4; CA 73-76; CAAS 33-36R;
CANR 35; CLR 36; CP 1; CWRI 5; DLB
19; MAICYA 1, 2; MTCW 1; RGEL 2;
SATA 15; WCH

Colvin, James
See Moorcock, Michael

Colwin, Laurie (E.) 1944-1992 .... CLC 5, 13,
23, 84
See also CA 89-92; CAAS 139; CANR 20,
46; DLB 218; DLBY 1980; MTCW 1

Comfort, Alex(ander) 1920-2000 .... CLC 7
See also CA 1-4R; CAAS 190; CANR 1,
45; CN 1, 2, 3, 4; CP 1, 2, 3, 4, 5, 6, 7;
DAM POP; MTCW 2

Comfort, Montgomery
See Campbell, (John) Ramsey

Compton-Burnett, I(vy)
1892(?)-1969 .... CLC 1, 3, 10, 15, 34;
TCLC 180
See also BRW 7; CA 1-4R; CAAS 25-28R;
CANR 4; DAM NOV; DLB 36; EWL 3;
MTCW 1, 2; RGEL 2

Comstock, Anthony 1844-1915 ...... TCLC 13
See also CA 169; CAAE 110

Comte, Auguste 1798-1857 .... NCLC 54

Conan Doyle, Arthur
See Doyle, Sir Arthur Conan
See also BPFB 1; BYA 4, 5, 11

Conde (Abellan), Carmen
1901-1996 .... HLCS 1
See also CA 177; CWW 2; DLB 108; EWL
3; HW 2

Conde, Maryse 1937- ..... BLCS; CLC 52, 92
See also BW 2, 3; CA 190; 110, 190; CANR
30, 53, 76; CWW 2; DAM MULT; EWL
3; MTCW 2; MTFW 2005

Condillac, Etienne Bonnot de
1714-1780 .... LC 26
See also DLB 313

Condon, Richard (Thomas)
1915-1996 .... CLC 4, 6, 8, 10, 45, 100
See also BEST 90:3; BPFB 1; CA 1-4R; 1;
CAAS 151; CANR 2, 23; CMW 4; CN 1,
2, 3, 4, 5, 6; DAM NOV; INT CANR-23;
MAL 5; MTCW 1, 2

Condorcet .... LC 104
See Condorcet, marquis de Marie-Jean-
Antoine-Nicolas Caritat
See also GFL Beginnings to 1789

Condorcet, marquis de
Marie-Jean-Antoine-Nicolas Caritat
1743-1794
See Condorcet
See also DLB 313

Confucius 551B.C.-479B.C. .... CMLC 19, 65;
WLCS
See also DA; DA3; DAB; DAC; DAM
MST

Congreve, William 1670-1729 ... DC 2; LC 5,
21; WLC 2
See also BRW 2; CDBLB 1660-1789; DA;
DAB; DAC; DAM DRAM, MST, POET;
DFS 15; DLB 39, 84; RGEL 2; WLIT 3

Conley, Robert J(ackson) 1940- .... NNAL
See also CA 41-44R; CANR 15, 34, 45, 96;
DAM MULT; TCWW 2

Connell, Evan S., Jr. 1924- .... CLC 4, 6, 45
See also AAYA 7; AMWS 14; CA 1-4R; 2;
CANR 2, 39, 76, 97, 140; CN 1, 2, 3, 4,
5, 6; DAM NOV; DLB 2, 335; DLBY
1981; MAL 5; MTCW 1, 2; MTFW 2005

Connelly, Marc(us Cook) 1890-1980 . CLC 7
See also CA 85-88; CAAS 102; CAD;
CANR 30; DFS 12; DLB 7; DLBY 1980;
MAL 5; RGAL 4; SATA-Obit 25

Cowper, William 1731-1800 ..... **NCLC 8, 94;**
PC 40
See also BRW 3; DA3; DAM POET; DLB
104, 109; RGEL 2

Cox, William Trevor 1928-
See Trevor, William
See also CA 9-12R; CANR 4, 37, 55, 76,
102, 139; DAM NOV; INT CANR-37;
MTCW 1, 2; MTFW 2005; TEA

Coyne, P. J.
See Masters, Hilary

Cozzens, James Gould 1903-1978 . **CLC 1, 4,**
11, 92
See also AMW; BPFB 1; CA 9-12R; CAAS
81-84; CANR 19; CDALB 1941-1968;
CN 1, 2; DLB 9, 294; DLBD 2; DLBY
1984, 1997; EWL 5; MAL 5; MTCW 1,
2; MTFW 2005; RGAL 4

Crabbe, George 1754-1832 .... **NCLC 26, 121**
See also BRW 3; DLB 93; RGEL 2

Crace, Jim 1946- .... **CLC 157; SSC 61**
See also CA 135; CAAE 128; CANR 55,
70, 123; CN 5, 6, 7; DLB 231; INT CA-
135

Craddock, Charles Egbert
See Murfree, Mary Noailles

Craig, A. A.
See Anderson, Poul

Craik, Mrs.
See Craik, Dinah Maria (Mulock)
See also RGEL 2

Craik, Dinah Maria (Mulock)
1826-1887 .... **NCLC 38**
See Craik, Mrs.; Mulock, Dinah Maria
See also DLB 35, 163; MAICYA 1, 2;
SATA 34

Cram, Ralph Adams 1863-1942 ..... **TCLC 45**
See also CA 160

Cranch, Christopher Pearse
1813-1892 .... **NCLC 115**
See also DLB 1, 42, 243

Crane, (Harold) Hart 1899-1932 .... **PC 3;**
TCLC 2, 5, 80; WLC 2
See also AMW; AMWR 2; CA 127; CAAE
104; CDALB 1917-1929; DA; DA3;
DAB; DAC; DAM MST, POET; DLB 4,
48; EWL 3; MAL 5; MTCW 1, 2; MTFW
2005; RGAL 4; TUS

Crane, R(onald) S(almon)
1886-1967 .... **CLC 27**
See also CA 85-88; DLB 63

Crane, Stephen (Townley)
1871-1900 ...... **SSC 7, 56, 70; TCLC 11,**
17, 32; WLC 2
See also AAYA 21; AMW; AMWC 1; BPFB
1; BYA 3; CA 140; CAAE 109; CANR
84; CDALB 1865-1917; DA; DA3; DAB;
DAC; DAM MST, NOV, POET; DLB 12,
54, 78; EXPN; EXPS; LAIT 2; LMFS 2;
MAL 5; NFS 4, 20; PFS 9; RGAL 4;
RGSF 2; SSFS 4; TUS; WYA; YABC 2

Cranmer, Thomas 1489-1556 .... **LC 95**
See also DLB 132, 213

Cranshaw, Stanley
See Fisher, Dorothy (Frances) Canfield

Crase, Douglas 1944- .... **CLC 58**
See also CA 106

Crashaw, Richard 1612(?)-1649 .... **LC 24**
See also BRW 2; DLB 126; PAB; RGEL 2

Cratinus c. 519B.C.-c. 422B.C. ..... **CMLC 54**
See also LMFS 1

Craven, Margaret 1901-1980 .... **CLC 17**
See also BYA 2; CA 103; CCA 1; DAC;
LAIT 5

Crawford, F(rancis) Marion
1854-1909 .... **TCLC 10**
See also CA 168; CAAE 107; DLB 71;
HGG; RGAL 4; SUFW 1

Crawford, Isabella Valancy
1850-1887 .... **NCLC 12, 127**
See also DLB 92; RGEL 2

Crayon, Geoffrey
See Irving, Washington

Creasey, John 1908-1973 .... **CLC 11**
See Marric, J. J.
See also CA 5-8R; CAAS 41-44R; CANR
8, 59; CMW 4; DLB 77; MTCW 1

Crebillon, Claude Prosper Jolyot de (fils)
1707-1777 .... **LC 1, 28**
See also DLB 313; GFL Beginnings to 1789

Credo
See Creasey, John

Credo, Alvaro J. de
See Prado (Calvo), Pedro

Creeley, Robert 1926-2005 .... **CLC 1, 2, 4, 8,**
11, 15, 36, 78; PC 73
See also AMWS 4; CA 1-4R; 10; CAAS
237; CANR 23, 43, 89, 137; CP 1, 2, 3,
4, 5, 6, 7; DA3; DAM POET; DLB 5, 16,
169; DLBD 17; EWL 3; MAL 5; MTCW
1, 2; MTFW 2005; PFS 21; RGAL 4; WP

Creeley, Robert White
See Creeley, Robert

Crenne, Helisenne de 1510-1560 .... **LC 113**
See also DLB 327

Crevecoeur, Hector St. John de
See Crevecoeur, Michel Guillaume Jean de
See also ANW

Crevecoeur, Michel Guillaume Jean de
1735-1813 .... **NCLC 105**
See Crevecoeur, Hector St. John de
See also AMWS 1; DLB 37

Crevel, Rene 1900-1935 .... **TCLC 112**
See also GLL 2

Crews, Harry 1935- .... **CLC 6, 23, 49**
See also AITN 1; AMWS 11; BPFB 1; CA
25-28R; CANR 20, 57; CN 3, 4, 5, 6, 7;
CSW; DA3; DLB 6, 143, 185; MTCW 1,
2; MTFW 2005; RGAL 4

Crichton, Michael 1942- ..... **CLC 2, 6, 54, 90**
See also AAYA 10, 49; AITN 2; BPFB 1;
CA 25-28R; CANR 13, 40, 54, 76, 127;
CMW 4; CN 2, 3, 6, 7; CPW; DA3; DAM
NOV, POP; DLB 292; DLBY 1981; INT
CANR-13; JRDA; MTCW 1, 2; MTFW
2005; SATA 9, 88; SFW 4; YAW

Crispin, Edmund .... **CLC 22**
See Montgomery, (Robert) Bruce
See also DLB 87; MSW

Cristina of Sweden 1626-1689 .... **LC 124**

Cristofer, Michael 1945(?)- .... **CLC 28**
See also CA 152; CAAE 110; CAD; CANR
150; CD 5, 6; DAM DRAM; DFS 15;
DLB 7

Cristofer, Michael Ivan
See Cristofer, Michael

Criton
See Alain

Croce, Benedetto 1866-1952 .... **TCLC 37**
See also CA 155; CAAE 120; EW 8; EWL
3; WLIT 7

Crockett, David 1786-1836 .... **NCLC 8**
See also DLB 3, 11, 183, 248

Crockett, Davy
See Crockett, David

Crofts, Freeman Wills 1879-1957 .. **TCLC 55**
See also CA 195; CAAE 115; CMW 4;
DLB 77; MSW

Croker, John Wilson 1780-1857 .... **NCLC 10**
See also DLB 110

Crommelynck, Fernand 1885-1970 .. **CLC 75**
See also CA 189; CAAS 89-92; EWL 3

Cromwell, Oliver 1599-1658 .... **LC 43**

Cronenberg, David 1943- .... **CLC 143**
See also CA 138; CCA 1

Cronin, A(rchibald) J(oseph)
1896-1981 .... **CLC 32**
See also BPFB 1; CA 1-4R; CAAS 102;
CANR 5; CN 2; DLB 191; SATA 47;
SATA-Obit 25

Cross, Amanda
See Heilbrun, Carolyn G(old)
See also BPFB 1; CMW; CPW; DLB 306;
MSW

Crothers, Rachel 1878-1958 .... **TCLC 19**
See also CA 194; CAAE 113; CAD; CWD;
DLB 7, 266; RGAL 4

Croves, Hal
See Traven, B.

Crow Dog, Mary (?)- .... **CLC 93**
See Brave Bird, Mary
See also CA 154

Crowfield, Christopher
See Stowe, Harriet (Elizabeth) Beecher

Crowley, Aleister .... **TCLC 7**
See Crowley, Edward Alexander
See also GLL 1

Crowley, Edward Alexander 1875-1947
See Crowley, Aleister
See also CAAE 104; HGG

Crowley, John 1942- .... **CLC 57**
See also AAYA 57; BPFB 1; CA 61-64;
CANR 43, 98, 138; DLBY 1982; FANT;
MTFW 2005; SATA 65, 140; SFW 4;
SUFW 2

Crowne, John 1641-1712 .... **LC 104**
See also DLB 80; RGEL 2

Crud
See Crumb, R.

Crumarums
See Crumb, R.

Crumb, R. 1943- .... **CLC 17**
See also CA 106; CANR 107, 150

Crumb, Robert
See Crumb, R.

Crumbum
See Crumb, R.

Crumski
See Crumb, R.

Crum the Bum
See Crumb, R.

Crunk
See Crumb, R.

Crustt
See Crumb, R.

Crutchfield, Les
See Trumbo, Dalton

Cruz, Victor Hernandez 1949- ... **HLC 1; PC**
37
See also BW 2; CA 65-68; 17; CANR 14,
32, 74, 132; CP 1, 2, 3, 4, 5, 6, 7; DAM
MULT, POET; DLB 41; DNFS 1; EXPP;
HW 1, 2; LLW; MTCW 2; MTFW 2005;
PFS 16; WP

Cryer, Gretchen (Kiger) 1935- .... **CLC 21**
See also CA 123; CAAE 114

Csath, Geza .... **TCLC 13**
See Brenner, Jozef
See also CAAE 111

Cudlip, David R(ockwell) 1933- .... **CLC 34**
See also CA 177

Cullen, Countee 1903-1946 . **BLC 1; HR 1:2;**
PC 20; TCLC 4, 37; WLCS
See also AFAW 2; AMWS 4; BW 1; CA
124; CAAE 108; CDALB 1917-1929;
DA; DA3; DAC; DAM MST, MULT,
POET; DLB 4, 48, 51; EWL 3; EXPP;
LMFS 2; MAL 5; MTCW 1, 2; MTFW
2005; PFS 3; RGAL 4; SATA 18; WP

Culleton, Beatrice 1949- .... **NNAL**
See also CA 120; CANR 83; DAC

Cum, R.
See Crumb, R.

Cumberland, Richard
1732-1811 .... **NCLC 167**
See also DLB 89; RGEL 2
Cummings, Bruce F(rederick) 1889-1919
See Barbellion, W. N. P.
See also CAAE 123
Cummings, E(dward) E(stlin)
1894-1962 .. **CLC 1, 3, 8, 12, 15, 68; PC
5; TCLC 137; WLC 2**
See also AAYA 41; AMW; CA 73-76;
CANR 31; CDALB 1929-1941; DA;
DA3; DAB; DAC; DAM MST, POET;
DLB 4, 48; EWL 3; EXPP; MAL 5;
MTCW 1, 2; MTFW 2005; PAB; PFS 1,
3, 12, 13, 19; RGAL 4; TUS; WP
Cummins, Maria Susanna
1827-1866 .... **NCLC 139**
See also DLB 42; YABC 1
Cunha, Euclides (Rodrigues Pimenta) da
1866-1909 .... **TCLC 24**
See also CA 219; CAAE 123; DLB 307;
LAW; WLIT 1
Cunningham, E. V.
See Fast, Howard
Cunningham, J(ames) V(incent)
1911-1985 .... **CLC 3, 31**
See also CA 1-4R; CAAS 115; CANR 1,
72; CP 1, 2, 3, 4; DLB 5
Cunningham, Julia (Woolfolk)
1916- .... **CLC 12**
See also CA 9-12R; CANR 4, 19, 36; CWRI
5; JRDA; MAICYA 1, 2; SAAS 2; SATA
1, 26, 132
Cunningham, Michael 1952- .... **CLC 34**
See also AMWS 15; CA 136; CANR 96,
160; CN 7; DLB 292; GLL 2; MTFW
2005; NFS 23
Cunninghame Graham, R. B.
See Cunninghame Graham, Robert
(Gallnigad) Bontine
**Cunninghame Graham, Robert (Gallnigad)
Bontine** 1852-1936 .... **TCLC 19**
See Graham, R(obert) B(ontine) Cunning-
hame
See also CA 184; CAAE 119
Curnow, (Thomas) Allen (Monro)
1911-2001 .... **PC 48**
See also CA 69-72; CAAS 202; CANR 48,
99; CP 1, 2, 3, 4, 5, 6, 7; EWL 3; RGEL
2
Currie, Ellen 19(?)- .... **CLC 44**
Curtin, Philip
See Lowndes, Marie Adelaide (Belloc)
Curtin, Phillip
See Lowndes, Marie Adelaide (Belloc)
Curtis, Price
See Ellison, Harlan
Cusanus, Nicolaus 1401-1464 .... **LC 80**
See Nicholas of Cusa
Cutrate, Joe
See Spiegelman, Art
Cynewulf c. 770- .... **CMLC 23**
See also DLB 146; RGEL 2
Cyrano de Bergerac, Savinien de
1619-1655 .... **LC 65**
See also DLB 268; GFL Beginnings to
1789; RGWL 2, 3
Cyril of Alexandria c. 375-c. 430 . **CMLC 59**
Czaczkes, Shmuel Yosef Halevi
See Agnon, S(hmuel) Y(osef Halevi)
Dabrowska, Maria (Szumska)
1889-1965 .... **CLC 15**
See also CA 106; CDWLB 4; DLB 215;
EWL 3
Dabydeen, David 1955- .... **CLC 34**
See also BW 1; CA 125; CANR 56, 92; CN
6, 7; CP 5, 6, 7

Dacey, Philip 1939- .... **CLC 51**
See also CA 231; 37-40R, 231; 17; CANR
14, 32, 64; CP 4, 5, 6, 7; DLB 105
Dacre, Charlotte c. 1772-1825(?) . **NCLC 151**
Dafydd ap Gwilym c. 1320-c. 1380 ..... **PC 56**
Dagerman, Stig (Halvard)
1923-1954 .... **TCLC 17**
See also CA 155; CAAE 117; DLB 259;
EWL 3
D'Aguiar, Fred 1960- .... **CLC 145**
See also CA 148; CANR 83, 101; CN 7;
CP 5, 6, 7; DLB 157; EWL 3
Dahl, Roald 1916-1990 ...... **CLC 1, 6, 18, 79;
TCLC 173**
See also AAYA 15; BPFB 1; BRWS 4; BYA
5; CA 1-4R; CAAS 133; CANR 6, 32,
37, 62; CLR 1, 7, 41, 111; CN 1, 2, 3, 4;
CPW; DA3; DAB; DAC; DAM MST,
NOV, POP; DLB 139, 255; HGG; JRDA;
MAICYA 1, 2; MTCW 1, 2; MTFW 2005;
RGSF 2; SATA 1, 26, 73; SATA-Obit 65;
SSFS 4; TEA; YAW
Dahlberg, Edward 1900-1977 .. **CLC 1, 7, 14**
See also CA 9-12R; CAAS 69-72; CANR
31, 62; CN 1, 2; DLB 48; MAL 5; MTCW
1; RGAL 4
Daitch, Susan 1954- .... **CLC 103**
See also CA 161
Dale, Colin .... **TCLC 18**
See Lawrence, T(homas) E(dward)
Dale, George E.
See Asimov, Isaac
d'Alembert, Jean Le Rond
1717-1783 .... **LC 126**
Dalton, Roque 1935-1975(?) ..... **HLCS 1; PC
36**
See also CA 176; DLB 283; HW 2
Daly, Elizabeth 1878-1967 .... **CLC 52**
See also CA 23-24; CAAS 25-28R; CANR
60; CAP 2; CMW 4
Daly, Mary 1928- .... **CLC 173**
See also CA 25-28R; CANR 30, 62; FW;
GLL 1; MTCW 1
Daly, Maureen 1921-2006 .... **CLC 17**
See also AAYA 5, 58; BYA 6; CAAS 253;
CANR 37, 83, 108; CLR 96; JRDA; MAI-
CYA 1, 2; SAAS 1; SATA 2, 129; SATA-
Obit 176; WYA; YAW
Damas, Leon-Gontran 1912-1978 .... **CLC 84**
See also BW 1; CA 125; CAAS 73-76;
EWL 3
Dana, Richard Henry Sr.
1787-1879 .... **NCLC 53**
Daniel, Samuel 1562(?)-1619 .... **LC 24**
See also DLB 62; RGEL 2
Daniels, Brett
See Adler, Renata
Dannay, Frederic 1905-1982 .... **CLC 11**
See Queen, Ellery
See also CA 1-4R; CAAS 107; CANR 1,
39; CMW 4; DAM POP; DLB 137;
MTCW 1
D'Annunzio, Gabriele 1863-1938 ... **TCLC 6,
40**
See also CA 155; CAAE 104; EW 8; EWL
3; RGWL 2, 3; TWA; WLIT 7
Danois, N. le
See Gourmont, Remy(-Marie-Charles) de
Dante 1265-1321 .... **CMLC 3, 18, 39, 70; PC
21; WLCS**
See Alighieri, Dante
See also DA; DA3; DAB; DAC; DAM
MST, POET; EFS 1; EW 1; LAIT 1;
RGWL 2, 3; TWA; WP
d'Antibes, Germain
See Simenon, Georges (Jacques Christian)

Danticat, Edwidge 1969- . **CLC 94, 139, 228;
SSC 100**
See also AAYA 29; CA 192; 152, 192;
CANR 73, 129; CN 7; DNFS 1; EXPS;
LATS 1:2; MTCW 2; MTFW 2005; SSFS
1; YAW
Danvers, Dennis 1947- .... **CLC 70**
Danziger, Paula 1944-2004 .... **CLC 21**
See also AAYA 4, 36; BYA 6, 7, 14; CA
115; CAAE 112; CAAS 229; CANR 37,
132; CLR 20; JRDA; MAICYA 1, 2;
MTFW 2005; SATA 36, 63, 102, 149;
SATA-Brief 30; SATA-Obit 155; WYA;
YAW
Da Ponte, Lorenzo 1749-1838 .... **NCLC 50**
d'Aragona, Tullia 1510(?)-1556 .... **LC 121**
Dario, Ruben 1867-1916 .... **HLC 1; PC 15;
TCLC 4**
See also CA 131; CANR 81; DAM MULT;
DLB 290; EWL 3; HW 1, 2; LAW;
MTCW 1, 2; MTFW 2005; RGWL 2, 3
Darley, George 1795-1846 .... **NCLC 2**
See also DLB 96; RGEL 2
Darrow, Clarence (Seward)
1857-1938 .... **TCLC 81**
See also CA 164; DLB 303
Darwin, Charles 1809-1882 .... **NCLC 57**
See also BRWS 7; DLB 57, 166; LATS 1:1;
RGEL 2; TEA; WLIT 4
Darwin, Erasmus 1731-1802 .... **NCLC 106**
See also DLB 93; RGEL 2
Daryush, Elizabeth 1887-1977 ...... **CLC 6, 19**
See also CA 49-52; CANR 3, 81; DLB 20
Das, Kamala 1934- .... **CLC 191; PC 43**
See also CA 101; CANR 27, 59; CP 1, 2, 3,
4, 5, 6, 7; CWP; DLB 323; FW
Dasgupta, Surendranath
1887-1952 .... **TCLC 81**
See also CA 157
**Dashwood, Edmee Elizabeth Monica de la
Pasture** 1890-1943
See Delafield, E. M.
See also CA 154; CAAE 119
da Silva, Antonio Jose
1705-1739 .... **NCLC 114**
Daudet, (Louis Marie) Alphonse
1840-1897 .... **NCLC 1**
See also DLB 123; GFL 1789 to the Present;
RGSF 2
Daudet, Alphonse Marie Leon
1867-1942 .... **SSC 94**
See also CA 217
d'Aulnoy, Marie-Catherine c.
1650-1705 .... **LC 100**
Daumal, Rene 1908-1944 .... **TCLC 14**
See also CA 247; CAAE 114; EWL 3
Davenant, William 1606-1668 .... **LC 13**
See also DLB 58, 126; RGEL 2
Davenport, Guy (Mattison, Jr.)
1927-2005 .... **CLC 6, 14, 38; SSC 16**
See also CA 33-36R; CAAS 235; CANR
23, 73; CN 3, 4, 5, 6; CSW; DLB 130
David, Robert
See Nezval, Vitezslav
Davidson, Avram (James) 1923-1993
See Queen, Ellery
See also CA 101; CAAS 171; CANR 26;
DLB 8; FANT; SFW 4; SUFW 1, 2
Davidson, Donald (Grady)
1893-1968 .... **CLC 2, 13, 19**
See also CA 5-8R; CAAS 25-28R; CANR
4, 84; DLB 45
Davidson, Hugh
See Hamilton, Edmond
Davidson, John 1857-1909 .... **TCLC 24**
See also CA 217; CAAE 118; DLB 19;
RGEL 2

Davidson, Sara 1943- .... **CLC 9**
See also CA 81-84; CANR 44, 68; DLB
185

Davie, Donald (Alfred) 1922-1995 .... **CLC 5,
8, 10, 31; PC 29**
See also BRWS 6; CA 1-4R; 3; CAAS 149;
CANR 1, 44; CP 1, 2, 3, 4, 5, 6; DLB 27;
MTCW 1; RGEL 2

Davie, Elspeth 1918-1995 .... **SSC 52**
See also CA 126; CAAE 120; CAAS 150;
CANR 141; DLB 139

Davies, Ray(mond Douglas) 1944- ... **CLC 21**
See also CA 146; CAAE 116; CANR 92

Davies, Rhys 1901-1978 .... **CLC 23**
See also CA 9-12R; CAAS 81-84; CANR
4; CN 1, 2; DLB 139, 191

Davies, Robertson 1913-1995 .. **CLC 2, 7, 13,
25, 42, 75, 91; WLC 2**
See Marchbanks, Samuel
See also BEST 89:2; BPFB 1; CA 33-36R;
CAAS 150; CANR 17, 42, 103; CN 1, 2,
3, 4, 5, 6; CPW; DA; DA3; DAB; DAC;
DAM MST, NOV, POP; DLB 68; EWL 3;
HGG; INT CANR-17; MTCW 1, 2;
MTFW 2005; RGEL 2; TWA

Davies, Sir John 1569-1626 .... **LC 85**
See also DLB 172

Davies, Walter C.
See Kornbluth, C(yril) M.

Davies, William Henry 1871-1940 ... **TCLC 5**
See also BRWS 11; CA 179; CAAE 104;
DLB 19, 174; EWL 3; RGEL 2

Davies, William Robertson
See Davies, Robertson

Da Vinci, Leonardo 1452-1519 ..... **LC 12, 57,
60**
See also AAYA 40

Davis, Angela (Yvonne) 1944- .... **CLC 77**
See also BW 2, 3; CA 57-60; CANR 10,
81; CSW; DA3; DAM MULT; FW

Davis, B. Lynch
See Bioy Casares, Adolfo; Borges, Jorge
Luis

Davis, Frank Marshall 1905-1987 ...... **BLC 1**
See also BW 2, 3; CA 125; CAAS 123;
CANR 42, 80; DAM MULT; DLB 51

Davis, Gordon
See Hunt, E. Howard

Davis, H(arold) L(enoir) 1896-1960 . **CLC 49**
See also ANW; CA 178; CAAS 89-92; DLB
9, 206; SATA 114; TCWW 1, 2

Davis, Hart
See Poniatowska, Elena

Davis, Natalie Zemon 1928- .... **CLC 204**
See also CA 53-56; CANR 58, 100

Davis, Rebecca (Blaine) Harding
1831-1910 .... **SSC 38; TCLC 6**
See also AMWS 16; CA 179; CAAE 104;
DLB 74, 239; FW; NFS 14; RGAL 4;
TUS

Davis, Richard Harding
1864-1916 .... **TCLC 24**
See also CA 179; CAAE 114; DLB 12, 23,
78, 79, 189; DLBD 13; RGAL 4

Davison, Frank Dalby 1893-1970 ..... **CLC 15**
See also CA 217; CAAS 116; DLB 260

Davison, Lawrence H.
See Lawrence, D(avid) H(erbert Richards)

Davison, Peter (Hubert) 1928-2004 . **CLC 28**
See also CA 9-12R; 4; CAAS 234; CANR
3, 43, 84; CP 1, 2, 3, 4, 5, 6, 7; DLB 5

Davys, Mary 1674-1732 .... **LC 1, 46**
See also DLB 39

Dawson, (Guy) Fielding (Lewis)
1930-2002 .... **CLC 6**
See also CA 85-88; CAAS 202; CANR 108;
DLB 130; DLBY 2002

Dawson, Peter
See Faust, Frederick (Schiller)
See also TCWW 1, 2

Day, Clarence (Shepard, Jr.)
1874-1935 .... **TCLC 25**
See also CA 199; CAAE 108; DLB 11

Day, John 1574(?)-1640(?) .... **LC 70**
See also DLB 62, 170; RGEL 2

Day, Thomas 1748-1789 .... **LC 1**
See also DLB 39; YABC 1

Day Lewis, C(ecil) 1904-1972 . **CLC 1, 6, 10;
PC 11**
See Blake, Nicholas; Lewis, C. Day
See also BRWS 3; CA 13-16; CAAS 33-
36R; CANR 34; CAP 1; CP 1; CWRI 5;
DAM POET; DLB 15, 20; EWL 3;
MTCW 1, 2; RGEL 2

Dazai Osamu .... **SSC 41; TCLC 11**
See Tsushima, Shuji
See also CA 164; DLB 182; EWL 3; MJW;
RGSF 2; RGWL 2, 3; TWA

de Andrade, Carlos Drummond
See Drummond de Andrade, Carlos

de Andrade, Mario 1892(?)-1945
See Andrade, Mario de
See also CA 178; HW 2

Deane, Norman
See Creasey, John

Deane, Seamus (Francis) 1940- ...... **CLC 122**
See also CA 118; CANR 42

de Beauvoir, Simone
See Beauvoir, Simone de

de Beer, P.
See Bosman, Herman Charles

De Botton, Alain 1969- .... **CLC 203**
See also CA 159; CANR 96

de Brissac, Malcolm
See Dickinson, Peter (Malcolm de Brissac)

de Campos, Alvaro
See Pessoa, Fernando (Antonio Nogueira)

de Chardin, Pierre Teilhard
See Teilhard de Chardin, (Marie Joseph)
Pierre

de Crenne, Helisenne c. 1510-c.
1560 .... **LC 113**

Dee, John 1527-1608 .... **LC 20**
See also DLB 136, 213

Deer, Sandra 1940- .... **CLC 45**
See also CA 186

De Ferrari, Gabriella 1941- .... **CLC 65**
See also CA 146

de Filippo, Eduardo 1900-1984 ... **TCLC 127**
See also CA 132; CAAS 114; EWL 3;
MTCW 1; RGWL 2, 3

Defoe, Daniel 1660(?)-1731 .... **LC 1, 42, 108;
WLC 2**
See also AAYA 27; BRW 3; BRWR 1; BYA
4; CDBLB 1660-1789; CLR 61; DA;
DA3; DAB; DAC; DAM MST, NOV;
DLB 39, 95, 101, 336; JRDA; LAIT 1;
LMFS 1; MAICYA 1, 2; NFS 9, 13;
RGEL 2; SATA 22; TEA; WCH; WLIT 3

de Gouges, Olympe
See de Gouges, Olympe

de Gouges, Olympe 1748-1793 .... **LC 127**
See also DLB 313

de Gourmont, Remy(-Marie-Charles)
See Gourmont, Remy(-Marie-Charles) de

de Gournay, Marie le Jars
1566-1645 .... **LC 98**
See also DLB 327; FW

de Hartog, Jan 1914-2002 .... **CLC 19**
See also CA 1-4R; CAAS 210; CANR 1;
DFS 12

de Hostos, E. M.
See Hostos (y Bonilla), Eugenio Maria de

de Hostos, Eugenio M.
See Hostos (y Bonilla), Eugenio Maria de

Deighton, Len .... **CLC 4, 7, 22, 46**
See Deighton, Leonard Cyril
See also AAYA 6; BEST 89:2; BPFB 1; CD-
BLB 1960 to Present; CMW 4; CN 1, 2,
3, 4, 5, 6, 7; CPW; DLB 87

Deighton, Leonard Cyril 1929-
See Deighton, Len
See also AAYA 57; CA 9-12R; CANR 19,
33, 68; DA3; DAM NOV, POP; MTCW
1, 2; MTFW 2005

Dekker, Thomas 1572(?)-1632 ..... **DC 12; LC
22**
See also CDBLB Before 1660; DAM
DRAM; DLB 62, 172; LMFS 1; RGEL 2

de Laclos, Pierre Ambroise Franois
See Laclos, Pierre-Ambroise Francois

Delacroix, (Ferdinand-Victor-)Eugene
1798-1863 .... **NCLC 133**
See also EW 5

Delafield, E. M. .... **TCLC 61**
See Dashwood, Edmee Elizabeth Monica
de la Pasture
See also DLB 34; RHW

de la Mare, Walter (John)
1873-1956 ..... **PC 77; SSC 14; TCLC 4,
53; WLC 2**
See also CA 163; CDBLB 1914-1945; CLR
23; CWRI 5; DA3; DAB; DAC; DAM
MST, POET; DLB 19, 153, 162, 255, 284;
EWL 3; EXPP; HGG; MAICYA 1, 2;
MTCW 2; MTFW 2005; RGEL 2; RGSF
2; SATA 16; SUFW 1; TEA; WCH

de Lamartine, Alphonse (Marie Louis Prat)
See Lamartine, Alphonse (Marie Louis Prat)
de

Delaney, Franey
See O'Hara, John (Henry)

Delaney, Shelagh 1939- .... **CLC 29**
See also CA 17-20R; CANR 30, 67; CBD;
CD 5, 6; CDBLB 1960 to Present; CWD;
DAM DRAM; DFS 7; DLB 13; MTCW 1

Delany, Martin Robison
1812-1885 .... **NCLC 93**
See also DLB 50; RGAL 4

Delany, Mary (Granville Pendarves)
1700-1788 .... **LC 12**

Delany, Samuel R., Jr. 1942- ... **BLC 1; CLC
8, 14, 38, 141**
See also AAYA 24; AFAW 2; BPFB 1; BW
2, 3; CA 81-84; CANR 27, 43, 116; CN
2, 3, 4, 5, 6, 7; DAM MULT; DLB 8, 33;
FANT; MAL 5; MTCW 1, 2; RGAL 4;
SATA 92; SCFW 1, 2; SFW 4; SUFW 2

de la Parra, (Ana) Teresa (Sonojo)
1890(?)-1936 .... **TCLC 185**
See Parra Sanojo, Ana Teresa de
See also CA 178; HW 2

De La Ramee, Marie Louise 1839-1908
See Ouida
See also CA 204; SATA 20

de la Roche, Mazo 1879-1961 .... **CLC 14**
See also CA 85-88; CANR 30; DLB 68;
RGEL 2; RHW; SATA 64

De La Salle, Innocent
See Hartmann, Sadakichi

de Laureamont, Comte
See Lautreamont

Delbanco, Nicholas 1942- ..... **CLC 6, 13, 167**
See also CA 189; 17-20R, 189; 2; CANR
29, 55, 116, 150; CN 7; DLB 6, 234

Delbanco, Nicholas Franklin
See Delbanco, Nicholas

del Castillo, Michel 1933- .... **CLC 38**
See also CA 109; CANR 77

Deledda, Grazia (Cosima)
1875(?)-1936 .... **TCLC 23**
See also CA 205; CAAE 123; DLB 264,
329; EWL 3; RGWL 2, 3; WLIT 7

Deleuze, Gilles 1925-1995 .... **TCLC 116**
See also DLB 296

Delgado, Abelardo (Lalo) B(arrientos)
1930-2004 .... **HLC 1**
See also CA 131; 15; CAAS 230; CANR
90; DAM MST, MULT; DLB 82; HW 1,
2

Delibes, Miguel .... **CLC 8, 18**
See Delibes Setien, Miguel
See also DLB 322; EWL 3

Delibes Setien, Miguel 1920-
See Delibes, Miguel
See also CA 45-48; CANR 1, 32; CWW 2;
HW 1; MTCW 1

DeLillo, Don 1936- ..... **CLC 8, 10, 13, 27, 39,
54, 76, 143, 210, 213**
See also AMWC 2; AMWS 6; BEST 89:1;
BPFB 1; CA 81-84; CANR 21, 76, 92,
133; CN 3, 4, 5, 6, 7; CPW; DA3; DAM
NOV, POP; DLB 6, 173; EWL 3; MAL 5;
MTCW 1, 2; MTFW 2005; RGAL 4; TUS

de Lisser, H. G.
See De Lisser, H(erbert) G(eorge)
See also DLB 117

De Lisser, H(erbert) G(eorge)
1878-1944 .... **TCLC 12**
See de Lisser, H. G.
See also BW 2; CA 152; CAAE 109

Deloire, Pierre
See Peguy, Charles (Pierre)

Deloney, Thomas 1543(?)-1600 .... **LC 41**
See also DLB 167; RGEL 2

Deloria, Ella (Cara) 1889-1971(?) ..... **NNAL**
See also CA 152; DAM MULT; DLB 175

Deloria, Vine, Jr. 1933-2005 .... **CLC 21, 122;
NNAL**
See also CA 53-56; CAAS 245; CANR 5,
20, 48, 98; DAM MULT; DLB 175;
MTCW 1; SATA 21; SATA-Obit 171

Deloria, Vine Victor, Jr.
See Deloria, Vine, Jr.

del Valle-Inclan, Ramon (Maria)
See Valle-Inclan, Ramon (Maria) del
See also DLB 322

Del Vecchio, John M(ichael) 1947- .. **CLC 29**
See also CA 110; DLBD 9

de Man, Paul (Adolph Michel)
1919-1983 .... **CLC 55**
See also CA 128; CAAS 111; CANR 61;
DLB 67; MTCW 1, 2

DeMarinis, Rick 1934- .... **CLC 54**
See also CA 184; 57-60, 184; 24; CANR 9,
25, 50, 160; DLB 218; TCWW 2

de Maupassant, (Henri Rene Albert) Guy
See Maupassant, (Henri Rene Albert) Guy
de

Dembry, R. Emmet
See Murfree, Mary Noailles

Demby, William 1922- .... **BLC 1; CLC 53**
See also BW 1, 3; CA 81-84; CANR 81;
DAM MULT; DLB 33

de Menton, Francisco
See Chin, Frank (Chew, Jr.)

Demetrius of Phalerum c.
307B.C.- .... **CMLC 34**

Demijohn, Thom
See Disch, Thomas M.

De Mille, James 1833-1880 .... **NCLC 123**
See also DLB 99, 251

Deming, Richard 1915-1983
See Queen, Ellery
See also CA 9-12R; CANR 3, 94; SATA 24

Democritus c. 460B.C.-c. 370B.C. .. **CMLC 47**

de Montaigne, Michel (Eyquem)
See Montaigne, Michel (Eyquem) de

de Montherlant, Henry (Milon)
See Montherlant, Henry (Milon) de

Demosthenes 384B.C.-322B.C. ...... **CMLC 13**
See also AW 1; DLB 176; RGWL 2, 3;
WLIT 8

de Musset, (Louis Charles) Alfred
See Musset, Alfred de

de Natale, Francine
See Malzberg, Barry N(athaniel)

de Navarre, Marguerite 1492-1549 ... **LC 61;
SSC 85**
See Marguerite d'Angouleme; Marguerite
de Navarre
See also DLB 327

Denby, Edwin (Orr) 1903-1983 .... **CLC 48**
See also CA 138; CAAS 110; CP 1

de Nerval, Gerard
See Nerval, Gerard de

Denham, John 1615-1669 .... **LC 73**
See also DLB 58, 126; RGEL 2

Denis, Julio
See Cortazar, Julio

Denmark, Harrison
See Zelazny, Roger

Dennis, John 1658-1734 .... **LC 11**
See also DLB 101; RGEL 2

Dennis, Nigel (Forbes) 1912-1989 ...... **CLC 8**
See also CA 25-28R; CAAS 129; CN 1, 2,
3, 4; DLB 13, 15, 233; EWL 3; MTCW 1

Dent, Lester 1904-1959 .... **TCLC 72**
See also CA 161; CAAE 112; CMW 4;
DLB 306; SFW 4

De Palma, Brian 1940- .... **CLC 20**
See also CA 109

De Palma, Brian Russell
See De Palma, Brian

de Pizan, Christine
See Christine de Pizan
See also FL 1:1

De Quincey, Thomas 1785-1859 ..... **NCLC 4,
87**
See also BRW 4; CDBLB 1789-1832; DLB
110, 144; RGEL 2

Deren, Eleanora 1908(?)-1961
See Deren, Maya
See also CA 192; CAAS 111

Deren, Maya .... **CLC 16, 102**
See Deren, Eleanora

Derleth, August (William)
1909-1971 .... **CLC 31**
See also BPFB 1; BYA 9, 10; CA 1-4R;
CAAS 29-32R; CANR 4; CMW 4; CN 1;
DLB 9; DLBD 17; HGG; SATA 5; SUFW
1

Der Nister 1884-1950 .... **TCLC 56**
See Nister, Der

de Routisie, Albert
See Aragon, Louis

Derrida, Jacques 1930-2004 ...... **CLC 24, 87,
225**
See also CA 127; CAAE 124; CAAS 232;
CANR 76, 98, 133; DLB 242; EWL 3;
LMFS 2; MTCW 2; TWA

Derry Down Derry
See Lear, Edward

Dersonnes, Jacques
See Simenon, Georges (Jacques Christian)

Der Stricker c. 1190-c. 1250 .... **CMLC 75**
See also DLB 138

Desai, Anita 1937- .... **CLC 19, 37, 97, 175**
See also BRWS 5; CA 81-84; CANR 33,
53, 95, 133; CN 1, 2, 3, 4, 5, 6, 7; CWRI
5; DA3; DAB; DAM NOV; DLB 271,
323; DNFS 2; EWL 3; FW; MTCW 1, 2;
MTFW 2005; SATA 63, 126

Desai, Kiran 1971- .... **CLC 119**
See also BYA 16; CA 171; CANR 127

de Saint-Luc, Jean
See Glassco, John

de Saint Roman, Arnaud
See Aragon, Louis

Desbordes-Valmore, Marceline
1786-1859 .... **NCLC 97**
See also DLB 217

Descartes, Rene 1596-1650 .... **LC 20, 35**
See also DLB 268; EW 3; GFL Beginnings
to 1789

Deschamps, Eustache 1340(?)-1404 .. **LC 103**
See also DLB 208

De Sica, Vittorio 1901(?)-1974 .... **CLC 20**
See also CAAS 117

Desnos, Robert 1900-1945 .... **TCLC 22**
See also CA 151; CAAE 121; CANR 107;
DLB 258; EWL 3; LMFS 2

Destouches, Louis-Ferdinand
1894-1961 .... **CLC 9, 15**
See Celine, Louis-Ferdinand
See also CA 85-88; CANR 28; MTCW 1

de Tolignac, Gaston
See Griffith, D(avid Lewelyn) W(ark)

Deutsch, Babette 1895-1982 .... **CLC 18**
See also BYA 3; CA 1-4R; CAAS 108;
CANR 4, 79; CP 1, 2, 3; DLB 45; SATA
1; SATA-Obit 33

Devenant, William 1606-1649 .... **LC 13**

Devkota, Laxmiprasad 1909-1959 . **TCLC 23**
See also CAAE 123

De Voto, Bernard (Augustine)
1897-1955 .... **TCLC 29**
See also CA 160; CAAE 113; DLB 9, 256;
MAL 5; TCWW 1, 2

De Vries, Peter 1910-1993 ..... **CLC 1, 2, 3, 7,
10, 28, 46**
See also CA 17-20R; CAAS 142; CANR
41; CN 1, 2, 3, 4, 5; DAM NOV; DLB 6;
DLBY 1982; MAL 5; MTCW 1, 2;
MTFW 2005

Dewey, John 1859-1952 .... **TCLC 95**
See also CA 170; CAAE 114; CANR 144;
DLB 246, 270; RGAL 4

Dexter, John
See Bradley, Marion Zimmer
See also GLL 1

Dexter, Martin
See Faust, Frederick (Schiller)

Dexter, Pete 1943- .... **CLC 34, 55**
See also BEST 89:2; CA 131; CAAE 127;
CANR 129; CPW; DAM POP; INT CA-
131; MAL 5; MTCW 1; MTFW 2005

Diamano, Silmang
See Senghor, Leopold Sedar

Diamant, Anita 1951- .... **CLC 239**
See also CA 145; CANR 126

Diamond, Neil 1941- .... **CLC 30**
See also CA 108

Diaz del Castillo, Bernal c.
1496-1584 .... **HLCS 1; LC 31**
See also DLB 318; LAW

di Bassetto, Corno
See Shaw, George Bernard

Dick, Philip K. 1928-1982 ... **CLC 10, 30, 72;
SSC 57**
See also AAYA 24; BPFB 1; BYA 11; CA
49-52; CAAS 106; CANR 2, 16, 132; CN
2, 3; CPW; DA3; DAM NOV, POP; DLB
8; MTCW 1, 2; MTFW 2005; NFS 5;
SCFW 1, 2; SFW 4

Dick, Philip Kindred
See Dick, Philip K.

Dickens, Charles (John Huffam)
1812-1870 .... **NCLC 3, 8, 18, 26, 37, 50,
86, 105, 113, 161; SSC 17, 49, 88; WLC
2**
See also AAYA 23; BRW 5; BRWC 1, 2;
BYA 1, 2, 3, 13, 14; CDBLB 1832-1890;
CLR 95; CMW 4; DA; DA3; DAB; DAC;
DAM MST, NOV; DLB 21, 55, 70, 159,
166; EXPN; GL 2; HGG; JRDA; LAIT 1,

Dorfman, Ariel 1942- .... **CLC 48, 77, 189; HLC 1**
See also CA 130; CAAE 124; CANR 67, 70, 135; CWW 2; DAM MULT; DFS 4; EWL 3; HW 1, 2; INT CA-130; WLIT 1

Dorn, Edward (Merton) 1929-1999 .... **CLC 10, 18**
See also CA 93-96; CAAS 187; CANR 42, 79; CP 1, 2, 3, 4, 5, 6, 7; DLB 5; INT CA-93-96; WP

Dor-Ner, Zvi .... **CLC 70**

Dorris, Michael 1945-1997 .... **CLC 109; NNAL**
See also AAYA 20; BEST 90:1; BYA 12; CA 102; CAAS 157; CANR 19, 46, 75; CLR 58; DA3; DAM MULT, NOV; DLB 175; LAIT 5; MTCW 2; MTFW 2005; NFS 3; RGAL 4; SATA 75; SATA-Obit 94; TCWW 2; YAW

Dorris, Michael A.
See Dorris, Michael

Dorsan, Luc
See Simenon, Georges (Jacques Christian)

Dorsange, Jean
See Simenon, Georges (Jacques Christian)

Dorset
See Sackville, Thomas

Dos Passos, John (Roderigo) 1896-1970 ... **CLC 1, 4, 8, 11, 15, 25, 34, 82; WLC 2**
See also AMW; BPFB 1; CA 1-4R; CAAS 29-32R; CANR 3; CDALB 1929-1941; DA; DA3; DAB; DAC; DAM MST, NOV; DLB 4, 9, 274, 316; DLBD 1, 15; DLBY 1996; EWL 3; MAL 5; MTCW 1, 2; MTFW 2005; NFS 14; RGAL 4; TUS

Dossage, Jean
See Simenon, Georges (Jacques Christian)

Dostoevsky, Fedor Mikhailovich 1821-1881 .. **NCLC 2, 7, 21, 33, 43, 119, 167; SSC 2, 33, 44; WLC 2**
See Dostoevsky, Fyodor
See also AAYA 40; DA; DA3; DAB; DAC; DAM MST, NOV; EW 7; EXPN; NFS 3, 8; RGSF 2; RGWL 2, 3; SSFS 8; TWA

Dostoevsky, Fyodor
See Dostoevsky, Fedor Mikhailovich
See also DLB 238; LATS 1:1; LMFS 1, 2

Doty, M. R.
See Doty, Mark

Doty, Mark 1953(?)- .... **CLC 176; PC 53**
See also AMWS 11; CA 183; 161, 183; CANR 110; CP 7

Doty, Mark A.
See Doty, Mark

Doty, Mark Alan
See Doty, Mark

Doughty, Charles M(ontagu) 1843-1926 .... **TCLC 27**
See also CA 178; CAAE 115; DLB 19, 57, 174

Douglas, Ellen .... **CLC 73**
See Haxton, Josephine Ayres; Williamson, Ellen Douglas
See also CN 5, 6, 7; CSW; DLB 292

Douglas, Gavin 1475(?)-1522 .... **LC 20**
See also DLB 132; RGEL 2

Douglas, George
See Brown, George Douglas
See also RGEL 2

Douglas, Keith (Castellain) 1920-1944 .... **TCLC 40**
See also BRW 7; CA 160; DLB 27; EWL 3; PAB; RGEL 2

Douglas, Leonard
See Bradbury, Ray

Douglas, Michael
See Crichton, Michael

Douglas, (George) Norman 1868-1952 .... **TCLC 68**
See also BRW 6; CA 157; CAAE 119; DLB 34, 195; RGEL 2

Douglas, William
See Brown, George Douglas

Douglass, Frederick 1817(?)-1895 ..... **BLC 1; NCLC 7, 55, 141; WLC 2**
See also AAYA 48; AFAW 1, 2; AMWC 1; AMWS 3; CDALB 1640-1865; DA; DA3; DAC; DAM MST, MULT; DLB 1, 43, 50, 79, 243; FW; LAIT 2; NCFS 2; RGAL 4; SATA 29

Dourado, (Waldomiro Freitas) Autran 1926- .... **CLC 23, 60**
See also CA 25-28R, 179; CANR 34, 81; DLB 145, 307; HW 2

Dourado, Waldomiro Freitas Autran
See Dourado, (Waldomiro Freitas) Autran

Dove, Rita 1952- .. **BLCS; CLC 50, 81; PC 6**
See also AAYA 46; AMWS 4; BW 2; CA 109; 19; CANR 27, 42, 68, 76, 97, 132; CDALBS; CP 5, 6, 7; CSW; CWP; DA3; DAM MULT, POET; DLB 120; EWL 3; EXPP; MAL 5; MTCW 2; MTFW 2005; PFS 1, 15; RGAL 4

Dove, Rita Frances
See Dove, Rita

Doveglion
See Villa, Jose Garcia

Dowell, Coleman 1925-1985 .... **CLC 60**
See also CA 25-28R; CAAS 117; CANR 10; DLB 130; GLL 2

Dowson, Ernest (Christopher) 1867-1900 .... **TCLC 4**
See also CA 150; CAAE 105; DLB 19, 135; RGEL 2

Doyle, A. Conan
See Doyle, Sir Arthur Conan

Doyle, Sir Arthur Conan 1859-1930 ..... **SSC 12, 83, 95; TCLC 7; WLC 2**
See Conan Doyle, Arthur
See also AAYA 14; BRWS 2; CA 122; CAAE 104; CANR 131; CDBLB 1890-1914; CLR 106; CMW 4; DA; DA3; DAB; DAC; DAM MST, NOV; DLB 18, 70, 156, 178; EXPS; HGG; LAIT 2; MSW; MTCW 1, 2; MTFW 2005; RGEL 2; RGSF 2; RHW; SATA 24; SCFW 1, 2; SFW 4; SSFS 2; TEA; WCH; WLIT 4; WYA; YAW

Doyle, Conan
See Doyle, Sir Arthur Conan

Doyle, John
See Graves, Robert

Doyle, Roddy 1958- .... **CLC 81, 178**
See also AAYA 14; BRWS 5; CA 143; CANR 73, 128; CN 6, 7; DA3; DLB 194, 326; MTCW 2; MTFW 2005

Doyle, Sir A. Conan
See Doyle, Sir Arthur Conan

Dr. A
See Asimov, Isaac; Silverstein, Alvin; Silverstein, Virginia B(arbara Opshelor)

Drabble, Margaret 1939- ...... **CLC 2, 3, 5, 8, 10, 22, 53, 129**
See also BRWS 4; CA 13-16R; CANR 18, 35, 63, 112, 131; CDBLB 1960 to Present; CN 1, 2, 3, 4, 5, 6, 7; CPW; DA3; DAB; DAC; DAM MST, NOV, POP; DLB 14, 155, 231; EWL 3; FW; MTCW 1, 2; MTFW 2005; RGEL 2; SATA 48; TEA

Drakulic, Slavenka 1949- .... **CLC 173**
See also CA 144; CANR 92

Drakulic-Ilic, Slavenka
See Drakulic, Slavenka

Drapier, M. B.
See Swift, Jonathan

Drayham, James
See Mencken, H(enry) L(ouis)

Drayton, Michael 1563-1631 .... **LC 8**
See also DAM POET; DLB 121; RGEL 2

Dreadstone, Carl
See Campbell, (John) Ramsey

Dreiser, Theodore 1871-1945 .... **SSC 30; TCLC 10, 18, 35, 83; WLC 2**
See also AMW; AMWC 2; AMWR 2; BYA 15, 16; CA 132; CAAE 106; CDALB 1865-1917; DA; DA3; DAC; DAM MST, NOV; DLB 9, 12, 102, 137; DLBD 1; EWL 3; LAIT 2; LMFS 2; MAL 5; MTCW 1, 2; MTFW 2005; NFS 8, 17; RGAL 4; TUS

Dreiser, Theodore Herman Albert
See Dreiser, Theodore

Drexler, Rosalyn 1926- .... **CLC 2, 6**
See also CA 81-84; CAD; CANR 68, 124; CD 5, 6; CWD; MAL 5

Dreyer, Carl Theodor 1889-1968 ...... **CLC 16**
See also CAAS 116

Drieu la Rochelle, Pierre 1893-1945 .... **TCLC 21**
See also CA 250; CAAE 117; DLB 72; EWL 3; GFL 1789 to the Present

Drieu la Rochelle, Pierre-Eugene 1893-1945
See Drieu la Rochelle, Pierre

Drinkwater, John 1882-1937 .... **TCLC 57**
See also CA 149; CAAE 109; DLB 10, 19, 149; RGEL 2

Drop Shot
See Cable, George Washington

Droste-Hulshoff, Annette Freiin von 1797-1848 .... **NCLC 3, 133**
See also CDWLB 2; DLB 133; RGSF 2; RGWL 2, 3

Drummond, Walter
See Silverberg, Robert

Drummond, William Henry 1854-1907 .... **TCLC 25**
See also CA 160; DLB 92

Drummond de Andrade, Carlos 1902-1987 .... **CLC 18; TCLC 139**
See Andrade, Carlos Drummond de
See also CA 132; CAAS 123; DLB 307; LAW

Drummond of Hawthornden, William 1585-1649 .... **LC 83**
See also DLB 121, 213; RGEL 2

Drury, Allen (Stuart) 1918-1998 .... **CLC 37**
See also CA 57-60; CAAS 170; CANR 18, 52; CN 1, 2, 3, 4, 5, 6; INT CANR-18

Druse, Eleanor
See King, Stephen

Dryden, John 1631-1700 ..... **DC 3; LC 3, 21, 115; PC 25; WLC 2**
See also BRW 2; CDBLB 1660-1789; DA; DAB; DAC; DAM DRAM, MST, POET; DLB 80, 101, 131; EXPP; IDTP; LMFS 1; RGEL 2; TEA; WLIT 3

du Bellay, Joachim 1524-1560 .... **LC 92**
See also DLB 327; GFL Beginnings to 1789; RGWL 2, 3

Duberman, Martin 1930- .... **CLC 8**
See also CA 1-4R; CAD; CANR 2, 63, 137; CD 5, 6

Dubie, Norman (Evans) 1945- .... **CLC 36**
See also CA 69-72; CANR 12, 115; CP 3, 4, 5, 6, 7; DLB 120; PFS 12

Du Bois, W(illiam) E(dward) B(urghardt) 1868-1963 ..... **BLC 1; CLC 1, 2, 13, 64, 96; HR 1:2; TCLC 169; WLC 2**
See also AAYA 40; AFAW 1, 2; AMWC 1; AMWS 2; BW 1, 3; CA 85-88; CANR 34, 82, 132; CDALB 1865-1917; DA; DA3; DAC; DAM MST, MULT, NOV;

Early, Jack
See Scoppettone, Sandra
See also GLL 1

East, Michael
See West, Morris L(anglo)

Eastaway, Edward
See Thomas, (Philip) Edward

Eastlake, William (Derry)
1917-1997 .... **CLC 8**
See also CA 5-8R; 1; CAAS 158; CANR 5,
63; CN 1, 2, 3, 4, 5, 6; DLB 6, 206; INT
CANR-5; MAL 5; TCWW 1, 2

Eastman, Charles A(lexander)
1858-1939 .... **NNAL; TCLC 55**
See also CA 179; CANR 91; DAM MULT;
DLB 175; YABC 1

Eaton, Edith Maude 1865-1914 .... **AAL**
See Far, Sui Sin
See also CA 154; DLB 221, 312; FW

Eaton, (Lillie) Winnifred 1875-1954 .... **AAL**
See also CA 217; DLB 221, 312; RGAL 4

Eberhart, Richard 1904-2005 ...... **CLC 3, 11,
19, 56; PC 76**
See also AMW; CA 1-4R; CAAS 240;
CANR 2, 125; CDALB 1941-1968; CP 1,
2, 3, 4, 5, 6, 7; DAM POET; DLB 48;
MAL 5; MTCW 1; RGAL 4

Eberhart, Richard Ghormley
See Eberhart, Richard

Eberstadt, Fernanda 1960- .... **CLC 39**
See also CA 136; CANR 69, 128

**Echegaray (y Eizaguirre), Jose (Maria
Waldo)** 1832-1916 .... **HLCS 1; TCLC 4**
See also CAAE 104; CANR 32; DLB 329;
EWL 3; HW 1; MTCW 1

Echeverria, (Jose) Esteban (Antonino)
1805-1851 .... **NCLC 18**
See also LAW

Echo
See Proust, (Valentin-Louis-George-Eugene)
Marcel

Eckert, Allan W. 1931- .... **CLC 17**
See also AAYA 18; BYA 2; CA 13-16R;
CANR 14, 45; INT CANR-14; MAICYA
2; MAICYAS 1; SAAS 21; SATA 29, 91;
SATA-Brief 27

Eckhart, Meister 1260(?)-1327(?) .. **CMLC 9,
80**
See also DLB 115; LMFS 1

Eckmar, F. R.
See de Hartog, Jan

Eco, Umberto 1932- .... **CLC 28, 60, 142**
See also BEST 90:1; BPFB 1; CA 77-80;
CANR 12, 33, 55, 110, 131; CPW; CWW
2; DA3; DAM NOV, POP; DLB 196, 242;
EWL 3; MSW; MTCW 1, 2; MTFW
2005; NFS 22; RGWL 3; WLIT 7

Eddison, E(ric) R(ucker)
1882-1945 .... **TCLC 15**
See also CA 156; CAAE 109; DLB 255;
FANT; SFW 4; SUFW 1

Eddy, Mary (Ann Morse) Baker
1821-1910 .... **TCLC 71**
See also CA 174; CAAE 113

Edel, (Joseph) Leon 1907-1997 .. **CLC 29, 34**
See also CA 1-4R; CAAS 161; CANR 1,
22, 112; DLB 103; INT CANR-22

Eden, Emily 1797-1869 .... **NCLC 10**

Edgar, David 1948- .... **CLC 42**
See also CA 57-60; CANR 12, 61, 112;
CBD; CD 5, 6; DAM DRAM; DFS 15;
DLB 13, 233; MTCW 1

Edgerton, Clyde (Carlyle) 1944- ...... **CLC 39**
See also AAYA 17; CA 134; CAAE 118;
CANR 64, 125; CN 7; CSW; DLB 278;
INT CA-134; TCLE 1:1; YAW

Edgeworth, Maria 1768-1849 ... **NCLC 1, 51,
158; SSC 86**
See also BRWS 3; DLB 116, 159, 163; FL
1:3; FW; RGEL 2; SATA 21; TEA; WLIT
3

Edmonds, Paul
See Kuttner, Henry

Edmonds, Walter D(umaux)
1903-1998 .... **CLC 35**
See also BYA 2; CA 5-8R; CANR 2; CWRI
5; DLB 9; LAIT 1; MAICYA 1, 2; MAL
5; RHW; SAAS 4; SATA 1, 27; SATA-
Obit 99

Edmondson, Wallace
See Ellison, Harlan

Edson, Margaret 1961- ...... **CLC 199; DC 24**
See also CA 190; DFS 13; DLB 266

Edson, Russell 1935- .... **CLC 13**
See also CA 33-36R; CANR 115; CP 2, 3,
4, 5, 6, 7; DLB 244; WP

Edwards, Bronwen Elizabeth
See Rose, Wendy

Edwards, G(erald) B(asil)
1899-1976 .... **CLC 25**
See also CA 201; CAAS 110

Edwards, Gus 1939- .... **CLC 43**
See also CA 108; INT CA-108

Edwards, Jonathan 1703-1758 .... **LC 7, 54**
See also AMW; DA; DAC; DAM MST;
DLB 24, 270; RGAL 4; TUS

Edwards, Sarah Pierpont 1710-1758 .. **LC 87**
See also DLB 200

Efron, Marina Ivanovna Tsvetaeva
See Tsvetaeva (Efron), Marina (Ivanovna)

Egeria fl. 4th cent. - .... **CMLC 70**

Egoyan, Atom 1960- .... **CLC 151**
See also AAYA 63; CA 157; CANR 151

Ehle, John (Marsden, Jr.) 1925- ...... **CLC 27**
See also CA 9-12R; CSW

Ehrenbourg, Ilya (Grigoryevich)
See Ehrenburg, Ilya (Grigoryevich)

Ehrenburg, Ilya (Grigoryevich)
1891-1967 .... **CLC 18, 34, 62**
See Erenburg, Il'ia Grigor'evich
See also CA 102; CAAS 25-28R; EWL 3

Ehrenburg, Ilyo (Grigoryevich)
See Ehrenburg, Ilya (Grigoryevich)

Ehrenreich, Barbara 1941- .... **CLC 110**
See also BEST 90:4; CA 73-76; CANR 16,
37, 62, 117; DLB 246; FW; MTCW 1, 2;
MTFW 2005

Eich, Gunter
See Eich, Gunter
See also RGWL 2, 3

Eich, Gunter 1907-1972 .... **CLC 15**
See Eich, Gunter
See also CA 111; CAAS 93-96; DLB 69,
124; EWL 3

Eichendorff, Joseph 1788-1857 .... **NCLC 8**
See also DLB 90; RGWL 2, 3

Eigner, Larry .... **CLC 9**
See Eigner, Laurence (Joel)
See also CA 23; CP 1, 2, 3, 4, 5, 6; DLB 5;
WP

Eigner, Laurence (Joel) 1927-1996
See Eigner, Larry
See also CA 9-12R; CAAS 151; CANR 6,
84; CP 7; DLB 193

Eilhart von Oberge c. 1140-c.
1195 .... **CMLC 67**
See also DLB 148

Einhard c. 770-840 .... **CMLC 50**
See also DLB 148

Einstein, Albert 1879-1955 .... **TCLC 65**
See also CA 133; CAAE 121; MTCW 1, 2

Eiseley, Loren
See Eiseley, Loren Corey
See also DLB 275

Eiseley, Loren Corey 1907-1977 .... **CLC 7**
See Eiseley, Loren
See also AAYA 5; ANW; CA 1-4R; CAAS
73-76; CANR 6; DLBD 17

Eisenstadt, Jill 1963- .... **CLC 50**
See also CA 140

Eisenstein, Sergei (Mikhailovich)
1898-1948 .... **TCLC 57**
See also CA 149; CAAE 114

Eisner, Simon
See Kornbluth, C(yril) M.

Eisner, Will 1917-2005 .... **CLC 237**
See also AAYA 52; CA 108; CAAS 235;
CANR 114, 140; MTFW 2005; SATA 31,
165

Eisner, William Erwin
See Eisner, Will

Ekeloef, (Bengt) Gunnar
1907-1968 .... **CLC 27; PC 23**
See Ekelof, (Bengt) Gunnar
See also CA 123; CAAS 25-28R; DAM
POET

Ekelof, (Bengt) Gunnar 1907-1968
See Ekeloef, (Bengt) Gunnar
See also DLB 259; EW 12; EWL 3

Ekelund, Vilhelm 1880-1949 .... **TCLC 75**
See also CA 189; EWL 3

Ekwensi, C. O. D.
See Ekwensi, Cyprian (Odiatu Duaka)

Ekwensi, Cyprian (Odiatu Duaka)
1921- .... **BLC 1; CLC 4**
See also AFW; BW 2, 3; CA 29-32R;
CANR 18, 42, 74, 125; CDWLB 3; CN 1,
2, 3, 4, 5, 6; CWRI 5; DAM MULT; DLB
117; EWL 3; MTCW 1, 2; RGEL 2; SATA
66; WLIT 2

Elaine .... **TCLC 18**
See Leverson, Ada Esther

El Crummo
See Crumb, R.

Elder, Lonne III 1931-1996 ..... **BLC 1; DC 8**
See also BW 1, 3; CA 81-84; CAAS 152;
CAD; CANR 25; DAM MULT; DLB 7,
38, 44; MAL 5

Eleanor of Aquitaine 1122-1204 ... **CMLC 39**

Elia
See Lamb, Charles

Eliade, Mircea 1907-1986 .... **CLC 19**
See also CA 65-68; CAAS 119; CANR 30,
62; CDWLB 4; DLB 220; EWL 3; MTCW
1; RGWL 3; SFW 4

Eliot, A. D.
See Jewett, (Theodora) Sarah Orne

Eliot, Alice
See Jewett, (Theodora) Sarah Orne

Eliot, Dan
See Silverberg, Robert

Eliot, George 1819-1880 ...... **NCLC 4, 13, 23,
41, 49, 89, 118, 183; PC 20; SSC 72;
WLC 2**
See Evans, Mary Ann
See also BRW 5; BRWC 1, 2; BRWR 2;
CDBLB 1832-1890; CN 7; CPW; DA;
DA3; DAB; DAC; DAM MST, NOV;
DLB 21, 35, 55; FL 1:3; LATS 1:1; LMFS
1; NFS 17, 20; RGEL 2; RGSF 2; SSFS
8; TEA; WLIT 3

Eliot, John 1604-1690 .... **LC 5**
See also DLB 24

Eliot, T(homas) S(tearns)
1888-1965 ...... **CLC 1, 2, 3, 6, 9, 10, 13,
15, 24, 34, 41, 55, 57, 113; PC 5, 31;
WLC 2**
See also AAYA 28; AMW; AMWC 1;
AMWR 1; BRW 7; BRWR 2; CA 5-8R;
CAAS 25-28R; CANR 41; CBD; CDALB
1929-1941; DA; DA3; DAB; DAC; DAM
DRAM, MST, POET; DFS 4, 13; DLB 7,
10, 45, 63, 245, 329; DLBY 1988; EWL

Erskine, John 1879-1951 .... **TCLC 84**
See also CA 159; CAAE 112; DLB 9, 102;
FANT
Erwin, Will
See Eisner, Will
Eschenbach, Wolfram von
See von Eschenbach, Wolfram
See also RGWL 3
Eseki, Bruno
See Mphahlele, Ezekiel
Esenin, S.A.
See Esenin, Sergei
See also EWL 3
Esenin, Sergei 1895-1925 .... **TCLC 4**
See Esenin, S.A.
See also CAAE 104; RGWL 2, 3
Esenin, Sergei Aleksandrovich
See Esenin, Sergei
Eshleman, Clayton 1935- .... **CLC 7**
See also CA 212; 33-36R, 212; 6; CANR
93; CP 1, 2, 3, 4, 5, 6, 7; DLB 5
Espada, Martin 1957- .... **PC 74**
See also CA 159; CANR 80; CP 7; EXPP;
LLW; MAL 5; PFS 13, 16
Espriella, Don Manuel Alvarez
See Southey, Robert
Espriu, Salvador 1913-1985 .... **CLC 9**
See also CA 154; CAAS 115; DLB 134;
EWL 3
Espronceda, Jose de 1808-1842 ..... **NCLC 39**
Esquivel, Laura 1950(?)- ... **CLC 141; HLCS 1**
See also AAYA 29; CA 143; CANR 68, 113,
161; DA3; DNFS 2; LAIT 3; LMFS 2;
MTCW 2; MTFW 2005; NFS 5; WLIT 1
Esse, James
See Stephens, James
Esterbrook, Tom
See Hubbard, L. Ron
Estleman, Loren D. 1952- .... **CLC 48**
See also AAYA 27; CA 85-88; CANR 27,
74, 139; CMW 4; CPW; DA3; DAM
NOV, POP; DLB 226; INT CANR-27;
MTCW 1, 2; MTFW 2005; TCWW 1, 2
Etherege, Sir George 1636-1692 . **DC 23; LC 78**
See also BRW 2; DAM DRAM; DLB 80;
PAB; RGEL 2
Euclid 306B.C.-283B.C. .... **CMLC 25**
Eugenides, Jeffrey 1960(?)- ...... **CLC 81, 212**
See also AAYA 51; CA 144; CANR 120;
MTFW 2005; NFS 24
Euripides c. 484B.C.-406B.C. .... **CMLC 23, 51; DC 4; WLCS**
See also AW 1; CDWLB 1; DA; DA3;
DAB; DAC; DAM DRAM, MST; DFS 1,
4, 6; DLB 176; LAIT 1; LMFS 1; RGWL
2, 3; WLIT 8
Evan, Evin
See Faust, Frederick (Schiller)
Evans, Caradoc 1878-1945 ... **SSC 43; TCLC 85**
See also DLB 162
Evans, Evan
See Faust, Frederick (Schiller)
Evans, Marian
See Eliot, George
Evans, Mary Ann
See Eliot, George
See also NFS 20
Evarts, Esther
See Benson, Sally
Everett, Percival
See Everett, Percival L.
See also CSW
Everett, Percival L. 1956- .... **CLC 57**
See Everett, Percival
See also BW 2; CA 129; CANR 94, 134;
CN 7; MTFW 2005

Everson, R(onald) G(ilmour)
1903-1992 .... **CLC 27**
See also CA 17-20R; CP 1, 2, 3, 4; DLB 88
Everson, William (Oliver)
1912-1994 .... **CLC 1, 5, 14**
See Antoninus, Brother
See also BG 1:2; CA 9-12R; CAAS 145;
CANR 20; CP 2, 3, 4, 5; DLB 5, 16, 212;
MTCW 1
Evtushenko, Evgenii Aleksandrovich
See Yevtushenko, Yevgeny (Alexandrovich)
See also CWW 2; RGWL 2, 3
Ewart, Gavin (Buchanan)
1916-1995 .... **CLC 13, 46**
See also BRWS 7; CA 89-92; CAAS 150;
CANR 17, 46; CP 1, 2, 3, 4, 5, 6; DLB
40; MTCW 1
Ewers, Hanns Heinz 1871-1943 ..... **TCLC 12**
See also CA 149; CAAE 109
Ewing, Frederick R.
See Sturgeon, Theodore (Hamilton)
Exley, Frederick (Earl) 1929-1992 .... **CLC 6, 11**
See also AITN 2; BPFB 1; CA 81-84;
CAAS 138; CANR 117; DLB 143; DLBY
1981
Eynhardt, Guillermo
See Quiroga, Horacio (Sylvestre)
Ezekiel, Nissim (Moses) 1924-2004 .. **CLC 61**
See also CA 61-64; CAAS 223; CP 1, 2, 3,
4, 5, 6, 7; DLB 323; EWL 3
Ezekiel, Tish O'Dowd 1943- .... **CLC 34**
See also CA 129
Fadeev, Aleksandr Aleksandrovich
See Bulgya, Alexander Alexandrovich
See also DLB 272
Fadeev, Alexandr Alexandrovich
See Bulgya, Alexander Alexandrovich
See also EWL 3
Fadeyev, A.
See Bulgya, Alexander Alexandrovich
Fadeyev, Alexander .... **TCLC 53**
See Bulgya, Alexander Alexandrovich
Fagen, Donald 1948- .... **CLC 26**
Fainzil'berg, Il'ia Arnol'dovich
See Fainzilberg, Ilya Arnoldovich
Fainzilberg, Ilya Arnoldovich
1897-1937 .... **TCLC 21**
See Il'f, Il'ia
See also CA 165; CAAE 120; EWL 3
Fair, Ronald L. 1932- .... **CLC 18**
See also BW 1; CA 69-72; CANR 25; DLB
33
Fairbairn, Roger
See Carr, John Dickson
Fairbairns, Zoe (Ann) 1948- .... **CLC 32**
See also CA 103; CANR 21, 85; CN 4, 5,
6, 7
Fairfield, Flora
See Alcott, Louisa May
Fairman, Paul W. 1916-1977
See Queen, Ellery
See also CAAS 114; SFW 4
Falco, Gian
See Papini, Giovanni
Falconer, James
See Kirkup, James
Falconer, Kenneth
See Kornbluth, C(yril) M.
Falkland, Samuel
See Heijermans, Herman
Fallaci, Oriana 1930-2006 .... **CLC 11, 110**
See also CA 77-80; CAAS 253; CANR 15,
58, 134; FW; MTCW 1
Faludi, Susan 1959- .... **CLC 140**
See also CA 138; CANR 126; FW; MTCW
2; MTFW 2005; NCFS 3
Faludy, George 1913- .... **CLC 42**
See also CA 21-24R

Faludy, Gyoergy
See Faludy, George
Fanon, Frantz 1925-1961 ... **BLC 2; CLC 74; TCLC 188**
See also BW 1; CA 116; CAAS 89-92;
DAM MULT; DLB 296; LMFS 2; WLIT
2
Fanshawe, Ann 1625-1680 .... **LC 11**
Fante, John (Thomas) 1911-1983 .... **CLC 60; SSC 65**
See also AMWS 11; CA 69-72; CAAS 109;
CANR 23, 104; DLB 130; DLBY 1983
Far, Sui Sin .... **SSC 62**
See Eaton, Edith Maude
See also SSFS 4
Farah, Nuruddin 1945- ...... **BLC 2; CLC 53, 137**
See also AFW; BW 2, 3; CA 106; CANR
81, 148; CDWLB 3; CN 4, 5, 6, 7; DAM
MULT; DLB 125; EWL 3; WLIT 2
Fargue, Leon-Paul 1876(?)-1947 .... **TCLC 11**
See also CAAE 109; CANR 107; DLB 258;
EWL 3
Farigoule, Louis
See Romains, Jules
Farina, Richard 1936(?)-1966 .... **CLC 9**
See also CA 81-84; CAAS 25-28R
Farley, Walter (Lorimer)
1915-1989 .... **CLC 17**
See also AAYA 58; BYA 14; CA 17-20R;
CANR 8, 29, 84; DLB 22; JRDA; MAI-
CYA 1, 2; SATA 2, 43, 132; YAW
Farmer, Philip Jose 1918- .... **CLC 1, 19**
See also AAYA 28; BPFB 1; CA 1-4R;
CANR 4, 35, 111; DLB 8; MTCW 1;
SATA 93; SCFW 1, 2; SFW 4
Farquhar, George 1677-1707 .... **LC 21**
See also BRW 2; DAM DRAM; DLB 84;
RGEL 2
Farrell, J(ames) G(ordon)
1935-1979 .... **CLC 6**
See also CA 73-76; CAAS 89-92; CANR
36; CN 1, 2; DLB 14, 271, 326; MTCW
1; RGEL 2; RHW; WLIT 4
Farrell, James T(homas) 1904-1979 . **CLC 1, 4, 8, 11, 66; SSC 28**
See also AMW; BPFB 1; CA 5-8R; CAAS
89-92; CANR 9, 61; CN 1, 2; DLB 4, 9,
86; DLBD 2; EWL 3; MAL 5; MTCW 1,
2; MTFW 2005; RGAL 4
Farrell, Warren (Thomas) 1943- ...... **CLC 70**
See also CA 146; CANR 120
Farren, Richard J.
See Betjeman, John
Farren, Richard M.
See Betjeman, John
Fassbinder, Rainer Werner
1946-1982 .... **CLC 20**
See also CA 93-96; CAAS 106; CANR 31
Fast, Howard 1914-2003 .... **CLC 23, 131**
See also AAYA 16; BPFB 1; CA 181; 1-4R;
181; 18; CAAS 214; CANR 1, 33, 54, 75,
98, 140; CMW 4; CN 1, 2, 3, 4, 5, 6, 7;
CPW; DAM NOV; DLB 9; INT CANR-
33; LATS 1:1; MAL 5; MTCW 2; MTFW
2005; RHW; SATA 7; SATA-Essay 107;
TCWW 1, 2; YAW
Faulcon, Robert
See Holdstock, Robert
Faulkner, William (Cuthbert)
1897-1962 .... **CLC 1, 3, 6, 8, 9, 11, 14, 18, 28, 52, 68; SSC 1, 35, 42, 92, 97; TCLC 141; WLC 2**
See also AAYA 7; AMW; AMWR 1; BPFB
1; BYA 5, 15; CA 81-84; CANR 33;
CDALB 1929-1941; DA; DA3; DAB;
DAC; DAM MST, NOV; DLB 9, 11, 44,
102, 316, 330; DLBD 2; DLBY 1986,
1997; EWL 3; EXPN; EXPS; GL 2; LAIT

Forster, Margaret 1938- .... **CLC 149**
See also CA 133; CANR 62, 115; CN 4, 5, 6, 7; DLB 155, 271

Forsyth, Frederick 1938- .... **CLC 2, 5, 36**
See also BEST 89:4; CA 85-88; CANR 38, 62, 115, 137; CMW 4; CN 3, 4, 5, 6, 7; CPW; DAM NOV, POP; DLB 87; MTCW 1, 2; MTFW 2005

Forten, Charlotte L. 1837-1914 .... **BLC 2; TCLC 16**
See Grimke, Charlotte L(ottie) Forten
See also DLB 50, 239

Fortinbras
See Grieg, (Johan) Nordahl (Brun)

Foscolo, Ugo 1778-1827 .... **NCLC 8, 97**
See also EW 5; WLIT 7

Fosse, Bob 1927-1987
See Fosse, Robert L.
See also CAAE 110; CAAS 123

Fosse, Robert L. .... **CLC 20**
See Fosse, Bob

Foster, Hannah Webster
1758-1840 .... **NCLC 99**
See also DLB 37, 200; RGAL 4

Foster, Stephen Collins
1826-1864 .... **NCLC 26**
See also RGAL 4

Foucault, Michel 1926-1984 . **CLC 31, 34, 69**
See also CA 105; CAAS 113; CANR 34; DLB 242; EW 13; EWL 3; GFL 1789 to the Present; GLL 1; LMFS 2; MTCW 1, 2; TWA

Fouque, Friedrich (Heinrich Karl) de la Motte 1777-1843 .... **NCLC 2**
See also DLB 90; RGWL 2, 3; SUFW 1

Fourier, Charles 1772-1837 .... **NCLC 51**

Fournier, Henri-Alban 1886-1914
See Alain-Fournier
See also CA 179; CAAE 104

Fournier, Pierre 1916-1997 .... **CLC 11**
See Gascar, Pierre
See also CA 89-92; CANR 16, 40

Fowles, John 1926-2005 .... **CLC 1, 2, 3, 4, 6, 9, 10, 15, 33, 87; SSC 33**
See also BPFB 1; BRWS 1; CA 5-8R; CAAS 245; CANR 25, 71, 103; CDBLB 1960 to Present; CN 1, 2, 3, 4, 5, 6, 7; DA3; DAB; DAC; DAM MST; DLB 14, 139, 207; EWL 3; HGG; MTCW 1, 2; MTFW 2005; NFS 21; RGEL 2; RHW; SATA 22; SATA-Obit 171; TEA; WLIT 4

Fowles, John Robert
See Fowles, John

Fox, Paula 1923- .... **CLC 2, 8, 121**
See also AAYA 3, 37; BYA 3, 8; CA 73-76; CANR 20, 36, 62, 105; CLR 1, 44, 96; DLB 52; JRDA; MAICYA 1, 2; MTCW 1; NFS 12; SATA 17, 60, 120, 167; WYA; YAW

Fox, William Price (Jr.) 1926- .... **CLC 22**
See also CA 17-20R; 19; CANR 11, 142; CSW; DLB 2; DLBY 1981

Foxe, John 1517(?)-1587 .... **LC 14**
See also DLB 132

Frame, Janet .. **CLC 2, 3, 6, 22, 66, 96, 237; SSC 29**
See Clutha, Janet Paterson Frame
See also CN 1, 2, 3, 4, 5, 6, 7; CP 2, 3, 4; CWP; EWL 3; RGEL 2; RGSF 2; TWA

France, Anatole .... **TCLC 9**
See Thibault, Jacques Anatole Francois
See also DLB 123, 330; EWL 3; GFL 1789 to the Present; RGWL 2, 3; SUFW 1

Francis, Claude .... **CLC 50**
See also CA 192

Francis, Dick
See Francis, Richard Stanley
See also CN 2, 3, 4, 5, 6

Francis, Richard Stanley 1920- ... **CLC 2, 22, 42, 102**
See Francis, Dick
See also AAYA 5, 21; BEST 89:3; BPFB 1; CA 5-8R; CANR 9, 42, 68, 100, 141; CD-BLB 1960 to Present; CMW 4; CN 7; DA3; DAM POP; DLB 87; INT CANR-9; MSW; MTCW 1, 2; MTFW 2005

Francis, Robert (Churchill)
1901-1987 .... **CLC 15; PC 34**
See also AMWS 9; CA 1-4R; CAAS 123; CANR 1; CP 1, 2, 3, 4; EXPP; PFS 12; TCLE 1:1

Francis, Lord Jeffrey
See Jeffrey, Francis
See also DLB 107

Frank, Anne(lies Marie)
1929-1945 .... **TCLC 17; WLC 2**
See also AAYA 12; BYA 1; CA 133; CAAE 113; CANR 68; CLR 101; DA; DA3; DAB; DAC; DAM MST; LAIT 4; MAI-CYA 2; MAICYAS 1; MTCW 1, 2; MTFW 2005; NCFS 2; RGHL; SATA 87; SATA-Brief 42; WYA; YAW

Frank, Bruno 1887-1945 .... **TCLC 81**
See also CA 189; DLB 118; EWL 3

Frank, Elizabeth 1945- .... **CLC 39**
See also CA 126; CAAE 121; CANR 78, 150; INT CA-126

Frankl, Viktor E(mil) 1905-1997 ...... **CLC 93**
See also CA 65-68; CAAS 161; RGHL

Franklin, Benjamin
See Hasek, Jaroslav (Matej Frantisek)

Franklin, Benjamin 1706-1790 .. **LC 25, 134; WLCS**
See also AMW; CDALB 1640-1865; DA; DA3; DAB; DAC; DAM MST; DLB 24, 43, 73, 183; LAIT 1; RGAL 4; TUS

Franklin, (Stella Maria Sarah) Miles (Lampe) 1879-1954 .... **TCLC 7**
See also CA 164; CAAE 104; DLB 230; FW; MTCW 2; RGEL 2; TWA

Franzen, Jonathan 1959- .... **CLC 202**
See also AAYA 65; CA 129; CANR 105

Fraser, Antonia 1932- .... **CLC 32, 107**
See also AAYA 57; CA 85-88; CANR 44, 65, 119; CMW; DLB 276; MTCW 1, 2; MTFW 2005; SATA-Brief 32

Fraser, George MacDonald 1925- ...... **CLC 7**
See also AAYA 48; CA 180; 45-48, 180; CANR 2, 48, 74; MTCW 2; RHW

Fraser, Sylvia 1935- .... **CLC 64**
See also CA 45-48; CANR 1, 16, 60; CCA 1

Frayn, Michael 1933- .... **CLC 3, 7, 31, 47, 176; DC 27**
See also AAYA 69; BRWC 2; BRWS 7; CA 5-8R; CANR 30, 69, 114, 133; CBD; CD 5, 6; CN 1, 2, 3, 4, 5, 6, 7; DAM DRAM, NOV; DFS 22; DLB 13, 14, 194, 245; FANT; MTCW 1, 2; MTFW 2005; SFW 4

Fraze, Candida (Merrill) 1945- .... **CLC 50**
See also CA 126

Frazer, Andrew
See Marlowe, Stephen

Frazer, J(ames) G(eorge)
1854-1941 .... **TCLC 32**
See also BRWS 3; CAAE 118; NCFS 5

Frazer, Robert Caine
See Creasey, John

Frazer, Sir James George
See Frazer, J(ames) G(eorge)

Frazier, Charles 1950- .... **CLC 109, 224**
See also AAYA 34; CA 161; CANR 126; CSW; DLB 292; MTFW 2005; NFS 25

Frazier, Ian 1951- .... **CLC 46**
See also CA 130; CANR 54, 93

Frederic, Harold 1856-1898 ... **NCLC 10, 175**
See also AMW; DLB 12, 23; DLBD 13; MAL 5; NFS 22; RGAL 4

Frederick, John
See Faust, Frederick (Schiller)
See also TCWW 2

Frederick the Great 1712-1786 .... **LC 14**

Fredro, Aleksander 1793-1876 .... **NCLC 8**

Freeling, Nicolas 1927-2003 .... **CLC 38**
See also CA 49-52; 12; CAAS 218; CANR 1, 17, 50, 84; CMW 4; CN 1, 2, 3, 4, 5, 6; DLB 87

Freeman, Douglas Southall
1886-1953 .... **TCLC 11**
See also CA 195; CAAE 109; DLB 17; DLBD 17

Freeman, Judith 1946- .... **CLC 55**
See also CA 148; CANR 120; DLB 256

Freeman, Mary E(leanor) Wilkins
1852-1930 .... **SSC 1, 47; TCLC 9**
See also CA 177; CAAE 106; DLB 12, 78, 221; EXPS; FW; HGG; MBL; RGAL 4; RGSF 2; SSFS 4, 8; SUFW 1; TUS

Freeman, R(ichard) Austin
1862-1943 .... **TCLC 21**
See also CAAE 113; CANR 84; CMW 4; DLB 70

French, Albert 1943- .... **CLC 86**
See also BW 3; CA 167

French, Antonia
See Kureishi, Hanif

French, Marilyn 1929-.. **CLC 10, 18, 60, 177**
See also BPFB 1; CA 69-72; CANR 3, 31, 134, 163; CN 5, 6, 7; CPW; DAM DRAM, NOV, POP; FL 1:5; FW; INT CANR-31; MTCW 1, 2; MTFW 2005

French, Paul
See Asimov, Isaac

Freneau, Philip Morin 1752-1832 .. **NCLC 1, 111**
See also AMWS 2; DLB 37, 43; RGAL 4

Freud, Sigmund 1856-1939 .... **TCLC 52**
See also CA 133; CAAE 115; CANR 69; DLB 296; EW 8; EWL 3; LATS 1:1; MTCW 1, 2; MTFW 2005; NCFS 3; TWA

Freytag, Gustav 1816-1895 .... **NCLC 109**
See also DLB 129

Friedan, Betty 1921-2006 .... **CLC 74**
See also CA 65-68; CAAS 248; CANR 18, 45, 74; DLB 246; FW; MTCW 1, 2; MTFW 2005; NCFS 5

Friedan, Betty Naomi
See Friedan, Betty

Friedlander, Saul 1932- .... **CLC 90**
See also CA 130; CAAE 117; CANR 72; RGHL

Friedman, B(ernard) H(arper)
1926- .... **CLC 7**
See also CA 1-4R; CANR 3, 48

Friedman, Bruce Jay 1930- ...... **CLC 3, 5, 56**
See also CA 9-12R; CAD; CANR 25, 52, 101; CD 5, 6; CN 1, 2, 3, 4, 5, 6, 7; DLB 2, 28, 244; INT CANR-25; MAL 5; SSFS 18

Friel, Brian 1929- .... **CLC 5, 42, 59, 115; DC 8; SSC 76**
See also BRWS 5; CA 21-24R; CANR 33, 69, 131; CBD; CD 5, 6; DFS 11; DLB 13, 319; EWL 3; MTCW 1; RGEL 2; TEA

Friis-Baastad, Babbis Ellinor
1921-1970 .... **CLC 12**
See also CA 17-20R; CAAS 134; SATA 7

Frisch, Max 1911-1991 ...... **CLC 3, 9, 14, 18, 32, 44; TCLC 121**
See also CA 85-88; CAAS 134; CANR 32, 74; CDWLB 2; DAM DRAM, NOV; DLB 69, 124; EW 13; EWL 3; MTCW 1, 2; MTFW 2005; RGHL; RGWL 2, 3

Fromentin, Eugene (Samuel Auguste)
1820-1876 .... **NCLC 10, 125**
See also DLB 123; GFL 1789 to the Present

Frost, Frederick
See Faust, Frederick (Schiller)

Frost, Robert 1874-1963 . **CLC 1, 3, 4, 9, 10, 13, 15, 26, 34, 44; PC 1, 39, 71; WLC 2**
See also AAYA 21; AMW; AMWR 1; CA 89-92; CANR 33; CDALB 1917-1929; CLR 67; DA; DA3; DAB; DAC; DAM MST, POET; DLB 54, 284; DLBD 7; EWL 3; EXPP; MAL 5; MTCW 1, 2; MTFW 2005; PAB; PFS 1, 2, 3, 4, 5, 6, 7, 10, 13; RGAL 4; SATA 14; TUS; WP; WYA

Frost, Robert Lee
See Frost, Robert

Froude, James Anthony
1818-1894 .... **NCLC 43**
See also DLB 18, 57, 144

Froy, Herald
See Waterhouse, Keith (Spencer)

Fry, Christopher 1907-2005 ... **CLC 2, 10, 14**
See also BRWS 3; CA 17-20R; 23; CAAS 240; CANR 9, 30, 74, 132; CBD; CD 5, 6; CP 1, 2, 3, 4, 5, 6, 7; DAM DRAM; DLB 13; EWL 3; MTCW 1; MTFW 2005; RGEL 2; SATA 66; TEA

Frye, (Herman) Northrop
1912-1991 .... **CLC 24, 70; TCLC 165**
See also CA 5-8R; CAAS 133; CANR 8, 37; DLB 67, 68, 246; EWL 3; MTCW 1, 2; MTFW 2005; RGAL 4; TWA

Fuchs, Daniel 1909-1993 .... **CLC 8, 22**
See also CA 81-84; 5; CAAS 142; CANR 40; CN 1, 2, 3, 4, 5; DLB 9, 26, 28; DLBY 1993; MAL 5

Fuchs, Daniel 1934- .... **CLC 34**
See also CA 37-40R; CANR 14, 48

Fuentes, Carlos 1928- .. **CLC 3, 8, 10, 13, 22, 41, 60, 113; HLC 1; SSC 24; WLC 2**
See also AAYA 4, 45; AITN 2; BPFB 1; CA 69-72; CANR 10, 32, 68, 104, 138; CDWLB 3; CWW 2; DA; DA3; DAB; DAC; DAM MST, MULT, NOV; DLB 113; DNFS 2; EWL 3; HW 1, 2; LAIT 3; LATS 1:2; LAW; LAWS 1; LMFS 2; MTCW 1, 2; MTFW 2005; NFS 8; RGSF 2; RGWL 2, 3; TWA; WLIT 1

Fuentes, Gregorio Lopez y
See Lopez y Fuentes, Gregorio

Fuertes, Gloria 1918-1998 .... **PC 27**
See also CA 178, 180; DLB 108; HW 2; SATA 115

Fugard, (Harold) Athol 1932- . **CLC 5, 9, 14, 25, 40, 80, 211; DC 3**
See also AAYA 17; AFW; CA 85-88; CANR 32, 54, 118; CD 5, 6; DAM DRAM; DFS 3, 6, 10, 24; DLB 225; DNFS 1, 2; EWL 3; LATS 1:2; MTCW 1; MTFW 2005; RGEL 2; WLIT 2

Fugard, Sheila 1932- .... **CLC 48**
See also CA 125

Fujiwara no Teika 1162-1241 .... **CMLC 73**
See also DLB 203

Fukuyama, Francis 1952- .... **CLC 131**
See also CA 140; CANR 72, 125

Fuller, Charles (H.), (Jr.) 1939- .... **BLC 2; CLC 25; DC 1**
See also BW 2; CA 112; CAAE 108; CAD; CANR 87; CD 5, 6; DAM DRAM, MULT; DFS 8; DLB 38, 266; EWL 3; INT CA-112; MAL 5; MTCW 1

Fuller, Henry Blake 1857-1929 .... **TCLC 103**
See also CA 177; CAAE 108; DLB 12; RGAL 4

Fuller, John (Leopold) 1937- .... **CLC 62**
See also CA 21-24R; CANR 9, 44; CP 1, 2, 3, 4, 5, 6, 7; DLB 40

Fuller, Margaret
See Ossoli, Sarah Margaret (Fuller)
See also AMWS 2; DLB 183, 223, 239; FL 1:3

Fuller, Roy (Broadbent) 1912-1991 ... **CLC 4, 28**
See also BRWS 7; CA 5-8R; 10; CAAS 135; CANR 53, 83; CN 1, 2, 3, 4, 5; CP 1, 2, 3, 4, 5; CWRI 5; DLB 15, 20; EWL 3; RGEL 2; SATA 87

Fuller, Sarah Margaret
See Ossoli, Sarah Margaret (Fuller)

Fuller, Sarah Margaret
See Ossoli, Sarah Margaret (Fuller)
See also DLB 1, 59, 73

Fuller, Thomas 1608-1661 .... **LC 111**
See also DLB 151

Fulton, Alice 1952- .... **CLC 52**
See also CA 116; CANR 57, 88; CP 5, 6, 7; CWP; DLB 193; PFS 25

Furphy, Joseph 1843-1912 .... **TCLC 25**
See Collins, Tom
See also CA 163; DLB 230; EWL 3; RGEL 2

Fuson, Robert H(enderson) 1927- .... **CLC 70**
See also CA 89-92; CANR 103

Fussell, Paul 1924- .... **CLC 74**
See also BEST 90:1; CA 17-20R; CANR 8, 21, 35, 69, 135; INT CANR-21; MTCW 1, 2; MTFW 2005

Futabatei, Shimei 1864-1909 .... **TCLC 44**
See Futabatei Shimei
See also CA 162; MJW

Futabatei Shimei
See Futabatei, Shimei
See also DLB 180; EWL 3

Futrelle, Jacques 1875-1912 .... **TCLC 19**
See also CA 155; CAAE 113; CMW 4

Gaboriau, Emile 1835-1873 .... **NCLC 14**
See also CMW 4; MSW

Gadda, Carlo Emilio 1893-1973 ...... **CLC 11; TCLC 144**
See also CA 89-92; DLB 177; EWL 3; WLIT 7

Gaddis, William 1922-1998 ... **CLC 1, 3, 6, 8, 10, 19, 43, 86**
See also AMWS 4; BPFB 1; CA 17-20R; CAAS 172; CANR 21, 48, 148; CN 1, 2, 3, 4, 5, 6; DLB 2, 278; EWL 3; MAL 5; MTCW 1, 2; MTFW 2005; RGAL 4

Gage, Walter
See Inge, William (Motter)

Gaiman, Neil 1960- .... **CLC 195**
See also AAYA 19, 42; CA 133; CANR 81, 129; CLR 109; DLB 261; HGG; MTFW 2005; SATA 85, 146; SFW 4; SUFW 2

Gaiman, Neil Richard
See Gaiman, Neil

Gaines, Ernest J. 1933- .. **BLC 2; CLC 3, 11, 18, 86, 181; SSC 68**
See also AAYA 18; AFAW 1, 2; AITN 1; BPFB 2; BW 2, 3; BYA 6; CA 9-12R; CANR 6, 24, 42, 75, 126; CDALB 1968-1988; CLR 62; CN 1, 2, 3, 4, 5, 6, 7; CSW; DA3; DAM MULT; DLB 2, 33, 152; DLBY 1980; EWL 3; EXPN; LAIT 5; LATS 1:2; MAL 5; MTCW 1, 2; MTFW 2005; NFS 5, 7, 16; RGAL 4; RGSF 2; RHW; SATA 86; SSFS 5; YAW

Gaitskill, Mary 1954- .... **CLC 69**
See also CA 128; CANR 61, 152; DLB 244; TCLE 1:1

Gaitskill, Mary Lawrence
See Gaitskill, Mary

Gaius Suetonius Tranquillus
See Suetonius

Galdos, Benito Perez
See Perez Galdos, Benito
See also EW 7

Gale, Zona 1874-1938 .... **TCLC 7**
See also CA 153; CAAE 105; CANR 84; DAM DRAM; DFS 17; DLB 9, 78, 228; RGAL 4

Galeano, Eduardo 1940- ... **CLC 72; HLCS 1**
See also CA 29-32R; CANR 13, 32, 100, 163; HW 1

Galeano, Eduardo Hughes
See Galeano, Eduardo

Galiano, Juan Valera y Alcala
See Valera y Alcala-Galiano, Juan

Galilei, Galileo 1564-1642 .... **LC 45**

Gallagher, Tess 1943- .... **CLC 18, 63; PC 9**
See also CA 106; CP 3, 4, 5, 6, 7; CWP; DAM POET; DLB 120, 212, 244; PFS 16

Gallant, Mavis 1922- ..... **CLC 7, 18, 38, 172; SSC 5, 78**
See also CA 69-72; CANR 29, 69, 117; CCA 1; CN 1, 2, 3, 4, 5, 6, 7; DAC; DAM MST; DLB 53; EWL 3; MTCW 1, 2; MTFW 2005; RGEL 2; RGSF 2

Gallant, Roy A(rthur) 1924- .... **CLC 17**
See also CA 5-8R; CANR 4, 29, 54, 117; CLR 30; MAICYA 1, 2; SATA 4, 68, 110

Gallico, Paul (William) 1897-1976 ...... **CLC 2**
See also AITN 1; CA 5-8R; CAAS 69-72; CANR 23; CN 1, 2; DLB 9, 171; FANT; MAICYA 1, 2; SATA 13

Gallo, Max Louis 1932- .... **CLC 95**
See also CA 85-88

Gallois, Lucien
See Desnos, Robert

Gallup, Ralph
See Whitemore, Hugh (John)

Galsworthy, John 1867-1933 .... **SSC 22; TCLC 1, 45; WLC 2**
See also BRW 6; CA 141; CAAE 104; CANR 75; CDBLB 1890-1914; DA; DA3; DAB; DAC; DAM DRAM, MST, NOV; DLB 10, 34, 98, 162, 330; DLBD 16; EWL 3; MTCW 2; RGEL 2; SSFS 3; TEA

Galt, John 1779-1839 .... **NCLC 1, 110**
See also DLB 99, 116, 159; RGEL 2; RGSF 2

Galvin, James 1951- .... **CLC 38**
See also CA 108; CANR 26

Gamboa, Federico 1864-1939 .... **TCLC 36**
See also CA 167; HW 2; LAW

Gandhi, M. K.
See Gandhi, Mohandas Karamchand

Gandhi, Mahatma
See Gandhi, Mohandas Karamchand

Gandhi, Mohandas Karamchand
1869-1948 .... **TCLC 59**
See also CA 132; CAAE 121; DA3; DAM MULT; DLB 323; MTCW 1, 2

Gann, Ernest Kellogg 1910-1991 ..... **CLC 23**
See also AITN 1; BPFB 2; CA 1-4R; CAAS 136; CANR 1, 83; RHW

Gao Xingjian 1940- .... **CLC 167**
See Xingjian, Gao
See also MTFW 2005

Garber, Eric 1943(?)-
See Holleran, Andrew
See also CANR 89, 162

Garcia, Cristina 1958- .... **CLC 76**
See also AMWS 11; CA 141; CANR 73, 130; CN 7; DLB 292; DNFS 1; EWL 3; HW 2; LLW; MTFW 2005

Garcia Lorca, Federico 1898-1936 ...... **DC 2; HLC 2; PC 3; TCLC 1, 7, 49, 181; WLC 2**
See Lorca, Federico Garcia
See also AAYA 46; CA 131; CAAE 104; CANR 81; DA; DA3; DAB; DAC; DAM DRAM, MST, MULT, POET; DFS 4, 10; DLB 108; EWL 3; HW 1, 2; LATS 1:2; MTCW 1, 2; MTFW 2005; TWA

Gertler, T. .... **CLC 34**
See also CA 121; CAAE 116

Gertsen, Aleksandr Ivanovich
See Herzen, Aleksandr Ivanovich

Ghalib .... **NCLC 39, 78**
See Ghalib, Asadullah Khan

Ghalib, Asadullah Khan 1797-1869
See Ghalib
See also DAM POET; RGWL 2, 3

Ghelderode, Michel de 1898-1962 ..... **CLC 6, 11; DC 15; TCLC 187**
See also CA 85-88; CANR 40, 77; DAM DRAM; DLB 321; EW 11; EWL 3; TWA

Ghiselin, Brewster 1903-2001 .... **CLC 23**
See also CA 13-16R; 10; CANR 13; CP 1, 2, 3, 4, 5, 6, 7

Ghose, Aurabinda 1872-1950 .... **TCLC 63**
See Ghose, Aurobindo
See also CA 163

Ghose, Aurobindo
See Ghose, Aurabinda
See also EWL 3

Ghose, Zulfikar 1935- .... **CLC 42, 200**
See also CA 65-68; CANR 67; CN 1, 2, 3, 4, 5, 6, 7; CP 1, 2, 3, 4, 5, 6, 7; DLB 323; EWL 3

Ghosh, Amitav 1956- .... **CLC 44, 153**
See also CA 147; CANR 80, 158; CN 6, 7; DLB 323; WWE 1

Giacosa, Giuseppe 1847-1906 .... **TCLC 7**
See also CAAE 104

Gibb, Lee
See Waterhouse, Keith (Spencer)

Gibbon, Edward 1737-1794 .... **LC 97**
See also BRW 3; DLB 104, 336; RGEL 2

Gibbon, Lewis Grassic .... **TCLC 4**
See Mitchell, James Leslie
See also RGEL 2

Gibbons, Kaye 1960- .... **CLC 50, 88, 145**
See also AAYA 34; AMWS 10; CA 151; CANR 75, 127; CN 7; CSW; DA3; DAM POP; DLB 292; MTCW 2; MTFW 2005; NFS 3; RGAL 4; SATA 117

Gibran, Kahlil 1883-1931 . **PC 9; TCLC 1, 9**
See also CA 150; CAAE 104; DA3; DAM POET, POP; EWL 3; MTCW 2; WLIT 6

Gibran, Khalil
See Gibran, Kahlil

Gibson, Mel 1956- .... **CLC 215**

Gibson, William 1914- .... **CLC 23**
See also CA 9-12R; CAD; CANR 9, 42, 75, 125; CD 5, 6; DA; DAB; DAC; DAM DRAM, MST; DFS 2; DLB 7; LAIT 2; MAL 5; MTCW 2; MTFW 2005; SATA 66; YAW

Gibson, William 1948- .... **CLC 39, 63, 186, 192; SSC 52**
See also AAYA 12, 59; AMWS 16; BPFB 2; CA 133; CAAE 126; CANR 52, 90, 106; CN 6, 7; CPW; DA3; DAM POP; DLB 251; MTCW 2; MTFW 2005; SCFW 2; SFW 4

Gibson, William Ford
See Gibson, William

Gide, Andre (Paul Guillaume)
1869-1951 ...... **SSC 13; TCLC 5, 12, 36, 177; WLC 3**
See also CA 124; CAAE 104; DA; DA3; DAB; DAC; DAM MST, NOV; DLB 65, 321, 330; EW 8; EWL 3; GFL 1789 to the Present; MTCW 1, 2; MTFW 2005; NFS 21; RGSF 2; RGWL 2, 3; TWA

Gifford, Barry (Colby) 1946- .... **CLC 34**
See also CA 65-68; CANR 9, 30, 40, 90

Gilbert, Frank
See De Voto, Bernard (Augustine)

Gilbert, W(illiam) S(chwenck)
1836-1911 .... **TCLC 3**
See also CA 173; CAAE 104; DAM DRAM, POET; RGEL 2; SATA 36

Gilbert of Poitiers c. 1085-1154 .... **CMLC 85**

Gilbreth, Frank B(unker), Jr.
1911-2001 .... **CLC 17**
See also CA 9-12R; SATA 2

Gilchrist, Ellen (Louise) 1935- .. **CLC 34, 48, 143; SSC 14, 63**
See also BPFB 2; CA 116; CAAE 113; CANR 41, 61, 104; CN 4, 5, 6, 7; CPW; CSW; DAM POP; DLB 130; EWL 3; EXPS; MTCW 1, 2; MTFW 2005; RGAL 4; RGSF 2; SSFS 9

Giles, Molly 1942- .... **CLC 39**
See also CA 126; CANR 98

Gill, Eric .... **TCLC 85**
See Gill, (Arthur) Eric (Rowton Peter Joseph)

Gill, (Arthur) Eric (Rowton Peter Joseph)
1882-1940
See Gill, Eric
See also CAAE 120; DLB 98

Gill, Patrick
See Creasey, John

Gillette, Douglas .... **CLC 70**

Gilliam, Terry 1940- .... **CLC 21, 141**
See Monty Python
See also AAYA 19, 59; CA 113; CAAE 108; CANR 35; INT CA-113

Gilliam, Terry Vance
See Gilliam, Terry

Gillian, Jerry
See Gilliam, Terry

Gilliatt, Penelope (Ann Douglass)
1932-1993 .... **CLC 2, 10, 13, 53**
See also AITN 2; CA 13-16R; CAAS 141; CANR 49; CN 1, 2, 3, 4, 5; DLB 14

Gilligan, Carol 1936- .... **CLC 208**
See also CA 142; CANR 121; FW

Gilman, Charlotte (Anna) Perkins (Stetson)
1860-1935 ...... **SSC 13, 62; TCLC 9, 37, 117**
See also AAYA 75; AMWS 11; BYA 11; CA 150; CAAE 106; DLB 221; EXPS; FL 1:5; FW; HGG; LAIT 2; MBL; MTCW 2; MTFW 2005; RGAL 4; RGSF 2; SFW 4; SSFS 1, 18

Gilmour, David 1946- .... **CLC 35**

Gilpin, William 1724-1804 .... **NCLC 30**

Gilray, J. D.
See Mencken, H(enry) L(ouis)

Gilroy, Frank D(aniel) 1925- .... **CLC 2**
See also CA 81-84; CAD; CANR 32, 64, 86; CD 5, 6; DFS 17; DLB 7

Gilstrap, John 1957(?)- .... **CLC 99**
See also AAYA 67; CA 160; CANR 101

Ginsberg, Allen 1926-1997 .... **CLC 1, 2, 3, 4, 6, 13, 36, 69, 109; PC 4, 47; TCLC 120; WLC 3**
See also AAYA 33; AITN 1; AMWC 1; AMWS 2; BG 1:2; CA 1-4R; CAAS 157; CANR 2, 41, 63, 95; CDALB 1941-1968; CP 1, 2, 3, 4, 5, 6; DA; DA3; DAB; DAC; DAM MST, POET; DLB 5, 16, 169, 237; EWL 3; GLL 1; LMFS 2; MAL 5; MTCW 1, 2; MTFW 2005; PAB; PFS 5; RGAL 4; TUS; WP

Ginzburg, Eugenia .... **CLC 59**
See Ginzburg, Evgeniia

Ginzburg, Evgeniia 1904-1977
See Ginzburg, Eugenia
See also DLB 302

Ginzburg, Natalia 1916-1991 .... **CLC 5, 11, 54, 70; SSC 65; TCLC 156**
See also CA 85-88; CAAS 135; CANR 33; DFS 14; DLB 177; EW 13; EWL 3; MTCW 1, 2; MTFW 2005; RGHL; RGWL 2, 3

Giono, Jean 1895-1970 .... **CLC 4, 11; TCLC 124**
See also CA 45-48; CAAS 29-32R; CANR 2, 35; DLB 72, 321; EWL 3; GFL 1789 to the Present; MTCW 1; RGWL 2, 3

Giovanni, Nikki 1943- ...... **BLC 2; CLC 2, 4, 19, 64, 117; PC 19; WLCS**
See also AAYA 22; AITN 1; BW 2, 3; CA 29-32R; 6; CANR 18, 41, 60, 91, 130; CDALBS; CLR 6, 73; CP 2, 3, 4, 5, 6, 7; CSW; CWP; CWRI 5; DA; DA3; DAB; DAC; DAM MST, MULT, POET; DLB 5, 41; EWL 3; EXPP; INT CANR-18; MAICYA 1, 2; MAL 5; MTCW 1, 2; MTFW 2005; PFS 17; RGAL 4; SATA 24, 107; TUS; YAW

Giovene, Andrea 1904-1998 .... **CLC 7**
See also CA 85-88

Gippius, Zinaida (Nikolaevna) 1869-1945
See Hippius, Zinaida (Nikolaevna)
See also CA 212; CAAE 106

Giraudoux, Jean(-Hippolyte)
1882-1944 .... **TCLC 2, 7**
See also CA 196; CAAE 104; DAM DRAM; DLB 65, 321; EW 9; EWL 3; GFL 1789 to the Present; RGWL 2, 3; TWA

Gironella, Jose Maria (Pous)
1917-2003 .... **CLC 11**
See also CA 101; CAAS 212; EWL 3; RGWL 2, 3

Gissing, George (Robert)
1857-1903 .... **SSC 37; TCLC 3, 24, 47**
See also BRW 5; CA 167; CAAE 105; DLB 18, 135, 184; RGEL 2; TEA

Gitlin, Todd 1943- .... **CLC 201**
See also CA 29-32R; CANR 25, 50, 88

Giurlani, Aldo
See Palazzeschi, Aldo

Gladkov, Fedor Vasil'evich
See Gladkov, Fyodor (Vasilyevich)
See also DLB 272

Gladkov, Fyodor (Vasilyevich)
1883-1958 .... **TCLC 27**
See Gladkov, Fedor Vasil'evich
See also CA 170; EWL 3

Glancy, Diane 1941- .... **CLC 210; NNAL**
See also CA 225; 136, 225; 24; CANR 87, 162; DLB 175

Glanville, Brian (Lester) 1931- .... **CLC 6**
See also CA 5-8R; 9; CANR 3, 70; CN 1, 2, 3, 4, 5, 6, 7; DLB 15, 139; SATA 42

Glasgow, Ellen (Anderson Gholson)
1873-1945 .... **SSC 34; TCLC 2, 7**
See also AMW; CA 164; CAAE 104; DLB 9, 12; MAL 5; MBL; MTCW 2; MTFW 2005; RGAL 4; RHW; SSFS 9; TUS

Glaspell, Susan 1882(?)-1948 ..... **DC 10; SSC 41; TCLC 55, 175**
See also AMWS 3; CA 154; CAAE 110; DFS 8, 18, 24; DLB 7, 9, 78, 228; MBL; RGAL 4; SSFS 3; TCWW 2; TUS; YABC 2

Glassco, John 1909-1981 .... **CLC 9**
See also CA 13-16R; CAAS 102; CANR 15; CN 1, 2; CP 1, 2, 3; DLB 68

Glasscock, Amnesia
See Steinbeck, John (Ernst)

Glasser, Ronald J. 1940(?)- .... **CLC 37**
See also CA 209

Glassman, Joyce
See Johnson, Joyce

Gleick, James (W.) 1954- .... **CLC 147**
See also CA 137; CAAE 131; CANR 97; INT CA-137

Glendinning, Victoria 1937- .... **CLC 50**
See also CA 127; CAAE 120; CANR 59, 89; DLB 155

Hall, Donald 1928- ... **CLC 1, 13, 37, 59, 151, 240; PC 70**
  See also AAYA 63; CA 5-8R; 7; CANR 2, 44, 64, 106, 133; CP 1, 2, 3, 4, 5, 6, 7; DAM POET; DLB 5; MAL 5; MTCW 2; MTFW 2005; RGAL 4; SATA 23, 97

Hall, Donald Andrew, Jr.
  See Hall, Donald

Hall, Frederic Sauser
  See Sauser-Hall, Frederic

Hall, James
  See Kuttner, Henry

Hall, James Norman 1887-1951 ..... **TCLC 23**
  See also CA 173; CAAE 123; LAIT 1; RHW 1; SATA 21

Hall, Joseph 1574-1656 .... **LC 91**
  See also DLB 121, 151; RGEL 2

Hall, Marguerite Radclyffe
  See Hall, Radclyffe

Hall, Radclyffe 1880-1943 .... **TCLC 12**
  See also BRWS 6; CA 150; CAAE 110; CANR 83; DLB 191; MTCW 2; MTFW 2005; RGEL 2; RHW

Hall, Rodney 1935- .... **CLC 51**
  See also CA 109; CANR 69; CN 6, 7; CP 1, 2, 3, 4, 5, 6, 7; DLB 289

Hallam, Arthur Henry
  1811-1833 .... **NCLC 110**
  See also DLB 32

Halldor Laxness .... **CLC 25**
  See Gudjonsson, Halldor Kiljan
  See also DLB 293; EW 12; EWL 3; RGWL 2, 3

Halleck, Fitz-Greene 1790-1867 .... **NCLC 47**
  See also DLB 3, 250; RGAL 4

Halliday, Michael
  See Creasey, John

Halpern, Daniel 1945- .... **CLC 14**
  See also CA 33-36R; CANR 93; CP 3, 4, 5, 6, 7

Hamburger, Michael 1924-2007 ... **CLC 5, 14**
  See also CA 196; 5-8R; 4; CANR 2, 47; CP 1, 2, 3, 4, 5, 6, 7; DLB 27

Hamburger, Michael Peter Leopold
  See Hamburger, Michael

Hamill, Pete 1935- .... **CLC 10**
  See also CA 25-28R; CANR 18, 71, 127

Hamilton, Alexander
  1755(?)-1804 .... **NCLC 49**
  See also DLB 37

Hamilton, Clive
  See Lewis, C.S.

Hamilton, Edmond 1904-1977 .... **CLC 1**
  See also CA 1-4R; CANR 3, 84; DLB 8; SATA 118; SFW 4

Hamilton, Elizabeth 1758-1816 ... **NCLC 153**
  See also DLB 116, 158

Hamilton, Eugene (Jacob) Lee
  See Lee-Hamilton, Eugene (Jacob)

Hamilton, Franklin
  See Silverberg, Robert

Hamilton, Gail
  See Corcoran, Barbara (Asenath)

Hamilton, (Robert) Ian 1938-2001 . **CLC 191**
  See also CA 106; CAAS 203; CANR 41, 67; CP 1, 2, 3, 4, 5, 6, 7; DLB 40, 155

Hamilton, Jane 1957- .... **CLC 179**
  See also CA 147; CANR 85, 128; CN 7; MTFW 2005

Hamilton, Mollie
  See Kaye, M.M.

Hamilton, (Anthony Walter) Patrick
  1904-1962 .... **CLC 51**
  See also CA 176; CAAS 113; DLB 10, 191

Hamilton, Virginia 1936-2002 .... **CLC 26**
  See also AAYA 2, 21; BW 2, 3; BYA 1, 2, 8; CA 25-28R; CAAS 206; CANR 20, 37, 73, 126; CLR 1, 11, 40; DAM MULT; DLB 33, 52; DLBY 2001; INT CANR-

20; JRDA; LAIT 5; MAICYA 1, 2; MAICYAS 1; MTCW 1, 2; MTFW 2005; SATA 4, 56, 79, 123; SATA-Obit 132; WYA; YAW

Hammett, (Samuel) Dashiell
  1894-1961 .... **CLC 3, 5, 10, 19, 47; SSC 17; TCLC 187**
  See also AAYA 59; AITN 1; AMWS 4; BPFB 2; CA 81-84; CANR 42; CDALB 1929-1941; CMW 4; DA3; DLB 226, 280; DLBD 6; DLBY 1996; EWL 3; LAIT 3; MAL 5; MSW; MTCW 1, 2; MTFW 2005; NFS 21; RGAL 4; RGSF 2; TUS

Hammon, Jupiter 1720(?)-1800(?) .... **BLC 2; NCLC 5; PC 16**
  See also DAM MULT, POET; DLB 31, 50

Hammond, Keith
  See Kuttner, Henry

Hamner, Earl (Henry), Jr. 1923- ...... **CLC 12**
  See also AITN 2; CA 73-76; DLB 6

Hampton, Christopher 1946- .... **CLC 4**
  See also CA 25-28R; CD 5, 6; DLB 13; MTCW 1

Hampton, Christopher James
  See Hampton, Christopher

Hamsun, Knut .... **TCLC 2, 14, 49, 151**
  See Pedersen, Knut
  See also DLB 297, 330; EW 8; EWL 3; RGWL 2, 3

Handke, Peter 1942- .... **CLC 5, 8, 10, 15, 38, 134; DC 17**
  See also CA 77-80; CANR 33, 75, 104, 133; CWW 2; DAM DRAM, NOV; DLB 85, 124; EWL 3; MTCW 1, 2; MTFW 2005; TWA

Handy, W(illiam) C(hristopher)
  1873-1958 .... **TCLC 97**
  See also BW 3; CA 167; CAAE 121

Hanley, James 1901-1985 ..... **CLC 3, 5, 8, 13**
  See also CA 73-76; CAAS 117; CANR 36; CBD; CN 1, 2, 3; DLB 191; EWL 3; MTCW 1; RGEL 2

Hannah, Barry 1942- .. **CLC 23, 38, 90; SSC 94**
  See also BPFB 2; CA 110; CAAE 108; CANR 43, 68, 113; CN 4, 5, 6, 7; CSW; DLB 6, 234; INT CA-110; MTCW 1; RGSF 2

Hannon, Ezra
  See Hunter, Evan

Hansberry, Lorraine (Vivian)
  1930-1965 ... **BLC 2; CLC 17, 62; DC 2**
  See also AAYA 25; AFAW 1, 2; AMWS 4; BW 1, 3; CA 109; CAAS 25-28R; CABS 3; CAD; CANR 58; CDALB 1941-1968; CWD; DA; DA3; DAB; DAC; DAM DRAM, MST, MULT; DFS 2; DLB 7, 38; EWL 3; FL 1:6; FW; LAIT 4; MAL 5; MTCW 1, 2; MTFW 2005; RGAL 4; TUS

Hansen, Joseph 1923-2004 .... **CLC 38**
  See Brock, Rose; Colton, James
  See also BPFB 2; CA 29-32R; 17; CAAS 233; CANR 16, 44, 66, 125; CMW 4; DLB 226; GLL 1; INT CANR-16

Hansen, Karen V. 1955- .... **CLC 65**
  See also CA 149; CANR 102

Hansen, Martin A(lfred)
  1909-1955 .... **TCLC 32**
  See also CA 167; DLB 214; EWL 3

Hanson, Kenneth O(stlin) 1922- .... **CLC 13**
  See also CA 53-56; CANR 7; CP 1, 2, 3, 4, 5

Hardwick, Elizabeth 1916- .... **CLC 13**
  See also AMWS 3; CA 5-8R; CANR 3, 32, 70, 100, 139; CN 4, 5, 6; CSW; DA3; DAM NOV; DLB 6; MBL; MTCW 1, 2; MTFW 2005; TCLE 1:1

Hardy, Thomas 1840-1928 .... **PC 8; SSC 2, 60; TCLC 4, 10, 18, 32, 48, 53, 72, 143, 153; WLC 3**
  See also AAYA 69; BRW 6; BRWC 1, 2; BRWR 1; CA 123; CAAE 104; CDBLB 1890-1914; DA; DA3; DAB; DAC; DAM MST, NOV, POET; DLB 18, 19, 135, 284; EWL 3; EXPN; EXPP; LAIT 2; MTCW 1, 2; MTFW 2005; NFS 3, 11, 15, 19; PFS 3, 4, 18; RGEL 2; RGSF 2; TEA; WLIT 4

Hare, David 1947- . **CLC 29, 58, 136; DC 26**
  See also BRWS 4; CA 97-100; CANR 39, 91; CBD; CD 5, 6; DFS 4, 7, 16; DLB 13, 310; MTCW 1; TEA

Harewood, John
  See Van Druten, John (William)

Harford, Henry
  See Hudson, W(illiam) H(enry)

Hargrave, Leonie
  See Disch, Thomas M.

Hariri, Al- al-Qasim ibn 'Ali Abu Muhammad al-Basri
  See al-Hariri, al-Qasim ibn 'Ali Abu Muhammad al-Basri

Harjo, Joy 1951- ..... **CLC 83; NNAL; PC 27**
  See also AMWS 12; CA 114; CANR 35, 67, 91, 129; CP 6, 7; CWP; DAM MULT; DLB 120, 175; EWL 3; MTCW 2; MTFW 2005; PFS 15; RGAL 4

Harlan, Louis R(udolph) 1922- .... **CLC 34**
  See also CA 21-24R; CANR 25, 55, 80

Harling, Robert 1951(?)- .... **CLC 53**
  See also CA 147

Harmon, William (Ruth) 1938- .... **CLC 38**
  See also CA 33-36R; CANR 14, 32, 35; SATA 65

Harper, F. E. W.
  See Harper, Frances Ellen Watkins

Harper, Frances E. W.
  See Harper, Frances Ellen Watkins

Harper, Frances E. Watkins
  See Harper, Frances Ellen Watkins

Harper, Frances Ellen
  See Harper, Frances Ellen Watkins

Harper, Frances Ellen Watkins
  1825-1911 ..... **BLC 2; PC 21; TCLC 14**
  See also AFAW 1, 2; BW 1, 3; CA 125; CAAE 111; CANR 79; DAM MULT, POET; DLB 50, 221; MBL; RGAL 4

Harper, Michael S(teven) 1938- ... **CLC 7, 22**
  See also AFAW 2; BW 1; CA 224; 33-36R, 224; CANR 24, 108; CP 2, 3, 4, 5, 6, 7; DLB 41; RGAL 4; TCLE 1:1

Harper, Mrs. F. E. W.
  See Harper, Frances Ellen Watkins

Harpur, Charles 1813-1868 .... **NCLC 114**
  See also DLB 230; RGEL 2

Harris, Christie
  See Harris, Christie (Lucy) Irwin

Harris, Christie (Lucy) Irwin
  1907-2002 .... **CLC 12**
  See also CA 5-8R; CANR 6, 83; CLR 47; DLB 88; JRDA; MAICYA 1, 2; SAAS 10; SATA 6, 74; SATA-Essay 116

Harris, Frank 1856-1931 .... **TCLC 24**
  See also CA 150; CAAE 109; CANR 80; DLB 156, 197; RGEL 2

Harris, George Washington
  1814-1869 .... **NCLC 23, 165**
  See also DLB 3, 11, 248; RGAL 4

Harris, Joel Chandler 1848-1908 ..... **SSC 19; TCLC 2**
  See also CA 137; CAAE 104; CANR 80; CLR 49; DLB 11, 23, 42, 78, 91; LAIT 2; MAICYA 1, 2; RGSF 2; SATA 100; WCH; YABC 1

Herriot, James 1916-1995 .... **CLC 12**
See Wight, James Alfred
See also AAYA 1, 54; BPFB 2; CAAS 148;
CANR 40; CLR 80; CPW; DAM POP;
LAIT 3; MAICYA 2; MAICYAS 1;
MTCW 2; SATA 86, 135; TEA; YAW

Herris, Violet
See Hunt, Violet

Herrmann, Dorothy 1941- .... **CLC 44**
See also CA 107

Herrmann, Taffy
See Herrmann, Dorothy

Hersey, John 1914-1993 .. **CLC 1, 2, 7, 9, 40,**
81, 97
See also AAYA 29; BPFB 2; CA 17-20R;
CAAS 140; CANR 33; CDALBS; CN 1,
2, 3, 4, 5; CPW; DAM POP; DLB 6, 185,
278, 299; MAL 5; MTCW 1, 2; MTFW
2005; RGHL; SATA 25; SATA-Obit 76;
TUS

Herzen, Aleksandr Ivanovich
1812-1870 .... **NCLC 10, 61**
See Herzen, Alexander

Herzen, Alexander
See Herzen, Aleksandr Ivanovich
See also DLB 277

Herzl, Theodor 1860-1904 .... **TCLC 36**
See also CA 168

Herzog, Werner 1942- .... **CLC 16, 236**
See also CA 89-92

Hesiod c. 8th cent. B.C.- .... **CMLC 5**
See also AW 1; DLB 176; RGWL 2, 3;
WLIT 8

Hesse, Hermann 1877-1962 ... **CLC 1, 2, 3, 6,**
11, 17, 25, 69; SSC 9, 49; TCLC 148;
WLC 3
See also AAYA 43; BPFB 2; CA 17-18;
CAP 2; CDWLB 2; DA; DA3; DAB;
DAC; DAM MST, NOV; DLB 66, 330;
EW 9; EWL 3; EXPN; LAIT 1; MTCW
1, 2; MTFW 2005; NFS 6, 15, 24; RGWL
2, 3; SATA 50; TWA

Hewes, Cady
See De Voto, Bernard (Augustine)

Heyen, William 1940- .... **CLC 13, 18**
See also CA 220; 33-36R, 220; 9; CANR
98; CP 3, 4, 5, 6, 7; DLB 5; RGHL

Heyerdahl, Thor 1914-2002 .... **CLC 26**
See also CA 5-8R; CAAS 207; CANR 5,
22, 66, 73; LAIT 4; MTCW 1, 2; MTFW
2005; SATA 2, 52

Heym, Georg (Theodor Franz Arthur)
1887-1912 .... **TCLC 9**
See also CA 181; CAAE 106

Heym, Stefan 1913-2001 .... **CLC 41**
See also CA 9-12R; CAAS 203; CANR 4;
CWW 2; DLB 69; EWL 3

Heyse, Paul (Johann Ludwig von)
1830-1914 .... **TCLC 8**
See also CA 209; CAAE 104; DLB 129,
330

Heyward, (Edwin) DuBose
1885-1940 .... **HR 1:2; TCLC 59**
See also CA 157; CAAE 108; DLB 7, 9,
45, 249; MAL 5; SATA 21

Heywood, John 1497(?)-1580(?) .... **LC 65**
See also DLB 136; RGEL 2

Heywood, Thomas 1573(?)-1641 .... **LC 111**
See also DAM DRAM; DLB 62; LMFS 1;
RGEL 2; TEA

Hiaasen, Carl 1953- .... **CLC 238**
See also CA 105; CANR 22, 45, 65, 113,
133; CMW 4; CPW; CSW; DA3; DLB
292; MTCW 2; MTFW 2005

Hibbert, Eleanor Alice Burford
1906-1993 .... **CLC 7**
See Holt, Victoria
See also BEST 90:4; CA 17-20R; CAAS
140; CANR 9, 28, 59; CMW 4; CPW;
DAM POP; MTCW 2; MTFW 2005;
RHW; SATA 2; SATA-Obit 74

Hichens, Robert (Smythe)
1864-1950 .... **TCLC 64**
See also CA 162; DLB 153; HGG; RHW;
SUFW

Higgins, Aidan 1927- .... **SSC 68**
See also CA 9-12R; CANR 70, 115, 148;
CN 1, 2, 3, 4, 5, 6, 7; DLB 14

Higgins, George V(incent)
1939-1999 .... **CLC 4, 7, 10, 18**
See also BPFB 2; CA 77-80; 5; CAAS 186;
CANR 17, 51, 89, 96; CMW 4; CN 2, 3,
4, 5, 6; DLB 2; DLBY 1981, 1998; INT
CANR-17; MSW; MTCW 1

Higginson, Thomas Wentworth
1823-1911 .... **TCLC 36**
See also CA 162; DLB 1, 64, 243

Higgonet, Margaret .... **CLC 65**

Highet, Helen
See MacInnes, Helen (Clark)

Highsmith, Patricia 1921-1995 ...... **CLC 2, 4,**
14, 42, 102
See Morgan, Claire
See also AAYA 48; BRWS 5; CA 1-4R;
CAAS 147; CANR 1, 20, 48, 62, 108;
CMW 4; CN 1, 2, 3, 4, 5; CPW; DA3;
DAM NOV, POP; DLB 306; MSW;
MTCW 1, 2; MTFW 2005

Highwater, Jamake (Mamake)
1942(?)-2001 .... **CLC 12**
See also AAYA 7, 69; BPFB 2; BYA 4; CA
65-68; 7; CAAS 199; CANR 10, 34, 84;
CLR 17; CWRI 5; DLB 52; DLBY 1985;
JRDA; MAICYA 1, 2; SATA 32, 69;
SATA-Brief 30

Highway, Tomson 1951- ...... **CLC 92; NNAL**
See also CA 151; CANR 75; CCA 1; CD 5,
6; CN 7; DAC; DAM MULT; DFS 2;
DLB 334; MTCW 2

Hijuelos, Oscar 1951- .... **CLC 65; HLC 1**
See also AAYA 25; AMWS 8; BEST 90:1;
CA 123; CANR 50, 75, 125; CPW; DA3;
DAM MULT, POP; DLB 145; HW 1, 2;
LLW; MAL 5; MTCW 2; MTFW 2005;
NFS 17; RGAL 4; WLIT 1

Hikmet, Nazim 1902-1963 .... **CLC 40**
See Nizami of Ganja
See also CA 141; CAAS 93-96; EWL 3;
WLIT 6

Hildegard von Bingen 1098-1179 . **CMLC 20**
See also DLB 148

Hildesheimer, Wolfgang 1916-1991 .. **CLC 49**
See also CA 101; CAAS 135; DLB 69, 124;
EWL 3; RGHL

Hill, Geoffrey (William) 1932- ...... **CLC 5, 8,**
18, 45
See also BRWS 5; CA 81-84; CANR 21,
89; CDBLB 1960 to Present; CP 1, 2, 3,
4, 5, 6, 7; DAM POET; DLB 40; EWL 3;
MTCW 1; RGEL 2; RGHL

Hill, George Roy 1921-2002 .... **CLC 26**
See also CA 122; CAAE 110; CAAS 213

Hill, John
See Koontz, Dean R.

Hill, Susan 1942- .... **CLC 4, 113**
See also CA 33-36R; CANR 29, 69, 129;
CN 2, 3, 4, 5, 6, 7; DAB; DAM MST,
NOV; DLB 14, 139; HGG; MTCW 1;
RHW

Hill, Susan Elizabeth
See Hill, Susan

Hillard, Asa G. III .... **CLC 70**

Hillerman, Tony 1925- .... **CLC 62, 170**
See also AAYA 40; BEST 89:1; BPFB 2;
CA 29-32R; CANR 21, 42, 65, 97, 134;
CMW 4; CPW; DA3; DAM POP; DLB
206, 306; MAL 5; MSW; MTCW 2;
MTFW 2005; RGAL 4; SATA 6; TCWW
2; YAW

Hillesum, Etty 1914-1943 .... **TCLC 49**
See also CA 137; RGHL

Hilliard, Noel (Harvey) 1929-1996 ... **CLC 15**
See also CA 9-12R; CANR 7, 69; CN 1, 2,
3, 4, 5, 6

Hillis, Rick 1956- .... **CLC 66**
See also CA 134

Hilton, James 1900-1954 .... **TCLC 21**
See also CA 169; CAAE 108; DLB 34, 77;
FANT; SATA 34

Hilton, Walter (?)-1396 .... **CMLC 58**
See also DLB 146; RGEL 2

Himes, Chester (Bomar) 1909-1984 .. **BLC 2;**
CLC 2, 4, 7, 18, 58, 108; TCLC 139
See also AFAW 2; AMWS 16; BPFB 2; BW
2; CA 25-28R; CAAS 114; CANR 22, 89;
CMW 4; CN 1, 2, 3; DAM MULT; DLB
2, 76, 143, 226; EWL 3; MAL 5; MSW;
MTCW 1, 2; MTFW 2005; RGAL 4

Himmelfarb, Gertrude 1922- .... **CLC 202**
See also CA 49-52; CANR 28, 66, 102

Hinde, Thomas .... **CLC 6, 11**
See Chitty, Thomas Willes
See also CN 1, 2, 3, 4, 5, 6; EWL 3

Hine, (William) Daryl 1936- .... **CLC 15**
See also CA 1-4R; 15; CANR 1, 20; CP 1,
2, 3, 4, 5, 6, 7; DLB 60

Hinkson, Katharine Tynan
See Tynan, Katharine

Hinojosa, Rolando 1929- .... **HLC 1**
See Hinojosa-Smith, Rolando
See also CA 131; 16; CANR 62; DAM
MULT; DLB 82; HW 1, 2; LLW; MTCW
2; MTFW 2005; RGAL 4

Hinton, S.E. 1950- .... **CLC 30, 111**
See also AAYA 2, 33; BPFB 2; BYA 2, 3;
CA 81-84; CANR 32, 62, 92, 133;
CDALBS; CLR 3, 23; CPW; DA; DA3;
DAB; DAC; DAM MST, NOV; JRDA;
LAIT 5; MAICYA 1, 2; MTCW 1, 2;
MTFW 2005; NFS 5, 9, 15, 16; SATA 19,
58, 115, 160; WYA; YAW

Hippius, Zinaida (Nikolaevna) .... **TCLC 9**
See Gippius, Zinaida (Nikolaevna)
See also DLB 295; EWL 3

Hiraoka, Kimitake 1925-1970
See Mishima, Yukio
See also CA 97-100; CAAS 29-32R; DA3;
DAM DRAM; GLL 1; MTCW 1, 2

Hirsch, E.D., Jr. 1928- .... **CLC 79**
See also CA 25-28R; CANR 27, 51, 146;
DLB 67; INT CANR-27; MTCW 1

Hirsch, Edward 1950- .... **CLC 31, 50**
See also CA 104; CANR 20, 42, 102; CP 6,
7; DLB 120; PFS 22

Hirsch, Eric Donald, Jr.
See Hirsch, E.D., Jr.

Hitchcock, Alfred (Joseph)
1899-1980 .... **CLC 16**
See also AAYA 22; CA 159; CAAS 97-100;
SATA 27; SATA-Obit 24

Hitchens, Christopher 1949- .... **CLC 157**
See also CA 152; CANR 89, 155

Hitchens, Christopher Eric
See Hitchens, Christopher

Hitler, Adolf 1889-1945 .... **TCLC 53**
See also CA 147; CAAE 117

Hoagland, Edward (Morley) 1932- .. **CLC 28**
See also ANW; CA 1-4R; CANR 2, 31, 57,
107; CN 1, 2, 3, 4, 5, 6, 7; DLB 6; SATA
51; TCWW 2

Hoban, Russell 1925- .... **CLC 7, 25**
See also BPFB 2; CA 5-8R; CANR 23, 37,
66, 114, 138; CLR 3, 69; CN 4, 5, 6, 7;
CWRI 5; DAM NOV; DLB 52; FANT;
MAICYA 1, 2; MTCW 1, 2; MTFW 2005;
SATA 1, 40, 78, 136; SFW 4; SUFW 2;
TCLE 1:1

Hobbes, Thomas 1588-1679 .... **LC 36**
See also DLB 151, 252, 281; RGEL 2

Hobbs, Perry
  See Blackmur, R(ichard) P(almer)

Hobson, Laura Z(ametkin)
  1900-1986 .... **CLC 7, 25**
  See also BPFB 2; CA 17-20R; CAAS 118;
  CANR 55; CN 1, 2, 3, 4; DLB 28; SATA
  52

Hoccleve, Thomas c. 1368-c. 1437 ...... **LC 75**
  See also DLB 146; RGEL 2

Hoch, Edward D(entinger) 1930-
  See Queen, Ellery
  See also CA 29-32R; CANR 11, 27, 51, 97;
  CMW 4; DLB 306; SFW 4

Hochhuth, Rolf 1931- .... **CLC 4, 11, 18**
  See also CA 5-8R; CANR 33, 75, 136;
  CWW 2; DAM DRAM; DLB 124; EWL
  3; MTCW 1, 2; MTFW 2005; RGHL

Hochman, Sandra 1936- .... **CLC 3, 8**
  See also CA 5-8R; CP 1, 2, 3, 4, 5; DLB 5

Hochwaelder, Fritz 1911-1986 .... **CLC 36**
  See Hochwalder, Fritz
  See also CA 29-32R; CAAS 120; CANR
  42; DAM DRAM; MTCW 1; RGWL 3

Hochwalder, Fritz
  See Hochwaelder, Fritz
  See also EWL 3; RGWL 2

Hocking, Mary (Eunice) 1921- .... **CLC 13**
  See also CA 101; CANR 18, 40

Hodgins, Jack 1938- .... **CLC 23**
  See also CA 93-96; CN 4, 5, 6, 7; DLB 60

Hodgson, William Hope
  1877(?)-1918 .... **TCLC 13**
  See also CA 164; CAAE 111; CMW 4; DLB
  70, 153, 156, 178; HGG; MTCW 2; SFW
  4; SUFW 1

Hoeg, Peter 1957- .... **CLC 95, 156**
  See also CA 151; CANR 75; CMW 4; DA3;
  DLB 214; EWL 3; MTCW 2; MTFW
  2005; NFS 17; RGWL 3; SSFS 18

Hoffman, Alice 1952- .... **CLC 51**
  See also AAYA 37; AMWS 10; CA 77-80;
  CANR 34, 66, 100, 138; CN 4, 5, 6, 7;
  CPW; DAM NOV; DLB 292; MAL 5;
  MTCW 1, 2; MTFW 2005; TCLE 1:1

Hoffman, Daniel (Gerard) 1923- . **CLC 6, 13, 23**
  See also CA 1-4R; CANR 4, 142; CP 1, 2,
  3, 4, 5, 6, 7; DLB 5; TCLE 1:1

Hoffman, Eva 1945- .... **CLC 182**
  See also AMWS 16; CA 132; CANR 146

Hoffman, Stanley 1944- .... **CLC 5**
  See also CA 77-80

Hoffman, William 1925- .... **CLC 141**
  See also CA 21-24R; CANR 9, 103; CSW;
  DLB 234; TCLE 1:1

Hoffman, William M.
  See Hoffman, William M(oses)
  See also CAD; CD 5, 6

Hoffman, William M(oses) 1939- ..... **CLC 40**
  See Hoffman, William M.
  See also CA 57-60; CANR 11, 71

Hoffmann, E(rnst) T(heodor) A(madeus)
  1776-1822 ..... **NCLC 2, 183; SSC 13, 92**
  See also CDWLB 2; DLB 90; EW 5; GL 2;
  RGSF 2; RGWL 2, 3; SATA 27; SUFW
  1; WCH

Hofmann, Gert 1931-1993 .... **CLC 54**
  See also CA 128; CANR 145; EWL 3;
  RGHL

Hofmannsthal, Hugo von 1874-1929 ... **DC 4; TCLC 11**
  See also CA 153; CAAE 106; CDWLB 2;
  DAM DRAM; DFS 17; DLB 81, 118; EW
  9; EWL 3; RGWL 2, 3

Hogan, Linda 1947- ..... **CLC 73; NNAL; PC 35**
  See also AMWS 4; ANW; BYA 12; CA 226;
  120, 226; CANR 45, 73, 129; CWP; DAM
  MULT; DLB 175; SATA 132; TCWW 2

Hogarth, Charles
  See Creasey, John

Hogarth, Emmett
  See Polonsky, Abraham (Lincoln)

Hogarth, William 1697-1764 .... **LC 112**
  See also AAYA 56

Hogg, James 1770-1835 .... **NCLC 4, 109**
  See also BRWS 10; DLB 93, 116, 159; GL
  2; HGG; RGEL 2; SUFW 1

Holbach, Paul-Henri Thiry
  1723-1789 .... **LC 14**
  See also DLB 313

Holberg, Ludvig 1684-1754 .... **LC 6**
  See also DLB 300; RGWL 2, 3

Holcroft, Thomas 1745-1809 .... **NCLC 85**
  See also DLB 39, 89, 158; RGEL 2

Holden, Ursula 1921- .... **CLC 18**
  See also CA 101; 8; CANR 22

Holderlin, (Johann Christian) Friedrich
  1770-1843 .... **NCLC 16; PC 4**
  See also CDWLB 2; DLB 90; EW 5; RGWL
  2, 3

Holdstock, Robert 1948- .... **CLC 39**
  See also CA 131; CANR 81; DLB 261;
  FANT; HGG; SFW 4; SUFW 2

Holdstock, Robert P.
  See Holdstock, Robert

Holinshed, Raphael fl. 1580- .... **LC 69**
  See also DLB 167; RGEL 2

Holland, Isabelle (Christian)
  1920-2002 .... **CLC 21**
  See also AAYA 11, 64; CA 181; 21-24R;
  CAAS 205; CANR 10, 25, 47; CLR 57;
  CWRI 5; JRDA; LAIT 4; MAICYA 1, 2;
  SATA 8, 70; SATA-Essay 103; SATA-Obit
  132; WYA

Holland, Marcus
  See Caldwell, (Janet Miriam) Taylor
  (Holland)

Hollander, John 1929- .... **CLC 2, 5, 8, 14**
  See also CA 1-4R; CANR 1, 52, 136; CP 1,
  2, 3, 4, 5, 6, 7; DLB 5; MAL 5; SATA 13

Hollander, Paul
  See Silverberg, Robert

Holleran, Andrew .... **CLC 38**
  See Garber, Eric
  See also CA 144; GLL 1

Holley, Marietta 1836(?)-1926 .... **TCLC 99**
  See also CAAE 118; DLB 11; FL 1:3

Hollinghurst, Alan 1954- .... **CLC 55, 91**
  See also BRWS 10; CA 114; CN 5, 6, 7;
  DLB 207, 326; GLL 1

Hollis, Jim
  See Summers, Hollis (Spurgeon, Jr.)

Holly, Buddy 1936-1959 .... **TCLC 65**
  See also CA 213

Holmes, Gordon
  See Shiel, M(atthew) P(hipps)

Holmes, John
  See Souster, (Holmes) Raymond

Holmes, John Clellon 1926-1988 ...... **CLC 56**
  See also BG 1:2; CA 9-12R; CAAS 125;
  CANR 4; CN 1, 2, 3, 4; DLB 16, 237

Holmes, Oliver Wendell, Jr.
  1841-1935 .... **TCLC 77**
  See also CA 186; CAAE 114

Holmes, Oliver Wendell
  1809-1894 .... **NCLC 14, 81; PC 71**
  See also AMWS 1; CDALB 1640-1865;
  DLB 1, 189, 235; EXPP; PFS 24; RGAL
  4; SATA 34

Holmes, Raymond
  See Souster, (Holmes) Raymond

Holt, Victoria
  See Hibbert, Eleanor Alice Burford
  See also BPFB 2

Holub, Miroslav 1923-1998 .... **CLC 4**
  See also CA 21-24R; CAAS 169; CANR
  10; CDWLB 4; CWW 2; DLB 232; EWL
  3; RGWL 3

Holz, Detlev
  See Benjamin, Walter

Homer c. 8th cent. B.C.- .... **CMLC 1, 16, 61; PC 23; WLCS**
  See also AW 1; CDWLB 1; DA; DA3;
  DAB; DAC; DAM MST, POET; DLB
  176; EFS 1; LAIT 1; LMFS 1; RGWL 2,
  3; TWA; WLIT 8; WP

Hongo, Garrett Kaoru 1951- .... **PC 23**
  See also CA 133; 22; CP 5, 6, 7; DLB 120,
  312; EWL 3; EXPP; PFS 25; RGAL 4

Honig, Edwin 1919- .... **CLC 33**
  See also CA 5-8R; 8; CANR 4, 45, 144; CP
  1, 2, 3, 4, 5, 6, 7; DLB 5

Hood, Hugh (John Blagdon) 1928- . **CLC 15, 28; SSC 42**
  See also CA 49-52; 17; CANR 1, 33, 87;
  CN 1, 2, 3, 4, 5, 6, 7; DLB 53; RGSF 2

Hood, Thomas 1799-1845 .... **NCLC 16**
  See also BRW 4; DLB 96; RGEL 2

Hooker, (Peter) Jeremy 1941- .... **CLC 43**
  See also CA 77-80; CANR 22; CP 2, 3, 4,
  5, 6, 7; DLB 40

Hooker, Richard 1554-1600 .... **LC 95**
  See also BRW 1; DLB 132; RGEL 2

Hooker, Thomas 1586-1647 .... **LC 137**
  See also DLB 24

hooks, bell 1952(?)- .... **CLC 94**
  See also BW 2; CA 143; CANR 87, 126;
  DLB 246; MTCW 2; MTFW 2005; SATA
  115, 170

Hooper, Johnson Jones
  1815-1862 .... **NCLC 177**
  See also DLB 3, 11, 248; RGAL 4

Hope, A(lec) D(erwent) 1907-2000 .... **CLC 3, 51; PC 56**
  See also BRWS 7; CA 21-24R; CAAS 188;
  CANR 33, 74; CP 1, 2, 3, 4, 5; DLB 289;
  EWL 3; MTCW 1, 2; MTFW 2005; PFS
  8; RGEL 2

Hope, Anthony 1863-1933 .... **TCLC 83**
  See also CA 157; DLB 153, 156; RGEL 2;
  RHW

Hope, Brian
  See Creasey, John

Hope, Christopher (David Tully)
  1944- .... **CLC 52**
  See also AFW; CA 106; CANR 47, 101;
  CN 4, 5, 6, 7; DLB 225; SATA 62

Hopkins, Gerard Manley
  1844-1889 ...... **NCLC 17; PC 15; WLC 3**
  See also BRW 5; BRWR 2; CDBLB 1890-
  1914; DA; DA3; DAB; DAC; DAM MST,
  POET; DLB 35, 57; EXPP; PAB; RGEL
  2; TEA; WP

Hopkins, John (Richard) 1931-1998 .. **CLC 4**
  See also CA 85-88; CAAS 169; CBD; CD
  5, 6

Hopkins, Pauline Elizabeth
  1859-1930 .... **BLC 2; TCLC 28**
  See also AFAW 2; BW 2, 3; CA 141; CANR
  82; DAM MULT; DLB 50

Hopkinson, Francis 1737-1791 .... **LC 25**
  See also DLB 31; RGAL 4

Hopley-Woolrich, Cornell George 1903-1968
  See Woolrich, Cornell
  See also CA 13-14; CANR 58, 156; CAP 1;
  CMW 4; DLB 226; MTCW 2

Horace 65B.C.-8B.C. .... **CMLC 39; PC 46**
  See also AW 2; CDWLB 1; DLB 211;
  RGWL 2, 3; WLIT 8

Horatio
  See Proust, (Valentin-Louis-George-Eugene)
  Marcel

Horgan, Paul (George Vincent O'Shaughnessy) 1903-1995 .. **CLC 9, 53**
See also BPFB 2; CA 13-16R; CAAS 147; CANR 9, 35; CN 1, 2, 3, 4, 5; DAM NOV; DLB 102, 212; DLBY 1985; INT CANR-9; MTCW 1, 2; MTFW 2005; SATA 13; SATA-Obit 84; TCWW 1, 2

Horkheimer, Max 1895-1973 .... **TCLC 132**
See also CA 216; CAAS 41-44R; DLB 296

Horn, Peter
See Kuttner, Henry

Horne, Frank (Smith) 1899-1974 ...... **HR 1:2**
See also BW 1; CA 125; CAAS 53-56; DLB 51; WP

Horne, Richard Henry Hengist 1802(?)-1884 .... **NCLC 127**
See also DLB 32; SATA 29

Hornem, Horace Esq.
See Byron, George Gordon (Noel)

Horney, Karen (Clementine Theodore Danielsen) 1885-1952 .... **TCLC 71**
See also CA 165; CAAE 114; DLB 246; FW

Hornung, E(rnest) W(illiam) 1866-1921 .... **TCLC 59**
See also CA 160; CAAE 108; CMW 4; DLB 70

Horovitz, Israel (Arthur) 1939- .... **CLC 56**
See also CA 33-36R; CAD; CANR 46, 59; CD 5, 6; DAM DRAM; DLB 7; MAL 5

Horton, George Moses 1797(?)-1883(?) .... **NCLC 87**
See also DLB 50

Horvath, odon von 1901-1938
See von Horvath, Odon
See also EWL 3

Horvath, Oedoen von -1938
See von Horvath, Odon

Horwitz, Julius 1920-1986 .... **CLC 14**
See also CA 9-12R; CAAS 119; CANR 12

Horwitz, Ronald
See Harwood, Ronald

Hospital, Janette Turner 1942- .... **CLC 42, 145**
See also CA 108; CANR 48; CN 5, 6, 7; DLB 325; DLBY 2002; RGSF 2

Hostos, E. M. de
See Hostos (y Bonilla), Eugenio Maria de

Hostos, Eugenio M. de
See Hostos (y Bonilla), Eugenio Maria de

Hostos, Eugenio Maria
See Hostos (y Bonilla), Eugenio Maria de

Hostos (y Bonilla), Eugenio Maria de 1839-1903 .... **TCLC 24**
See also CA 131; CAAE 123; HW 1

Houdini
See Lovecraft, H. P.

Houellebecq, Michel 1958- .... **CLC 179**
See also CA 185; CANR 140; MTFW 2005

Hougan, Carolyn 1943-2007 .... **CLC 34**
See also CA 139; CAAS 257

Household, Geoffrey (Edward West) 1900-1988 .... **CLC 11**
See also CA 77-80; CAAS 126; CANR 58; CMW 4; CN 1, 2, 3, 4; DLB 87; SATA 14; SATA-Obit 59

Housman, A(lfred) E(dward) 1859-1936 .... **PC 2, 43; TCLC 1, 10; WLCS**
See also AAYA 66; BRW 6; CA 125; CAAE 104; DA; DA3; DAB; DAC; DAM MST, POET; DLB 19, 284; EWL 3; EXPP; MTCW 1, 2; MTFW 2005; PAB; PFS 4, 7; RGEL 2; TEA; WP

Housman, Laurence 1865-1959 .... **TCLC 7**
See also CA 155; CAAE 106; DLB 10; FANT; RGEL 2; SATA 25

Houston, Jeanne Wakatsuki 1934- .... **AAL**
See also AAYA 49; CA 232; 103, 232; 16; CANR 29, 123; LAIT 4; SATA 78, 168; SATA-Essay 168

Howard, Elizabeth Jane 1923- ..... **CLC 7, 29**
See also BRWS 11; CA 5-8R; CANR 8, 62, 146; CN 1, 2, 3, 4, 5, 6, 7

Howard, Maureen 1930- .... **CLC 5, 14, 46, 151**
See also CA 53-56; CANR 31, 75, 140; CN 4, 5, 6, 7; DLBY 1983; INT CANR-31; MTCW 1, 2; MTFW 2005

Howard, Richard 1929- .... **CLC 7, 10, 47**
See also AITN 1; CA 85-88; CANR 25, 80, 154; CP 1, 2, 3, 4, 5, 6, 7; DLB 5; INT CANR-25; MAL 5

Howard, Robert E 1906-1936 .... **TCLC 8**
See also BPFB 2; BYA 5; CA 157; CAAE 105; CANR 155; FANT; SUFW 1; TCWW 1, 2

Howard, Robert Ervin
See Howard, Robert E

Howard, Warren F.
See Pohl, Frederik

Howe, Fanny (Quincy) 1940- .... **CLC 47**
See also CA 187; 117, 187; 27; CANR 70, 116; CP 6, 7; CWP; SATA-Brief 52

Howe, Irving 1920-1993 .... **CLC 85**
See also AMWS 6; CA 9-12R; CAAS 141; CANR 21, 50; DLB 67; EWL 3; MAL 5; MTCW 1, 2; MTFW 2005

Howe, Julia Ward 1819-1910 .... **TCLC 21**
See also CA 191; CAAE 117; DLB 1, 189, 235; FW

Howe, Susan 1937- .... **CLC 72, 152; PC 54**
See also AMWS 4; CA 160; CP 5, 6, 7; CWP; DLB 120; FW; RGAL 4

Howe, Tina 1937- .... **CLC 48**
See also CA 109; CAD; CANR 125; CD 5, 6; CWD

Howell, James 1594(?)-1666 .... **LC 13**
See also DLB 151

Howells, W. D.
See Howells, William Dean

Howells, William D.
See Howells, William Dean

Howells, William Dean 1837-1920 ... **SSC 36; TCLC 7, 17, 41**
See also AMW; CA 134; CAAE 104; CDALB 1865-1917; DLB 12, 64, 74, 79, 189; LMFS 1; MAL 5; MTCW 2; RGAL 4; TUS

Howes, Barbara 1914-1996 .... **CLC 15**
See also CA 9-12R; 3; CAAS 151; CANR 53; CP 1, 2, 3, 4, 5, 6; SATA 5; TCLE 1:1

Hrabal, Bohumil 1914-1997 ...... **CLC 13, 67; TCLC 155**
See also CA 106; 12; CAAS 156; CANR 57; CWW 2; DLB 232; EWL 3; RGSF 2

Hrabanus Maurus 776(?)-856 .... **CMLC 78**
See also DLB 148

Hrotsvit of Gandersheim c. 935-c. 1000 .... **CMLC 29**
See also DLB 148

Hsi, Chu 1130-1200 .... **CMLC 42**

Hsun, Lu
See Lu Hsun

Hubbard, L. Ron 1911-1986 .... **CLC 43**
See also AAYA 64; CA 77-80; CAAS 118; CANR 52; CPW; DA3; DAM POP; FANT; MTCW 2; MTFW 2005; SFW 4

Hubbard, Lafayette Ronald
See Hubbard, L. Ron

Huch, Ricarda (Octavia) 1864-1947 .... **TCLC 13**
See also CA 189; CAAE 111; DLB 66; EWL 3

Huddle, David 1942- .... **CLC 49**
See also CA 57-60; 20; CANR 89; DLB 130

Hudson, Jeffrey
See Crichton, Michael

Hudson, W(illiam) H(enry) 1841-1922 .... **TCLC 29**
See also CA 190; CAAE 115; DLB 98, 153, 174; RGEL 2; SATA 35

Hueffer, Ford Madox
See Ford, Ford Madox

Hughart, Barry 1934- .... **CLC 39**
See also CA 137; FANT; SFW 4; SUFW 2

Hughes, Colin
See Creasey, John

Hughes, David (John) 1930-2005 ..... **CLC 48**
See also CA 129; CAAE 116; CAAS 238; CN 4, 5, 6, 7; DLB 14

Hughes, Edward James
See Hughes, Ted
See also DA3; DAM MST, POET

Hughes, (James Mercer) Langston 1902-1967 ..... **BLC 2; CLC 1, 5, 10, 15, 35, 44, 108; DC 3; HR 1:2; PC 1, 53; SSC 6, 90; WLC 3**
See also AAYA 12; AFAW 1, 2; AMWR 1; AMWS 1; BW 1, 3; CA 1-4R; CAAS 25-28R; CANR 1, 34, 82; CDALB 1929-1941; CLR 17; DA; DA3; DAB; DAC; DAM DRAM, MST, MULT, POET; DFS 6, 18; DLB 4, 7, 48, 51, 86, 228, 315; EWL 3; EXPP; EXPS; JRDA; LAIT 3; LMFS 2; MAICYA 1, 2; MAL 5; MTCW 1, 2; MTFW 2005; NFS 21; PAB; PFS 1, 3, 6, 10, 15; RGAL 4; RGSF 2; SATA 4, 33; SSFS 4, 7; TUS; WCH; WP; YAW

Hughes, Richard (Arthur Warren) 1900-1976 .... **CLC 1, 11**
See also CA 5-8R; CAAS 65-68; CANR 4; CN 1, 2; DAM NOV; DLB 15, 161; EWL 3; MTCW 1; RGEL 2; SATA 8; SATA-Obit 25

Hughes, Ted 1930-1998 . **CLC 2, 4, 9, 14, 37, 119; PC 7**
See Hughes, Edward James
See also BRWC 2; BRWR 2; BRWS 1; CA 1-4R; CAAS 171; CANR 1, 33, 66, 108; CLR 3; CP 1, 2, 3, 4, 5, 6; DAB; DAC; DLB 40, 161; EWL 3; EXPP; MAICYA 1, 2; MTCW 1, 2; MTFW 2005; PAB; PFS 4, 19; RGEL 2; SATA 49; SATA-Brief 27; SATA-Obit 107; TEA; YAW

Hugo, Richard
See Huch, Ricarda (Octavia)

Hugo, Richard F(ranklin) 1923-1982 .... **CLC 6, 18, 32; PC 68**
See also AMWS 6; CA 49-52; CAAS 108; CANR 3; CP 1, 2, 3; DAM POET; DLB 5, 206; EWL 3; MAL 5; PFS 17; RGAL 4

Hugo, Victor (Marie) 1802-1885 .... **NCLC 3, 10, 21, 161; PC 17; WLC 3**
See also AAYA 28; DA; DA3; DAB; DAC; DAM DRAM, MST, NOV, POET; DLB 119, 192, 217; EFS 2; EW 6; EXPN; GFL 1789 to the Present; LAIT 1, 2; NFS 5, 20; RGWL 2, 3; SATA 47; TWA

Huidobro, Vicente
See Huidobro Fernandez, Vicente Garcia
See also DLB 283; EWL 3; LAW

Huidobro Fernandez, Vicente Garcia 1893-1948 .... **TCLC 31**
See Huidobro, Vicente
See also CA 131; HW 1

Hulme, Keri 1947- .... **CLC 39, 130**
See also CA 125; CANR 69; CN 4, 5, 6, 7; CP 6, 7; CWP; DLB 326; EWL 3; FW; INT CA-125; NFS 24

Innis, Harold Adams 1894-1952 .... **TCLC 77**
See also CA 181; DLB 88

Insluis, Alanus de
See Alain de Lille

Iola
See Wells-Barnett, Ida B(ell)

Ionesco, Eugene 1912-1994 ... **CLC 1, 4, 6, 9, 11, 15, 41, 86; DC 12; WLC 3**
See also CA 9-12R; CAAS 144; CANR 55, 132; CWW 2; DA; DA3; DAB; DAC; DAM DRAM, MST; DFS 4, 9; DLB 321; EW 13; EWL 3; GFL 1789 to the Present; LMFS 2; MTCW 1, 2; MTFW 2005; RGWL 2, 3; SATA 7; SATA-Obit 79; TWA

Iqbal, Muhammad 1877-1938 .... **TCLC 28**
See also CA 215; EWL 3

Ireland, Patrick
See O'Doherty, Brian

Irenaeus St. 130- .... **CMLC 42**

Irigaray, Luce 1930- .... **CLC 164**
See also CA 154; CANR 121; FW

Iron, Ralph
See Schreiner, Olive (Emilie Albertina)

Irving, John 1942- . **CLC 13, 23, 38, 112, 175**
See also AAYA 8, 62; AMWS 6; BEST 89:3; BPFB 2; CA 25-28R; CANR 28, 73, 112, 133; CN 3, 4, 5, 6, 7; CPW; DA3; DAM NOV, POP; DLB 6, 278; DLBY 1982; EWL 3; MAL 5; MTCW 1, 2; MTFW 2005; NFS 12, 14; RGAL 4; TUS

Irving, John Winslow
See Irving, John

Irving, Washington 1783-1859 . **NCLC 2, 19, 95; SSC 2, 37; WLC 3**
See also AAYA 56; AMW; CDALB 1640-1865; CLR 97; DA; DA3; DAB; DAC; DAM MST; DLB 3, 11, 30, 59, 73, 74, 183, 186, 250, 254; EXPS; GL 2; LAIT 1; RGAL 4; RGSF 2; SSFS 1, 8, 16; SUFW 1; TUS; WCH; YABC 2

Irwin, P. K.
See Page, P(atricia) K(athleen)

Isaacs, Jorge Ricardo 1837-1895 ... **NCLC 70**
See also LAW

Isaacs, Susan 1943- .... **CLC 32**
See also BEST 89:1; BPFB 2; CA 89-92; CANR 20, 41, 65, 112, 134; CPW; DA3; DAM POP; INT CANR-20; MTCW 1, 2; MTFW 2005

Isherwood, Christopher 1904-1986 ... **CLC 1, 9, 11, 14, 44; SSC 56**
See also AMWS 14; BRW 7; CA 13-16R; CAAS 117; CANR 35, 97, 133; CN 1, 2, 3; DA3; DAM DRAM, NOV; DLB 15, 195; DLBY 1986; EWL 3; IDTP; MTCW 1, 2; MTFW 2005; RGAL 4; RGEL 2; TUS; WLIT 4

Ishiguro, Kazuo 1954- . **CLC 27, 56, 59, 110, 119**
See also AAYA 58; BEST 90:2; BPFB 2; BRWS 4; CA 120; CANR 49, 95, 133; CN 5, 6, 7; DA3; DAM NOV; DLB 194, 326; EWL 3; MTCW 1, 2; MTFW 2005; NFS 13; WLIT 4; WWE 1

Ishikawa, Hakuhin
See Ishikawa, Takuboku

Ishikawa, Takuboku 1886(?)-1912 ..... **PC 10; TCLC 15**
See Ishikawa Takuboku
See also CA 153; CAAE 113; DAM POET

Iskander, Fazil (Abdulovich) 1929- .. **CLC 47**
See Iskander, Fazil' Abdulevich
See also CA 102; EWL 3

Iskander, Fazil' Abdulevich
See Iskander, Fazil (Abdulovich)
See also DLB 302

Isler, Alan (David) 1934- .... **CLC 91**
See also CA 156; CANR 105

Ivan IV 1530-1584 .... **LC 17**

Ivanov, V.I.
See Ivanov, Vyacheslav

Ivanov, Vyacheslav 1866-1949 .... **TCLC 33**
See also CAAE 122; EWL 3

Ivanov, Vyacheslav Ivanovich
See Ivanov, Vyacheslav

Ivask, Ivar Vidrik 1927-1992 .... **CLC 14**
See also CA 37-40R; CAAS 139; CANR 24

Ives, Morgan
See Bradley, Marion Zimmer
See also GLL 1

Izumi Shikibu c. 973-c. 1034 .... **CMLC 33**

J. R. S.
See Gogarty, Oliver St. John

Jabran, Kahlil
See Gibran, Kahlil

Jabran, Khalil
See Gibran, Kahlil

Jackson, Daniel
See Wingrove, David

Jackson, Helen Hunt 1830-1885 .... **NCLC 90**
See also DLB 42, 47, 186, 189; RGAL 4

Jackson, Jesse 1908-1983 .... **CLC 12**
See also BW 1; CA 25-28R; CAAS 109; CANR 27; CLR 28; CWRI 5; MAICYA 1, 2; SATA 2, 29; SATA-Obit 48

Jackson, Laura (Riding) 1901-1991 .... **PC 44**
See Riding, Laura
See also CA 65-68; CAAS 135; CANR 28, 89; DLB 48

Jackson, Sam
See Trumbo, Dalton

Jackson, Sara
See Wingrove, David

Jackson, Shirley 1919-1965 . **CLC 11, 60, 87; SSC 9, 39; TCLC 187; WLC 3**
See also AAYA 9; AMWS 9; BPFB 2; CA 1-4R; CAAS 25-28R; CANR 4, 52; CDALB 1941-1968; DA; DA3; DAC; DAM MST; DLB 6, 234; EXPS; HGG; LAIT 4; MAL 5; MTCW 2; MTFW 2005; RGAL 4; RGSF 2; SATA 2; SSFS 1; SUFW 1, 2

Jacob, (Cyprien-)Max 1876-1944 .... **TCLC 6**
See also CA 193; CAAE 104; DLB 258; EWL 3; GFL 1789 to the Present; GLL 2; RGWL 2, 3

Jacobs, Harriet A(nn) 1813(?)-1897 .... **NCLC 67, 162**
See also AFAW 1, 2; DLB 239; FL 1:3; FW; LAIT 2; RGAL 4

Jacobs, Jim 1942- .... **CLC 12**
See also CA 97-100; INT CA-97-100

Jacobs, W(illiam) W(ymark) 1863-1943 .... **SSC 73; TCLC 22**
See also CA 167; CAAE 121; DLB 135; EXPS; HGG; RGEL 2; RGSF 2; SSFS 2; SUFW 1

Jacobsen, Jens Peter 1847-1885 .... **NCLC 34**

Jacobsen, Josephine (Winder) 1908-2003 .... **CLC 48, 102; PC 62**
See also CA 33-36R; 18; CAAS 218; CANR 23, 48; CCA 1; CP 2, 3, 4, 5, 6, 7; DLB 244; PFS 23; TCLE 1:1

Jacobson, Dan 1929- ...... **CLC 4, 14; SSC 91**
See also AFW; CA 1-4R; CANR 2, 25, 66; CN 1, 2, 3, 4, 5, 6, 7; DLB 14, 207, 225, 319; EWL 3; MTCW 1; RGSF 2

Jacqueline
See Carpentier (y Valmont), Alejo

Jacques de Vitry c. 1160-1240 ...... **CMLC 63**
See also DLB 208

Jagger, Michael Philip
See Jagger, Mick

Jagger, Mick 1943- .... **CLC 17**
See also CA 239

Jahiz, al- c. 780-c. 869 .... **CMLC 25**
See also DLB 311

Jakes, John 1932- .... **CLC 29**
See also AAYA 32; BEST 89:4; BPFB 2; CA 214; 57-60, 214; CANR 10, 43, 66, 111, 142; CPW; CSW; DA3; DAM NOV, POP; DLB 278; DLBY 1983; FANT; INT CANR-10; MTCW 1, 2; MTFW 2005; RHW; SATA 62; SFW 4; TCWW 1, 2

James I 1394-1437 .... **LC 20**
See also RGEL 2

James, Andrew
See Kirkup, James

James, C(yril) L(ionel) R(obert) 1901-1989 .... **BLCS; CLC 33**
See also BW 2; CA 125; CAAE 117; CAAS 128; CANR 62; CN 1, 2, 3, 4; DLB 125; MTCW 1

James, Daniel (Lewis) 1911-1988
See Santiago, Danny
See also CA 174; CAAS 125

James, Dynely
See Mayne, William (James Carter)

James, Henry Sr. 1811-1882 .... **NCLC 53**

James, Henry 1843-1916 .... **SSC 8, 32, 47; TCLC 2, 11, 24, 40, 47, 64, 171; WLC 3**
See also AMW; AMWC 1; AMWR 1; BPFB 2; BRW 6; CA 132; CAAE 104; CDALB 1865-1917; DA; DA3; DAB; DAC; DAM MST, NOV; DLB 12, 71, 74, 189; DLBD 13; EWL 3; EXPS; GL 2; HGG; LAIT 2; MAL 5; MTCW 1, 2; MTFW 2005; NFS 12, 16, 19; RGAL 4; RGEL 2; RGSF 2; SSFS 9; SUFW 1; TUS

James, M. R. .... **SSC 93**
See James, Montague (Rhodes)
See also DLB 156, 201

James, Montague (Rhodes) 1862-1936 .... **SSC 16; TCLC 6**
See James, M. R.
See also CA 203; CAAE 104; HGG; RGEL 2; RGSF 2; SUFW 1

James, P. D. .... **CLC 18, 46, 122, 226**
See White, Phyllis Dorothy James
See also BEST 90:2; BPFB 2; BRWS 4; CDBLB 1960 to Present; CN 4, 5, 6; DLB 87, 276; DLBD 17; MSW

James, Philip
See Moorcock, Michael

James, Samuel
See Stephens, James

James, Seumas
See Stephens, James

James, Stephen
See Stephens, James

James, William 1842-1910 .... **TCLC 15, 32**
See also AMW; CA 193; CAAE 109; DLB 270, 284; MAL 5; NCFS 5; RGAL 4

Jameson, Anna 1794-1860 .... **NCLC 43**
See also DLB 99, 166

Jameson, Fredric (R.) 1934- .... **CLC 142**
See also CA 196; DLB 67; LMFS 2

James VI of Scotland 1566-1625 .... **LC 109**
See also DLB 151, 172

Jami, Nur al-Din 'Abd al-Rahman 1414-1492 .... **LC 9**

Jammes, Francis 1868-1938 .... **TCLC 75**
See also CA 198; EWL 3; GFL 1789 to the Present

Jandl, Ernst 1925-2000 .... **CLC 34**
See also CA 200; EWL 3

Janowitz, Tama 1957- .... **CLC 43, 145**
See also CA 106; CANR 52, 89, 129; CN 5, 6, 7; CPW; DAM POP; DLB 292; MTFW 2005

Jansson, Tove (Marika) 1914-2001 ... **SSC 96**
See also CA 17-20R; CAAS 196; CANR 38, 118; CLR 2; CWW 2; DLB 257; EWL 3; MAICYA 1, 2; RGSF 2; SATA 3, 41

Kops, Bernard 1926- .... **CLC 4**
See also CA 5-8R; CANR 84, 159; CBD;
CN 1, 2, 3, 4, 5, 6, 7; CP 1, 2, 3, 4, 5, 6,
7; DLB 13; RGHL

Kornbluth, C(yril) M. 1923-1958 .... **TCLC 8**
See also CA 160; CAAE 105; DLB 8;
SCFW 1, 2; SFW 4

Korolenko, V.G.
See Korolenko, Vladimir G.

Korolenko, Vladimir
See Korolenko, Vladimir G.

Korolenko, Vladimir G.
1853-1921 .... **TCLC 22**
See also CAAE 121; DLB 277

Korolenko, Vladimir Galaktionovich
See Korolenko, Vladimir G.

Korzybski, Alfred (Habdank Skarbek)
1879-1950 .... **TCLC 61**
See also CA 160; CAAE 123

Kosinski, Jerzy 1933-1991 ..... **CLC 1, 2, 3, 6,
10, 15, 53, 70**
See also AMWS 7; BPFB 2; CA 17-20R;
CAAS 134; CANR 9, 46; CN 1, 2, 3, 4;
DA3; DAM NOV; DLB 2, 299; DLBY
1982; EWL 3; HGG; MAL 5; MTCW 1,
2; MTFW 2005; NFS 12; RGAL 4;
RGHL; TUS

Kostelanetz, Richard (Cory) 1940- .. **CLC 28**
See also CA 13-16R; 8; CANR 38, 77; CN
4, 5, 6; CP 2, 3, 4, 5, 6, 7

Kostrowitzki, Wilhelm Apollinaris de
1880-1918
See Apollinaire, Guillaume
See also CAAE 104

Kotlowitz, Robert 1924- .... **CLC 4**
See also CA 33-36R; CANR 36

Kotzebue, August (Friedrich Ferdinand) von
1761-1819 .... **NCLC 25**
See also DLB 94

Kotzwinkle, William 1938- ..... **CLC 5, 14, 35**
See also BPFB 2; CA 45-48; CANR 3, 44,
84, 129; CLR 6; CN 7; DLB 173; FANT;
MAICYA 1, 2; SATA 24, 70, 146; SFW
4; SUFW 2; YAW

Kowna, Stancy
See Szymborska, Wislawa

Kozol, Jonathan 1936- .... **CLC 17**
See also AAYA 46; CA 61-64; CANR 16,
45, 96; MTFW 2005

Kozoll, Michael 1940(?)- .... **CLC 35**

Kramer, Kathryn 19(?)- .... **CLC 34**

Kramer, Larry 1935- .... **CLC 42; DC 8**
See also CA 126; CAAE 124; CANR 60,
132; DAM POP; DLB 249; GLL 1

Krasicki, Ignacy 1735-1801 .... **NCLC 8**

Krasinski, Zygmunt 1812-1859 .... **NCLC 4**
See also RGWL 2, 3

Kraus, Karl 1874-1936 .... **TCLC 5**
See also CA 216; CAAE 104; DLB 118;
EWL 3

Kreve (Mickevicius), Vincas
1882-1954 .... **TCLC 27**
See also CA 170; DLB 220; EWL 3

Kristeva, Julia 1941- .... **CLC 77, 140**
See also CA 154; CANR 99; DLB 242;
EWL 3; FW; LMFS 2

Kristofferson, Kris 1936- .... **CLC 26**
See also CA 104

Krizanc, John 1956- .... **CLC 57**
See also CA 187

Krleza, Miroslav 1893-1981 .... **CLC 8, 114**
See also CA 97-100; CAAS 105; CANR
50; CDWLB 4; DLB 147; EW 11; RGWL
2, 3

Kroetsch, Robert (Paul) 1927- .... **CLC 5, 23,
57, 132**
See also CA 17-20R; CANR 8, 38; CCA 1;
CN 2, 3, 4, 5, 6, 7; CP 6, 7; DAC; DAM
POET; DLB 53; MTCW 1

Kroetz, Franz
See Kroetz, Franz Xaver

Kroetz, Franz Xaver 1946- .... **CLC 41**
See also CA 130; CANR 142; CWW 2;
EWL 3

Kroker, Arthur (W.) 1945- .... **CLC 77**
See also CA 161

Kroniuk, Lisa
See Berton, Pierre (Francis de Marigny)

Kropotkin, Peter (Aleksieevich)
1842-1921 .... **TCLC 36**
See Kropotkin, Petr Alekseevich
See also CA 219; CAAE 119

Kropotkin, Petr Alekseevich
See Kropotkin, Peter (Aleksieevich)
See also DLB 277

Krotkov, Yuri 1917-1981 .... **CLC 19**
See also CA 102

Krumb
See Crumb, R.

Krumgold, Joseph (Quincy)
1908-1980 .... **CLC 12**
See also BYA 1, 2; CA 9-12R; CAAS 101;
CANR 7; MAICYA 1, 2; SATA 1, 48;
SATA-Obit 23; YAW

Krumwitz
See Crumb, R.

Krutch, Joseph Wood 1893-1970 ..... **CLC 24**
See also ANW; CA 1-4R; CAAS 25-28R;
CANR 4; DLB 63, 206, 275

Krutzch, Gus
See Eliot, T(homas) S(tearns)

Krylov, Ivan Andreevich
1768(?)-1844 .... **NCLC 1**
See also DLB 150

Kubin, Alfred (Leopold Isidor)
1877-1959 .... **TCLC 23**
See also CA 149; CAAE 112; CANR 104;
DLB 81

Kubrick, Stanley 1928-1999 .... **CLC 16;
TCLC 112**
See also AAYA 30; CA 81-84; CAAS 177;
CANR 33; DLB 26

Kumin, Maxine 1925- .... **CLC 5, 13, 28, 164;
PC 15**
See also AITN 2; AMWS 4; ANW; CA
1-4R; 8; CANR 1, 21, 69, 115, 140; CP 2,
3, 4, 5, 6, 7; CWP; DA3; DAM POET;
DLB 5; EWL 3; EXPP; MTCW 1, 2;
MTFW 2005; PAB; PFS 18; SATA 12

Kundera, Milan 1929- . **CLC 4, 9, 19, 32, 68,
115, 135, 234; SSC 24**
See also AAYA 2, 62; BPFB 2; CA 85-88;
CANR 19, 52, 74, 144; CDWLB 4; CWW
2; DA3; DAM NOV; DLB 232; EW 13;
EWL 3; MTCW 1, 2; MTFW 2005; NFS
18; RGSF 2; RGWL 3; SSFS 10

Kunene, Mazisi 1930-2006 .... **CLC 85**
See also BW 1, 3; CA 125; CAAS 252;
CANR 81; CP 1, 6, 7; DLB 117

Kunene, Mazisi Raymond
See Kunene, Mazisi

Kunene, Mazisi Raymond Fakazi Mngoni
See Kunene, Mazisi

Kung, Hans .... **CLC 130**
See Kung, Hans

Kung, Hans 1928-
See Kung, Hans
See also CA 53-56; CANR 66, 134; MTCW
1, 2; MTFW 2005

Kunikida Doppo 1869(?)-1908
See Doppo, Kunikida
See also DLB 180; EWL 3

Kunitz, Stanley 1905-2006 ..... **CLC 6, 11, 14,
148; PC 19**
See also AMWS 3; CA 41-44R; CAAS 250;
CANR 26, 57, 98; CP 1, 2, 3, 4, 5, 6, 7;
DA3; DLB 48; INT CANR-26; MAL 5;
MTCW 1, 2; MTFW 2005; PFS 11;
RGAL 4

Kunitz, Stanley Jasspon
See Kunitz, Stanley

Kunze, Reiner 1933- .... **CLC 10**
See also CA 93-96; CWW 2; DLB 75; EWL
3

Kuprin, Aleksander Ivanovich
1870-1938 .... **TCLC 5**
See Kuprin, Aleksandr Ivanovich; Kuprin,
Alexandr Ivanovich
See also CA 182; CAAE 104

Kuprin, Aleksandr Ivanovich
See Kuprin, Aleksander Ivanovich
See also DLB 295

Kuprin, Alexandr Ivanovich
See Kuprin, Aleksander Ivanovich
See also EWL 3

Kureishi, Hanif 1954- .. **CLC 64, 135; DC 26**
See also BRWS 11; CA 139; CANR 113;
CBD; CD 5, 6; CN 6, 7; DLB 194, 245;
GLL 2; IDFW 4; WLIT 4; WWE 1

Kurosawa, Akira 1910-1998 ..... **CLC 16, 119**
See also AAYA 11, 64; CA 101; CAAS 170;
CANR 46; DAM MULT

Kushner, Tony 1956- .... **CLC 81, 203; DC 10**
See also AAYA 61; AMWS 9; CA 144;
CAD; CANR 74, 130; CD 5, 6; DA3;
DAM DRAM; DFS 5; DLB 228; EWL 3;
GLL 1; LAIT 5; MAL 5; MTCW 2;
MTFW 2005; RGAL 4; RGHL; SATA 160

Kuttner, Henry 1915-1958 .... **TCLC 10**
See also CA 157; CAAE 107; DLB 8;
FANT; SCFW 1, 2; SFW 4

Kutty, Madhavi
See Das, Kamala

Kuzma, Greg 1944- .... **CLC 7**
See also CA 33-36R; CANR 70

Kuzmin, Mikhail (Alekseevich)
1872(?)-1936 .... **TCLC 40**
See also CA 170; DLB 295; EWL 3

Kyd, Thomas 1558-1594 .. **DC 3; LC 22, 125**
See also BRW 1; DAM DRAM; DFS 21;
DLB 62; IDTP; LMFS 1; RGEL 2; TEA;
WLIT 3

Kyprianos, Iossif
See Samarakis, Antonis

L. S.
See Stephen, Sir Leslie

Labe, Louise 1521-1566 .... **LC 120**
See also DLB 327

Labrunie, Gerard
See Nerval, Gerard de

La Bruyere, Jean de 1645-1696 .... **LC 17**
See also DLB 268; EW 3; GFL Beginnings
to 1789

LaBute, Neil 1963- .... **CLC 225**
See also CA 240

Lacan, Jacques (Marie Emile)
1901-1981 .... **CLC 75**
See also CA 121; CAAS 104; DLB 296;
EWL 3; TWA

Laclos, Pierre-Ambroise Francois
1741-1803 .... **NCLC 4, 87**
See also DLB 313; EW 4; GFL Beginnings
to 1789; RGWL 2, 3

Lacolere, Francois
See Aragon, Louis

La Colere, Francois
See Aragon, Louis

La Deshabilleuse
See Simenon, Georges (Jacques Christian)

Lady Gregory
See Gregory, Lady Isabella Augusta (Persse)

Lady of Quality, A
See Bagnold, Enid

**La Fayette, Marie-(Madelaine Pioche de la
Vergne)** 1634-1693 .... **LC 2**
See Lafayette, Marie-Madeleine
See also GFL Beginnings to 1789; RGWL
2, 3

Levin, Ira 1929- .... **CLC 3, 6**
See also CA 21-24R; CANR 17, 44, 74,
139; CMW 4; CN 1, 2, 3, 4, 5, 6, 7; CPW;
DA3; DAM POP; HGG; MTCW 1, 2;
MTFW 2005; SATA 66; SFW 4

Levin, Meyer 1905-1981 .... **CLC 7**
See also AITN 1; CA 9-12R; CAAS 104;
CANR 15; CN 1, 2, 3; DAM POP; DLB
9, 28; DLBY 1981; MAL 5; RGHL; SATA
21; SATA-Obit 27

Levine, Albert Norman
See Levine, Norman
See also CN 7

Levine, Norman 1923-2005 .... **CLC 54**
See Levine, Albert Norman
See also CA 73-76; 23; CAAS 240; CANR
14, 70; CN 1, 2, 3, 4, 5, 6; CP 1; DLB 88

Levine, Norman Albert
See Levine, Norman

Levine, Philip 1928- .. **CLC 2, 4, 5, 9, 14, 33,
118; PC 22**
See also AMWS 5; CA 9-12R; CANR 9,
37, 52, 116, 156; CP 1, 2, 3, 4, 5, 6, 7;
DAM POET; DLB 5; EWL 3; MAL 5;
PFS 8

Levinson, Deirdre 1931- .... **CLC 49**
See also CA 73-76; CANR 70

Levi-Strauss, Claude 1908- .... **CLC 38**
See also CA 1-4R; CANR 6, 32, 57; DLB
242; EWL 3; GFL 1789 to the Present;
MTCW 1, 2; TWA

Levitin, Sonia (Wolff) 1934- .... **CLC 17**
See also AAYA 13, 48; CA 29-32R; CANR
14, 32, 79; CLR 53; JRDA; MAICYA 1,
2; SAAS 2; SATA 4, 68, 119, 131; SATA-
Essay 131; YAW

Levon, O. U.
See Kesey, Ken

Levy, Amy 1861-1889 .... **NCLC 59**
See also DLB 156, 240

Lewes, George Henry 1817-1878 ... **NCLC 25**
See also DLB 55, 144

Lewis, Alun 1915-1944 .... **SSC 40; TCLC 3**
See also BRW 7; CA 188; CAAE 104; DLB
20, 162; PAB; RGEL 2

Lewis, C. Day
See Day Lewis, C(ecil)
See also CN 1

Lewis, Cecil Day
See Day Lewis, C(ecil)

Lewis, Clive Staples
See Lewis, C.S.

Lewis, C.S. 1898-1963 ... **CLC 1, 3, 6, 14, 27,
124; WLC 4**
See also AAYA 3, 39; BPFB 2; BRWS 3;
BYA 15, 16; CA 81-84; CANR 33, 71,
132; CDBLB 1945-1960; CLR 3, 27, 109;
CWRI 5; DA; DA3; DAB; DAC; DAM
MST, NOV, POP; DLB 15, 100, 160, 255;
EWL 3; FANT; JRDA; LMFS 2; MAI-
CYA 1, 2; MTCW 1, 2; MTFW 2005;
NFS 24; RGEL 2; SATA 13, 100; SCFW
1, 2; SFW 4; SUFW 1; TEA; WCH;
WYA; YAW

Lewis, Janet 1899-1998 .... **CLC 41**
See Winters, Janet Lewis
See also CA 9-12R; CAAS 172; CANR 29,
63; CAP 1; CN 1, 2, 3, 4, 5, 6; DLBY
1987; RHW; TCWW 2

Lewis, Matthew Gregory
1775-1818 .... **NCLC 11, 62**
See also DLB 39, 158, 178; GL 3; HGG;
LMFS 1; RGEL 2; SUFW

Lewis, (Harry) Sinclair 1885-1951 . **TCLC 4,
13, 23, 39; WLC 4**
See also AMW; AMWC 1; BPFB 2; CA
133; CAAE 104; CANR 132; CDALB
1917-1929; DA; DA3; DAB; DAC; DAM

MST, NOV; DLB 9, 102, 284, 331; DLBD
1; EWL 3; LAIT 3; MAL 5; MTCW 1, 2;
MTFW 2005; NFS 15, 19, 22; RGAL 4;
TUS

Lewis, (Percy) Wyndham
1884(?)-1957 .. **SSC 34; TCLC 2, 9, 104**
See also BRW 7; CA 157; CAAE 104; DLB
15; EWL 3; FANT; MTCW 2; MTFW
2005; RGEL 2

Lewisohn, Ludwig 1883-1955 .... **TCLC 19**
See also CA 203; CAAE 107; DLB 4, 9,
28, 102; MAL 5

Lewton, Val 1904-1951 .... **TCLC 76**
See also CA 199; IDFW 3, 4

Leyner, Mark 1956- .... **CLC 92**
See also CA 110; CANR 28, 53; DA3; DLB
292; MTCW 2; MTFW 2005

Lezama Lima, Jose 1910-1976 .... **CLC 4, 10,
101; HLCS 2**
See also CA 77-80; CANR 71; DAM
MULT; DLB 113, 283; EWL 3; HW 1, 2;
LAW; RGWL 2, 3

L'Heureux, John (Clarke) 1934- ...... **CLC 52**
See also CA 13-16R; CANR 23, 45, 88; CP
1, 2, 3, 4; DLB 244

Li Ch'ing-chao 1081(?)-1141(?) .... **CMLC 71**

Liddell, C. H.
See Kuttner, Henry

Lie, Jonas (Lauritz Idemil)
1833-1908(?) .... **TCLC 5**
See also CAAE 115

Lieber, Joel 1937-1971 .... **CLC 6**
See also CA 73-76; CAAS 29-32R

Lieber, Stanley Martin
See Lee, Stan

Lieberman, Laurence (James)
1935- .... **CLC 4, 36**
See also CA 17-20R; CANR 8, 36, 89; CP
1, 2, 3, 4, 5, 6, 7

Lieh Tzu fl. 7th cent. B.C.-5th cent.
B.C. .... **CMLC 27**

Lieksman, Anders
See Haavikko, Paavo Juhani

Lifton, Robert Jay 1926- .... **CLC 67**
See also CA 17-20R; CANR 27, 78, 161;
INT CANR-27; SATA 66

Lightfoot, Gordon 1938- .... **CLC 26**
See also CA 242; CAAE 109

Lightfoot, Gordon Meredith
See Lightfoot, Gordon

Lightman, Alan P(aige) 1948- .... **CLC 81**
See also CA 141; CANR 63, 105, 138;
MTFW 2005

Ligotti, Thomas (Robert) 1953- ...... **CLC 44;
SSC 16**
See also CA 123; CANR 49, 135; HGG;
SUFW 2

Li Ho 791-817 .... **PC 13**

Li Ju-chen c. 1763-c. 1830 .... **NCLC 137**

Lilar, Francoise
See Mallet-Joris, Francoise

Liliencron, Detlev
See Liliencron, Detlev von

Liliencron, Detlev von 1844-1909 .. **TCLC 18**
See also CAAE 117

Liliencron, Friedrich Adolf Axel Detlev von
See Liliencron, Detlev von

Liliencron, Friedrich Detlev von
See Liliencron, Detlev von

Lille, Alain de
See Alain de Lille

Lillo, George 1691-1739 .... **LC 131**
See also DLB 84; RGEL 2

Lilly, William 1602-1681 .... **LC 27**

Lima, Jose Lezama
See Lezama Lima, Jose

Lima Barreto, Afonso Henrique de
1881-1922 .... **TCLC 23**
See Lima Barreto, Afonso Henriques de
See also CA 181; CAAE 117; LAW

Lima Barreto, Afonso Henriques de
See Lima Barreto, Afonso Henrique de
See also DLB 307

Limonov, Eduard
See Limonov, Edward
See also DLB 317

Limonov, Edward 1944- .... **CLC 67**
See Limonov, Eduard
See also CA 137

Lin, Frank
See Atherton, Gertrude (Franklin Horn)

Lin, Yutang 1895-1976 .... **TCLC 149**
See also CA 45-48; CAAS 65-68; CANR 2;
RGAL 4

Lincoln, Abraham 1809-1865 .... **NCLC 18**
See also LAIT 2

Lind, Jakov 1927-2007 ... **CLC 1, 2, 4, 27, 82**
See Landwirth, Heinz
See also CA 4; CAAS 257; DLB 299; EWL
3; RGHL

Lindbergh, Anne Morrow
1906-2001 .... **CLC 82**
See also BPFB 2; CA 17-20R; CAAS 193;
CANR 16, 73; DAM NOV; MTCW 1, 2;
MTFW 2005; SATA 33; SATA-Obit 125;
TUS

Lindsay, David 1878(?)-1945 .... **TCLC 15**
See also CA 187; CAAE 113; DLB 255;
FANT; SFW 4; SUFW 1

Lindsay, (Nicholas) Vachel
1879-1931 .... **PC 23; TCLC 17; WLC 4**
See also AMWS 1; CA 135; CAAE 114;
CANR 79; CDALB 1865-1917; DA;
DA3; DAC; DAM MST, POET; DLB 54;
EWL 3; EXPP; MAL 5; RGAL 4; SATA
40; WP

Linke-Poot
See Doeblin, Alfred

Linney, Romulus 1930- .... **CLC 51**
See also CA 1-4R; CAD; CANR 40, 44,
79; CD 5, 6; CSW; RGAL 4

Linton, Eliza Lynn 1822-1898 .... **NCLC 41**
See also DLB 18

Li Po 701-763 .... **CMLC 2, 86; PC 29**
See also PFS 20; WP

Lipsius, Justus 1547-1606 .... **LC 16**

Lipsyte, Robert 1938- .... **CLC 21**
See also AAYA 7, 45; CA 17-20R; CANR
8, 57, 146; CLR 23, 76; DA; DAC; DAM
MST, NOV; JRDA; LAIT 5; MAICYA 1,
2; SATA 5, 68, 113, 161; WYA; YAW

Lipsyte, Robert Michael
See Lipsyte, Robert

Lish, Gordon 1934- .... **CLC 45; SSC 18**
See also CA 117; CAAE 113; CANR 79,
151; DLB 130; INT CA-117

Lish, Gordon Jay
See Lish, Gordon

Lispector, Clarice 1925(?)-1977 .... **CLC 43;
HLCS 2; SSC 34, 96**
See also CA 139; CAAS 116; CANR 71;
CDWLB 3; DLB 113, 307; DNFS 1; EWL
3; FW; HW 2; LAW; RGSF 2; RGWL 2,
3; WLIT 1

Littell, Robert 1935(?)- .... **CLC 42**
See also CA 112; CAAE 109; CANR 64,
115, 162; CMW 4

Little, Malcolm 1925-1965
See Malcolm X
See also BW 1, 3; CA 125; CAAS 111;
CANR 82; DA; DA3; DAB; DAC; DAM
MST, MULT; MTCW 1, 2; MTFW 2005

Littlewit, Humphrey Gent.
See Lovecraft, H. P.

Lowell, Robert (Traill Spence, Jr.)
1917-1977 .... **CLC 1, 2, 3, 4, 5, 8, 9, 11, 15, 37, 124; PC 3; WLC 4**
See also AMW; AMWC 2; AMWR 2; CA 9-12R; CAAS 73-76; CABS 2; CAD; CANR 26, 60; CDALBS; CP 1, 2; DA; DA3; DAB; DAC; DAM MST, NOV; DLB 5, 169; EWL 3; MAL 5; MTCW 1, 2; MTFW 2005; PAB; PFS 6, 7; RGAL 4; WP

Lowenthal, Michael (Francis)
1969- .... **CLC 119**
See also CA 150; CANR 115

Lowndes, Marie Adelaide (Belloc)
1868-1947 .... **TCLC 12**
See also CAAE 107; CMW 4; DLB 70; RHW

Lowry, (Clarence) Malcolm
1909-1957 .... **SSC 31; TCLC 6, 40**
See also BPFB 2; BRWS 3; CA 131; CAAE 105; CANR 62, 105; CDBLB 1945-1960; DLB 15; EWL 3; MTCW 1, 2; MTFW 2005; RGEL 2

Lowry, Mina Gertrude 1882-1966
See Loy, Mina
See also CA 113

Lowry, Sam
See Soderbergh, Steven

Loxsmith, John
See Brunner, John (Kilian Houston)

Loy, Mina .... **CLC 28; PC 16**
See Lowry, Mina Gertrude
See also DAM POET; DLB 4, 54; PFS 20

Loyson-Bridet
See Schwob, Marcel (Mayer Andre)

Lucan 39-65 .... **CMLC 33**
See also AW 2; DLB 211; EFS 2; RGWL 2, 3

Lucas, Craig 1951- .... **CLC 64**
See also CA 137; CAD; CANR 71, 109, 142; CD 5, 6; GLL 2; MTFW 2005

Lucas, E(dward) V(errall)
1868-1938 .... **TCLC 73**
See also CA 176; DLB 98, 149, 153; SATA 20

Lucas, George 1944- .... **CLC 16**
See also AAYA 1, 23; CA 77-80; CANR 30; SATA 56

Lucas, Hans
See Godard, Jean-Luc

Lucas, Victoria
See Plath, Sylvia

Lucian c. 125-c. 180 .... **CMLC 32**
See also AW 2; DLB 176; RGWL 2, 3

Lucilius c. 180B.C.-102B.C. .... **CMLC 82**
See also DLB 211

Lucretius c. 94B.C.-c. 49B.C. .... **CMLC 48**
See also AW 2; CDWLB 1; DLB 211; EFS 2; RGWL 2, 3; WLIT 8

Ludlam, Charles 1943-1987 .... **CLC 46, 50**
See also CA 85-88; CAAS 122; CAD; CANR 72, 86; DLB 266

Ludlum, Robert 1927-2001 .... **CLC 22, 43**
See also AAYA 10, 59; BEST 89:1, 90:3; BPFB 2; CA 33-36R; CAAS 195; CANR 25, 41, 68, 105, 131; CMW 4; CPW; DA3; DAM NOV, POP; DLBY 1982; MSW; MTCW 1, 2; MTFW 2005

Ludwig, Ken 1950- .... **CLC 60**
See also CA 195; CAD; CD 6

Ludwig, Otto 1813-1865 .... **NCLC 4**
See also DLB 129

Lugones, Leopoldo 1874-1938 .... **HLCS 2; TCLC 15**
See also CA 131; CAAE 116; CANR 104; DLB 283; EWL 3; HW 1; LAW

Lu Hsun .... **SSC 20; TCLC 3**
See Shu-Jen, Chou
See also EWL 3

Lukacs, George .... **CLC 24**
See Lukacs, Gyorgy (Szegeny von)

Lukacs, Gyorgy (Szegeny von) 1885-1971
See Lukacs, George
See also CA 101; CAAS 29-32R; CANR 62; CDWLB 4; DLB 215, 242; EW 10; EWL 3; MTCW 1, 2

Luke, Peter (Ambrose Cyprian)
1919-1995 .... **CLC 38**
See also CA 81-84; CAAS 147; CANR 72; CBD; CD 5, 6; DLB 13

Lunar, Dennis
See Mungo, Raymond

Lurie, Alison 1926- ..... **CLC 4, 5, 18, 39, 175**
See also BPFB 2; CA 1-4R; CANR 2, 17, 50, 88; CN 1, 2, 3, 4, 5, 6, 7; DLB 2; MAL 5; MTCW 1; NFS 24; SATA 46, 112; TCLE 1:1

Lustig, Arnost 1926- .... **CLC 56**
See also AAYA 3; CA 69-72; CANR 47, 102; CWW 2; DLB 232, 299; EWL 3; RGHL; SATA 56

Luther, Martin 1483-1546 .... **LC 9, 37**
See also CDWLB 2; DLB 179; EW 2; RGWL 2, 3

Luxemburg, Rosa 1870(?)-1919 ..... **TCLC 63**
See also CAAE 118

Luzi, Mario (Egidio Vincenzo)
1914-2005 .... **CLC 13**
See also CA 61-64; CAAS 128; CANR 9, 70; CWW 2; DLB 128; EWL 3

L'vov, Arkady .... **CLC 59**

Lydgate, John c. 1370-1450(?) .... **LC 81**
See also BRW 1; DLB 146; RGEL 2

Lyly, John 1554(?)-1606 .... **DC 7; LC 41**
See also BRW 1; DAM DRAM; DLB 62, 167; RGEL 2

L'Ymagier
See Gourmont, Remy(-Marie-Charles) de

Lynch, B. Suarez
See Borges, Jorge Luis

Lynch, David 1946- .... **CLC 66, 162**
See also AAYA 55; CA 129; CAAE 124; CANR 111

Lynch, David Keith
See Lynch, David

Lynch, James
See Andreyev, Leonid (Nikolaevich)

Lyndsay, Sir David 1485-1555 .... **LC 20**
See also RGEL 2

Lynn, Kenneth S(chuyler)
1923-2001 .... **CLC 50**
See also CA 1-4R; CAAS 196; CANR 3, 27, 65

Lynx
See West, Rebecca

Lyons, Marcus
See Blish, James (Benjamin)

Lyotard, Jean-Francois
1924-1998 .... **TCLC 103**
See also DLB 242; EWL 3

Lyre, Pinchbeck
See Sassoon, Siegfried (Lorraine)

Lytle, Andrew (Nelson) 1902-1995 ... **CLC 22**
See also CA 9-12R; CAAS 236; CANR 70; CN 1, 2, 3, 4, 5, 6; CSW; DLB 6; DLBY 1995; RGAL 4; RHW

Lyttelton, George 1709-1773 .... **LC 10**
See also RGEL 2

Lytton of Knebworth, Baron
See Bulwer-Lytton, Edward (George Earle Lytton)

Maas, Peter 1929-2001 .... **CLC 29**
See also CA 93-96; CAAS 201; INT CA-93-96; MTCW 2; MTFW 2005

Mac A'Ghobhainn, Iain
See Smith, Iain Crichton

Macaulay, Catherine 1731-1791 .... **LC 64**
See also DLB 104, 336

Macaulay, (Emilie) Rose
1881(?)-1958 .... **TCLC 7, 44**
See also CAAE 104; DLB 36; EWL 3; RGEL 2; RHW

Macaulay, Thomas Babington
1800-1859 .... **NCLC 42**
See also BRW 4; CDBLB 1832-1890; DLB 32, 55; RGEL 2

MacBeth, George (Mann)
1932-1992 .... **CLC 2, 5, 9**
See also CA 25-28R; CAAS 136; CANR 61, 66; CP 1, 2, 3, 4, 5; DLB 40; MTCW 1; PFS 8; SATA 4; SATA-Obit 70

MacCaig, Norman (Alexander)
1910-1996 .... **CLC 36**
See also BRWS 6; CA 9-12R; CANR 3, 34; CP 1, 2, 3, 4, 5, 6; DAB; DAM POET; DLB 27; EWL 3; RGEL 2

MacCarthy, Sir (Charles Otto) Desmond
1877-1952 .... **TCLC 36**
See also CA 167

MacDiarmid, Hugh .... **CLC 2, 4, 11, 19, 63; PC 9**
See Grieve, C(hristopher) M(urray)
See also BRWS 12; CDBLB 1945-1960; CP 1, 2; DLB 20; EWL 3; RGEL 2

MacDonald, Anson
See Heinlein, Robert A.

Macdonald, Cynthia 1928- .... **CLC 13, 19**
See also CA 49-52; CANR 4, 44, 146; DLB 105

MacDonald, George 1824-1905 .... **TCLC 9, 113**
See also AAYA 57; BYA 5; CA 137; CAAE 106; CANR 80; CLR 67; DLB 18, 163, 178; FANT; MAICYA 1, 2; RGEL 2; SATA 33, 100; SFW 4; SUFW; WCH

Macdonald, John
See Millar, Kenneth

MacDonald, John D. 1916-1986 .. **CLC 3, 27, 44**
See also BPFB 2; CA 1-4R; CAAS 121; CANR 1, 19, 60; CMW 4; CPW; DAM NOV, POP; DLB 8, 306; DLBY 1986; MSW; MTCW 1, 2; MTFW 2005; SFW 4

Macdonald, John Ross
See Millar, Kenneth

Macdonald, Ross ..... **CLC 1, 2, 3, 14, 34, 41**
See Millar, Kenneth
See also AMWS 4; BPFB 2; CN 1, 2, 3; DLBD 6; MAL 5; MSW; RGAL 4

MacDougal, John
See Blish, James (Benjamin)

MacDougal, John
See Blish, James (Benjamin)

MacDowell, John
See Parks, Tim(othy Harold)

MacEwen, Gwendolyn (Margaret)
1941-1987 .... **CLC 13, 55**
See also CA 9-12R; CAAS 124; CANR 7, 22; CP 1, 2, 3, 4; DLB 53, 251; SATA 50; SATA-Obit 55

Macha, Karel Hynek 1810-1846 .... **NCLC 46**

Machado (y Ruiz), Antonio
1875-1939 .... **TCLC 3**
See also CA 174; CAAE 104; DLB 108; EW 9; EWL 3; HW 2; PFS 23; RGWL 2, 3

Machado de Assis, Joaquim Maria
1839-1908 .... **BLC 2; HLCS 2; SSC 24; TCLC 10**
See also CA 153; CAAE 107; CANR 91; DLB 307; LAW; RGSF 2; RGWL 2, 3; TWA; WLIT 1

Machaut, Guillaume de c.
1300-1377 .... **CMLC 64**
See also DLB 208

Mattheson, Rodney
See Creasey, John

Matthews, (James) Brander
1852-1929 .... **TCLC 95**
See also CA 181; DLB 71, 78; DLBD 13

Matthews, Greg 1949- .... **CLC 45**
See also CA 135

Matthews, William (Procter III)
1942-1997 .... **CLC 40**
See also AMWS 9; CA 29-32R; 18; CAAS
162; CANR 12, 57; CP 2, 3, 4, 5, 6; DLB
5

Matthias, John (Edward) 1941- .... **CLC 9**
See also CA 33-36R; CANR 56; CP 4, 5, 6,
7

Matthiessen, F(rancis) O(tto)
1902-1950 .... **TCLC 100**
See also CA 185; DLB 63; MAL 5

Matthiessen, Peter 1927- ... **CLC 5, 7, 11, 32,
64**
See also AAYA 6, 40; AMWS 5; ANW;
BEST 90:4; BPFB 2; CA 9-12R; CANR
21, 50, 73, 100, 138; CN 1, 2, 3, 4, 5, 6,
7; DA3; DAM NOV; DLB 6, 173, 275;
MAL 5; MTCW 1, 2; MTFW 2005; SATA
27

Maturin, Charles Robert
1780(?)-1824 .... **NCLC 6, 169**
See also BRWS 8; DLB 178; GL 3; HGG;
LMFS 1; RGEL 2; SUFW

Matute (Ausejo), Ana Maria 1925- ... **CLC 11**
See also CA 89-92; CANR 129; CWW 2;
DLB 322; EWL 3; MTCW 1; RGSF 2

Maugham, W. S.
See Maugham, W(illiam) Somerset

Maugham, W(illiam) Somerset
1874-1965 .. **CLC 1, 11, 15, 67, 93; SSC
8, 94; WLC 4**
See also AAYA 55; BPFB 2; BRW 6; CA
5-8R; CAAS 25-28R; CANR 40, 127;
CDBLB 1914-1945; CMW 4; DA; DA3;
DAB; DAC; DAM DRAM, MST, NOV;
DFS 22; DLB 10, 36, 77, 100, 162, 195;
EWL 3; LAIT 3; MTCW 1, 2; MTFW
2005; NFS 23; RGEL 2; RGSF 2; SATA
54; SSFS 17

Maugham, William Somerset
See Maugham, W(illiam) Somerset

Maupassant, (Henri Rene Albert) Guy de
1850-1893 . **NCLC 1, 42, 83; SSC 1, 64;
WLC 4**
See also BYA 14; DA; DA3; DAB; DAC;
DAM MST; DLB 123; EW 7; EXPS; GFL
1789 to the Present; LAIT 2; LMFS 1;
RGSF 2; RGWL 2, 3; SSFS 4, 21; SUFW;
TWA

Maupin, Armistead 1944- .... **CLC 95**
See also CA 130; CAAE 125; CANR 58,
101; CPW; DA3; DAM POP; DLB 278;
GLL 1; INT CA-130; MTCW 2; MTFW
2005

Maupin, Armistead Jones, Jr.
See Maupin, Armistead

Maurhut, Richard
See Traven, B.

Mauriac, Claude 1914-1996 .... **CLC 9**
See also CA 89-92; CAAS 152; CWW 2;
DLB 83; EWL 3; GFL 1789 to the Present

Mauriac, Francois (Charles)
1885-1970 .... **CLC 4, 9, 56; SSC 24**
See also CA 25-28; CAP 2; DLB 65, 331;
EW 10; EWL 3; GFL 1789 to the Present;
MTCW 1, 2; MTFW 2005; RGWL 2, 3;
TWA

Mavor, Osborne Henry 1888-1951
See Bridie, James
See also CAAE 104

Maxwell, Glyn 1962- .... **CLC 238**
See also CA 154; CANR 88; CP 6, 7; PFS
23

Maxwell, William (Keepers, Jr.)
1908-2000 .... **CLC 19**
See also AMWS 8; CA 93-96; CAAS 189;
CANR 54, 95; CN 1, 2, 3, 4, 5, 6, 7; DLB
218, 278; DLBY 1980; INT CA-93-96;
MAL 5; SATA-Obit 128

May, Elaine 1932- .... **CLC 16**
See also CA 142; CAAE 124; CAD; CWD;
DLB 44

Mayakovski, Vladimir (Vladimirovich)
1893-1930 .... **TCLC 4, 18**
See Maiakovskii, Vladimir; Mayakovsky,
Vladimir
See also CA 158; CAAE 104; EWL 3;
MTCW 2; MTFW 2005; SFW 4; TWA

Mayakovsky, Vladimir
See Mayakovski, Vladimir (Vladimirovich)
See also EW 11; WP

Mayhew, Henry 1812-1887 .... **NCLC 31**
See also DLB 18, 55, 190

Mayle, Peter 1939(?)- .... **CLC 89**
See also CA 139; CANR 64, 109

Maynard, Joyce 1953- .... **CLC 23**
See also CA 129; CAAE 111; CANR 64

Mayne, William (James Carter)
1928- .... **CLC 12**
See also AAYA 20; CA 9-12R; CANR 37,
80, 100; CLR 25, 123; FANT; JRDA;
MAICYA 1, 2; MAICYAS 1; SAAS 11;
SATA 6, 68, 122; SUFW 2; YAW

Mayo, Jim
See L'Amour, Louis

Maysles, Albert 1926- .... **CLC 16**
See also CA 29-32R

Maysles, David 1932-1987 .... **CLC 16**
See also CA 191

Mazer, Norma Fox 1931- .... **CLC 26**
See also AAYA 5, 36; BYA 1, 8; CA 69-72;
CANR 12, 32, 66, 129; CLR 23; JRDA;
MAICYA 1, 2; SAAS 1; SATA 24, 67,
105, 168; WYA; YAW

Mazzini, Guiseppe 1805-1872 .... **NCLC 34**

McAlmon, Robert (Menzies)
1895-1956 .... **TCLC 97**
See also CA 168; CAAE 107; DLB 4, 45;
DLBD 15; GLL 1

McAuley, James Phillip 1917-1976 .. **CLC 45**
See also CA 97-100; CP 1, 2; DLB 260;
RGEL 2

McBain, Ed
See Hunter, Evan
See also MSW

McBrien, William (Augustine)
1930- .... **CLC 44**
See also CA 107; CANR 90

McCabe, Patrick 1955- .... **CLC 133**
See also BRWS 9; CA 130; CANR 50, 90;
CN 6, 7; DLB 194

McCaffrey, Anne 1926- .... **CLC 17**
See also AAYA 6, 34; AITN 2; BEST 89:2;
BPFB 2; BYA 5; CA 227; 25-28R, 227;
CANR 15, 35, 55, 96; CLR 49; CPW;
DA3; DAM NOV, POP; DLB 8; JRDA;
MAICYA 1, 2; MTCW 1, 2; MTFW 2005;
SAAS 11; SATA 8, 70, 116, 152; SATA-
Essay 152; SFW 4; SUFW 2; WYA; YAW

McCaffrey, Anne Inez
See McCaffrey, Anne

McCall, Nathan 1955(?)- .... **CLC 86**
See also AAYA 59; BW 3; CA 146; CANR
88

McCann, Arthur
See Campbell, John W(ood, Jr.)

McCann, Edson
See Pohl, Frederik

McCarthy, Charles, Jr.
See McCarthy, Cormac

McCarthy, Cormac 1933- .... **CLC 4, 57, 101,
204**
See also AAYA 41; AMWS 8; BPFB 2; CA
13-16R; CANR 10, 42, 69, 101, 161; CN
6, 7; CPW; CSW; DA3; DAM POP; DLB
6, 143, 256; EWL 3; LATS 1:2; MAL 5;
MTCW 2; MTFW 2005; TCLE 1:2;
TCWW 2

McCarthy, Mary (Therese)
1912-1989 .. **CLC 1, 3, 5, 14, 24, 39, 59;
SSC 24**
See also AMW; BPFB 2; CA 5-8R; CAAS
129; CANR 16, 50, 64; CN 1, 2, 3, 4;
DA3; DLB 2; DLBY 1981; EWL 3; FW;
INT CANR-16; MAL 5; MBL; MTCW 1,
2; MTFW 2005; RGAL 4; TUS

McCartney, James Paul
See McCartney, Paul

McCartney, Paul 1942- .... **CLC 12, 35**
See also CA 146; CANR 111

McCauley, Stephen (D.) 1955- .... **CLC 50**
See also CA 141

McClaren, Peter .... **CLC 70**

McClure, Michael (Thomas) 1932- ... **CLC 6,
10**
See also BG 1:3; CA 21-24R; CAD; CANR
17, 46, 77, 131; CD 5, 6; CP 1, 2, 3, 4, 5,
6, 7; DLB 16; WP

McCorkle, Jill (Collins) 1958- .... **CLC 51**
See also CA 121; CANR 113; CSW; DLB
234; DLBY 1987; SSFS 24

McCourt, Frank 1930- .... **CLC 109**
See also AAYA 61; AMWS 12; CA 157;
CANR 97, 138; MTFW 2005; NCFS 1

McCourt, James 1941- .... **CLC 5**
See also CA 57-60; CANR 98, 152

McCourt, Malachy 1931- .... **CLC 119**
See also SATA 126

McCoy, Horace (Stanley)
1897-1955 .... **TCLC 28**
See also AMWS 13; CA 155; CAAE 108;
CMW 4; DLB 9

McCrae, John 1872-1918 .... **TCLC 12**
See also CAAE 109; DLB 92; PFS 5

McCreigh, James
See Pohl, Frederik

McCullers, (Lula) Carson (Smith)
1917-1967 .... **CLC 1, 4, 10, 12, 48, 100;
SSC 9, 24, 99; TCLC 155; WLC 4**
See also AAYA 21; AMW; AMWC 2; BPFB
2; CA 5-8R; CAAS 25-28R; CABS 1, 3;
CANR 18, 132; CDALB 1941-1968; DA;
DA3; DAB; DAC; DAM MST, NOV;
DFS 5, 18; DLB 2, 7, 173, 228; EWL 3;
EXPS; FW; GLL 1; LAIT 3, 4; MAL 5;
MBL; MTCW 1, 2; MTFW 2005; NFS 6,
13; RGAL 4; RGSF 2; SATA 27; SSFS 5;
TUS; YAW

McCulloch, John Tyler
See Burroughs, Edgar Rice

McCullough, Colleen 1937- ...... **CLC 27, 107**
See also AAYA 36; BPFB 2; CA 81-84;
CANR 17, 46, 67, 98, 139; CPW; DA3;
DAM NOV, POP; MTCW 1, 2; MTFW
2005; RHW

McCunn, Ruthanne Lum 1946- .... **AAL**
See also CA 119; CANR 43, 96; DLB 312;
LAIT 2; SATA 63

McDermott, Alice 1953- .... **CLC 90**
See also CA 109; CANR 40, 90, 126; CN
7; DLB 292; MTFW 2005; NFS 23

McElroy, Joseph 1930- .... **CLC 5, 47**
See also CA 17-20R; CANR 149; CN 3, 4,
5, 6, 7

McElroy, Joseph Prince
See McElroy, Joseph

Mendelsohn, Jane 1965- .... **CLC 99**
    See also CA 154; CANR 94

Mendoza, Inigo Lopez de
    See Santillana, Inigo Lopez de Mendoza, Marques de

Menton, Francisco de
    See Chin, Frank (Chew, Jr.)

Mercer, David 1928-1980 .... **CLC 5**
    See also CA 9-12R; CAAS 102; CANR 23; CBD; DAM DRAM; DLB 13, 310; MTCW 1; RGEL 2

Merchant, Paul
    See Ellison, Harlan

Meredith, George 1828-1909 .. **PC 60; TCLC 17, 43**
    See also CA 153; CAAE 117; CANR 80; CDBLB 1832-1890; DAM POET; DLB 18, 35, 57, 159; RGEL 2; TEA

Meredith, William 1919-2007 ...... **CLC 4, 13, 22, 55; PC 28**
    See also CA 9-12R; 14; CANR 6, 40, 129; CP 1, 2, 3, 4, 5, 6, 7; DAM POET; DLB 5; MAL 5

Meredith, William Morris
    See Meredith, William

Merezhkovsky, Dmitrii Sergeevich
    See Merezhkovsky, Dmitry Sergeyevich
    See also DLB 295

Merezhkovsky, Dmitry Sergeevich
    See Merezhkovsky, Dmitry Sergeyevich
    See also EWL 3

Merezhkovsky, Dmitry Sergeyevich 1865-1941 .... **TCLC 29**
    See Merezhkovsky, Dmitrii Sergeevich; Merezhkovsky, Dmitry Sergeevich
    See also CA 169

Merimee, Prosper 1803-1870 ... **NCLC 6, 65; SSC 7, 77**
    See also DLB 119, 192; EW 6; EXPS; GFL 1789 to the Present; RGSF 2; RGWL 2, 3; SSFS 8; SUFW

Merkin, Daphne 1954- .... **CLC 44**
    See also CA 123

Merleau-Ponty, Maurice 1908-1961 .... **TCLC 156**
    See also CA 114; CAAS 89-92; DLB 296; GFL 1789 to the Present

Merlin, Arthur
    See Blish, James (Benjamin)

Mernissi, Fatima 1940- .... **CLC 171**
    See also CA 152; FW

Merrill, James 1926-1995 ...... **CLC 2, 3, 6, 8, 13, 18, 34, 91; PC 28; TCLC 173**
    See also AMWS 3; CA 13-16R; CAAS 147; CANR 10, 49, 63, 108; CP 1, 2, 3, 4; DA3; DAM POET; DLB 5, 165; DLBY 1985; EWL 3; INT CANR-10; MAL 5; MTCW 1, 2; MTFW 2005; PAB; PFS 23; RGAL 4

Merrill, James Ingram
    See Merrill, James

Merriman, Alex
    See Silverberg, Robert

Merriman, Brian 1747-1805 .... **NCLC 70**

Merritt, E. B.
    See Waddington, Miriam

Merton, Thomas (James) 1915-1968 . **CLC 1, 3, 11, 34, 83; PC 10**
    See also AAYA 61; AMWS 8; CA 5-8R; CAAS 25-28R; CANR 22, 53, 111, 131; DA3; DLB 48; DLBY 1981; MAL 5; MTCW 1, 2; MTFW 2005

Merwin, W.S. 1927- ..... **CLC 1, 2, 3, 5, 8, 13, 18, 45, 88; PC 45**
    See also AMWS 3; CA 13-16R; CANR 15, 51, 112, 140; CP 1, 2, 3, 4, 5, 6, 7; DA3; DAM POET; DLB 5, 169; EWL 3; INT CANR-15; MAL 5; MTCW 1, 2; MTFW 2005; PAB; PFS 5, 15; RGAL 4

Metastasio, Pietro 1698-1782 .... **LC 115**
    See also RGWL 2, 3

Metcalf, John 1938- .... **CLC 37; SSC 43**
    See also CA 113; CN 4, 5, 6, 7; DLB 60; RGSF 2; TWA

Metcalf, Suzanne
    See Baum, L(yman) Frank

Mew, Charlotte (Mary) 1870-1928 .. **TCLC 8**
    See also CA 189; CAAE 105; DLB 19, 135; RGEL 2

Mewshaw, Michael 1943- .... **CLC 9**
    See also CA 53-56; CANR 7, 47, 147; DLBY 1980

Meyer, Conrad Ferdinand 1825-1898 .... **NCLC 81; SSC 30**
    See also DLB 129; EW; RGWL 2, 3

Meyer, Gustav 1868-1932
    See Meyrink, Gustav
    See also CA 190; CAAE 117

Meyer, June
    See Jordan, June

Meyer, Lynn
    See Slavitt, David R(ytman)

Meyers, Jeffrey 1939- .... **CLC 39**
    See also CA 186; 73-76, 186; CANR 54, 102, 159; DLB 111

Meynell, Alice (Christina Gertrude Thompson) 1847-1922 .... **TCLC 6**
    See also CA 177; CAAE 104; DLB 19, 98; RGEL 2

Meyrink, Gustav .... **TCLC 21**
    See Meyer, Gustav
    See also DLB 81; EWL 3

Michaels, Leonard 1933-2003 ..... **CLC 6, 25; SSC 16**
    See also AMWS 16; CA 61-64; CAAS 216; CANR 21, 62, 119; CN 3, 45, 6, 7; DLB 130; MTCW 1; TCLE 1:2

Michaux, Henri 1899-1984 .... **CLC 8, 19**
    See also CA 85-88; CAAS 114; DLB 258; EWL 3; GFL 1789 to the Present; RGWL 2, 3

Micheaux, Oscar (Devereaux) 1884-1951 .... **TCLC 76**
    See also BW 3; CA 174; DLB 50; TCWW 2

Michelangelo 1475-1564 .... **LC 12**
    See also AAYA 43

Michelet, Jules 1798-1874 .... **NCLC 31**
    See also EW 5; GFL 1789 to the Present

Michels, Robert 1876-1936 .... **TCLC 88**
    See also CA 212

Michener, James A. 1907(?)-1997 . **CLC 1, 5, 11, 29, 60, 109**
    See also AAYA 27; AITN 1; BEST 90:1; BPFB 2; CA 5-8R; CAAS 161; CANR 21, 45, 68; CN 1, 2, 3, 4, 5, 6; CPW; DA3; DAM NOV, POP; DLB 6; MAL 5; MTCW 1, 2; MTFW 2005; RHW; TCWW 1, 2

Mickiewicz, Adam 1798-1855 . **NCLC 3, 101; PC 38**
    See also EW 5; RGWL 2, 3

Middleton, (John) Christopher 1926- .... **CLC 13**
    See also CA 13-16R; CANR 29, 54, 117; CP 1, 2, 3, 4, 5, 6, 7; DLB 40

Middleton, Richard (Barham) 1882-1911 .... **TCLC 56**
    See also CA 187; DLB 156; HGG

Middleton, Stanley 1919- .... **CLC 7, 38**
    See also CA 25-28R; 23; CANR 21, 46, 81, 157; CN 1, 2, 3, 4, 5, 6, 7; DLB 14, 326

Middleton, Thomas 1580-1627 ...... **DC 5; LC 33, 123**
    See also BRW 2; DAM DRAM, MST; DFS 18, 22; DLB 58; RGEL 2

Mieville, China 1972(?)- .... **CLC 235**
    See also AAYA 52; CA 196; CANR 138; MTFW 2005

Migueis, Jose Rodrigues 1901-1980 . **CLC 10**
    See also DLB 287

Mikszath, Kalman 1847-1910 .... **TCLC 31**
    See also CA 170

Miles, Jack .... **CLC 100**
    See also CA 200

Miles, John Russiano
    See Miles, Jack

Miles, Josephine (Louise) 1911-1985 .... **CLC 1, 2, 14, 34, 39**
    See also CA 1-4R; CAAS 116; CANR 2, 55; CP 1, 2, 3, 4; DAM POET; DLB 48; MAL 5; TCLE 1:2

Militant
    See Sandburg, Carl (August)

Mill, Harriet (Hardy) Taylor 1807-1858 .... **NCLC 102**
    See also FW

Mill, John Stuart 1806-1873 ... **NCLC 11, 58, 179**
    See also CDBLB 1832-1890; DLB 55, 190, 262; FW 1; RGEL 2; TEA

Millar, Kenneth 1915-1983 .... **CLC 14**
    See Macdonald, Ross
    See also CA 9-12R; CAAS 110; CANR 16, 63, 107; CMW 4; CPW; DA3; DAM POP; DLB 2, 226; DLBD 6; DLBY 1983; MTCW 1, 2; MTFW 2005

Millay, E. Vincent
    See Millay, Edna St. Vincent

Millay, Edna St. Vincent 1892-1950 ..... **PC 6, 61; TCLC 4, 49, 169; WLCS**
    See Boyd, Nancy
    See also AMW; CA 130; CAAE 104; CDALB 1917-1929; DA; DA3; DAB; DAC; DAM MST, POET; DLB 45, 249; EWL 3; EXPP; FL 1:6; MAL 5; MBL; MTCW 1, 2; MTFW 2005; PAB; PFS 3, 17; RGAL 4; TUS; WP

Miller, Arthur 1915-2005 ..... **CLC 1, 2, 6, 10, 15, 26, 47, 78, 179; DC 1; WLC 4**
    See also AAYA 15; AITN 1; AMW; AMWC 1; CA 1-4R; CAAS 236; CABS 3; CAD; CANR 2, 30, 54, 76, 132; CD 5, 6; CDALB 1941-1968; DA; DA3; DAB; DAC; DAM DRAM, MST; DFS 1, 3, 8; DLB 7, 266; EWL 3; LAIT 1, 4; LATS 1:2; MAL 5; MTCW 1, 2; MTFW 2005; RGAL 4; RGHL; TUS; WYAS 1

Miller, Henry (Valentine) 1891-1980 .... **CLC 1, 2, 4, 9, 14, 43, 84; WLC 4**
    See also AMW; BPFB 2; CA 9-12R; CAAS 97-100; CANR 33, 64; CDALB 1929-1941; CN 1, 2; DA; DA3; DAB; DAC; DAM MST, NOV; DLB 4, 9; DLBY 1980; EWL 3; MAL 5; MTCW 1, 2; MTFW 2005; RGAL 4; TUS

Miller, Hugh 1802-1856 .... **NCLC 143**
    See also DLB 190

Miller, Jason 1939(?)-2001 .... **CLC 2**
    See also AITN 1; CA 73-76; CAAS 197; CAD; CANR 130; DFS 12; DLB 7

Miller, Sue 1943- .... **CLC 44**
    See also AMWS 12; BEST 90:3; CA 139; CANR 59, 91, 128; DA3; DAM POP; DLB 143

Miller, Walter M(ichael, Jr.) 1923-1996 .... **CLC 4, 30**
    See also BPFB 2; CA 85-88; CANR 108; DLB 8; SCFW 1, 2; SFW 4

Millett, Kate 1934- .... **CLC 67**
    See also AITN 1; CA 73-76; CANR 32, 53, 76, 110; DA3; DLB 246; FW; GLL 1; MTCW 1, 2; MTFW 2005

Millhauser, Steven 1943- ... **CLC 21, 54, 109; SSC 57**
See also CA 111; CAAE 110; CANR 63, 114, 133; CN 6, 7; DA3; DLB 2; FANT; INT CA-111; MAL 5; MTCW 2; MTFW 2005

Millhauser, Steven Lewis
See Millhauser, Steven

Millin, Sarah Gertrude 1889-1968 ... **CLC 49**
See also CA 102; CAAS 93-96; DLB 225; EWL 3

Milne, A. A. 1882-1956 .... **TCLC 6, 88**
See also BRWS 5; CA 133; CAAE 104; CLR 1, 26, 108; CMW 4; CWRI 5; DA3; DAB; DAC; DAM MST; DLB 10, 77, 100, 160; FANT; MAICYA 1, 2; MTCW 1, 2; MTFW 2005; RGEL 2; SATA 100; WCH; YABC 1

Milne, Alan Alexander
See Milne, A. A.

Milner, Ron(ald) 1938-2004 ..... **BLC 3; CLC 56**
See also AITN 1; BW 1; CA 73-76; CAAS 230; CAD; CANR 24, 81; CD 5, 6; DAM MULT; DLB 38; MAL 5; MTCW 1

Milnes, Richard Monckton
1809-1885 .... **NCLC 61**
See also DLB 32, 184

Milosz, Czeslaw 1911-2004 .... **CLC 5, 11, 22, 31, 56, 82; PC 8; WLCS**
See also AAYA 62; CA 81-84; CAAS 230; CANR 23, 51, 91, 126; CDWLB 4; CWW 2; DA3; DAM MST, POET; DLB 215, 331; EW 13; EWL 3; MTCW 1, 2; MTFW 2005; PFS 16; RGHL; RGWL 2, 3

Milton, John 1608-1674 ..... **LC 9, 43, 92; PC 19, 29; WLC 4**
See also AAYA 65; BRW 2; BRWR 2; CDBLB 1660-1789; DA; DA3; DAB; DAC; DAM MST, POET; DLB 131, 151, 281; EFS 1; EXPP; LAIT 1; PAB; PFS 3, 17; RGEL 2; TEA; WLIT 3; WP

Min, Anchee 1957- .... **CLC 86**
See also CA 146; CANR 94, 137; MTFW 2005

Minehaha, Cornelius
See Wedekind, Frank

Miner, Valerie 1947- .... **CLC 40**
See also CA 97-100; CANR 59; FW; GLL 2

Minimo, Duca
See D'Annunzio, Gabriele

Minot, Susan (Anderson) 1956- ...... **CLC 44, 159**
See also AMWS 6; CA 134; CANR 118; CN 6, 7

Minus, Ed 1938- .... **CLC 39**
See also CA 185

Mirabai 1498(?)-1550(?) .... **PC 48**
See also PFS 24

Miranda, Javier
See Bioy Casares, Adolfo
See also CWW 2

Mirbeau, Octave 1848-1917 .... **TCLC 55**
See also CA 216; DLB 123, 192; GFL 1789 to the Present

Mirikitani, Janice 1942- .... **AAL**
See also CA 211; DLB 312; RGAL 4

Mirk, John (?)-c. 1414 .... **LC 105**
See also DLB 146

Miro (Ferrer), Gabriel (Francisco Victor)
1879-1930 .... **TCLC 5**
See also CA 185; CAAE 104; DLB 322; EWL 3

Misharin, Alexandr .... **CLC 59**

Mishima, Yukio ... **CLC 2, 4, 6, 9, 27; DC 1; SSC 4; TCLC 161; WLC 4**
See Hiraoka, Kimitake
See also AAYA 50; BPFB 2; GLL 1; MJW; RGSF 2; RGWL 2, 3; SSFS 5, 12

Mistral, Frederic 1830-1914 .... **TCLC 51**
See also CA 213; CAAE 122; DLB 331; GFL 1789 to the Present

Mistral, Gabriela
See Godoy Alcayaga, Lucila
See also DLB 283, 331; DNFS 1; EWL 3; LAW; RGWL 2, 3; WP

Mistry, Rohinton 1952- ... **CLC 71, 196; SSC 73**
See also BRWS 10; CA 141; CANR 86, 114; CCA 1; CN 6, 7; DAC; DLB 334; SSFS 6

Mitchell, Clyde
See Ellison, Harlan

Mitchell, Emerson Blackhorse Barney
1945- .... **NNAL**
See also CA 45-48

Mitchell, James Leslie 1901-1935
See Gibbon, Lewis Grassic
See also CA 188; CAAE 104; DLB 15

Mitchell, Joni 1943- .... **CLC 12**
See also CA 112; CCA 1

Mitchell, Joseph (Quincy)
1908-1996 .... **CLC 98**
See also CA 77-80; CAAS 152; CANR 69; CN 1, 2, 3, 4, 5, 6; CSW; DLB 185; DLBY 1996

Mitchell, Margaret (Munnerlyn)
1900-1949 .... **TCLC 11, 170**
See also AAYA 23; BPFB 2; BYA 1; CA 125; CAAE 109; CANR 55, 94; CDALBS; DA3; DAM NOV, POP; DLB 9; LAIT 2; MAL 5; MTCW 1, 2; MTFW 2005; NFS 9; RGAL 4; RHW; TUS; WYAS 1; YAW

Mitchell, Peggy
See Mitchell, Margaret (Munnerlyn)

Mitchell, S(ilas) Weir 1829-1914 .... **TCLC 36**
See also CA 165; DLB 202; RGAL 4

Mitchell, W(illiam) O(rmond)
1914-1998 .... **CLC 25**
See also CA 77-80; CAAS 165; CANR 15, 43; CN 1, 2, 3, 4, 5, 6; DAC; DAM MST; DLB 88; TCLE 1:2

Mitchell, William (Lendrum)
1879-1936 .... **TCLC 81**
See also CA 213

Mitford, Mary Russell 1787-1855 ... **NCLC 4**
See also DLB 110, 116; RGEL 2

Mitford, Nancy 1904-1973 .... **CLC 44**
See also BRWS 10; CA 9-12R; CN 1; DLB 191; RGEL 2

Miyamoto, (Chujo) Yuriko
1899-1951 .... **TCLC 37**
See Miyamoto Yuriko
See also CA 170, 174

Miyamoto Yuriko
See Miyamoto, (Chujo) Yuriko
See also DLB 180

Miyazawa, Kenji 1896-1933 .... **TCLC 76**
See Miyazawa Kenji
See also CA 157; RGWL 3

Miyazawa Kenji
See Miyazawa, Kenji
See also EWL 3

Mizoguchi, Kenji 1898-1956 .... **TCLC 72**
See also CA 167

Mo, Timothy (Peter) 1950- .... **CLC 46, 134**
See also CA 117; CANR 128; CN 5, 6, 7; DLB 194; MTCW 1; WLIT 4; WWE 1

Modarressi, Taghi (M.) 1931-1997 ... **CLC 44**
See also CA 134; CAAE 121; INT CA-134

Modiano, Patrick (Jean) 1945- .... **CLC 18, 218**
See also CA 85-88; CANR 17, 40, 115; CWW 2; DLB 83, 299; EWL 3; RGHL

Mofolo, Thomas (Mokopu)
1875(?)-1948 .... **BLC 3; TCLC 22**
See also AFW; CA 153; CAAE 121; CANR 83; DAM MULT; DLB 225; EWL 3; MTCW 2; MTFW 2005; WLIT 2

Mohr, Nicholasa 1938- .... **CLC 12; HLC 2**
See also AAYA 8, 46; CA 49-52; CANR 1, 32, 64; CLR 22; DAM MULT; DLB 145; HW 1, 2; JRDA; LAIT 5; LLW; MAICYA 2; MAICYAS 1; RGAL 4; SAAS 8; SATA 8, 97; SATA-Essay 113; WYA; YAW

Moi, Toril 1953- .... **CLC 172**
See also CA 154; CANR 102; FW

Mojtabai, A(nn) G(race) 1938- ..... **CLC 5, 9, 15, 29**
See also CA 85-88; CANR 88

Moliere 1622-1673 ..... **DC 13; LC 10, 28, 64, 125, 127; WLC 4**
See also DA; DA3; DAB; DAC; DAM DRAM, MST; DFS 13, 18, 20; DLB 268; EW 3; GFL Beginnings to 1789; LATS 1:1; RGWL 2, 3; TWA

Molin, Charles
See Mayne, William (James Carter)

Molnar, Ferenc 1878-1952 .... **TCLC 20**
See also CA 153; CAAE 109; CANR 83; CDWLB 4; DAM DRAM; DLB 215; EWL 3; RGWL 2, 3

Momaday, N. Scott 1934- ...... **CLC 2, 19, 85, 95, 160; NNAL; PC 25; WLCS**
See also AAYA 11, 64; AMWS 4; ANW; BPFB 2; BYA 12; CA 25-28R; CANR 14, 34, 68, 134; CDALBS; CN 2, 3, 4, 5, 6, 7; CPW; DA; DA3; DAB; DAC; DAM MST, MULT, NOV, POP; DLB 143, 175, 256; EWL 3; EXPP; INT CANR-14; LAIT 4; LATS 1:2; MAL 5; MTCW 1, 2; MTFW 2005; NFS 10; PFS 2, 11; RGAL 4; SATA 48; SATA-Brief 30; TCWW 1, 2; WP; YAW

Monette, Paul 1945-1995 .... **CLC 82**
See also AMWS 10; CA 139; CAAS 147; CN 6; GLL 1

Monroe, Harriet 1860-1936 .... **TCLC 12**
See also CA 204; CAAE 109; DLB 54, 91

Monroe, Lyle
See Heinlein, Robert A.

Montagu, Elizabeth 1720-1800 .... **NCLC 7, 117**
See also FW

Montagu, Mary (Pierrepont) Wortley
1689-1762 .... **LC 9, 57; PC 16**
See also DLB 95, 101; FL 1:1; RGEL 2

Montagu, W. H.
See Coleridge, Samuel Taylor

Montague, John (Patrick) 1929- ..... **CLC 13, 46**
See also CA 9-12R; CANR 9, 69, 121; CP 1, 2, 3, 4, 5, 6, 7; DLB 40; EWL 3; MTCW 1; PFS 12; RGEL 2; TCLE 1:2

Montaigne, Michel (Eyquem) de
1533-1592 .... **LC 8, 105; WLC 4**
See also DA; DAB; DAC; DAM MST; DLB 327; EW 2; GFL Beginnings to 1789; LMFS 1; RGWL 2, 3; TWA

Montale, Eugenio 1896-1981 ... **CLC 7, 9, 18; PC 13**
See also CA 17-20R; CAAS 104; CANR 30; DLB 114, 331; EW 11; EWL 3; MTCW 1; PFS 22; RGWL 2, 3; TWA; WLIT 7

Montesquieu, Charles-Louis de Secondat
1689-1755 .... **LC 7, 69**
See also DLB 314; EW 3; GFL Beginnings to 1789; TWA

Montessori, Maria 1870-1952 ...... **TCLC 103**
See also CA 147; CAAE 115

Montgomery, (Robert) Bruce 1921(?)-1978
See Crispin, Edmund
See also CA 179; CAAS 104; CMW 4

Montgomery, L(ucy) M(aud)
1874-1942 .... **TCLC 51, 140**
See also AAYA 12; BYA 1; CA 137; CAAE
108; CLR 8, 91; DA3; DAC; DAM MST;
DLB 92; DLBD 14; JRDA; MAICYA 1,
2; MTCW 2; MTFW 2005; RGEL 2;
SATA 100; TWA; WCH; WYA; YABC 1

Montgomery, Marion, Jr. 1925- .... **CLC 7**
See also AITN 1; CA 1-4R; CANR 3, 48,
162; CSW; DLB 6

Montgomery, Marion H. 1925-
See Montgomery, Marion, Jr.

Montgomery, Max
See Davenport, Guy (Mattison, Jr.)

Montherlant, Henry (Milon) de
1896-1972 .... **CLC 8, 19**
See also CA 85-88; CAAS 37-40R; DAM
DRAM; DLB 72, 321; EW 11; EWL 3;
GFL 1789 to the Present; MTCW 1

Monty Python
See Chapman, Graham; Cleese, John
(Marwood); Gilliam, Terry; Idle, Eric;
Jones, Terence Graham Parry; Palin,
Michael (Edward)
See also AAYA 7

Moodie, Susanna (Strickland)
1803-1885 .... **NCLC 14, 113**
See also DLB 99

Moody, Hiram 1961-
See Moody, Rick
See also CA 138; CANR 64, 112; MTFW
2005

Moody, Minerva
See Alcott, Louisa May

Moody, Rick .... **CLC 147**
See Moody, Hiram

Moody, William Vaughan
1869-1910 .... **TCLC 105**
See also CA 178; CAAE 110; DLB 7, 54;
MAL 5; RGAL 4

Mooney, Edward 1951-
See Mooney, Ted
See also CA 130

Mooney, Ted .... **CLC 25**
See Mooney, Edward

Moorcock, Michael 1939- ...... **CLC 5, 27, 58,**
236
See Bradbury, Edward P.
See also AAYA 26; CA 45-48; 5; CANR 2,
17, 38, 64, 122; CN 5, 6, 7; DLB 14, 231,
261, 319; FANT; MTCW 1, 2; MTFW
2005; SATA 93, 166; SCFW 1, 2; SFW 4;
SUFW 1, 2

Moorcock, Michael John
See Moorcock, Michael

Moore, Alan 1953- .... **CLC 230**
See also AAYA 51; CA 204; CANR 138;
DLB 261; MTFW 2005; SFW 4

Moore, Brian 1921-1999 ... **CLC 1, 3, 5, 7, 8,**
19, 32, 90
See Bryan, Michael
See also BRWS 9; CA 1-4R; CAAS 174;
CANR 1, 25, 42, 63; CCA 1; CN 1, 2, 3,
4, 5, 6; DAB; DAC; DAM MST; DLB
251; EWL 3; FANT; MTCW 1, 2; MTFW
2005; RGEL 2

Moore, Edward
See Muir, Edwin
See also RGEL 2

Moore, G. E. 1873-1958 .... **TCLC 89**
See also DLB 262

Moore, George Augustus
1852-1933 .... **SSC 19; TCLC 7**
See also BRW 6; CA 177; CAAE 104; DLB
10, 18, 57, 135; EWL 3; RGEL 2; RGSF
2

Moore, Lorrie .... **CLC 39, 45, 68**
See Moore, Marie Lorena
See also AMWS 10; CN 5, 6, 7; DLB 234;
SSFS 19

Moore, Marianne (Craig)
1887-1972 .... **CLC 1, 2, 4, 8, 10, 13, 19,**
47; PC 4, 49; WLCS
See also AMW; CA 1-4R; CAAS 33-36R;
CANR 3, 61; CDALB 1929-1941; CP 1;
DA; DA3; DAB; DAC; DAM MST,
POET; DLB 45; DLBD 7; EWL 3; EXPP;
FL 1:6; MAL 5; MBL; MTCW 1, 2;
MTFW 2005; PAB; PFS 14, 17; RGAL 4;
SATA 20; TUS; WP

Moore, Marie Lorena 1957- .... **CLC 165**
See Moore, Lorrie
See also CA 116; CANR 39, 83, 139; DLB
234; MTFW 2005

Moore, Michael 1954- .... **CLC 218**
See also AAYA 53; CA 166; CANR 150

Moore, Thomas 1779-1852 .... **NCLC 6, 110**
See also DLB 96, 144; RGEL 2

Moorhouse, Frank 1938- .... **SSC 40**
See also CA 118; CANR 92; CN 3, 4, 5, 6,
7; DLB 289; RGSF 2

Mora, Pat 1942- .... **HLC 2**
See also AMWS 13; CA 129; CANR 57,
81, 112; CLR 58; DAM MULT; DLB 209;
HW 1, 2; LLW; MAICYA 2; MTFW
2005; SATA 92, 134

Moraga, Cherrie 1952- ...... **CLC 126; DC 22**
See also CA 131; CANR 66, 154; DAM
MULT; DLB 82, 249; FW; GLL 1; HW 1,
2; LLW

Morand, Paul 1888-1976 .... **CLC 41; SSC 22**
See also CA 184; CAAS 69-72; DLB 65;
EWL 3

Morante, Elsa 1918-1985 .... **CLC 8, 47**
See also CA 85-88; CAAS 117; CANR 35;
DLB 177; EWL 3; MTCW 1, 2; MTFW
2005; RGHL; RGWL 2, 3; WLIT 7

Moravia, Alberto .... **CLC 2, 7, 11, 27, 46;**
SSC 26
See Pincherle, Alberto
See also DLB 177; EW 12; EWL 3; MTCW
2; RGSF 2; RGWL 2, 3; WLIT 7

More, Hannah 1745-1833 ...... **NCLC 27, 141**
See also DLB 107, 109, 116, 158; RGEL 2

More, Henry 1614-1687 .... **LC 9**
See also DLB 126, 252

More, Sir Thomas 1478(?)-1535 ... **LC 10, 32,**
140
See also BRWC 1; BRWS 7; DLB 136, 281;
LMFS 1; RGEL 2; TEA

Moreas, Jean .... **TCLC 18**
See Papadiamantopoulos, Johannes
See also GFL 1789 to the Present

Moreton, Andrew Esq.
See Defoe, Daniel

Morgan, Berry 1919-2002 .... **CLC 6**
See also CA 49-52; CAAS 208; DLB 6

Morgan, Claire
See Highsmith, Patricia
See also GLL 1

Morgan, Edwin (George) 1920- .... **CLC 31**
See also BRWS 9; CA 5-8R; CANR 3, 43,
90; CP 1, 2, 3, 4, 5, 6, 7; DLB 27

Morgan, (George) Frederick
1922-2004 .... **CLC 23**
See also CA 17-20R; CAAS 224; CANR
21, 144; CP 2, 3, 4, 5, 6, 7

Morgan, Harriet
See Mencken, H(enry) L(ouis)

Morgan, Jane
See Cooper, James Fenimore

Morgan, Janet 1945- .... **CLC 39**
See also CA 65-68

Morgan, Lady 1776(?)-1859 .... **NCLC 29**
See also DLB 116, 158; RGEL 2

Morgan, Robin (Evonne) 1941- .... **CLC 2**
See also CA 69-72; CANR 29, 68; FW;
GLL 2; MTCW 1; SATA 80

Morgan, Scott
See Kuttner, Henry

Morgan, Seth 1949(?)-1990 .... **CLC 65**
See also CA 185; CAAS 132

Morgenstern, Christian (Otto Josef
Wolfgang) 1871-1914 .... **TCLC 8**
See also CA 191; CAAE 105; EWL 3

Morgenstern, S.
See Goldman, William

Mori, Rintaro
See Mori Ogai
See also CAAE 110

Mori, Toshio 1910-1980 .... **AAL; SSC 83**
See also CA 244; CAAE 116; DLB 312;
RGSF 2

Moricz, Zsigmond 1879-1942 .... **TCLC 33**
See also CA 165; DLB 215; EWL 3

Morike, Eduard (Friedrich)
1804-1875 .... **NCLC 10**
See also DLB 133; RGWL 2, 3

Mori Ogai 1862-1922 .... **TCLC 14**
See Ogai
See also CA 164; DLB 180; EWL 3; RGWL
3; TWA

Moritz, Karl Philipp 1756-1793 .... **LC 2**
See also DLB 94

Morland, Peter Henry
See Faust, Frederick (Schiller)

Morley, Christopher (Darlington)
1890-1957 .... **TCLC 87**
See also CA 213; CAAE 112; DLB 9; MAL
5; RGAL 4

Morren, Theophil
See Hofmannsthal, Hugo von

Morris, Bill 1952- .... **CLC 76**
See also CA 225

Morris, Julian
See West, Morris L(anglo)

Morris, Steveland Judkins (?)-
See Wonder, Stevie

Morris, William 1834-1896 . **NCLC 4; PC 55**
See also BRW 5; CDBLB 1832-1890; DLB
18, 35, 57, 156, 178, 184; FANT; RGEL
2; SFW 4; SUFW

Morris, Wright (Marion) 1910-1998 . **CLC 1,**
3, 7, 18, 37; TCLC 107
See also AMW; CA 9-12R; CAAS 167;
CANR 21, 81; CN 1, 2, 3, 4, 5, 6; DLB
2, 206, 218; DLBY 1981; EWL 3; MAL
5; MTCW 1, 2; MTFW 2005; RGAL 4;
TCWW 1, 2

Morrison, Arthur 1863-1945 .... **SSC 40;**
TCLC 72
See also CA 157; CAAE 120; CMW 4;
DLB 70, 135, 197; RGEL 2

Morrison, Chloe Anthony Wofford
See Morrison, Toni

Morrison, James Douglas 1943-1971
See Morrison, Jim
See also CA 73-76; CANR 40

Morrison, Jim .... **CLC 17**
See Morrison, James Douglas

Morrison, John Gordon 1904-1998 ... **SSC 93**
See also CA 103; CANR 92; DLB 260

Morrison, Toni 1931- ..... **BLC 3; CLC 4, 10,**
22, 55, 81, 87, 173, 194; WLC 4
See also AAYA 1, 22, 61; AFAW 1, 2;
AMWC 1; AMWS 3; BPFB 2; BW 2, 3;
CA 29-32R; CANR 27, 42, 67, 113, 124;
CDALB 1968-1988; CLR 99; CN 3, 4, 5,

Murry, John Middleton
1889-1957 .... **TCLC 16**
See also CA 217; CAAE 118; DLB 149
Musgrave, Susan 1951- .... **CLC 13, 54**
See also CA 69-72; CANR 45, 84; CCA 1; CP 2, 3, 4, 5, 6, 7; CWP
Musil, Robert (Edler von)
1880-1942 .... **SSC 18; TCLC 12, 68**
See also CAAE 109; CANR 55, 84; CDWLB 81; DLB 81, 124; EW 9; EWL 3; MTCW 2; RGSF 2; RGWL 2, 3
Muske, Carol .... **CLC 90**
See Muske-Dukes, Carol (Anne)
Muske-Dukes, Carol (Anne) 1945-
See Muske, Carol
See also CA 203; 65-68, 203; CANR 32, 70; CWP; PFS 24
Musset, Alfred de 1810-1857 . **DC 27; NCLC 7, 150**
See also DLB 192, 217; EW 6; GFL 1789 to the Present; RGWL 2, 3; TWA
Musset, Louis Charles Alfred de
See Musset, Alfred de
Mussolini, Benito (Amilcare Andrea)
1883-1945 .... **TCLC 96**
See also CAAE 116
Mutanabbi, Al-
See al-Mutanabbi, Ahmad ibn al-Husayn Abu al-Tayyib al-Jufi al-Kindi
See also WLIT 6
My Brother's Brother
See Chekhov, Anton (Pavlovich)
Myers, L(eopold) H(amilton)
1881-1944 .... **TCLC 59**
See also CA 157; DLB 15; EWL 3; RGEL 2
Myers, Walter Dean 1937- .. **BLC 3; CLC 35**
See Myers, Walter M.
See also AAYA 4, 23; BW 2; BYA 6, 8, 11; CA 33-36R; CANR 20, 42, 67, 108; CLR 4, 16, 35, 110; DAM MULT, NOV; DLB 33; INT CANR-20; JRDA; LAIT 5; MAICYA 1, 2; MAICYAS 1; MTCW 2; MTFW 2005; SAAS 2; SATA 41, 71, 109, 157; SATA-Brief 27; WYA; YAW
Myers, Walter M.
See Myers, Walter Dean
Myles, Symon
See Follett, Ken
Nabokov, Vladimir (Vladimirovich)
1899-1977 .... **CLC 1, 2, 3, 6, 8, 11, 15, 23, 44, 46, 64; SSC 11, 86; TCLC 108, 189; WLC 4**
See also AAYA 45; AMW; AMWC 1; AMWR 1; BPFB 2; CA 5-8R; CAAS 69-72; CANR 20, 102; CDALB 1941-1968; CN 1, 2; CP 2; DA; DA3; DAB; DAC; DAM MST, NOV; DLB 2, 244, 278, 317; DLBD 3; DLBY 1980, 1991; EWL 3; EXPS; LATS 1:2; MAL 5; MTCW 1, 2; MTFW 2005; NCFS 4; NFS 9; RGAL 4; RGSF 2; SSFS 6, 15; TUS
Naevius c. 265B.C.-201B.C. .... **CMLC 37**
See also DLB 211
Nagai, Kafu .... **TCLC 51**
See Nagai, Sokichi
See also DLB 180
Nagai, Sokichi 1879-1959
See Nagai, Kafu
See also CAAE 117
Nagy, Laszlo 1925-1978 .... **CLC 7**
See also CA 129; CAAS 112
Naidu, Sarojini 1879-1949 .... **TCLC 80**
See also EWL 3; RGEL 2
Naipaul, Shiva 1945-1985 .... **CLC 32, 39; TCLC 153**
See also CA 112; CAAE 110; CAAS 116; CANR 33; CN 2, 3; DA3; DAM NOV; DLB 157; DLBY 1985; EWL 3; MTCW 1, 2; MTFW 2005

Naipaul, V.S. 1932- .. **CLC 4, 7, 9, 13, 18, 37, 105, 199; SSC 38**
See also BPFB 2; BRWS 1; CA 1-4R; CANR 1, 33, 51, 91, 126; CDBLB 1960 to Present; CDWLB 3; CN 1, 2, 3, 4, 5, 6, 7; DA3; DAB; DAC; DAM MST, NOV; DLB 125, 204, 207, 326, 331; DLBY 1985, 2001; EWL 3; LATS 1:2; MTCW 1, 2; MTFW 2005; RGEL 2; RGSF 2; TWA; WLIT 4; WWE 1
Nakos, Lilika 1903(?)-1989 .... **CLC 29**
Napoleon
See Yamamoto, Hisaye
Narayan, R.K. 1906-2001 ...... **CLC 7, 28, 47, 121, 211; SSC 25**
See also BPFB 2; CA 81-84; CAAS 196; CANR 33, 61, 112; CN 1, 2, 3, 4, 5, 6, 7; DA3; DAM NOV; DLB 323; DNFS 1; EWL 3; MTCW 1, 2; MTFW 2005; RGEL 2; RGSF 2; SATA 62; SSFS 5; WWE 1
Nash, (Frediric) Ogden 1902-1971 . **CLC 23; PC 21; TCLC 109**
See also CA 13-14; CAAS 29-32R; CANR 34, 61; CAP 1; CP 1; DAM POET; DLB 11; MAICYA 1, 2; MAL 5; MTCW 1, 2; RGAL 4; SATA 2, 46; WP
Nashe, Thomas 1567-1601(?) .... **LC 41, 89**
See also DLB 167; RGEL 2
Nathan, Daniel
See Dannay, Frederic
Nathan, George Jean 1882-1958 .... **TCLC 18**
See Hatteras, Owen
See also CA 169; CAAE 114; DLB 137; MAL 5
Natsume, Kinnosuke
See Natsume, Soseki
Natsume, Soseki 1867-1916 .... **TCLC 2, 10**
See Natsume Soseki; Soseki
See also CA 195; CAAE 104; RGWL 2, 3; TWA
Natsume Soseki
See Natsume, Soseki
See also DLB 180; EWL 3
Natti, (Mary) Lee 1919-
See Kingman, Lee
See also CA 5-8R; CANR 2
Navarre, Marguerite de
See de Navarre, Marguerite
Naylor, Gloria 1950- ..... **BLC 3; CLC 28, 52, 156; WLCS**
See also AAYA 6, 39; AFAW 1, 2; AMWS 8; BW 2, 3; CA 107; CANR 27, 51, 74, 130; CN 4, 5, 6, 7; CPW; DA; DA3; DAC; DAM MST, MULT, NOV, POP; DLB 173; EWL 3; FW; MAL 5; MTCW 1, 2; MTFW 2005; NFS 4, 7; RGAL 4; TCLE 1:2; TUS
Neal, John 1793-1876 .... **NCLC 161**
See also DLB 1, 59, 243; FW; RGAL 4
Neff, Debra .... **CLC 59**
Neihardt, John Gneisenau
1881-1973 .... **CLC 32**
See also CA 13-14; CANR 65; CAP 1; DLB 9, 54, 256; LAIT 2; TCWW 1, 2
Nekrasov, Nikolai Alekseevich
1821-1878 .... **NCLC 11**
See also DLB 277
Nelligan, Emile 1879-1941 .... **TCLC 14**
See also CA 204; CAAE 114; DLB 92; EWL 3
Nelson, Willie 1933- .... **CLC 17**
See also CA 107; CANR 114
Nemerov, Howard 1920-1991 .... **CLC 2, 6, 9, 36; PC 24; TCLC 124**
See also AMW; CA 1-4R; CAAS 134; CABS 2; CANR 1, 27, 53; CN 1, 2, 3; CP 1, 2, 3, 4; DAM POET; DLB 5, 6; DLBY 1983; EWL 3; INT CANR-27; MAL 5; MTCW 1, 2; MTFW 2005; PFS 10, 14; RGAL 4

Nepos, Cornelius c. 99B.C.-c. 24B.C. .... **CMLC 89**
See also DLB 211
Neruda, Pablo 1904-1973 .. **CLC 1, 2, 5, 7, 9, 28, 62; HLC 2; PC 4, 64; WLC 4**
See also CA 19-20; CAAS 45-48; CANR 131; CAP 2; DA; DA3; DAB; DAC; DAM MST, MULT, POET; DLB 283, 331; DNFS 2; EWL 3; HW 1; LAW; MTCW 1, 2; MTFW 2005; PFS 11; RGWL 2, 3; TWA; WLIT 1; WP
Nerval, Gerard de 1808-1855 ... **NCLC 1, 67; PC 13; SSC 18**
See also DLB 217; EW 6; GFL 1789 to the Present; RGSF 2; RGWL 2, 3
Nervo, (Jose) Amado (Ruiz de)
1870-1919 .... **HLCS 2; TCLC 11**
See also CA 131; CAAE 109; DLB 290; EWL 3; HW 1; LAW
Nesbit, Malcolm
See Chester, Alfred
Nessi, Pio Baroja y
See Baroja, Pio
Nestroy, Johann 1801-1862 .... **NCLC 42**
See also DLB 133; RGWL 2, 3
Netterville, Luke
See O'Grady, Standish (James)
Neufeld, John (Arthur) 1938- .... **CLC 17**
See also AAYA 11; CA 25-28R; CANR 11, 37, 56; CLR 52; MAICYA 1, 2; SAAS 3; SATA 6, 81, 131; SATA-Essay 131; YAW
Neumann, Alfred 1895-1952 .... **TCLC 100**
See also CA 183; DLB 56
Neumann, Ferenc
See Molnar, Ferenc
Neville, Emily Cheney 1919- .... **CLC 12**
See also BYA 2; CA 5-8R; CANR 3, 37, 85; JRDA; MAICYA 1, 2; SAAS 2; SATA 1; YAW
Newbound, Bernard Slade 1930-
See Slade, Bernard
See also CA 81-84; CANR 49; CD 5; DAM DRAM
Newby, P(ercy) H(oward)
1918-1997 .... **CLC 2, 13**
See also CA 5-8R; CAAS 161; CANR 32, 67; CN 1, 2, 3, 4, 5, 6; DAM NOV; DLB 15, 326; MTCW 1; RGEL 2
Newcastle
See Cavendish, Margaret Lucas
Newlove, Donald 1928- .... **CLC 6**
See also CA 29-32R; CANR 25
Newlove, John (Herbert) 1938- .... **CLC 14**
See also CA 21-24R; CANR 9, 25; CP 1, 2, 3, 4, 5, 6, 7
Newman, Charles 1938-2006 .... **CLC 2, 8**
See also CA 21-24R; CAAS 249; CANR 84; CN 3, 4, 5, 6
Newman, Charles Hamilton
See Newman, Charles
Newman, Edwin (Harold) 1919- ...... **CLC 14**
See also AITN 1; CA 69-72; CANR 5
Newman, John Henry 1801-1890 . **NCLC 38, 99**
See also BRWS 7; DLB 18, 32, 55; RGEL 2
Newton, (Sir) Isaac 1642-1727 ...... **LC 35, 53**
See also DLB 252
Newton, Suzanne 1936- .... **CLC 35**
See also BYA 7; CA 41-44R; CANR 14; JRDA; SATA 5, 77
New York Dept. of Ed. .... **CLC 70**
Nexo, Martin Andersen
1869-1954 .... **TCLC 43**
See also CA 202; DLB 214; EWL 3
Nezval, Vitezslav 1900-1958 .... **TCLC 44**
See also CAAE 123; CDWLB 4; DLB 215; EWL 3

Ng, Fae Myenne 1957(?)- .... **CLC 81**
    See also BYA 11; CA 146

Ngema, Mbongeni 1955- .... **CLC 57**
    See also BW 2; CA 143; CANR 84; CD 5,
    6

Ngugi, James T(hiong'o) . **CLC 3, 7, 13, 182**
    See Ngugi wa Thiong'o
    See also CN 1, 2

Ngugi wa Thiong'o
    See Ngugi wa Thiong'o
    See also CD 3, 4, 5, 6, 7; DLB 125; EWL 3

Ngugi wa Thiong'o 1938- ... **BLC 3; CLC 36,**
    182
    See Ngugi, James T(hiong'o); Ngugi wa
    Thiong'o
    See also AFW; BRWS 8; BW 2; CA 81-84;
    CANR 27, 58; CDWLB 3; DAM MULT,
    NOV; DNFS 2; MTCW 1, 2; MTFW
    2005; RGEL 2; WWE 1

Niatum, Duane 1938- .... **NNAL**
    See also CA 41-44R; CANR 21, 45, 83;
    DLB 175

Nichol, B(arrie) P(hillip) 1944-1988 . **CLC 18**
    See also CA 53-56; CP 1, 2, 3, 4; DLB 53;
    SATA 66

Nicholas of Cusa 1401-1464 .... **LC 80**
    See also DLB 115

Nichols, John 1940- .... **CLC 38**
    See also AMWS 13; CA 190; 9-12R; 190;
    2; CANR 6, 70, 121; DLBY 1982; LATS
    1:2; MTFW 2005; TCWW 1, 2

Nichols, Leigh
    See Koontz, Dean R.

Nichols, Peter (Richard) 1927- .... **CLC 5, 36,**
    65
    See also CA 104; CANR 33, 86; CBD; CD
    5, 6; DLB 13, 245; MTCW 1

Nicholson, Linda .... **CLC 65**

Ni Chuilleanain, Eilean 1942- .... **PC 34**
    See also CA 126; CANR 53, 83; CP 5, 6, 7;
    CWP; DLB 40

Nicolas, F. R. E.
    See Freeling, Nicolas

Niedecker, Lorine 1903-1970 ..... **CLC 10, 42;**
    PC 42
    See also CA 25-28; CAP 2; DAM POET;
    DLB 48

Nietzsche, Friedrich (Wilhelm)
    1844-1900 .... **TCLC 10, 18, 55**
    See also CA 121; CAAE 107; CDWLB 2;
    DLB 129; EW 7; RGWL 2, 3; TWA

Nievo, Ippolito 1831-1861 .... **NCLC 22**

Nightingale, Anne Redmon 1943-
    See Redmon, Anne
    See also CA 103

Nightingale, Florence 1820-1910 ... **TCLC 85**
    See also CA 188; DLB 166

Nijo Yoshimoto 1320-1388 .... **CMLC 49**
    See also DLB 203

Nik. T. O.
    See Annensky, Innokenty (Fyodorovich)

Nin, Anais 1903-1977 ..... **CLC 1, 4, 8, 11, 14,**
    60, 127; SSC 10
    See also AITN 2; AMWS 10; BPFB 2; CA
    13-16R; CAAS 69-72; CANR 22, 53; CN
    1, 2; DAM NOV, POP; DLB 2, 4, 152;
    EWL 3; GLL 2; MAL 5; MBL; MTCW 1,
    2; MTFW 2005; RGAL 4; RGSF 2

Nisbet, Robert A(lexander)
    1913-1996 .... **TCLC 117**
    See also CA 25-28R; CAAS 153; CANR
    17; INT CANR-17

Nishida, Kitaro 1870-1945 .... **TCLC 83**

Nishiwaki, Junzaburo 1894-1982 .... **PC 15**
    See Junzaburo, Nishiwaki
    See also CA 194; CAAS 107; MJW; RGWL
    3

Nissenson, Hugh 1933- .... **CLC 4, 9**
    See also CA 17-20R; CANR 27, 108, 151;
    CN 5, 6; DLB 28, 335

Nister, Der
    See Der Nister
    See also DLB 333; EWL 3

Niven, Larry 1938-
    See Niven, Laurence VanCott
    See also CA 207; 21-24R, 207; 12; CANR
    14, 44, 66, 113, 155; CPW; DAM POP;
    MTCW 1, 2; SATA 95, 171; SFW 4

Niven, Laurence VanCott .... **CLC 8**
    See Niven, Larry
    See also AAYA 27; BPFB 2; BYA 10; DLB
    8; SCFW 1, 2

Nixon, Agnes Eckhardt 1927- .... **CLC 21**
    See also CA 110

Nizan, Paul 1905-1940 .... **TCLC 40**
    See also CA 161; DLB 72; EWL 3; GFL
    1789 to the Present

Nkosi, Lewis 1936- .... **BLC 3; CLC 45**
    See also BW 1, 3; CA 65-68; CANR 27,
    81; CBD; CD 5, 6; DAM MULT; DLB
    157, 225; WWE 1

Nodier, (Jean) Charles (Emmanuel)
    1780-1844 .... **NCLC 19**
    See also DLB 119; GFL 1789 to the Present

Noguchi, Yone 1875-1947 .... **TCLC 80**

Nolan, Christopher 1965- .... **CLC 58**
    See also CA 111; CANR 88

Noon, Jeff 1957- .... **CLC 91**
    See also CA 148; CANR 83; DLB 267;
    SFW 4

Norden, Charles
    See Durrell, Lawrence (George)

Nordhoff, Charles Bernard
    1887-1947 .... **TCLC 23**
    See also CA 211; CAAE 108; DLB 9; LAIT
    1; RHW 1; SATA 23

Norfolk, Lawrence 1963- .... **CLC 76**
    See also CA 144; CANR 85; CN 6, 7; DLB
    267

Norman, Marsha (Williams) 1947- . **CLC 28,**
    186; DC 8
    See also CA 105; CABS 3; CAD; CANR
    41, 131; CD 5, 6; CSW; CWD; DAM
    DRAM; DFS 2; DLB 266; DLBY 1984;
    FW; MAL 5

Normyx
    See Douglas, (George) Norman

Norris, (Benjamin) Frank(lin, Jr.)
    1870-1902 .... **SSC 28; TCLC 24, 155**
    See also AAYA 57; AMW; AMWC 2; BPFB
    2; CA 160; CAAE 110; CDALB 1865-
    1917; DLB 12, 71, 186; LMFS 2; MAL
    5; NFS 12; RGAL 4; TCWW 1, 2; TUS

Norris, Leslie 1921-2006 .... **CLC 14**
    See also CA 11-12; CAAS 251; CANR 14,
    117; CAP 1; CP 1, 2, 3, 4, 5, 6, 7; DLB
    27, 256

North, Andrew
    See Norton, Andre

North, Anthony
    See Koontz, Dean R.

North, Captain George
    See Stevenson, Robert Louis (Balfour)

North, Captain George
    See Stevenson, Robert Louis (Balfour)

North, Milou
    See Erdrich, Louise

Northrup, B. A.
    See Hubbard, L. Ron

North Staffs
    See Hulme, T(homas) E(rnest)

Northup, Solomon 1808-1863 ...... **NCLC 105**

Norton, Alice Mary
    See Norton, Andre
    See also MAICYA 1; SATA 1, 43

Norton, Andre 1912-2005 .... **CLC 12**
    See Norton, Alice Mary
    See also AAYA 14; BPFB 2; BYA 4, 10,
    12; CA 1-4R; CAAS 237; CANR 2, 31,
    68, 108, 149; CLR 50; DLB 8, 52; JRDA;
    MAICYA 2; MTCW 1; SATA 91; SUFW
    1, 2; YAW

Norton, Caroline 1808-1877 .... **NCLC 47**
    See also DLB 21, 159, 199

Norway, Nevil Shute 1899-1960
    See Shute, Nevil
    See also CA 102; CAAS 93-96; CANR 85;
    MTCW 2

Norwid, Cyprian Kamil
    1821-1883 .... **NCLC 17**
    See also RGWL 3

Nosille, Nabrah
    See Ellison, Harlan

Nossack, Hans Erich 1901-1977 .... **CLC 6**
    See also CA 93-96; CAAS 85-88; CANR
    156; DLB 69; EWL 3

Nostradamus 1503-1566 .... **LC 27**

Nosu, Chuji
    See Ozu, Yasujiro

Notenburg, Eleanora (Genrikhovna) von
    See Guro, Elena (Genrikhovna)

Nova, Craig 1945- .... **CLC 7, 31**
    See also CA 45-48; CANR 2, 53, 127

Novak, Joseph
    See Kosinski, Jerzy

Novalis 1772-1801 .... **NCLC 13, 178**
    See also CDWLB 2; DLB 90; EW 5; RGWL
    2, 3

Novick, Peter 1934- .... **CLC 164**
    See also CA 188

Novis, Emile
    See Weil, Simone (Adolphine)

Nowlan, Alden (Albert) 1933-1983 ... **CLC 15**
    See also CA 9-12R; CANR 5; CP 1, 2, 3;
    DAC; DAM MST; DLB 53; PFS 12

Noyes, Alfred 1880-1958 .... **PC 27; TCLC 7**
    See also CA 188; CAAE 104; DLB 20;
    EXPP; FANT; PFS 4; RGEL 2

Nugent, Richard Bruce
    1906(?)-1987 .... **HR 1:3**
    See also BW 1; CA 125; DLB 51; GLL 2

Nunn, Kem .... **CLC 34**
    See also CA 159

Nussbaum, Martha Craven 1947- .. **CLC 203**
    See also CA 134; CANR 102

Nwapa, Flora (Nwanzuruaha)
    1931-1993 .... **BLCS; CLC 133**
    See also BW 2; CA 143; CANR 83; CD-
    WLB 3; CWRI 5; DLB 125; EWL 3;
    WLIT 2

Nye, Robert 1939- .... **CLC 13, 42**
    See also BRWS 10; CA 33-36R; CANR 29,
    67, 107; CN 1, 2, 3, 4, 5, 6, 7; CP 1, 2, 3,
    4, 5, 6, 7; CWRI 5; DAM NOV; DLB 14,
    271; FANT; HGG; MTCW 1; RHW;
    SATA 6

Nyro, Laura 1947-1997 .... **CLC 17**
    See also CA 194

Oates, Joyce Carol 1938- .. **CLC 1, 2, 3, 6, 9,**
    11, 15, 19, 33, 52, 108, 134, 228; SSC 6,
    70; WLC 4
    See also AAYA 15, 52; AITN 1; AMWS 2;
    BEST 89:2; BPFB 2; BYA 11; CA 5-8R;
    CANR 25, 45, 74, 113, 129; CDALB
    1968-1988; CN 1, 2, 3, 4, 5, 6, 7; CP 5,
    6, 7; CPW; CWP; DA; DA3; DAB; DAC;
    DAM MST, NOV, POP; DLB 2, 5, 130;
    DLBY 1981; EWL 3; EXPS; FL 1:6; FW;
    GL 3; HGG; INT CANR-25; LAIT 4;
    MAL 5; MBL; MTCW 1, 2; MTFW 2005;
    NFS 8, 24; RGAL 4; RGSF 2; SATA 159;
    SSFS 1, 8, 17; SUFW 2; TUS

O'Brian, E. G.
    See Clarke, Arthur C.

O'Brian, Patrick 1914-2000 .... **CLC 152**
See also AAYA 55; BRWS 12; CA 144;
CAAS 187; CANR 74; CPW; MTCW 2;
MTFW 2005; RHW

O'Brien, Darcy 1939-1998 .... **CLC 11**
See also CA 21-24R; CAAS 167; CANR 8,
59

O'Brien, Edna 1932- ..... **CLC 3, 5, 8, 13, 36,
65, 116, 237; SSC 10, 77**
See also BRWS 5; CA 1-4R; CANR 6, 41,
65, 102; CDBLB 1960 to Present; CN 1,
2, 3, 4, 5, 6, 7; DA3; DAM NOV; DLB
14, 231, 319; EWL 3; FW; MTCW 1, 2;
MTFW 2005; RGSF 2; WLIT 4

O'Brien, Fitz-James 1828-1862 ..... **NCLC 21**
See also DLB 74; RGAL 4; SUFW

O'Brien, Flann .... **CLC 1, 4, 5, 7, 10, 47**
See O Nuallain, Brian
See also BRWS 2; DLB 231; EWL 3;
RGEL 2

O'Brien, Richard 1942- .... **CLC 17**
See also CA 124

O'Brien, Tim 1946- .... **CLC 7, 19, 40, 103,
211; SSC 74**
See also AAYA 16; AMWS 5; CA 85-88;
CANR 40, 58, 133; CDALBS; CN 5, 6,
7; CPW; DA3; DAM POP; DLB 152;
DLBD 9; DLBY 1980; LATS 1:2; MAL
5; MTCW 2; MTFW 2005; RGAL 4;
SSFS 5, 15; TCLE 1:2

Obstfelder, Sigbjoern 1866-1900 .... **TCLC 23**
See also CAAE 123

O'Casey, Sean 1880-1964 .... **CLC 1, 5, 9, 11,
15, 88; DC 12; WLCS**
See also BRW 7; CA 89-92; CANR 62;
CBD; CDBLB 1914-1945; DA3; DAB;
DAC; DAM DRAM, MST; DFS 19; DLB
10; EWL 3; MTCW 1, 2; MTFW 2005;
RGEL 2; TEA; WLIT 4

O'Cathasaigh, Sean
See O'Casey, Sean

Occom, Samson 1723-1792 .... **LC 60; NNAL**
See also DLB 175

Occomy, Marita (Odette) Bonner
1899(?)-1971
See Bonner, Marita
See also BW 2; CA 142; DFS 13; DLB 51,
228

Ochs, Phil(ip David) 1940-1976 .... **CLC 17**
See also CA 185; CAAS 65-68

O'Connor, Edwin (Greene)
1918-1968 .... **CLC 14**
See also CA 93-96; CAAS 25-28R; MAL 5

O'Connor, (Mary) Flannery
1925-1964 .... **CLC 1, 2, 3, 6, 10, 13, 15,
21, 66, 104; SSC 1, 23, 61, 82; TCLC
132; WLC 4**
See also AAYA 7; AMW; AMWR 2; BPFB
3; BYA 16; CA 1-4R; CANR 3, 41;
CDALB 1941-1968; DA; DA3; DAB;
DAC; DAM MST, NOV; DLB 2, 152;
DLBD 12; DLBY 1980; EWL 3; EXPS;
LAIT 5; MAL 5; MBL; MTCW 1, 2;
MTFW 2005; NFS 3, 21; RGAL 4; RGSF
2; SSFS 2, 7, 10, 19; TUS

O'Connor, Frank .... **CLC 23; SSC 5**
See O'Donovan, Michael Francis
See also DLB 162; EWL 3; RGSF 2; SSFS
5

O'Dell, Scott 1898-1989 .... **CLC 30**
See also AAYA 3, 44; BPFB 3; BYA 1, 2,
3, 5; CA 61-64; CAAS 129; CANR 12,
30, 112; CLR 1, 16; DLB 52; JRDA;
MAICYA 1, 2; SATA 12, 60, 134; WYA;
YAW

Odets, Clifford 1906-1963 ..... **CLC 2, 28, 98;
DC 6**
See also AMWS 2; CA 85-88; CAD; CANR
62; DAM DRAM; DFS 3, 17, 20; DLB 7,
26; EWL 3; MAL 5; MTCW 1, 2; MTFW
2005; RGAL 4; TUS

O'Doherty, Brian 1928- .... **CLC 76**
See also CA 105; CANR 108

O'Donnell, K. M.
See Malzberg, Barry N(athaniel)

O'Donnell, Lawrence
See Kuttner, Henry

O'Donovan, Michael Francis
1903-1966 .... **CLC 14**
See O'Connor, Frank
See also CA 93-96; CANR 84

Oe, Kenzaburo 1935- .. **CLC 10, 36, 86, 187;
SSC 20**
See Oe Kenzaburo
See also CA 97-100; CANR 36, 50, 74, 126;
DA3; DAM NOV; DLB 182, 331; DLBY
1994; LATS 1:2; MJW; MTCW 1, 2;
MTFW 2005; RGSF 2; RGWL 2, 3

Oe Kenzaburo
See Oe, Kenzaburo
See also CWW 2; EWL 3

O'Faolain, Julia 1932- .... **CLC 6, 19, 47, 108**
See also CA 81-84; 2; CANR 12, 61; CN 2,
3, 4, 5, 6, 7; DLB 14, 231, 319; FW;
MTCW 1; RHW

O'Faolain, Sean 1900-1991 ...... **CLC 1, 7, 14,
32, 70; SSC 13; TCLC 143**
See also CA 61-64; CAAS 134; CANR 12,
66; CN 1, 2, 3, 4; DLB 15, 162; MTCW
1, 2; MTFW 2005; RGEL 2; RGSF 2

O'Flaherty, Liam 1896-1984 .... **CLC 5, 34;
SSC 6**
See also CA 101; CAAS 113; CANR 35;
CN 1, 2, 3; DLB 36, 162; DLBY 1984;
MTCW 1, 2; MTFW 2005; RGEL 2;
RGSF 2; SSFS 5, 20

Ogai
See Mori Ogai
See also MJW

Ogilvy, Gavin
See Barrie, J(ames) M(atthew)

O'Grady, Standish (James)
1846-1928 .... **TCLC 5**
See also CA 157; CAAE 104

O'Grady, Timothy 1951- .... **CLC 59**
See also CA 138

O'Hara, Frank 1926-1966 .... **CLC 2, 5, 13,
78; PC 45**
See also CA 9-12R; CAAS 25-28R; CANR
33; DA3; DAM POET; DLB 5, 16, 193;
EWL 3; MAL 5; MTCW 1, 2; MTFW
2005; PFS 8, 12; RGAL 4; WP

O'Hara, John (Henry) 1905-1970 . **CLC 1, 2,
3, 6, 11, 42; SSC 15**
See also AMW; BPFB 3; CA 5-8R; CAAS
25-28R; CANR 31, 60; CDALB 1929-
1941; DAM NOV; DLB 9, 86, 324; DLBD
2; EWL 3; MAL 5; MTCW 1, 2; MTFW
2005; NFS 11; RGAL 4; RGSF 2

O'Hehir, Diana 1929- .... **CLC 41**
See also CA 245

Ohiyesa
See Eastman, Charles A(lexander)

Okada, John 1923-1971 .... **AAL**
See also BYA 14; CA 212; DLB 312; NFS
25

Okigbo, Christopher 1930-1967 .... **BLC 3;
CLC 25, 84; PC 7; TCLC 171**
See also AFW; BW 1, 3; CA 77-80; CANR
74; CDWLB 3; DAM MULT, POET; DLB
125; EWL 3; MTCW 1, 2; MTFW 2005;
RGEL 2

Okigbo, Christopher Ifenayichukwu
See Okigbo, Christopher

Okri, Ben 1959- .... **CLC 87, 223**
See also AFW; BRWS 5; BW 2, 3; CA 138;
CAAE 130; CANR 65, 128; CN 5, 6, 7;
DLB 157, 231, 319, 326; EWL 3; INT
CA-138; MTCW 2; MTFW 2005; RGSF
2; SSFS 20; WLIT 2; WWE 1

Olds, Sharon 1942- .. **CLC 32, 39, 85; PC 22**
See also AMWS 10; CA 101; CANR 18,
41, 66, 98, 135; CP 5, 6, 7; CPW; CWP;
DAM POET; DLB 120; MAL 5; MTCW
2; MTFW 2005; PFS 17

Oldstyle, Jonathan
See Irving, Washington

Olesha, Iurii
See Olesha, Yuri (Karlovich)
See also RGWL 2

Olesha, Iurii Karlovich
See Olesha, Yuri (Karlovich)
See also DLB 272

Olesha, Yuri (Karlovich) 1899-1960 . **CLC 8;
SSC 69; TCLC 136**
See Olesha, Iurii; Olesha, Iurii Karlovich;
Olesha, Yury Karlovich
See also CA 85-88; EW 11; RGWL 3

Olesha, Yury Karlovich
See Olesha, Yuri (Karlovich)
See also EWL 3

Oliphant, Mrs.
See Oliphant, Margaret (Oliphant Wilson)
See also SUFW

Oliphant, Laurence 1829(?)-1888 .. **NCLC 47**
See also DLB 18, 166

Oliphant, Margaret (Oliphant Wilson)
1828-1897 .... **NCLC 11, 61; SSC 25**
See Oliphant, Mrs.
See also BRWS 10; DLB 18, 159, 190;
HGG; RGEL 2; RGSF 2

Oliver, Mary 1935- ... **CLC 19, 34, 98; PC 75**
See also AMWS 7; CA 21-24R; CANR 9,
43, 84, 92, 138; CP 4, 5, 6, 7; CWP; DLB
5, 193; EWL 3; MTFW 2005; PFS 15

Olivier, Laurence (Kerr) 1907-1989 . **CLC 20**
See also CA 150; CAAE 111; CAAS 129

Olsen, Tillie 1912-2007 .... **CLC 4, 13, 114;
SSC 11**
See also AAYA 51; AMWS 13; BYA 11;
CA 1-4R; CAAS 256; CANR 1, 43, 74,
132; CDALBS; CN 2, 3, 4, 5, 6, 7; DA;
DA3; DAB; DAC; DAM MST; DLB 28,
206; DLBY 1980; EWL 3; EXPS; FW;
MAL 5; MTCW 1, 2; MTFW 2005;
RGAL 4; RGSF 2; SSFS 1; TCLE 1:2;
TCWW 2; TUS

Olson, Charles (John) 1910-1970 .. **CLC 1, 2,
5, 6, 9, 11, 29; PC 19**
See also AMWS 2; CA 13-16; CAAS 25-
28R; CABS 2; CANR 35, 61; CAP 1; CP
1; DAM POET; DLB 5, 16, 193; EWL 3;
MAL 5; MTCW 1, 2; RGAL 4; WP

Olson, Toby 1937- .... **CLC 28**
See also CA 65-68; 11; CANR 9, 31, 84;
CP 3, 4, 5, 6, 7

Olyesha, Yuri
See Olesha, Yuri (Karlovich)

Olympiodorus of Thebes c. 375-c.
430 .... **CMLC 59**

Omar Khayyam
See Khayyam, Omar
See also RGWL 2, 3

Ondaatje, Michael 1943- ..... **CLC 14, 29, 51,
76, 180; PC 28**
See also AAYA 66; CA 77-80; CANR 42,
74, 109, 133; CN 5, 6, 7; CP 1, 2, 3, 4, 5,
6, 7; DA3; DAB; DAC; DAM MST; DLB
60, 323, 326; EWL 3; LATS 1:2; LMFS
2; MTCW 2; MTFW 2005; NFS 23; PFS
8, 19; TCLE 1:2; TWA; WWE 1

Ondaatje, Philip Michael
See Ondaatje, Michael

Oneal, Elizabeth 1934-
See Oneal, Zibby
See also CA 106; CANR 28, 84; MAICYA
1, 2; SATA 30, 82; YAW

Paine, Thomas 1737-1809 .... **NCLC 62**
　See also AMWS 1; CDALB 1640-1865;
　DLB 31, 43, 73, 158; LAIT 1; RGAL 4;
　RGEL 2; TUS

Pakenham, Antonia
　See Fraser, Antonia

Palamas, Costis
　See Palamas, Kostes

Palamas, Kostes 1859-1943 .... **TCLC 5**
　See Palamas, Kostis
　See also CA 190; CAAE 105; RGWL 2, 3

Palamas, Kostis
　See Palamas, Kostes
　See also EWL 3

Palazzeschi, Aldo 1885-1974 .... **CLC 11**
　See also CA 89-92; CAAS 53-56; DLB 114,
　264; EWL 3

Pales Matos, Luis 1898-1959 .... **HLCS 2**
　See Pales Matos, Luis
　See also DLB 290; HW 1; LAW

Paley, Grace 1922- .. **CLC 4, 6, 37, 140; SSC
　8**
　See also AMWS 6; CA 25-28R; CANR 13,
　46, 74, 118; CN 2, 3, 4, 5, 6, 7; CPW;
　DA3; DAM POP; DLB 28, 218; EWL 3;
　EXPS; FW; INT CANR-13; MAL 5;
　MBL; MTCW 1, 2; MTFW 2005; RGAL
　4; RGSF 2; SSFS 3, 20

Palin, Michael (Edward) 1943- .... **CLC 21**
　See Monty Python
　See also CA 107; CANR 35, 109; SATA 67

Palliser, Charles 1947- .... **CLC 65**
　See also CA 136; CANR 76; CN 5, 6, 7

Palma, Ricardo 1833-1919 .... **TCLC 29**
　See also CA 168; LAW

Pamuk, Orhan 1952- .... **CLC 185**
　See also CA 142; CANR 75, 127; CWW 2;
　WLIT 6

Pancake, Breece Dexter 1952-1979
　See Pancake, Breece D'J
　See also CA 123; CAAS 109

Pancake, Breece D'J .... **CLC 29; SSC 61**
　See Pancake, Breece Dexter
　See also DLB 130

Panchenko, Nikolai .... **CLC 59**

Pankhurst, Emmeline (Goulden)
　1858-1928 .... **TCLC 100**
　See also CAAE 116; FW

Panko, Rudy
　See Gogol, Nikolai (Vasilyevich)

Papadiamantis, Alexandros
　1851-1911 .... **TCLC 29**
　See also CA 168; EWL 3

Papadiamantopoulos, Johannes 1856-1910
　See Moreas, Jean
　See also CA 242; CAAE 117

Papini, Giovanni 1881-1956 .... **TCLC 22**
　See also CA 180; CAAE 121; DLB 264

Paracelsus 1493-1541 .... **LC 14**
　See also DLB 179

Parasol, Peter
　See Stevens, Wallace

Pardo Bazan, Emilia 1851-1921 .... **SSC 30;
　TCLC 189**
　See also EWL 3; FW; RGSF 2; RGWL 2, 3

Pareto, Vilfredo 1848-1923 .... **TCLC 69**
　See also CA 175

Paretsky, Sara 1947- .... **CLC 135**
　See also AAYA 30; BEST 90:3; CA 129;
　CAAE 125; CANR 59, 95; CMW 4;
　CPW; DA3; DAM POP; DLB 306; INT
　CA-129; MSW; RGAL 4

Parfenie, Maria
　See Codrescu, Andrei

Parini, Jay (Lee) 1948- .... **CLC 54, 133**
　See also CA 229; 97-100, 229; 16; CANR
　32, 87

Park, Jordan
　See Kornbluth, C(yril) M.; Pohl, Frederik

Park, Robert E(zra) 1864-1944 ..... **TCLC 73**
　See also CA 165; CAAE 122

Parker, Bert
　See Ellison, Harlan

Parker, Dorothy (Rothschild)
　1893-1967 . **CLC 15, 68; PC 28; SSC 2,
　101; TCLC 143**
　See also AMWS 9; CA 19-20; CAAS 25-
　28R; CAP 2; DA3; DAM POET; DLB 11,
　45, 86; EXPP; FW; MAL 5; MBL;
　MTCW 1, 2; MTFW 2005; PFS 18;
　RGAL 4; RGSF 2; TUS

Parker, Robert B. 1932- .... **CLC 27**
　See also AAYA 28; BEST 89:4; BPFB 3;
　CA 49-52; CANR 1, 26, 52, 89, 128;
　CMW 4; CPW; DAM NOV, POP; DLB
　306; INT CANR-26; MSW; MTCW 1;
　MTFW 2005

Parker, Robert Brown
　See Parker, Robert B.

Parker, Theodore 1810-1860 .... **NCLC 186**
　See also DLB 1, 235

Parkin, Frank 1940- .... **CLC 43**
　See also CA 147

Parkman, Francis, Jr. 1823-1893 .. **NCLC 12**
　See also AMWS 2; DLB 1, 30, 183, 186,
　235; RGAL 4

Parks, Gordon 1912-2006 .... **BLC 3; CLC 1,
　16**
　See also AAYA 36; AITN 2; BW 2, 3; CA
　41-44R; CAAS 249; CANR 26, 66, 145;
　DA3; DAM MULT; DLB 33; MTCW 2;
　MTFW 2005; SATA 8, 108; SATA-Obit
　175

Parks, Suzan-Lori 1964(?)- .... **DC 23**
　See also AAYA 55; CA 201; CAD; CD 5,
　6; CWD; DFS 22; RGAL 4

Parks, Tim(othy Harold) 1954- ...... **CLC 147**
　See also CA 131; CAAE 126; CANR 77,
　144; CN 7; DLB 231; INT CA-131

Parmenides c. 515B.C.-c.
　450B.C. .... **CMLC 22**
　See also DLB 176

Parnell, Thomas 1679-1718 .... **LC 3**
　See also DLB 95; RGEL 2

Parr, Catherine c. 1513(?)-1548 .... **LC 86**
　See also DLB 136

Parra, Nicanor 1914- ... **CLC 2, 102; HLC 2;
　PC 39**
　See also CA 85-88; CANR 32; CWW 2;
　DAM MULT; DLB 283; EWL 3; HW 1;
　LAW; MTCW 1

Parra Sanojo, Ana Teresa de la
　1890-1936 .... **HLCS 2**
　See de la Parra, (Ana) Teresa (Sonojo)
　See also LAW

Parrish, Mary Frances
　See Fisher, M(ary) F(rances) K(ennedy)

Parshchikov, Aleksei 1954- .... **CLC 59**
　See Parshchikov, Aleksei Maksimovich

Parshchikov, Aleksei Maksimovich
　See Parshchikov, Aleksei
　See also DLB 285

Parson, Professor
　See Coleridge, Samuel Taylor

Parson Lot
　See Kingsley, Charles

Parton, Sara Payson Willis
　1811-1872 .... **NCLC 86**
　See also DLB 43, 74, 239

Partridge, Anthony
　See Oppenheim, E(dward) Phillips

Pascal, Blaise 1623-1662 .... **LC 35**
　See also DLB 268; EW 3; GFL Beginnings
　to 1789; RGWL 2, 3; TWA

Pascoli, Giovanni 1855-1912 .... **TCLC 45**
　See also CA 170; EW 7; EWL 3

Pasolini, Pier Paolo 1922-1975 .. **CLC 20, 37,
　106; PC 17**
　See also CA 93-96; CAAS 61-64; CANR
　63; DLB 128, 177; EWL 3; MTCW 1;
　RGWL 2, 3

Pasquini
　See Silone, Ignazio

Pastan, Linda (Olenik) 1932- .... **CLC 27**
　See also CA 61-64; CANR 18, 40, 61, 113;
　CP 3, 4, 5, 6, 7; CSW; CWP; DAM
　POET; DLB 5; PFS 8, 25

Pasternak, Boris 1890-1960 ... **CLC 7, 10, 18,
　63; PC 6; SSC 31; TCLC 188; WLC 4**
　See also BPFB 3; CA 127; CAAS 116; DA;
　DA3; DAB; DAC; DAM MST, NOV,
　POET; DLB 302, 331; EW 10; MTCW 1,
　2; MTFW 2005; RGSF 2; RGWL 2, 3;
　TWA; WP

Patchen, Kenneth 1911-1972 .... **CLC 1, 2, 18**
　See also BG 1:3; CA 1-4R; CAAS 33-36R;
　CANR 3, 35; CN 1; CP 1; DAM POET;
　DLB 16, 48; EWL 3; MAL 5; MTCW 1;
　RGAL 4

Pater, Walter (Horatio) 1839-1894 . **NCLC 7,
　90, 159**
　See also BRW 5; CDBLB 1832-1890; DLB
　57, 156; RGEL 2; TEA

Paterson, A(ndrew) B(arton)
　1864-1941 .... **TCLC 32**
　See also CA 155; DLB 230; RGEL 2; SATA
　97

Paterson, Banjo
　See Paterson, A(ndrew) B(arton)

Paterson, Katherine 1932- .... **CLC 12, 30**
　See also AAYA 1, 31; BYA 1, 2, 7; CA 21-
　24R; CANR 28, 59, 111; CLR 7, 50;
　CWRI 5; DLB 52; JRDA; LAIT 4; MAI-
　CYA 1, 2; MAICYAS 1; MTCW 1; SATA
　13, 53, 92, 133; WYA; YAW

Paterson, Katherine Womeldorf
　See Paterson, Katherine

Patmore, Coventry Kersey Dighton
　1823-1896 .... **NCLC 9; PC 59**
　See also DLB 35, 98; RGEL 2; TEA

Paton, Alan 1903-1988 ..... **CLC 4, 10, 25, 55,
　106; TCLC 165; WLC 4**
　See also AAYA 26; AFW; BPFB 3; BRWS
　2; BYA 1; CA 13-16; CAAS 125; CANR
　22; CAP 1; CN 1, 2, 3, 4; DA; DA3;
　DAB; DAC; DAM MST, NOV; DLB 225;
　DLBD 17; EWL 3; EXPN; LAIT 4;
　MTCW 1, 2; MTFW 2005; NFS 3, 12;
　RGEL 2; SATA 11; SATA-Obit 56; TWA;
　WLIT 2; WWE 1

Paton Walsh, Gillian
　See Paton Walsh, Jill
　See also AAYA 47; BYA 1, 8

Paton Walsh, Jill 1937- .... **CLC 35**
　See Paton Walsh, Gillian; Walsh, Jill Paton
　See also AAYA 11; CANR 38, 83, 158; CLR
　2, 65; DLB 161; JRDA; MAICYA 1, 2;
　SAAS 3; SATA 4, 72, 109; YAW

Patsauq, Markoosie 1942- .... **NNAL**
　See also CA 101; CLR 23; CWRI 5; DAM
　MULT

Patterson, (Horace) Orlando (Lloyd)
　1940- .... **BLCS**
　See also BW 1; CA 65-68; CANR 27, 84;
　CN 1, 2, 3, 4, 5, 6

Patton, George S(mith), Jr.
　1885-1945 .... **TCLC 79**
　See also CA 189

Paulding, James Kirke 1778-1860 ... **NCLC 2**
　See also DLB 3, 59, 74, 250; RGAL 4

Paulin, Thomas Neilson
　See Paulin, Tom

Paulin, Tom 1949- .... **CLC 37, 177**
　See also CA 128; CAAE 123; CANR 98;
　CP 3, 4, 5, 6, 7; DLB 40

Pausanias c. 1st cent. - .... **CMLC 36**

Paustovsky, Konstantin (Georgievich)
1892-1968 .... **CLC 40**
See also CA 93-96; CAAS 25-28R; DLB
272; EWL 3

Pavese, Cesare 1908-1950 .... **PC 13; SSC 19;**
TCLC 3
See also CA 169; CAAE 104; DLB 128,
177; EW 12; EWL 3; PFS 20; RGSF 2;
RGWL 2, 3; TWA; WLIT 7

Pavic, Milorad 1929- .... **CLC 60**
See also CA 136; CDWLB 4; CWW 2; DLB
181; EWL 3; RGWL 3

Pavlov, Ivan Petrovich 1849-1936 . **TCLC 91**
See also CA 180; CAAE 118

Pavlova, Karolina Karlovna
1807-1893 .... **NCLC 138**
See also DLB 205

Payne, Alan
See Jakes, John

Payne, Rachel Ann
See Jakes, John

Paz, Gil
See Lugones, Leopoldo

Paz, Octavio 1914-1998 . **CLC 3, 4, 6, 10, 19,**
51, 65, 119; HLC 2; PC 1, 48; WLC 4
See also AAYA 50; CA 73-76; CAAS 165;
CANR 32, 65, 104; CWW 2; DA; DA3;
DAB; DAC; DAM MST, MULT, POET;
DLB 290, 331; DLBY 1990, 1998; DNFS
1; EWL 3; HW 1, 2; LAW; LAWS 1;
MTCW 1, 2; MTFW 2005; PFS 18;
RGWL 2, 3; SSFS 13; TWA; WLIT 1

p'Bitek, Okot 1931-1982 .... **BLC 3; CLC 96;**
TCLC 149
See also AFW; BW 2, 3; CA 124; CAAS
107; CANR 82; CP 1, 2, 3; DAM MULT;
DLB 125; EWL 3; MTCW 1, 2; MTFW
2005; RGEL 2; WLIT 2

Peabody, Elizabeth Palmer
1804-1894 .... **NCLC 169**
See also DLB 1, 223

Peacham, Henry 1578-1644(?) .... **LC 119**
See also DLB 151

Peacock, Molly 1947- .... **CLC 60**
See also CA 103; 21; CANR 52, 84; CP 5,
6, 7; CWP; DLB 120, 282

Peacock, Thomas Love
1785-1866 .... **NCLC 22**
See also BRW 4; DLB 96, 116; RGEL 2;
RGSF 2

Peake, Mervyn 1911-1968 .... **CLC 7, 54**
See also CA 5-8R; CAAS 25-28R; CANR
3; DLB 15, 160, 255; FANT; MTCW 1;
RGEL 2; SATA 23; SFW 4

Pearce, Philippa 1920-2006
See Christie, Philippa
See also CA 5-8R; CAAS 255; CANR 4,
109; CWRI 5; FANT; MAICYA 2; SATA-
Obit 179

Pearl, Eric
See Elman, Richard (Martin)

Pearson, T. R. 1956- .... **CLC 39**
See also CA 130; CAAE 120; CANR 97,
147; CSW; INT CA-130

Pearson, Thomas Reid
See Pearson, T. R.

Peck, Dale 1967- .... **CLC 81**
See also CA 146; CANR 72, 127; GLL 2

Peck, John (Frederick) 1941- .... **CLC 3**
See also CA 49-52; CANR 3, 100; CP 4, 5,
6, 7

Peck, Richard 1934- .... **CLC 21**
See also AAYA 1, 24; BYA 1, 6, 8, 11; CA
85-88; CANR 19, 38, 129; CLR 15; INT
CANR-19; JRDA; MAICYA 1, 2; SAAS
2; SATA 18, 55, 97, 110, 158; SATA-
Essay 110; WYA; YAW

Peck, Richard Wayne
See Peck, Richard

Peck, Robert Newton 1928- .... **CLC 17**
See also AAYA 3, 43; BYA 1, 6; CA 182;
81-84, 182; CANR 31, 63, 127; CLR 45;
DA; DAC; DAM MST; JRDA; LAIT 3;
MAICYA 1, 2; SAAS 1; SATA 21, 62,
111, 156; SATA-Essay 108; WYA; YAW

Peckinpah, David Samuel
See Peckinpah, Sam

Peckinpah, Sam 1925-1984 .... **CLC 20**
See also CA 109; CAAS 114; CANR 82

Pedersen, Knut 1859-1952
See Hamsun, Knut
See also CA 119; CAAE 104; CANR 63;
MTCW 1, 2

Peele, George 1556-1596 .... **DC 27; LC 115**
See also BRW 1; DLB 62, 167; RGEL 2

Peeslake, Gaffer
See Durrell, Lawrence (George)

Peguy, Charles (Pierre)
1873-1914 .... **TCLC 10**
See also CA 193; CAAE 107; DLB 258;
EWL 3; GFL 1789 to the Present

Peirce, Charles Sanders
1839-1914 .... **TCLC 81**
See also CA 194; DLB 270

Pelecanos, George P. 1957- .... **CLC 236**
See also CA 138; CANR 122; DLB 306

Pelevin, Victor 1962- .... **CLC 238**
See Pelevin, Viktor Olegovich
See also CA 154; CANR 88, 159

Pelevin, Viktor Olegovich
See Pelevin, Victor
See also DLB 285

Pellicer, Carlos 1897(?)-1977 .... **HLCS 2**
See also CA 153; CAAS 69-72; DLB 290;
EWL 3; HW 1

Pena, Ramon del Valle y
See Valle-Inclan, Ramon (Maria) del

Pendennis, Arthur Esquir
See Thackeray, William Makepeace

Penn, Arthur
See Matthews, (James) Brander

Penn, William 1644-1718 .... **LC 25**
See also DLB 24

PEPECE
See Prado (Calvo), Pedro

Pepys, Samuel 1633-1703 ... **LC 11, 58; WLC**
4
See also BRW 2; CDBLB 1660-1789; DA;
DA3; DAB; DAC; DAM MST; DLB 101,
213; NCFS 4; RGEL 2; TEA; WLIT 3

Percy, Thomas 1729-1811 .... **NCLC 95**
See also DLB 104

Percy, Walker 1916-1990 .... **CLC 2, 3, 6, 8,**
14, 18, 47, 65
See also AMWS 3; BPFB 3; CA 1-4R;
CAAS 131; CANR 1, 23, 64; CN 1, 2, 3,
4; CPW; CSW; DA3; DAM NOV, POP;
DLB 2; DLBY 1980, 1990; EWL 3; MAL
5; MTCW 1, 2; MTFW 2005; RGAL 4;
TUS

Percy, William Alexander
1885-1942 .... **TCLC 84**
See also CA 163; MTCW 2

Perec, Georges 1936-1982 .... **CLC 56, 116**
See also CA 141; DLB 83, 299; EWL 3;
GFL 1789 to the Present; RGHL; RGWL
3

Pereda (y Sanchez de Porrua), Jose Maria
de 1833-1906 .... **TCLC 16**
See also CAAE 117

Pereda y Porrua, Jose Maria de
See Pereda (y Sanchez de Porrua), Jose
Maria de

Peregoy, George Weems
See Mencken, H(enry) L(ouis)

Perelman, S(idney) J(oseph)
1904-1979 .. **CLC 3, 5, 9, 15, 23, 44, 49;**
SSC 32
See also AITN 1, 2; BPFB 3; CA 73-76;
CAAS 89-92; CANR 18; DAM DRAM;
DLB 11, 44; MTCW 1, 2; MTFW 2005;
RGAL 4

Peret, Benjamin 1899-1959 .... **PC 33; TCLC**
20
See also CA 186; CAAE 117; GFL 1789 to
the Present

Peretz, Isaac Leib
See Peretz, Isaac Loeb
See also CA 201; DLB 333

Peretz, Isaac Loeb 1851(?)-1915 ...... **SSC 26;**
TCLC 16
See Peretz, Isaac Leib
See also CAAE 109

Peretz, Yitzkhok Leibush
See Peretz, Isaac Loeb

Perez Galdos, Benito 1843-1920 ..... **HLCS 2;**
TCLC 27
See Galdos, Benito Perez
See also CA 153; CAAE 125; EWL 3; HW
1; RGWL 2, 3

Peri Rossi, Cristina 1941- .. **CLC 156; HLCS**
2
See also CA 131; CANR 59, 81; CWW 2;
DLB 145, 290; EWL 3; HW 1, 2

Perlata
See Peret, Benjamin

Perloff, Marjorie G(abrielle)
1931- .... **CLC 137**
See also CA 57-60; CANR 7, 22, 49, 104

Perrault, Charles 1628-1703 .... **LC 2, 56**
See also BYA 4; CLR 79; DLB 268; GFL
Beginnings to 1789; MAICYA 1, 2;
RGWL 2, 3; SATA 25; WCH

Perry, Anne 1938- .... **CLC 126**
See also CA 101; CANR 22, 50, 84, 150;
CMW 4; CN 6, 7; CPW; DLB 276

Perry, Brighton
See Sherwood, Robert E(mmet)

Perse, St.-John
See Leger, (Marie-Rene Auguste) Alexis
Saint-Leger

Perse, Saint-John
See Leger, (Marie-Rene Auguste) Alexis
Saint-Leger
See also DLB 258, 331; RGWL 3

Persius 34-62 .... **CMLC 74**
See also AW 2; DLB 211; RGWL 2, 3

Perutz, Leo(pold) 1882-1957 .... **TCLC 60**
See also CA 147; DLB 81

Peseenz, Tulio F.
See Lopez y Fuentes, Gregorio

Pesetsky, Bette 1932- .... **CLC 28**
See also CA 133; DLB 130

Peshkov, Alexei Maximovich 1868-1936
See Gorky, Maxim
See also CA 141; CAAE 105; CANR 83;
DA; DAC; DAM DRAM, MST, NOV;
MTCW 2; MTFW 2005

Pessoa, Fernando (Antonio Nogueira)
1888-1935 ..... **HLC 2; PC 20; TCLC 27**
See also CA 183; CAAE 125; DAM MULT;
DLB 287; EW 10; EWL 3; RGWL 2, 3;
WP

Peterkin, Julia Mood 1880-1961 ...... **CLC 31**
See also CA 102; DLB 9

Peters, Joan K(aren) 1945- .... **CLC 39**
See also CA 158; CANR 109

Peters, Robert L(ouis) 1924- .... **CLC 7**
See also CA 13-16R; 8; CP 1, 5, 6, 7; DLB
105

Petofi, Sandor 1823-1849 .... **NCLC 21**
See also RGWL 2, 3

Powys, John Cowper 1872-1963 ... **CLC 7, 9, 15, 46, 125**
See also CA 85-88; CANR 106; DLB 15, 255; EWL 3; FANT; MTCW 1, 2; MTFW 2005; RGEL 2; SUFW

Powys, T(heodore) F(rancis)
1875-1953 .... **TCLC 9**
See also BRWS 8; CA 189; CAAE 106; DLB 36, 162; EWL 3; FANT; RGEL 2; SUFW

Pozzo, Modesta
See Fonte, Moderata

Prado (Calvo), Pedro 1886-1952 ... **TCLC 75**
See also CA 131; DLB 283; HW 1; LAW

Prager, Emily 1952- .... **CLC 56**
See also CA 204

Pratchett, Terry 1948- .... **CLC 197**
See also AAYA 19, 54; BPFB 3; CA 143; CANR 87, 126; CLR 64; CN 6, 7; CPW; CWRI 5; FANT; MTFW 2005; SATA 82, 139; SFW 4; SUFW 2

Pratolini, Vasco 1913-1991 .... **TCLC 124**
See also CA 211; DLB 177; EWL 3; RGWL 2, 3

Pratt, E(dwin) J(ohn) 1883(?)-1964 . **CLC 19**
See also CA 141; CAAS 93-96; CANR 77; DAC; DAM POET; DLB 92; EWL 3; RGEL 2; TWA

Premchand .... **TCLC 21**
See Srivastava, Dhanpat Rai
See also EWL 3

Prescott, William Hickling
1796-1859 .... **NCLC 163**
See also DLB 1, 30, 59, 235

Preseren, France 1800-1849 .... **NCLC 127**
See also CDWLB 4; DLB 147

Preussler, Otfried 1923- .... **CLC 17**
See also CA 77-80; SATA 24

Prevert, Jacques (Henri Marie)
1900-1977 .... **CLC 15**
See also CA 77-80; CAAS 69-72; CANR 29, 61; DLB 258; EWL 3; GFL 1789 to the Present; IDFW 3, 4; MTCW 1; RGWL 2, 3; SATA-Obit 30

Prevost, (Antoine Francois)
1697-1763 .... **LC 1**
See also DLB 314; EW 4; GFL Beginnings to 1789; RGWL 2, 3

Price, Reynolds 1933- .. **CLC 3, 6, 13, 43, 50, 63, 212; SSC 22**
See also AMWS 6; CA 1-4R; CANR 1, 37, 57, 87, 128; CN 1, 2, 3, 4, 5, 6, 7; CSW; DAM NOV; DLB 2, 218, 278; EWL 3; INT CANR-37; MAL 5; MTFW 2005; NFS 18

Price, Richard 1949- .... **CLC 6, 12**
See also CA 49-52; CANR 3, 147; CN 7; DLBY 1981

Prichard, Katharine Susannah
1883-1969 .... **CLC 46**
See also CA 11-12; CANR 33; CAP 1; DLB 260; MTCW 1; RGEL 2; RGSF 2; SATA 66

Priestley, J(ohn) B(oynton)
1894-1984 .... **CLC 2, 5, 9, 34**
See also BRW 7; CA 9-12R; CAAS 113; CANR 33; CDBLB 1914-1945; CN 1, 2, 3; DA3; DAM DRAM, NOV; DLB 10, 34, 77, 100, 139; DLBY 1984; EWL 3; MTCW 1, 2; MTFW 2005; RGEL 2; SFW 4

Prince 1958- .... **CLC 35**
See also CA 213

Prince, F(rank) T(empleton)
1912-2003 .... **CLC 22**
See also CA 101; CAAS 219; CANR 43, 79; CP 1, 2, 3, 4, 5, 6, 7; DLB 20

Prince Kropotkin
See Kropotkin, Peter (Aleksieevich)

Prior, Matthew 1664-1721 .... **LC 4**
See also DLB 95; RGEL 2

Prishvin, Mikhail 1873-1954 .... **TCLC 75**
See Prishvin, Mikhail Mikhailovich

Prishvin, Mikhail Mikhailovich
See Prishvin, Mikhail
See also DLB 272; EWL 3

Pritchard, William H(arrison)
1932- .... **CLC 34**
See also CA 65-68; CANR 23, 95; DLB 111

Pritchett, V(ictor) S(awdon)
1900-1997 ... **CLC 5, 13, 15, 41; SSC 14**
See also BPFB 3; BRWS 3; CA 61-64; CAAS 157; CANR 31, 63; CN 1, 2, 3, 4, 5, 6; DA3; DAM NOV; DLB 15, 139; EWL 3; MTCW 1, 2; MTFW 2005; RGEL 2; RGSF 2; TEA

Private 19022
See Manning, Frederic

Probst, Mark 1925- .... **CLC 59**
See also CA 130

Procaccino, Michael
See Cristofer, Michael

Proclus c. 412-c. 485 .... **CMLC 81**

Prokosch, Frederic 1908-1989 ...... **CLC 4, 48**
See also CA 73-76; CAAS 128; CANR 82; CN 1, 2, 3, 4; CP 1, 2, 3, 4; DLB 48; MTCW 2

Propertius, Sextus c. 50B.C.-c.
16B.C. .... **CMLC 32**
See also AW 2; CDWLB 1; DLB 211; RGWL 2, 3; WLIT 8

Prophet, The
See Dreiser, Theodore

Prose, Francine 1947- .... **CLC 45, 231**
See also AMWS 16; CA 112; CAAE 109; CANR 46, 95, 132; DLB 234; MTFW 2005; SATA 101, 149

Protagoras c. 490B.C.-420B.C. ...... **CMLC 85**
See also DLB 176

Proudhon
See Cunha, Euclides (Rodrigues Pimenta) da

Proulx, Annie
See Proulx, E. Annie

Proulx, E. Annie 1935- .... **CLC 81, 158**
See also AMWS 7; BPFB 3; CA 145; CANR 65, 110; CN 6, 7; CPW 1; DA3; DAM POP; DLB 335; MAL 5; MTCW 2; MTFW 2005; SSFS 18, 23

Proulx, Edna Annie
See Proulx, E. Annie

Proust, (Valentin-Louis-George-Eugene)
Marcel 1871-1922 ..... **SSC 75; TCLC 7, 13, 33; WLC 5**
See also AAYA 58; BPFB 3; CA 120; CAAE 104; CANR 110; DA; DA3; DAB; DAC; DAM MST, NOV; DLB 65; EW 8; EWL 3; GFL 1789 to the Present; MTCW 1, 2; MTFW 2005; RGWL 2, 3; TWA

Prowler, Harley
See Masters, Edgar Lee

Prudentius, Aurelius Clemens 348-c.
405 .... **CMLC 78**
See also EW 1; RGWL 2, 3

Prudhomme, Rene Francois Armand
1839-1907
See Sully Prudhomme, Rene-Francois-Armand
See also CA 170

Prus, Boleslaw 1845-1912 .... **TCLC 48**
See also RGWL 2, 3

Pryor, Aaron Richard
See Pryor, Richard

Pryor, Richard 1940-2005 .... **CLC 26**
See also CA 152; CAAE 122; CAAS 246

Pryor, Richard Franklin Lenox Thomas
See Pryor, Richard

Przybyszewski, Stanislaw
1868-1927 .... **TCLC 36**
See also CA 160; DLB 66; EWL 3

Pseudo-Dionysius the Areopagite fl. c. 5th
cent. - .... **CMLC 89**
See also DLB 115

Pteleon
See Grieve, C(hristopher) M(urray)
See also DAM POET

Puckett, Lute
See Masters, Edgar Lee

Puig, Manuel 1932-1990 .... **CLC 3, 5, 10, 28, 65, 133; HLC 2**
See also BPFB 3; CA 45-48; CANR 2, 32, 63; CDWLB 3; DA3; DAM MULT; DLB 113; DNFS 1; EWL 3; GLL 1; HW 1, 2; LAW; MTCW 1, 2; MTFW 2005; RGWL 2, 3; TWA; WLIT 1

Pulitzer, Joseph 1847-1911 .... **TCLC 76**
See also CAAE 114; DLB 23

Purchas, Samuel 1577(?)-1626 .... **LC 70**
See also DLB 151

Purdy, A(lfred) W(ellington)
1918-2000 .... **CLC 3, 6, 14, 50**
See also CA 81-84; 17; CAAS 189; CANR 42, 66; CP 1, 2, 3, 4, 5, 6, 7; DAC; DAM MST, POET; DLB 88; PFS 5; RGEL 2

Purdy, James (Amos) 1923- .... **CLC 2, 4, 10, 28, 52**
See also AMWS 7; CA 33-36R; 1; CANR 19, 51, 132; CN 1, 2, 3, 4, 5, 6, 7; DLB 2, 218; EWL 3; INT CANR-19; MAL 5; MTCW 1; RGAL 4

Pure, Simon
See Swinnerton, Frank Arthur

Pushkin, Aleksandr Sergeevich
See Pushkin, Alexander (Sergeyevich)
See also DLB 205

Pushkin, Alexander (Sergeyevich)
1799-1837 .... **NCLC 3, 27, 83; PC 10; SSC 27, 55, 99; WLC 5**
See Pushkin, Aleksandr Sergeevich
See also DA; DA3; DAB; DAC; DAM DRAM, MST, POET; EW 5; EXPS; RGSF 2; RGWL 2, 3; SATA 61; SSFS 9; TWA

P'u Sung-ling 1640-1715 .... **LC 49; SSC 31**

Putnam, Arthur Lee
See Alger, Horatio, Jr.

Puttenham, George 1529(?)-1590 ...... **LC 116**
See also DLB 281

Puzo, Mario 1920-1999 .... **CLC 1, 2, 6, 36, 107**
See also BPFB 3; CA 65-68; CAAS 185; CANR 4, 42, 65, 99, 131; CN 1, 2, 3, 4, 5, 6; CPW; DA3; DAM NOV, POP; DLB 6; MTCW 1, 2; MTFW 2005; NFS 16; RGAL 4

Pygge, Edward
See Barnes, Julian

Pyle, Ernest Taylor 1900-1945
See Pyle, Ernie
See also CA 160; CAAE 115

Pyle, Ernie .... **TCLC 75**
See Pyle, Ernest Taylor
See also DLB 29; MTCW 2

Pyle, Howard 1853-1911 .... **TCLC 81**
See also AAYA 57; BYA 2, 4; CA 137; CAAE 109; CLR 22, 117; DLB 42, 188; DLBD 13; LAIT 1; MAICYA 1, 2; SATA 16, 100; WCH; YAW

Pym, Barbara (Mary Crampton)
1913-1980 .... **CLC 13, 19, 37, 111**
See also BPFB 3; BRWS 2; CA 13-14; CAAS 97-100; CANR 13, 34; CAP 1; DLB 14, 207; DLBY 1987; EWL 3; MTCW 1, 2; MTFW 2005; RGEL 2; TEA

Pynchon, Thomas 1937- .. **CLC 2, 3, 6, 9, 11, 18, 33, 62, 72, 123, 192, 213; SSC 14, 84; WLC 5**
See also AMWS 2; BEST 90:2; BPFB 3; CA 17-20R; CANR 22, 46, 73, 142; CN 1, 2, 3, 4, 5, 6, 7; CPW 1; DA; DA3; DAB; DAC; DAM MST, NOV, POP; DLB 2, 173; EWL 3; MAL 5; MTCW 1, 2; MTFW 2005; NFS 23; RGAL 4; SFW 4; TCLE 1:2; TUS

Pythagoras c. 582B.C.-c. 507B.C. . **CMLC 22**
See also DLB 176

Q
See Quiller-Couch, Sir Arthur (Thomas)

Qian, Chongzhu
See Ch'ien, Chung-shu

Qian, Sima 145B.C.-c. 89B.C. .... **CMLC 72**

Qian Zhongshu
See Ch'ien, Chung-shu
See also CWW 2; DLB 328

Qroll
See Dagerman, Stig (Halvard)

Quarles, Francis 1592-1644 .... **LC 117**
See also DLB 126; RGEL 2

Quarrington, Paul (Lewis) 1953- ..... **CLC 65**
See also CA 129; CANR 62, 95

Quasimodo, Salvatore 1901-1968 .... **CLC 10; PC 47**
See also CA 13-16; CAAS 25-28R; CAP 1; DLB 114, 332; EW 12; EWL 3; MTCW 1; RGWL 2, 3

Quatermass, Martin
See Carpenter, John (Howard)

Quay, Stephen 1947- .... **CLC 95**
See also CA 189

Quay, Timothy 1947- .... **CLC 95**
See also CA 189

Queen, Ellery .... **CLC 3, 11**
See Dannay, Frederic; Davidson, Avram (James); Deming, Richard; Fairman, Paul W.; Flora, Fletcher; Hoch, Edward D(entinger); Kane, Henry; Lee, Manfred B.; Marlowe, Stephen; Powell, (Oval) Talmage; Sheldon, Walter J(ames); Sturgeon, Theodore (Hamilton); Tracy, Don(ald Fiske); Vance, Jack
See also BPFB 3; CMW 4; MSW; RGAL 4

Queen, Ellery, Jr.
See Dannay, Frederic; Lee, Manfred B.

Queneau, Raymond 1903-1976 ..... **CLC 2, 5, 10, 42**
See also CA 77-80; CAAS 69-72; CANR 32; DLB 72, 258; EW 12; EWL 3; GFL 1789 to the Present; MTCW 1, 2; RGWL 2, 3

Quevedo, Francisco de 1580-1645 .... **LC 23**

Quiller-Couch, Sir Arthur (Thomas) 1863-1944 .... **TCLC 53**
See also CA 166; CAAE 118; DLB 135, 153, 190; HGG; RGEL 2; SUFW 1

Quin, Ann 1936-1973 .... **CLC 6**
See also CA 9-12R; CAAS 45-48; CANR 148; CN 1; DLB 14, 231

Quin, Ann Marie
See Quin, Ann

Quincey, Thomas de
See De Quincey, Thomas

Quindlen, Anna 1953- .... **CLC 191**
See also AAYA 35; CA 138; CANR 73, 126; DA3; DLB 292; MTCW 2; MTFW 2005

Quinn, Martin
See Smith, Martin Cruz

Quinn, Peter 1947- .... **CLC 91**
See also CA 197; CANR 147

Quinn, Peter A.
See Quinn, Peter

Quinn, Simon
See Smith, Martin Cruz

Quintana, Leroy V. 1944- ...... **HLC 2; PC 36**
See also CA 131; CANR 65, 139; DAM MULT; DLB 82; HW 1, 2

Quintilian c. 40-c. 100 .... **CMLC 77**
See also AW 2; DLB 211; RGWL 2, 3

Quintillian 0035-0100 .... **CMLC 77**

Quiroga, Horacio (Sylvestre) 1878-1937 ... **HLC 2; SSC 89; TCLC 20**
See also CA 131; CAAE 117; DAM MULT; EWL 3; HW 1; LAW; MTCW 1; RGSF 2; WLIT 1

Quoirez, Francoise 1935-2004 .... **CLC 9**
See Sagan, Francoise
See also CA 49-52; CAAS 231; CANR 6, 39, 73; MTCW 1, 2; MTFW 2005; TWA

Raabe, Wilhelm (Karl) 1831-1910 . **TCLC 45**
See also CA 167; DLB 129

Rabe, David (William) 1940- .. **CLC 4, 8, 33, 200; DC 16**
See also CA 85-88; CABS 3; CAD; CANR 59, 129; CD 5, 6; DAM DRAM; DFS 3, 8, 13; DLB 7, 228; EWL 3; MAL 5

Rabelais, Francois 1494-1553 .... **LC 5, 60; WLC 5**
See also DA; DAB; DAC; DAM MST; DLB 327; EW 2; GFL Beginnings to 1789; LMFS 1; RGWL 2, 3; TWA

Rabi'a al-'Adawiyya c. 717-c. 801 .... **CMLC 83**
See also DLB 311

Rabinovitch, Sholem 1859-1916
See Sholom Aleichem
See also CAAE 104

Rabinyan, Dorit 1972- .... **CLC 119**
See also CA 170; CANR 147

Rachilde
See Vallette, Marguerite Eymery; Vallette, Marguerite Eymery
See also EWL 3

Racine, Jean 1639-1699 .... **LC 28, 113**
See also DA3; DAB; DAM MST; DLB 268; EW 3; GFL Beginnings to 1789; LMFS 1; RGWL 2, 3; TWA

Radcliffe, Ann (Ward) 1764-1823 ... **NCLC 6, 55, 106**
See also DLB 39, 178; GL 3; HGG; LMFS 1; RGEL 2; SUFW; WLIT 3

Radclyffe-Hall, Marguerite
See Hall, Radclyffe

Radiguet, Raymond 1903-1923 ...... **TCLC 29**
See also CA 162; DLB 65; EWL 3; GFL 1789 to the Present; RGWL 2, 3

Radnoti, Miklos 1909-1944 .... **TCLC 16**
See also CA 212; CAAE 118; CDWLB 4; DLB 215; EWL 3; RGHL; RGWL 2, 3

Rado, James 1939- .... **CLC 17**
See also CA 105

Radvanyi, Netty 1900-1983
See Seghers, Anna
See also CA 85-88; CAAS 110; CANR 82

Rae, Ben
See Griffiths, Trevor

Raeburn, John (Hay) 1941- .... **CLC 34**
See also CA 57-60

Ragni, Gerome 1942-1991 .... **CLC 17**
See also CA 105; CAAS 134

Rahv, Philip .... **CLC 24**
See Greenberg, Ivan
See also DLB 137; MAL 5

Raimund, Ferdinand Jakob 1790-1836 .... **NCLC 69**
See also DLB 90

Raine, Craig (Anthony) 1944- .. **CLC 32, 103**
See also CA 108; CANR 29, 51, 103; CP 3, 4, 5, 6, 7; DLB 40; PFS 7

Raine, Kathleen (Jessie) 1908-2003 .. **CLC 7, 45**
See also CA 85-88; CAAS 218; CANR 46, 109; CP 1, 2, 3, 4, 5, 6, 7; DLB 20; EWL 3; MTCW 1; RGEL 2

Rainis, Janis 1865-1929 .... **TCLC 29**
See also CA 170; CDWLB 4; DLB 220; EWL 3

Rakosi, Carl .... **CLC 47**
See Rawley, Callman
See also CA 5; CAAS 228; CP 1, 2, 3, 4, 5, 6, 7; DLB 193

Ralegh, Sir Walter
See Raleigh, Sir Walter
See also BRW 1; RGEL 2; WP

Raleigh, Richard
See Lovecraft, H. P.

Raleigh, Sir Walter 1554(?)-1618 .... **LC 31, 39; PC 31**
See Ralegh, Sir Walter
See also CDBLB Before 1660; DLB 172; EXPP; PFS 14; TEA

Rallentando, H. P.
See Sayers, Dorothy L(eigh)

Ramal, Walter
See de la Mare, Walter (John)

Ramana Maharshi 1879-1950 .... **TCLC 84**

Ramoacn y Cajal, Santiago 1852-1934 .... **TCLC 93**

Ramon, Juan
See Jimenez (Mantecon), Juan Ramon

Ramos, Graciliano 1892-1953 .... **TCLC 32**
See also CA 167; DLB 307; EWL 3; HW 2; LAW; WLIT 1

Rampersad, Arnold 1941- .... **CLC 44**
See also BW 2, 3; CA 133; CAAE 127; CANR 81; DLB 111; INT CA-133

Rampling, Anne
See Rice, Anne
See also GLL 2

Ramsay, Allan 1686(?)-1758 .... **LC 29**
See also DLB 95; RGEL 2

Ramsay, Jay
See Campbell, (John) Ramsey

Ramuz, Charles-Ferdinand 1878-1947 .... **TCLC 33**
See also CA 165; EWL 3

Rand, Ayn 1905-1982 ...... **CLC 3, 30, 44, 79; WLC 5**
See also AAYA 10; AMWS 4; BPFB 3; BYA 12; CA 13-16R; CAAS 105; CANR 27, 73; CDALBS; CN 1, 2, 3; CPW; DA; DA3; DAC; DAM MST, NOV, POP; DLB 227, 279; MTCW 1, 2; MTFW 2005; NFS 10, 16; RGAL 4; SFW 4; TUS; YAW

Randall, Dudley (Felker) 1914-2000 . **BLC 3; CLC 1, 135**
See also BW 1, 3; CA 25-28R; CAAS 189; CANR 23, 82; CP 1, 2, 3, 4, 5; DAM MULT; DLB 41; PFS 5

Randall, Robert
See Silverberg, Robert

Ranger, Ken
See Creasey, John

Rank, Otto 1884-1939 .... **TCLC 115**

Ransom, John Crowe 1888-1974 .. **CLC 2, 4, 5, 11, 24; PC 61**
See also AMW; CA 5-8R; CAAS 49-52; CANR 6, 34; CDALBS; CP 1, 2; DA3; DAM POET; DLB 45, 63; EWL 3; EXPP; MAL 5; MTCW 1, 2; MTFW 2005; RGAL 4; TUS

Rao, Raja 1908-2006 .... **CLC 25, 56; SSC 99**
See also CA 73-76; CAAS 252; CANR 51; CN 1, 2, 3, 4, 5, 6; DAM NOV; DLB 323; EWL 3; MTCW 1, 2; MTFW 2005; RGEL 2; RGSF 2

Raphael, Frederic (Michael) 1931- ... **CLC 2, 14**
See also CA 1-4R; CANR 1, 86; CN 1, 2, 3, 4, 5, 6, 7; DLB 14, 319; TCLE 1:2

Raphael, Lev 1954- .... **CLC 232**
See also CA 134; CANR 72, 145; GLL 1

Ratcliffe, James P.
See Mencken, H(enry) L(ouis)

Rathbone, Julian 1935- .... **CLC 41**
See also CA 101; CANR 34, 73, 152

Rattigan, Terence (Mervyn)
1911-1977 .... **CLC 7; DC 18**
See also BRWS 7; CA 85-88; CAAS 73-76; CBD; CDBLB 1945-1960; DAM DRAM; DFS 8; DLB 13; IDFW 3, 4; MTCW 1, 2; MTFW 2005; RGEL 2

Ratushinskaya, Irina 1954- .... **CLC 54**
See also CA 129; CANR 68; CWW 2

Raven, Simon (Arthur Noel)
1927-2001 .... **CLC 14**
See also CA 81-84; CAAS 197; CANR 86; CN 1, 2, 3, 4, 5, 6; DLB 271

Ravenna, Michael
See Welty, Eudora

Rawley, Callman 1903-2004
See Rakosi, Carl
See also CA 21-24R; CAAS 228; CANR 12, 32, 91

Rawlings, Marjorie Kinnan
1896-1953 .... **TCLC 4**
See also AAYA 20; AMWS 10; ANW; BPFB 3; BYA 3; CA 137; CAAE 104; CANR 74; CLR 63; DLB 9, 22, 102; DLBD 17; JRDA; MAICYA 1, 2; MAL 5; MTCW 2; MTFW 2005; RGAL 4; SATA 100; WCH; YABC 1; YAW

Ray, Satyajit 1921-1992 .... **CLC 16, 76**
See also CA 114; CAAS 137; DAM MULT

Read, Herbert Edward 1893-1968 ..... **CLC 4**
See also BRW 6; CA 85-88; CAAS 25-28R; DLB 20, 149; EWL 3; PAB; RGEL 2

Read, Piers Paul 1941- .... **CLC 4, 10, 25**
See also CA 21-24R; CANR 38, 86, 150; CN 2, 3, 4, 5, 6, 7; DLB 14; SATA 21

Reade, Charles 1814-1884 .... **NCLC 2, 74**
See also DLB 21; RGEL 2

Reade, Hamish
See Gray, Simon (James Holliday)

Reading, Peter 1946- .... **CLC 47**
See also BRWS 8; CA 103; CANR 46, 96; CP 5, 6, 7; DLB 40

Reaney, James 1926- .... **CLC 13**
See also CA 41-44R; 15; CANR 42; CD 5, 6; CP 1, 2, 3, 4, 5, 6, 7; DAC; DAM MST; DLB 68; RGEL 2; SATA 43

Rebreanu, Liviu 1885-1944 .... **TCLC 28**
See also CA 165; DLB 220; EWL 3

Rechy, John 1934- ..... **CLC 1, 7, 14, 18, 107; HLC 2**
See also CA 195; 5-8R, 195; 4; CANR 6, 32, 64, 152; CN 1, 2, 3, 4, 5, 6, 7; DAM MULT; DLB 122, 278; DLBY 1982; HW 1, 2; INT CANR-6; LLW; MAL 5; RGAL 4

Rechy, John Francisco
See Rechy, John

Redcam, Tom 1870-1933 .... **TCLC 25**

Reddin, Keith 1956- .... **CLC 67**
See also CAD; CD 6

Redgrove, Peter (William)
1932-2003 .... **CLC 6, 41**
See also BRWS 6; CA 1-4R; CAAS 217; CANR 3, 39, 77; CP 1, 2, 3, 4, 5, 6, 7; DLB 40; TCLE 1:2

Redmon, Anne .... **CLC 22**
See Nightingale, Anne Redmon
See also DLBY 1986

Reed, Eliot
See Ambler, Eric

Reed, Ishmael 1938- ..... **BLC 3; CLC 2, 3, 5, 6, 13, 32, 60, 174; PC 68**
See also AFAW 1, 2; AMWS 10; BPFB 3; BW 2, 3; CA 21-24R; CANR 25, 48, 74, 128; CN 1, 2, 3, 4, 5, 6, 7; CP 1, 2, 3, 4, 5, 6, 7; CSW; DA3; DAM MULT; DLB 2, 5, 33, 169, 227; DLBD 8; EWL 3; LMFS 2; MAL 5; MSW; MTCW 1, 2; MTFW 2005; PFS 6; RGAL 4; TCWW 2

Reed, John (Silas) 1887-1920 .... **TCLC 9**
See also CA 195; CAAE 106; MAL 5; TUS

Reed, Lou .... **CLC 21**
See Firbank, Louis

Reese, Lizette Woodworth
1856-1935 .... **PC 29; TCLC 181**
See also CA 180; DLB 54

Reeve, Clara 1729-1807 .... **NCLC 19**
See also DLB 39; RGEL 2

Reich, Wilhelm 1897-1957 .... **TCLC 57**
See also CA 199

Reid, Christopher (John) 1949- .... **CLC 33**
See also CA 140; CANR 89; CP 4, 5, 6, 7; DLB 40; EWL 3

Reid, Desmond
See Moorcock, Michael

Reid Banks, Lynne 1929-
See Banks, Lynne Reid
See also AAYA 49; CA 1-4R; CANR 6, 22, 38, 87; CLR 24; CN 1, 2, 3, 7; JRDA; MAICYA 1, 2; SATA 22, 75, 111, 165; YAW

Reilly, William K.
See Creasey, John

Reiner, Max
See Caldwell, (Janet Miriam) Taylor (Holland)

Reis, Ricardo
See Pessoa, Fernando (Antonio Nogueira)

Reizenstein, Elmer Leopold
See Rice, Elmer (Leopold)
See also EWL 3

Remarque, Erich Maria 1898-1970 . **CLC 21**
See also AAYA 27; BPFB 3; CA 77-80; CAAS 29-32R; CDWLB 2; DA; DA3; DAB; DAC; DAM MST, NOV; DLB 56; EWL 3; EXPN; LAIT 3; MTCW 1, 2; MTFW 2005; NFS 4; RGHL; RGWL 2, 3

Remington, Frederic S(ackrider)
1861-1909 .... **TCLC 89**
See also CA 169; CAAE 108; DLB 12, 186, 188; SATA 41; TCWW 2

Remizov, A.
See Remizov, Aleksei (Mikhailovich)

Remizov, A. M.
See Remizov, Aleksei (Mikhailovich)

Remizov, Aleksei (Mikhailovich)
1877-1957 .... **TCLC 27**
See Remizov, Alexey Mikhaylovich
See also CA 133; CAAE 125; DLB 295

Remizov, Alexey Mikhaylovich
See Remizov, Aleksei (Mikhailovich)
See also EWL 3

Renan, Joseph Ernest 1823-1892 . **NCLC 26, 145**
See also GFL 1789 to the Present

Renard, Jules(-Pierre) 1864-1910 .. **TCLC 17**
See also CA 202; CAAE 117; GFL 1789 to the Present

Renart, Jean fl. 13th cent. - .... **CMLC 83**

Renault, Mary .... **CLC 3, 11, 17**
See Challans, Mary
See also BPFB 3; BYA 2; CN 1, 2, 3; DLBY 1983; EWL 3; GLL 1; LAIT 1; RGEL 2; RHW

Rendell, Ruth 1930- .... **CLC 28, 48**
See Vine, Barbara
See also BPFB 3; BRWS 9; CA 109; CANR 32, 52, 74, 127, 162; CN 5, 6, 7; CPW; DAM POP; DLB 87, 276; INT CANR-32; MSW; MTCW 1, 2; MTFW 2005

Rendell, Ruth Barbara
See Rendell, Ruth

Renoir, Jean 1894-1979 .... **CLC 20**
See also CA 129; CAAS 85-88

Rensie, Willis
See Eisner, Will

Resnais, Alain 1922- .... **CLC 16**

Revard, Carter 1931- .... **NNAL**
See also CA 144; CANR 81, 153; PFS 5

Reverdy, Pierre 1889-1960 .... **CLC 53**
See also CA 97-100; CAAS 89-92; DLB 258; EWL 3; GFL 1789 to the Present

Rexroth, Kenneth 1905-1982 .... **CLC 1, 2, 6, 11, 22, 49, 112; PC 20**
See also BG 1:3; CA 5-8R; CAAS 107; CANR 14, 34, 63; CDALB 1941-1968; CP 1, 2, 3; DAM POET; DLB 16, 48, 165, 212; DLBY 1982; EWL 3; INT CANR-14; MAL 5; MTCW 1, 2; MTFW 2005; RGAL 4

Reyes, Alfonso 1889-1959 .... **HLCS 2; TCLC 33**
See also CA 131; EWL 3; HW 1; LAW

Reyes y Basoalto, Ricardo Eliecer Neftali
See Neruda, Pablo

Reymont, Wladyslaw (Stanislaw)
1868(?)-1925 .... **TCLC 5**
See also CAAE 104; DLB 332; EWL 3

Reynolds, John Hamilton
1794-1852 .... **NCLC 146**
See also DLB 96

Reynolds, Jonathan 1942- .... **CLC 6, 38**
See also CA 65-68; CANR 28

Reynolds, Joshua 1723-1792 .... **LC 15**
See also DLB 104

Reynolds, Michael S(hane)
1937-2000 .... **CLC 44**
See also CA 65-68; CAAS 189; CANR 9, 89, 97

Reznikoff, Charles 1894-1976 .... **CLC 9**
See also AMWS 14; CA 33-36; CAAS 61-64; CAP 2; CP 1, 2; DLB 28, 45; RGHL; WP

Rezzori, Gregor von
See Rezzori d'Arezzo, Gregor von

Rezzori d'Arezzo, Gregor von
1914-1998 .... **CLC 25**
See also CA 136; CAAE 122; CAAS 167

Rhine, Richard
See Silverstein, Alvin; Silverstein, Virginia B(arbara Opshelor)

Rhodes, Eugene Manlove
1869-1934 .... **TCLC 53**
See also CA 198; DLB 256; TCWW 1, 2

R'hoone, Lord
See Balzac, Honore de

Rhys, Jean 1890-1979 .... **CLC 2, 4, 6, 14, 19, 51, 124; SSC 21, 76**
See also BRWS 2; CA 25-28R; CAAS 85-88; CANR 35, 62; CDBLB 1945-1960; CDWLB 3; CN 1, 2; DA3; DAM NOV; DLB 36, 117, 162; DNFS 2; EWL 3; LATS 1:1; MTCW 1, 2; MTFW 2005; NFS 19; RGEL 2; RGSF 2; RHW; TEA; WWE 1

Ribeiro, Darcy 1922-1997 .... **CLC 34**
See also CA 33-36R; CAAS 156; EWL 3

Ribeiro, Joao Ubaldo (Osorio Pimentel)
1941- .... **CLC 10, 67**
See also CA 81-84; CWW 2; EWL 3

Ribman, Ronald (Burt) 1932- .... **CLC 7**
See also CA 21-24R; CAD; CANR 46, 80; CD 5, 6

Robinson, Edwin Arlington
1869-1935 .... **PC 1, 35; TCLC 5, 101**
See also AAYA 72; AMW; CA 133; CAAE
104; CDALB 1865-1917; DA; DAC;
DAM MST, POET; DLB 54; EWL 3;
EXPP; MAL 5; MTCW 1, 2; MTFW
2005; PAB; PFS 4; RGAL 4; WP

Robinson, Henry Crabb
1775-1867 .... **NCLC 15**
See also DLB 107

Robinson, Jill 1936- .... **CLC 10**
See also CA 102; CANR 120; INT CA-102

Robinson, Kim Stanley 1952- .... **CLC 34**
See also AAYA 26; CA 126; CANR 113,
139; CN 6, 7; MTFW 2005; SATA 109;
SCFW 2; SFW 4

Robinson, Lloyd
See Silverberg, Robert

Robinson, Marilynne 1944- ...... **CLC 25, 180**
See also AAYA 69; CA 116; CANR 80, 140;
CN 4, 5, 6, 7; DLB 206; MTFW 2005;
NFS 24

Robinson, Mary 1758-1800 .... **NCLC 142**
See also DLB 158; FW

Robinson, Smokey .... **CLC 21**
See Robinson, William, Jr.

Robinson, William, Jr. 1940-
See Robinson, Smokey
See also CAAE 116

Robison, Mary 1949- .... **CLC 42, 98**
See also CA 116; CAAE 113; CANR 87;
CN 4, 5, 6, 7; DLB 130; INT CA-116;
RGSF 2

Roches, Catherine des 1542-1587 ...... **LC 117**
See also DLB 327

Rochester
See Wilmot, John
See also RGEL 2

Rod, Edouard 1857-1910 .... **TCLC 52**

Roddenberry, Eugene Wesley 1921-1991
See Roddenberry, Gene
See also CA 110; CAAS 135; CANR 37;
SATA 45; SATA-Obit 69

Roddenberry, Gene .... **CLC 17**
See Roddenberry, Eugene Wesley
See also AAYA 5; SATA-Obit 69

Rodgers, Mary 1931- .... **CLC 12**
See also BYA 5; CA 49-52; CANR 8, 55,
90; CLR 20; CWRI 5; INT CANR-8;
JRDA; MAICYA 1, 2; SATA 8, 130

Rodgers, W(illiam) R(obert)
1909-1969 .... **CLC 7**
See also CA 85-88; DLB 20; RGEL 2

Rodman, Eric
See Silverberg, Robert

Rodman, Howard 1920(?)-1985 .... **CLC 65**
See also CAAS 118

Rodman, Maia
See Wojciechowska, Maia (Teresa)

Rodo, Jose Enrique 1871(?)-1917 .... **HLCS 2**
See also CA 178; EWL 3; HW 2; LAW

Rodolph, Utto
See Ouologuem, Yambo

Rodriguez, Claudio 1934-1999 .... **CLC 10**
See also CA 188; DLB 134

Rodriguez, Richard 1944- .... **CLC 155; HLC 2**
See also AMWS 14; CA 110; CANR 66,
116; DAM MULT; DLB 82, 256; HW 1,
2; LAIT 5; LLW; MTFW 2005; NCFS 3;
WLIT 1

Roelvaag, O(le) E(dvart) 1876-1931
See Rolvaag, O(le) E(dvart)
See also AAYA 75; CA 171; CAAE 117

Roethke, Theodore (Huebner)
1908-1963 .... **CLC 1, 3, 8, 11, 19, 46,
101; PC 15**
See also AMW; CA 81-84; CABS 2;
CDALB 1941-1968; DA3; DAM POET;
DLB 5, 206; EWL 3; EXPP; MAL 5;
MTCW 1, 2; PAB; PFS 3; RGAL 4; WP

Rogers, Carl R(ansom)
1902-1987 .... **TCLC 125**
See also CA 1-4R; CAAS 121; CANR 1,
18; MTCW 1

Rogers, Samuel 1763-1855 .... **NCLC 69**
See also DLB 93; RGEL 2

Rogers, Thomas Hunton 1927-2007 . **CLC 57**
See also CA 89-92; CANR 163; INT CA-
89-92

Rogers, Will(iam Penn Adair)
1879-1935 .... **NNAL; TCLC 8, 71**
See also CA 144; CAAE 105; DA3; DAM
MULT; DLB 11; MTCW 2

Rogin, Gilbert 1929- .... **CLC 18**
See also CA 65-68; CANR 15

Rohan, Koda
See Koda Shigeyuki

Rohlfs, Anna Katharine Green
See Green, Anna Katharine

Rohmer, Eric .... **CLC 16**
See Scherer, Jean-Marie Maurice

Rohmer, Sax .... **TCLC 28**
See Ward, Arthur Henry Sarsfield
See also DLB 70; MSW; SUFW

Roiphe, Anne 1935- .... **CLC 3, 9**
See also CA 89-92; CANR 45, 73, 138;
DLBY 1980; INT CA-89-92

Roiphe, Anne Richardson
See Roiphe, Anne

Rojas, Fernando de 1475-1541 ... **HLCS 1, 2;
LC 23**
See also DLB 286; RGWL 2, 3

Rojas, Gonzalo 1917- .... **HLCS 2**
See also CA 178; HW 2; LAWS 1

Roland (de la Platiere), Marie-Jeanne
1754-1793 .... **LC 98**
See also DLB 314

**Rolfe, Frederick (William Serafino Austin
Lewis Mary)** 1860-1913 .... **TCLC 12**
See Al Siddik
See also CA 210; CAAE 107; DLB 34, 156;
RGEL 2

Rolland, Romain 1866-1944 .... **TCLC 23**
See also CA 197; CAAE 118; DLB 65, 284,
332; EWL 3; GFL 1789 to the Present;
RGWL 2, 3

Rolle, Richard c. 1300-c. 1349 ...... **CMLC 21**
See also DLB 146; LMFS 1; RGEL 2

Rolvaag, O(le) E(dvart) .... **TCLC 17**
See Roelvaag, O(le) E(dvart)
See also DLB 9, 212; MAL 5; NFS 5;
RGAL 4

Romain Arnaud, Saint
See Aragon, Louis

Romains, Jules 1885-1972 .... **CLC 7**
See also CA 85-88; CANR 34; DLB 65,
321; EWL 3; GFL 1789 to the Present;
MTCW 1

Romero, Jose Ruben 1890-1952 .... **TCLC 14**
See also CA 131; CAAE 114; EWL 3; HW
1; LAW

Ronsard, Pierre de 1524-1585 . **LC 6, 54; PC
11**
See also DLB 327; EW 2; GFL Beginnings
to 1789; RGWL 2, 3; TWA

Rooke, Leon 1934- .... **CLC 25, 34**
See also CA 25-28R; CANR 23, 53; CCA
1; CPW; DAM POP

Roosevelt, Franklin Delano
1882-1945 .... **TCLC 93**
See also CA 173; CAAE 116; LAIT 3

Roosevelt, Theodore 1858-1919 ..... **TCLC 69**
See also CA 170; CAAE 115; DLB 47, 186,
275

Roper, William 1498-1578 .... **LC 10**

Roquelaure, A. N.
See Rice, Anne

Rosa, Joao Guimaraes 1908-1967 ... **CLC 23;
HLCS 1**
See Guimaraes Rosa, Joao
See also CAAS 89-92; DLB 113, 307; EWL
3; WLIT 1

Rose, Wendy 1948- . **CLC 85; NNAL; PC 13**
See also CA 53-56; CANR 5, 51; CWP;
DAM MULT; DLB 175; PFS 13; RGAL
4; SATA 12

Rosen, R. D.
See Rosen, Richard (Dean)

Rosen, Richard (Dean) 1949- .... **CLC 39**
See also CA 77-80; CANR 62, 120; CMW
4; INT CANR-30

Rosenberg, Isaac 1890-1918 .... **TCLC 12**
See also BRW 6; CA 188; CAAE 107; DLB
20, 216; EWL 3; PAB; RGEL 2

Rosenblatt, Joe .... **CLC 15**
See Rosenblatt, Joseph
See also CP 3, 4, 5, 6, 7

Rosenblatt, Joseph 1933-
See Rosenblatt, Joe
See also CA 89-92; CP 1, 2; INT CA-89-92

Rosenfeld, Samuel
See Tzara, Tristan

Rosenstock, Sami
See Tzara, Tristan

Rosenstock, Samuel
See Tzara, Tristan

Rosenthal, M(acha) L(ouis)
1917-1996 .... **CLC 28**
See also CA 1-4R; 6; CAAS 152; CANR 4,
51; CP 1, 2, 3, 4, 5, 6; DLB 5; SATA 59

Ross, Barnaby
See Dannay, Frederic; Lee, Manfred B.

Ross, Bernard L.
See Follett, Ken

Ross, J. H.
See Lawrence, T(homas) E(dward)

Ross, John Hume
See Lawrence, T(homas) E(dward)

Ross, Martin 1862-1915
See Martin, Violet Florence
See also DLB 135; GLL 2; RGEL 2; RGSF
2

Ross, (James) Sinclair 1908-1996 ... **CLC 13;
SSC 24**
See also CA 73-76; CANR 81; CN 1, 2, 3,
4, 5, 6; DAC; DAM MST; DLB 88;
RGEL 2; RGSF 2; TCWW 1, 2

Rossetti, Christina 1830-1894 ... **NCLC 2, 50,
66, 186; PC 7; WLC 5**
See also AAYA 51; BRW 5; BYA 4; CLR
115; DA; DA3; DAB; DAC; DAM MST,
POET; DLB 35, 163, 240; EXPP; FL 1:3;
LATS 1:1; MAICYA 1, 2; PFS 10, 14;
RGEL 2; SATA 20; TEA; WCH

Rossetti, Christina Georgina
See Rossetti, Christina

Rossetti, Dante Gabriel 1828-1882 . **NCLC 4,
77; WLC 5**
See also AAYA 51; BRW 5; CDBLB 1832-
1890; DA; DAB; DAC; DAM MST,
POET; DLB 35; EXPP; RGEL 2; TEA

Rossi, Cristina Peri
See Peri Rossi, Cristina

Rossi, Jean-Baptiste 1931-2003
See Japrisot, Sebastien
See also CA 201; CAAS 215

Saba, Umberto 1883-1957 .... **TCLC 33**
    See also CA 144; CANR 79; DLB 114;
    EWL 3; RGWL 2, 3
Sabatini, Rafael 1875-1950 .... **TCLC 47**
    See also BPFB 3; CA 162; RHW
Sabato, Ernesto 1911- ... **CLC 10, 23; HLC 2**
    See also CA 97-100; CANR 32, 65; CD-
    WLB 3; CWW 2; DAM MULT; DLB 145;
    EWL 3; HW 1, 2; LAW; MTCW 1, 2;
    MTFW 2005
Sa-Carneiro, Mario de 1890-1916 . **TCLC 83**
    See also DLB 287; EWL 3
Sacastru, Martin
    See Bioy Casares, Adolfo
    See also CWW 2
Sacher-Masoch, Leopold von
    1836(?)-1895 .... **NCLC 31**
Sachs, Hans 1494-1576 .... **LC 95**
    See also CDWLB 2; DLB 179; RGWL 2, 3
Sachs, Marilyn 1927- .... **CLC 35**
    See also AAYA 2; BYA 6; CA 17-20R;
    CANR 13, 47, 150; CLR 2; JRDA; MAI-
    CYA 1, 2; SAAS 2; SATA 3, 68, 164;
    SATA-Essay 110; WYA; YAW
Sachs, Marilyn Stickle
    See Sachs, Marilyn
Sachs, Nelly 1891-1970 .. **CLC 14, 98; PC 78**
    See also CA 17-18; CAAS 25-28R; CANR
    87; CAP 2; DLB 332; EWL 3; MTCW 2;
    MTFW 2005; PFS 20; RGHL; RGWL 2,
    3
Sackler, Howard (Oliver)
    1929-1982 .... **CLC 14**
    See also CA 61-64; CAAS 108; CAD;
    CANR 30; DFS 15; DLB 7
Sacks, Oliver 1933- .... **CLC 67, 202**
    See also CA 53-56; CANR 28, 50, 76, 146;
    CPW; DA3; INT CANR-28; MTCW 1, 2;
    MTFW 2005
Sacks, Oliver Wolf
    See Sacks, Oliver
Sackville, Thomas 1536-1608 .... **LC 98**
    See also DAM DRAM; DLB 62, 132;
    RGEL 2
Sadakichi
    See Hartmann, Sadakichi
Sa'dawi, Nawal al-
    See El Saadawi, Nawal
    See also CWW 2
Sade, Donatien Alphonse Francois
    1740-1814 .... **NCLC 3, 47**
    See also DLB 314; EW 4; GFL Beginnings
    to 1789; RGWL 2, 3
Sade, Marquis de
    See Sade, Donatien Alphonse Francois
Sadoff, Ira 1945- .... **CLC 9**
    See also CA 53-56; CANR 5, 21, 109; DLB
    120
Saetone
    See Camus, Albert
Safire, William 1929- .... **CLC 10**
    See also CA 17-20R; CANR 31, 54, 91, 148
Sagan, Carl 1934-1996 .... **CLC 30, 112**
    See also AAYA 2, 62; CA 25-28R; CAAS
    155; CANR 11, 36, 74; CPW; DA3;
    MTCW 1, 2; MTFW 2005; SATA 58;
    SATA-Obit 94
Sagan, Francoise .... **CLC 3, 6, 9, 17, 36**
    See Quoirez, Francoise
    See also CWW 2; DLB 83; EWL 3; GFL
    1789 to the Present; MTCW 2
Sahgal, Nayantara (Pandit) 1927- .... **CLC 41**
    See also CA 9-12R; CANR 11, 88; CN 1,
    2, 3, 4, 5, 6, 7; DLB 323
Said, Edward W. 1935-2003 .... **CLC 123**
    See also CA 21-24R; CAAS 220; CANR
    45, 74, 107, 131; DLB 67; MTCW 2;
    MTFW 2005

Saint, H(arry) F. 1941- .... **CLC 50**
    See also CA 127
St. Aubin de Teran, Lisa 1953-
    See Teran, Lisa St. Aubin de
    See also CA 126; CAAE 118; CN 6, 7; INT
    CA-126
Saint Birgitta of Sweden c.
    1303-1373 .... **CMLC 24**
Sainte-Beuve, Charles Augustin
    1804-1869 .... **NCLC 5**
    See also DLB 217; EW 6; GFL 1789 to the
    Present
Saint-Exupery, Antoine de
    1900-1944 .... **TCLC 2, 56, 169; WLC**
    See also AAYA 63; BPFB 3; BYA 3; CA
    132; CAAE 108; CLR 10; DA3; DAM
    NOV; DLB 72; EW 12; EWL 3; GFL
    1789 to the Present; LAIT 3; MAICYA 1,
    2; MTCW 1, 2; MTFW 2005; RGWL 2,
    3; SATA 20; TWA
Saint-Exupery, Antoine Jean Baptiste Marie
    Roger de
    See Saint-Exupery, Antoine de
St. John, David
    See Hunt, E. Howard
St. John, J. Hector
    See Crevecoeur, Michel Guillaume Jean de
Saint-John Perse
    See Leger, (Marie-Rene Auguste) Alexis
    Saint-Leger
    See also EW 10; EWL 3; GFL 1789 to the
    Present; RGWL 2
Saintsbury, George (Edward Bateman)
    1845-1933 .... **TCLC 31**
    See also CA 160; DLB 57, 149
Sait Faik .... **TCLC 23**
    See Abasiyanik, Sait Faik
Saki .... **SSC 12; TCLC 3; WLC 5**
    See Munro, H(ector) H(ugh)
    See also BRWS 6; BYA 11; LAIT 2; RGEL
    2; SSFS 1; SUFW
Sala, George Augustus 1828-1895 . **NCLC 46**
Saladin 1138-1193 .... **CMLC 38**
Salama, Hannu 1936- .... **CLC 18**
    See also CA 244; EWL 3
Salamanca, J(ack) R(ichard) 1922- .. **CLC 4,**
    15
    See also CA 193; 25-28R, 193
Salas, Floyd Francis 1931- .... **HLC 2**
    See also CA 119; 27; CANR 44, 75, 93;
    DAM MULT; DLB 82; HW 1, 2; MTCW
    2; MTFW 2005
Sale, J. Kirkpatrick
    See Sale, Kirkpatrick
Sale, John Kirkpatrick
    See Sale, Kirkpatrick
Sale, Kirkpatrick 1937- .... **CLC 68**
    See also CA 13-16R; CANR 10, 147
Salinas, Luis Omar 1937- ... **CLC 90; HLC 2**
    See also AMWS 13; CA 131; CANR 81,
    153; DAM MULT; DLB 82; HW 1, 2
Salinas (y Serrano), Pedro
    1891(?)-1951 .... **TCLC 17**
    See also CAAE 117; DLB 134; EWL 3
Salinger, J.D. 1919- . **CLC 1, 3, 8, 12, 55, 56,**
    138; SSC 2, 28, 65; WLC 5
    See also AAYA 2, 36; AMW; AMWC 1;
    BPFB 3; CA 5-8R; CANR 39, 129;
    CDALB 1941-1968; CLR 18; CN 1, 2, 3,
    4, 5, 6, 7; CPW 1; DA; DA3; DAB; DAC;
    DAM MST, NOV, POP; DLB 2, 102, 173;
    EWL 3; EXPN; LAIT 4; MAICYA 1, 2;
    MAL 5; MTCW 1, 2; MTFW 2005; NFS
    1; RGAL 4; RGSF 2; SATA 67; SSFS 17;
    TUS; WYA; YAW
Salisbury, John
    See Caute, (John) David

Sallust c. 86B.C.-35B.C. .... **CMLC 68**
    See also AW 2; CDWLB 1; DLB 211;
    RGWL 2, 3
Salter, James 1925- .. **CLC 7, 52, 59; SSC 58**
    See also AMWS 9; CA 73-76; CANR 107,
    160; DLB 130
Saltus, Edgar (Everton) 1855-1921 . **TCLC 8**
    See also CAAE 105; DLB 202; RGAL 4
Saltykov, Mikhail Evgrafovich
    1826-1889 .... **NCLC 16**
    See also DLB 238:
Saltykov-Shchedrin, N.
    See Saltykov, Mikhail Evgrafovich
Samarakis, Andonis
    See Samarakis, Antonis
    See also EWL 3
Samarakis, Antonis 1919-2003 .... **CLC 5**
    See Samarakis, Andonis
    See also CA 25-28R; 16; CAAS 224; CANR
    36
Sanchez, Florencio 1875-1910 .... **TCLC 37**
    See also CA 153; DLB 305; EWL 3; HW 1;
    LAW
Sanchez, Luis Rafael 1936- .... **CLC 23**
    See also CA 128; DLB 305; EWL 3; HW 1;
    WLIT 1
Sanchez, Sonia 1934- .... **BLC 3; CLC 5, 116,**
    215; PC 9
    See also BW 2, 3; CA 33-36R; CANR 24,
    49, 74, 115; CLR 18; CP 2, 3, 4, 5, 6, 7;
    CSW; CWP; DA3; DAM MULT; DLB 41;
    DLBD 8; EWL 3; MAICYA 1, 2; MAL 5;
    MTCW 1, 2; MTFW 2005; SATA 22, 136;
    WP
Sancho, Ignatius 1729-1780 .... **LC 84**
Sand, George 1804-1876 ..... **NCLC 2, 42, 57,**
    174; WLC 5
    See also DA; DA3; DAB; DAC; DAM
    MST, NOV; DLB 119, 192; EW 6; FL 1:3;
    FW; GFL 1789 to the Present; RGWL 2,
    3; TWA
Sandburg, Carl (August) 1878-1967 . **CLC 1,**
    4, 10, 15, 35; PC 2, 41; WLC 5
    See also AAYA 24; AMW; BYA 1, 3; CA
    5-8R; CAAS 25-28R; CANR 35; CDALB
    1865-1917; CLR 67; DA; DA3; DAB;
    DAC; DAM MST, POET; DLB 17, 54,
    284; EWL 3; EXPP; LAIT 2; MAICYA 1,
    2; MAL 5; MTCW 1, 2; MTFW 2005;
    PAB; PFS 3, 6, 12; RGAL 4; SATA 8;
    TUS; WCH; WP; WYA
Sandburg, Charles
    See Sandburg, Carl (August)
Sandburg, Charles A.
    See Sandburg, Carl (August)
Sanders, (James) Ed(ward) 1939- .... **CLC 53**
    See Sanders, Edward
    See also BG 1:3; CA 13-16R; 21; CANR
    13, 44, 78; CP 1, 2, 3, 4, 5, 6, 7; DAM
    POET; DLB 16, 244
Sanders, Edward
    See Sanders, (James) Ed(ward)
    See also DLB 244
Sanders, Lawrence 1920-1998 .... **CLC 41**
    See also BEST 89:4; BPFB 3; CA 81-84;
    CAAS 165; CANR 33, 62; CMW 4;
    CPW; DA3; DAM POP; MTCW 1
Sanders, Noah
    See Blount, Roy (Alton), Jr.
Sanders, Winston P.
    See Anderson, Poul
Sandoz, Mari(e Susette) 1900-1966 .. **CLC 28**
    See also CA 1-4R; CAAS 25-28R; CANR
    17, 64; DLB 9, 212; LAIT 2; MTCW 1,
    2; SATA 5; TCWW 1, 2
Sandys, George 1578-1644 .... **LC 80**
    See also DLB 24, 121
Saner, Reg(inald Anthony) 1931- .... **CLC 9**
    See also CA 65-68; CP 3, 4, 5, 6, 7

Schnitzler, Arthur 1862-1931 ..... **DC 17; SSC 15, 61; TCLC 4**
See also CAAE 104; CDWLB 2; DLB 81, 118; EW 8; EWL 3; RGSF 2; RGWL 2, 3

Schoenberg, Arnold Franz Walter 1874-1951 .... **TCLC 75**
See also CA 188; CAAE 109

Schonberg, Arnold
See Schoenberg, Arnold Franz Walter

Schopenhauer, Arthur 1788-1860 . **NCLC 51, 157**
See also DLB 90; EW 5

Schor, Sandra (M.) 1932(?)-1990 ..... **CLC 65**
See also CAAS 132

Schorer, Mark 1908-1977 .... **CLC 9**
See also CA 5-8R; CAAS 73-76; CANR 7; CN 1, 2; DLB 103

Schrader, Paul (Joseph) 1946- . **CLC 26, 212**
See also CA 37-40R; CANR 41; DLB 44

Schreber, Daniel 1842-1911 .... **TCLC 123**

Schreiner, Olive (Emilie Albertina) 1855-1920 .... **TCLC 9**
See also AFW; BRWS 2; CA 154; CAAE 105; DLB 18, 156, 190, 225; EWL 3; FW; RGEL 2; TWA; WLIT 1; WWE 1

Schulberg, Budd (Wilson) 1914- .. **CLC 7, 48**
See also BPFB 3; CA 25-28R; CANR 19, 87; CN 1, 2, 3, 4, 5, 6, 7; DLB 6, 26, 28; DLBY 1981, 2001; MAL 5

Schulman, Arnold
See Trumbo, Dalton

Schulz, Bruno 1892-1942 .. **SSC 13; TCLC 5, 51**
See also CA 123; CAAE 115; CANR 86; CDWLB 4; DLB 215; EWL 3; MTCW 2; MTFW 2005; RGSF 2; RGWL 2, 3

Schulz, Charles M. 1922-2000 .... **CLC 12**
See also AAYA 39; CA 9-12R; CAAS 187; CANR 6, 132; INT CANR-6; MTFW 2005; SATA 10; SATA-Obit 118

Schulz, Charles Monroe
See Schulz, Charles M.

Schumacher, E(rnst) F(riedrich) 1911-1977 .... **CLC 80**
See also CA 81-84; CAAS 73-76; CANR 34, 85

Schumann, Robert 1810-1856 ...... **NCLC 143**

Schuyler, George Samuel 1895-1977 . **HR 1:3**
See also BW 2; CA 81-84; CAAS 73-76; CANR 42; DLB 29, 51

Schuyler, James Marcus 1923-1991 .. **CLC 5, 23**
See also CA 101; CAAS 134; CP 1, 2, 3, 4, 5; DAM POET; DLB 5, 169; EWL 3; INT CA-101; MAL 5; WP

Schwartz, Delmore (David) 1913-1966 ... **CLC 2, 4, 10, 45, 87; PC 8**
See also AMWS 2; CA 17-18; CAAS 25-28R; CANR 35; CAP 2; DLB 28, 48; EWL 3; MAL 5; MTCW 1, 2; MTFW 2005; PAB; RGAL 4; TUS

Schwartz, Ernst
See Ozu, Yasujiro

Schwartz, John Burnham 1965- .... **CLC 59**
See also CA 132; CANR 116

Schwartz, Lynne Sharon 1939- .... **CLC 31**
See also CA 103; CANR 44, 89, 160; DLB 218; MTCW 2; MTFW 2005

Schwartz, Muriel A.
See Eliot, T(homas) S(tearns)

Schwarz-Bart, Andre 1928-2006 .... **CLC 2, 4**
See also CA 89-92; CAAS 253; CANR 109; DLB 299; RGHL

Schwarz-Bart, Simone 1938- . **BLCS; CLC 7**
See also BW 2; CA 97-100; CANR 117; EWL 3

Schwerner, Armand 1927-1999 .... **PC 42**
See also CA 9-12R; CAAS 179; CANR 50, 85; CP 2, 3, 4, 5, 6; DLB 165

Schwitters, Kurt (Hermann Edward Karl Julius) 1887-1948 .... **TCLC 95**
See also CA 158

Schwob, Marcel (Mayer Andre) 1867-1905 .... **TCLC 20**
See also CA 168; CAAE 117; DLB 123; GFL 1789 to the Present

Sciascia, Leonardo 1921-1989 .. **CLC 8, 9, 41**
See also CA 85-88; CAAS 130; CANR 35; DLB 177; EWL 3; MTCW 1; RGWL 2, 3

Scoppettone, Sandra 1936- .... **CLC 26**
See Early, Jack
See also AAYA 11, 65; BYA 8; CA 5-8R; CANR 41, 73, 157; GLL 1; MAICYA 2; MAICYAS 1; SATA 9, 92; WYA; YAW

Scorsese, Martin 1942- .... **CLC 20, 89, 207**
See also AAYA 38; CA 114; CAAE 110; CANR 46, 85

Scotland, Jay
See Jakes, John

Scott, Duncan Campbell 1862-1947 .... **TCLC 6**
See also CA 153; CAAE 104; DAC; DLB 92; RGEL 2

Scott, Evelyn 1893-1963 .... **CLC 43**
See also CA 104; CAAS 112; CANR 64; DLB 9, 48; RHW

Scott, F(rancis) R(eginald) 1899-1985 .... **CLC 22**
See also CA 101; CAAS 114; CANR 87; CP 1, 2, 3, 4; DLB 88; INT CA-101; RGEL 2

Scott, Frank
See Scott, F(rancis) R(eginald)

Scott, Joan .... **CLC 65**

Scott, Joanna 1960- .... **CLC 50**
See also CA 126; CANR 53, 92

Scott, Paul (Mark) 1920-1978 ...... **CLC 9, 60**
See also BRWS 1; CA 81-84; CAAS 77-80; CANR 33; CN 1, 2; DLB 14, 207, 326; EWL 3; MTCW 1; RGEL 2; RHW; WWE 1

Scott, Ridley 1937- .... **CLC 183**
See also AAYA 13, 43

Scott, Sarah 1723-1795 .... **LC 44**
See also DLB 39

Scott, Sir Walter 1771-1832 .... **NCLC 15, 69, 110; PC 13; SSC 32; WLC 5**
See also AAYA 22; BRW 4; BYA 2; CD-BLB 1789-1832; DA; DAB; DAC; DAM MST, NOV, POET; DLB 93, 107, 116, 144, 159; GL 3; HGG; LAIT 1; RGEL 2; RGSF 2; SSFS 10; SUFW 1; TEA; WLIT 3; YABC 2

Scribe, (Augustin) Eugene 1791-1861 . **DC 5; NCLC 16**
See also DAM DRAM; DLB 192; GFL 1789 to the Present; RGWL 2, 3

Scrum, R.
See Crumb, R.

Scudery, Georges de 1601-1667 .... **LC 75**
See also GFL Beginnings to 1789

Scudery, Madeleine de 1607-1701 .. **LC 2, 58**
See also DLB 268; GFL Beginnings to 1789

Scum
See Crumb, R.

Scumbag, Little Bobby
See Crumb, R.

Seabrook, John
See Hubbard, L. Ron

Seacole, Mary Jane Grant 1805-1881 .... **NCLC 147**
See also DLB 166

Sealy, I(rwin) Allan 1951- .... **CLC 55**
See also CA 136; CN 6, 7

Search, Alexander
See Pessoa, Fernando (Antonio Nogueira)

Sebald, W(infried) G(eorg) 1944-2001 .... **CLC 194**
See also BRWS 8; CA 159; CAAS 202; CANR 98; MTFW 2005; RGHL

Sebastian, Lee
See Silverberg, Robert

Sebastian Owl
See Thompson, Hunter S.

Sebestyen, Igen
See Sebestyen, Ouida

Sebestyen, Ouida 1924- .... **CLC 30**
See also AAYA 8; BYA 7; CA 107; CANR 40, 114; CLR 17; JRDA; MAICYA 1, 2; SAAS 10; SATA 39, 140; WYA; YAW

Sebold, Alice 1963(?)- .... **CLC 193**
See also AAYA 56; CA 203; MTFW 2005

Second Duke of Buckingham
See Villiers, George

Secundus, H. Scriblerus
See Fielding, Henry

Sedges, John
See Buck, Pearl S(ydenstricker)

Sedgwick, Catharine Maria 1789-1867 .... **NCLC 19, 98**
See also DLB 1, 74, 183, 239, 243, 254; FL 1:3; RGAL 4

Sedulius Scottus 9th cent. -c. 874 .. **CMLC 86**

Seelye, John (Douglas) 1931- .... **CLC 7**
See also CA 97-100; CANR 70; INT CA-97-100; TCWW 1, 2

Seferiades, Giorgos Stylianou 1900-1971
See Seferis, George
See also CA 5-8R; CAAS 33-36R; CANR 5, 36; MTCW 1

Seferis, George .... **CLC 5, 11; PC 66**
See Seferiades, Giorgos Stylianou
See also DLB 332; EW 12; EWL 3; RGWL 2, 3

Segal, Erich (Wolf) 1937- .... **CLC 3, 10**
See also BEST 89:1; BPFB 3; CA 25-28R; CANR 20, 36, 65, 113; CPW; DAM POP; DLBY 1986; INT CANR-20; MTCW 1

Seger, Bob 1945- .... **CLC 35**

Seghers, Anna .... **CLC 7**
See Radvanyi, Netty
See also CDWLB 2; DLB 69; EWL 3

Seidel, Frederick (Lewis) 1936- .... **CLC 18**
See also CA 13-16R; CANR 8, 99; CP 1, 2, 3, 4, 5, 6, 7; DLBY 1984

Seifert, Jaroslav 1901-1986 . **CLC 34, 44, 93; PC 47**
See also CA 127; CDWLB 4; DLB 215, 332; EWL 3; MTCW 1, 2

Sei Shonagon c. 966-1017(?) ..... **CMLC 6, 89**

Sejour, Victor 1817-1874 .... **DC 10**
See also DLB 50

Sejour Marcou et Ferrand, Juan Victor
See Sejour, Victor

Selby, Hubert, Jr. 1928-2004 ..... **CLC 1, 2, 4, 8; SSC 20**
See also CA 13-16R; CAAS 226; CANR 33, 85; CN 1, 2, 3, 4, 5, 6, 7; DLB 2, 227; MAL 5

Selzer, Richard 1928- .... **CLC 74**
See also CA 65-68; CANR 14, 106

Sembene, Ousmane
See Ousmane, Sembene
See also AFW; EWL 3; WLIT 2

Senancour, Etienne Pivert de 1770-1846 .... **NCLC 16**
See also DLB 119; GFL 1789 to the Present

Sender, Ramon (Jose) 1902-1982 ...... **CLC 8; HLC 2; TCLC 136**
See also CA 5-8R; CAAS 105; CANR 8; DAM MULT; DLB 322; EWL 3; HW 1; MTCW 1; RGWL 2, 3

Shepard, James R.
See Shepard, Jim

Shepard, Jim 1956- .... **CLC 36**
See also AAYA 73; CA 137; CANR 59, 104, 160; SATA 90, 164

Shepard, Lucius 1947- .... **CLC 34**
See also CA 141; CAAE 128; CANR 81, 124; HGG; SCFW 2; SFW 4; SUFW 2

Shepard, Sam 1943- .... **CLC 4, 6, 17, 34, 41, 44, 169; DC 5**
See also AAYA 1, 58; AMWS 3; CA 69-72; CABS 3; CAD; CANR 22, 120, 140; CD 5, 6; DA3; DAM DRAM; DFS 3, 6, 7, 14; DLB 7, 212; EWL 3; IDFW 3, 4; MAL 5; MTCW 1, 2; MTFW 2005; RGAL 4

Shepherd, Jean (Parker)
1921-1999 .... **TCLC 177**
See also AAYA 69; AITN 2; CA 77-80; CAAS 187

Shepherd, Michael
See Ludlum, Robert

Sherburne, Zoa (Lillian Morin)
1912-1995 .... **CLC 30**
See also AAYA 13; CA 1-4R; CAAS 176; CANR 3, 37; MAICYA 1, 2; SAAS 18; SATA 3; YAW

Sheridan, Frances 1724-1766 .... **LC 7**
See also DLB 39, 84

Sheridan, Richard Brinsley
1751-1816 . **DC 1; NCLC 5, 91; WLC 5**
See also BRW 3; CDBLB 1660-1789; DA; DAB; DAC; DAM DRAM, MST; DFS 15; DLB 89; WLIT 3

Sherman, Jonathan Marc 1968- .... **CLC 55**
See also CA 230

Sherman, Martin 1941(?)- .... **CLC 19**
See also CA 123; CAAE 116; CAD; CANR 86; CD 5, 6; DFS 20; DLB 228; GLL 1; IDTP; RGHL

Sherwin, Judith Johnson
See Johnson, Judith (Emlyn)
See also CANR 85; CP 2, 3, 4, 5; CWP

Sherwood, Frances 1940- .... **CLC 81**
See also CA 220; 146, 220; CANR 158

Sherwood, Robert E(mmet)
1896-1955 .... **TCLC 3**
See also CA 153; CAAE 104; CANR 86; DAM DRAM; DFS 11, 15, 17; DLB 7, 26, 249; IDFW 3, 4; MAL 5; RGAL 4

Shestov, Lev 1866-1938 .... **TCLC 56**

Shevchenko, Taras 1814-1861 .... **NCLC 54**

Shiel, M(atthew) P(hipps)
1865-1947 .... **TCLC 8**
See Holmes, Gordon
See also CA 160; CAAE 106; DLB 153; HGG; MTCW 2; MTFW 2005; SCFW 1, 2; SFW 4; SUFW

Shields, Carol 1935-2003 .. **CLC 91, 113, 193**
See also AMWS 7; CA 81-84; CAAS 218; CANR 51, 74, 98, 133; CCA 1; CN 6, 7; CPW; DA3; DAC; DLB 334; MTCW 2; MTFW 2005; NFS 23

Shields, David 1956- .... **CLC 97**
See also CA 124; CANR 48, 99, 112, 157

Shields, David Jonathan
See Shields, David

Shiga, Naoya 1883-1971 .... **CLC 33; SSC 23; TCLC 172**
See Shiga Naoya
See also CA 101; CAAS 33-36R; MJW; RGWL 3

Shiga Naoya
See Shiga, Naoya
See also DLB 180; EWL 3; RGWL 3

Shilts, Randy 1951-1994 .... **CLC 85**
See also AAYA 19; CA 127; CAAE 115; CAAS 144; CANR 45; DA3; GLL 1; INT CA-127; MTCW 2; MTFW 2005

Shimazaki, Haruki 1872-1943
See Shimazaki Toson
See also CA 134; CAAE 105; CANR 84; RGWL 3

Shimazaki Toson .... **TCLC 5**
See Shimazaki, Haruki
See also DLB 180; EWL 3

Shirley, James 1596-1666 .... **DC 25; LC 96**
See also DLB 58; RGEL 2

Shirley Hastings, Selina
See Hastings, Selina

Sholokhov, Mikhail (Aleksandrovich)
1905-1984 .... **CLC 7, 15**
See also CA 101; CAAS 112; DLB 272, 332; EWL 3; MTCW 1, 2; MTFW 2005; RGWL 2, 3; SATA-Obit 36

Sholom Aleichem 1859-1916 .... **SSC 33; TCLC 1, 35**
See Rabinovitch, Sholem
See also DLB 333; TWA

Shone, Patric
See Hanley, James

Showalter, Elaine 1941- .... **CLC 169**
See also CA 57-60; CANR 58, 106; DLB 67; FW; GLL 2

Shreve, Susan
See Shreve, Susan Richards

Shreve, Susan Richards 1939- .... **CLC 23**
See also CA 49-52; 5; CANR 5, 38, 69, 100, 159; MAICYA 1, 2; SATA 46, 95, 152; SATA-Brief 41

Shue, Larry 1946-1985 .... **CLC 52**
See also CA 145; CAAS 117; DAM DRAM; DFS 7

Shu-Jen, Chou 1881-1936
See Lu Hsun
See also CAAE 104

Shulman, Alix Kates 1932- .... **CLC 2, 10**
See also CA 29-32R; CANR 43; FW; SATA 7

Shuster, Joe 1914-1992 .... **CLC 21**
See also AAYA 50

Shute, Nevil .... **CLC 30**
See Norway, Nevil Shute
See also BPFB 3; DLB 255; NFS 9; RHW; SFW 4

Shuttle, Penelope (Diane) 1947- .... **CLC 7**
See also CA 93-96; CANR 39, 84, 92, 108; CP 3, 4, 5, 6, 7; CWP; DLB 14, 40

Shvarts, Elena 1948- .... **PC 50**
See also CA 147

Sidhwa, Bapsi 1939-
See Sidhwa, Bapsi (N.)
See also CN 6, 7; DLB 323

Sidhwa, Bapsy (N.) 1938- .... **CLC 168**
See Sidhwa, Bapsi
See also CA 108; CANR 25, 57; FW

Sidney, Mary 1561-1621 .... **LC 19, 39**
See Sidney Herbert, Mary

Sidney, Sir Philip 1554-1586 .... **LC 19, 39, 131; PC 32**
See also BRW 1; BRWR 2; CDBLB Before 1660; DA; DA3; DAB; DAC; DAM MST, POET; DLB 167; EXPP; PAB; RGEL 2; TEA; WP

Sidney Herbert, Mary
See Sidney, Mary
See also DLB 167

Siegel, Jerome 1914-1996 .... **CLC 21**
See Siegel, Jerry
See also CA 169; CAAE 116; CAAS 151

Siegel, Jerry
See Siegel, Jerome
See also AAYA 50

Sienkiewicz, Henryk (Adam Alexander Pius)
1846-1916 .... **TCLC 3**
See also CA 134; CAAE 104; CANR 84; DLB 332; EWL 3; RGSF 2; RGWL 2, 3

Sierra, Gregorio Martinez
See Martinez Sierra, Gregorio

Sierra, Maria de la O'LeJarraga Martinez
See Martinez Sierra, Maria

Sigal, Clancy 1926- .... **CLC 7**
See also CA 1-4R; CANR 85; CN 1, 2, 3, 4, 5, 6, 7

Siger of Brabant 1240(?)-1284(?) . **CMLC 69**
See also DLB 115

Sigourney, Lydia H.
See Sigourney, Lydia Howard (Huntley)
See also DLB 73, 183

Sigourney, Lydia Howard (Huntley)
1791-1865 .... **NCLC 21, 87**
See Sigourney, Lydia H.; Sigourney, Lydia Huntley
See also DLB 1

Sigourney, Lydia Huntley
See Sigourney, Lydia Howard (Huntley)
See also DLB 42, 239, 243

Siguenza y Gongora, Carlos de
1645-1700 .... **HLCS 2; LC 8**
See also LAW

Sigurjonsson, Johann
See Sigurjonsson, Johann

Sigurjonsson, Johann 1880-1919 ... **TCLC 27**
See also CA 170; DLB 293; EWL 3

Sikelianos, Angelos 1884-1951 .... **PC 29; TCLC 39**
See also EWL 3; RGWL 2, 3

Silkin, Jon 1930-1997 .... **CLC 2, 6, 43**
See also CA 5-8R; 5; CANR 89; CP 1, 2, 3, 4, 5, 6; DLB 27

Silko, Leslie 1948- ...... **CLC 23, 74, 114, 211; NNAL; SSC 37, 66; WLCS**
See also AAYA 14; AMWS 4; ANW; BYA 12; CA 122; CAAE 115; CANR 45, 65, 118; CN 4, 5, 6, 7; CP 4, 5, 6, 7; CPW 1; CWP; DA; DA3; DAC; DAM MST, MULT, POP; DLB 143, 175, 256, 275; EWL 3; EXPP; EXPS; LAIT 4; MAL 5; MTCW 2; MTFW 2005; NFS 4; PFS 9, 16; RGAL 4; RGSF 2; SSFS 4, 8, 10, 11; TCWW 1, 2

Sillanpaa, Frans Eemil 1888-1964 ... **CLC 19**
See also CA 129; CAAS 93-96; DLB 332; EWL 3; MTCW 1

Sillitoe, Alan 1928- .. **CLC 1, 3, 6, 10, 19, 57, 148**
See also AITN 1; BRWS 5; CA 191; 9-12R, 191; 2; CANR 8, 26, 55, 139; CDBLB 1960 to Present; CN 1, 2, 3, 4, 5, 6; CP 1, 2, 3, 4, 5; DLB 14, 139; EWL 3; MTCW 1, 2; MTFW 2005; RGEL 2; RGSF 2; SATA 61

Silone, Ignazio 1900-1978 .... **CLC 4**
See also CA 25-28; CAAS 81-84; CANR 34; CAP 2; DLB 264; EW 12; EWL 3; MTCW 1; RGSF 2; RGWL 2, 3

Silone, Ignazione
See Silone, Ignazio

Silver, Joan Micklin 1935- .... **CLC 20**
See also CA 121; CAAE 114; INT CA-121

Silver, Nicholas
See Faust, Frederick (Schiller)

Silverberg, Robert 1935- .... **CLC 7, 140**
See also AAYA 24; BPFB 3; BYA 7, 9; CA 186; 1-4R, 186; 3; CANR 1, 20, 36, 85, 140; CLR 59; CN 6, 7; CPW; DAM POP; DLB 8; INT CANR-20; MAICYA 1, 2; MTCW 1, 2; MTFW 2005; SATA 13, 91; SATA-Essay 104; SCFW 1, 2; SFW 4; SUFW 2

Silverstein, Alvin 1933- .... **CLC 17**
See also CA 49-52; CANR 2; CLR 25; JRDA; MAICYA 1, 2; SATA 8, 69, 124

Smart, Elizabeth 1913-1986 .... **CLC 54**
See also CA 81-84; CAAS 118; CN 4; DLB 88

Smiley, Jane 1949- ...... **CLC 53, 76, 144, 236**
See also AAYA 66; AMWS 6; BPFB 3; CA 104; CANR 30, 50, 74, 96, 158; CN 6, 7; CPW 1; DA3; DAM POP; DLB 227, 234; EWL 3; INT CANR-30; MAL 5; MTFW 2005; SSFS 19

Smiley, Jane Graves
See Smiley, Jane

Smith, A(rthur) J(ames) M(arshall)
1902-1980 .... **CLC 15**
See also CA 1-4R; CAAS 102; CANR 4; CP 1, 2, 3; DAC; DLB 88; RGEL 2

Smith, Adam 1723(?)-1790 .... **LC 36**
See also DLB 104, 252, 336; RGEL 2

Smith, Alexander 1829-1867 .... **NCLC 59**
See also DLB 32, 55

Smith, Anna Deavere 1950- .... **CLC 86**
See also CA 133; CANR 103; CD 5, 6; DFS 2, 22

Smith, Betty (Wehner) 1904-1972 .... **CLC 19**
See also AAYA 72; BPFB 3; BYA 3; CA 5-8R; CAAS 33-36R; DLBY 1982; LAIT 3; RGAL 4; SATA 6

Smith, Charlotte (Turner)
1749-1806 .... **NCLC 23, 115**
See also DLB 39, 109; RGEL 2; TEA

Smith, Clark Ashton 1893-1961 .... **CLC 43**
See also CA 143; CANR 81; FANT; HGG; MTCW 2; SCFW 1, 2; SFW 4; SUFW

Smith, Dave .... **CLC 22, 42**
See Smith, David (Jeddie)
See also CA 7; CP 3, 4, 5, 6, 7; DLB 5

Smith, David (Jeddie) 1942-
See Smith, Dave
See also CA 49-52; CANR 1, 59, 120; CSW; DAM POET

Smith, Iain Crichton 1928-1998 .... **CLC 64**
See also BRWS 9; CA 21-24R; CAAS 171; CN 1, 2, 3, 4, 5, 6; CP 1, 2, 3, 4, 5, 6; DLB 40, 139, 319; RGSF 2

Smith, John 1580(?)-1631 .... **LC 9**
See also DLB 24, 30; TUS

Smith, Johnston
See Crane, Stephen (Townley)

Smith, Joseph, Jr. 1805-1844 .... **NCLC 53**

Smith, Kevin 1970- .... **CLC 223**
See also AAYA 37; CA 166; CANR 131

Smith, Lee 1944- .... **CLC 25, 73**
See also CA 119; CAAE 114; CANR 46, 118; CN 7; CSW; DLB 143; DLBY 1983; EWL 3; INT CA-119; RGAL 4

Smith, Martin
See Smith, Martin Cruz

Smith, Martin Cruz 1942- .. **CLC 25; NNAL**
See also BEST 89:4; BPFB 3; CA 85-88; CANR 6, 23, 43, 65, 119; CMW 4; CPW; DAM MULT, POP; HGG; INT CANR-23; MTCW 2; MTFW 2005; RGAL 4

Smith, Patti 1946- .... **CLC 12**
See also CA 93-96; CANR 63

Smith, Pauline (Urmson)
1882-1959 .... **TCLC 25**
See also DLB 225; EWL 3

Smith, Rosamond
See Oates, Joyce Carol

Smith, Sheila Kaye
See Kaye-Smith, Sheila

Smith, Stevie 1902-1971 .... **CLC 3, 8, 25, 44; PC 12**
See also BRWS 2; CA 17-18; CAAS 29-32R; CANR 35; CAP 2; CP 1; DAM POET; DLB 20; EWL 3; MTCW 1, 2; PAB; PFS 3; RGEL 2; TEA

Smith, Wilbur 1933- .... **CLC 33**
See also CA 13-16R; CANR 7, 46, 66, 134; CPW; MTCW 1, 2; MTFW 2005

Smith, William Jay 1918- .... **CLC 6**
See also AMWS 13; CA 5-8R; CANR 44, 106; CP 1, 2, 3, 4, 5, 6, 7; CSW; CWRI 5; DLB 5; MAICYA 1, 2; SAAS 22; SATA 2, 68, 154; SATA-Essay 154; TCLE 1:2

Smith, Woodrow Wilson
See Kuttner, Henry

Smith, Zadie 1975- .... **CLC 158**
See also CA 50; CANR 93; MTFW 2005

Smolenskin, Peretz 1842-1885 .... **NCLC 30**

Smollett, Tobias (George) 1721-1771 ... **LC 2, 46**
See also BRW 3; CDBLB 1660-1789; DLB 39, 104; RGEL 2; TEA

Snodgrass, W.D. 1926- .... **CLC 2, 6, 10, 18, 68; PC 74**
See also AMWS 6; CA 1-4R; CANR 6, 36, 65, 85; CP 1, 2, 3, 4, 5, 6, 7; DAM POET; DLB 5; MAL 5; MTCW 1, 2; MTFW 2005; RGAL 4; TCLE 1:2

Snorri Sturluson 1179-1241 .... **CMLC 56**
See also RGWL 2, 3

Snow, C(harles) P(ercy) 1905-1980 ... **CLC 1, 4, 6, 9, 13, 19**
See also BRW 7; CA 5-8R; CAAS 101; CANR 28; CDBLB 1945-1960; CN 1, 2; DAM NOV; DLB 15, 77; DLBD 17; EWL 3; MTCW 1, 2; MTFW 2005; RGEL 2; TEA

Snow, Frances Compton
See Adams, Henry (Brooks)

Snyder, Gary 1930- . **CLC 1, 2, 5, 9, 32, 120; PC 21**
See also AAYA 72; AMWS 8; ANW; BG 1:3; CA 17-20R; CANR 30, 60, 125; CP 1, 2, 3, 4, 5, 6, 7; DA3; DAM POET; DLB 5, 16, 165, 212, 237, 275; EWL 3; MAL 5; MTCW 2; MTFW 2005; PFS 9, 19; RGAL 4; WP

Snyder, Zilpha Keatley 1927- .... **CLC 17**
See also AAYA 15; BYA 1; CA 252; 9-12R, 252; CANR 38; CLR 31, 121; JRDA; MAICYA 1, 2; SAAS 2; SATA 1, 28, 75, 110, 163; SATA-Essay 112, 163; YAW

Soares, Bernardo
See Pessoa, Fernando (Antonio Nogueira)

Sobh, A.
See Shamlu, Ahmad

Sobh, Alef
See Shamlu, Ahmad

Sobol, Joshua 1939- .... **CLC 60**
See Sobol, Yehoshua
See also CA 200; RGHL

Sobol, Yehoshua 1939-
See Sobol, Joshua
See also CWW 2

Socrates 470B.C.-399B.C. .... **CMLC 27**

Soderberg, Hjalmar 1869-1941 ...... **TCLC 39**
See also DLB 259; EWL 3; RGSF 2

Soderbergh, Steven 1963- .... **CLC 154**
See also AAYA 43; CA 243

Soderbergh, Steven Andrew
See Soderbergh, Steven

Sodergran, Edith (Irene) 1892-1923
See Soedergran, Edith (Irene)
See also CA 202; DLB 259; EW 11; EWL 3; RGWL 2, 3

Soedergran, Edith (Irene)
1892-1923 .... **TCLC 31**
See Sodergran, Edith (Irene)

Softly, Edgar
See Lovecraft, H. P.

Softly, Edward
See Lovecraft, H. P.

Sokolov, Alexander V(sevolodovich) 1943-
See Sokolov, Sasha
See also CA 73-76

Sokolov, Raymond 1941- .... **CLC 7**
See also CA 85-88

Sokolov, Sasha .... **CLC 59**
See Sokolov, Alexander V(sevolodovich)
See also CWW 2; DLB 285; EWL 3; RGWL 2, 3

Solo, Jay
See Ellison, Harlan

Sologub, Fyodor .... **TCLC 9**
See Teternikov, Fyodor Kuzmich
See also EWL 3

Solomons, Ikey Esquir
See Thackeray, William Makepeace

Solomos, Dionysios 1798-1857 .... **NCLC 15**

Solwoska, Mara
See French, Marilyn

Solzhenitsyn, Aleksandr I. 1918- .. **CLC 1, 2, 4, 7, 9, 10, 18, 26, 34, 78, 134, 235; SSC 32; WLC 5**
See Solzhenitsyn, Aleksandr Isayevich
See also AAYA 49; AITN 1; BPFB 3; CA 69-72; CANR 40, 65, 116; DA; DA3; DAB; DAC; DAM MST, NOV; DLB 302, 332; EW 13; EXPS; LAIT 4; MTCW 1, 2; MTFW 2005; NFS 6; RGSF 2; RGWL 2, 3; SSFS 9; TWA

Solzhenitsyn, Aleksandr Isayevich
See Solzhenitsyn, Aleksandr I.
See also CWW 2; EWL 3

Somers, Jane
See Lessing, Doris

Somerville, Edith Oenone
1858-1949 .... **SSC 56; TCLC 51**
See also CA 196; DLB 135; RGEL 2; RGSF 2

Somerville & Ross
See Martin, Violet Florence; Somerville, Edith Oenone

Sommer, Scott 1951- .... **CLC 25**
See also CA 106

Sommers, Christina Hoff 1950- ...... **CLC 197**
See also CA 153; CANR 95

Sondheim, Stephen (Joshua) 1930- . **CLC 30, 39, 147; DC 22**
See also AAYA 11, 66; CA 103; CANR 47, 67, 125; DAM DRAM; LAIT 4

Sone, Monica 1919- .... **AAL**
See also DLB 312

Song, Cathy 1955- .... **AAL; PC 21**
See also CA 154; CANR 118; CWP; DLB 169, 312; EXPP; FW; PFS 5

Sontag, Susan 1933-2004 ... **CLC 1, 2, 10, 13, 31, 105, 195**
See also AMWS 3; CA 17-20R; CAAS 234; CANR 25, 51, 74, 97; CN 1, 2, 3, 4, 5, 6, 7; CPW; DA3; DAM POP; DLB 2, 67; EWL 3; MAL 5; MBL; MTCW 1, 2; MTFW 2005; RGAL 4; RHW; SSFS 10

Sophocles 496(?)B.C.-406(?)B.C. .... **CMLC 2, 47, 51, 86; DC 1; WLCS**
See also AW 1; CDWLB 1; DA; DA3; DAB; DAC; DAM DRAM, MST; DFS 1, 4, 8, 24; DLB 176; LAIT 1; LATS 1:1; LMFS 1; RGWL 2, 3; TWA; WLIT 8

Sordello 1189-1269 .... **CMLC 15**

Sorel, Georges 1847-1922 .... **TCLC 91**
See also CA 188; CAAE 118

Sorel, Julia
See Drexler, Rosalyn

Sorokin, Vladimir .... **CLC 59**
See Sorokin, Vladimir Georgievich
See also CA 258

Sorokin, Vladimir Georgievich
See Sorokin, Vladimir
See also DLB 285

Starbuck, George (Edwin)
1931-1996 .... **CLC 53**
See also CA 21-24R; CAAS 153; CANR 23; CP 1, 2, 3, 4, 5, 6; DAM POET

Stark, Richard
See Westlake, Donald E.

Statius c. 45-c. 96 .... **CMLC 91**
See also AW 2; DLB 211

Staunton, Schuyler
See Baum, L(yman) Frank

Stead, Christina (Ellen) 1902-1983 ... **CLC 2, 5, 8, 32, 80**
See also BRWS 4; CA 13-16R; CAAS 109; CANR 33, 40; CN 1, 2, 3; DLB 260; EWL 3; FW; MTCW 1, 2; MTFW 2005; RGEL 2; RGSF 2; WWE 1

Stead, William Thomas
1849-1912 .... **TCLC 48**
See also CA 167

Stebnitsky, M.
See Leskov, Nikolai (Semyonovich)

Steele, Richard 1672-1729 .... **LC 18**
See also BRW 3; CDBLB 1660-1789; DLB 84, 101; RGEL 2; WLIT 3

Steele, Timothy (Reid) 1948- .... **CLC 45**
See also CA 93-96; CANR 16, 50, 92; CP 5, 6, 7; DLB 120, 282

Steffens, (Joseph) Lincoln
1866-1936 .... **TCLC 20**
See also CA 198; CAAE 117; DLB 303; MAL 5

Stegner, Wallace (Earle) 1909-1993 .. **CLC 9, 49, 81; SSC 27**
See also AITN 1; AMWS 4; ANW; BEST 90:3; BPFB 3; CA 1-4R; 9; CAAS 141; CANR 1, 21, 46; CN 1, 2, 3, 4, 5; DAM NOV; DLB 9, 206, 275; DLBY 1993; EWL 3; MAL 5; MTCW 1, 2; MTFW 2005; RGAL 4; TCWW 1, 2; TUS

Stein, Gertrude 1874-1946 .... **DC 19; PC 18; SSC 42; TCLC 1, 6, 28, 48; WLC 5**
See also AAYA 64; AMW; AMWC 2; CA 132; CAAE 104; CANR 108; CDALB 1917-1929; DA; DA3; DAB; DAC; DAM MST, NOV, POET; DLB 4, 54, 86, 228; DLBD 15; EWL 3; EXPS; FL 1:6; GLL 1; MAL 5; MBL; MTCW 1, 2; MTFW 2005; NCFS 4; RGAL 4; RGSF 2; SSFS 5; TUS; WP

Steinbeck, John (Ernst) 1902-1968 ... **CLC 1, 5, 9, 13, 21, 34, 45, 75, 124; SSC 11, 37, 77; TCLC 135; WLC 5**
See also AAYA 12; AMW; BPFB 3; BYA 2, 3, 13; CA 1-4R; CAAS 25-28R; CANR 1, 35; CDALB 1929-1941; DA; DA3; DAB; DAC; DAM DRAM, MST, NOV; DLB 7, 9, 212, 275, 309, 332; DLBD 2; EWL 3; EXPS; LAIT 3; MAL 5; MTCW 1, 2; MTFW 2005; NFS 1, 5, 7, 17, 19; RGAL 4; RGSF 2; RHW; SATA 9; SSFS 3, 6, 22; TCWW 1, 2; TUS; WYA; YAW

Steinem, Gloria 1934- .... **CLC 63**
See also CA 53-56; CANR 28, 51, 139; DLB 246; FL 1:1; FW; MTCW 1, 2; MTFW 2005

Steiner, George 1929- .... **CLC 24, 221**
See also CA 73-76; CANR 31, 67, 108; DAM NOV; DLB 67, 299; EWL 3; MTCW 1, 2; MTFW 2005; RGHL; SATA 62

Steiner, K. Leslie
See Delany, Samuel R., Jr.

Steiner, Rudolf 1861-1925 .... **TCLC 13**
See also CAAE 107

Stendhal 1783-1842 .... **NCLC 23, 46, 178; SSC 27; WLC 5**
See also DA; DA3; DAB; DAC; DAM MST, NOV; DLB 119; EW 5; GFL 1789 to the Present; RGWL 2, 3; TWA

Stephen, Adeline Virginia
See Woolf, (Adeline) Virginia

Stephen, Sir Leslie 1832-1904 .... **TCLC 23**
See also BRW 5; CAAE 123; DLB 57, 144, 190

Stephen, Sir Leslie
See Stephen, Sir Leslie

Stephen, Virginia
See Woolf, (Adeline) Virginia

Stephens, James 1882(?)-1950 .... **SSC 50; TCLC 4**
See also CA 192; CAAE 104; DLB 19, 153, 162; EWL 3; FANT; RGEL 2; SUFW

Stephens, Reed
See Donaldson, Stephen R(eeder)

Stephenson, Neal 1959- .... **CLC 220**
See also AAYA 38; CA 122; CANR 88, 138; CN 7; MTFW 2005; SFW 4

Steptoe, Lydia
See Barnes, Djuna
See also GLL 1

Sterchi, Beat 1949- .... **CLC 65**
See also CA 203

Sterling, Brett
See Bradbury, Ray; Hamilton, Edmond

Sterling, Bruce 1954- .... **CLC 72**
See also CA 119; CANR 44, 135; CN 7; MTFW 2005; SCFW 2; SFW 4

Sterling, George 1869-1926 .... **TCLC 20**
See also CA 165; CAAE 117; DLB 54

Stern, Gerald 1925- .... **CLC 40, 100**
See also AMWS 9; CA 81-84; CANR 28, 94; CP 3, 4, 5, 6, 7; DLB 105; RGAL 4

Stern, Richard (Gustave) 1928- ... **CLC 4, 39**
See also CA 1-4R; CANR 1, 25, 52, 120; CN 1, 2, 3, 4, 5, 6, 7; DLB 218; DLBY 1987; INT CANR-25

Sternberg, Josef von 1894-1969 .... **CLC 20**
See also CA 81-84

Sterne, Laurence 1713-1768 .... **LC 2, 48; WLC 5**
See also BRW 3; BRWC 1; CDBLB 1660-1789; DA; DAB; DAC; DAM MST, NOV; DLB 39; RGEL 2; TEA

Sternheim, (William Adolf) Carl
1878-1942 .... **TCLC 8**
See also CA 193; CAAE 105; DLB 56, 118; EWL 3; IDTP; RGWL 2, 3

Stevens, Margaret Dean
See Aldrich, Bess Streeter

Stevens, Mark 1951- .... **CLC 34**
See also CA 122

Stevens, Wallace 1879-1955 . **PC 6; TCLC 3, 12, 45; WLC 5**
See also AMW; AMWR 1; CA 124; CAAE 104; CDALB 1929-1941; DA; DA3; DAB; DAC; DAM MST, POET; DLB 54; EWL 3; EXPP; MAL 5; MTCW 1, 2; PAB; PFS 13, 16; RGAL 4; TUS; WP

Stevenson, Anne (Katharine) 1933- .. **CLC 7, 33**
See also BRWS 6; CA 17-20R; 9; CANR 9, 33, 123; CP 3, 4, 5, 6, 7; CWP; DLB 40; MTCW 1; RHW

Stevenson, Robert Louis (Balfour)
1850-1894 ...... **NCLC 5, 14, 63; SSC 11, 51; WLC 5**
See also AAYA 24; BPFB 3; BRW 5; BRWC 1; BRWR 1; BYA 1, 2, 4, 13; CD-BLB 1890-1914; CLR 10, 11, 107; DA; DA3; DAB; DAC; DAM MST, NOV; DLB 18, 57, 141, 156, 174; DLBD 13; GL 3; HGG; JRDA; LAIT 3; MAICYA 1, 2; NFS 11, 20; RGEL 2; RGSF 2; SATA 100; SUFW; TEA; WCH; WLIT 4; WYA; YABC 2; YAW

Stewart, J(ohn) I(nnes) M(ackintosh)
1906-1994 .... **CLC 7, 14, 32**
See also Innes, Michael
See also CA 85-88; 3; CAAS 147; CANR 47; CMW 4; CN 1, 2, 3, 4, 5; MTCW 1, 2

Stewart, Mary (Florence Elinor)
1916- .... **CLC 7, 35, 117**
See also AAYA 29, 73; BPFB 3; CA 1-4R; CANR 1, 59, 130; CMW 4; CPW; DAB; FANT; RHW; SATA 12; YAW

Stewart, Mary Rainbow
See Stewart, Mary (Florence Elinor)

Stifle, June
See Campbell, Maria

Stifter, Adalbert 1805-1868 .. **NCLC 41; SSC 28**
See also CDWLB 2; DLB 133; RGSF 2; RGWL 2, 3

Still, James 1906-2001 .... **CLC 49**
See also CA 65-68; 17; CAAS 195; CANR 10, 26; CSW; DLB 9; DLBY 01; SATA 29; SATA-Obit 127

Sting 1951-
See Sumner, Gordon Matthew
See also CA 167

Stirling, Arthur
See Sinclair, Upton

Stitt, Milan 1941- .... **CLC 29**
See also CA 69-72

Stockton, Francis Richard 1834-1902
See Stockton, Frank R.
See also AAYA 68; CA 137; CAAE 108; MAICYA 1, 2; SATA 44; SFW 4

Stockton, Frank R. .... **TCLC 47**
See Stockton, Francis Richard
See also BYA 4, 13; DLB 42, 74; DLBD 13; EXPS; SATA-Brief 32; SSFS 3; SUFW; WCH

Stoddard, Charles
See Kuttner, Henry

Stoker, Abraham 1847-1912
See Stoker, Bram
See also CA 150; CAAE 105; DA; DA3; DAC; DAM MST, NOV; HGG; MTFW 2005; SATA 29

Stoker, Bram . **SSC 62; TCLC 8, 144; WLC 6**
See Stoker, Abraham
See also AAYA 23; BPFB 3; BRWS 3; BYA 5; CDBLB 1890-1914; DAB; DLB 304; GL 3; LATS 1:1; NFS 18; RGEL 2; SUFW; TEA; WLIT 4

Stolz, Mary 1920-2006 .... **CLC 12**
See also AAYA 8, 73; AITN 1; CA 5-8R; CAAS 255; CANR 13, 41, 112; JRDA; MAICYA 1, 2; SAAS 3; SATA 10, 71, 133; YAW

Stolz, Mary Slattery
See Stolz, Mary

Stone, Irving 1903-1989 .... **CLC 7**
See also AITN 1; BPFB 3; CA 1-4R; 3; CAAS 129; CANR 1, 23; CN 1, 2, 3, 4; CPW; DA3; DAM POP; INT CANR-23; MTCW 1, 2; MTFW 2005; RHW; SATA 3; SATA-Obit 64

Stone, Oliver 1946- .... **CLC 73**
See also AAYA 15, 64; CA 110; CANR 55, 125

Stone, Oliver William
See Stone, Oliver

Stone, Robert 1937- .... **CLC 5, 23, 42, 175**
See also AMWS 5; BPFB 3; CA 85-88; CANR 23, 66, 95; CN 4, 5, 6, 7; DLB 152; EWL 3; INT CANR-23; MAL 5; MTCW 1; MTFW 2005

Stone, Ruth 1915- .... **PC 53**
See also CA 45-48; CANR 2, 91; CP 5, 6, 7; CSW; DLB 105; PFS 19

Sutcliff, Rosemary 1920-1992 .... **CLC 26**
See also AAYA 10; BYA 1, 4; CA 5-8R; CAAS 139; CANR 37; CLR 1, 37; CPW; DAB; DAC; DAM MST, POP; JRDA; LATS 1:1; MAICYA 1, 2; MAICYAS 1; RHW; SATA 6, 44, 78; SATA-Obit 73; WYA; YAW

Sutro, Alfred 1863-1933 .... **TCLC 6**
See also CA 185; CAAE 105; DLB 10; RGEL 2

Sutton, Henry
See Slavitt, David R(ytman)

Suzuki, D. T.
See Suzuki, Daisetz Teitaro

Suzuki, Daisetz T.
See Suzuki, Daisetz Teitaro

Suzuki, Daisetz Teitaro
1870-1966 .... **TCLC 109**
See also CA 121; CAAS 111; MTCW 1, 2; MTFW 2005

Suzuki, Teitaro
See Suzuki, Daisetz Teitaro

Svevo, Italo .... **SSC 25; TCLC 2, 35**
See Schmitz, Aron Hector
See also DLB 264; EW 8; EWL 3; RGWL 2, 3; WLIT 7

Swados, Elizabeth 1951- .... **CLC 12**
See also CA 97-100; CANR 49, 163; INT CA-97-100

Swados, Elizabeth A.
See Swados, Elizabeth

Swados, Harvey 1920-1972 .... **CLC 5**
See also CA 5-8R; CAAS 37-40R; CANR 6; CN 1; DLB 2, 335; MAL 5

Swados, Liz
See Swados, Elizabeth

Swan, Gladys 1934- .... **CLC 69**
See also CA 101; CANR 17, 39; TCLE 1:2

Swanson, Logan
See Matheson, Richard (Burton)

Swarthout, Glendon (Fred)
1918-1992 .... **CLC 35**
See also AAYA 55; CA 1-4R; CAAS 139; CANR 1, 47; CN 1, 2, 3, 4, 5; LAIT 5; SATA 26; TCWW 1, 2; YAW

Swedenborg, Emanuel 1688-1772 ..... **LC 105**

Sweet, Sarah C.
See Jewett, (Theodora) Sarah Orne

Swenson, May 1919-1989 ...... **CLC 4, 14, 61, 106; PC 14**
See also AMWS 4; CA 5-8R; CAAS 130; CANR 36, 61, 131; CP 1, 2, 3, 4; DA; DAB; DAC; DAM MST, POET; DLB 5; EXPP; GLL 2; MAL 5; MTCW 1, 2; MTFW 2005; PFS 16; SATA 15; WP

Swift, Augustus
See Lovecraft, H. P.

Swift, Graham 1949- .... **CLC 41, 88, 233**
See also BRWC 2; BRWS 5; CA 122; CAAE 117; CANR 46, 71, 128; CN 4, 5, 6, 7; DLB 194, 326; MTCW 2; MTFW 2005; NFS 18; RGSF 2

Swift, Jonathan 1667-1745 ..... **LC 1, 42, 101; PC 9; WLC 6**
See also AAYA 41; BRW 3; BRWC 1; BRWR 1; BYA 5, 14; CDBLB 1660-1789; CLR 53; DA; DA3; DAB; DAC; DAM MST, NOV, POET; DLB 39, 95, 101; EXPN; LAIT 1; NFS 6; RGEL 2; SATA 19; TEA; WCH; WLIT 3

Swinburne, Algernon Charles
1837-1909 ... **PC 24; TCLC 8, 36; WLC 6**
See also BRW 5; CA 140; CAAE 105; CD-BLB 1832-1890; DA; DA3; DAB; DAC; DAM MST, POET; DLB 35, 57; PAB; RGEL 2; TEA

Swinfen, Ann .... **CLC 34**
See also CA 202

Swinnerton, Frank (Arthur)
1884-1982 .... **CLC 31**
See also CA 202; CAAS 108; CN 1, 2, 3; DLB 34

Swinnerton, Frank Arthur
1884-1982 .... **CLC 31**
See also CAAS 108; DLB 34

Swithen, John
See King, Stephen

Sylvia
See Ashton-Warner, Sylvia (Constance)

Symmes, Robert Edward
See Duncan, Robert

Symonds, John Addington
1840-1893 .... **NCLC 34**
See also DLB 57, 144

Symons, Arthur 1865-1945 .... **TCLC 11**
See also CA 189; CAAE 107; DLB 19, 57, 149; RGEL 2

Symons, Julian (Gustave)
1912-1994 .... **CLC 2, 14, 32**
See also CA 49-52; 3; CAAS 147; CANR 3, 33, 59; CMW 4; CN 1, 2, 3, 4, 5; CP 1, 3, 4; DLB 87, 155; DLBY 1992; MSW; MTCW 1

Synge, (Edmund) J(ohn) M(illington)
1871-1909 .... **DC 2; TCLC 6, 37**
See also BRW 6; BRWR 1; CA 141; CAAE 104; CDBLB 1890-1914; DAM DRAM; DFS 18; DLB 10, 19; EWL 3; RGEL 2; TEA; WLIT 4

Syruc, J.
See Milosz, Czeslaw

Szirtes, George 1948- .... **CLC 46; PC 51**
See also CA 109; CANR 27, 61, 117; CP 4, 5, 6, 7

Szymborska, Wislawa 1923- ... **CLC 99, 190; PC 44**
See also CA 154; CANR 91, 133; CDWLB 4; CWP; CWW 2; DA3; DLB 232, 332; DLBY 1996; EWL 3; MTCW 2; MTFW 2005; PFS 15; RGHL; RGWL 3

T. O., Nik
See Annensky, Innokenty (Fyodorovich)

Tabori, George 1914- .... **CLC 19**
See also CA 49-52; CANR 4, 69; CBD; CD 5, 6; DLB 245; RGHL

Tacitus c. 55-c. 117 .... **CMLC 56**
See also AW 2; CDWLB 1; DLB 211; RGWL 2, 3; WLIT 8

Tagore, Rabindranath 1861-1941 .... **PC 8; SSC 48; TCLC 3, 53**
See also CA 120; CAAE 104; DA3; DAM DRAM, POET; DLB 323, 332; EWL 3; MTCW 1, 2; MTFW 2005; PFS 18; RGEL 2; RGSF 2; RGWL 2, 3; TWA

Taine, Hippolyte Adolphe
1828-1893 .... **NCLC 15**
See also EW 7; GFL 1789 to the Present

Talayesva, Don C. 1890-(?) .... **NNAL**

Talese, Gay 1932- .... **CLC 37, 232**
See also AITN 1; CA 1-4R; CANR 9, 58, 137; DLB 185; INT CANR-9; MTCW 1, 2; MTFW 2005

Tallent, Elizabeth 1954- .... **CLC 45**
See also CA 117; CANR 72; DLB 130

Tallmountain, Mary 1918-1997 .... **NNAL**
See also CA 146; CAAS 161; DLB 193

Tally, Ted 1952- .... **CLC 42**
See also CA 124; CAAE 120; CAD; CANR 125; CD 5, 6; INT CA-124

Talvik, Heiti 1904-1947 .... **TCLC 87**
See also EWL 3

Tamayo y Baus, Manuel
1829-1898 .... **NCLC 1**

Tammsaare, A(nton) H(ansen)
1878-1940 .... **TCLC 27**
See also CA 164; CDWLB 4; DLB 220; EWL 3

Tam'si, Tchicaya U
See Tchicaya, Gerald Felix

Tan, Amy 1952- ...... **AAL; CLC 59, 120, 151**
See also AAYA 9, 48; AMWS 10; BEST 89:3; BPFB 3; CA 136; CANR 54, 105, 132; CDALBS; CN 6, 7; CPW 1; DA3; DAM MULT, NOV, POP; DLB 173, 312; EXPN; FL 1:6; FW; LAIT 3, 5; MAL 5; MTCW 2; MTFW 2005; NFS 1, 13, 16; RGAL 4; SATA 75; SSFS 9; YAW

Tandem, Carl Felix
See Spitteler, Carl

Tandem, Felix
See Spitteler, Carl

Tanizaki, Jun'ichiro 1886-1965 ... **CLC 8, 14, 28; SSC 21**
See Tanizaki Jun'ichiro
See also CA 93-96; CAAS 25-28R; MJW; MTCW 2; MTFW 2005; RGSF 2; RGWL 2

Tanizaki Jun'ichiro
See Tanizaki, Jun'ichiro
See also DLB 180; EWL 3

Tannen, Deborah 1945- .... **CLC 206**
See also CA 118; CANR 95

Tannen, Deborah Frances
See Tannen, Deborah

Tanner, William
See Amis, Kingsley

Tante, Dilly
See Kunitz, Stanley

Tao Lao
See Storni, Alfonsina

Tapahonso, Luci 1953- .... **NNAL; PC 65**
See also CA 145; CANR 72, 127; DLB 175

Tarantino, Quentin (Jerome)
1963- .... **CLC 125, 230**
See also AAYA 58; CA 171; CANR 125

Tarassoff, Lev
See Troyat, Henri

Tarbell, Ida M(inerva) 1857-1944 . **TCLC 40**
See also CA 181; CAAE 122; DLB 47

Tardieu d'Esclavelles,
 Louise-Florence-Petronille
See Epinay, Louise d'

Tarkington, (Newton) Booth
1869-1946 .... **TCLC 9**
See also BPFB 3; BYA 3; CA 143; CAAE 110; CWRI 5; DLB 9, 102; MAL 5; MTCW 2; RGAL 4; SATA 17

Tarkovskii, Andrei Arsen'evich
See Tarkovsky, Andrei (Arsenyevich)

Tarkovsky, Andrei (Arsenyevich)
1932-1986 .... **CLC 75**
See also CA 127

Tartt, Donna 1964(?)- .... **CLC 76**
See also AAYA 56; CA 142; CANR 135; MTFW 2005

Tasso, Torquato 1544-1595 .... **LC 5, 94**
See also EFS 2; EW 2; RGWL 2, 3; WLIT 7

Tate, (John Orley) Allen 1899-1979 .. **CLC 2, 4, 6, 9, 11, 14, 24; PC 50**
See also AMW; CA 5-8R; CAAS 85-88; CANR 32, 108; CN 1, 2; CP 1, 2; DLB 4, 45, 63; DLBD 17; EWL 3; MAL 5; MTCW 1, 2; MTFW 2005; RGAL 4; RHW

Tate, Ellalice
See Hibbert, Eleanor Alice Burford

Tate, James (Vincent) 1943- ..... **CLC 2, 6, 25**
See also CA 21-24R; CANR 29, 57, 114; CP 1, 2, 3, 4, 5, 6, 7; DLB 5, 169; EWL 3; PFS 10, 15; RGAL 4; WP

Tate, Nahum 1652(?)-1715 .... **LC 109**
See also DLB 80; RGEL 2

Tauler, Johannes c. 1300-1361 ...... **CMLC 37**
See also DLB 179; LMFS 1

Thomas, Ross (Elmore) 1926-1995 .. **CLC 39**
See also CA 33-36R; CAAS 150; CANR 22, 63; CMW 4

Thompson, Francis (Joseph)
1859-1907 .... **TCLC 4**
See also BRW 5; CA 189; CAAE 104; CD-BLB 1890-1914; DLB 19; RGEL 2; TEA

Thompson, Francis Clegg
See Mencken, H(enry) L(ouis)

Thompson, Hunter S. 1937(?)-2005 .. **CLC 9, 17, 40, 104, 229**
See also AAYA 45; BEST 89:1; BPFB 3; CA 17-20R; CAAS 236; CANR 23, 46, 74, 77, 111, 133; CPW; CSW; DA3; DAM POP; DLB 185; MTCW 1, 2; MTFW 2005; TUS

Thompson, James Myers
See Thompson, Jim (Myers)

Thompson, Jim (Myers)
1906-1977(?) .... **CLC 69**
See also BPFB 3; CA 140; CMW 4; CPW; DLB 226; MSW

Thompson, Judith (Clare Francesca)
1954- .... **CLC 39**
See also CA 143; CD 5, 6; CWD; DFS 22; DLB 334

Thomson, James 1700-1748 .... **LC 16, 29, 40**
See also BRWS 3; DAM POET; DLB 95; RGEL 2

Thomson, James 1834-1882 .... **NCLC 18**
See also DAM POET; DLB 35; RGEL 2

Thoreau, Henry David 1817-1862 .. **NCLC 7, 21, 61, 138; PC 30; WLC 6**
See also AAYA 42; AMW; ANW; BYA 3; CDALB 1640-1865; DA; DA3; DAB; DAC; DAM MST; DLB 1, 183, 223, 270, 298; LAIT 2; LMFS 1; NCFS 3; RGAL 4; TUS

Thorndike, E. L.
See Thorndike, Edward L(ee)

Thorndike, Edward L(ee)
1874-1949 .... **TCLC 107**
See also CAAE 121

Thornton, Hall
See Silverberg, Robert

Thorpe, Adam 1956- .... **CLC 176**
See also CA 129; CANR 92, 160; DLB 231

Thorpe, Thomas Bangs
1815-1878 .... **NCLC 183**
See also DLB 3, 11, 248; RGAL 4

Thubron, Colin 1939- .... **CLC 163**
See also CA 25-28R; CANR 12, 29, 59, 95; CN 5, 6, 7; DLB 204, 231

Thubron, Colin Gerald Dryden
See Thubron, Colin

Thucydides c. 455B.C.-c. 395B.C. . **CMLC 17**
See also AW 1; DLB 176; RGWL 2, 3; WLIT 8

Thumboo, Edwin Nadason 1933- .... **PC 30**
See also CA 194; CP 1

Thurber, James (Grover)
1894-1961 .. **CLC 5, 11, 25, 125; SSC 1, 47**
See also AAYA 56; AMWS 1; BPFB 3; BYA 5; CA 73-76; CANR 17, 39; CDALB 1929-1941; CWRI 5; DA; DA3; DAB; DAC; DAM DRAM, MST, NOV; DLB 4, 11, 22, 102; EWL 3; EXPS; FANT; LAIT 3; MAICYA 1, 2; MAL 5; MTCW 1, 2; MTFW 2005; RGAL 4; RGSF 2; SATA 13; SSFS 1, 10, 19; SUFW; TUS

Thurman, Wallace (Henry)
1902-1934 ..... **BLC 3; HR 1:3; TCLC 6**
See also BW 1, 3; CA 124; CAAE 104; CANR 81; DAM MULT; DLB 51

Tibullus c. 54B.C.-c. 18B.C. .... **CMLC 36**
See also AW 2; DLB 211; RGWL 2, 3; WLIT 8

Ticheburn, Cheviot
See Ainsworth, William Harrison

Tieck, (Johann) Ludwig
1773-1853 ..... **NCLC 5, 46; SSC 31, 100**
See also CDWLB 2; DLB 90; EW 5; IDTP; RGSF 2; RGWL 2, 3; SUFW

Tiger, Derry
See Ellison, Harlan

Tilghman, Christopher 1946- .... **CLC 65**
See also CA 159; CANR 135, 151; CSW; DLB 244

Tillich, Paul (Johannes)
1886-1965 .... **CLC 131**
See also CA 5-8R; CAAS 25-28R; CANR 33; MTCW 1, 2

Tillinghast, Richard (Williford)
1940- .... **CLC 29**
See also CA 29-32R; 23; CANR 26, 51, 96; CP 2, 3, 4, 5, 6, 7; CSW

Tillman, Lynne (?)- .... **CLC 231**
See also CA 173; CANR 144

Timrod, Henry 1828-1867 .... **NCLC 25**
See also DLB 3, 248; RGAL 4

Tindall, Gillian (Elizabeth) 1938- ...... **CLC 7**
See also CA 21-24R; CANR 11, 65, 107; CN 1, 2, 3, 4, 5, 6, 7

Tiptree, James, Jr. .... **CLC 48, 50**
See Sheldon, Alice Hastings Bradley
See also DLB 8; SCFW 1, 2; SFW 4

Tirone Smith, Mary-Ann 1944- .... **CLC 39**
See also CA 136; CAAE 118; CANR 113; SATA 143

Tirso de Molina 1580(?)-1648 .... **DC 13; HLCS 2; LC 73**
See also RGWL 2, 3

Titmarsh, Michael Angelo
See Thackeray, William Makepeace

Tocqueville, Alexis (Charles Henri Maurice Clerel Comte) de 1805-1859 .. **NCLC 7, 63**
See also EW 6; GFL 1789 to the Present; TWA

Toer, Pramoedya Ananta
1925-2006 .... **CLC 186**
See also CA 197; CAAS 251; RGWL 3

Toffler, Alvin 1928- .... **CLC 168**
See also CA 13-16R; CANR 15, 46, 67; CPW; DAM POP; MTCW 1, 2

Toibin, Colm 1955- .... **CLC 162**
See also CA 142; CANR 81, 149; CN 7; DLB 271

Tolkien, John Ronald Reuel
See Tolkien, J.R.R

Tolkien, J.R.R 1892-1973 ...... **CLC 1, 2, 3, 8, 12, 38; TCLC 137; WLC 6**
See also AAYA 10; AITN 1; BPFB 3; BRWC 2; BRWS 2; CA 17-18; CAAS 45-48; CANR 36, 134; CAP 2; CDBLB 1914-1945; CLR 56; CN 1; CPW 1; CWRI 5; DA; DA3; DAB; DAC; DAM MST, NOV, POP; DLB 15, 160, 255; EFS 2; EWL 3; FANT; JRDA; LAIT 1; LATS 1:2; LMFS 2; MAICYA 1, 2; MTCW 1, 2; MTFW 2005; NFS 8; RGEL 2; SATA 2, 32, 100; SATA-Obit 24; SFW 4; SUFW; TEA; WCH; WYA; YAW

Toller, Ernst 1893-1939 .... **TCLC 10**
See also CA 186; CAAE 107; DLB 124; EWL 3; RGWL 2, 3

Tolson, M. B.
See Tolson, Melvin B(eaunorus)

Tolson, Melvin B(eaunorus)
1898(?)-1966 .... **BLC 3; CLC 36, 105**
See also AFAW 1, 2; BW 1, 3; CA 124; CAAS 89-92; CANR 80; DAM MULT, POET; DLB 48, 76; MAL 5; RGAL 4

Tolstoi, Aleksei Nikolaevich
See Tolstoy, Alexey Nikolaevich

Tolstoi, Lev
See Tolstoy, Leo (Nikolaevich)
See also RGSF 2; RGWL 2, 3

Tolstoy, Aleksei Nikolaevich
See Tolstoy, Alexey Nikolaevich
See also DLB 272

Tolstoy, Alexey Nikolaevich
1882-1945 .... **TCLC 18**
See Tolstoy, Aleksei Nikolaevich
See also CA 158; CAAE 107; EWL 3; SFW 4

Tolstoy, Leo (Nikolaevich)
1828-1910 . **SSC 9, 30, 45, 54; TCLC 4, 11, 17, 28, 44, 79, 173; WLC 6**
See Tolstoi, Lev
See also AAYA 56; CA 123; CAAE 104; DA; DA3; DAB; DAC; DAM MST, NOV; DLB 238; EFS 2; EW 7; EXPS; IDTP; LAIT 2; LATS 1:1; LMFS 1; NFS 10; SATA 26; SSFS 5; TWA

Tolstoy, Count Leo
See Tolstoy, Leo (Nikolaevich)

Tomalin, Claire 1933- .... **CLC 166**
See also CA 89-92; CANR 52, 88; DLB 155

Tomasi di Lampedusa, Giuseppe 1896-1957
See Lampedusa, Giuseppe (Tomasi) di
See also CAAE 111; DLB 177; EWL 3; WLIT 7

Tomlin, Lily 1939(?)-
See Tomlin, Mary Jean
See also CAAE 117

Tomlin, Mary Jean .... **CLC 17**
See Tomlin, Lily

Tomline, F. Latour
See Gilbert, W(illiam) S(chwenck)

Tomlinson, (Alfred) Charles 1927- .... **CLC 2, 4, 6, 13, 45; PC 17**
See also CA 5-8R; CANR 33; CP 1, 2, 3, 4, 5, 6, 7; DAM POET; DLB 40; TCLE 1:2

Tomlinson, H(enry) M(ajor)
1873-1958 .... **TCLC 71**
See also CA 161; CAAE 118; DLB 36, 100, 195

Tonna, Charlotte Elizabeth
1790-1846 .... **NCLC 135**
See also DLB 163

Tonson, Jacob fl. 1655(?)-1736 .... **LC 86**
See also DLB 170

Toole, John Kennedy 1937-1969 ..... **CLC 19, 64**
See also BPFB 3; CA 104; DLBY 1981; MTCW 2; MTFW 2005

Toomer, Eugene
See Toomer, Jean

Toomer, Eugene Pinchback
See Toomer, Jean

Toomer, Jean 1894-1967 .. **BLC 3; CLC 1, 4, 13, 22; HR 1:3; PC 7; SSC 1, 45; TCLC 172; WLCS**
See also AFAW 1, 2; AMWS 3, 9; BW 1; CA 85-88; CDALB 1917-1929; DA3; DAM MULT; DLB 45, 51; EWL 3; EXPP; EXPS; LMFS 2; MAL 5; MTCW 1, 2; MTFW 2005; NFS 11; RGAL 4; RGSF 2; SSFS 5

Toomer, Nathan Jean
See Toomer, Jean

Toomer, Nathan Pinchback
See Toomer, Jean

Torley, Luke
See Blish, James (Benjamin)

Tornimparte, Alessandra
See Ginzburg, Natalia

Torre, Raoul della
See Mencken, H(enry) L(ouis)

Torrence, Ridgely 1874-1950 .... **TCLC 97**
See also DLB 54, 249; MAL 5

Turner, Frederick 1943- .... **CLC 48**
See also CA 227; 73-76, 227; 10; CANR
12, 30, 56; DLB 40, 282

Turton, James
See Crace, Jim

Tutu, Desmond M(pilo) 1931- .. **BLC 3; CLC
80**
See also BW 1, 3; CA 125; CANR 67, 81;
DAM MULT

Tutuola, Amos 1920-1997 ..... **BLC 3; CLC 5,
14, 29; TCLC 188**
See also AFW; BW 2, 3; CA 9-12R; CAAS
159; CANR 27, 66; CDWLB 3; CN 1, 2,
3, 4, 5, 6; DA3; DAM MULT; DLB 125;
DNFS 2; EWL 3; FW; MTCW 1, 2; MTFW
2005; RGEL 2; WLIT 2

Twain, Mark .... **SSC 6, 26, 34, 87; TCLC 6,
12, 19, 36, 48, 59, 161, 185; WLC 6**
See Clemens, Samuel Langhorne
See also AAYA 20; AMW; AMWC 1; BPFB
3; BYA 2, 3, 11, 14; CLR 58, 60, 66; DLB
11; EXPN; EXPS; FANT; LAIT 2; MAL
5; NCFS 4; NFS 1, 6; RGAL 4; RGSF 2;
SFW 4; SSFS 1, 7, 16, 21; SUFW; TUS;
WCH; WYA; YAW

Tyler, Anne 1941- . **CLC 7, 11, 18, 28, 44, 59,
103, 205**
See also AAYA 18, 60; AMWS 4; BEST
89:1; BPFB 3; BYA 12; CA 9-12R; CANR
11, 33, 53, 109, 132; CDALBS; CN 1, 2,
3, 4, 5, 6, 7; CPW; CSW; DAM NOV,
POP; DLB 6, 143; DLBY 1982; EWL 3;
EXPN; LATS 1:2; MAL 5; MBL; MTCW
1, 2; MTFW 2005; NFS 2, 7, 10; RGAL
4; SATA 7, 90, 173; SSFS 17; TCLE 1:2;
TUS; YAW

Tyler, Royall 1757-1826 .... **NCLC 3**
See also DLB 37; RGAL 4

Tynan, Katharine 1861-1931 .... **TCLC 3**
See also CA 167; CAAE 104; DLB 153,
240; FW

Tyndale, William c. 1484-1536 .... **LC 103**
See also DLB 132

Tyutchev, Fyodor 1803-1873 .... **NCLC 34**

Tzara, Tristan 1896-1963 .... **CLC 47; PC 27;
TCLC 168**
See also CA 153; CAAS 89-92; DAM
POET; EWL 3; MTCW 2

Uchida, Yoshiko 1921-1992 .... **AAL**
See also AAYA 16; BYA 2, 3; CA 13-16R;
CAAS 139; CANR 6, 22, 47, 61;
CDALBS; CLR 6, 56; CWRI 5; DLB 312;
JRDA; MAICYA 1, 2; MTCW 1, 2;
MTFW 2005; SAAS 1; SATA 1, 53;
SATA-Obit 72

Udall, Nicholas 1504-1556 .... **LC 84**
See also DLB 62; RGEL 2

Ueda Akinari 1734-1809 .... **NCLC 131**

Uhry, Alfred 1936- .... **CLC 55**
See also CA 133; CAAE 127; CAD; CANR
112; CD 5, 6; CSW; DA3; DAM DRAM,
POP; DFS 11, 15; INT CA-133; MTFW
2005

Ulf, Haerved
See Strindberg, (Johan) August

Ulf, Harved
See Strindberg, (Johan) August

Ulibarri, Sabine R(eyes)
1919-2003 .... **CLC 83; HLCS 2**
See also CA 131; CAAS 214; CANR 81;
DAM MULT; DLB 82; HW 1, 2; RGSF 2

Unamuno (y Jugo), Miguel de
1864-1936 .. **HLC 2; SSC 11, 69; TCLC
2, 9, 148**
See also CA 131; CAAE 104; CANR 81;
DAM MULT, NOV; DLB 108, 322; EW
8; EWL 3; HW 1, 2; MTCW 1, 2; MTFW
2005; RGSF 2; RGWL 2, 3; SSFS 20;
TWA

Uncle Shelby
See Silverstein, Shel

Undercliffe, Errol
See Campbell, (John) Ramsey

Underwood, Miles
See Glassco, John

Undset, Sigrid 1882-1949 .. **TCLC 3; WLC 6**
See also CA 129; CAAE 104; DA; DA3;
DAB; DAC; DAM MST, NOV; DLB 293,
332; EW 9; EWL 3; FW; MTCW 1, 2;
MTFW 2005; RGWL 2, 3

Ungaretti, Giuseppe 1888-1970 ... **CLC 7, 11,
15; PC 57**
See also CA 19-20; CAAS 25-28R; CAP 2;
DLB 114; EW 10; EWL 3; PFS 20;
RGWL 2, 3; WLIT 7

Unger, Douglas 1952- .... **CLC 34**
See also CA 130; CANR 94, 155

Unsworth, Barry (Forster) 1930- .... **CLC 76,
127**
See also BRWS 7; CA 25-28R; CANR 30,
54, 125; CN 6, 7; DLB 194, 326

Updike, John 1932- . **CLC 1, 2, 3, 5, 7, 9, 13,
15, 23, 34, 43, 70, 139, 214; SSC 13, 27;
WLC 6**
See also AAYA 36; AMW; AMWC 1;
AMWR 1; BPFB 3; BYA 12; CA 1-4R;
CABS 1; CANR 4, 33, 51, 94, 133;
CDALB 1968-1988; CN 1, 2, 3, 4, 5, 6,
7; CP 1, 2, 3, 4, 5, 6, 7; CPW 1; DA;
DA3; DAB; DAC; DAM MST, NOV,
POET, POP; DLB 2, 5, 143, 218, 227;
DLBD 3; DLBY 1980, 1982, 1997; EWL
3; EXPP; HGG; MAL 5; MTCW 1, 2;
MTFW 2005; NFS 12, 24; RGAL 4;
RGSF 2; SSFS 3, 19; TUS

Updike, John Hoyer
See Updike, John

Upshaw, Margaret Mitchell
See Mitchell, Margaret (Munnerlyn)

Upton, Mark
See Sanders, Lawrence

Upward, Allen 1863-1926 .... **TCLC 85**
See also CA 187; CAAE 117; DLB 36

Urdang, Constance (Henriette)
1922-1996 .... **CLC 47**
See also CA 21-24R; CANR 9, 24; CP 1, 2,
3, 4, 5, 6; CWP

Urfe, Honore d' 1567(?)-1625 .... **LC 132**
See also DLB 268; GFL Beginnings to
1789; RGWL 2, 3

Uriel, Henry
See Faust, Frederick (Schiller)

Uris, Leon 1924-2003 .... **CLC 7, 32**
See also AITN 1, 2; BEST 89:2; BPFB 3;
CA 1-4R; CAAS 217; CANR 1, 40, 65,
123; CN 1, 2, 3, 4, 5, 6; CPW 1; DA3;
DAM NOV, POP; MTCW 1, 2; MTFW
2005; RGHL; SATA 49; SATA-Obit 146

Urista (Heredia), Alberto (Baltazar)
1947- .... **HLCS 1**
See Alurista
See also CA 182; CANR 2, 32; HW 1

Urmuz
See Codrescu, Andrei

Urquhart, Guy
See McAlmon, Robert (Menzies)

Urquhart, Jane 1949- .... **CLC 90**
See also CA 113; CANR 32, 68, 116, 157;
CCA 1; DAC; DLB 334

Usigli, Rodolfo 1905-1979 .... **HLCS 1**
See also CA 131; DLB 305; EWL 3; HW 1;
LAW

Usk, Thomas (?)-1388 .... **CMLC 76**
See also DLB 146

Ustinov, Peter (Alexander)
1921-2004 .... **CLC 1**
See also AITN 1; CA 13-16R; CAAS 225;
CANR 25, 51; CBD; CD 5, 6; DLB 13;
MTCW 2

U Tam'si, Gerald Felix Tchicaya
See Tchicaya, Gerald Felix

U Tam'si, Tchicaya
See Tchicaya, Gerald Felix

Vachss, Andrew 1942- .... **CLC 106**
See also CA 214; 118, 214; CANR 44, 95,
153; CMW 4

Vachss, Andrew H.
See Vachss, Andrew

Vachss, Andrew Henry
See Vachss, Andrew

Vaculik, Ludvik 1926- .... **CLC 7**
See also CA 53-56; CANR 72; CWW 2;
DLB 232; EWL 3

Vaihinger, Hans 1852-1933 .... **TCLC 71**
See also CA 166; CAAE 116

Valdez, Luis (Miguel) 1940- ..... **CLC 84; DC
10; HLC 2**
See also CA 101; CAD; CANR 32, 81; CD
5, 6; DAM MULT; DFS 5; DLB 122;
EWL 3; HW 1; LAIT 4; LLW

Valenzuela, Luisa 1938- .... **CLC 31, 104;
HLCS 2; SSC 14, 82**
See also CA 101; CANR 32, 65, 123; CD-
WLB 3; CWW 2; DAM MULT; DLB 113;
EWL 3; FW; HW 1, 2; LAW; RGSF 2;
RGWL 3

Valera y Alcala-Galiano, Juan
1824-1905 .... **TCLC 10**
See also CAAE 106

Valerius Maximus fl. 20- .... **CMLC 64**
See also DLB 211

Valery, (Ambroise) Paul (Toussaint Jules)
1871-1945 .... **PC 9; TCLC 4, 15**
See also CA 122; CAAE 104; DA3; DAM
POET; DLB 258; EW 8; EWL 3; GFL
1789 to the Present; MTCW 1, 2; MTFW
2005; RGWL 2, 3; TWA

Valle-Inclan, Ramon (Maria) del
1866-1936 .... **HLC 2; TCLC 5**
See del Valle-Inclan, Ramon (Maria)
See also CA 153; CAAE 106; CANR 80;
DAM MULT; DLB 134; EW 8; EWL 3;
HW 2; RGSF 2; RGWL 2, 3

Vallejo, Antonio Buero
See Buero Vallejo, Antonio

Vallejo, Cesar (Abraham)
1892-1938 .... **HLC 2; TCLC 3, 56**
See also CA 153; CAAE 105; DAM MULT;
DLB 290; EWL 3; HW 1; LAW; RGWL
2, 3

Valles, Jules 1832-1885 .... **NCLC 71**
See also DLB 123; GFL 1789 to the Present

Vallette, Marguerite Eymery
1860-1953 .... **TCLC 67**
See Rachilde
See also CA 182; DLB 123, 192

Valle Y Pena, Ramon del
See Valle-Inclan, Ramon (Maria) del

Van Ash, Cay 1918-1994 .... **CLC 34**
See also CA 220

Vanbrugh, Sir John 1664-1726 .... **LC 21**
See also BRW 2; DAM DRAM; DLB 80;
IDTP; RGEL 2

Van Campen, Karl
See Campbell, John W(ood, Jr.)

Vance, Gerald
See Silverberg, Robert

Vance, Jack 1916-
See Queen, Ellery; Vance, John Holbrook
See also CA 29-32R; CANR 17, 65, 154;
CMW 4; MTCW 1

Villiers de l'Isle Adam, Jean Marie Mathias Philippe Auguste 1838-1889 ... **NCLC 3; SSC 14**
See also DLB 123, 192; GFL 1789 to the Present; RGSF 2

Villon, Francois 1431-1463(?) . **LC 62; PC 13**
See also DLB 208; EW 2; RGWL 2, 3; TWA

Vine, Barbara .... **CLC 50**
See Rendell, Ruth
See also BEST 90:4

Vinge, Joan (Carol) D(ennison) 1948- .... **CLC 30; SSC 24**
See also AAYA 32; BPFB 3; CA 93-96; CANR 72; SATA 36, 113; SFW 4; YAW

Viola, Herman J(oseph) 1938- .... **CLC 70**
See also CA 61-64; CANR 8, 23, 48, 91; SATA 126

Violis, G.
See Simenon, Georges (Jacques Christian)

Viramontes, Helena Maria 1954- .... **HLCS 2**
See also CA 159; DLB 122; HW 2; LLW

Virgil
See Vergil
See also CDWLB 1; DLB 211; LAIT 1; RGWL 2, 3; WLIT 8; WP

Visconti, Luchino 1906-1976 .... **CLC 16**
See also CA 81-84; CAAS 65-68; CANR 39

Vitry, Jacques de
See Jacques de Vitry

Vittorini, Elio 1908-1966 .... **CLC 6, 9, 14**
See also CA 133; CAAS 25-28R; DLB 264; EW 12; EWL 3; RGWL 2, 3

Vivekananda, Swami 1863-1902 .... **TCLC 88**

Vizenor, Gerald Robert 1934- .... **CLC 103; NNAL**
See also CA 205; 13-16R, 205; 22; CANR 5, 21, 44, 67; DAM MULT; DLB 175, 227; MTCW 2; MTFW 2005; TCWW 2

Vizinczey, Stephen 1933- .... **CLC 40**
See also CA 128; CCA 1; INT CA-128

Vliet, R(ussell) G(ordon) 1929-1984 .... **CLC 22**
See also CA 37-40R; CAAS 112; CANR 18; CP 2, 3

Vogau, Boris Andreyevich 1894-1938
See Pilnyak, Boris
See also CA 218; CAAE 123

Vogel, Paula A. 1951- .... **CLC 76; DC 19**
See also CA 108; CAD; CANR 119, 140; CD 5, 6; CWD; DFS 14; MTFW 2005; RGAL 4

Voigt, Cynthia 1942- .... **CLC 30**
See also AAYA 3, 30; BYA 1, 3, 6, 7, 8; CA 106; CANR 18, 37, 40, 94, 145; CLR 13, 48; INT CANR-18; JRDA; LAIT 5; MAICYA 1, 2; MAICYAS 1; MTFW 2005; SATA 48, 79, 116, 160; SATA-Brief 33; WYA; YAW

Voigt, Ellen Bryant 1943- .... **CLC 54**
See also CA 69-72; CANR 11, 29, 55, 115; CP 5, 6, 7; CSW; CWP; DLB 120; PFS 23

Voinovich, Vladimir 1932- .. **CLC 10, 49, 147**
See also CA 81-84; 12; CANR 33, 67, 150; CWW 2; DLB 302; MTCW 1

Voinovich, Vladimir Nikolaevich
See Voinovich, Vladimir

Vollmann, William T. 1959- ...... **CLC 89, 227**
See also CA 134; CANR 67, 116; CN 7; CPW; DA3; DAM NOV, POP; MTCW 2; MTFW 2005

Voloshinov, V. N.
See Bakhtin, Mikhail Mikhailovich

Voltaire 1694-1778 . **LC 14, 79, 110; SSC 12; WLC 6**
See also BYA 13; DA; DA3; DAB; DAC; DAM DRAM, MST; DLB 314; EW 4; GFL Beginnings to 1789; LATS 1:1; LMFS 1; NFS 7; RGWL 2, 3; TWA

von Aschendrof, Baron Ignatz
See Ford, Ford Madox

von Chamisso, Adelbert
See Chamisso, Adelbert von

von Daeniken, Erich 1935- .... **CLC 30**
See also AITN 1; CA 37-40R; CANR 17, 44

von Daniken, Erich
See von Daeniken, Erich

von Eschenbach, Wolfram c. 1170-c. 1220 .... **CMLC 5**
See Eschenbach, Wolfram von
See also CDWLB 2; DLB 138; EW 1; RGWL 2

von Hartmann, Eduard 1842-1906 .... **TCLC 96**

von Hayek, Friedrich August
See Hayek, F(riedrich) A(ugust von)

von Heidenstam, (Carl Gustaf) Verner
See Heidenstam, (Carl Gustaf) Verner von

von Heyse, Paul (Johann Ludwig)
See Heyse, Paul (Johann Ludwig von)

von Hofmannsthal, Hugo
See Hofmannsthal, Hugo von

von Horvath, Odon
See von Horvath, Odon

von Horvath, Odon
See von Horvath, Odon

von Horvath, Odon 1901-1938 .... **TCLC 45**
See von Horvath, Oedoen
See also CA 194; CAAE 118; DLB 85, 124; RGWL 2, 3

von Horvath, Oedoen
See von Horvath, Odon
See also CA 184

von Kleist, Heinrich
See Kleist, Heinrich von

Vonnegut, Kurt, Jr.
See Vonnegut, Kurt

Vonnegut, Kurt 1922-2007 .... **CLC 1, 2, 3, 4, 5, 8, 12, 22, 40, 60, 111, 212; SSC 8; WLC 6**
See also AAYA 6, 44; AITN 1; AMWS 2; BEST 90:4; BPFB 3; BYA 3, 14; CA 1-4R; CANR 1, 25, 49, 75, 92; CDALB 1968-1988; CN 1, 2, 3, 4, 5, 6, 7; CPW 1; DA; DA3; DAB; DAC; DAM MST, NOV, POP; DLB 2, 8, 152; DLBD 3; DLBY 1980; EWL 3; EXPN; EXPS; LAIT 4; LMFS 2; MAL 5; MTCW 1, 2; MTFW 2005; NFS 3; RGAL 4; SCFW; SFW 4; SSFS 5; TUS; YAW

Von Rachen, Kurt
See Hubbard, L. Ron

von Sternberg, Josef
See Sternberg, Josef von

Vorster, Gordon 1924- .... **CLC 34**
See also CA 133

Vosce, Trudie
See Ozick, Cynthia

Voznesensky, Andrei (Andreievich) 1933- .... **CLC 1, 15, 57**
See Voznesensky, Andrey
See also CA 89-92; CANR 37; CWW 2; DAM POET; MTCW 1

Voznesensky, Andrey
See Voznesensky, Andrei (Andreievich)
See also EWL 3

Wace, Robert c. 1100-c. 1175 .... **CMLC 55**
See also DLB 146

Waddington, Miriam 1917-2004 .... **CLC 28**
See also CA 21-24R; CAAS 225; CANR 12, 30; CCA 1; CP 1, 2, 3, 4, 5, 6, 7; DLB 68

Wagman, Fredrica 1937- .... **CLC 7**
See also CA 97-100; INT CA-97-100

Wagner, Linda W.
See Wagner-Martin, Linda (C.)

Wagner, Linda Welshimer
See Wagner-Martin, Linda (C.)

Wagner, Richard 1813-1883 ..... **NCLC 9, 119**
See also DLB 129; EW 6

Wagner-Martin, Linda (C.) 1936- .... **CLC 50**
See also CA 159; CANR 135

Wagoner, David (Russell) 1926- .... **CLC 3, 5, 15; PC 33**
See also AMWS 9; CA 1-4R; 3; CANR 2, 71; CN 1, 2, 3, 4, 5, 6, 7; CP 1, 2, 3, 4, 5, 6, 7; DLB 5, 256; SATA 14; TCWW 1, 2

Wah, Fred(erick James) 1939- .... **CLC 44**
See also CA 141; CAAE 107; CP 1, 6, 7; DLB 60

Wahloo, Per 1926-1975 .... **CLC 7**
See also BPFB 3; CA 61-64; CANR 73; CMW 4; MSW

Wahloo, Peter
See Wahloo, Per

Wain, John (Barrington) 1925-1994 . **CLC 2, 11, 15, 46**
See also CA 5-8R; 4; CAAS 145; CANR 23, 54; CDBLB 1960 to Present; CN 1, 2, 3, 4, 5; CP 1, 2, 3, 4, 5; DLB 15, 27, 139, 155; EWL 3; MTCW 1, 2; MTFW 2005

Wajda, Andrzej 1926- .... **CLC 16, 219**
See also CA 102

Wakefield, Dan 1932- .... **CLC 7**
See also CA 211; 21-24R, 211; 7; CN 4, 5, 6, 7

Wakefield, Herbert Russell 1888-1965 .... **TCLC 120**
See also CA 5-8R; CANR 77; HGG; SUFW

Wakoski, Diane 1937- ...... **CLC 2, 4, 7, 9, 11, 40; PC 15**
See also CA 216; 13-16R, 216; 1; CANR 9, 60, 106; CP 1, 2, 3, 4, 5, 6, 7; CWP; DAM POET; DLB 5; INT CANR-9; MAL 5; MTCW 2; MTFW 2005

Wakoski-Sherbell, Diane
See Wakoski, Diane

Walcott, Derek 1930- ... **BLC 3; CLC 2, 4, 9, 14, 25, 42, 67, 76, 160; DC 7; PC 46**
See also BW 2; CA 89-92; CANR 26, 47, 75, 80, 130; CBD; CD 5, 6; CDWLB 3; CP 1, 2, 3, 4, 5, 6, 7; DA3; DAB; DAC; DAM MST, MULT, POET; DLB 117, 332; DLBY 1981; DNFS 1; EFS 1; EWL 3; LMFS 2; MTCW 1, 2; MTFW 2005; PFS 6; RGEL 2; TWA; WWE 1

Waldman, Anne (Lesley) 1945- .... **CLC 7**
See also BG 1:3; CA 37-40R; 17; CANR 34, 69, 116; CP 1, 2, 3, 4, 5, 6, 7; CWP; DLB 16

Waldo, E. Hunter
See Sturgeon, Theodore (Hamilton)

Waldo, Edward Hamilton
See Sturgeon, Theodore (Hamilton)

Walker, Alice 1944- ...... **BLC 3; CLC 5, 6, 9, 19, 27, 46, 58, 103, 167; PC 30; SSC 5; WLCS**
See also AAYA 3, 33; AFAW 1, 2; AMWS 3; BEST 89:4; BPFB 3; BW 2, 3; CA 37-40R; CANR 9, 27, 49, 66, 82, 131; CDALB 1968-1988; CN 4, 5, 6, 7; CPW; CSW; DA; DA3; DAB; DAC; DAM MST, MULT, NOV, POET, POP; DLB 6, 33, 143; EWL 3; EXPN; EXPS; FL 1:6; FW; INT CANR-27; LAIT 3; MAL 5; MBL; MTCW 1, 2; MTFW 2005; NFS 5; RGAL 4; RGSF 2; SATA 31; SSFS 2, 11; TUS; YAW

Waugh, Evelyn (Arthur St. John)
1903-1966 .. **CLC 1, 3, 8, 13, 19, 27, 44, 107; SSC 41; WLC 6**
See also BPFB 3; BRW 7; CA 85-88; CAAS 25-28R; CANR 22; CDBLB 1914-1945; DA; DA3; DAB; DAC; DAM MST, NOV, POP; DLB 15, 162, 195; EWL 3; MTCW 1, 2; MTFW 2005; NFS 13, 17; RGEL 2; RGSF 2; TEA; WLIT 4

Waugh, Harriet 1944- .... **CLC 6**
See also CA 85-88; CANR 22

Ways, C. R.
See Blount, Roy (Alton), Jr.

Waystaff, Simon
See Swift, Jonathan

Webb, Beatrice (Martha Potter)
1858-1943 .... **TCLC 22**
See also CA 162; CAAE 117; DLB 190; FW

Webb, Charles (Richard) 1939- .... **CLC 7**
See also CA 25-28R; CANR 114

Webb, Frank J. .... **NCLC 143**
See also DLB 50

Webb, James, Jr.
See Webb, James

Webb, James 1946- .... **CLC 22**
See also CA 81-84; CANR 156

Webb, James H.
See Webb, James

Webb, James Henry
See Webb, James

Webb, Mary Gladys (Meredith)
1881-1927 .... **TCLC 24**
See also CA 182; CAAS 123; DLB 34; FW; RGEL 2

Webb, Mrs. Sidney
See Webb, Beatrice (Martha Potter)

Webb, Phyllis 1927- .... **CLC 18**
See also CA 104; CANR 23; CCA 1; CP 1, 2, 3, 4, 5, 6, 7; CWP; DLB 53

Webb, Sidney (James) 1859-1947 .. **TCLC 22**
See also CA 163; CAAE 117; DLB 190

Webber, Andrew Lloyd .... **CLC 21**
See Lloyd Webber, Andrew
See also DFS 7

Weber, Lenora Mattingly
1895-1971 .... **CLC 12**
See also CA 19-20; CAAS 29-32R; CAP 1; SATA 2; SATA-Obit 26

Weber, Max 1864-1920 .... **TCLC 69**
See also CA 189; CAAE 109; DLB 296

Webster, John 1580(?)-1634(?) ...... **DC 2; LC 33, 84, 124; WLC 6**
See also BRW 2; CDBLB Before 1660; DA; DAB; DAC; DAM DRAM, MST; DFS 17, 19; DLB 58; IDTP; RGEL 2; WLIT 3

Webster, Noah 1758-1843 .... **NCLC 30**
See also DLB 1, 37, 42, 43, 73, 243

Wedekind, Benjamin Franklin
See Wedekind, Frank

Wedekind, Frank 1864-1918 .... **TCLC 7**
See also CA 153; CAAE 104; CANR 121, 122; CDWLB 2; DAM DRAM; DLB 118; EW 8; EWL 3; LMFS 2; RGWL 2, 3

Wehr, Demaris .... **CLC 65**

Weidman, Jerome 1913-1998 .... **CLC 7**
See also AITN 2; CA 1-4R; CAAS 171; CAD; CANR 1; CD 1, 2, 3, 4, 5; DLB 28

Weil, Simone (Adolphine)
1909-1943 .... **TCLC 23**
See also CA 159; CAAE 117; EW 12; EWL 3; FW; GFL 1789 to the Present; MTCW 2

Weininger, Otto 1880-1903 .... **TCLC 84**

Weinstein, Nathan
See West, Nathanael

Weinstein, Nathan von Wallenstein
See West, Nathanael

Weir, Peter (Lindsay) 1944- .... **CLC 20**
See also CA 123; CAAE 113

Weiss, Peter (Ulrich) 1916-1982 .. **CLC 3, 15, 51; TCLC 152**
See also CA 45-48; CAAS 106; CANR 3; DAM DRAM; DFS 3; DLB 69, 124; EWL 3; RGHL; RGWL 2, 3

Weiss, Theodore (Russell)
1916-2003 .... **CLC 3, 8, 14**
See also CA 189; 9-12R, 189; 2; CAAS 216; CANR 46, 94; CP 1, 2, 3, 4, 5, 6, 7; DLB 5; TCLE 1:2

Welch, (Maurice) Denton
1915-1948 .... **TCLC 22**
See also BRWS 8, 9; CA 148; CAAE 121; RGEL 2

Welch, James (Phillip) 1940-2003 ..... **CLC 6, 14, 52; NNAL; PC 62**
See also CA 85-88; CAAS 219; CANR 42, 66, 107; CN 5, 6, 7; CP 2, 3, 4, 5, 6, 7; CPW; DAM MULT, POP; DLB 175, 256; LATS 1:1; NFS 23; RGAL 4; TCWW 1, 2

Weldon, Fay 1931- . **CLC 6, 9, 11, 19, 36, 59, 122**
See also BRWS 4; CA 21-24R; CANR 16, 46, 63, 97, 137; CDBLB 1960 to Present; CN 3, 4, 5, 6, 7; CPW; DAM POP; DLB 14, 194, 319; EWL 3; FW; HGG; INT CANR-16; MTCW 1, 2; MTFW 2005; RGEL 2; RGSF 2

Wellek, Rene 1903-1995 .... **CLC 28**
See also CA 5-8R; 7; CAAS 150; CANR 8; DLB 63; EWL 3; INT CANR-8

Weller, Michael 1942- .... **CLC 10, 53**
See also CA 85-88; CAD; CD 5, 6

Weller, Paul 1958- .... **CLC 26**

Wellershoff, Dieter 1925- .... **CLC 46**
See also CA 89-92; CANR 16, 37

Welles, (George) Orson 1915-1985 .. **CLC 20, 80**
See also AAYA 40; CA 93-96; CAAS 117

Wellman, John McDowell 1945-
See Wellman, Mac
See also CA 166; CD 5

Wellman, Mac .... **CLC 65**
See Wellman, John McDowell; Wellman, John McDowell
See also CAD; CD 6; RGAL 4

Wellman, Manly Wade 1903-1986 ... **CLC 49**
See also CA 1-4R; CAAS 118; CANR 6, 16, 44; FANT; SATA 6; SATA-Obit 47; SFW 4; SUFW

Wells, Carolyn 1869(?)-1942 .... **TCLC 35**
See also CA 185; CAAE 113; CMW 4; DLB 11

Wells, H(erbert) G(eorge) 1866-1946 . **SSC 6, 70; TCLC 6, 12, 19, 133; WLC 6**
See also AAYA 18; BPFB 3; BRW 6; CA 121; CAAE 110; CDBLB 1914-1945; CLR 64; DA; DA3; DAB; DAC; DAM MST, NOV; DLB 34, 70, 156, 178; EWL 3; EXPS; HGG; LAIT 3; LMFS 2; MTCW 1, 2; MTFW 2005; NFS 17, 20; RGEL 2; RGSF 2; SATA 20; SCFW 1, 2; SFW 4; SSFS 3; SUFW; TEA; WCH; WLIT 4; YAW

Wells, Rosemary 1943- .... **CLC 12**
See also AAYA 13; BYA 7, 8; CA 85-88; CANR 48, 120; CLR 16, 69; CWRI 5; MAICYA 1, 2; SAAS 1; SATA 18, 69, 114, 156; YAW

Wells-Barnett, Ida B(ell)
1862-1931 .... **TCLC 125**
See also CA 182; DLB 23, 221

Welsh, Irvine 1958- .... **CLC 144**
See also CA 173; CANR 146; CN 7; DLB 271

Welty, Eudora 1909-2001 .... **CLC 1, 2, 5, 14, 22, 33, 105, 220; SSC 1, 27, 51; WLC 6**
See also AAYA 48; AMW; AMWR 1; BPFB 3; CA 9-12R; CAAS 199; CABS 1; CANR 32, 65, 128; CDALB 1941-1968; CN 1, 2, 3, 4, 5, 6, 7; CSW; DA; DA3; DAB; DAC; DAM MST, NOV; DLB 2, 102, 143; DLBD 12; DLBY 1987, 2001; EWL 3; EXPS; HGG; LAIT 3; MAL 5; MBL; MTCW 1, 2; MTFW 2005; NFS 13, 15; RGAL 4; RGSF 2; RHW; SSFS 2, 10; TUS

Welty, Eudora Alice
See Welty, Eudora

Wen I-to 1899-1946 .... **TCLC 28**
See also EWL 3

Wentworth, Robert
See Hamilton, Edmond

Werfel, Franz (Viktor) 1890-1945 ... **TCLC 8**
See also CA 161; CAAE 104; DLB 81, 124; EWL 3; RGWL 2, 3

Wergeland, Henrik Arnold
1808-1845 .... **NCLC 5**

Wersba, Barbara 1932- .... **CLC 30**
See also AAYA 2, 30; BYA 6, 12, 13; CA 182; 29-32R, 182; CANR 16, 38; CLR 3, 78; DLB 52; JRDA; MAICYA 1, 2; SAAS 2; SATA 1, 58; SATA-Essay 103; WYA; YAW

Wertmueller, Lina 1928- .... **CLC 16**
See also CA 97-100; CANR 39, 78

Wescott, Glenway 1901-1987 .. **CLC 13; SSC 35**
See also CA 13-16R; CAAS 121; CANR 23, 70; CN 1, 2, 3, 4; DLB 4, 9, 102; MAL 5; RGAL 4

Wesker, Arnold 1932- .... **CLC 3, 5, 42**
See also CA 1-4R; 7; CANR 1, 33; CBD; CD 5, 6; CDBLB 1960 to Present; DAB; DAM DRAM; DLB 13, 310, 319; EWL 3; MTCW 1; RGEL 2; TEA

Wesley, Charles 1707-1788 .... **LC 128**
See also DLB 95; RGEL 2

Wesley, John 1703-1791 .... **LC 88**
See also DLB 104

Wesley, Richard (Errol) 1945- .... **CLC 7**
See also BW 1; CA 57-60; CAD; CANR 27; CD 5, 6; DLB 38

Wessel, Johan Herman 1742-1785 ...... **LC 7**
See also DLB 300

West, Anthony (Panther)
1914-1987 .... **CLC 50**
See also CA 45-48; CAAS 124; CANR 3, 19; CN 1, 2, 3, 4; DLB 15

West, C. P.
See Wodehouse, P(elham) G(renville)

West, Cornel 1953- .... **BLCS; CLC 134**
See also CA 144; CANR 91, 159; DLB 246

West, Cornel Ronald
See West, Cornel

West, Delno C(loyde), Jr. 1936- .... **CLC 70**
See also CA 57-60

West, Dorothy 1907-1998 ...... **HR 1:3; TCLC 108**
See also BW 2; CA 143; CAAS 169; DLB 76

West, (Mary) Jessamyn 1902-1984 ... **CLC 7, 17**
See also CA 9-12R; CAAS 112; CANR 27; CN 1, 2, 3; DLB 6; DLBY 1984; MTCW 1, 2; RGAL 4; RHW; SATA-Obit 37; TCWW 2; TUS; YAW

West, Morris L(anglo) 1916-1999 ..... **CLC 6, 33**
See also BPFB 3; CA 5-8R; CAAS 187; CANR 24, 49, 64; CN 1, 2, 3, 4, 5, 6; CPW; DLB 289; MTCW 1, 2; MTFW 2005

Wilbur, Richard 1921- .. **CLC 3, 6, 9, 14, 53, 110; PC 51**
See also AAYA 72; AMWS 3; CA 1-4R; CABS 2; CANR 2, 29, 76, 93, 139; CDALBS; CP 1, 2, 3, 4, 5, 6, 7; DA; DAB; DAC; DAM MST, POET; DLB 5, 169; EWL 3; EXPP; INT CANR-29; MAL 5; MTCW 1, 2; MTFW 2005; PAB; PFS 11, 12, 16; RGAL 4; SATA 9, 108; WP

Wilbur, Richard Purdy
See Wilbur, Richard

Wild, Peter 1940- .... **CLC 14**
See also CA 37-40R; CP 1, 2, 3, 4, 5, 6, 7; DLB 5

Wilde, Oscar (Fingal O'Flahertie Wills)
1854(?)-1900 .... **DC 17; SSC 11, 77; TCLC 1, 8, 23, 41, 175; WLC 6**
See also AAYA 49; BRW 5; BRWC 1, 2; BRWR 2; BYA 15; CA 119; CAAE 104; CANR 112; CDBLB 1890-1914; CLR 114; DA; DA3; DAB; DAC; DAM DRAM, MST, NOV; DFS 4, 8, 9, 21; DLB 10, 19, 34, 57, 141, 156, 190; EXPS; FANT; GL 3; LATS 1:1; NFS 20; RGEL 2; RGSF 2; SATA 24; SSFS 7; SUFW; TEA; WCH; WLIT 4

Wilder, Billy .... **CLC 20**
See Wilder, Samuel
See also AAYA 66; DLB 26

Wilder, Samuel 1906-2002
See Wilder, Billy
See also CA 89-92; CAAS 205

Wilder, Stephen
See Marlowe, Stephen

Wilder, Thornton (Niven)
1897-1975 .. **CLC 1, 5, 6, 10, 15, 35, 82; DC 1, 24; WLC 6**
See also AAYA 29; AITN 2; AMW; CA 13-16R; CAAS 61-64; CAD; CANR 40, 132; CDALBS; CN 1, 2; DA; DA3; DAB; DAC; DAM DRAM, MST, NOV; DFS 1, 4, 16; DLB 4, 7, 9, 228; DLBY 1997; EWL 3; LAIT 3; MAL 5; MTCW 1, 2; MTFW 2005; NFS 24; RGAL 4; RHW; WYAS 1

Wilding, Michael 1942- ...... **CLC 73; SSC 50**
See also CA 104; CANR 24, 49, 106; CN 4, 5, 6, 7; DLB 325; RGSF 2

Wiley, Richard 1944- .... **CLC 44**
See also CA 129; CAAE 121; CANR 71

Wilhelm, Kate .... **CLC 7**
See Wilhelm, Katie
See also AAYA 20; BYA 16; CA 5; DLB 8; INT CANR-17; SCFW 2

Wilhelm, Katie 1928-
See Wilhelm, Kate
See also CA 37-40R; CANR 17, 36, 60, 94; MTCW 1; SFW 4

Wilkins, Mary
See Freeman, Mary E(leanor) Wilkins

Willard, Nancy 1936- .... **CLC 7, 37**
See also BYA 5; CA 89-92; CANR 10, 39, 68, 107, 152; CLR 5; CP 2, 3, 4, 5; CWP; CWRI 5; DLB 5, 52; FANT; MAICYA 1, 2; MTCW 1; SATA 37, 71, 127; SATA-Brief 30; SUFW 2; TCLE 1:2

William of Malmesbury c. 1090B.C.-c. 1140B.C. .... **CMLC 57**

William of Moerbeke c. 1215-c. 1286 .... **CMLC 91**

William of Ockham 1290-1349 ..... **CMLC 32**

Williams, Ben Ames 1889-1953 ..... **TCLC 89**
See also CA 183; DLB 102

Williams, Charles
See Collier, James Lincoln

Williams, Charles (Walter Stansby)
1886-1945 .... **TCLC 1, 11**
See also BRWS 9; CA 163; CAAE 104; DLB 100, 153, 255; FANT; RGEL 2; SUFW 1

Williams, C.K. 1936- .... **CLC 33, 56, 148**
See also CA 37-40R; 26; CANR 57, 106; CP 1, 2, 3, 4, 5, 6, 7; DAM POET; DLB 5; MAL 5

Williams, Ella Gwendolen Rees
See Rhys, Jean

Williams, (George) Emlyn
1905-1987 .... **CLC 15**
See also CA 104; CAAS 123; CANR 36; DAM DRAM; DLB 10, 77; IDTP; MTCW 1

Williams, Hank 1923-1953 .... **TCLC 81**
See Williams, Hiram King

Williams, Helen Maria
1761-1827 .... **NCLC 135**
See also DLB 158

Williams, Hiram Hank
See Williams, Hank

Williams, Hiram King
See Williams, Hank
See also CA 188

Williams, Hugo (Mordaunt) 1942- ... **CLC 42**
See also CA 17-20R; CANR 45, 119; CP 1, 2, 3, 4, 5, 6, 7; DLB 40

Williams, J. Walker
See Wodehouse, P(elham) G(renville)

Williams, John A(lfred) 1925- . **BLC 3; CLC 5, 13**
See also AFAW 2; BW 2, 3; CA 195; 53-56, 195; 3; CANR 6, 26, 51, 118; CN 1, 2, 3, 4, 5, 6, 7; CSW; DAM MULT; DLB 2, 33; EWL 3; INT CANR-6; MAL 5; RGAL 4; SFW 4

Williams, Jonathan (Chamberlain)
1929- .... **CLC 13**
See also CA 9-12R; CANR 8, 108; CP 1, 2, 3, 4, 5, 6, 7; DLB 5

Williams, Joy 1944- .... **CLC 31**
See also CA 41-44R; CANR 22, 48, 97; DLB 335

Williams, Norman 1952- .... **CLC 39**
See also CA 118

Williams, Roger 1603(?)-1683 .... **LC 129**
See also DLB 24

Williams, Sherley Anne 1944-1999 ... **BLC 3; CLC 89**
See also AFAW 2; BW 2, 3; CA 73-76; CAAS 185; CANR 25, 82; DAM MULT, POET; DLB 41; INT CANR-25; SATA 78; SATA-Obit 116

Williams, Shirley
See Williams, Sherley Anne

Williams, Tennessee 1911-1983 . **CLC 1, 2, 5, 7, 8, 11, 15, 19, 30, 39, 45, 71, 111; DC 4; SSC 81; WLC 6**
See also AAYA 31; AITN 1, 2; AMW; AMWC 1; CA 5-8R; CABS 3; CAD; CANR 31, 132; CDALB 1941-1968; CN 1, 2, 3; DA; DA3; DAB; DAC; DAM DRAM, MST; DFS 17; DLB 7; DLBD 4; DLBY 1983; EWL 3; GLL 1; LAIT 4; LATS 1:2; MAL 5; MTCW 1, 2; MTFW 2005; RGAL 4; TUS

Williams, Thomas (Alonzo)
1926-1990 .... **CLC 14**
See also CA 1-4R; CAAS 132; CANR 2

Williams, William C.
See Williams, William Carlos

Williams, William Carlos
1883-1963 .... **CLC 1, 2, 5, 9, 13, 22, 42, 67; PC 7; SSC 31; WLC 6**
See also AAYA 46; AMW; AMWR 1; CA 89-92; CANR 34; CDALB 1917-1929; DA; DA3; DAB; DAC; DAM MST,

POET; DLB 4, 16, 54, 86; EWL 3; EXPP; MAL 5; MTCW 1, 2; MTFW 2005; NCFS 4; PAB; PFS 1, 6, 11; RGAL 4; RGSF 2; TUS; WP

Williamson, David (Keith) 1942- ..... **CLC 56**
See also CA 103; CANR 41; CD 5, 6; DLB 289

Williamson, Ellen Douglas 1905-1984
See Douglas, Ellen
See also CA 17-20R; CAAS 114; CANR 39

Williamson, Jack .... **CLC 29**
See Williamson, John Stewart
See also CA 8; DLB 8; SCFW 1, 2

Williamson, John Stewart 1908-2006
See Williamson, Jack
See also CA 17-20R; CAAS 255; CANR 23, 70, 153; SFW 4

Willie, Frederick
See Lovecraft, H. P.

Willingham, Calder (Baynard, Jr.)
1922-1995 .... **CLC 5, 51**
See also CA 5-8R; CAAS 147; CANR 3; CN 1, 2, 3, 4, 5; CSW; DLB 2, 44; IDFW 3, 4; MTCW 1

Willis, Charles
See Clarke, Arthur C.

Willy
See Colette, (Sidonie-Gabrielle)

Willy, Colette
See Colette, (Sidonie-Gabrielle)
See also GLL 1

Wilmot, John 1647-1680 .... **LC 75; PC 66**
See Rochester
See also BRW 2; DLB 131; PAB

Wilson, A.N. 1950- .... **CLC 33**
See also BRWS 6; CA 122; CAAE 112; CANR 156; CN 4, 5, 6, 7; DLB 14, 155, 194; MTCW 2

Wilson, Andrew Norman
See Wilson, A.N.

Wilson, Angus (Frank Johnstone)
1913-1991 . **CLC 2, 3, 5, 25, 34; SSC 21**
See also BRWS 1; CA 5-8R; CAAS 134; CANR 21; CN 1, 2, 3, 4; DLB 15, 139, 155; EWL 3; MTCW 1, 2; MTFW 2005; RGEL 2; RGSF 2

Wilson, August 1945-2005 .. **BLC 3; CLC 39, 50, 63, 118, 222; DC 2; WLCS**
See also AAYA 16; AFAW 2; AMWS 8; BW 2, 3; CA 122; CAAE 115; CAAS 244; CAD; CANR 42, 54, 76, 128; CD 5, 6; DA; DA3; DAB; DAC; DAM DRAM, MST, MULT; DFS 3, 7, 15, 17, 24; DLB 228; EWL 3; LAIT 4; LATS 1:2; MAL 5; MTCW 1, 2; MTFW 2005; RGAL 4

Wilson, Brian 1942- .... **CLC 12**

Wilson, Colin (Henry) 1931- .... **CLC 3, 14**
See also CA 1-4R; 5; CANR 1, 22, 33, 77; CMW 4; CN 1, 2, 3, 4, 5, 6; DLB 14, 194; HGG; MTCW 1; SFW 4

Wilson, Dirk
See Pohl, Frederik

Wilson, Edmund 1895-1972 .. **CLC 1, 2, 3, 8, 24**
See also AMW; CA 1-4R; CAAS 37-40R; CANR 1, 46, 110; CN 1; DLB 63; EWL 3; MAL 5; MTCW 1, 2; MTFW 2005; RGAL 4; TUS

Wilson, Ethel Davis (Bryant)
1888(?)-1980 .... **CLC 13**
See also CA 102; CN 1, 2; DAC; DAM POET; DLB 68; MTCW 1; RGEL 2

Wilson, Harriet
See Wilson, Harriet E. Adams
See also DLB 239

Wilson, Harriet E.
See Wilson, Harriet E. Adams
See also DLB 243

Wilson, Harriet E. Adams
  1827(?)-1863(?) .... **BLC 3; NCLC 78**
  See Wilson, Harriet; Wilson, Harriet E.
  See also DAM MULT; DLB 50
Wilson, John 1785-1854 .... **NCLC 5**
Wilson, John (Anthony) Burgess 1917-1993
  See Burgess, Anthony
  See also CA 1-4R; CAAS 143; CANR 2,
  46; DA3; DAC; DAM NOV; MTCW 1,
  2; MTFW 2005; NFS 15; TEA
Wilson, Katharina .... **CLC 65**
Wilson, Lanford 1937- .. **CLC 7, 14, 36, 197;**
  DC 19
  See also CA 17-20R; CABS 3; CAD; CANR
  45, 96; CD 5, 6; DAM DRAM; DFS 4, 9,
  12, 16, 20; DLB 7; EWL 3; MAL 5; TUS
Wilson, Robert M. 1941- .... **CLC 7, 9**
  See also CA 49-52; CAD; CANR 2, 41; CD
  5, 6; MTCW 1
Wilson, Robert McLiam 1964- .... **CLC 59**
  See also CA 132; DLB 267
Wilson, Sloan 1920-2003 .... **CLC 32**
  See also CA 1-4R; CAAS 216; CANR 1,
  44; CN 1, 2, 3, 4, 5, 6
Wilson, Snoo 1948- .... **CLC 33**
  See also CA 69-72; CBD; CD 5, 6
Wilson, William S(mith) 1932- .... **CLC 49**
  See also CA 81-84
Wilson, (Thomas) Woodrow
  1856-1924 .... **TCLC 79**
  See also CA 166; DLB 47
Winchilsea, Anne (Kingsmill) Finch
  1661-1720
  See Finch, Anne
  See also RGEL 2
Winckelmann, Johann Joachim
  1717-1768 .... **LC 129**
  See also DLB 97
Windham, Basil
  See Wodehouse, P(elham) G(renville)
Wingrove, David 1954- .... **CLC 68**
  See also CA 133; SFW 4
Winnemucca, Sarah 1844-1891 .... **NCLC 79;**
  NNAL
  See also DAM MULT; DLB 175; RGAL 4
Winstanley, Gerrard 1609-1676 .... **LC 52**
Wintergreen, Jane
  See Duncan, Sara Jeannette
Winters, Arthur Yvor
  See Winters, Yvor
Winters, Janet Lewis .... **CLC 41**
  See Lewis, Janet
  See also DLBY 1987
Winters, Yvor 1900-1968 .... **CLC 4, 8, 32**
  See also AMWS 2; CA 11-12; CAAS 25-
  28R; CAP 1; DLB 48; EWL 3; MAL 5;
  MTCW 1; RGAL 4
Winterson, Jeanette 1959- .... **CLC 64, 158**
  See also BRWS 4; CA 136; CANR 58, 116;
  CN 5, 6, 7; CPW; DA3; DAM POP; DLB
  207, 261; FANT; FW; GLL 1; MTCW 2;
  MTFW 2005; RHW
Winthrop, John 1588-1649 .... **LC 31, 107**
  See also DLB 24, 30
Wirth, Louis 1897-1952 .... **TCLC 92**
  See also CA 210
Wiseman, Frederick 1930- .... **CLC 20**
  See also CA 159
Wister, Owen 1860-1938 ..... **SSC 100; TCLC**
  21
  See also BPFB 3; CA 162; CAAE 108;
  DLB 9, 78, 186; RGAL 4; SATA 62;
  TCWW 1, 2
Wither, George 1588-1667 .... **LC 96**
  See also DLB 121; RGEL 2
Witkacy
  See Witkiewicz, Stanislaw Ignacy

Witkiewicz, Stanislaw Ignacy
  1885-1939 .... **TCLC 8**
  See also CA 162; CAAE 105; CDWLB 4;
  DLB 215; EW 10; EWL 3; RGWL 2, 3;
  SFW 4
Wittgenstein, Ludwig (Josef Johann)
  1889-1951 .... **TCLC 59**
  See also CA 164; CAAE 113; DLB 262;
  MTCW 2
Wittig, Monique 1935-2003 .... **CLC 22**
  See also CA 135; CAAE 116; CAAS 212;
  CANR 143; CWW 2; DLB 83; EWL 3;
  FW; GLL 1
Wittlin, Jozef 1896-1976 .... **CLC 25**
  See also CA 49-52; CAAS 65-68; CANR 3;
  EWL 3
Wodehouse, P(elham) G(renville)
  1881-1975 . **CLC 1, 2, 5, 10, 22; SSC 2;**
  TCLC 108
  See also AAYA 65; AITN 2; BRWS 3; CA
  45-48; CAAS 57-60; CANR 3, 33; CD-
  BLB 1914-1945; CN 1, 2; CPW 1; DA3;
  DAB; DAC; DAM NOV; DLB 34, 162;
  EWL 3; MTCW 1, 2; MTFW 2005; RGEL
  2; RGSF 2; SATA 22; SSFS 10
Woiwode, L.
  See Woiwode, Larry (Alfred)
Woiwode, Larry (Alfred) 1941- ... **CLC 6, 10**
  See also CA 73-76; CANR 16, 94; CN 3, 4,
  5, 6, 7; DLB 6; INT CANR-16
Wojciechowska, Maia (Teresa)
  1927-2002 .... **CLC 26**
  See also AAYA 8, 46; BYA 3; CA 183;
  9-12R, 183; CAAS 209; CANR 4, 41;
  CLR 1; JRDA; MAICYA 1, 2; SAAS 1;
  SATA 1, 28, 83; SATA-Essay 104; SATA-
  Obit 134; YAW
Wojtyla, Karol (Jozef)
  See John Paul II, Pope
Wojtyla, Karol (Josef)
  See John Paul II, Pope
Wolf, Christa 1929- .... **CLC 14, 29, 58, 150**
  See also CA 85-88; CANR 45, 123; CD-
  WLB 2; CWW 2; DLB 75; EWL 3; FW;
  MTCW 1; RGWL 2, 3; SSFS 14
Wolf, Naomi 1962- .... **CLC 157**
  See also CA 141; CANR 110; FW; MTFW
  2005
Wolfe, Gene 1931- .... **CLC 25**
  See also AAYA 35; CA 57-60; 9; CANR 6,
  32, 60, 152; CPW; DAM POP; DLB 8;
  FANT; MTCW 2; MTFW 2005; SATA
  118, 165; SCFW 2; SFW 4; SUFW 2
Wolfe, Gene Rodman
  See Wolfe, Gene
Wolfe, George C. 1954- .... **BLCS; CLC 49**
  See also CA 149; CAD; CD 5, 6
Wolfe, Thomas (Clayton)
  1900-1938 ...... **SSC 33; TCLC 4, 13, 29,**
  61; WLC 6
  See also AMW; BPFB 3; CA 132; CAAE
  104; CANR 102; CDALB 1929-1941;
  DA; DA3; DAB; DAC; DAM MST, NOV;
  DLB 9, 102, 229; DLBD 2, 16; DLBY
  1985, 1997; EWL 3; MAL 5; MTCW 1,
  2; NFS 18; RGAL 4; SSFS 18; TUS
Wolfe, Thomas Kennerly, Jr.
  1931- .... **CLC 147**
  See Wolfe, Tom
  See also CA 13-16R; CANR 9, 33, 70, 104;
  DA3; DAM POP; DLB 185; EWL 3; INT
  CANR-9; MTCW 1, 2; MTFW 2005; TUS
Wolfe, Tom .... **CLC 1, 2, 9, 15, 35, 51**
  See Wolfe, Thomas Kennerly, Jr.
  See also AAYA 8, 67; AITN 2; AMWS 3;
  BEST 89:1; BPFB 3; CN 5, 6, 7; CPW;
  CSW; DLB 152; LAIT 5; RGAL 4
Wolff, Geoffrey 1937- .... **CLC 41**
  See also CA 29-32R; CANR 29, 43, 78, 154

Wolff, Geoffrey Ansell
  See Wolff, Geoffrey
Wolff, Sonia
  See Levitin, Sonia (Wolff)
Wolff, Tobias 1945- .... **CLC 39, 64, 172; SSC**
  63
  See also AAYA 16; AMWS 7; BEST 90:2;
  BYA 12; CA 117; 22; CAAE 114; CANR
  54, 76, 96; CN 5, 6, 7; CSW; DA3; DLB
  130; EWL 3; INT CA-117; MTCW 2;
  MTFW 2005; RGAL 4; RGSF 2; SSFS 4,
  11
Wolitzer, Hilma 1930- .... **CLC 17**
  See also CA 65-68; CANR 18, 40; INT
  CANR-18; SATA 31; YAW
Wollstonecraft, Mary 1759-1797 .... **LC 5, 50,**
  90
  See also BRWS 3; CDBLB 1789-1832;
  DLB 39, 104, 158, 252; FL 1:1; FW;
  LAIT 1; RGEL 2; TEA; WLIT 3
Wonder, Stevie 1950- .... **CLC 12**
  See also CAAE 111
Wong, Jade Snow 1922-2006 .... **CLC 17**
  See also CA 109; CAAS 249; CANR 91;
  SATA 112; SATA-Obit 175
Wood, Ellen Price
  See Wood, Mrs. Henry
Wood, Mrs. Henry 1814-1887 ...... **NCLC 178**
  See also CMW 4; DLB 18; SUFW
Wood, James 1965- .... **CLC 238**
  See also CA 235
Woodberry, George Edward
  1855-1930 .... **TCLC 73**
  See also CA 165; DLB 71, 103
Woodcott, Keith
  See Brunner, John (Kilian Houston)
Woodruff, Robert W.
  See Mencken, H(enry) L(ouis)
Woodward, Bob
  See Woodward, Robert Upshur
Woodward, Robert Upshur 1943- .. **CLC 240**
  See also CA 69-72; CANR 31, 67, 107;
  MTCW 1
Woolf, (Adeline) Virginia 1882-1941 .. **SSC 7,**
  79; TCLC 1, 5, 20, 43, 56, 101, 123,
  128; WLC 6
  See also AAYA 44; BPFB 3; BRW 7;
  BRWC 2; BRWR 1; CA 130; CAAE 104;
  CANR 64, 132; CDBLB 1914-1945; DA;
  DA3; DAB; DAC; DAM MST, NOV;
  DLB 36, 100, 162; DLBD 10; EWL 3;
  EXPS; FL 1:6; FW; LAIT 3; LATS 1:1;
  LMFS 2; MTCW 1, 2; MTFW 2005;
  NCFS 2; NFS 8, 12; RGEL 2; RGSF 2;
  SSFS 4, 12; TEA; WLIT 4
Woollcott, Alexander (Humphreys)
  1887-1943 .... **TCLC 5**
  See also CA 161; CAAE 105; DLB 29
Woolrich, Cornell .... **CLC 77**
  See Hopley-Woolrich, Cornell George
  See also MSW
Woolson, Constance Fenimore
  1840-1894 .... **NCLC 82; SSC 90**
  See also DLB 12, 74, 189, 221; RGAL 4
Wordsworth, Dorothy 1771-1855 . **NCLC 25,**
  138
  See also DLB 107
Wordsworth, William 1770-1850 .. **NCLC 12,**
  38, 111, 166; PC 4, 67; WLC 6
  See also AAYA 70; BRW 4; BRWC 1; CD-
  BLB 1789-1832; DA; DA3; DAB; DAC;
  DAM MST, POET; DLB 93, 107; EXPP;
  LATS 1:1; LMFS 1; PAB; PFS 2; RGEL
  2; TEA; WLIT 3; WP
Wotton, Sir Henry 1568-1639 .... **LC 68**
  See also DLB 121; RGEL 2

Literary Criticism Series
Cumulative Topic Index

This index lists all topic entries in Thomson Gale's *Children's Literature Review* (CLR), *Classical and Medieval Literature Criticism* (CMLC), *Contemporary Literary Criticism* (CLC), *Drama Criticism* (DC), *Literature Criticism from 1400 to 1800* (LC), *Nineteenth-Century Literature Criticism* (NCLC), *Short Story Criticism* (SSC), and *Twentieth-Century Literary Criticism* (TCLC). The index also lists topic entries in the Gale Critical Companion Collection, which includes the following publications: *The Beat Generation* (BG), *Feminism in Literature* (FL), *Gothic Literature* (GL), and *Harlem Renaissance* (HR).

Topic Index

NCLC Cumulative Nationality Index

NCLC-185 Title Index

ISBN-13: 978-0-7876-9856-0
ISBN-10: 0-7876-9856-3